# Contemporary Europe

# Contemporary Europe

## Economics, Politics and Society

DAVID EDYE

VALERIO LINTNER

**PRENTICE HALL**

London   New York   Toronto   Sydney   Tokyo   Singapore
Madrid   Mexico City   Munich

First published 1996 by
Prentice Hall Europe
Campus 400, Maylands Avenue
Hemel Hempstead
Hertfordshire, HP2 7EZ
A division of
Simon & Schuster International Group

Typeset in 9½/12pt Palatino by
Hands Fotoset, Leicester

Printed and bound in Great Britain by
Redwood Books, Trowbridge, Wiltshire

Library of Congress Cataloging-in-Publication Data

Available from the Publisher

British Library Cataloguing in Publication Data

A catalogue record for this book is available from
The British Library

ISBN 0 13 355827 4

1   2   3   4   5       00   99   98   97   96

*to Anna, Dominic, Sasha and Shamima*

# Contents

# Acknowledgements

The idea for this book originated in the early 1990s while we were both lecturers in European Politics and European Economics, respectively, at the University of North London. However, its first seeds were probably sown in the late 1970s when, as researchers at the European University Institute in Florence, we discovered the delights of Europe and discussed the necessity of an interdisciplinary approach to the understanding of European societies over a few leisurely glasses of wine in the University's Bar Fiasco.

Many people made contributions to the book's appearance. We must first of all thank Sue Lintner and Kika Lindner for their patience and support. Additionally, we would like to thank Farida Kulasi, the research assistant in the Department of Economics at London Guildhall University (LGU) for all her help in collating data, Ben Wynne at the University of North London (UNL) European Documentation Centre for helping us find our way around the maze of EU publications, Phil Pothen from LGU library for unravelling the mysteries of CD-ROM, Professor Mike Newman for his constant help, encouragement and patient reading of the various drafts, Professor Clive Church for his helpful comments, Professor George Hadjimatheou for his general support, Peter Gowan for his incisive comments on elites, Mike Koupland for his Herculean efforts in printing the various drafts, Frank Brouwer for keeping true to his name, Tony Conibear for his invaluable insights into regulation theory, Professor Alain Marchand for his comments on France, Rafael Ramos Garcia, Vince Wilkins, Sarah Podro, Simon Carroll, Jonathan Pass, Gerry Garby-Czerniawski and Henrike Bauer for their invaluable comments on the draft, Sergio Sacchi for his insights into contemporary Italy, Harold Wong Chee for his detailed knowledge of the Pacific Rim, Khatijah Ruhomutally for her invaluable clerical assistance, as well as other colleagues in European Studies at the UNL and in Economics at LGU. As ever, the responsibility for the views expressed, as well as for any errors and omissions, is solely ours.

David Edye
Valerio Lintner

London September 1995

# Map of the European Union

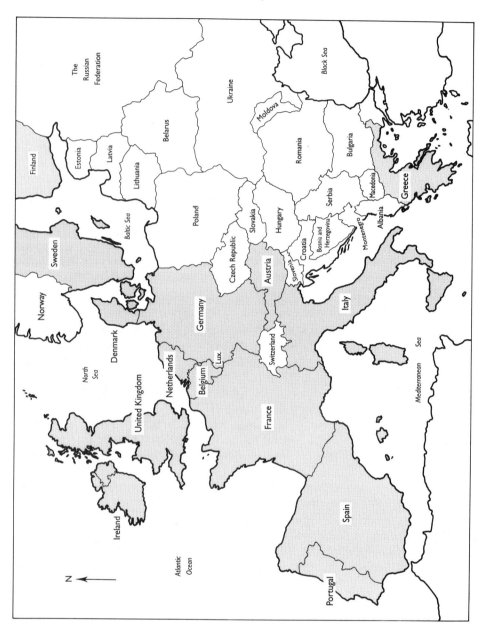

# CHAPTER ONE

# Contemporary Europe

## An Introduction

Europe ce petit cap d'Asie

PAUL VALÉRY

## 1.1 Scope and method

The fundamental objective of this book is to provide the reader with a rounded and comprehensive, but at the same time accessible, picture of the nature of modern European societies. The basic premise is that to understand a complex issue such as the nature of contemporary European society the view from one traditional subject discipline is not enough. The book therefore seeks to provide a view of Europe which is broadly interdisciplinary. We seek to look at contemporary Europe from an economic, political and social perspective.[1]

Politics is indeed distinguishable from economics and social life – but it cannot be understood as a distinct 'field' of activity, occurring in a separate realm or region of its own. It needs to be grasped, rather, as an aspect of all social relations (including economic relations), the aspect of conflict and struggle.[2]

Our approach is based within the general framework of the unity and diversity of the European experience. Any comparative analysis will tend to focus on the general at the expense of the particular, but there are sufficient common experiences and influences to be able to reach conclusions about the general direction of European societies.

We have been able to find and assess a great deal of both national and EU-generated data which have enabled us to analyse the most important trends in economics, politics and society throughout Western Europe and to a certain extent in East/Central Europe.

The book is intended to be of interest to economists, political scientists, sociologists and to students of emerging interdisciplinary areas such as European Studies, Policy Studies and International Relations alike, as well as to the general reader. This implies that in writing the book we assume limited prior knowledge of the specific concepts and techniques of each of these disciplines. In particular, our experience tends to suggest that economic analysis is an area that is particularly problematic for the non-specialist, and that many potential readers might suffer from a form of 'economic phobia'. The economics sections, therefore, are carefully devised so as to introduce the reader gently into the essence of the subject, at least in so far as it is required in order to understand the issues with which we deal.

The process of economic and political integration is of course a significant dimension of contemporary Europe. This supranational context is covered in the book, but our main emphasis is on Europe at the level of the nation state, and in particular the United Kingdom, France, Germany, Italy and Spain. Other countries are considered; for example, there are sections on Scandinavia, the Benelux countries and East/Central Europe in various parts of the book. The reality is that Europe still consists of a series of nation states, and will continue to do so for the foreseeable future. Even in the context of any European federal state that might emerge in the future, nation states or regions are likely to remain the focal point of many aspects of economic, political and social organisation. In any case a new federal Europe would inevitably be a product of the tastes, preferences, ideas and practices of the states that have formed it, hence our interest in the 'Europe of the Nations'. In examining Europe from this perspective, we have in mind a number of questions. The principal ones can be listed as follows:

- What is contemporary Europe like, and what are its fundamental economic, political and social characteristics?
- How and why did Europe develop into what it is?
- What are the similarities and differences between the different European nation states (the unity and diversity of contemporary Europe)?
- What influence do the individual features of the different European countries have on economic performance, on the sociopolitical arena, and on the general quality of life of European citizens?
- What are the emerging issues in today's Europe and how can they be interpreted and analysed?
- What is the external environment in which European states have to operate in the modern world?
- What is the role of the European nation state in the late twentieth century? What are the limits to its powers to control its own economic, political and social destiny in the context of an increasingly interdependent world (the national as opposed to supranational dimension of contemporary Europe)?
- What are the implications of the above for the future, and in particular for the possibility of further European integration, whatever the form that this might take?

The book is intended to shed some light on these matters and to promote a debate.

The contents of the book can be broadly seen as consisting of two parts. In the first part we seek to provide a theoretical context, in the second part we seek to apply the context to the analysis of specific issues, developments and policy areas. The context is essentially provided in the first four chapters. These are in some ways the 'core' of the text, and they are based on the principle that in order to understand what is happening in Europe we need to have a background which includes the essential dimensions of history and theory. In this, the first chapter, we examine what Europe is and survey the principal features of post-1945 European development. In the next three chapters we analyse the theoretical frameworks which underpin the choices that are open to European societies from an economic, political and social perspective. Thus Chapter 2 provides the essential economic theory required to understand modern Europe, concentrating on the theoretical basis of the mixed economy, while Chapter 3 examines the necessary political theory. Chapter 4 then considers the social basis of European societies.

From Chapter 5 onwards we apply what has come before to the analysis of structures and of particularly significant areas and developments. It is beyond the scope of this, or for that matter any other single book, to provide a comprehensive analysis of all the applied issues that arise from the framework we have developed previously. Our objective is thus to be selective, in the sense that we deal with the issues and areas that we feel are of particular significance to understanding the essential nature of contemporary Europe. We hope to whet the appetite sufficiently for readers to follow up issues and policies in which they become interested through further reading. An important objective of the book is to provide a framework which makes this possible.

Thus, Chapters 5 and 6 look at economic organisation and policy in the broad sense, deepening some of the issues raised in Chapter 2 and broadly highlighting how the issues raised therein have been resolved in various European countries. Chapter 5 outlines the common experiences and convergent parameters within which the European economies operate. It also introduces the increasingly important supra-national dimension to organisation and policy-making. Chapter 6 is a comparative study of the various interpretations one finds of the mixed economy, and of the essential 'cultures' of European capitalism. Chapter 7 discusses labour markets and labour market policies in European countries, while Chapter 8 looks at party systems and at mainstream political parties in various countries. Chapter 9 examines the emergence of alternative political parties and new social movements as actors in Europe. Chapter 10 then analyses government structures and executive power at national and regional levels. The penultimate chapter studies the social dimension of contemporary Europe. In this way we present a balanced coverage of the developments and policy issues that are most central to the understanding of the essential features of contemporary Europe. In Chapter 12 we provide a conclusion, in which we review the themes of the book, examine the implications and results of the unity and diversity that exists and has existed in Europe.

Additionally, there is an extensive Statistical Appendix which provides the data which are an essential background to understanding the issues covered in the book. The impact of the fundamental changes that have occurred in the former Soviet colonies in East/Central Europe since the late 1980s is not covered in a specific chapter, but is mentioned throughout.

## 1.2  What is Europe?

It is naturally difficult to delineate where Europe begins and ends. At the most basic level it is not clear whether it should be defined as a geographical zone, an historically determined area, an ethnically coherent area, an economically compatible space, or some mixture of all these elements. For example, is Turkey, a predominantly Muslim country with numerous unsuccessful applications to join the European Union, a part of Europe? Do we stop at the Urals, and only consider that part of Russia as part of Europe? Is Israel, a contestant in the Eurovision Song Contest, part of Europe? What about Malta and Cyprus, or Albania? The questions are fraught with difficulty.

Historically speaking, we could say that Europe stretches up to the Urals and is bounded by the Rome–Istanbul (Constantinople) axis; but with the collapse of the Soviet Empire all those supposedly fixed boundaries are shifting. For the purposes of this book, however, and so that we do not end up at the Kurile Islands in the Pacific Ocean, we have to make some choices.

Our instincts are to take a very wide view of Europe, but these ideological and philosophical positions must be tempered by practical imperatives. For the former Italian foreign minister Gianni de Michelis, Europe or the European Union (EU) consisted of a number of concentric circles, the widest of which included the United States! This position may be appealing to Atlantic internationalists, but it is impractical for our purposes. The emphasis of the book, therefore, is on the European 'core' where we live and work and the main area of preoccupation for our readership. We can define this as follows:

- The 12 states that constituted the European Community ([EC], or European Union [EU] in the post-Maastricht scenario) since the early 1980s, i.e. Germany, France, Italy, the United Kingdom, Spain, Netherlands, Belgium, Luxembourg, Denmark, Ireland, Portugal and Greece.
- The three new members of the EU that were previously European Free Trade Area (EFTA) members and, more recently, part of the European Economic Area (EEA), i.e. Austria, Sweden and Finland.[3] Switzerland, on the other hand, has rejected the EEA and thus the possibility of accession to the EU in the foreseeable future, while the Norwegian people for the second time in their history rejected the membership of the EU that their leaders had negotiated at a referendum in 1994.

This group, including Switzerland and Norway, can be regarded as the 'inner core' of contemporary Europe. To these groups can be added an 'outer core' of European states which consists of:

- the former Council for Mutual Economic Assistance (COMECON) countries that are geographically closest to the EU, i.e. Poland, Hungary, The Czech Republic, The Slovak Republic (which make up the Visegrad states), and Bulgaria and Romania. The first four countries currently have Europe agreements with the EU. These will be discussed in later chapters, but they essentially consist of trade agreements in which the principle of eventual full EU membership at some unspecified date in the future is accepted. The latter two states are also in the process of negotiating agreements with the EU, and will also probably seek full membership at some stage. These are all relatively small states, but they pose interesting problems and opportunities as they attempt a rapid transformation from communist centrally planned states to pluralist democracies with market economies. In any event, Table 1.1 shows the basic characteristics of most of the core countries with which we are concerned in the context of the situation in the United States and Japan.

From Table 1.1 it can be seen that the total Gross Domestic Product (GDP) of the Union is around 10 per cent greater than that of the United States, and about 64 per cent higher than that of Japan. Within the EU, Germany accounts for nearly 28 per cent of total GDP, followed by France (18.1 per cent), Italy (14.3 per cent) and the United Kingdom (13.7 per cent). The new entrants, although generally prosperous, are small countries that have only added marginally to total EU GDP. The tiny state of Luxembourg is the richest country in the EU in terms of per capita GDP. Of the larger countries, Germany is the richest in these terms, followed by Denmark, France and Austria. Greece, Portugal, Spain and Ireland are, in order, the poorest EU countries, while the United Kingdom has a per capita GDP which is now significantly below the EU average. Of the former EFTA entrants, Austria and Sweden have levels of national income per head above the EU average, while Finland's is below the EU average. In terms of the rest of the world, the EU average per capita GDP is still significantly below that of the United States, and even further below that of Japan, although the richest EU countries have a level of GDP per inhabitant which matches that of the United States.

In purely geographical area terms France is the largest of the EU countries, followed by Spain, Sweden, Germany, Finland, Italy and the United Kingdom. Apart from Luxembourg, Belgium is the smallest country in the EU, closely followed by the Netherlands, Denmark and Ireland. Germany, on the other hand, has the largest population in the EU, followed by the United Kingdom, Italy and France. The newly enlarged EU has a population roughly equivalent to that of the United States and Japan put together, making it in economic terms the most important market in the world. If we include the other European countries that we have not included in our 'core', then the importance of Europe as a market and as an economic entity in general is even further enhanced.

## 1.3 Post-1945 European development: how we arrived where we are

Europe, or at least the European Union is, as we have seen, now one of the richest and most sophisticated parts of the world. EU per capita income is far in excess of the average for the world as a whole. In economic terms, its societies enjoy a high standard of living, characterised by good diets (often too good in terms of obesity and heart disease), high consumption of consumer durables as well as leisure services such as entertainment and holidays abroad. Its citizens enjoy the relative security

**Table 1.1** Basic data of the European Union of '12' and of '15' compared with the United States and Japan (1993)

| | Area | | | Population* | | | Gross Domestic Product (GDP) | | | | GDP per inhabitant | |
|---|---|---|---|---|---|---|---|---|---|---|---|---|
| | 1000 km² | Eur12=100 | Eur15=100 | 1000 | Eur12=100 | Eur15=100 | Mrd. ECU | Eur12=100 | Eur15=100 | ECU/head | Eur12=100 | Eur15=100 |
| Belgium | 31 | 1.3 | 1.0 | 10 085 | 2.9 | 2.7 | 180.0 | 3.3 | 3.0 | 17 849 | 113 | 112 |
| Denmark | 43 | 1.8 | 1.3 | 5189 | 1.5 | 1.4 | 115.5 | 2.1 | 2.0 | 22 253 | 140 | 140 |
| Germany | 357 | 15.1 | 11.0 | 81 180 | 23.3 | 21.9 | 1631.5 | 29.5 | 27.6 | 20 097 | 127 | 126 |
| Greece | 132 | 5.6 | 4.1 | 10 362 | 3.0 | 2.8 | 76.7 | 1.4 | 1.3 | 7406 | 47 | 46 |
| Spain | 505 | 21.4 | 15.6 | 39 141 | 11.2 | 10.6 | 408.4 | 7.4 | 6.9 | 10 434 | 66 | 65 |
| France | 544 | 23.0 | 16.8 | 57 327 | 16.4 | 15.5 | 1068.6 | 19.3 | 18.1 | 18 640 | 118 | 117 |
| Ireland | 69 | 2.9 | 2.1 | 3561 | 1.0 | 1.0 | 40.4 | 0.7 | 0.7 | 11 334 | 72 | 71 |
| Italy | 301 | 12.7 | 9.3 | 58 098 | 16.7 | 15.7 | 847.3 | 15.3 | 14.3 | 14 584 | 92 | 91 |
| Luxembourg | 3 | 0.1 | 0.1 | 398 | 0.1 | 0.1 | 10.7 | 0.2 | 0.2 | 26 859 | 170 | 168 |
| Netherlands | 42 | 1.8 | 1.3 | 15 290 | 4.4 | 4.1 | 264.0 | 4.8 | 4.5 | 17 268 | 109 | 108 |
| Portugal | 92 | 3.9 | 2.8 | 9877 | 2.8 | 2.7 | 72.3 | 1.3 | 1.2 | 7323 | 46 | 46 |
| United Kingdom | 244 | 10.3 | 7.5 | 58 168 | 16.7 | 15.7 | 807.8 | 14.6 | 13.7 | 13 887 | 88 | 87 |
| Europe of 12 | 2363 | 100.0 | x | 348 676 | 100.0 | x | 5523.2 | 100.0 | x | 15 840 | 100 | x |
| Austria | 84 | x | 2.6 | 7991 | x | 2.2 | 155.5 | x | 2.6 | 19 453 | x | 122 |
| Finland | 338 | x | 10.4 | 5066 | x | 1.4 | 71.5 | x | 1.2 | 14 110 | x | 88 |
| Sweden | 450 | x | 13.9 | 8719 | x | 2.4 | 159.2 | x | 2.7 | 18 256 | x | 114 |
| Europe of 15 | 3235 | x | 100.0 | 370 452 | x | 100.0 | 5909.3 | x | 100.0 | 15 951 | x | 100.0 |
| United States | 9373 | 396.7 | 289.7 | 258 311 | 74.1 | 69.7 | 5367.4 | 97.2 | 90.8 | 20 779 | 131 | 130 |
| Japan | 378 | 16.0 | 11.7 | 124 674 | 35.8 | 33.7 | 3600.6 | 65.2 | 60.9 | 28 880 | 182 | 182 |

* The population data with regard to the concepts of National Accounts.
Source: Eurostat.

offered by historically high degrees of welfare provision. There is considerable variation across the countries in terms of this provision but nobody dies of hunger, although there is homelessness and outdoor sleeping in most of the major European cities. There is fairly general access to pension rights, although these again vary in their generosity. The political systems based on various forms of pluralist democracy provide government that is broadly functional and representative. The mass media ensure that information is presented about major events, despite obvious partisanship and over-concentration on particular issues. Social mores are, on the whole, influenced by liberal traditions. There is no death penalty in any EU state, and murders are sufficiently rare to merit large-scale media attention. Human rights are generally respected, and citizens are protected from exploitation and abuses under the law.

However, although this may be the general picture, there are serious imbalances in the distribution of privilege and material benefits within Europe. Poverty is widespread and increasing, equality before the law is often a myth, a large amount of resources are wasted on armaments, and the democratic system is under increasing strain in many countries. The rise and electoral success of extreme right wing parties is giving new impetus to expressions and practice of sexism and racism. Furthermore, Europe is a key player in the attempt to resolve the problem of growth and environmental degradation. Furthermore, the growing gap between the wealthy nations and those in the poorer regions of the world is of crucial significance as the continent increasingly resembles a fortress.

On the whole, however, people in Europe are beneficiaries of a comfortable material system. We consider next how good the real standard of living is, how the material benefits are distributed (unity and diversity) and thirdly, how Europe developed into what it is now. The objective is to trace the main trends that have shaped the nature of the continent, rather than provide a comprehensive account of the post-war development of Europe. Marginally greater weight is given to economic developments in this analysis.

### 1.3.1   The evolution of modern Europe: the economic dimension

The data collated in the Statistical Appendix to this book reveal a remarkable increase in the per capita income of all European countries during the years up to the early 1990s. These stark statistics encompass the extent of the economic development that has taken place in the continent over the last half-century or so. Needless to say, this development has been far from even. Some countries, notably Germany but also France, the Benelux countries and the Scandinavian countries have grown from the ashes of the war to become among the richest and most economically powerful countries in the world. Others, notably Italy and Spain, have grown from, essentially, a position among the most developed of the Less Developed Countries (LDCs) to advanced economies with, in Italy's case, a place in the G7 group of the most developed industrial countries in the world. Britain has continued on its long established path of relative decline in economic power, and has now been well and truly overtaken by the majority of continental European Union member states as the leading economic power in the continent. Here too, however, material standards of living have risen more or less consistently throughout the post-war period; nor have the fruits of economic growth been equally distributed geographically within countries. Most European states are characterised by substantial regional disparities and consequent 'regional problems', the Italian Mezzogiorno and the North and West of England being obvious examples. In addition, growing prosperity has not been shared evenly between citizens, and modern European countries are also characterised by substantial inequalities in the personal distribution of income and by the existence of a substantial incidence of poverty, not surprisingly often denied by governments.

There may not have been equal distribution, but there most certainly has been economic development, and it has been substantial in its dimensions. This section outlines the principal economic characteristics of this development and thus provides a broad sketch of the economic history of Europe since the Second World War.

If we trace the economic history of Europe from 1945 to the present day we can discern three distinct phases: a period of reconstruction to the early 1950s, a period of economic boom during the 'Keynesian consensus' of the 1950s and 1960s, and a period of crisis, introspection and neo-liberal revisionism during the 1980s and 1990s. We shall examine each in turn.

## Reconstruction

As one might expect, Europe emerged from the Second World War in a state of general economic devastation. War on the continent had raged for 6 years. This had of course resulted in massive death (around 40 million people were killed, including 17 million Russians and 6 million Jews), hardship and suffering, but it had also entailed widespread destruction of the economic infrastructure such as factories and communication systems, and the concentration of production on the goods required to wage hostilities: tanks, guns, ships, aeroplanes, uniforms and other military paraphernalia. In addition, agricultural output had collapsed because of shortages of labour and other resources, and distribution systems had all but broken down. The European economy thus could not produce enough of the goods and services required for normal life, and it urgently needed to be rebuilt and redirected.

Yet, out of these ashes, the phoenix of economic recovery rose far more rapidly than anyone had dared hope. There were of course differences in growth rates, but by the early 1950s industrial production was back to pre-war levels in all European countries. The star performer was West Germany, where by 1951 industrial output was 50 per cent higher than in 1936. Here, inflation was curtailed by a currency reform in 1948, while capitalists were encouraged to invest by substantial concessions granted by the government. At the same time wages were kept low by a mixture of compliant trade unions who accepted moderate wage settlements and who went on strike infrequently, and by a mass of skilled, mobile and willing refugee workers prepared to work long hours for low renumeration. Many West European countries followed analogous paths of restraining consumption and channelling resources into investment. There were, it has to be said, plenty of investment opportunities available because of the need to rebuild after the war, and because there was a backlog from the depressed 1930s. These parameters provided the historical conditions under which such a development strategy might work, and in post-war Europe it did.

Two other factors facilitated the reconstruction of Europe:

(a) Europe during this period benefited substantially from American aid under the Marshall Plan.[4] This has been criticised as an instrument of American imperialism in some quarters, and it is true that the United States needed an economically strong and ideologically compatible West Europe as a bulwark against what it regarded as the threat of the Communist Eastern Bloc, which had emerged during this period. Nevertheless, US injections of resources undoubtedly did play a significant role in the economic successes of the period, mainly by helping to reduce supply bottlenecks and by avoiding some of the short-term crises that would otherwise have constrained growth.

(b) The period saw the emergence of a new way of economic thinking.[5] The philosophical approach that was adopted towards economic affairs was a traditional capitalist one in many ways, but it was also different from that of the 1930s. The latter were years of *laissez-faire* liberal economics, in which the economic system was seen as being self-regulating, and in which the role of the state in controlling its outcomes was regarded as being strictly limited. Faith in this free market system had been shaken by the depression of the 1920s and 1930s, which brought with it mass unemployment and poverty and which spawned the Jarrow hunger marches in Britain, the legendary 'brother can you spare a dime' syndrome in the United States, and arguably the Second World War itself. But the war was, by necessity, a period of intervention in the economy in which governments directly controlled production and distribution in order to ensure the economic outcomes that were necessary in order to wage hostilities. After the war the feeling remained that if this had been done with some success to tackle the problems of war, then surely some form of intervention, albeit different and more limited in its extent, was surely appropriate in order to solve the problems of the peace. This, together with a greater interest in distribution and mass welfare that had emerged from the collective efforts and spirit that wartime perforce requires, made the time ripe for the economics of John Maynard Keynes, whose approach had been developed in the pre-war years. The basis of Keynesianism, as it has come to be known, is that governments are not necessarily helpless before the natural forces of capitalism, the 'hidden hand' as Adam Smith famously called it, but can take steps to alter outcomes such as high unemployment if they so desire. This was a message of hope, and it was embraced by West European societies. The basis of the European 'mixed economies', market systems with extensive state involvement, was thus laid. Different countries interpreted the mixed economy in different ways, and the various interpretations of the mixed economy is a central concern of this book.

In Britain the new Labour government significantly extended the role of the state in economic affairs. It implemented an ambitious programme of nationalisation, and above all it laid the foundations of the welfare state, creating the National Health

Service and establishing a comprehensive system of social security by implementing much of the Beveridge report.[6] At the same time reconstruction was slow for a country that had triumphed in the war, and Britain's position of economic pre-eminence was beginning to show signs of fading. Food was rationed until 1954, an attempt to restore the convertibility of sterling in 1947 failed as holders of the currency rushed into dollars and, above all, the United Kingdom's external position came under threat. Britain had traditionally been a net overseas creditor, but the American Lend Lease programme increased external debt to the point that for the first time since the eighteenth century the country became a net debtor. This increased the vulnerability of the British economy to short-term balance of payments fluctuations and laid the basis for the external constraints to growth and the consequent stop–go policies that were henceforth to condition the country's economic performance.

France suffered serious instability during this period, but managed to put into place the systems and institutions which were to facilitate rapid economic development in later years. The most important of these was the planning system. This was strongly influenced by the work of Etienne Clementel, who had helped to organise France's recovery from World War I. It originated as an emergency measure to manage the immediate post-war crisis, but eventually developed into a permanent means of influencing the economy. Le Plan, as it came to be known, has in one way or another dominated the French post-war economic scenario. French planning will be referred to in subsequent chapters. However, it is important at this stage to emphasise that it was essentially both non-socialist and flexible, without the firm production quotas such as were employed in the Soviet Union, but with sectoral targets which were then disaggregated to individual firm level, and with a fundamental reliance on cooperation rather than compulsion. It is no coincidence that the system came to be known as 'indicative planning' and was to be used as a model (with no great success) by other countries such as the United Kingdom. The system's success in France probably relied a great deal on the individuals involved (for example, Jean Monnet, who was to become one of the founding fathers of the European Economic Community), and on the fact that relations between leading industrialists and civil servants were traditionally cordial, both attending the same elite schools and frequenting similar circles.

In Belgium, reconstruction was facilitated by large dollar reserves that had built up from the sale of colonial (Congolese) uranium to the United States. This permitted the Belgians to set up a generous system of social security. In the Netherlands and Luxembourg the situation was more problematic, since resources were more scarce and the destruction of the war had been greater. Nevertheless, recovery there was, and the process was facilitated by the Benelux Agreement which had been concluded in 1944 by the Dutch, Belgian and Luxembourg governments in exile in London. This created a customs union between the three countries, and was to significantly influence subsequent European integration.

Of the Nordic countries, Finland emerged from the war in the worst position, having made the mistake of allying itself with the losing side. The consequent reparations, in the form of the compulsory supply of capital equipment, that had to be paid to the Soviet Union proved a hindrance to the process of reconstruction.

Raw materials and machinery had to be imported to meet Soviet demands, with predictable effects on the balance of payments. There was also a substantial resettlement problem caused by the surrender of territory gained from the Russians during the war. Sweden, on the other hand, emerged the strongest of the Scandinavian countries, using its neutrality to sell goods such as ball bearings to both sides of the conflict. The Swedes actually managed to increase national income during the war. Norway and Denmark, despite German occupation, also emerged relatively unscathed from the hostilities.

In Southern Europe the Iberian states of Spain and Portugal enjoyed the easiest recovery process, being poor and not very industrialised in the first place, having maintained their neutrality, and having benefited substantially from US aid as a result of the staunch anti-communism of their Fascist dictators Franco and Salazar. Italy and Greece had been occupied and had been the scene of substantial guerilla warfare, and in the case of Greece, civil war as well. Their problems were therefore commensurately greater.

The countries of East/Central Europe fell under the control of the Soviet Union during this period, and planned economies were established in all of them, in the context of Communist states and the ownership by the state of the means of production.

An important feature of the reconstruction period was that it saw the emergence of a new international economic order which was to facilitate the subsequent economic boom. In the West, the the basis of a new international economic system was laid down at Bretton Woods in New Hampshire in July 1944, where the 44 participating countries set up the basis of a regime aimed at achieving stable exchange rates, avoiding destabilising capital movements, liberalising trade and promoting international investment.

What emerged from Bretton Woods was a system of fixed exchange rates, whereby countries agreed to maintain the value of their currencies within 1 per cent of a par value expressed in gold or US$. There was a commitment on the part of countries to avoid the competitive devaluations which characterised the pre-war period, and short-term balance of payments deficits and exchange rate pressures were to be dealt by borrowing from a pool of foreign currency administered by the new International Monetary Fund (IMF), to which all members had to contribute part of their reserves according to their economic weight. Borrowing was to be conditional on members abiding by the 'rules of the game', which discouraged devaluation and encouraged countries to deal with external imbalances by deflationary internal policies, much as in the days of the pre-war Gold Standard. The system was underpinned by the United States, which agreed to peg the price of gold (at $32 per ounce) by selling gold at this price to all comers. Subsequently, the Organisation for European Economic Cooperation (OEEC), the forerunner of the Present Organisation for Economic Cooperation and Development (OECD), was set up to administer Marshall Aid. Economic development in the rest of the world was to be facilitated through the International Bank for Reconstruction and Development (IBRD, or World Bank).

Trade was to be liberalised through The General Agreement on Tariffs and Trade (GATT), which was set up in October 1947,[7] and which was to oversee a host of multilateral tariff reductions at various 'rounds' of negotiations, beginning with the Geneva Round in 1947. GATT is based on the 'most favoured nation' principle, whereby any tariff reductions have to be extended to all GATT members. Of particular significance for Europe was the creation of the European Coal and Steel Community (ECSC) in 1952, which was to prove the predecessor of the European Economic Community (EEC) and the present European Union (EU).

In East/Central Europe, the Council for Mutual Economic Assistance (CMEA, or COMECON) was created to promote cooperation and balanced exchange, always of course under the control of the former Soviet Union.

While the Russians were busy building their new empire, West European countries during this period were busy with the process of begining to shed their old ones. Thus former colonies in India, South-East Asia, Africa and the Middle East began to emerge as sovereign and independent nations, several to become Newly Industrialised Countries (NICs) in subsequent years. While formal political control over former colonies was gradually severed, in general important economic links with former colonies remained throughout this period, and they continued to be a source of cheap food, raw materials and even labour for European states.

## Keynesian consensus and economic boom

This period can be seen as covering the time from the early/mid-1950s to the late 1960s. It was a period of rapid economic growth in most countries under the umbrella of almost universal acceptance of the Keynesian model of how economies work and how economic policy should be conducted. This period of growth was probably kick-started by the Korean War of 1950–51 and by the subsequent US rearmament, which provided a Keynesian stimulus to the world economy. The boom continued throughout most of two decades, marginally interrupted by recessions in 1952, 1956–58, 1963 and 1967.[8] It was facilitated by:

(a) A plentiful supply of labour that was available in the agricultural sector of most European countries[9] for the expanding and more productive industries in the cities. When this source dried up, any possibility of a labour supply constraint to growth was obviated by an influx into the central European industrial heartland of migrant workers, at first from Southern Italy and then from Spain, Turkey and former colonies such as the British West Indies and the French Mahgreb.

(b) A plentiful supply of cheap energy, raw materials and food, often from existing and former colonies.

(c) An ever-growing demand for consumer durable and other goods by an increasing population and the hordes of new, often highly paid, industrial workers.

(d) The increased international trade which followed in the wake of the various GATT rounds and the creation of the EEC in 1957 and the European Free Trade Association (EFTA)[10] in 1959.

An indication of the dimension of the economic growth that was experienced during this period can be had if we consider that industrial output in France increased at an annual rate of 8–9 per cent during the 1950s and 1960s, while total output went up by around 5 per cent each year in the same period. In Germany, output rose 6.2 per cent annually and manufacturing production rose by 8 per cent a year during the 1950s and 1960s. Investment in West Germany averaged a remarkable 27 per cent of gross national product, increasing the capital stock fourfold, in the course of these two decades. Performance in the Benelux countries, Italy, Spain, Portugal, Austria, Switzerland and, to a slightly lesser extent, the Nordic countries was equally impressive. Only Britain lagged somewhat behind, industrial output growing at around half the European average during the boom. Britain's relatively poor performance has been commented on at length, and has been attributed to a host of factors ranging from the power of its organised labour, the deficiencies of its entrepreneurial classes and of its class system; through the difficulties it experienced in shedding its pretensions to world influence, which led to defence spending far greater than that of other European countries; to the small size of its agricultural sector; and the fact that its industrial infrastructure was not destroyed in the war, and thus did not have to be modernised to the same extent afterwards. The country's stop–go macroeconomic policies, necessitated by a serious balance of payments constraint to growth, which in turn grew from its structural weaknesses, certainly did not help. When the UK economy expanded it sucked in extra imports and had to be deflated to correct the consequent balance of payments deficit. Nevertheless, even the UK economy delivered unprecedented increases in the prosperity of its citizens.

Different interpretations of the mixed economy were, as we shall see, adopted by different countries, with France in particular experimenting with 'indicative planning'. However, there was widespread consensus along Keynesian lines as to how economies functioned and what was the appropriate way of managing them. The period was characterised by a widening of the definition of public and merit goods (see Chapter 3) and a rapid increase in public expenditure in all countries, generally concentrated and in particular in the Nordic states, on expanded welfare provision. It was also characterised by the widespread adoption of the **Fordist** model of mass production and consumption, and by the adoption of **Taylorism** as a means of work organisation (see Chapters 2, 5 and 7).

It should be noted that in this period it was not only the West European economies that grew at such a rapid rate, for the COMECON countries also experienced rapid industrialisation and growth, even allowing for difficulties in measuring its extent and the low base from which these countries started. Many developed from poor agricultural into substantial industrial economies during this period. The big structural problem was agriculture, which consistently failed to deliver the goods despite, or perhaps because of, attempts to collectivise the sector.

The party had to come to an end, and this duly occurred around the end of the 1960s and the beginning of the 1970s. The late 1960s saw increasing strains placed on the international monetary system that had served Europe and the rest of the world so well. The United States started running a large balance of payments deficit, and a lack of confidence in its ability to underpin the international system developed. In 1965 President DeGaulle began to exercise France's right to buy gold from the United States at the official price of $32 an ounce (considerably less that its real market value), and other countries followed suit until by 1971 the fixed price of the dollar in terms of gold collapsed and with it, in effect, went much of the Bretton Woods system, to be replaced eventually by a regime of flexible exchange rates.

Against this background of crisis in the international monetary system came internal crisis in Europe. This was probably precipitated by three factors:

1   Increased internal struggle over the distribution of income. The Fordist system of production had resulted in widespread disenchantment among European workforces, and more powerful trade unions began to win greater benefits for their members, at the expense of company profits. In Italy, for example, the 'hot autumn' of 1969 brought in its wake not only higher wages but also a plethora of rights, including indexation and the *Cassa Integrazione Guadagni*, which guaranteed an earnings replacement rate of 80 per cent for redundant workers, thus creating the 'Pompeiian economy', its workers frozen in place like the dead citizens of the famous Roman city. There was frequent industrial disruption, as in the Italian *autunno caldo* and in May 1968 in Paris, when workers and disaffected students joined forces to put the state under pressure of an unprecedented dimension in the post-war period.

2   Increased energy, raw material and commodity prices, typified of course by the leap in oil prices, which trebled during a brief period in 1973 and jumped again in 1979, as a result of the operation of the cartel run by the Organisation of Petroleum Exporting Countries (OPEC). This led to a substantial increase in input prices and a commensurate upward pressure on inflation, which was exacerbated by expansions in the money supply partly as a result of the need on the part of the United States to finance war in Vietnam.

3   The gradual shift in the comparative advantage in manufacturing which Europe had traditionally enjoyed away from the continent and towards the NICs, and in particular Japan, a trend which was to continue and intensify in subsequent years.

Panic reactions on the part of European governments, which deflated economies in response to the balance of payments problems which followed the oil price rise, did not help. In any case, profits were squeezed, growth slowed, and the early 1970s saw the emergence of the phenomenon of 'stagflation', unemployment and inflation increasing at the same time, contrary in principle to the basic predictions of the Keynesian system.

Many interpreted this as a shifting out of countries' Phillips curves[11] because of the worsening parameters within which economies had to operate, and tried to reverse the process by the use of, *inter alia*, incomes policies. Some renewed their interest in long-wave cycles of capitalism, such as those postulated by Kondratieff and Schumpeter (see Chapter 2), according to which the 1950s and 1960s had been an upswing phase, while the 1970s constituted the start of a downswing. Many others began to question the very basis of Keynesian economics, which was felt to have contributed to an excessive shift away from the market as an allocator of resources (see Chapter 2). The 'excessive' role for government, and consequently excessive public spending and taxation and loss of incentive, particularly for the middle classes, also came under attack. From this there gradually emerged a shift in economic consensus away from Keynesianism and back towards the classical belief in markets and liberal economics. The world had, in the previous 30 years or so, moved away from the classical model. Many believed that what was wrong was not the model but the world. It is this reinterpretation of the classical model which characterises the period from the late 1970s to the present day.

## Neo-liberalism

Neo-liberal economics originally took the label of 'monetarism', and was inspired by new interest in the Austrian economists such as Hayek and by the work of the American economist Milton Friedman. The precise nature of this and other forms of neo-liberal economic thinking which emerged during the course of the 1970s and 1980s will be considered in detail in Chapters 3 and 6. However, it was fundamentally based on a belief in the market as a basis for economic organisation. Keynesianism and interventionism in general had misguidedly interfered with the efficient functioning of the market system, and Europe and the world was paying the price in the form of economic stagnation. The answer was to cut the role of government and 'free the market'.

Hence the 1980s and 1990s have been the period of change, characterised by:

(a) attempts to cut public spending and the Keynesian welfare state, and a narrowing definition of what constitute public and merit goods (see Chapter 2);

(b) attempts to cut taxation;

(c) the acceptance of low inflation as the main objective of economic policy to be pursued by tight monetary policies, and at the expense of unemployment, which has risen steeply in the period;

(d) privatisation and deregulation. All this intensified by the collapse of communism and central planning in Eastern Europe, which has left the market unchallenged as a system of economic organisation, and has precipitated a rush to set up market economies at a frenetic pace in the former Soviet Union and the newly independent countries of Eastern and Central Europe.

(e) changes in the structure of production and employment, gradually moving away from the Fordist model of mass production and consumption towards some sort of post-Fordist paradigm based on specialisation and flexibility (see Chapter 2). Among other things, this has precipitated a large increase in outworking and in part-time (and often low-paid) work. It has also been a period of:

(f) increased economic interdependence caused by greatly increased trade and capital movements, in turn facilitated by financial market deregulation, by reductions in tariffs and non-tariff barriers to trade (NTBs) as a result of the GATT and European integration, and by a 'communications revolution'. Nation states have lost more of the ability to control their own economic destinies independently in isolation of what is happening elsewhere. Perhaps as a result of this, and in an attempt to recapture some of the lost economic sovereignty, there has been:

(g) an increasing tendency for countries to form regional blocs, in Europe's case of course the EC and subsequent EU.

European countries have operated within a framework of very stable European exchange rates under the aegis of the European Monetary System (EMS).[12] They have also faced increasingly serious competition in domestic and export markets from an expanding group of NICs, particularly from the countries around the 'Pacific Rim'.

Judgement of the success of the neo-liberal economic agenda is perhaps a little premature, but the signs so far are decidedly mixed. Rates of inflation in Europe have certainly fallen and converged. Growth has been steady, apart from recessions at the beginning of the 1980s and 1990s, but relatively slow, despite the early impetus to demand provided by arms spending in the Cold War. The increase in the trend growth of GDP which was supposed to result from the 'new realism' and from the move towards 'flexible specialisation' does not appear to have materialised. Profits have increased, but at the expense of economic equality. Unemployment has emerged as a major problem, arguably exacerbated by the restrictive policies that have been pursued, by the deregulation of labour markets, by the decline in the state as a job provider, as well as by the technological revolution that has taken place.

An interesting and radical interpretation of post-war European economic development is provided by what has come to be known as the **regulation** school of thought, which from an often neo-Marxian perspective attempts to provide some explanations for the cyclical and spatially uneven development of capitalist economies. According to this approach, the boom of the 1950s and 1960s fundamentally reflected a period when social institutions and structures, based on corporatism, Fordism, the welfare state and the Bretton Woods international system, succeeded in mediating and regulating the underlying conflicts which exist in capitalist economies, thus allowing accumulation and growth to take place in a relatively steady and unhindered fashion. The crisis of the 1970s, on the other hand, was precipitated when this institutional and structural balance broke down. There were essentially four dimensions to this collapse:

1. The decline of the Fordist/Taylorist method of production which slowed the rate of change of productivity.
2. The dismantling of the Bretton Woods system, which had regulated international economic relations.
3. The fiscal crisis of the state, which had previously provided a welfare system capable of containing conflict, but which was no longer in a position to do so at an acceptable cost in terms of taxation.
4. The expansion in the power of the NICs, who were now themselves adopting Fordist models of production.

Regulation theorists tend to regard the current situation as a period of restructuring (rather like the 1920s and 1930s), pending the emergence of a new order, the precise nature of which is uncertain. Some claim that this will be based on some kind of post-Fordist model, others that it will be based on 'flexible specialisation'.[13]

Whatever the view one chooses to take the future looks challenging, with increased competition from the NICs a certainty, with the problem of accommodating the East/Central states into the European System, with an increasing inability or unwillingness on the part of the United States to prop up the international economic system, with uncertainty surrounding the future of the European integration project, with threats to welfare provision arising partly from ageing populations, with increasing social problems, with the loss of the Cold War as a Keynesian stimulus to demand, and so on. One of the big issues concerns the future of employment on the continent, and how best to promote it: low wages and deregulation or investment in people and equipment? This is a microcosm of what is perhaps the biggest issue: the future of the neo-liberal agenda. Will the move towards unregulated markets intensify, or will a new and more eclectic order emerge out of the current situation? There is certainly some evidence of the re-emergence of a form of Keynesianism in some European countries. We shall see. These developments and issues will be taken up further in subsequent chapters of this book.

## 1.3.2   The evolution of modern Europe: the political dimension

The economic developments outlined above have taken place in the context of, and hand in hand with, developments in the political sphere. The post-1945 period has been characterised by continuity and change. The emergence of mainly liberal–democratic systems built around notions of consensual corporatism or enlightened *dirigisme* and the recent challenge of neo-liberalism are key features of these decades. Furthermore, there has been, more recently, the growth of new politics in the form of new social movements which have challenged traditional forms of participation and process.

The effect of the French Revolution is critical as the bench-mark against which the republican ideal was developed, and the threat against which monarchist states sought to defend themselves.[14] The first main expression of modern British conservative ideology was written by Edmund Burke, the Bristol MP, in 1790, entitled *Reflections on the Revolution in France*, in which he sought to outline and defend notions of custom, deference and traditional order against the Revolutionary programme. Other writers such as Thomas Paine, William Godwin and Mary Woolstonecraft presented clear support and commitment to the ideals of the Revolution. Even in 1989, during the celebrations to mark the bicentenary of the Revolution, the British Prime Minister on her visit to Paris challenged the notion that the Revolution had been an unqualified success, citing the massacres of pro-Royalist groups in the Vendée area of Western France as an eighteenth century equivalent of modern terrorism. Finally, the French Revolution is important in giving us the terms Left and Right, which referred to the position of the various parties in the semicircle of the National Assembly. Those parties most opposed to the monarchy sat on the left.

However, although the form of the State in terms of republic or monarchy has differed since 1789, there has been a growing similarity in the kinds of liberal democratic structures that have been introduced throughout Western Europe since 1945. Within Europe there are states with old established monarchies such as the United Kingdom, the Netherlands, Denmark and Sweden and, more recently, Spain, together with republics such as France, Italy, Ireland, the Federal Republic of Germany, and more recently the Czech Republic, Slovakia, Hungary and Poland.

All states in western and East/Central Europe now have political systems which can be defined as liberal–democratic. Since 1945 the number of such states in western

Europe has grown to include all countries, the most recent being Spain (1978). The East/Central European states have only joined this club since 1989. Although this is the contemporary situation, and suggests a certain uniformity between these states, the similarities and differences in their development will be assessed.

Questions of power and how the state is organised have concerned political scientists for thousands of years. Ever since human beings came to live together in communities and cities, attempts have been made to propose the most ideal form of political organisation. These issues are still alive in contemporary Europe and Chapter 3 begins by examining traditional and recent views on power and authority, as well as the debate about democracy. There are also very different views about how the state is organised and whose interests it serves. Since 1945 the importance of the state has grown in terms of its involvement in economic, political and social life. In many West European countries the proportion of GNP accounted for by the state sector has been consistently more than 40 per cent and in some countries, for example Sweden, it is much greater. The theories that are considered in Chapter 3 focus on the nature and role of the state, and the chapter ends with an analysis of what the state is and how it differs from civil society.

One result of this increased role of the state has been the growth of a bureaucracy, or civil service in British parlance, to manage it. The concentration of power in the hands of the executive has led many commentators to consider what the implications have been, first on the way in which policy is formulated and implemented and more generally on the democratic process. Questions about accountability and participation have been raised, and in Chapter 10 we look at these issues mainly in the West European context, making reference also to the role that interest and pressure groups may play in the policy making process. The second part of the chapter considers the nature and style of national governing processes based on our recurrent theme of unity and diversity, and the relative importance of subnational or regional structures of government.

The classic divide between left and right within the context of the Cold War has been one of the primary features of the post-1945 party system, but other major cleavages such as region, ethnicity, religion, language and, to a lesser extent, post-materialism have also come to play a significant role. Cleavages do not exist as isolated and exclusive categories, but should be seen operating in combinations, changing over time and varying in intensity. Lipset and Rokkan (1967) have explained the development of the party system in terms of cleavages between Centre/Periphery, State/Church, Urban/Rural and Labour/Capital.[15] The features of this system emerged after the First World War, and as a result of universal suffrage have remained more or less frozen to the present day. The same emphasis on stability of political systems was presented by Rose and Urwin.[16]

The events of the 1970s, which coincided with the end of the post-war boom, challenged this notion of 'frozen' party systems. The clear divide between left and right has diminished in importance, long-term voter alignments have declined, there is increasing electoral volatility and with the emergence of new parties and new social movements the question now is whether the party system is undergoing a process of dealignment from old positions to a possible realignment.[17] In discussing these various approaches we are concerned that we do not lose sight of the very real divides that existed and continue to exist within these supposedly 'stable' political systems, that may indicate a degree of fragility which terms like 'frozen' do not convey. Let us remember that a thaw usually follows a 'freeze', and there may be more thin ice around than we imagine. We consider these developments in Chapter 8.

In the 30 years from 1945 there appeared to be a growing consensus in the middle ground of politics expressed in the term 'Butskellism' in Britain (an amalgamation of the names of the two leading centrist politicians Conservative Butler and Labour leader Gaitskell). The middle way between Communism and capitalism was being defined in a social democratic and Christian democratic fashion. The oldest social democratic party in the world, the German Social Democrats (SPD), abandoned their overtly Marxist orientation at their party congress in Bad Godesberg in 1959 and moved towards the centre ground. They embraced the 'Social Market' philosophy expounded by Christian democrat Erhard, of mixing the market with public sector involvement. Three years previously Labour's Anthony Crosland had written a book entitled *The Future of Socialism* in which he stated that capitalism had undergone fundamental changes since the 1930s, and that Britain in 1956 was not capitalist in the nineteenth century sense of the term. The achievements of socialist governments had succeeded in getting right-wing parties to accept the basic tenets of intervention in terms of planning and the need to maintain full employment. The consequences of these developments for socialist parties implied a revision of standard party doctrine on key elements such as nationalisation.[18]

This continual tension between the various wings of the socialist movement, which lasted to 1989 and still echoes through to the present day, had its origins in the late nineteenth century debate among German socialists between reform and revolution. It began with the role set out for social democratic parties from the 1891 Erfurt programme.[19] The disagreements between Eduard Bernstein and August Bebel on the one hand and Rosa Luxemburg and Karl Liebknecht on the other, led to the eventual split in the SPD during the First World War, and the founding of the German Communist Party (KPD) by Luxemburg and Liebknecht in 1919. But most European social democratic and socialist parties held on to certain tenets of Marxism until the 1970s, particularly in their definition of being a party of the 'working class' and in controlling the command sectors of the economy through a comprehensive programme of nationalisation. These parties began to abandon their role as parties primarily of the working class, and become 'catch-all' (Kirchheimer, 1968) in the decades after 1959. The process of reform that was initiated by the SPD in that year spread beyond the socialist and social democratic parties to the West European communist parties. By the mid-1970s, the Spanish and Italian communist parties had developed a form of communism known as Euro-communism, which recognised the reality that the working class had changed and old ideas about revolution needed modifying.

On the centre right of the political spectrum, the Christian democratic parties of Germany (CDU) and Italy (DC) founded in the wake of the defeat of Fascism in 1945, as well as the British Conservative Party until 1979, were also concerned to mitigate the harshest effects of capitalism. The Italian DC, with the legacy of Mussolini's corporate state, developed into a party with a strong statist ideology whereas the West German CDU embraced a more free market approach, although in the classic formulation of *Soziale Markt* (The Social Market).[20] The Conservative Party in the United Kingdom accepted the basic tenets of the post-1945 consensus that the state had a role to play in managing the economy and trying to avoid the worst effects of unemployment.

For Fogarty, Christian democracy is:

a movement of those who aim to solve – with the aid of Christian principles and 'democratic' techniques – that range of temporal problems which the Church has repeatedly and solemnly declared to lie within the 'supreme' competence of the lay society, and outside direct ecclesiastical control.[21]

The challenge to Christian democracy and 'Butskellism' came during the 1970s and 1980s from the right of the political spectrum in the form of neo-liberalism. The United Kingdom has been the main centre for the neo-liberal experiment during the period of Conservative government from 1979 onwards. In essence, neo-liberals consider that the state has become too big and distant from the citizens it is supposed to serve and so needs to be cut back. Policies such as privatisation which are designed to reduce the role of the state in the economy are reflected by similar approaches in the political sphere. For example, the process of giving individual schools control over their budgets has been seen as a way of freeing them from the control of local government. However, one problem that has arisen from the whole neo-liberal experiment has been the need for a great deal of government legislation from the centre, which implies an increased rather than a reduced role for the state, so that in the example of autonomy for local schools above, control has passed from local government to central government. Many of these policies, particularly in the economic sphere, have found favour with other the major European governments.[22] We consider these issues in more detail in Chapter 2.

Among other explanations of what kinds of changes may take place within a country is the focus on a country's political culture in terms of its institutions, ideological orientation and general values that distinguish it from other states. Almond and Verba's (1965) major work *The Civic Culture* can be seen as the first comparative attempt to analyse and define the nature of each country's particular political system in terms of the components of its political culture; but their explanation tends to overstate the importance of the cultural over the economic as a determinant of a country's political system. It is similar to the explanation that there is some kind of national character which can be determined as the factor explaining why and how change takes place.[23] Furthermore, this kind of analysis does not take account of the way in which change results from the clash of opposing interests, and the resolution of those conflicts, which seems to us a more useful way to approach the whole question of how and why change takes place within a political system. Moreover, as Mény indicates, a presentation of one political culture within a particular country ignores the very real role played by subcultures within the national political culture, as for example in Italy until recently, with the Catholic and communist subcultures.[24]

In general, the overall approach that states have taken since 1945 can be categorised in two ways. The first group of countries, for example Sweden, the Federal Republic of Germany, and Britain until the late 1970s, followed a path of consensual corporatism in contrast to the enlightened *dirigisme*, or interventionism, as in the case of France, where the state played a very central role in directing the economy (*etatist*). The future is uncertain in terms of the nature of the political systems that will develop both at national and European level. The liberal-democratic state will continue, with debates over where and how power should be exercised. The issue of regional participation will become more important. The ideological divide between left and right seems to have almost disappeared, which raises questions about whether other kinds of ideas will lead to the formation of new parties or movements. All these issues are considered throughout the book.

### 1.3.3 The evolution of modern Europe: the social dimension

Together with this approach we shall also be trying to locate contemporary Europe within the context of the development of industrial societies over the last 200 years. For Giddens 'modernity' representing a new social order developed in Europe from the eighteenth century onwards and was characterised by four institutional dimensions: capitalism, industrialism, surveillance (the state control of information and monitoring) and military power.[25] In Chapter 4 we explore the way in which European societies have developed in the light of these four dimensions and present theories concerning class, gender and race to examine the nature of stability and change in any society. We will try to examine the course of events to see whether any pattern is emerging about the way in which these industrial societies are developing. Primarily we are concerned to see whether they are all becoming increasingly similar. This suggestion stems from some writers' belief that technological factors are the key determinants of society, and the more these or any other societies industrialise the more they converge (Kumar, 1978).

We shall also look at the way in which in the last decades of the twentieth century the whole basis of 'modernity' and progress is being challenged.[26] Are we living, in Beck's terms, in an orderly society which is progressing in a harmonious and stable manner, or are we rather living on the edge of a volcano which may erupt at any time? Perhaps a more vivid image of our progress is that of a runaway juggernaut called progress/modernity careering down into our world. We shall also consider whether terms such as 'post-modernism' and 'post-industrial society' are useful ways of describing our societies. Europe has a semblance of unity in its development in terms of notions of progress, the control of nature and the importance of technology, but it has also an experience of diversity, which will be highlighted.

The role of the state in the provision of welfare will be discussed in Chapter 11. This has been an important part of the social landscape in western European countries. Changes in the age structure of the population, together with increasing affluence and the reluctance of the new middle class to bear the required tax burden have brought into question the whole concept of the welfare state. The issues that arise in this context concern the social cohesion of European societies. The welfare state has been seen in the post-1945 period as the main guarantor of the necessary elements to hold society together. Ideas about social solidarity all stem from a belief that the state has a key role to play in ensuring that even those at the bottom of the pile do at least have some chances (i.e. provision of free health care, free education and cheap housing), and are not left completely to the mercies of the economic effects of capitalism.

The effect of a decline in social cohesion in a society is social exclusion, where large numbers of people are excluded from the benefits of the society. This happens because they are unemployed, partly employed, or in low-paid occupations, and the previous welfare provision has been systematically cut back so that there are no longer any 'cushions' against harsh economic circumstances. We treat these themes in terms of looking at the social exclusion of certain groups and the whole issue of whether an 'underclass' is forming.

Other key developments in the social arena have been the disappearance of the traditional blue collar working class and the emergence of a large middle class. Urbanisation, the increasing secularisation of European societies and the growing participation of women in the labour market have been important changes in the post-1945 period. The effect that all these developments have had on family life is an important factor in determining how people live together. The salience of migration, ethnicity and racism as issues that straddle economic, political and social boundaries will be examined.

The main social developments that have taken place in this period have been influenced by the process of increased industrialisation and urbanisation. The social dislocation that has resulted from the large-scale movements of people on a national level from the countryside to the towns and cities has been significant in terms of the effects on family structure and traditional domestic roles.

The growing participation of women in the labour force has been an important and growing feature, a new peacetime phenomenon, although a common feature of many wartime economies. The effect of this has been to force governments to provide child care and nursery education provision to varying degrees. In addition, international migration has also been a major influence on European societies, providing the necessary extra labour force for the 30-year post-war boom, and changing the ethnic composition of European societies.

This period has also seen a decline in religious participation, and with secularisation has meant that many European societies have become more materialist and consumerist, as people have distanced themselves from traditional beliefs. Many more couples are living together and having children out of wedlock, and there appears to be some change in who does what at home in terms of child care and household chores: in other words, the domestic division of labour. We shall attempt to examine all these trends in European societies to see whether they are leading to a harmonised and standardised kind of society.

# Further reading

Aldcroft, D. (1980) *The European Economy 1914–1980*, London: Croom Helm.

Almond, G. and Verba, S. (1965) *The Civic Culture Political Attitudes and Democracy in Five Nations*, Princeton, NJ: Princeton University Press.

Armstrong, P., Glyn, A. and Harrison, J. (1991) *Capitalism Since 1945*, Oxford: Blackwell.

Bailey, J. (ed.) (1992) *Social Europe*, London: Longman Sociology Series.

Blondel, J. (1990) *Comparative Government*, London: Philip Allan.

Calvert, P. (1993) *An Introduction to Comparative Politics*, Hemel Hempstead: Harvester Wheatsheaf.

Cipolla, C. (ed.) (1976) *The Fontana Economic History of Europe*, vols 5, 6, Glasgow: Fontana.

Dahl, R. A. (ed.) (1966) *Political Oppositions in Western Democracies*, New Haven: Yale University Press.

Giddens, A. (1981) *A Contemporary Critique of Historical Materialism*, London: Macmillan.

Giddens, A. (1985) *The Nation State and Violence*, Cambridge: Polity Press.

Giddens, A. (1987) *The Consequences of Modernity*, Cambridge: Polity Press.

Hague, R. and Harrop, M. (1988) *Comparative Politics and Government: An Introduction*, London: Macmillan.

Jones, C. (1993) *New Perspectives on the Welfare State in Europe*, London: Routledge.

Kavanagh, D. and Peele, G. (1984) *Comparative Government and Politics*, London: Heinemann.

Kirchheimer, O. (1968) in Dahl, R. A. (ed.) *Political Oppositions in Western Democracies*, New Haven: Yale University Press.

Kumar, K. (1978) *Prophecy and Progress, the Sociology of Industrial and Post-industrial Society*, London: Allen Lane.

Lash, S. and Urry, J. (1987) *The End of Organised Capitalism*, Cambridge: Polity Press.

Leys, C. (1989) *Politics in Britain*, London: Verso.

Maddison, A. (1982) *Phases of Capitalist Development*, Oxford: OUP.

Marglin, S. and Schor, J. (1990) *The Golden Age of Capitalism; Reinterpreting the Post-War Experience*, Oxford: OUP.

Mayer, L. and Burnett, J. (1993) *Comparative Politics*, London: Prentice Hall.

Mény, Y. (1993) *Government and Politics in Western Europe, Britain, France, Italy, Germany*, Oxford: OUP.

Milward, A. S. (1984) *The Reconstruction of Western Europe, 1945–51*, London: Methuen.

Nove, A. (1981) *An Economic History of the USSR*, Harmondsworth: Penguin.

Nove, A. (ed.) (1981) *The East European Economies in the 1970s*, London.

Paxman, J. (1990) *Friends in High Places*, London: Michael Joseph.

Sampson, A. (1971) *The New Anatomy of Britain*, London: Hodder & Stoughton.

Sampson, A. (1992) *The Essential Anatomy of Britain*, London: Hodder & Stoughton.

Tipton, F. B. and Aldrich, R. (1987) *An Economic and Social History of Europe: From 1939 to the Present*, London: Macmillan.

Van der Wee, H. (1986) *Prosperity and Upheaval: The World Economy 1945–1980*, Harmondsworth: Penguin.

Wilson, F. L. (1990) *European Politics Today*, London: Prentice Hall.

# Notes

1. In making this statement we are acutely aware that we are bound by the intellectual baggage that we have accumulated in our separate subject disciplines (politics and economics) over

the years, and that true interdisciplinarity is an elusive concept that possesses no real paradigm. Much of what we actually achieve may thus be regarded by some as multidisciplinarity rather than interdisciplinarity. Nevertheless, we feel that the issues are so important and the potential rewards so satisfying that we are keen to attempt this more rounded approach. For an interesting analysis and critique of the development of separate 'disciplines' in the social sciences see Wallerstein, I. (1990) 'World systems analysis' in *Social Theory Today*, Giddens, A. and Turner, J. (eds) Cambridge: Polity Press.

2. Leys, C. (1989) *Politics in Britain*, London: Verso, p. 12.
3. The EEA consisted essentially of an arrangement whereby the four freedoms contained in the EU Common Market and consolidated by the EC's 1992 programme (freedom of movement for goods, services, capital and labour) was extended to cover the EFTA area as well.
4. More than $13 billion was spent through the Marshall Aid programme, three-quarters of it going to Britain, France, Italy, West Germany and the Netherlands.
5. The detailed theoretical issues which need to be understood in this context are discussed at some length in Chapter 2.
6. William Beveridge's report in 1942 is widely held to have laid the foundations of the modern British welfare state.
7. At the subsequent Havana Conference in 1947–48 the USA and Britain had tried to set up a more ambitious system of trade liberalisation with an International Trade Organisation (ITO). Interestingly enough this idea has recently been revived following the belated signing of the Uruguay Round of the GATT. When the original ITO collapsed, the GATT took over the mantle with considerable success.
8. Interpreted by some as perhaps the ascending part of a long-run cycle, such as the 50-year cycles of capitalist economies postulated by the Russian economist Kondratieff.
9. Agricultural employment fell from 5.1 million to 3.9 million in West Germany between 1950–61, and from 8.3 million to 5.6 million in Italy over roughly the same period, for example. The exception was Britain where, significantly, the industrial revolution had happened earlier than in the rest of Europe and where the flight from the land had therefore already largely taken place.
10. Austria, Britain, Denmark, Norway, Portugal, Sweden and Switzerland.
11. The famous trade-off between inflation and unemployment which A. W. Phillips had first postulated in 1956, and which became the accepted wisdom during the 15 or 20 years that followed.
12. Despite periods of instability such the turbulence in the EMS in 1992 that eventually resulted in the exit of sterling and the lira from the system.
13. The nature of Regulation Theory will be considered in more detail in Chapter 2 of this book.
14. The 'politics and ideology [of the 19th century] were formed mainly by the French . . . a tricolour of some kind became the emblem of virtually every emerging nation, and European (or indeed world) politics between 1789 and 1917 were largely the struggle for and against the principles of 1789, or even the more incendiary ones of 1793'. Hobsbawm, E. J. (1980) *The Age of Revolution*, London: Sphere, p. 73.
15. Lipset, S. and Rokkan, S. (1967) *Party Systems and Voter Alignments: Cross National Perspectives*, New York: Free Press.
16. Rose, R. and Urwin, D. (1969) 'Social cohesion, political parties and strains in regimes' *Comparative Political Studies* 2, pp. 7–67.
17. Flanagan, S. C. and Dalton, R. J. (1984) Parties under stress: realignment and dealignment in advanced industrial societies, *WEP* 7.

18. Crosland, C. A. R. (1967) *The Future of Socialism*, London: Jonathan Cape.
19. Paterson, W. (1993) 'Reprogramming social democracy' in *Rethinking Social Democracy in Western Europe*, London: Frank Cass.
20. It was this emphasis on the market underpinned with strong elements of Christian notions of social solidarity that was embraced by the SPD after their Bad Godesberg conversion in the expression 'Soviel Markt wie möglich, soviel Staat wie nötig' [As much market as possible, as much state as necessary].
21. Fogarty in Smith, G. (1990) *Policy in Western Europe*, Aldershot: Gower, p. 54.
22. The French government led by the RPR (Gaullist) Prime Minister Chirac between 1986–88 began a series of privatisations.
23. Leys, C. (1989) p. 15.
24. Mény, Y. (1993) p. 2.
25. Giddens, A. (1981, 1985).
26. See Beck, W. (1992) *Risk Society*, London: Sage; Lash, S. and Urry, J. (1987) *The End of Organised Capitalism*. Cambridge: Polity Press.

CHAPTER TWO

---

# Market or state

## The theory of economic organisation in Europe

### 2.1  Background: fundamental economic problems and alternative means of solving them

We now turn to the first of the fundamental factors that determine the nature of European societies – economic organisation – before exploring the theoretical underpinnings of European societies from a political and social perspective in Chapters 3 and 4. This chapter thus seeks to analyse the theoretical background to the economic choices that contemporary European societies have made. The objective is to analyse the general features of the theoretical debate in this area, so as to provide the reader with some of the economic background required to make sense of what follows in the rest of the book. No prior knowledge of economic analysis is assumed. More specific analysis which is relevant to particular issues covered in the book is presented in the context of the relevant chapters.

At the very basis of this issue lies what economists are fond of calling the 'economic problem'. This arises from **scarcity**, i.e. the fact that the planet on which we live does not have sufficient resources (raw materials, people, etc.) to satisfy the wants and demands of its inhabitants. The word **want** is used advisedly here, since the more commonly used alternative, need, is a somewhat loaded concept. What we really **need** to satisfy the basic imperatives of existence is limited (food, clothing, shelter and the like), and in a Utopian universe there would be enough to go around and scarcity and world hunger would not exist. However, as commentators from Marx onwards have long pointed out, need is a relative concept which is fundamentally determined by nature of the society in which we operate. Hence in Europe we feel that we need televisions and (perhaps) cars and holidays, while in the third world the concept of need is of course much more modest.[1] Be that as it may, the existence of a mismatch between our wants and what the planet can deliver is the fundamental *raison d'être* for economics. We need to organise our societies in such a way as to make the most of what we have got. In other words we need to set up a system to **allocate scarce resources**, in order to achieve the best we can in terms of **efficiency** (maximising the relationship between inputs and outputs in production, and making what people really want to have) and **equity** (sharing out what we have produced in a way that we consider appropriate and fair). This will inevitably involve making choices, and

26

each item we produce and consume will have an **opportunity cost**, i.e. what we have to sacrifice in order to be able to enjoy it.

This economic problem is common to all societies whatever their nature and political basis. We need to solve it whether we live or want to live in a capitalist society, or a communist one, or for that matter a Maoist, Trotskyist, Anarchist, Fascist, totalitarian or democratic one. No matter what one's approach to life, this issue is quite simply inescapable. It is also a problem that is mind-bogglingly complex in its nature. Just consider how many millions of different goods and services are consumed in modern European societies on a daily basis and how many millions more primary and intermediate goods and services are required to produce these final products. How are we to decide just what is to be produced and in what quantities? And how are we to decide how what is produced is to be shared out among the millions of people and the multitude of groupings that constitute the population?

In the course of this century one can identify three approaches to solving this problem: **the market**, central **planning**, and **the mixed economy**. The first, in its purest form, represents the epitome of non-interventionism by the state; the second is its diametric opposite, with the state taking all the economic decisions; the third is a varying mixture of the first two. We shall briefly examine the essential nature of the market and planning mechanisms in turn from a theoretical standpoint, and we shall then proceed to evaluate the strengths and weaknesses of each and examine the case for the mixed economy – the model of economic organisation which has been preferred by the European countries with which we are most concerned in this book.

## 2.2   The market

In a market economy, resources are allocated on the basis of the disaggregated decisions of consumers deciding what they want to buy (**demand**), and of producers deciding what they wish to sell (**supply**).

Consumers make their decisions on the basis of the **utility** that they obtain from consuming a good or service, while the incentive for producers to produce arises from the desire to make as much **profit** as possible. The interaction of supply and demand takes place within a market and will determine just which goods and services are to be produced and how much of each of them will be made. There are in principle many millions of such markets, each determining the production and distribution of different goods and services in particular areas or localities. It is beyond the scope of this book to provide a detailed theoretical explanation of how markets operate.[2] It is nevertheless desirable to review the essence of the analysis, which is illustrated in Fig. 2.1. This illustrates the hypothetical case of a free market for spaghetti in Italy.

In the figure, the price of spaghetti (P) is measured along the vertical axis, while the quantity of spaghetti bought and sold (Q) is measured along the horizontal axis. DD is the demand curve for spaghetti. It slopes downwards from left to right, since according to the **law of demand** price is inversely related to demand, i.e. people buy more as prices fall and vice-versa. The position of the curve in the graph is determined by the **conditions of demand**, i.e. factors such as people's incomes, tastes, the price

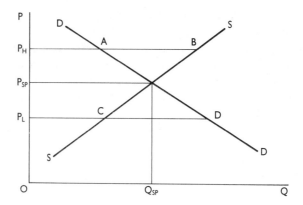

***Figure 2.1***   How markets allocate resources. A product market: the market for spaghetti in Italy

and availability of alternative goods that can be used to satisfy the same wants
(e.g. rice, potatoes, types of pasta), as well as a variety of other factors. If any of the
conditions of demand change, this will shift the curve as a whole. For example, if
spaghetti becomes more fashionable (e.g. as a part of the much vaunted
'Mediterranean diet') more spaghetti will be eaten at any given price, and DD will
shift to the right. If the price of rice falls, people will buy more rice and thus less
spaghetti at any given price, and DD will shift to the left. The shape and slope of the
curve, i.e. the extent that the demand for spaghetti is responsive to changes in price,
is measured by **price elasticity of demand**.

SS represents the supply curve for spaghetti. This slopes upwards from left to right,
since, according to the **law of supply**, it is assumed that producers will find it
profitable to offer more for sale at higher prices. The position of SS on the graph will
be determined by the **conditions of supply** (the price of inputs, technology, etc.). A
change in any of these will change how much spaghetti is offered for sale at various
prices, and will thus shift SS as a whole. The responsiveness of supply to changes in
price, and thus the shape and slope of the curve is determined by the **price elasticity
of supply**.

In Fig 2.1 the amount of spaghetti bought and sold, and thus the resources that are
allocated to its production, will be O–Qsp, where supply is equal to demand. Here
everybody is, in principle, satisfied: consumers can obtain all that they want at the
prevailing price, and producers can sell all that they want to produce at this price. It
is important to note that in this scenario it is price that plays a rationing role and brings
demand and supply together. O–Psp is the **equilibrium price** of spaghetti, the only
price that is stable and from which there is no tendency to change. A price higher
than Psp (for example O–PH) will result in a surplus of spaghetti (A–B), since
producers of spaghetti would wish to offer for sale more than consumers would wish
to buy and price will tend to fall to equilibrium; while a price lower than O–Psp (for
example O–PL) will result in shortage of spaghetti (C–D) thus inducing price to rise
towards equilibrium, and bringing supply and demand back into equality.

In this way the market resolves the efficiency aspect of the resource allocation problem; but what determines the equity aspect, or the **distribution** of what is produced? If price plays a rationing role in a market system, then it is the amount of money that one has which will determine the access of individuals to the fruits of the system. In a pure market economy, personal incomes will be in principle determined by a market process through the operation of **factor markets**, and in particular **capital markets** and **labour markets**. In the latter people supply their skills and labour, which are demanded by producers who want to use these to produce the goods and services to be sold in **product markets**.

The essential principles behind this are illustrated in Fig. 2.2, which shows a hypothetical **labour market** for workers in the Italian spaghetti industry. Here we measure the wage rate (W) which Italian spaghetti workers are paid (the price of labour) along the vertical axis, and employment (N) in the spaghetti industry (the quantity of labour) along the horizontal axis. DL represents the demand for labour. This is said to be in **derived demand**, that is labour demanded not for its own sake but for what it can produce. The demand for labour reflects its productivity (or marginal productivity,[3] to be more precise). The curve is downward-sloping because of the **law of diminishing returns**, i.e. increasing amounts of labour combined with a fixed amount of capital produce smaller and smaller additions to total production. The slope (elasticity) of the demand curve will be determined by factors such as the elasticity of demand for spaghetti in the product market, and will be greater in the long term than in the short term, reflecting the employers' greater ability to substitute capital for labour in the production process over a longer period. The position of the demand curve in the graph reflects the inherent productivity of spaghetti workers which is determined by a number of factors, one of which is the amount of **human capital** (education and training) embedded in the workers concerned. The greater the human capital the further to the right will be the demand curve, and thus the greater the wage it will be able to command. SL is the supply of labour curve, which is sometimes thought to bend backwards at higher wage rates. The interaction of the demand and supply of labour determines equilibrium wages for workers in the Italian spaghetti industry (O–Wsp) and thus the access of these workers to product markets, while O–Nsp represents the equilibrium number of people 'bought and sold' (i.e. employed) in this occupation.

The system can lay some claims to being 'fair', or at least meritocratic, in that the demand for labour is supposed to reflect its productivity and thus wages should reflect the economic worth of working people. In addition, if the labour market works as it is meant to there should be no such thing as unemployment, since at the equilibrium wage all who want to work are employed. In this scenario, unemployment can only occur in principle if there are 'imperfections' such as trade union power which cause the market not to clear and wages to remain above equilibrium. In Fig. 2.2, the persistence of the wage WH results in unemployment equivalent to A–B.

Similarly, the returns to capital are determined in **capital markets** by the interaction of supply and demand for the factor. The access of the owners of capital to the 'goodies' available in product markets is determined by the equilibrium **rental** or price of capital, which reflects the productivity of the factor of production. The alleged

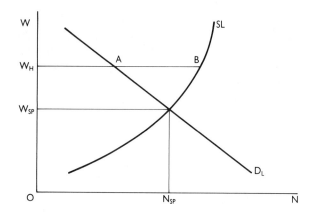

**Figure 2.2** How markets allocate resources. A factor market: the market for spaghetti workers in Italy

fairness of this lies in the fact that returns to the owners of capital reflect the inherent economic worth of the factor that they control.

Thus, in a pure market economy resources are allocated by what Adam Smith referred to as the 'invisible hand' through which people acting purely in their own individual interests and without regard to the common good of society 'promote an end (the public interest) which was no part of their intention'. The attraction of this lies in the fact that it is an automatic and self-regulating mechanism which, on the face of it, requires no action on the part of governments or anybody else in order to function. In fact in this world interference with the natural laws of the market serve only to reduce the overall level of welfare. This has led some commentators and politicians to associate pure markets with the appealing concept of **freedom**, since the system operates without compulsion on the part of the state. Others, as we shall see, would beg to differ.

In a pure market system the economic role of government is thus strictly limited. There is in principle no need for macroeconomic policy, since the economy as a whole regulates itself through the interaction of **aggregate demand** and **aggregate supply** much in the same fashion that individual markets do. This is simply illustrated in Fig. 2.3, which continues our hypothetical Italian example.

Here we measure the overall price level (P) along the vertical axis, and the level of GNP (Y) along the horizontal axis. AD represents aggregate (total) demand in the Italian economy. It slopes downwards from left to right partly because people's real income and thus their ability to buy declines as the price level increases, and partly because at higher price levels there will be more import penetration and lower exports. SAS represents the aggregate supply curve, which in the short term slopes upwards from left to right, reflecting the fact that real wage costs and profits are lower at higher price levels (assuming wages do not increase), and thus producers will want to produce more at these higher price levels. LAS is the Italian aggregate supply curve in the long term, and it is arguably vertical on the assumption that workers succeed

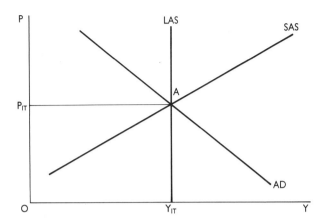

***Figure 2.3*** The Italian economy as a whole: aggregate demand and aggregate supply

in keeping their wages in line with rises in the price level (inflation). In these circumstances there is no incentive for firms to hire more employees and produce more as the price level increases. Macroeconomic equilibrium in Italy occurs at point A, at a price level O–PIt and a level of GNP O–YIt.

In this scenario, **economic growth** occurs automatically as a result of exogenous factors such as technical progress, and would be depicted by the LAS curve as a whole shifting to the right. Experience has shown that the path which growth follows in market economies is far from even, but in fact tends to occur in a cyclical manner characterised by periods of slow or negative growth (recession) followed by periods of boom. This is usually known as the **trade cycle**.

The system is thus often referred to as *laissez-faire*. It depends centrally on **competition** in order to achieve maximum efficiency: competitive producers need to minimise costs in order to survive and prosper. The penalty for failing to be efficient is bankruptcy. The writers and theoreticians who historically developed the intellectual basis of the market system, for example Pareto and Walras, have shown (under very restrictive assumptions) that perfect competition in all product and factor markets is a necessary condition for the maximisation of economic welfare in such a system. This is often referred to as **Pareto optimality**. To maximise welfare on a world scale, the *laissez-faire* system must operate in a context of free international exchange, that is **free trade**.

In practice, however, even the most diehard proponents of the market system would concede that the government has an important role to play in the operation of a successful market economy of even the purest kind. In essence, there are at least three essential structural prerequisites for such a market economy to function properly – even a free market economy cannot be fully free from any interference. These parameters in most cases can only be delivered by a government, and they will be considered in turn.

First, and perhaps most significantly, **property rights and private ownership must be guaranteed**. Governments in market economies need to legislate to ensure this, for without private property and the ability to pass it on to subsequent generations there would be no incentive for capitalists to accumulate capital.

Secondly, **competition and the operation of a free marketplace must be ensured**. Some of the basic arguments for this have been considered above, but it is a basic feature of capitalist economies that businessmen have every incentive to limit competition in their own markets so as to acquire the ability to raise prices and earn **supernormal** or **monopoly profits**. Governments therefore need to legislate to ensure that **monopolies** and **restrictive practices** are controlled. Failure to so do impairs the efficiency of resource allocation and results in welfare losses for the economy as a whole. A difficulty here is the possibility that in some cases monopoly power may actually be beneficial. This arises from the possible presence of **economies of scale**[4] and the need to promote the growth necessary for the dynamic efficiency of the system by facilitating **innovation through Research and Development** (R&D).[5] These imperatives may justify, in some industries, the existence of monopoly power and the large firms which accompany it. It renders the operation of anti-trust or anti-monopoly policy by governments a necessarily eclectic process. Competition, of course, is not solely a phenomenon relevant to the production side of the economy. It is also important for a government to ensure that consumers operate within a market which allows them to make 'rational' economic choices and put them into operation. Information is a key issue here. An additional aspect of this issue concerns free trade. Although many of today's capitalist economies developed into what they now are against a background of autarky, the logic of the market system would necessitate (increasingly so in today's shrinking and highly interdependent world) free international exchange in order to ensure competition and 'rational' resource allocation.

Finally, **the moral parameters within which the system works must be agreed and policed**. Totally unregulated, a capitalist system might come to resemble a jungle as both consumers and producers vie with each other for increased shares of the fruits of the planet: after all, the system is based on the concept that the greatest happiness of the greatest number can be achieved by everybody acting exclusively in their own private interests. The dangers of this for both equity and social harmony are evident. Unscrupulous and exploitative competitive behaviour may develop among producers, while consumers are likely to be tempted to resort to less than ethical means to improve their claims over the material fruits of the system. Additionally, because the market system relies fundamentally on inequality for its incentive structures, there is theoretically no real limit to the extent of poverty and deprivation which it may precipitate.[6] Assuming that a society believes that corruption (as well as other dubious forms of behaviour) and poverty are undesirable, or at least threaten the political permanence of the system, then it is incumbent on the government to make sure that economic activity takes place within an agreed and enforceable set of legal (or, at a pinch, self-regulated) parameters. An ancillary aspect of this issue is that **bankruptcies must be regulated**. As we have seen, the possibility of going out of business provides the incentive necessary to ensure efficiency within a capitalist system. Typically, between 2–6 per cent of firms in a market economy tend to become bankrupt in the course of any year, and the government of such a system consequently needs to ensure that these bankruptcies are not only a real threat, but that they occur within an organised and agreed framework.

Whether governments succeed in regulating the market or not, the above discussion can serve to provide us with important insights into the kind of society we can expect if we choose the free market as a means of allocating resources. Historically, of course, there have been other agencies and forces apart from the government which have provided checks and balances to the effects of the free market. For example, in Adam Smith's time this function was performed partly by the prevailing religious climate, which provided some moral parameters within which capitalists were obliged to operate. Today, however, it is difficult to envisage alternatives to the state and, as we shall discuss subsequently, perhaps even supranational governmental bodies, as a means of controlling the effects of the market.

## 2.3  Planning

The real alternative to the market as a means of resource allocation in the twentieth century has been planning. There are a number of variants of planning as a means of economic organisation, the best known of which is the **centrally planned economy**. The principles behind a centrally planned economy are diametrically opposed to those which underpin a pure market economy. The essence of this system is that the key decisions about what should be produced, in what quantities each good and service is produced, what prices should be charged and what wage each employee is to be paid are taken by bureaucrats operating through planning agencies or whatever organisation is charged with the task of allocating the resources that are available. Hence the association of this type of economic system with the concept of **control**. It follows that a prerequisite of such an economic set-up is complete or at least very widespread **ownership by the state of the means of production**. The essential principles of the operation of this are illustrated in Fig. 2.4, which shows the hypothetical allocation environment for cars in the centrally planned economy of the imaginary state of Trotskia.

Here, as in previous cases dealt with in this section, price (P) is measured along the vertical axis, quantity bought and sold (Q) is measured along the horizontal axis, and there is a downward-sloping demand curve (DD). The difference lies in the supply curve, which is vertical, the planning authorities having decreed that O–Qpl cars should be produced in Trotskia in a given period of time. The authorities also set the price of cars, which in our example would have to be O–Ppl if all the cars that consumers would want to purchase are to be available in the shops.

In light of this, it is not difficult to identify the fundamental prerequisites for the successful functioning of a planning system. In essence these are two:

(a)   The planning authorities have to be able to **estimate accurately how many** cars need to be produced (as well as precisely the millions of other goods and services that should be produced, and in which quantities each should be made). In our example, they have to be clear that O–Qpl represents a suitable number of cars to meet the needs of the population, bearing in mind the general constraints and competing

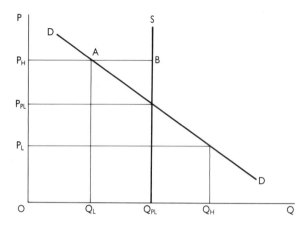

**Figure 2.4** Prices and production in a centrally planned economy: care in Trotskia

demands which inevitably face the economic system as a whole. In a market economy, of course, this problem does not in principle exist.

(b)   The planning authorities need to **determine a suitable price** to charge for cars. In our example, problems arise if the centrally determined price is different from O–Ppl. If it were set at, for instance, O–Ph, then there would be a surplus of cars equivalent to A–B, since supply (O–Qpl) would exceed demand (O–Ql) at this price. On the other hand if price was set below O–Ppl (O–Pl), then there would be a shortage of cars, since demand (O–Qh) would exceed supply (O–Qpl). In the case of a market system, these surpluses and shortages would be dynamically and automatically eliminated by the operation of the market mechanism. In a centrally planned economy, however, no such mechanism exists and therefore the imbalances between supply and demand can both exist and persist.

These are both essentially issues of **information**, which in theory should be eminently solvable. Planners need to be highly competent at their jobs and in touch with people's desires and the requirements of the economic system, but if they are not and their initial price and quantity estimates prove to be inappropriate, then a suitable **feedback mechanism** should be able to remedy matters. Large numbers of unsold cars would be a signal to cut prices in the short term and reduce production in the longer term, while long waiting list for cars would entail an increase in prices and (if this is possible) an increase in production in the long term. Even with such a feedback mechanism the problem of flexibility and adjustment arises, for although prices may be changed quickly, output targets might not be so easy to vary in a suitably rapid fashion. Changing the output of cars involves also changing the planned production of tyres, metals, plastics, glass and a host of other raw materials and intermediate products, for example.

This brings into focus another feature of planned economies, the large level of **inventories**, or stocks of goods, that they require. Inventories build up when prices have been set too high or output has been overestimated by the planners, and a surplus ensues. There is also every encouragement for enterprises to hoard inputs in order to be able to vary production in the context of the **uncertainty** which they face.

The basic macroeconomics of such a planned economy are, on the surface at least, simple to depict. The aggregate supply curve we discussed above (see Fig. 2.3) would be vertical (for example, LAS), since supply is in principle centrally determined by the authorities and thus independent of the price level. Given that the planning authorities also control the price level in a planned economy, overall imbalances between demand and supply can occur in much the same way as described in our microeconomic example above.

Central planning is not the only type of planning that has either been attempted or is conceivable. An interesting variant is the **market socialism** that has been experimented with during the post-war period in Yugoslavia and Hungary. This involves leaving allocation decisions to a market mechanism, while keeping the ownership of the means of production in public hands. The state's planners do not set production targets, but they determine prices to which public enterprises respond. A market mechanism is thus simulated. Such a system is perhaps superficially attractive to many as a potential means of achieving a degree of equity and efficiency at the same time, but unfortunately experience has shown that it does not work particularly well. The reasons for this are evident from our earlier discussions in this chapter. In reality the 'market mechanism' which is simulated is not really a market mechanism at all. For a start, planners rather than consumers determine prices in such a system, and thus the state, to a large extent, continues to control what is produced. This method of allocation also lacks the incentive mechanism of a true market system since there is no private ownership to reward accumulation, and the threat of bankruptcy as an incentive to efficiency is effectively removed because the state will ultimately subsidise loss-making firms (as well as taxing profitable ones).

It should be noted that forms of planning can also take place within market or mixed economies. For example, later in this book we shall discuss French Indicative Planning, the British attempts at a National Plan, and regional planning.

However, if we eliminate hybrid systems such as market socialism, and in the absence of a completely different model of how economic systems should be organised, then it is clear that the effective choice with which European societies have been faced has been between a market mechanism characterised by private ownership of the means of production, and a planned economy with ownership firmly in the hands of the state. We shall next discuss the relative merits of the two systems, and then the case for the mixed economy as a 'third way' of tackling the economic problem.

## 2.4   The relative merits of market and plan

Having considered the theoretical basis of Markets and Planning as means of allocating resources we now need to evaluate how each tends to work in practice, for the choice of how to organise an economy is a highly practical one: we are not interested in a system that looks extremely elegant on paper; rather, we want one which is going to deliver the goods (and the services!).

The first point to make in this context is that although twentieth century examples of more-or-less pure planning mechanisms abound,[7] there are no examples available of a textbook market economy. Even the economies that come closest to the model outlined above, such as the United States, have state sectors that are far larger and more active than the pure model would imply.

Nevertheless, one can come to some tentative conclusions, given what we can deduce from the theory which underpins each system, and given what we have been able to observe from the operation of each system in practice. The debate in this area is a long-standing one. In the 1930s, for example, the Polish economist Oscar Lange claimed that planning mechanisms would allocate resources more effectively by a continual process of changing prices and by ensuring that all resources were utilised, thus avoiding the mass unemployment that was experienced in market economies during the great depression. On the other hand, the Austrian school led by Ludwig von Mises and Friedrich von Hayek extolled the technical superiority of the market system. In general, the consensus would seem to be that market economies tend to be good at delivering efficiency, but not so effective when it comes to ensuring equity. Planned economies, on the other hand, tend to be less able to satisfy efficiency criteria, but perform better on equity; or, as Winston Churchill put it in a slightly jaundiced manner: 'The inherent vice of capitalism is the unequal sharing of blessings; the inherent virtue of socialism is the equal sharing of misery'.

The reasons for this are clear. Market economies tend to perform well on the **efficiency** front since the price mechanism, if it works properly, is inherently more flexible and thus responsive to demand. It is based on what is sometimes referred to as **consumer sovereignty**, the ability of consumers to determine what is produced by means of their purchasing power. A market mechanism thus does not have to rely on the ability of planners to get things right. The latter may well be able to predict reasonably accurately what the consumption and investment requirements of the state are. However, no matter how well-meaning and able they might be, they are unlikely to be able to forecast as accurately what many millions of private consumers will want to buy, or to react sufficiently swiftly to changes in the consumption patterns of citizens.

A further key point here concerns the issue of **incentives** to perform efficiently within the economic system. On a personal level, the incentive to perform well in one's employment is provided at the most basic level in a market system by the need to work to earn a living – no income is guaranteed to the unemployed in a pure market economy – and then by the possibility of enhancing one's standard of living by earning higher rewards for higher productivity.[8] On an enterprise or firm level, the incentive to be efficient is provided by the profit motive and by a well-defined penalty for failure, i.e. bankruptcy. In a planned economy, however, personal incentive is probably reduced by the fact that everyone is guaranteed a minimum standard of living no matter how productive they are.[9] This may be considered desirable on other grounds, but it is probably realistic to assume that in purely economic terms it does have a disincentive effect. At enterprise level, much incentive is removed by the absence of bankruptcy as a penalty for failure. In fact, inefficient enterprises are the ones that end up receiving subsidies from the state, while successful ones are taxed for their efficiency. In addition, enterprises have every interest in pushing for low targets that they can easily meet: hardly an incentive to enterprise.

This assumes, of course, that people are motivated solely by money and material considerations. It is perfectly possible to conceive of a situation where people positively believe in, for example, the communist system in which they live, and that the success of this system and a desire to promote the common good provides the incentive to be productive and responsible in the workplace. This position captures the moral high ground, but unfortunately the experience of planned communist economies this century has shown that such a belief in the system tends to break down – market economies do not have a monopoly in alienation – and when this happens we are left with base materialism as the source of incentive. Here market economies hold most of the trumps.

A further issue to consider in this context concerns the **size** of enterprises in planned economies. Experience has shown that planned economic systems tend to rely on extremely large production units,[10] which may in certain circumstances yield **economies of scale**, but which also tend to be unwieldy. This is not to say that size and dominant positions are not, as we shall see, a problem in market economies, but the fact is that planned economies tend to result in unbalanced productive structures, lacking small and medium-sized firms. Another issue here concerns the internal operation of enterprises under central planning. We have seen above how enterprises tend to hold a wastefully high level of **inventories** in order to tackle the problem of uncertainty of supply of intermediate goods. In addition there is little incentive to innovate and to develop and adopt advanced technologies (at least in the non-military sector), since there is the imperative to utilise the plentiful supply of labour. Finally, there is the issue of **quality**, or lack of it, due to the absence of incentive and to the phenomenon of **storming**, enterprises rushing to produce quantities of goods of dubious quality at the last moment in order to meet production targets before the end of a planning period.

Planned economies perform better than market economies in terms of **equity**, since the central planning authorities determine earnings and can thus engineer the distribution of income to meet this objective. In addition the lack of private property and of accumulation means that wealth cannot in principle become concentrated in the hands of a few. This is not to say that there will be complete equality, for in practice there will be a tendency for a privileged elite, such as the Communist Party hierarchy in the former Soviet Union, to develop; but the fundamental nature of a planning system is such that it should be possible to achieve a relatively equal and just society. On the other hand, inequality lies at the very heart of market economies. The pursuit of private income and wealth (or greed, to express the issue starkly) is, as we have seen, the basic incentive which makes the market system function, and it therefore follows that a pure market economy will be fundamentally characterised by great wealth co-existing alongside abject poverty. Indeed, it is often claimed that there is a trade-off between equity and efficiency in such an economy: the more equality there is, the less well the system functions. Be that as it may, it is generally held that weaknesses in efficiency have been the root cause of the apparent triumph of market economies which has occurred in recent years.

This issue is not quite as clear-cut as many would have us believe, or as a superficial analysis of events over the last 10 years or so might indicate. It is certainly true that the vast majority of planning systems have collapsed during this period, and that there seems at present little realistic alternative to the market as a system of resource allocation. However, planning does have some virtues. One should not forget that for a considerable period of time planning did succeed in raising living standards in countries such as Russia and in transforming them from a state of virtual feudalism into advanced industrial societies. It was in the next phase of development, when the demands of consumers became more ambitious and sophisticated, and when the associated planning decisions became commensurately more complex, that the systems really began to fail. Nor should it be assumed that the collapse of planning mechanisms was due to factors that are purely economic, for their demise was probably accelerated by the arms race of the Cold War, which forced the Soviet Union and its satellite states to forgo the production of consumer goods in order to produce weapons. Equally, the populations of East/Central European planned economies were clearly no longer willing to accept factors such as restrictions on mobility, human rights abuses and subjugation to Soviet imperialism.

A tentative conclusion might be that planning mechanisms in general work well enough from the point of view of efficiency as long as the decisions to be made are clear-cut and not too numerous. After all, all societies make widespread use of planning in times of crisis such as war. They fail to deliver, however, in situations where the decisions to be made are complex and numerous, where a market mechanism's automatic adjustment processes are more likely to ensure responsiveness to what consumers want.

## 2.5   The mixed economy

One important conclusion from the analysis presented above is that, although on balance one might prefer a market economy to a planned economy on the grounds of economic efficiency, there are serious problems associated with the pure *laissez-faire* approach we have discussed. A balanced view might be that neither system in its pure form is acceptable as a means of economic organisation in a society that seeks material prosperity, but not at the price of divisiveness and social disharmony. It is possibly because of this that the European countries with which we are concerned in this book during the post-war period have chosen in essence to organise their economies on the basis of an adapted form of the market, which has come to be known as **the mixed economy**. In this section we analyse the precise nature of the problems with markets, and in the process we examine the case for the adoption of one or other variant of the mixed economy model of economic organisation. In such a model resources are allocated essentially by a market mechanism, and the means of production are predominantly in the hands of private individuals and private enterprises, but the state plays a significant role in the functioning of the economy in order to achieve certain agreed social and political objectives, to correct some of the deficiencies of the free market and to make the market mechanism work better. Thus in many ways **the case for the mixed economy is the same as the case for varying degrees of state intervention in the functioning of a market economy**.

It is worth remembering that in this section we are concerned with a critique of the market from an economic point of view. There is more to this, and the debate here should be seen in the context of objections that have been levelled at the market from other perspectives. For example, the philosophical basis of the market has been criticised by various writers.[11]

The issue can be seen as consisting of microeconomic aspects as well as macroeconomic aspects, and the discussion will follow this division. Finally, some modern radical critiques of the operation of markets will be discussed.

### 2.5.1 The microeconomic case for mixed economies: market failure

Microeconomics concerns the study of economic behaviour at the level of individual decision makers, i.e. individual consumers and individual firms or producers. In a pure market system microeconomics is a more important explicator of economic outcomes than macroeconomics. At this level, the problems that a free market system throws up can be largely subsumed under the heading of **market failure**,[12] and from a broad neoclassical tradition it is this that provides the theoretical basis for government intervention in the market. One could identify very many types of market failure. Here we shall identify some of the principal ones which are relevant to our analysis of European societies in recent years.

#### Unequal distribution of personal income and wealth

As we have seen, the unhindered operation of markets leads necessarily to inequality. There are moral, political and economic reasons why societies might wish to engineer a more equitable distribution of income and wealth than the one which a free market provides. For example, if we return to the concept of freedom mentioned above, there is a case for claiming that economic freedom in the form of consumer sovereignty is of little use to people who do not have the economic means to exercise it. If it is true that inequality is an essential prerequisite for the efficient operation of a pure market economy, then those without economic means will constitute a sizeable proportion of the population, and a *laissez-faire* system will thus only work for a limited section of the population. This may reduce social cohesion and may in certain circumstances endanger the political stability of the society itself.[13] Thus even the 'winners' in a capitalist system may have a vested interest in promoting greater equality.

The classic means which can be used to attempt to reduce inequality consist of:

(a)  Use of a **progressive tax system** such as income tax, wealth tax or inheritance tax to raise money from the better off which can be used to:

(b)  **Redistribute** resources directly to the less well off, principally through direct cash payments via the social security system. Progressive taxation can also be used to provide goods and services for:

(c)  **Collective consumption**. For example, the state may provide **public goods** or **merit goods**. Public goods were defined in somewhat abstract fashion by Paul Samuelson in 1954 as goods and services which can be consumed by one individual without preventing their consumption by other individuals. This in contrast to private goods, whose consumption by an individual reduces the supply available to others. 'Pure' public goods, such as defence or law and order are made available to all consumers at zero direct cost; they are indivisible in that the benefits which accrue to each individual user are not measurable, and they are non-exclusive since all have access to them. Less pure public goods are subject to spatial limitations (they can only be enjoyed by people in a particular area), or to capacity limitations which reduce the non-competitive access of all to their benefits. The British National Health Service, for example, does not have the resources to treat all patients for all complaints, and resorts to implicit rationing of its provision. In practice, there are few public goods which can in all ways satisfy the conditions for 'purity', and most such goods would be regarded as 'mixed', to the extent that they contain private as well as public elements. For example, the use of public roads by motorists may affect the supply of the road system to other motorists by contributing to traffic congestion. Merit goods are goods that it is felt should be made available to as many people as possible because of the social benefits which their provision confers. Education and health provision are examples of such goods, but there are many others: social security entitlements, a fire-fighting service, cheap housing, public libraries, parks, and even subsidised food might be examples.

There are, by the same token, 'demerit' goods, the wide availability of which is considered harmful to the collective interest. An obvious example would be tobacco. It is important to note that there is no hard and fast definition of what should be provided by the state as a public good or a merit good, since many of these can be provided by both the public sector or the private sector.[14] The provision by the state of these goods is a result of preferences expressed through the political process, and the comprehensiveness of the definition of these goods can be seen as one indicator of the degree of 'mixedness' of an economy.

Be that as it may, by paying for public and merit goods through a progressive tax system and by providing them for free or for little cost, the state can in principle redistribute real income in a market economy, for many of the goods in question might be affordable in appropriate quantities only by the better off in a pure market system. They would thus in an overall sense be under-supplied by the market. This is not to say that the desire to promote greater equality is the sole reason for the state providing public or merit goods from the public purse. The state might want to provide public goods in order to rectify another aspect of market failure: **indivisibilities**, i.e. goods that are considered desirable but will not be provided by the market in response to demand by individuals. An example is defence – one cannot conceive of individuals going into a shop and wanting to buy an amount protection against aggression by a foreign power!

Similarly, it should also not be assumed that the provision of public goods and merit goods always redistributes income in favour of the less well off. Money spent by the state on defence and law and order, for example, favours predominantly the interests of those who own most property and thus have most to lose by lawlessness and political instability. Similarly, grants given to such institutions as the London Royal Opera House have been criticised as regressive since they subsidise artistic pursuits that are (unhappily) the domain of the better off in society. Given that the provision of public and merit goods is the result of the political process, one should not be surprised if the most powerful sections of a community often manage to skew provision of these goods in favour of their own interests.

(d)   Public ownership. State-owned industries can be operated in such a way as to charge lower prices than the free market would produce, any financial deficits then being made up by subsidies from progressive taxation. For example, nationalised industries have, at various times since the war, set prices equal to marginal cost, much lower than profit-maximising prices. Since the activities that have been taken into state hands tend to be utilities and so on, whose products account for a significant proportion of the expenditures of people on low incomes, this is one possible means of redistributing income, even though current economic orthodoxies would tend to preclude any extension of public ownership.[15]

(e)   Regulation. When (as has, of course, been the case recently) former nationalised activities are privatised, some of the controls discussed above can in principle be exercised by a regulator, although in practice the scope for action available to a regulator is likely to be much more limited. Naturally in a mixed economy a significant proportion of output will always be in the private sector. The activities of private sector firms can be controlled by means of a system of regulation, either directly enforceable through the legal framework or voluntary and monitored and policed by relevant industrial and professional bodies. In this context, the regulation would naturally have the objective of controlling commercial activity in order to produce a more just or more equitable society. To this end, the most important sphere for regulation is likely to be the labour market, where governments may wish to influence parameters such as maximum working hours, and minimum social entitlements. In general, the issue of regulation and how much of it there should be is, as we shall see in later chapters, a central area of debate concerning the operation of the European mixed economies.

(f)   **Direct intervention in the operation of the price mechanism**. Governments can attempt to redistribute income by controlling important prices through legislation. Examples of this are the rent controls which have operated in various European countries during the post-war period, and the minimum wage legislation which has similarly been operated in several European countries during this time. Economic liberals would claim that distorting the operation of markets in this way merely leads to resource misallocation and undesirable secondary effects, accommodation shortages and unemployment in the case of our two examples. To counter this possibility, the state may choose to let the market determine the prices of key goods and services and then ensure access to them by the less well off by means of a **subsidy**, in our examples a housing benefit and an income subsidy for low-paid employees.

## Unemployment

Experience has shown that market economies cannot guarantee full utilisation of a country's productive capacity and in fact unemployment, with all its economic wastefulness and social costs, has been a constant problem. There are essentially two views on the causes of unemployment. One would suggest that unemployment is fundamentally microeconomically determined in a situation where labour markets do not function properly and wages fail to fall towards equilibrium (see Fig. 2.2 above). In this case the role of the state would be to remove the factors that stop the market clearing (trade union power, restrictive practices, minimum wage mechanisms and so on). The alternative view is the Keynesian one, that unemployment is fundamentally macroeconomically determined by insufficient demand. This will be discussed in the section below on macroeconomic aspects. Both approaches will be further explored in Chapter 7 on labour markets, along with other aspects of labour market failure such as imperfect mobility of labour, mismatches between the demand and supply of particular skills, etc.

## Externalities

In a market system, decisions about what to produce and in what quantities are, as we have seen, taken by individual producers on the basis of their own internal private calculations, i.e. it is **private costs** and **private benefits**, usually of a purely financial kind, that determine these crucial allocative decisions. However, it is clear that economic activity in many instances has indirect effects on others, described also in the literature as 'spillover effects', 'third party effects', 'neighbourhood effects' or, in Pigou's parlance, 'uncompensated services or disservices'. These factors, however, do not enter into the private calculus. A privately run urban transport system will decide how many buses and trains to run and what fares to charge according to what will maximise the profits of the organisation. However, a public transport system also results in **social benefits** or **external economies** which do not influence the decisions of the transport organisation. For example, a cheap and effective urban transport system is likely to result in fewer private cars on the roads, and thus reduced pollution, less congestion, shorter journey times and perhaps even a reduced number of road accidents. Thus there is a divergence between private and social benefits in this case. If these externalities are taken into account and allocative decisions are taken on the more complete and socially desirable basis of their **social costs and benefits**, then the likelihood is that more transport services would be provided at a cheaper price. The existence of social benefits may in this way lead to a good or service being under-supplied.

Conversely, the existence of **social costs** may lead to a divergence between these and private costs which results in over-supply. For example, a chemical firm may discharge toxic waste into a river, killing wildlife, endangering human health and preventing local fishermen from exercising their trade. If these **external diseconomies** were taken into account, the ideal output of the chemical firm would be reduced.

A particular case of this type of market failure is the so-called **short-termism** which has been identified by some commentators[16] as particularly relevant to the United Kingdom (and will be considered in more detail in Chapter 6). The basis of it is that economic agents may take decisions over such factors as investment pay-back periods, dividend payments and so on which are designed to maximise returns to the individual organisation over the short term, while from the point of view of society as a whole a longer-term outlook might be more desirable. A further topical and absolutely crucial issue which can be analysed in terms of market failure concerns the **environment**. From an economic perspective, the root of our current environmental problems arises from the tradition of treating the 'biosphere'[17] as a free good, i.e. something that need not enter either the private (or the social) calculus in economic decision making. This was fine as long as the global level of economic activity was modest; but with world output now producing a level of pollution which potentially threatens the very future of life on earth, it has become vital for the biosphere to be treated as a scarce good, and priced as such.

Another issue which can be analysed in this fashion is **industrial policy**. This may take a variety of forms. On the most basic level, the external social benefits of economic activity in general may justify the facilitation of such activity by government. In particular, certain types of economic activity such as the development of small and medium-sized enterprises (SMEs), the promotion of export activities, or the establishment of 'national champions'[18] may be considered of particular strategic importance to warrant special treatment. Additionally, investment (especially in new technologies) and research and development (R&D) may be under-supplied as a result of allocative decisions made on the basis of the private internal calculus of industrial concerns. Yet R&D and investment may be considered to confer external benefits to society in the form of innovation and future employment,[19] such that governments may be justified in intervening to increase their provision. In addition to these proactive aspects of industrial policy, governments might feel justified in pursuing defensive industrial policies, aimed at protecting vulnerable firms from external competition or managing the rate of decline of certain industries (steel, shipbuilding, textiles, for example). This is in response to the external costs to society (unemployment, regional imbalances, etc.[20]) which result from economic adjustment that occurs at an excessively rapid pace.[21] A particular issue here concerns **de-industrialisation**, the process by which employment in manufacturing industry (the secondary sector) declines while employment in the service (or tertiary) sector expands. This is a secular trend in all European societies, and follows the historical shift that has already occurred away from the primary sector (argriculture, raw materials) and into the secondary sector. It brings with it many advantages: service sector activities often enhance the quality of life for consumers, employment in the tertiary sector is often (but not always) more pleasant. However, when the speed of this type of economic adjustment is so great that new jobs in services are insufficient to absorb the labour that is being shed by manufacturing, unemployment will result.[22] There is thus a case for using industrial policy to correct this particular form of negative externality. Similarly, **social regulation** (for example of labour markets) to eliminate factors such as discrimination and to encourage minimum standards for conditions of employment (see Chapter 7).

Accordingly, there is a case for the state to intervene to correct such imbalances between what is optimal from a private point of view and what is best from a collective perspective. The state could intervene in a number of ways. It could:

(a)  **Use taxes and subsidies** to correct the imbalances. This was first suggested by the economist Pigou, and involves taxing activities that generate negative externalities to reduce the quantity of these that is produced, and subsidising activities that result in positive externalities to increase their output. In our example, the government might tax the production of chemicals and subsidise urban transport. A further topical example is the carbon tax that is widely canvassed by environmentalists and others. Subsidies can take a number of forms: obvious ones such as direct cash payments or tax breaks, as well as less slightly less obvious ones such as the provision of social infrastructure (communications, training, etc.) which reduces internal costs to firms.

(b)  **Provide an activity directly as a public or merit good** (see above). In our example above, urban transport would be wholly or partly supplied by the state and supplied and priced according to social criteria.

(c)  **Regulate**, or intervene to ensure minimum standards. This could be done either by bargaining and voluntary agreement (**self-regulation**) or by legislation (**direct regulation**). In our examples, the chemical firm might be forced by law not to discharge waste into the river, and the urban transport corporation might be obliged to provide a minimum level of service at a fixed price.

## Information

If economic agents are to behave in a rational way, they require knowledge of the possibilities and of what is happening in the rest of the market. Such complete knowledge is rarely available, however, and imperfect information is a major factor which prevents the efficient functioning of markets as allocators of resources. There are clearly many ways in which the state could intervene to improve the quality of information available to economic agents. For example, the provision of vacancy information would allow the labour market to function more effectively, while measures to improve knowledge of technological developments might help product markets to work better.

## Instability

Markets, and especially financial markets, have a tendancy to overshoot – to rise too high in times of excess optimism, and to fall too low in more pessimistic periods. This can occur because of the 'sheep' mentality of some economic agents who merely follow what everyone else is doing, rather than attempt their own objective evaluation of situations. History is full of examples of this kind of 'stupid capitalism',[23] which is typically characterised by speculative bubbles that swell up only to burst leaving economic problems in their wake. Such instability can also result from **speculation**,[24] the incidence of which has been increased by the growth of trade in **financial derivatives**. The collapse of Barings Bank in 1995 is a case in point (see Fig. 2.5).

# The Barings crisis: why it happened

## FT writers explain the background to the great banking collapse

**Q: Why has Barings Bank collapsed?**
A: Apparently because of dealings by Nick Leeson, a 28-year-old trader employed by Barings in Singapore. Leeson is alleged to have acted without authorisation in trading huge numbers of Japanese futures and options contracts, the value of which fell sharply when the Tokyo stock market declined.

By the end of last week, his losses amounted to £625m, exceeding the bank's capital of £541m. As a result, Barings was unable to meet payments necessary to allow it to resume trading on Monday. Worse, the losses had the potential to rise further, undermining rescue efforts.

A syndicate of more than a dozen leading UK clearing and investment banks responded to calls from the Bank of England to organise a "lifeboat". They were prepared to re-capitalise Barings, but the fear of potential further losses on futures scuppered the deal.

**Q: How could a single trader run up such huge losses?**
A: We may not know until the administrator, Ernst & Young, and the Bank of England have completed their separate investigations.

The loss-making deals involved derivatives with a value reflecting that of the Nikkei 225, one of the Japanese equity market's main stock indices. Leeson traded futures contracts on both the Singapore International Monetary Exchange (Simex) and the Osaka Securities Exchange. Barings' Singapore office developed a profitable business by taking advantage of small price differences between the two, buying the contract on one exchange and selling it on the other.

In the past few months, Leeson appears to have shifted this strategy and amassed a huge "long" position at a time when Japanese stock prices were falling.

Because the contracts were traded on a derivatives exchange, Barings had to lodge collateral – known as the "variation margin" – at the end of each day, based on the difference between the amount paid for the contracts and their market value then. As a result, huge losses accumulated.

**Q: Why did Barings' management not spot what was happening?**
A: The evidence points to weak management controls. In Singapore, Leeson appears to have been in charge of both trading (agreeing and executing trades) and settlement (recording trades and monitoring the payment of collateral) – a highly unusual arrangement. This apparently allowed him to hide loss-making transactions in a secret account numbered 88888 – a Chinese lucky number. Senior executives of Barings in London were told by internal auditors last August that there was a risk Leeson could over-ride controls.

**Q: Who has profited from Barings' trading mistakes?**
A: Many international banks and securities firms which were trading on the same derivatives markets as Barings. Just as Leeson was a heavy buyer of the Nikkei 225 contracts, many other traders were big sellers.

When Barings was forced to post losses on the Singapore and Osaka exchanges, these traders made money – although it is difficult to be more specific than that. But some of these same firms could end up paying out to meet calls Barings is now unable to make.

Both exchanges, like many other international futures and options exchanges, are linked to clearing houses, which effectively guarantee trades. If a member defaults – as in this case – the exchanges make good the margin calls through a central clearing fund made up from members' contributions.

The exchanges also have their own resources from which payments can be made. And if these two tranches of protection are exhausted, the clearing house can call on its members to meet losses.

**Q: Who has lost money?**
A: The owners of the group – the Baring Foundation and senior executive management – have almost certainly lost their equity in the bank. British charities and the arts will lose out because the foundation, the UK's ninth largest grant-making trust, expects its annual income to fall from £14m to just over £2m because of the bank's collapse.

The position of depositors with the bank and other creditors depends on what deal Ernst & Young can strike with buyers of Barings' assets. If, as seemed possible yesterday, it sells the Barings Group to ING, a Dutch banking and insurance group – even for £1 – then any losses may be slight or even non-existent.

Those most at risk are Barings' depositors, whose £2.5bn of funds has been frozen. If the worst happened, other banks (which account for about £1bn of the deposits) would get nothing. Other depositors such as local councils, pension funds, charities and building societies, would get 75 per cent of their deposits back, but only up to a maximum of £15,000.

Clients of Baring Asset Management, the group's fund management arm, have their investments "ring fenced": that is, protected legally against creditors. But Barings has an in-house custodian which holds some clients' assets in trust – and the Custodian uses Barings Bank as the depositor for client cash balances. The clients must stand in line with other creditors to get these cash balances back.

Although Barings' unit trusts were suspended during the week, dealing resumed on Thursday. Since then there have been negligible withdrawals from Barings by unit-holders. The position of offshore investment companies – the Dublin-based funds and the Guernsey-based Baring Chrysalis and Baring Emerging Europe – is more complex.

**Q: Could this happen to another bank? Should I be concerned about my savings?**
A: Don't panic. High street banks have billions of pounds of assets. They could sustain heavy losses in one or another area of business without being at risk.

As for very small banks, the failure to launch a lifeboat has undoubtedly caused a frisson through the City. But it could mean that banks generally become

*Figure 2.5* The Barings crisis: why it happened
*Source: Financial Times, 4/3/95*

more secure as supervisors recommend improvements in control systems.

**Q: Should the Bank have done more to save Barings?**
A: The case for the Bank putting taxpayers' money at risk was weak because Barings was too small to pose a serious threat to the banking system as a whole. But some argue that the Bank should have stepped in to save the good name of the City. Yet the depositors were mainly City professionals who knew that the Bank's implicit guarantee for the accepting houses had been removed long ago. And, given the circumstances the politics of bailing out depositors would have been difficult.

**Q: Has the collapse damaged the world's financial system?**
A: The chief impact has been felt in Japan, where equities fell initially by 3.8 per cent on the news. Since Japanese banks have large equity holdings, this posed a modest threat to their capital.

In the UK, sterling and equities weakened a little after the collapse but, if there has been contagion at other UK merchant banks, it appears to have been contained so far. In the longer run, it seems likely depositors will demand higher interest rates from UK merchant banks.

Greater polarisation of big and small institutions is a probable consequence of the Bank's decision not to act as a lender of last resort.

**Q: This surely underlines the dangers to the global**

**financial system of futures and other derivative products?**
A: Yes. The global banking system is already accident prone, having experienced crises with property lending in 1974, third world debt in 1982, and more property and financial trouble in the early 1990s.

Banks look increasingly to speculative trading activity in the markets for their profits, and the widespread assumption that central banks will stand behind large banks that run into trouble has encouraged risk-taking. The growth of derivatives against this unstable background is clearly a worry.

**Q: What does Barings' collapse tell us about Britain's much vaunted competitiveness in the global financial services industry?**
A: Britain's strength in this area derives only marginally from the activities of British-owned merchant banks. Its competitive edge comes mainly from the activities of the (mainly foreign) investment and commercial banks that choose London as their base to do euromarket business in the European time zone.

All investment banks across the world have been finding the going tough of late. It could be that Barings tells us more about the future polarisation of banking between big and small banks than about the competitiveness of the UK in financial services.

■ **Contributors:** *John Plender, Richard Lapper, Alison Smith, Peter Montagnon and John Gapper.*

**Figure 2.5** *Continued*

In such circumstances the role of the state is to set rules for the market designed to prevent such events from occurring, and to intervene at appropriate times. A further dimension of the inherent instability of market economies concerns the **trade cycles** referred to above. This is essentially an issue of macroeconomic management (with the objective of evening out the cyclical swings), which is discussed below.

## Monopoly

We have seen above how the existence of competition is an essential prerequisite for the achievement of the 'Pareto optimality' we discussed above, and thus of a welfare maximising allocation of resources in a market economy. However, as various commentators have observed,[25] there is a tendency in market economies for monopoly power to develop, reducing overall welfare in market economies and transferring resources from consumers to producers. Monopoly power can take the form of dominant positions in markets (textbook monopoly), or of price fixing or market sharing cartels in oligopolistic markets. In this context one can observe that the state can attempt to correct this type of market failure by pursuing a competition or anti-trust policy.

## Imbalance in the spatial distribution of economic activity

The free operation of market economies tends to result in the concentration of economic activity in certain areas to the relative detriment of others, thus resulting in what are generally referred to as 'regional problems'. Again, this will be examined in some detail in subsequent chapters and in the context of the radical critiques discussed later in this chapter, but here it can be noted that the obvious solution might be to pursue some form of regional policy designed to shift economic activity to less prosperous areas. Such a policy might consist of a 'work-to workers' approach (encouraging investment in the regions or in inner cities) and/or a 'workers-to-work' approach (encouraging labour mobility).

Before we leave this consideration of market failure and state intervention in the operation of markets, it is worth noting that there is a theoretical problem associated with partial and piecemeal intervention by governments in the operation of markets at the microeconomic level. This is generally referred to as the **theory of second best**. Developed originally by Lipsey and Lancaster (1957) in the context of the theory of international trade, this demonstrates mathematically and under restrictive assumptions that, in the presence of a number of market imperfections, intervention to correct one of them does not necessarily make the overall allocation of resources and thus the level of welfare better. In fact it could make the overall situation worse. Taken at face value, the theory of second best would be a recipe for total inaction by the state. However, it is a highly abstract proposition that in practice has been largely ignored by policy makers. Nevertheless, its existence does provide a challenge of sorts to the theory of government intervention in market economies.

### 2.5.2 Macroeconomic dimensions of the mixed economy: Keynesianism and its neo-liberal critique

The aim of this section is to examine briefly the essence of the case for government intervention in a market economy at the macroeconomic level.[26] Macroeconomics deals with the functioning of the economy as a whole. As such it concerns issues such as the level of employment and unemployment, the level of National Income, the rate of growth, the balance of payments and the rate of inflation in an economy.

The pure market approach to macroeconomics was to an extent outlined above (see Fig. 2.3), and in essence it consists of the view that macroeconomic outcomes are determined by the aggregated operation of the various markets that make the basic allocation decisions in different parts of the economy. The policy implication of the pure market position at a macroeconomic level is thus similar to the one we have discussed at the microeconomic level, that is that the best possible outcome will be achieved when markets are left well alone by the state. There is thus little or no role for government intervention in the operation of the economy at the macroeconomic level. The role of the state is limited to policing the free operation of markets and ensuring 'sound money', that is an acceptable rate of inflation. This is the *laissez-faire* position that was taken by the so-called **classical** school of economists who dominanted economic thinking until the Second World War. Their position can best be illustrated by means of a simple **circular flow model** such as the one shown in Fig. 2.6, which examines the hypothetical case of the Italian economy following the example we have established in this chapter.

Figure 2.6 illustrates the fundamental macroeconomic relationships which exist in the Italian or any other economy. The 'firms' box represents the basic production side of the economy, while households are the basic consumption unit. Italian people live in households, and they work in and provide other factor services to firms. In return for their efforts they receive income which is equivalent to the value of what is produced by the firms. This income is then naturally spent on the goods and services that are produced, and so on. The fundamental proposition here is that the supply of goods and services in the Italian economy creates its own demand, since the income which is generated through production leads to expenditure which is just sufficient to buy the goods and services that are produced. This is generally known as **Say's law**, after the nineteenth century French economist Jean Baptiste Say. There may be leakages from this circular flow in the form of savings, but these are exactly compensated by injections into the flow in the form of investment spending. Savings and investment are determined in the capital market and kept constantly equal to one another by changes in the rate of interest. It is the equilibrium level of employment generated in the labour market (see Fig. 2.2 above) that determines the level of output in the Italian economy, and thus the volume of money flowing around the circular flow. In this world the economy will always operate at full employment and there can thus be no unemployment, since the free operation of the labour market ensures the equality of the demand for and the supply of labour (see Fig. 2.2); nor can there be over-production. The model is crucially dependent on three assumptions: that savings and investment are determined by the rate of interest, that wages, prices and interest rates are flexible in both directions, and that a high degree of competition exists in the economy.

This *laissez-faire* approach to the economy at the macro level began to be questioned during the great depression of the 1930s, which was characterised by the kind of mass

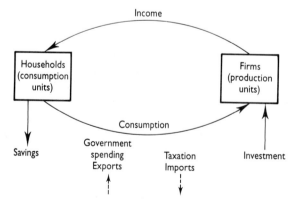

**Figure 2.6**　A simple circular flow of income model of the Italian economy

unemployment which should have been impossible according to the classical model. From the debate that ensued there emerged a new approach to macroeconomics, which has come to be known as Keynesianism after its initiator John Maynard Keynes,[27] and it is this that provides the basic case for government intervention at the macroeconomic level.

According to Keynes, classical theory is flawed in two senses:

(a)  It ignores monopoly and other imperfections in product and factor (particularly labour) markets. These make it likely that prices and wages will be inflexible, particularly downwards and in the short term.

(b)  It wrongly assumes that savings will always be kept equal to investment by movements in the rate of interest. Savings and investment are influenced by factors other than the rate of interest (for example the level of national income and business expectations). In any case there are other injections into the circular flow (demand from abroad in the form of exports and expenditure by governments) as well as other withdrawals from the circular flow (demand for goods and services produced abroad, and taxation by the state).

Because of this, Say's law does not hold, and it is perfectly possible for total demand in the economy to be less than the total value of production. In this case firms will lay off workers and there will be **demand deficient unemployment**. According to Keynes, the overall level of economic activity, of production and of employment in the economy, will depend on the level of (aggregate) demand. If we want to have full employment we must have a level of aggregate demand sufficient to generate it. If aggregate demand is insufficient to generate an amount of production which will secure full employment, then the state has the power to intervene to correct the situation. This can be done by taking measures to increase the level of demand, which in turn can be achieved by increasing one or more of the constituent parts of aggregate demand in an economy. These consist of private consumption, investment spending, government spending and the net effect of the foreign sector (exports minus imports). These can be increased principally by the use of appropriate fiscal policies (government spending and taxation) and/or monetary policies (policies which affect money markets and the rate of interest), although the extreme Keynesian position would favour using the former. For example, demand could be stimulated and unemployment reduced by one or more of the following:

(a)  direct increases in government spending, 'paying people to dig holes and then paying them to fill them in again' to paraphrase a famous quotation by Keynes;
(b)  cuts in taxation, which increase people's disposable income and thus stimulate consumption;
(c)  reductions in the rate of interest, which stimulate investment and consumption;
(d)  any other measure which increases exports and encourages import substitution (e.g. devaluation of the currency); and
(e)  any other measure which leads to an increase in consumption and investment or a fall in savings (e.g. relaxation in the legal framework for borrowing, investment subsidies).

Whatever method of intervention is adopted, the initial stimulation of demand is amplified by a **multiplier effect** on national income. The size of the multiplier depends on the **marginal propensities to save, tax and import**, i.e. the proportion of any increase in national income which goes on saving, taxation or purchases from abroad. The larger these withdrawals from the circular flow, the smaller the multiplier.

Naturally, in this model of the world policy has sometimes to be deployed in a deflationary direction. If demand in the economy exceeds production, then firms will expand output until all available resources are deployed, but after this point the economy will not be able to meet the demands of its citizens and and either a balance of payments deficit or demand–pull inflation will result. In these circumstances, the Keynesian prescription would consist of reducing demand by appropriate fiscal and monetary policies.[28] Given that capitalist economies are subject to the trade cycle with its upswings and downturns, one of the objectives of discretionary macroeconomic policy should be to even out the cyclical swings of the economy, by increasing demand in the downswing and deflating demand in the upturn.

In any case, the essence of Keynesian economics is that the market, if left to its own devices, is unlikely to deliver the goods in terms of the four traditional objectives for an economy: full employment, price stability, balance of payments equilibrium and an acceptable rate of growth. It may in practice be impossible to achieve all of these at once,[29] but if we are to have any chance of coming somewhere close to doing so, then intervention by the state is an absolute necessity. Keynesian economics is thus very much the economics of intervention in the operation of the market. It may be interpreted as a message of hope: that we can to an extent influence our economic destinies, and are not completely at the mercy of the vagaries of the market.

As was discussed in Chapter 1, Keynesian economics was very much the accepted wisdom in Europe and elsewhere throughout the post-war period until the early 1970s. During the 1970s it came to be challenged as a result of the poor performance of European economies in the wake of the oil price rises and the sociopolitical instability which characterised this period. An alternative emerged, which came to be known broadly as **monetarism**. Many of the basic principles of this have become the accepted wisom on economics and economic policy in the 1980s and 1990s, and they have therefore largely driven economic developments in Europe during this period. There are many versions of monetarism,[30] but its fundamental principles form a coherent set of opinions which are sometimes referred to as **neo-liberal economics**. Monetarism's basic original features consisted of:

(a)  a belief in pure markets as the best possible allocators of resources;
(b)  a consequent belief that the growth of the mixed economy during the post-war years and the expansion of the role of government that accompanied it had diminished the efficiency of the market system;[31]
(c)  a belief in what has become known as **supply-side economics**, based on the principle that governments can only really act to stimulate the production side of the economy, rather than the demand side. Hence tax cuts to increase incentive, privatisation, deregulation, cuts in government expenditure and other measures to facilitate the free functioning of markets and 'roll back the frontiers of the state', in Margaret Thatcher's parlance.

(d) a rejection of Keynesian macroeconomics as ineffective in anything but the short term, and as a precipitator of high inflation;[32]
(e) a belief that the priority in economic policy should be to provide 'sound money', i.e. low inflation.
(f) a belief that low inflation could be achieved by restricting the supply of money in the economy, since, according to the work of Milton Friedman, there was a direct relationship between the amount of money in circulation and the rate of inflation. Hence the term monetarism. Control of the supply of money was to be achieved by high interest rates, the elimination of budget deficits, and by measures such as the 'Medium Term Financial Strategy' in the United Kingdom, a curious kind of collective psychological engineering aimed at predicting low inflation, government borrowing and money supply into the future in an attempt to create a self-fulfilling prophesy among economic agents – the principle that if you tell people enough times that green is red, they will eventually believe it.

Neo-liberal economics is thus based on many of the principles of the classical school which dominated economic thinking prior to the Second World War, to that extent it can be considered to be revisionist. It implies a very different vision of the mixed economy to the one adopted during the Keynesian heyday: much more market and much less state, to put it succinctly.

Pure monetarism was abandoned in the early 1980s by those such as the United Kingdom who attempted to implement it, when it became clear that in a world of interdependent and deregulated capital markets it was extremely difficult to control the money supply at a national level. Furthermore, the costs in terms of lost output and unemployment of restrictive monetary policies proved to be high, as experience in the United Kingdom tends to demonstrate. However, much of the neo-liberal agenda remains: the control of inflation through monetary policies (now adopting other policy targets such as the exchange rate), supply-side policies, liberalisation of markets, etc.

In practice this has involved microeconomic policies designed to attempt to cut taxes (especially for higher earners); to attempt to reduce public expenditure (especially on welfare); to deregulate markets; and notably **privatisation**. The latter, according to its proponents, increases economic welfare by making formerly state owned concerns market responsive and thus more efficient. It can also reduce public expenditure and be used to promote 'popular capitalism', if privatisation shares are distributed among a wide range of the population. In practice many privatisations have involved transferring public sector monopolies into the private sector, with the result that any efficiency gains have benefited share owners (in the form of high dividends) at the expense of consumers (who often have had to pay higher prices). Moreover, privatisation may contribute to greater economic and social inequality by reducing access to basic goods and services (since these are provided by the market only in accordance with firms' internal calculus – see 3.5.1), as well as by increasing income disparities in employment and indeed unemployment itself.[33]

European countries have interpreted the basic neo-liberal agenda in various ways, but this approach to economics has fundamentally conditioned economic developments and policies in Europe over the years since the late 1970s. The other development that has fundamentally conditioned economic events in Europe in this period has been European integration. We shall take both these themes up in Chapters 5 and 6 and in other, subsequent chapters.

An interesting and challenging supplement to the analysis discussed above is provided by what are usually referred to as **long wave theories**. These attempt to analyse the long-term development of capitalism in terms of cycles. These cycles tend to last around 55 years, interspersed with shorter cycles (usually known as Kuznetz or Juglar cycles), and they are generally named after Kondratieff, the Russian economist who first wrote about them. According to Kondratieff, these cycles are caused by long-term changes in fixed capital formation on major infrastructure projects, for example railway building. Interest in Kondratieff cycles was revived by by the American economist Schumpeter, who in 1939 identified similar cyclical movements, identifying three waves: one at the time of the industrial revolution (1787–1842), another at the time of railway building (1843–97), and a final ('neo-mercantilist') one beginning in 1898.[34] Schumpeter's view is that the upswing of cycles are connected with periods of innovation, which then lead to new industries and growth, which then in turn peter out and a downswing results, a process of 'creative destruction', as he referred to it. More recently, Schumpeter's analysis has been refined by Freeman *et al.* (1982), who suggest that it is not merely the number of innovations that determine long wave cycles, but also the interrelationship and linkages between innovations that matter. According to this approach, the European boom of the 1950s and 1960s was due to the emergence of new technologies and new industries such as electronics, drugs, petrochemicals, cars and consumer durables, while the crisis that followed can be explained by the development of a mismatch between the emerging new technologies and the social and institutional structures (industrial relations, management structures, etc.) in which they have to operate. International differences in economic performance can thus be explained by the extent of mismatch between technology and structures in different countries. The Schumpeterian view would imply that the fundamental development which has conditioned the European (and other) economies since the 1970s is the emergence of revolutionary information and communications technologies.

### 2.5.3   Radical critiques of free markets

The case for government intervention and thus for the mixed economy that we have thus far developed is based fundamentally on the so-called 'neo-classical' proposition that markets basically do work, and that what is required from government is therefore a 'helping hand'. There are, however, more radical critiques of the operation of markets, and it to these that we now turn. Some reject capitalism and the market totally, others would imply a high degree of government intervention to influence their outcomes.

The most radical critique of free markets has come from the different categories of fundamental **Marxists** and from various types of **Anarchists** and radical **Greens**. The analysis here is in many ways straightforward. Put bluntly, the market produces outcomes which are so far removed from anything that can vaguely be considered as socially acceptable that the only solution is to do away with it altogether, replacing it with (perhaps) some type of communist planning, and some kind of (perhaps very locally based) system of cooperatives, or syndicalism, self-sufficiency, ecologically sustainable and personally fulfilling production and work and (perhaps moneyless) trade.[35] The stark Marxian alternative has, however, been somewhat discredited by the collapse of Soviet planning, while the Green and Anarchist alternative, although in many ways idealistic and attractive, seems clearly impractical in anything but local contexts. Most such groups have an interim strategy to manage the transition from capitalism to the chosen alternative.

An interesting recent development in radical analysis has emanated from **regulation theorists** (economists[36] and others, such as geographers). One of the intellectual attractions of this lies in its interdisciplinary nature, for it tends to stress the interrelationship of the various aspects of society in explaining economic performance. Regulation theory rejects neoclassical notions of economic equilibrium and theories based on individual choice. Like the Schumpetarian school discussed above, it seeks to explain the uneven development of market economies over time. It also seeks to analyse the reasons for the uneven spatial development of economies. Regulation theories view long-term economic development as a cyclical process whose nature is determined by the type of social and structural parameters that prevail. Literature on regulation theory tends to be written in its own, often inaccessible, code. This is a pity, since some of the insights that it offers are extremely useful. Regulation theory varies in its emphasis according to whom you read. Essentially, however, it is based on four concepts:[37]

1. 'Regimes of Accumulation'. These consist of the way in which production, income distribution, exchange and consumption is systematically organised in a society. The effective and harmonious interaction of all these factors provides a system of accumulation that is conducive to growth and economic success.

2. 'Industrial Trajectories' or paradigms. This refers to the way in which production and work are essentially organised. Examples would be Taylorism and Fordism and, since the 1970s, the automation that has resulted from the development of new technologies.

3. 'Modes of Regulation'. These are the 'rules of the game', or the set of structural and institutional arangements within which the economic system operates. In a capitalist system they tend to cover four broad areas:

    (a)  the monetary system;
    (b)  the wage determination system;[38]
    (c)  the type of competition and of relationship between firms; and
    (d)  the nature and role of the state.

A system of regulation basically arbitrates and mediates between the various parties that are likely to be in conflict within a society: different social classes, social groups, enterprises, sectors of the economy, etc. It consists mainly of:

    (a)  a legal and structural framework;
    (b)  collective agreements; and

(c)  a shared system of values and mores.

4.  'Hegemonic Structures'. These consist of the broad political and institutional policy or strategy which a country adopts and then identifies with the general interest of the community as a whole. It is based on economic imperatives, but also affects all aspects of society. For example, the period of Keynesian hegemony involved not only economic policy but a whole series of political and social developments, centred mainly around the welfare state, that involved incorporating working people into an 'historic compromise' with industrial management. In this way underlying tensions between labour and capital were avoided, permitting economic activity to proceed unhindered.

All of the above are closely interrelated and both determine and reflect economic performance in an advanced industrial society. Regulation theory, however, emphasises the importance of the mode of regulation in determining economic outcomes in the long term. It is this that determines the regime of accumulation, given a particular form of industrialisation. When the mode of regulation succeeds in mediating and pacifying the contraditions that arise between groups and interests within an economic system, as in the case of the post-war boom, steady economic growth occurs. Crises, or periods of stagnation and instability, on the other hand, occur when the system of regulation breaks down, when a model of economic organisation and development runs out of steam, or for reasons associated with cycles of technological development.

We have briefly discussed in Chapter 1 the regulation theory interpretation of the post-war European boom and of the period of neo-liberalism that succeeded it. One should add that Boyer, one of the leading regulation theorists, considers that in the 1970s and 1980s the 'monopolistic' model of wage determination, based on trade union power and regulated labour markets, was the factor that prevented a repetition of the 1930s slump by keeping wages and thus demand high. This is quite at odds, of course, with the neo-liberal analysis of 'rigidities' in the labour market being a major cause of weak economic performance. We shall return to this in Chapter 7.

Regulation theorists regard the current period as one of restructuring after the crisis, characterised by the rapid emergence of revolutionary new technologies. Out of this will emerge a new economic status quo with a new mode of regulation, new hegemonic structures and a new type of labour process or work organisation. How good the new status quo adopted by each country or region is in meeting the requirements of the new world in which we live will determine the future economic success or failure of countries or regions. The nature of the new order in each country will be determined by the political process, both within the country itself and in an international context.

Regulation theorists would favour the development of supranational modes of regulation to recapture some control over international (predominantly capital) markets. They advocate the adoption of internal policies designed to intervene in the operation of markets and regulate their outcomes, pointing out that organised societies (Germany, Sweden, Japan) tend to perform better than those who allow markets to function freely (the United States and Britain). In particular, they would support approaches that promote investment in human capital, that facilitate innovation and the development of new industries, that socially regulate market behaviour, that result in consensual management styles and that encourage industrial democracy. As far as the new system of work organisation based on high technology is concerned, the choice lies between some kind post-Fordist model and a model based on 'flexible specialisation' as described by Piore and Sabel (1984).[39] Which one of these emerges will in part determine the nature of the system of regulation and macroeconomic framework to be adopted. In the context of the discussion in this chapter, regulation theory would imply a heavily regulated form of the mixed economy, stressing the fact that regulation involves areas that are outside the economic arena, as well as those that fall directly within it. Social Democracy rather than Social Darwinism, to put it starkly.

In addition there are a number of other radical critiques of the way markets operate, one implicit in the work of the Swedish economist Gunnar Myrdal.[40] Writing originally in the context of development economics, Myrdal suggests that markets do not necessarily work in the way that neoclassical theory would predict. The latter would suggest that the free operation of markets and the free movement of the factors of production will tend to equalise factor earnings between different countries and different regions. Myrdal, however, postulates that free markets, and in particular free capital markets, lead to 'polarisation' effects as a result of a process of 'cumulative causation'.

According to this approach, capital will tend to flow towards the areas where it is most productive, i.e. areas which are more prosperous and which benefit from external economies. This increases the prosperity of these areas, reinforces their attractiveness to capital, and in turn causes more capital to flow from poorer areas to more prosperous ones. Thus rich areas become involved in a benign cycle and grow gradually more prosperous, at the expense of poorer areas which gradually become relatively pauperised. Free labour markets, and in particular the free movement of labour, might lead to similar effects, since it may drain relatively poor areas of human capital and 'entrepreneurial verve'. There may be some movement of capital from prosperous areas of the 'economic core' towards the less prosperous periphery as a result of factors such as congestion and differentials in labour costs, but this 'spillover effect' is most unlikely to outweigh the polarization effects. It is of course very difficult to test this hypothesis empirically, but there is evidence to suggest there is considerable substance to it. This approach to how markets work is particularly relevant, in a European context, to the issue of regional policy, but there are other implications. In any case Myrdal's analysis provides a powerful agument for a strong level of government intervention in a mixed economy.

A further critique of free market capitalism emenates from Karl Polanyi (1957). He argues, among other things, that the unhindered functioning of markets may lead paradoxically to their ultimate restriction, as societies strive to protect themselves against the potentially destructive and anarchic results by setting up closed economies and authoritarian societies. This, argues Polanyi, is what happened in the early part of the twentieth century, and what others[41] fear might happen again at the start of the next century unless we succeeed in regulating the kind of capitalist forces that will be discussed in subsequent chapters.

## 2.6   Summary and conclusions

In this chapter we have reviewed the basic functioning of both market economies and planned economies, and have surveyed some aspects of their respective strengths and weaknesses. The conclusions is that, while a market system of economic organisation is on balance preferable on the grounds of its superior performance in terms of efficiency, the market in its pure and unregulated form exhibits serious weaknesses. There are those who advocate some limited intervention by the state to correct the various types of market failure at a micro or macroeconomic level, while a more radical viewpoint would suggest that the market is fundamentally flawed and requires widespread state intervention to produce an acceptable outcome. Either way, the conclusion is that what is required is some form of mixed economy.

The importance of this chapter in the context of the book is that it provides an overview of the rationale for the type of economic organisation which has been adopted by the European countries with which we are principally concerned in the years following the Second World War, i.e. allocation of resources by the market and predominantly private ownership of the means of production, albeit with a varying but significant degree of government intervention in the functioning of the economic system.

This is not to imply that the decision to adopt the mixed economy model after 1945 was in any way the result of open choice, for in reality the adoption of a centrally planned economy in West Europe was never a realistic possibility, given the international political scene at the time. However, the analysis presented in this chapter is essential to understanding the nature of the economic systems which have existed in European countries over the last 50 or so years, and thus to understanding the nature of these societies. It may also serve as a salutary reminder that, in the period following the triumph of the market and the collapse of planning systems throughout East/Central Europe and elsewhere, we need to be aware of the limitations of the market. It may be the only realistic means we have available of allocating resources, but on its own it will not solve all our basic economic problems.

## Further reading

Aglietta, M. (1979) *A Theory of Capitalist Regulation*, London: New Left Books.

Atkinson, A. B. (1984) *The Economics of Inequality*, 2nd edn, Oxford: Oxford University Press.

Bacon, R. and Eltis, W. (1974) *Britain's Economic Problem: too Few Producers?* 2nd ed., Basingstoke: Macmillan.

Baran, P. A. and Sweezey, P. M. (1966) *Monopoly Capital*, New York: Monthly Review Press.

Benko, G. and Dunford, M. (eds) (1991) *Industrial Change and Regional Development*, London: Belhaven.

Boyer, R. (1986) *La Théorie de la Régulation: une Analyse Critique*, Paris: La Découverte.

Boyer, R. (ed.) (1988) *The Search for Labour Market Flexibility: The European Economies in Transition*, Oxford: Clarendon Press.

Brouwer, F., Lintner, V. and Newman M. (eds) (1994) *Economic Policy Making and the European Union*, London: Federal Trust.

Buxton, A., Chapman, P. and Temple, P. (eds) (1994) *Britain's Economic Performance*, London: Routledge.

Freeman, C., Clark, C. and Soete, L. (1982) 'Unemployment and technical innovation: a study of long waves and economic development', London: Pinter.

Haworth, A. (1994) *Anti-Libertarianism: Markets Philosophy and Myth*, London: Routledge.

Hunt, E. K. and Sherman, H. J. (1990) *Economics: An Introduction to Traditional and Radical Views*, 6th edn, New York: HarperCollins.

Hutton, W. (1995) *The State We're In*, London: Jonathan Cape.

Isachsen, A. J., Hamilton, C. and Gylfason, T. (1992) *Understanding the Market Economy*, Oxford: Oxford University Press.

Lipietz, A. (1987) *Mirages and Miracles: the Crises of Global Fordism*, London: Verso.

Lipsey, R. G. and Lancaster, K. (1957) 'The general theory of second best', *Review of Economic Studies* 2, pp. 249–62.

Meade, J. (1975) *The Intelligent Radical's Guide to Economic Policy*, London: Allen & Unwin.

Meade, J. (1976) *The Just Economy*, London: Allen & Unwin.

Mishan, E. J. (1981) *Introduction to Normative Economics*, Oxford: Oxford University Press.

Myrdal, G. (1957) *Economic Theory and Underdeveloped Regions*, London: Duckworth.

Ormerod, P. (1995) *The Death of Economics*, London: Faber & Faber.

Pareto, V. (1909) *Manuel d'Economie Politique*, edited by Schwier, A. S. and Page, A. N., New York: A. M. Kelly, 1971.

Piore, M. and Sabel, C. F. (1984) *The Second Industrial Divide: Possibilities for Prosperity*, New York: Basic Books.

Pigou, A. C. (1946) *The Economics of Welfare* 4th edn, London: Macmillan.

Polanyi, K. (1957) *The Great Transformation*, New York: Octagon.

Samuelson, P. A. (1954) 'The Pure Theory of Public Expenditure', *Review of Economics and Statistics* 7, pp. 347–63.

Schumpeter (1939) *Business Cycles*, New York: McGraw-Hill.

Sen, A. K. (1973) *On Economic Inequality*, Oxford: Clarendon Press.

Servan-Schreiber, J.-J. (1969) *Le Défi Americain*, Harmondsworth: Penguin.

Sloman, J. (1994) *Economics* 2nd ed., Hemel Hempstead: Harvester Wheatsheaf.

## Notes

1. Satisfying the perceived needs of the developed world has a cost in terms of pollution, exhaustion of resources, stress, the stark inequalities between the first and third world etc. Some, notably in the Green movement, find this cost unacceptable and are striving to redefine our concept of need. These issues are explored in detail in subsequent chapters.
2. There are many good undergraduate textbooks which examine this in great detail; for example, Sloman, J. (1994) *Economics*, 2nd edn, Hemel Hempstead: Harvester Wheatsheaf.
3. The additions to total production that result from hiring one more worker, see any basic economics text.
4. The possibility that allowing large firms to exist may, in some industries, result in reductions in average costs of production, as a result of factors such as increased scope for the division of labour (which speeds up the overall production process), spreading of overhead or fixed costs and managerial specialisation. Examples would include the computer industry, the car industry, aeroplanes, etc.
5. This, according to some commentators such as Schumpeter, is facilitated by the presence

of monopoly power in certain sectors of the economy, since this ensures the resources and rewards required to give firms the incentive to spend money on research and development.

6. Capitalism, of course, is not the only system that can lead to corruption, as experience in the former Soviet Union and elsewhere has demonstrated.

7. The Soviet Union and its East/Central European satellite states, Cuba, Maoist China, etc.

8. This also provides the incentive for people to become involved in education and training, or to acquire **human capital**, since this in principle enhances personal productivity and thus allows the individual concerned to command higher earnings in the labour market.

9. One could, of course, attempt to introduce productivity bonuses in order to increase incentive, but there is likely to be a limit to how effective these can be.

10. Average employment in industrial enterprises in the Soviet Union was around 1000, while collective farms employed on average around 600 workers each – very high figures indeed by Western standards.

11. For example, Alan Haworth (1994) attacks the model of 'mutually beneficial' exchanges which underpins libertarian philosophy, and in the process questions the whole philosophical basis of the market.

12. For a full and technically sophisticated analysis of the concept of market failure see Mishan (1981).

13. A related issue concerns poverty, which will be discussed in Chapter 11.

14. For example, health is a merit good largely provided by the state in the United Kingdom through the National Health Service, while in the United States it is (largely) provided by the private sector. Public preference in this area changes: in the 1950s and 1960s the definition of merit and public goods that it was appropriate for the state to provide was extensive and growing, while the 1980s were characterised by a marked shift in public preference towards goods and services provided by the private sector.

15. The current trend is, particularly in the United Kingdom, to privatise activities wherever possible. In parts of the public sector where privatisation is not possible, the basic objective is to introduce internal markets.

16. See, for example, Buxton, *et al.* (1994) and Hutton (1995).

17. The complex ecological interactions which permit life on earth to function.

18. This has been an approach traditionally adopted by France – see Servan-Schreiber (1969) and Chapter 6.

19. Which need to promote what the American economist Schumpeter refers to as the 'dynamic efficiency of capitalism'.

20. The costs of unemployment (apart from the personal ones), it should be remembered, are largely borne by the community in the form of social security payments and forgone tax revenues.

21. Regional policy can be seen as representing a specific example of industrial policy (see below and Chapter 10).

22. There may also be a 'critical mass' of manufacturing, below which it would be strategically unwise for European countries to fall. This debate over this has been keen in the United Kingdom, where the rate of de-industrialisation has been particularly rapid.

23. The most notable historically being 'tulipmania', the bout of frenzied trading of flower bulbs in seventeenth century Amsterdam, and the 'South Sea Bubble' share price boom and bust in eighteenth century London. More recent, and perhaps less spectacular, have been the 1980s stock market crashes in Europe and the United States, the property market crash in the United Kingdom and so on.

24. In the presence of government policy, this can also subvert the wishes of democratically

elected governments, as arguably happened in the context of the United Kingdom's exit from the ERM in 1992 – see Chapter 5.

25. For example, Baran and Sweezey (1966).

26. The analysis presented here is by necessity very brief and selective. Readers who are interested in a full exposition of macroeconomic ideas can refer to one of the many economics textbooks, for example Sloman (1994).

27. His seminal work work being *The General Theory of Employment, Interest and Money*, published in 1936.

28. The above is necessarily a very simple and sketchy outline of the principles of Keynesianism. There is a mountain of literature on the subject for those who wish to know more. The best starting point is one of the major textbooks, for example Sloman (1994).

29. For example, the trade-off between inflation and unemployment postulated by the Phillips curve analysis would suggest that these two objects are to an extent mutually exclusive.

30. For example the **new classicist** school and the **rational expectations** school. See any modern economics textbook.

31. See Bacon and Eltis (1974).

32. For the archetypal critique of Keynesian demand management and its effects on inflation, see the analysis surrounding the 'expectations augmented Phillips Curve' in many economic principles texts.

33. The UK experience has shown that the earnings of top executives increase substantially after privatisation, while privatised firms shed significant amounts of labour (see the example of British Gas, British Telecom, etc.). The promotion of popular capitalism has also proved to be somewhat of a myth, since privatisation shares end up in the hands of a limited amount of investors (although it could be claimed that a wide section of the population depends on the investments of financial institutions for their savings and pensions), while small investors have little impact on companies' decision making.

34. A rapid, 'back-of-the-envelope' calculation would suggest that the current Kondratieff cycle began in 1953, and will end in 2008, when the next upswing is due to begin!

35. For a full treatment of the principles of Marxian economics and other alternative approaches to economics see, for example, Hunt and Sherman (1990).

36. Notably French economists such as Aglietta, Boyer and Lipiez.

37. A good exposition of regulation theory is to be found in Benko and Dunford (1991), which influenced parts of this section.

38. Widely defined as including a variety of factors such as conditions of employment, recruitment methods and methods of skill acquisition.

39. This issue will be discussed further in Chapter 7.

40. See Myrdal (1957).

41. For example, Hutton (1995).

# CHAPTER THREE

# Freedom and control

## The theoretical basis of European political choices

## 3.1   Introduction

This chapter aims to present the main theoretical approaches to understanding European societies from a political perspective. We begin with an analysis of power and authority and then present critiques of liberal democracy, looking closely at the notions of representation, association and participation. This is followed by a presentation of various theories about how the state operates within liberal democracies in order to provide a context within which the later chapters will fit. We shall be looking, therefore, at **pluralist**, **neo-pluralist**, **elitist**, **corporatist** and **Marxist** theories, and their explanation of the way liberal democracies are organised and run. In the penultimate section we look at what the state is and present the debate about the state and civil society.

Francis Fukuyama argues that the demise of communism represents the triumph of liberal democracy.[1] This triumph indicates that liberal democracy is the best possible form of state in which people can choose to be governed; it is the pinnacle of human achievement in terms of the organisation and running of politics in a society. This enormous assumption is based on the argument that liberal democracies in whatever form allow the best possible representation of people's wishes, and since everyone is free to vote for whomever they like it allows for the representation of all sections of society in the popular assembly of a country. So what it is that is so special about liberal democracy?

In Chapter 1 we stated that liberal democracy was now a common feature of nation states in Europe. Underpinning the whole structure of liberal democracy is the notion of pluralism, which includes not only the political but also the economic and social spheres. However, the notion that liberal democracies are necessarily pluralistic has been challenged by theorists from many different schools. The terms used to describe liberal democracy can become varied and confusing; so, for instance, we can have a pluralist liberal democracy or a corporatist liberal democracy, and other forms of pluralism have been defined as 'limited pluralism' (Hayward, 1986) or 'biased pluralism' (Ham and Hill, 1993).

What do all these terms mean? This chapter aims to provide a guide through the maze by outlining the main strands of the debate about liberal democracy, and thereby to have some kind of framework to analyse contemporary European societies. The summary gives a brief assessment of the various theories and their usefulness in explaining the way in which states are governed.

## 3.2 Power and authority

This will o' the wisp pursuit of power

ANEURIN BEVAN

There are three main ways in which social scientists have defined power (Hague *et al.*, 1992):

- the achievement of shared goals;
- the ability to impose your will on someone else against their opposition; and
- the ability to affect the way people live against their own interests.

The **first** definition is very much one which sees society based on the notion of consensus, where there are shared goals common to all members of that society.[2] The **second** view is more linked to an analysis that recognises an element of coercion in the relationship but also implies that there can be some negotiation between the holder and subject in the power relationship.[3] The **final** idea of power suggests that power is exercised where people's interests are not taken into consideration even though they may not know that they have those interests.[4] This is Lukes's view, which has its origins in a Marxist analysis of power, and seems a useful way of looking at power since it goes beyond an explanation of power in terms of individual behaviour and takes into account the way in which groups and institutions act within particular structures. It also takes into account the way in which power may be exercised in a non-overt way by highlighting the hidden mechanisms which allow some groups to influence and dominate the decision-making process in democratic societies, concealed from public gaze and scrutiny. Finally it is useful to consider 'power as neither static nor locational; attempts to use power at different levels may also lead to shifts in power relationships'.[5]

Although this argument may relativise the notion of power, it does at least open up the possibility of understanding power and its operation in modern societies in terms of coalescences of centres of influence. This process is ongoing, dynamic and open to negotiation and change at each and every moment. This point of view does not ignore the fact that such coalescences do tend to develop into solid structures and become institutionalised, but nevertheless are open to change and modification.

The writings of Max Weber (1864–1920) and Michel Foucault (1926–84) provide a useful comparison of different views on power and how it is exercised in society.

### Weber on power and authority

Weber presented three different types of authority which explained how obedience to a particular ruler or ruling group was ensured: **traditional**, **charismatic** and **legal-rational**.

Traditional authority is usually based on a hereditary ruler relying on a long and distant past to ensure people's obedience. For example, monarchies throughout the world use the weight of history to justify their position, although in the modern world their actual position of power has become increasingly tenuous (e.g. the monarchy in Britain).

Charismatic authority is based on a leader's ability to rouse and inspire the people, but is usually very dependent on the individual and tends to disappear once they are gone. Figures such as Mahatma Gandhi, Martin Luther King, Ayatollah Khomeini and Nelson Mandela are examples of such leaders.

Legal-rational authority is based on people's obedience to a set of objective rules beyond any one individual, and as such is completely different to **charismatic** authority. Weber had in mind modern forms of the bureaucratic state where there existed a set of clear rules and regulations governing the way in which the state operated, and which people obeyed because they recognised the need for a set of impartial rules. Weber believed that this third type of authority was becoming increasingly prevalent in the modern world. The concept of **Rechtsstaat** in Germany sums up the nature of this kind of state.[6]

Weber's categories are useful in trying to analyse the way in which societies may be ruled, but he recognised that power underlies all forms of authority. The state in the final analysis has a monopoly over the forms of coercion it can use (see our definition of the state in Chapter 1) so that if a group refuses to obey, measures can be taken to ensure obedience. However, this can only happen when the opposition is small and isolated; if the groups grow into some kind of large movement, as for instance the Northern Leagues in Italy or other regional groups, then the power of the state can be undermined.

In industrial disputes, also, the state may accept that it has lost its authority and so either force its opponents back to work or accept their demands as, for example, the French government did in the autumn of 1993 when it acceded to Air France workers' demands to withdraw redundancy plans. However, a subsequent appeal to all the workforce by the management in April 1994 to accept a restructuring plan that would entail at least 5000 redundancies was accepted in a secret vote by more than 80 per cent of the workforce.[7]

An important development in this whole area is to recognise that all sorts of other individuals and groups have power and authority in the modern world, apart from the traditional groups such as politicians, industrialists, financiers and priests, and particularly those in the entertainment and sporting world. Furthermore, when this is coupled with financial power it is a formidable force. The ability of someone like Silvio Berlusconi in Italy to use the media channels at his disposal to become a key figure in politics says a great deal about power and authority in the modern world. The mass media play a key role in ensuring the 'hegemony' of certain ideas in society, and the position of the dominant groups. Some writers have also stressed the way in which the media plays an influential role in presenting not only those issues which are deemed to be important, but also in keeping such issues off the agenda. Hood

(1989) refers to 'gatekeepers', who ensure that only certain issues appear on the agenda, and Chomsky's *Necessary Illusions* (1989) demonstrates the way the media acts very much at the behest of powerful groups within the state in the way it portrays or does not portray certain events, and the way in which it unquestioningly accepts official explanations of events (see Chapter 12).

## Michel Foucault on power

Foucault has provided one of the more provocative analyses of power in modern societies, with a view of power that challenges accepted notions that power is a thing or possession which one person or group has over another.

He argues that power relations exist at all levels of society, and they are experienced as 'micro-powers'. We experience power in many different ways on a daily basis, when a particular power is exercised over us, or when we ourselves may exercise some kind of power over others. Rather than a hierarchical notion of power, a dominator–dominated dynamic, Foucault considers power to be more like a network or grid.

In this much broader conception of power, Foucault has links with the feminist movement's insistence that the personal is political, and that power relations exist in all arenas of human experience including the most intimate. He can also be seen as a kind of pluralist in terms of his ideas that power is somehow not concentrated, but dispersed through its operations in many different arenas of human interaction.[8] Unlike the American pluralists who consider power is dispersed but then refocused into a central point so that sovereignty can be exercised, Foucault's notion of power is characterised by no centre, just a never-ending series of networks:

Power is not something located in and symbolised by the sovereign, but permeates society in such a way that taking over the state apparatus (through political revolution or coup) does not in itself change the power network.[9]

It simply produces different knowledges and techniques of power. It becomes very difficult, therefore, to carry out a revolution because you cannot be sure where your efforts at taking over power should be directed. If there is no centre then what do you overthrow?[10] All you are left with in the Foucault struggle is a series of local resistances. However, it is possible to think critically about the exercise of 'freedom'. If we can understand how we have become these contingent subjects, then we may be able to exercise some freedom in relation to the subjects that we might come to be.[11]

The traditional notion of examining power has been limited, merely asking questions about how legitimacy is created in society or the nature of the state in terms of its coercive powers. Power is not some kind of abstract entity, but only has meaning in terms of the way in which it is exercised and experienced. For writers like Lukes, power is exercised by one person or agent over another individual or group. For Foucault the main point is that power is not something (a possession) that one agent has and another lacks, but power is exercised, as the quotation below indicates, in the effect of one action on another action. Power relations and the context in which those relations operate are the most crucial aspects of any analysis of power. Furthermore, power relations are rooted in all aspects of human interaction.

> Power exists only when it is put into action . . . what defines a relationship of power is that it is a mode of action which does not act directly and immediately on others. Instead it acts upon their actions.[12]

Foucault uses the concept of pastoral power to define the exercise of another kind of power through what are defined as technologies of care (education, health and social services and mass media). The Church was the initial provider of care in western Europe. In some countries such as Germany (**Kirchensteuer** – church tax), Spain and Italy the church still plays a crucial role in the provision of health and social services. In Britain, the church is heavily involved in the education system, particularly at primary school level; but, in general, since the eighteenth century the church has lost this role, and the state has taken over these functions. Moreover, the growth of these institutions, according to Foucault, has invaded every aspect of our lives and turned us from human beings into subjects.

These institutions control our lives even to the extent that we ourselves actually collude in the control that these agencies have over us. This has been achieved by controlling the body, either as labour power in terms of economic control, or as reproductive power in terms of control over expressions of desire. Our innermost desires seem to be defined by these technologies of care and where they appear to transgress society's norms, as in the case of homosexuality, then they are labelled as 'deviant' and subject to intense psychiatric analysis in terms of disorder.

Although there has been the growth of the concept of individual human rights since the eighteenth century, at the same time the state has increasingly taken on the function of integrating individuals totally into society through these agencies. The growth of the welfare state has meant that we are 'controlled' in a greater way than any other time in history. From birth onwards, one or other of the technologies of care assesses us (postnatal check-up/physically fit or unfit/mental health), classifies us (streaming in schools/access to further or higher education), numbers us (NHS number, National Insurance number, driving licence number, passport number, social security card, student enrolment number, office number, and so on), or influences us (mass media).

This process relates to the key aspect of Foucault's notion of power, contained in his analysis of the power/knowledge relationship.[13] Foucault develops Nietzsche's notion that knowledge is gained by human beings to the extent to which it can be used to achieve power and domination over things and people. It is a function of human interests and power relations. Knowledge according to this view is not something that can be separated from power.[14]

The goal of his work has been to create a history of how human beings are made into the subjects of one form or another of power relation.[15] Foucault's main concerns are how the more obvious disciplining institutions in society, such as prisons, asylums and hospitals, are reflected in other institutions such as the armed services, education and factories.[16] The most useful way to analyse power relations in society is by looking at the forms of resistance that exist against different forms of power (Foucault's accounts of power always include resistance). For example, to understand and develop a critique of what society means by sanity and legality, it is useful to look at madness (asylums) or illegality (prisons and prisoners).

Furthermore, accepted notions of hierarchy have become subject recently to different kinds of challenges, which help to highlight power relations; for example, struggles which are about challenging 'the power of men over women, parents over children, psychiatry over the mentally ill, of medicine over the whole population, of administration over the ways people live'.[17]

Every power relation implies a strategy of struggle. There have been three types of struggles throughout history, against ethnic, social, or religious domination, against economic exploitation (class struggle), and against individual subjection and submission. If the nineteenth century was characterised by the second form of struggle, then our contemporary world is characterised predominantly by the third form. Foucault answers the criticism that all struggles are the product of economic and social structures, by stressing that the exercise of power is more complex than simply a reduction to those two factors. No matter what kind of economic and social structures there are, what ethnic, social or religious affiliation people may have, the same struggle exists about identity, about how to answer the question: **Who are we?**

Power is not seen wholly as a negative force which has tended to underpin the attitude of Marxists to discussions of power, for whom power exists in terms of domination or repression. For Foucault power can be a positive and productive force. Finally Foucault questions the Enlightenment project, as have many post-modernist thinkers, arguing that is there is no necessary progress or meaning to be gained from history. Rather than society evolving towards more freedom and self-expression, the reverse is the case with the development of a more repressive and imprisoned society.

Critics of Foucault have argued that, first, he underestimates the nature of the dominant power structures in society. A strong centre exists in all societies which determines people's behaviour even down to micro-levels. He seems to disregard the way in which power can coalesce into a central force. It is the state that 'establishes the general framework within which all other disciplinary institutions operate'.[18] There are also differences between states. The liberal state attempts to limit the arbitrary exercise of all kinds of power, while the totalitarian state removes these limits and promotes indoctrination, repression and concentration camps. Secondly, his expressed 'anarchism' is 'self-indulgent radical chic'.[19] Finally there is a distinction to be made between being in or out of prison. His suggestion that, since we all live in this 'carceral' (prison-like) society, there is really no difference between inside and outside prison is, according to critics, flawed.

Power is evident in the interaction of people and agencies and reflected in the ability to get your own way (even by coercion) in spite of opposition and even where implementing any decision may adversely affect people's interests.[20] The problem with the exercise of power on the macro-political level is when it is seen in its naked form, for example when someone uses violence or force to impose their will on a group of people, thereby rendering their position inherently unstable. The aim, therefore, for any ruler or group is to get people to obey them, that is to accept their power, without too much questioning, in other words to establish their hegemony.

All groups, therefore, seek **authority** because it is the legitimate form of power and is more stable.

In our discussion of power and authority, then, we have presented the classic and modern views of these terms, and we would also emphasise the importance of looking beyond the usual range of actors in the visible political world at a wider range of individuals and groups in trying to decide where power lies. Furthermore, it is important to consider Foucault's ideas about power, which are an attempt to define the concept more broadly than has been usual in political science, by introducing ideas about the omnipresence of power relations in all aspects of daily life.

## 3.3  Democracy

Democracy is not a religion

DR MAHATHIR MOHAMED, PRIME MINISTER OF MALAYSIA 1994

It is better to have ten devils fighting amongst themselves,
than one devil with absolute power

STUDENT, TIEN AN MEN SQUARE, MAY 1989

Before dealing with the types of liberal democracies we comment briefly on the debate surrounding democracy in general. As Parry and Moran (1994) indicate, the definition of what constitutes a democracy is extremely problematic.[21] The origin of the word is Greek, meaning 'rule of the people', and was used to define the way in which the Greek city states in classical times were organised and run. However, the franchise at that time was limited, excluding women, immigrants and slaves. Sartori (1987) is quite clear that although we use the term democracy to define systems both ancient and modern, there is nothing for us to learn from classical times about running a modern democratic state. It is really only in the twentieth century that full participation by the people has taken place, with the franchise won by all social classes and particularly women in all West European states (NB: the vote for women in Switzerland was only won in 1971. In many parts of the world women are still disenfranchised, for example in Kuwait and Saudi Arabia).

The debate since Rousseau, Marx and J. S. Mill has concentrated on the participatory or representative nature of democracy. For Rousseau representative democracy is not really democracy, since it entails people giving up their power to others who govern them. For Marx bourgeois democracy is not real democracy, since real democracy can only exist when equality prevails in the economic and social sphere and people can 'participate in making decisions not only over what are conventionally termed governmental issues but over matters affecting workplace and leisure activities'.[22] The failure of so-called Marxist regimes to increase participation by the people in any meaningful way has led to new discussion about participatory democracy by Marxist and non-Marxist thinkers alike.

Poulantzas, writing from within a neo-Marxist perspective, and Macpherson, from a radical perspective, have developed their respective ideas about democracy from Marx and Mill. Poulantzas criticises Lenin for not being able to accept the notion of competing centres of power expressed within the soviets, and its subsequent legacy in the over-centralised state. He calls for an opening-up of state institutions and the greater participation of groups within the arena of civil society.

Macpherson stresses the importance of making political parties more open and promoting the notion of direct democracy. The question arises as to whether these types of ideas would be practicable within large-scale societies, but it is not a question that deters or should deter discussion about the nature of democracy. We are far from Rousseau's romantic notion of gathering beneath the oak tree, but none the less these remain key issues in thinking about democracy. There is also the idea that increasing the possibility of participation will develop people's sense of being able to influence their own lives, and therefore promote a real sense of democracy (Pateman, 1970).

## Feminism and democracy

Pursuing the notions of the relativism of political and other fundamental beliefs, Phillips (1993) argues that the importance of new developments in thinking about democracy is the recognition that all concepts are contested. Furthermore the new democracy rejects monolithic solutions and recognises the importance of subgroups based on gender, ethnicity, religion, sexuality, language and disability. The politics of these new social movements is discussed more fully in Chapter 9. As she notes:

What distinguishes a radical perspective on democracy is not its expectation of future homogeneity and consensus, but its commitment to a politics of solidarity and challenge and change.[23]

The feminist critique of liberal democracy centres on notions of citizenship, participation and heterogeneity.[24] The first point that needs to be made is the massive under-representation of women in elected assemblies all over the world (see Fig. 3.1).[25] There are institutional and cultural reasons for this absence of elected women representatives. Women are still considered to have the primary responsibility for care of all dependants, thus restricting the amount of other time to devote to activities outside the home environment. Other obstacles are the way in which assemblies work, in terms of their hours, location and procedures, and cultural factors such as politics being the domain of the man because in the classical formulation politics is about the public sphere outside the home, women's place is inside the home. Feminism has fought long and hard to introduce the notion of the personal as political in order to break down this rigid separation of what is considered to be politics.

In terms of citizenship, then, the creation of the welfare state in the post-1945 world has led to a differentiation between the active employed citizen and the citizen dependent on welfare provision. As Phillips notes, the formulation of this notion of citizenship was taking place just as the respective roles of man = breadwinner and woman = dependent wife were being reasserted after the Second World War[26] (see Chapter 11). The immediate consequence of this, then, was to categorise women as second-class citizens, if citizens at all.[27]

## Women and electoral representation

There have been substantial increases in the numbers of women elected to public office in some European countries. The most spectacular increases have been in the Scandinavian countries.[28] In the 1970s the percentage of women elected to office in Sweden at all levels was about 14–15 per cent, but by the end of the 1980s it has risen to around 40 per cent. The major reason for this increase has been as much to do with women's own motivation to improve their representation as the nature of the various electoral systems.

As far as practical measures go, many political parties have now instituted quotas in order to increase the presence of women in political parties. The first major problem has been to ensure that enough women are willing to put themselves forward to be considered as candidates, and then to overcome the hold by men on the key economic posts. Women generally tend to be placed in charge of those portfolios that are considered more 'feminine', for example family affairs, social issues or health care.

The social democratic parties have started the process of introducing quotas in order to increase the participation of women. The German SPD, after its party congress in Münster in 1988, agreed that by 1994 women should hold no less than 40 per cent of all party offices. By 1998 this quota should also apply to candidate lists and parliamentary representation.[29] But it has been the Green parties that have been the most insistent on parity between women and men in all areas of the party.[30]

## Participatory democracy

Green thinkers have been in the forefront of this debate with their ideas about grass roots decision making and rotating leadership. There has also been a recognition of the lack of real democracy in the economic sphere by the neo-pluralist thinkers we mentioned above (Dahl, 1985).

Hirst's (1994) ideas about associative democracy are an attempt to find ways of making modern representative institutions more accountable to their electorate. One of the key issues within Britain is the 'democratic deficit', which refers to the way in which democratic accountability has become increasingly diminished. He argues against the New Right's belief that the market can solve the problems of regulation of the economy and the provision of welfare.

Instead he reformulates long-standing arguments about pluralism, cooperation and voluntary associations and maintains that democracy can provide the necessary information and efficiency to make society operate better. He also offers a new way to think about the state in terms of a network of voluntary associations made up of freely associating individual citizens. The left also comes in for criticism for its over-dependence on the state in providing welfare. Original socialist aspirations about self-organisation, reflected in the nineteenth century Friendly Societies and Mutual Associations have been lost, and the present situation of a culture of dependency on the welfare state could be replaced by more cooperative and self-generated processes. It is in the key area of civil society that Hirst argues that socialists ignored the very

## I. Comparative Data 1985–1994

| Parliamentary population in the 54 ECE member countries | 1985* | 1994 |
|---|---|---|
| Total parliamentarians | 12 583 | 16 043 |
| Data available on | 12 583 | 16 043 |
| Men | 10 552 | 14 235 |
| Women | 2 031 | 1 808 |
| **% Women** | **16.14%** | **11.27%** |

| **Single or lower chambers** | 1985* | 1994 |
|---|---|---|
| Total parliamentarians | 10 093 | 12 722 |
| Data available on | 10 093 | 12 722 |
| Men | 8 443 | 11 193 |
| Women | 1 650 | 1 529 |
| **% Women** | **16.35%** | **12.02%** |

| **Other chambers** | 1985* | 1994 |
|---|---|---|
| Total parliamentarians | 2 490 | 3 321 |
| Data available on | 2 490 | 3 321 |
| Men | 2 109 | 3 042 |
| Women | 381 | 279 |
| **% Women** | **15.30%** | **8.40%** |

* Figures corresponding to the Parliaments of the sovereign States at that date.

## II. Country breakdown as at 30 June 1994

*The date of the latest elections or of the appointment as well as the number of women out of the total membership of the House are indicated in brackets*

**Albania**
People's Assembly (March 1992) ........................................... 5.7   (8/140)
**Andorra**
General Council (December 1993) ......................................... 3.6   (1/28)
**Armenia**
Supreme Council (May 1990) .............................................. 3.1   (8/260)
**Austria**
Federal Council (varying dates according to the provinces) .................... 20.6   (13/63)
National Council (October 1990) ........................................... 21.3   (39/183)
**Azerbaijan**
National Council (September 1990) ........................................ 2.0   (1/50)
**Belarus**
Supreme Soviet (March 1990) ............................................. 3.8   (13/346)
**Belgium**
Senate (November 1991) ................................................. 10.9   (20/184)
House of Representatives (November 1991) ................................. 9.4   (20/212)
**Bosnia and Herzegovina**
Assembly of the Republic (Nov./Dec. 1990) ................................. 4.5   (7/156)
**Bulgaria**
National Assembly (October 1991) ........................................ 12.9   (31/240)
**Canada**
Senate (all appointed for a continuous term) .............................. 15.4   (16/104)
House of Commons (November 1993) ..................................... 18.0   (53/295)

***Figure 3.1***   Distribution of seats between men and women in the national parliaments of the 54 member countries of the Economic Commission for Europe
*Source:* Inter-parliamentary Union (1994)

**Croatia**
    House of Zupanije (February 1993) ...................................................... 4.8   (3/63)
    House of Representatives (August 1992) ............................................... 5.8   (8/138)
**Cyprus**
    House of Representatives (May 1991) ................................................... 5.4   (3/56)
**Czech republic**
    Chamber of Deputies (June 1992) ...................................................... 10.0   (20/200)
**Denmark**
    Folketinget (December 1990) ........................................................... 33.0   (59/179)
**Estonia**
    State Assembly (September 1992) ....................................................... 13.7   (14/102)
**Finland**
    Eduskunta – Riksdagen (March 1991) ................................................... 39.0   (78/200)
**France**
    Senate (September 1992) ................................................................ 5.0   (16/321)
    National Assembly (March 1993) ........................................................ 6.1   (35/577)
**Georgia**
    Supreme Soviet (October 1992) ........................................................ 6.3   (14/222)
**Germany**
    Bundesrat (varying dates) ............................................................. 14.7   (10/68)
    Bundestag (December 1990) ........................................................... 20.5   (136/662)
**Greece**
    Greek Chamber of Deputies (October 1993) ........................................... 6.0   (18/300)
**Hungary**
    National Assembly (May 1994) ......................................................... 10.9   (42/386)
**Iceland**
    Althingi (April 1991) .................................................................. 23.8   (15/63)
**Ireland**
    Senate (February 1992) ................................................................ 13.3   (8/60)
    House of Representatives (November 1992) ........................................... 12.0   (20/166)
**Israel**
    Knesset (June 1992) ................................................................... 9.2   (11/120)
**Italy**
    Senate (March 1994) .................................................................. 8.9   (29/326)
    Chamber of Deputies (March 1994) .................................................... 15.1   (95/630)
**Kazakhstan**
    Supreme Soviet (March 1994) ......................................................... 11.9   (21/177)
**Kyrghyzstan**
    Supreme Soviet (February 1990) ....................................................... 6.3   (22/350)
**Latvia**
    Supreme Council (June 1993) .......................................................... 15.0   (15/100)
**Liechtenstein**
    Diet (October 1993) .................................................................. 8.0   (2/25)
**Lithuania**
    Seimas (Oct./Nov. 1992) .............................................................. 7.1   (10/141)
**Luxembourg**
    Chamber of Deputies (June 1994) ..................................................... 20.0   (12/60)
**Malta**
    House of Representatives (February 1992) ............................................. 1.5   (1/65)
**Moldova**
    Parliament (February 1994) ............................................................ 4.8   (5/104)
**Monaco**
    National Council (January 1993) ....................................................... 5.6   (1/18)
**Norway**
    Stortinget (September 1993) ........................................................... 39.4   (65/165)

*Figure 3.1*   Continued

**Netherlands**
   First Chamber (May 1991) . . . . . . . . . . . . . . . . . . . . . . . . . . . . . . . . . . . . . . . 25.3  (19/75)
   Second Chamber (May 1994) . . . . . . . . . . . . . . . . . . . . . . . . . . . . . . . . . . 31.3  (47/150)
**Poland**
   Senate (September 1993) . . . . . . . . . . . . . . . . . . . . . . . . . . . . . . . . . . . . 13.0  (13/100)
   Sejm (September 1993) . . . . . . . . . . . . . . . . . . . . . . . . . . . . . . . . . . . . . . 13.0  (60/460)
**Portugal**
   Assembly of the Republic (October 1991) . . . . . . . . . . . . . . . . . . . . . . . . 8.7  (20/230)
**Romania**
   Senate (September 1992) . . . . . . . . . . . . . . . . . . . . . . . . . . . . . . . . . . . . . 1.4  (2/143)
   House of Deputies (September 1992) . . . . . . . . . . . . . . . . . . . . . . . . . . . 3.5  (12/341)
**Russian Federation**
   Council of the Federation (December 1993) . . . . . . . . . . . . . . . . . . . . . . 5.1  (9/178)
   State Duma (December 1993) . . . . . . . . . . . . . . . . . . . . . . . . . . . . . . . . . 9.6  (43/448)
**San Marino**
   Great Central Council (May 1993) . . . . . . . . . . . . . . . . . . . . . . . . . . . . . 11.7  (7/60)
**Slovak Republic**
   National Council (June 1992) . . . . . . . . . . . . . . . . . . . . . . . . . . . . . . . . . 18.1  (23/127)
**Slovenia**
   National Assembly (December 1992) . . . . . . . . . . . . . . . . . . . . . . . . . . 14.4  (13/90)
**Spain**
   Senate (June 1993) . . . . . . . . . . . . . . . . . . . . . . . . . . . . . . . . . . . . . . . . . 12.6  (32/254)
   Congress of Deputies (June 1993) . . . . . . . . . . . . . . . . . . . . . . . . . . . . 16.0  (56/350)
**Sweden**
   Riksdagen (September 1991) . . . . . . . . . . . . . . . . . . . . . . . . . . . . . . . . . 33.5  (117/349)
**Switzerland**
   Council of States (October 1991) . . . . . . . . . . . . . . . . . . . . . . . . . . . . . 8.7  (4/46)
   National Council (October 1991) . . . . . . . . . . . . . . . . . . . . . . . . . . . . . 17.5  (35/200)
**The Former Yugoslav Republic of Macedonia**
   National Assembly (Nov./Dec. 1990). . . . . . . . . . . . . . . . . . . . . . . . . . . 4.2  (5/120)
**Turkey**
   Grand National Assembly (October 1991) . . . . . . . . . . . . . . . . . . . . . . 1.8  (8/450)
**Turkmenistan**
   Supreme Soviet (January 1990) . . . . . . . . . . . . . . . . . . . . . . . . . . . . . . . 4.6  (8/175)
**Ukraine**
   Parliament (April 1994) . . . . . . . . . . . . . . . . . . . . . . . . . . . . . . . . . . . . . 3.6  (12/337)
**United Kingdom**
   House of Lords. . . . . . . . . . . . . . . . . . . . . . . . . . . . . . . . . . . . . . . . . . . . 6.4  (77/1196)
   House of Commons (April 1992) . . . . . . . . . . . . . . . . . . . . . . . . . . . . . 9.2  (60/651)
**United States of America**
   Senate (November 1992) . . . . . . . . . . . . . . . . . . . . . . . . . . . . . . . . . . . 7.0  (7/100)
   House of Representatives (November 1992). . . . . . . . . . . . . . . . . . . . . 11.0  (48/435)
**Uzbekistan**
   Supreme Council (February 1990) . . . . . . . . . . . . . . . . . . . . . . . . . . . . 9.6  (48/500)
**Yugoslavia**
   Chamber of Republics (December 1993) . . . . . . . . . . . . . . . . . . . . . . . 2.5  (1/40)
   Chamber of Citizens (December 1992) . . . . . . . . . . . . . . . . . . . . . . . . 3.0  (4/133)

*Figure 3.1*  Continued

real possibilities of building socialism. He does not reject the role of the state but merely wishes to re-emphasise the role of voluntarism, so that there is an equal and supportive relationship between the two. This model combines the benefits of encompassing both the voluntary and decentralised local approach which was replaced by the welfare state, and the idea of 'comprehensive well-funded public services which the national state appeared to provide and localism and mutual aid could not' (Hirst, 1994).

This view of reorganising the political system is based around a strong notion of the community; but it is different to another concept of 'communitarian' which is used to describe the kind of society where moral values are re-emphasised. The basis of this society is a strengthening of the family as the provider of a strong moral framework to the new generation. The schools are the next arena where these moral values can be inculcated, located within the context of a third arena, the community. The state is seen as the fourth part of this society, which provides the overall framework for ensuring commitment to democratic values and respect for other groups.[32] These kinds of ideas have been around for a long time, for example, Robert Owen's New Lanarkshire communities of the early nineteenth century espoused similar notions of the community. Their reappearance now is in response to an Anglo-American concern that their societies are no longer cohesive and in some danger of disintegrating. One key fear is that the traditional family structure is disappearing. However, the reality is that families are now constituted in many different forms and moral indignation at single parent families, which in most cases, are run by women, is misplaced.

Communitarians, then, need to embrace a very broad definition of the family. Furthermore, the concept of the community can be used both by the left and the right. It can be used as a way of empowering people to increase participation in the democratic process and thereby challenge national and international sources of power, or as a way to divert people into small-scale individualised and localised activity which allows the main national or international structures of society to continue in the same way as before with even less scrutiny and accountability.[33]

In Britain, for example, one way to promote this kind of community would be to reform political institutions and introduce more democratically accountable and transparent procedures. Other measures that would be necessary include the provision of low cost industrial finance, regional networks of collaborative public–private partnerships to provide collective services, and legislation to facilitate the setting up of mutual firms and worker cooperatives. The emphasis is to devolve decision-making and the economy to regional and local level.

## 3.4  Pluralism and neo-pluralism

The free market system with its emphasis on the free activity of individuals competing in the market place (economic pluralism) promoted the growth of interest groups eventually coalescing into competing political parties (political pluralism). Prior to the free market system and in tandem with its development came the growth of ideas about the protection of individual rights against the power of the absolutist state, based largely on the defence of private property against the powers of an absolute monarchy (Macpherson, 1964).

Locke and Montesquieu and subsequent political theorists also stressed the importance of separating the powers of the state (legislative, executive and judicial) in order to prevent concentration of power in one branch of government.[34] This feature is best known in the US system of checks and balances. De Tocqueville and J. S. Mill argued for the protection of individual liberty through a series of interest groups against the encroaching powers of the state.[35] So we have three important elements of a liberal democracy: **competition**, **individual rights** and a **balanced political system**.

Social pluralism refers to the plethora of different interest and pressure groups which exist within any liberal democratic state, and which operate within civil society. The most important interest groups are trade unions and employers' organisations, which may or may not have a role to play in the governing of a country. The role of the mass media is also crucial in influencing and determining policy outcomes. More distant from the centres of decision making and usually outside any formal role in the governing process are pressure groups. These encompass every aspect of activity, for example environmental groups such as Greenpeace or anti-racist organisations such as SOS-Racisme. There is continuing debate over the role and influence of both interest groups and pressure groups (see the section on Corporatism below).

De Tocqueville was one of the first writers to recognise the importance of interest groups within the US political system.[36] Democracy required intermediate associations between the state and the citizenry, commonly known as factions. The American philosopher John Dewey referred to these groups as 'publics', and to society as being made up of a 'universe of many publics'.

The whole debate about pluralism in the post-1945 world was sparked off by the publication in 1956 of American sociologist C. Wright Mills's *The Power Elite*. Mills argued that the United States is governed by three interlocking elite groups, the military, the business and the political elite. President Eisenhower had already warned in the early 1950s of the growing influence of the 'military–industrial complex'. Mills emphasised the elite groups' similarity of educational and social background and permeability. He dismissed the notion that within liberal democracy all groups might have equal access to and control of the levers of power. We deal with these points in more detail later in this chapter.

In response to this indictment of the United States and by implication other Western liberal democracies, Dahl produced his classic defences of pluralism.[37] In these books he refutes the ideas of Mills, by showing that in a small- to medium-sized American town, New Haven, the notion that there were a series of interlocking elites who controlled all decision making was erroneous. He argues that this may have been the case in the nineteenth century but in the contemporary world the real picture was different.

The process of decision making was complex and, depending on the particular decision being taken, different groups had access and power to control the outcome. These groups are referred to as 'minorities', and democracy is defined in Dahl's terms as 'minorities government'. Democracy is protected from one faction gaining too much power and becoming oppressive by what Dahl refers to as **polyarchy**, whereby these groups have to compete in an 'open contest for electoral support, which balances out one group against another'.[38]

A further contribution that Dahl has made to this discussion about democracy concerns the way in which a legitimate **opposition** has become part of the structure of liberal democracies. He refers to it as one of the great 'social discoveries' of the human race, because it means that political competition, at the heart of the pluralist argument, is guaranteed. **Oppositions** can come to power in a peaceful and legitimate way and this is accepted by opponents, as their chance to govern may come around again soon. Through such a mechanism power can become dispersed (Dahl, 1966); although, as Mény (1993) points out, it was not really until 1981 and 1986 in France that the process of alternation and then 'cohabitation' became established so that a legitimate **opposition** came to be accepted. For the pluralists, then, power is 'non-hierarchically and competitively arranged'; it is dispersed and non-cumulative.[39]

The pluralist argument stresses the importance of individuals and groups representing different interests engaged in an 'endless process of bargaining' (Dahl, 1957). These groups may cluster around particular cleavages, as Dahl's fourfold categorisation of associations indicates: **cultural** (family, religious and educational, e.g. universities), **governmental** (Parliament, the executive and the judiciary, including local government), **political** (political parties, pressure groups) and finally **economic** (employers' organisations and trade unions).[40] The debate has continued, with Samuel H. Beer (1974) arguing that liberal democracy is based on three main economic groups, business, labour and agriculture which act in rough equilibrium, and J. K. Galbraith (1984) highlighting the way in which these groups provide countervailing power. The fact that very few people actually participate actively in the political process is not an issue for pluralists, as everyone has the chance to participate if they choose to do so.[41] In Dahl's words they can become 'activated' whenever they choose, and so the element of choice which is a central feature of liberal democratic states is therefore maintained.

The initial assumptions that pluralist political theory made began to be seriously undermined by the conflicts that arose in Europe and the United States during the 1960s, and particularly by the lack of democracy in the economic sphere, where concern was expressed at the overwhelming and unaccountable power of Trans-National Corporations (TNCs). A revised theory was needed to explain the inability of certain groups to prevail in this key area of the decision-making process. **Pluralism** evolved into **neo-pluralism** to try to come to terms with these new developments.

The work of the neo-pluralists, including Dahl, concentrates on the need for democracy in the economic sphere.[42] There needs to be change from 'stockholder democracy to owner-worker democracy' whereby employees have a direct say in the running of their firms so that they become 'democratically governed enterprises'.[43] The neo-pluralists argue that the same kind of democratic accountability in the political system needs to be extended to the economic sphere (Lindblom, 1977).

In conclusion, then, neo-pluralists argue like pluralists, that the policy outcomes in any liberal democratic state reflect the state's basic neutrality in dealing with opposing opinions and being able to come to some kind of compromise between the demands of various groups.

## Criticisms of pluralism and neo-pluralism

Critics of pluralist and neo-pluralist theory have focused on a number of areas:

(i)   Methods. The methods used by the pluralists have been open to criticism in terms of their focus on overt political conflict, on certain key issues, and the micro nature of their studies. Their assumptions that all political conflict is overt has been criticised by those who argue that it is not necessarily those issues which are visible which hold the key as to who has power but it is the power to influence the agenda so that certain issues never reach the light of day that is crucial. Bachrach and Baratz use Schattschneider's concept of the 'mobilisation of bias', which results in issues being prevented from coming into the public domain and open to public gaze and scrutiny.[44] Opponents of the micro nature of the pluralists' studies argue that this ignores the wider structural nature of society within which these groups exercise their power, whereby some groups have greater resources and fuller access to knowledge and information, that leads to 'systematic imbalance'.[45]

(ii)   State as neutral. This assumption by pluralists has been characterised by Dunleavy and O'Leary in a threefold way: the 'weathervane', 'neutral' and 'broker' state, which has been challenged by the radical elite and Marxist theorists.[46] For pluralists, there is no single powerful decision-making centre but a diffuse power structure open to influence and change, depending on the relative weight that each particular group has at any particular time. Political parties operate therefore in an open and competitive arena with equal access to the electorate.

The debate has also to be situated in the context of the Cold War and the need to highlight the important differences between the Western pluralistic liberal democratic states and the monolithic command economy states of the Soviet bloc. The debate has continued since then and has involved questions about whether the elite groups in society form a ruling class, how open the societies really are, and the role of the state. Hayward refers to 'limited pluralism' to define the way in which industrial societies are structured and managed.[47]

## 3.5   Elite theory

**Classical elite** theories were formulated by Vilfredo Pareto (1848–1923), Gaetano Mosca (1858–1941) and Robert Michels (1876–1936).[48] All three writers emphasise the inevitable tendency for any society to throw up an elite group which will dominate and determine the direction of that society. Their theories about the way in which societies developed and were governed grew out of a rejection of Marx's ideas about classes and the way in which progress took place in human societies. Underlying their work there is also a fear and hatred of the masses. Marx's ideas about a classless (i.e. non-elite) society and the mass participation of people in the political process were seen as Utopian by these writers. Marx's notion of a 'vanguard' party made up of professional revolutionaries, later developed by Lenin into the leading role of the Party, led to the institutionalisation of an elite group within the party structure.[49] Nevertheless, Marx stressed that everyone could have power by participating fully in society and determining their own life, whereas the elite theorists argue that it is only ever a small group of people in leading positions in society that determine what everyone else should do.

Elite theory relies heavily on psychological interpretations of human behaviour using stereotyped behaviour from the animal kingdom. Pareto, borrowing heavily from Machiavelli, sees human societies led by people with lion-like (decisive and bold) or fox-like (cunning and guile) characteristics. Change comes about when one elite loses its vitality, becomes decadent and is replaced by another elite, the 'circulation of elites'. History is seen as cyclical and characterised as 'a graveyard of aristocracies'.

For Mosca there is a small group of people in any society who possess a material, intellectual and moral superiority that gives them the right to lead the masses, who have a psychological need to be led. Mosca also recognised the role that education and training could play in forming an elite, and the way that such institutions were always 'more open to the rich than to the poor'.[50]

Michels, writing in 1911, based his notion of an inevitability of elite rule from an analysis he made of the German Social Democratic Party (SPD). He showed that even within an organisation such as the SPD, which was supposedly committed to notions of participation and representing members' interests, a hierarchical and bureaucratic organisation became established. Michels refers to this process as the 'iron law of oligarchy', which stems from the need for groups to become organised in modern democratic societies in order to promote their interests. Once established the organisation is taken over by paid officials, it becomes a rigid hierarchy and displays all those 'petty, narrow and illiberal' tendencies found in any such bureaucratic organisation, when an elite or oligarchy comes into being and starts to dominate. The overriding concern of the elite is to hold on to their positions and power within whatever type of society, capitalist or communist. Michels also stresses the psychological need for the masses to be led.

Schumpeter's analysis of modern democracies, originally published in 1943, led him to similar conclusions. Like Weber, Schumpeter sees capitalism as accelerating a process of increasing rationalisation through the growth of large-scale bureaucratic organisations. Unlike Weber, however, Schumpeter does not regard this process as necessarily threatening to democracy. It is an inevitable, and acceptable, development in organising the running of society. The subsequent increase in technical experts who act in an impartial way to run the society has great implications for society. Socialism, then, merely becomes another way of managing an already existing bureaucracy, created by capitalism. Democracy is therefore about gaining power to control these large organisations. The particular form that it needs to take is defined as 'leadership democracy' or 'competitive elitism'. The role for the people is to choose those who will rule them. There is no space in Schumpeter's model for any real participation by the people, only limited discussion and the odd vote now and again.[51] Weber also saw the need for strong leadership to fight bureaucratic greyness and bureaucracy in order to inculcate national values.

Criticisms of classic elite theory have been based on their over-pessimistic analysis of human nature, which they see as dangerous and needing to be controlled. There also seems to exist a shared contempt for the masses which has its modern form in the New Right theories, which are basically anti-democratic. The almost biological formulation of the state as a strong organism which needs to be protected from the weakness and feebleness of the masses found echoes later in the Fascist notion of the strong leader and the cult of the master race.

## Radical elite theory

C. Wright Mills's analysis concentrates solely on elites in the United States. He rejects the classical elite theorists' notion that the elites have special psychological capabilities that make them superior to the rest of society. Instead Mills focuses on the institutional structures that allow them to prevail. There are three key institutions: the major corporations, the military and the federal government. The leading actors in these institutions form part of what Mills terms the 'power elite', an interlocking group which joins together the economic, military and political power of the United States, which takes all the major decisions that affect national and, given the predominance of the United States, international issues.

As the economy has become more global so economic power has become concentrated in the TNCs, many of whom, like General Motors, are more powerful than most other nation states. This concentration of economic power has been reflected in the increasing centralisation of power at the federal government level. The final piece in the interlocking jigsaw is the social background of the elite, most of whom are male, white Anglo-Saxon Protestant (WASPs) in leading executive positions.

Mills differs from classic elite theorists in arguing that there is no inevitability in this process, it is a product of a particular industrial and historical process. Since Mills wrote, debate has focused on whether this elite always acts in a coherent and unified manner. Much of Dahl's political theory was based on the need to refute Mills's ideas, and debate continues on the whole nature of the elite.

## Elites in Western Europe

Terms such as the political class, the dominant class and the Establishment all refer to the same broad group of people at the top of any society in the modern state. The question in which political scientists are interested is whether these groups all share the same background, values and outlook. Most importantly, do these groups all act with one voice? In other words, is there one centre of power, exercised by people from similar backgrounds with similar views? Or are there several competing groups of power? Even if there are several competing elites, do they not all subscribe more or less to the same underlying economic, political and cultural values?

In the United Kingdom, there is the view that the leading groups who run the economics, politics and culture of the country are made up of a series of interlocking circles of people who know how to make connections.[52] Power in this model is diffused, but only really to a limited extent. As Paxman notes, most leading groups in British society are made up of white, university educated (mainly Oxbridge) men.[53] It is this same Oxbridge elite that Tony Benn finds within the 'core executive in Britain who make all the decisions'.[54] In France it is suggested that the social and cultural elite is composed of 500 important families, mainly Paris-based, the political elite is made up of the Grand Corps, graduates of the leading bureaucrat-training colleges, like the ENA and the Ecole Polytechnique, and the economic elite from the long-established families such as Dassault and Peugeot. There is, however, considerable overlap between these various elites in France, according to a recent survey of French business elites.[55] The number of former pupils of the ENA and the Ecole Polytechnique who had previously worked in government, and then taken up leading posts in one of France's 200 largest companies, had increased from 41 per cent in 1983 to 47 per cent in 1993.

In our search for the most powerful and influential governing groups in contemporary western Europe, we shall be using the term elite to cover three kinds of groups. First of all there are the officials and leading members of established political parties and organisations who form the **political elites**. Linked to this group are the **bureaucratic elites**, who in many countries, particularly France and Germany, are often although not exclusively interchangeable (see Chapter 10). Then there are the **social elites**, which refers to leaders of business, media owners and presenters and leading members of social organisations such as Employers Associations, Trade Unions and other peak interest groups. These are the groups with a great deal of economic power. Not all these elites have equal power, and the purpose of this book will be to come to some kind of assessment of their relative power.

## Elites in East/Central Europe (ECE)

This section examines the whole debate about elites in the countries of East/Central Europe (ECE) (Poland, Hungary, and the Czech and Slovak Republics).[56] The socialist system that existed for about 40 years in those countries threw up a political, and smaller dominant governing, elite based exclusively on membership of the Communist Party. This group controlled the 'iron triangle of power', which represents the coalition of political (party), administrative and technocratic elites'.[57] Political elites, techno-bureaucracies and organised interests operate everywhere, including western Europe. Under the system of state socialism everyone was dependent on the Communist Party. As a result of the transition, these close linkages have been broken and these groups have developed their own power centres. It is important to note also that many changes both in the economic and political sphere pre-dated the complete collapse of the old regimes in 1989. The strength of the Solidarity movement had already forced the Polish government to agree to a set of reforms designed to introduce democracy. In Hungary, there was in existence a buoyant small business sector.[58] However, there has been some institutional and cultural continuity post-1989 although great change in terms of personnel in the political elite.

The transition in ECE has been from a highly centralised one-party state based on a dogmatic political philosophy to a more pluralist liberal democratic form of state. In the economic sphere the transition has been from a command economy (state-owned and centrally controlled) to a market economy based on private ownership and driven by profit and competition. The process of transition has been variable and none of the ECE states has arrived fully at the Western Capitalist Liberal Democratic model. Indeed, each of these new 'democratic' states is proceeding at its own pace of reform.

The single most significant factor in elite composition has been the infusion of completely new personnel into leading positions within the state. In Hungary, the top political elite is estimated at 1200 people with about 10 000 members of the middle to high level administrative–technocratic elite. Between 1989 and 1990 practically the whole of this elite was replaced by new personnel.[59] Furthermore, in pre-1989 ECE a counter-elite, made up of intellectuals, writers, church leaders and workers' organisations (for example, **Solidarnosc** (Solidarity) in Poland) developed out of conflict with the authoritarian state. Many of these people, like Walesa in Poland and Havel in the Czech Republic, now have prominent roles in the new democracies.

One feature of the transition, however, has been the continuing struggle between this new elite and a new counter-elite, made up of the old elite. The danger presented by this sudden change of personnel is the development of a clientelistic state.[60] The new political leaders find themselves in positions where they can gain influence through the appointment of sympathetic supporters in the bureaucracy. In addition, many of the previous bureaucrats had skills which are still valuable, for example foreign languages and knowledge of the administrative system. This group forms one part of the new counter-elite.

Much of the state-led privatisation has led to the emergence of an economic elite dependent on the favours of the political elite. Contracts have tended to be awarded to supporters of this or that party, which have in their turn had their campaigns financed by those people they have helped set up in business in the first place. The three elite groups, then, are made up of a new political elite, the dependent bureaucrats who owe their position to their new masters, and the newly created economic bourgeoisie.

Opposition to these developments has come from the nationalist–populist parties and the pure free marketeers. A crucial element lacking in the economic transition is the emergence of small-scale entrepreneurs. One result of the lack of agreed goals has been a fragmentation of the political system, and the development of a clientelistic system.

The elites are disunited and Agh argues that in ECE what is needed is a 'consensually united elite', a new professional political elite, which should develop 'an articulated relationship with organised interests and with civil society'.[61] The same point is raised by Szablowski concerning the dissension that has arisen within the Solidarity movement:

The outbursts of personal animosities which gradually turned into non-negotiable matters of principle were perfectly in keeping with the absence of a mature democratic elite culture.[62]

The kind of features of such an elite culture are notions of accommodation, bargain and compromise to resolve key policy differences. Szablowski argues that these features are absent in contemporary Polish political culture. The Polish political elite is made up of the intelligentsia, whose values of 'collective mission' and notions of 'didactic functions' does not accord well with a middle class which is much more orientated towards economic achievement, and a democratic elite culture whose values stress more individualism, adversarial politics and compromise.[63]

## 3.6   Corporatism and neo-corporatism

Corporatism explores the nature of the relationship between the state and organised interests. It is based on the assumption that in recent years there has been growing state intervention in the management of the economy. This has resulted in the incorporation of the two main economic interest groups, employers' organisations and trade unions, into the realm of economic management to create a tripartite structure. An example in Britain was the role of the National Economic Development Council (NEDO, more affectionately known as 'Neddy'), and in Germany the notion of *Konziertierte Aktion*, which together with the *Sozialgesprächsrunde* (Social Partners' Round Table Discussions), brought together the state, employers' organisations and trade unions to discuss economic and social policy. Although the state may set the overall context for economic management, tripartism often becomes bipartism, with employers and trade unions engaged in direct negotiation.

According to this theory the state:

is not controlled by any particular economic class or group, but plays an independent and dominant role in its relationship with capital and labour.[64]

The interest groups it deals with tend to be led from the top and are hierarchical and bureaucratic organisations. They may represent their members in these corporatist structures, but they are also obliged to discipline their members should they part from the accepted policy. There is, therefore, a price to pay in becoming incorporated. These interest groups, according to Schmitter, are organised:

into a limited number of singular, compulsory, non-competitive, hierarchically ordered and functionally differentiated categories, recognised or licensed (if not created) by the state and granted a deliberate representational monopoly within their respective categories in exchange for observing certain controls on their selection of leaders and articulation of demands and supports.[65]

For Panitch, corporatism:

integrates organised socio-economic producer groups through a system of representation and cooperative mutual interaction at the leadership level and mobilisation and social control at the mass level.[66]

Towards the end of the last century it became clear to everyone that industrial society was here to stay. Many people, however, bemoaned the fact that the supposedly cosy medieval relationship between landlord and peasant and that ordered and supposedly harmonious society had been destroyed by capitalism. Society had become too atomised, in their view, as a result of liberalism with its glorification of the rights of the individual. So corporatism came to define those societies which tried to recreate the social bonds of solidarity that existed in pre-capitalist times.

The importance of Catholicism in this respect needs to be considered in its espousal of a social order based on harmony and an integrated polity. Although some of the corporatist criticisms of industrial capitalist society are similar to the Marxist critique, a key point of difference is the importance corporatist thinkers attach to private property. In countries such as Italy of the 1920s and 1930s under Mussolini, and Portugal between 1933–1974 (Estado Novo) under Salazar, the term corporatism was used to describe the particular form taken by the state in the way in which it was organised and run. In particular, this kind of corporatism refers to the combined role of big business, large landowners and the state, where the state tries to 'guide' the economy and protect it from the effects of international competition on the one hand and the challenge of organised labour in the form of trade unions on the other hand.[67] What, then, are the characteristics of the modern-day corporatism and how do these differ from the pluralism?

The impetus to the new debate about **corporatism** or, strictly speaking, **neo-corporatism**, to distinguish it from its pre-1945 being, came from Philippe Schmitter's work in the 1970s, which he saw as offering:

to the political analyst an explicit alternative to the paradigm of interest politics which has here-tofore completely dominated the discipline of North American political science: pluralism.[68]

However, the actual distinction between these two approaches may lie more in form than actual content. The corporatist model does not necessarily exclude elements of pluralism. As Schmitter has explained, corporatist patterns very over time and place. Other writers have also leaned towards this view, notably Lehmbruch.[69] Perhaps the most useful analysis of this relationship between pluralism and corporatism is Cawson and Saunders' dual state thesis.[70]

The dual state thesis argues that the relations between the state and organised interests are not all of the same degree. At the macroeconomic national level, the central state is involved in helping promote the accumulation of capital, in conjunction with other leading producer groups. These groups are usually the large employers' associations and trade unions, and this kind of activity can be seen as corporatist. However, at a local or regional level where the state is more closely related to consumption, for instance of welfare (e.g. housing benefits), the local state becomes involved with many different kinds of groups, and so reflects a more pluralist pattern.[71]

For Schmitter there are two kinds of corporatism, state and societal. Examples of the first type, which is authoritarian, include Fascist Italy, Nazi Germany and Salazar's Portugal. The second type refers to the societies of western Europe and the United States, where corporatist structures have grown up as elements of pluralism have declined. The reason for this decline in the pluralist nature of western democracies is the need to continue to ensure the most suitable conditions for the accumulation of capital. This has meant that the state has had to become far more involved in economic management, and become directly involved with negotiating policy outcomes with peak interest groups. As public and private monopolies have come to dominate the economic landscape, so the state has become increasingly involved in detailed issues concerning the economy (promoting investment, prices and incomes policy and interest rate management). The effect of neo-liberalism is to try to reduce the state component in this equation, but which paradoxically has increased state involvement in the United Kingdom by the creation of state organisations such as QUANGOs (quasi-autonomous non-governmental organisations).

## 3.7  Marxist theory

The executive of the modern state is but a committee for running the common affairs of the bourgeoisie

MARX AND ENGELS, *The Communist Manifesto*

The basic elements of Marxism concern the overwhelming importance that the organisation of the economy has over all other aspects of society. For Marx, the **bourgeoisie** (ruling class or capitalist class) as the owners and controllers of capital (finance, land, mines, factories, and shops) were the predominant group in a capitalist society, and society was run in all its aspects, economic as well as political, social and cultural, in order to serve their interests first and foremost. The opening quote is a reflection of that analysis, which indicates that the business of government was basically to run a system in favour of the bourgeoisie, to protect and promote their private property and create the conditions whereby they could accumulate as much capital and make as much profit as possible. On the other side of this equation were the working class (**proletariat**), who have nothing to sell except their labour power, and who were kept in barely subsistence conditions in order for the bourgeoisie to be able to maintain healthy profits. For the proletariat, it was important to try to gain as much from the system as possible in terms of better wages and conditions at work, and better housing, education and health care.

Society was divided into these two opposing classes, whose interests were diametrically opposed, and who existed in an antagonistic relationship. Particular social classes have arisen throughout human history depending on the nature of the agricultural, or in the nineteenth century, industrial production system that was predominant. The relationship between the classes, for example serfs and their masters in the Middle Ages, was antagonistic. For Marx and Engels, and Marxists generally, the way in which the antagonism between social classes resolves itself explains the development of history. Under capitalism, we find the bourgeoisie and the proletariat opposing each other and in Marx's prediction, as a result of the tensions between the two groups, and the fact that the proletariat is a much larger class, it will eventually overcome the bourgeoisie and a classless society will arrive.

The debate among neo-Marxist writers concerns the explanations for the domination of the state by the interests of capital. Is it as a result of the common social and educational background of the elite and the demands of capital, or is it wholly a result of the objective forces of capital that forces the elite to act in a certain way? There is a further question concerning the 'relative autonomy' of the state. Does economic and political power always go hand in hand, with political power always acting at the behest of economic power? In other words, does the state always act in the interests of one united dominant economic class? Or does it act sometimes only in favour of one particular group within the dominant class? For example, high interest rates favour those in the insurance and banking world, but makes it very difficult and expensive to expand for those with a business who need to borrow that money. Furthermore, some would argue that at other times the state acts in the interests of the dominated class, by providing state insurance schemes to which employers have to make a contribution.

Miliband's original argument was that the state is not neutral and acts in the interests of the dominant economic class. It operates in this way because the social class that runs the political and economic organisations in capitalist society is interlinked socially and educationally, and furthermore is dependent on being successful in the economic sphere in order to maintain their dominant position. Capital is a powerful objective force which straitjackets the officials of the state, such as civil servants, to work in a way that promotes the most effective form of capital accumulation. The state therefore serves the long-term interests of the bourgeoisie by providing an infrastructure within which the economy can function, for instance schooling, for the next generation of workers and tax breaks to promote investment. As we mentioned in Chapter 1 it also controls the means of coercion in order to ensure conformity to its requirements.

Poulantzas takes issue with Miliband's emphasis on the class background of state officials as an important explanation for the domination of one class. Instead he argues that it is the objective power of capital that determines the relationship between the state and the bourgeoisie. This is a structuralist argument, which says that the behaviour of individuals or groups within the capitalist state is as a result of the demands made upon them by the objective power of capital. Both writers agree that the state is not neutral: their differences are really a matter of emphasis.

Furthermore, they also accept that there is some kind of 'relative autonomy' within the system, that allows groups some measure of choice as to how to act. However, this element of their argument would then deny the force of the structuralist argument that explains groups' behaviour purely as a result of objective forces acting on them. Furthermore, if capitalists are a divided group then a monocausal explanation based on a structural analysis is not adequate, and it may be necessary to include an element of pluralism even if only in terms of competitive elites.

For Louis Althusser, the state ensured obedience through coercion in the form of repressive state apparatuses, such as the army and police force, and ideological state apparatuses, such as the education system and the mass media. This is another structuralist viewpoint which concentrates on the way in which human beings are compelled to act based on the direction of these various institutions.

## 3.8   The state and civil society

A key factor in helping to understand the way in which European development has taken place is the nature and role of the state. We take as our starting point that it is the organisation and control of production processes that determines to a large extent the nature of any individual state. Furthermore, by stressing the importance of the production process, we are also highlighting the relevance of social classes and the interrelationship and conflict between them. We consider the whole debate between those who argue that the state is nothing more than the political expression of ruling groups in society, and those who argue that it is more important to focus on interest groups and the whole nature of civil society, in order to understand better how society is run.

## What is the state?

The state has a dual structure and purpose. It is all those institutions which ensure obedience through coercion (political, legal, judicial, administrative, including the police and the military) and also those institutions which 'manufacture consent' (Chomsky) through influencing and controlling public opinion, for instance the education system, the mass media and government propaganda agencies. Gramsci's notion of hegemony is useful in explaining how this process operates, whereby the state is able to ensure consent not only by having the actual physical means i.e. the police or the army, but also by the way in which people's/our minds are influenced and directed from birth by the agencies of opinion-forming listed above.[72] In fact, the state has become and remains all-intrusive, in spite of neo-liberal attempts to reduce its role; for example, measures such as giving every citizen in Britain a National Health number at birth, and a National Insurance number as soon as we are employed, to more universal features such as deciding how much tax we should pay, what kind of education we should receive, inducements to use private cars or public transport, and whether we should have to do military service or not. Briefly, then, the state is active in the whole area of welfare, economic management, and areas concerning planning and consumer protection (Ham and Hill, 1993).

## Actors in the state

Within, between and outside those structures there is an ongoing dynamic process between social classes, negotiated by political parties, interest groups such as trade unions and employers' organisations, and to a lesser extent pressure groups.

'classes' are perhaps best thought of as expressing the constant interaction between socio-economic structure and political process, and between what is determined and what can be, and is, changed by human agency.[73]

These social classes are in Gramsci's (1971) terms 'historic blocs' made up of groups in society which occupy certain positions within the hierarchy of the state in terms of a dominant and subordinate relationship. The dominant social class is one such 'historic bloc' which has at its disposal all the means detailed above to ensure conformity to its demands. These social classes can be made up of different groups and it is important to see whether they perceive themselves as acting in concert so that they actually constitute a distinct social class. Cox (1987) has highlighted the mediating role of classes in the relation between production and the state, and he goes on to indicate that this operates not only at the national level but also at the global level. Within this global map of social classes the **dominant** groups are made up of:

1. The controllers of large Trans-National Corporations (TNCs).
2. Controllers of large national enterprises and industrial groups.
3. Locally based smaller scale industrialists.

Included in 1 are also members of the Trilateral Commission (composed of national political and bureaucratic elites), the OECD, the IMF, the World Bank, as well as a transnational managerial class and public officials in national and international agencies, particularly in the area of 'high finance' (leading merchant bankers, national and international bankers, insurance managers and other large-scale financiers).[74]

These views echo those of Karl Polanyi (1968) on the dominating role of **haute finance** in the nineteenth century, which is relevant to the continuing role played by this group in the contemporary world. He considered that the reason for decades of relative peace between nation states in Europe during the nineteenth century was largely a result of **haute finance** needing peace to maintain and protect their investments.[75]

Cox outlines five different categories which make up the **subordinate** groups: those people involved in technical, scientific and supervisory occupations closely linked to 'the functions of industrial management', 'established' workers in fairly secure employment and usually unionised, 'nonestablished' workers in insecure, casual and non-unionised employment, industrial workers in the newly industrialising countries (NICs) such as Taiwan, South Korea and Malaysia, and the large group of landless people who are fitfully employed in the informal sector of the economy in many countries of the South. To this last group can also be added the small-scale farmers of the South who produce most of the food and whose livelihood, particularly in subSaharan Africa and India, is likely to be adversely affected by the latest GATT round.

The dominant groups reinforce their positions within the global and national economic and political structures by the ownership and control of mass media organisations, which have become huge TNCs. In Sklair's words these groups have a 'cultural–ideological' project, which is to persuade people to become ever-greater consumers of the goods produced by other TNCs which they are either owned by or own themselves:

The culture-ideology of consumerism is, as it were, the fuel that powers the motor of global capitalism. The driver is the transnational capitalist class. But the vehicle itself is the mighty transnational corporation.[76]

In the 30 years after 1945 the dominant influence in the western world was the United States, and van der Pijl (1984) has outlined the way in which an Atlantic ruling class has developed. Atlanticism as both ideology and an actual process of class formation was based on liberalisation and state intervention, the two pillars of corporate liberalism which developed hand in hand. It was initiated by Roosevelt's **Atlantic Universalism** brought about by the European focus of World War II, followed by the **Atlantic Union** which arose from the Marshall Plan as an anti-Soviet bloc, then Kennedy's **Atlantic Partnership** (1961) to restore unity of purpose to an Atlantic world given the rise of the EEC and its break from American domination. The effect of Nixon's removal of the dollar from the Gold Standard in 1971, with the growth in international liquidity, then allowed TNCs to relocate their enterprises in the periphery which together with the effect of the oil price rises of the early 1970s, led to the breakdown of the capital–labour compromise (**corporatism**) and the dissolution of the 'hegemonial strategy of the Atlantic bourgeoisie'.

In discussing the nature and role of the state, we will focus our attention on the way in which interest groups and social classes operate within these structures. As we have indicated previously, unity and diversity of experience are present within all western European states. It is useful to examine, as far as possible, how the state is organised by analysing models of coordination: market coordination, coordination by hierarchy and network coordination. Despite the two different views on power, which are presented in Section 3.2, it is still valuable to analyse how power is exercised by highlighting those groups that have the most influence and power within the context of each nation state, and then to see whether we can discern a pattern emerging of groups at a European level which operate in a similar way to national groups.

The role of the state at a national level is crucial, therefore, in setting out the parameters of action in all areas of activity. However, it is important to emphasise that in the period which we are considering the international context has provided the general framework within which nation states have operated and been constrained:

There is a practical connection between the effort of a state to organise its society and its effort to maintain itself and pursue its goals in the interstate context.[77]

Therefore, over a period of time the role of the state is crucial in the economic sphere where, for example, it can actively set an agenda to attract foreign investment by allowing tax breaks, the example of Nissan in Sunderland or establishing, in the British case, enterprise zones (EZ). In the EZs, companies can be given up to a 10-year break from paying local taxes. It can also favour accumulation by finance capital over industrial capital by raising interest rates, or in other sectors by creating subsidies. In the social arena policies can be introduced that promote child care facilities which can have an effect not only on the ability of many women to join the labour market, but also can in time lead to changes in the way in which the family is structured and the division of labour in the domestic sphere/who does what in the home family environment.

Cox considers that there have been two main types of state in western Europe this century: the 'welfare-nationalist' state, which was 'built to protect the national economy from outside influences and to enhance national power in relation to rivals', and the more recent 'neoliberal state', which 'sought its security as a member of a stable alliance system and its economic growth as a participant in an open world economy'.[78]

In deciding where to focus our attention in order to provide a satisfactory answer to the question 'where does power lie in Europe?' we shall consider the interrelationship between various structures and actors at nation state and supranational level. Does power lie with political parties, as representatives of the people's will according to classic theories about liberal democracies may suggest? Or does power lie outside the formal structures of representation within a constellation of bankers, industrialists and bureaucrats, and in Brussels?

Hayward (1986) seems clear on this point:

Most of those who are essential to liberal, social and economic democracy are excluded from the economic policy community, whereas most of those included – notably the elite economic bureaucrats and the select business leaders – have no democratic legitimacy . . . among those excluded for most purposes are: the voters, political parties and parliament; the local authorities; the trade unions; the press; the mass of consumers.[79]

These public policy partners, in Hayward's view, allow these groups occasional participation, but see themselves as the only true 'guardians of an enduring public interest'. We should distinguish, further, between actors in the debate around issues concerning the operation of the welfare state, and those involved in influencing and making decisions about macroeconomic planning. In the first case we find fragmented pressure groups operating according to partial and contradictory agendas, while in the second we perceive a much more coordinated approach run by bankers, industrialists and bureaucrats in different combinations and with different relative powers, according to the particular nation state under consideration. So, for instance, in Germany it is the three leading banks the Deutsche Bank, the Commerzbank and the Dresdner Bank with their massive holdings and presence on the boards of leading German companies that control the economic planning. In France it is the Grand Corps within the ministries who direct planning, in Italy it is Confindustria, and in Britain, it is an interlocking arrangement between the City, the Bank of England and the Treasury: 'spider's web but no spider'. It is Cawson and Saunders' dual state thesis which relates closely to this point about the differing importance of interest and other groups depending on the issues being decided. The specific role of the state in economic affairs is considered in some detail throughout the book.

## What is civil society?

The concept of civil society has a long history, with political theorists trying to separate out the state from all the other activities that went on in a society. The state was seen in its formal terms as the legislature, the executive and the judiciary, fulfilling the role described in the last section, with the activities of various interest groups as representing civil society. For Marx and neo-Marxists, the state is the expression of the interests of the bourgeoisie and:

Civil society is the state-guaranteed realm of commodity production and exchange – of private property, greedy market competition and private rights.[80]

There is no distinction, then, between these spheres of activity, with civil society merely an adjunct of the state. Keane (1988) argues, however, that not only does civil society predate capitalism, but with the failure of state socialism in eastern Europe and the Soviet Union, and liberal democracy in the West unable to promote broad democracy by increasing citizens' participation, the concept is in need of reassessment.[81]

Civil society, then, is all those spheres of activity undertaken by citizens, either linked to the state like peak interest groups (e.g. trade unions, employers' groups) but not subordinate to it. It also includes all those other interest groups on a national basis, such as the National Trust, pressure groups such as Greenpeace, social, cultural and sporting associations, and the myriad local and community groups. Civil society also implies a certain set of organising principles based on notions of self-help, mutuality voluntarism and cooperation. It is predicated on equality between citizens and also reflects the real aspirations of people in terms of their self-identity as human beings, which may not necessarily be expressed through their work (economic relation to the state) or their social position in terms of hierarchy.[82]

Another challenge to Marx's arguments came from Marshall (1950), who reasserted the ancient notion of citizenship, which has three crucial components: civil rights, political rights and social rights. Each of these rights has developed out of particular historical circumstances:

- Civil rights refers to all those individual rights such as freedom of speech and faith, and the right to own property which writers like Locke championed against the absolutist state in the seventeenth century. It took until the last decades of the eighteenth century for these rights to be codified, as for instance, in the US constitution and the Declaration of Rights that accompanied the French Revolution. These rights formed the basis for the growth of capitalism and led to class inequalities.
- Political rights arose during the nineteenth century, when struggles were fought to ensure a greater franchise and greater representation for the people in elected assemblies.
- Social rights refer to all those rights, such as health care education and benefits, that citizens have demanded under the provisions of the welfare state, which has been a twentieth century development.

For Marshall, these rights have gone a long way to mitigating the worst effects of capitalism and although they have not brought about full equality they have at least improved all citizens' participation in the social world. Critics of Marshall have focused on his rather rosy view of the way in which rights have evolved and may continue to evolve, but all have agreed on the importance of stressing the link and interdependence of these rights.[83] The subsequent debate surrounding Marshall's ideas has given rise to notions of **social citizenship**, which refers to the extent to which people are entitled to support from the provisions of the welfare state. If social citizenship defines a particular relationship to the welfare state then **social exclusion** defines those people who are excluded in one way or another from enjoying the benefits available from a welfare system.

This whole debate is at the heart of the nature of the relationship between the state and civil society. By emphasising these rights, what Marshall does is to show the dynamic of the relationship between the state and civil society, and the importance of the demands that citizens make on the state from their position in civil society. At the same time it is the state that defines the parameters of citizenship in terms of legal rights, but it is important to realise that this whole arena is part of a contest which is ongoing between these two entities (see Fig. 3.2).

| **State**<br>(Public sphere) | **Civil Society**<br>(Private sphere) | |
|---|---|---|
| *National* – Legislature<br>Executive<br>Judiciary | Political parties | |
| *Obligations/duties*<br>Income tax<br>Conscription | *Interest groups*<br>Trade unions<br>Employers' organisations<br>+ Industrial lobbies, e.g.<br>transport/chemicals/steel | *Obligations/duties*<br>Subscriptions |
| *The mass media*<br>State-owned media | Private media | |
| *Education*<br>Schools, colleges, universities | | |
| Army/police | *Church/synagogue/mosque/temple* | |
| *Regional* – Regional assembly<br>Regional government | *Pressure groups*<br>Environmental/social<br>charities | |
| *Duties*<br>Local tax | *Associations*<br>Cultural/sporting | |
| *Local* – Local government | | |
| *Services* – e.g. health/education | | |

**Figure 3.2** Parameters of citizenship: the state versus civil society

It is difficult to draw a hard and fast distinction between the state and civil society, hence in Fig. 3.2 many groups such as political parties straddle the divide. According to Katz and Mair the role of political parties has changed over the last century from their original task of representing the interests of civil society to the state, via a situation of being:

. . . independent brokers between the state and civil society (the classic 'catch-all party' phase) . . . to a new and more recent stage, in which they actually move closer to becoming part of the state, and remain at quite a remove from civil society.[84]

It is useful to bear in mind the nature of the relationship, then, between the state and civil society, as a way of analysing the current structure of contemporary European societies.

## 3.9   Summary

All these theories of the state attempt to explain the way in which liberal democracies function in contemporary Europe. It is difficult to point to any one of these theories and say it provides *the* answer to our concern about explaining how the state is organised and run. Even within each of these theoretical perspectives there is considerable debate among the protagonists as we have seen. The Marxist debate between Miliband and Poulantzas over the relative autonomy of the state, and the debate among the corporatist school over whether Great Britain once displayed signs of corporatism which are long gone, should alert us to the difficulty of searching for monocausal explanations. It is the interconnectedness and the unity and diversity of experience in Europe that leads us to a position of 'mosaic eclecticism' as the basis of our theory. This path provides us with both a certain illumination and a healthy scepticism of a monoparadigmatic approach, although we would emphasise that such an approach should in no way be seen as the 'pick and mix' approach to social sciences. We are close to the thinking of Ham and Hill:

that to search for a single theory of the state is less useful than adopting a more eclectic approach which draws on the strengths of different theories.[85]

This point is echoed by Jessop; although he is referring specifically to Marxist theories of the state, it nevertheless holds for all mono-causal explanations:

For while any attempt to analyse the world must assume that it is determinate and determined, it does not follow that a single theory can comprehend the totality of its determinations without resorting to reductionism of one kind or another.[86]

Each theory that we have discussed, then, provides us with a certain useful way of analysing contemporary European states. The pluralist approach is useful in explaining the role of the state in those areas outside of macro economic management, for instance in the case of personal behaviour concerning the age of consent for gay men, or the choice women may or may not have concerning childbirth arrangements. Elitist theory helps us understand the way in which particular educational and social elites may be perpetuated, while corporatist theory has shed light on the role of interest groups and their preponderance in many areas of decision making. Marxist theory is still crucial in terms of emphasising the key role played by economic factors in structuring the range of policies and responses to that policy, but it does not fully explain the role of state when it appears to act in ways contrary to the wishes and needs of the ruling or dominant class.

Furthermore, the impact of nationalism on the way the state has acted in recent years and the issues of race and gender sit uncomfortably with a purely economic approach. Jessop argues that the state must be viewed as 'a set of institutions involving conflicts between a range of interests not just social classes'.[87] For instance, conflict between state officals (at national or local level) and citizens: in disputes over entitlement to benefits, local tax charges (e.g. Council Tax), access to health records and choice of school.

Issues of dominance, accountability and participation will be explored throughout subsequent chapters as we focus on substantive areas such as the labour market, industry, local and regional government and the welfare state. What we are concerned to find out is in whose interests are policies formulated and implemented, and how this process operates.

## Further reading

For a clear and succinct presentation of all these theories see:

Dunleavy, P. and O'Leary, B. (1987) *Theories of the State, the Politics of Liberal Democracy*, London: Macmillan.

Ham, C. and Hill, M. (1993) *The Policy Process in the Modern Capitalist State*, Hemel Hempstead: Harvester Wheatsheaf.

Hayward, J. (1986) *The State and Market Economy: Industrial patriotism and economic intervention in France*, Hemel Hempstead: Harvester Wheatsheaf.

### Power and authority

Chomsky, N. (1989) *Necessary Illusions. Thought Control in Democratic Societies*, London: Pluto.

Gerth, H. and Wright Mills, C. (1974) *From Max Weber*, London: RKP.

Giddens, A. and Held, D. (1982) *Classes, Power and Conflict*, Basingstoke: Macmillan.

Hague, R., Harrop, M. and Breslin, S. (1992) *Comparative Government and Politics, An Introduction*, London: Macmillan.

Lukes, S. (ed.) (1986) *Power*, Oxford: Blackwell.

### Democracy

Held, D. (1989) *Models of Democracy*, Cambridge: Polity Press.

Parry, G. and Moran, M. (1994) *Democracy and Democratisation*, London: Routledge.

Sartori, G. (1987) *The Theory of Democracy Revisited*, Chatham NJ: Chatham House Publishers.

### Specialist reading on democracy

Dahl, R. A. (1966) *Political Opposition in Western Democracies*, New Haven: Yale University Press.

Etzioni, A. (1995) *The Spirit of Community*, New York: Simon & Schuster.

Habermas, J. (1984) *The Theory of Communicative Action II: Lifeworld and System*, Boston MA: Beacon Press.

Hirst, P. (1994) *Associative Democracy: New Forms of Economic and Social Governance*, Cambridge: Polity Press.

Hood, S. (1989) *On Television*, London: Pluto Press.

Keane, J. (1988) *Democracy and Civil Society*, London: Verso.
Lovenduski, J. (1986) *Women and European Politics*, Hemel Hempstead: Harvester Wheatsheaf.
Lovenduski, J. and Norris, P. (1993) *Gender and Party Politics*, London: Sage.
Offe, C. (1984) *Contradictions of the Welfare State*, Cambridge, MA: MIT Press.
Pateman, C. (1970) *Participation and Democratic Theory*, Cambridge: Cambridge University Press.
Phillips, A. (1992) *Engendering Democracy*, Cambridge, Polity Press.
Randall, V. (1987) *Women and Politics. An International Perspective*, London: Macmillan.

## Pluralism and neo-pluralism

Beer, S. (ed.) (1974) *Modern Political Development*, New York: Random House.
Dahl, R. (1956) *A Preface to Democratic Theory*, Chicago: University of Chicago Press.
Dahl, R. (1961) *Who Governs? Democracy and power in an American city*, New Haven: Yale University Press.
Dahl, R. (1985) *A Preface to Economic Democracy*, Cambridge: Polity Press.
Galbraith, J. K. (1984) *Anatomy of Power*, New York: Hamilton.
Lindblom, C. (1977) *Politics and Markets*, London: Basic Books.
Macpherson, C. B. (1964) *The Political Theory of Possessive Individualism*, Oxford: Oxford University Press.
Mény, Y. (1993) *Government and Politics in Western Europe, Britain, France, Italy, Germany*, Oxford: Oxford University Press.

## Elites

Higley, J. and Gunther. R. (eds) (1992) *Elites and Democratic Consolidation in Latin America and Southern Europe*, Cambridge: Cambridge University Press.
Leif, T., Legrand, H.-J. and Klein, K. (eds) (1992) *Die Politische Klasse in Deutschland. Eliten auf dem Prüfstand*, Bonn: Bouvier Verlag.
Meisel, J. (1965) *Pareto and Mosca*, New York: Prentice Hall.
Nye, R. (1977) *The Anti-democratic Sources of Elite Theory, Pareto, Mosca and Michels*, London: Sage.
Paxman, J. (1990) *Friends In High Places. Who runs Britain?* London: Michael Joseph.
Sampson, A. (1992) *The Essential Anatomy of Britain*, London: Hodder & Stoughton.

## East/Central Europe

Agh, A. (1994) 'From Nomenklatura to Clientura: The emergence of new political elites in Eastern Europe' *Labour Focus on Eastern Europe* 47, pp. 58–77.
Derlien, H.-V. and Szablowski, G. J. (eds) (1993) 'Regime transitions, elites and bureaucracies in Eastern Europe' *Governance, Special Issue* 6(3) July.

## Corporatism

Lehmbruch, G. and Schmitter, P. C. (eds) (1982) *Patterns of Corporatist Policy Making*, London: Sage.
Lehmbruch, G. (1982) 'Introduction: neo-corporatism in comparative perspective' in *Patterns of Corporatist Policy-Making* Lehmbruch, G. and Schmitter, P. (eds), London: Sage.

Williamson, P. J. (1989) *Corporatism in Perspective*, London: Sage.
Winkler, J. (1976) 'Corporatism' *Archives Europeénnes de Sociologie*, XVII (1), pp. 65–80.


## Marxism

Benton, T. (1984) *The Rise and Fall of Structural Marxism, Althusser and his Influence*, London: Macmillan.
Miliband, R. (1969) *The State in Capitalist Society*, London: Weidenfeld & Nicholson.
Poulantzas, N. (1969) 'The problem of the capitalist state' *New Left Review* 58, pp. 75–89.


## The State and Civil Society

Cox, R. (1987) *Production, Power and World Order. Social Forces in the Making of History*, New York: Columbia University Press.
Gramsci, A. (1971) *Prison Notebooks*, London: Lawrence & Wishart.
Hayward, J. E. S. (1986) *The State and The Market Economy: Industrial Patriotism and Economic Intervention in France*, Hemel Hempstead: Harvester Wheatsheaf.
Keane, J. (1988) *Democracy and Civil Society*, London: Verso.
Leys, C. (1989) *Politics in Britain*, London: Verso.
Marshall, T. H. (1950) *Citizenship and Social Class*, Cambridge: Cambridge University Press.
Polanyi, K. (1968) *The Great Transformation*, Boston: Beacon Press.
Sklair, L. (1991) *The Sociology of the Global System*, Hemel Hempstead: Harvester Wheatsheaf.
van der Pijl, K. (1984) *The Making of an Atlantic Ruling Class*, London: Verso.


## Notes

1. Fukuyama, F. (1992) *The End of History and the Last Man*, Harmondsworth: Penguin. For a refutation of the Fukuyama thesis see Callinicos, A. (1992) *The Revenge of History*, Cambridge: Polity Press. See also the *History Today* collection of articles: Ryan, A. (1992) *Introduction. After the End of History*, London: Collins & Brown.
2. Parsons, T. (1969) *Politics and Social Structure*, New York: Free Press.
3. Dahl, R. (1957) 'The concept of power', *Behavioural Science* (3) pp. 201–15.
4. Lukes, S. (1974) *Power: A Radical View*, London: Macmillan.
5. Newman, M. (1994) 'Sovereignty, public power and the economy' in *Economic Policy Making in the European Union*, Brouwer, F., Lintner, V. and Newman, M. (eds), London: Federal Trust.
6. This concept, originally devised in the late nineteenth century, implied the impartial administration of justice, and the respect for that system by all state officials and judges. Unfortunately this concept did not prevent the rise of the Nazi party and the destruction of all the values implied in **Rechtsstaat**, but it nevertheless has been revived with stronger safeguards in the very successful **Basic Law** of the Federal Republic (**Grundgesetz**) (see also Chapter 10).
7. There seems to be a general acceptance by employees all over Europe that these kinds of measures are inevitable, as has been demonstrated by the widespread acceptance by miners in Britain of redundancy packages. Some isolated opposition does occur, as in S. Wales in April 1994 and Air France in late 1993, but it is sporadic and sooner or later peters out.

8. Michael Walzer in Hoy, D. (ed.) (1986) Foucault: A Critical Reader, Blackwell.

9. Hoy, 1986, p. 134.

10. Foucault does not believe in the sovereign state or the ruling class, and since the people do not exist as an entity (a demos), there can be no democratic revolution. Walzer in Hoy op. cit., p. 55.

11. Foucault, M. (1984) 'What is Enlightenment?' in *The Foucault Reader*, Dreyfus, H. and Rabinow, P. (eds), Harmondsworth: Penguin.

12. Foucault in Dreyfus, H. and Rabinow, P. 1984, p. 220.

13. Foucault, M. (1980) *Power/Knowledge*, Hemel Hempstead: Harvester Wheatsheaf.

14. Hoy, D. (1991) *Foucault: A Critical Reader*, Oxford: Blackwell.

15. Foucault identifies two meanings of the word 'subject': subject to someone else by control and dependence, and tied to his own identity by a conscience or self-knowledge.

16. For many writers this is capitalist society, but Foucault prefers to use terms like the 'disciplinary society', or the 'carceral archipelago'.

17. Foucault, M. (1982) 'The subject and power' in *Michel Foucault* Dreyfus, H. and Rabinow, P. (eds) Hemel Hempstead: Harvester Wheatsheaf, p. 211.

18. Walzer in Hoy, 1991, p. 66.

19. Rorty, R. (1991) in Hoy, D. (ed.) *Foucault: A Critical Reader*, Oxford: Blackwell.

20. For Bertrand Russell:

'Power over human beings may be classified by the manner of influencing individuals, or by the type of organisation'.
   This view is illustrated in the following way, by reference to our behaviour towards animals:
   'When a pig with a rope round its middle is hoisted squealing into a ship, it is subject to direct physical power (military or police power). On the other hand, when the proverbial donkey follows the proverbial carrot, we induce him to act as we wish by persuading him that it is in his interest to do so (power of propaganda). Intermediate between these two cases is that of performing animals, in whom habits have been formed by rewards and punishments (power of education); also, in a different way, that of sheep induced to embark on a ship, when the leader has to be dragged across the gangplank by force, and the rest then follow willingly (party politics, when a leader is bound to a clique or party bosses).'
   In conclusion, economic organisations use rewards and punishments as incentives and deterrents; schools, churches and political parties aim at influencing opinion.
   Russell, B. (1986) 'The forms of power' in *Power* Lukes, S. (ed.), Oxford: Blackwell.

21. Parry, G. and Moran, M. (1994) *Democracy and Democratization*, London: Routledge.

22. Parry and Moran, 1994, p. 4.

23. Phillips, A. (1993) *Democracy and Difference*, Cambridge: Polity Press, p. 161.

24. Phillips, 1993, p. 105.

25. See also the 1992 UN study, *Women in Politics and Decision-Making in the late Twentieth Century*, The Hague: Martinus Nijhoff.

26. Phillips, 1993, pp. 75–89. See also Walby, S. (1994) 'Is the concept of citizenship gendered?' *Sociology* 28 No. 2, pp. 379–95.

27. See also the conclusion for a more detailed analysis of the issue of citizenship.

28. Salisbury, D. (1993) 'The politics of increased representation: the Swedish case' in *Gender and Party Politics*, Lovenduski, J. and Norris, P. (eds) London: Sage.

29. Kolinsky, E. (1993) 'Party change and women's representation in Unified Germany', in *Gender and Party Politics*, Lovenduski, J. and Norris, P., London: Sage.

30. Kolinsky, 1993, p. 131.

31. Inter-Parliamentary Union, Place du Petit-Saconnex 1211 Geneva 19 Switzerland. There are many groups campaigning for increased participation of women in representative assemblies, such as Emily's List and the 300 Group in Britain and L'Assemblée des Femmes in France.

32. Etzioni, A. (1995) *The Spirit of Community*, New York: Simon & Schuster.

33. *Guardian*, 18/02/95.

34. John Locke (1924) *Second Treatise on Government*, London: Dent; Montesquieu (1746) *The Spirit of the Laws*.

35. De Tocqueville (1843) *Democracy in America*; J. S. Mill (1861) *On Representative Government*.

36. De Tocqueville saw the main threat to liberty as being the growing power of the state in terms of the number of people in its service and its conforming pressures, hence the need for interest groups to come between the state and the individual to protect the interests of individuals against the state. De Tocqueville also considered the demand for equality by the growing strength of the industrial working class as the threat to liberty.

37. Dahl, R. A. (1956) *A Preface to Democratic Theory*, Chicago: University of Chicago Press and (1961) *Who governs? Democracy and Power in an American City*, New Haven: Yale University Press.

38. Held, D. (1989) *Models of Democracy*, Cambridge: Polity Press, p. 193.

39. Held, 1989, p. 189.

40. Dunleavy, P. and O'Leary, B. (1987) *Theories of the State*, London: Macmillan.

41. Only a very few people belong to political parties, and from whom the governing political class is composed. Data from a number of EU countries.

42. Lindblom, C. (1977) *Politics and Markets*, New York: Basic Books; Dahl, R. (1985) *A Preface to Economic Democracy*, Cambridge: Polity Press and (1989) *Democracy and its Critics*, New Haven: Yale University Press.

43. Dahl, 1985, p. 332.

44. Bachrach, P. and Baratz, M. (1970) *Power and Poverty*, New York: Oxford University Press; Schattschneider, E. F. (1960) *The Semi-Sovereign People: A Realist View of Democracy in America*, New York: Rinehart and Winston.

45. Held, 1989, p. 195.

46. Dunleavy and O'Leary, 1987, p. 43 on the pluralist kind of state.

47. Hayward, 1986, p. 18.

48. Pareto, V. (1966) in Finer, S. E. *Sociological Writings*, London: Pall Mall Press; Mosca, G. (1939) *Elements di scienza politica. The Ruling Class*, New York: McGraw-Hill; Michels, R. (1977) in Nye, R. *The Anti-democratic Sources of Elite Theory, Pareto, Mosca, Michels*, London: Sage.

49. It was Lenin's notion of 'democratic centralism' that has been blamed for the development of these elite groups. The emphasis tended to be on centralism rather than on democracy. The *Nomenklatura* were the Party elite who had more privileges than everyone else and created a self-perpetuating ruling elite. In order to progress into any leading position in those societies it was necessary to become a member of the Party.

50. Mosca, G. (1939) *The Ruling Class*, New York: McGraw-Hill, p. 58.

51. Schumpeter, J. A. (1961) *Capitalism, Socialism and Democracy*, London: Allen & Unwin.

52. For Useem there is an inner circle of finance capitalists, which forms a cohesive group influencing not just financial policy but all areas of public policy. In Britain, the inner circle is made up of organisations such as the CBI, the Association of British Chambers of Commerce, the Institute of Directors, and the British Institute of Management. Members of these groups, it is argued, have good access to government ministers, indeed some of them usually have been government ministers or leading civil servants. Useem, M. (1991) 'Inner circle' in *Who Rules Britain?* Scott, J. (ed.) Cambridge: Polity Press, pp. 149–50.

53. Sampson, A. (1971) *The New Anatomy of Britain*, London: Hodder & Stoughton; Paxman, J. (1990) *Friends in High Places*, Harmondsworth: Penguin.

54. Mullin, C. and Benn, T. (eds) (1984) *Arguments for Democracy*, Harmondsworth: Penguin.

55. Bauer, M. and Bertin-Mourot, B. (1995) Boyden Executive Search, *Guardian*, 11/03/95.

56. This section relies heavily on the works of Atilla Agh, the special issue of *Governance*, and Peter Gowan of the London European Research Centre at the University of North London.
57. Agh, 1994, p. 69.
58. Andorka, R. (1993) 'Regime transitions in Hungary in the 20th century: the role of national counter-elites', in Derlien and Szablowski, 1993, pp. 358–71.
59. Agh, 1994, p. 71.
60. 'Italianisation' a clientelistic state is created where personal preference and patronage play a crucial role in how the state is organised and managed, rather than another possible pathway westernised and professionalised, i.e. professional bureaucracy and other elites based on merit and competence: Agh, 1994, p. 74.
61. Agh, 1994, p. 77.
62. Szablowski, G. (1993) 'Governing and competing elites in Poland' in Derlien and Szablowski, 1993, p. 351.
63. Szablowski, 1993, p. 354.
64. Ham and Hill (1993), p. 39.
65. Ideal type of Corporatism: Schmitter, P. (1974) 'Still the century of corporatism?' *Review of Politics* 36 pp. 93–4.
66. Panitch, L. (1980) 'Recent theorisations of corporatism: reflections on a growth industry *British Journal of Sociology* 31(92) p. 173.
67. Williamson, 1989, p. 42.
68. Schmitter in Williamson, 1989, p. 49.
69. Lehmbruch, 1982, pp. 16–25.
70. Cawson, A. and Saunders P. (1983) *Corporatism, Competitive Politics and Class Struggle* in *Capital and Politics*, King, R. (ed.) London: Routledge and Kegan Paul.
71. Cawson and Saunders in Williamson, 1989, p. 124.
72. Gramsci, A. (1971) *Prison Notebooks*, London: Lawrence & Wishart.
73. Leys, 1989, p. 160.
74. Cox, 1987, p. 357.
75. Polanyi (1968) Chapter 1: The Hundred Years Peace. The collapse in 1995 of one of the oldest merchant banks in the world, Barings, recalled Cardinal Richelieu's statement in the eighteenth century that the bank was the sixth great power of Europe after England, France, Austria, Prussia and Russia. *Independent*, 04/03/95.
76. Sklair, 1991, p. 53.
77. Cox, 1987, p. 106.
78. Cox, 1987, p. 219.
79. Hayward, 1986, p. 18.
80. Keane, 1988, p. 32.
81. See also the collection of articles in Andrews, G. (ed.) (1991) *Citizenship*, London: Lawrence & Wishart.
82. For a more Utopian view of the way in which civil society could operate see Gorz, A. (1989) *A Critique of Economic Rationality*, London: Verso.
83. Walby, S. (1994) 'Is citizenship gendered?' *Sociology* 28(2) pp. 379–95.
84. Katz, R. and Mair, P. (1994) *How Parties Organise: Change and Adaptation in Party Organisations in Western Democracies*, London: Sage, p. 8.
85. Ham and Hall, 1993, p. 46.
86. Jessop, B. (1982) *The Capitalist State*, Oxford: Martin Robertson, p. 221.
87. Jessop in Ham and Hill, 1993, p. 47.

# CHAPTER FOUR

# Unity and diversity

## The social basis of European societies

### 4.1 Introduction: social theory

We begin with a question: does the drinking of a global brand of cola, the wearing of a global brand of blue jeans, the watching of a TV series that is seen worldwide and the desire to listen to a particular kind of global music mean that we are all becoming the same? At a superficial level the answer is yes, and it has been suggested that this is part of the universalising tendency of capitalism to incorporate and dominate all areas of human activity. The processes of globalisation at the economic and political levels, which are outlined elsewhere in this book, also have their effect in the social world. Most West European societies have undergone similar experiences of increasing industrialisation, urbanisation and growing secularisation since 1945, and are now part of the European Union with its emphasis on economic and political integration. The effect of the development towards greater integration within the European Union coupled with the wider globalisation process may mean that our societies will become increasingly uniform.

Another part of this process of growing uniformity is illustrated by the debate since the 1960s, about whether industrial societies are becoming identical (Kerr *et al.*, 1960; Rootes and Davis, 1994). There has been talk of the 'logic of industrialism' leading to the convergence of industrial societies, on the basis of similar economic and political institutions which give rise to similar behaviour in the social sphere. For example, smaller family units mean an end to the old idea of the extended family. Greater emancipation of women stemming from increased economic, political and social status is a common feature of industrialised societies although it has not developed uniformly. In considering our general theme of unity and diversity this chapter aims to provide some comment on that debate.

It is also important to recognise that historical and cultural factors still play a part in differentiating people in terms of their identity. Some groups find the necessary justification for promoting and defending particularities to the extent of fighting for their own specific beliefs and territories, for example the horror of 'ethnic cleansing' in Bosnia. Fortunately this kind of violent nationalism is rare in contemporary Europe, and there are other more positive aspects of what has been termed 'civic nationalism'.[1] The kinds of differences that are highlighted between different people, whether at a national or subnational/regional level, tend to be based on one nation or region or group maintaining that it has had a particular history, which is often reinforced by having a different language, or a different religion. Within nations or regions there may be other factors that promote differences between people for example class, gender and race.

We are all individuals and yet as human beings we live as members of wider social groups such as the family and within a given territorial space (region or nation). The societies in which we are brought up influence us by the way in which we are educated, whether we are part of a religious group, what kind of mass media we have, and the nature of the particular economic and political institutions. Social theory seeks to explain the way in which individuals in groups organise themselves and fit into society, and how society affects them. It also tries to show how various factors, for example such as social class, gender, race, age, and sexual orientation, may affect the life chances of an individual or group.

Our anlysis of the social world is based on the view that various forces interact and conflict in a dynamic fashion to produce what we call society. In Chapter 9, we see how political parties reflect and mould their programmes depending on the social composition of and aspirations of people in society. Our social identity is partly given to us (from our family), partly from our income and status position, and partly from how we see ourselves. Certain aspects may be more important than others at different times in our lives.[2]

For example, if you are a woman from an Asian background, who has been born and brought up in western Europe and you want to go to university, you may encounter support in your educational aspirations (or disapproval if your family wants you to get married). You may gain a degree and find a good job, and you may also decide to follow custom and practice by agreeing to an arranged marriage at a later date; but as a woman, you may have to face barriers to a career choice if, for instance, it is in medicine as a doctor or a surgeon (a heavily male dominated profession). There may be other barriers to entry or progress once in the profession from your ethnic origin (racism), or you or your family may not know the right people in the medical world's network who can assist your career (class background). Your identity and life chances, then, come out of the interaction between the kind of person you are and the influences of gender, race and class, which are key factors in explaining and understanding how society operates (Mirza, 1992).

A final point to be made about social theory is that it contains very different explanations about how society is structured and how it works. In the chapters on economic and political theory, we presented various different interpretations of how the economy functioned, and how the political system was organised and run. Social theory can be divided into three broad approaches. First of all there are those theorists who see society working rather like the human body, with each of the main parts/institutions having its own particular function and acting in balance and harmony with each other (Functionalist approach). Then there are those theorists who take the opposite view and see society as being based on conflict, with institutions in society acting in the interests of one particular class and in antagonism to other classes (Marxist or conflict approach). Finally there are those who reject both these kinds of large-scale and total explanations of how individuals and groups live and operate in the world. They insist that a much better way of finding out and explaining how society works is to focus on interpreting the small-scale interactions that take place between people in their everyday lives (symbolic-interaction approach). The debate is also based in general terms between those who insist that individuals have some kind of a free hand in deciding how they live their lives and that they are the 'agents' of their own destinies, and those who maintain that our actions are heavily dependent or subject to the influences of the much larger institutions or structures in society.[3] For example, if you are unemployed is it your own fault? Is it because you did not work hard enough at school or your attitude is difficult? Or are you unemployed because of larger issues concerning government policy on education and the kind of schooling you received? Finally, in a globalised economy you may be unemployed as a result of investment decisions taken thousands of miles away. Social theory aims to provide a way of understanding that relationship between the individual and the broader social context, and developing the ability within people to make those kinds of links between individual experience and the wider influences from national and global structures.

This chapter begins by presenting the general trends in the development of European societies, and raising issues about culture and identity which give people a sense of belonging. These processes may be leading to growing uniformity or alternatively they may be the basis on which people may like to differentiate themselves from others. Then we examine theories about class, gender and race to demonstrate the way in which these factors cause differences and divides within societies.[4]

## Modernity

This first section will begin with a brief historical introduction and then will highlight the overall trends that have affected contemporary European societies since 1945. There has been some kind of world economic system for centuries, with European nations developing trading links from the fourteenth century onwards; for example, Marco Polo's journeys to China, and the exploits of Vasco da Gama, Columbus and Raleigh, in the fifteenth and sixteenth centuries. This was followed by conquest in Latin America for gold and silver, West Africa for slaves, and the territorial colonisation of most parts of the world at the end of the nineteenth century.[5] European and North American economic growth was financed by a combination of all those factors together with the technological achievements of the Industrial Revolution.

Our modern 'western' world which has been created out of those developments has revealed a number of common processes: in the political arena there has been the development of the secular state with its citizenry. The ideas among others of Machiavelli, Hobbes, Locke and Montesquieu were crucial in changing perceptions of the role the state and promoting the rights of the individual against the overwhelming power of the monarch (see Chapter 3 for further discussion on the issues concerning the nature of democracy and participation). A second process has been the establishment of the global capitalist economy, which after the recent demise of most 'socialist' states since 1989 has become supreme. The development of this economic system led to a third process shaping the social composition of society, in particular the formation of social classes, and gender and ethnic divisions in the labour market. The final process has been the decline in religion and the rise of a secular culture (Hall 1992).

Most of the processes of modernity have affected other societies as well, but to differing degrees. For example, many of the new industrialising countries (NICs) such as China, Taiwan, Malaysia or Singapore have shown enormous economic growth in recent years, but this has not necessarily meant that they have become more democratic (in the western liberal democratic sense) or that their cultures have become less religiously based. The common features of these societies and 'western' societies is their industrialism, that is, advanced industrial development. Nevertheless, the rapid economic expansion experienced in the NICs has created tensions over these very issues, for example of democracy, as the events of Tien an Men square in China in 1989 show.

Other common features of industrialised societies concern the growth in the interventionist and regulatory role of the state, to facilitate the running of the economic system. This intervention takes a number of forms, from ensuring the public health of the population, providing its education and establishing a transport infrastructure, to direct fiscal and macroeconomic management. Although the neo-liberal agenda has set itself the task of reducing the role of the state, it still plays an important part in all aspects of society. Indeed, it could be argued that the neo-liberal agenda actually increases the role of the state.

Overshadowing this whole process has been the Enlightenment project in Europe, with its emphasis on the beneficial effects of progress, as reason comes to dominate over religion, magic and superstition. However, the European culture that produced Beethoven also produced Belsen, and the Declaration of the Rights of Man in 1789 excluded women and most colonial peoples from its benefits. So there is at the heart of modernity and progress, as a European venture, a contradiction between positive and negative processes.

Globalisation is the relatively new term used to describe these processes which have led some writers to talk about a global village, where electronic media can give us up to the minute information about events worldwide, controlled by a few large transnational corporations. The information superhighway (Internet) which has become an increasing focus for states' infrastructural development is another feature of this process. At the same time we are witnessing a growth in people's need for particularism that is to relate to a local community often in the form of a nation or region based largely on invented histories (see below). This need is reinforced by many people's demands in large states such as the United States, India and increasingly the EU that human progress should imply greater participation, which should take place at as local a level as possible; so a common feature of the modern world and our European experience is the global and the local. Despite previous divisions of the world into First, Second and Third World categories, everyone and everything is interconnected and interdependent. From the food we eat, the clothes we wear and the news we watch, we have all become part of a global economic and political network.[6] This network, run largely in the economic sphere by powerful transnational corporations, has its political counterpart in the much less powerful United Nations, still dominated by western powers, particularly the United States.[7]

There is, also, the whole question of people's identity as growing secularisation, the decline of Cold War certainties and individualisation proceed:

Just now everybody wants to talk about 'identity'. . . it has taken on so many different connotations . . . but one thing is clear – identity only becomes an issue when it is in crisis, when something assumed to be fixed, coherent and stable is displaced by the experience of doubt and uncertainty.[8]

Great importance is placed by people on being free to establish their own individual identity. The increasing demands for equal treatment from the women's movement and the gay movement have raised precisely those doubts and challenged traditional and fixed notions of personal and social identity.

For Beck (1992), the reasons for this growth in demands for self-expression stem from the fragmentation and dissolution of traditional social structures. Social identity is not as dependent as it was on class, family or neighbourhood, as we have all become more liberated in the West from those ties and live more individualised lives. But this emancipation brings risks, and we have to undertake an ongoing calculation on an individual basis every time we enter into a social situation. We cannot take anything for granted any more or rely on fixed points of reference. Such demands for greater individuality come up against the pressure for greater standardisation of identities from our exposure to the global mass media, work organisations and mass consumerism.

Sennett (1993) outlines the development of a secular capitalist urban culture with a mass consumer society, where the satisfaction of sensations has to become increasingly immediate (fast food/touch of the button technology). As people become more and more concerned with their own individual preoccupations so they lose touch with the social space around them which declines in importance. This endless and obsessive preoccupation with self leads to a form of 'social narcissism' where experiences are sought out which help the self to develop. In their personal lives people seek what is denied to them in their public life from the breakdown of family, class and community. The result is a frail, brittle, fractured and fragmented self, which Sennett argues results in a crisis of social identity. In this situation people may therefore seek solace, comfort and escape in any one of a number of different forms, from drug use to violence. The dangers of this kind of breakdown on a larger scale are considered by Hobsbawm (see Chapter 12).

One way in which this search for identity is expressed is through nationalisms of whatever kind, which rely on cultural factors as a key motivating force for their dynamism.[9] By culture we are referring to all those attributes of a society which give its members some sense of identity and belonging: language and literature, religion or a code of ethics, art, architecture, music and food. These elements have developed over time and are usually tied for their origins to a particular place, but as a result of migration and diaspora cultures can and do develop when they are not fixed to some territory. These uprooted cultures, then, become part of and interact with other environments and cultures to produce variations of their original forms. We are born into a culture (primordiality) and culture helps us to make sense of the world. We tend to accept this culture as fixed, as part of an unchanging and essential part of our existence; but even something as fundamental as language can and does change over time.

Toffler (1983) identifies three stages in terms of locations of identity through which humans have progressed into modern times. In the period of the agricultural revolution attachment was to family, clans or villages. During the Industrial Revolution, class relations became predominant. Now in what he calls the Third Wave, a more heterogeneous and differentiated society is developing with international travel, trade and the global economy where individuals are freer to choose their identities. This individualisation of experience may reflect the experience of those in the industrialised world, but it is not an accurate description of the kinds of choices available to most of the people living on this planet (Toffler, 1983).

Nevertheless, the decline of the nation state has led to an increase in the number and importance of various different regional or subnational groups and parties which attempt to provide a secure identity. Although this phenomenon may be more obvious in eastern Europe and particularly in former Yugoslavia, similar developments are taking place within western Europe. We aim here to show how cultural differentiation arises and why it assumes such importance in people's lives.

All of us seem to need some kind of fixed and essential place or idea to guide us through the insecurities of personal, political and social life. With the great diaspora of modern times, caused by war, famine or economic necessity, people have moved across continents to search for a better life. This process of migration is ages old and has meant the transfer of cultures across continents. People have carried their culture with them rather like their luggage and as it is unwrapped it comes into interaction with the culture of their new home.

Some groups have managed to maintain their cultural traditions more or less intact, but there are always modifications as people adapt to their new environments and in many cases the new environment adapts to this new influx, which in turn changes the host culture. The process is therefore ongoing and dynamic, which makes it very difficult to say that one culture is particular or pure, given its centuries-long interaction with other influences. An obvious example of this process is in music, where different forms of music interact and produce hybrid versions such as Bhangra rock, Jazz funk or Rai music.

The other important point to emphasise is that all notions of special characteristics of a people or a special territory are social constructions.[10] This means that it has been human beings that came up with these ideas in the first place and although over time they have taken on the idea of permanence and become almost 'natural', they are still basically something which human beings have created. The implication of all this is that what human beings have created they can also change; things do not always have to be as they were, and in fact most human societies have evolved a great deal over time.

In Edward Said's words:

No one today is purely **one** thing. Labels like Indian, or woman, or Muslim, or American are no more than starting points, which if followed into actual experience for only a moment are quickly left behind. Imperialism consolidated the mixture of cultures and identities on a global scale. But its most paradoxical gift was to allow people to believe that they were only, mainly, exclusively white, or black, or Western, or Oriental. Yet just as human beings make their own history, they also make their cultures and ethnic identities.[11]

The very success of the human race has been as a result of its ongoing capacity to adapt to new environments, whether those environments have been created by nature or other human beings. The problem is, however, that all human beings seem to need fixed categories of some kind to make sense of the world, and to have some notion of belonging. When a group or community feels under threat then it resorts to its traditional modes of living as a defence mechanism against danger, whether economic, political or social. Ideas about culture are important in motivating and legitimating human behaviour, but cultural bases are not natural, essential or immutable, they are constructed and promoted as being essential to human beings. The wholesale dismissal of essentialism is problematic because, first, many human beings believe some things are essential, secondly the processes which give rise to categories are essential to human beings (e.g. ongoing attempt to generate sense of identity through in-group/out-group dichotomy, present in most human relationships), and finally the creation of categories is essential to human beings.

Language, religion and traditions are all examples of categories which become cultures, and which are then defined and named and take on life of their own; they become taken-for-granted aspects of our world, almost 'natural':

Overall what is important is the process of category formation, and sense of belonging; of belonging is essential rather than the categories/products themselves, and this process is ongoing all the time and gives cultures their dynamism and change. (Jackson & Penrose, 1993)

Nationalism is the motivating ideology of modern world, and the idea of culture is integral to any request for secession. There are two cultural bases: primary, which includes language, religion and tradition and ancillary, which refers to history, its symbols and shared meanings. The use of the ancillary base to legitimise a nationalist movement may increase substantially when primary bases are under threat or diminishing. The key factor is nation and nationalism, but nationalism legitimises only specific elements of culture. Cultural bases are very powerful motivators, but the way in which they are operationalised and ideologically essentialised is directly linked to power, particularly the elite's need to maintain power.

Culture is essential; therefore, nations are essential since culture forms the basis of nation. Both sources are seen as necessary and inevitable, so claims of common ancestry based on pseudo-biological grounds are used. For example, Germany's nationality laws are based on the notion of *jus sanguinis*. That means it is very difficult to become a German national if you cannot show some bloodlink to Germany. Consequently, after the break-up of the Soviet Union many ethnic Germans from the

Volga region of Russia claimed German citizenship, even though neither they nor their ancestors had been back to Germany for centuries. In many cases, also, they did not even speak German.

Within Europe both East and West, the prominence of all these groups is one indication of the start of the decline of the nation state's cultural homogeneity. Under totalitarian regimes the centre dominates and stifles, excludes or banishes those who pronounce regional particularisms. The most extreme case of the break-up of a nation state in Europe is the war in former Yugoslavia, but the fragmentation of the former Soviet Union is another example of this process. Within western Europe, there are also numerous examples of a similar process occurring. The United Kingdom as it currently exists is less than 80 years old, and it is likely that within the next few decades it may change again. The construction of one British identity may become more difficult, as each constituent part develops in its own way. Under Franco, Spain was a heavily centralised state where the Catalan and Basque provinces were dominated by Madrid, and where language and other cultural expressions were forbidden. The way in which the Spanish state is currently developing suggests that in the near future Catalonia and the Basque province may become increasingly independent of Madrid's control.

## Language

One area in which culture is strongly defended is language, with groups set up to keep the language 'pure'.[12] A French government proposal in 1994 to ban about 3500 foreign, mainly English, words from official use is one recent indication of this desire to protect the cultural heritage. The French minister of culture who spearheaded this move, Jacques Toubon, or 'Mr Allgood' as the French media dubbed him, came up against a constitutional court decision declaring the move unconstitutional as it interfered with the right of people to express themselves as they wished. Nevertheless, in terms of official government publications, academic papers, conferences and advertising, French words must be used.[13] The government, however, immediately fell foul of its own proposals in a poster campaign exhorting the use of condoms (préservatif) as protection against Aids during the summer of 1994: 'Utilisez les préservatifs! Fuck Aids!'.

It is becoming increasingly difficult to maintain such watertight boundaries, and any historical analysis would indicate that language is continually evolving as human beings interact and move. It is, however, interesting to note that it is English which seems to be a dominant force affecting languages around the world and which reflects not just the imperial past of the United Kingdom, but more importantly the hegemonic role of the United States since the end of the Second World War. So at the same time that demands are made to give more political and economic weight to regional and local particularisms, there are other tendencies strengthening global institutions and structures, of which the increasing use of the English language is one example.

## Challenges to modernity

There have been several challenges to the way in which some traditional theories have analysed and interpreted the modern world. The changes that have taken place in the economic and political worlds have had implications for the social world, and forced people to take account of new forms of social organisation and identification. Most importantly the period of post-war affluence in the industrialised countries of the capitalist world challenged the Marxist view that society was based on two opposing classes locked in a duel to the death, with the working class about to appear as the final victor.

These new approaches to explaining the world have come under the heading of **post-modernism**. Elsewhere, we have seen that the large-scale type of industrial production (characterised by Gramsci as **Fordist**, after the mass production techniques of Henry Ford) has given way to a more small-scale and flexible way of production known as **post-Fordism**. In the political sphere there is evidence of new forms of politics that attempt to go beyond traditional categories of left and right. In the social sphere the decline of more stable reference points for our identity, such as family, religion or neighbourhood mean that new kinds of attitudes and ways of living are developing. It is these changes that post-modernist thinkers aim to identify and explain.

Characteristics of post-modernism are 'ephemerality, fragmentation, discontinuity and the chaotic', preferring difference over uniformity, implying an analysis of the world from previously ignored or forgotten perspectives (Harvey, 1989). The focus changes from capitalism and class, and exploitation on a macroscale to the individual, the local and the particular. So, for instance, in politics it involves looking away from the main political parties and traditional actors within the political system, to other groups such as women, ethnic groups and the gay movement. Michel Foucault, whose view on power was presented in Chapter 3, is seen as a post-modernist. Rather than talk about power as a thing controlled by a small elite in its own interests, he broadens out the discussion. Power is present in all human relations, particularly at the local level. This view of the world seeks to explain the way society operates in terms of a more multidimensional and multilayered approach, and is suspicious of the totalising approaches and explanations found in Marxism or in Freud. Critics of post-modernism argue that ignoring comprehensive approaches leads to small-scale and unconnected analysis, and neglects the large-scale exploitation and oppression that is present in the world (Callinicos, 1989). In considering the next section, post-modernists might argue that categories such as class, gender and race need to be broken down in order to really understand how the world operates. It is important to recognise the limitations of these categories but they are nevertheless still useful in explaining very real divides that exist in society.

## 4.2  Class, gender and race – introduction

In this section we consider just three factors that form part of social cleavages. However, we are aware that cleavages such as region, religion and rural–urban divides which have affected and continue to influence the political system are also significant in the social world.[14] It should be remembered that just as political cleavages have differing intensities and durations and have a tendency to overlap, so these social cleavages function in the same way. Furthermore, our approach is based on the view that society is best explained in terms of conflict, which is rarely violent, between various groups and the factors which we present in the next section should be seen within this context.

## 4.3 Social class and stratification

An important way in which societies are organised is dependent on factors such as income and wealth. There is no doubt that all societies are stratified to some extent, that is to say there is a hierarchy within that society which involves some people in the top layer owning more wealth and having more status and power than others. The means by which those people arrive at such positions is also subject to variables such as their social class position at birth and their subsequent chances in education and occupation.

According to classic Marxist theory society is divided into two opposing classes, although Marx did allow for the presence of intermediary classes (but he saw these classes merging into one or other of the two opposing classes). It is an unequal society with those at the top owning more, earning more and benefiting from all the advantages that wealth provides. The only way to overcome these inequalities was for the working class to gain or seize power (via revolution) and then, since it was the largest class, it could distribute all the benefits of society equally among its members. A model of this kind of society is a pyramid with a large base, the working class (proletariat) and then tapering up to a small elite group (bourgeoisie) at the pinnacle. The main problem with the Marxist analysis of social class in the post-1945 period is that it has found it difficult to find a place for the growing middle class, as this section of society does not fit neatly into either of the two classic categories.

Other writers such as Weber saw society divided into classes based not solely on income, but also status and party (political power). This analysis allows us to have a much broader idea of how society is divided. It is a 'multidimensional' (Saunders, 1990) approach that goes beyond a narrow class explanation of inequality. For example, trade unions may not be as wealthy as TNCs, but they do exercise some kind of political power. Another example is the clergy which, in most European societies, may not be very wealthy, but their position in terms of status is quite high and they command a certain amount of influence, although it is important to differentiate between the individual priest, a relatively poor person, and the Church, a relatively rich institution.

The classification of groups into social classes has been undertaken for more than 100 years. In the maps of areas of poverty in London in the mid-nineteenth century, eight areas are defined according to the classes living there. There are the middle classes through to the 'vicious criminal classes' (the lumpenproletariat in Marx's terms, and now part of the 'underclass').

The official classification of social class in the United Kingdom has tended to rely on the occupation of the father:

I.   Professionals
II.  Managerial and technical
III. (N) Skilled occupations – non-manual
III. (M) Skilled occupations – manual
IV.  Partly skilled occupations
V.   Unskilled

These categories have endured a great deal of criticism for being too crude as indicators of social class position. Why should a non-manual occupation like a clerk, for example, be in category III, while a skilled worker who would probably earn more be located in IV? Furthermore, if occupation is the sole indicator of social class position what about those, usually wealthy, members of society who live on income from property or investments?[15] The classification also relies on the male breadwinner, and so tends to exclude nearly half the population (see section below on Gender for more details of this critique). In 1995 the government agreed to change these categories, because it was clear that the world of the early 1900s, when this classification was first devised, had now changed.[16]

Another way to look at stratification is in terms of elites and their networks (see Chapter 3). In Britain, an elite has been created and maintained through a network of public schools, Oxbridge and landed wealth. In France an elite is formed via a network based on education at one of the top Paris lycées and then one of the elite administrative schools such as the ENA or l'Ecole Polytechnique, which dominate political, social and academic life. This is almost exclusively based in Paris, and also includes some of the old family firm industrialists such as Dassault. In Italy the role of the parties, and until recently the Christian Democratic Party (DC) in particular, has been instrumental in ensuring that particular groups remain at the apex of the economic, political and social hierarchy. In Germany as a result of the effects of the Nazi period and the post-1945 settlement there has not arisen the same kind of closed hierarchy, so that we can conclude that there is still relative openness in the access of individuals to positions of political although not economic power, with the administrative and political ruling elite increasingly coming from the law faculties of all universities, which do not have anything resembling the same hierarchy as in other major European countries. Certainly to progress anywhere within those state structures, including the academic world, a doctorate is essential, but there is no established elite in the same sense as the British public school/Oxbridge elite or the Grandes Ecoles and the top Paris lycées.[17]

In Spain and Greece a more personalist social structure exists, which means that adherents of the successful political parties gain access to important positions within society. Industrial and economic wealth, including landed property, is maintained within extended family networks, but then this is also the case elsewhere in Europe. One other kind of network of elites in Spain is operated by the Opus Dei, which runs the University of Navarra. It is neither a religious order nor a secular institution (perhaps a think tank), but its members have played and continue to play a leading role in Spanish society. For example, many Opus Dei members were in Franco's cabinets in the late 1960s and were largely responsible for masterminding the country's economic growth during that period. This influence filtered through journalism, including the editors of El País, El Mundo and controllers of some radio stations.[18]

How can we measure whether one society is more divided than another? Strictly speaking what we are concerned with is economic stratification, which includes factors such as distribution of wealth and income and the nature and scale of welfare benefits. Distribution of income statistics are one way in which some idea of how many people fall into the general category of 'middle class' can be made. Obviously the figures have to be adjusted country by country for cost of living indices, and the nature of social welfare support has to be calculated, but it can be generally assumed that a person's income and wealth will be a good indicator of their 'social position, life-style, status and even state of health' (Davis, 1992:19). The other side of this coin is an attempt to measure the incidence of poverty in any society and the amount of social exclusion. More detailed analysis of poverty is provided in Chapter 11.

In post-1945 western Europe there has been significant social mobility and society may now reflect a rugby ball with a large middle class and a small lower income group at the bottom with an equivalent small group at the top. This middle class now accounts for between 45 per cent and 50 per cent of the societies in western Europe. The decline in traditional blue collar employment and the growth of service industries has led to the increase in this sector of society. The period of practically full employment in the 30 years from 1945 and a comprehensive welfare state led to an absolute increase in affluence, and the coining of such terms as the 'affluent society' (Galbraith) expressing 'contentment' at their new higher standards of living. The 'embourgeoisement' thesis maintained that working class was becoming middle class, in both lifestyle and aspirations.[19] This view was challenged by several studies which aimed to show how that, despite rising affluence, the traditional working class was still more collectively minded and had not completely accepted the values and norms of capitalism,[20] with its emphasis on individualism. More recent studies show it is a result of the lack of support from the two main vehicles of working class organisation, the trade unions and the Labour Party, that has meant less collective action. In other words, the values and aspirations may have apparently become more individualised, but in fact middle class values have not become wholly accepted (Devine, 1992).

Hutton (1995) offers a model for British society which is divided according to a 30:30:40 schema. Thirty per cent are the very poor, the long-term unemployed or never-employed and those on low or fixed benefits. The next 30 per cent are those in employment, whether full-time, part-time or intermittent, but whose jobs are poorly paid and with poor prospects. The 40 per cent are the relatively affluent in more secure and better-paid employment, and the wealthy.

Ardagh (1991) considered that income levels for the working class have been so high that 'a semi-classless society' had developed in West Germany. Certainly average wage rates are very high and the standard of living one of the highest in Europe. Those who perform the least well-paid jobs tend to come from one or another immigrant or refugee community, and virtually none of them are German. Despite the levelling out of incomes in many areas some kind of class distinction is maintained through the education system, with only about 15 per cent of university students from a working class background.[21]

French society has undergone massive transformation since 1945, with the accelerated decline of the *paysans* (small-scale farmers), and in common with other European societies the reduction in the primary and secondary sectors of the economy has led to the demise of the working-class as a significant part of the labour force and as a political force. Nevertheless, disparities in income remain and for Forbes and Hewlett:

... virtually everyone in France has become richer and the general standard of living has risen ... and while the society has become much less obviously hierarchical and rigid, social mobility is not as great as might have been hoped or expected.[22]

According to one measure of income distribution used by Lane and Ersson (1987), Scandinavian countries have a more even distribution of income than anywhere else in Europe. The greater degree of inequality is found in Southern Europe.[23] The post-war trend in most European countries has been towards a more equitable distribution of income, but this has tended to take place in terms of redistribution among the more affluent sections of society. The poor have not benefited and recent studies in the United Kingdom indicate that poverty has increased in the last decade (see Chapter 11).

## The underclass

Recent debates in the United States and Europe, particularly in Britain, have focused on the existence of what has been called an 'underclass'. This term refers to those people who form part of the most excluded and marginalised sections of society, for example the long-term unemployed, the sick and single parents, usually women, who live on social welfare benefits. For Murray, three main phenomena define the underclass, 'illegitimacy, violent crime and drop out from the labour force'.[24] The concern is that there is now a whole new group of people who have no vested interest in society.

It is important to realise that concern about the danger or presence of this 'underclass' has been around for a long time. In Elizabethan England, measures were taken to try to keep the poor from becoming too much of a burden on society. Thomas Malthus, in his writings on population at the end of the eighteenth century, warned of the corrosive effect on social solidarity of large numbers of the poor producing too many children, perpetuating their situation of poverty and spreading disease.[25] Blame has always tended to be dished out on to the poor, for their lack of self-control (producing too many children), for their wanton excesses (too much drinking), and their danger to public health from their prevalence to contagious diseases and its spread to other sections of society.

The economic crisis in many industrialised countries since the mid-1970s has led to increasing numbers of people becoming part of a casualised and insecure working population. Through no fault of their own industrial structures are changing, production is becoming more global and more and more, people are no longer guaranteed a job for life. Unemployment has remained at high levels for years and increasing social exclusion has developed. The same group, then, who have been at the sharpest receiving end of economic changes are now being blamed for being in that situation, and are finding that the social welfare safety net is being slowly removed. This process is part of the logic of neo-liberal economics which sees the need for a cheap and flexible labour force (see Chapter 2). It seems odd, therefore, that those who are fulfilling a key role in maintaining the low level of wages and providing the necessary background for increased profits and expansion should then be blamed if they are unable to keep up to the standards which society expects of them.

Another dimension to this debate is the situation of immigrant communities. People came to Europe after 1945 to contribute to the post-war reconstruction, and were recognised by such leaders as the former German Chancellor, Willy Brandt, as having played a key role in enabling Europe to achieve such sustained high levels of economic growth. The unemployment rate among members of those communities is now greater than for others and so they are found disproportionately in conditions of economic and social precariousness.

Two key givens of industrialised societies, namely full-time and long-term employment for men, and the nuclear household are now increasingly open to question.[26] The effect of all of this is the creation of a group of people in some state of social exclusion. In an attempt to continue to blame the poor for their misfortune writers tend to miss how the situation has developed from changes in the global system of production. There may also be another element in the debate, which is evidence of a backlash from writers about the changing composition of western industrialised societies from the presence of large numbers of people in them from different ethnic origins, and the challenge to traditional power structures from the increasing emancipation and participation of women.[27]

## 4.4   Gender and stratification

Social class theories have been challenged on the grounds that whereas those theories consider occupational class inequalities as the fundamental cleavage in society, feminist writers argue that sexual inequality is the key and determining cleavage in society. Patriarchy is the system which, according to feminist writers, transcends class and racial divisions in society. Patriarchy is defined as:

A system of social structures, and practices in which men dominate, oppress and exploit women.[28]

Patriarchy has been a feature of all European societies and other societies for centuries. It existed before capitalism arrived in the eighteenth century and hence the argument that it is a more persistent form of social division than class and, to a certain extent, race. It has also been a feature of those countries that call or have called themselves socialist, despite the political rhetoric of equality between men and women. There is, however, an ongoing debate among feminists as to the degree to which it is exclusively patriarchy or capitalism or racism that can explain social structures and how they operate. The various perspectives of feminism below reflect the nature of this debate.

A fundamental problem with most of social stratification theory, then, is that women have been excluded from the analysis. According to these theories social position is determined by the occupation of the 'breadwinner', which has been traditionally assumed to be the male head of a household. Social class therefore is assumed on the basis of household rather than on an individual basis. The effect of this approach, according to Abbott and Sapsford (1987), is that women's position in society is seen as dependent on men, and less value is attached to the whole range of women's experiences. Feminist writers have challenged the whole basis of the class analyses that are outlined in the previous section, on the grounds that those theories are inadequate in explaining both gender inequalities and failure to incorporate women adequately into the explanation of class inequalities.

The critique of traditional theories and research into social inequality by feminist writers has formed part of a wide-ranging critique of the 'male-stream' bias in much of social science thinking and writing until recently. The main points of this critique focus on the traditional omission of women within the framework of studies in social sciences, the perception of women solely in terms of their importance for men and not in their own right, and finally the acceptance that the standard of male is superior and the norm.[29] This situation of omission or neglect is part of a more universal process of discrimination against women, which has been reinforced by religious and other authorities and practice through the centuries and legitimised by nineteenth-century pseudo-scientific explanations of the 'female' temperament expressed in terms such as 'the weaker sex'.

Within the feminist analysis of this social reality various strands seek to explain stratification by giving weight to some factors over others. There are three main feminist schools of thought:

1. Radical feminists argue that women's oppression is the main dividing feature of social reality. The writings of Christine Delphy (1977) have attempted to demonstrate that women are opposed to men as a class, since the nature of the relationship is basically one of exploitation. The way this oppression is carried out is through the family, in terms of 'sexual slavery and forced motherhood'.[30] Patriarchy, therefore, is the fundamental cleavage in society, greater than economic or racial divides.
2. Marxist and socialist feminists maintain that women's oppression is tied up with the exploitative nature of capitalism. Once these oppressive structures are removed then other forms of oppression will disappear. They also stress the importance of linking up issues concerning gender with those of class and race.
3. Liberal feminists are concerned to gain increasing rights from within the system, in terms of equal legal status.

The importance of this approach is that it adds another dimension to the debate about the way in which societies are structured and are developing. In our analysis of various issues concerned primarily with women's situation in society, which is contained in Chapter 11, it becomes clear that there is a long way to go until any kind of equality is achieved between men and women in their ability to participate fully in all aspects of the public and private spheres of human activity.

## 4.5   Ethnicity and racism

The third way in which societies can be divided is on ethnic or racial grounds. Within the Anglo-American world this division has been expressed in terms of black and white. In other West European countries these terms are not used so frequently, with ethnic or cultural factors being highlighted. Despite the difference in terminology and approaches to issues of racism and discrimination, ethnic communities' experience of the reality of discrimination is very similar throughout Europe.

The growth of natural sciences during the eighteenth and nineteenth centuries, with their attempts to discover fixed laws governing the operation of nature and the greater classification of animal species, led eventually to the articulation of differences between the human species. Fichte, in the early nineteenth century, was followed by Gobineau some decades later, who put forward the view that rather than one human race there were different human species and that some races, notably the Europeans, were superior to others. These views had a great influence on subsequent political movements such as the Nazi party, which used similar classifications showing the superiority of the Aryan race over inferior races such Jewish and other races.[31] The example of Nazism also shows that race is not only about colour, but also about ethnicity which encompasses a person's language, religion and other aspects of culture (music, dress, food).[32]

Although the category of race has been shown to be worthless, the experience of racism is still very real. Racism exists where one group of people dominate another group on the basis of their perceived physical or cultural attributes, and where the subordinate group suffers discrimination as a result of this unfair use of power. It takes many forms, from the casual verbal insult in the street or workplace to the actual physical violence encountered, for example, by immigrant workers being firebombed in their hostels in Germany, Romany gypsies being hounded out of their homes in Hungary and Asian people being attacked in London. It also refers to the systematic exclusion from the benefits of the society of those people both directly and indirectly, on the grounds that they are 'racially' or in more modern terms 'ethnically' different (usually known as 'institutional or structural racism'). Whereas in the past justification was based on 'racial' grounds, now that these differences have proved to be unscientific, cultural or ethnic differences are now used to justify exclusion.[33]

In contemporary Europe racism tends to be based on this notion of perceived cultural differences, but at an immediate level the phenotypical characteristics are still predominant. For example, attacks or harassment against certain groups of people are based on how they appear as much as the fact of their cultural background. Police checks on identity papers in France, or immigration controls at British sea and airports operate as much on a person's appearance as their culture; in Sivanandan's words: 'Our faces are our passports'.

It is also important to note that in many cases nationalism and racism are closely linked. As Miles notes:

. . . racism is the lining of the cloak of nationalism which surrounds and defines the boundaries of England as an imagined community.[34]

Nationalism is an ideology which seeks to develop an exclusive category of people who belong to one territory based on long-term presence or occupation. According to this view the world is divided into various nations, with their own particular culture, and each group of people should live in their own nation. The dominant national group therefore will seek to exclude or marginalise others in its territory who are not members of the nation. The assumption on which nationalism is based, in a similar manner to racism, is that there are 'natural' differences to people living in different parts of the world and that therefore people should stay in their 'natural' environment.

In all these debates we should remember that all these categories of race and nation are 'social constructs', that is they are categories invented by people for particular reasons. They may want to hold on to power and so find it useful to create an 'in-group' and an 'out-group'. Rather than seeking common ground between people and nations they seek out differences and, through a process of inventing a particular kind of history, develop notions of heroic deeds and selfless sacrifice.

The presence of large numbers of people from different European and non-European cultures residing and working within the boundaries of Western and East/Central Europe is one of the most significant features of post-1945 European societies, but we should not forget that people from all over the world have been residing in western Europe for centuries.[35] Their presence has altered forever the notion that 'European' can now be defined solely in terms of skin colour (white), or exclusively Christian. Being 'European', or 'French', or 'English', or 'German' now encompasses, to a greater or lesser extent, those people from all over the world who have become nationals of the various EU countries or who as non-EU nationals have chosen permanent residence here, many having been born and grown up here (Said, 1994).[36]

The question of colour has been at the forefront of the debate in the United Kingdom. This is a result of the influence of the main paradigm of race relations in the United States, although as we point out above, racism does not simply manifest itself in discrimination against people of different colour. The use of the term 'black' to describe most immigrant groups to the United Kingdom is now considered problematic. In the rest of Europe the use of the term black does not carry the same significance, where discrimination is expressed much more around notions of ethnic/cultural differentiation.

Black as a term was originally used to create a sense of solidarity among Asian and Afro-Caribbeans in Britain struggling against the effects of racism in the United Kingdom. It is an exclusive representation of men and women of subSaharan African origin and, Modood argues, too loose a concept because first it sometimes refers simply to Afro-Caribbeans and sometimes to other categories. Secondly, a concept based on colour is too narrow when discrimination can be based on cultural differences, for example in the case of the Irish in Britain, the experience of Slavonic and Jewish people in Germany and elsewhere in Europe. Thirdly, it creates a false essentialism and suggests common characterisitics of Afro-Caribbean and Asian communities, when they are from different cultures and have had different experiences. Finally, it accepts a definition based on skin colour alone. This is too negative and uses, as a basis of identity, a definition from nineteenth century racial ideologies.[37] Stuart Hall has also questioned the use of the term as an over-generalised concept, which does not take account of the 'extraordinary diversity' of experiences contained within the category 'black' and fails to recognise that 'black' is 'essentially a politically and culturally constructed category, which . . . has no guarantees in Nature'.[38]

## 4.6  Summary

This chapter has shown how the changes associated with modernity and post-modernity have affected European societies. Within the framework of those analyses, we have presented some theoretical outlooks on how societies are divided, using the main cleavages of class, gender and race. These concepts are all problematic and it has not been our intention to be exclusive in such a presentation, by suggesting that only these factors are important. People may experience social exclusion also as a result of how old they are (age), where they live (region), or their desires (sexual orientation). Nevertheless the three categories of class, gender and race do represent a useful way of understanding how these societies operate and the context in which they will develop. The more empirical data relating to these ideas is contained in Chapter 11, and is used to indicate how these divides may be expressed in social reality.

## Further reading

### Modernity and postmodernity

Beck, U. (1992) *Risk Society: Towards a New Modernity*, London: Sage.
Callinicos, A. (1989) *Against Post-modernism: A Marxist Critique*, Cambridge: Polity Press.
Clarke, J. and Saunders, P. (1991) 'Who are you and what are you?' *Sociology Review* September, pp. 15–20.
Forbes, J. and Hewlett, N. (1994) *Contemporary France*, London: Longman.
Hall, S. (1992) 'The question of cultural identity' in *Modernity and its Futures* Hall, S., Held, D. and McGrew, T., Cambridge: Polity Press.
Harvey, D. (1989) *The Condition of Postmodernity*, Oxford: Blackwell.
Jackson, P. and Penrose, J. (1993) *Constructions of Race, Place and Nation*, London: UCL Press.
Keating, M. (1988) *State and Regional Nationalism*, Hemel Hempstead: Harvester Wheatsheaf.
Kerr, C., Dunlop, T., Harbison, F. and Mayers, C. A. (1960) *Industrialism and Industrial Man*, Cambridge, MA: Harvard University Press.
Lash, S. and Urry, J. (1987) *The End of Organised Capitalism*, Cambridge: Polity Press.
Rootes, C. and Davis, H. (eds) (1994) *Social Change and Political Transformation*, London: UCL Press.

Said, E. (1993) *Culture and Imperialism*, London: Chatto & Windus.
Sennett, R. (1993) *The Fall of Public Man*, London: Faber & Faber.
Toffler, A. (1983) *Previews and Premises*, New York: Chaucer Press.
Warde, A. (1994) 'Consumption, identity-formation and uncertainty', *Sociology* 28 (4), pp. 877–98.

## Social stratification and social class

Ardagh, J. (1991) *Germany and the Germans*, London: Penguin.
Bottomore, T. B. (1970) *Classes in Modern Societies*, London: Allen & Unwin.
Davis, H. (1992) 'Social Stratification in Europe' in *Social Europe* Bailey, J. (ed.), London: Longman.
Devine, F. (1992) *Affluent Workers Revisited: Privatism and the Working Class*, Edinburgh: Edinburgh University Press.
Hutton, W. (1995) *The State We're In*, London: Jonathan Cape.
Saunders, P. (1990) *Social Class and Stratification*, London: Routledge.

## Gender and stratification

Abbott, P. and Sapsford, R. (1987) *Women and Social Class*, London: Tavistock Press.
Crompton, R. and Mann, M. (eds) (1986) *Gender and Stratification*, Cambridge: Polity Press.
Delphy, C. (1977) *The Main Enemy*, London: Women's Research and Resources Centre Publications.
Millett, K. (1991) *Sexual Politics*, London: Virago.

## Ethnicity and racism

Anderson, B. (1991) *Imagined Communities*, London: Verso.
Donald, J. and Rattansi, A. (eds) (1992) *Race, Culture and Difference*, London: Sage.
Fryer, P. (1984) *Staying Power*, London: Pluto.
Miles, R. (1993) *Racism after 'race relations'*, London: Routledge.
Mirza, H. (1992) *Young, Female and Black*, London: Routledge.
Rattansi, A. and Westwood, S. (eds) (1994) *Racism, Modernity and Identity on the Western Front*, Cambridge: Polity Press.
Rex, J. (1992) 'Race and Ethnicity in Europe' in *Social Europe* Bailey, J. (ed.) London: Longman.
Said, E. (1994) *Representations of the Intellectual*, New York: Vintage.

## Notes

1. For consideration of the possibility of a progressive form of nationalism, see Nairn, T. (1983) *The Break-up of Britain, Crisis and Neo-nationalism*, London: Verso and Ignatieff, M. (1993) *Blood and Belonging. Journeys into the new nationalism*, London: BBC Books.
2. We are aware also that another important cleavage in all societies is the age-cycle. This cleavage is reflected in the fact that many older people have formed their own political

parties to promote their interests. The 1994 general election in the Netherlands saw the Union 55+ party win one seat.

3. For a much more detailed guide throughout the social theory jungle see Craib, I. (1992) *Modern Social Theory*, Hemel Hempstead: Harvester Wheatsheaf. The first chapter in Haralambos, M. and Holborn, M. (1995) *Sociology. Themes and Perspectives*, London: Collins Educational is an excellent introduction to social theory.

4. There are also some writers, for example Cox (1987) and Sklair (1991), who consider that as a result of globalisation these factors are useful ways of explaining differences at the international level.

5. For example, the carving-up of Africa by the major European powers at the Congress of Berlin in 1883.

6. The driving force for most people in most societies throughout history is the desire for relative comfort and material wellbeing, however basic. The consumption desires and patterns of spending of many people all over the world is becomingly similar. Shopping malls are a popular global experience from Los Angeles to Leeds, Cologne to Kuala Lumpur and Singapore to Shanghai. Perhaps we are becoming undifferentiated global consumers!

7. For a more complete sociology of globalisation see Sklair, L. (1991) *Sociology of the Global System*, Hemel Hempstead: Harvester Wheatsheaf.

8. Mercer, K. (1990) 'Welcome to the Jungle: Identity and Diversity in Postmodern Politics' in *Identity: Community, Culture, Difference* Rutherford, J. (ed.), London: Lawrence & Wishart.

9. The difference between a 'nation' and a 'state' refers largely to this cultural element. A nation combines the political with the cultural within an historic territory, while the state refers usually just to the institutional forms of economic and political management of a territory. The two do overlap, but there are very few countries where the nation and the state are the same, and can be justifiably called a nation-state. Most states have several different nations within them, as for example the historic nations of Catalonia and the Basque province in Spain, and Scotland and Wales within the United Kingdom. See Smith, A. D. (1991) *National Identity*, Harmondsworth: Penguin, Chs. 1–3.

10. Most European nations created their identities during the nineteenth century, and so the appeal for example to a 1000-year-old tradition is based largely on selective and exaggerated interpretation of history: Hobsbawm, E. and Ranger, T. (eds) (1983) *The Invention of Tradition*, Cambridge: Cambridge University Press.

11. Said, E. (1993) *Culture and Imperialism*, London: Chatto & Windus, p. 407.

12. Where groups of people sharing cultural, linguistic, or religious traits or common economic interests are concentrated in particular territories, a sense of collective identity may develop. Keating, M. (1988) *State and Regional Nationalism*, Hemel Hempstead: Harvester Wheatsheaf, p. 16.

13. *Financial Times*, 01/08/94 and 06/08/94. Mr Toubon is quoted as saying that 'French must not become to English what today Latin and Greek are to French'.

14. For a more detailed discussion of the these issues see Cole, M. (1989) '"Race" and Class or "race", class, gender and community?: a critical appraisal of the radicalised fraction of the working-class thesis' *British Journal of Sociology* 40 (1).

15. Advertisers tend to use an A–E classification system based more on spending and consumption patterns than occupation.

16. *Guardian*, 17/07/95.

17. Ardagh, J. (1988) *Germany and the Germans*, London: Penguin, p. 177.

18. Members hand over their salaries except for personal modest needs, full members are celibate, others are married. John Hooper, 'The Holy and the Ivy League' *Guardian*, 19/4/94. Opus Dei is strong in other countries, for instance a recent Irish Chief Justice is a

member. For more details of elite networks and their influence, see the *Economist's Good Network Guide*, 26/12/92–08/01/93. See also Lannon, F. and Preston, P. (1990) *Elites and Power in Twentieth Century Spain*, Oxford: Clarendon.

19. Zweig, F. (1961) *The Worker in an Affluent Society*, London: Heinemann. See also Galbraith, J. K. (1993) *The Culture of Contentment*, Harmondsworth: Penguin.
20. The 'affluent worker' studies led by John Goldthorpe revealed changes in the outlook and aspirations of the working class. See, for example, Goldthorpe, J. *et al.* (1969) *The Affluent Worker in the Class Structure*, Cambridge: Cambridge University Press.
21. Ardagh, 1991, p. 175.
22. Forbes and Hewlett, 1994, p. 377.
23. Data quoted by Davis, H. (1992) 'Social Stratification in Europe' in *Social Europe* Bailey, J. (ed.), London: Longman.
24. Murray, C. (1990) 'The Emerging British Underclass' *Choice in Welfare Series 2*, London: Health and Welfare Unit, Institute of Economic Affairs. p. 4.
25. For an excellent account of recent debates and their historical roots, see Morris, L. (1994) *Dangerous Classes. The Underclass and Social Citizenship*, London: Routledge.
26. Morris, 1994, p. 157.
27. For an excellent critique of 'underclass' theories, see Mann, K. (1992) *The Making of an English 'Underclass'? The social divisions of welfare and labour*, Milton Keynes: Open University Press.
28. Walby, S. (1989) 'Theorising patriarchy' *Sociology* 23 (2) pp. 213–34.
29. For further discussion of these issues see Randall, V. (1987) *Women and Politics*, London: Macmillan and Abbott, P. and Wallace, C. (1992) *An Introduction to Sociology. Feminist Perspectives*, London: Macmillan.
30. Abbott and Wallace, 1992, p. 14.
31. It has only been very recently that South Africa has become a multicultural democratic state. Previously under the apartheid regime, the state was founded upon this notion that human beings could be classified into separate races.
32. The experience of the Irish in Britain is another indication of the way in which racial discrimination exists based not on colour but on ethnic/cultural differences. The claims that there was some scientific basis to the concept of 'race' have been shown to be totally false. There are no fixed measurable characteristics of any group of human beings which can then be classified into races, and so in common with many other other writers we use the term phenotype which describes the visible markers of a person (i.e. skin colour, features, hair colour) which may be used as the basis for discrimination (Castles and Miller, 1993).
33. The whole process of 'ethnic cleansing' in the former Yugoslavia is based on this notion that one ethnic group is superior to another, and is therefore justified in removing them. This has taken place despite centuries of intercommunal marriage and co-existence.
34. Miles, R. (1989) 'Recent Marxist theories of nationalism and the issue of racism' *British Journal of Sociology* 38 (24–43).
35. Evidence exists that centurions from Africa formed part of the Roman force of occupation in Britain after 55 BC. Since Elizabethan times most of the large ports, particularly London, have been home to large numbers of people from Asia, Africa and the Caribbean. See Fryer, P. (1984) *Staying Power*, London: Pluto Press.
36. Said, 1994, p. 28. See also Pieterse, J. N. (1994) 'Unpacking the West: How European is Europe?' in *Racism, Modernity and Identity on the Western Front* Rattansi, A. and Westwood, S. (eds) Cambridge: Polity Press.
37. Modood, T. (1994) 'Political blackness and Asian identity' *Sociology* 28 (4). Some caution is necessary concerning Modood's attempts to define 'Asian' in terms of the risk of falling back on the same kind of 'essentialism' that, he argues, underlines the use of the term 'black'.
38. Hall in Donald and Rattansi, 1992, p. 254.

CHAPTER FIVE

# The European mixed economies in practice

## The unity of experiences

### 5.1 Introduction

Having examined the theoretical underpinning of the European mixed economies, we now discuss some of the essential aspects of their operation in practice. The aim of this chapter and of Chapter 6, in conjunction with which it should be read, is to consider the interpretations of the mixed economy that have been adopted by European countries, in the context of the parameters within which the European economy has been obliged to operate. The objective of the chapters is not to provide a detailed account of economic developments and policies in each each economy – this is impossible in the space available, and in any case is documented elsewhere.[1] Rather it is intended to give a broad and analytical picture of the fundamental economic direction which different countries have taken and of the forces, the ideas, the developments, the structures and the policies that have to a large extent conditioned such choices, and thus have conditioned the nature and development of contemporary European societies. To this end the two chapters seek to examine three interrelated themes:

(a)  the essential economic characteristics of European mixed economies;
(b)  the impact of changes in the external and internal parameters within which the the European economies have had to function; and
(c)  the influence of the process of European integration on the European economy.

   Thus, while in Chapter 2 we analysed the rationale for and the consequences of alternative approaches to economic organisation, and we outlined the case for the mixed economy model that has been adopted by West European countries in the post-war period, here we examine how European countries have adapted the basic idea of the mixed economy to their own particular circumstances. We shall do so by examining the similarities and differences in their experiences and approaches: the former (unity) in this chapter and the latter (diversity) in Chapter 6.

### 5.2  Common parameters and the extent of convergence

In many ways, there are considerable similarities (**unity**) in the European national experience at present and over recent years, at least as far as West Europe is concerned.[2] The principal dimensions of this are discussed below.

At the most basic and obvious level, the countries with which we are mainly concerned have, as we have seen, adopted broadly **similar models of economic organisation**, based as we have said on the principle of the mixed economy.[3] This is in contrast to, for example, the United States which has adopted a much 'purer' form of capitalism, based to a greater extent on *laissez-faire*. In doing so, the European economies have developed a distinctive, perhaps specifically 'European', model of economic organisation. In the parlance of regulation theory, they have adopted regimes of accumulation and modes of regulation that, although different in detail, follow the same broad lines.

European countries have all experienced **similar trends in their economic histories**, or at least they have moved in roughly the same direction during the various phases of post-war economic history. These were outlined in Chapter 1, but it is clear that all countries had to go through a reconstruction period from 1945–50/2, then all went through a period of rapid economic growth until the late 1960s, a period of crisis in the 1970s, and then the current period of slower growth and retrenchment into neo-liberal economics and increased reliance on market forces. If one examines this issue from the perspective of long wave theory, European countries have ridden roughly the same phase of the Kondratieff or Schumpeterian cycle (see Chapter 2), even if long-term trends have been experienced differently in different countries.

Similarly, they have all been subject to similar **trends in economic ideology** and the consequent changes in the climate of mainstream economic thinking. They all espoused Keynesianism, all abandoned it at roughly the same time, and then all embraced in differing degrees the neo-liberal agenda (see Chapters 1, 2 and 6). It has been rare for individual countries to follow lines of economic policy which have been substantially out of line with those pursued by their neighbours. The 1981–83 Mitterrand government in France, which was elected to carry out a Keynesian expansion of the economy and an interventionist industrial strategy at a time when other countries were busy experimenting with monetarism and other aspects of neo-liberalism represents an obvious exception.[4] At present, the neo-liberal belief in free markets and *laissez-faire* is still the dominant economic framework, even though there is some evidence of a renewed interest in Keynesianism and other forms of intervention and regulation of the economy, as the neo-liberal momentum runs somewhat out of steam in European countries such as the United Kingdom.

They are all faced with a number of contemporary **internal challenges**, the response to which will largely determine the nature of life in European countries into the next century. The first of these concerns the **environment**, which we discuss elsewhere in the book. Perhaps even more important, at least in the short term, is the issue of **employment**, or how best to ensure work and prosperity for their population into the future, in the light of the changing environment we are here discussing. Over recent years the latter has developed into a major problem for the European economies, all of which have suffered, albeit in different degrees, from having large numbers of their citizens on the dole. This too is an issue to which we will return in Chapter 7. Similarly, the **age structure** of the population in EU countries raises important issues for the future. Most EU countries are characterised by low birth rates[5] and increased longevity, presenting the prospect of ageing populations, increased dependency ratios,[6] and the associated problems concerning issues such as the finance of future pensions, and probable increased demands on health services.

In addition to the above, European countries are faced with a **similar external environment**, having to work within similar parameters and having to adapt to changes in these parameters. The principal dimensions of this have included increasing competition, technology, international economic arrangements, increased mobility of capital, economic interdependence, economic and political integration and economic convergence, all of which are now discussed.

They all face **increasing competition** in internal and world markets, particularly from the NICs in the Pacific Rim who have challenged Europe's traditional economic strength, not only in manufacturing, but also increasingly in service areas such as banking. The most successful of the NICs over the last 30 or so years have been the eight East Asian countries studied recently by the World Bank (1993), i.e. Hong Kong, Indonesia, Japan, Malaysia, Singapore, South Korea, Taiwan and Thailand. These countries together grew at an average annual rate of 5.5 per cent between 1965 and 1990, more than twice as fast as the OECD countries and three times faster than Latin America. Their share of world manufacturing exports increased from 9 per cent to 21 per cent over the same period. Interestingly enough, the World Bank points out that this growth was achieved hand in hand with relatively low and declining inequality of income in some countries, and with policies that mixed free markets with substantial intervention in the form of subsidies, tax incentives, export promotion, import barriers and substantial investment in human capital (an East Asian model of the mixed economy?). The establishment of market economies in East/Central Europe and indeed in China (which presently has strong trade links with Japan), if succcessful, may provide further challenges of a similar kind over coming years.

Perhaps the principal challenge which Europe thus far has faced in manufacturing, its traditional area of strength, has come from the the first and the most advanced of the NICs, Japan. An idea of the magnitude of this challenge may be gained from Figs 5.1 and 5.2, the first showing the EU countries' current account position *vis-à-vis* Japan in the 1980s and early 1990s, and the latter showing similar data for the most recent years.

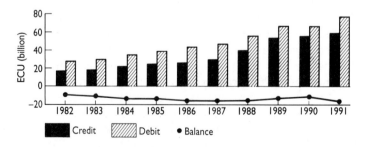

**Figure 5.1**   EU–Japan current account flows 1982–91. *Source: Eurostat.*

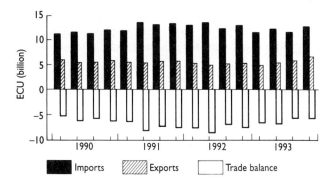

*Figure 5.2* EU trade flows with Japan 1990–93. *Source: Eurostat.*

Japan–EU trade is almost exclusively in manufactured products, and from the graphs it is clear that the members of the EU have run a sizeable and consistent deficit on such trade with Japan over this period. In absolute terms, the EU trade deficit with Japan amounted to ECU31 bn in 1992, and ECU25.1 bn in 1993. The total value of imports into the EC from Japan increased by 230.9 per cent between 1980 and 1990, from ECU13 968 m to ECU46 224 m. The main EU imports from Japan are road vehicles (ECU11.8 bn in 1993), office machinery (ECU6.5 bn), electrical machinery (ECU5.5 bn), and telecommunications and sound equipment (ECU5.1 bn). Trade with the ASEAN states of Hong Kong, South Korea, Singapore and Taiwan has also grown in importance, but in these cases the EU countries have managed to maintain a rough balance between imports and exports.[7] The increased penetration of European markets for manufactured goods by Japan fundamentally reflects the superior record of the Japanese over both the EU 12 countries and the United States in investment in this field, as is shown in Fig. 5.3.

The growing relative strength of the Japanese economy *vis-à-vis* Europe is in turn reflected by the secular decline in the exchange rate for the DM against the yen, as is

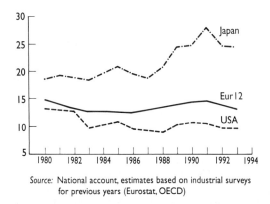

*Source:* National account, estimates based on industrial surveys for previous years (Eurostat, OECD)

*Figure 5.3* Comparison of investment as a percentage of Gross Value Added in manufacturing at current market prices. *Source: Eurostat.*

shown in Table 5.1 While the exchange rate for the DM has virtually trebled against sterling, and virtually doubled against the currencies of other EC countries since 1972, it has in fact fallen by one-third against the yen. The long-term relationship between the yen and other European currencies such as sterling can be readily deduced. The increasing penetration of European markets by imports from all sources can be readily observed from Table 5.2.

This shows the penetration of markets between 1980 and 1991 by types of industry. Overall there has been an increase in penetration from 14.2 per cent to 18.9 per cent over this period, with particularly large increases in mechanical engineering (12.6–19.0 per cent), electrical engineering (13.6–20.9 per cent), motor vehicles and transport equipment (30.9–51.5 per cent), leather goods (26.7–45.2 per cent) and footware and clothing (21.3–37.8 per cent). The greatest level of import penetration is in chemicals (including man-made fibres, 87.5 per cent in 1991), cars and transport equipment (51.5 per cent), leather goods (45.2 per cent) and office machinery (37.8 per cent).

European countries have all been affected by the fundamental changes that have taken place and continue to occur in **technology**, from the early post-war development of mechanisation and automation to the current information and communications 'revolution'. They will naturally also be affected by future developments in emerging fields such as biotechnologies. Changes in technology have precipitated fundamental changes in the manner of production, in general away from a **Fordist** way of operating towards to a broadly **post-Fordist** one, or one based on **flexible specialisation**,[8] altering the nature of work accordingly (see Chapters 2 and 7). Regulation theorists would say that they have been subject to broadly similar industrial trajectories.

They have all had to operate within the context of the changing **international economic arrangements** that have characterised the post-war period, from the Bretton Woods system of fixed exchange rates, through the period of flexible exchange rates that followed the break up of the Bretton Woods system, and back to the fixed exchange rates of the Exchange Rate Mechanism (ERM) of the EU's European Monetary System (EMS). In addition, they have been subject to an increasingly liberal world trade regime as a result of the various rounds of the GATT and of the internal tariff and NTB elimination that has come with the EU customs union.[9] This of course

**Table 5.1**   DM exchange rate. *Source: European Economy, 1994–92.*                     (End 1972 = 100)

|           | USD | FF  | HFL | LIT | UKL | YEN | EC  | 18 ICs |
|-----------|-----|-----|-----|-----|-----|-----|-----|--------|
| end of:   |     |     |     |     |     |     |     |        |
| 1975      | 123 | 108 | 102 | 144 | 142 | 122 | 121 | 117    |
| 1980      | 165 | 146 | 108 | 263 | 162 | 108 | 163 | 145    |
| 1985      | 131 | 193 | 112 | 378 | 213 | 85  | 215 | 162    |
| 1988      | 181 | 215 | 112 | 408 | 236 | 74  | 231 | 176    |
| 1989      | 190 | 215 | 112 | 416 | 278 | 89  | 240 | 186    |
| 1990      | 216 | 214 | 112 | 418 | 262 | 95  | 237 | 189    |
| 1991      | 213 | 215 | 112 | 420 | 266 | 86  | 238 | 188    |
| 1992      | 200 | 215 | 112 | 506 | 310 | 81  | 256 | 195    |
| 11/1993   | 188 | 218 | 111 | 551 | 297 | 68  | 263 | 193    |

*Source: Eurostat.*

**Table 5.2** Import penetration of the EC market. Source: *European Economy*

| NACE code | | 1980 | 1981 | 1982 | 1983 | 1984 | 1985 | 1986 | 1987 | 1988 | 1989 | 1990 | 1991 |
|---|---|---|---|---|---|---|---|---|---|---|---|---|---|
| | | | | | | | | | (extra-EC) imports as a percentage of apparent consumption[1] | | | | |
| 22 | Metals | 21.3 | 19.5 | 20.4 | 22.1 | 21.6 | 21.8 | 21.4 | 21.5 | 25.5 | 23.8 | 23.3 | 24.8 |
| 24 | Non-metallic minerals | 3.5 | 3.8 | 3.7 | 3.9 | 4.4 | 4.6 | 4.7 | 4.8 | 5.1 | 5.4 | 5.5 | 6.1 |
| 25+26 | Chemicals[2] | 105.8 | 115.5 | 99.6 | 109.6 | 123.3 | 127.4 | 106.9 | 104.9 | 97.4 | 95.7 | 85.0 | 87.5 |
| 31 | Manufacturing of metal articles | 4.0 | 4.3 | 4.4 | 4.4 | 4.7 | 4.7 | 4.7 | 4.9 | 5.3 | 5.6 | 5.6 | 6.2 |
| 32 | Mechanical engineering | 12.6 | 14.3 | 14.3 | 13.9 | 14.8 | 16.5 | 16.1 | 16.8 | 17.2 | 17.8 | 18.1 | 19.0 |
| 33 | Office mach. and data proc. equip. | 30.3 | 33.4 | 30.7 | 32.0 | 36.8 | 35.5 | 33.7 | 36.2 | 36.4 | 38.2 | 36.8 | 37.8 |
| 34 | Electrical engineering | 13.6 | 15.9 | 15.9 | 16.4 | 18.4 | 18.7 | 17.6 | 18.0 | 19.2 | 20.2 | 19.9 | 20.9 |
| 35 | Motor vehicles and parts | 7.5 | 8.1 | 8.3 | 9.4 | 10.9 | 11.2 | 11.4 | 11.0 | 11.1 | 11.3 | 11.6 | 13.1 |
| 36 | Other transport equipment | 23.4 | 27.2 | 27.5 | 27.8 | 31.2 | 24.0 | 19.3 | 20.5 | 31.5 | 33.3 | 33.8 | 38.4 |
| 37 | Instrument engineering | 30.9 | 35.0 | 35.6 | 38.2 | 42.0 | 40.7 | 39.5 | 38.7 | 39.4 | 42.4 | 41.7 | 42.7 |
| 41/42 | Food, drink and tobacco | 6.7 | 7.0 | 6.9 | 6.9 | 7.3 | 7.0 | 6.1 | 5.9 | 6.2 | 6.1 | 5.8 | 5.7 |
| 43 | Textiles | 8.9 | 9.9 | 9.8 | 9.6 | 9.5 | 9.4 | 10.3 | 12.0 | 12.5 | 12.8 | 14.0 | 16.8 |
| 44 | Leather goods | 26.7 | 27.1 | 27.6 | 25.8 | 27.7 | 31.4 | 30.7 | 32.9 | 36.4 | 42.1 | 43.7 | 45.2 |
| 45 | Footwear and clothing | 21.3 | 24.0 | 24.0 | 22.7 | 24.8 | 25.3 | 26.6 | 28.8 | 29.7 | 32.7 | 34.1 | 37.8 |
| 46 | Timber and wooden furniture | 18.2 | 18.1 | 18.3 | 19.3 | 19.6 | 18.7 | 18.2 | 18.5 | 18.4 | 19.0 | 18.6 | 17.5 |
| 47 | Paper, printing and publishing | 12.2 | 13.4 | 13.1 | 12.9 | 14.2 | 13.5 | 13.0 | 13.3 | 13.6 | 14.2 | 13.2 | 12.5 |
| 48 | Rubber and plastics | 6.1 | 6.8 | 7.3 | 7.3 | 7.7 | 8.0 | 7.7 | 8.0 | 8.7 | 9.0 | 9.1 | 9.6 |
| | Total | 14.2 | 15.1 | 15.2 | 15.5 | 16.9 | 16.9 | 16.2 | 16.4 | 17.7 | 18.3 | 18.1 | 18.9 |

1. Gross output plus total imports minus total exports. The Community is defined as EUR 9 during the entire period.
2. Includes man-made fibres.
*Source:* VISA databank, *Eurostat.*

partly accounts for the increased trade flows to be observed in the above tables and figures. In this context one might also mention the economic challenge European countries face from the results of the **break-up of the Soviet Union**, and its former empire in East/Central Europe. Furthermore, we should bear in mind that part of the international context in which European countries operate includes the issue of **world development**. Hunger and poverty in the third world throws up a series of moral, economic and political issues that cannot forever be ducked.

European countries are all having to come to terms with the vastly **increased mobility of capital** we have experienced in the post-war period, and especially in more recent years. This is perhaps the most important external development which has affected the European economies in the late twentieth century. Learning to cope with its effects will in all probability dominate the debate over economic policy well into the next century. Increased capital mobility has resulted from a variety of developments: the 'information revolution', the growth in foreign direct and portfolio investment, the emergence of 'petrodollars'[10] and speculation, as well as from the deregulation of capital markets that has come partly in the wake of the general global movement towards free market ideals and partly as a result of EU attempts to complete the internal market. This increased mobility of capital has contributed to the enhanced interdependence of European economies, making the conduct of economic policy at the purely national level problematic. It has thus also contributed to the reduction in national economic sovereignty and to the movement towards economic integration discussed later in this chapter. Data on capital flows is notoriously unreliable, but Fig. 5.4 gives a good idea of the startling increase that has occurred over the last few years.

From this we can see that the stock of international bank lending increased from $324 bn in 1980 to $7.5 trillion in 1991, from 4 per cent to 44 per cent of the OECD's

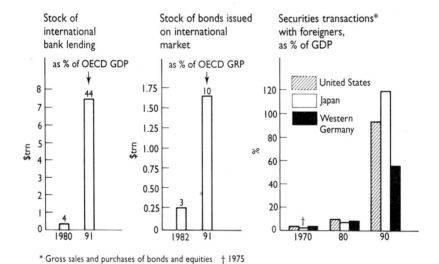

* Gross sales and purchases of bonds and equities   † 1975

**Figure 5.4** Indicators of international capital flows. *Source: Economist,* 19/9/92.

GDP. The stock of bonds issued on international markets similarly increased from 3 per cent to 10 per cent of OECD GDP between 1982 and 1991, while the third segment of the figure shows the massive increase that has taken place in the importance of securities transactions with foreigners. This is reinforced when one considers that during the 1980s the volume of global securities transactions in equities alone increased at an annual compound rate of 28 per cent per annum. We now live in a genuinely global capital market.

A somewhat anecdotal impression of the influence of capital mobility in the modern world can be had if we consider that the investments of the UK financial services industry alone are roughly equivalent to 100 per cent of the country's GDP.[11] A mere precautionary shift of 5 per cent of these out of sterling is therefore sufficient to neutralise the whole of the United Kingdom's foreign exchange reserves, as we saw at the time of the United Kingdom's and Italy's ignominious exit from the ERM in 1992 (see Fig. 5.5 and Section 5.5 of this chapter). This represents a good example of the extent to which the power of uncontrolled capital markets can effectively subvert the wishes of democratically elected governments, and indeed whole communities: in both Italy and the United Kingdom in 1992 membership of the ERM was a central parameter of economic policy.[12] The increase that has occurred in foreign direct investment by multinational corporations (MNCs) is well known,[13] but Fig. 5.6 illustrates the increase that has taken place over the last decade in flows of portfolio investment between selected EC countries.

European countries are all experiencing increased **economic interdependence** not only among themselves but also *vis-à-vis* other parts of the world economy, partly because of the greater mobility of capital discussed above, and partly because of increased trade, particularly intra-European Union trade. Table 5.3 shows the extent to which intra-trade among the EC of 12 countries has grown in importance during the years between 1980 and 1992. It will be noted that for the 12 countries as a whole the proportion of intra-trade in total trade has risen from 49.2 per cent to 61.3 per cent during these 13 years. The latest enlargement will, of course, further substantially increase the proportion of intra-trade for the new EU of 15 countries, given that nearly a quarter of non-intra trade was with the ex-EFTA countries in the early 1990s. Table 5.4, on the other hand, demonstrates the increase that has taken place in the volume of EC trade with countries outside the integration scheme between 1970 and 1990.

From Table 5.4 one should note the huge increase (roughly by a factor of eight) in the total value of this trade, reflecting the general increase in world trade, and the change in the proportional direction of trade, towards Japan and the other NICs and away from Latin America, the ACP countries and the OPEC countries.[14]

They all have been involved in the process of **economic** (and **political**) **integration**. This has been the case not only for the current 15 members of the EU, but also for the former members of EFTA and for the East/Central European states who now aspire to EU membership. One of the features of integration has been an increased recent propensity to accept leadership on economic policy from Germany, which has now emerged as the most influential economic power in the region. Again, this will be taken up below.

# Black Wednesday massacre

Will Hutton has written this account from interviews and briefings obtained from officials and ministers involved in the events leading up to Black Wednesday by Alex Brummer, John Glover, John Hooper, Ruth Kelly, Mark Milner and John Palmer in Belgium, Germany, France, Ireland, Portugal, Italy, Spain and Britain.

Speculators began taking scalps and the pound was next in the firing line. The die for British disaster was cast as eleventh-hour talks produced only Italian devaluation and a small German interest rate cut. Guardian investigations reveal how sterling made its inglorious exit from the ERM.

The 11 other EC central bank governors were appalled. There is a convention that no-one speaks to the press after the regular second Tuesday of the month meetings at the Bank for International Settlements in Basle, but on September 8 Dr Helmut Schlesinger insisted that he was going to put the record straight.

What has upset him was the supposed guarantee he had offered at the Bath summit that the Bundesbank would not raise interest rates. He could make no such cast iron guarantee; nor had he any confidence that the existing parties inside the ERM would survive. He wanted to attack the way the Bath summit had been presented.

There was widespread consternation. The prospect of his telling the press these things would provoke the crisis that had been looming for weeks. Dr Schlessinger said that of course he was not going to talk about currencies but he had to reassure the German public that the Bundesbank still reserved its rights over interest rate policy. He was not to be deterred.

Warming to his theme as the meeting progressed he said that the level of Bundesbank support for the lira, approaching DM100 billion and with no end in sight, was unsustainable. He reminded his peers that the ERM had responded to similar crises in 1986 and 1987 with a realignment. He did not signal that he would be making a formal request for a realignment conference over the coming weekend but, as one participant said "We were put on notice."

Even as they were talking the foreign exchange markets were in the process of taking the first of the many scalps they were to claim over the next two months – the Finnish markka.

The Finns had pegged the markka to the ecu as their own version of a markka "fort" policy, informally shadowing the ERM but without any of the ERM's support mechanisms. Interest rates had been forced up to 18 per cent the previous Thursday, but by that Tuesday evening the force of speculation forced Finland to abandon the peg.

On Wednesday the markka fell by nearly 15 per cent, giving the speculators an instant huge profit: the hunt was now on for bigger game, with banks' foreign exchange departments around the globe who had not made a killing holding inquisitions, and those who had scenting blood.

There could be no more obvious tarket than the lira. The markets had got wind of realignment talk, and selling the lira seemed a one-way bet. The austerity package was bogged down in parliament, forcing the government to defer vital decisions for a week; Italy's foreign exchange reserves were falling rapidly and the Bundesbank had made no secret of its view that Italy should devalue. On Wednesday the waves of selling reached new peaks. The following day the Italian government, amid further massive intervention, announced that it would seek emergency powers in the event of an economic crisis. The "announcement effect" was tiny, and by Thursday evening it was clear in Frankfurt, Bonn and Rome that Italy's position was no longer tenable. The lira would have to be devalued.

At this stage the Guardian understands the Italians let it be known that they wanted the EC Monetary Committee, which governs the ERM and is composed of senior finance ministry and central bank representatives from all members, to hold a full meeting over the coming weekend.

From Bath the Italians knew that the Dutch and Belgians would support a realignment; and the German position could hardly be clearer.

Even though the British and Spanish had signalled their opposition surely they would see that, if the lira devalued alone, they would be in the same position as the lira when the markka was knocked off its perch – the next in the firing line.

Although accounts have focused on the weekend of September 12/13 it was the events of Thursday morning to Friday evening that made a solo Italian devaluation certain. The Italian request to hold a full monetary committee meeting was obstructed in London, Paris and Madrid; although it is not clear whether the request was ever clearly communicated. Certainly the Treasury do not consider that any such request came before Saturday night.

Even then it would have not been too late for the British to signal their readiness for a full meeting, forcing Spain to abandon its opposition. The way would have been open to discuss, if not a general realignment, then what Horst Köhler, the German state secretary for finance, calls a "broad" realignment. The guilder, mark, and Belgian and French francs would have revalued and some other currencies,

*Figure 5.5* Black Wednesday massacre
*Source: Guardian, 1/12/92*

including sterling, would have moved lower with a German interest rate cut to lubricate the process. It was not to be.

The British line was that with the French referendum only seven trading days away sterling could survive unscathed. What happened afterwards would very much depend on the vote – giving lots of political cover if, for example, a "no" vote forced a general realignment. Indeed, the British had already decided that if such a realignment was on offer, with the mark unilaterally revaluing against the rest of the ERM, they would go along with it.

For months certain British officials had been increasingly convinced that sterling devaluation was inevitable. A difference of opinion was emerging between a still confident Treasury and more sceptical Bank of England, who could see the scale of the support required to support the lira and knew that for sterling, much more widely traded, the scale of the speculative attack would be colossal.

But the official line remained that the problem was the strains thrown up by the divergence between high German and low US interest rates rather than sterling's parity with the mark. Devaluation was off the agenda.

The Prime Minister's support could be taken for granted – that summer he had taken out a fixed rate mortgage at 9.8 per cent – and Andrew Crockett, executive director at the Bank of England, had informed central bank deputies in Basle only on Monday that the Government was under immense political constraint. If it raised interest rates support for the Maastricht treaty would evaporate. Equally, as Mr Major's famous "no devaluation" speech to the Scottish CBI explained, it was so far out on a limb that anything less than a general realignment was politically impossible.

Moreover, although the lira was under terrible pressure, sterling seemed to be holding comparatively well, even if it was at the bottom of its permitted ERM band. What point was there in joining a realignment now? The manifesto, the repeated commitments not to devalue, the joint EC finance ministers' statement that Mr Lamont had initiated, the ecu loan, and Mr. Lamont's chairmanship of the Bath summit could not be repudiated.

The Germans knew they had a first-class crisis on their hands; they accepted that if Italy devalued alone not only would it be bad for the Italians but also for those weaker currencies who had passed up the opportunity, and the Germans would be faced with a mark intervention running to tens of billions.

A "general" realignment against the mark was impossible for the French to accept before the Maastricht referendum but what about a "broad" realignment, in which the pound joined the lira, peseta, escudo, and even the Irish punt and Danish krone, in moving down against a mark block, including the franc and perhaps the Dutch guilder?

To sweeten the deal Germany was prepared to lower its interest rates, but it is not clear from telephone calls made between Rome, Frankfurt, Bonn, London, Paris and Madrid how far advanced was the Germans' thinking or how explicit their offer. Certainly Carlo Ciampi, governor of the Bank of Italy,

believes that with a "broad" realignment the Bundesbank could have lowered German short-term interest rates by a full percentage point instead of the quarter percentage point that emerged. The idea may have been floated but never became a hard bargaining position.

Horst Köhler is on record as saying that the British were offered a "broad" realignment but did not accept. Nigel Wicks, Köhler's opposite number at the Treasury, is known to have received a telephone call from him on Friday but says it concerned arrangements for the visit of Treasury officials to Germany the following week. Both men's coolness during the biggest financial crisis the ERM had yet encountered can only be admired.

By Friday afternoon it was likely that further realignment negotiations were going to take place over the weekend by telephone, rather than the full EC Monetary Committee meeting which might have produced a "broad" realignment. The exchange of views initiated by the Germans had not produced any basis on which to proceed. As Chancellor Kohl, finance minister Theo Waigel and Horst Köhler met Dr Schlesinger and his number two, Hans Tietmeyer, at the Bundesbank on Friday evening it was clear that the cumulative Bundesbank intervention, totalling around DM290 billion (£107 billion) had to be staunched.

Mr Kohl agreed; and Mr Köhler and Mr Tietmeyer were deputed to go to Rome on Saturday to negotiate an Italian devaluation. Mr Köhler would first fly to Paris and ask Jean-Claude Trichet, head of the French finance ministry and chair of the EC Monetary Committee, to contact other members and try to keep open the options of "broad" realignment and a Sunday committee meeting. But realistically the Germans had already conceded that the most likely outcome would be a unilateral Italian devaluation.

On Saturday evening Nigel Wicks, the Treasury's representative on the committee, was contacted by Mr Trichet and told the outcome of the Rome discussions. The lira was to be devalued by 7 per cent. The Germans would lower their Lombard rate by 0.25 per cent and their discount and money market intervention rates by 0.5 per cent. It was a "done deal", as one British source said.

Formal British assent required a meeting, and Mr Wicks attempted to round up the key players for 7.45am on Sunday at the Treasury. He could only contact Sir Terence Burns, Permanent Secretary to the Treasury by mobile phone and, frightened of security, talked eliptically of "problems with our sick patient" (Italy).

At the Treasury on Sunday morning the Bank of England team, Professor Alan Budd, the Government's chief economic adviser, and other Treasury officials were assembling as an upbeat Sir Terence and the Chancellor entered the room. One participant describes them as "cock-a-hoop"; another no more than "relieved". But there was no disguising their welcome for the German interest rate cut as the signal that might see sterling safety through the next week.

The Bank of England representatives were more cautious, worried that the devaluation left the pound exposed and that the speculation might be irresistible.

**Figure 5.5** *Continued*

As the implications were discussed Sir Terence called the meeting to order.

His questions were – do we object?, and do we want to join in? Everyone, whatever their private misgivings, knew the answers and the decisions were almost instantaneous. Britain could hardly object, and at this late stage there was no point in reversing the longstanding policy of resisting a broad realignment without the French. Even had bigger German interest rate reductions been available with British participation there was no forum to discuss them, and Britain had no intention of calling for one in the form of a full meeting of the EC Monetary Committee. Agreement could be done by telephone, and anyway time was running short; the Irish had only been informed at 11pm on Saturday and the Bank of Holland was ignorant as late as midday on Sunday.

There was the question of how the devaluation should be presented and confirmation needed from the Germans that Mr Trichet's description of the deal was accurate but within 45 minutes Mr Wicks was in a position to give British assent.

In retrospect almost everybody believes that not holding a full EC Monetary Committee meeting was a mistake. The Italians are still smarting from the insult, with Guillano Amato, the Italian Prime Minister saying it was "scandalous" that the lira's devaluation was treated as an everyday matter. Some Bank of England officials felt at the time and still do that it would have been better to get the whole issue into the open.

The reception of the deal on Monday morning was better than the pessimists had feared, although there was Bank of England unease at the way Downing Street sources expressed such jubilation at the prospect of immediately lower British interest rates. Like the withdrawal of the high interest National Savings instrument First Option, because it might have led to higher mortgage rates, it was another reminder to the markets of how anxious the Government was to lower interest rates and how resistant it was to increases.

As Tuesday wore on the danger signals multiplied. The selling of sterling was becoming intense and the pound was at its floor. The markets were increasingly convinced that whatever the result of the French vote sterling was a one-way bet. If there was a "no" vote the ERM would break down and sterling would devalue. If there was a "yes" vote, a general, or at least very broad realignment including sterling looked equally certain. The markets were right; and the British had walked knowingly into the trap.

Inside the Treasury the strain was intense. With the peseta feeling the fallout Carlos Solchaga, the Spanish finance minister, telephoned Norman Lamont to ask him how things were. "Awful", came the reply, "I'm just living from day to day." Many others echoed this.

At 6.45pm that Tuesday there was a stock-taking meeting at the Treasury to report on the last few hours trading and decide the strategy for Wednesday. The Governor and Deputy Governor of the Bank of England were there, along with two or three other senior officials; the Treasury team included, as always, Sir Terence Burns and the Chancellor.

Would raising interest rates be a warning of distress, a signal to the markets that the end was nigh, or a pre-emptive strike? It was clear that as trading began the Bank of England should intervene by buying sterling as aggressively and openly as possible but what should follow?

Although Eddie George, the Deputy Governor, laid out the classic intervention strategy culminating in higher interest rates, the Bank team was clear what it wanted – agreement in principle that interest rates could be lifted on the Wednesday if necessary, with some prepared to argue for a pre-emptive rise when the markets opened.

It was while the discussion was in full flow that the Governor read out loud the message from his press office. Helmut Schlesinger had given an interview casting doubt about whether existing parities would hold – a clear hint that he thought sterling would devalue.

The meeting was stunned. The Governor, Robin Leigh Pemberton, was asked to make immediate contact with Dr Schlesinger to ask for clarification and rebuttal of the news if true. At least one member present was heard to have said that the news was devastating; the game was up. In the centre of the table, where the principal decision-makers sat, there was extreme concern but no open admission that defeat was staring them in the face – rather a recognition that the witching hour was fast approaching.

The following morning at 9am Mr Leigh Pemberton, Mr George, Mr Burns, and the Chancellor met at the Treasury. Overt intervention was not going well – indeed in one exchange that morning a senior official is known to have counselled that the entire exercise would be fruitless. The selling pressure was growing with the pound still at its ERM floor. At 11am interest rates were lifted to 12 per cent; and by 11.30am the same four had decided they would have to tell the Prime Minister, esconced in Admiralty House, that in the face of overwhelming selling the pound's parity could not be held.

Europe's central bankers, who held two telephone conferences that day, discerned a "sense of panic" in the British camp by mid-morning; the scale of selling was outside the British experience. At lunchtime first the Prime Minister himself and then his conclave of inner ministers, including Douglas Hurd, Michael Heseltine and Kenneth Clarke, learnt the news. A decision to hike rates to 15 per cent was taken and announced at 2.15pm with hopes not completely dead, but when that failed the denouement was inevitable.

It was not even clear that the pound could get through the day without its membership of the ERM being suspended. Other ERM countries urged Britain to hold on, to go for a unilateral devaluation rather than suspension, or simply to announce a temporary suspension.

Pierre Bérégovoy, the French Prime Minister, rang John Major twice encouraging him to stay in the ERM rather than leave it. But by 5pm the decision was taken to rescind the 15 per cent minimum lending rate (MLR), and by 7.45pm the Chancellor announced sterling's suspension from the ERM.

At the hastily convened European Monetary Committee meeting in Brussels that night Nigel Wicks from the Treasury and Andrew Crockett from the Bank of England explained the British decision. Mr Wicks

**Figure 5.5**  *Continued*

began by confessing that the last hour before the market closed had been the worst in his life, while Crockett explained that Britain had spent £11 billion in reserves, nearly half its total.

They wanted a complete suspension of the ERM until after the French vote, arguing that a simple sterling devaluation was impossible because any medium-term defensible exchange rate was so dependent on the referendum result.

Indeed the Dutch had told the Bank of England during the afternoon that any devaluation would have to be over 10 per cent to be credible – outside ERM rules. And what if the market judged any devaluation to be insufficient? That would mean a rout. By Wednesday afternoon the trap had snapped shut; there was no way out. British membership of the ERM had come to an inglorious end.

## Tactics that failed to save sterling

September 7–8: Central bank governors and deputies meet in Basle.

September 8: Finnish authorities forced to float the markka after it is heavily sold in the market.

September 9: Italian lira comes under a wave of heavy selling pressure.

September 10: Italian government takes on emergency powers to cut the budget deficit.

September 10–11: Germany initiates extensive bilateral talks.

September 12: Tietmayer and Köhler in Rome negotiate the Italian devaluation due to be announced the following day.

September 13: Treasury at 7.45am meeting agrees to unilateral Italian devaluation which is announced in the evening. Bundesbank says it will reduce interest rates.

September 14: German rates come down by 0.25 percentage points, providing brief respite for sterling.

September 15: Sterling and lira sold heavily in foreign exchange markets. Pound closes barely above ERM floor.

Early evening meeting between Treasury and Bank to discuss strategy for next day. Some Bank officials propose pre-emptive two-point rise in base rates to 12 per cent before markets open next day. News agencies carry reports saying Dr Schlesinger believed weekend realignment of ERM did not go far enough.

September 16: Black Wednesday opens with sterling under intense pressure. Bank's first line of defence is heavy intervention – buying pounds with UK's reserves of foreign currency – in attempt to push up price. Tactic fails to lift sterling off ERM floor. At 11am Bank announces minimum lending rate (MLR) to be set at 12 per cent. High street banks put up base rates to 12 per cent.

Despute further intervention, pound remains under severe pressure in late morning and early afternoon. By 11.30am Treasury realises position is hopeless.

But crisis meeting of inner group of Cabinet ministers sanctions 2.15pm announcement that MLR will be set at 15 per cent from following morning.

Financial markets see 15 per cent MLR as admission of defeat and assume devaluation, now inevitable. Pressure on sterling abates in anticipation of announcement. Soon after 7.30pm Chancellor announces suspension of ERM membership and rescinds 15 per cent MLR.

Late evening: EC's monetary committee meets in Brussels. Lira also leaves ERM, Spanish peseta devalued by 5 per cent.

September 17: MLR reduced to 10 per cent at 9.30am. Pound falls sharply.

September 18: Pound ends the week at DM2.61, 6 per cent below old ERM floor.

September 20: French vote yes to Maastricht by narrow margin.

**Figure 5.5**  *Continued*

In the light of such fundamental shared experiences, it is not surprising that there has been substantial **economic convergence** among West and some Southern European countries. Figures 5.7 and 5.8 provide us with an indication of the convergence that has taken place since 1980 in two important monetary variables: inflation and long-term interest rates, respectively. This is not say that there are not still substantial **divergences** or differences in the European economy, and this is a factor that will render moves towards a monetary union in Europe problematic. These differences are naturally partly the result of the diversity between European countries that we shall discuss below (in Chapter 6). An obvious dimension of these differences is the divide between the mainly 'northern' countries in the centre or core of the EU, and the predominantly 'Southern' states on the periphery. The latter tend to have different structures and in some ways weaker economic performance than the former, opening up the possibility of integration based on a 'two-speed Europe': Germany,

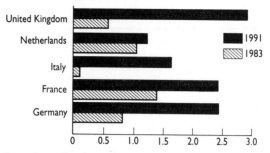

Portfolio investment from other EC countries

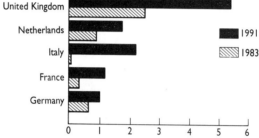

Portfolio investment in other EC countries

**Figure 5.6**   Intra-EC portfolio investment in selected European countries
*Source: European Economy.*

France, Austria, the Benelux countries and perhaps the United Kingdom proceding towards closer integration, while the others join in if and when they are ready to do so. One indication of this diversity is the far from complete factor price equalisation (convergence of wage rates and returns to capital) that has occurred among European countries, at least as far as labour is concerned. In fact, a recent econometric study[15] suggests that the creation of the customs union resulted in a substantial convergence in wages among EC members, but only under the assumption of purchasing power parity exchange rates. Without this assumption there is no clear evidence of wage conversion, and in fact there is a suggestion that wage dispersion may have taken place. According to the same study there is no evidence that the 1992 programme increased wage conversion in Europe. What is more, there are substantial differences in the prices of similar goods and services in European countries, as persistent differences in car prices between the United Kingdom and the rest of the EC demonstrate.

***Table 5.3*** Share of intra-trade in total trade: imports and exports by member state.
Source: *European Economy.* (%)

| | 1980 | | 1985 | | 1990 | | 1992 | |
|---|---|---|---|---|---|---|---|---|
| | Imports | Exports | Imports | Exports | Imports | Exports | Imports | Exports |
| **Original six member states** | | | | | | | | |
| B/L | 61.6 | 73.2 | 68.6 | 70.2 | 70.7 | 75.1 | 71.2 | 74.8 |
| F | 52.0 | 55.4 | 59.4 | 53.7 | 64.9 | 62.7 | 65.7 | 63.1 |
| D | 49.4 | 51.1 | 53.1 | 49.7 | 54.3 | 54.3 | 54.7 | 54.1 |
| I | 46.2 | 51.6 | 47.1 | 48.2 | 57.4 | 58.2 | 58.8 | 57.7 |
| NL | 54.7 | 73.5 | 55.8 | 74.7 | 59.9 | 76.5 | 58.8 | 75.4 |
| **First enlargement** | | | | | | | | |
| DK | 50.3 | 51.6 | 50.7 | 44.8 | 53.8 | 52.1 | 55.4 | 54.5 |
| IRL | 75.3 | 76.0 | 71.7 | 68.9 | 70.8 | 74.8 | 71.9 | 74.2 |
| UK | 40.9 | 45.0 | 47.3 | 48.8 | 51.0 | 52.6 | 50.7 | 55.5 |
| **Second and third enlargements** | | | | | | | | |
| GR | 40.9 | 48.2 | 48.1 | 54.2 | 64.1 | 64.0 | 62.8 | 64.2 |
| P | 45.3 | 58.6 | 45.9 | 62.5 | 69.1 | 73.5 | 73.6 | 74.8 |
| E | 31.3 | 52.2 | 37.9 | 53.3 | 59.1 | 65.0 | 60.3 | 66.3 |
| EUR 12 | 49.2 | 55.7 | 53.4 | 54.9 | 58.8 | 61.0 | 59.3 | 61.3 |

*Source:* Eurostat. The former system of statistics collection based on customs declarations at intra-Community frontiers was replaced on 1 January 1993 by Intrastat. For structural reasons. Intrastat results for the first quarter of 1993 cannot be compared with statistics collected under the former system.

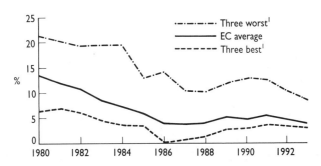

[1] Unweighted avarege of the three worst- or best-performing countries.

***Figure 5.7*** EC inflation 1980–93
Source: *European Economy.*

A further indication of the differences, this time in real variables, which persists among the countries with which we are concerned can be seen in Tables 5.5 and 5.6. These reveal little evidence of convergence over the years since 1980 in both unemployment rates and in real unit labour costs in manufacturing industry.

**Table 5.4**  Community trade by major groups of countries[1]. *Source: European Economy*

**Imports**

| Year | Industrialised countries | | | | | Developing countries | | | | | | | Eastern Europe[6] | STEs[7] | Total extra-EC (billion ECU) (%) |
|---|---|---|---|---|---|---|---|---|---|---|---|---|---|---|---|
| | USA | Japan | EFTA | Other | Total | Latin America | ODs[2] | Mediter-ranean[3] | Asian NIEs[4] | ACP | OPEC[5] | Total | | | |
| 1970 | 21.7 | 3.4 | 17.4 | 12.1 | 54.6 | 7.9 | 0.7 | 9.4 | 1.5 | 8.9 | 16.3 | 38.0 | 6.4 | 0.8 | 61.8 |
| 1975 | 17.6 | 4.2 | 15.6 | 8.3 | 45.7 | 5.7 | 0.7 | 7.5 | 2.4 | 7.4 | 27.9 | 45.7 | 6.9 | 0.9 | 132.9 |
| 1980 | 16.9 | 4.9 | 17.0 | 7.3 | 46.1 | 5.8 | 0.4 | 8.3 | 2.2 | 7.3 | 27.2 | 45.7 | 7.3 | 0.9 | 282.5 |
| 1981 | 17.2 | 5.4 | 16.8 | 7.1 | 46.4 | 6.4 | 0.5 | 8.9 | 3.3 | 6.0 | 27.0 | 45.4 | 7.3 | 0.9 | 318.3 |
| 1982 | 17.7 | 5.7 | 17.2 | 7.1 | 47.8 | 6.5 | 0.5 | 10.0 | 3.2 | 6.0 | 24.6 | 43.2 | 8.2 | 0.9 | 335.4 |
| 1983 | 17.2 | 6.4 | 19.2 | 7.1 | 49.8 | 7.2 | 0.4 | 10.3 | 3.7 | 6.5 | 21.0 | 40.6 | 8.6 | 1.0 | 341.7 |
| 1984 | 17.2 | 6.6 | 19.4 | 7.8 | 51.0 | 7.1 | 0.4 | 10.2 | 3.6 | 7.2 | 18.5 | 38.9 | 9.2 | 1.0 | 390.6 |
| 1985 | 17.0 | 7.0 | 20.2 | 8.0 | 52.1 | 7.3 | 0.4 | 10.9 | 3.5 | 7.5 | 17.8 | 38.4 | 8.4 | 1.1 | 406.6 |
| 1986 | 16.9 | 9.9 | 23.5 | 8.6 | 59.0 | 6.0 | 0.4 | 8.5 | 4.9 | 5.9 | 11.5 | 32.2 | 7.4 | 1.1 | 334.6 |
| 1987 | 16.5 | 10.2 | 24.3 | 8.2 | 59.2 | 5.7 | 0.5 | 8.6 | 6.0 | 4.9 | 10.3 | 31.9 | 7.2 | 1.4 | 340.1 |
| 1988 | 17.6 | 10.7 | 23.4 | 9.9 | 61.6 | 5.9 | 0.5 | 7.8 | 6.3 | 4.5 | 8.2 | 30.1 | 6.4 | 1.7 | 387.9 |
| 1989 | 18.7 | 10.4 | 23.0 | 8.6 | 60.6 | 5.8 | 0.5 | 8.3 | 6.0 | 4.4 | 9.1 | 30.7 | 6.5 | 1.9 | 446.7 |
| 1990 | 18.4 | 10.0 | 23.5 | 7.9 | 59.7 | 5.5 | 0.5 | 9.1 | 5.7 | 4.3 | 9.7 | 31.1 | 6.8 | 2.2 | 462.7 |

**Exports**

| Year | Industrialised countries | | | | | Developing countries | | | | | | | Eastern Europe[6] | STEs[7] | Total extra-EC (billion ECU) (%) |
|---|---|---|---|---|---|---|---|---|---|---|---|---|---|---|---|
| | USA | Japan | EFTA | Other | Total | Latin America | ODs[2] | Mediter-ranean[3] | Asian NIEs[4] | ACP | OPEC[5] | Total | | | |
| 1970 | 18.0 | 2.6 | 25.1 | 13.6 | 59.3 | 6.7 | 1.7 | 10.3 | 2.1 | 7.6 | 7.5 | 31.0 | 7.3 | 1.5 | 54.2 |
| 1975 | 11.9 | 2.0 | 22.4 | 11.9 | 48.1 | 6.6 | 1.2 | 14.1 | 2.0 | 7.5 | 16.4 | 38.5 | 10.3 | 1.6 | 118.5 |
| 1980 | 12.8 | 1.0 | 25.5 | 10.3 | 49.6 | 6.1 | 1.1 | 13.4 | 2.7 | 7.9 | 18.1 | 41.2 | 8.0 | 1.2 | 216.7 |
| 1981 | 14.5 | 2.2 | 21.5 | 9.2 | 47.5 | 6.2 | 1.2 | 14.4 | 2.7 | 7.8 | 21.2 | 44.6 | 6.8 | 1.0 | 265.3 |
| 1982 | 15.7 | 2.3 | 22.1 | 8.9 | 48.9 | 5.2 | 1.2 | 12.9 | 3.0 | 7.2 | 20.7 | 43.8 | 6.3 | 1.0 | 284.1 |
| 1983 | 17.4 | 2.6 | 22.0 | 8.7 | 50.7 | 4.1 | 1.2 | 13.2 | 3.1 | 5.9 | 18.4 | 41.1 | 7.0 | 1.2 | 300.6 |
| 1984 | 21.0 | 2.7 | 21.8 | 9.5 | 55.0 | 4.1 | 1.2 | 12.3 | 3.3 | 5.2 | 15.6 | 37.4 | 6.3 | 1.3 | 350.9 |
| 1985 | 22.6 | 2.8 | 22.4 | 9.8 | 57.6 | 3.9 | 1.1 | 11.7 | 3.5 | 5.2 | 12.8 | 34.0 | 6.2 | 2.2 | 378.7 |
| 1986 | 22.0 | 3.3 | 25.5 | 9.6 | 60.5 | 4.0 | 1.3 | 11.1 | 3.7 | 4.8 | 10.3 | 31.5 | 5.9 | 2.2 | 341.9 |
| 1987 | 21.2 | 4.0 | 26.6 | 9.9 | 61.7 | 4.0 | 2.4 | 10.1 | 4.4 | 4.2 | 8.7 | 30.8 | 5.7 | 1.8 | 339.3 |
| 1988 | 19.8 | 4.7 | 26.6 | 10.1 | 61.2 | 3.6 | 2.4 | 9.8 | 5.4 | 4.3 | 8.6 | 31.3 | 5.7 | 1.8 | 362.9 |
| 1989 | 18.9 | 5.1 | 26.1 | 10.1 | 60.2 | 3.7 | 2.4 | 9.9 | 5.5 | 4.0 | 8.5 | 31.8 | 6.3 | 1.7 | 413.0 |
| 1990 | 18.2 | 5.4 | 26.5 | 9.6 | 59.8 | 3.6 | 2.4 | 10.9 | 5.5 | 4.0 | 8.4 | 32.0 | 6.7 | 1.5 | 419.8 |

1. The country groupings are not mutually exclusive, thereby giving rise to some double counting as well as exclusions of trade flows. OPEC includes Nigeria and Gabon whose trade flows are also recorded under the ACP. Turkey, the former Yugoslavia and Malta appear under the industrialised countries as well as under the Mediterranean countries. The excluded countries concern in particular some South Asian countries (India, Pakistan, Sri Lanka, etc.) as well as some South-East Asian countries (Malaysia, Thailand, Philippines, etc.). These countries are, however, included in the developing countries total.
2. Overseas departments and territories of the Member States of the European Community.
3. Ceuta and Melilla, Gibraltar, Malta, Yugoslavia, Turkey, Albania, Morocco, Algeria, Tunisia, Libya, Egypt, Cyprus, Lebanon, Syria, Israel and Jordan.
4. Newly industrialising economies of Hong Kong, South Korea, Singapore and Taiwan.
5. Algeria, Libya, Nigeria, Gabon, Venezuela, Ecuador, Iraq, Saudi Arabia, Kuwait, Bahrain, Qatar, United Arab Emirates and Indonesia.
6. Former USSR and GDR, CSFR, Hungary, Romania, Bulgaria, Albania and Poland.
7. State-trading economies of America and Asia: Cuba, Vietnam, Mongolia, China and North Korea.

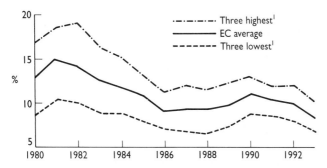

Three highest[1]
EC average
Three lowest[1]

[1] Unweighted average of the three countries with the highest or lowest rates;
Greece and Portugal excluded because of missing data.

*Figure 5.8* EC long-term interest rates 1980–93
*Source: European Economy.*

*Table 5.5* Unemployment rates of EC member states 1980–93[1]

| | | | | | *(% of civilian labour force)* | |
|---|---|---|---|---|---|---|
| *Source: European Economy.* | | | | | | |
| | 1980 | 1985 | 1990 | 1991 | 1992 | 1993 |
| B | 7.4 | 11.8 | 7.6 | 7.5 | 8.2 | 9.5 |
| DK | 5.2 | 7.2 | 8.1 | 8.9 | 9.5 | 10.5 |
| WD[2] | 2.7 | 7.1 | 4.8 | 4.2 | 4.5 | 5.6 |
| D[2] | – | – | – | 5.1 | 5.9 | 6.8 |
| GR | 2.7 | 7.7 | 7.0 | 7.7 | 7.7 | 7.8 |
| E | 11.6 | 21.6 | 16.1 | 16.3 | 18.0 | 21.2 |
| F | 6.2 | 10.1 | 9.0 | 9.5 | 10.0 | 10.8 |
| IRL | 8.0 | 18.2 | 14.5 | 16.2 | 17.8 | 18.4 |
| I | 7.1 | 9.9 | 10.0 | 10.0 | 10.3 | 11.0 |
| L | 2.4 | 2.9 | 1.7 | 1.6 | 1.9 | 2.6 |
| NL | 6.4 | 10.5 | 7.5 | 7.0 | 6.7 | 8.2 |
| P | 7.6 | 8.8 | 4.6 | 4.1 | 4.7 | 5.2 |
| UK | 5.6 | 11.4 | 7.0 | 8.8 | 10.0 | 10.4 |
| EUR $-$[2] | 6.0 | 10.8 | 8.3 | 8.7 | 9.3 | 10.4 |
| EUR $+$[2] | – | – | – | 8.8 | 9.5 | 10.6 |

1. Eurostat definition.
2. WD = West Germany, D = unified Germany, EUR $-$ = EUR 12 including West
Germany, EUR $+$ = EUR 12 including unified Germany.

## 5.3 Supranationalism in the European economy: the process of European integration

We now turn to discuss European integration. This is arguably, along with the increased capital mobility to which its most recent development is partly a response, the most fundamental development which conditions the nature of the European economy in the late twentieth century. As such it merits a section of its own within this chapter. In this section we will examine some of the basic characterisics of the

***Table 5.6***   Real Unit labour cost performance in manufacturing 1980–93[1]
Source: European Economy.                              *(Index 1987 = 100)*

|       | 1980  | 1985  | 1990  | 1991  | 1992  | 1993  |
|-------|-------|-------|-------|-------|-------|-------|
| B     | 109.6 | 99.3  | 92.4  | 100.9 | 103.8 | 103.8 |
| DK    | 104.8 | 95.3  | 85.5  | 85.9  | 84.4  | 82.7  |
| WD[2] | 103.9 | 100.0 | 100.3 | 103.6 | 107.5 | 110.5 |
| D[2]  | –     | –     | :     | :     | :     | :     |
| GR    | :     | :     | :     | :     | :     | :     |
| E     | 112.2 | 96.5  | 106.3 | 109.7 | 114.9 | 110.4 |
| F     | 108.9 | 106.5 | 91.4  | 94.1  | 94.0  | 96.4  |
| IRL   | 141.8 | 111.8 | 98.3  | 98.3  | :     | :     |
| I     | 104.0 | 103.1 | 102.9 | 107.7 | 109.5 | 106.4 |
| L     | 116.7 | 90.7  | 89.0  | 92.0  | 89.6  | 90.6  |
| NL    | 116.1 | 101.4 | 88.7  | 91.0  | 93.4  | 94.6  |
| P     | 115.3 | 100.0 | 93.7  | 93.9  | 99.2  | 100.5 |
| UK    | 113.1 | 103.2 | 106.6 | 114.0 | 110.0 | 110.1 |
| EUR −[2] | :  | :     | :     | :     | :     | :     |
| EUR +[2] | –  | –     | :     | :     | :     | :     |

1. 1992–93: estimates for B, DK, WD, E, F, I, NL. 1991–93: estimates for P, UK.
2. WD = West Germany, D = unified Germany, EUR − = EUR 12 including West Germany, EUR + = EUR 12 including unified Germany.

process of economic integration in Europe under the aegis of the EU. The objective is not to cover in detail all aspects of the nature and operation of the EU, but rather to discuss the impact which events within the EU are having and are likely to have in the future on the European economies and on the conduct of economic policy in Europe.

Bound up inexorably with this is some consideration of the effect of the changes that are taking place in the European (and indeed the world) economy on the level of government at which economic policy is most efficiently and appropriately conducted. The discussion elsewhere in this book, to an extent, takes for granted that European nation states are sovereign economic entities that are basically in a position to make their own choices regarding the conduct of economic policy. Countries having made these choices are then in a position to implement them by means of their own policy actions. In other words, it has been broadly assumed that the principal level at which economic decisions are made and at which economic policy is conducted is the individual nation state itself. The alert reader, however, will note that a recurring theme of recent economic developments in European countries is their internationalisation.

A fundamental feature of today's world is that events outside the nation state increasingly condition economic choices in Europe. As we have seen, substantial international economic interdependence is now a reality in a world of ever greater free exchange and of deregulated international capital markets. Of particular significance as far as Europe is concerned is the fact that contemporary European economic developments and policies are increasingly conditioned by the process of economic (and political, for the two are inextricably interrelated) integration in the continent. What is more, there is every prospect that over the coming years the development of European integration will fundamentally shift the locus of economic decision and policy making away from the individual nation state acting on its own, and towards the supranational level. Intriguingly, there are also forces present in contemporary Europe that would imply that some aspects of economic policy might best be conducted at the subnational or regional levels. Some scenarios beg the question of the future of the European nation state as we now know it. It is with these and related issues that we deal in this section of the chapter.[16] To facilitate our understanding of European integration under the aegis of the EU, it is important to note a few essential points from the outset.

The integration of European countries is a process that seems to be **cyclical** in its development. Over the years since the signing of the Treaty of Rome in 1957, one can broadly identify phases of rapid progress, followed by periods of stagnation or even reversal of the process. These cycles of development seem to be related to an extent to the economic cycle. Thus the early 1980s were a period when little happened in the EC (apart from the uncertain start of the EMS). Yet the mid- and late 1980s were a period of hectic development characterised by the implementation of the '1992' programme to complete the internal market and by the Maastricht blueprint for monetary union by the millenium. The early 1990s have been a period of slowdown, with the Maastricht process called into question by the deflationary nature of the convergence criteria, during a recession, by German unification, by the power of capital markets and by uncertainty surrounding the democratic control of the institutions that are contemplated.

The process of integration is essentially **cumulative** in nature, to the extent that each developement provides the rationale for and strengthens the case for further ones. Thus the completion of the internal market gave more weight to the arguments in favour of monetary union and resulted in this revolutionary development being placed firmly on the EU agenda. It is also probably fair to say that there is a strong link between economic integration and political integration. Monetary union in particular is difficult to envisage without some development of integration in the political field.

The process of economic integration is in some senses a **circular** one. Integration is to an extent a reaction to the growing openness and interdependence of the European economies, but at the same time reinforces the processes that are making the European economies interdependent. To this extent the process of integration is an important source of **unity** in Europe.

The institutional structure of the EU is such that at this juncture **nation states retain most of the power**. The real decision-making power lies with the Councils of Ministers, which are intergovernmental bodies rather than supranational councils. Of the supranational bodies in the EU, the Commission of course plays a significant role in proposing and policing legislation, but as the 'civil service' of the EU it does not take decisions. The European Parliament is not a legislative body,[17] despite its name, and the European Court of Justice interprets and enforces EU law (which, however, supercedes national law). Individual countries can still exercise a veto over fundamental developments, although decisions are being increasingly taken by (qualified) majorities. In fact, an interesting aspect of the debate surrounding the future of the EU concerns the extent to which decision making should be transferred from an intergovernmental basis to a supranational one. The outcome of this debate will determine and reflect the essential nature of the EU of the future: whether we will have a Europe of independent but interrelated nation states (the model favoured by the right, and a few of the left, of UK politics), or a Europe based on some sort of federalism (the model favoured by most others).[18] A starting point in our analysis concerns the forces that have caused the EU to be set up in the first place and then conditioned its development into what it is now. Many of these are essentially political in nature:

- a basic desire, in the immediate post-war period, to prevent another war between France, Germany and Britain;
- the perceived need, during the years between 1945 and the late 1980s, to establish a capitalist bloc in West Europe as a bulwark against Soviet Communism;
- the wish for the continent to collectively wield greater power in international relations;
- the later imperative for newly established democracies such as Greece, Spain and Portugal, to anchor their political systems by linking with more established democratic states;
- the fundamental idea that cooperation, interchange, mobility and access on a Europe-wide scale was eminently desirable; and so on.

Others are more economic, for example:

- a desire to reap whatever rewards might be available from internal trade liberalisation (gains in economic welfare as a result of better allocation of resources, economies of scale);
- a wish to benefit from greater X-efficiency[19] resulting from increased competition;
- a wish to obtain any gains in efficiency that might result from increased intra-union labour and capital mobility;
- the benefits to be had from coordinating policies in various areas (despite the losses inherent in the CAP – see below);
- the desire to protect the European economy from external challenges, for example from the NICs;
- the wish to follow 'best practice' (i.e. German practice) in macroeconomic management.

There have also been costs which have arisen from the process:

- changes in the structure and location of economic activity (structural change and economic adjustment) lie at the very heart of the resource allocation gains that may result from the process of integration.[20] However, the distribution of any economic gains, and thus the impact of the structural change that follows, has not been even. Some countries and regions within countries (particularly at the periphery of the EU) have not benefited as much as areas at the core of the Union, and they may even have suffered in absolute terms;[21]

- the Common Agricultural Policy (CAP) is irrational and results in high food prices, regressive income distribution effects, environmental damage, and dumping of surpluses on world markets, to the detriment of food producers in the rest of the planet;
- involvement in the EU integration project inevitably involves some surrender of economic sovereignty at the national level, although the real extent of such losses may be not as great as it is perceived in some quarters, as we shall discuss below.

Regardless of all this, it is important to reiterate that the very process of integration has itself increased the vulnerability of European countries to economic events outside of the nation state, and has made these countries more interdependent with each other. In addition, it must be stressed again that participation in the process of integration in the EU necessarily involves surrendering controls over important aspects of economic policy making and policy implementation – an issue discussed below. Latterly, one of the main economic arguments in favour of economic integration in Europe has become the perceived need for European countries to act in concert in order to attempt to recapture some of the economic sovereignty that has been ceded to (mainly international financial) markets.

### 5.3.1   The EU: fundamental economic characteristics and effects

Be that as it may, the original European Economic Community set up by the six countries[22] who signed the Treaty of Rome of 1957[23] has grown, via the EC, into the current EU of 15 countries.[24] The economic arrangements which form part of the *acquis communautaire*, the range of legislation and regulations contained in the Treaty of Rome and developed since then, can be conveniently divided into four categories. The first three we shall deal with here, the last is particularly significant and as such merits a section (5.5) of its own:

### The customs union

This involves establishing and policing **internal free trade between members**, that is EU members removing all tariff as well as substantial non-tariff barriers (NTBs) to intra-union trade in goods and services. Explicit tariffs on trade between EU members have all long since been removed, but in any case the importance of tariffs as sources of trade distortion have been greatly diminished on a global scale. NTBs have become more important impediments to trade, and some of these have been removed or reduced as a result of the EC's ubiquitous '1992' programme. Membership of the customs union also necessitates adopting a **common external trade policy** *vis-à-vis* the rest of the world. This involves both common external tariffs and common NTBs, as well as adopting a common stance in trade negotiations such as the recent Uruguay round of the GATT.

## The common market

In addition to the trade measures discussed above, membership of the EU common market (sometimes referred to as the 'internal market' or the 'level playing field') also involves accepting the **free movement of labour and capital** within the union, while adopting common policies and stances towards inflows and outflows of labour and capital from and to the rest of the world. The freedom of movement clauses of the Treaty of Rome established legal rights in this area right from the outset, but efforts to increase mobility were intensified in the course of the '1992' programme to complete the internal market. It is fair to say, however, that at present the mobility of capital within Europe and between Europe and the rest of the world is substantially greater that is the mobility of labour. The steps contained in the '1992' and subsequent programme (ERASMUS, LINGUA, SOCRATES, etc.) concentrated on enhancing the mobility of people with substantial educational backgrounds and professional skills. While it is true that the actions of the EU (for example, the abolition of all foreign exchange controls) have contributed to the increased mobility of capital in Europe, it is also probably fair to say that this is something that would have happened anyway, EU or no EU. At the same time, the control of immigration into the EU has been developed largely outside the official structures of the EU, as evidenced by the activities of the Trevi group of internal affairs ministers and by the Schengen Treaty.[25]

## Common policies

The third category is the development of **common policies** in important areas of the European economy. Clearly the most significant of these has been the **common agricultural policy (CAP)**. This consists in essence of a system of subsidy for agriculture that operates through the price mechanism: the EU farming ministers set minimum prices for most (but not all) above world market prices, so they are kept up to the desired level by a tariff[26] which is calculated on a daily basis to allow just enough imports into the EU to bridge any gap between internal demand and internal production. Prices are often set without much regard for what people actually want to buy, and so frequently they have been set above internal equilibrium between supply and demand. The result has been not only expensive food but also surpluses, which have been mopped up by the EU's 'intervention buying', in order to prevent prices from falling below the desired level. These surpluses have been stored, generating the infamous 'butter mountains' and 'wine lakes' which have scarred the public image of the EC and EU in recent years. Alternatively they have been 'dumped' (exported at below cost price) on world markets, to the detriment of food producers elsewhere and to the delight of sections of the populist press which has used the anomalies created to lambast the whole European integration project. Furthermore the CAP, it should be noted, has redistributed resources between states and individuals in member countries in a generally regressive fashion. It has also arguably contributed to the continent's ecological degradation by promoting the indiscriminate use of chemical additives, since the subsidy system rewards quantity of production rather than the quality of what is produced.

The CAP has resulted in some benefits to European societies: Europe is now a substantial net exporter of food where once it was a net importer; food is plentiful, if you can afford it; agricultural incomes have been increased, however inefficiently and inequitably this may have been done; there have been vast improvements in agricultural technologies and in agricultural productivity, even at the cost of the environmental damage referred to above and the threat to the purity of what we eat that has resulted from the use of pesticides and the like. Nevertheless, the consumer has had to pay heavily and twice over for the policy, mainly through high food prices, but also via the EU budget, 60–70 per cent of which has typically been swallowed up by the CAP. There have been attempts to modify the excesses of the policy: in 1989 in the wake of the budget reforms that doubled the size of the structural funds following the establishment of the '1992' programme, and through the McSharry Plan and the Uruguay GATT round. In general one can say that reform from inside the Community has proved to be difficult, and real change has been precipitated by external forces such as pressure from the United States and others in the GATT negotiations. Over the last few years prices have fallen, surpluses have been reduced and the budgetary cost of the CAP has been moderated to an extent. The fundamental problem lies, however, in the very nature of the policy which is based on the 'tail wagging the dog', millions of consumers paying heavily to protect the interests of a minority of large farmers. Such regulation has been distinctly unavailable to other industries such as steel and coal mining, which have had to live (and die) in the free market. Nevertheless, there is a shortage of alternatives available. The obvious other approach to agricultural protection is through some system of direct cash transfers on the model of the former UK 'deficiency payments' system, which would probably be politically unacceptable because of its tax implications and because of the transfer of direct spending power to the EU that it would involve.[27]

The CAP is of course not the only common policy to be pursued at EU level, although one could be forgiven for thinking that it is, given the (mostly adverse) publicity that it generates and the huge proportion of the budget that it accounts for. Other major policies are operated at EU level through the 'structural funds': the European Regional Development Fund (ERDF), which is the main instrument of the EU's regional policy, and the European Social Fund (ESF), the principal means of implementing the Union's social policy.[28] In addition, important aspects of European industrial and competition policy, fiscal policy, transport policy, environmental policy and fisheries policy are now conducted at EU level, while the common regulatory frameworks established by the 1992 programme affect a wide range of aspects of economic and political life, from employment contracts to the cleanliness of beaches, from local economic development to government subsidies to industry. We shall return to many of these in other parts of the book.

### 5.3.2 *Monetary integration*

Monetary integration was not originally an explicit aim of the then EEC, to the extent that there was no mention of it in the Treaty of Rome. However, it has now moved to the very centre of the European agenda, with a single currency for Europe by the millenium envisaged in the Maastricht Treaty.

There are a variety of forms that monetary integration can take, but the limiting case is a complete **monetary union**. This is popularly conceived as consisting of a situation in which countries agree to dispense with their own national currencies and replace them with a single common currency: the ECU, the Europa, the Jean Monnet, or whatever. However, from a strictly economic point of view one could argue that a European single currency is not strictly an essential prerequisite for a monetary union, which would *de facto* exist in the presence of:

(a)  irrevocably fixed exchange rates between the European countries;
(b)  full convertibility of national currencies, which can be exchanged for each other in any quantity and at any time at the fixed rate; and
(c)  a completed European common market.

A **single currency** would, however, certainly constitute a desirable or even crucial addition to the above. It would be an important symbol of the monetary union (creating a 'European monetary identity'), it would save on the transaction costs of changing currencies, it would make the common market and other joint policies work better by increasing the transparency of prices. Most crucially, the single currency might safeguard the long-term integrity of the European monetary union. While different currencies exist, there will always be a doubt about the truly irrevocable nature of fixed exchange rates, given the political temptation to engineer a 'quick fix' for the economy via a devaluation.

The points outlined above do provide economic arguments for a monetary union, but the fundamental argument in favour of such a union is rooted in the belief that it would **increase the efficacy of European economic policy making** in certain areas (see below). The arguments against monetary union essentially concern two areas:

(a)  The *distribution* of any economic gains that result from the union is likely to be uneven,[29] or the costs of structural change that are likely to result from a monetary union may be concentrated in some regions of the union. This has led many people to consider some form of effective redistribution mechanism as essential within a European monetary union.

(b)  A possible **loss of national economic sovereignty**, or national control over economic policy making and implementation. This too is discussed below, but the key issue here is whether countries lose sovereignty by pooling it, or in fact enhance it through cooperation.

The most important point about monetary union in the context of our discussion, however, lies in the fact that it necessitates substantial amounts of coordination or **joint determination of economic policies** at the supranational level in order to exist at an acceptable political cost. Among other things, a monetary union would involve substantial structural change in the European economy, especially as far as the weaker economies are concerned. Minimising the costs of such change would require substantial convergence in economic objectives and outcomes among European countries. This cannot be achieved without some kind of formal policy coordination and cooperation at the supranational level excercised through EU organisations such as a European Central Bank. The critical point here is that, as we have mentioned, this in turn inevitably involves some surrender of **economic sovereignty** on the part of nation states to the supranational level. The economic and institutional arrangements implicit in a complete monetary union would mean to a large extent the establishment of a *de facto* **economic union**. Surrender of economic sovereignty inevitably involves surrender of political sovereignty, some form of **political union** would probably follow, and thus the position of the nation state as we have come to know it is called into question.[30]

Specifically, involvement in a complete monetary union in the EU and all the developments that go with it means that participating European countries cede varying degrees of control over policy in the following areas:

(a) Trade policy, including tariffs and NTBs. This involves the some surrender of such policy tools as industrial subsidies, indirect taxes and the use of public procurement to promote local economic development. It also means that the regulation of important markets, including the labour market, is undertaken at Union level.
(b) Capital market regulation, including exchange controls.
(c) Immigration policy, which must be harmonised for the union in the absence of national frontiers.
(d) The areas of EU common policies, such as the CAP and competition.

These are largely to do with the common market, and a monetary union would of course intensify the effect of the processes involved. In addition, a monetary union would specifically necessitate some surrender of national control over important objectives of economic policy, as well as the tools required to implement these policy preferences. A body of economic theory, pioneered by Fleming and Corden in the early 1970s, examines the welfare costs involved in terms of countries having to accept second best preferences in the Phillips trade-off between inflation and unemployment.[31] For example, a country involved in a monetary union cannot pursue a policy designed to reduce unemployment when its partners are involved in pursuing policies designed primarily to reduce the level of inflation. If a country wants to pursue its preferred policy stance it must first of all win the political argument in the union over the fundamental objectives of economic policy. The distribution of any welfare costs will be determined by the nature of the joint decision making process. If common EU policy objectives are determined by leadership, then the leader (Germany) suffers no welfare losses, which are shared by other countries in relation to how close each country's preferences are in relation to Germany's. If objectives are determined by negotiation the losses of this kind will be shared, each country's individual loss being determined by how close its own preferences are to EU collective preferences. The main policy areas affected would be:

(a) **Exchange rates** as a tool of economic management. Exchange rate policy *vis-à-vis* the rest of the world has to be determined at EU level, and there are of course no internal exchange rates because there are no internal currencies, or at least the internal currencies are irrevocably pegged against one another and cannot be altered. This is potentially particularly serious if we consider the experience of, for example, the

United Kingdom in the post war period. Here we have the case of a country that has lost competitiveness steadily throughout the period, and to an extent has safeguarded its level of production, employment and wealth by a steady devaluation of sterling against the DM and other European currencies (see Table 5.1 above).[32] Without the possibility of devaluation, future differentials in UK competitiveness would have to be borne at the cost of relative stagnation and/or outward migration. The alternative is to achieve convergence in productivity, employment and inflation between European countries.

(b)    Aspects of **monetary policy**. The current ideological consensus is that inflation is the most important aspect of a country's economic performance, and that inflation can best be controlled by monetary policy. Thus in order to achieve convergence in rates of inflation European countries need to follow similar or common monetary policies and interest rates and the supply of money (assuming this is possible), for example, would need to be determined at Union level. This would require accepting common stances on policy objectives, as well as ceding powers to EU organisations such as the European Monetary Institute (EMI), the European Central Bank (ECB) and the European System of Central Banks (ESCB). This in turn then begs the question of how collective EU preferences and policy stances are to be determined (see above), and of how these supranational institutions (that are to be independent) can be politically controlled.

(c)    As we shall see, the Maastricht blueprint for EMU concentrates on inflation and monetary aggregates. Differences in rates of inflation are not, however, the only indicator of divergence, and a balanced view would suggest that other variables apart from monetary aggregates impact on inflation. Therefore other aspects of economic policy may additionally have to be coordinated or jointly determined. The obvious example is aspects of **fiscal policy**, but also **microeconomic policies** such as labour market policies may have to be conducted to an extent at the supranational level.

At first glance, the above would tend to suggest that involvement in the integration process involves serious losses of economic sovereignty on the part of the European countries that are ceding all these powers to the EU. However, in order to arrive at a judgement here one needs to consider two points:

1.  how much of the power that is on the surface being transferred from nation states to the supranational level really exists in practice at the national level? And, related to this,
2.  to what extent will transfer of power to the supranational level result in a real increase in the collective influence of European nation states over economic forces and in economic arenas?

Expressed in another way, to what extent could individual European nation states hope to exercise their own policy preferences outside the EU? The answer to these questions is not empirically verifiable and is to a large extent based on one's own subjective view of the nature of the world around us, but it is nevertheless extremely important to the future of the European economy. A tentative conclusion might be based on the following considerations.[33]

## The size of the country and its economic strength

In general one could postulate that the smaller a country is, and the less economic weight it carries, the less control it is likely to have over the external parameters that constrain local decision making. Some small countries such as the Netherlands and Belgium have never suffered illusions about their economic independence. Others, such as the Scandinavian countries are in the process of abandoning their own specific high welfare approach to the mixed economy. Medium-sized countries such as the United Kingdom and France come from a colonialist tradition. They are used to a degree of economic autonomy which may now be fading, and many in these countries have not found the process easy to accept. Economic power increases the propensity for economic self-determination and it also confers leadership, as is the case of Germany within the EU.[34] In the broadest sense, the relationship between the size and economic power of countries and sovereignty losses could be illustrated in Fig. 5.9.

## The nature of the policy area involved

In general, policies which are essentially macroeconomic in nature (attempts to control inflation, unemployment, growth and the balance of payments by monetary and fiscal policies) do not involve significant sovereignty losses. This is because it is probable that in these areas small and medium-sized countries do not possess very much sovereignty to start with. There would seem to be plenty of evidence of this in the recent experience of such economies: the experience of the Mitterrand government in France between 1981–83, the vain attempts on the part of the UK government to control the domestic money in the early 1980s and, above all, the ignominious exit of sterling and the lira from the ERM in late 1992 being classic examples. All these are discussed elsewhere in this book.

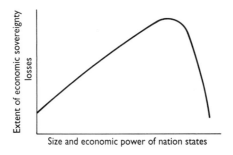

**Figure 5.9** The relationship between country size and losses in economic sovereignty in the EU

## The timescale involved

In the short term, there may be greater scope for conducting an independent approach to policy than in the long run. For example, the 1992 devaluation of sterling provided an instant boost to the UK economy, although it is arguable that the United Kingdom is, as a result, still stuck in its old vicious cycle of devaluation, inflation, loss of competitiveness and more devaluation that ERM membership was intended to break.

## The extent to which policies are consistent with those being pursued elsewhere

For example, it is difficult to envisage any one EU country pursuing a policy of reflation on its own in a context of most other EU states implementing policies designed to control inflation by using monetary and fiscal policies to restrict demand. Put another way, the economic sovereignty losses involved in the process of integration are likely to be greatest for dissident states and dissenting ideas (the Mitterrand case). Take the case of left of centre ideas within Europe: the only prospect of these being implemented is now at the EU rather than at the national level. Most left of centre politicians now seem to have realised this.[35]

Whatever one's own personal feelings on this issue, it is clear that the globalisation of world economic relations and, in particular, the vast increase in the international mobility of capital, have ushered in an era in which the ability of European citizens to exercise control over the economic aspects of their lives through the democratic process now requires certain economic policies to be conducted at a level above that of the nation state. This in many ways provides the essential rationale for economic integration in the EU. There are still many unanswered questions, however, about which economic policies should be pursued at which level of government. The study of fiscal federalism[36] attempts to address such questions. It needs to be extended and applied to the current situation in Europe. The principle of **subsidiarity**, ironically championed by the UK government as a diversionary tactic to slow down the deepening of the EU, is a good starting point. According to this, policies should be pursued at the lowest level of government which is compatible with their efficient implementation. In this way, democratic accountability is maximised. However, if one adopts this idea, then it is not at all clear that there will be an objective case in terms of efficiency and democracy for action at the national level in, say, 50 years' time: subsidiarity may well mark the beginning of the end of the nation state in Europe. Then another question arises concerning the size of the EU and its relationship with other major international actors such as the United States, Japan and the NICs. Is the EU really the appropriate level for supranational policy making? Finally, assuming that the EU can replace the nation state as the agent for some types of policy-making, how can democratic control over its actions be established? These are the real questions that surround the future of monetary union in Europe.

We can now examine the **EU's attempts to move towards EMU** over the last 30 or so years. These can be divided conveniently into three phases:

## EMU

The issue of monetary integration first appeared on the European agenda at the Hague summit in 1969, partly as a strategy aimed at restoring stability after the political events of May 1968. The debate at the time centred on the extent to which Europe was in fact an 'optimum currency area',[37] and on the best strategy for constructing a monetary union. On the latter issue there were two points of view, which came to be referred to as the 'economist' approach and the 'monetarist' position (nothing to do with Milton Friedman). The former, mainly supported by the Dutch and the Germans through the Schiller Plan, favoured a gradualist approach to EMU, involving the promotion of harmonisation and convergence in order to prepare the ground for the single currency. The latter, canvassed by the Commission, France and Belgium through the Barre Plan, supported a 'shock theory' approach, involving the introduction of fixed exchange rates at as a *fait accompli*, leaving countries to adjust to these ex-post.

The outcome was predictably a compromise between the two, in the shape of the Werner Plan of 1970, most of which was adopted by the Council of Ministers in March 1971 and which came into effect in March 1972. It provided for efforts to harmonise economic policies, but also created the 'snake in the tunnel' system of fixed exchange rates. The 'snake' consisted of fixing the exchange rates between the 10 participants (the original six plus Britain, Denmark and Ireland who were in the process of joining the then EEC) within bands of ±2.25 per cent. The 'tunnel' involved fixing the parity of the snake currencies against the dollar and other world currencies within the 4.5 per cent bands established in the Smithsonian Agreements of December 1991. The overall objective was a 'monetary union by 1980'. The observant reader will conclude therefore that the plan failed, collapsing in the wake of the disarray which followed the oil crisis. When the chips were down, European nation states were fundamentally unwilling to subordinate their own interests to those of the EEC. Thus sterling floated away in June 1972, Italy left in February 1973, France in January 1974 and again in March 1976, and the dream of EMU faded away.

## EMS

The impetus towards monetary integration was revived in 1977 by Roy Jenkins, and the EMS was set up at the Bremen and Copenhagen Councils of 1978, coming into existence in March 1979. The EMS basically has two features:

(a) the European Currency Unit (ECU), which is the European 'currency in waiting' and is the fulcrum of the ERM. It is based on a 'weighted basket' of all the currencies involved; and

(b) the Exchange Rate Mechanism (ERM), which attempts to fix the exchange rates between the participating countries and between these currencies and the ECU within a band of ±15 per cent (= −6 per cent for weaker currencies such as the lira and sterling). There is thus a 'snake', but this time no 'tunnel', since the

European currencies involved can float *vis-à-vis* the dollar, the yen and other world currencies. The mechanism for maintaining exchange rates within the system exchange consists of agreements for supportive central bank intervention in foreign exchange markets, a (limited) reserve pooling obligation, and a (largely unused) divergence indicator. This is backed up by some measures to promote policy convergence and by a limited redistributive mechanism.

There was considerable scepticism about the EMS at the time of its launch, and it encountered early instabilities. However, to many people's surprise it weathered the storm in the early 1980s and proved to be a considerable success. It:

(a) Promoted exchange stability in Western Europe. There were only 11 realignments (12 if one includes the exit of sterling and the lira in late 1992) altogether, and none at all between January 1987 and the exit of sterling, while currencies outside the ERM experienced considerably greater instability.

(b) Contributed to lower and increasingly convergent rates of inflation in Europe, although it must be said that price stability was also facilitated by the neo-liberal consensus on economic policy in this period.

(c) Managed to establish an increasing role for the ECU as a private sector currency during the course of the 1980s.

However, the EMS was weakened by the United Kingdom's refusal to join the ERM (although sterling was always part of the ECU basket) until 'the time was right' in October 1990,[38] and arguably by excessive reliance on German leadership. Nevertheless, it paved the way for what was to follow.


## Maastricht

The very success of the EMS provided the stimulus in the late 1980s for a debate on the way forward for the the system. The Commission's response was to set up the Delors Committee which produced what is usually referred to as the Delors Report in April 1989, calling for a full monetary union to be set up in three stages. This spawned two Inter-Governmental Conferences (IGCs, one of which was on the subject of political union, which had not originally been on the agenda) then the Maastricht Treaty, which has now been tortuously ratified in EU member states. It is important to note that the Maastricht Treaty deals with more than just monetary union, for it constitutes a wide-ranging reform of the Community and a significant step forward for European integration on a number of fronts. Its principal feature is the **Treaty on European Union**, but there are also 17 assorted protocols (additional agreements not signed by all members) as well as 33 Declarations (guidelines on the interpretation and implementation of the Treaty which, however, are not legally binding).[39]

The Treaty of European Union amends the Treaty of Rome and it consists of five aspects:

(a) Naturally, a **European Union** based on:
  (i) the current EC and its institutions;
  (ii) a common intergovernmental foreign and security policy;

(iii) a common home affairs and justice policy, again conducted on an intergovernmental basis

(iv) a number of common policies in areas such as education, training, youth, public health, the labour market, industrial policy, communications, research and development, regional policy, environmental policy and development policy.

(b) **Subsidiarity**, which was introduced into the Treaty largely to allay fears in certain quarters that too much power might be transferred to the EU level. As discussed above, it might also pave the way for regionalism and the marginalisation of the nation state in the (very) long term.

(c) A **Committee of the Regions**, with solely advisory powers.[40]

(d) **EMU**, as we shall discuss below.

(e) **European citizenship**, which is considered in many quarters to be a somewhat controversial concept, but the proposals include giving European citizens the right to stand for election and vote in local and European elections in all EU states, to be represented by the consuls of all EU states, and to complain to the European Ombudsman about deficiencies in EU institutions.[41]

All this is to be supplemented by some limited institutional reform granting a little more power to the European Parliament, some provisions for tackling fraud and ensuring financial rectitude (the Court of Auditors becomes a full EC institution), and an enhancement in the powers of the European Court of Justice to improve the implementation of EU legislation. Finally there is the Social Chapter, a separate Protocol to which the United Kingdom has not adhered. The United Kingdom and Denmark also have the right to 'opt out' of the provisions for EMU.

The specific proposals and timetable for EMU are shown below. The first of the three stages are undertaken under existing Community powers, while the final two stages require an ammendment to the Treaty of Rome.

**Stage one** consists of the completion of the single market, increased coordination and cooperation in economic and monetary fields, strengthening the EMS, an extended role for the ECU and an enhanced role for the Committee of Governors of EU members' central banks. This stage began in July 1990 and should have been completed by January 1993.

**Stage two** essentially involves the groundwork for the single currency: all members are to be included in the narow band of the ERM, the European Monetary Institute (EMI) is to be set up to promote the coordination necessary for EMU. This stage began in January 1994.

**Stage three** is then complete monetary union, with the introduction of the ECU as the single currency for Europe. A specific agenda has been prepared for this, with deadlines and convergence criteria that are to be met. The timetable is as follows: **by December 1996**, if the EC Council of Finance Ministers decide by a qualified majority that a 'critical mass' of seven states (six if the United Kingdom opts out) have met the convergence criteria, then a date is to be set for introducing the ECU in relevant states. Failing that, **by December 1997** will see the start of an automatic process leading to complete monetary union among a minimum of five states by January 1999. Additionally, **1998** is to herald:

(i) the start of the creation of the European central bank (ECB), which takes over from the EMI, and is seen as the independent issuer of currency, and of
(ii) the European System of Central banks (ESCB), the independent conductor of monetary policy and foreign exchange operations.

If these institutions are not yet in place, then national central banks are to become independent at this time.

The Maastricht **convergence criteria** are as follows:

(a)   states must have a maximum budget deficit of 3 per cent of GDP per annum;
(b)   countries must having a maximum total public sector debt of 60 per cent of GDP;
(c)   there are to be no realignments within the ERM;
(d)   countries are to have a rate of inflation a maximum of 1.5 per cent above the average rate in the three lowest inflation EU countries in the year before the decision (1996 or 1998). This qualification rate (4.7 per cent when the Treaty was signed) must be judged as 'sustainable'.
(e)   long-term (government bond) interest rates should be a maximum of 2 per cent above the average of those in the three lowest rate countries.

Table 5.7 shows the position with these convergence criteria in 1993, as well as the prospects of EU member states meeting them by 1999.

The future of EMU is uncertain. There are many difficulties, a point emphasised by factors such as British reluctance, the difficulties in ratifying Maastricht, the difficulties Germany has experienced over unification, the costs involved for some of the outlying states in meeting the convergence criteria in a recession, and the disarray within the ERM that turbulent foreign exchange markets has precipitated.[42] However, a rump of the most economically advanced countries in the EU (Germany, France, Austria, Belgium, Luxembourg, the Netherlands, and perhaps Sweden, Norway and even the United Kingdom) seem to be both ready and willing to proceed within something like the conditions and timetable set out in the Maastricht Treaty. The Commission, meanwhile, has been busy preparing the transition to the single currency. Their proposals are shown in Table 5.8 below, and they envisage a slippage in the Maastricht timetable. Various outcomes are possible, including a two-speed or even a 'variable geometry'[43] Europe. The view taken here is that it is by no means certain[44] that EMU will take place as envisaged in the Maastricht Treaty, but that in the long term such a development is both likely and desirable. It will in turn inevitably hasten the process of convergence between the European economies.

## 5.4   Conclusion

In this chapter we have reviewed the factors of unity, or the similar internal, external and historical parameters within which the experience of the European mixed economies has been framed, and we have seen how these have contributed to considerable convergence between them. We have discussed, among other factors, the influence of increased international mobility of capital, of technological changes,

**Table 5.7** Current position on, and prospects for, the Maastricht convergence criteria.

| Member state | Inflation in 1993 % | Pass test by 1999? | Public deficit 1993 % of GDP | Pass test by 1999? | Long-term interest rate 1993, % | Pass test by 1999? | Public debt 1993 % of GDP | Pass test by 1999? | Feasible to join EMU by 1999? |
|---|---|---|---|---|---|---|---|---|---|
| Belgium | 2.8 | √ | 7.4 | ≈ | 7.3 | √ | 138 | ⊙ | √ |
| Denmark | 1.4 | √ | 4.4 | √ | 8.9 | √ | 79 | √ | √ |
| Germany | 4.3 | √ | 4.2 | √ | 6.3 | ⊙ | 50 | ⊙ | ⊙ |
| Greece | 13.7 | ⊙ | 15.5 | ⊙ | 23.9 | ⊙ | 114 | ⊙ | ≈ |
| Spain | 4.7 | ≈ | 7.2 | ≈ | 10.2 | ≈ | 56 | √ | ≈ |
| France | 2.3 | √ | 5.9 | √ | 6.8 | √ | 45 | √ | √ |
| Ireland | 2.3 | √ | 3.0 | √ | 7.7 | √ | 93 | ≈ | √ |
| Italy | 4.4 | ≈ | 10.0 | ⊙ | 11.3 | ⊙ | 116 | ⊙ | ⊙ |
| Luxembourg | 3.6 | √ | 2.5 | √ | 6.9 | √ | 10 | √ | √ |
| Netherlands | 2.1 | √ | 4.0 | √ | 6.7 | √ | 83 | √ | √ |
| Portugal | 6.7 | ⊙ | 8.9 | ⊙ | 12.4 | ⊙ | 70 | √ | ≈ |
| UK | 3.4 | ≈ | 7.6 | √ | 7.9 | √ | 53 | √ | √ |
| EU average | 3.8 | | 6.4 | | 8.1 | | 66 | | |
| Target | <1.5% above 3 best | | 3.0% | | <2% above 3 best | | 60% | | |
| Austria | 3.7 | √ | 2.9 | √ | 6.6 | √ | 57 | √ | √ |
| Finland | 2.2 | ≈ | 9.1 | ⊙ | 10.0 | ≈ | 60 | √ | ≈ |
| Norway | 2.3 | √ | 3.2 | √ | 6.9 | √ | 47 | √ | √ |
| Sweden | 4.5 | ≈ | 14.7 | ≈ | 8.8 | √ | 67 | ≈ | ≈ |

√ Should achieve the criterion relatively easily.

≈ Will have difficulties meeting the criterion and may not manage to do so.

⊙ Unlikely to meet the criterion.

Source: European Parliament (1994).

**Table 5.8**  Introduction of a single currency/sequence of events

| Phase A<br>Launch of EMU | Phase B<br>Start of EMU | Phase C<br>Single currency fully introduced |
|---|---|---|
| *Start of the phase:* | *Start of the phase:* | *Start of the phase:* |
| • List of participating Member States<br>• Date of start of EMU announced (or confirmed)<br>• Deadline for the final changeover to the single currency<br>• Setting up of the ESCB and the ECB<br>• Start of production of notes and coins | • Fixing of conversion rates<br>• ECU becomes a currency in its own right<br>• Monetary and exchange-rate policy in ECU<br>• Inter bank, monetary, capital, and exchange markets in ECU<br>• New government debt issued in ECU<br>• Corresponding wholesale payment systems in ECU | • ECU notes and coins introduced<br>• Banks have completed the changeover (retail business payment systems)<br>• Notes and coins denominated in national currency are withdrawn<br>• Public and private operators complete the changeover<br>• Only the ECU is used |
| *Throughout the phase:* | *Throughout the phase:* | |
| Stepping-up of preparations and implementation of measures that will, if possible, have been adopted beforehand<br>• Legal framework<br>• National steering structure<br>• Banking and financial community changeover plan | • Banks and financial institutions continue the changeover<br>• Public and private operators other than banks proceed with the changeover circumstances permitting | |
| 1 year maximum | 3 years maximum | Several weeks |

*Source:* EC Commission (1995)

of increased external competition, and of changes in opinion regarding what constitutes appropriate economic policy. In particular we have examined the influence of European integration under the aegis of the EU on the European economic scene. However, as we have seen, there remain substantial differences between countries in economic outcomes and in interpretation of how a mixed economy should be structured and operated. This is the subject of the chapter which follows.

# Further reading

Bacon, R. and Eltis, W. (1974) *Britain's Economic Problem: too Few Producers?* 2nd ed., Basingstoke: Macmillan.

Boltho, A. (ed.) (1982) *The European Economy: Growth and Crisis*, Oxford: Oxford University Press.

Brouwer, F., Lintner, V. and Newman, M. (eds) (1994) *Economic Policy and the European Union*, London: Federal Trust.

Buxton, T., Chapman, P. and Temple, P. (eds) (1994) *Britain's Economic Performance*, London: Routledge.

Church, C. H. and Phinnemore, D. (1994) *European Union and European Community*, Hemel Hempstead: Harvester Wheatsheaf.

Coates, K. and Barrett-Brown, M. A. (1993) *European Recovery Programme*, Nottingham: Spokesman.

Corden, W. M. (1972) 'Monetary Integration' *Princeton Essays in International Finance*, No. 73, Princeton, NJ.

Dyker, D. (ed.) (1971) *The National Economies of Europe*, London: Longman.

El-Agraa, A. (1994) *The Economics of the European Community* 4th ed., Hemel Hempstead: Harvester Wheatsheaf.

European Commission (1995). *One Currency for Europe*, Green Paper on the Practical Arrangements for the Introduction of the Single Currency, Brussels.

European Parliament (1994), *The Social Consequences of Economic and Monetary Union*, Working Paper, Social Affairs Series, Luxembourg.

Fleming, M. (1971) 'On exchange rate unification' *Economic Journal* 81, pp. 467–88.

Grilli, V., Masciandro, D. and Tabellini, G. (1991) 'Political and monetary institutions and public financial policies in the industrial countries' *Economic Policy*, 13, pp. 428–45.

Hampden-Turner, C. and Trompenaars, A. (1994) *The Seven Cultures of Capitalism*, London: Piatkus.

Holland, S. (1983) *Out of Crisis*, Nottingham: Spokesman.

Holland, S. (1993) *The European Imperative*, Nottingham: Spokesman.

Hutton, W. (1995) *The State We're In*, London: Jonathan Cape.

Lintner, V. and Mazey, S. (1991) *The European Community: Economic and Political Aspects*, Maidenhead: McGraw-Hill.

Milward, A. S. (1992) *The European Rescue of the Nation State*, London: Routledge.

Milward, A. S., Lynch, F. M., Romero, F., Ranieri, R. and Soerensen, V. (1993) *The Frontier of National Sovereignty*, London: Routledge.

Mundell, R. A. (1961) 'A theory of optimum currency areas' *American Economic Review* 51, 657–65.

Newman, M. (1996) *Democracy, Sovereignty and the European Union*, London: Hurst.

Oates, W. (1972) *Fiscal Federalism*, New York: Harcourt Brace Jovanovitch.

Somers, F. (ed.) (1994) *European Economies: A Comparative Study* 2nd ed., London: Pitman.

Tsoukalis, L. (1993) *The New European Economy*, 2nd ed., Oxford: Oxford University Press.

Van Mourik, A. (1994) *Wages and European Integration*, Maastricht: BIV Publications.

World Bank (1993) *The East Asian Miracle*, Washington DC.

## Notes

1. See, for example, Somers (1991), Dyker (1992), Boltho (1982), as well as other documentary sources such as the OECD annual country reports for various countries.
2. East/Central European countries also underwent their own form of unitary economic experience with membership of COMECON and the establishment of centrally planned economies.
3. Although, as we shall see, the United Kingdom in particular has in the 1980s and 1990s attempted to give markets a free hand in every possible fashion. The former Soviet Union and its satellite states up to the late 1980s, of course, adopted centrally planned economies, which they are now often feverishly attempting to replace with market systems.
4. Although the British Labour Party would have attempted something similar with its 'alternative economic strategy', had it been elected to power in 1983.
5. For example, women in Italy now have on average 1.2 children each, the lowest fertility rate in the world.
6. According to Eurostat, the proportion of the population over 65 (expressed as a percentage

of the population aged 15–64 years) of European countries is forecasted to rise dramatically: to around 50 per cent by 2040 in the Netherlands (from 18 per cent in 1990); to around 40 per cent in the United Kingdom (from about 23 per cent in 1990); to 44 per cent in Denmark (from 22 per cent); to 48 per cent in Germany (from 23 per cent); to 40 per cent in Portugal (from 18 per cent); to 40 per cent in France (from 22 per cent); to 43 per cent in Belgium and Spain (from 22 per cent and 17 per cent respectively); to 50 per cent in Italy (from 21 per cent; and 27 per cent in Ireland (from 18 per cent) – these rough estimates, like all population forecasts should, however, be treated with some caution, since much can change in the space of almost half a century.

7. These countries accounted for 1.5 per cent of total EC imports and 2.1 per cent of EC exports in 1970. By 1990, this had risen to 5.7 of imports and 5.5 per cent of exports. The total value of EC imports from Taiwan, for example, increased by 308.7 per cent between 1980 and 1990, from 2241m ECU to 9159m ECU.

8. Fordist methods of production are based on the division of the production process into increasingly small and discrete sections and on mass production in long production runs. The advantage of this is that workers become specialised and more efficient at the limited range of functions they perform, and unit costs of production fall accordingly. The disadvantages concern the fact that products that are made in this fashion tend to be uniform ('you can have cars in any colour you want as long as it is black', as Henry Ford is reputed to have said). Also, Fordist production tends to de-skill workforces and it often renders work monotonous, with the result that workers can become alienated, precipitating poor quality goods and services and industrial relations problems. Post-Fordist methods of production often result from the new technologies, and emphasise small-batch production which can be customised to individual consumers' requirements.

9. For example, according to UNCTAD, the average tariff rate on manufactured products in the EC countries in 1990 amounted to 5.9 per cent in 1990. In 1950 it had been 18 per cent in France, 26 per cent in Germany, 25 per cent in Italy, 11 per cent in the Netherlands and 23 per cent in the United Kingdom. Between the same years manufacturing tariffs also fell from 14 per cent to 4.8 per cent in the United States and from 9 per cent to 4.4 per cent in Sweden.

10. Predominantly the balance of payments surpluses of the oil producing countries, referred to in the press as 'hot money', because of the volatile way in which they are shifted around international money markets.

11. The assets of UK pension funds alone amounted to $717.3 bn in 1993, about 75 per cent of GDP. In other EU countries, apart from the Netherlands, the importance of the financial services industry is considerably less: in Germany pension fund assets amounted in 1993 to only $106bn (±5 per cent of GDP), in France to $41.1bn, in Italy $11.7bn, and in Spain to $10.1bn.

12. In the case of the United Kingdom, ERM membership was supported by HM government, HM opposition, the Liberal Democrat Party, the TUC and the CBI. The only group who openly opposed membership at the time was what remained of the Communist Party of Great Britain. Expulsion from the ERM, despite subsequent rhetoric by ministers, was a great blow which effectively left the United Kingdom without an economic policy for a period of time.

13. The world stock of foreign direct investment was estimated to be in the region of $1.7 trillion in the early 1990s, when there were about 35 000 transnational corporations with 147 000 foreign affiliates.

14. The latter largely reflecting the fall in the real price of oil that has taken place since the late 1970s.

15. Aad van Mourik, 1994.
16. It is of course beyond the scope of this chapter to provide a detailed analysis of the operations of the EU. For this see, for example, Lintner and Mazey, 1991, El-Agraa, 1994 or Tsoukalis, 1993.
17. Despite the existence of some cooperation and co-decision procedures.
18. Despite doubts about federalism in Sweden and Denmark, and among some of the French political parties.
19. According to the American economist Harvey Liebenstein, economic actors are faced with a trade-off between income and leisure, and competition forces people away from an X-inefficient position where they choose a quiet life and towards an X-efficient one in which they have to work harder to survive. This proposition is naturally impossible to test empirically, which is perhaps why it has proved so attractive to politicians.
20. See Lintner and Mazey, 1991, among others.
21. This is very difficult to ascertain empirically, since it is very problematic to construct what is referred to as an 'anti-monde', an estimate of what would have in any case occurred in the absence of the EU. The latter is needed in order to attempt to isolate the effect of integration from that of a myriad of other variables.
22. Germany, France, Italy, Belgium, the Netherlands and Luxembourg.
23. It actually came into operation in 1958.
24. Britain, Ireland and Denmark joined in 1973, Greece in 1981, Spain and Portugal in 1986, and finally Finland, Sweden and Austria became members on the 1st January 1995.
25. For further consideration of these and issues surrounding labour mobility, migration, assylum, ethnicity and racism see Chapters 7 and 11.
26. The variable levy.
27. For a fuller consideration of the impact of the CAP, see Lintner and Mazey, 1991.
28. There is also a structural element to the CAP. This is, however, insignificant in relation to the price support aspect of agricultural policy.
29. Unless we completely accept the pure neo-liberal analysis: see Chapter 2.
30. The issue of nation states, national sovereignty and their relationship to European integration, apart from being of great importance, is also extremely complex – see, Brouwer *et al.*, 1994; Milward, 1992; Milward *et al.*, 1993; and Newman, 1995.
31. Whatever form this trade-off takes, and indeed whether it exists at all, the expectations augmented approach would imply that common rates of inflation can be achieved without serious long-term unemployment effects.
32. Devaluation cuts the price of exports and increases the price of imports, thus compensating for lost competitiveness.
33. See Brouwer *et al.*, 1994.
34. It could be argued, however, that large states who are *de facto* leaders may suffer sovereignty losses too as a result of integration, to the extent that they have to surrender some of their leadership position. For example, it has been argued that Germany will suffer losses in the context of the EMU envisaged in the Maastricht Treaty, since its leadership position in determining European macroeconomic policy will be moderated within the ECB and the ESCB.
35. Work is beginning to appear on alternative economic strategies at the EU level; see for example Coates, K. and Barrett-Brown, M. (1993) and Holland, S. (1983, 1993). At the same time there are some embryonic signs of movement in this direction within the EU itself; see the 1994 (Jacques Delors) White Paper on employment creation.
36. See Oates, 1972.
37. An area in which it is possible and beneficial to have fixed exchange rates; see Mundell, 1961.

38. Arguably the worst time immaginable, in the context of German unification and the coming recession.
39. For an excellent interpretation of the Maastricht Treaty see Church and Phinnemore, 1994.
40. See Brouwer *et al.*, 1994.
41. Non-EU citizens who are legally resident in the EU also have this right.
42. At the time of writing the ERM technically continues to exist without sterling and the lira, and with fluctuation bands of ±15 per cent.
43. Countries being left, to an extent, free to opt in and out of various EU developments.
44. Or even necessarily desirable, given that (a) the convergence criteria are rigid and ideologically biased to the exclusion of real criteria such unemployment and regional disparities; (b) the issue of the democratic accountability of EU institutions such as the ECB remains unresolved; and (c) there is a largely insufficient redistribution mechanism within the EU.

CHAPTER SIX

# Diversity

## The different interpretations of
## the mixed economy in Europe

### 6.1   Introduction: diverse national approaches to the mixed economy

In Chapter 5 we examined the unity of experience among the European mixed economies. We now continue with our analysis of how the European mixed economies have fared in practice by examining the other side of this coin. Along with considerable unity has come substantial **diversity**, for different European countries have chosen to interpret the mixed economy model in different ways. This diversity has arisen partly out of the different characteristics and the different circumstances to be found in each country, and partly from different preferences regarding the type of society considered desirable in various countries. It is to this that we now turn.

The aim of this chapter is thus to discuss the essential nature of the various interpretations, models or even cultures based on the mixed economy that have been developed in European countries. Again we emphasise that the objective of the chapter is not to provide a detailed account of the precise economic developments and policies in each each European economy, but rather to give a broad and analytical picture of the fundamental economic direction which different countries have taken now and over recent years. In this context, it is important to note three points from the outset:

1.   The specific ways in which the mixed economy has been interpreted in different countries is fundamentally the product of more than just economic forces, historical patterns, the political process and the social preferences of communities being influences that are just as significant. Equally, the economic organisation and policies that have been developed in each country have far-ranging consequences outside the economic arena, affecting the very fabric of these societies. Hence the interdisciplinary approach of this book. In this particular context, we shall tend to concentrate on the economic aspects of this issue.

2.   Although the policy orientation in most countries has changed over the post-war years roughly in line with the trends described above and in preceding chapters, nevertheless there have been significant differences in emphasis between countries, which have resulted from and indeed reinforced their basic diversity.

3.   The experience of most countries has depended to a varying but significant degree on their size. Large countries have naturally wielded more economic influence

155

and have at various times assumed leadership roles in the European economy. Smaller countries on the other hand often have had to follow more powerful neighbours and adopt policy stances which have recognised their openness and dependence on outside developments. This is not to say that small countries have been unable to adopt their own specific preferences in the economic arena. The experience of the Nordic countries, which until recently managed to build their economies around very comprehensive welfare systems financed by high taxation, are a case in point, but the evidence is mounting that even they are finding it extremely difficult to maintain their individual stances in the face of what is happening in the rest of the region, and indeed the world.

In this chapter we shall discuss some aspects of diversity that are of fundamental significance. Other significant areas of diversity, such as approaches to the labour market, social policy and regional policy, are then discussed in later chapters.

A convenient means of analysing the basic nature of diversity in the European economies is to attempt a classification of the different approaches that we can observe to economic organisation. These will inevitably contain broad generalisations, but they will nevertheless provide an overview of the issues involved, and of what is sometimes referred to as the 'culture' of the different capitalist systems.[1] Here we will identify five essential approaches to the European mixed economy:

(a) the 'British model';
(b) the 'social market model' adopted by Germany and others;
(c) the 'French model', which is now converging with the German approach to the social market;
(d) the 'Scandinavian model', which was until recently quite distinct, but which is now also moving towards the German paradigm; and
(e) the 'Southern model' which, if it exists at all, has characteristics which often seem idiosyncratic, at least from a north European perspective.

There is substantial overlap between at least some of these basic models of economic organisation and intervention, and the evidence is that in the 1990s Europe is being polarised into two camps, based around the 'social market' approach and the 'British' approach. However, there are also fundamental differences in approach and philosophy between them. We shall now examine each in turn, and then briefly consider the implications for the posible emergence of a 'European model' of economic organisation.

## 6.2   The British model

We start with the British approach to the economy, since this is the closest to home. It is important to note from the outset that this model is probably the one that has undergone the most fundamental change during the post-war period. Here we shall consider both the old and the new, but we shall naturally concentrate on the current situation. The big change in the United Kingdom occurred with the election of the

Conservative government in 1979. Up to this point the UK economy had been characterised:

(i)  by active Keynesian demand management on the part of both Conservative and Labour governments,[2] sometimes following the electoral cycle;

(ii)  by a firm belief that full employment should be the main objective of economic policy;

(iii)  by 'stop–go' macroeconomic policies, exacerbated by the United Kingdom's high marginal propensity to import[3] – expansions of the economy would invariably be brought to a juddering halt by balance of payments problems;

(iv)  by a substantial degree of government involvement in the economy at the microeconomic level, including a large number of nationalised industries,[4] a high degree of public and merit good provision (free education, free health, libraries, free school milk, etc.), and the widespread regulation of markets in a variety of areas, extending as far as direct attempts to alter prices. For example, there were attempts to control the price of basic foodstuffs and rents at various times during the Labour governments of the 1960s and 1970s. There was even an unsuccessful dalliance with planning, on the lines of the French system of 'indicative planning' (see below) during the Wilson administrations of the 1960s;

(v)  by a relatively comprehensive welfare state, based on the principle of the social security 'safety net', the universal entitlement to a minimum standard of living established in the wake of the Beveridge Report; and

(vi)  by strong trade unions with both considerable industrial muscle and significant political influence. 'Beer and sandwiches' with trade union leaders at 10 Downing Street during the Wilson governments were symptomatic of a corporatist approach to problem solving and decision making. Perhaps the zenith of this was represented by the incomes policies of the 1970s, which were agreed between the Labour government of the time and the main trade union leaders.[5]

The result was, as we have seen, steady economic growth, gradually increasing living standards and a generally cohesive society, but also relative economic decline in comparison to other European countries, a fact that would always be difficult to accept by what was formerly an imperial power and the richest nation in the world. The advent of the Thatcher governments saw a shift, then taken as far as considered electorally possible, towards a different model, partly in an attempt to reverse this long-term trend. This model is exceedingly neo-liberal in nature, and is based to a considerable extent on the United States' interpretation of the free market economy. Its main features are similar to those of the neo-liberal agenda discussed in Chapters 1, 2 and 5, and they include:

(i)  An abandonment of Keynesian economic management in anything but the short-term.[6] Keynesianism was claimed by its critics to have been ineffectual in securing full employment, and indeed to have worsened economic performance by 'crowding out' private sector investment, and by precipitating high levels of inflation (the 'expectations augmented' Phillips Curve analysis[7]).

(ii)  The adoption of the control of inflation as the principal objective of economic policy to be achieved up to the mid-1980s by controlling the money supply and by the 'medium term financial strategy', thereafter by targeting other variables but still adopting tight monetary policies.

(iii) 'Supply-side economics', based on measures designed to enhance the productivity of the economy by measures such as cuts in (principally the higher rates of) taxation to increase incentive. These reductions in taxation[8] are made possible by:

(iv)  A major increase in the role of free markets as allocators of resources, and a commensurate reduction in the involvement of the state in the economy (and thus in public expenditure[9]), under the banner of such slogans as Thatcher's soundbite 'rolling back the frontiers of the state'. An excessively large state sector, and an unduly small market-orientated private sector were responsible, it was argued, for the United Kingdom's relatively weak economic performance (see Bacon and Eltis, 1976). This change in emphasis has manifested itself in the form of action in various interrelated areas:

(a) A far-ranging privatisation programme, to an extent subsequently imitated by other European countries. It is beyond the scope of this book to explore this in detail. Suffice to say that UK privatisation has covered virtually all of the basic utilities and basic industries previously in state hands: telecommunications, gas, electricity generation and retail, water, airlines, petroleum, freight, coal, steel, etc. The intention is to follow these with the privatisation of more difficult areas such as the railways and postal services. The UK approach to privatisation has been based on a (futile) attempt to promote mass share ownership through (arguably) under-priced and highly publicised flotations.[10] The market behaviour of privatised firms is, then, to an extent controlled by the appointment of regulators.[11] It is worth noting in this context, however, that, apart from industries, the UK government has also taken steps to move substantial aspects of pension provision into the private sector, and to privatise many of the functions of local (and indeed central) government. There has also been a substantial reduction in what Hutton (1995) refers to as the 'social space', parks, etc., which may have had an impact on social problems such as crime.

(b) Deregulation of markets. Some examples of this include the following:

- in the labour market, eliminating wage councils that previously regulated wages, reducing the power of trade unions by legislation and by taking on powerful unions in industrial disputes (for example, the miners' strike, the steelworkers' strike and the Grunwick newspaper dispute in the 1980s), facilitating the adoption of American-style management methods which emphasise the 'right to manage', reducing (to the extent that this is politically possible) unemployment benefits to encourage people to take the jobs that are available, generally reducing employment rights, with far-reaching consequences for the nature of employment and indeed the very fabric of UK society (see below and Chapters 11 and 12);
- in the housing market: abolishing rent controls, and reducing local government involvement in the provision of housing;
- in financial markets: eliminating exchange controls and controls on credit, as well as deregulating the City of London (the famous 'Big Bang');

- in general: taking a minimalist approach to regulation areas such as health and safety, disabled rights and environmental protection. Hence, for example, the refusal by the Thatcher and Major governments to have anything to do with the EU's social legislation in the form of the 'Social Charter' and the 'Social Chapter' of the Maastricht Treaty.

(c) A reduction (again taken to the limits of the politically possible) in the extent of public and merit goods provision. Thus there has been a significant decrease in the public provision of services in areas ranging from education and health[12] to public libraries, social amenities and transport. There has also been an increase in private sector provision in these areas, as the people who can afford it have been forced to into the private sector in response to crumbling public sector provision. The strategy has basically consisted in privatising (or forcing competitive tender in the case of local government provision) whenever possible, and in other cases (the National Health service, schools and universities, where there is widespread public resistance to reducing public provision) attempting to create internal markets in order to achieve similar effects. All in all, one can conclude that the United Kingdom has experienced attempts to gradually break down the welfare state which had been constructed in the post-1945 period.

(d) A substantial reduction[13] in industrial policy and regional policy. Industrial and regional development were now largely to be left to the market, which would ensure that 'lame ducks' did not survive, that appropriate levels of R&D and innovation would be undertaken, that regional disparities would be eliminated. Surviving government expenditure in the regions was administered through development agencies and QUANGOs such as the (albeit successful) Welsh Development Agency. The rest was replaced by initiatives such as totally deregulated and tax exempt 'enterprise zones' and the creation of public gardens in places such as Liverpool.[14] Regionalism and regional policy are considered further in Chapter 10.

(v) The abandonment of the corporatist approach to decision making in general, and industrial relations in particular, in favour a more conflictual approach, based on firm but autocratic government ('there is no alternative') and on US-style managerialism ('the right to manage').

Contemporary Britain under the Conservative governments of Margaret Thatcher and John Major has come to be regarded very firmly as the leading exponent of the neo-liberal approach to the mixed economy among the European nation states. However, it should be noted that in many ways it has fallen between two stools: political resistance among the population[15] has precluded a full implementation of the neo-liberal agenda in the same way as has been done in the United States. At the same time the country has naturally not enjoyed the benefits of a more 'social market' form of organisation, since the UK government has of course explicitly rejected this way forward.

As ever, economic structures are inextricably related to social and political ones, and they in turn impact on them and on the general nature of the society in which people live. Thus in the United Kingdom change in the regulatory framework and in other aspects of economic organisation involve changes in the social institutions and practices that provided the framework for British society during most of the post-war period. It has been widely argued that the very essence and value system of British society has changed in the process, from a cooperative one to one based on individualism ('there is no such thing as society', as Margaret Thatcher once iterated), and to what Hutton (1995) refers to as the '40:30:30' society. The latter consists of a fundamentally marginalised and disenfranchised 30 per cent of the population, with a further 40 per cent in traditional secure and established 'primary' labour market positions, and a further 30 per cent in jobs that are transitory and insecure, based on part-time and short-term contracts.

Both the 'old-style' and the 'new-style' British capitalism have been based on a number of essential structural features, which have fundamentally conditioned its nature and results. Foremost among these are the following.

## The financial sector

The pre-eminent position of the **financial sector** in the City of London is of great significance. Britain, as the European country with historically the longest capitalist tradition, has the largest stock exchange among the European states, the most developed financial services industry, the most efficient and evolved banking sector. This is both welcomed as a source of strength and criticised as a source of weakness. It is a strength to the extent that an evolved financial sector is a source of potential comparative advantage, and it is therefore to an extent a wealth creator and an employment generator for the country. The limitations of the UK financial sector have also been the object of considerable comment in recent years.[16] The essence of the criticism consists of:

(a)   the claim that the nature of the system damages the manufacturing sector in the United Kingdom by encouraging 'short-termism' and discouraging investment. There are two dimensions to this:

(i)   the principal shareholders in UK firms are in fact the pension and other mutual funds, which are administered by fund managers who in turn depend on high dividends in order to achieve satisfactory rates of return and keep their jobs. These fund managers thus require high dividend payments from UK industry, and therefore put pressure on boards of directors (who in turn depend on shareholding fund managers to keep their own positions) to distribute a high proportion of profits in the form of dividends. This naturally means that there is less left over than in other countries to finance investment projects; and

(ii)   apart from reinvested profits, the other principal source of funds for industrial investment is money borrowed from the banking system. The UK banks are also fundamentally owned by institutional shareholders, and they too are therefore under pressure to deliver high dividends. Partly because of this, they tend to insist on high rates of return and short pay-back periods on the investment that they finance, certainly in comparison with other European countries. This, naturally, disqualifies many investment projects that might otherwise have taken place.

As such, it can be argued that the financial sector in the United Kingdom has contributed to the particularly rapid process of **de-industrialisation** that has occurred in the United Kingdom over recent years (see Chapter 2).

(b)    Although the United Kingdom probably does have a comparative advantage in the financial sector, the advantages that ensue from this are arguably limited by:

(i)    the comparatively low, and falling, level of employment that this sector generates. Concentration on finance as the lead sector in an economy therefore has its limitations in terms of employment;

(ii)    the fact that non-tariff barriers to trade in financial products tend to be relatively intractible, thus reducing the scope for trade in this field. The extent to which UK firms will benefit from the creation of an EU internal market in financial services remains to be seen. The evidence from 'big bang'[17] suggests that this has disproportionately benefited non-UK providers at the expense of UK firms. In addition,

(iii)    the increasingly 'footloose' nature of many capital markets, which increases the risk involved in putting too many of the country's eggs into this particular basket.

(c)    That such a reliance on the stock exchange results in enhanced degrees of instability in the economic system, by arguably engendering a 'casino' mentality based on speculation for individual profit rather than a system which serves to facilitate genuine wealth generation. This has been exacerbated by the emergence of the **financial derivatives** market. Some would claim that this provides a necessary means of hedging against future risk. To others it provides a further vehicle for speculation in which enormous sums of money can be won or lost in brief periods of time, as the recent collapse of Barings Bank has demonstrated (see Chapter 2).

## Central bank

A **central bank**, the Bank of England, has been under the direct control of government. It has thus been the instrument of monetary policy, implementing decisions that have been taken by ministers, rather than determining policy on its own account. This is in contrast to the situation of, for example, the Bundesbank, which in principle runs German monetary policy on the basis of the objectives contained in its statute and without explicit political influence. The UK system does have some positive effects in that economic policy can claim to be, to an extent at least, democratically accountable. Nevertheless, it carries with it certain disadvantages since governments have been tempted to determine monetary policy on the basis of their own imperatives (i.e. getting re-elected), rather than on the basis of the objective requirements of the economy, assuming that one can determine what these might be. Thus we have experienced a stop–go electoral cycle of economic policy in the United Kingdom: governments are elected, deflate the economy at an early stage in the life of the parliament in order to get unpopular decisions out of the way, and then reflate the economy in order to generate a 'feelgood factor' in time for the next general election. According to the Maastricht Treaty (see Chapter 5) central banks of all EU members, or at least the ones that participate in EMU, are due to become independent by 1998 at the latest, and there have been some attempts to move the operations of the Bank of England in this direction. Nevertheless, the status of the Bank of England has been fundamental to the nature of UK economic policy making.

The issue of central bank independence is not a clear-cut one, since this system throws up the problem of democratic accountability. It also begs the question of the appropriateness of the objectives contained in the Banks' statutes,[18] and of the ability of 'experts' to determine what is best for a country's citizens. Nevertheless, there does seem to be a strong correlation between central bank independence and price stability in various countries, as Fig. 6.1 demonstrates. Table 6.1 then shows some details of the different models of central bank governance as it existed in pre-Maastricht times.

## 'Property owning democracy'

The United Kingdom has developed a **property owning democracy**, i.e. a situation in which a large proportion (around 60 per cent) of the population own their own dwellings, often with the help of large mortgages. This is in contrast to the situation in other European countries, where ownership of housing is less prevalent and where there is a greater propensity to rent accommodation. This structural peculiarity has

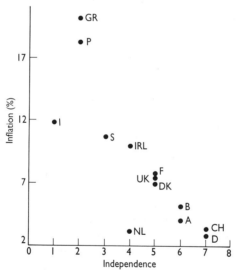

Average Annual Rate of Inflation and Central Bank Independence, OECD countries 1980–1989

The horizontal axis reports a measure of central bank independence ranging from 0 (not independent) to 8 (perfectly independent). Inflation tends to be higher, over a 10-year period, where the central bank is less independent.

**Figure 6.1**   The relationship between central bank independence and inflation in European countries. *Source:* Adapted from Grilli *et al.* (1991).

***Table 6.1*** Aspects of central bank independence
Source: *Adapted from Grilli et al. (1991).*

| | Governor | | Government on board | Overdraft facilities to Treasury | Independence index* | |
|---|---|---|---|---|---|---|
| | Term (yrs) | Renew- able | | | Econ. | Polit. |
| Belgium | 5 | yes | yes | Limited automatic | 6 | 1 |
| Denmark | ∞ | – | yes | Unlimited automatic | 5 | 3 |
| France | ∞ | – | yes | Limited automatic | 5 | 2 |
| Germany | 8 | no | no | Limited non-automatic | 7 | 6 |
| Greece | 4 | yes | yes | Limited automatic | 2 | 2 |
| Ireland | 7 | yes | yes | Limited automatic | 4 | 3 |
| Italy | ∞ | – | no | Limited automatic | 1 | 4 |
| Netherlands | 7 | yes | no | Limited automatic | 4 | 6 |
| Portugal | 5 | yes | no | Limited automatic | 2 | 1 |
| UK | 5 | yes | no | None | 5 | 1 |
| Spain | 4 | yes | no | Limited automatic | 3 | 2 |
| Switzerland | 6 | yes | no | Limited automatic | 7 | 5 |
| Japan | 5 | yes | yes | Limited non-automatic | 5 | 1 |
| USA | 4 | yes | no | None | 7 | 5 |

* Indices of economic and political independence base on the criteria mentioned in the text.
Scale: 0–8 (economic independence largest with a score of 8).
    0–8 (political independence largest with a score of 8).
Source: Grilli et al. *(1991).*

been consistently encouraged by governments who have subsidised home ownership (in the form of tax relief on the first tranche of mortgage payments), perhaps in the hope of courting electoral advantage. It has also proved to be highly lucrative for lenders, at least in more recent years. In this period real interest rates (the difference between interest rates and the rate of inflation) have been high, and mortgages are secured against the property they are used to purchase. Thus lenders have been able to obtain substantial returns without incurring substantial risk. The result has not always been positive:

(a)  It has facilitated a high level of indebtedness. In the years following the 'big bang', debt in the United Kingdom increased substantially as people took out ever-larger mortgages to keep up with the property boom of the late 1980s, and then borrowed increasing amounts secured against the equity in their homes to maintain consumption levels when interest rates and mortgage repayments were increased to dampen down the boom.

(b)  It has arguably crowded out 'productive' investment in areas such as manufacturing. For a long time many British people believed that house prices could only go in one direction: up. As a result housing was regarded as the most desirable avenue for investment, safer and more profitable than industry.

(c)  It has limited labour mobility, since there are lags and costs involved in buying and selling houses, and prices differ across the country.

(d)  It has led to difficulties in implementing monetary policy. The tendency referred to above for UK consumers to borrow to maintain consumption when mortgage rates increase has resulted in a low elasticity of demand for money with respect to the rate of interest,[19] i.e. big rises in interest rates are required to achieve falls in demand in the UK economy.

(e) Finally, it has precipitated considerable social costs as a result of 'negative equity'[20] and repossessions of property by lenders, as UK house buyers have discovered that in a market economy the price of assets can go down as well as up.

The recent crisis in the UK housing market and the policy of gradually reducing government subsidies to private house buyers is likely to change some of the above in the medium term.

## North Sea oil

The discovery of oil under the North Sea has also had a mixed effect on the UK economy. The positive aspects have consisted of:

(a) a considerable increase in output that has resulted from production in the North Sea;

(b) the increase in government tax revenues that has ensued, which were largely used, however, to finance the mitigation of the social costs of the monetarist experiment in order to render these politically acceptable – another example of the interrelationship between economics and politics in policy making; and

(c) the boost to the UK balance of payments that has resulted from import displacement and from exports of oil.

On the other hand, critics claim that North Sea oil was partly responsible in the 1980s (along with the high interest rate policy of the period) for an exchange rate for sterling that was arguably too high for UK manufacturing industry, increasing its lack of competitiveness and accelerating the process of UK de-industrialisation.

## Concentration of economic power

The **Concentration of economic power** (as well as political power) in the South of England, is reflected in the lack of economic and political devolution and in regional problems of substantial proportions.[21]

## Political system

A **political system** which is based on the first-past-the-post electoral system, which tends to ensure parliamentary majorities and which, together with the United Kingdom's lack of a written constitution and of an effective second chamber, gives (almost) absolute power to the Party that wins general elections. This naturally renders consensual politics unnecessary.

## Defence expenditure

The United Kingdom has maintained a very high level of **defence expenditure**, certainly in comparison with other major European countries. Although this may have precipitated indirect benefits in terms of innovation and employment, it has arguably also crowded out other forms of government expenditure, particularly in R&D in areas relevant to consumer goods. In addition, it may have displaced private sector R&D in this field. As such it may have contributed to the process of de-industrialisation in the United Kingdom. Recently, the UK government has been forced to cut defence spending as part of its public expenditure limitations.

## European integration

Finally, one should note the awkward relationship that the United Kingdom has had with the process of **European integration**. The country missed the boat when the EEC was first established in the 1950s, with the result that when it eventually did join it had to put up with policies such as the CAP that were decidedly not in its interests. The incredible antagonism towards monetary and other forms of integration, often verging on xenophobia, which is being displayed by the so-called 'Eurosceptics' in the Conservative Party may be pushing the country into similar mistakes in the late twentieth century. Britain is paying a high price for 'getting out of empire', shedding the delusions of grandeur that are a leftover fron its imperial past. One of the ironies of the United Kingdom's relationship with Europe, however, lies in the fact that Margaret Thatcher, for all her Euro-antagonism, is often cited as a prime motivator of the recent progress of the European integration project. To begin with, her antagonistic approach to the EC probably served to unite the other powers concerned, and in addition it was she who was a key motivator in launching the '1992' programme (see Chapter 5) – possibly a case of the economic liberal taking precedence over the nationalist.

## 6.3　The German social market model

The model of European capitalism with which the UK approach is often compared and indeed juxtaposed is the social market, and it is to this that we now turn. The social market model is most closely associated with Germany, but variants of it are the norm in a variety of European countries, notably Austria, the Netherlands and, to an extent, Switzerland. Other countries such as France, Sweden and the southern European states are engaged in adopting some of its most successful aspects to their own require- ments. In fact, German leadership in the context of the EU has meant that many European countries are converging around the German model of the social market.

　The social market model is essentially based on the concept that if the market is the fundamental means of allocating resources, then, in order to work properly, it must be regulated and administered in such a fashion as to produce a socially acceptable outcome. This is not merely a matter of equity or social justice, but also a matter of efficiency. The productive potential of an economy and how well it fulfils its potential depends in no small way on the people that work in it, and people have a greater propensity to work hard and are more committed to making a system work when they have a stake in it, when they see it working to the benefit of the majority, and when they feel that they have a say in the nature of the system and its development. Thus, according to this perspective, the social market is an effective way of creating wealth, while at the same time producing a cohesive and just society. This would suggest that the trade-off between equity and efficiency that we discussed in Chapter 3 may be a complex one, for in the case of the social market equity and efficiency can, to an extent, be seen to co-exist in a way that some economics textbooks would suggest is not possible. Once more it must be stressed that we are not simply considering the functioning of an economic system in isolation, for the social market 'system' consists of an interdependent set of economic, political and social institutions and practices.

The social market in Germany (**Soziale Marktwirtschaft**) was established after the Second World War. The German constitution (**Grundgesetz** of 1949) does not directly provide for such a system of economic organisation, but it does define Germany as a democratic and social federal state, thereby emphasising the importance of social justice to the long-term success of the market economy. Out of this principle has emerged a market system which is highly organised, extensively regulated and which broadly emphasises cooperation and partnership rather than divisiveness. The German social market is fundamentally characterised by the following features:

(a)   Cooperation and partnership between employers and trade unions in the **labour market** and in **industrial affairs**. This is embodied in **mitbestimmung**, or co-decision making, which operates at the level of the boardroom and of the works council. This is essentially a compromise between capital and labour, between workers and their managers, whereby both recognise each other's rights and interests, and follow an agreed path for the common good. Workers thus benefit from having managers who agree not to run their firms in a purely top–down fashion and solely for the narrow interest of shareholders. The **wage bargaining** mechanism is also collective and consensual in nature. The great majority of German workers are represented by large trade unions, while employers' organisations represent most employers. Both make concessions to each other's interests. Workers renounce the right to strike and to pursue wage claims which may be inappropriate to the circumstances of the firm they work for. They are covered by legally enforceable agreements that forbid strike action during their period of operation. In return 75 per cent of German workers are covered by industry-wide wage agreements which produce wage rates that are considerably greater than probably would otherwise be generated. These collective agreements between employers and trade unions (**tarifvertrage**) can only be altered locally when it is in the interests of employees to do so (**gunstigkeitsprinzip**).

Thus both industrial relations and wages are to a large extent managed, to the benefit of both labour and capital. Workers have relatively high wages and job security, managers enjoy low labour turnover rates and no disruption to the process of production by organised labour. The whole system is underpinned by an extensive system of regulation covering the labour market and industrial co-determination. This is discussed further in subsequent chapters. The German paradigm can be contrasted with the United Kingdom's essentially conflictual industrial relations system and the autocratic management methods of many UK employers. The latter has usually resulted in relatively low wages. In the past it produced high levels of industrial action and it now arguably relies on the threat of unemployment to maintain industrial peace.

(b)  A **financial system**, which provides the parameters within which this industrial cooperation can operate. The central feature of the German financial system is that it does not insist on the maximisation of short-term returns. It pivots around the German banks, who are the main sources of finance for firms. The Frankfurt stock exchange, like those in Amsterdam, Stockholm, Vienna and Zürich, are small in comparison with the London stock market, and are commensurately less important to firms.[22] The banks not only loan money to German industry but they are significant shareholders in German firms, both on their own behalf and on behalf of their clients. They take a direct interest in the running of the firms, frequently having representatives on boards of directors. The banks are often regionally based, and as such can claim to be close to small and medium-sized firms and to be aware of local needs. They therefore have an intimate knowledge of the prospects and requirements of firms, and are in many ways their partners and cooperators. Because of this they can take a long-term view, and facilitate the objective of long-term growth and stability. This system is conducive to high rates of investment, since there is not so much pressure to continually pay high dividends, and since it is often in the interests of the banks themselves, as owners of firms, to accept longer payback periods and lower rates of return on loans for investment projects. This is in contrast to the 'short-termism' that, as we have seen, the British financial system tends to produce. The German banking system is regulated by one of the autonomous government agencies discussed below (**Bundesaufsichsamt fur das Kreditwesen**).

(c)  A generous **social welfare system**, or **sozialstaat**. This is based on:

(i)  A contributory pension system, membership of which is mandatory for most workers. Half of all contributions are paid by employers, and pensions are dependent on one's contribution record. Pensions are index-linked to the level of average incomes, and tend to be relatively generous.[23]

(ii)  Mandatory health insurance for most workers, again with half the contributions paid by employers.

(iii)  Compulsory unemployment insurance for all, the cost of which is again equally shared between employers and employees. This provides a high ratio of income replacement in the case of unemployment.[24]

(iv)  Compulsory insurance against workplace injury (**Berufsgenossenschaften**), paid for by employers.

(v)  A 'safety net' system of social aid, paid by local authorities to those with no other source of income.

This comprehensive system is naturally very expensive. Pension contributions amount to 19.5 per cent of gross incomes, health insurance to 13 per cent, unemployment insurance to 6.5 per cent, for example. An important by-product, however, is the creation of a sense of social solidarity. Another is low labour turnover, and the ability of firms to hold on to employees in times of recession, when part of their wages are paid by social insurance.

(d)   A comprehensive **education and training system**. In the German system the two are strongly interlinked, and a 'dual vocational system' combines academic education with workplace experience, with the result that 70 per cent of German employees are technically qualified (compared to a mere 30 per cent in the United Kingdom). Germany enjoys the highest number of apprentices per head of the population of any country in the world, many of whom then graduate to the status of craftsmen (**handwerke**) and master-craftsmen (**meister**). As a result German employers benefit from a constant supply of highly skilled labour, which has contributed to high levels of German productivity.

(e)   A **political system** based on a high degree of decentralisation, and a specific system of proportional representation. This is discussed elsewhere in the book, but in this context it is important to note that the former brings government closer to the people, while the latter fosters the need for cooperation and power sharing in order to work towards the 'common good'.

(f)   A series of **independent government agencies**.[25] The most famous of these is the independent central bank (**Bundesbank**) which runs monetary policy for the republic in line with its statute, which in turn establishes the control of inflation as the sole objective of the bank's policy – the bank is only obliged to support the economic policies of the government to the extent that these are compatible with price stability, and it can only provide credit for state budgets within strict limits. The bank attempts to make policy by building the greatest possible degree of consensus – the membership of its governing council includes the presidents of the state banks of each of the German regions (**Bundesländer**), each of whom is appointed by regional governments, for example. This type of model for a central bank does have its problems (see Chapter 5 and Section 6.2 above), but it has to a large extent ensured that the conduct of monetary policy is removed from the direct political process, avoiding the electoral cycle of economic policy that has been experienced in the United Kingdom. It has also ensured a significant degree of price stability, which has contributed considerably to the post-war successes of the German economy. It is because of this[26] that the Bundesbank has been used as the model for the putative European Central Bank (ECB, see Chapter 5).

Apart from the Bundesbank, there are a number of other independent government agencies that control and regulate important areas of economic life, always on the principles of building consensus, cooperation and partnership in whatever area they happen to operate by representing a wide range of opinion and geographical interests. There is the regulator of competition (**Bundeskartellamt**, which regulates mergers),[27] and there are also **regulatory authorities** that control the operation of a wide variety of industries such as transport, telecommunications, public utilities, banking, insurance and agriculture.

(g)   A culture of determining a broad range of **economic policy** on the basis of consensus, as a result of 'concerted action', negotiations between the country's different social partners. The system is broadly that the government comes up with policy proposals that are then the subject of negotiation with employers and trade unions, as well as discussion with regional governments and opposition parties, before implementation. The Chancellor is the conductor of this 'concert', while the Bundesbank ultimately guarantees price stability. To some this might appear a rather messy form of corporatism. To others it represents an effective means of ensuring consensus and social cohesion.

(h)   A large **Mittelstand**, or medium-sized firm sector, which is roughly twice as big as that in the United Kingdom. The success of German small entrepreneurs is facilitated by the support of the regional banks, by the plentiful supply of skilled labour, and by:

(i)   An active **industrial policy**. This is often locally based, and offers the *mittelstand* in particular considerable protection from external forces by providing technological support and so on.

The German mixed economy is fundamentally underpinned by the country's value system and political culture, which tends to emphasise order, solidarity, discipline, subsidiarity (**subsidiaritätsprinzip**), equalisation across the *Länder*, and a general emphasis on the production side of the economy in preference to the financial sector. The weaknesses of the social market as a model for the mixed economy are essentially:

1.   That it is expensive, and thus requires high levels of taxes and social contributions on the part of both employers and employees, a weakness that is particularly relevant in times of high unemployment and of public resistance to high levels of taxation.

2.   That its high social contributions and its regulatory framework may discourage direct investment from abroad, from multinational firms that are seeking a more deregulated environment in which to operate and who might prefer to locate in, for example, the United Kingdom.

3.   That it can be inflexible in the face of the often rapid changes that market economies have to undergo. Restructuring the system can be slow since power is spread widely, and the extensive regulatory system can slow down firms' responses to change in their external environment. Some claim that excessive policy continuity effectively precludes any form of radical change. Nevertheless change does eventually occur, and when it happens it is generally less painful. In the early 1990s Volkswagen managed to negotiate wage and working time reductions with its unions, for example.

A particular issue with which Germany has had to deal over recent years, and which has tested the solidity of its social market economy, has been **unification**. The incorporation of the former East Germany into the new Germany from 1 July 1990 has conferred even greater potential economic power on Germany, but it has also produced considerable problems. Monetary union on the basis of parity between the DM and the Ost Mark confronted Germany with the gross uncompetitiveness and consequent economic collapse of the former German Democratic Republic (GDR). In 1990 alone GNP in the East fell by 20 per cent, and industrial output halved. Unemployment in the new *Länder* rose to over 800 000, 9.2 per cent of the workforce, with an estimated 2 million more people on short-time working. The cost of social security transfers and of additional industrial policy and infrastructural expenditure drove the federal budget into a deficit of DM14 bn in 1991, from a position of balance in 1989, bringing the federal government into conflict with the Bundesbank (which had proposed a monetary union on the basis of 2 Ost Marks to DM1). Eventually taxes and social contributions were increased from July 1991, to the extent of DM48 bn over 2 years. This was supplemented by increases in interest rates by the Bundesbank, the knock-on effects of which probably served to exacerbate the European recession of the early 1990s.

The latter has been cited by some as an example of Germany placing its own interests ahead of any European ideals when the chips are down, revealing the potential dangers involved in accepting German leadership too uncritically. In this context it should also be noted that the strength of the German economy was in many ways historically built on the 'beggar-thy-neighbour' policy of promoting exports by keeping an over-valued exchange rate for the DM.

These potential disadvantages of the social market and the recent difficulties that Germany has faced have led some to suggest that the social market model may be on the edge of crisis in the context of the rapid changes in the world economy to which we have referred above. In the United Kingdom it has been argued that the British free market, deregulated approach to the mixed economy is better able to adapt to and withstand the external challenges we now face. This remains to be seen. What is clear is that Germany is in fact in the process of moving to an extent towards greater allocation of resources by the market, as demonstrated by its privatisation programme encompassing, for example, the national airline Lufthansa in 1994, as well as plans to sell off Deutsche Telekom in 1996.

It is in many ways the main issue facing the European economies at present: should the way forward be to follow the social market model, or to follow the British model? Most are voting with their feet and in different ways and at differing speeds are trying to adopt the main points of strength of the former. The consequence is that the broad social market approach has become in many ways the basis of much of the convergence that is currently occurring among the European economies under the aegis of the EU.[28] It should nevertheless be emphasised that the social market itself may well be forced to lean increasingly towards the market and less towards the social, as the European economies face the external challenges which are in the pipeline. Indeed, there is a case for arguing that this process is already well under way.

## The Netherlands

Another example of the social market model of the mixed economy is to be found in **the Netherlands**. Like Germany, Holland has a comprehensive social security system, developed over the years as a result of the country's strong religious traditions. This provides comprehensive coverage for virtually the entire population throughout their lives, and it has largely been responsible for the huge size of the public sector in the Netherlands, which accounted for 61 per cent of GDP in 1983 but to an extent has been reduced since then. Holland is traditionally a trading nation with a very open economy, used to the limits to economic sovereignty imposed by its size and geographical location. It also has the largest service sector in any European country (precipitating the term 'Dutch disease'), which reflects its status as a centre for distribution (the 'gateway to Europe') and its emphasis on non-market services such as health, education and social provision. Manufacturing industry is therefore of relatively small importance to the Dutch economy, despite the influence of large multinational firms such as Philips.

There is no great tradition of direct government intervention in the economy, but the social market principle manifests itself clearly in the areas of social security and wage determination. In the case of the latter area, wages negotiation is conducted on a corporatist tripartite basis between government employers and the trade unions. Often the negotiations conclude in central agreements, which then act as a basis for detailed local agreements. As in the German case, the emphasis is on cooperation and consultation with the government contributing centrally to the process, especially since many social benefits and contributions are based on levels of pay. In addition, one should note that in the Netherlands most socioeconomic policy making is conducted in consultation with the Social Economic Council (**Sociaal Economische Raad**), emphasising the cooperative nature of the Dutch decision-making process. As in Germany, the economic system is supported by appropriate political structures. The Amsterdam stock exchange is small and is dominated by four large multinational firms: Royal Dutch, Unilever, Philips and AKZO. The banking sector is advanced and concentrated, and it is dominated by the giant ABM AMRO group. Again, the financial sector is subject to considerable regulation, although here too we have seen a recent relaxation in the regulatory climate. Macroeconomic policy in the Netherlands closely follows German leadership. The Dutch central bank (**De Nederlandsche Bank**, DNB) closely follows German interest rates, only rarely changing rates independently of the Bundesbank. This has worked well, for inflation in the Netherlands has been the lowest in the EU and the guilder the second strongest currency after the DM. Recently the Netherlands has also faced the problem of the spiralling cost of its high level of welfare, and there have been some attempts to scale down its cost.

## Belgium and Luxembourg

Belgium and Luxembourg are small countries which fall within the social market tradition. Luxembourg is very much a special case, a tiny country that has achieved a universally high standard of living and of social cohesion by exploiting its particular position as a principality at the centre of mainland Europe. It is in a monetary union with Belgium. Ironically, in this context, one of the features of the Luxembourg economy is a liberal and deregulated financial services sector that has permitted the principality to become a centre of activity in this field. A central feature of the Belgian experience arises from the fact that the country is ethnically polarised between the Flemings in the north of the country and the Walloons in the south. Some of the problems that have arisen from this have been tackled by the regionalisation laws that came into effect in 1982. The Belgian economy is also a very open one and is dominated by services (65.5 per cent of GDP in 1989), reflecting partly its position as the headquarters of the European Commission and of NATO. It has a comprehensive welfare system with generous pension and employment benefits and universal health care. The predictable implication of this is high public expenditure and substantial government debt, among the highest in Europe as a proportion of GDP. The Belgian central bank (*Banque Nationale de Belgique*) is 50 per cent government owned and is thus subject to political control, even though it has considerable economic autonomy. The stock exchange is small, and recently subject to attempts at deregulation.

### Switzerland

**Switzerland** is another small country that has adopted this broad type of approach. This is a very particular country that has made its fortune from its expertise in banking and, some would argue, its ability to free-ride the regulatory systems set up in the rest of Europe by providing discrete but secure banking services and remaining outside the EU. Switzerland is of course a highly decentralised federal state comprising German, French and Italian speaking 'cantons'. It is very much a socially regulated economy with comprehensive welfare provision. Space precludes an examination of other broadly social market economies such as **Austria**, but the corporatist model adopted in this country is very similar to that in Germany.[29]

## 6.4   The Scandinavian model

**Sweden**, together with the other Scandinavian countries, has long been regarded as the very epitome of a socially regulated state in which economic policy is determined by a process of collaboration. For most of the post-war period it is probably fair to say that the 'Swedish model' represented an extreme version of the social market approach, much more interventionist and corporatist than the German version. More recent events suggest that the innovative interpretation of the mixed economy developed by Nordic countries is in the process of being pulled towards the mainstream social market model.

Swedish policy was based on the model of economic policy put forward by the economists Gosta Rehn and Rudolph Meidner at the Swedish Trade Union Congress (**LO-Kongress**) of 1951. This had the potentially contradictory joint objectives of full employment, price stability and rapid growth in the context of a small, highly open and interdependent economy. It represented, however, an inventive piece of economic and social engineering, and it formed the basis of the 'Swedish model'. This in essence consisted of:

(a)   Wages that were determined not by the market, but by a form of planning process. There were central agreements on wages, which were based on consensus between unions, employers and government as to the total wages bill that the nation could afford. Individual wages were then be on the **solidarist wage policy** principle, according to which there would be equal pay for equal work regardless of the sector or firm in which one was employed.

(b) **'Planned industrial Darwinism'**. The lack of market-determined wages in the economy inevitably meant that only the most efficient firms would survive, since marginal firms would not be able to afford the high centrally determined wages, that on the other hand might be appropriate for parts of the economy with higher productivity. The rate of decline of marginal industries was controlled by the extensive use of **subsidies**. In order to allow the most efficient sectors of the economy to expand without meeting labour supply and skill supply bottlenecks, the government would provide a 'rationalisation reserve' of human capital by implementing:

(c) An **active education and training policy**, aimed at both educating all the population to a high standard and at training workers made redundant in low productivity firms to fill jobs in expanding firms. The latter objective involved considerable amounts of industrial vocational traning, especially among the less skilled, in order to ensure a good supply of technicians. This was supplemented by:

(d) An active **labour market policy**, administered by a central employment service, and aimed principally at promoting the mobility of labour by means of relocation grants and so on.

(e) A generous and encompassing **welfare system**, including a system of subsidised housing, which made it possible for people to undergo retraining, and also naturally served to create social cohesion.

(f) An active **regional policy** to provide in cases where the decline low productivity industries was regionally concentrated. This naturally involved a widespread use of subsidies.

(g) A comprehensive system of **social regulation** of the private sector.

The system was underpinned by the state, which was meant to preserve price stability by pursuing **tight financial policies**, while financing the huge expense of the system by **high taxation** (the highest in the world) on individuals and on the successful parts of the corporate sector. The cohesion and widespread popular acceptance of the Swedish model was such that people were prepared to pay high taxes in order to benefit from the eminently desirable results.

The Swedish model of the mixed economy enabled the population to achieve one of the highest material standards of living in the world, as well as a substantial degree of economic justice. It effectively divided the economy into two sectors: a 'competitive' manufacturing sector,[30] which effectively competed on world markets on the basis of the high productivity and quality that resulted from high investment, high levels of R&D and the high human capital embedded in the workforce, and a 'protected' sector (housing, defence, education, etc., both in the private and the public sector) which provide 'quality-of life' goods and services and human capital development. The export-orientated competitive sector was in many ways the engine of growth, providing the wealth to underpin the high standard of living that the Swedish people enjoyed.

This approach to the social market proved remarkably successful for much of the post-war period, despite a notable propensity for cyclical swings in Swedish economic performance.[31] However, its fortunes began to wane from the 1970s. In terms of internal events, this was mainly due to two factors:

1. The state was ultimately unwilling or unable to keep financial policy sufficiently

tight to ensure price stability running, for example, a substantial public sector deficit. As a result, Sweden experienced a rate of inflation (12–16 per cent for much of the decade) which was significantly above that of other European countries.

2.    The size of the protected sector expanded too rapidly relative to the competitive sector during the 1970s. This was partly due to the lack of pay differentials, which enhanced the attractiveness of working in the protected sector,[32] and partly because the competitive sector failed to produce sufficient new firms. The result was that the elimination of less competitive firms produced unemployment, de-industrialisation and balance of payments problems.

Thus the Swedish model had to be reformed, and it duly was after a substantial devaluation in 1982. The 'third way', as this reform came to be known, consisted of an attempt to reconcile the principles of the Rhen-Meidner approach with a tighter approach to financial policy and a certain degree of deregulation. In addition, measures were introduced to stimulate private savings and to increase the mobility of labour. The overall objectives were to control inflation and to shift resources from the protected sector into the competitive sector. These measures seemed to work to an extent for a few years, but from around 1985 it became clear that no real change had been precipitated. The protected sector, both public and private, remained strong, its position cushioned by strong trade unions who resisted the introduction of wage differentials *vis-à-vis* the competitive sector. Instead, what emerged from deregulation of credit markets was a growing financial sector, which began to compete with manufacturing for the best labour and other resources, and a form of the 'British disease' began to emerge in Sweden.

By the early 1990s it had become clear that the Swedish model was in severe difficulty, perhaps no longer able to cope in the same way with the external challenges that were emerging in the increasingly interdependent world economy. A new policy stance was adopted which effectively shifted the emphasis of the social market in the country more towards the European mainstream, and paved the way for entry into the EU in 1995. This was typified by the decision to link the krone to the ECU in May 1991, removing devaluation as the obvious means of restoring lost competitiveness and forcing the population to accept the burden of inflation control more directly. From now on interest rates would be determined more by the Bundesbank than by the Swedish government. The Swedish model now seems to be losing its distinctive character and to be very much moving towards the German interpretation of the social market.

Other Scandinavian countries have pusued variants of the Swedish model, notably **Denmark**. Space precludes a detailed examination of these in this context.[33]

## 6.5    The French model

Like the Swedes and most other European countries, the French approach towards the mixed economy has converged over the last few years in the general direction of the European model of the social market. However, France is a major European country that over the years has had its distinctive approach to the mixed economy. As such it merits an albeit brief section of its own within this chapter.

Pre-war France had been characterised by high levels of protection (particularly for agriculture), and by state intervention to prop up fundamentally uncompetitive industries. It thus entered the post-war period with a dual economy with a relatively large agricultural sector and a need to restructure. The mixed economy that France built up during the post-war period to the 1980s was founded on familiar principles of considerable state intervention in the functioning of the economy (**dirigisme**). As such it contrasted quite sharply with the more (social) market-orientated approach adopted by Germany. Another contrast was the emphasis that was placed on economic growth at the expense of price stability.[34] A similarity with Germany, however, was the beggar-thy-neighbour policy of promoting exports by keeping the franc undervalued, as is demonstrated by the arguably excessive devaluations of 1958 and 1969. Specifically, French *dirigisme* took the form of:

(a) widespread regulation of the economy, in particular of capital markets, of nationalised industries and of the labour market practices of private firms. A particularly significant aspect of this was a vitual monopoly for many years of the sources of finance for industrial expansion, which facilitated the success of:
(b) the system of **indicative planning**, through which the state sought to influence the direction and structure of the economy;[35]
(c) a high degree of centralisation of policy making, based naturally around Paris;
(d) the extensive subsidies to industry, and
(e) promoting industrial concentration, in an attempt to develop national champions in industry to counter *le défi Americain* (the American challenge, as Servan-Schreiber called it).[36]

France's rapid post-war period of growth (often referred to as *Les Trentes Glorieuses*) was somewhat marred by a small business sector that was concentrated in declining sectors of the economy, as well as by substantial spatial inequalities in the distribution of economic activity, parts of the south, the east, Brittany and the north faring less well than the central regions. In addition, the agricultural sector remained relatively large in France, despite the reduction in employment that occurred in this area. Eventually, as in other countries, growth petered out. The Barre government of the late 1970s failed to reverse the trend, and was replaced by the Mitterrand regime of 1981–84, which attempted to pursue an 'alternative economic policy' based on Keynesian reflation and increased state intervention in industrial affairs. This shift in policy occurred at a time when other European countries, and notably the United Kingdom, were pursuing diametrically opposite approaches to economic policy based on the neo-liberal agenda. Accordingly, it fell flat on its face when France sucked in extra imports that it could not finance by greater exports to its neighbours who were busy limiting internal demand. The franc was devalued three times within the ERM between October 1981 and March 1983, and this whole period represents a fine case study in the limits to national economic sovereignty in a Europe that is now highly interdependent and which is characterised by a high degree of capital mobility.

There followed a distinct shift in policy by the Fabius government, with the support of the employers' association (*Conseil National du Patronat Francais*, CNPF) away from the traditional *dirigiste* line and towards a more market-orientated position. Subsidies were reduced, the regulation and control of nationalised industries was pared away, rules covering the dismissal of workers by the private sector were liberalised, capital markets were deregulated. More market, certainly, but still a broadly socially regulated market on German lines, the basis of which was to an extent laid by the reforms introduced by Mitterrand in the 1980s. The essence of these is shown in Fig. 6.2 (which also shows some of the political and social dimensions of these reforms) and the broad imprint they have given to the French economy will be difficult to reverse. Deregulation was supplemented by privatisation on the part of the Rocard government and followed by more of the same during the Chirac government. An interesting feature of the French privatisation programme, and an indication of the Gallic interpretation of capitalism, lies in the way that the French government initially attempted to 'protect' its privatised companies by establishing the principle of the **noyau dur** aimed at encouraging long-term investors to take strategic stakes in the former state companies. This was then revived by the Balladur government which, however, stated that the 20 per cent limit on foreign stakes which existed in the previous round of privatisations will be scrapped, thus opening such shareholder groups to foreign companies. In any case, in 1993 the Balladur government announced a far-ranging privatisation programme encompassing 21 companies, 12 of which were due for privatisation in 1986 before the stock market crashed in 1987 and the Socialist Government was elected in 1988. The details of this are shown below:

## French companies due to be privatised (1993 list)

**Postponed from 1986:**

| | |
|---|---|
| AGF | Crédit Lyonnais |
| GAN | Banque Nationale de Paris |
| UAP | Péchiney |
| Bull | Rhône-Poulenc |
| Thomson | Elf-Acquitaine |
| Banque Hervet | Société Marseillaise de Crédit |

**1993 additions**

| | |
|---|---|
| Aerospatiale | Cie Generale Maritime |
| Air France | Renault |
| Caisse Centrale de Réassurance | SEITA |
| Caisse Nationale de | SNECMA |
|    Prévoyance-Assurances | Usinor-Sacilor |

The other plank on which the new approach was based was a policy of 'franc fort', rejecting devaluation and adhering to a fixed exchange rate within the ERM, thus forcing internal economic agents to adjust to the new realities rather than rely on continuing devaluations in order to restore lost competitiveness. Membership of the ERM was, *inter alia*, used by the state as a *force majeur* argument for encouraging the country to accept the costs of restructuring. There duly followed a period of considerable pain, and the franc had in fact to be marginally devalued *vis-à-vis* the

| Proposed aims | Policies adopted |
|---|---|
| **Participation/Autogestion** | |
| 1.  Workers' rights | Auroux Laws |
| | i.  On collective bargaining: obligatory annual pay negotiations. Nov. 82. |
| | ii.  Workers' representation on works committees. Protection for part-time and short-term contract workers. Dec. 82. |
| | iii.  Freedom of expression – consultation with management. Aug. 82. |
| | iv.  Workers' democracy in public firms. Representation on boards. |
| | |
| 2.  Decentralisation | Defferre Laws 1982–86 |
| | i.  Prefects and prefectoral control over local government abolished. |
| | ii.  26 regional governments established (four overseas territories) plus Corsica given special status. |
| | iii.  New powers and resources devolved to all levels of local government. |
| | iv.  Administrative decentralisation. |
| | |
| **Liberalisation** | |
| 1.  Civil liberties | a)  Abolition of death penalty in 1981. |
| | b)  Reform of public order laws (including police stop and search powers). |
| | c)  Citizens given right to go directly to European Court of Justice. |
| | d)  Relaxation of attitude to homosexuals. |
| | |
| 2.  Media/cultural reform | a)  Creation of High Authority to control TV. |
| | b)  Legalisation of private/local radio and TV stations. |
| | c)  Increase in culture budget and support for 'socialist' projects: *Institut du Monde Arabe*, regional cultures, popular theatre, etc. |

ASSESSMENT

Several of the above reforms, while arguably not inherently 'socialist' in character, were important changes. In many ways they were modernising steps. In practice, their impact was limited by unemployment financial constraints and informal resistance to reforms. Equally, in the case of cultural policy, government subsidies remained weighted towards traditional activities – opera, concerts and focused upon Paris.

*Figure 6.2*  French socialist policies 1981–86

DM twice between April 1986 and January 1987. Thereafter it has remained fixed against the DM and a considerable economic recovery has ensued which, in terms of many economic indicators,[37] has rendered the French economy one of the strongest in Europe.

The major reservation that one has to place on this optimistic judgement of the French economy concerns the fact that, like other European countries, it continues to suffer from high levels of unemployment (officially around 12 per cent in mid-1995) which will be very difficult to reduce, and which were a major bone of contention duting the 1995 presidential election. With the victory of the right, in the shape of the Gaullist Jacques Chirac, in the 1995 Presidential elections we may well see further moves towards a more free market, but still distinctly Gallic, interpretation of the mixed economy in France.

## 6.6   The Southern model

The first issue to explore in this section is whether there is indeed a 'Southern model', for in the case of Italy, Spain, Portugal and Greece we are dealing with countries with often very discrete characteristics. Nevertheless there are links between them, and it is convenient to discuss them as a group. The factors they have in common are:

1. These four countries all emerged from the Second World War as relatively poor and undeveloped, with large agricultural sectors.
2. They have all had recent experience of Fascist governments, some more recent than others, the Franco, Salazar and the Colonels' regimes lasting well into the post-war period in Spain, Portugal and Greece, respectively.
3. They have all experienced rapid economic growth, again some (Italy, Spain) more than others, and some (Italy) sooner than others.
4. They all have what are sometimes regarded from a northern European perspective as somewhat idiosyncratic economic and state systems.
5. They all characterised by significant economic, administrative and political distortions and problems.
6. They are all keen to participate fully in the European integration project, perhaps in order to use the EU as an external stimulus to internal modernisation. As a result, they are all engaged in attempts to move their various interpretations of the mixed economy towards the northern European social market paradigm, a process that frequently is proving painful.

In this context we shall use Italy as a case study of this particular appoach to the mixed economy.


### Italy

Italy's post-war economic progress has been dramatic – the country has developed from what Ezio Tarantelli[38] was fond of describing as 'the most developed of the less developed countries' into a major industrialised country with a seat on the G7 group of leading world economies.

The Italian version of the mixed economy that has delivered this degree of economic success has consisted of a curious and sometimes idiosyncratic mixture of market and state, at least if it is viewed from a northern European perspective. The country represents perhaps a unique interdisciplinary case study, for one cannot hope to understand the Italian economy without reference to the country's political and social characteristics. On the one hand, Italy has been characterised by many of the features one would associate with a modern and successful free market economy:

   1.   A dynamic and competitive small and medium-sized business sector (SMEs), from which originated much of the impetus for the 'economic miracles' of the 1960s and (arguably) the 1980s.[39] In the mid-1980s 59 per cent of manufacturing employment was located in firms of less than 100 employees, compared with 16 per cent in Germany, 27.7 per cent in France, 22 per cent in the United Kingdom, and

16.5 per cent in the United States. What is more, the average size of all firms in Italy has been falling.[40] The role of SMEs in the 1980s economic success is particularly interesting. During this period some of the SMEs (particularly in the North around Turin) that emerged in Italy were the result of subcontracting by large firms seeking to escape the regulation and high labour costs which followed the 'hot autumn',[41] and they thus constituted a 'dependent' sector. Others, mainly in the central regions such as Emilia-Romagna and in the Veneto were technologically sophisticated firms that were independent of larger producers. The development of the latter was considerably facilitated by the interventionist approach of regional governments and they have come to be known as **terza Italia**, the engine of Italian growth and possibly a model of 'flexible specialisation' for the rest of Europe.

2.   Large and internationally competitive 'national champions' such as FIAT, the Finninvest group, Olivetti, Montedison, Indesit, Zanussi and Benetton.

3.   Associated with this, a steady supply of high profile elite entrepreneurs such as the Agnelli family, Carlo de Benedetti, Raoul Gardini, Luciano Benetton and, of course, Silvio Berlusconi.[42]

4.   A strong 'enterprise culture', which does not always pay much attention to such niceties as the legal framework. This is to an extent reflected by the existence of a large 'informal economy', whose size is estimated to be as great as 30 per cent of GDP.

On the other hand, at the same time Italy has experienced widespread state involvement in the operation of its market economy:

1.   There has been significant direct ownership of industry, mainly through two **enti publici**, effectively state-holding companies, IRI (**Istituto per la Ricostruzione Industriale**) and ENI (**Ente Nazionale Idrocarburi**). Between them these have controlled large sections of the Italian economy, including Alfa-Romeo, the telecommunications company SIP (now Telecom Italia), the electricity company ENEL, as well as a range of interests in areas such as engineering, steel, shipbuilding, motorways and hydrocarbons.

2.   There has been widespread direct and indirect subsidy of industry by the state, especially of loss-making companies in the IRI and ENI groups. A vivid example of this occurred in 1980, when IRI alone lost a staggering 2200 bn lire, equivalent to about 6 per cent of national income. At one stage in the early 1980s each Alfasud car that was sold was subsidised to the tune of around £1000.

3.   There has been widespread social regulation of industry and of the labour market, the latter typified by the concessions to organised labour by the state in the wake of the 'hot autumn' of industrial and political unrest in 1969. In 1972 the majority of the Italian workforce was given entitlement to 150 annual hours of paid education. In 1975 the right to avoid dismissal on purely economic grounds was established by the extension of the **Cassa Integrazione Guadagni** to guarantee at least 80 per cent of full pay to workers who were laid off.[43]

4.   There has been widespread direct interference by the state in the functioning of the price mechanism. Two examples of this are the **scala mobile**, which from 1975 automatically index-linked the earnings of most employees, and the **Equo Canone** which has fixed rents in the housing market. In addition, before the completion of

the EC's '1992' programme (see Chapter 5), the Italian state had operated stringent exchange controls to protect the value of the lira.

5.   The state has held monopolies in the sale of certain goods such as tobacco and salt.[44]

6.   There has been considerable explicit or implicit employment creation by the state, which has used its bureacracy and industries such as the railways to provide an arguably inflated number of jobs for Italian citizens.[45]

7.   There has been a very active and expensive regional policy. Italy is essentially a dual economy, with the south or **Mezzogiorno** consistently under-developed and poor in contrast with the highly industrialised and prosperous north, and large transfers have been made throughout the post-war period to the south by the state corporations and through the **Cassa per il Mezzogiorno**.[46]

8.   The state has provided a welfare system which is relatively generous, if not at all comprehensive. This has been achieved either directly or through the social regulation of the private sector. Public welfare has been provided through the social *enti publici*: **Istituto Nazionale per la Previdenza Sociale (INPS)** for social security, **INAM** for health insurance and **INAIL** for insurance against accidents at work. State pensions in Italy are on the whole generous, as are maternity rights and so on, and employees generally enjoy favourable conditions of employment. However, the Italian social security system in general only covers people in employment, and what it does not provide is any form of 'social safety net' along the lines of that introduced in the United Kingdom following the Beveridge Report.[47] Furthermore many pensions, and especially the ubiquitous invalidity pensions, have tended to be used as a means of patronage, being distributed by a system of **raccomandazioni**, i.e. on political criteria rather than on the basis of need (see below).

9.   The provision of some public merit goods by the Italian state has also been limited in its scope. Considerable quantities of economic infrastructure such as motorways and railways have been provided at considerable cost, but the same cannot be said for provision of a social nature. For much of the post-war period education and health were under-supplied and inefficient, and access to them was often a lottery.[48] Recently there have been attempts at reform, for example an attempt to create a UK-style national health service, but provision remains low by international standards.[49]

All this has taken place in the context of a number of very particular and sometimes destructive structural features:

1.   An inefficient and ineffective bureaucracy, which until recently was even incapable of collecting taxes properly.

2.   A political system which, despite recent reforms has, at least at first glance, failed to produce stable government.

3.   Widespread organised crime, especially in the south where the Sicilian Mafia, the Neapolitan Camorra and the Calabrian Ndraghetta have enormous influence.

4.   Endemic corruption. This has been highlighted in the 1990s by **'operation clean hands'**, the investigations of the magistrature which led to the demise of Italy's traditional political parties and the emergence of their current (sometimes merely renamed) substitutes.[50] However, corruption existed long before this and became

institutionalised into the Italian political system. For example, Italy has the highest proportion of invalidity pensioners in Europe,[51] largely as a result of the Christian Democrat Party's practice of using them to bribe their supporters, especially in the Mezzogiorno.

5.   A protected, fragmented and relatively inefficient financial system. For example, Italian banks tend to be small and often cumbersome (although their record of lending to industry is relatively good), and the Italian stock exchange is relatively insignificant.

6.   Strong trade unions, divided along political lines (see Chapter 7) who, at least until recently, succeeded in achieving particularly favourable conditions of employment for their members.

So why is it that the Italian model of the mixed economy has proved to be so successful? The answer probably lies in the fact that many entrepreneurs in Italy have consistently found ways of coping with or of avoiding the formal restrictions and regulations imposed by the Italian system, and thus in whole sectors of the economy a free market has operated in practice. For example, until recently the state bureaucracy was palpably incapable of collecting taxes from the richest in society, and so many simply did not pay any. At the same time some of the albeit idiosyncratic aspects of the Italian state and of Italian society have succeeded in providing a degree of social protection sufficient to ensure social cohesion.[52] Thus the Italians arguably have had their own type of social market, with an efficient market sector and an, albeit limited, degree of social protection as well.

The quality and adaptability of Italian capitalism can be seen in the way that the economy has restructured after the 'hot autumn', with the emergence of the *Terza Italia* in the 1980s, as well in the development of a large 'informal economy', estimated to account for up to 30 per cent of the country's GDP. The latter has been seen as a reaction on the part of economic agents to the arguably restrictive formal regulations within which the Italian state has attempted to make them operate.

The state has ensured social protection for those fortunate enough to work in the formal sector of the economy, while a strange combination of the informal economy, the system of patronage in pension provision, the family,[53] the Catholic Church and (perversely) even organised crime and corruption (the Mafia is said to provide a form of social security for its supporters in the poor parts of the south) have acted as social shock-absorbers for the remainder of the population.

All this, allied to a host of historically favourable conditions during the post-war period (for example low wages, a plentiful supply of labour from the south, the discovery of gas in the Adriatic), a low base to start with and some staunch monetary management by the Bank of Italy, has resulted in a successful economy in terms of high growth rates and rapidly increasing standards of living. This despite rates of inflation that have been consistently above the EU average and reached its highest level of 21.1 per cent in 1980.[54] It has also left Italy with a number of outstanding economic problems, notably:

- the *Mezzogiorno*;
- a large public sector debt (as high as 11 per cent of GDP in 1990) that has resulted from high expenditure and low tax revenues; and

- high unemployement, in common with the rest of Europe.

In addition one could add factors which are not specifically economic, such as the need to modernise the state bureaucracy, the need to tackle organised crime and corruption, etc., to the list of pressing issues. An interesting side issue here concerns Italy's tranformation over the last few years from a labour exporting country into, for the first time in its history, a labour importing country, attracting an estimated 2 million largely illegal migrants from North Africa and from the Slav and Baltic states. These migrants exist largely within the informal economy, and are forming part of what many see as a new underclass. Here is an economic, political and indeed social issue that the Italian state will have to face into the next century.[55]

Attempts to tackle these issues, and in particular the size of the public debt, have been going on since the mid-1980s. As far as the deficits of the state are concerned, the possible solutions are essentially three: to cut expenditure, to increase taxes or to privatise. All are fraught with difficulty, given the nature of Italian society, and they would accordingly require substantial institutional, social and political reform. Taxes are difficult to increase because of the size of the informal economy and the inefficiency of the state bureaucracy. Cuts in expenditure involve cutting subsidies (relatively straightforward) or cutting pensions and social provision (very painful and socially dangerous). There is widespread political opposition to privatisation. Nevertheless, Romano Prodi at IRI virtually eliminated the *ente publico*'s deficit between 1983–89, and privatised 17 firms with a labour force of 64 000 (including Alfa-Romeo, which was sold to FIAT, and Montedison) during this period. He also presided over large inflows of private capital into state owned banks. Franco Reviglio managed a similar if less spectacular task at ENI during this period, as well as reforming aspects of tax collection while Minister of Finance.

Real pressure for reform, however, has come since the signing of the Maastricht Treaty (see Chapter 5), which has established low inflation and low public sector debt as preconditions for participation in any future monetary union in the EU. It intensified following the lira's ejection from the ERM (along with sterling) in September 1992. The Amato government of 1992–93, the 'government of technocrats' led by Carlo Azeglio Ciampi from 1993–94, the Berlusconi government of 1994–95 and the technocratic government of Lamberto Dini have all attempted a mixture of privatisation, limited tax increases and expenditure cuts. As part of this process two publically owned banks, Credito Italiano and Banca Commerciale Italiana, were privatised in 1993 and 1994, respectively. Interestingly, foreign involvement in privatisations has been strongly discouraged, and efforts have been made to prevent the companies involved from being broken up.[56] The recent emphasis has been on pensions reform, which has proved to being a political minefield.[57] Thus Italy is desperately attempting to move its model of the economy closer to the north European social market. The extent to which this will prove in the long term to be possible or even entirely desirable remains to be seen.

Space precludes a detailed study of the other southern European economies of **Spain**, **Portugal** and **Greece**, even though each provide fascinating case studies.[58] These are all countries which have recently emerged from Fascism to experience rapid growth and modernisation within the EU. The economic performance of Spain has been particularly impressive, while Greece is the economy with the greatest problems of the the three, at least in terms of its ability to qualify for any future EU monetary union.

## 6.7 Conclusion: towards a European model?

What, then, can we conclude about the diverse approaches to the mixed economy in Europe? It is certainly true that the various countries with which we are concerned adopted their own distinctive interpretations of the problem of economic organisation for most of the post-war period. However, over the last decade or so there has been considerable **convergence around the German social market** approach to the mixed economy. Most European countries naturally retain their own emphases, preferences and diversity, but the adoption of German leadership in key aspects of macro-economic management has led to the emergence of what increasingly resembles a 'European model'. The only 'alternative', if this is the right word, is represented by the British neo-liberal approach which, as we have seen, emphasises the market over the social. Some of the main differences between the two approaches is summarised in Table 6.2 below, which emphasises the interrelationship between the economic, social and political factors that determine the nature of a mixed economy.

The fundamental question for the future is whether the two models discussed above are compatible and can be fused over time into a single 'European model' that is capable of coping with the external challenges and that, as we have seen, face the European economies. Or, whether one approach is so superior to the other that it will eventually prevail. A third possibility is that the two approaches are so incompatible that the European economies will polarise, with the bulk of Europe continuing to integrate around the German model and the United Kingdom going its own way. The outcome will naturally depend on the political situation, particularly in the United Kingdom, as much as on the inherent superiority of one model over the other. After all, what is at stake is the kind of society in which people want to live. The balance of probabilities, and the preference of the authors, is clearly for the second solution. The latter is probably an outcome that is less than likely, given that all countries are engaged in a general process of movement towards more of the market, and that in many ways the future may well be about emphases rather than absolutes. We shall see.

Having examined some of the principal elements of unity and diversity in the economic preferences, organisation and policies of various European countries, we now return briefly to differences in economic performance. The general performance of the countries with which we are principally concerned has been alluded to throughout this book, and the reader should by now be aware of the basic shape of the 'league table' of post-war national performance (see the Statistical Appendix, and in particular the national income tables). In Chapter 12 we will return briefly to some of the aspects of national economic performance, and we will also attempt to make some connections between the diversity of national structures and policies and

**Table 6.2**   British and social market models of the mixed economy compared
*Source:* Adapted from Grilli *et al.* (1991)

| Characteristic | European social market | British capitalism |
|---|---|---|
| **Basic principle** | | |
| Dominant factor of production | partnership | capital |
| 'Public' tradition | high | low |
| Centralisation | medium | high |
| Reliance on price-mediated markets | medium | high |
| Supply relations | bureaucracy planned | arms-length price-driven |
| Industrial groups | high | low |
| Extent privatised | medium | high |
| **Financial system** | | |
| Market structure | bureaucracy committed | uncommitted marketised |
| Banking system | traditional regulated regional | advanced marketised centralised |
| Stock market | unimportant | very important |
| Required returns | medium | high |
| **Labour market** | | |
| Job security | high | low |
| Labour mobility | medium | medium |
| Labour/management | cooperative | adversarial |
| Pay differential | medium | large |
| Turnover | medium | medium |
| Skills | high | poor |
| Union structure | industry-wide | craft |
| Strength | high | low |
| **The firm** | | |
| Main goal | market share fulfilment | profits |
| Role top manager | consensus | boss-king hierarchy |
| Social overheads | high | medium, down |
| **Welfare system** | | |
| Basic principle | corporatist social democracy | mixed |
| Universal transfers | high | medium, down |
| Means-testing | low | medium, up |
| Degree education tiered by class | medium | high |
| Private welfare | low | medium, up |
| **Government policies** | | |
| Role of government | encompassing | strong adversarial |
| Openness to trade | quite open | open |
| Industrial policy | high | non-existent |
| Top income tax | high | medium |

national economic performance. Again, we shall stress the interdisciplinary nature of the latter, for political and social structures affect economic performance and vice versa. In this context, however, it is sufficient to note that in general socially regulated economies have performed better than those based more on neo-liberal free market principles.

This naturally has interesting implications for the new democracies that have emerged since the late 1980s in East/Central Europe. We will return briefly to these in Chapter 12. It is interesting to note here that these countries, having rejected communism, are now in the process of establishing market economies in somewhat of a hurry, encountering many fundamental problems in the process. For example, how does one privatise without the existence of a capital market? The question here concerns what type of market economy they should adopt: those based on the neo-liberal model, or on their own versions of the social market approach? It would seem that in general they are being pushed towards the former, although many countries still maintain some of the more enlightened aspects of previous social provision. It will be fascinating to see what finally emerges. The above should help to shed some light on the possible consequences of the choices that are now being made.

## Further reading

Bacon, R. and Eltis, W. (1976) *Britain's Economic Problem: too Few Producers?*, 2nd edn, London: Macmillan.

Bishop, M., Kay, J. and Mayer, C. (1994) *Privatisation and Economic Performance*, Oxford: Oxford University Press.

Bishop, M., Kay. J. and Mayer, C. (1995) *The Regulatory Challenge*, Oxford: Oxford University Press.

Boltho, A. (ed.) (1982) *The European Economy: Growth and Crisis*, Oxford: Oxford University Press.

Brouwer, F., Lintner, V. and Newman, M. (eds) (1994) *Economic Policy and the European Union*, London: Federal Trust.

Buxton, A., Chapman, P. and Temple, P. (eds) (1994) *Britain's Economic Performance*, London: Routledge.

Coates, K. and Barrett-Brown, M. (1993) *A European Recovery Programme*, Nottingham: Spokesman.

Corden, M. (1972) 'Monetary Integration' *Princeton Essays in International Finance* 73.

Dyker, D. (ed.) (1992) *The National Economies of Europe*, London: Longman.

Elstrin, S. and Holmes, P. (1983) *French Planning in Theory and Practice*, London: Allen & Unwin.

Fleming, M. (1971) 'On exchange rate unification' *Economic Journal* 81, 467–88.

Ginsborg, P. (1990) *A History of Contemporary Italy*, Harmondsworth: Penguin.

Grilli, V., Masciandro, D. and Tabellini, G. (1991) 'Political and monetary institutions and public financial policies in the industrial countries' *Economic Policy* 13, 428–45.

Hampden-Turner, C. and Trompenaars, A. (1994) *The Seven Cultures of Capitalism*, London: Piatkus.

Holland, S. (1983) *Out of Crisis*, Nottingham: Spokesman.

Holland, S. (1993) *The European Imperative*, Nottingham: Spokesman.

Hough, J. R. (1982) *The French Economy*, London: Croom Helm.

Hutton, W. (1995) *The State We're In*, London: Jonathan Cape.

Leaman, J. (1988) *The Political Economy of West Germany, 1945–1985*, London: Macmillan.

Lieberman, S. (1982) *The Contemporary Spanish Economy*, London: Allen & Unwin.

Lintner, V. and Mazey, S. (1996) *The European Community: Economic and Political Aspects*, Maidenhead: McGraw-Hill.

Majone, G. (ed.) (1990) *Deregulation of Regulation? Regulatory reform in Europe and the United States*, London: Pinter.

Mundell, R. A. (1951) 'A theory of optimum currency areas' *American Economic Review* 51, 657–65.

Oates, W. (1993) *Fiscal Federalism*, New York: Harcourt Brace Jovanovitch.

Padoa-Schioppa Kostoris, F. (1993) *Italy, the Sheltered Economy*, Oxford: Clarendon Press.

Somers, F. (ed.) (1991) *European Economies: A Comparative Study*, 2nd ed., London: Pitman.

Van Mourik, A. (1994) *Wages and European Integration*, Maastricht: BIV Publications.

World Bank (1993) *The East Asian Miracle*, Washington DC.

# Notes

1. See Hampden-Turner and Trompenaars, 1994 and Hutton, 1995.
2. Often referred to as the 'Butskellist consensus', after the Conservative and Labour politicians Butler and Gaitskell.
3. The proportion of any increases in national income that are spent on imported goods and services.
4. All the basic utilities: gas, water, electricity, the General Post Office, British Telecom (originally part of the GPO), British Airways, British Rail(ways), coal, steel, some freight carriers, British Petroleum, etc.
5. And which eventually broke down after grass roots resistance during the 'winter of discontent' of 1978–79.
6. Cynics would claim that Keynesian demand management resurfaces around election times!
7. According to this, Keynesian demand management designed to reduce unemployment merely has the effect of increasing inflation (by moving along the trade-off between inflation and unemployment that is postulated by the traditional Phillips curve and thus augmenting inflationary expectations), while failing to reduce unemployment (which in this model is determined microeconomically in the labour market – see Chapter 2). The traditional Phillips analysis thus only works in the short term, and the long-term Expectations Augmented Phillips curve is really a vertical straight line.
8. In fact, although there have been cuts in (particularly the higher) rates of income tax, there is evidence that the overall incidence of taxation in the United Kingdom has actually increased.
9. Although this has in fact remained a fairly constant proportion of GDP, largely because of the high levels of unemployment which the United Kingdom has experienced.
10. For example, trying to persuade 'Sid' to buy shares in British Telecom.
11. For example, OFTEL for telecommunication, OFWAT for water, OFGAS, etc. See Bishop *et al.* 1994, 1995 for an analysis of the economic results of some UK privatisations and indeed UK deregulation.
12. Although the UK government has shied away from overt privatisation of the National Health Service, since this would be likely to prove politically disastrous for them.
13. Some would say 'dismantlement of'.
14. Although an indirect effect of this might have been to recreate some of the lost social space – see below.
15. As well as reservations among some within the government itself. For example, the

Chancellor of the Exchequer Kenneth Clarke, in rejecting welfare cuts to fund pre-election tax cuts, is quoted as saying:

'I don't want to see the development of an underclass, where part of the population is dispossessed; a part that regards itself as not belonging to the aspirations and way of life of the rest of society.' (*Guardian*, 20.7.1995).

16. See Hutton, 1995 and Buxton, *et al.*, 1994, for example.
17. The much-vaunted deregulation of the City of London in the 1980s.
18. For example, is the control of inflation above all other economic objectives always the best policy for a country to pursue? Also, where do the objectives to be pursued by central banks originate? Are they not in some way or other the product of a political process at a specific point in time, and as such determined by the prevailing ideological climate of the time?
19. The extent to which the demand for money and the amount that people wish to borrow is responsive or otherwise to changes in rates of interest.
20. A situation where, as a result of falls in property prices, the loan taken out to buy property exceeds the market value of the property itself.
21. See Chapter 10.
22. For example, contested takeovers, so common in the United Kingdom, are vitually non-existent in social market countries.
23. The average pension for a German married couple in 1994 amounted to around 1600 ECU (±£1000) per month.
24. Up to 68 per cent in the first year, and up to 58 per cent thereafter.
25. Sometimes referred to as the 'para-state'.
26. As well German insistence that this model be adopted.
27. Cartels and restrictive practices are specifically against the law, while the behaviour of monopolies (*marktbeherrschende Unternnehmen*) is controlled to prevent abuse of dominant positions.
28. Given the reality of German leadership within the EU, many would argue that there is no effective choice involved here.
29. For details of the Austrian corporatist approach to industrial relations see Chapter 7.
30. See Lars Pettersson in Dyker, 1992. The competitive sector is mainly manufacturing based, containing such multinationals as Volvo and Saab.
31. Boom up to 1962, relative stagnation at high levels of prosperity from 1962–75, a mild boom at the end of the latter period, stagnation and relative crisis between 1975–82, boom between 1982–89, and stagnation from around 1989.
32. The protected sector was in any case a preferred place to work for many young Swedes, who increasingly eschewed technocratically based economic activity in favour of more pleasant and secure employment in the protected sector, even though earnings were more modest in the latter: a phenomenon that is also familiar in the United Kingdom.
33. But see Dyker, 1992.
34. For example, between 1974 and 1979 inflation in France averaged nearly 11 per cent, compared to 5 per cent in Germany over the same period.
35. See, for example, Elstrin and Holmes, 1983.
36. Ironically, despite the nationalist rhetoric of the period, between 1960 and 1980 the proportion of French output in foreign hands increased from 8 per cent to around 25 per cent, mainly as a result of US foreign direct investment.
37. See the Statistical Appendix.
38. The economist who was subsequently murdered by the Red Brigades.
39. If we take the example of the domestic 'white goods' industrial sector, in 1947 Candy were producing one washing machine a day, yet by 1967 they were producing one every

15 seconds. In 1947 Zanussi employed a mere 250 people. Between 1951 and 1967 annual production of fridges increased from 18 500 to 3 200 000, the third largest fridge output in the world after the United States and Japan (Ginsborg, 1990).

40. See the chapter by Paci in Dyker, 1992.

41. According to the Italian statistical agency ISTAT, in 1983 labour costs in large firms were 40 per cent greater than in small firms.

42. Who is discussed elsewhere in the book, but who established the Finninvest group of media and other interests before setting up the Forza Italia political party and becoming Prime Minister in 1994.

43. For a considerable period of time, workers who had been made redundant could turn up to the workplace, play cards all day, and go home vitually with a full wage packet. In this period Italy became known as the 'Pompeiian economy', its workers frozen into place like the statues of the famous Roman city.

44. A leftover from the Fascist era.

45. Often employment in the state sector has been used as a means of patronage and has been distributed according to political allegiances. The system of **lottizzazione**, has pervaded Italian society: the three trade union confederations are split on political lines (see Chapter 7), the three state TV channels are controlled by different political parties, for example.

46. Often these resources have been inappropriately used as a result of corruption, the Mafia, bureaucratic inefficiency and policy confusion. They have had mixed results: the south is now more prosperous than it was, and is no longer a major labour exporting area, but it is still much poorer than the north. Expressed in index numbers (Italy = 100), gross GDP per head in the south was 67.3 in 1987, while in the centre/north it was 118.8. Disaffection with the extent of the resources which the state has transferred to the Mezzogiorno, as well a degree of racism, has been partly responsible for the emergence of the seperatist Northern Leagues led by Umberto Bossi.

47. This function is largely performed by the family and by charitable bodies.

48. Although Italy has statistically had a very high participation rate in higher education, this has been largely a myth. Many have been working students taking many years to graduate, while being registered at a university is one way of avoiding military service.

49. For example, the proportion of Italian GNP which is spent on health is the third lowest in the OECD.

50. These investigations at first revealed widespread municipal corruption, for example in Milan, which came to be known as **tangentopoli** (bribesville), and then they implicated household names from all major political parties (except the old PCI) such as the Socialist Bettino Craxi and Giulio Andreotti, the doyen of the Christian Democrats and many times Prime Minister, who is accused of actually being a member of the Mafia. Thousands of people have been indicted and hundreds have ended up in jail. Even members of the new guard, such as Silvio Berlusconi, have been under investigation. There is is currently an attempt to compromise and call a halt to the investigations, which at one stage threatened to involve a large proportion of the Italian ruling class.

51. Of a population of 59 million, 19 million Italians receive pensions, and around half of these are invalidity pensions.

52. In particular periods social cohesion in Italy has been strained. For example, during the years following the *autunno caldo* of 1969, when Italian society was under challenge from a number of developments, including the terrorism of the Red Brigades and Fascist groups during the 1970s and early 1980s.

53. Which is now in decline, following the social changes that have occurred in Italy over the

last few years, including a decline in the Italian birth rate to 1.2 children per female – the lowest in the world.

54. And a steadily depreciating currency that has restored lost competitiveness.

55. These people make their living as **'vu cumprá'** (peddlers), agricultural labourers, windscreen washers etc., and often live in the bidonvilles that are mushrooming on the edge of many large towns. They sometimes have to suffer the racism of an indigenous population unused to black people. The attitude of the state to them was at first liberal (around 1 million were granted citizenship), but has lately become restrictive and protectionist, under pressure from some parts of the electorate and from other EU governments.

56. The *Economist* (9.9.1995) has referred to this as the 'Italian solution' to privatisation.

57. This and other aspects of the Italian reform process have been facilitated by rapid economic growth since the lira's exit from the ERM: the month-on-month rate of growth reached nearly 25 per cent in mid-1995. This might, however, merely represent a temporary 'quick-fix' following devaluation.

58. See Dyker, 1992 and Summers, 1994 for brief introductions to these economies.

# CHAPTER SEVEN

# European labour markets and industrial relations

## 7.1  Introduction

This chapter deals with an area that is of central importance to European societies, since the labour market is instrumental in determining the livelihood of most Europeans, and thus their life chances, their material standard of living and important aspects of the general quality of their lives. Labour market developments and policies increasingly both reflect and determine how European countries are facing the challenges of the present and indeed the future (see Chapter 5).

In this chapter we will outline the nature of labour market structures, developments and policies in a range of European countries, as ever emphasising the unity and diversity of experiences and approaches, and evaluating what has been most successful and holds the best prospects for the future. In this context we will examine the increasingly worrying problem of unemployment. We will then examine some aspects of comparative European industrial relations, and then some particular issues of labour market policy concerning migrant workers.

## 7.2  European labour markets and labour market policies

The basic principles of the neoclassical view of how labour markets function in a market economy was outlined in Chapter 2. It will be recalled that wage rates and the level of employment in a free market are determined by the interaction of the demand for labour (how many people employers wish to hire at various wage rates) and the supply of labour (how many people wish to work in various activities at different wage rates).[1]

Because of the central economic, political and social importance of labour markets, governments in Europe and elsewhere have consistently intervened in a particularly active way in their operation. Intervention in the labour market occurs in order to affect a range of outcomes, for example earnings levels and structures, employment volumes, conditions of employment and the quality of the workforce. Labour market policy is typically implemented by governments by means of legislative activities and by administrative mechanisms that use existing institutional structures. What emerges is a kind of regulatory framework within which the labour market operates. It is important to note that these systems of labour market regulation do not emerge solely as a result of actions on the part of governments, but also as a result of bargaining processes between employers and employees. It should be stressed that, as in other spheres, labour market policies and outcomes are fundamentally shaped by the economic and political climate in general, and in particular by the nature of the state and by the relative strength of labour (usually in the form of trade unions – see below) and capital, the two main actors in the labour market.

Thus, during the post-war period European countries have in essence experienced two distinct approaches to labour market policy and regulation, reflecting the changes in the ideological and policy-making climate which have taken place following the move from what Sengenberger (1984) and others have termed **welfare capitalism** to **free market capitalism**.[2]

## Welfare capitalism

**Welfare capitalism** was the dominant model in Europe up to the mid-1970s. Its features have been discussed elsewhere in the book (see Chapters 1 and 2 in particular); it is sufficient to point out here that these years were characterised by high economic growth, rising material prosperity and general agreement on how European economies should best be structured and managed: a mixed economy, with high degree of state intervention, of varying nature but based broadly on hands-on Keynesian principles. Production was predominantly based on Fordist mass production and Taylorist work practices (see Chapters 1 and 5), which created the conditions for the emergence of powerful labour organisations able to negotiate labour contracts at an industry-wide level, often covering the earnings and conditions of hundreds of thousands of workers at a time. This spawned labour market structures, practices and policies that were in essence both corporatist and interventionist.

**Corporatism** involved the participation of organised labour in decisions that affected not only the labour market but also the economy in general (see Chapter 3). Decisions would typically be made on a tripartite basis, involving employers, employees and the government. This was typified by the system of co-determinism in Austria and Germany and the 'beer and sandwiches at Number 10' style of decision making in the United Kingdom (see Chapter 6). Forms of corporatism were also to be found in other European countries such as Italy, the Benelux countries and (in arguably an extreme form, see Chapter 6 and below) Scandinavia. In France, however, practice was not explicitly corporatist, although implicitly the power of organised labour was of course taken into account in decision making. The essence of corporatism is a compromise between labour and capital: workers obtain rising living standards, improved working conditions and secure, stable and socially protected full time employment. In return they assure employers, often (notably in Germany) through legally binding agreements, cooperation in achieving stability, continuity of production, increases in productivity and the modernisation of production. As we have seen (Chapter 6) the compromise worked less satisfactorily in the United Kingdom than in other European countries.

**Intervention** by governments in the labour market had the basic objective of sheltering labour as much as possible from the worst aspects of the free market. It took a variety of forms, including:

(a)  setting minimum wages,[3] for example the RMI (previously SMIC) in France and the activities of the Wages Councils in the United Kingdom;[4]
(b)  indexation of wages, for example the *scala mobile* introduced in Italy after the *autunno caldo* (see Chapter 6);
(c)  direct intervention in earnings determination, notably through the incomes policies that were adopted, for example by the 1970s Labour governments in Great Britain,[5] and more starkly and directly by the Scandinavian system of wage determination (see Chapter 6);
(d)  regulation to promote social protection for employees, such as the compulsory contributory social insurance shemes and the compulsory redundancy payments introduced in most countries;
(e)  regulation to set minimum standards for conditions of employment in areas such as job security, pensions, maternity pay and even rights to education (in Italy);
(f)  facilitating the acquisition of human capital, through the provision of education, training and apprenticeship schemes;
(g)  measures to promote the geographical mobility of labour, often as part of a regional policy; and
(h)  on a macroeconomic level, direct influence over the level of employment by the use of Keynesian policies of demand management (see Chapters 2 and 5).

Labour markets under welfare capitalism provided many advantages for the populations of Europe, not the least of which was full employment, and generally (but to varying extents) succeeded in facilitating economic progress. However, they also resulted in high wage (and non-wage) costs, and in European labour markets that were characterised by significant **rigidities**. Shared decision making and active intervention by the state reduce competition in the labour market and therefore the possibility and flexibility of downward adjustment, i.e. the ability of employers to reduce wages, lay off employees and reduce the non-wage social costs of employment in response to competition and changes in demand patterns.[6] This in turn can damage economic performance, to the extent that it may slow down the response of economies to changes in the parameters within which they have to operate.

The nature of labour market rigidities varies between European countries, and its extent is difficult to quantify. Lane (1989), in a study of Britain, Germany and France, suggests that the 'quantitative' rigidity of labour[7] was greater in France and in Germany than in the United Kingdom. In France this developed as a result of state controls over large-scale redundancies that were introduced in 1969, extended in 1974 and by legislation in 1973 and 1975. In Germany, co-determination and the involvement of works councils in the redundancy process ensured considerable job security, as did the 1972 amendment of the Works Constitution Act. In both countries employers took to making long-term employment plans rather than short-term adjustments to their levels of employment. In the United Kingdom, despite a legal framework laid down by the Redundancy Payments Act of 1965 and by the

Employment Protection Act of 1978, employers found it much easier to lay off workers and did so much more often. The Scandinavian model of the mixed economy (Chapter 6) ensured high levels of quantitative rigidity, while in Italy rigidity in the formal sector of the economy became so great in the 1970s (notably through the operation of the Cassa Integrazione Guadagni – see Chapter 6) that it came to be known as the 'Pompeiian economy', frozen in place like the statues in the Roman city overcome by lava from Mount Vesuvius. External rigidity in Germany was counterbalanced by high levels of flexibility in the deployment of labour within firms. To an extent this was also the case in France, but the British economy was characterised by significant internal rigidities, typified by an inflexible demarcation of jobs. All economies experienced significant wage rigidities as a result of factors such as indexation and industry-wide pay bargaining. In the United Kingdom this led to wages rising consistently faster than productivity, while in Germany there were greater pay differentials and lower wage inflation. The social costs of employment rose rapidly everywhere, particularly in France and in Scandinavia.

## Free market capitalism

While the post-war boom continued, no one was unduly worried by these labour market rigidities. In addition some European countries, notably Germany, used migrant workers as the flexible part of their workforce: hiring them in times of labour shortage and sending them home in times of falling demand.[8] However, the deterioration in general economic conditions in the 1970s precipitated a change from welfare capitalism to free market capitalism; their removal or reduction became a prominent part of the new (neo-liberal) economic agenda. The principal economic features of free market capitalism have been discussed in Chapters 1, 2 and 5, but in essence neo-liberalism involves a general freeing of markets and a reduction in the involvement of governments in the functioning of the economic system. The reasons for the shift in emphasis towards this form of the mixed economy have also been discussed, but of particular importance in this context are increased external competition, particularly from the NICs,[9] as well as the emergence of new technologies. It should also be remembered that the neo-liberal free market agenda has been applied with greater enthusiasm and purity in some European countries (particularly the United Kingdom) than in others. Hand in hand with this new phase in the approach to the mixed economy has come mass unemployment (see below), that has both partly resulted from market capitalism and has also greatly facilitated its operation.

As far as the labour market is concerned, market capitalism has manifested itself in distinct changes in approach and policy on the part of governments. These have included:

(a) Particularly in the United Kingdom, a retreat from corporatism and a reduction in the influence of organised labour in decision-making processes within and without firms. The power of organised labour itself has been restricted by rising unemployment, falling trade union membership and (in the United Kingdom) legislative change and failed industrial disputes such as the miners' strike of the 1980s. Elsewhere in Europe, the tradition of cooperation in employment affairs is on the wane but remains distinctly stronger.

(b)   A process of **deregulation** of the labour market. This has had the effect of removing or reducing legislative and other controls over the way that labour markets operate in determining wage levels, employment levels, employment rights and so on. An example is the abolition of Wages Councils in the United Kingdom and the retreat from indexation in Italy.

(c)   Privatisation, which has affected the labour market by permitting the introduction of new labour practices (see below) into large parts of what was previously the relatively protected public sector.[10] Where it has proved politically impossible to privatise (for example, in the case of the British NHS), governments have attempted to simulate similar effects by introducing internal markets.

(d)   A retreat from macroeconomic intervention designed to impact on the labour market by the use of Keynesian demand management policies. Labour markets are affected heavily, as we have seen, by the 'supply-side' policies (see Chapter 2) of deregulation and tax reduction that are now in favour. They have also been affected by the various employment subsidies, apprenticeship schemes and job creation schemes that have facilitated the labour market changes discussed below by often providing firms with cheap labour.

This change in the policy climate *vis-à-vis* labour markets has varied between countries in its nature and intensity (see Chapter 6) with, as ever, the United Kingdom the leading enthusiast for the free market. The United Kingdom's position is typified by the Conservative government's refusal to accept the 'social chapter' of the Maastricht Treaty (see Section 7.5 below). These relatively modest proposals for minimum social and other standards in employment would be a levelling down in most European countries. For the United Kingdom, however, they represent a levelling up, and some UK employers fear that increased social overheads would reduce their competitiveness. Nevertheless, the change in policy climate has both reflected and in turn facilitated a marked change in employment practices among European employers. This change has in turn reflected the adoption of new cost-cutting production methods and practices which employers have felt obliged to adopt in response to changes in the parameters within which they function (see Chapter 5) and in particular (as we have seen) in response to increased external competition and to changes in technology. These new practices have included:

(a)   'downsizing', that is shedding labour, introducing more efficient work practices and new technologies, both of which require the use of a smaller number of employees;

(b)   attempting to cut wages and to reduce the social provision in work contracts, partly by some of the methods discussed below;

(c)   devolving parts of the production process outside the firm. This has mainly taken the form of subcontracting by large firms. Smaller firms can often produce specific items more cheaply than larger ones by avoiding the overheads of a large firm, by paying lower wages to their non-unionised employees who are not covered by the collective agreements of the primary sector, and by taking advantage of the incentives and subsidies that are often available to small firms;

(d)   the increased use of part-time workers and workers on fixed-term contracts. These are regarded as more flexible workers, since they are[11] less expensive than full-time workers and are less protected by labour market regulation and therefore easier to dispense with in times of falling demand;

(e)   an increase in 'management culture',[12] managers using new management techniques and styles, sometime imported from the United States, having greater freedom in how they wish to deploy labour and capital, and making decisions unhindered by such practices as the need to consult other actors in the work process. With the latter, of course, comes a reduction in workplace democracy.

All this has naturally changed the **nature of work**, more so in countries such as the United Kingdom that have adopted the market capitalism model with the most enthusiasm. To begin with, there is now as we have mentioned large-scale unemployment in all European countries, the presence of which has been one of the factors that have made increasingly insecure workforces accept the changes discussed above. There has been an increase in part-time and fixed term employment. Proponents of the dual labour market approach (see Section 7.5 below) would regard this as an extension of the relative size of the secondary labour market. Those who are in full-time work are often insecure about their future employment prospects,[13] less socially protected, paid lower wages, have to work harder and have less control over their work environment.[14]

Also important to the nature of work in contemporary Europe is the increase in what Piore and Sabel (1984) refer to as **flexible specialisation** in production. Again, this has occurred in response to the changes in firms' external environment discussed above. Essentially it consists of a move away from Fordist and Taylorist forms of production and work organisation, based on mass production of standardised products and using unskilled labour and specific and inflexible machinery. Europe is often no longer competitive in this form of production, having been displaced in world markets by the NICs, and in any case many domestic European markets are to an extent saturated with this type of product. In its place has come (to an extent) production which is customised, frequently of high quality and based on short production runs. This has been made possible by the emergence of new technologies such as Computer Aided Design and Manufacturing (CAD/CAM), Flexible Manufacturing Systems (FMS) and robots, which enable production to be customised quickly and cheaply, removing the need for long production runs and diminishing the importance of economies of scale. In terms of the labour market, flexible specialisation has meant a movement towards the utilisation of skilled labour organised flexibly along traditional 'craft' lines,[15] in contrast with the Taylorist system of using unskilled labour to perform highly specialised, repetitive, low discretion tasks which offer low job satisfaction and often led to alienation.

Some form of flexible specialisation is often seen as one way in which European countries can replace the competitiveness they have lost in Fordist production. It is dificult to estimate the extent to which production is now organised along these lines in contemporary Europe, although interesting examples of it can be found, for example in central Italy (see Chapter 6). Lane (1989) suggests that in Germany, France and Britain it is only an emergent trend rather than a fully fledged alternative to mass production. The impetus for its introduction has been technology-led in Germany, whereas in the United Kingdom it has been precipitated by changes in labour market regulation and in the industrial relations system. In France the emergence of manpower with new skills is taken to have been the impetus for change. Lane also suggests that the impediments to change (in terms of management methods, education and training and industrial relations systems[16]) in the direction of flexible specialisation are considerably greater in Britain and France than they are in Germany, which has a highly educated and skilled workforce and will therefore have a head start in this area.

In any case, the changes to the nature of work induced by these emerging production methods seem likely to continue. They will clearly have to be taken into account in the formulation of employment policy into the twenty-first century; so must the well-documented secular shift in European countries away from agriculture and manufacturing and towards services.[17] Finally, one should mention in this context the trend towards the increased 'delocalisation' production. Manufacturing has long been subject to delocalisation but now technological change, and in particular information technology (IT), has increased the tradeability of service activities, thus creating the prospect of the 'global service village' (Soete, 1994).

## 7.3  Unemployment in Europe

As we have mentioned, one of the most important features of the the 1980s and 1990s has been the emergence of mass unemployment in Europe. In the 1960s unemployment in Europe hovered around 2–3 per cent (virtually full employment). It then increased steadily throughout the 1970s, and since 1981 it has never been less than 8 per cent.[18] In 1994, according to official statistics, the rate of unemployment in the EU as a whole had risen to 12 per cent of the labour force, with approximately 18 million people on the dole. Figure 7.1 shows unemployment rates in various European countries according to the OECD standardised definition (which is a useful measure since national definitions of unemployment vary and often tend to underestimate the true level[19]).

It can be seen from Fig. 7.1 that Spain has the highest rate of unemployment in Europe at 23.4 per cent. Of the larger European countries, France has the highest rate of unemployment (around 12 per cent), while Germany has the lowest (around 6 per cent). Britain's unemployment rate was about 10 per cent.[20] Much of the unemployment in European countries is now long term:[21] in Spain 54 per cent, in France 36.1 per cent, in Italy 58.2 per cent, in the United Kingdom 35.4 per cent, in the Netherlands 44 per cent, in Germany 46.3 per cent (OECD, 1993 and Symes 1995 – in Sweden long-term unemployment is still low at only 8 per cent of the total). Furthermore, the incidence of unemployment in Europe has a regional bias and is greatest in women, the young and ethnic minorities, all of whom are more likely to be unemployed than prime-age white males.[22] For example, according to Eurostat the

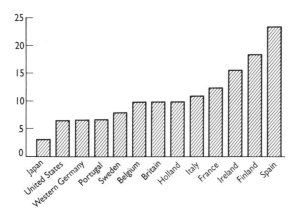

**Figure 7.1**   European unemployment 1993
         *Source:* OECD.

unemployment rate for women in the EC 12 countries in 1990 was 11.2 per cent, compared with 6.6 per cent for men.[23] Unemployment rates for the young (under 25) in the EC 12 countries were 16.5 per cent in 1990, compared with total unemployment of 8.5 per cent. Again there are national variations – in Germany youth unemployment (4.5 per cent) was actually lower than total unemployment (5.1 per cent).

There is naturally considerable debate as to the causes of such unemployment, and the debate has tended to polarise along familiar neo-liberal versus (broadly) Keynesian lines. During the Keynesian heyday, unemployment was thought to consist of four types:

1. **Seasonal** unemployment, caused by seasonal differences in economic activity in various industries such as tourism.
2. **Frictional or search** unemployment, consisting of people between jobs.
3. **Structural** unemployment, caused by such factors as the decline of industries and changes in technologies.
4. **Keynesian, cyclical or demand deficient** unemployment, caused by a level of aggregate demand in the economy insufficient to produce full employment (see Chapter 2).

The emphasis was on the latter cause, and solutions accordingly emphasised demand management as a means of securing full employment. More recently, neo-liberals have tended to talk in terms of **voluntary** and **involuntary** unemployment, most unemployment consisting of the former, since if labour markets worked according to the free market model (see Chapter 2) and people were willing to work at (lower) market wages, then there would be no such thing as unemployment, or at any rate large-scale unemployment. This approach has referred to the **natural** rate of unemployment or the **non-accelerating inflation rate of unemployment (NAIRU)** which is determined by the extent of imperfections or rigidities in the labour market.[24] Neo-liberals have therefore concentrated their solutions for unemployment on measures designed to reduce labour market rigidities, to reduce wages and to increase incentives. Hence deregulation, trade union 'reform', cuts in unemployment benefit and so on have been the order of the day, as have been supply-side policies such as tax cuts (usually for the better off). An interesting aside here concerns the fact that, in a Keynesian world, reducing wages and particularly those of the lower-paid can actually reduce employment by reducing aggregate demand. The approach one adopts is therefore crucial, for the wrong analysis of the causes of unemployment can be tragically counter-productive.

Nevertheless, the big increase in unemployment in Europe over the last two decades has been fundamentally precipitated by changes in a number of structural features:

(a)   The peculiarities of birth rates and age structures of the population in some countries, which have at various times increased the labour force disproportionately. An example are the 'baby boomers' who reached working age in the 1970s and 1980s.

(b)   Increased labour force participation rates, particularly among women. Between 1973 and 1990 female participation rates in France increased from 50.1 per cent to 56.6 per cent, in Germany from 50.3 per cent to 57 per cent, in the United Kingdom from 53.2 per cent to 64.8 per cent, in Spain from 33.4 per cent to 41.1 per cent, and in the Netherlands from 29.2 per cent to 53 per cent (OECD). These last two points (a and b) have fundamentally meant that there has been an increase in the overall **supply of labour**, requiring an increase in employment just to keep unemployment from rising. This naturally means that increases in GDP are no longer necessarily accompanied by growth in employment.

(c)   The introduction of new technologies which almost invariably mean fewer people are needed to perform the same tasks.

(d)   Increased competition from outside the Continent, and particularly from the Pacific Rim countries, in relatively labour-intensive types of production. This has particularly affected blue-collar employment in Europe.

(e)   The secular change that has occurred from the primary and secondary sectors of the economy into the tertiary sector. This has often resulted in regional and industrial mismatches between the supply and demand for labour.

(f)   The change from a welfare capitalism approach to labour markets to a free market capitalism approach (see 7.2 above). Points c–f have been factors which have basically tended to reduce or limit the growth in the overall **demand for labour**.

The fact is that in contemporary Europe unemployment has become an intractable problem, which must clearly be tackled if we are to avoid the creation of an underclass in Europe. We have seen that there is no consensus on the best way forward, although for the moment it is neo-liberal views that tend to prevail, particularly in the United Kingdom. It seems clear that free market solutions at the very least need to be supplemented by more interventionist forms of policy, for example by public works, widespread investment in human capital and job creation (particularly) for the most vulnerable groups in society. It also seems clear that there must be an increasingly supranational dimension to any solutions for unemployment, given the limits to the economic sovereignty and power of the individual European nation states (see Chapter 5), and given the need to avoid competitive beggar-my-neighbour employment creation policies between European countries.[25] The debate on the best way forward for employment policy is one, albeit important, aspect of the broader underlying issue of how best to organise European societies in order to meet the challenges of the future.

## 7.4  Comparative industrial relations

This section aims to provide an overview of the situation of trade unionism in Europe. There has been a clear reduction in the influence of the trade unions throughout this period in most of the countries we shall examine, but there are some countries, such as Denmark, where trade union membership has actually increased during the 1980s. Many governments have pursued a neo-liberal policy that increased the direct intervention of the state in all aspects of industrial relations. The best example of this process has been the United Kingdom, where the Conservative government has introduced a range of measures designed to reduce and in some cases remove altogether the role and influence of the trade unions. We begin, however, with those countries where unions are considered part and parcel of the political and social culture.

Countries where corporatism in terms of tripartite approaches to organisation and resolution of economic and social issues is at its most developed (see above and Chapter 3). The best examples of this situation are the Scandinavian countries, as well as Austria, Belgium and Ireland, then the particular case of Germany, followed by France, Italy, Spain and Portugal, and then the United Kingdom and the Netherlands.

### The context

There have been three main changes since the 1970s in the area of industrial relations:

1.   The change in the relationship between the economy and the amount and nature of work, with consequences such as mass and long-term unemployment, the division of the labour market into secure and insecure employment sectors and particularly the increase in the number of part-time casual jobs, mainly done by women (see above and Chapter 11, Section 11.5).

2.   The role of the state has been reduced in the provision of social policy. The effect of this on public expenditure has been to cut many areas of welfare, including unemployment and sickness benefits (these benefits are sometimes referred to as the 'social wage').

3.   Finally, more automated technology has replaced human beings in many production areas causing unemployment, and led to different forms of production methods (see Chapter 5). This has led to more decentralised decision-making (local) and at the same time led to the globalisation of the economy, where firms can produce their goods anywhere in the world. In many traditional industrialised economies, there has been a huge shift from manufacturing to services sector employment. More than half the workforce in the EU is now engaged in this sector, except in Greece and Portugal.

The experience for West Europeans has been the internationalisation of their economies and societies into supranational spaces equipped with a corresponding infrastructure of ever more integrated social, legal and employment structures.[26]

The effect on trade unions, their membership levels and practice, has been enormous. Table 7.1 indicates the relative proportion of the workforce that is unionised.

**Table 7.1**  Trade unions in the European Union

| Country | (percentage) | Type of union |
|---|---|---|
| Austria | 47% | Craft-based |
| Belgium | 55% | Ideologically and religiously divided: Christian and socialist |
| Denmark | 80% | Craft-based |
| Finland | 72% | Craft-based |
| France | 10% | Ideologically divided: communist and socialist |
| Germany | 34% | 17 industry unions (craft-based). Largest in Germany and the world is IG Metall, covers those in manufacturing industry c. 3.4 m members. |
| Greece | 25% | Ideologically divided: communist and socialist |
| Ireland | 53% | Craft-based |
| Italy | 39% | Ideologically and religiously divided: Democratic left (communist), socialist and Christian democrat. |
| Luxembourg | 50% | Ideologically divided: socialist and Christian democrat |
| Netherlands | 25% | Ideologically and religiously divided: Catholic, liberal and socialist |
| Portugal | 30% | Ideologically divided: communist and socialist |
| Spain | 12% | Ideologically divided: Communist and socialist |
| Sweden | 86% | Craft-based |
| UK | 33% | Craft-based |

*Source*: ETUI Trade Union Membership in Western Europe (Brussels, 1993) and Lecher (1994), p. 91.
*Comment*: In those countries where there has been a strong communist leadership of trade unions, ideological (communist vs. socialist) and religious (Catholic vs. communist) divides have determined union membership. France's exceptionally low level of unionisation is partly explained by the presence of 'in-house unions'.

Women's share of total union membership is highest in the Scandinavian countries, at about 50 per cent of total union members, followed by the United Kingdom with 38 per cent, France with 30 per cent, Germany 25 per cent and the Netherlands 18 per cent.

Table 7.1 indicates the high level of unionisation in most of the Scandinavian countries. The nature of the employer–union cooperation has meant that despite high levels of unemployment, social protection has survived. These countries, together with Austria, Belgium and to a certain extent Germany and Ireland, have developed a political culture where trade unions exist in a framework of partnership with other social partners, notably the employers and government, rather than in antagonism which characterises industrial relations elsewhere. This is not to say that strikes never take place in those countries, but one feature of the period since the early 1980s is the decline in the rate of disputes overall and by sector, as Figs 7.2, 7.3 and 7.4 show, particularly in the cases of the United Kingdom, Finland, Denmark and Italy. This can be explained in the main by the growth in unemployment leading to the fear of

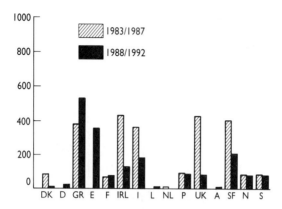

**Figure 7.2** Days of work lost per 1000 workers: total
Source: Eurostat.

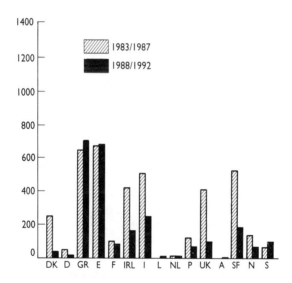

**Figure 7.3** Days of work lost per 1000 workers: industry
Source: Eurostat.

losing a job and so less industrial militancy. Partly also, some governments, as in the United Kingdom, have introduced legislation to restrict the scope for industrial action. There are, however, exceptions to this decline of union action, as the cases of Sweden, Greece and to a certain extent Spain indicate.

Neo-liberal policies were introduced by the Belgian government during the 1980s, but this has not led to any great decline in the influence of the trade unions or a massive drop in membership, which has been the effect in the United Kingdom. There are three reasons for this continued importance of trade unions in Belgium: first the trade unions, despite their religious divisions, managed to stay united and produce

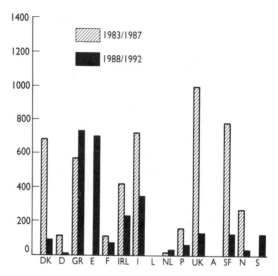

**Figure 7.4**  Days of work lost per 1000 workers: services
*Source: Eurostat.*

an alternative economic programme that was generally popular throughout the country; secondly, the notion of joint employer–employee collective bargaining with a government-appointed independent chairperson is well embedded within the political culture of industrial relations, and has survived the neo-liberal onslaught. Finally, the trade unions enjoy a special role in terms of receiving additional social benefits and in being exclusively responsible for paying out unemployment benefit.[27]

The same experience of a corporatist approach to industrial relations and wider issues of economic and social planning is a key feature of Austrian political culture. The system of 'social partnership' (*Sozialpartnerschaft*) is evident in the role of the four main interest associations.[28] An important feature of this set-up and that of the other 'corporatist' states is the regulatory role that these peak organisations are expected to play. This means that once an agreement is reached within the various fora, then all parties are obliged to accept the decisions collectively reached.

Recent experience in Ireland has demonstrated the growing nature of attempts to reinvigorate a framework of social partnership, after a period of recession and neo-liberal policies that effectively broke the corporatist consensus of the 1970s. In 1987 employers and unions agreed on a Programme for National Recovery (PNR) which was followed in January 1991 by a more widespread agreement that included govern-ment on a Programme for Economic and Social Progress (PESP), covering a wide range of social and economic issues. However, the attempt to construct a comprehensive and centralised system of national collective bargaining has come up against the particular nature of Ireland's political history, in terms of its political cleavages (see Chapter 8, Section 3), and the emergence of new political parties such as the Labour Party. This has meant that strong local pressures exist that affect the overall nationally negotiated agreements, which in turn contain more 'market-driven rules'.[29]

Germany's system of industrial relations, that has led many writers to characterise it as the model of consensus, has been seriously affected by the effects of unemployment and particularly the whole process of unification. There have beeen a number of increasingly bitter disputes and several large-scale strikes, as the trade union movement attempts to counter the effects of the recession and the cost of unification. Nevertheless there are strong elements of corporatism within the system, reflected in the whole programme of Concerted Action (*Konzertierte Aktion*). This process results in extensive consultation with all the social partners, and was particularly marked during the coalition government led by the SPD between 1969–82, when a whole series of round table discussions took place between the leading social partners (*Soziale Gesprächsrunde*).

The unions have been organised since 1945 into unitary trade unions, covering various sectors of the economy such as manufacturing, the service sector and mining, and there have been very few inter-union wrangles over membership recruitment and demarcation disputes which have been a debilitating feature of British industrial relations. There are 16 sector unions which are members of the DGB (*Deutscher Gewerschaftsbund* – equivalent to the British TUC), including the Police Trade Union. The employers are similarly organised into federation groups, which has led to the development of these large and concentrated sector groups, centralised bargaining covering a large number of employees.

The most important employers' confederations are the BDI (*Bundesverband der Deutschen Industrie*), covering employers in the major manufacturing sectors such as car production and food production, and the BDA (*Bundesvereinigung der Deutschen Arbeitgeberverbände*), which coordinates practically all German employers' organisations, about 760 in total. Then there are three smaller federal groups: the *Deutsche Industrie-und Handelstag*, coordinating the various chambers of commerce, the *Zentralverband des Deutschen Handwerks*, coordinating craft groups, and finally the *Deutscher Bauernverband e. V.* which represents more than 90 per cent of all Germany's farmers.[30]

Two key elements in German industrial relations are first the separation between the trade unions and the elected workplace representatives on the works councils, and then the comprehensive codification of how disputes should be managed. During collective bargaining disputes can arise between a nationally negotiated industry-wide agreement and individual works agreements from works councils. Furthermore, unions have the right to strike whereas works councils' duty is to maintain industrial peace.

A classic feature of the German system is this whole process of codetermination (*Mitbestimmung*) via the works' councils, which aims to create the framework for a consensus approach to the resolution of industrial disputes. This highly legalised form of industrial relations has meant that the government has not intervened too directly in the process of collective bargaining unlike, for example, in the United Kingdom where such intervention is frequent and intrusive, as the signalworkers' dispute of 1994 indicated. The whole emphasis of the system is to reduce tensions and channel disputes into legal resolutions, hence the crucial role played by lawyers within the system. However, there has been increasing interference by government in negotiations on pay, conditions and the length of the working week in terms of the situation of the former East Germany (new federal states).

The threat to the consensus and stability of the industrial relations scene in Germany stems from the government's policies of neo-liberalism and the heavy costs of unification. As the global effects of increased competition become more evident, there are increasing pressures on governments to reduce production costs. Numerous measures have been attempted from reducing wage increases, cutting the social wage (i.e. unemployment, sickness and other benefits) and direct reductions on unions' powers. In Germany, the government has launched a campaign against the 'pampered' status of employees, arguing that Germany's industrial competitiveness is threatened by its high labour and attendant costs compared to the lower costs of production in the East/Central European states and elsewhere. The *Deutsche Industrie-und Handelstag* published a report in 1993 indicating that in a survey of leading employers, most indicated that they were going to transfer production to peripheral states and overseas to avoid high costs in Germany. Despite these policies there has been a minimal loss of members in West Germany compared to the United Kingdom and France, but the effect of unemployment in the new federal states has caused an overall loss of members.[31]

Trade unions in France, Italy and Spain are divided more or less on ideological and religious grounds and share similar problems in terms of organisation and influence. In France a coherent and widespread national approach to collective bargaining has not really developed, a result of ideological differences, lack of coordination between various levels and a hostile employer attitude to the role of trade unions, resulting in frequent conflictual situations developing.[32] Collective bargaining tends to take place at company level where the real negotiating is done by works committees (so-called 'house' unions), which have no trade union status. Citroën, for example, has a large such 'house' union with whom most of the negotiating takes place.[33]

The debate between the left and the right in France has turned on whether bargaining should take place at local or industry level. During the 1980s the trend was for more and more local bargaining, a trend which was apparent all over Europe. However, after 1988 the Rocard Government, tried increasingly to promote collective bargaining and some employers' organisations, including the employers' confederation, the CNPF, have been in favour of industry-wide agreements as a more harmonious way of restructuring their industries. The socialist-led CFDT has also been influential at the European level in promoting the development of measures contained in the social chapter, including the German-influenced idea of works councils, and it has been supported by the CNPF which has taken a more progressive role at the supranational level than the national level.

Italy has a much higher level of unionisation than France, although similar ideological divides, but has suffered a steady decline in members for all three main unions. There were periods of tripartite cooperation until the mid-1980s, but organised labour is now forming alliances to the Northern League and the *Alleanza Nazionale*. In July 1993 *Confindustria*, the employers' confederation, the three main TU confederations and the government agreed a new structure for collective bargaining, with industry-level bargaining scheduled to take place every 4 years.

Spain was divided between the UGT (socialist) and the CC.OO (Communist) who led the General Strike in December 1988. There was, however, loss of support for both trade union organisations in the 1980s as the UGT was perceived to be too close to PSOE and and the CC.OO too close to the Communist Party. After 1988 the trade unions combined in order to challenge the PSOE government. The General Strike in the autumn of 1988 was an attempt to force the government to call a halt to its neo-liberal policies of wage restraint and welfare cutbacks.

The trade unions have accepted new legislation for maintenance of essential services during industrial action in return for the establishment of an Economic and Social Council in 1992, and the establishment of works councils (modelled on similar councils in Germany). However, the low level of unionisation in Spain effectively means that non-union workers dominate these councils.

In January 1994 another General Strike was called by UGT and CC.OO to protest at PSOE's neo-liberal policy and in favour of employment and solidarity. The unions challenged the new labour market reforms, which would increase casualisation of the labour market particularly for young people, and sanction payments below minimum wage level.[34]

The CGTP-IN (communist) is the largest and most representative confederation in Portugal but it is the only major union in western Europe not represented in the ETUC. There are two other unions the UGT, set up by the socialist party and the neo-liberal social democratic party (PSD) formed in 1978. In Greece, the development of independent trade unions has been hampered by their incorporation by the state during the period of the military dictatorship between 1967–73. The presence of this kind of 'state syndicalism' has endured, particularly within the socialist trade union.

The system of industrial relations in the United Kingdom has been been in many ways the complete opposite of that in Germany. Until 1982 British unions enjoyed immunity from the law, and rules governing collective bargaining have been loosely defined and established by custom and practice. Agreements were not legally binding, and workers had few legally guaranteed rights. British unions operate on a variety of bases: craft, industry, general and white collar, with the result that there have traditionally been large numbers of unions (up to 113 affiliated to the TUC in the 1970s), and in addition multi-unionism in many workplaces. Bargaining has shifted in recent years from industry level to a more decentralised basis, usually in the form of plant bargaining. Organisation at plant level has centred around the system of shop stewards, while at a national level the Trades Union Congress (TUC) has been the sole umbrella body. This system is complex and ambiguous. It has been essentially conflictual in nature, and up to the 1980s precipitated levels of industrial action well above the European average.

In line with the general shift from welfare capitalism towards free market capitalism, there have been attempts at fundamental reform of the British industrial relations system by the Conservative governments of the 1980s, which have been facilitated by a considerable drop in union membership, largely as result of industrial decline in the United Kingdom during this period. The Employment Acts of 1980 and 1982 attempted to restrict union rights in areas such as picketing, the closed shop and secondary action, as well as rendering unions legally liable for damages in cases of illegal action, and introducing large fines for contempt of court. The Trade Union Act 1984 introduced compulsory strike ballots and rules for the election of union officials. As important as changes in the legal framework has been the government's willingness to take on powerful unions in direct confrontations such as the steelworkers' strike, the miners' strike and the Grunwick dispute in the 1980s. British unions are now considerably less influential and the frequency of industrial disputes is far lower, although this is probably due as much to lower membership, unemployment and the introduction of new practices by employers (for example the no-strike agreements introduced by Japanese multinationals locating in the United Kingdom) as to trade union reform. The United Kingdom is still a long way from a cooperative system of industrial relations.

## 7.5  Immigrants in the labour market

We called for workers, human beings came instead

MAX FRISCH

The period of reconstruction in western Europe during the post-war period necessitated the import of large numbers of migrant labour. The United Kingdom, France and the Netherlands relied on their existing and former colonies as the major source of that labour, while Germany initially relied on the influx of refugees from its former territories in the East, and then signed bilateral agreements with Turkey, Greece and Yugoslavia to satisfy its labour needs. The availability of this source of cheap labour, young, fit and willing to do the jobs at low wages that the indigenous workers were not prepared to do, played a crucial role in creating the high level of economic growth enjoyed by most countries in the period up to 1973 (Kindleberger, 1967; Barnabé, 1988). The presence of these populations has had enormous economic, political and social effects in western Europe (see also Chapter 4, Section 4.5 and Chapter 11, Section 11.6).

As far as the European Union is concerned, provisions within the Treaty of Rome (Articles 48–51) and subsequent regulations and directives provided for the free movement of labour and other factors within the Common Market. Apart from some migration from the Mezzogiorno to Germany and small-scale cross border movements along the French/German and Benelux borders, the effect of these provisions in terms of impact on labour flows has been minimal.[35] Most of the major labour flows have been from outside the Community and subject to different political and economic regulation (Miller, 1981; Edye, 1987). Table 7.2 shows the number of foreign workers in the EC 12 countries to 1992. Although overall figures appear low, the significant aspect of foreign workers in the EU, both EU-nationals and non-EU nationals, lies in their relatively younger age, which means they are more likely to be economically active.

In the EU as a whole the breakdown of the foreign population shows that 52 per cent of that population is made up of workers (Table 7. 3). Table 7.4 indicates the four most common nationalities in a selection of member states. It is interesting to note

***Table 7.2*** Number of foreign worker, 1983–92 (1000)
Source: Eurostat

| Country | 1983 | 1984 | 1985 | 1986 | 1987 | 1988 | 1989 | 1990 | 1991 | 1992 |
|---|---|---|---|---|---|---|---|---|---|---|
| EUR 12 | 4776 | 4811 | 4869 | 4688 | 4946 | 4893 | 4999 | 5123 | 5271 | 5931 |
| Belgium | 246 | 229 | 209 | 244 | 217 | 216 | 218 | 236 | 243 | 271 |
| Denmark | 37 | 38 | 40 | 38 | 38 | 36 | 44 | 45 | 53 | 49 |
| Germany | 2024 | 2063 | 1966 | 1970 | 2044 | 1937 | 2143 | 2310 | 2484 | 2836 |
| Greece | 24 | 23 | 24 | 20 | 20 | 24 | 21 | 23 | 30 | 44 |
| Spain | : | : | : | : | 37 | 35 | 34 | 33 | 49 | 69 |
| France | 1332 | 1383 | 1344 | 1268 | 1237 | 1271 | 1313 | 1287 | 1253 | 1230 |
| Ireland | 26 | 27 | 26 | 25 | 26 | 28 | 27 | 29 | 32 | 32 |
| Italy | : | : | : | : | : | : | : | : | : | 188 |
| Luxembourg | 43 | 44 | 46 | 46 | 48 | 48 | 49 | 52 | 53 | 60 |
| Netherlands | 165 | : | 155 | : | 168 | 175 | 185 | 189 | 202 | 224 |
| Portugal | : | : | : | 18 | 14 | 24 | 28 | 25 | 28 | 19 |
| United Kingdom | 878 | 1006 | 1060 | 1059 | 1096 | 1100 | 937 | 893 | 843 | 908 |

*Source:* Eurostat, Community labour force surveys.

***Table 7.3*** Proportion of foreign workers in the total non-national population, 1983–92

| Country | 1983 | 1984 | 1985 | 1986 | 1987 | 1988 | 1989 | 1990 | 1991 | 1992 |
|---|---|---|---|---|---|---|---|---|---|---|
| EUR 12 | 53.2 | 53.3 | 55.2 | 51.4 | 50.1 | 50.7 | 51.6 | 51.9 | 51.3 | 52.3 |
| Belgium | 39.2 | 37.9 | 39.2 | 38.6 | 35.8 | 34.9 | 35.0 | 35.6 | 37.5 | 38.5 |
| Denmark | 55.2 | 52.0 | 59.3 | 58.2 | 58.8 | 51.8 | 53.7 | 53.0 | 53.1 | 56.7 |
| Germany | 61.0 | 61.5 | 59.8 | 57.5 | 56.6 | 57.6 | 58.4 | 58.2 | 57.8 | 60.0 |
| Greece | 38.8 | 35.6 | 39.1 | 36.2 | 36.7 | 40.0 | 38.7 | 41.0 | 44.5 | 49.1 |
| Spain | : | : | : | : | 38.1 | 36.3 | 34.4 | 34.9 | 39.4 | 47.6 |
| France | 49.3 | 48.3 | 46.9 | 46.8 | 45.6 | 45.7 | 46.1 | 46.6 | 46.1 | 45.9 |
| Ireland | 40.9 | 39.2 | 39.6 | 38.5 | 38.7 | 40.6 | 40.1 | 41.7 | 43.4 | 40.2 |
| Italy | : | : | : | : | : | : | : | : | : | 47.6 |
| Luxembourg | 60.2 | 61.7 | 60.8 | 62.1 | 62.6 | 61.2 | 61.0 | 60.0 | 61.6 | 64.7 |
| Netherlands | 44.0 | : | 40.8 | : | 41.3 | 41.3 | 41.7 | 41.1 | 40.0 | 43.8 |
| Portugal | : | : | : | 51.4 | 51.5 | 48.3 | 56.6 | 50.7 | 54.6 | 43.4 |
| United Kingdom | 52.2 | 52.0 | 52.2 | 51.4 | 51.5 | 53.9 | 56.2 | 56.9 | 52.8 | 51.4 |

*Source:* Eurostat, Community labour force surveys.

that whereas in some EU countries the predominant foreign worker group or groups are from outside the Union, for example in Germany, Spain and the Netherlands, in countries like the United Kingdom, for example, the largest group of foreign workers are EU citizens from Ireland.

In terms of explaining how and why people migrate, migration theory differentiates between 'push' and 'pull' factors to analyse motivation for migratory movements. Push factors are those which cause migrants to leave their countries and may be defined as poverty, unemployment or underemployment. Pull factors refer to a 'combination of economic, demographic and social developments',[36] which meant that western Europe had to import a large amount of labour in order to cope with its reconstruction. In addition to economic factors prompting people to migrate, substantial numbers of people left countries such as Portugal, Spain and Greece during the 1950s and 1960s for political reasons to escape the dictatorships.

**Table 7.4**  Non-national workers by largest citizenship groups in a selection of member states, 1992
*Source: Eurostat.*

| Denmark | % | Germany | % | Greece | % | Spain | % |
|---|---|---|---|---|---|---|---|
| Turks | 14 | Turks | 33 | British | 33 | Moroccans | 27 |
| British | 10 | Former Yugoslavs | 18 | Germans | 13 | Portuguese | 6 |
| Germans | 9 | Italians | 8 | French | 10 | British | 5 |
| Former Yugoslavs | 8 | Greeks | 5 | Italians | 5 | Germans | 4 |
| Other EU | 9 | Other EU | 9 | Other EU | 10 | Other EU | 8 |
| Other non-EU | 51 | Other non-EU | 25 | Other non-EU | 29 | Other non-EU | 50 |
| Total non-nationals | 100 | Total non-nationals | 100 | Total non-nationals | 100 | Total non-nationals | 100 |

| Italy | % | Luxembourg | % | Netherlands | % | Portugal | % | United Kingdom | % |
|---|---|---|---|---|---|---|---|---|---|
| Moroccans | 14 | French | 27 | Turks | 21 | Spanish | 6 | Irish | 26 |
| Tunisians | 7 | Portuguese | 27 | Moroccans | 14 | British | 5 | Italians | 5 |
| Former Yugoslavs | 5 | Belgians | 17 | Belgians | 10 | Germans | 3 | French | 3 |
| British | 4 | Germans | 11 | British | 9 | USA citizens | 3 | Spanish | 2 |
| Other EU | 11 | Other EU | 13 | Other EU | 21 | Other EU | 6 | Other EU | 6 |
| Other non-EU | 59 | Other non-EU | 6 | Other non-EU | 23 | Other non-EU | 76 | Other non-EU | 55 |
| Total non-nationals | 100 | Total non-nationals | 100 | Total non-nationals | 100 | Total non-nationals | 100 | Total non-nationals | 100 |

NB: Due to rounding, total non-national workers might not equal 100%.
*Source:* Eurostat, Community labour force surveys, 1992.

In overall terms, most migration does not take place as a result of some kind of free choice, where individuals are out to 'maximise their wellbeing', and where both migrant and host country benefit. It seems more useful to see labour migration as:

a movement of workers propelled by the dynamics of the transnational capitalist economy, which simultaneously determines both the 'push' and the 'pull'.[37]

Migrations are, therefore, part and parcel of the increasingly global economic and political system (Castles and Miller, 1993). Collinson (1993) categorises four types of migration:

1. Voluntary economic migration (e.g. worker migration into western Europe during the 1950s and 1960s).
2. Clearly political and voluntary migration (e.g. Jews to Israel).
3. Political and involuntary or forced migration (asylum seekers and refugees).
4. Economic and involuntary or forced migration (refugees from famine).

However, these are often overlapping categories and someone who migrates as a voluntary economic migrant may also have strong political reasons for wishing to leave their country. Sociocultural factors such as family reunification and linguistic links also need to be considered, as well as the different categories of workers such as professional and unskilled, documented and illegal (Collinson. 1993). Finally we should add to these models the way in which gender differences, patriarchal structures, networks and global trends interact to create female patterns of migration.[38]

## The dual labour market

Piore (1980) highlights the role of migrant labour in a dual labour market. Production under capitalism requires both capital-intensive and labour-intensive production methods. The economy operates in this way as a result of the flux and uncertainty of economic activity. Jobs in the secondary sector are more vulnerable to seasonal factors, changes in fashions and taste and the wider effects of boom and recession. Access to the primary sector of the labour market is dependent on a combination of skill, stability of demand and worker organisation. The secondary labour market is characterised by low pay, poor conditions, poor promotional chances and low or no trade union organisation. It is the part-time casualised sector of the labour market, highly flexible in terms of employers' ability to hire and fire dependent on levels of demand. Piore (1980) and Goldthorpe (1984) identify migrant labour and women as making up a large percentage of those employed in the secondary sector of the labour market. The primary sector is made up predominantly of indigenous workers. The whole debate between the UK government and the other EU governments concerning this section of the labour market in the EU rests on the amount of protection in terms of rights allowed to workers in this sector. Although the social chapter provisions in the Maastricht Treaty provide only the basic level of protection mainly in terms of health and safety at work, nevertheless the divide demonstrates the different approaches to industrial relations. Neo-liberals want to have a completely free labour market; corporatists and neo-corporatists favour some kind of, albeit minimum, social protection.

In terms of future labour market demands concern is being expressed about the ageing population in western Europe tied in with the falling birth rate. In order to resolve the lack of new workers which is projected to occur within the next 20 years, various estimates exist as to the likely growth in the population of North Africa, a possible source of new labour (see Chapter 11, Section 11.3).

Initially labour-importing countries welcomed the presence of these workers, who it was imagined would return home once they had made enough money. In Germany this was known as the 'rotation principle' (**Rotationsprinzip**) and in France the process of extracting as much useful labour from these workers as possible was referred to as the lemon-squeezer (**presse-citron**). Once the labourer had been squeezed dry, then it was time to hire new workers.

The downturn in the west European economies during the 1970s and 1980s resulted in the introduction of increasingly restrictive immigration regulations (see further Chapter 11, Section 11.6). The attempt was made to halt any further entry of workers and at the same time to make it difficult for those who had been resident to be joined by their families and to enjoy full civic rights. Numerous efforts were made, particularly by the French and German governments, to offer inducements to certain migrant groups to return to their countries of origin. It has always been clear that it is those groups who are considered culturally non-assimilable, for example Turkish people in Germany and Maghrebins and west Africans in France, who are offered inducements to leave.

The presence of these groups has also had repercussions in the political arena. The effect of the rise in unemployment and the general assumption that there were too many immigrants in western Europe provided fertile ground on which parties and movements of the Far Right could try to cultivate their populist support. The *Front National* in France, the *Republikaner* and the *Deutsche Volks Union* (DVU) in Germany, and the *Vlaams Blok* in Belgium, have all been successful in using immigrant groups as scapegoats for a whole range of economic and social problems (see Chapter 8, Section 8.6.2). Mainstream politicians across the political spectrum have also contributed to these fears, and very few have challenged the nature and basis of the Far Right's statements. Many parties have, instead, incorporated parts of the Far Right programmes into their own policies. One of the dangers from such lack of political courage is the difficulty in controlling these parties once they become firmly entrenched in the political system. These tensions are just as prevalent in the countries of East and Central Europe, with events in Ketegyhaza, Hungary where a group of gypsies were attacked and their houses set on fire, reflecting popular discontent. Populist currents within the Hungarian Democratic Forum (MDF), whose deputy president Istvan Csurka expressed the view that the Magyar nation had been coexisting too long with: 'disadvantaged strata and groups . . . to whom the laws of natural selection do not apply'. The MDF has a popularity rating of around 20 per cent.[39]

The presence of large numbers of people who have come to work in Europe since 1945, and who are now settled in those countries, raises all kinds of questions about Europe's degree of tolerance, adaptability and respect for basic human rights. Massive repatriation of these people, which seems the favoured policy of the extreme right, is not possible and policies that turn on ever-increasing restrictions merely create insecurity. Migration has been an integral part of European development for centuries and given, now, its ageing population and the increasing globalisation of the economy, it is likely to remain a necessity in the future. It becomes a priority that immigration policies reflect that reality, and measures are implemented for the already settled populations that ensure greater social cohesion.

## 7.6   Summary

In this chapter we have reviewed some of the salient features and developments in the labour markets of European countries. The debate between the welfare capitalism and the free market capitalism models of labour market organisation and policies continues to dominate the agenda. Increased globalisation and technological change have provided new challenges within which European labour markets will have to operate into the next century. In this context it will be imperative for the future of European populations to find a way of ensuring the maintenance of their standards of living, and in particular to secure personally fulfilling and socially productive employment for the mass of the population. This will entail a number of policy developments, but in particular policies designed to substantially increase the human capital embedded in Europe's people, for this seems the best way of maintaining Europe's competitiveness in a changing world. The need to maintain international competitiveness will entail more substantial welfare cuts and possible relocation of production outside the EU. The implications for industrial relations and social cohesion will require careful consideration. Given the ageing population in Europe, the need will persist for widespread migration. It remains to be seen which path European countries choose to follow to meet the challenges ahead.

## Further reading

Barnabé, F. (1988) 'The labour market and unemployment' in *The European Economy Growth and Crisis*, Oxford: Oxford University Press.

Blanchard, O. J. and Summers, L. H. (1896) 'Hysteresis and the European unemployment problem' in *National Bureau of Economic Research Macro Economica Annual*, Cambridge, Mass: MIT Press.

Bocock, R. and Thompson, K. (eds) (1992) *Social & Cultural Forms of Modernity*, Cambridge: Polity Press.

Bovenkerk, F. *et al.* (1990) 'Racism, migration and the state in western Europe' *International Sociology* 5 (4), December, 380–93.

Brouwer, F., Lintner, V. and Newman, M. (1994) *Economic Policy and the European Union*, London: Federal Trust.

Castles, S., Booth, H. and Wallace, T. (1984) *Here for Good. W. Europe's New Ethnic Minorities*, London: Pluto Press.

Castles, S. and Kosack, G. (1985) *Immigrant Workers & Class Structure in Western Europe*, Oxford: Oxford University Press.

Castles, S. and Miller, M. J. (1993) *The Age of Migration*, New York: Guilford Press.

Coates, K. and Barrett Brown, M. (eds) (1993) *A European Recovery Programme*, Nottingham: Spokesman.

Collinson, S. (1993) *Beyond Borders: West European Migration Policy Towards the 21st Century*, London: RIIA, Wyndham Trust.

Edye, D. (1987) *Immigrant Labour and Government Policy*, Aldershot: Gower.

Employment Department Group (1995) *Labour Market and Skill Trends 1994/5*, London: Department of Employment.

Ferner, A. and Hyman, R. (1992) *Industrial Relations in the New Europe*, Oxford: Blackwell.

Flanagan, R. J. (1987) 'Labour market behaviour and European economic growth' in *Barriers to European Growth: a Transatlantic View* Lawrence, R. Z. and Schultz, C. L. (eds), Washington: Brookings Institution.

Freeman, C. and Soete, L. (1994) *Work for all or Mass Unemployment*, London: Frances Pinter.

Goldthorpe, J. H. (ed.) (1984) *Order and Conflict in Contemporary Capitalism*, Oxford: Oxford University Press.

Hammar, T. (ed.) (1985) *European Immigration Policy: A Comparative Study*, Cambridge: Cambridge University Press.

Holland, S. (1983) *Out of Crisis*, Nottingham: Spokesman.

Holland, S. (1993) *The European Imperative*, Nottingham: Spokesman.

Hutton, W. (1995) *The State We're In*, London: Jonathan Cape.

Hyman, R. (1991) 'European unions: towards 2000' *Work, Employment and Society* 5 (4) pp. 621–39.

Kindleberger, C. P. (1967) *Europe's Post-War Growth: The Role of Labor Supply*, Oxford: Oxford University Press.

Kreile, M. (1988) 'The Crisis of Italian Trade Unionism in the 1980s', *WEP* 11, pp. 54–67.

Lane, C. (1989) *Management and Labour in Europe*, London: Edward Elgar.

Lange, P. and Regini, M. (eds) (1989) *State, Market and Social Regulation. New Perspectives on Italy*. Cambridge: Cambridge University Press.

Layton-Henry, Z. (ed.) (1990) *The Political Rights of Migrant Workers in Western Europe*, London: Sage.

Lecher, W. (ed.) (1994) *Trade Unions in the European Union. A Handbook*, London: Lawrence & Wishart.

Lintner, V. G., Pokorny, M., Woods, M. M. and Blinkhorn, M. R. (1987) 'Trade unions and technological change in the UK mechanical engineering industry' *British Journal of Industrial Relations* XXV (1) March, 235–54.

Miller, M. J. (1981) *Foreign Workers in Europe. An Emerging Political Force*, New York: Praeger.

OECD (1977) *The Cyclically Determined Homeward Flow of Migrant Workers*, Paris.

OECD Employment Outlook (1993), Paris.

Phizacklea, A. (ed.) (1983) *One Way Ticket? Migration and Female Labour*, London: Routledge & Kegan Paul.

Piore, M. J. (1980) *Birds of Passage. Migrant Labor and Industrial Societies*, Cambridge: Cambridge University Press.

Piore, M. J. and Sabel, C. (1984) *The Second Industrial Divide*, New York: Basic Books.

Rowbotham, S. and Mitter, J. (eds) (1994) *Dignity and Daily Bread*, London: Routledge.

Sengenberger, W. (1984) 'West German employment policy: restoring worker competition' *Industrial Relations* 23 (3), 323–56.

Sloman, J. (1994) *Economics*, 2nd edn, Hemel Hempstead: Harvester Wheatsheaf.

Soete, L. (1994) 'European Integration and Strategies for Employment', in Brouwer, F., Lintner, V. and Newman, M. 'Economic Policy and the European Union', London: Federal Trust.

Symes, V. (1995) *Unemployment in Europe*, London: Routledge.

Taylor, R. (1994) *The Future of the Trade Unions*, London: André Deutsch.

## Notes

1. For a fuller analysis of the functioning of labour markets, see the relevant chapters of Sloman, 1994.

2. Senenberger was referring to the German case, but others (Lane, 1989) have used these terms to discuss developments on a wider basis. In earlier chapters we also refer to these as concepts as Keynesianism and neo-liberalism – see Chapters 1 and 2.

3. This is an issue that is very much back on the agenda in the United Kingdom. Minimum wages are criticised, particularly from a neo-liberal perspective, as leading to job losses in low-paid sectors (see the section on labour markets in Chapter 2 for an illustration of the process through which this might occur). The argument, however, is complex and difficult to resolve empirically.

4. Wages Councils sought to control minimum wages in particularly low paid sectors of the economy. For example, one of the longest standing of these operated in the agricultural sector. They were also important in service sectors such as hotel and catering and hairdressing.

5. In addition, governments often became directly involved in the wage determination process by intervening in industrial disputes and urging (usually) moderation in wage settlements. These forms of intervention were even supplemented by attempts to control the price of basic consumption goods, for example in the United Kingdom during the 1970s.

6. In particular this affects quantitative adjustments of wages and employment, since qualitative adjustments concerning skill levels are usually determined within firms.

7. That is the extent to which, because of increased employment rights, labour had become a fixed factor of production.

8. OECD, 1993, 197.

9. And the shift in competitive advantage in mass Fordist manufacturing from Europe to the NICs.

10. Also, cynics might add, by contributing to the increase in the remuneration packages available to higher managers in the UK utility industries.

11. Especially in the case of part-time workers, many of whom are women.

12. Typified by the catch phrase 'the right to manage' which was popular in the United Kingdom in the 1980s.

13. Hutton (1995) refers to this as the 40:30:30 society in the United Kingdom.

14. It should be noted that the shift from manufacturing to services that has occurred in most European countries has exacerbated this trend – see below.

15. Employees are required to perform a greater range of skilled tasks, providing more job satisfaction as well as more workplace autonomy.

16. Although evidence suggests that UK trade unions, contrary to some expectations, have not had a negative influence on the introduction of the technologies required for flexible specialisation – see Lintner *et al.* 1987.

17. For a detailed study of this see Freeman and Soete, 1994 and Soete in Brouwer *et al.*, 1994.

18. Around 2 per cent higher than the OECD average.

19. Furthermore many people have given up looking for jobs and do not enter the statistics, and many who are employed are working in part-time jobs when they would prefer full-time employment.

20. And had fallen somewhat since, following the 1992 devaluation.

21. People out of work for more than 12 months. This is important since unemployment statistics measure a flow rather than a stock of people – the unemployed are not always the same, since people move in and out of jobs.

22. Some of the higher unemployment among ethnic minorities and women is no doubt due to discrimination in the labour market, although the extent to which this is so is notoriously difficult to estimate.

23. Although there are considerable national variations. For example in the United Kingdom male unemployment (7.4 per cent) was greater than female unemployment (6.6 per cent).

24. The NAIRU is very difficult to define and measure. Nevertheless, according to Blanchard and Summers (1986) between 1967–69 and 1981–83 it increased from 2.4 per cent to 9.2 per cent in the United Kingdom, from 1.3 per cent to 6.2 per cent in Germany and from 2.2 per cent to 6.9 per cent in France. According to Flanagan (1987) between 1983–87 the NAIRU for France and Germany was 6 per cent, and it had increased more in most European countries than in the United States.

25. There has already been some work carried out on the possibility of an EU role in job creation, and the form this might take – see Coates and Barratt Brown, 1993; Holland, 1983, 1993.

26. Lecher and Naumann in Lecher (1994), p. 4.

27. Joint committees exist in more than 80 branches of industry, and cover practically all employees' and employers' organisations. Furthermore, the National Labour Council (*Conseil National de Travail*) first set up in 1952 and composed of employees' and employers' representatives covering the whole of the economy to advise the government on social issues, has now expanded its role into the whole arena of collective agreements. As it is a legally constituted body protected by statute its deliberations and decisions have been

crucial in maintaining the strength of the trade union movement and preventing its fragmentation and decentralisation as has happened in other countries (Lecher and Naumann, 1994, p. 9).

28. The four are: the Federal Chamber of Business (BWK), the Federation of Chambers of Agriculture, the Austrian Trade Union Federation (ÖGB) and the Austrian Central Chamber of Labour (ÖAKT). For further information see Franz Taxler in Ferner and Hyman, 1992.

29. Ferdinand von Prondzynski in Ferner and Hyman, 1992.

30. This information is taken from Rolfs, H.-H. and Schäfer, U. (1993) *Jahrbuch der Bundesrepublik Deutschland*, Hamburg: Beck/dtv.

31. Jacobi, Keller and Müller-Jentsch in Ferner and Hyman, 1992.

32. Goetschy and Rozenblatt in Ferner and Hyman, 1992.

33. Although the level of union membership is very low in France, the Socialist government gave the trade unions the right to negotiate on behalf of workers even though they were not union members. The actual level of membership is therefore no indicator of the amount of influence that the unions wield. Furthermore the strike weapon is still resorted to, although the characteristic of strikes in France is that they are short but intense.

34. Gillespie, R. in Urwin, D. and Paterson, W. E. (1990) *Politics in Western Europe Today: perspectives, policies and problems*. London: Longman, p. 209.

35. For more recent developments in EU policy towards immigration and asylum seekers, see *Immigration and Asylum Policies*, Brussels: European Commission, ISEC/B14 09/08/94.

36. Castles, S. and Kosack, G. (1973) *Immigrant Workers and Class Structure in Western Europe*, Oxford: Oxford University Press, p. 26.

37. Zolberg in Castles and Miller, 1993, p. 22.

38. Podro, S. (1994) 'Third World Women and Immigration Policy in Spain: The Pressures of a Free World Market on Immigration Control', unpublished MA Dissertation University of North London.

39. *Independent*, 25/10/92.

**CHAPTER EIGHT**

---

# Party systems and mainstream parties

## 8.1  Introduction

In the next three chapters we aim to analyse the nuts and bolts of the state, by examining the development of party systems and parties, cleavages, electoral systems together with an analysis of whether there has been a change in party systems via a process of realignment and dealignment.

A common assumption is that scarcity is a feature of all societies, and disputes arise over how those scarce resources should be distributed. It is also evident, however, that abundance is a feature of some societies or among certain sections of some societies. However, in any situation either of scarcity or abundance, negotiation has to take place over distribution of those resources. Politics is concerned with the way in which that negotiation takes place to reach some kind of generally acceptable resolution to the question of the use, production and distribution of resources.

When this process breaks down, as it does during times of unrest, then other methods are introduced to allocate resources. As von Clausewitz said: 'War is politics carried out by other means'. Conflict, then, is at the basis of all political processes, but it does not necessarily always lead to violence. More often than not a resolution is found that can be maintained for a period, until new issues arise to be resolved. The process is therefore ongoing and dynamic, and open to constant negotiation and renegotiation, conflict and resolution. These conflicts arise from divisions or cleavages in society which have led to the growth of parties and groups formed to aggregate particular interests. We begin by defining what a party system is, then examine cleavages, and finally look at the major ideologies and parties within western Europe, and the changes affecting the kind of party systems that exist.

## 8.2  Typology of party systems

A party system refers to the way political parties interact within a political system. From this definition what is important is the number of parties, their size and influence and their position along the ideological spectrum. Changes within parties do not necessarily affect the party system; for example in Britain, despite the Labour

Party undergoing a radical change in its ideological make-up, the party system remains firmly unchanged.[1] However, the party system may have changed in the early 1980s if the Social Democratic Party (SDP) led by the 'Gang of Four' had succeeded in becoming a major party.[2] The details of the current debate over the electoral system in the United Kingdom are discussed in the next section.[3]

Similarly in Germany after the 1959 Bad Godesberg conference, when the SPD dropped its strongly socialist orientation, there was no dramatic change to the party system. It was only as a result of the arrival of the Greens in the early 1980s that commentators began to discuss the way in which the party system might change. Even with the somewhat different party systems which existed in Greece, Spain and Portugal in the mid- to late 1970s there were certain common characteristics of all three systems including, most importantly: centre-right and centre-left domination and competition for centre ground; jettisoning of strong ideological baggage by the socialist parties; decline of communist parties; difficulty of centre-right parties to project their new role, arising partly from identification with the recently discredited authoritarian regimes; and charismatic politicians such as González in Spain and Papandreou in Greece.[4] A common feature of these three systems is their high degree of personalism tied to a clientelistic state structure, similar until recently to the Italian model.

All political systems in western and East Central Europe are liberal democratic, with a plurality of political parties (see below for comment on **singularism**) operating within a party system, organised according to transparent rules governing the nature and conduct of the electoral process. This does not preclude governing parties attempting occasionally to abolish countervailing centres of democratically elected power, which happened in the United Kingdom in the mid-1980s with the demise of certain metropolitan authorities, notably in London, Manchester and Sheffield.

There have been two key developments in western Europe, according to Lipset and Rokkan, which have shaped those societies: the national revolution and the industrial revolution. The national revolution led to the formation of unitary nation states and broke up local and regional autonomy and affinities, and the industrial revolution destroyed the traditional agricultural semi-feudal relationships between owner and peasant to be replaced by classes organised along economic lines.[5] Rokkan adds a third revolution: the international revolution, which led to the split between the communist and socialist parties,[6] but the sharp ideological divides have now softened and in many cases the programmes of communist and socialist parties have become indistinguishable.[7]

Lipset and Rokkan describe how the party systems in western Europe were formed based on a historical analysis of their development (Lipset and Rokkan, 1967). Their main hypothesis is that the party system has been 'frozen' in western Europe since the end of the First World War. This was a result of the fact that the main cleavages in industrial societies, socioeconomic, religious, linguistic and territorial had all developed before the introduction of universal mass suffrage (see below). They attempt to find a relationship between the cleavages in society and the way in which people vote. There appears to be a strong link between those who are employers voting for right-wing parties and those who are workers voting for left-wing parties.

However, all right-wing parties have been successful at one time or another in capturing an important part of the working-class vote.[8]

The classic cleavages, then, which Lipset and Rokkan identify of class and religion do not have the same importance as previously (Bartoloni and Mair, 1984). We examine below the classic cleavages of class and religion.

## Party systems and polarisation

Party systems are also referred to in terms of the degree of polarisation that exists in them. If there is a sharp ideological divide between the parties with little middle ground then we can refer to such a system as being polarised. A continuum can be established along which parties are placed; in this context it is important to be aware that these positions are not fixed in stone. The experience of socialist parties has been to move to the centre, so that the gap between party programmes of the mainstream parties in western Europe is not that great. Furthermore the change within communist parties has also mirrored the move to the centre, with wholescale jettisoning of classic ideology and tactics.

Sartori's model of party systems is based on two axes: one charts the number of parties, the other the degree of ideological difference between them.[9] Centripetal and centrifugal polarisation describe whether the parties have a tendency to coalesce towards the centre or gravitate towards the extremes, thereby creating a much greater degree of polarisation. There are, however, problems with all these attempts to categorise party systems for a number of reasons.

First of all, how do you measure the degree of ideological difference between parties? Usually this is done on the basis of the manifesto, speeches or actual programmes in government, but perhaps a more useful, more difficult, way to measure the distance between parties would be to question voters as to their perceptions of the differences between parties.

Secondly, does a mere counting of the number of parties really tell us how fragmented or polarised a party system is? A more valuable measure of stability may be to consider other historical factors and the kind of political culture that exists in any one country. For example, in the Netherlands general election of 3 May 1994, 12 parties won seats in the 150-seat Lower House of parliament (**Tweede Kamer**), with the most successful party the Labour Party (PvdA) winning 37 seats. Although the overall result led to some concern about the stability of Dutch politics, the political culture and tradition meant that coalition government is accepted as the norm, there was no run on the guilder and government continues to function much as before.

There are also many ways in which the party system in any one country may be characterised. For example, the French party system under the current Fifth Republic has been defined as bipolar (Wright, 1989), coalescing around the left and the right. This situation contrasts with the experiences of the Fourth Republic (1946–58), where there were multiple party coalitions and no stable poles of political focus. Wright indicates that in France there have been four main factors that produced bipolarisation in that system: institutional, electoral, societal and cultural, and presidential and party strategies.[10] All these factors are important in other European countries in forming the party system, although not all lead to bipolarisation.

Institutional factors refer to the way in which the executive takes on an increasing role in the decision-making process to the detriment of the national assemblies.[11] This is a feature of most West European states (see Chapter 10). Electoral factors concern the voting system which, depending on whether it is a form of PR or first-past-the-post, can have a decisive influence on the party system (see section below on electoral systems). Societal and cultural factors include political traditions, such as the large communist tradition in France and Italy, or the strong role of the political parties with very little countervailing centres of power in terms of civil society in Spain, Portugal, or Greece. Presidential and party strategies are, to a certain extent, dependent on these other factors, forcing parties to seek coalitions in order to capture key political positions.

A term that may be useful in defining the current party systems of western Europe is **singularism** rather than pluralism. As a result of the decline in ideological distance between the established parties, which is largely a result of the decline in the left, there appears to be a great deal of common ground in the policies promoted by the large established parties. The traditional division of left and right loses its substance, with each major party producing a version of more or less the same way to manage the economic and social life of a country. This is not the same situation as existed in the Soviet Union or eastern Europe with only one party dominating the political landscape, and no regular elections with alternating parties. Pluralism still exists, but now refers to the presence, role and influence of marginal political parties, which may become incorporated into the mainstream, such as the *Alleanza Nazionale* (AN) in Italy after the March 1994 election.[12] It also refers to the role of interest groups within the political process.

This feature of modern liberal-democratic systems is also the result of the decline in the role and effectiveness of parliament, coupled with the extensive and intrusive role of the state, which means more and more power resting with the executive and its bureaucratic structures. The real tension that exists is between centralisation and participation, between the metropole and the region or locality, between government-appointed commissions and representative assemblies, and between singularity and plurality. Each European country demonstrates these tensions to a greater or lesser degree.

It is also more generally a consequence of the greater speed of communication and need for instant solutions in the modern world. These demands conflict with the desire to allow a greater degree of participation, which necessarily entails a much slower process of consultation before any decision is reached. The contradiction, then, is between a world where information (although controlled by a few large transnational conglomerates) has never been more easily available and accessible, allowing individuals greater choice and by implication greater control over their lives, and the demands for rapid action from the global economic system, where decisions affecting the lives of everyone are taken quickly and without much consultation.[13]

The nature of the relationship between the parties and the various cleavages in society is important in determining the kind of party system that develops. As Mény notes:

While cleavage structures may help to create or transform political parties, political parties are also vital to the perpetuation of cleavage structures.[14]

## 8.3 Cleavages

This section analyses the presence, persistence and possible changes to cleavages within western European states.[15] There have been four main areas around which cleavages traditionally developed within western Europe, which have affected the formation of the party system:

- class;
- religion;
- region including language; and
- rural–urban.

There is a further, more recent, cleavage around 'post-material' values, which has found its expression in the growth of New Social Movements and Green Parties (see Chapter 9), although it remains to be seen whether this particular cleavage can have the same mobilising intensity as the other cleavages. These cleavages, although apparently distinct in many countries, do overlap, so that a political party whose power base is primarily regional will appeal across class, religious and rural–urban divides, as for example the Northern League in Italy. Furthermore, within many states, even being part of one social class or another does not necessarily indicate voting intentions.

The history of such cleavages within western Europe has revealed a constant negotiation and tension between these elements, reflecting the effects of industrial-isation and democratisation in each particular society. There are similarities and differences between individual European countries concerning the way in which these cleavages have been expressed and their relative importance over time.

Traditional cleavages may also disappear when a major issue presents itself, as the issue of Europe has done, particularly in the United Kingdom and France. Supporters of the various EC developments have tended to come from the centre ground of the political spectrum, with opposition from both ends of the spectrum. In the 1975 referendum debate in the United Kingdom on whether the country should remain in the EEC, the right wing of the Conservative Party and the left wing of the Labour Party both campaigned for a No vote. Their reasons were different but their objective position was similar. The same phenomenon could be observed in France during the debate in the 1992 referendum over ratification of the Maastricht Treaty. Left-wing campaigners such as Jean-Pierre Chevènement and the PCF, and right-wing organisations such as the Gaullist Pasqua and the neo-Fascist Front National all campaigned for a No vote.[16]

The case of Ireland since 1922 illustrates another way in which cleavages have developed. In 1921 there was really only one major political party in the South, Sinn Fein, which as a nationalist party denied all cleavages based on class or the rural–urban divide. However, as the new Irish State was coming into being after the Treaty of 1921 with the British, so two new political parties emerged, divided not along classic lines but according to their respective acceptance or rejection of the Treaty. Cummann Gael which later became Fine Gael accepted the division of the country enshrined in the Treaty, and was supported mainly by men of property 'the social snobs', and was strong on stability and law and order. In the 1930s, the party's 'Blue Shirts' movement was close to the ideas of Continental Fascism, which also included support from the poet W. B. Yeats.

Fianna Fail, led originally by De Valera, rejected the Treaty and drew its support from business, small farmers and workers and was conservative on social issues. It has been Fianna Fail, as a Catholic and nationalist party, that has dominated the political scene in Ireland until recently and with the development of a clientelist state structure has managed to maintain its dominance in a similar way to the Italian DC. Overall, the differences now between these two parties is negligible. In the last 10 years, a more ideologically based Labour Party has emerged with its support among the urban, mainly Dublin, middle class and social liberals. Fine Gael and Fianna Fail gain about 65 per cent of the vote with the Labour Party gaining around 20 per cent. In addition, there is the left-wing Workers' Party/Democratic Left which participated in government for the first time in 1995.

## Class

The industrialisation of western Europe during the nineteenth and early twentieth centuries, led to the growth of large political parties representing the two main groups in society, divided along class lines. The working class began to organise politically through combinations, trade unions and finally formed political parties.[17] The German Social Democratic Party (the SPD) founded in 1875 was the first major party established to represent workers' interests. The owners and controllers of capital, the bourgeoisie, sought to protect and promote their interests through parties such as the Tory Party in Britain (founded in the late eighteenth century).[18]

The salience of class as a key factor explaining voting behaviour has long been a source of debate about political systems. Within the British political system there has traditionally been a close correlation between social class and political expression. It was seen as the factor above all others that explained people's political orientation and voting behaviour. The link between social class and voting intentions now seems less close both in Britain and elsewhere in western Europe.[19] In other European countries class has also played a crucial role in determining political affiliation. For example in France, numerous studies have shown that blue collar workers tend to vote for the party of the left.[20]

In the nineteenth century, Toryism as expressed by Disraeli stressed the 'one nation' aspect of its policies, which survived at various times and in various guises until 1979. One of its most renowned periods was the 1945–79 period of consensus known as 'Butskellism' (see Chapter 6). It was replaced by Thatcherism during the 1980s, which was none the less able to maintain Conservative Party support among working-class voters.[21] Recent debates have considered whether class is declining in importance as a factor in explaining political behaviour.[22] The authors of a recent study on the 1992 General Election in the United Kingdom dispute the view that social class no longer matters, and that increasing affluence has 'detached' working-class voters from their traditional roots and voting habits.[23]

In the wider European context several authors suggest that a simple class-based explanation is too crude, since identity with the interests of one class is changing as a larger middle class emerges. This new social formation becomes better educated, more professionally qualified and more affluent and is likely to consider non-material factors as important. Issues such as a quality of life, related to leisure and environment, are becoming increasingly crucial. Political behaviour is becoming more complex and so parties are having to go beyond simple and traditional class based loyalties to win support. This process has led to a 'modernisers' versus 'traditionalists' split evident in all socialist, social democratic and communist parties in Europe.

The modernisers recognise the changing composition of society and want their parties to embrace these new middle-class groups. At the same time they are prepared to promote politics that stress individualism and socially managed or responsible capitalism. Traditionalists tend to want to keep certain tenets of socialist faith such as nationalisation and full employment policies, and are wary of wholescale embrace of new social market and non-collectivist policies.

This change in the socioeconomic structure of most western European countries has led to the phenomenon of the 'catch-all' party, a result of the fact that declining social polarisation has led to reduced political polarisation.[24] The 'catch-all' party aims to transcend not only the traditional left–right ideological divide, but also the Catholic–Protestant, clerical–anti-clerical, regional and rural–urban cleavages.

## Religion

Despite the almost universal decline in religious affiliation and church-going in western Europe, religion and religious values still have an impact on political life (Mény, 1993; Smith, 1990). Whereas in the past clericalism was associated with conservative parties and anti-clericalism closely associated with socialist and communist party supporters, now these distinctions are not so strong, except perhaps in Switzerland. On the whole other cleavages such as region have become more important.

However, there are still important areas where the church–state relationship is embedded into the institutional framework of a country, although it may not directly influence the way in which people vote.[25] For example, in Germany the government collects the church tax (**Kirchensteuer**) on behalf of the churches, which is then used for the provision of many social services. In both England and Ireland there are established churches, an issue that in the Irish case represents one of the main stumbling blocks in terms of an acceptable constitutional settlement to the Unionists in Northern Ireland. Secondly, there is the tension between religious ethics and morality and political values. The debates over the last 30 years in all European countries to liberalise the laws concerning divorce, abortion and contraception have seen the churches leading campaigns against these measures. In Chapter 11 we outline the way in which abortion became a central issue in the West German–East German unification negotiations, and still remains a hotly contested area. In Poland, too, abortion remains an important source of divide between the church and the secular authorities, with the pro-abortion lobby tending to be located on the left. Education is another area where church–state relations are contested.

In France most private schools are Catholic-run, and attempts to interfere with their organisation by the socialist government in the early 1990s led to huge protests. Defenders of the state system, however, mounted their own huge demonstration in 1994 against the right-wing government's proposals to increase finance for private schools. Conflict has arisen also between religious practice over the wearing of the veil by Muslim girls in schools. The whole basis of the French republican tradition is that no preference is given by the state to any particular religion or group within the public arena of state education. All are considered equal citizens, and so the wearing of a garment that indicates religious affiliation is seen as a challenge to that republican tradition which developed out of a strong anti-clericalism in the nineteenth century. In Britain it is interesting to note that although religious schools are permitted to run within the state sector, so far this possibility has not been extended to Muslim schools.

The Christian Democratic parties of Europe also profess to be based on Christian values, and certainly in their early years they were strongly supported by the churches, who were vocal on their behalf (see section below on parties of the right); but religious values are declining and less significance is attached to those values in explaining voting behaviour. Perhaps most noticeable is the case of the Netherlands, where confessional parties now no longer play the dominant role that they used to play, and the CDA includes both Catholics and Protestants (see section below on realignment and dealignment).

The importance of religion as a defining cleavage within contemporary western Europe is less influential than before in terms of explaining how people vote. This is in contrast with the United States, where the Christian Coalition played a significant role in helping the right-wing Republican Party to victory in the legislative elections of November 1994. Furthermore, states such as Iran base much of their system of government on the *Sharia*, or Islamic Law. In this case the distinction between civil society and the state is all but lost.

## Region and rural–urban

In terms of regions and the rural–urban divides, the overall tendency within western Europe is for the rural–urban divide to have diminished as a significant cleavage, while regions and regionalism have become an increasingly important cleavage. For a time the centralising tendencies of the nation-state overwhelmed and suppressed, in some cases, the demand for more regional autonomy for example in Spain until Franco's death in 1975. In France, rural-based farmer parties no longer have the same influence as in the 1940s and 1950s: a reflection of the growing urbanisation of French society, although farmers do still play a significant role in national politics and in the national psyche, rather like coalminers have done in the United Kingdom.

In Italy regional parties played a minor role until the rise of the Lega Lombarda in the 1980s, which articulated protest against the over-centralisation of the Italian state, and a reluctance to pay taxes to subsidise the poorer south of the country. The Italian election of March 1994 revealed the strength of these regional cleavages with the success of the Northern League (*Lega Nord*) and the National Alliance (*Alleanza Nazionale*) in the south. Other examples of parties which attempt to transcend the classic cleavages are nationalist parties such as the Scottish National Party (SNP), the Basque National Party (PNV) and Sinn Fein. For a more detailed analysis of the effect of these cleavages see the section below on regional movements and parties.

## Summary

Although on the whole western Europe has witnessed a change in the nature and intensity of the traditional cleavages, there is still a continuing debate about the precise effect each of these cleavages has on the party system. It may be that with the stronger regionalist and separatist movements in Italy, Spain and the United Kingdom and developments at the EU level, that there will be a subnational revolution that will transform the nation state. For some the nation state still has plenty of life left in it yet.

There is no doubt, however, that party systems have been affected by the reduction in ideological distance between the left and the right. Parties no longer define themselves as offering different models of society but versions of the same model. The parties, themselves, have also been affected by another major institutional development in western Europe since 1945, namely the increasing role of the state at both local and national level in the provision of services and the employment of large numbers of people. The effect of this development has led to the need for political parties to occupy the main positions within these bureaucracies. It has also led to a new cleavage between public and private sector employees. This development has been compounded in those countries with an underdeveloped civil society, particularly in the form of independent trade unions and mass media.

The main feature of these clientelistic states is the way in which political parties become part and parcel of the state structure at both national and local level, including the media. In reality clientelism goes beyond defining the party system as such, and becomes a much wider definition of the way in which the state operates under the strict control of political party domination. In addition it refers to the favours given to party supporters in terms of jobs and contracts in the public sector. Clientelism tends to develop in those countries where political parties play the predominant role, not only at the level of local and national government but also in many areas of civil society. Italy has been considered the main country to exhibit these characteristics, but similar characteristics are noticeable in Spain, Greece and Portugal.[26] However, this is not exclusively a Southern European phenomenon, as the Gaullist/Giscardian/ Mitterrand state in France shows and recent experience in the United Kingdom reveals. The reduction in the autonomy of local government in Britain and the increasing centralisation of power at the centre has meant that government ministers now have enormous powers of patronage at their disposal. The growth of QUANGOs with their system of political appointees, who are mainly Conservative party supporters, bears witness to the growth of a clientelistic state in the United Kingdom with similarities to the Southern European model.[27]

The party system, then, has had to adapt to the scope of the civil service/ bureaucracy, and the influence of extra-parliamentary interest groups such as transnational companies (TNCs) in constraining elected governments' room for manoeuvre. The role of interest groups and to a certain extent pressure groups, may reveal more about how the modern state operates than a strict concentration on political parties. The overwhelming presence of the state may decline as a result of the neo-liberal agenda of privatisation, but although this may reduce the role of the state in the economic sphere it is compensated for by the increased role of the state in areas such as managing the criminal justice system, including prisons.

These institutional factors combine with the electoral system in playing a key role in influencing the party system, as the section below indicates. Societal and cultural factors refer to changes in society such as growing emancipation for women, more regional consciousness and calls for more participation in the democratic process. The arrival of the Greens on the political scene has changed the party system, as movements attempt to overcome the widespread alienation that many voters feel with the political system.

## 8.4   Electoral systems

The debate about electoral systems revolves around the relative influence the party system has on the electoral system, and vice versa. A further issue concerns which kind of system allows for the broadest form of representation. In this section we will look at the two main types of electoral system in operation in western Europe, beginning with the most common form, proportional representation (PR), and then analysing the preferred form in the United Kingdom, and the more developed form in France, of a simple plurality system or first-past-the-post (FPTP), as it is more commonly known. The section will outline the elements of the two systems, then present the relative merits of the two systems.[28]

### Proportional representation (PR)

This system usually operates under a **list system**, which involves large multimember constituencies, sometimes grouped into regions. The voter selects from a party list of candidates rather than a single individual. The Netherlands is the only country in western Europe where the whole country is taken as one constituency. This form of PR is considered to be the purest, since parliamentary representation is calculated according to national votes. Other countries such as Belgium, Luxembourg, Spain, Portugal and Greece operate other versions of PR based on regions, and in Ireland the single transferable vote system is used.

### Additional member system

Germany operates this kind of system, whereby half the seats in the *Bundestag* (the Lower House) are single member constituency seats, elected on a first-past-the-post system. The other half are allocated to parties on a regional list basis, with the intention of arriving at a proportional result overall. Each voter has two votes, one for the candidate in the constituency, the other for the party list. The final distribution of seats is decided by the second vote for the party list, and so Germany has a PR system even though it contains elements of the FPTP. The two major parties, the SPD and the CDU–CSU, tend to win all the constituency seats, and so smaller parties only have a chance of representation via the list system. To prevent the kind of splintering of the party system that occurred under the Weimar Republic there is a threshold requirement of three constituency seats or 5 per cent of valid votes cast in the whole of the country.[29] The advantages of this kind of system are that it allows, first, for some kind of voter identification on a constituency basis, although the major parties tend to dominate, and also permits smaller party representation on a regional basis, thereby reinforcing the federal element of the German party system. Voter choice is also enhanced, since someone can vote for a candidate from one party in the constituency and then choose another party from the list. The German Liberal Party (FDP) and the Greens have both benefited from this kind of split voting.

### Arguments in favour of PR

- It allows for fairer representation overall – i.e. a greater degree of pluralism.
- It allows for representation of small parties such as liberal and green parties in Germany, and all kinds of parties in the Netherlands and Denmark.
- It fosters government by consent, since major parties need to form coalitions to govern effectively.
- Decentralisation is promoted where regional lists are used, therefore allowing greater devolution of power from the centre.
- It reflects European-wide practice and reinforces the tendency within Europe of power going up to the supranational level and down to the regional level (linked to subsidiarity – see Chapter 12).
- It is overall more democratic.

### Arguments against PR

- No clear majority government (although this may depend on party system), and government formations decided behind closed doors. Sometimes there can be a majority government.
- Unstable government – too many parties leads to unstable and frequent changes in government; but the experience of the Netherlands, Denmark and Switzerland, with multiparty coalitions, does not bear this out.
- It allows smaller parties a disproportionate influence over the larger parties.

- It permits smaller parties to change allegiance in order to ensure their continuation in a governing coalition. For example, the FDP has remained intermittently part of the governing coalition since the founding of the Federal Republic in 1949, and uninterruptedly first with the SPD and then with the CDU–CSU since 1969. If the United Kingdom had operated a similar system then the Liberal Party would have played the same role since 1951 (Plant Commission Labour Party, 1993).
- It allows parties to determine who is elected by their control of the listing positions.

## Majority voting system

The simple plurality system or first-past-the-post (FPTP) system, as it is more commonly called, is used for elections in the United Kingdom (except for local government and European elections in Northern Ireland). In parliamentary elections single member constituencies are used, but in local government elections multi-member constitutencies exist where there can be three-member wards. In this case the three candidates with the highest number of votes are elected.

A development of this system is the two-ballot system used in France for National Assembly and Presidential Elections. In the first round of voting only a candidate getting an absolute majority of votes is elected. In the National Assembly elections, candidates at the end of the first ballot who poll more than 12.5 per cent of the total number of registered voters in a constituency are entitled to go through to the second round where FPTP operates, but many withdraw because of electoral pacts. In the Presidential election, only the two leading candidates go through to the second round. For European, regional, and local elections France uses a list system.[30]

### Arguments for FPTP

- Constituency accountability – voters have a much closer contact with their elected representative in a constituency than under a national or regional list system.
- Effective government – governing with a clear programme unhindered by the need to compromise with a coalition partner provides for a clearer voter choice and more effective pursuit of policy objectives. Clearer consent and legitimacy is ensured under this system.
- Stable government – overall majority leads to stability, but as David Butler says: 'political culture and tradition is far more important than the electoral system in determining the stability of a government'.[31] The events following the change of system from PR to more FPTP in Italy for the 1994 elections shows that FPTP does not logically lead to clear majority government or stop the behind-closed-door bargaining process.
- Excludes extreme elements, such as neo-Fascist parties.

An issue that concerns electoral systems is their influence on parties and party systems. Does PR mean a greater number of parties and therefore fairer represen-tation of the people? Most countries which operate a PR system have some kind of percentage threshold above which a party must score in order to gain a seat in the parliament. In the Netherlands this is very low, where a party has only to gain 0.67 per cent of the national vote to win a seat. In Denmark it is 2 per cent and in Germany 5 per cent. The effect of this kind of threshold is to prevent too much fragmentation of the party system, which it is considered would lead to instability from too many parties unable to agree, and unable to form a workable coalition. However, the presence of at least 10 parties in the Dutch parliament has not led to suggestions that the Dutch party system is unstable, although the the May 1994 elections may herald a period of relative instability. As Butler, quoted above, has noted stability is more a result of historical and political culture factors rather than the presence of a large number of parties. The example of PR leading to multiparty systems during the Weimar period in Germany, or during the Fourth Republic in France (1946–58), seems to bear out Butler's comments. Overwhelming economic factors in the Weimar case, and the refusal of Gaullist movement and the French Communist Party (PCF) to accord the constitution any legitimacy, were key factors in undermining parliament's effectiveness, not the mere presence of many different parties.

The ability of PR to fragment the party system and allow in smaller parties is graphically illustrated in the elections to the French National Assembly in 1986. As a result of fears that the governing party, the PS (*Parti Socialiste*) might not win the forthcoming election, the French electoral system was changed from the simple plurality FPTP to PR. The move initiated by President Mitterrand was calculated to allow the FN a number of seats, in the hope of depriving the mainstream right of a majority. The move failed, as the right gained enough seats to form a government, and it permitted the entry of the far right *Front National* (FN) into the National Assembly with 34 seats. The experiment was short-lived and during the right's term of office the system reverted to the previous one.[32]

The example of Italy from 1948 to 1994 provides an example of a PR system where one single party was able to dominate simply by changing its coalition partners, and the crucial reason for this was the need to exclude the PCI. The DC was the main party in the Italian government from 1945 until 1994. It presided over the development of a clientelistic state, where everything depended on party membership or acquaintance with party officials. The term *partitocrazia*, rule by party as opposed to rule by parliament, defined the Italian party system.

The system (which has now changed) used a form of PR with a very low threshold, one constituency seat, or 300 000 votes nationwide. Each party's total list vote was divided by the quota to determine the number of seats it was entitled to in any constituency. Remainders were aggregated nationally to help smaller parties gain representation. The overall result meant that the number of seats gained by a party in the Chamber of Deputies was close in terms of proportion to its national share of the vote.[33] Electoral volatility has always been difficult to measure in Italy until recently, when it has become apparent that the major parties are losing out to the regional and other parties. Coalitions have been an important part of governing Italy. Understanding the construction of Italian coalitions is thus a complex process. History, ideology, intra-party conflicts and institutional rules all play a role.[34]

In Spain, the system was characterised by a strong degree of *personalismo*, which basically means that preferment for contracts and individual promotion within the public service is dependent not on any objective and transparent examinations of merit but on who you happen to know. The basis of this system was established under the Franco dictatorship, and although there has been some attempt to change this structure under the government of the socialist party (PSOE) since 1982, most commentators tend to highlight this element as a continuing major feature of the political system (see Chapter 10).

Overall, however, the party system in Spain has developed since 1975 along standard West European lines. There has been a traditional left–right ideological divide between PSOE and the various right-wing parties. Under the PR voting system, there has also been representation of other parties; at the national level the Left Unity party (IU) acting as the guardian of socialism as PSOE has moved to the right, and as important the strong regional parties particularly in Catalonia, the CiU,[35] and the Basque province PNV (*Partido Nacionalista Vasco*) and HB (*Herri Batasuna*) (for further information on these parties see below). The conservative parties have until recently been too closely associated with the discredited Franco regime to have any real electoral chance, but this now appears to be changing as corruption charges against the incumbent socialists begin to increase. The UCD, led by Suarez, one of the key figures in the transition, has now faded with the PP which emerged from the AP, and led by a post-Franco politician José-Maria Aznar. The importance of the regional parties became clear after the 1993 elections when PSOE lost its overall majority and became dependent on them, particularly the CiU for its continued majority in the Chamber of Deputies.

In conclusion the party system can be described as balanced with little ideological distance between the two main parties and between PSOE and the CiU. Furthermore, the three main national parties, the PSOE, PP, and the IU together with the nationalist CiU, won more than 85 per cent of the popular vote at the 1993 elections.

One effect of PR may be that groups seek parliamentary status as a channel of influencing policy rather than rely on interest group or pressure group activity to forward their interests. Although the Green Party in the United Kingdom won about 15 per cent of the vote in the 1989 European election, it gained no seat. It is perhaps no wonder that, given the refusal of either of the two main political parties to introduce a PR system, membership of groups such as Greenpeace and Friends of the Earth is so high in the United Kingdom. Furthermore, it could be argued that any element of PR allows groups a much wider forum to put forward their case, so that in the Netherlands or Germany environmental groups have their pressure groups as one source of influence, and their parliamentary representation as another. In the Netherlands, also, parties representing the elderly gained seats for the first time in the May 1994 election. However, the greater degree of representation also means that extreme right-wing parties have a presence in national parliaments.

## 8.5   Realignment and dealignment

Increasing stability and consolidation of established political parties seemed to be the one feature which came to characterise the western European party systems in the post-1945 world. Political scientists pointed to growing ideological similarity stemming from a growth in the numbers of middle-income earners (the *embourgeoisement* thesis), and a consensus among the left and the right over policy concerning the role of the state in providing full employment, education, housing, health and the whole range of welfare benefits. The middle ground of politics had been secured and the new middle class in terms of its income, outlook and aspirations reigned supreme, reflected in the orientation of the mainstream social democratic and Christian democratic parties. The expansion of this middle class looked unstoppable and this would come to be reflected in a wider and more solid base for their respective political parties. This analysis was based on the notion that party systems reflect social cleavages, and as these cleavages diminished in importance so would the differences between the parties and thereby the nature of the party system in terms of polarised groups. Partly, also, as Flanagan and Dalton explain, sharp cleavages become blurred as a party becomes institutionalised.[36] Moreover, class was becoming a declining cleavage even during the economic crisis of the 1970s. Inglehart's work also showed that a more important cleavage was the generational cleavage, based on age and education, a factor also considered crucially important by Allardt.[37]

The economic crisis of the 1970s and the influence of New Right thought and its practical application by governments in the United Kingdom and the United States during the 1980s has challenged this overall prediction of stability and consolidation. In addition the rise of new social movements and extreme right-wing parties have led to a debate about whether there is a realignment taking place in western European party systems. This realignment is reflected by instability and increasing electoral volatility, but is considered to be a temporary phenomenon. A much deeper process has also been suggested: that of dealignment, which throws into question the whole role of political parties and their role as mediators and vehicles of representation between government and the people. This view raises the issue about whether other groups such as interest groups, pressure groups and particularly industrial and finance interests are now more important than political parties in negotiating and settling the political agenda. This analysis is also tied into a view that sees the operation of power in much larger terms than simply the purely party political. Our comments concerning the pluralist and corporatist view of the state are also relevant in this context (see Chapter 3).

Dalton *et al.* (1984) list seven factors that they see as influencing change in party systems: *embourgeoisement*, social mobility, mass society (atomised society), community integration, cognitive mobilisation (political sophistication), ageing party system (cyclical party success) and value change (cf. Inglehart and Flanagan decline in respect for authority, conformity, religiosity and work ethic).[38]

They raise the question about whether a new phase of post-industrial society is developing, with an industrial/post-industrial cleavage and also in Rose's terms a new cleavage between public sector and private sector:

one can see signs that the structure of democratic party systems, frozen for so much of our lifetime, is beginning to thaw.[39]

Numerous studies of different countries by Dalton *et al.* show the decline of traditional voting patterns which have impacted on the party system. In the Netherlands, for example, Irwin and Dittrich demonstrate how the traditional cleavages in Dutch society have declined in importance.[40] The classic representation of the Netherlands has referred to a four way **verzuiling** (segmentation or pillarisation) of the society into Catholic, Protestant, socialist and liberal (neutral) political subcultures. Factors such as the decline in confessional politics, decline in religious attendance and the rise of new parties has changed this four-way split. Seip has also pointed to the end of compulsory voting, which loosened the ties between some parties and voters, and individual voter change as the most important factors in explaining party system change in the Netherlands.[41] The most important factor of dealignment is 'the decrease in the party-affiliated portion of the electorate', the floating voters. The General Election of May 1994 seems to confirm this analysis with both main parties, the Christian Democrats (CDA) and the socialists, losing more than 30 seats between them to the strongly pro-European left of centre Democrats.[42]

In contrast to the Netherlands the traditional cleavages of religion, region and class are still strong in Spain, although McDonough and Pina argue that there is a process of loosening up taking place.[43] Three factors account for this change: age, the changing role of the state and the absorption of Spain into the capitalist subsystem. However, 'primordial bonds and personalism' are still strong, with the army, the Church and banks playing a predominant role in the country. The presence of regional cleavages is reflected in the significant role played by the Catalan Nationalist Party, the CiU, in giving Felipe Gonzalez a majority of one in the Congress of Deputies (Lower House) after the election of 1993. Although Spain's mainstream parties are divided along classic left–right lines, localism continues to play an important role. The same phenomenon has become apparent again in Italy, with the growth of the Northern League, and the predominantly southern-based Freedom Alliance (AN + *Forza Italia*).[44]

Perhaps the most important element that has given rise to this whole debate has been the growth of 'new politics', expressed particularly in the work of Inglehart. He argues that intergenerational value change, a result of increasing affluence, absence of war and sociocultural changes have produced the 'new politics'. His view suggests that these phenomena will become permanent, while his opponents argue that these movements are the result of the socioeconomic crisis of the late 1970s and 1980s. Once the crisis is over we can expect this kind of politics to diminish in importance.[45]

'New politics' groups tend to be composed of those under 45 years who have undergone higher education, with an emphasis on neglected areas of the political agenda such as the environment (although it is a measure of their success that this issue is now very much part of mainstream debate), participative politics, disarmament and third world development. Furthermore, their tactics are based on a wide range of direct-action measures such as squatting, blockading roads and other developments, non-payment of taxes and more traditional approaches such as demonstrations and boycotts. Such extra-parliamentary activities tend to differentiate out the 'new politics' groups from other groups who seek to influence through usual channels. Values are a key feature of these groups, based as they are on attempts to counter consumerism, decentralise production and prioritise other kinds of economic structures. Such programmes do challenge generally accepted ideas about the nature of liberal democracy as currently practised, and question the need for continued economic growth, large-scale armaments production and excessive consumption patterns. We look in more detail at 'new politics' in the next chapter when we discuss new social movements.

Gordon Smith takes issue with the Dalton thesis arguing that provided both mainstream parties gain more than 80 per cent of the national vote then really the party system is still stable.[46] Although this argument explains stability in a formalistic sense it does not reveal how the parties may have undergone some kind of ideological or programmatic change, which is itself a product of instability. For instance, the threat of the extreme right in France and Germany, and to a lesser extent the United Kingdom in the late 1970s has impacted on the mainstream parties to such an extent that they have borrowed from those parties to implement new harsh measures against immigrants and immigration.

The issue of immigration also appears to be a significant factor in changing the nature of the party system. It is not a cleavage as such but it plays a key role in explaining the popularity of extreme right-wing party programmes, and is used by mainstream parties of the left and right as a way of securing votes. The examples in France of the socialist government, during the premiership of Edith Cresson, the speeches of the leaders of the UDF (Valéry Giscard d'Estaing) and RPR (Jacques Chirac) in 1992 and the campaign leaflets of the Social and Liberal Democrats in the Tower Hamlets by-election in October 1993, all indicate the way such parties play the race card. Within the party programmes themselves, there is clear echoing of extreme right-wing rhetoric by the mainstream parties, in terms of calling for restrictions on further immigration and encouragements to repatriation.

Overall, what is discernible in analysing changes in western European party systems is our common theme of unity and diversity. There are general factors hastening the process, such as *embourgeoisement* and generational change, and then more particular factors such as religion and region which have a differing salience depending on the particular country in question. The effect on the party system will be dependent on the extent to which the mainstream parties can incorporate elements of these demands into their programmes.

## 8.6 Political parties

The growth in the number of political parties at the end of the last century and the first two decades of this century and competing in the political marketplace has been a product of the competition of people and groups in the economic sphere. The classic notions of liberal democracy have been reflected in the plurality of parties in open competition, with freedom of opinion, expression, organisation and assembly subject to an agreed set of rules. The ability of different parties, for example socialist and communist parties, to participate in this kind of system has been restricted since the last century. During Bismarck's time as German Chancellor anti-socialist laws were enacted to restrict the SPD and similar organisations from participating in the political process, and in the 1950s the Supreme Court in the Federal Republic of Germany, The Federal Constitutional Court (*Bundesverfassungsgericht*), banned the Communist Party as well as an extreme right-wing party, Socialist Republican Party (SRP).[47] Political parties play a fourfold role within liberal democratic societies, as discussed below.

## Legitimating role

By participating in the democratic process they give the system its validity. When, for example, Sinn Fein agreed in August 1994 to accept to end its support for an armed resolution to the situation in Northern Ireland, it became accepted within the framework of the democratic system. It agreed to be bound by the rules of that process. Non-violent tactics such as participating in debates, using means of publicity to persuade and accepting the ultimate decision of the ballot box are the key features of this process. Parties play a stabilising role within the political system.

## Organisational role

Aspiring politicians need some kind of party label if they want to ensure their success in the long term. Mitterrand fashioned the Socialist Party in France very much in his own image, and used it as his base to win the presidency. Even Berlusconi in Italy needed to create some kind of party structure with *Forza Italia* to win the elections of 1994.

They provide on the whole the political leadership although often people are brought in from outside (for example Lord Young, a businessman, brought in to the Cabinet during Mrs Thatcher's premiership). The centrality of parties to the democratic system is outlined in the German Basic Law (**Grundgesetz**) where it states that parties form the basis of government. Furthermore the state financing of parties, provided they poll sufficient votes, highlights the important role of parties.

## Representative

They are the vehicles of representation for people in a society and a way for grievances to be channelled, but since most major parties in Europe have become 'catch-all' parties they perform this function in an imperfect manner. They act merely as a forum for aggregating diverse interests, which are then processed into a party manifesto on which to fight an election. Parties can, therefore, be seen as playing a unifying rather than a divisive role in the political system. Some Green parties could be seen as more representative in the sense that they tend to be more single-issue orientated and therefore perform a more direct representative role.

## Educational and integrative

This role refers to the issues and values that parties express which form part of the political culture of a society.[48] The educational role was seen as being crucial to parties and resulted in the creation of book clubs, welfare agencies, newspapers, leisure clubs for sporting groups and young people. This used to be one of the most important roles for a political party, in recruiting members and persuading people of its ideology and programme, but in contemporary Europe the decline in party membership and the growth of the mass media have taken over this educative role. Very few people, outside party activists, read party publications on policy, and with fewer members internal party debate is restricted. However, the political affiliation of newspapers, even though no longer party newspapers, is still important, particularly in Britain.

The major tendency within political parties during this period has been towards a greater professionalisation, reflected in the growth of a hierarchy of paid officials, resulting in a significant bureaucratisation of parties and their structures. This has been a long term process as Michels noted in his 1911 study of the German SPD, but it has become a common feature of all mainstream parties from the British Labour Party and the French Gaullist Party *Rassemblement pour la République* (RPR). The use of all kinds of marketing strategies, particularly advertising, more usually associated with the commercial sector, has also become a vital part of selling parties.

Overall the mainstream parties of the centre-left and centre-right have won the allegiance of the overwhelming majority of the electorate which votes, in some cases gaining up to 90 per cent of those voting but never falling below 75 per cent. However, these statistics mask the nature of the differences that may exist even within political parties which, for electoral reasons, have to present a united face in order to win elections.

Concern has also been expressed about the declining importance of political parties within western European liberal democracies. Recent evidence indicates, however, that the overall picture in western Europe points to a greater role for parties (Katz and Mair, 1994). Moreover, parties are also maintaining or increasing their membership, and giving those members a greater say in how policy should be formulated and leaders elected. State funding of parties has also given them a much more central role within the whole political system.

Political parties, then, have developed as the main forum through which this process of representation has been undertaken. There has been a common background to the development of political parties in western Europe stemming from a shared historical, political, social, economic, religious, ideological and cultural process. The next three sections look at the main groupings of political parties under the headings of left, right and centre. As this section has indicated, these are not fixed categories, changing over time and place both between and within parties.

### 8.6.1 *Parties and movements of the left*

#### Mainstream left

The left in Europe encompasses a wide spectrum including the social democracy of the German Social Democratic Party (SPD), the former Eurocommunism of the Italian Party of the Democratic Left (PDS), the post-communist Democratic Left Alliance (SLD) and the PSL (Polish Peasant Party) in Poland, the range of small traditional and reformed communist parties and Trotskyist groups. Our concern in this section will be to present the ideological and organisational developments that have taken place in the mainstream parties in recent decades.

In Chapter 1 we outlined the way in which the debate between socialism and social democracy has been around for over a century. Since 1945 the key ideological change that has overtaken socialist and social democratic parties has been the jettisoning of crucial tenets of the socialist faith. In particular, as a result of growing affluence, the parties have abandoned policies promoting wholescale nationalisation, full employment, expansion of the welfare state and increasing industrial democratisation. The French Socialist Party (PS) was one of the last socialist governments in western Europe to attempt elements of this kind of policy between 1981–83, together with a form of Keynesian policy in terms of increasing government spending. The experiment was abandoned in favour of austerity measures.[49] It is also interesting to note that the attempt to devolve some levels of government down to the regional and departmental level in France indicates the move away from one of the traditional socialist notions of using the power of the central state to introduce reforms. This tendency reflects one of the other early socialist idea about self-help and organisation at local and community level.

All the socialist parties in government in western Europe during the 1980s have moved to the centre. In fact the process began with the move by the SPD from a class party to a catch-all party at their Bad Godesberg party conference of 1959. With the demise of their traditional constituencies of manual blue collar workers, the parties have embraced an eclectic ideology that brings them close to other mainstream parties of the traditional right. In key areas of fiscal policy, macroeconomic policy, foreign policy, social security and over Europe, the differences are of degree rather than substance. The Labour Party in Britain, as well as the SPD in Germany, both in opposition for most of the 1980s and 1990s now have a programme of promising tax cuts and restraining spending on welfare, very similar to aspects of their opponents' policies. The only difference between the two parties' approach to government is in the SPD's concern to revive the grand corporate partnership of government, employers, unions and the Bundesbank (*Konzertierte Aktion*), while the Labour Party is doing its best to shed any vestige of the notion that it may still be controlled by the trade unions. Nevertheless, both parties are committed to switching spending on unemployment benefits to financing jobs, which marks them out to a certain extent from their right wing opponents.[50] The Labour Party's programme for constitutional reform within the United Kingdom is another defining characteristic.

The situation in Southern Europe has followed a similar pattern with the Spanish Socialist party (PSOE) in government moving steadily to the right since the mid-1980s, and using cuts in welfare spending as one way to control the budget deficit.[51] The result has been a split with its own trade union support in the UGT, and the creation of a more socialist party to the left, the United Left (*Izquierda Unida*, IU), including the reformed PCE. Two general strikes in November 1988 and February 1993 were called by the trade unions to protest against the government's austerity measures. The Portuguese Socialist Party (PS), in opposition for nearly 10 years, is similarly engaged in defining itself as party of the centre-left, dedicated to making the market run more efficiently. It sees the differences between itself and the governing right-wing Social Democrats (PSD) as one of degree, not substance, and defines its ideological position as a synthesis of European social democracy and left-wing liberalism of the United States variety.[52] The socialist party in Greece, PASOK, has maintained a strong line in Marxist rhetoric, but has moved from implementing a policy that could be described as 'left Keynesianism' in the early 1980s to an austerity policy that resulted in higher unemployment particularly among the young.[53]

The *Sozialdemokratische Partei Österreichs* (SPÖ) is one of the oldest, founded in 1889, and since 1970 it has won the largest number of votes of any Austrian Party and has held the Chancellorship since that time. The SPÖ have a traditional social democratic programme stressing freedom, equality, justice and solidarity, and use the concept of 'ecological circulation-flow economy', which reflects an attempt to reconcile economic growth with environmental concerns. The incorporation of concerns for the environment into social democratic party programmes has been a result of the influence and success of green parties in the 1980s. This has led to Red–Green alliances at local and regional level, although sometimes not altogether harmonious.

The experience of the Social Democratic Labour Party (SAP) in Sweden is significant for all other social democratic parties. The party was in power from the 1930s until it was ousted by the conservatives in the 1991 general election.[54] During almost 60 years of power the party created one of the most extensive welfare systems in the world: a universal catch-all safety net, with high levels of child care provision and increasing participation of women at all levels of society. The 1991 conservative government set out to privatise some of these social services and cut public sector jobs. The result was the loss of 100 000 public sector jobs, mainly affecting women. In the September 1994 election, the left was returned to power with the biggest swing since the 1930s, promising Keynesian measures of state spending on training and job creation schemes with the aim of full employment. However, this kind of programme is not a tax and spend policy, as some of the other elements of the Social Democrats' programme includes cuts in child benefits and pensions. Furthermore there is evidence that many younger voters were attracted to the former Communist Left Party and the Green Party.[55]

The debate about the future of social democracy still divides interventionists from market socialists, those who see a central role for the state in terms of economic planning and those who favour a more relaxed regulatory role for the state in terms of making capitalism work better. There is also evidence of a resurgence in discussion about ethical values for social democracy. These ideas concern promoting support and protection for the family and community. The influence of Christian notions of social solidarity and community, based around inculcating ideas about right and wrong, and maintaining and improving the role of the family and the schools, finds expression in the Christian Socialist Movement in the British Labour Party and the approach of people such as Jacques Delors in France and Oskar Lafontaine in Germany.[56]

## Other left

### Communist parties and Eurocommunism

The communist parties in western Europe were founded in the aftermath of the Russian Revolution in 1917. They developed out of splits with the leading social democratic parties, and almost immediately became part of the wider communist movement directed from Moscow.[57] The Yugoslav Communist Party led by Tito and the Italian Communist Party (PCI) led by Togliatti were the only two communist parties that attempted to follow a more independent path in the period after 1945.[58] In the 1960s and 1970s Santiago Carrillo, the exiled leader of the Spanish Communist Party (PCE), began formulating a new ideological programme which culminated in the PCE's form of Eurocommunism.

In terms of their founding ideology, most parties considered themselves the political expression of the working class. They were class parties with an explicitly Marxist programme that implied their sole control over the state ('dictatorship of the proletariat'), and the nationalisation of all the major economic forces in society ('the Command Economy'). The party organisation was based on Lenin's notion of 'democratic centralism', which meant some internal party debate, but once a decision had been reached then absolute loyalty to the party line was enforced. Many writers have suggested that there was a great deal more centralism than democracy in this model, the proof of which lies in the undemocratic nature of most of the regimes of Eastern Europe, and the almost complete obedience that western European Parties had to show to Moscow. These parties had to accept that the Soviet model of communism was the one and true model which all other parties had to follow.

This over-centralised party structure and closely managed command economy became two of the main points of criticism of the Soviet model as other parties tried to establish a more independent model. Furthermore, the notion that violent revolution was the only way to seize state power became increasingly unlikely in the western European democracies.[59] The PCI, therefore, together with the PCE chose, a more Eurocommunist line. The main elements of Eurocommunism were an acceptance that socialism could be achieved via the means of parliamentary democracy. A pluralist political system, with competing parties in open and free elections was the main point. Furthermore, the market had a role to play in the economy, and not just a centralised state controlled system.[60] The success of this policy was evident in Italy during the 1970s when the PCI almost overtook the DC as the main party. However, the success of the 1970s was matched by a decline in membership during the 1980s.

Although the PCF had managed to gain four ministerial posts in the first socialist government formed after the elections in 1981 in France, they did not last long in their posts and resigned in protest at the government's austerity policy in 1983. Under the leadership of Georges Marchais for most of the 1970s and 1980s, the PCF maintained a hot and cold commitment to supporting the Soviet Union. They were less than vociferous in their condemnation of the Soviet invasion of Afghanistan in 1979 (Marchais supported it), and after their ejection from the coalition government, still held to policies, for example, of full-scale nationalisation. Unsuccessful attempts were made by Charles Fiterman, a former transport minister in the coalition cabinet, to change the party's doctrine to a more Eurocommunist line. Subsequently, they have continued to lose support and now are lucky to score above 10 per cent.

After the events of 1989 and the failed Communist coup in Russia in 1991, all western European communist parties have had to consider further their role. In the post-1989 world with the collapse of the Soviet Union, many communist parties have metamorphosed into socialist parties of one sort or another. For example, the Italian Communist Party (PCI) one of the strongest Communist parties in western Europe in the post-1945 world, has become the PDS (the Party of the Democratic Left), although a smaller group has **Rifondazione**, which holds more closely to traditional communist ideology.[61]

For former communist parties in the 'East', there has been a shift to more social democratic orientation. As a result of disillusionment with the slow process of tangible benefits from the unification of Germany many people in the new Federal states (former East Germany), have swung back to support for the reconstructed Communist Party, now called the PDS (the Democratic Socialist Party), led by Gregor Gysi. During the general election campaign in the autumn of 1994, the party campaigned effectively in its eastern stronghold and won more than three constituency seats, thereby allowing it to benefit from the proportional distribution of seats, which meant it finally gained 30 seats in the Bundestag.

The experience of the ex-communist parties in other ECE countries, for example the Democratic Left Alliance (SLD) and the Polish Peasant Party (PSL) in Poland, reflects the same kind of disillusionment with capitalism.[62] However, many of these reformed ex-communist parties have followed a policy programme of financial orthodoxy, similar to those of the social democratic parties in government in western Europe. These measures indicate an overall social democratic orientation rather than any old-style socialist or communist state interventionism. The SLD relies heavily on the ex-communist dominated trade union, the OPZZ, for its organisational support but, like the Labour Party in Britain, it is engaged in a process of loosening its ties with the trade union. Much of its important electoral support comes from former Communist Party *apparatchiks*, who have benefited directly from the sale of state enterprises to become the business class.[63] The result has been a policy of corporatism in terms of reorganising the trade union movement into fewer federations and the creation of a procedure of centralised collective bargaining. Overall, however, given Poland's recent history in terms of the strength of the Solidarity trade union movement, the general consensus is that the state still has a key role to play in macroeconomic management. Hence the slowing down of some of the privatisation programme, and the support for continued provision of a national health programme and other welfare benefits.[64] The only cloud on the SLD–PSL coalition's horizon is over entry to the European Union, which the PSL is less keen on, fearing its members will be unable to compete with the large agro-industry in the EU. A counterpoint to this fear is the concern of French agricultural interests that the entry of Poland and other East/Central states will affect their farmers by a flood of cheap imports. In Hungary, the Czech Republic and Slovakia the story is similar with variations on the social democratic theme being played by new centre-left parties and reformed ex-communist party members. The overall problem for these ex-communist parties, as they splinter more and more, is to find some kind of coherent ideology that both gives some sense to their existence and has the chance of electoral success. The difficulties are manifold, and as Bull notes:

The idea of a 'new democratic left' . . . seems to symbolise the fact that ultimately the problems faced by both political worlds ('refounded' communism and the non-communist left) amount to the same thing: the crisis of the democratic-socialist project itself.[65]

Nevertheless, the left in Europe, however defined, is not totally on the ropes. Despite the fragile hold on power of PSOE, the social democrats in Sweden have regained power and the results for the socialist candidate, Lionel Jospin, in the French presidential elections, winning the first round and scoring a respectable 47.4 per cent of the vote in the second round, indicate a modest upswing in fortunes. Furthermore, the PDS's (former PCI) successes in the May 1995 Italian local elections point to a recovery that could be sustained.

## The left at the European level

This section looks briefly at the role of the socialist parties in the European Parliament (EP), and their attempts to create a united and common programme at EU level. At the annual congress of the Confederation of European Socialist Parties in November 1992, the socialist and social democratic parties in the EU decided to create the Party of European Socialists (PES), to decide action on key issues affecting the EU. The first major step of the new party was to agree to a common party manifesto for the European elections in June 1994.[66]

After both the 1989 and 1994 European elections the socialists formed the largest bloc in the EP. The 1994 manifesto reflected the usual social democratic approach calling for a coordinated European strategy to combat unemployment and social exclusion, and more action on equal opportunities and protection of the environment. Matters of controversy for national parties such as the British Labour Party may turn on the call for greater democratisation of European institutions, particularly the European Parliament.[67]

These agreements are the first steps towards creating a cohesive transnational party structure, but it is too early to speculate on their possible future role, given the strength of the national parties. As Bardi notes:

. . . the transnational federations themselves, in terms of political relevance and organisational structure, appear to be little more than expressions of a generic sense of commonality shared by other parties with comparable histories and similar sets of values . . . Given the present institutional arrangements in the EC, the formation of genuine 'Europarties' is thus rather unlikely.[68]

The effect of closer links with other European parties may affect internal party orientations, as for example with the Labour Party in Britain. It has undergone a radical change of heart as far as the European Community and now the European Union is concerned. In its manifesto for the 1983 general election the party was calling for withdrawal from the EC, and even in 1991 the then leader (Neil Kinnock – now a European Commissioner) rejected other European socialist parties' moves towards creating a common European defence programme.[69] The realisation has dawned on Labour that in terms of social protection, the standards being set by the EU are more in keeping with their own policies than anything being proposed on a national level.

## 8.6.2  Parties and movements of the right

This section will examine all aspects of the right in western Europe in two main parts, beginning with an analysis of the mainstream right and then considering the rise and presence of the extreme right.

### Mainstream Right

#### Christian Democracy and Conservatism

Our analysis in this part will be mainly a comparative treatment of the respective differences between Christian Democracy and Conservatism. We will begin with an examination of the ideology and orientation of Christian Democracy by looking at the German Christian Democratic Party (CDU) and its sister party in Bavaria the Christian Social Union (CSU), and the Italian Christian Democrats (DC), which has ceased to exist, but which dominated post-1945 Italian politics until 1993. We shall also make reference to the Austrian ÖVP (*Österreichische Volkspartei* – Austrian People's Party) and Eastern European parties. The British Conservative Party will be the main focus of our treatment of conservatism, but in order to provide a comprehensive comparison we will also look at other right-wing parties, in particular the French UDF and RPR, as well as the PP in Spain and the coalition of right-wing parties in Italy, to attempt to discern common threads.

#### Christian Democracy

Christian Democracy is essentially a post-1945 phenomenon although antecedents can be found in nineteenth century parties. In the immediate aftermath of the Second World War certain factors combined to contribute to the emergence of Christian Democracy as the guiding ideology of the right, particularly in Germany and Italy:[70]

- the Catholic Church still retained its mass base;
- most traditional forces of the right had been discredited from their acquiescence or lukewarm opposition to Fascism;
- resistance forces contained Catholics and Protestants;
- development of new political thinking by Catholic intellectuals; and
- United States support for Christian Democratic parties.

The major changes concerned the way in which these parties were able to create a distinctive identity separate from that of the Catholic hierarchy. It is important to note that the Vatican had never countenanced any temporal opposition to its authority, and was as such actively hostile to the basic principles of the liberal democratic state, based as it is on notions of individual rights within a secular state and loyalty to that state and not to Rome. The doctrine of **ultramontanism** refers to this idea of prime and unquestioning loyalty to Rome and not to the local state.

These parties were designed to appeal across denominational, class, regional and ethnic cleavages. Their ideology is based on the notion of politics being governed by laws gained from Christianity; in particular, the dignity of the human individual with a moral and spiritual dimension gained from God, within the context of a family, community and social environment, with its responsibilities of maintaining social solidarity.[71] There exists an anti-acquisitive, anti-consumerist tendency in this philosophy. The implications of this ideology for practical politics is seen from the way in which these parties have promoted certain policies.

There has been a strong emphasis on the social welfare provision of the state and the church. In Germany, for example, the churches have a special status as public corporate entities which are in partnership with the state. Everyone (other than those who ask to be exempted) pays 2 per cent of their income in a tax (*Kirchensteuer*) that goes to finance the churches' role in the provision of social services, such as homes for the elderly, care for the disabled and hostels for the homeless as well as kindergartens and schools.[72] Furthermore the state contributes to the salaries of priests.

This close involvement of the church with the state has been reflected in the way in which the Christian democratic parties have viewed the role of the state in running society. The notion of corporatism is very strong, with ideas about social partnership as the cornerstone. The state should be involved with both sides of industry in initiating policy, not just concerning industrial relations but across other areas. There has been in Italy, too, a large trade union which was tied to the DC, the CISL, which indicates both the desire to reflect the aspirations of the working class and a fear of the influence of communism (CISL moved away from the DC in the 1970s).

Anti-communism has been one of the main binding forces in the make-up of these parties, with both the immediate post-war leaders Adenauer in Germany and de Gasperi in Italy firmly nailing their colours to this mast. With this orientation, there has been a consistent and strong pro-European stance, with both parties playing a central role in the construction of the European Community.

In terms of other areas of policy, the parties have promoted traditional Christian values, which have brought them into conflict with the desires and aspirations of their constituency. Their views on marriage, divorce and abortion have come into conflict as the societies have become more secular. In Italy the DC was opposed to any liberalisation of these fundamental aspects of family life, and campaigned actively against a Yes vote in the divorce referendum of 1974. In Germany, the unification process after 1989 brought out clearly the CDU-CSU's opposition to abortion. In the former DDR (East Germany) abortion had been obtainable virtually on demand, whereas in the Federal Republic there were certain restrictions, particularly in Bavaria under the CSU.[73] The controversy over paragraph 218 indicates the continuing relevance of religious values at the heart of the parties' ideology.

The internal structure of both parties has reflected their desire to be movements of all sections of society rather than parties in the strict sense of the word (like the RPR in France, and the Green Parties). The CDU has been federalist, and given the nature of the political system in the Federal Republic, many of its leading figures have come up from the regional level.

Within the DC, there existed currents (*correnti*) of opinion, which formed into strong factions within the party itself. These groups spanned more or less the ideological spectrum from extreme right to centre left, and explain the way in which the DC was able to form coalitions with parties of the centre and left. In the 1960s the DC opened to the left, when the PSI (Socialist Party) entered into coalition, and for a period during the 1980s Bettino Craxi of the PSI was the prime minister. There are also suggestions that the murder of one of the DC's leading figures in 1978, Aldo Moro, was linked to his attempts to bring into government the Italian Communist Party (PCI).

The Christian Democrats' support has been based on practising Christians, rural populations, urban lower-middle-class, women and certain regional centres such as Bavaria and North East Italy. This profile is also reflected in the type of support for Christian Democratic parties in the Benelux countries. In recent years there has been erosion of this support from the growth of secularism, more consumerist attitudes, decline of the rural vote and changing attitudes among women. The Catholic subculture, particularly in Italy, has also lost its importance, with its provision of social and sporting clubs losing out to the growth of other forms of entertainment and family leisure patterns.

An overall assessment must recognise the success of the Christian Democrats in Germany and Italy in integrating most forces of the right, and giving a legitimacy to liberal democracy. Furthermore, they have been at the forefront of efforts to European integration at the national and European level, as the section below on the European People's Party demonstrates. But their predominant position must be seen in the context of the immediate post-1945 settlement, and the crucial support they received from western governments and particularly the United States (Ginsborg, 1990). The anti-communist card allowed them enduring support in the fixed positions of the ideological divide of the Cold War.

The fortunes of Christian Democracy in the mid-1990s are mixed. The DC has been virtually wiped off the political map in Italy, although the CDU has maintained itself as the pre-eminent political party in Germany. In France there is no Christian Democratic party as such, but the UDF (*Union pour la Démocratie Française*), set up by Giscard d'Estaing in the mid-1970s, espoused initially much of the same social market philosophy and notions of social solidarity. Like their coalition partners on the right the Gaullist RPR (*Rassemblement pour la République*), they began to accept a more neo-liberal line in the mid-1980s.[74]

The RPR, although still committed to some notion of the **dirigiste** state, began to follow a clearer neo-liberal path in the mid-1980s, particularly in government from 1986–88, and as the largest party in the coalition right-wing government after 1993. Like their conservative counterparts across the Channel, there were calls for more

deregulation and privatisation, spiced up by traditional right-wing demands for
stronger law and order, tighter immigration controls and possible link-ups with the
*Front National*. Some of these policies were opposed by the UDF, in particular the idea
of alliance with the FN. As with the British conservative party, the RPR is split over
Europe. During the 1992 referendum debate leading figures in the party such as
Charles Pasqua and Philippe Séguin opposed the Maastricht Treaty.

The RPR leader Jacques Chirac succeeded François Mitterrand as President in May
1995, on a platform that seemed to combine both a commitment to financial rigour
and state intervention to reduce the high levels of unemployment in France. Other
aspects of his programme promised a continuation of the conservative agenda of
deregulation and emphasis on law and order and tougher immigration controls. The
decision to resume nuclear testing is a standard populist flag-wrapping exercise, in
the line of promoting the long-standing French independent nuclear capability. The
reversal of the free movement provisions of the Schengen treaty (see Chapter 11) is
another populist measure designed to toughen up on immigration, and at the same
time send a signal to France's Eurosceptics that the new President can be tough on
Brussels. In many of these policy areas the RPR is closer to British conservatism than
Continental Christian Democracy.

### Conservatism

British Toryism has almost nothing in common with Christian Democracy in Europe, and the
spirit in which Christian Democracy proceeds to European construction is almost the opposite
of Conservative pragmatism. Peregrine Worsthorne[75]

The main reasons for this difference, he argues, stem from the social teachings of the
Catholic church which contain anti-capitalist elements, doctrines of corporatism and
defence of agriculture. British conservatism, on the other hand, is characterised by a
more individualistic, pragmatic ideology. This expresses itself in a strong belief in the
free market against any state intervention, a legacy of nineteenth century liberalism
and a more emotional, nostalgic belief in Britain's unique greatness as an island power
that makes it difficult to join in a more united economic and political framework.

This particular view of British conservatism is conditioned by the experience of the
party during the heyday of neo-liberalism in the 1980s. The experience of Disraeli's
'one nation' in the nineteenth century, and the 1945–79 period of 'Butskellism'
indicates that there are many other strands of conservatism which are closer in
thinking to Continental Christian Democracy.

British Conservatism is not an -ism. It is not a system of ideas . . . It is not an ideology a doctrine.[76]

### The new right in Italy

*Forza Italia*, the political party created by Silvio Berlusconi just a few months before
the 1994 Italian elections and which won an overwhelming mandate at those elections
to govern in coalition with the Northern League (*Lega Nord*/LN) and the National
Alliance (*Alleanza Nazionale*/AN), represents the ascendancy of neo-liberalism in Italy.

However, the various strains in the coalition are apparent from conflicting ideological strands and the government lasted less than a year. The Northern League and *Forza Italia* are inclined towards a Thatcherite neo-liberalism while the AN maintains a statist and *dirigiste* stance towards the role of the state, echoing very strongly the corporatist philosophy of Mussolini's strong state. The notion of a strong centralised state and continued help for the south (AN's power base) is directly at odds with the Northern League's federalist policy, and its open hostility to the south. In Guido Passalacqua's prescient words, 'the partners are like snakes, entwined together but striking at each other continually'.[77]

The dominant force is *Forza Italia*, whose policy of neo-liberalism implies tax cuts, privatisation and the promise of a good life for all Italians. Perhaps the single most important factor in selling their programme has been the fact that Berlusconi's conglomerate business empire Fininvest controls almost 90 per cent of Italian private television, reaching almost half the total population. Together with a string of publishing companies and one of Italy's most successful football clubs, AC Milan, this apparent success story has persuaded many Italians that a similar approach can rejuvenate the Italian economy by reducing public debt and creating employment. It is a populist message very similar to the one promoted by the British Conservative Party during the 1980s.

The triumph of *Forza Italia* was also a result of the corruption of the old dominant political elites in the DC and Socialist Party (PSI), and the inability of the new Left to shake off their past. It also represents the changing allegiance of the leaders of most of Italy's large corporations from the DC to *Forza Italia*. Another factor appears to be the electorate's concern that the anti-corruption drive was becoming too destabilising, hence the explanation why so many people changed from voting for anti-corruption candidates in the December 1993 municipal elections to *Forza Italia* or other allied parties.

It is important to note that although this particular message may have the air of a 'new' right about it, Berlusconi has many links with the corrupt previous political elite, notably Bettino Craxi and the socialist party (PSI) which ran Milan. Many of these former political allies have changed allegiances to *Forza Italia*. He joined the illegal P2 Masonic Lodge in 1978, set up to preserve Italy from communism. The activities of this group include collusion with the Mafia, and various shadowy relations with extreme right terrorist groups.[78] Overall, however, the success of Berlusconi has been to draw these disparate elements together into a governing coalition, which given its apparently contradictory elements has managed to form a government.

The inherent instability of the coalition led to its collapse within a year, and the formation of a new government led by Lamberto Dini, previously Berlusconi's finance minister. The apogee of *Forza Italia*'s electoral success came with its 32 per cent score in the European elections in 1994, but with corruption scandals lapping around Berlusconi's door and the ideological disputes between the coalition partners, the opposition has bounced back. In local elections in May 1995, the PDS won 46 of the 54 provinces where elections took place, and the *Partito Popolare* (PP), heirs to the DC legacy, increased their share of the vote from 1994. Despite this electoral setback, the

11 June 1995 referendum results meant that Berlusconi could keep control of two of his three national TV channels.[79] There is no doubt that *Forza Italia* will remain a key player on the Italian political scene, and the extent of the revival in fortunes of the PP remains to be seen.

### The right at the EU level: European People's Party (EPP)

The EPP groups together the main Christian Democratic parties of European Union in the European Parliament. Despite its claims to have created a 'veritable supra-national party',[80] it is not likely to become a mass party; it is rather:

. . . an organisation which unites national parties of similar style into a loose framework for political cooperation within European institutions for the pursuit of broad goals (economic and political integration).[81]

Its general orientation is very much in line with mainstream Christian Democratic thinking, combining the strands of economic and social justice (former DC and Benelux parties), with emphasis on market values and individualistic liberalism (CDU and Austrian ÖVP). This tension has always been at the heart of Christian Democratic ideology and Hanley indicates, in common with other writers, that the tendency has recently been to move towards the more liberal-conservative position.

One of its major problems has been the relationship with the British Conservative Party, on several issues concerning both the future integration of the European Union in terms of moves towards federalism, and issues concerning social policy. Nevertheless, it is an important political grouping, led by national elites, which coordinates approaches to issues within the European institutions, to achieve consensus.

[These elites are] . . . a highly cultivated, multilingual set of European professionals, buttressed by a common set of religious values . . . such an elite, which lives out in its daily life the reality of an integrated Europe, is far ahead ideologically of its national party activists, let alone voters.[82]

### Far right

Whatever the roots of the current rise in far right-wing parties in Europe, there is no doubt from their electoral success since 1983 the last decade or so, that we are witnessing the acceptance by mainstream parties of some of the ideas of neo-Fascism and the election and appointment of members of neo-Fascist parties in government.[83] Some of these parties, particularly the Italian National Alliance, are direct descendants of the Fascist parties of the 1930s and 1940s. (The forerunner of the National Alliance the MSI was formed by former members of Mussolini's *Salo Republic*.) In northern Europe these parties more or less disappeared from the official scene, and only became a presence again with the rise of the FN to prominence in 1983 at Dreux near Paris. The FN represents, however, part of a far right tradition that encompasses the movements against Dreyfus at the end of the nineteenth century, the Vichy period and the Poujadists of the 1950s. Throughout continental Europe such parties are increasingly popular and have commanded up to 15 per cent of the popular vote in some elections. The causes are discussed below:

- Economic crisis has led to mass unemployment and increasing poverty.
- Established political parties have become over-bureaucratised and seem unable to provide solutions to these great economic and social problems.
- There has also been the presence of large numbers of different ethnic groups who immigrated into western Europe during the boom years of the 1950s and 1960s, and who are now used as the scapegoat for many of society's ills, particularly unemployment and drug-related criminality. In eastern Europe, the rise of such groups stems from similar, and even more severe economic and social problems, and in addition a virulent anti-Semitic and anti-gypsy outlook.
- A final explanation for the rise of the far right in recent years concerns the benefits those parties have gained from a change in allegiance by certain political and social elites (Gowan, 1993). These elite groups have switched because they consider the far right as being more willing to pursue neo-liberal economic policy; at the same time these groups, particularly the Republikaner in Germany and the *Vlaams Blok* (Flemish Block) in Belgium, have managed to catch a public mood of disenchantment with established parties. It has also been suggested that some of the support for the far right has come from disenchanted working-class voters.[84]

### Programme

The ideology of the far right is based to a certain extent on ideas from the Fascist parties of the 1930s repackaged to blend in more with post-1945 developments. Perhaps the most significant aspect of this approach has been a total absence of the anti-capitalist rhetoric of the inter-war Fascist parties, both in terms of a critique of economics and liberal democracy. The programme is pure neo-liberalism, no taxation, privatisation and a rhetoric about freeing the entrepreneurial spirit. However, this may merely be a tactical ploy, as the party programmes themselves display clear anti-capitalist and anti-liberal democratic trends. In terms of economic policy there is a harking back to autarkic policy which is formulated in terms of an anti-EU position, and the development of national economic policies behind fairly closed tariff barriers. Unions have no role to play in this system other than as party authorised workers' associations. There is also strong criticism of the failure of political elites within the liberal democratic framework.

Some of the current ideas were not monopolised just by the inter-war Fascist parties but were standard ideas of the authoritarian Catholic right and the nationalist conservative parties at that time. In general, this new ideology has been characterised as national liberal by Bruno Mégret of the FN, where there is an emphasis on using the liberal democratic state to introduce a neo-liberal economic programme and curtail countervailing powers either in local government or the trade unions. As Gowan indicates, the liberal in national liberal 'stands to political liberalism as National Socialism stands to socialism'.[85] The experience in Britain since 1979 demonstrates another attempt to use the institutions of a liberal democratic state to pursue such a programme, although it may prove more difficult in decentralised states.

There is considerable opposition to the notion of the post-war welfare state, with the programme linked to a notion of popular capitalism. Social policy is concerned to return women to their perceived traditional role at home, with a ban on contraception and abortion. Crime is to be fought by stringent punishment and the death penalty. All of this is designed to promote and protect the indigenous nationals, and is permeated by a notion of ethnic purity.

The FN, in common with other far right parties such as the *Republikaner*, the DVU, the *Vlaams Blok* and the *Northern League*,[86] promotes the notion of a homogeneous ethnic identity against any attempt to suggest a multiethnic and multicultural society. Bruno Mégret, one of the FN's leading ideologues, has drawn up a list of measures to counter 'cosmopolitanism', which is code for racial impurity and was used both in France during the Dreyfus era, and by the Nazis to attack Jewish people. The suggestion is that such people cannot be trusted because their allegiance is international and not national patriotic. The further implication of this notion of purity is that other races are impure and therefore inferior, and are easily used as scapegoats for everything from unemployment and lack of housing to crime.

The anti-immigrant approach of the far right has been the most successful plank of their programme, influencing other more established parties across the political spectrum, particularly in France. Charles Pasqua, the Interior Minister in the 1993–95 French government, borrowed both the rhetoric and the ideas of the FN in pursuing stricter immigration policies.

The recent electoral successes of the far right in western Europe began in earnest with the election of a FN councillor at a by-election in Dreux in 1983. At the next year's European election the FN won 11.4 per cent of the vote, and in 1986 at the general election 34 FN deputies were elected to the National Assembly under a PR system. The FN's national support continued at around 10 per cent throughout the 1980s and early 1990s. However, it is important to note also that the established parties of the right entered into coalitions with the FN at regional level in Provence–Alpes–Côte d'Azur during the 1980s and many local politicians have expressed their close affinity with the FN. The FN position as a force in French politics has been maintained with its 15 per cent in the first round of the presidential election in April 1995.

The *Republikaner* first gained prominence in January 1989 at the Berlin elections when they gained about 9 per cent of the vote, and 7.2 per cent at the European elections 6 months later. The effect of the German unification process was to cause splits within the far right and the *Republikaner* only managed 2 per cent at the all-German elections of 1990. These splits were short-lived and by 1992 they were back to their former popular support gaining 11 per cent in the Baden-Würtemberg *Landtag* elections, and nearly 9 per cent in similar elections in Hesse in spring 1993. Another far right party, the DVU (German People's Union), with support mainly in North West Germany, also broke throught the 5 per cent barrier in 1992 and won representation in Bremen with 8 per cent and Frankfurt 10 per cent. Both parties base their appeal on a very strong anti-immigrant programme, and the promotion of an 'ethnic-territorial' policy. This principle involves the protection of the pure Germans, and a warning of the dangers of multiculturalism, particularly from the large numbers of Turkish immigrants in Germany.

The more overt neo-Fascist group in the Italian parliament after the elections of March 1994 is the National Alliance, with a direct link via the MSI to the Salo Republic, the last government of Mussolini. The MSI has been close to the right wing of the DC for a number of years, and allegedly implicated in certain attempts to destabilise the Italian Republic in the 1970s. It has been a small if influential opposition force on the far right of Italian politics. The elections of March 1994 have returned this far right element in Italian politics to the government. Their programme is based on a clear statist vision of Italy and as such is in direct conflict with the more federalist outlook of the Northern League and their proposal for different minimum wages in the North and the South. However, the AN has managed to attract members from a wider spectrum than just the traditional supporters of the Mussolini corporatist state philosophy. For example, in common with all far right parties in Europe and the Northern League they are opposed to any further immigration into Italy, and want to institute a policy of repatriation. Overall the Alliance considers itself a neo-liberal party along the lines of the British Conservative Party in its Thatcherite heyday, no longer neo-Fascist but post-Fascist. It is difficult to make an assessment as the party has been reluctant to commit its 'new' ideas to paper in the form of a manifesto, but a proposal for an American-style presidential system seems to hark back to the days of Il Duce and strong leadership.[87] In the first session of the Italian Senate, the upper house in the Italian parliament, the AN unsuccessfully attempted to get the Senate to rescind the 1948 ban on Fascist parties.

The AN are in the main line of the far right in the rest of Europe, and in their call for the return of women to their traditional roles reflect the traditional conservative social policy underlying their neo-liberalism. The problem with this call for a return of women to the home is that it is an attempt to turn the clock back on three decades of growing women's participation in the labour market, a process which looks like increasing in Italy as elsewhere in western Europe.

In terms of formations of 'Europarties', the very nationalistic and xenophobic tendencies of the far right has made it almost impossible for them to form any kind of transnational groupings. The German *Republikaner* have long disputed the status of the Alto Adige/South Tyrol with the Italian MSI (now AN), and the French FN have been unable to agree with the *Republikaner* on a common language to be used at meetings of the European Far Right in the European Parliament.

### 8.6.3  Parties and movements of the centre

One way of looking at the centre ground in European politics would concentrate on the number of small and, in some cases, extremely influential parties, such as the German FDP (*Freie Demokratische Partei*), which are placed in the middle part of the political spectrum.[88] The problem in trying to define the centre as a distinct ideological space comes from the increasing overlap of Social Democracy and Christian Democracy. On the one hand, therefore, there is some kind of ideological centre which the main parties may seek to occupy, and also there are those smaller parties which are in the centre, such as the German FDP, and the British Liberal Democrats.

In France the centre-right umbrella group is the UDF (see section on the right above) with the PR (*Parti Républicain*), and the CDS (*Centre des Démocrates Sociaux*), occupying the space closest to the centre.

These parties are situated more or less in the middle of the multiparty system, and according to Keman must have a distinctive electoral and policy position. Given all the changes in European politics, and the more fluid ideological positions of all the mainstream parties, it is difficult to pin these 'centre' parties down as fixed very firmly to the centre. Nevertheless many commentators tend to use the labels centre-left, centre and centre-right when describing them. Keman estimates that about a third of West European parties are located within the centre ground. Keman further uses the term 'pivot parties' in his analysis of the role that centre parties can play, only if they can be seen as playing a 'central' and 'dominant' role.[89] He suggests that many of these parties occupy the centre ground according to principles of self-interest, rather than strictly being accountable or responsive to the people's will.

Certain smaller parties do play such a 'pivot' role, for example the German FDP, but this position is inherently unstable and dependent on a multiplicity of political factors. Most importantly the number of seats that a party wins in terms of the balance of power within any coalition is crucial. Since they occupy the centre these parties run the risk of ideological squeeze from bigger partners on either side. This kind of embrace can be damaging, and leads to big swings in electoral support. In the 1983 general election in the United Kingdom, the SDP/Liberal Alliance polled nearly as many votes as the Labour Party, but by 1987 this massive support had been squeezed out. In the 1990 Bundestag elections in Germany, the FDP gained 11 per cent of the vote gaining nearly 79 seats, but by the 1994 elections it had dropped to 6.9 per cent giving it 47 seats, and had polled under the 5 per cent hurdle in several *Land* elections. Both the PR and CDS in France increased the number of deputies they had in the National Assembly elections of 1993, to 106 and 60, respectively. Both parties, although formally under the UDF umbrella, have threatened to break away, using this new-found level of support to assert a more independent line. They could claim to hold some kind of 'pivot' position, in terms of trying to influence the policies of the larger coalition partner the RPR.

In terms of ideological orientation, all these parties are in favour of the free market but have a social conscience attached to that belief, but their economic ideology may have different shades of liberalism and neo-liberalism. On privatisation, for example, the PR in France is more in favour of that policy than, for example, the Liberal Democrats. On issues concerning tax, the FDP in Germany is very much a low tax party, while the Liberal Democrats are committed to raising income tax to fund greater education provision in Britain. The Dahrendorf Commission, sponsored by the Liberal Democrat Party, envisages a key role for the state in providing, for example, a basic income guarantee or minimum wage.[90]

In terms of state power, they tend to favour greater transparency in the way the government is run, the decentralisation of power to local level, and hence are supporters of greater regional autonomy. In Britain the party has a strong community orientation. All parties under consideration here are ardent Europeans and in favour of a federal Europe. They hold to traditional notions of the freedom of the individual and in the British case are socially progressive, concerning issues like divorce and abortion. The Bill and subsequent Act to reform the law on abortion (1967) in Britain was proposed by the former Liberal Party leader, David Steel.

Their future is uncertain given the decline in sharp ideological differences of the major left and right parties. Since many of the social democratic parties of western Europe, both in government and in opposition, have espoused a pale version of neo-liberal economics, the role of these parties in some countries may be to keep the flame of neo-Keynesianism alive. Their commitment to the concept of liberty, however vague, has always been seen as a healthy counter to the more statist and bureaucratic approaches of their ideological neighbours.

### 8.6.4 Regional parties and movements

In this section we will look at the main regional and subnational movements and parties which have gained increasing popularity over the last few decades. There is a range of demands that regional movements and parties have put forward. Outright demands for secession from the nation state are common to the programmes of the Scottish National Party (SNP), *Partido Nacional Vaisco* (Basque) (PNV), *Convergència i Unió* (CiU – The Catalan Nationalist Party) and to a certain extent the *Lega Nord* (Italy). The case of Belgium is particular since political parties in both halves of the country, Wallonia in the south and the Flemish-speaking region of the north, have demanded separate status but so far the nation state has remained intact within a federalist structure (Belgium is considered in greater detail in Chapter 10 under federalism). Then there are those parties which claim some greater form of autonomy but wish to remain within the current state, proposing a federal solution like Plaid Cymru.

### Lega Nord (LN)

The *Lega Nord* (The Northern League) grew out of the *Lega Lombarda* (formed in 1984), and is an alliance of various different regional groups in Northern Italy based on anti-*partitocrazia*, anti-southernism and anti-immigration. Their first success was the election of Umberto Bossi, the *Lega Nord*'s leader as Senator in 1987. The success of the LN was based on the failure of the established parties, particularly the DC and to a certain extent the PSI and the PCI to:

respond to the electorate's desire for modernity and a European style of political competition in line with the level of socio-economic development manifested in Italy.[91]

The appeal of the LN is in terms of its catch-all political programme, based neither on class nor single issue politics.

In an interview in 1992 Bossi and Gianfranco Miglio characterised the League's position as an essentially federalist, populist, freemarket movement concerned to bring about widespread share ownership and opposed to private monopolies. They pointed to the need to change the constitution, because in giving the DC continuing power it had allowed corruption, nepotism and a decline in effective legislation to take place.[92] The LN argue for three macro-regions, the North, the Centre and the South, and by 'emphasising regional identity in terms of cultural and socio-economic differences, the LN has provided the basis for a new collective identity to fill the gap left by the disappearance of the traditional cleavages of class, religion and ideology'.[93]

There is also a strong anti-centralist anti-Rome element to their programme as they consider that taxes paid by northern Italians have gone via the DC-dominated government to the DC and Mafia-dominated south. In discussing their membership, Miglio states that members 'are citizens who have not yet been contaminated by the advantages of political power'. The honeymoon period for the new coalition after the 1994 elections did not last very long and with the taste of political power the coalition of the League with *Forza Italia* and the National Alliance (a predominantly southern group) soon foundered on the rocks of unbridgeable ideological differences. Both men denied the charge that they were leading a Fascist group, although the new speaker of the Chamber of Deputies, Irene Pivetti, a League member, has openly stated her support for some of the 'positive things that Fascism achieved before the disastrous pact with Hitler'.[94]

Nevertheless, Bossi rejected initially any possibility that his movement would join the government if it contained National Alliance members, but eventually agreed to participate despite numerous AN ministers and deputy ministers: another strand to the LN's politics is its strong anti-immigrant stance, and its emphasis on law and order.

## Spain

> Convergència i Unió (CiU) Catalan Nationalist Party
> Partido Nacionalista Vasco (PNV) Basque Nationalists
> Herri Batasuna (HB) + Euskadi Ta Askatasuna ETA

The regional parties in Spain have had a long fight in claiming their legitmate role within the framework of the Spanish state. Two centralising tendencies can be identified, liberalism and the army. The liberals of the nineteenth century were committed to the notion that a centralised state represented progress, and the army considered it as a 'sacred duty' to maintain the integrity of Spain particularly after its defeats in Cuba and the Philippines at the end of the nineteenth century.[95]

The CiU arose out from the conservative *Lliga Catalana* of the 1930s. It is strong in the countryside, with the socialists controlling the urban areas. Unlike the experience of the PNV in the Basque province, CiU has maintained a steady support of around 45 per cent, and became a key player in the coalition maintaining PSOE in power at a national level after the 1993 general election. It is basically a conservative party although close to the Continental strand of Christina Democracy, like the PNV, which makes its alliance with the PSOE understandable.[96]

The PNV was founded at the turn of the century as a nationalist confessional party, with one of its main demands independent diplomatic links with the Vatican. Like the CiU in Catalonia it was a right-wing party led by the petit-bourgeoisie, with its roots in the Carlist movement of the 19th century in Spain, opposed to the liberalism of the 1870s. Carlism was a romantic movement of extreme clericalism and conservatism, but also with a demand for devolution and local liberties. One of the leading ideologues at the end of the nineteenth century, who created the modern notion of Basque identity *Euskadi,* was Sabino de Arana, who warned the Basques of the dangers of dilution of their race and culture by the influx of immigrants from other parts of Spain who had come to work in the shipbuilding and other industries around Bilbao.[97] The PNV reluctantly supported the Republican side in the civil war and suffered the bombing of their ancient centre at Guernica and, as a result of Franco's victory, were heavily punished. The language and the culture were suppressed, and Franco maintained constant pressure during the whole of his dictatorship against any nationalist movement. Between 1968–75 a state of emergency and the suspension of even limited human rights was declared no less than 18 times in parts of the province.[98] Despite moving away from its Carlist and overtly racist origins the PNV, however, steadily lost support during this period as younger members began in the 1960s to doubt the effectiveness of the policy of gradualism, giving rise to ETA and its political wing HB, organised around a new policy of radical left-wing nationalism.

ETA was committed to the armed struggle as a way to liberate their country from Spain. Their spectacular assassination and bombing campaign led to increased repression, and the cycle of violence continued. The advent of parliamentary democracy in 1977 presented ETA with a dilemma, which resulted in some members leaving to form *Euskadiko Eskerra* (the Basque Left), a party committed to the democratic process, and which accepted the new government's programme for regional devolution. Support for HB has decreased from a high of 25 per cent to around 10–15 per cent. It is important to note in this context that the main political parties in Spain PSOE and the PP, both committed to maintaining the centralised state, are well organised both in the Basque province and Catalonia. Support for these parties and other parties such as IU (*Izquierda Unida*: United Left, the Communist-dominated coalition) in favour of state unity is often over 50 per cent.

In recent years support for the armed struggle has declined and there has been a concerted effort by both the Spanish and French governments against the leading members of ETA. There are also indications that ETA may be willing to renounce the armed struggle. One of HB's veteran leaders, Jon Idigoras, stated before the regional elections of 23 October 1994 that anyone in HB 'can play the role of Gerry Adams'.[99]

## United Kingdom (UK)

### *The Scottish National Party (SNP)/Plaid Cymru/SDLP/Sinn Fein*

The Scottish National Party (SNP) was founded in 1934 out of the remains of the Scottish Home Rule Association (SHRA), and after its successes in the 1970s has declined in popularity, but maintained a steady 20–25 per cent of the popular vote.

The SNP describes itself as a moderate, left-of-centre political party committed to the establishment of an independent Scottish parliament. Their programme is still for an independent Scotland, within the EU. In the last hundred years there have been 34 bills presented in the House of Commons to establish a devolved Scotish assembly of parliament. Currently opposition to the government in London is expressed more widely by support for the Labour Party and to small extent the LD. The SNP attacks both these parties for their weak defence of Scottish interests whether as MPs or as MEPs. The SNP is also critical about both those parties' conclusion that Scottish interests can best be represented from London and within the structure of the Committee of the Regions (COR).

For Scotland participation in the COR is seen as a kind of humiliation, since it reduces its claim to full statehood. Central government in London has a budget of £12 bn per annum administered by a Secretary of State, and three junior ministers, but the country has fewer powers of how to spend that money than a German *Land* government or a Spanish region.[100] Most of the Scottish members of the COR see it as a vehicle to promote devolution in their country and pressure the UK government to create autonomous and viable regions. The SNP's attitude to the COR is that while it can provide:

a useful opportunity for Scottish local authorities to develop closer European ties, it can never be a substitute for Scotland as a nation being represented in the Council of Ministers.[101]

The nationalist parties now see bodies like the COR as a way of 'circumventing a British State committed to political centralisation and the sway of unrestrained market forces',[102] but only as a prelude to full statehood, as Alex Salmond, their leader, stated after their 32.6 per cent share of the vote in the 1994 European election,

. . . the SNP have emerged as clear winners with a vision of Scotland as a first-class nation in Europe rather than a second-class region in Britain'.[103]

## Northern Ireland

### SDLP

The largest nationalist party in Northern Ireland is the Social Democratic and Labour Party (SDLP). The name indicates its ideological orientation as a moderate left-of-centre party, which has as one of its long-term policy aims a united Ireland. It has always been totally opposed, however, to any non-democratic means to hasten this end, and it has consequently often been at odds with Sinn Fein.[104] In the 1992 general election, the SDLP increased its percentage of the vote at the expense of Sinn Fein.

### Sinn Fein

Sinn Fein is one of the leading nationalist parties in Northern Ireland, and is the political wing of the Irish Republican Army (IRA). It has been involved in the struggle for a free and united Ireland since the nineteenth century. At present it is in negotiation with the British government over the Downing Street Declaration of

15 December 1993 signed between the Irish and British governments. This declaration is designed to provide some kind of framework to pursue an agreed settlement to the issue of the North.

## 8.7 Summary

The development of cleavages within all European societies is an ongoing process. The big freeze is over, and although the major parties of the mainstream left and right continue to attract the largest number of votes, support for the Greens and the Far Right in particular suggests that new kinds of cleavages may be in the process of being formed. The classic divides between left and right have diminished in intensity, as have the religious and rural–urban cleavages. There are two relatively new cleavages over the future of the European Union and regionalism that have affected the party system. Europe is likely to continue as a significant cleavage, and the rise of regional parties and movements will have a long-term and important role to play in the changes to the party system at national and European level. Part of the Flanagan and Dalton thesis concerning electoral volatility seems to be a strong feature of contemporary European politics. The future of the nation state is secure for the time being but in the course of the next few decades, the changes in the global economy together with demands for local and regional territorial unit identification may undermine the kind of national politics based on the nation state in Europe, as it has been fixed over the last 200 years.

# Appendix I

**Table 8.1A** Political parties in the European Union.

| | Communist | Independent Socialist | Social Democrats | Liberal–Radicals | Centre | Christian Christian-Dem | Liberal Conservative | Conservative ('National') | Right Wing | Ethnic/Regional | 'New Parties' |
|---|---|---|---|---|---|---|---|---|---|---|---|
| Austria | KPÖ | | SPÖ | | | ÖVP | | | FPÖ | | Green Alt. VGO |
| Belgium | | | BSP/PSB | | | CVP/PSC | VLD(PVV)/ PRL–FDF | | Vlaams Blok | VB/Volksunie | Ecology/Alt Agalev |
| Denmark | | Socialist (SF) | Social Democrats | Radical Venstre (RV) | Centre (CD) | Christian (KrF) | Venstre | Conservative (KF) | Progress | | |
| Finland | | | Social (SSDP) Democrats | | Centre (KESK) | Christian (SKL) | | Conservative | Rural (SMP) | Swedish (SFP) | Greens |
| France | PCF | | PS | Left–Rads (MRG) | | | UDF | RPR | FN | | Greens/Ecol MdC |
| Germany | | PDS | SPD | | | CDU | FDP | CSU | Republikaner DVU | | Greens Bundnis '90 |
| Greece | KKE | Synaspismos | Pasok | | | | POLA | New Democracy | | | |
| Ireland | | Democratic Left/Workers Party | Labour | Fine Gael | | | Prog.Dems | Fianna Fail | | Sinn Fein | Green Alliance |
| Italy | PDS(ex PCI) | La Rete | PSI | PRI PSDI | | PPI (formerly DC) | PLI | Forza Italia | A.N. (formerly MSI/DN) | South Tyrol/ SVP Lega Nord | Radical Greens |
| Luxembourg | Communist | | LSAP/PSOL | | | Christian Social CSV/PCS | | | | | Greens |
| Netherlands | | | PvdA | Dem.'66 Radical | | CDA | VVD | | | | |
| Portugal | Communist (PCP) | | Socialist (PS) | | Soc–Dem Centre | CDS | PSD | | | | |
| Spain | IU (United Left) | | PSE (PSOE) | | Centre | | | Popular Party (PP) | FN | PNV/HB CIU | Union 55 + Green Left |
| Sweden | Comm. | | Soc. Dem. (SAP) | | Centre | | Liberal | Conservative | | | Greens/Ecol |
| UK | | | Labour SDLP (N Ireland) | Lib-Dems. | | | | Conservative | | SNP UUP DUP N.Sinn Plaid Cymru | Green Party |

Sources: 1. Keesings Record of World Events.   2. Gordon Smith (1990) *Politics in Western Europe*, Aldershot: Dartmouth.   3. Party manifestos.

## Appendix II

### *Election results in EU Member States*

*Sources:* Keesings Record of World Events, press reports, embassies.

**Table 8.2A**   (a) Austria (Nationalrat) 1983, 1986.

| Party | 1983 | | 1986 | |
|---|---|---|---|---|
| | Vote (%) | Seats | Vote (%) | Seats |
| Socialist Party (SPÖ) | 47.7 | 90 | 43.1 | 80 |
| People's Party (ÖVP) | 43.0 | 81 | 41.3 | 77 |
| Freedom Party (FPÖ) | 5.0 | 12 | 9.7 | 18 |
| United Greens (VPÖ) | 1.9 | 0 ⎫ | 4.8 | 8 |
| Alternative List (AL) | 1.4 | 0 ⎭ | | |
| Communist Party (KPÖ) | 0.7 | 0 | 0.7 | 0 |
| Others | 0.2 | 0 | 0.3 | 0 |
| Totals | 100.0 | 183 | 100.0 | 183 |

**Table 8.2A**   (b) Austrian general election results, 1990.

| Party | Seats | Percentage of valid votes |
|---|---|---|
| SPÖ | 80 | 42.8 |
| ÖVP | 60 | 32.1 |
| FPÖ | 33 | 16.6 |
| Green Alternative | 10 | 4.8 |
| Others* | 0 | 3.8 |

* Including Communists (KPÖ) and United Greens (VPÖ).
*Turnout:* 86 per cent of total electorate of 5 600 000.

**Table 8.2A**   (c) Austrian general election, 1994.

| Party | Percentage of votes | | Seats | |
|---|---|---|---|---|
| | 1994 | 1990 | 1994 | 1990 |
| SPÖ | 35.23 | 42.78 | 65 | 80 |
| ÖVP | 27.74 | 32.06 | 52 | 60 |
| FPÖ | 22.64 | 16.63 | 42 | 33 |
| Greens | 7.01 | 4.78 | 13 | 10 |
| Liberal Forum | 5.74 | – | 11 | – |
| Others | 1.64 | 3.75 | 0 | 0 |
| Total | 100.00 | 100.00 | 183 | 183 |

*Turnout:* 78.06 per cent of electorate of 5 773 660 (86 per cent in 1990).

**Table 8.3A**　(a) Belgium (Kamer des Volksvertegenwoordigers/Chambre des Representants) 1981, 1985.

| | 1981 | | 1985 | |
|---|---|---|---|---|
| Party | Vote (%) | Seats | Vote (%) | Seats |
| Christian People's Party | 19.7 | 43 | 21.3 | 49 |
| Flemish Socialist Party | 12.6 | 26 | 14.5 | 32 |
| Francophone Socialist | 12.6 | 35 | 13.8 | 35 |
| Party of Liberty and Progress | 13.1 | 28 | 10.7 | 22 |
| Reform Liberal Party | 8.2 | 24 | 10.2 | 24 |
| Social Christian Party | 6.7 | 18 | 8.0 | 20 |
| Volksunie | 9.9 | 20 | 8.0 | 16 |
| Agalev | 4.4 | 4 | 3.7 | 4 |
| Ecolo | | | 2.5 | 5 |
| Francophone Democratic Front | 4.2 | 6 | 1.2 | 3 |
| Walloon Rally | | 2 | 0.1 | 0 |
| Democratic Union for the Respect of Labour | 2.7 | 3 | 1.1 | 1 |
| Communist Party | 2.3 | 2 | 1.2 | 0 |
| Flemish Bloc | 1.1 | 1 | 1.4 | 1 |
| Others | 2.5 | 0 | 2.3 | 0 |
| Totals | 100.0 | 212 | 100.0 | 212 |

**Table 8.3A**　(b) Elections to Belgian Chamber of Representatives.

| Party | Seats | | Percentage of votes | |
|---|---|---|---|---|
| | 1991 | 1987 | 1991 | 1987 |
| *CVP | 39 | 43 | 16.7 | 19.5 |
| *PS | 35 | 40 | 13.6 | 15.6 |
| *SP | 28 | 32 | 12.0 | 14.0 |
| PVV | 26 | 25 | 11.9 | 11.5 |
| PRL | 20 | 23 | 8.2 | 9.4 |
| *PSC | 18 | 19 | 7.8 | 8.0 |
| Vlaams Bloc | 12 | 2 | 6.6 | 1.9 |
| *Volksunie | 10 | 16 | 5.9 | 8.1 |
| Ecolo | 10 | 3 | 5.1 | 2.6 |
| Agalev | 7 | 6 | 4.9 | 4.5 |
| **Van Rossem list | 3 | – | 3.2 | – |
| FDF | 3 | 3 | 1.5 | 1.2 |
| Others | 1† | 0 | 2.6 | 3.7 |

* Member of outgoing Martens coalition.
** List headed by Jean-Pierre Van Rossem, 46, an anarchist and former multi-millionaire, who was arrested for fraud immediately before the election.
† Seat won by Front national, with 1.1 per cent of vote. Half a dozen other parties also contested the elections without securing representation.

***Table 8.3A***　　(c) Belgian general election, 1995.

| Party | Percentage of vote | Seats Chamber* | Senate |
|---|---|---|---|
| †Christian People's Party (CVP) | 17.2 | 29 | 7 |
| †Social Christian Party (PSC) | 7.7 | 12 | 3 |
| Flemish Liberals and Democrats (VLD) | 13.1 | 21 | 6 |
| Liberal Reform Party (PRL–FDF) | 10.3 | 18 | 5 |
| †Socialist Party (SP) | 12.6 | 20 | 6 |
| †Socialist Party (PS) | 11.9 | 21 | 5 |
| *Vlaams Bloc* | 7.8 | 11 | 3 |
| *Volksunie* | 4.7 | 5 | 2 |
| National Front (FN) | 2.3 | 2 | – |
| *Agalev* | 4.4 | 5 | 1 |
| *Ecolo* | 4.0 | 6 | 2 |

\* In 1991 the Chamber of Representatives had 208 seats as compared with 150 in the new Chamber.
† Member of outgoing ruling coalition.　　*Electorate: 7 200 000.*

***Table 8.4A***　　(a) Denmark (*Folketing*)\*.

| Party | 1981 Vote (%) | Seats | 1984 Vote (%) | Seats | 1987 Vote (%) | Seats | 1988 Vote (%) | Seats |
|---|---|---|---|---|---|---|---|---|
| Social Democrats | 32.9 | 59 | 31.6 | 56 | 29.3 | 54 | 29.8 | 55 |
| Conservatives | 14.5 | 26 | 23.4 | 42 | 20.8 | 38 | 19.3 | 35 |
| Socialist People's Party | 11.3 | 21 | 11.5 | 21 | 14.6 | 27 | 13.0 | 24 |
| Liberals | 11.3 | 20 | 12.1 | 22 | 10.5 | 19 | 11.8 | 22 |
| Progress Party | 8.9 | 16 | 3.6 | 6 | 4.8 | 9 | 9.0 | 16 |
| Centre Democrats | 8.3 | 15 | 4.6 | 8 | 4.9 | 9 | 4.7 | 9 |
| Radicals | 5.1 | 9 | 5.5 | 10 | 6.2 | 11 | 5.6 | 10 |
| Left Socialists | 2.7 | 5 | 2.7 | 5 | 1.4 | 0 | 0.6 | 0 |
| Christian People's Party | 2.3 | 4 | 2.7 | 5 | 2.4 | 4 | 2.0 | 4 |
| Justice Party | 1.5 | 0 | 1.5 | 0 | 0.5 | 0 | – | 0 |
| Communist Party | 1.1 | 0 | 0.7 | 0 | 0.9 | 0 | 0.8 | 0 |
| Common Course | – | – | – | – | 2.2 | 4 | 1.9 | 0 |
| Greens | – | – | – | – | 1.3 | 0 | 1.3 | 0 |
| Others | 1.0 | 0 | 0.1 | 0 | 0.2 | 0 | 0.0 | 0 |
| Totals | 100.0 | 175 | 100.0 | 175 | 100.0 | 175 | 100.0 | 175 |

\* Metropolitan Denmark only. In addition the Faroe Islands and Greenland each return two Members to the *Folketing*.

***Table 8.4A***　　(b) Danish general election

| Party | Percentage of votes 1994 | 1990 | Seats† 1994 | 1990 |
|---|---|---|---|---|
| *Social Democrats | 34.6 | 37.4 | 62 | 69 |
| Liberals | 23.3 | 15.8 | 42 | 29 |
| Conservatives | 15.0 | 16.0 | 27 | 30 |
| Socialist People's Party | 7.3 | 8.3 | 13 | 15 |
| Progress Party | 6.4 | 6.4 | 11 | 12 |
| *Social Liberals | 4.6 | 3.5 | 8 | 7 |
| Unity List | 3.1 | 1.7 | 6 | 0 |
| *Centre Democrats | 2.8 | 5.1 | 5 | 9 |
| *Christian People's Party | 1.8 | 2.3 | 0 | 4 |
| Independents | 1.0 | 3.6 | **1 | 0 |

\* Member of outgoing government coalition.
† In addition to the 175 seats listed here, the Faroes and Greenland each sent two deputies to the *Folketing*.
\*\* Seat won by comedian Jakob Haugaard.

**Table 8.5A**   (a) Finland (*Eduskunta*), 1982.

| Party | Vote (%) | Seats |
|---|---|---|
| Social Democrats | 26.7 | 57 |
| National Coalition | 22.1 | 44 |
| Centre Party ⎫ | | |
| Liberal People's Party ⎭ | 17.6 | 38 |
| Finnish People's Democratic Union | 13.8 | 27 |
| Rural Party | 9.7 | 17 |
| Swedish People's Party | 4.9 | 11 |
| Christian League | 3.0 | 3 |
| Greens | 1.4 | 2 |
| Pensioners' Party | – | – |
| Democratic Alternative | – | – |
| Others | 0.8 | 1 |
| Totals | 100.0 | 200 |

**Table 8.5A**   (b) Finnish election results

| Party | Percentage of votes | | Seats | |
|---|---|---|---|---|
| | 1991 | 1987 | 1991 | 1987 |
| KESK Centre Party/Liberal People's Party | 24.8 | 17.6 | 55 | 40 |
| SSDP Social Democrats | 22.1 | 24.1 | 48 | 56 |
| *Kokoomus* National Coalition | 19.3 | 23.1 | 40 | 53 |
| Left-Wing Alliance (VL)* | 10.1 | 13.4 | 19 | 20 |
| Green Alliance | 6.8 | 4.0 | 10 | 4 |
| Swedish People's Party (SFP)† | 5.5 | 5.3 | 12 | 13 |
| Finnish Rural Party (SMP) | 4.8 | 6.3 | 7 | 9 |
| Finnish Christian Union (SKL) | 3.1 | 2.6 | 8 | 5 |
| Liberal People's Party (LKP) | 1.2 | 1.0 | 1 | 0 |
| Others | 2.3 | 2.6 | 0 | 0 |

* 1987 figures are combined totals for Finnish People's Democratic League (SKDL) and Democratic Alternative (DEVA).

† Including one representative for the autonomous Åland Islands.

**Table 8.5A**   (c) Finnish election results

| Party | Percentage of vote | | Seats | |
|---|---|---|---|---|
| | 1995 | 1991 | 1995 | 1991 |
| Finnish Social Democratic Party (SDP) | 28.3 | 22.1 | 63 | 48 |
| Centre Party (KESK) | 19.9 | 24.8 | 44 | 55 |
| National Coalition Party (*Kokoomus* – KOK) | 17.9 | 19.3 | 39 | 40 |
| Left-Wing Alliance (VL) | 11.2 | 10.1 | 22 | 19 |
| Swedish People's Party (SFP)* | 5.1 | 5.5 | 12 | 12 |
| Greens (*Vihreāt*) | 6.5 | 6.8 | 9 | 10 |
| Finnish Christian League (SKL) | 3.0 | 3.1 | 7 | 8 |
| Young Finns (NS) | 2.8 | – | 2 | – |
| Finnish Rural Party (SMP) | 1.3 | 4.8 | 1 | 7 |
| Ecological Party (EP) | 0.3 | – | 1 | – |
| Others | 3.7 | 3.5 | 0 | 1 |

* Including one representative for the autonomous Åland Islands.

***Table 8.6A***    (a) France – presidential elections

| | 1981 | | | 1988 | |
| --- | --- | --- | --- | --- | --- |
| | Round I | Round II | | Round I | Round II |
| Candidates | Vote (%) | Vote (%) | Candidates | Vote (%) | Vote (%) |
| François Mitterrand (Socialist) | 25.8 | 51.8 | François Mitterrand (Socialist) | 34.1 | 54.0 |
| Valéry Giscard d'Estaing (Union for French Democracy) | 28.3 | 48.2 | Jacques Chirac (Gaullist RPR) | 19.9 | 46.0 |
| Jacques Chirac (Gaullist RPR) | 18.0 | – | Raymond Barre (Union for French Democracy) | 16.5 | – |
| Georges Marchais (Communist) | 15.3 | – | Jean-Marie Le Pen (National Front) | 14.4 | – |
| Brice Lalonde (Ecologist) | 3.9 | – | André Lajoinie (Communist) | 6.8 | – |
| Arlette Laguiller (Trotskyist) | 2.3 | – | Antoine Waechter (Greens) | 3.8 | – |
| Michel Crépeau (Left Radical) | 2.2 | – | Pierre Juquin (Independent Communist) | 2.1 | – |
| Michel Debré (Independent Gaullist) | 1.7 | – | Arlette Laguiller (Trotskyist) | 2.0 | – |
| Marie-France Garaud (Independent Gaullist) | 1.3 | – | Pierre Boussel (Trotskyist) | 0.4 | – |
| Huguette Bouchard (Unified Socialist Party) | 1.1 | – | | | |
| Totals | 100.0 | 100.0 | | 100.0 | 100.0 |

***Table 8.6A***    (b) First round of French presidential elections, 1995

| | Votes | Percentage of valid votes |
| --- | --- | --- |
| Lionel Jospin | 7 101 992 | 23.30 |
| Jacques Chirac | 6 351 672 | 20.84 |
| Edouard Balladur | 5 662 116 | 18.58 |
| Jean-Marie Le Pen | 4 573 202 | 15.00 |
| Robert Hue | 2 634 187 | 8.64 |
| Arlette Laguiller | 1 616 546 | 5.30 |
| Philippe de Villiers | 1 444 053 | 4.74 |
| Dominique Voynet | 1 011 373 | 3.32 |
| Jacques Cheminade | 85 070 | 0.28 |
| Total | 30 480 211 | 100.00 |

*Votes cast:* 31 369 029 (78.37 per cent) out of electorate of 40 026 937. Of votes cast 2.83 per cent were void, leaving 30 480 211 valid votes cast.
*Source: Le Monde,* 26 April 1995.

| Second round of French presidential elections, 1995 | |
| --- | --- |
| Jacques Chirac | 52.64 per cent |
| Lionel Jospin | 47.36 per cent |

**Table 8.7A**    (a) France (Assemblée Nationale) National Assembly.

| Party | 1981 Vote (%) | 1981 Seats | 1986 Vote (%) | 1986 Seats | 1988 Vote (%) | 1988 Seats |
|---|---|---|---|---|---|---|
| Extreme left parties | 1.4 | 0 | 1.7 | 0 | 0.4 | 0 |
| Communist Party | 16.1 | 44 | 9.8 | 35 | 11.3 | 27 |
| Socialist Party and other candidates supporting President Mitterrand | 38.2 | 289 | 32.7 | 216 | 37.6 | 280 |
| Rally for the Republic | 20.8 | 85 } | 41.0 | 277 | 19.2 | 128 |
| Union for French Democracy | 19.2 | 61 } | | | 18.5 | 129 |
| Other right-wing candidates | 2.8 | 12 | 3.8 | 14 | 2.8 | 12 |
| National Front | 0.2 | 0 | 9.7 | 35 | 9.6 | 1 |
| Greens | 1.1 | 0 | 1.2 | 0 | 0.4 | 0 |
| Others | 0.2 | 0 | 0.1 | 0 | 0.2 | 0 |
| Totals | 100.0 | 491 | 100.0 | 577 | 100.0 | 577 |

**Table 8.7A**    (b) First and second rounds of French legislative elections (1993)

| Party | Percentage of vote 1st round (1988 figure in parentheses) | 2nd round | Distribution of seats New Assembly | At dissolution |
|---|---|---|---|---|
| Extreme left | 1.77  (0.36) | 0.10 | 0 | 0 |
| PCF | 9.18 (11.32) | 4.61 | 23 | 26 |
| PS | 17.59 (34.76) | 28.25 | 54 | 252 |
| *MRG | 0.89  (1.14) | 1.15 | 6 | 10 |
| †Presidential majority | 1.79  (1.65) | 2.17 | 10 | 20 |
| GE | 3.62    (–) | 0.08 | 0 | – |
| *les Verts* | 4.01  (0.35) | 0.09 | 0 | – |
| Regionalists | 0.45  (0.07) | 0.17 | 0 | 0 |
| Others | 3.76    (–) | 0.00 | 0 | 0 |
| RPR | 20.39 (19.18) | 28.27 | 247 | 126 |
| UDF | 19.08 (18.49) | 25.84 | 213 | 131 |
| Various right | 4.71  (2.85) | 3.56 | 24 | 11 |
| *Front National* | 12.41  (9.65) | 5.66 | 0 | 1 |
| Extreme right | 0.27  (0.13) | 0.00 | 0 | 0 |

* *Mouvement des radicaux de gauche.*
† Comprised various left candidates.
There were 5319 candidates for the 577 National Assembly seats (as compared with 2880 in 1988).
In the new National Assembly there were 35 women.

**Table 8.7A**    (c) Presidents and Prime Ministers 1981–1995

| | President | Prime Minister |
|---|---|---|
| 1981 | F. Mitterrand I (PS) | P. Mauroy (PS) |
| 1983 | | L. Fabius (PS) |
| 1986–88 Cohabitation I | | J. Chirac (RPR) |
| 1988 | F. Mitterrand II | M. Rocard (PS) |
| 1991 | | E. Cresson (PS) |
| 1992 | | P. Bérégovey (PS) |
| 1993–95 Cohabitation II | | E. Balladur (RPR) |
| 1995 | J. Chirac (RPR) | A. Juppé (RPR) |

**Table 8.8A** (a) Greece, 1974

| Party | Seats | Votes | Per cent |
|---|---|---|---|
| New Democracy | 220 | 2 670 804 | 54.37 |
| Centre Union–New Forces | 60 | 1 002 908 | 20.42 |
| Pan-Hellenic Socialist Movement | 12 | 666 806 | 13.58 |
| United Left | 8 | 464 331 | 9.45 |
| National Democratic Union | – | 54 162 | 1.10 |
| Others | – | 53 345 | 1.08 |

**Table 8.8A** (b) 1977

| Party | Seats | Votes | Per cent |
|---|---|---|---|
| New Democracy | 172 | 2 146 687 | 41.85 |
| Pasok | 93 | 1 299 196 | 25.33 |
| EDHK | 15 | 613 113 | 11.95 |
| KKE (exterior) | 11 | 480 188 | 9.36 |
| National Front | 5 | 349 851 | 6.82 |
| APLF | 2 | 139 762 | 2.72 |
| New Liberal Party | 2 | 55 560 | 1.08 |
| EKKE | 0 | 11 962 | 0.23 |
| Others | 0 | 33 565 | 0.66 |

**Table 8.8A** (a) 1981

| Party | Seats | Votes | Per cent |
|---|---|---|---|
| Pasok | 172 | 2 725 395 | 48.06 |
| New Democracy | 115 | 2 033 774 | 35.86 |
| KKE (exterior) | 13 | 619 296 | 10.92 |
| Progressive Party | 0 | 95 697 | 1.69 |
| KKE (interior) | 0 | 77 465 | 1.37 |
| Democratic Unity | 0 | 40 553 | 0.72 |
| Union of the Democratic Centre | 0 | 23 735 | 0.42 |
| Liberal Party | 0 | 20 726 | 0.37 |
| Christian Democracy | 0 | 8709 | 0.15 |
| Revolutionary Left | 0 | 6540 | 0.12 |
| Revolutionist Communist Party/ Marxist–Leninist Communist Party | 0 | 4734 | 0.08 |
| International Labour Union | 0 | 1643 | 0.03 |
| Others | 0 | 12 674 | 0.21 |

**(d)** Greek Parliamentary Election Results, October 1993

| Party | Seats | % Vote 1993 | 1990 | Nov. 1989 | June 1989 | 1985 |
|---|---|---|---|---|---|---|
| Pasok | 170 | 46.88 | 38.61 | 40.67 | 39.15 | 45.82 |
| New Democracy | 110 | 39.30 | 46.88 | 46.19 | 44.25 | 40.85 |
| Political Spring[1] | 11 | 4.87 | – | – | – | – |
| KKE | 9 | 4.54 | – | – | – | 9.89 |
| Synaspismos[2] | 0 | 2.94 | 10.28 | 10.96 | 13.12 | – |
| KKE (Interior) | 0 | – | – | – | – | 1.84 |
| Other | 0 | 1.47 | 4.23 | 2.18 | 3.48 | 1.60 |

1. Founded 1993.
2. Founded in 1989, *Synaspismos* was an electoral alliance between the KKE and the Greek Left Party. The KKE left the coalition after the 1990 election.

**Table 8.9A**  (a) Ireland (the *Dáil*)

|  | 11.6.1981 | | 18.2.1982 | | 24.11.1982 | |
|---|---|---|---|---|---|---|
| Party | Vote (%) | Seats | Vote (%) | Seats | Vote (%) | Seats |
| *Fianna Fáil* | 45.3 | 78 | 47.3 | 81 | 45.2 | 75 |
| *Fine Gael* | 36.5 | 65 | 37.3 | 63 | 39.2 | 70 |
| Labour | 9.9 | 15 | 9.1 | 15 | 9.4 | 16 |
| Workers' Party | 1.7 | 1 | 2.2 | 3 | 3.3 | 2 |
| National H-Block Committee | 2.5 | 2 | – | – | – | – |
| *Sinn Féin* | – | – | – | – | – | – |
| Greens | – | – | – | – | – | – |
| Progressive Democrats | – | – | – | – | – | – |
| Others | 4.2 | 5 | 4.1 | 4 | 2.9 | 3 |
| Totals | 100.0 | 166 | 100.0 | 166 | 100.0 | 166 |

**Table 8.9A**  (b)

|  | Seats at dissolution | | Percentage of votes* | |
|---|---|---|---|---|
| Party | 1989 | 1987 | 1989 | 1987 |
| *Fianna Fáil* | 77 | 80** | 43.7 | 44.1 |
| *Fine Gael* | 55 | 51 | 29.6 | 27.1 |
| Labour Party | 15 | 12 | 8.0 | 6.5 |
| Workers' Party | 7 | 4 | 5.6 | 3.8 |
| Progressive Democrats | 6 | 14 | 5.0 | 11.9 |
| Others | 6† | 4 | 8.2 | 6.6 |

\* First preference votes.

\*\* 81 seats won in 1987, but one vacant at the dissolution following the appointment of Ray MacSharry to the European Commission from January 1989.

† Four as in 1987 plus Roger Garland, who became the first Green Party representative in the *Dáil*, and Tom Fox, an independent.

**Table 8.9A**  (c) Election to *Dáil Éireann* (Lower House), 1992.

| No | Party | Votes N | % | Change since 1989 | Seats N | % | Change since 1989 |
|---|---|---|---|---|---|---|---|
| 10 | *Fianna Fáil* | 674 650 | 39.1 | −5.0 | 68 | 41.0 | − 5.4 |
| 14 | *Fine Gael* | 422 106 | 24.5 | −4.8 | 45 | 27.1 | − 6.0 |
| 8 | Labour Party | 333 013 | 19.3 | +9.8 | 33 | 19.9 | −10.9 |
| 25 | Progressive Democrats | 80 787 | 4.7 | −0.8 | 10 | 6.0 | + 2.4 |
|  | Democratic Left | 47 945 | 2.8 | +2.8 | 4 | 2.4 | − 2.4 |
| 22 | *Sinn Féin* | 27 809 | 1.6 | +0.4 | 0 | 0 | – |
| 24 | Green Party | 24 110 | 1.4 | −0.1 | 1 | 0.6 | 0 |
| 19 | The Workers' Party | 11 533 | 0.7 | −4.3 | 0 | 0 | − 4.2 |
|  | Christian Centrist Party | 3413 | 0.2 | +0.2 | 0 | 0 | – |
|  | Others | 99 487 | 5.8 | +1.9 | 5 | 3.0 | − 0.6 |

Total number of seats: 166.

*Table 8.10A* (a) Federal German Republic (*Bundestag*)

| Party | 1980 Vote (%) | 1980 Seats | 1983 Vote (%) | 1983 Seats | 1987 Vote (%) | 1987 Seats |
|---|---|---|---|---|---|---|
| Christian Democratic Union ⎫ | 44.5 | 174 ⎫ | 48.8 | 191 ⎫ | 44.3 | 174 |
| Christian Social Union ⎭ | | 52 ⎭ | | 53 ⎭ | | 49 |
| Social Democrats | 42.9 | 218 | 38.2 | 193 | 37.0 | 186 |
| Free Democrats | 10.6 | 53 | 7.0 | 34 | 9.1 | 46 |
| Greens | 1.5 | 0 | 5.6 | 27 | 8.3 | 42 |
| Communist Party | 0.2 | 0 | 0.2 | 0 | – | – |
| National Democrats | 0.2 | 0 | 0.2 | 0 | 0.6 | 0 |
| Others | 0.1 | 0 | 0.0 | 0 | 0.7 | 0 |
| Totals | 100.0 | 497 | 100.0 | 498 | 100.0 | 497 |

*Table 8.10A* (b) German general election

| Party | Percentage of vote 1994 | 1990 | Seats 1994 | 1990 |
|---|---|---|---|---|
| CDU | 34.2 | 36.7 | 244 | 268 |
| CSU | 7.3 | 7.1 | 50 | 51 |
| FDP | 6.9 | 11.0 | 47 | 79 |
| SPD | 36.4 | 33.5 | 252 | 239 |
| Greens | 7.3 | 3.9 | 49 | – |
| PDS | 4.4 | 2.4 | 30 | 17 |
| Republicans | 1.9 | 2.1 | 0 | – |
| Alliance 90/Greens | – | 1.2 | – | 8 |
| Others | 1.6 | 2.1 | 0 | 0 |
| Totals | 100.0 | 100.0 | 672 | 662 |

*Turnout:* 79.1 per cent (77.8 per cent in 1990).

*Table 8.10A* (c) Chancellors and Coalitions in the Federal Republic

| | | |
|---|---|---|
| September 1949 | Adenauer I | CDU–CSU, FDP, DP |
| October 1953 | Adenauer II | CDU–CSU, FDP/FVP, DP, BHE |
| October 1957 | Adenauer III | CDU–CSU, DP |
| November 1961 | Adenauer IV | CDU–CSU, FDP |
| October 1963 | Erhard I | CDU–CSU, FDP |
| October 1965 | Erhard II | CDU–CSU, FDP |
| December 1966 | Kiesinger | CDU–CSU, SDP |
| October 1969 | Brandt I | SPD, FDP |
| December 1972 | Brandt II | SPD, FDP |
| May 1974 | Schmidt I | SPD, FDP |
| December 1976 | Schmidt II | SPD, FDP |
| November 1980 | Schmidt III | SPD, FDP |
| October 1982 | Kohl I | CDU–CSU, FDP |
| March 1983 | Kohl II | CDU–CSU, FDP |
| January 1987 | Kohl III | CDU–CSU, FDP |
| October 1990 | Kohl IV | CDU–CSU, FDP |
| October 1994 | Kohl V | CDU–CSU, FDP |

***Table 8.11A***    (a) Luxembourg (Chambre des Deputés), 1984

| Party | Vote (%) | Seats |
|---|---|---|
| Christian Social Party | 36.6 | 25 |
| Socialist Workers' Party | 31.8 | 21 |
| Democratic Party | 20.4 | 14 |
| Communist Party | 4.4 | 2 |
| Green Alternative | 4.2 | 2 |
| Independent Socialist Party | 2.4 | 0 |
| Others | 0.2 | 0 |
| Total | 100.0 | 64 |

***Table 8.11A***    (b) General election results

| Party | Seats | | Percentage | |
|---|---|---|---|---|
| | 1989 | 1984 | 1989 | 1984 |
| Christian Socials | 22 | 25 | 31.67 | 34.9 |
| Socialists | 18 | 21 | 27.23 | 33.6 |
| Democratic Party | 11 | 14 | 16.17 | 18.7 |
| Greens* | 4 | 2 | 8.36 | 5.2 |
| Five-sixths action committee | 4 | – | 7.31 | – |
| Communists | 1 | 2 | 5.11 | 5.0 |
| Others** | 0 | 0 | 4.16 | 2.7 |

* Represents in 1989 seats won and percentage of votes polled by both *Déi Gréng Alternativ* and *Gréng Lëscht Ekologesch Initiativ*, two separate environmentalist lists which each won two seats. In 1984 only *Déi Gréng Alternativ* contested the election.
** There were nine other party lists (including a number of smaller environmentalist lists) contesting the 1989 election. Of the electorate of 218 940, 191 332 or 87.39% went to the polls.

***Table 8.11A***    (c) 1994

| Party | Seats |
|---|---|
| Christian Social People's Party (CSU/PCS) | 21 |
| Luxembourg Socialist Workers Party (LSAP/POSL) | 17 |
| Liberal Democratic Party (DP/PD) | 12 |
| Green Alternative | 5 |

***Table 8.12A*** (a) Italy (Chamber of Deputies) election results, 1985–1992 (percentages)

| Party | Regional 1985 | Regional 1990 | Provincial 1985 | Provincial 1990 | Communal 1985 | Communal 1990 | National 1987 | National 1992 |
|---|---|---|---|---|---|---|---|---|
| Christian Democrats (DC) | 34.7 | 33.4 | 33.5 | 31.6 | 33.8 | 33.9 | 34.2 | 29.7 |
| Communists (PCI) | 30.8 | 24.0 | 29.8 | 23.8 | 28.7 | 22.9 | 26.6 | – |
| Democratic Left (PDS)[a] | – | – | – | – | – | – | – | 16.1 |
| Communist Refoundation | – | – | – | – | – | – | – | 5.6 |
| Socialists (PSI) | 13.1 | 15.3 | 13.7 | 15.7 | 15.4 | 17.8 | 14.3 | 13.6 |
| Northern Leagues | – | 5.4 | 0.4 | 4.4 | 0.2 | 2.5 | 0.6 | 8.7 |
| Neo-Fascists (MSI) | 6.3 | 3.9 | 7.3 | 4.7 | 4.8 | 3.1 | 5.9 | 5.4 |
| Republicans (PRI) | 4.1 | 3.6 | 4.4 | 4.1 | 4.8 | 4.2 | 3.7 | 4.4 |
| Social Democrats (PSDI) | 3.4 | 2.8 | 4.1 | 3.4 | 4.3 | 3.4 | 3.0 | 2.7 |
| Liberals (PLI) | 2.2 | 2.0 | 2.6 | 2.4 | 2.4 | 2.2 | 2.1 | 2.8 |
| Green Lists | 1.8 | 2.4 | 1.0 | 2.4 | 0.9 | 1.3 | 2.5 | – |
| Rainbow Greens [b] | – | 1.4 | – | 1.1 | – | 0.5 | – | 2.8 |
| Green Alliance | – | 1.2 | – | 1.7 | – | 1.9 | – | – |
| Radicals | – | – | – | – | – | – | 2.6 | 1.2 |
| Proletarian Democrats | 1.6 | 1.0 | 1.6 | 0.9 | 1.1 | 0.6 | 1.7 | – |
| Anti-Prohibitionists | 1.1 | 1.0 | – | 0.9 | – | 0.3 | – | – |
| La Rete | – | – | – | – | – | – | – | 1.9 |

*Notes:*
[a] The Italian Communist Party (PCI) split into the Democratic Left Party (PDS) (the social democratic majority) and *Rifondazione Comunista* (Communist Refoundation) (the left-wing rump) in 1990.
[b] In many areas the Green Lists and Rainbow Greens campaigned together.
Radical Party's founder, Marco Pannella, led a personal list (the *Lista Pannella*) including the Anti-Prohibitionists.

***Table 8.12A*** (b) Italian election results 1994

| Bloc | Chamber of Deputies Percentage of PR vote | Seats |
|---|---|---|
| Freedom Alliance | 42.9 | 366 |
| Direct votes | | 302 |
| *Forza Italia* | 21.0 | 30 |
| National Alliance | 13.5 | 23 |
| Northern League | 8.4 | 11 |
| Progressive Alliance | 34.4 | 213 |
| Direct votes | | 164 |
| Democratic Party of the Left | 20.4 | 38 |
| Communist Refoundation | 6.0 | 11 |
| Greens | 2.7 | 0 |
| Socialists | 2.2 | 0 |
| The Network | 1.9 | 0 |
| Democratic Alliance | 1.2 | 0 |
| Pact for Italy | 15.7 | 46 |
| Direct votes | | 4 |
| Italian Popular Party | 11.1 | 29 |
| *Segni Pact* | 4.6 | 13 |
| Others | 8.0 | 5 |

Electorate: 48 300 000 (minimum voting age 18). Turnout: 86.1 per cent.

| Bloc | Senate Percentage of vote | Seats |
|---|---|---|
| Freedom Alliance | 42.0 | 156 |
| Progressive Alliance | 33.0 | 122 |
| Pact for Italy | 17.0 | 31 |
| Others | 8.0 | 6 |

Electorate: 42 700 000 (minimum voting age 25). Turnout: 85.5 per cent.
*Sources:* Ministry of Interior, *Financial Times*, *Guardian*.

**Table 8.12A**    (c) Italian election alliances, 1994

| Party and provenance | Orientation | Leader |
|---|---|---|
| Right-wing Freedom Alliance | | |
| Christian Democratic Centre (CCD), right-wing of Christian Democratic Party | Conservative | Pierferdinando Casini |
| *Forza Italia* (Go, Italy!), founded in January 1994 | Free-market | Silvio Berlusconi |
| National Alliance (AN), formerly Italian Social Movement (MSI) | Neo-Fascist | Gianfranco Fini |
| Northern League (LN), unchanged | Federalist | Umberto Bossi |
| Pannella List, Radical Party | Libertarian | Marco Pannella |
| Union of the Democratic Centre (UDC), Italian Liberal Party | Centre right | Unknown |
| Centrist Pact for Italy | | |
| Italian Popular Party (PPI), Christian Democratic Party | Catholic Centrist | Mino Martinazzoli |
| Pact for Italy (*Patto per l'Italia, also called Patto Segni*), Christian Democratic Party | Reformist | Mario Segni |
| Left-wing Progressive Alliance | | |
| Communist Reformation (RC), Italian Communist Party | Marxist | Fausto Bertinotti |
| Democratic Alliance (AD), Italian Socialist and Republican Parties | Left-wing | Ferdinando Adornato |
| Democratic Party of the Left (PDS), Italian Communist Party | Social democratic | Achille Occhetto |
| Greens (*Verdi*), unchanged | Ecologist | Carlo Ripa di Meana |
| Italian Socialist Party (PSI), remnants of Italian Socialist Party | Social democratic | Ottaviano del Turco |
| Network (*La Rete*), left-wing Catholic anti-Mafia Resigned post-elections | Unchanged | Leoluca Orlando |

**Table 8.13A**    (a) The Netherlands (*Tweede Kamer*)

| Party | 1981 | | 1982 | | 1986 | |
|---|---|---|---|---|---|---|
| | Vote (%) | Seats | Vote (%) | Seats | Vote (%) | Seats |
| Christian Democrat Appeal | 30.8 | 48 | 30.4 | 47 | 34.6 | 54 |
| Labour Party | 28.3 | 44 | 29.4 | 45 | 33.3 | 52 |
| Liberal Party | 17.3 | 26 | 23.1 | 36 | 17.4 | 27 |
| Democrats '66 | 11.1 | 17 | 4.3 | 6 | 6.1 | 9 |
| Pacifist Socialist Party | 2.1 | 3 | 2.3 | 3 | 1.2 | 1 |
| Communist Party | 2.1 | 3 | 1.8 | 3 | 0.6 | 0 |
| Political Reformed Party | 2.0 | 3 | 1.9 | 3 | 1.7 | 3 |
| Radical Political Party | 2.0 | 3 | 1.7 | 2 | 1.3 | 2 |
| Reformed Political Federation | 1.5 | 2 | 1.5 | 2 | 0.9 | 1 |
| Greens | – | – | – | – | 0.2 | 0 |
| Centre Party (extreme right) | 0.1 | 0 | 0.5 | 1 | 0.4 | 0 |
| Others | 2.7 | 1 | 3.1 | 2 | 2.3 | 1 |
| Totals | 100.0 | 150 | 100.0 | 150 | 100.0 | 150 |

**Table 8.13A**    (b) Netherlands general election

| Party | Seats | | Percentage of votes | |
|---|---|---|---|---|
| | 1994 | 1989 | 1994 | 1989 |
| PvdA | 37 | 49 | 24.0 | 31.9 |
| CDA | 34 | 54 | 22.2 | 35.3 |
| VVD | 31 | 22 | 19.9 | 14.6 |
| D66 | 24 | 12 | 15.5 | 7.9 |
| *SGP/RPF/GPV | 7 | 6 | 4.8 | 4.1 |
| AOV | 6 | – | 3.6 | – |
| Groen Links | 5 | 6 | 3.5 | 4.1 |
| CD | 3 | 1 | 2.5 | 0.9 |
| †SP | 2 | 0 | 1.3 | 0.4 |
| 55+ Union | 1 | – | 0.9 | – |
| Others | 0 | 0 | 1.8 | 0.8 |

* Political Reformed Party/Reformational Political Federation/Reformed Political Association (right-wing Protestant parties).

†Socialist Party.

***Table 8.13A*** (c) Results of General Elections in The Netherlands for the Lower House of Parliament, 3 May 1994, 150 seats

| Party | 1989 | 1994 |
|---|---|---|
| Christian Democratic Alliance (CDA) | 54 | 34 |
| Labour Party (PvdA) | 49 | 37 |
| People's Party for Freedom and Democracy (Liberals) (VVD) | 22 | 31 |
| Democrats '66 (D'66) | 12 | 24 |
| Green Left (Grl) | 6 | 5 |
| Calvinist Party (SGP) | 3 | 2 |
| Reformed Political League (GPV) | 2 | 2 |
| Evangelical Political Federation (RPF) | 1 | 3 |
| Socialist Party (SP) | – | 2 |
| General Association for the Elderly | – | 6 |
| Union 55+ | – | 1 |
| Centre Democrats (CD) | 1 | 3 |

***Table 8.14A*** (a) Portugal (Assembleia da Republica), 1975

| Party | Votes | Percentage | Number of Deputies |
|---|---|---|---|
| Portuguese Socialist Party, PSP (22) | 2 145 392 | 37.87 | 115 |
| Popular Democratic Party, PPD (22) | 1 494 575 | 26.38 | 80 |
| Portuguese Communist Party, PCP (22) | 709 639 | 12.53 | 30 |
| Social Democratic Centre, CDS (21) | 433 153 | 7.65 | 16 |
| Portuguese Democratic Movement–Democratic Electoral Committee, MDP–CDE (22) | 233 362 | 4.12 | 5 |
| Popular Socialist Front, FSP (15) | 66 161 | 1.17 | – |
| Movement of the Socialist Left, MES (15) | 57 682 | 1.02 | – |
| Popular Democratic Union, UDP (10) | 44 546 | 0.79 | 1 |
| Electoral Front of Communists (Marxist-Leninist), FEC–ML (12) | 32 508 | 0.57 | – |
| Monarchist Party, PPM (14) | 31 809 | 0.56 | – |
| Popular United Party, PUP (7) | 12 984 | 0.23 | – |
| International Communist League, LCI (4) | 10 732 | 0.19 | – |

***Table 8.14A*** (b) 1979

| Party | 1979 | 1976 |
|---|---|---|
| Democratic Alliance (total) | 128 | – |
|     PSD | 75 | 73 |
|     CDS | 42 | 42 |
|     PPM | 5 | 0 |
|     Reformists | 5 | – |
|     Independents | 1 | – |
|     Socialist Party | 74 | 107 |
| United People's Alliance (total) | 47 | – |
|     PCP | 44 | 40 |
|     MDP | 3 | – |
| Popular Democratic Union | 1 | 1 |
| Total | 250 | 263 |

**Table 8.14A** (c) Portugal (*Assembleia da Republica*).

| Party | 1980 Vote (%) | 1980 Seats | 1983 Vote (%) | 1983 Seats | 1985 Vote (%) | 1985 Seats | 1987 Vote (%) | 1987 Seats |
|---|---|---|---|---|---|---|---|---|
| Centre Social Democrats ⎫ | | 82 | 12.9 | 30 | 10.2 | 22 | 4.4 | 4 |
| Social Democrats ⎬ | 48.3 | 46 | 27.2 | 75 | 30.6 | 88 | 51.3 | 148 |
| Popular Monarchists ⎭ | | 6 | 0.5 | 0 | | | 0.4 | 0 |
| Socialist Party | 28.7 | 74 | 36.1 | 101 | 21.3 | 57 | 22.8 | 60 |
| Communist Party | 17.3 | 41 | 18.1 | 44 | 15.9 | 38 | 12.5 | 31 |
| Popular Democratic Union | 1.4 | 1 ⎫ | 1.2 | 0 | 1.3 | 0 | 0.9 | 0 |
| Revolutionary Socialist Party | 1.0 | 0 ⎭ | | | 0.6 | 0 | 0.6 | 0 |
| Socialist Unity Party | 1.4 | 0 | 0.3 | 0 | | | 0.2 | 0 |
| Democratic Renewal Party | – | – | – | – | 18.4 | 45 | 5.0 | 7 |
| Others | 1.9 | 0 | 3.7 | 0 | 1.7 | 0 | 1.9 | 0 |
| Totals | 100.0 | 250 | 100.0 | 250 | 100.0 | 250 | 100.0 | 250 |

**Table 8.14A** (d) Elections to the *Assembleia da Republica* (unicameral parliament) 1991

| No. | Party | Votes | % | Change | Seats | % | Change |
|---|---|---|---|---|---|---|---|
| 3 | *Partido Social Democrata*/Social Democratic Party (PPD/PSD) | 2 861 430 | 50.4 | +0.3 | 132 | 58.4 | −0.5 |
| 4 | *Partido Socialista*/Socialist Party (PS) | 1 659 881 | 29.3 | +7.0 | 71 | 31.4 | +7.4 |
| 19 | *Caligação Democrático Unitária*/United Democratic Coalition (CDU) | 502 804 | 8.8 | −3.4 | 17 | 7.5 | −5.1 |
| 1 | *Partido do Centro Democrático Social*/Centre Social Democrats (CDS) | 248 781 | 4.4 | +0.1 | 5 | 2.2 | +0.6 |
| 20 | *Partido do Solidariadade Nacional*/Party of National Solidarity (PSN) | 95 735 | 1.7 | +1.7 | 1 | 0.4 | +0.4 |
| 17 | *Partido Renovador Democrático*/Democratic Renewal Party (PRD) | 34 700 | 0.6 | −4.3 | 0 | 0 | −2.8 |
| 7 | *União Democrática Popular*/Popular Democratic Union (UDP) | 6169 | 0.1 | −0.8 | 0 | 0 | 0 |
| | Total | | | | 226 | | |

**Table 8.15A** (a) Spain (*Congreso de Diputados*) and Senate.

| | Votes 1982 | Seats in Congress 1982 | Seats in Congress 1979 | Seats in Senate 1982 | Seats in Senate 1979 |
|---|---|---|---|---|---|
| PSOE/PSC–PSOE | 10 127 392 | 202 | 121 | 134 | 68 |
| AP/AP–PDP | 5 543 107* | 106 | 9† | 54 | 3† |
| UCD | 1 425 093 | 12 | 168‡ | 4 | 120 |
| CiU | 772 726 | 12 | 8 | § | 1 |
| PNV | 395 656 | 8 | 7 | 7 | 8 |
| PCE–PSUC | 844 976 | 4 | 23 | 0 | 0 |
| CDS | 600 842 | 2 | – | 0 | – |
| HB | 210 601 | 2 | 3 | 0 | 1 |
| ERC | 138 116 | 1 | 1 | § | 1 |
| EE | 100 326 | 1 | 1 | 0 | 0 |
| Independents and others | 648 346 | 0 | 9 | 2 | 6 |

\* Includes 139 148 votes won in coalition with UCD in the Basque region.
† Seats won by Democratic Coalition in 1979.
‡ Reduced to 122 by end of August 1982.
§ Combined to form *Catalunya al Senat* with 7 members.

**Table 8.15A** (b) Spain (*Congreso de Diputados*), 1986.

| Party | Percentage | Seats |
|---|---|---|
| Socialist Party | 44.3 | 184 |
| Popular Alliance ⎫ Popular Democrats ⎭ | 26.1 | 105 |
| Union of the Democratic Centre (UCD) | – | – |
| Democratic and Social Centre (CDS) | 9.3 | 19 |
| Communist Party and allies | 4.6 | 7 |
| Major Catalan parties | | |
| Convergence and Unity | 5.0 | 18 |
| Catalan Republican Left | 0.5 | 0 |
| Major Basque parties | | |
| Basque Nationalists | 1.5 | 6 |
| Herri Batasuna | 1.2 | 5 |
| Basque Left | 0.5 | 2 |
| Other regional parties | 3.1 | 4 |
| Democratic Reformist Party | 1.0 | 0 |
| Greens | 0.4 | 0 |
| Others | 2.5 | 0 |
| Totals | 100.0 | 350 |

**Table 8.15A** (c) Spanish election results.

| | Chamber of Deputies | | | | | Senate | | | |
|---|---|---|---|---|---|---|---|---|---|
| | | | | | | | Seats | | |
| | | Seats | | % of vote | | Elected | Ap-pointed* | Total | |
| Party | 1996 | 1993 | 1989 | 1993 | 1989 | 1993 | 1993 | 1993 | 1989 |
| Socialist Workers' Party (PSOE) | 141 | 159 | 175 | 38.68 | 39.55 | 96 | 21 | 117 | 128 |
| Popular Party (PP) | 156 | 141 | 107 | 34.82 | 25.83 | 93 | 14 | 107 | 92 |
| United Left (IU) | 21 | 18 | 17 | 9.57 | 9.05 | – | 2 | 2 | 4 |
| Convergence and Union (CiU) | 16 | 17 | 18 | 4.95 | 5.04 | 10 | 5 | 15 | 12 |
| Basque Nationalist Party (PNV) | 5 | 5 | 5 | 1.24 | 1.24 | 3 | 2 | 5 | 6 |
| Canarian Coalition (CC) | – | 4 | – | 0.88 | – | 1 | – | 1 | – |
| *Herri Batasuna* (HB) | – | 2 | 4 | 0.88 | 1.06 | 1 | – | 1 | 3 |
| Catalan Republican Party (ERC) | – | 1 | – | 0.80 | – | – | – | – | – |
| Aragon Party (PAR) | – | 1 | 1 | 0.61 | 0.35 | – | 1 | 1 | 1 |
| *Eusko Alkartasuna* (EA) | – | 1 | 2 | 0.55 | 0.67 | – | 1 | 1 | – |
| Valencian Union (UV) | – | 1 | 2 | 0.48 | 0.71 | – | 1 | 1 | 1 |
| Others | 11 | – | – | – | – | – | – | – | 5 |
| Total | 350 | 350 | 350 | 100.00 | 100.00 | 204 | 47 | 251 | 254 |

* By Autonomous Communities.

**Table 8.16A**    (a) Sweden (*Riksdag*)

| Party | 1982 Vote (%) | Seats | 1985 Vote (%) | Seats | 1988 Vote (%) | Seats |
|---|---|---|---|---|---|---|
| Social Democrats | 45.6 | 166 | 44.7 | 156 | 43.2 | 156 |
| Moderate Unity Party | 23.6 | 86 | 21.3 | 76 | 18.3 | 66 |
| Centre Party | 15.5 | 56 | 12.4 | 43 | 11.3 | 42 |
| Christian Democrats | 1.9 | 0 | | 1 | 2.9 | 0 |
| People's Party | 5.9 | 21 | 14.2 | 51 | 12.2 | 44 |
| Left Party Communists | 5.6 | 20 | 5.4 | 19 | 5.8 | 21 |
| Greens | 1.7 | 0 | 1.5 | 0 | 5.5 | 20 |
| Others | 0.2 | 0 | 0.5 | 0 | 0.7 | 0 |
| Totals | 100.0 | 349 | 100.0 | 349 | 100.0 | 349 |

**Table 8.16A**    (b) Swedish general election

| Party | 1994 % of vote | Seats | 1991 % of vote | Seats |
|---|---|---|---|---|
| Social Democrats (SAP) | 45.25 | 161 | 37.7 | 138 |
| Left Party (Vp) | 6.17 | 22 | 4.5 | 16 |
| Ecology Party (MpG) | 5.02 | 18 | 3.4 | 0 |
| *Moderates (M) | 22.37 | 80 | 21.9 | 80 |
| *Liberal Party (Fp) | 7.19 | 26 | 9.1 | 33 |
| *Centre Party (C) | 7.65 | 27 | 8.5 | 31 |
| *Christian Democratic Community Party (KdS) | 4.06 | 15 | 7.1 | 26 |
| New Democracy (ND) | 1.23 | 0 | 6.7 | 25 |
| Others | 1.06 | 0 | 1.1 | 0 |

* Member of outgoing coalition.
*Turnout:* 86.0 per cent (86.7 per cent in 1991).

**Table 8.17A**    (a) United Kingdom (House of Commons), 1983.

| Party | Vote (%) | Seats |
|---|---|---|
| Conservatives | 42.4 | 397 |
| Labour Party | 27.6 | 209 |
| Liberal Party | 25.4 | 17 |
| Social Democratic Party | | 6 |
| Scottish National Party | 1.1 | 2 |
| *Plaid Cymru* | 0.4 | 2 |
| Greens | 0.2 | 0 |
| Communist Party | 0.0 | 0 |
| Northern Irish parties | | |
|    Ulster Unionist Party | 0.8 | 11 |
|    Democratic Unionist Party | 0.5 | 3 |
|    Social Democratic and Labour Party | 0.4 | 1 |
|    *Sinn Féin* | 0.3 | 1 |
|    Alliance Party | 0.1 | 0 |
| Others | 0.8 | 1 |
| Totals | 100.0 | 650 |

***Table 8.17A*** (b) UK general election.

| Party | Percentage of votes | | Seats | | |
|---|---|---|---|---|---|
| | 1992 | 1987 | 1992 election | 1987 election | at dissolution |
| Conservative Party | 41.93 | 42.22 | 336 | 375 | 367 |
| Labour Party | 34.39 | 30.83 | 271 | 229 | 227 |
| Liberal Democrats | 17.85 | – | 20 | 0 | 22 |
| Social Democrats | – | – | 0 | 0 | 3 |
| Liberal–SDP Alliance | – | 22.57 | 0 | 22 | 0 |
| SNP | 1.87 | 1.28 | 3 | 3 | 5 |
| *Plaid Cymru* | 0.47 | 0.38 | 4 | 3 | 3 |
| Official Ulster Unionists | 0.81 | 0.85 | 9 | 9 | 9 |
| Democratic Unionists | 0.31 | 0.26 | 3 | 3 | 3 |
| Ulster Popular Unionist | 0.06 | 0.06 | 1 | 1 | 1 |
| Social Democratic and Labour Party | 0.55 | 0.47 | 4 | 3 | 3 |
| *Sinn Féin* | 0.23 | 0.26 | 0 | 1 | 1 |
| Others* | 1.43 | 0.82 | 0 | 1 | 6 |
| Total | 100.00 | 100.00 | **651 | 650 | 650 |

* Included the Green Party with 0.51 per cent of the vote in 1992 (0.26 in 1987). The 'other' seat in 1987 comprised the Speaker; those at dissolution comprised the Speaker, three Deputy Chairmen of Ways and Means and two former Labour MPs who were expelled from the party in December 1991 and who were sitting as independents.
** The number of parliamentary seats was increased by one in 1992 with the division of the Milton Keynes constituency into two.
Regionally, *Plaid Cymru* got 9.0 per cent of the vote in Wales; the SNP got 21.5 per cent of votes in Scotland; in Northern Ireland the three unionist parties together got 50.2 per cent (52 in 1987); the SDLP 23.5 per cent (21.1); and *Sinn Féin* 10.0 per cent (11.4).
*Source:* House of Commons Public Information Office.

***Table 8.18A*** European Elections. Electorate and turnout in EC states in 1979 and 1984.

| Country | | Electorate | Turnout | Valid votes |
|---|---|---|---|---|
| Belgium | 1984 | 6 975 677 | 92.2 | 5 725 837 |
| | 1979 | 6 800 584 | 91.4 | 5 442 867 |
| Luxembourg | 1984 | 214 434 | 87.0 | 162 898 |
| | 1979 | 212 740 | 88.9 | 169 787 |
| Italy | 1984 | 44 446 614 | 83.9 | 34 957 759 |
| | 1979 | 42 193 369 | 86.0 | 35 042 601 |
| Greece | 1984 | 7 790 309 | 77.2 | 5 956 060 |
| | 1979 | 6 806 951 | 78.6 | 5 753 478 |
| Germany | 1984 | 44 451 981 | 56.8 | 24 841 306 |
| | 1979 | 42 751 940 | 65.7 | 27 847 109 |
| France | 1984 | 36 836 544 | 56.7 | 20 119 200 |
| | 1979 | 35 180 531 | 60.7 | 20 253 307 |
| Denmark | 1984 | 3 804 660 | 52.3 | 1 988 791 |
| | 1979 | 3 725 235 | 47.8 | 1 754 850 |
| Netherlands | 1984 | 10 700 000 | 50.5 | 5 292 557 |
| | 1979 | 9 808 176 | 58.1 | 5 666 403 |
| Ireland | 1984 | 2 413 404 | 47.6 | 1 120 516 |
| | 1979 | 2 188 798 | 63.6 | 1 339 072 |
| United Kingdom | 1984 | 42 984 998 | 32.56 | 13 998 171 |
| | 1979 | 42 559 460 | 31.6 | 13 446 091 |
| Total | 1984 | 199 485 841 | 59.0 | 114 163 095 |
| | 1979 | 192 227 784 | 62.5 | 116 715 565 |

***Table 8.19A***   European Parliament – Distribution of seats after June 1979 elections

| Country | Soc | EPP | EDG | Com | LD | DEP | TCDI | Others | Total |
|---|---|---|---|---|---|---|---|---|---|
| Belgium (91.6%) | 7 | 10 | – | – | 4 | – | 1 | 2 | 24 |
| Denmark (47.1%) | 4 | – | 3 | 1 | 3 | 1 | 4 | – | 16 |
| France (60.7%) | 21 | 9 | – | 19 | 17 | 15 | – | – | 81 |
| Ireland (63.6%) | 4 | 4 | – | – | 1 | 5 | 1 | – | 15 |
| Italy (85.5%) | 13 | 30 | – | 24 | 5 | – | 5 | 4 | 81 |
| Luxembourg (88.9%) | 1 | 3 | – | – | 2 | – | – | – | 6 |
| Netherlands (57.8%) | 9 | 10 | – | – | 4 | – | – | 2 | 25 |
| United Kingdom (31.8%) | 18 | – | 61 | – | – | 1 | – | 1 | 81 |
| West Germany (61.5%) | 35 | 42 | – | – | 4 | – | – | – | 81 |
| Totals | 112 | 108 | 64 | 44 | 40 | 22 | 11 | 9 | 410 |

| | |
|---|---|
| Socialists (Soc) | 112 |
| European People's Party (EPP) | 108 |
| European Democrats (EDG) (European Conservative Group) | 64 |
| Communists (Com) | 44 |
| Liberals and Democrats (LD) | 40 |
| Progressive Democrats (DEP) | 22 |
| Independents | 20 |
| | 410 |

***Table 8.20A***   1994 European Elections
**European Parliament election results in all 12 EU member countries**
* Member of current government.
In results columns of all tables: – did not contest election; 0 won no seats.
*Sources:* European Parliament Directorate-General for Information and Public Relations; *Süddeutsche Zeitung* June 14; *Financial Times* June 14; *Le Monde* June 15; *Economist* June 18.

**Belgium** (June 12)

| Party | 1994 % | 1994 Seats | 1989 % | 1989 Seats |
|---|---|---|---|---|
| *Christian People's Party (CVP) | 17.0 | 4 | 21.1 | 5 |
| *Christian Social Party (PSC) | 6.9 | 2 | 8.1 | 2 |
| Christian Social Party (CSP) | 0.2 | 1 | – | – |
| *Socialist Party (PS–Walloon) | 11.3 | 3 | 14.5 | 5 |
| *Socialist Party (SP–Flemish) | 10.8 | 3 | 12.4 | 3 |
| Flemish Liberals and Democrats (VLD)[2] | 11.4 | 3 | 10.6 | 2 |
| Liberal Reform Party (PRL) | 9.0 | 3 | 8.7 | 2 |
| Flemish Bloc (*Vlaams Bloc*) | 7.8 | 2 | 4.1 | 1 |
| National Front (FN) | 2.9 | 1 | – | – |
| Live Differently (*Agalev*) | 6.7 | 1 | 7.6 | 1 |
| Ecology Party (*Ecolo*) | 4.8 | 1 | 6.3 | 2 |
| People's Union (*Volksunie*) | 4.4 | 1 | 5.4 | 1 |
| Others | 6.8 | 0 | 1.2 | 0 |
| Total | 100.0 | 25 | 100.0 | 24 |

[1] Party of German-speaking minority.
[2] Called Freedom and Progress Party (PVV) in 1989.
*Turnout:* 90.7 per cent (90.7 per cent in 1989).

**Denmark** (June 9)

| Party | 1994 % | Seats | 1989 % | Seats |
|---|---|---|---|---|
| *Venstre* Liberals | 19.0 | 4 | 16.6 | 3 |
| Conservative People's Party (KF) | 17.7 | 3 | 13.3 | 2 |
| *Social Democrats (SD) | 15.8 | 3 | 23.3 | 4 |
| June Movement (JB) | 15.2 | 2 | – | – |
| People's Movement against the EU | 10.3 | 2 | 18.9 | 4 |
| Socialist People's Party (SF) | 8.6 | 1 | 9.1 | 1 |
| *Social Liberals (*Radikale Venstre*) | 8.5 | 1 | 2.8 | 0 |
| Progress Party (FP) | 2.9 | 0 | 5.3 | 0 |
| *Christian People's Party (KrF) | 1.1 | 0 | 2.7 | 0 |
| *Centre Democrats (CD) | 0.9 | 0 | 8.0 | 2 |
| Total | 100.0 | 16 | 100.0 | 16 |

*Turnout:* 52.5 per cent (46.2 per cent in 1989).

**France** (June 12)

| Party | 1994 % | Seats | 1989 % | Seats |
|---|---|---|---|---|
| *Union for French Democracy/Rally for the Republic (UDF/RPR) | 25.58 | 28 | 28.9 | 26 |
| *Centre of Social Democrats (CDS)[1] | – | – | 8.4 | 7 |
| Socialist Party (PS) | 14.49 | 15 | 23.6 | 22 |
| Another Europe | 12.33 | 13 | – | – |
| Radical Energy | 12.03 | 13 | – | – |
| National Front (FN) | 10.52 | 11 | 11.7 | 10 |
| French Communist Party (PCF) | 6.88 | 7 | 7.7 | 7 |
| Union of Ecologists[2] | 2.94 | 0 | 10.6 | 8 |
| *Génération Écologie*[2] | 2.01 | 0 | | 1 |
| Pro-hunting list | 3.9 | 0 | – | – |
| Alternative politics (*Chevènement*) | 2.5 | 0 | – | – |
| Sarajevo list | 1.6 | 0 | – | – |
| Others | 5.2 | 0 | 9.1 | 0 |
| Total | 100.0 | 87 | 100.0 | 81 |

[1] Campaigned separately from UDF/RPR in 1989.
[2] Contested as *les Verts* in 1989.
*Turnout:* 53.7 per cent (48.7 per cent in 1989).

**Germany** (June 12)

| Party | 1994 % | Seats | 1989 % | Seats |
|---|---|---|---|---|
| Social Democratic Party (SPD) | 32.2 | 40 | 37.3 | 31 |
| *Christian Democratic Union (CDU) | 32.0 | 39 | 29.5 | 25 |
| Alliance 90/Greens | 10.1 | 12 | 8.4 | 8 |
| *Christian Social Union (CSU) | 6.8 | 8 | 8.2 | 7 |
| Party of Democratic Socialism (PDS) | 4.7[1] | 0 | – | – |
| *Free Democratic Party (FDP) | 4.1 | 0 | 5.6 | 4 |
| Republicans | 3.9 | 0 | 7.1 | 6 |
| Others | 6.2[2] | 0 | 3.9 | 0 |
| Total | 100.0 | 99 | 100.0 | 81 |

[1] Polled between 15 and 27 per cent in eastern *Länder* (states) and just over 40 per cent in east Berlin.
[2] Federation of Free Citizens (*Bund freier Bürger*, an anti-Maastricht party also known as the Brunner Party) 1.1 per cent, others less than 1 per cent.
*Turnout:* 60.1 per cent (62.3 per cent in 1989).

**Greece** (June 12)

| Party | 1994 | | 1989 | |
|---|---|---|---|---|
| | % | Seats | % | Seats |
| *Panhellenic Socialist Movement (Pasok) | 37.64 | 10 | 36.0 | 9 |
| New Democracy (ND) | 32.66 | 9 | 40.4 | 10 |
| Political Spring (POLA) | 8.65 | 2 | – | – |
| Communist Party of Greece (KKE)[1] | 6.29 | 2 | – | – |
| Alliance of Left and Progressive Forces (*Synaspismos*) | 6.25 | 2 | – | – |
| Communist Alliance[1] | – | – | 14.3 | 4 |
| Democratic Renewal (Diana) | 2.79 | 0 | 1.4 | 1 |
| Others | 5.72[2] | 0 | 7.9 | 0 |
| Total | 100.0 | 25 | 100.0 | 24 |

[1] In 1989 the orthodox communist KKE-Exterior and the Eurocommunist KKE-Interior contested the elections jointly as the Communist Alliance.
[2] Including environmental groups, right-wing extremists and recently formed Left-wing Resistance to the EU.
*Turnout:* 71.2 per cent (79.9 per cent in 1989).

**Ireland** (June 9)

| Party | 1994 | | 1989 | |
|---|---|---|---|---|
| | % | Seats | % | Seats |
| *Fianna Fáil* | 35.00 | 7 | 31.5 | 6 |
| *Fine Gael* | 24.27 | 4 | 21.6 | 4 |
| *Labour Party | 10.99 | 1 | 9.5 | 1 |
| Green Alliance | 7.92 | 2 | 3.8 | 0 |
| Independents | 6.94 | 1 | 11.9 | 2 |
| Progressive Democrats | 6.48 | 0 | 11.9 | 1 |
| Democratic Left[1] | 3.49 | – | – | – |
| *Sinn Féin* | 2.97 | 0 | 2.3 | 0 |
| Workers' Party | 1.94 | 0 | 7.5 | 1 |
| Total | 100.0 | 15 | 100.0 | 15 |

[1] Founded 1992 by breakaway faction of Workers' Party.
*Turnout:* 44.0 per cent (68.3 per cent in 1989).

**Italy** (June 12)

| Party | 1994 | | 1989 | |
|---|---|---|---|---|
| | % | Seats | % | Seats |
| *Forza Italia* | 30.6 | 27 | – | – |
| Democratic Party of the Left (PDS)[1] | 19.1 | 16 | 27.6 | 22 |
| *National Alliance (AN)[2] | 12.5 | 11 | 5.5 | 4 |
| Italian Popular Party (PPI)[3] | 10.0 | 8 | 32.9 | 26 |
| *Northern League (LN)[4] | 6.6 | 6 | 1.8 | 2 |
| Communist Refoundation (RC) | 6.1 | 5 | – | – |
| *Segni Pact* | 3.3 | 3 | – | – |
| Federation of Greens[5] | 3.2 | 3 | 3.8 | 5 |
| *Pannella Riformatori* (PR)[6] | 2.1 | 2 | 4.4 | 4 |
| Italian Socialist Party (PSI) | 1.8 | 2 | 14.8 | 12 |
| Network (*La Rete*) | 1.1 | 1 | – | – |
| Italian Republican Party (PRI)[6] | 0.7 | 1 | – | – |
| Italian Democratic Socialist Party (PSDI) | 0.7 | 1 | 2.7 | 2 |
| Southern League (*Lega Meridionale*) | 0.7 | 0 | – | – |
| South Tyrol People's Party (SVP) | 0.6 | 1 | 0.5 | 1 |
| Val d'Aosta (UV) | 0.4 | 0 | 0.6 | 1 |
| Others | 0.5[7] | 0 | 5.4 | 2 |
| Total | 100.0 | 87 | 100.0 | 81 |

**Italy** Continued

(For March 1994 general election and table of recent party political changes see pp. 39918–20.)
[1] Italian Communist Party (PCI) in 1989.
[2] Formerly Italian Social Movement–National Right (MSI–DN).
[3] Formerly Christian Democratic Party (CD).
[4] Formerly Lombardy League.
[5] Called simply the Greens (*Verdi*) in 1989.
[6] In 1989 three centre parties stood jointly: the Radical Party (PR), the Italian Liberal Party (PLI) and the Italian Republican Party (PRI). In 1994 the PR list was headed by Marco Pannella, while the PLI and PRI stood separately.
[7] Lombardy Alpine League (*Lega Alpina Lombarda*) (0.3 per cent), PLI (0.2 per cent) and Solidarity (0.045 per cent).
*Turnout:* 74.8 per cent (81.5 per cent in 1989).

**Luxembourg** (June 12)

| Party | 1994 | | 1989 | |
|---|---|---|---|---|
| | % | Seats | % | Seats |
| *Christian Social People's Party (CSV/PCS) | 31.4 | 2 | 34.9 | 3 |
| *Luxembourg Socialist Workers' Party (LSAP/POSL) | 24.8 | 2 | 25.4 | 2 |
| Democratic Party (DP/PD) | 18.9 | 1 | 20.0 | 1 |
| Greens[1] | 10.9 | 1 | 6.1 | 0 |
| Others | 14.0 | 0 | 13.6 | 0 |
| Total | 100.0 | 6 | 100.0 | 6 |

[1] Campaigned as two separate lists in 1989.
*Turnout:* 86.6 per cent (87.4 per cent in 1989).

**Netherlands** (June 9)

| Party | 1994 | | 1989 | |
|---|---|---|---|---|
| | % | Seats | % | Seats |
| *Christian Democratic Appeal (CDA) | 30.8 | 10 | 34.6 | 10 |
| *Labour Party (PvdA) | 22.9 | 8 | 30.7 | 8 |
| People's Party for Freedom and Democracy (VVD) | 17.9 | 6 | 13.6 | 3 |
| Democrats 66 (D66) | 11.7 | 4 | 5.9 | 1 |
| Confessional parties[1] | 7.8 | 2 | 5.9 | 1 |
| *Groen Links*[2] | 6.1 | 1 | 7.0 | 2 |
| Others | 2.8[3] | 0 | 2.3 | 0 |
| Total | 100.0 | 31 | 100.0 | 25 |

*Caretaker government following May general election – see pp. 40024–25.
[1] Comprising Political Reformed Party (SGP), Reformational Political Federation (RPF) and Reformed Political Association (GPV) (campaigned as Coalition of Calvinists in 1989).
[2] Called Green Progressive Alliance (GPA) in 1989.
[3] Included Socialist Party (1.3 per cent); Centre Democrats (1.0 per cent) and List 9 (0.2 per cent).
*Turnout:* 35.6 per cent (47.2 per cent in 1989).

**Portugal** (June 12)

| Party | 1994 | | 1989 | |
|---|---|---|---|---|
| | % | Seats | % | Seats |
| Socialist Party (PS) | 34.79 | 10 | 28.5 | 8 |
| *Social Democratic Party (PSD) | 34.36 | 9 | 32.7 | 9 |
| Democratic Social Centre (CDS) | 12.48 | 3 | 14.1 | 3 |
| Unified Democratic Coalition (CDU) | 11.22 | 3 | 14.4 | 4 |
| Democratic Renewal Party (PRD) | 0.19 | 0 | – | – |
| Others | 6.96 | 0 | 10.3 | 0 |
| Total | 100.0 | 25 | 100.0 | 24 |

*Turnout:* 35.6 per cent (51.2 per cent in 1989).

**Spain** (June 12)

| Party | 1994 % | 1994 Seats | 1989 % | 1989 Seats |
|---|---|---|---|---|
| Popular Party (PP) | 40.21 | 28 | 21.7 | 15 |
| *Spanish Socialist Workers' Party (PSOE) | 30.67 | 22 | 40.2 | 27 |
| United Left (IU) | 13.46 | 9 | 6.2 | 4 |
| Convergence and Union (CiU) | 4.67 | 3 | 4.3 | 2 |
| Nationalist Coalition (CN) | 2.80 | 2 | 1.9 | 1 |
| People's European Coalition (CEP) | 1.29 | 0 | 1.5 | 1 |
| Democratic and Social Centre (CDS) | 0.99 | 0 | 7.2 | 5 |
| *Herri Batasuna* (HB) | 0.97 | 0 | 1.7 | 1 |
| People's Left (IP) | – | – | 1.9 | 1 |
| Andalucia Regional Party (Capa) | 0.76 | 0 | 1.9 | 1 |
| Galician Nationalist Bloc (BNG) | 0.76 | 0 | – | – |
| Greens | 0.68 | 0 | – | – |
| *Ruiz Mateos* | 0.44 | 0 | 3.9 | 2 |
| Others | 2.30 | 0 | 7.6 | 0 |
| Total | 100.0 | 64 | 100.0 | 60 |

*Turnout:* 59.58 per cent (54.6 per cent in 1989).

**United Kingdom** (June 9)

*Great Britain*

| Party | 1994 % | 1994 Seats | 1989 % | 1989 Seats |
|---|---|---|---|---|
| Labour Party | 44.24 | 62 | 40.1 | 45 |
| *Conservative Party | 27.83 | 18 | 34.1 | 32 |
| Liberal Democrats[1] | 16.72 | 2 | 6.4 | 0 |
| Greens | 3.24 | 0 | 15.0 | 0 |
| Scottish National Party (SNP) | 3.19[2] | 2 | 2.7 | 1 |
| *Plaid Cymru* | 1.06[3] | 0 | 0.8 | 0 |
| Others | 3.72 | 0 | 0.9 | 0 |
| Total | 100.0 | 84 | 100.0 | 78 |

[1] In 1989 the Social and Liberal Democratic Party (SLDP).
[2] Won 32.6 per cent of the vote in Scotland.
[3] Won 17 per cent of the vote in Wales.
*Turnout:* 36.1 per cent (35.9 per cent in 1989).

*Northern Ireland*

| Party | 1994 % | 1994 Seats | 1989 % | 1989 Seats |
|---|---|---|---|---|
| Democratic Unionist Party (DUP) | 29.16 | 1 | 29.9 | 1 |
| Social Democratic and Labour Party (SDLP) | 28.93 | 1 | 25.5 | 1 |
| (Official) Ulster Unionist Party (OUP) | 23.84 | 1 | 22.2 | 1 |
| *Sinn Féin* | 9.86 | 0 | 9.1 | 0 |
| Others | 8.21 | 0 | 13.3 | 0 |
| Total | 100.0 | 3 | 100.0 | 3 |

*Turnout:* 48.67 per cent (47.7 per cent in 1989).

*Turnout for the UK as a whole:* 36.4 per cent (36.2 per cent in 1989).

# Further reading

## Party systems

Katz, R. and Mair, P. (1994) *How Parties Organise: Change and Adaptation in Party Organisations in Western Democracies*, London: Sage.
Lane, J.-E. and Ersson, P. (1991) *Politics in Western Europe*, London: Sage.
Mény, Y. (1993) *Government and Politics in Western Europe*, Oxford: Oxford University Press.
Plant, R. (1993) *Report of the Plant Commission*, London: Labour Party.
Smith, G. (1990) *Politics in Western Europe*, Aldershot: Dartmouth.
Urwin, D. and Paterson, W. (eds) (1990) *Politics in Western Europe Today, Perspectives, Policies and Problems Since 1980*, London: Longman.
Wright, V. (1989) *The Government and Politics of France*, London: Unwin Hayman.

## The left

Gillespie, R. and Paterson, W. (1993) *Rethinking Social Democracy in Western Europe*, London: Frank Cass.
Koelble, T. (1991) *The Left Unraveled, Social Democracy and the New Left Challenge in Britain and Germany*, Brookfields, VT: Duke University Press.
Oberreuter, H. and Mintzel, A. (1990) *Parteien in der Bundesrepublik Deutschland*, Bonn: Olzog Verlag.
Paterson, W. and Gillespie, R. (eds), (1993) 'Rethinking social democracy in western Europe' *West European Politics (WEP)* 16 (1), 60–75.
Shaw, E. (1994) *The Labour Party Since 1979*, London: Routledge.
von Beyme, K. (1985) *Political Parties in Western Europe*, Aldershot: Gower.
Wilde, L. (1994) *Modern European Socialism*, Durham, NC: Dartmouth.

## Other left

Agh, A. (1994) 'From Nomenclatura to Clientura: The Emergence of New Political Elites in Eastern Europe', *Labour Focus on Eastern Europe* 47, pp. 58–77.
McLellan, D. (1980) *Marxism after Marx*, Basingstoke: Macmillan.
Machin, H. (1983) *National Communism in Western Europe*, London: Methuen.
Schwab, G. (ed.) (1981) *Eurocommunism*, London: Aldwych Press.

## Christian Democracy

Ginsborg, P. (1990) *A History of Contemporary Italy*, London: Penguin.
Hanley, D. (ed.) (1994) *Christian Democracy in Europe*, London: Pinter.
Henig, S. (ed.) *Political Parties in the European Community*, London: Allen & Unwin.
Irving, R. E. M. (1979) *The Christian Democratic Parties of Western Europe*, London: Allen & Unwin.
Irving, R. E. M. (1979) 'Christian Democracy in post-war Europe: conservatism writ large or distinctive political phenomenon?' *West European Politics (WEP)*, 2 (1), pp. 53–68.
Layton-Henry, Z. (1982) *Conservative Politics in Western Europe*, London: Macmillan.
Pridham, G. (1976) 'Christian Democracy in Italy and West Germany: a comparative analysis'

in *Social and Political Movements in Western Europe*, Kolinsky, M. and Paterson, W. (eds), London: Croom Helm.


## Conservatism

Gilmour, I. (1978) *Inside Right*, London: Hutchinson.
Gilmour, I. (1992) *Dancing with Dogma*, London: Simon and Schuster.
Goldthorpe, J. and Lockwood, D. (1968), *The Affluent Worker, Political Attitudes and Behaviour*, Cambridge: Cambridge University Press.
Young, H. (1990) *One of Us*, London: Pan.


## Far Right

Cheles, K., Ferguson, R. and Vaughan, M. (1991) *Neo-Fascism in Europe*, London: Longman.
Funken, K. and Deckers, W. (1993) *The Revival of Right-Wing Movements in Europe*, London: Friedrich Ebert Foundation and Richmond College.
'Extreme Right in Europe' (1992) *Race & Class*, Special Issue, March.
Gower, C. (1993) 'The New Far Right in Western Europe' in Funken, K. and Deckers, W. (1993).
Schain, M. (1987) 'Racial politics: the rise of the National Front', in *The French Socialists in Power*, McCarthy, P. (ed.), New York: Greenwood Press.
von Beyme, K. (1988) *West European Politics*, Special Issue 11 (2), (whole issue) pp. 1–142.


## Regional parties and movements

Hooper, J. (1995) *The New Spaniards*, London: Penguin.
Leonardi, R. and Kovacs, M. (1993) 'The Lega Nord: the rise of a new catch-all party' in *Italian Politics: A Review*, vol. 8 Hellman, S. and Pasquino, G. (eds), London: Pinter.
Sullivan, J. (1988) *ETA and Basque Nationalism*, London: Routledge.
Woods, D. (1992) 'The Centre no longer holds: The Rise of Regional Leagues in Italian Politics', *WEP* 15 (2), pp. 56–76.

## Notes

1. This internal change in parties may itself be due to systemic change, for example the rise of the SDP/Liberals.
2. The 'Gang of Four' referred to David Owen, Roy Jenkins, Shirley Williams and Bill Rogers, founders of the SDP.
3. For further analysis of party change, see Bartolini, S. and Mair, P. (1984) *Party Politics in Contemporary Europe*, London: Frank Cass.
4. Gillespie in Urwin and Paterson, 1990, p. 228.
5. Lane and Ersson, 1991, p. 44.
6. Rokkan in Mény, 1993, p. 44.
7. Some communist parties still survive attached to traditional ideology like PCF in France, PCP in Portugal, KKE in Greece and the Rifondazione in Italy.
8. 'In the inarticulate mass of the English populace, [Disraeli] discerned the Conservative

workingman as the sculptor perceives the angel prisoned in a block of marble', *The Times* 18/04/1883 in McKenzie, R. and Silver, A. (1968) *Angels in Marble. Working Class Conservatives in Urban England*, London: Heinemann Educational.

9.  Sartori, G. (1968) 'European political parties: the case of polarised pluralism' in *Readings in Modern Political Analysis*, Dahl, R. A. and Neubauer, D. E. (eds) (1968) London: Prentice Hall, p. 122.

10. Wright, 1989, pp. 162–80.

11. Paterson and Urwin, 1990, p. 234.

12. The *Alleanza Nazionale* is the new name for the *Movimento Sociale Italiano* (MSI), which was the direct descendant of Mussolini's Fascist party.

13. The decision of the UK government, for example, to support Sterling to the tune of around £5 bn during Wednesday 16 September 1992 and then later that day to leave the European Exchange Rate Mechanism was taken by only a few ministers and officials.

14. Mény, 1993, p. 47.

15. 'Cleavages are the criteria which divide the members of a community or subcommunity into groups, and the relevant cleavages are those which divide members into groups with important political differences at specific times and places'. Rae, D. W. and Taylor, M. (1970) *The Analysis of Political Cleavages*, New Haven: Yale University Press.

16. The whole debate about whether there is any significant ideological distance between the left and the right any more is discussed by Imbert, C. and Julliard, J. (1995) *La droite et la gauche. Qu'est-ce qui les distingue encore?* Paris: Robert Laffont/Grasset.

17. See Thompson, E. P. (1991) *The Making of the English Working Class*, London: Penguin.

18. The exact formation of the modern Tory or Conservative party is uncertain. A Tory party did exist during the eighteenth century, but the party system was such that political parties and a party system as such did not really develop until after 1832. Gilmour, I. (1978) *Inside Right. A Study of Conservatism*, London: Hutchinson.

19. This process, known as **embourgeoisement**, refers to the changing composition of the working class whereby traditional blue-collar jobs became scarcer and white-collar jobs increased in the service sector. It has been argued that this process of embourgeoisement together with increased social mobility has affected the traditional support of the working class for left-wing parties. Goldthorpe and Lockwood noted this phenomenon in their 1960s studies of *The Affluent Worker*.

20. Mény, 1993, p. 22.

21. Gilmour, I. (1978) and *Dancing with Dogma* (1992) for discussion about ideology and conservatism.

22. Heath, A., Jowell, R., Curtice, J., Evans, G., Field, J. and Witherspoon, S. (1991) *Understanding Political Change: The British Voter 1964–87*, Oxford: Pergamon Press.

23. Heath, A., Jowell, R., Curtice, J. (1994) *Labour's Lost Chance*, Aldershot: Dartmouth Press.

24. Kirchheimer, O. (1966) 'The transformation of western European party systems' in LaPalombara, J. and Weiner, M. (eds) *Political Parties and Political Development*, Princeton NJ: Princeton University Press, and in Smith, G. (1990) *Politics in Western Europe*, Aldershot: Dartmouth Press, p. 55.

25. It is worth noting in this context that the Catholic church did not really accept the legitimacy of the secular state until the Lateran Pact in 1929. Even then this pact was not signed with a liberal democratic state but with Mussolini's government.

26. Gillespie, R. *The Consolidation of New Democracies* in Urwin and Paterson, 1990, *Politics in Western Europe*, London: Longman, p. 227.

27. Despite promises to 'roll back the frontiers of the state', what has actually happened is that there has been very little diminution in the size or role of the state. Instead the state has

been maintained, with a proliferation of parastatal and quasi-state organisations, with the real change being in the reduction of these bodies' public accountability.

28. For more discussion of these systems see the *Economist*, 01/05/93.
29. This threshold limit was used by the PDS (former SED: East German Communist Party) to gain members in the Bundestag after the 1994 German general election.
30. For a succinct presentation and analysis of all the different kinds of voting systems see the Report of the Working Party on Electoral Systems, ('Plant Commission') (1993) Labour Party, 150 Walworth Road, London SE17 1JT.
31. Butler in Plant Commission, 1993.
32. Knapp, A. (1987) 'Proportional but bipolar: France's Electoral System in 1986' *WEP* 10 (1), pp. 89–114.
33. Hine, D. (1993) *Governing Italy The Politics of Bargained Pluralism*, Oxford: Oxford University Press, pp. 88–90.
34. Hine, 1993, pp. 96–106. The new Italian voting system allows for a mixture of PR and FPTP.
35. The CiU is actually a coalition of two parties, the *Convergencia Democrática de Catalunya* (CDC) and the *Uniò Democrática de Catalunya* (UDC).
36. Flanagan, S. and Dalton, R. (1984) 'Parties under stress: realignment and dealignment in advanced industrial societies' *WEP* 7, pp. 7–23.
37. Inglehart, R. (1977) *The Silent Revolution*, Princeton: Princeton University Press; Allardt, E. 'Past and emerging political cleavages' in *Party Organisation and the Politics of the New Masses* (ed.) Berlin: Free University.
38. Dalton, R., Flanagan, S. and Beck, P. (1984) *Electoral Change in Advanced Industrial Democracies: Realignment or Dealignment*, Princeton: Princeton University Press.
39. Dalton *et al.*, 1984, p. 459.
40. Irwin and Dittrich in Dalton *et al.*, 1984.
41. Seip, D. (1979) in *European Electoral Systems Handbook* Sasse, C., Georgel, J. and Hand, G. (eds), *Changes in Dutch Politics*, London: Butterworths.
42. *Guardian*, 04/05/94.
43. McDonough and López Pina in Dalton *et al.*, 1984.
44. The *Alleanza Nazionale* is the renamed MSI.
45. Poguntke, T. (1987) 'New politics and party systems: the emergence of a new type of party?' *WEP* 10 (1), pp. 76–88.
46. Smith, G. (1993) 'Dimensions of change in the German party system', in *Parties and Party Systems in the New Germany*, Padgett, S. (ed.), Aldershot: Dartmouth.
47. The German Communist Party, known at the time as the KPD (Communist Party of Germany) then promptly changed its name to the DKP (German Communist Party), without incurring another ban.
48. 'A political culture is the totality of ideas and attitudes towards authority, discipline, governmental responsibilities and entitlements, and associated patterns of cultural transmission, like the educational system and even family life'. David Robertson (1990), *Dictionary of Politics*, Harmondsworth: Penguin.
49. Wilde, L. (1994) *Modern European Socialism*, Aldershot: Dartmouth.
50. For an analysis of recent programmatic change in West European Social Democratic Parties see Gillespie, R. and Paterson, W. *Rethinking Social Democracy in Western Europe*, London: Frank Cass.
51. Gillespie, R. and Williams, A. (eds) (1989) *Southern European Socialism*, Manchester: Manchester University Press.
52. *Financial Times*, 28/10/94.
53. Wilde, 1994.

54. For more detailed analysis of the reasons for the party's defeat in the 1991 election, see Chapter 4.
55. *Guardian*, 01/10/94.
56. The work of the American sociologist Amitai Etzioni has stressed the need for societies to create awareness for others and prioritise family and community responsibilities over individualist desires: *Economist*, 11/06/94.
57. The German Communist (KPD) was formed by Rosa Luxemburg and Karl Liebknecht as a split from the SPD. They led the party to prominence in the ill-fated German revolution of 1919, and were subsequently executed.
58. Some of the inspiration for the PCI's more flexible programme stemmed from the ideas of one of its founders Antonio Gramsci. In *Prison Notebooks* (see Chapter 3, Section 3.8) written while incarcerated by the Fascist authorities in Turin prison during the late 1920s and early 1930s, Gramsci developed a strategy that involved parties manoeuvring for position in a period before they could actually seize power. His argument was based on an analysis that western communist parties were unlikely to achieve power via insurrection as the Bolshevik Party had done in 1917. The tactic, therefore, was to think more long term, build up support, enter into alliances and thereby create the base for gaining power.
59. Enrico Berlinguer, leader of the PCI in the 1970s, considered that the lessons of the Chilean coup of September 1973 had shown what could happen to a democratically elected Marxist government. The need for some kind of tactical and ideological change therefore became imperative, which became known as the 'historic compromise'. It is the case that most western European communist parties had tacitly accepted in the 1950s that there would be no violent overthrow of the state.
60. The main elements of the Eurocommunism programme were: 1. democracy; 2. party puluralism; 3. parliament and representative institutions; 4. popular sovereignty exercised regularly via ballot box and universal suffrage; 5. trade unions independent of the state and parties; 6. freedom for an opposition; 7. human rights; 8. freedom of cultural, scientific and artistic pursuits; 9. religious freedoms; 10. broad participation by people in social life; 11. national independence from international control (reference to subordination from Moscow); 12. solidarity with Third World countries; 13. end to foreign bases everywhere; 14. ban on nuclear weapons. Carrillo, S. (1977) *Eurocommunism and the State*, London: Lawrence and Wishart.
61. The PDS must identify social and political allies quickly, or else 'it runs the risk of finding itself with a reduced institutional presence, less political power, and limited political influence'. Pasquino, G. (1993) 'Programmatic renewal, and much more: from the PCI to the PDS' in *Rethinking Social Democracy in Western Europe* Gillespie, R. and Paterson. W. (eds) London: Frank Cass.
62. These parties have been influenced in terms of their ideological make-up by the changes in the Italian Communist Party.
63. This process, whereby former leading Party officials have moved directly into leading positions in the old state enterprises which have become newly privatised, is a common phenomenon throughout East/Central Europe. See Agh, A. (1994).
64. *Guardian*, 01/10/94.
65. Bull, M. (1995) 'The West European Communist Movement in the late twentieth century' *West European Politics* 18 (1), pp. 78–97.
66. *Guardian*, 05/11/93.
67. Party of European Socialists, Manifesto for 1994 European Elections adopted 06/11/93.
68. Bardi, L. (1994) 'Transitional party federations, European parliamentary party groups, and the building of Europarties' in Katz, R. and Mair, P. (eds) (1994), p. 369.

69. *Guardian*, 05/12/91.
70. Although we concentrate in this section on Germany and Italy, it is important to note the dominant role played by Christian Democratic parties in other parts of Europe, particularly in the Benelux countries. In Belgium, the CVP, the Flemish Christian Democratic party, has provided the prime minister in all governments apart from a period of 2 years since 1968. See Paul Lucardie and Hans-Martien ten Napel in Hanley, 1994.
71. Hanley: 'Introduction' in Hanley 1994, pp. 3–5. Hanley uses the term 'personalism' to emphasise the central importance of the individual in Christan Democratic thinking. NB: This is different to the use of the term *personalismo* in the Spanish political context, which refers to the preferment of party members or family into positions of influence.
72. In Spain church tax is 6 per cent of income.
73. The CSU which arose from the old Centrum party has always reflected the independence of Bavaria. It follows a more conservative line in representing this largely Catholic federal state (*Land*) although the policy of its long-time leader Franz Josef Strauss led to the opening up of links to the Soviet Union in the 1980s to promote economic growth. Some overtures have been made to consider the almost unthinkable idea of an alliance with the Greens in the light of the indecisive general election of 1994. *Independent on Sunday*, 20/11/94.
74. Raymond Barre, the former Prime Minister, set out his moderate ideas of economic liberalism in his 1984 book, *Refléxions pour Demain*, Paris: Hachette.
75. Worsthorne, P. (1991) 'Unnatural Bedfellows' *Sunday Telegraph*, 21/1/91.
76. Gilmour, 1978, p. 121. See also *Dancing with Dogma*, 1992.
77. *Independent*, 3/4/94.
78. *Independent*, 02/04/94.
79. *Economist*, 13/05/95.
80. For more details on the EPP, see Hanley in Hanley, 1994.
81. Hanley, 1994, p. 194.
82. Hanley, 1994, p. 196.
83. The link between mainstream parties and the far right in the immediate post-1945 period is mentioned by Gowan in Funken and Deckers, 1993, and more extensively in Blinkhorn, M. (ed.) (1990) *Fascists and Conservatives. The Radical Right and the Establishment in the 20th Century*, London: Unwin Hyman.
84. Mény, 1993, p. 23.
85. Gowan, 1993, p. 52.
86. The inclusion of the Leagues as part of the far right is disputed by some commentators.
87. John Hooper, *Guardian*, 14/05/94.
88. The FDP has been part of the governing coalition since 1969, at first with the SPD, then it changed sides in 1982 to the CDU-CSU. The West German foreign minister for almost 20 years was Hans-Dietrich Genscher, a member of the FDP, whose longevity in office prompted some commentators to characterise German foreign policy during that period as 'Genscherism'. In terms of his own political philosophy, he once said: 'I was taught that liberalism is the best way of fighting anti-liberalism'. *Guardian*, 04/12/90.
89. Keman, H. (1994) 'The search for the centre: pivot parties in the West European party systems' *West European Politics* 17 (4), pp. 124–48.
90. Commission on Wealth Creation and Social Cohesion, *Guardian*, 25/07/95.
91. Leonardi, R. and Kovacs, M. (1993) 'The Lega Nord: The rise of a new Italian catch-all party' in *Italian Politics. A Review* vol. 8, (eds), London: Pinter.
92. *Guardian*, 29/05/92.
93. Leonardi and Kovacs, 1993, p. 61.
94. *Independent*, 23/04/94.

95. The progressive idea of the modernising role of the centralised state was also a strong element in socialist thinking, and PSOE was as opposed as the liberals to the separatism of Catalonia and the Basque province.

96. In Germany between 1966–69, the CDU governed in a 'Grand coalition' with the SPD, and in Italy there were frequent coalitions between the DC and the PSI (Socialist Party).

97. Arana created the new Basque province out of selective interpretation of its historical roots. He included the four provinces of Spain with three French provinces as the heartland of this old nation.

98. The army and the Guardia Civil were considered by the Basques as an army and police force of occupation, in much the same way that many Nationalists in the North of Ireland considered the British Army and the Royal Ulster Constabulary as an enemy force.

99. *Financial Times*, 21/10/94.

100. *Guardian*, 08/03/94.

101. SNP Manifesto for the European Elections, 1994.

102. Keating, M. and Jones, B. (1991) 'Scotland and Wales: peripheral assertion and European integration' *Parliamentary Affairs*, 44, pp. 311–24.

103. *Guardian*, 14/06/94.

104. *The Times*, 21/03/92.

___

# CHAPTER NINE

# New social movements and alternative parties

## 9.1 Introduction

This chapter looks at the rise of the new social movements (NSMs) and the role and influence of these various movements, particularly the various environmental and peace movements, the women's movements, anti-racist and the lesbian and gay movement. We begin by tracing their origins, and outline some of the main analyses for their rise and popularity. The membership of these NSMs overlaps considerably with single-issue pressure groups and green political parties. For example, someone may be a member of Greenpeace (and/or another single-issue pressure group) as well as the Green Party or other political party.[1] Although NSMs are now more usually linked with green parties and their current ideology with a left-of-centre orientation, this has not always been the case. Ecologism as an ideology was popular among the Fascist and extreme right parties and movements of the pre-1945 period.

The word 'movement' is used to describe these various groups, as they are not part of any identifiable political ideology and aim to avoid the hierarchical structure of political parties.[2] They aim also not only to transcend the classic left–right ideological divide, but also to go beyond that cleavage. They have seen themselves as forming part of a rainbow coalition of different groups outside the mainstream political process. The issue of whether they can avoid all the problems associated with becoming a mainstream political party, particularly creating a hierarchy of party professionals, has been a source of constant concern for all green parties in Europe, and most especially for the Green Party in Germany, as we shall see below.[3]

There can also be other kinds of social movements, for instance groups of people sharing a common industrial position, who come together to pressurise governments from outside of the formal political process and with no direct links to any political party. Tarrow defines social movements as:

collective challenges by groups with common purposes and solidarity in sustained and mainly contentious interaction with elites, opponents and authorities.[4]

The example he uses is of the various groups involved in the tuna-fishing disputes in the Bay of Biscay in 1994, which could be considered a social movement. Not all social movements are as formally constituted as the women's movement or the peace movement. Furthermore, a social movement may evolve into an interest group that is more concerned with becoming part of the institutional decision making process than mounting protests. The environmental movement has by and large followed this path.

The rise of NSMs has been attributed to changes in values in the younger generation, based on a long period of 'affluence, the absence of war and socio-cultural changes' (Inglehart, 1977), and to changes in the nature of work and the workforce. A major characteristic of European societies has been a declining blue-collar working class with diminishing industrial and political power. Several authors have noted the effect that this change has had on the political landscape with the rise of these movements.[5] They pose fundamental challenges to the whole basis of industrial societies, going beyond merely focusing on redistribution, which has been the main motor of left/right political struggles. The importance of such movements, therefore, lies in the way they confront existing parties and their ideologies, which may bring about a realignment of party systems along new cleavages. This has been an ongoing process in western Europe over the last few decades with the decline in class-based voting. The evidence from Germany and Sweden, where the ideas of NSMs have found expession in the green parties, indicates a level of electoral support of around 10 per cent nationally and higher at local level.[6] Certainly the efforts that mainstream parties of both right and left have made to take on board some new social movement issues, concerning the environment for example, is an indication of their influence. Richardson (1995) suggest that new social movements and single issue organisations have been able to influence the political process:

Interest groups and new social movements have come to present a major challenge to parties as channels of participation and for the resources which citizens are willing to donate . . . citizens are increasingly willing to use other channels of participation, reflecting a very strong and vibrant market for poltical activism in Western Democracies. Decline in the market share of political parties may, therefore, be as much a sign of vitality than of depoliticisation.[7]

In the first all German general election of 1990, the various green parties did very badly and it was suggested that in times of economic crisis the electorate was more interested in employment above all else. The green parties, stereotyped as the parties of no growth, did not seem to be the likely promoters of economic growth to increase employment. However, the results of the Swedish election of September 1994 and second all-German election a month later indicate that those issues closest to the programme of the green parties still command support. The continued pressure of new social movements, therefore, on green parties and other parties continues to be important.

## 9.2 The rise of new social movements – theoretical considerations

There have been four main factors influencing the rise of NSMs:

- Popular dissatisfaction with the form of politics in terms of over reliance on technology as solution to problems.

- Greater awareness of new political issues, environment gender, race, peace, third world development and social issues.
- New definition of democracy, more participatory politics.
- Growing interest in local politics, seen as a way to test out new politics before the national level. The particular nature of the German electoral system (see Chapter 6 and Chapter 10 on the federal structure of Germany) favoured the election of citizens' action groups (*Bürgerinitiative Gruppen*) to local and regional council parliaments.[8]

For Offe the new social movements share the same analytical insight with the new right that:

> the conflicts and contradictions of advanced industrial society can no longer be resolved by the state or by increasing bureaucracy.[9]

However, they reach quite different conclusions as to how to resolve this problem. For conservatives the emphasis is to depoliticise everything (for example take the politics out of education), while new social movements seek to politicise all relations, at however small a level, and to reconstitute a civil society not regulated by bureaucracy and the state.[10] There has also been a change in values, from the traditional values of capitalist society to another set of values. The old values of social mobility, private life, consumption, instrumental rationality, respect for authority and de-emphasised political participation have been replaced by concerns about the environment, human rights (women's movement, anti-racist movements), peace and alternative or communal styles of life. The new values stress autonomy and self-realisation and therefore imply a greater degree of control by all people over their lives. This means greater participation in decision making at levels which are manageable, that is at local and regional level. These movements would aim to make the notion of subsidiarity really mean devolution of power to the most local level.

In his analysis of the problems facing capitalism, Habermas outlined the increasing difficulty some groups were facing in accepting that it was the fairest and most beneficial way to organise production in society. As more and more people came to question the very basis of this kind of society, and the society itself was unable to provide everyone or most people with a satisfactory standard of living, then it faced a crisis of legitimacy.[11] Given the high degree of inequality generated by capitalism on a worldwide scale and concomitant problems such as pollution and natural and social degradation, he foresaw two ways in which protest against the prevailing values of the system would be expressed. There was the **retreatist** path towards drugs and dropping out of society, and there was the **activist** path involving various student, women and other movements.[12]

André Gorz, in tandem with Habermas and others, has developed a critique of modern industrial society in which he sees similar aspects of crisis. This crisis is represented by the continuous chase after growth and the constant creation of new needs more quickly than society can satisfy them. The physical limits to growth are becoming apparent in the environmental and social degradation of the planet.[13] He suggests the category of the **sufficient** should be the basis on which society should be run. This is not an economic category, but a cultural or existential category.

To say what is enough is enough is to imply that no good would be served by having any more; and that more would not be better . . . 'Enough is as good as a feast' as the English say.[14]

This forms part of a generalised critique of capitalism's expansionary tendencies, excessive private accumulation and modern consumer society. These ideas are at the heart of the new social movements' programme of low or no growth, and also reflect experiences in other societies where work is directed towards sufficient satisfaction of essential needs, and then the rest of the time is spent in leisure pursuits or play.[15]

Gorz has also analysed the whole nature of work in the modern world.[16] His main ideas concern the liberation of time, the abolition of work and the development of autonomous activity. For Gorz, work in the modern sense bears no relation to the tasks, repeated day after day, which are indispensable to the maintenance and reproduction of our individual lives. Nor should work be confused with toil which individuals undertake on their own initiative for themselves or their families, for example housework or artistic work. This kind of work is fundamentally different from the kind of work around which society currently revolves. His solution, then, to free up people's time is to organise production and consumption on the basis of needs. This means decentralised production which can be more responsive to a locality's needs and a reduction in the amount of time people have to go out to do what is currently defined as work. He suggests that this could be reduced to about 25 hours per week, leaving people to perform about 5 hours of socially useful work per week for their community, and then the rest of the time for themselves. The attraction of such ideas has never really met the full test of practice, but they remain nevertheless part of the way in which new social movements consider issues around growth.

Gorz is also critical of the green parties for their almost exclusive focus on ecologism. Ecology by itself will not end the great inequalities which exist. It is necessary to confront the whole notion that more equals better, and accept that 'it is possible to be happier with less affluence'.[17]

Anna Bramwell has demonstrated that a history of ecological thinking since the nineteenth century shows how basket weavers and organic farmers in the 1930s, for example, were in favour of smallholdings and against centralisation of production by the state. They were strongly against mechanisation, racial contamination of native stock and alien imports, for example bamboos and corned beef. These ideas were influential on people in the Third Reich such as Walter Darré, Hitler's agricultural minister, who espoused ecologism. These ideas of a pure agriculture tied in with Nazi ideals about a pure race, and their general obsession with health and physical fitness.[18] The Nazi taint on all soil-centred tradition remained until rescued by the left in the 1960s, which was more favourable to state intervention, and had a global rather than national outlook.

We examine next the kinds of problems that these movements have faced in the world of electoral politics in negotiating their programme with other political parties and within their own ranks.

## 9.2.1  Composition and tactics of NSMs

### Membership

The profile of members of NSMs suggests that they are mainly from the middle class, and have completed at least 13 years of education. In other words most of the leading members have reached university entrance level and usually are or have been students in higher education. The level of affluence, for example in West German society after the 1950s, meant that a whole group of young people had no experience of war or associated hardships, and their values therefore were different to those of their parents. Less emphasis was placed on material progress and more on intellectual and creative fulfilment. These sets of values have been characterised as post-materialist. The first flowering of these movements began in the 1950s with the Beat Poets such as Allen Ginsberg and Jack Kerouac, and then the Hippy movement of the 1960s and early 1970s. The context of the civil rights movements in the United States as well as the protests against US involvement in the Vietnam War gave the movements a sharper edge. May 1968 in France and the 'hot autumn' in Italy in 1969 were also important in the way student protesters linked up with workers' movements to oppose the whole nature of exploitation under capitalism. Some protesters ended up espousing revolutionary violence as the way to overthrow capitalism, like the Weathermen in the United States, the Angry Brigade in Britain and more spectacularly, the Red Army Faction (Baader-Meinhof Group) in West Germany and the Red Brigades in Italy. Others 'retreated', and others joined emerging alternative lifestyle counter-culture groups.

### Tactics

Some protesters rejected the violent path and were inspired rather by the non-violent tactics used by Gandhi in the struggle he led for Indian independence (*Satyagraha*), and the Civil Rights movement in the United States of the 1950s and 1960s led by Martin Luther King. This has involved, therefore, tactics of mass protest such as demonstrations, sit-ins and obstruction (to prevent road building), including use of chains, a tactic used by the suffragettes in Britain in the early part of this century to win the vote. There have been high profile media publicity exploits, such as Greenpeace's attempts to block the outflow from the Sellafield Nuclear Reprocessing Plant in northern England, and a systematic and at times successful lobbying of government and industry to modify policies.

## 9.2.2  Types of movements

### Peace

In the post-1945 world, opposition to the manufacture and threatened use of weapons of mass destruction (nuclear and biological) resulted, in Britain, with the formation of the 'Committee of 100' led among others by philosopher Bertrand Russell, historian A. J. P. Taylor and future Labour Party leader Michael Foot. The creation of the Campaign for Nuclear Disarmament (CND), whose Aldermaston marches (centre for Britain's nuclear weapons research) became a feature of every anti-war protester's Easter diary, focused the campaign on the nuclear weapons, and by implication the growth of the military–industrial complex that came to dominate much of the West's economic and political organisation during the Cold War. The peace movements experienced a huge growth in membership during the late 1970s and early 1980s as the West rapidly increased its military expenditure and threatened to use nuclear force.

Added to this, the United States and the United Kingdom were led by two of the most anti-Soviet leaders in the post-1945 world, one of whom President Reagan couched his verbal attacks on the Soviet Union in terms of Armageddon and Doomsday scenarios, and people became seriously frightened. The 'Star Wars' scenario seemed to have leapt straight off the cinema screen into practical policy, which may be understandable given the president's original profession, and shrewd calculation of many people's mind-set at that time.

## Environment

If the peace movement was the catalyst for the rise of NSMs, then it has been concern about the environment which has provided the most popular mass support for their development. Great pollution disasters from oil spillage such as the *Torrey Canyon* tanker disaster off the Isles of Scilly in 1967, the *Amoco Cadiz* off Brittany in 1978 and the worry over the effects of increasing pollution raised the issue of the environment.[19] Linked to concern about the environment, movements dedicated to the protection of animal rights have grown enormously in Britain and elsewhere in the EU.

## Women's movements

Most writers consider the women's movement to be a new social movement (Jenson, 1985; Andreasen *et al.*, 1990), although some argue that it is not so new, and indeed in an active political form has been around since the early 1900s (Spender, 1983). In Jenson's words:

the women's movement is defined as a social movement whose actions resulted – either by design or chance – in the emergence of a new collective identity . . .[20]

If the women's movement is the practical expression of women demanding equal status, then its ideological underpinning comes from feminism, which according to Bhasin and Khan, is:

an awareness of women's oppression and exploitation in society, at work and within the family, and conscious action by women and men to change this situation . . . a struggle for the achievement of women's equality, dignity and freedom of choice to control our lives and bodies within and outside the home . . . for a just and equitable society for women and men both.[21]

It is true that issues concerning greater rights for women and greater participation in all spheres of society have been around for a long time. In the age of the French Revolution, demands were being made in Britain for greater equality by, among others, Mary Wollstonecraft,[22] but it has not really been until this century that any leaps forward have been made in terms of equal rights for women. The major development in these feminist struggles for autonomy came during the 1960s, around the areas controlling sexuality and reproduction. Campaigns were launched to liberalise contraception and abortion, and to fight for more child care facilities. The issue of violence against women both within and outside marriage and relationships was also part of a long-term demand for equal protection and changes in the law.

Issues concerning sex had seemed irrelevant to many radical thinkers and activists, and subordinate to the class struggle (see Chapter 4). The change in that attitude arose from the women's movement in the 1960s, whose slogan 'The personal is political' encapsulated the idea that all relations, even the most intimate, were the proper subject of debate and action. The effect that this movement has had on the traditional concept of power is also important. In most previous political theory, power is considered very much in terms of relations in the public sphere, that is between groups debating and struggling over the share of material and other resources in society. The various arenas were among the political and other elites in parliament, in the courts, in industrial relations and in conflict between nation states. The women's movement has stressed the importance of bringing that whole debate into an analysis of power relations in the domestic environment and in sexual behaviour. The fight against patriarchy, therefore, both within the domestic context and wider society has been at the forefront of the women's movement. During this century, then, and particularly since the 1960s, the scope of action has broadened to include all aspects of relations between men and women. The women's movement represents part of a conscious and collective effort to change women's position, which includes a challenge to male dominance and the values and norms which oppress women (Dahlerup, 1986).

Since the mid-nineteenth century the fight has been for equal social and political rights, beginning with demands for equal rights in education, marriage and divorce, then the right to vote (the suffragette movement). In the post-1945 world, the demand has been for equal rights at work in terms of equal pay (Article 119 of the 1957 Rome Treaty setting up the EEC which made the UK government introduce the 1975 Equal Pay Act), and greater protection in terms of working conditions and benefits, for example maternity benefit and child benefit.[23] At the same time, women were also demanding more control over their bodies in terms of contraception and abortion, and new definitions concerning violent behaviour against them; for the first time in the early 1990s in the United Kingdom, a charge of rape can be brought against a violent partner within marriage.

The first major breakthrough in political rights was the almost universal acceptance of voting rights for women, won mostly within western Europe by 1939 (except Switzerland where the vote was not won until 1971). Then there are the huge transformations that are currently taking place within all western European societies, which began to occur from the 1960s onwards. Books such as *The Second Sex* by Simone de Beauvoir first published in 1949 were crucial in terms of preparing the ground for these changes. In addition there are other factors which have been important, namely:

- rapid urbanisation that has required greater participation by women in the labour market and thereby permitted a greater degree of financial independence;
- changing family structures;
- greater social and sexual independence;
- growing secularisation which led to changing attitudes concerning the position of women in society;
- the spread of mass higher education; and
- the growth of womens' movements throughout the industrialised world articulating and demanding equal rights has been the motor force in terms of promoting the changes that still being worked out.

## Women's organisations

Campaigning organisations have been set up in all European countries to defend and promote issues concerning women. These organisations range from those that campaign to increase representation of women in elected office (the 300 Group, Emily's List in the United Kingdom, **Clár na mBan** in Ireland, and *L'Assemblée des Femmes* in France[24]), to groups that campaign over issues concerning rights for single parents, in terms of benefit rights.

## Anti-racism

There has been a great deal of academic literature and some government action trying to anlayse the causes and to suggest solutions to reduce the level and intensity of racism and nationalism in western Europe. As Blaut states:

even if all the roots are torn out, the vine (of cultural racism) will not wither: it will grow other roots, a new theory of racism, unless racism is attacked, not as theory but as practice.[25]

The growth of the anti-racist movements during the 1970s was a direct response to the rise of racist movements and neo-Fascist political parties.[26] The diversity of the various groups involved, from immigrant workers' associations, civil rights groups, local church and citizens action groups, as well as groups based around music, led to a massive response on the part of immigrant workers and their families and other organisations to counter the growing threat posed by racist ideas and subsequent violent actions.[27]

The success of these movements has waxed and waned according to the perceived threat from the extreme right. From the height of their popularity in the 1970s and 1980s, they have become less visible in terms of street demonstrations as the leaders become more integrated within the political hierarchies of various parties and organisations. Their ability to mobilise thousands of people is undiminished, although it remains to be seen whether the formal expression and protection of rights in terms of equal opportunities' policies, which was an indirect part of their efforts will be maintained and strengthened or fall into neglect.

## Anti-racism and the EU

The prevalence of racism in the EU countries has prompted the various EU institutions to consider ways in which the rise in popularity of the various neo-Fascist and racist groups can be stemmed. Two reports from committees of the European Parliament led by Evrigenis (1985) and Ford (1990) have noted the extent of racism and xenophobia in the EU, and proposed certain ways of tackling the issue. However, the split within the Ford committee over the recommendations contained in it indicate that the general political will in this area is still not very strong.

An anti-racism commission was set up at the Heads of Government Summit in Corfu in 1994 to report by March 1995 on ideas to 'encourage tolerance and understanding of foreigners'.[28] At the same time tighter restrictions on immigration and asylum, in particular a common set of regulations for work permits to non-EU nationals. The EU Heads of Government Summit in Essen in December 1994 considered what action was necessary to combat racism, in response to a report on the growth of racism which stemmed from an initiative of Chancellor Kohl and President Mitterrand.[29] Governments in the EU are reluctant to accept that the EU has competence in this area, as they have always argued that such issues are a matter for national competence.

## Lesbian and gay movements

The lesbian and gay movement is another part of the diverse composition of NSMs. In this section we look at issues concerning homosexuality in modern European societies, and consider the whole issue of sexual politics and sexual orientation as it has formed part of a critique of modern society both in terms of what are considered 'normal' relationships and respective domestic roles (i.e. heterosexual nuclear family unit, male breadwinner/female homemaker) (see also Chapter 11 on the family).[30]

It is now possible within the EU for a homosexual couple to have the right to a civil marriage at a registry office, for example in Denmark. Marriages blessed by the church, although not officially sanctioned by any religious organisation in contemporary Europe, was common practice for a thousand years until the eighteenth century in Europe.[31] Other issues concern the possibility for lesbian and gay couples to foster or adopt children,[32] the discussion of sexual diversity in schools and the acceptance of lesbian and gay people within the public services, for example the armed forces and youth work. The whole issue remains highly charged, and is the scene for continuing battles both within Europe and the United States between equal rights campaigners and extreme religious organisations from all faiths.[33]

The concept of 'homosexual' was first used in the mid- to late nineteenth century and thereafter became part of a defined identity.[34] Around the turn of this century, as Michel Foucault indicates, the growth of psychoanalysis led to the labelling of 'perverse' forms of pleasure, including homosexuality, so that it became susceptible to analysis in terms of psychic disorder.[35] In most European countries there has been widespread acceptance that discrimination against people on the basis of their sexuality contravenes fundamental human rights; but as Table 9.1 on age of consent shows, there is still not complete equality in all European countries.

There are three issues which seem to be at the heart of the debate about homosexuality in modern societies, linked also to the debate about feminism. The first concerns the whole nature of what is meant by masculine and feminine. The second concerns the challenge (or threat) that homosexuality presents to society in terms of the usually religious based ideals about the sanctity of the heterosexual family and its function as the sole reproductive and child-rearing unit. The third issue is the fear that widespread acceptance and discussion about homosexuality will somehow

**Table 9.1**   Age of consent in European countries

| | Heterosexual | Homosexual |
|---|---|---|
| Albania | 14 | 14 |
| Austria | 15 | 15 |
| Belgium | 16 | 16 |
| Czech Republic | 15 | 15 |
| Denmark | 15 | 15 |
| Finland | 15 | 15 |
| France | 15 | 15 |
| Germany | 16 | 16 |
| Greece | 15 | 15 |
| Hungary | 15 | 15 |
| Ireland | 16 | * |
| Italy | 16 | 16 |
| Luxembourg | 15 | 15 |
| Malta | 12 | 12 |
| Netherlands | 12 | 12 |
| Norway | 16 | 16 |
| Poland | 15 | 15 |
| Portugal | 16 | 16 |
| Slovakia | 15 | 15 |
| Spain | 12 | 12 |
| Sweden | 15 | 15 |
| Switzerland | 16 | 16 |
| United Kingdom | 16 | 18 |

* – the age is being debated.
Sources: House of Commons Hansard 21/2/94 cols. 75–86
P. Tatchell. *Europe in the Pink* (GMP Press, 1992).

lead to more 'corruption of the nation's morals' than similar attention and discussion about straight sexual behaviour.[36]

Definitions of gender are socially constructed, so that what is meant by masculine and feminine changes over time and from society to society.[37] The importance of our personal identity is very intimately tied into our perception also of our sexual identity; but none of these categories is wholly fixed. Rather, there is a continuum from homosexuality via bisexuality and heterosexuality to celibacy. There are strong pressures in society to conform to accepted notions of behaviour, so that men should display aggression and women should appear to be more caring. Furthermore, in terms of sexual behaviour definitions are used to categorise people who cross or transgress the borders of behaviour with terms like 'butch' applied to 'masculine' women and 'effeminate' used for 'feminine' men.

### Fostering and adoption

In Denmark, the Netherlands, Norway, Sweden and Germany a homosexual couple may foster but not jointly adopt a child. The rule allows only individual homosexuals to adopt, not couples. In Britain, only heterosexual married couples are allowed to adopt, but there are no restrictions on homosexuals fostering either as individuals or as couples.

### Public service

Anti-discrimination legislation exists in Denmark, France, the Netherlands, Norway and Sweden. Membership of the armed forces is open to homosexuals in Austria, Belgium, Denmark, Germany, Finland, France, the Netherlands, Norway, Spain, Sweden and Switzerland. In Germany homosexuals are barred from the officer ranks.[38]

### Promotion of homosexuality (see section below on European Parliament)

The International Lesbian and Gay Association coordinates action at the EU level in liaison with national groups, to promote and defend equal rights for gay and lesbian people. In each country, apart from those countries where homosexuality is still illegal,[39] these organisations are part of the diverse composition of new social movements which aim to influence policy outside the traditional party structures.

### *9.2.3  The European Union*

The European Parliament has been active in the defence and promotion of Gay rights throughout the EU.[40] In February 1994 the parliament approved action to combat discrimination against homosexuals, and called for a revision of the Maastricht Treaty to set up a new body to fight discrimination on the grounds of 'nationality, religious faith, colour, sex, sexual orientation or other differences'.[41] The United Kingdom was singled out for its illiberal laws (Austria, Finland and Turkey have similar provisions), and was called on to repeal Section 28 of the Local Government Act 1988 which forbids the promotion of homosexuality in schools.[42] Many groups argue that Section 28 is in breach of Britain's obligations under Article 8 of the European Convention on Human Rights, which provides that 'everyone has the right to respect for his private and family life, his home and correspondence'. Britain's age of consent for homosexual couples is also one of the highest in the EU. The Greek Cypriot government's ban on homosexual relations was deemed by the European Commission on Human Rights in Strasbourg in 1990 to contravene Article 8. The same article was also used by the Commission in 1982 to force the British government to change the law relating to homosexuality in Northern Ireland.

## 9.3  New social movements and green parties

Green politics and institutional party politics are anathema, incompatible in process, in means and in ends.

ANNA BRAMWELL[43]

The rise of green parties since the early 1980s as a force in European politics has been one of the most important new developments challenging the traditional party systems. These 'post-materialist' parties have attempted to change the political agenda by highlighting and campaigning on areas such as the environment, abolition of nuclear weapons and power, anti-militarism, equal rights for women, ethnic groups and other minorities, and demanding a wholescale change in the emphasis on growth that underpins all economic thinking. They argue instead for low or no growth based more on small-scale economic production, less waste and imbued with the spirit of sustainability. In this section we will look briefly at the reasons for the rise of these parties, and how they have fared in ideological and electoral terms since they first burst on the scene in any significant way at the 1983 German general election.

The context within which the green parties arose was the downturn in the European economies after the oil price shock in the early 1970s. Around the same time concern about the environment in terms of pollution, and growing alienation with the political system, led many voters to express their dissatisfaction by joining and voting for 'alternative' parties, which eventually became green parties.

The main themes of green thinking can be summarised as concerning participation, survival, emancipation and ecology.[44] The two themes of participation and emancipation can be traced back to the Enlightenment in the eighteenth century, and have been introduced by the 'new' left and other groups since the 1960s. New themes of survival also have a long history but are connected to other less progressive ideas about human beings, nature and society.

## Participation

Contemporary party politics and representative democracy have led to a situation where small groups of party professionals and politicians monopolise the organisation and expression of people's wishes (see Michels in section on elitism in Chapter 3). The structures of the representative institutions within nation states has led to a great distance opening up between the voters and those they elect and the site/locus of political power. Green ideas about participation are designed to bring about greater participation by people in the decision-making process and devolution of decision-making procedures down to the lowest practical level.

## Survival

The issue here concerns both the widespread use of nuclear power and the production of nuclear and chemical weapons, Furthermore opposition is growing to the increasing levels of pollution attendant on industrial processes, particularly in terms of nuclear waste disposal.

## Emancipation

One of the main results of the greater degree of participation in politics will be a greater voice and space given to groups who have tended to be marginalised within mainstream parties. Women, ethnic groups and the gay movment are seen as forming part of a 'rainbow' coalition, whose greater political voice and recognition will involve a more emancipated social environment.

## Ecology

**Small is Beautiful** is the title of E. F. Schumacher's book extolling the virtues and necessity of small-scale localised production. It sums up the basic ecological philosophy of the greens, concerned as it is to create a sustainable economic system, which is low polluting and based on principles of managed growth. The depth of attachment to this principle of 'ecology' has led to sharp divides in the green movement and within their political parties between the fundamentalist and realist wings. Depending on how pure you want your ecology to be determines whether you go for more total approaches or accept the constraints of current practice and push for more reforms. The most vocal exponent of the first tendency has been the German writer Rudolf Bahro, while Helmut Wiesenthal has put forward the necessity of compromise in terms of political programmes and action.[45]

## Green political parties

The British Green Party (the oldest in Europe) called itself People when it was formed in 1973 and changed its name to the Ecology Party in 1975, before using 'Green' in 1985. Although the first modern green party, it has been unable to translate longevity into electoral success, as we indicate below. This section, therefore, begins with the **Die Grünen**, the German Green Party, as it has been the most successful in electoral terms and its debates reflect most of the tensions that exist within green parties in other countries.

The party arose out of the combination of various citizens' action groups (**Bürgerinitiative**), rainbow alliances and anti-nuclear groups in the 1970s. Their first national success was at the 1983 West German general election, when they won 5.6 per cent of the vote and gained 27 seats in the Bundestag. The main parts of their programme included withdrawal from NATO, a complete halt to all nuclear power projects, emergency environmental action, greater decentralisation of political and economic power to increase participation, equal opportunities (gender and race) and greater democratisation of the media (no private TV or radio, no cable TV).

At regional (*Land*) and local level the greens came into coalitions with the SPD, for example in Hessen in the early 1980s and then again between 1990–94. They have also been in so-called 'traffic light' coalitions with the FDP and SPD.

The presence of the greens at local and regional level has resulted in issues being raised that might otherwise have been ignored by the other parties. These concern alternative energy projects, traffic abatement and cycle-way measures, positive discrimination for women in the job market and action to support foreigners and asylum seekers. Their appeal has also spread from beyond a narrow constituency of political activists and alternative lifestyle people to skilled workers, particularly in the high-tech industries and to white collar workers.[46] This support is reflected in terms of their relationship to the trade union movement, where they have tended to gain more support from the public service sector trade unions rather than the manufacturing trade unions.[47] Along with Bundnis '90, the umbrella green and civil rights group in the former East Germany, the green alliance in Germany has now become a key player in several *Land* governments.

The most divisive debate within the green movement has been over the kind of politics which should be pursued. The *fundis* are critical of coalitions with other parties, which implies more centralisation of the party organisation, and they are sceptical that radical change is possible by parliamentary means. The *realos* argue for an instru-mental parliamentary strategy to achieve certain limited objectives tied in with extra-parliamentary action and a more streamlined party machinery.[48] Originally, the greens proposed rotating parliamentary membership whereby an MP would sit for a 2-year period then give up their seat to a newcomer. In principle this was an excellent way to increase the number of people familiar with the Bundestag, but it meant that effective action was diminished because the new people took time to learn about parliamentary procedures. The *realos* argument has won the day, with many *fundis* leaving the movement. The greens are home to many former left-wing and anarchist political radicals, and the impression is that many of the left-wing radicals, who have jettisoned much of their ideology, have kept to the idea that some kind of structured organisation is necessary to achieve any results. The same split occurred in the British Green Party in 1992, but the *fundis* prevailed and the *realos* have left.

Similar tensions exist within and between the Green Parties in France. There is the original more 'fundamentalist' Green Party (**Les Verts**), founded in 1984, and the recent more pragmatic **Génération Ecologie**, founded in 1990.[49] In the 1970s the green parties were gaining about 10 per cent in opinion polls, but this levelled to a steady 7 per cent in the 1980s and stayed there until 1995 when it fell to around 3 per cent. The general reduction in the bipolar nature of the French system and the growth of the political ecology movement in Europe are two key factors explaining the growth in green support.[50] Their recent failure to make any electoral breakthrough is partly a result of their divided nature and the personality clash between their respective leaders, Waechter and Lalonde.

The electoral system in the United Kingdom does not allow small party representation, and so most environmental politics tend to be located in the other parties, mainly the Labour Party and Liberal Democrats, and smaller nationalist parties. The spectacular result the 1989 European election. There are some local councillors but the split at the 1992 Party Conference has left the party divided and weak.

In Italy the *Liste Verdi* and *Arcobaleno Verde* gained some success in their campaign against the corrupt nature of the traditional parties and their bureaucratic tendencies. They have joined in electoral campaigns with the Radical Party. Although the greens in Spain became the fifth largest national party at the general elections in 1993, their percentage of the vote both at national and local level has never risen above 5 per cent.

In East/Central Europe there appear to be no thriving green parties except in Bulgaria.[51] In a climate where there are pressing concerns about economic expansion to create growth and therefore jobs, green issues are seen as a luxury.

## 9.4   Summary

### New social movements and their influence and impact

Despite sociocultural and value changes and the increasing importance of the issues themselves, the impact of the 'new politics', in terms of influencing the political agenda and fulfilling its goals, has differed greatly between countries. These differences can be explained partly by the speed with which values in each society have changed, and also by the responsiveness of the various political systems to the new demands and the nature of the barriers that exist permitting or excluding small party representation. Clearly in those electoral systems such as the United Kingdom, green parties which are the main vehicle of NSMs have little or no chance of securing any local council, let alone national parliamentary seats. In countries which operate some form of PR, such as Germany, Denmark, Sweden or the Netherlands, NSMs find they can have a voice at all levels of the political system. The greens in the European Parliament have formed their own rainbow group, GVPE (*Groupe Vert du Parlement Européen*), and although relatively small in number compared to the EPP and the Socialist grouping have maintained a high profile in campaigns opposing road-building programmes, protecting public sector broadcasting and leading opposition to the French government's decision in 1995 to resume nuclear testing in the Pacific.

The impact of the NSMs concerns how much of their programme in forming the bedrock of ideas and support for green parties has really changed the nature of the major parties of the left and right, and the nature of politics generally. It is evident that in order not to lose some sections of their support, left-wing and right-wing parties have attempted to incorporate elements of these policies into their party statements, but most of the changes have been cosmetic and not real.

Nevertheless, the popular support for this kind of politics and for green parties does not seem to be diminishing and points the way to a more diverse polity in the next decade.

## Appendix 9.1

### Green parties' general and European election results (seats in parentheses)

*Germany*
| | | |
|---|---|---|
| 1983 – General | 5.6% | (27) |
| 1984 – Euro | 8.2% | (7) |
| 1987 – General | 8.3% | (42) |
| 1990 – General | 3.9% | (0) |
| 1994 – Euro | 10.1% | (12) |
| 1994 – General | 7.3% | (49) |

*France*
Les Verts
| | |
|---|---|
| 1984 – Euro | 3.4% |
| 1988 – Pres | 3.8% |
| 1993 – General | 7.6% (with GE) |
| 1994 – Euro | 2.94% (Verts) + 2.01% (GE) |
| 1995 – Pres | 3.3% |

Génération Ecologie (GE)

*United Kingdom*
| | | |
|---|---|---|
| 1987 – General | 1.4% | (0) |
| 1989 – Euro | 14.7% | (0) |
| 1992 – General | 1.3% | (0) |
| 1994 – Euro | 3.24% | (0) |

*Italy*
| | | |
|---|---|---|
| 1987 – General | 2.5% | (13) |
| 1989 – Euro | 6% | (5) |
| 1993 – Won seats in local elections with PDS in Rome, Naples, Genoa and Venice | | |
| 1994 – General | 2.7% | (0) |
| 1994 – Euro | 3.2% | (3) |

*Spain*

| | |
|---|---|
| 1989 – Euro | Los Verdes – Lista Verde   0.76% |
| | Los Verdes Ecologistas   0.66% |
| 1991 | Candidates in all seats at local elections |
| 1993 | No seat in the Cortes but with 184 000 votes = fifth largest national party |
| 1994 – Euro | 0.68%   (0) |

*European Parliament*   Green Parties in the European Parliament – Groupe Vert du Parlement Européen (GVPE)

| | |
|---|---|
| 1984 – Rainbow Coalition | 20 seats |
| 1989 – Green | 28 seats |
| 1994 – Green | 23 seats |

# Further reading

## New social movements and green parties

Bahro, R. (1984) *From Red to Green*, London: Verso.

Betz, H.-G. (1991) *Postmodern Politics in Germany. The Politics of Resentment*, London: Macmillan.

Bramwell, A. (1994) *The Fading of the Greens: the Decline of Environmental Politics in the West*, London: Yale University Press.

Dalton, R. J. (1994) *The Green Rainbow: Environmental Groups in Western Europe*, New Haven: Yale University Press.

Dalton, R. J. and Kuechler, M. (1990) *Challenging the Political Order. New Social Movements in Western Democracies*, Cambridge: Cambridge University Press.

Eckersley, R. (1992) *Environmentalism and Political Thought – Toward an ecocentric approach*, London: UCL Press.

Giddens, A. (1994) *Beyond Left and Right*, Cambridge: Polity Press.

Hulsberg, W. (1988) *The German Greens – A Social and Political Profile*, London: Verso.

Inglehart, R. (1977) *The Silent Revolution: Changing values and political styles among Western Publics*, Princeton: Princeton University Press.

Jacobs, F. (1989) *Western European Political Parties: A Comprehensive Guide*, London: Longman.

Judge, D. (ed.) (1993) *A Green Dimension for the EC*, London: Frank Cass.

Kolinsky, E. and Gaffney, J. (1991) *Political Culture in France and Germany*, London: Routledge.

Parkin, S. (1989) *Green Parties. An International Guide*, London: Heretic Books.

Parkin, S. (1994) *The Life and Death of Petra Kelly*, London: Pandora/HarperCollins.

Richardson, D. and Rootes, C. (1995) *The Green Challenge: the development of Green Parties in Europe*, London: Routledge.

Robinson, M. (1992) *The Greening of British Party Politics*, Manchester: Manchester University Press.

Scharf, T. (1994) *The German Greens*, London: Berg.

Scott, A. (1990) *Ideology and the New Social Movements*, London: Unwin Hyman.

Spretnak, C. and Capra, F. (1985) *Green Politics*, London: Paladin.

Wiesenthal, H. (1993) *Realism in Green Politics*, Manchester: Manchester University Press.

## Articles

Delwaide, J. (1993) 'Postmaterialism and politics: the Schmidt SPD and the greening of Germany' *German Politics* 2 August, 2.

Doherty, B. (1992) 'The fundi-realo controversy: an analysis of four European Green Parties' *Environmental Politics* 1 (1) Spring, pp. 25–40.

Hoffman-Martinot, V. (1991) 'Grüne and Verts: two faces of European Ecologism' *WEP* 14 (4) pp. 70–95.

Kvistad, G. (1987) 'Between state and society: Green political ideology in the mid-1980s' *WEP* 10 (2) pp. 211–28.

Ladrech, R. (1989) 'Social movements and party systems: the French Socialist Party and new social movements' *WEP* 12 (3) pp. 262–79.

Müller, F. (1985) 'Rommel NSM and smaller parties: a comparative perspective' *WEP* 8 (1) pp. 41–54.

Offe, C. (1985) 'New social movements: challenging the boundaries of institutional politics' *Social Research* 52 (4) pp. 35–45.

Poguntke, T. (1987) 'New politics and party systems: the emergence of a new type of party system?' *WEP* 10. pp. 76–88.

Poguntke, T. and Schmitt-Beck, R. (1994) 'Still the same with a new name? Bündnis 90/Die Grünen after the fusion' *German Politics* 3 (1) pp. 91–113.

Reiter, H. (1993) 'The Rise of the "New Agenda" and the decline of Partisanship' *WEP* 16 (2) pp. 66–80.

Rothacher, A. (1984) 'The Green Party in German Politics' *WEP* 7 (3) pp. 109–116.

Szarka, J. (1994) 'Green politics in France: the impasse of non-alignment' *Parliamentary Affairs* 47 (3) pp. 446–55.

## Women

Andreasen, T. (1990) *Moving On: New Perspectives on the Women's Movement*, Aarhus: Aarhus University Press.

Dahlerup, D. (1986) *The New Women's Movement, Feminism and Political Power in Europe and the USA*, London: Sage.

Einhorn, B. (1994) *Cinderella goes to Market: Citizenship, Gender and Women's Movements in East Central Europe*, London: Verso.

Jenson, J. (1985) 'Struggling for identity: the Women's Movement and the State in Western Europe' *West European Politics* 8 (4) pp. 5–18.

Spender, D. (1983) *There's always been a Women's Movement this Century*, London: Pandora Press.

'Women in Eastern and Western Europe – In Transition and Recession' *Journal of Area Studies* (Loughborough University) 6 Spring (1995).

## Anti-Racist

Bjorgo, T. and Witte, R. (1993) *Racist Violence in Europe*, London: Macmillan.

Gilroy, P. (1993) *There Ain't No Black in the Union Jack*, London: Routledge.

Wrench, J. and Solomos, J. (1993) *Racism and Migration in W. Europe*, London: Berg.

## Sexuality

Caplan, P. (ed.) (1989) *The cultural construction of sexuality*, London: Routledge.
Coward, R. (1984) *Female Desire: Women's sexuality today*, London: Paladin.
Dollimore, J. (1991) *Sexual Dissidence*, Oxford: Oxford University Press.
Foucault, M. (1981) *The History of Sexuality*, vol. 1, Harmondsworth: Penguin.
Simpson, M. (1994) *Male Impersonators: Men Performing Masculinity*, London: Cassell.
Tatchell, P. (1992) *Europe in the Pink*, London: GMP Publishers.
Tatchell, P. (1990) 'Out in Europe', London: Channel 4 Television.

## Notes

1. Müller-Rommel, F. 'New social movements and smaller parties: a comparative perspective' *WEP* 8 (1) pp. 41–54.
2. In this context it is also worth noting that a mainstream party like the French Gaullist party, the RPR, in all its guises, has always tried to avoid calling itself a party in the traditional sense. The reason for this is to be able to make a broad appeal to the electorate, and not be tied down by any ideological baggage.
3. The challenge that NSMs make to the whole structure of representative democratic political structures, particularly in terms of their control by elites, is undermined by the way these movements themselves become professionalised and develop hierarchical structures with an 'elite' making most decisions, although such tendencies are not apparent in all NSMs. Roth, R. (1992) 'Eliten und Gegeneliten. Neue Soziale Bewegungen als Herausforderung "demokratischer Elitenherrschaft"' in *Die Politische Klasse in Deutschland* Leif, T., Legrand, H.-J. and Klein, A., Bonn Berlin: Bouvier.
4. Tarrow, S. (1995) 'The Europeanisation of conflict: reflections from a social movement perspective' *WEP* 18 (2) pp. 223–51.
5. See further Gilroy, P (1993) *There Ain't No Black in the Union Jack*, London: Routledge. Touraine, A. (1981) *The Voice and the Eye. An Analysis of social movements*, Cambridge: Cambridge University Press.
6. Betz, H.-G. (1991) *Postmodern politics in Germany. The politics of resentment*, Macmillan.
7. Richardson, J. (1995) 'The market for political activism: interest groups as a challenge to political parties' *West European Politics* 18 (1) pp. 116–39.
8. Scharf, T. (1994) *The German Greens Challenging the Consensus*, London: Berg, pp. 57–59.
9. Offe, 1985, p. 819.
10. As Offe indicates, NSMs seek to break down the classical divide between the public and private spheres. For Aristotle, the domain of the political was the public sphere, where all free citizens participated in all aspects of decision making. The private sphere of the home with its domestic arrangements and interpersonal relations was outside the realm of the state and interference by it. Given that women were excluded from the public domain, this meant that men could do what they liked at home. For further discussion of this public/private sphere see Chapter 3, section on feminism and democracy, and Anne Phillips on Citizenship in Phillips, A. (1992) *Engendering Democracy*, Cambridge: Polity Press.
11. Habermas, J. (1989) *Legitimation Crisis*, Cambridge: Polity Press.
12. Habermas, J. (1974) What does a crisis mean today? 'Legitimation problems in late capitalism' *Social Research* 40. These two forms of protest occasionally coalesce, as for example in the opposition to the proposed Criminal Justice Bill in the United Kingdom in 1994, which threatened the activities of all these types of movements.

13. 'We know that for 150 years industrial society has developed through the looting of reserves whose creation required tens of millions of years; and that until very recently, all economists – whether classical or Marxist – have rejected such questions as irrelevant or "reactionary"'. Organisations such as the **New Economics Foundation** in Britain are also pursuing new ways of thinking about organising the economy. The whole issue of decentralisation and developing the local and economy are at the centre of their analysis. (NEF, Vine Court, 112–116 Whitechapel Road, London E1 1JE. Tel: 0171 377 5696.)

14. *Guardian*, 9–10/12/1989. Such ideas are also found in many of the world's major religions which all have some teaching about the rejection of material wealth through redistribution.

15. Sahlins, M. (1974) *Stone Age Economics*, London: Tavistock. Sahlins investigates societies where production is organised to provide enough for people's needs.

16. Gorz, A. (1989) *Critique of Economic Reason*, London: Verso.

17. *Guardian*, 9–10/12/1989.

18. The Nazi Party was strongly anti-smoking, which explains the reluctance that organisations in the Federal Republic now face in trying to promote anti-smoking policies. Hitler also banned fox-hunting.

19. Animal Rights campaigners can also be considered as forming part of a new social movement, but their current influence on policy remains to be determined. Some of their concerns are reflected in the programmes of the environment groups.

20. Jenson, J. (1985) 'Struggling for identity: the Women's Movement and the state in western Europe' *West European Politics* 8 (4) pp. 5–18. This article also charts the historical development of the women's movement in a number of West European countries.

21. Bhasin, K. and Khan, N. S. (1995) *A Diplomacy of the Oppressed. New Directions in International Feminism* in Ashworth, G. (ed.) London: Zed Books.

22. Wollstonecraft, M. (1992, originally published 1792) *A Vindication of the Rights of Women*, London: Penguin. She was referred to by Walpole at the time as a 'hyena in petticoats'. It is interesting to compare the views in this work on the role of women with those of Jean-Jacques Rousseau in his work *Emile*, written at more or less the same time and proposing quite a different, and traditional, view of women's role in society.

23. Despite the objections of the UK government, the member states of the EU finally agreed that women should be statutorily entitled to a minimum period of 14 weeks maternity benefit irrespective of employment or other status. This regulation entered into force on 1 November 1994.

24. **Clár na mBan** (Women's Agenda), was set up in the North of Ireland, and now covers the whole of Ireland, campaigning around issues of equality for women in all areas of society and greater representation for women in public life; *The Chartist* 151 (November–December) pp. 14–15.

25. Blaut, J. (1991) 'The theory of cultural racism' *Antipode* 24 pp. 289–99, (1993) in Jackson and Penrose *Race Place and Nation*, London: U.C.L. Press. p. 19.

26. Gilroy, 1991.

27. The list below is by no means exhaustive but indicates the range of groups involved:
UK – Rock against Racism, The Anti-Nazi League, Anti-Racist Alliance, The Runnymede Trust.
France – SOS Racisme, Touch pas à mon pôte.
Germany – SOS Rassismus, Pro-Asyl.

28. *Guardian*, 15/06/94.

29. The report drawn up by Jean Kahn, a political ally of the Edouard Balladur, calls for an EU race relations directive that would establish laws to prevent discrimination in employment and housing for the estimated 17 million people living in the EU but who do not have nationality of one or other Member State; *Guardian*, 17/11/94.

30. 'In our society, heterosexual relations are seen as the norm, and homosexual relations are stigmatised. Nonconformity to the norms of heterosexuality threatens the dominant ideology's view of sex as 'innate' and 'natural'. Male homosexuality threatens male solidarity and superordination because some men take on what are thought of as female characteristics. Lesbianism is similarly seen as threatening to male superiority because the women who enage in it appear not to need men.' Caplan, P. (1989) *The Cultural Construction of Sexuality*, London: Routledge.

31. Both Catholic and Eastern Orthodox churches blessed homosexual unions for a thousand years from the eighth century to the eighteenth century. Boswell, J. (1994) *The Marriage of Likeness. Same Sex Unions in pre-Modern Europe*, HarperCollins. Another major issue in this context is the debate over gay clergy and the attitude of the Church of England.

32. The Lesbian and Gay Christian Movement condemned The Children's Society, one of the leading voluntary agencies concerned with care for children, and run by the Church of England, for apparently operating a policy prohibiting homosexuals from acting as foster carers; *Guardian*, 27/10/94.

33. Homosexuality has become a lightning rod for the fears of those who wish that nothing had changed and that feminism had ever happened. The religious right knows very well that the laws against homosexuality are a way of regulating what is meant by masculine and feminine, not only in terms of the choice of sexual partner (someone of the opposite sex), but also in the wider sense of what is acceptable behaviour for men and women; *Guardian*, 13/01/94.

34. Caplan, 1989, p. 5.

35. Foucault in Caplan, 1989, pp. 7–8. The effects of this labelling continue to this day with suggestions that homosexuality is explained by some kind of different genetic make up to 'normal' human beings, rather than accepting it as one of the many diverse forms of human sexual expression.

36. This attitude was expressed forcefully in the House of Commons Debates by those MPs arguing against the lowering of the age of consent from 21 to 16 or even 18 years. See *Hansard Debates* 21/02/94, cols 74–86.

37. Giddens, A. (1992) *Sociology*, Cambridge: Polity Press, pp. 186–93.

38. Much of the detail in this section is from Tatchell, P. (1992) *Europe in the Pink*, London: GMP Press.

39. Estonia, Latvia, Lithuania, Romania, former Soviet Union, and Bosnia, Herzegovina, Macedonia and Serbia.

40. The Ford Report on Racism and Xenophobia (1990) made a recommendation that among the grounds for seeking asylum should include 'gender and sexual orientation'.

41. *Guardian*, 09/02/94.

42. Section 28 Local Government Act, 1988.

   (1) A Local Authority shall not:
      (a) intentionally promote homosexuality or publish material with the intention of promoting homosexuality;
      (b) promote the teaching in any maintained school of the acceptability of homosexuality as a pretended family relationship;

   (2) Nothing in subsection (1) above shall be taken to prohibit the doing of anything for the purpose of treating or preventing the spread of disease.

   (3) In any proceedings in connection with the application of this section a court shall draw such inferences as to the intention of the local authority as may reasonably be drawn from the evidence before it.

   Source: Colvin, M. and Hawskley, J. (1989) *Section 28. A Practical Guide to the Law and its Implications*, London: Liberty, NCCl.

43. *Guardian*, 15/10/94.
44. Eckersley, R. (1992) *Environmentalism and Political Thought – Toward an Ecocentric Approach*, London: UCL Press.
45. Bahro, 1984. Wiesenthal, H. (1993) *Realism in Green Politics*, Manchester: Manchester University Press.
46. Wiesenthal, 1993, pp. 101–3.
47. Hoffman-Martinot, 1991, p. 74.
48. Ferris in Weisenthal, 1993.
49. This party was led initially by Brice Lalonde, a former environment minister under Mitterrand, who gave his blessing to its creation. It was seen as an attempt by the Socialists to win more 'green' votes. In fact Lalonde proved to be more independent than Mitterrand had anticipated, but despite some initial successes, Génération Ecologie's showing at the 1995 presidential election was very poor, and it has been wracked by disputes with Les Verts. (See Appendix).
50. Cole, A. and Doherty, B. (1995) 'France. Pas comme les autres – the French Greens at the crossroads' *The Green Challenge* in Richardson, D. and Rootes, C. (eds), London: Routledge.
51. There was a popular Green party in Czechoslovakia in the immediate aftermath of the 1989 revolution, but with the divide of the country and other events its support has more or less vanished. See further Jehlicka and Kostelecky in Richardson and Rootes, 1995.

# CHAPTER TEN

# Executive power – actors and styles in government, national and regional

## 10.1  Introduction

This chapter focuses first on other groups, apart from political parties, that operate within the structures of the state, and then on those structures themselves. There are sections on the role of bureaucratic elites, the relative importance of interest groups, parliaments and governmental systems in the major western European countries, at both national and regional level. The nature of each country's system of government is a result of its historical experience and the development of its political culture. Although most European states are now heavily industrialised economies operating within liberal democratic political structures, that unity of experience can be contrasted with the diversity of governmental systems that operate.

One way to approach the nature of administration in European states and to see whether there is unity or diversity in the way these different systems operate, is to consider 'policy styles'. Policy style refers to the ways in which procedures operate in formulating and implementing policy.[1] First of all there appear to be certain common issues facing western European states in terms of public policy problems, for example environmental pollution, transport and dealing with the growing elderly population. Secondly, Richardson considers that there has been a huge expansion in the amount of policy being implemented, leading to 'overcrowding' of the policy-making process. This has both resulted from the increasing complexity of policy problems and led to an increasing role for interest groups in the policy-making process. Decision makers are having to take more divergent interests into account and therefore the process has become more complex and longer. This may have made the whole process more democratic in that there is more consultation and participation in the formulation and implementation of policy. A third and more recent factor is the growth of legislation emanating from the European Commission, which in the form of Treaty provisions and Regulations requires similar solutions from the member states. These three elements have led to the conclusion that problems and policy responses are converging. For Hayward:

As the pressure of events external to the national policy-making process increases in scale, intensity and tempo, the capacity of national policy styles to retain their distinctiveness can be expected to diminish.[2]

Furthermore, stemming from the 'overcrowding' of policy sectors, certain groups who consider themselves excluded from the policy-making process have developed new ways of influencing the agenda of government. 'Unconventional participation' fuelled by media attention refers to methods that do not follow traditional procedures. This approach has become more widespread throughout Europe partly as a result of the ineffectiveness of processes, which may allow some representation but not much power (see section below on interest groups). New social movements (NSMs) and other more *ad hoc* groups have developed these forms of protest, for example, to highlight opposition to roadbuilding projects.

Within this overall tendency to convergence there may still be some diversity both within states and between states. There may be overall differing national policy styles and within-states variation depending on which policy elites are involved. Hine's models, discussed below, point to differing ways in which the bureaucratic elite may work. The state structures within which policy-making takes place are different: the more balanced system between centre and region, for example the federal systems of Germany, Austria and Belgium may lead to a greater degree of involvement of groups than the more centralised and secretive British and French systems. The prevailing political ideology of the time, neo-liberal or corporatist, may determine the nature of the consultation procedure in terms of who is consulted and who is excluded. For example, the British Conservative government since 1979 has systematically avoided consultation with the trade union movement, which marked a fundamental change to the unions' close relations with previous conservative and labour administrations. Finally, the amount of secrecy involved in the policy-making process may differ from state to state, with Britain and France comparatively closed compared to the more open systems of Scandinavia and the Netherlands.

Overall, however, governments are now emphasising a consensus approach with different interest groups, and so have become reactive rather than anticipatory. The question still remains where the main locus of policy making is, parliament or the executive. It is perhaps useful to see the relationship in terms of a pendulum with each branch having more power at some times than the other. The complexity of the policy-making process, the 'overcrowding', and the growing sectorisation of the policy-making process, makes parliaments' scrutiny processes more and more stretched, and the pendulum tends to swing and stay longer with the executive in the modern state.

Other differences concern the characteristics of these particular systems. The terms 'presidentialism' or 'semi-presidentialism' have been used to describe the French system of government, 'Chancellor Democracy' the German system, and in the United Kingdom 'prime ministerial' government is applied. All these descriptions point to one striking factor, namely that the role of the executive in general and the chief executive in particular has become of overwhelming importance. In Italy, on the other hand, the system of government from 1948 to 1994 was characterised as *partitocrazia* (rule by the parties) and in Spain, as in Greece, there has been a strong element of *partitocrazia* infused with *personalismo* (cult of a charismatic leader). There seems to be a much closer identification of the party with the state in Southern Europe, although in northern Europe the nature of changes in the governmental system of the United Kingdom since 1979 points to a similar experience (see Chapter 3).

Every country in Europe, apart from the United Kingdom, has a written constitution, but constitutions are not tablets of stone that once written are forever unchanging. Constitutions exist within social, political and economic contexts and are open to amendment from legislative bodies, the judiciary and other pressures. Constitutional courts are given the job of interpreting the constitution, and what at one period of history may have seemed agreed becomes open to change.[3]

How does the state actually operate in the various European countries? That is dependent on the interplay between the various structures at national, regional and local level, the personnel in those structures (i.e. civil servants/bureaucrats), the geopolitical context (e.g. Cold War, or New World Order) and the role of transnational companies (TNCs) in influencing the national economies. The section on interest groups assesses the relative weight and influence of various groups within these structures.

## 10.2   Bureaucratic elites

The role of bureaucratic elites is crucial to understanding where power lies, and how power is exercised in contemporary western Europe. In the following pages we shall attempt to examine the nature and extent of the way these elites exercise that power in the major West European states and also in East/Central Europe. Some of the systems involve a high degree of overlap between political power and administrative action, others have created government-sponsored agencies with more freedom to act on their own initiative. All the systems, however, are characterised by a hierarchically ordered structure of personnel; but in France and Britain there is a narrow elite of state managers. Even with the reforms in the British civil service there will still be an elite of around 2500 policy-makers.[4] This in spite of perhaps the most far-reaching attempt to hive off government work to quasi-autonomous agencies (QUANGOs), and thereby reduce the number of civil servants.

One way to study key civil servants in state bureaucracies is to consider the role they play in terms of four models: pluralist, New Right, corporatist/elitist, and Marxist. Under the *pluralist* model they are seen as neutral administrators, little more than cyphers who carry out administration in terms of technical tasks that need to be undertaken. For the *New Right*, these bureaucrats are budget maximisers, who are partly responsible for the huge growth in the role of the state, and in whose interest it is to see that the state remains large. They make concessions to interest group demands which leads to the overloaded nature of government. The *corporatist/elitist* model considers this group in terms of their shared social, educational and cultural background. As a result of their training and this shared background and their longevity in post, they are the ones with the real power in terms of the way in which the state operates. They can be seen as state managers, pulling the strings of the politicians they purportedly serve. Finally, the *Marxist* model sees this group in Marx's classic formulation as managing the affairs of state in the interests of the capitalist class. The crucial question is whether state officials at senior levels are part of a neutral apparatus or perform a structural role in promoting and defending the running of a capitalist or communist economy, and therefore constitute part of a ruling class. Although the senior levels of the bureaucracy in West European states may not constitute a class in classic formulations, since they do not own much capital, none the less they control an enormous amount of power within the political and economic system. Particularly within both the British and French systems, the shared background and the flow of personnel from public administration to private enterprise can be seen as one way in which large-scale economic interests like TNCs can have influence. The suggestion is that these groups will do all in their power to prevent far-reaching reforms, mainly from a left-wing government, from ever seeing the light of day.

We begin by some observations on the way in which Weber saw bureaucracy developing, and then analyse more specifically the background, training and culture of bureaucratic elites within contemporary European governments. We conclude this section with a consideration of the way in which the neo-liberal approach has challenged the power of the bureaucracy but, using the particular case of the United Kingdom, we argue that despite the creation of privatised agencies the power of the bureaucracy is still formidable.

Weber's analysis of bureaucracy led him to believe that the process of bureaucratisation was becoming a universal feature of modern life, both of the modern state and of the capitalist enterprise.[5] The number of officials would continue to grow in both the public and private sectors, running national or local administration and private companies. As far as training and access to these official positions is concerned, Weber envisaged the development of a meritocratic system whereby people would enter and rise in the system according to talent and hard work rather than from family or class preference. Administration would be delivered impartially to ensure everyone gained equal treatment. This would result in a more democratic system, 'administration could no longer be preserved as the narrow privilege of traditional social groups'.[6]

Despite this move towards more democratic procedures Weber's analysis pointed to an elite democracy, not a full participatory democracy. Weber was also concerned that individual freedoms and the entrepreneurial spirit would be stifled by the weight of the bureaucratic machine. It was necessary therefore to have countervailing powers to balance the power of the bureaucracy with a system of plurality of institutions, but again only an elite kind of pluralism and subject to some kind of control by other centres of power, namely political parties. Weber also saw the need for some kind of charismatic figure to overcome the increasing drabness and greyness that modern life would come to resemble as the bureaucratic tendencies came to dominate all aspects of life.

Weber was aware that the overwhelming power of the bureaucracy, from its position of technical expertise and career longevity, made it very difficult for politicians to control. Furthermore, the political parties themselves were subject to the same bureaucratising tendencies, and became organisations not of the people they claimed to represent but for their own benefit and particularly the party leadership, which Robert Michels noted in his 1911 study of the way in which the SPD operated.

The presence of bureaucracy has been criticised by both left and right. The left argue that bureaucracy has grown too powerful and is beyond full democratic account-ability, and prevents the growth of full democracy, while the neo-liberals highlight the brake bureaucracy imposes on the free operation of the market, reflected in such phrases as 'rolling back the frontiers of the state'. The state is identified at both national and local level as employing officials who make up the bureaucracy. Most people's experience of the state is at this micro-level, whether trying to sort out social security benefits at a local benefits office, writing to tax officials or organising education for children.

Hine (1993) outlines three different models of the way in which the bureaucracy operates in western Europe. The **first** model is the German approach (also US practice) where the top layer of the bureaucracy is appointed by each incoming administration. These civil servants are usually known party loyalists, who take charge of the most important posts in terms of policy formulation and implementation. The previous occupants of these posts usually take early retirement at federal level, or at *Land* level remain as civil servants but are demoted to less important and less interesting posts.

The **second** model is practised in the United Kingdom, where the Civil Service is considered to be neutral, with prime loyalty to the Crown represented by the minister. This model is now open to some amendment, given the practice of recent senior appointments, and the direct interest taken in such appointments by Mrs Thatcher as prime minister. A more accurate assessment might suggest a hybrid model containing elements of the US/German model.

The **third** model is the process in France, whereby the civil service is nominally neutral and permanent but there is clear recognition of partisan loyalties, and where each minister has a personal 'cabinet' to liaise with top officials in other departments.[7] However, the Fifth Republic has seen an increasing politicisation of the civil service, reflected in the number of civil servants standing and elected in parliamentary elections. Almost half of the deputies after the 1986 elections to the National Assembly were civil servants. Teachers at all levels are also civil servants, but even if they are discounted the overall trend is to greater participation by civil servants in politics.[8] The concept of an administrative or bureaucratic elite refers not only to people holding top jobs in the civil service, but encompasses those who have made a lifetime career in government service.

In Germany, the organisation of the civil service tends to favour the creation of an elite within one particular ministry, based on technical expertise or a legal background. However, the overt politicisation of senior posts results in frequent changes of this top group according to whichever party is in government at *Bund* (federal) or *Land* (regional) level. Most senior civil servants have taken a law degree and undergone a period of apprenticeship in a *Land* government department. In addition, a doctorate is virtually an essential requirement to leading positions within the federal government. One hurdle to high level promotion is the **Berufsverbot**, whereby membership of certain political parties or sympathies with unconstitutional views are grounds for dismissal from the civil service. Introduced in the 1970s under an SPD-led government it affected those on the left and right of the political spectrum, particularly Communist Party members. Other countries operate similar kinds of screening processes, known in the United Kingdom as positive vetting ('the three wise men') designed to screen out those holding unacceptable political views, and whose sexual practices may lay them open to extortion.[9] The category of civil servant (*Beamte*) in Germany, as in France, is very wide including teachers and lecturers at all levels, and in Germany even train drivers.

Top civil servants in the federal ministries tend to stay in one ministry for most of their careers, unlike the United Kingdom or France.[10] This leads to a great deal of technical specialisation and reliance on the expert. A general issue concerning civil servants in all the countries we are examining is that technical expertise tends to provide the answer to all government decisions, sometimes to the detriment of other viewpoints. If expertise is too narrowly concentrated it can exclude wider participation in decision making. In France, the attempt to devolve power to local levels after the **Defferre** reforms for regional government in 1982 was excellent in theory, but in practice all the administrative experience and technical expertise remained within the national ministries, thereby perpetuating the traditional dependency.

The German civil service system, based as it is on a federal system, allows for a much broader social base to the civil service and a greater degree of elite turnover than in any of the other major countries of western Europe. Nevertheless, the top layers of the civil service are dominated in Germany as in France and the United Kingdom by the upper middle class. Moreover, in all countries the bureaucratic elite tends to reproduce itself. In Germany, half the top civil servants are the children of former top civil servants, a similar figure in Italy and the United Kingdom, and about a third in France.

The top civil servants in the United Kingdom, are still predominantly the products of public schools and Oxbridge, despite greater access from other entrants to the higher echelons during the 1980s. In the very top echelon, which is exclusively male, 16 of the 20 permanent secretaries in March 1994 went to public schools and 14 of the 20 to Oxbridge.

The Head of the Civil Service insists on the following principles that hold the civil service together: political neutrality or impartiality, integrity and objectivity, together with ministerial responsibility and recruitment through fair and open competition.[11] Teamwork is also stressed, with little of the competitive element that exists in the French system. Furthermore, the British civil service is run by a single corporate leadership structure of the super-elite with circulation of these senior officials across departments. The question of loyalty is crucial, and stems from changes instituted in 1979 which raised the profile of civil servants in outlining government policy through the departmentally related select committees, but it is a fine line to tread between outlining and defending policy. It is clear that civil servants are key players in the formulating of policy, but is unclear as to whether that loyalty should include silence when it is apparent that a minister is misleading parliament.

A former permanent secretary at the Department of Health is quoted as saying that 'economy with the truth is the essence of a reply to a parliamentary question'.[12] Perhaps one measure that would reduce this happening would be more open government. At present the Official Secrets Act, despite a recent overhaul, still puts enormous restrictions on transparency in government. This issue is tied up to more fundamental constitutional reform in the United Kingdom, which groups such as Charter 88 are demanding.

Ministers use a variety of measures, for example statutory instruments, to implement legislation, usually after the passage of an enabling law. This device removes the need for ministers to go again before parliament, and weakens accountability to the elected body. It is civil servants who form part and parcel of this exercise of executive privilege that may lead to conflicts with perceived notions of loyalty.

In France all senior positions within the civil service are filled by graduates of one of the elite civil service training schools. The most important of these are the *Ecole Nationale d'Administration* (ENA) which trains the generalist technocrats, and the *Ecole Polytechnique*, whose graduates tend to end up in more scientific technocratic posts. *Enarques* as the graduates of the ENA are called, and *les X* from the *Ecole Polytechnique* enjoy an almost total monopoly of top jobs in France – in the civil service, state-owned industries and politics. An important factor in their domination of the top posts is their mobility in and out of ministers' **cabinets** and ministries, rarely staying more than 3 years in one post.[13]

Ardagh (1988) characterises the system as an 'elitist technocracy' related to the notion of a *dirigiste* state where 'public life, both political and economic is dominated by the top level civil servants known as les Grands Corps de l'Etat'. The *Grands Corps* are formed from the 12 or so state collegiate bodies, for example Finance, Mines, Roads and Bridges that operate parallel to the ministries.[14] According to Ardagh the ENA equips its graduates with:

generalised skills which enable the elite to occupy posts that have little connection with their prior training. The members of the elite become politicians, bankers, industrialists, international civil servants.[15]

Three main ideas guide the role of these institutions: the importance of the role of the state and the high moral status of service to it, the primacy of the 'general interest' and the 'desire for efficiency'. These ideas are built on the notion of the impartiality of the administration, whose job it is to make objective decisions about how the country should be run.[16]

Wright stresses that despite this apparent hegemony of public life in France by top civil servants it is important not to consider the civil service as one large unified monolith. There are real internal divisions based on the rivalry between the various *Grands Corps*, the *Enarques* versus *les X*, the technical Corps, and by strong ideological cleavages (a pluralist model of competitive elites). The most important influence on the behaviour of the leading civil servants may be their position in any particular ministry and the role they are expected to carry out there, rather than their family, class or educational background.[17] Nevertheless, this group of about 3000 civil servants can be considered as an elite, not only in terms of size but also in terms of social background, education and training.

Wright points to the interpenetration of civil servants and politicians both at national, regional and local level, and where:

> it is difficult to know where the civil service starts and the government ends, and all the more so because the **fonctionnarisation du pouvoir politique** (the bureaucratisation of political power) has been accompanied by a **politicisation de la fonction publique** (politicisation of the civil service).[18]

In Italy the model of the civil service is the neutral profession, but whose members form part of the **cabinet** of ministerial advisers. There is an attempt by the civil service to keep policy and administration separate. Most senior civil servants have a legal training, and their social background is quite different to the administrative elites of France and the United Kingdom. They are not from the upper middle class, many are from the south, entering the service as law graduates from southern universities. The job is seen as one for life and there seem to be few incentives to show initiative.

Like other bureaucracies, there is a small group of top-level managers, then a 'relatively undifferentiated body of civil servants' characterised by a 'low level of pay differentials, which are below private sector rates'.[19]

After a new system was introduced in 1972 a *dirigenza* group of senior managers was created to relieve ministers of certain routine tasks. This group numbers about 6000 in total, and is selected via a *corso-concorso* (competitive entrance training programme). It was initially intended to operate outside main grades of the civil service, but it has now has been incorporated into the main civil service. Hine notes that the administrative elite in Italy is a 'closed and compartmentalised world' where horizontal recruitment is rare and there is little cross-fertilisation. Furlong comments that in terms of public policy in general there is no 'overall control or directive capacity over the central administration', and the system of government is characterised by a 'fragmented, uncoordinated and unresponsive' control. The primary role is played by individual ministers and their officials. Furthermore:

> Complex problems tend to be given to more specialised parastatal agencies, whose expertise is greater than that of the administrtation.[20]

It remains to be seen whether the recent changes in Italian politics will alter the fundamental nature of the way in which the country is governed.

In Spain the growth of political patronage has led to a similar kind of state structure as in Italy in terms of 'clientelism'.[21] The domination of the Socialist Party (PSOE) in government during most of the 1980s has led to the appointment of their supporters in all levels of the civil and public service.[22] Criticism of this kind of political patronage led the government to indicate in 1987 which posts were open to political appointment and which could be gained from usual career progression, but a real reform of recruitment to the public sector is still awaited.[23]

In Italy, Spain and Greece the maintenance of a large public sector is therefore in

314          Contemporary Europe

the interests of all parties as it is a useful mechanism of winning and maintaining support. However, the Italian example has shown that a bloated bureaucracy poses severe problems to any attempt to reduce public expenditure. Under the convergence terms of the Maastricht Treaty for economic and monetary union, these countries will find it extremely difficult to meet those requirements.

## Conclusion

The civil service becomes one of the prime targets that neo-liberals attack in their policy of reducing the power and role of the state. The over-bureaucratic, over-intrusive and ever-increasing way in which the state operates in contemporary societies needs to be diminished, expressed in slogans such as 'Roll back the frontiers of the state', and 'Get government off the backs of the people'. One practical way in which this policy has been undertaken in the British context has been the creation of more than 100 smaller government agencies to provide the specialist services previously carried out by large ministries.[24]

The introduction of market forces with the whole range of bonuses and performance-related pay has been seen as the precursor to privatisation of many of these agencies. The overall aim is to split the policy makers from those who provide services. The end result will be to keep about 12 000 senior civil servants in the main government departments in Whitehall to oversee policy and hive off the rest (about 600 000) to specialist agencies.[25]

Another part of this policy of rolling back the frontiers of the state lies in the reduction of government controls on the operation of business. This has taken the form of removing regulations on the way businesses should operate, the abolition of Wages Councils which regulated wages and by ensuring minimum wage levels, in the some of the worst-paid sectors of the economy such as catering and retailing.

Bureaucratic elites have by necessity a close relationship to politicians and the crucial question concerns the locus of their loyalty. The absence of a constitution regulating the behaviour of government, and the nature of the civil service in the United Kingdom, means that loyalties can be torn between the government of the day, parliament (the public interest), and the Crown (traditionally the Head of the Home Civil Service, but see the quote below). On this question the recent former Head of the Civil Service is quite clear:

Civil servants are servants of the Crown. For all practical purposes the Crown in this context means and is represented by the government of the day . . . in the determination of policy, the civil servant has no constitutional responsibility or role distinct from that of the minister.[26]

In Germany public servant behaviour is guided by more transparent rules and regulations, although this does not necessarily mean that the public interest is always protected. The different types of civil service, however, mean that political bias among civil servants is obvious rather than the notion of neutrality maintained in the British system.

A bureaucratic culture becomes established where the very permanence of their positions, longevity and their expertise tend to act as an effective brake on radical policies of their political masters and their relative impermanence. Many civil servants may have to carry out wishes against their better judgements, but as Wright and others have noted, in France their intense rivalry and the demands of various ministries may establish some kind of equilibrium.[27]

The desire for secrecy seems to be a universal part of bureaucracy's soul. Some governments in the EU, notably the UK government, are notorious for the wide definition of what constitutes an official secret. At the EU level, the question of official secrecy is becoming an issue in the way in which member states conduct their business whether in the Council of Ministers, or in matters concerning civil rights: for example, the *Ad Hoc* Committee on Immigration. The Dutch government has taken a case before the European Union Court in Luxembourg to demand more openness in EU proceedings, which the European Parliament has supported.[28]

The Code of Public Access to Documents drawn up by the EU's Council of Ministers meeting in December 1993 favoured disclosure of documents unless there were special reasons to keep them secret, such as public safety, monetary stability or personal privacy. In addition, however, there was a catch-all clause which allowed for material to be withheld to protect the confidentiality of the Council's deliberations.[29]

The Committee of Permanent Representatives (COREPER) is made up of ambassadorial-ranking officials from the member states permanently located in Brussels, precisely the same groups who occupy the most senior posts in the national bureaucracies. The growing interlocking of national and EU Commission bureaucracies has important implications for democratic acountability at all levels of government throughout the EU.[30] The German and US bureuacracy and the way they function at least have the transparency of more open government than the more closed hierarchies of the United Kingdom and, to a somewhat lesser extent, the French models.

## 10.3 Parliaments

There is considerable debate about the power of parliament and whether it is in decline. For some writers the days of parliaments' supreme power are over (Smith, 1990; Wright, 1990), but the jury is still out over whether this decline will become a permanent feature (Mény, 1993). As far as the case of Southern Europe is concerned, parliaments there appeared initially to be in the best of health:

The available evidence suggests a new trend particularly during the last decade and a half, towards reinforcement and strengthening of parliaments in this area (S. Europe).[31]

The main reason for this strengthening was the liberation from non-democratic government in these areas. Portugal freed itself from dictatorship in 1974, Spain developed democratic institutions after the death of Franco in 1975, and Greece became a democracy again in the mid-1970s after the toppling of the colonels who had been in power since 1967. However, the whole problem of *partitocrazia* described above tends to diminish parliaments' role, particularly when one party monopolises power for too long. Moreover, as Liebert indicates, subsequent developments have tended to subordinate parliament's role to the need for strong government, although this development has still meant that parliament has played a 'central' role in the periods of transition.[32]

The debate arises as a result of a comparative assessment of parliaments' role in the late twentieth century with power in the 'golden age' of the nineteenth century. In the post-1945 world with the huge growth in the role of the state and its attendant bureaucracy, the role of the legislature, it is argued, continues to decline in importance and relevance;[33] but every country's parliament continues to play a key role in legitimising the political system. Since the so-called heyday of parliaments' power, universal suffrage has been introduced and mass political parties representing all kinds of different groups have emerged in the parliamentary arena. Parliaments are still considered the most important site for democratic legitimation in new democracies.

It is important to bear in mind that:

Parliaments do not just perform a fixed set of functions, as the functionalist doctrine proposed, among them the functions of government formation, legislation, education, interest articulation and intermediation, publication. Parliaments possess an intriguing 'all-purpose flexibility' at different times and in different circumstances they do many different things.[34]

The influence of parliaments changes as a result of a number of factors, notably the presence or absence of coalition government, the size of a government's majority and the nature of the relationship between the legislature and the executive. Coalition government means that constant negotiation has to take place between the parties, which provides a focus for parliamentary activity. If a government has a small majority then the relative influence of its own party members in parliament becomes crucial. In commenting on the changing role of British MPs since the 1970s, Norton notes an increasing independence of voting behaviour which has made the House of Commons:

a more significant policy-influencing body . . . and they have served to generate parliamentary structures for subjecting government to more regular and sustained scrutiny.

Although, as Norton concedes, this is not the same as policy making.[35] Finally, parliament plays a significant role in those countries where its committees have wide powers of investigation into ministers' and bureaucrats' activities.

The overall context of the kind of state in which a parliament or an assembly operates is also critical. For instance, in federal systems like those in Germany or Austria the legislative system includes the regions right at the heart of the parliamentary process, whereas in the French or British systems the national parliament has a more predominant role. However, in terms of the actual day to day government of a country, much of the work is done in all countries by the executives at national or regional level. The important focus of attention should therefore be on the nature and way in which the bureaucracy operates and how accountable and transparent the whole executive is to democratic scrutiny. Berry's quotation in the section below gives an indication of one view on how the British system operates.

## 10.4 Interest groups, pressure groups and lobbying

In trying to decide where power lies, and which groups are able to wield more power than other groups, the influence of interest groups within liberal democracies is crucial. If most decisions that affect our lives are being taken by a bureaucratic elite in close liaison with political elites, then this section aims to reveal another angle to that decision-making process, namely the role of interest and pressure groups. We should remember that in using the notion of power we need to consider whether power is seen as a possession or whether in Foucault's terms it permeates all aspects of human relations at the individual and group level.

'Sleaze' and 'corruption' have become common terms to describe some of the activities and behaviour of parliamentary representatives, government ministers and senior civil servants in many EU member states. Issues such as favouring a particular company for a public works contract, paying to have questions asked in parliament and misuse of public funds have raised serious questions about the conduct and role of public officials within liberal democratic states. A related question about whether the overall running of government should be more widely revealed in order to prevent this kind of behaviour concerns how much of government activity should be transparent, that is in the public domain. The implication is that some people or organisations are gaining extra, exclusive or unfair favours as a result of inducements being made by interested parties to have issues raised with particular government departments, and policy considered for their benefit. These people or groups can gain the ear of the relevant officials because they are able to lobby effectively on their own behalf or can afford to pay someone else to do that job for them.

Lobbying covers a wide range of activities, from writing a letter to a government department to meeting a minister to press forward a particular issue or gain a particular contract. The concern arises primarily when lobbying takes place behind the scenes. For example, concern was shown at the decision to develop the Ebbsfleet site in Kent as the major terminus for the Channel Tunnel rail link. It only became apparent later that one of the directors of the company that lobbied the government about Ebbsfleet was also an MP and deputy chair of the Conservative Party. The other groups involved in lobbying for other sites, for example at Stratford in East London, did not have quite such a close link to centres of the decision-making process.

The whole idea of lobbying, particularly within the British political system, is considered as an 'essentially negative phenomenon',[36] and numerous writers have warned of the dangers of the British system succumbing to the influence of the professional lobbyist, as in the United States.[37] Much of this clamour is based on an overestimation of the influence and power of the British MP. In Berry's words:

Policy making in Britain remains highly centralised and effectively minimises the initiatory role of the ordinary MP. An emphasis on parliamentary democracy in the public domain, and a corresponding preoccupation with the activities of individual MPs, presents an essentially distorted view of the democratic process in Britain. It is a view which, although deeply embedded in the popular consciousness, is far removed from the reality of central government decision making and a largely rubber stamping legislature.[38]

The real focus of concern about lobbying concerns the growing links between the executive and interest groups, reinforced by the 'revolving door' syndrome, whereby ministers and middle- to senior-ranking civil servants take jobs in the private sector immediately after leaving their posts in the public sector, and often into those industries which they were previously responsible for regulating. A useful analytical approach in this context is to consider the whole issue in terms of contacts and transfers of elites from one zone or centre of influence (government) into another linked, albeit separate, zone of influence (business). These elites can then be analysed in terms of whether their actions then promote a pluralist or corporatist decision-making structure.

In terms of which interest groups do the lobbying, there have been several theories about their role and relative influence within liberal democracy. In the nineteenth century de Tocqueville considered such groups as crucial to the way in which citizens could channel their grievances. The main issues are to ascertain how much influence these groups have in the policy-making process. One key role interest groups have is lobbying policy makers on behalf of their members. As we indicate in the next chapter on governmental systems, the decline of parliaments' influence throughout liberal democratic states has meant that lobby groups now target not only parliamentary representatives but increasingly members of the executive, in order to influence policy. This process is observable at the national and European Community level. Wilson's definition is a useful starting point:

Interest groups are generally defined as organisations, separate from government though often in close partnership with government, which attempt to influence public policy.[39]

There is sometimes an overlap in the way in which interest groups and pressure groups operate. Generally speaking, however, interest groups tend to be multi-issue organisations and pressure groups single-issue bodies. Often this distinction is not strictly followed. Interest groups attempt to exert pressure on government to introduce, amend or remove legislation. Although they are outside the formal structures of government, they do form part of its institutional mechanism by their full-time presence on consultative bodies. Examples of peak interest groups are the trade union and employers' groups, such as the TUC and CBI in Britain and the DGB and BDA in Germany. These groups aim to influence the formulation of policy in a wide range of areas. As we have made clear elsewhere their role and power is extremely dependent on the political culture and ideological orientation of whatever government is in power. In Spain and Greece, for example, the trade union movement was heavily dominated by PSOE and PASOK, and acted for a long time as another arm of government.[40]

Pressure groups also aim to influence the policy-making process, but the difference to interest groups is their relative distance from the centres of the decision-making process and their single-issue orientation. For example, they are not part of the institutional framework and are not consulted as a matter of course by government. It may be the case that interest groups become more like pressure groups if their access to government decision-making becomes blocked.

For example, the trade unions in the United Kingdom had a close institutional link with government from 1945 until the the early 1980s, which was terminated as a result of the Conservative government's decision to abolish some of the consultative bodies on which they represented their members' interests.[41] They effectively became more like a pressure group in terms of their tactics, although they retained key features of an interest group in the general composition of their membership and their wide-ranging interests. Another difference is the relationship with political parties. Traditional peak interest groups may have some autonomy from political parties but this distinction may become very blurred, as in the case of trade union support for a political party; for example, the British Labour Party and, to a lesser extent, the German SPD. Pressure groups cherish their political independence and seek to influence whatever political party is in power. Finally, it is important to recognise that some interest groups are more powerful than others.

It is the nature of the partnership which is crucial. A government can be seen to consult widely, but in the final analysis there is a big difference between consultation and real decision making (Richardson, 1990). Those with higher socioeconomic status have greater representation than lower groups. The growing importance of such groups stems from the declining influence of parliaments, and the strong links between groups and government departments together with the growing inter-penetration of civil servants and industry. This has been particularly true of Britain during the last 15 years, but is also part of the wider European experience.

## Example of lobbying – the road lobby

At the national level in Britain, the Road Hauliers' Association and the British Road Federation exert considerable influence on governments in order to promote road building to facilitate the quicker movement of goods. The British government has also been concerned to remove unnecessary legislation on companies' activities through a process of deregulation. The task force set up to advise the government on deregulation in the Transport Industry consisted of representatives of companies which had between them contributed more than £1 m to the Conservative Party. The group was successful in persuading the government to scrap the ban, which limited heavy lorry movements in London.

At the EU level the European Round Table of Industrialists (ERT) set up by Pehr Gyllenhammer (former head of Volvo) after a request from Viscount Davignon (the then EC Commissioner for Industry) includes some EC commissioners and heads of 40 transnational companies. The Youth Environment Action Network (EYFA) opposed the ERT's call for spending 60 times more on EU road links than rail.[42] Their proposals relate to the implementation of Trans-European Networks of roads (TENs).[43]

Opposition to such schemes is usually organised on a local level by immediately concerned groups and sometimes coordinated by national or international groups such as Friends of the Earth or Greenpeace, or even local action groups.[44] The access to the decision-making process is crucial, and pressure groups tend to target access to media to publicise their campaign. The question is whether they do provide any real countervailing power. They depend on the accuracy of information available, challenging the need of all governments to operate in secrecy, particularly where national defence interests are concerned.

## The EU and the role of the lobby

According to Mazey and Richardson, there has been a large increase in the number and type of interest groups lobbying the EU, which is a development from previous lobbying done through national ministries. Since the adoption of the SEA in 1986 and more particularly as a result of the Maastricht Treaty, more decision-making power will transfer to EU institutions.[45]

The Commission is attempting to regularise the situation of 'special interest groups' (the official term) in Brussels. According to 1993 figures there are about 10 000 people working in Brussels for and on behalf of the 3000 special interest groups.[46] (The Commission itself employs about 12 000 people, of whom about half are actively engaged in the policy-making process.) About 50 per cent of the groups represent industrial and commercial employers' interests, 25 per cent represent agricultural and food producers' groups, 20 per cent represent the service sector including banking and finance and 5 per cent represent trade union, consumer and environmental groups.[47] There are also professional lobbying firms, and many local and regional authorities lobby in Brussels. Most of the French regions and the German *Länder* have permanent delegations in Brussels. Moreover, under agreements reached between the German *Länder* and the federal government, each time a federal minister goes to Brussels they are accompanied by a representative of the *Länder*.[48]

There are institutional and structural factors that determine the nature and role of the lobbying process, for example:

- the weak role of the European Parliament (EP), which has meant that groups focus more on a particular Directorate-General. This situation is changing, particularly since the EP is becoming more involved in the first reading stage of proposed legislation.
- No one single style of lobbying, as institutions are still in their early stages. The Commission is seen as an 'an adolescent bureaucracy'.
- The corporatist nature of the EU, and the desire to consult widely, means that lobbying has to be multipronged.

Overall, however, the growth of state, despite the attempt by neo-liberal governments to reduce its role and the complexity of government, mean that direct access to the relevant government departmental official or politician becomes a matter for professional organisations. This development does not necessarily have to have any sinister connotation, provided that the methods are subject to transparency and politicians are fully accountable.

## 10.5 Styles of government and state structures

### *10.5.1 The French model*

#### Presidentialism

The tendency of the Fifth Republic has been towards an increase in the power of the executive, and particularly the President at the expense of parliament, the National Assembly. This feature has its roots in the experience of the Fourth Republic where political parties were strong and instability was a feature of government. De Gaulle was hostile to the centrality of political parties within the democratic system, and so the Fifth Republic constitution of 1958 reflected this primacy of the executive. Presidentialism as a term must be considered as a flexible concept, since there have been times, particularly during the periods of **cohabitation**, when the power of the presidency has been trimmed.

Presidentialism can be considered in three main ways: the first where the President has a large parliamentary majority, for example De Gaulle (1962–69) and Mitterrand (1981–86). The second is where the President has a parliamentary majority but it is either fractious, as in Giscard d'Estaing's case (1974–81), or small as in Mitterrand's case (1988–93). Finally, there is qualified presidentialism or semi-presidentialism when the president faces a hostile parliamentary majority (Mitterrand 1986-88 and 1993–95).

De Gaulle's successful attempt in 1962 to have the president directly elected and therefore claim greater legitimacy within the system, as a result of a direct mandate, did strengthen presidential power. In the most common situation where the president has a supportive majority in the parliament, his power has been supreme.[49] But, as Wright notes:

> The central question of any Constitution – who rules? – is fudged . . . Certain articles of the constitution clearly suggest that the prime minister governs, while successive prime ministers until 1986 and Presidents of the Republic have so far claimed that the president rules: with the French Constitution of 1958 we enter the world not of Descartes but Lewis Carroll.[50]

Under Article 5, for example, the President's role is seen as the *arbitre*, the arbitrator or neutral referee with the nation's interests always primary;[51] but how does this interpretation of the article fit with the subsequent Articles 20 and 21 that state that the prime minister has the responsibility for running the government? The President also has the power to appoint the prime minister (Article 8) and the power to veto the prime minister's choice of ministers, which Mitterrand did to Premier Chirac's nominees for the foreign and defence posts in 1986.[52] Finally the President can also dissolve the National Assembly and call new elections, subject to certain conditions (Article 12).

Two other factors have also increased the focus of the political system on the Presidency. The first is the long 7-year term of office and the other is the personality of the incumbent.[53] Over 7 years a president can institutionalise a style and method of government which can dominate other political actors on the scene. Secondly, the nebulous area of actual powers has allowed presidents in the Fifth Republic to stamp their own personalities on the running of government.

The experience of **cohabitation** has revealed limits on the completely free hand that a president may have, and coined the new term 'semi-presidentialism'. Between 1986 and 1988 and again after the 1993 general election, the president had to work with a prime minister and parliamentary majority from the opposing parties. Mitterrand played a dual and effective role during the first period of **cohabitation**. Sometimes he was the detached Head of State above the party political fray, concerned more about France's position in the world. At other times he was more interventionist, defending the interests of all those not represented by the right-wing government. The social democracy of Mitterrand and the almost Christian Democracy of the government led by Prime Minister Balladur (1993–95) revealed itself in a fairly harmonious working relationship, unlike the more fractious relationship between the more conservative Gaullist prime minister Chirac in the 1986–88 period.[54]

Other factors contributed to this reversal in power, namely the president weakened by the overwhelming defeat of the PS at the general election in 1993, the fact that his own term in office was coming to an end with the presidential election in 1995, and his own ill health. Overall, however, the primary focus of executive power within the French system remains with the President.

## 10.5.2   The German model

### Chancellor democracy

With Basic Law (**Grundgesetz**) the situation in Germany reveals a different constitutional position of the leading executive position of Chancellor to that of French president. There are number of concepts that are useful in understanding how the German system of government works: **Kanzlerdemokratie** (Chancellor Democracy), **Rechtsstaat** (state based on the rule of law) and **Politikverflechtung** (intertwining of policy). The term 'Chancellor Democracy' has been used to define the German system of government. The term was originally developed in the 1950s as a way of describing Chancellor Adenauer's pre-eminence within the Federal government.[55] There are two different ways of looking at the relationship between the head of government and governing party elites: One is characterised by the figure who dominates his party executive and party and sees it as his instrument, the other is more like the 'chairman of a team of more or less equal party leaders, and the party elites inside and outside the legislature may play a greater role in fashioning government policy'.[56]

Article 65 of the Basic Law establishes the Chancellor's power to determine policy (**Richtlininenkompetenz**), and therefore to assume responsibility for the government before the **Bundestag** (Lower House in Parliament). This means the post-holder is more important than his/her colleagues. Article 64 gives the Chancellor the exclusive right to nominate federal ministers and to dismiss them.[57]

The office of chancellor, then, has been determined by the incumbent, in terms of how much attention they pay to the demands of their party. Konrad Adenauer and

Helmut Schmidt both took on a more autonomous role, while Willy Brandt tended to maintain closer ties with his party. Helmut Kohl has grown into the office but at the same time has maintained the party as his power base. Longevity in post gives any incumbent a certain aura of pre-eminence, which Kohl has enjoyed, but politics is full of banana-skins and the security of any chancellor can be easily undermined. The peak of political power is often followed by a rapid decline into powerlessness. The experience of Margaret Thatcher in 1990 and François Mitterrand in 1993–95 is evidence of how quickly the mighty can fall.

In terms of the office itself the chancellor is 'the outstanding political leader in the Federal Republic, but it is very far from a Chancellor Democracy'.[58] The tenure of a chancellor is also dependent on electoral and coalition considerations. The frequency of local and regional (*Land*) elections mean that any chancellor has to take into account the nature of his party's support, since the majority in the *Bundesrat* can change and have an effect on policy formulation.[59] In terms of the incumbency of Chancellor Kohl, Gow considers him as a 'dominant and domineering leader' and *Die Zeit* comments that 'the Chancellor is like an oak cupboard, which you're always running into, and which everybody's given up trying to move'.[60]

The notion of the **Rechtsstaat** – government based on a clear set of rules as laid down in the constitution and regulated by the Constitutional Court (since 1949 the Federal Constitutional Court: **Bundesverfassungsgericht**), has a long history in Germany. Unfortunately it was unable to resist the ravages of Nazism, but it has been reasserted in the Federal Republic and strengthened by the proactive role of the Court as independent guardian of the Constitution and a counterweight to executive power.[61] The Court has also been involved in underpinning the federal nature of Germany by supporting the regions (*Länder*) against the centre. For example, in the 1960s Adenauer tried to alter the federal nature of the country's broadcasting system and centralise it, but the Court ruled in favour of the *Länder*.

Another feature of the German system is known as **Politikverflechtung** (intertwining of policy), whereby any policy has to pass through an elaborate and wide range of consultative committees. The nature of this process involves many different kinds of regional government and interest group representation. The conciliation committee (*ausschuss*) and other procedures between the *Bundestag* and the *Bundesrat* attempt to ensure that consultation can remove potential disputes.

Perhaps the crucial aspect of the nature and style of government is the federal context within which government is exercised in the Federal Republic (see section below on federalism and regional government). **Bund-Länder Kommissions** are often set up as, for example, in 1976 to examine ways of developing long term and comprehensive integration policies for immigrant workers and their families.

### 10.5.3  The British model

#### Parliamentary sovereignty

The United Kingdom has no written constitution, and the way in which the state operates rests on the doctrine of **parliamentary sovereignty** within the framework of a constitutional monarchy. Under this doctrine each new parliament elected by the people is sovereign, and no parliament can bind its successor. Advantages of this system in the eyes of its supporters is its flexibility and responsiveness to political changes. The primary disadvantage is that the whole structure is only able to work with a high degree of consensus or deference. In 1924 and 1929, when the Labour Party formed the government, it accepted the basic tenets of this set-up out of a mixture of deference and agreement. In the post-1945 world the high degree of political consensus known as Butskellism meant that this method of procedure was able to continue. Obviously any government would be in favour of the doctrine of parliamentary sovereignty as it permits a large measure of autonomy in carrying out its programme. It could be termed parliamentary absolutism, and there are growing calls for a new constitutional settlement, which would include the incorporation of the European Convention on Human Rights into English Law, and the abolition of the House of Lords in its present state.

This system is underpinned by a notion of voluntarism and individualism, perhaps best exemplified in the practice of the City in its financial dealings, which has operated according to the notion of the gentleman's agreement ('my word is my bond'). Unfortunately, this way of working has led to substantial irregularities and the City's opposition to any form of regulation is now no longer tenable. General rules based on more transparent methods of behaviour have had to be introduced. The high degree of involvement by people in charities is also part of the tradition of voluntarism, but more importantly the whole system of common law which has grown up over the centuries.

This emphasis on pragmatism, which developed almost organically out of precedents into a set of unwritten rules has become the basis of what might loosely be termed a constitution. This is also the world of the gifted amateur, where there is no need to have a particular technical training, both in terms of the traditional background of the civil service elite in Whitehall (although this may now be changing) and the multiple portfolios any one individual may have performed as a government minister.[62] It is also reflected in the great degree of autonomy that a prime minister may exercise, provided they have the party on their side. It is imbued with the notion of the essential gentlemanly fairmindedness exemplified in cricketing metaphors such as 'keeping a straight bat'. However, just as cricket has undergone its own kind of revolution and become less 'gentlemanly', so the days of the 'good chaps' (incorruptible, steadfast and apolitical), have gone. The Thatcher revolution attempted to remove all the 'good chaps', in order to reverse the long period of economic decline.[63] It was successful in some aspects of personnel and institutional change, but instead of a new reinvigorated system of government the United Kingdom now has one of the most centralised and least democratic states in western Europe, with the almost complete removal of any kind of local autonomy. With no written constitution, the United Kingdom has become an 'elective dictatorship' in the words of one previous conservative Lord Chancellor.[64] State power without any control by elected bodies, and little accountability, has meant little protection for citizens.[65]

This kind of piecemeal, almost organic development of statutes, to create the basis of what might be termed a 'constitution' in the United Kingdom needs to be set in the wider framework of the monarchy, the unelected House of Lords and the use of the royal prerogative. Orders in Council, whereby a government minister can introduce legislation, have tended to increase the powers of the executive so that government ministers are able to introduce short bills before parliament, allowing themselves greater flexibility in enacting legislation. Together with the Official Secrets Act, the operation of the British Constitution is still based on the notion of deference to the monarchy and the greater wisdom of the executive, mostly carried out in secret.

A small group of people, then, a 'state within a state' (Benn), govern the country with no great challenges to this tradition. The experience of government since 1979 in the United Kingdom has been the ease with which a strong and determined government can ride roughshod over democratically accountable bodies and even abolish them (the example of the Greater London Council (GLC), and other metropolitan authorities). This centralised state, with increasing powers of the executive, are all tendencies which will be reinforced by civil service reforms and the growth of QUANGOs.

QUANGOs (quasi-autonomous non-governmental organisations) are unelected bodies, run by government-appointed members without any effective parliamentary, legal or democratic control. They represent the major way in which the Conservative Government is reducing the accountability of central government and the autonomy of local government. The destruction of the autonomy of local government in Britain and the increasing centralisation of power has meant that government ministers now have enormous powers of patronage at their disposal. The growth of QUANGOs with their system of political appointees, who are mainly Conservative Party supporters, bears witness to the growth of a clientelistic state in the United Kingdom very similar to the Southern European model.

There are now more than 5500 QUANGOs or extra-governmental organisations (EGOs) which are responsible for spending nearly £50 bn per year, one third of all public spending. There are 73 000 people appointed by the respective ministers to run QUANGOs, who are accountable to the minister and then to parliament.[66] The members of these bodies have been defined as the 'new magistracy', after the early nineteenth century way of having many areas of government run by magistrates appointed by the state in the days before democracy arrived in the shape of elected councillors.[67] There is no requirement for consultation and it is entirely up to the minister to decide who should sit on them. Recent investigations reveal that very few Labour Party or trade union members are appointed, and predominantly Conservative Party members or supporters tend to be preferred.[68] The attitude is best summed up by the then minister responsible for Open Government:

We have strengthened the formal line of accountability by making public services directly accountable to their customers . . . (the issue was not) . . . whether those who run our public services are elected but whether they are consumer responsive.[69]

In conclusion, it is clear that some kind of fundamental reorganisation of the state has been attempted by the policy of neo-liberalism since 1979. The aim has been to

reduce the importance of the state in all domains of public life. However, what seems
to have happened is that there has been very little reduction in the proportion of GNP
attributable to the activities of the state. At the same time there has been a massive
increase in the concentration of power at the centre by the state, both through direct
legislation, for example in terms of reducing local government autonomy and trade
union power, and indirectly through the promotion of QUANGOs.

The doctrine of parliamentary sovereignty, which gives inordinate power to the
executive, has been shown to lack any real effective safeguards, which may explain
the increasing calls for the United Kingdom to incorporate the European Convention
on Human Rights into its domestic law, and also consider the possibility of a written
constitution as the most effective way to protect citizens against the whims of over-
centralised government.

### 10.5.4   The Southern model

#### Clientelismo and personalismo

Most writers suggest that the power of the executive in the Italian experience since
1948 has been compounded by the way in which leading positions in the public sector
have been at the gift of political parties. This has led to the characterisation of that
system as *partitocrazia* (rule by the parties). The new Italy created from the defeat of
Mussolini and the new constitution of 1948 maintained a strong state sector and as
this increased so the power of patronage also increased with the consequent division
of spoils between the major political parties. Various terms have been used to describe
the way in which the Italian political system has operated until recently: *clientelismo*
(clientelism), oiled by the means of *tangentopoli* (kickbacks or bribes). The presence of
the state at national and local level with its enormous powers of patronage has led to
the growth of this kind of heavily bureaucratised system.

Italy had to contend with the legacy of a strong centralised state from the Fascist
era and political parties which operated on a national scale, all of which together with
the delay until 1970 in establishing the full apparatus of regional councils has meant
that the regions have played a lesser role until recently in the development of Italian
state.[70] Their relative importance is still evolving, which may increase with recent
political changes in Italy and European-wide developments. The success of the *Lega
Nord* as a regional political force indicates the way in which there has long been
resentment that the over-centralised state has not been sensitive to the demands from
its regions (see Chapter 8 on regional movements and parties).

The 1947 Italian Constitution reflects the tensions that existed between left and right
in the immediate post-1945 period. It is an attempt to find a compromise between the
ideology of *laissez-faire* economics and the responsibility of the state to provide some
kind of social infrastructure to protect its citizens from the worst effects of a free
market economy (Cotta, 1990). In terms of executive responsibilities, the constitution
gives the president the power to consult with all parties and then nominate a prime
minister, who will form a governing council of ministers (cabinet). As a result of the

number of political parties represented in parliament and the fluid nature of changing coalitions, there have been more than 60 governments since the war. The president, therefore, has come to play an important role within the Italian system, although the basic nature of **partitocrazia** has tended to dominate the style of government. The Italian system is far from the presidentialism of France or the prime ministerialism of the United Kingdom. However, in contrast to these executive dominated systems the nature of the key role played by parties has meant that the Italian parliament is the centre of institutional power. One further feature in terms of bicameralism is the equal powers between the Chamber of Deputies and the Senate, with very few institutional mechanisms to settle differences. This means that legislation must pass through both chambers in an identical form, with the consequent delay to implementation.

A similar process of institutional development can be observed in Spain since the demise of the Franco regime in the mid-1970s, where the accession to power of the Socialist party (PSOE) in 1982 has led to a huge expansion of PSOE appointees in the public sector. Up to that time the **Cortes** had played a dominant role after the constitutional settlement of 1978.[71] Furthermore, as the section on regional structures in Spain indicates below, the upper house of the Spanish parliament, the Senate, plays a role in bridging the divided between the centre and the regions (**autonomia**). The regions play a key role within the Spanish state structure, particularly as a strong counter to centralist tendencies from Madrid. However, the permanence of PSOE in power from 1982 for over a decade with no alternation has led to a situation where a form of *partitocrazia* exists, with all the attendant possibilities of abuse of power and systematic corruption.[72]

PSOE carried out a process of *occupacion institutional*, with the intention of ensuring that its members became heads of the most important state organisations and made up a large part of the leading posts within these organisations.[73] This also included the judicial system so that the usual separation of powers between the executive and the judiciary became extremely blurred.[74] By the late 1980s PSOE had its members in leading positions in the Bank of Spain and other financial institutions, leading Juan Carlos Escudier and Manuel Sanchez to coin the term *socialismo bancario*, to describe a situation where PSOE controlled 55 per cent of the Spanish financial system.[75] The Red Cross and the Spanish blind association *la ONCE* are controlled by PSOE, as are numerous other aspects of civil society in terms of associations. Most importantly, PSOE has kept very tight controls on the state radio and television system, causing the opposition parties to complain of undue bias.[76] PSOE also has an influence in Spain's most popular private radio station, *Onda Cero*, which is owned by ONCE.

An important feature of this occupation of key institutional positions by PSOE is that it is not the party as a whole but factions within the parties that controls these positions. This also compares to the previous Italian situation of the DC, with their *correnti* (currents or factions) who occupied certain positions and depending which current was in power would favour their supporters.

## 10.6  Regional government

The purpose of this section is to provide an analysis of the nature of government systems at the subnational, mainly regional level. The feature of many Continental European states is the presence of a strong regional element in the structure and running of the state. The importance of this regional level of government differs from country to country, but it is coming to play a significant part in the way these countries are governed.

France has traditionally been considered one of the most centralised states in western Europe, and despite recent attempts at decentralisation Paris will continue to remain the dominant focus of economic, political, social and cultural life.[77] Nevertheless, there are countervailing tendencies at various local levels of administration and government, which together with European-wide initiatives partly modify this picture.

The regions in France are basically aggregates of several départements and although they have been designated as such for some decades, their status and funding to operate planning, economic and cultural activities was only secured in 1982 by the **Loi Defferre**.[78] The regions and the **départements** now have increased autonomy in nine policy areas, including regional planning, urban policy, housing, transport, education, social security, the police, culture and the environment.

The regions' legitimacy has been assured by having their assemblies elected for the first time in 1986 and subsequently every 6 years. Unfortunately for the socialist government most regional assemblies have tended to have conservative majorities. Their other role is to help to coordinate local initiatives at lower levels of government.

The mayor is a key figure in French local government with important duties, first as the representative of the state in the **commune**, ensuring the implementation of legislation from Paris, then as the executive officer of the council. In this capacity they are responsible for implementing, supervising and overseeing all aspects of the council's work. Finally in the larger cities, for example such as Montpellier, they have an entrepreneurial role, which is evident from the council's promotion of the idea of Montpellier as the centre of a Mediterranean geographical rainbow with Barcelona at one pole and Genoa at the other.[79] This time the pot of gold is seen as being evenly distributed throughout the arc. The extension of the TGV line from Montpellier to Barcelona is part of this project, which fits into a wider EU concept of a **Europe of Regions** or a **Europe of City States** (see Chapter 12), along the Renaissance Italian model. One problem that is associated with the development of these high speed rail links is the so-called 'tunnel' effect whereby development takes place at the poles of the line, rather than all along the line. Hence, for example, Lille's insistence that it should be a main terminus for the 'Chunnel' link.

Most of this local intervention has taken place during the time of a socialist government. Undoubtedly this fact has contributed to the way in which a medium-sized city like Montpellier, for example, has been able to pursue its particular policy, but it is important to recognise various other factors in the structure and culture of the political system in France that facilitate this kind of approach.

First, there is the tradition since 1945 of accepting that the state has a key role to play in society. This policy known as **dirigisme** (interventionism) initiated by De Gaulle, no friend of socialism, nevertheless resulted in the nationalisation of various leading sectors of the French economy in the late 1940s.[80] Although often criticised as over-centralised power from Paris, it does mean that there has been strategic planning from the centre expressed in the various National Plans. The economic liberalism that is now current in French politics is a relatively new phenomenon, and must be differentiated from the extreme form of neo-liberalism that has taken root in Britain. The government, led by prime minister Balladur from 1993 to 1995, should be seen more in the Continental mode of Christian Democracy with its emphasis on social solidarity and community than as conservative in the current British sense. Even a right-wing politician like Jacques Chirac, who has subscribed to some of the tenets of neo-liberalism such as privatisation during his premiership between 1986 and 1988, would be unlikely to allow services in Paris, his personal fiefdom, to be contracted out to such an extent that as mayor he had no more role to play in local government. Since his election as President in May 1995, Chirac seems inclined to continue the policy of what might be termed neo-liberalism *à la française*, which involves a great deal of state direction in privatised industries (see Chapter 6 on the French Model).

Another reason for this was the existence of a multiple mandate system (**cumul des mandats**) whereby one person could hold numerous elected offices at the same time. For instance, at one stage Chirac held five different elected offices including the office of mayor of Paris. There are of course concerns about concentration of power under this system, and the socialist government restricted the number of such mandates to two; but it did and still does mean that there is great deal of interpenetration of local and national elites, with the obvious advantages of being able to promote local issues at the centre.[81] Even a number of top civil servants working in Paris become locally elected officials, and can use their expertise to lobby for their area in the central administration. Another effect of this system has been the development of a kind of local civic pride, perhaps chauvinism, which despite the centralised structure of the French administrative system has meant that local notables become engaged in a kind of competitive effort to ensure that their town or city receives all the possible grants to maintain its standing. The relationship, therefore, should be seen as a dynamic one, with the decentralisation measures for the regions, introduced by the socialist government in 1982, as one way of trying to redress the balance of this over-centralised structure.[82]

Overall the **Defferre** reforms have been welcomed, but they have not necessarily meant any great transfer of power from the national or regional to the local commune level.[83] Partly for reasons of lack of technical expertise and finance, the state at regional and national level has the controlling hand. Furthermore, the exercise of decentralisation democracy has not meant any greater participation by people in the new councils. What has happened is that the local notables now have one extra arena in which to perform.[84] In the municipalities like Montpellier the criticism is also levelled that the left-dominated council has reneged on its initial promise to consult and involve people more, by increasing participation in the decision-making process at the neighbourhood level in local communities. Nevertheless, by establishing effective regional administrations France, like most other Continental Member States of the European Union, is preparing itself for the possible future political structures of a **Europe of the Regions**, whereby power moves up to the supranational level in Brussels, Strasbourg and Luxembourg, and down to the regional level. The creation of **Euroregions** may be one way in which transfrontier groupings transcend national boundaries, but they will still remain beholden to their national governments for support.[85]

The issue of regional government in Germany and in Austria, Belgium and Switzerland is tied up with the federal nature of their government systems. Federalism represents one way in which the structure of a sovereign state allows its constituent states, regions or provinces a great deal of autonomy at the national and increasingly international level.

The basic structure of the German state is federal, which means that in theory at least the constituent parts of the state, the various *Länder* (federal states/regions) have an equal status with the federal government, the *Bund*. There are 16 *Länder* in Germany ranging from the largest North-Rhine Westphalia to the smallest the city state of Bremen. Apart from Hamburg, Bremen and Bavaria, all the *Länder* in the western zone were creations of the allied powers after 1945, although for centuries until the 1866–71 unification, Germany was composed of kingdoms, duchies and free cities of varying sizes.[86] The notion of a historic region with a secessionist claim has not been an issue so far in the post-1945 debate about German regionalism. However, with the newly unified state of Germany it may be that old particularisms arise based on historical areas such as Prussia and Bavaria, although this is doubtful. The major divide in Germany since 1990 is between the East and the West, the *Ossis* and the *Wessis*, which is likely to take a generation to resolve.

The federal nature of Germany is reflected in the structure of its Parliament. The Lower House, the *Bundestag*, is elected according to universal popular suffrage. The Upper House, the *Bundesrat* (BR), is made up of delegates from the governing party or coalitions from each of the *Bundesländer*. It has 68 members, and each state is entitled to between three to six delegates depending on population. The Upper House is important politically in the system of government since many bills need to be passed by the *Bundesrat* before they can become law. The *Bundesrat* also has influence over the federal budget, taxation and constitutional amendments. Since federal elections take place at different times to *Länder* elections, the majority in the *Bundesrat* often differs from that of the *Bundestag*. For example, since 1991 the BR has had a Social Democrat majority while in the *Bundestag* a CDU–CSU–FDP coalition has formed the government, and it has used this majority to alter some of the government's tax proposals to finance the costs of unification. Regional elections, then, are important in the way they can alter the balance of power in the BR and therefore at the federal level. They are also useful as a way of gauging opposition to the government and mean that any government has to be constantly sensitive to the impact of its policies. It is, therefore, a clear indication of the way in which the federal nature of the state is reinforced.[87]

Through the process of *Politikverflechtung*, there is a great deal of joint consultation at all stages of the policy-making process, which has led to a description of the system as 'cooperative federalism'. Essentially this means that although the *Bund* (federal government) may legislate it is up to the *Länder* to implement the policy.

The different competences of the *Bund* and the *Länder* are set out mainly in Articles 70–75 of the Basic Law (*Grundgesetz*). The exclusive competence of the *Bund* exists in the areas of foreign affairs, nationality, defence, railways, air traffic, postal services and telecommincations, currency, weights and measures, the economy and foreign trade. This exclusive competence is, however, being altered as the government proceeds with its privatisation plans. Already the Post Office has been split from telecommunications, and *Deutsche Telekom*, the new company, is about to undergo the same kind of progressive privatisation that characterised the privatisation of British Telecom in the United Kingdom. This means that the *Bund* will play a regulatory role in the provision of these services, and could therefore be considered as reducing its competence in these areas. Furthermore, the role of *Deutsche Telekom* in providing the infrastructure for cable and satellite channels has undermined the competence of the *Länder* in their area of broadcasting control. The main areas of *Länder* competence are in the areas of education, cultural and religious affairs, the police and local government. There is more a sharing of executive powers, with very few federal agencies.

In conclusion, then, the federal structure is still an important feature of the German state but it is clear that the *Bund* has intervened increasingly in those areas that may have been considered exclusively for the *Länder*. An example of this is in the area of higher education, where the federal government has become a joint partner with the *Länder*. In 1969, an amendment to the Basic Law outlined three areas where there were to be joint tasks, expansion of higher education, including teaching hospitals, improvements in the economic structure of the regions, and certain agricultural and environmental projects. In order to fund the huge increase in higher education it was necessary for the *Länder* to have financial support from the federal government. The result has been increasing participation and finance from the centre with the federal government also controlling the level of student grants.

Another feature of German federalism has been the absence of a capital as a strong focus for the country. Bonn is a medium-sized town in the Rhineland, and thus has managed to play the perfect role as the non-dominant seat of the government. The decision to move the capital back to Berlin has raised all sorts of fears about the growing centralisation tendencies that the move may entail, but it is unlikely that a mere geographic relocation will further centralising forces; the more important forces will come from policies agreed at EU level.

It is in relation to the institutions of the EU that the strength of the federal system will be tested. Already the *Länder* have equal status with federal ministers at Council of Ministers meetings, and they were among the first regions to set up permanent offices in Brussels to lobby on behalf of their interests.[88] Furthermore, with the developments taking place at the supranational level the recent formation of the Committee of the Regions (COR) presents the various regions in the EU with the possibility of even greater power within their own states as they deal directly with Brussels. There are even suggestions that the COR will become the second chamber of the European Parliament and so fulfil a similar role to that of the *Bundesrat* (see Chapter 12).

Austria's federal system has much in common with that of its bigger neighbour to the north. The state is a federal state divided into nine regions with each region having representation at the federal level through the *Bundesrat*, which performs much the same kind of role as in Germany. It has a delaying role in terms of objections to the legislation emanating from the lower house, the *Nationalrat*, but it can be overruled if the original legislation is then carried by the lower house.

'Ethnic federalism' has been the term used to define the system of government in Belgium. The country is basically divided between the Northern Flemish Flanders region and the Southern French Wallonia region; Brussels is a mainly French-speaking area within Flanders. For a long time the country considered it was a unitary state with a constitutional monarchy. The monarchy has remained as a popular unifying force, while the country has divided itself increasingly into these three areas or regions, Flemish, Walloon and Brussels and three linguistic communities, Flemish, Francophone and German-speaking. In order to remain as a state various federalist formula have been devised.

After the 1971 constitutional reforms, a certain amount of devolved power was given to the two main regions in the areas of culture, education and regional economic management. However, the issue of Brussels has remained contentious and most of the cleavages have followed the linguistic divide. Governments have tended to be composed of coalitions of the various ideological parties based on the linguistic divide. The new constitution was adopted by the House of Representatives and the Senate on 14 July 1993.

This constitution defines Belgium as a federal state made up of regions and communities, with the key feature being the greater autonomy for the regions and communities. This is an unusual feature of a federal state in that most tend to have just one form of devolved unit and not two based as they are in Belgium on areas (regions) and populations (communities) (see Table 10.1). Each of these two units has its own administrative competences, financial powers and democratic institutions.

*Table 10.1*    Administrative divisions in Belgium

**BELGIUM**
**Federal level**
The State – Belgium

**Community level**
Flemish community    French community    German community

**Regional level**
Flemish region    Brussels – Capital region    Wallonia region

**Linguistic Zones**
Flemish zone    Bilingual zone    French zone    German zone

*Source:* Adapted from De Boeck (ed.) (1993) 'Comprendre la Belgique', Ligue des Familles in *La Belgique Fédérale: une construction complexe, mais équilibrée*, Polet, R. (ed.) EIPASCOPE European Institute of Public Administration no. 1995/1.

Furthermore, the federal level is not set above the two other units but at the same level. There is no hierarchy of statutes between federal law and decrees or orders made by the other two units, hence the establishment of 'consultation committees' and, in the final domestic instance, a Court of Arbitration to settle matters between these various units.[89] Any decision of these bodies does not prevent one or other parties seeking recourse from international courts, such as the European Court of Justice, to resolve disputes.

The federal government still has responsibility for 60 per cent of federal income, and has full competence in areas of financial and monetary affairs, foreign policy, organisation of the judiciary, economic and social affairs.[90] This is a standard division of federal–region responsibilities, and the international treaty-signing competence that the new Belgium regions possess is similar to that of the German *Länder*.[91]

The other notable feature of the new Belgian set-up is the election of members to the upper house of the Belgian parliament, the Senate. There are now three categories of senator, one group directly elected from the regions, another group appointed from the regional and community parliaments and a further group coopted by these two groups. Overall there must be 41 Flemings (one from Brussels), 29 francophones (six from Brussels) and one German-speaking. In addition there is a system to prevent the Dutch-speaking majority in the parliament from pushing through legislation that the Francophone group considers is against its interests.[92]

Overall it may appear that Belgium is on the verge of 'drifting apart' as a state but, as Deelen argues, many of the consultation and cooperation procedures instituted actually force the respective parties to seek common and agreed policies.[93] Any such constitutional measures will not of themselves prevent a break-up of the state; rather it will depend at the national level on the will of the two main communities, and the way in which regional policy at the EU level is developed.

Although Switzerland is not a member of the EU its system of government, based as it is on a strong degree of federalism, has been suggested as a useful model for the EU to consider as the debate over the nature and character of the integration process develops. Switzerland is a federal state made up of three distinct linguistic groups and different religious groups, and the pivotal role of the cantons in national policy-making has drawn admirers over the centuries. Jean-Jacques Rousseau was among the first to praise the decentralised government, with its system of cantons each having a great deal of autonomy and the delicate balance between local and central powers.

The basis of the modern Swiss state is the 1874 constitution, and it has developed:

> a complex system of power sharing, not merely in terms of a simple division between centre and periphery but also in terms of the shared composition of central authority. Sovereignty is very much polyarchic. At the same time the mixture of vertical and horizontal federalism, with shared financing of most federal legislation, makes Switzerland very much an example of cooperative federalism. Moreover federalism interlocks with direct democracy and consensual politics so that it has been described as '**Konkordanzföderalismus**'.[94]

Church cautions against the transposition of the Swiss model directly to the EU on the grounds that, first, the much-praised model took hundreds of years to evolve and involved a degree of violence. Secondly, there are only a few distinct language groups compared to the vast range within the EU. Finally, federalism in Switzerland is so bound up with particular notions of direct democracy, consensus and even neutrality that it would not export well.[95] Nevertheless, even though each country's federalism is a result of its own historical development, the Swiss model does provide useful comparative standards of decentralisation and opposition to strong central control. In this respect, like the German example of federalism, it is the affirmation of the local and regional against the central that is its most important characteristic. This concept is, therefore, completely at odds with the British Europhobes' concept of federalism at the EU level as a step towards a over-centralised Eurostate.

The United Kingdom[96] is characterised by an absence of a regional level of government and very restricted powers of local government in comparison with Continental Europe. Unlike local authorities in practically every other European country, local authorities in the United Kingdom can only undertake those activities that have been given to them by parliament, rather than being the democratic forum which governs a locality. On the Continent, regional and local authorities operate under a **power of general competence**, which means that they can carry out any activity in the interests of their local communities, provided it does not go against the constitution.

For example, in order to provide Lille with an integrated public transport system with the Channel Tunnel TGV station at its hub, the city council levied a tax on local business for a period of 2 years. The result is a completely new city public transportation network and commercial centre. This kind of one-off taxation for a particular local project would be beyond any power that a local authority on its own initiative could undertake in the United Kingdom.[97] In fact, the opposite is likely with the very real prospect of its grant from central government being capped if it overshoots centrally determined levels of expenditure. There are, however, some proposals to allow some local authorities this kind of power of general competence. The very lack of a written constitution in the United Kingdom, means that central government can control tightly the activities of local authorities.

The debate about regionalism in the United Kingdom returned to prominence during the 1960s and 1970s when nationalist parties in Wales and Scotland won seats from the established Labour and Conservative parties on a programme calling for some kind of regional assembly by the Welsh Nationalists (*Plaid Cymru*) to full-scale independence by the Scottish National Party (SNP). Furthermore, 1968 marked the resumption of the centuries-old conflict in Ireland, this time in Northern Ireland, which is of course still part of the United Kingdom, leading eventually to the imposition of direct rule from London in 1972.[98]

The regions of the United Kingdom are often characterised, as is the case in other European countries, by distinct ethnic backgrounds and strong local identity. Scotland, Wales and Northern Ireland were, as we shall see, separate countries for centuries, while some of the regions of England possess their own discrete ethnicity. A good example is Cornwall and the South West, which regards itself as, and in fact is, substantially different from the rest of the United Kingdom and tends to regard rule from Westminster with a great deal of resentment.

As is the case in most other European countries, there is substantial economic inequality between the various UK regions. One important indicator of regional deprivation is the level of unemployment.[99] In 1992, for example, this stood at 11.2 per cent in the North, 14.5 per cent in Northern Ireland and 10.6 per cent in the North West, compared with an average of 9.4 per cent for the United Kingdom as a whole and only 7.2 per cent in East Anglia. Moreover, there are substantial variations in prosperity within regions themselves. For example in 1992 unemployment in South Yorkshire stood at 12.6 per cent, in Cornwall at 12.8 per cent and in Merseyside at 15.2 per cent – all considerably more than the levels for the respective regions as a whole. In addition, some urban areas are substantially more deprived than the regions in which they are located.[100]

In terms of regional development within England, a government White Paper on competitiveness (24 May 1994) proposed establishing 10 integrated regional offices (IRO) of four central government departments: Environment, Employment, Trade and Industry and Transport. The idea is to provide a coordinated approach to these issues. However, the overall role of these offices is consistent with the government's approach of maintaining central government control, since the staff will be civil servants, answerable to the Secretary of State for the Environment who will chair a new Cabinet Committee for their work. Furthermore, the way in which England has been divided into various regions under the May 1994 White Paper does not accord with other official designations of regions. For example, in the South East of England there is the London and South East Regional Planning Conference (SERPLAN), which brings together all the South East local authorities, including London, to report to the Secretary of State for the Environment on all issues affecting the economy, environment, housing and transport in the South East. Their reports form the basis for the government's guidance policy on the region, with the latest report 'Regional Planning Guidance for the South East' RPG 9 produced in March 1994, and covering the period 1991–2011. The creation of these 10 regions is part of an attempt to create the administrative basis for applications for grants to the EU's structural funds, but contains no democratic element. As the *Economist* stated:

In the European Community, Britain's government insists on subsidiarity. At home, it does nothing of the sort'.[101]

The neo-liberal policies of privatisation and tax cuts have also been part of a wider programme aimed at reducing or abolishing local and metropolitan centres of countervailing power, both in terms of the amount of revenue a local authority can raise on its own, and the kinds of services it may provide.

Under a slogan of 'rolling back the frontiers of the state', the Conservative Government strengthened the power of the state in the area of industrial relations, education and local government. This policy which has been referred to as administrative 'Jacobinism' and proclaimed as giving government back to the people, but a process of administrative privatisation has in fact resulted in the wholescale nationalisation of large areas of local government activities.[102] This is also, to a large extent, true of the Scottish Office and the Scottish Development Agency (SDA) now known as Scottish Enterprise, the Welsh Office and the Welsh Development Agency (WDA), and the Northern Ireland Office.

In general, the Conservative Party (the Conservative Party's full name is the Conservative and Unionist Party) is committed to the maintenance of the Union, that is the United Kingdom in its present form. It depends at present (1995) for its parliamentary majority on the support of the Ulster Unionists, but is the minority party in terms of seats in Wales and Scotland, having only six of 38 seats in Wales and 11 of 72 seats in Scotland. After the June 1994 European elections the Conservative Party had no MEPs in either Wales or Scotland. There has been a tradition of always having a Scot as Secretary of State for Scotland, but the same principle rarely applies to Wales.

Ireland shares with the United Kingdom the distinction of having one of the most centralised states in Europe, with little devolution of powers to the subnational county level of administration.[103] Local authorities have very limited functions and like their counterparts in the United Kingdom have no power of general competence. There is no regional structure of government or administration apart from health boards, regional tourism organisations and advisory bodies for the distribution of EU structural funds. In their analysis of issues concerning regions in Ireland, Coyle and Sinnott use the term 'sub-region' since the whole of Ireland has been designated as a region for the purposes of structural funding. There is, however, a National Development Plan which is considering the establishment of some kind of regional admininstrative structure.

In Italy, the regions form one part of a three-tier system of elected government below the national level of regions, provinces and municipalities. Under the 1948 Italian Constitution Articles 114–133, five special and 15 ordinary regions were set up, which were to be considered as autonomous territorial entities.[104] From 1977 onwards when the regions were finally able to enjoy their full constitutional status, their responsibilities were mainly in the region's economy and social services. Other duties include regulations covering local police force (not the *carabinieri*), town planning, tourism and agriculture. Each region has an assembly from which is elected a governing council and president, and a civil service, but 80 per cent of which is made up of national civil servants.[105] Furthermore, in parallel with the French **préfet** system, central government appoints a regional commissioner to oversee the operation of the regional council.

Regional dependence on Rome is exemplified by issues concerning finance, where their own taxation revenues bring in less than 10 per cent of their total budget. Furthermore, most of their other expenditure is determined by constraints imposed by Rome, whereby funds are provided for specific projects. As Hine notes:

Decentralisation of special regional funds . . . has thus not greatly added to the devolution of decision-making powers, merely to the devolution of the administration of centrally determined policies.[106]

One of the main reasons for the lack of success of the regions as genuine vehicles of devolved democratic fora and administrative units has stemmed from the nature of the Italian political system, whereby all levels of subnational government have been affected by **partitocrazia**. This has meant that allocation of posts in public service and expenditure of state funds has been more dependent on winning votes than in any overall strategic programme for regional development. There have been some exceptions to this rule, notably the regions of Tuscany and Emilia-Romagna in the former 'Red Belt' of Central Italy.

The regions do not have any exclusive powers, in the same way that the *Länder* in Germany or the *autonomia* in Spain possess. The same limited powers are a feature also of the provincial and municipal levels of government; but despite the fact that all these levels of subnational government possess restricted competence, they play an important role in terms of national political life at the symbolic level (Hine 1993). National politicians need a strong regional or local base to ensure re-election, and so they try to ensure that their constituencies and constituents benefit from state aid of one sort or another. Part of the reason for this strong local identification stems from Italy's relatively recent unification and despite huge internal migration since 1945 still remains a strong feature of Italian society.[107]

Although control from the centre has remained strong, some parts of Italy have developed practically their own semi-autonomous mini-states. The province of Bolzano, for example, in Northern Italy between Austria and Trento, has gone along more or less on its own way in becoming almost a province of Austria. The population of this area, known as the South Tyrol or Upper Adige, have their own German-speaking education and media system, their own separate political parties, strong economic ties with Austria and some of the same citizenship rights as Austrian citizens. The Italian-speaking minority has felt excluded in its own country, and responded by voting for neo-Fascist parties which are in favour of maintaining the unitary state. With the entry of Austria into the EU in January 1995 and the establishment of the Committee of the Regions (COR) the tensions between the two communities may now diminish.

The structure of regional government in Spain is new although the 'historic regions' like Catalonia and the Basque province had some degree of autonomy before the Civil War. The new configuration of the Spanish state has to be considered in the context of the 40-year period of the Franco dictatorship, when Spain was a highly centralised country, with regional languages and culture suppressed.[108] The issue of autonomy has been controversial since it hits directly at the notion of a strong state still supported by many right-wing groups.[109] Under the 1978 constitution Spain is defined as a unitary state with a strongly decentralised pattern of government, reflected in a new configuration of 17 'autonomous communities' (AC) which are in effect its regions. Under the regional level of government there are two further levels, the provinces and municipalities (local councils). The constitution, however, guarantees free movement for goods and people throughout Spain and does not permit any ACs forming confederations among themselves.[110]

There is a division of responsibilities between the central state and the ACs, and differing degrees of autonomy dependent upon the particular nature of each AC's agreement ('statute of autonomy') with central government. Each AC has its own government with a president, parliament, executive and judicial system.[111] They can introduce their own laws and implement them either directly or through the provincial level of government. The 'statute of autonomy' lays down which laws can be approved by the regional government without reference to Madrid. The AC's main areas of competence are in regional planning, education, housing, culture, tourism, environmental protection, water, agriculture and some powers over energy.

The Constitution guarantees financial self-sufficiency to each AC. They can raise their own taxes and receive central government funds. The 1980 Organic Law on the Financing of Autonomous Communities (LOFCA) laid down the ultimate target for distribution of spending, with 50 per cent for central government and 25 per cent each for the ACs and local government. There is also an equalisation fund to correct imbalances between the regions.

In terms of representation at the national level the Upper House in the Spanish Parliament, the Senate, is described officially as the 'House of Territorial Representation', designed to give the ACs effective representation at the centre, but its methods of election mean that the representatives from regional assemblies, about 25 per cent of the total seats, are heavily outnumbered by representatives from the provinces, generally favouring the conservative rural areas.

Membership of the EU has been generally welcomed by the ACs, with Catalonia and the Basque province intent on pursuing their desire for further autonomy firmly within the context of the EU. There has been some concern that there may be a loss of power via the process of the government implementation of EU regulations and directives. The ACs have therefore been asking for the same kind of representation in the various EU fora that the German *Länder* have gained. The government has responded by setting up a working group to consider whether AC ministers could attend Council of Minister meetings in Brussels as respresentatives of the Spanish State. Furthermore, a 'general commission on the autonomous communities' has been established to consider ways of making the Senate a more truly regional chamber, and to involve the ACs in the distribution of various EU funds. The ACs are wary that the Commission may reduce their ability to negotiate with government directly.

Overall this decentralised system was designed to allow a much greater degree of regional autonomy after 40 years of a highly centralised system. We can draw parallels with the way in which the West German system was constructed in the aftermath of the Second World War. Although the regional competences appear similar between the two countries, the ACs do not have anything approaching the structured federal–regional relationship that exists in Germany. The *Bundesrat* in the German parliament guarantees the *Länder* a key role in policy making at the federal level, unlike the Spanish Senate. Furthermore, the role of the *Länder* in terms of equal participation in negotiations at EU level is still some way off for the ACs. The EU may be the arena for resolving the issue of the Basque province, in terms of some kind of Basque independence within a 'Europe of the Regions'.[112] This suggestion has also been made as one way to resolve the issue of Northern Ireland for the United Kingdom. The political initiatives by the British and Irish governments to seek a peaceful solution to the Northern Ireland situation in 1993–94 prompted the leader of the Basque separatist group ETA to demand that the Spanish government consider similar moves.[113]

The differing regional systems within the West European political sphere and their growing importance indicate the degree to which the state at the centre is declining in terms of being able to make unilateral decisions. There are obvious limits to subnational governments' powers, but the regions play a crucial role in articulating demands from other sources, and can be seen as an integral part of increasing democratic participation. They also have a key economic role to play in terms of providing the effective forum for strategic decisions concerning inward investment and development of infrastructure. Those countries with such devolved systems seem to score better on most indices of economic, political and social performance.

## 10.7   Summary

The purpose of this chapter has been to present the structure of the state and the way that government is run in a selection of European states. The role of bureaucratic elites and interest groups is important in trying to ascertain where power lies. In outlining the main points of these systems and the various characteristics that they possess, we have aimed to provide a framework of comparative analysis. This has to be set, however, within the economic and social framework of contemporary European states which is provided in other chapters. There are certain common features of these systems that can be discerned.

Increasing collaboration between governments in Western Europe means that distinctive approaches to the policy-making process are becoming less pronounced in all areas. Common problems are being resolved with common solutions within a common framework. The growth of the legislative output of the EU and its impact in domestic policy fora has enormous implications for the future of the nation state.

The various kinds of regional structures that exist and the way in which the EU is moving towards an idea of a 'Europe of the Regions' are an indication that there is an attempt to decentralise power away from the centre. The relative success of these policies remains to be seen, but there appear to be strong movements within many of the EU member states for subsidiarity to mean something in practice (see Chapter 12). That tendency may have significant implications for the policy-making process, and all those involved in it both as participants and antagonists.

## Appendix

***Table 10.1A***   Regions

|  | Population 1991 (1000) | GDP 1991 (million ECU) | GDP 1991 (million PPS) | GDP per capita 1991 (ECU) | GDP per capita 1991 (PPS) | GDP per capita 1991 (PPS) EUR = 100 | GDP per capita 1980 (PPS) EUR = 100 |
|---|---|---|---|---|---|---|---|
| **EUR 12** | **344 704** | **5 172 447** | **5 166 869** | **15 005** | **14 989** | **100** | **100** |
| **Belgique–Belgie** | **9977** | **159 222** | **161 557** | **15 959** | **16 193** | **108** | **106** |
| Vlaams Gewest | 5759 | 93 083 | 94 448 | 16 162 | 16 399 | 109 | 105 |
| Region Wallonne | 3254 | 41 869 | 42 483 | 12 866 | 13 054 | 87 | 90 |
| Bruxelles–Brussel | 963 | 24 270 | 24 626 | 25 195 | 25 565 | 171 | 166 |

**Table 10.1A**   *Continued*

| | Population 1991 (1000) | GDP 1991 (million ECU) | GDP 1991 (million PPS) | GDP per capita 1991 (ECU) | GDP per capita 1991 (PPS) | GDP per capita 1991 (PPS) EUR = 100 | GDP per capita 1980 (PPS) EUR = 100 |
|---|---|---|---|---|---|---|---|
| Antwerpen | 1602 | 30 759 | 31 210 | 19 195 | 19 476 | 130 | 130 |
| Brabant | 2250 | 40 128 | 40 717 | 17 835 | 18 096 | 121 | 121 |
| Hainaut | 1280 | 15 210 | 15 433 | 11 879 | 12 053 | 80 | 84 |
| Liege | 1000 | 14 665 | 14 881 | 14 659 | 14 874 | 99 | 102 |
| Limburg (B) | 748 | 11 804 | 11 977 | 15 775 | 16 006 | 107 | 93 |
| Luxembourg (B) | 232 | 3002 | 3046 | 12 937 | 13 127 | 88 | 84 |
| Namur | 423 | 5335 | 5413 | 12 616 | 12 801 | 85 | 87 |
| Oost-Vlaanderen | 1335 | 20 355 | 20 654 | 15 248 | 15 472 | 103 | 97 |
| West-Vlaanderen | 1106 | 17 964 | 18 227 | 16 248 | 16 486 | 110 | 106 |
| **Danmark** | **5154** | **105 345** | **85 431** | **20 439** | **16 576** | **111** | **105** |
| **BR Deutschland** | **79 984** | **1 373 080** | **1 268 410** | **17 167** | **15 858** | **106** | **119** |
| Baden-Württemberg | 9852 | 207 270 | 191 471 | 21 038 | 19 434 | 130 | 125 |
| Stuttgart | 3697 | 85 987 | 79 433 | 23 261 | 21 488 | 143 | 137 |
| Karlsruhe | 2542 | 53 351 | 49 285 | 20 991 | 19 391 | 129 | 126 |
| Freiburg | 1983 | 36 834 | 34 026 | 18 578 | 17 161 | 114 | 112 |
| Tübingen | 1631 | 31 097 | 28 727 | 19 062 | 17 609 | 117 | 113 |
| Bayern | 11 482 | 236 304 | 218 292 | 20 581 | 19 012 | 127 | 115 |
| Oberbayern | 3810 | 96 132 | 88 804 | 25 230 | 23 307 | 155 | 139 |
| Niederbayern | 1082 | 17 757 | 16 403 | 16 417 | 15 165 | 101 | 89 |
| Oberpfalz | 1013 | 16 487 | 15 231 | 16 274 | 15 033 | 100 | 92 |
| Aberfranken | 1079 | 19 091 | 17 636 | 17 690 | 16 342 | 109 | 101 |
| Mittelfranken | 1603 | 34 584 | 31 948 | 21 575 | 19 930 | 133 | 121 |
| Unterfranken | 1263 | 21 420 | 19 787 | 16 958 | 15 665 | 105 | 97 |
| Schwaben | 1632 | 30 834 | 28 483 | 18 898 | 17 458 | 116 | 106 |
| Berlin | 3433 | 53 143 | 49 091 | 15 480 | 14 300 | 95 | 130 |
| Brandenburg | 2560 | 14 900 | 13 760 | 5820 | 5375 | 36 | : |
| Bremen | 688 | 17 717 | 16 367 | 25 754 | 23 791 | 159 | 150 |
| Hamburg | 1662 | 56 405 | 52 106 | 33 943 | 31 356 | 209 | 187 |
| Hessen | 5791 | 139 613 | 128 971 | 24 108 | 22 271 | 149 | 131 |
| Darmstadt | 3567 | 100 186 | 92 550 | 28 084 | 25 943 | 173 | 149 |
| Gießen | 1006 | 16 943 | 15 652 | 16 848 | 15 564 | 104 | 98 |
| Kassel | 1218 | 22 484 | 20 770 | 18 460 | 17 053 | 114 | 106 |
| Mecklenburg-Vorpommern | 1909 | 10 140 | 9370 | 5312 | 4908 | 33 | : |
| Niedersachsen | 7436 | 129 879 | 119 979 | 17 467 | 16 136 | 108 | 104 |
| Braunschweig | 1651 | 31 753 | 29 333 | 19 236 | 17 770 | 119 | 112 |
| Hannover | 2076 | 41 457 | 38 297 | 19 973 | 18 451 | 123 | 118 |
| Lüneburg | 1500 | 21 039 | 19 436 | 14 027 | 12 958 | 86 | 85 |
| Weser-Ems | 2209 | 35 629 | 32 913 | 16 127 | 14 898 | 99 | 96 |
| Nordrhein-Westfalen | 17 467 | 326 311 | 301 438 | 18 681 | 17 257 | 115 | 118 |
| Düsseldorf | 5267 | 109 174 | 100 852 | 20 726 | 19 146 | 128 | 131 |
| Köln | 4048 | 77 047 | 71 174 | 19 032 | 17 581 | 117 | 118 |
| Münster | 2491 | 40 097 | 37 040 | 16 097 | 14 870 | 99 | 106 |
| Detmold | 1899 | 33 899 | 31 315 | 17 847 | 16 487 | 110 | 111 |
| Arnsberg | 3761 | 66 094 | 61 056 | 17 572 | 16 233 | 108 | 113 |
| Rheinland-Pfalz | 3782 | 64 097 | 59 211 | 16 947 | 15 655 | 104 | 107 |
| Koblenz | 1408 | 21 846 | 20 181 | 15 513 | 14 331 | 96 | 97 |

**Table 10.1A** Continued

| | Population 1991 (1000) | GDP 1991 (million ECU) | GDP 1991 (million PPS) | GDP per capita 1991 (ECU) | GDP per capita 1991 (PPS) | GDP per capita 1991 (PPS) EUR = 100 | GDP per capita 1980 (PPS) EUR = 100 |
|---|---|---|---|---|---|---|---|
| Trier | 488 | 7086 | 6546 | 14 533 | 13 425 | 90 | 94 |
| Rheinhessen-Pfalz | 1887 | 35 165 | 32 485 | 18 640 | 17 220 | 115 | 117 |
| Saarland | 1084 | 19 694 | 18 193 | 18 165 | 16 781 | 112 | 107 |
| Sachsen | 4739 | 25 000 | 23 090 | 5275 | 4872 | 33 | : |
| Sachsen-Anhalt | 2856 | 16 100 | 14 870 | 5637 | 5207 | 35 | : |
| Schleswig-Holstein | 2648 | 43 876 | 40 531 | 16 569 | 15 306 | 102 | 103 |
| Thüringen | 2595 | 12 630 | 11 670 | 4867 | 4497 | 30 | : |
| **Ellada** | **10 153** | **57 116** | **75 105** | **5625** | **7397** | **49** | **52** |
| Voreia Ellada | 3296 | 17 381 | 22 855 | 5273 | 6934 | 46 | 49 |
| Anatoliki Makedonia, Thraki | 568 | 2895 | 3807 | 5101 | 6707 | 45 | 41 |
| Kentriki Makedonia | 1714 | 9183 | 12 075 | 5358 | 7045 | 47 | 52 |
| Dytiki Makedonia | 291 | 1595 | 2097 | 5483 | 7210 | 48 | 48 |
| Thessalia | 724 | 3708 | 4876 | 5125 | 6739 | 45 | 48 |
| Kentriki Ellada | 2389 | 12 976 | 17 063 | 5431 | 7142 | 48 | 52 |
| Ipeiros | 336 | 1436 | 1889 | 4277 | 5624 | 38 | 38 |
| Ionia Nisia | 189 | 939 | 1235 | 4969 | 6534 | 44 | 41 |
| Dytiki Ellada | 693 | 3360 | 4418 | 4845 | 6371 | 43 | 45 |
| Sterea Ellada | 571 | 3894 | 5121 | 6815 | 8962 | 60 | 72 |
| Peloponnisos | 599 | 3346 | 4400 | 5583 | 7341 | 49 | 52 |
| Attiki | 3487 | 21 849 | 28 730 | 6265 | 8238 | 55 | 59 |
| Nisia Aigaiou, Kriti | 981 | 4910 | 6457 | 5006 | 6582 | 44 | 42 |
| Voreio Aigaio | 197 | 810 | 1065 | 4115 | 5412 | 36 | 36 |
| Notio Aigaio | 254 | 1407 | 1850 | 5547 | 7294 | 49 | 45 |
| Kriti | 530 | 2693 | 3542 | 5077 | 6677 | 45 | 44 |
| **España** | **39 037** | **426 494** | **467 054** | **10 925** | **11 964** | **80** | **71** |
| Noroeste | 4466 | 40 537 | 44 392 | 9076 | 9939 | 66 | 67 |
| Galicia | 2810 | 23 435 | 25 664 | 8340 | 9134 | 61 | 61 |
| Asturias | 1128 | 11 556 | 12 655 | 10 243 | 11 217 | 75 | 77 |
| Cantabria | 528 | 5545 | 6073 | 10 498 | 11 496 | 77 | 78 |
| Noreste | 4131 | 51 877 | 56 810 | 12 557 | 13 751 | 92 | 85 |
| Pais Vasco | 2133 | 26 764 | 29 310 | 12 545 | 13 738 | 92 | 89 |
| Navarra | 522 | 7146 | 7826 | 13 682 | 14 983 | 100 | 90 |
| Rioja | 261 | 3118 | 3414 | 11 963 | 13 101 | 87 | 88 |
| Aragon | 1215 | 14 848 | 16 260 | 12 221 | 13 383 | 89 | 76 |
| Madrid | 4888 | 66 691 | 73 034 | 13 645 | 14 943 | 100 | 81 |
| Centro (E) | 5478 | 48 714 | 53 347 | 8892 | 9738 | 65 | 62 |
| Castilla – Leon | 2631 | 25 038 | 27 419 | 9516 | 10 421 | 70 | 70 |
| Castilla – La Mancha | 1717 | 15 614 | 17 099 | 9094 | 9959 | 66 | 61 |
| Extremadura | 1130 | 8062 | 8829 | 7133 | 7811 | 52 | 45 |
| Este | 10 498 | 132 015 | 144 569 | 12 576 | 13 772 | 92 | 79 |
| Cataluña | 6020 | 80 469 | 88 121 | 13 368 | 14 639 | 98 | 83 |
| Comunidad Valenciana | 3794 | 41 663 | 45 625 | 10 981 | 12 025 | 80 | 71 |
| Baleares | 684 | 9883 | 10 822 | 14 454 | 15 828 | 106 | 86 |
| Sur | 8088 | 70 547 | 77 256 | 8723 | 9552 | 64 | 57 |
| Andalucia | 6934 | 58 724 | 64 309 | 8469 | 9275 | 62 | 56 |
| Murcia | 1029 | 10 692 | 11 709 | 10 394 | 11 382 | 76 | 65 |

**Table 10.1A**  *Continued*

|  | Population 1991 (1000) | GDP 1991 (million ECU) | GDP 1991 (million PPS) | GDP per capita 1991 (ECU) | GDP per capita 1991 (PPS) | GDP per capita 1991 (PPS) EUR = 100 | GDP per capita 1980 (PPS) EUR = 100 |
|---|---|---|---|---|---|---|---|
| Ceuta y Melilla | 125 | 1131 | 1238 | 9012 | 9869 | 66 | 50 |
| Canarias | 1488 | 16 114 | 17 646 | 10 831 | 11 861 | 79 | 59 |
| **France** | **56 702** | **970 341** | **978 103** | **17 113** | **17 250** | **115** | **114** |
| Ile de France | 10 686 | 273 291 | 275 477 | 25 575 | 25 780 | 172 | 162 |
| Bassin Parisien | 10 278 | 160 606 | 161 891 | 15 627 | 15 752 | 105 | 109 |
| Champagne-Ardenne | 1347 | 23 004 | 23 188 | 17 074 | 17 211 | 115 | 119 |
| Picardie | 1813 | 26 445 | 26 657 | 14 586 | 14 702 | 98 | 109 |
| Haute-Normandie | 1740 | 28 992 | 29 224 | 16 663 | 16 797 | 112 | 117 |
| Centre | 2375 | 37 434 | 37 733 | 15 760 | 15 886 | 106 | 106 |
| Basse-Normandie | 1392 | 20 340 | 20 502 | 14 610 | 14 727 | 98 | 99 |
| Bourgogne | 1610 | 24 391 | 24 586 | 15 150 | 15 272 | 102 | 103 |
| Nord – Pas-de-Calais | 3964 | 54 607 | 55 044 | 13 774 | 13 884 | 93 | 99 |
| Est | 5028 | 78 881 | 79 512 | 15 688 | 15 814 | 106 | 111 |
| Lorraine | 2304 | 32 944 | 33 207 | 14 299 | 14 413 | 96 | 107 |
| Alsace | 1627 | 28 377 | 28 604 | 17 445 | 17 585 | 117 | 117 |
| Franche-Comté | 1097 | 17 562 | 17 702 | 16 004 | 16 132 | 108 | 109 |
| Ouest | 7457 | 107 037 | 107 893 | 14 354 | 14 469 | 97 | 96 |
| Pays de la Loire | 3063 | 45 823 | 46 189 | 14 961 | 15 080 | 101 | 100 |
| Bretagne | 2798 | 39 168 | 39 481 | 13 997 | 14 109 | 94 | 94 |
| Poitou-Charentes | 1596 | 22 046 | 22 222 | 13 816 | 13 927 | 93 | 92 |
| Sud-Ouest | 5959 | 89 593 | 90 310 | 15 035 | 15 155 | 101 | 97 |
| Aquitaine | 2801 | 44 354 | 44 709 | 15 833 | 15 959 | 106 | 103 |
| Midi-Pyrénées | 2436 | 35 610 | 35 894 | 14 621 | 14 738 | 98 | 92 |
| Limousin | 722 | 9630 | 9707 | 13 334 | 13 440 | 90 | 88 |
| Centre-Est | 6685 | 109 067 | 109 940 | 16 314 | 16 445 | 110 | 109 |
| Rhône-Alpes | 5365 | 90 481 | 91 205 | 16 865 | 17 000 | 113 | 114 |
| Auvergne | 1321 | 18 583 | 18 731 | 14 071 | 14 184 | 95 | 93 |
| Mediterranee | 6645 | 97 259 | 98 037 | 14 637 | 14754 | 98 | 99 |
| Languedoc-Roussillon | 2124 | 27 712 | 27 934 | 13 050 | 13 154 | 88 | 87 |
| Provence-Alpes-Côte d'Azur | 4271 | 66 466 | 66 998 | 15 562 | 15 686 | 105 | 111 |
| Corse | 250 | 3081 | 3106 | 12 316 | 12 415 | 83 | : |
| Departements d'Outre-Mer[1] | 1438 | 9038 | 8787 | 6283 | 6110 | 45 | : |
| Guadeloupe | 381 | 2003 | 1948 | 5259 | 5113 | 38 | : |
| Martinique | 356 | 2576 | 2505 | 7239 | 7038 | 52 | : |
| Guyane | 111 | 810 | 787 | 7286 | 7085 | 52 | : |
| Réunion | 590 | 3649 | 3548 | 6180 | 6008 | 45 | : |
| **Ireland** | **3524** | **35 144** | **38 113** | **9973** | **10 815** | **72** | **60** |
| **Italia** | **57 796** | **930 934** | **918 361** | **16 107** | **15 890** | **106** | **103** |
| Nord Ovest | 6210 | 115 432 | 113 873 | 18 588 | 18 336 | 112 | 119 |
| Piemonte | 4367 | 81 650 | 80 547 | 18 697 | 18 444 | 123 | 119 |
| Valle d'Aosta | 116 | 2339 | 2308 | 20 182 | 19 910 | 133 | 127 |
| Liguria | 1727 | 31 443 | 31 018 | 18 204 | 17 958 | 120 | 117 |
| Lombardia | 8947 | 188 572 | 186 025 | 21 078 | 20 793 | 139 | 135 |
| Nord Est | 6498 | 120 556 | 118 928 | 18 554 | 18 303 | 122 | 113 |
| Trentino-Alto Adige | 891 | 17 121 | 16 889 | 19 212 | 18 953 | 126 | 120 |

[1] 1989 data.

**Table 10.1A** *Continued*

| | Population 1991 (1000) | GDP 1991 (million ECU) | GDP 1991 (million PPS) | GDP per capita 1991 (ECU) | GDP per capita 1991 (PPS) | GDP per capita 1991 (PPS) EUR = 100 | GDP per capita 1980 (PPS) EUR = 100 |
|---|---|---|---|---|---|---|---|
| Veneto | 4402 | 80 462 | 79 375 | 18 279 | 18 032 | 120 | 111 |
| Friuli-Venezia Giulia | 1205 | 22 973 | 22 663 | 19 069 | 18 811 | 125 | 115 |
| Emilia-Romagna | 3934 | 78 713 | 77 650 | 20 007 | 19 737 | 132 | 134 |
| Centro (I) | 5830 | 97 497 | 96 180 | 16 724 | 16 498 | 110 | 111 |
| Toscana | 3570 | 61 156 | 60 330 | 17 131 | 16 900 | 113 | 113 |
| Umbria | 823 | 12 765 | 12 593 | 15 502 | 15 292 | 102 | 107 |
| Marche | 1436 | 23 576 | 23 258 | 16 412 | 16 191 | 108 | 108 |
| Lazio | 5193 | 95 771 | 94 477 | 18 442 | 18 193 | 121 | 107 |
| Campania | 5845 | 64 548 | 63 676 | 11 043 | 10 894 | 73 | 67 |
| Abruzzi-Molise | 1609 | 22 216 | 21 916 | 13 807 | 13 620 | 91 | 85 |
| Abruzzi | 1272 | 18 063 | 17 819 | 14 196 | 14 004 | 93 | 87 |
| Molise | 337 | 4154 | 4098 | 12 337 | 12 170 | 81 | 77 |
| Sud | 6868 | 72 842 | 71 858 | 10 605 | 10 462 | 70 | 68 |
| Puglia | 4085 | 47 315 | 46 676 | 11 583 | 11 426 | 76 | 73 |
| Basilicata | 625 | 6339 | 6253 | 10 137 | 10 000 | 67 | 70 |
| Calabria | 2158 | 19 188 | 18 929 | 8891 | 8771 | 59 | 58 |
| Sicilia | 5197 | 55 360 | 54 613 | 10 653 | 10 509 | 70 | 69 |
| Sardegna | 1665 | 19 426 | 19 164 | 11 668 | 11 511 | 77 | 74 |
| **Luxembourg (Grand-Duche)** | **387** | **7550** | **7599** | **19 509** | **19 636** | **131** | **116** |
| **Nederland** | **15 067** | **235 208** | **234 293** | **15 611** | **15 550** | **104** | **109** |
| Noord-Nederland | 1609 | 25 544 | 25 445 | 15 880 | 15 818 | 106 | 135 |
| Groningen | 559 | 11 728 | 11 683 | 20 997 | 20 915 | 140 | 210 |
| Friesland | 604 | 7761 | 7730 | 12 843 | 12 793 | 85 | 88 |
| Drenthe | 446 | 6055 | 6032 | 13 586 | 13 533 | 90 | 102 |
| Oost-Nederland | 3074 | 42 112 | 41 949 | 13 698 | 13 645 | 91 | 94 |
| Overijssel | 1031 | 14 325 | 14 270 | 13 890 | 13 836 | 92 | : |
| Gelderland | 1825 | 25 139 | 25 041 | 13 777 | 13 723 | 92 | : |
| Flevoland | 218 | 2648 | 2638 | 12 135 | 12 088 | 81 | : |
| West-Nederland | 7052 | 117 595 | 117 138 | 16 676 | 16 611 | 111 | 116 |
| Utrecht | 1029 | 16 927 | 16 861 | 16 447 | 16 383 | 109 | 107 |
| Noord-Holland | 2405 | 41 703 | 41 541 | 17 339 | 17 271 | 115 | 123 |
| Zuid-Holland | 3258 | 53 072 | 52 866 | 16 290 | 16 227 | 108 | 116 |
| Zeeland | 359 | 5894 | 5871 | 16 394 | 16 330 | 109 | 103 |
| Zuid-Nederland | 3332 | 49 956 | 49 762 | 14 993 | 14 935 | 100 | 95 |
| Noord-Brabant | 2216 | 33 736 | 33 605 | 15 221 | 15 162 | 101 | 97 |
| Limburg (NL) | 1116 | 16 220 | 16 157 | 14 540 | 14 483 | 97 | 91 |
| **Portugal** | **9362** | **55 502** | **84 859** | **5928** | **9064** | **60** | **53** |
| Continente | 9362 | 55 502 | 84 859 | 5928 | 9064 | 60 | 53 |
| Norte | 3450 | 18 101 | 27 676 | 5247 | 8022 | 54 | 44 |
| Centro (P) | 1725 | 7132 | 10 905 | 4135 | 6323 | 42 | 42 |
| Lisboa e Vale do Tejo | 3304 | 26 653 | 40 751 | 8067 | 12 334 | 82 | 69 |
| Alentejo | 545 | 1904 | 2911 | 3494 | 5343 | 36 | 49 |
| Algarve | 339 | 1711 | 2617 | 5052 | 7724 | 52 | 48 |
| Acores | 237 | : | : | : | : | : | : |
| Madeira | 253 | : | : | : | : | : | : |

**Table 10.1A**   *Continued*

| | Population 1991 (1000) | GDP 1991 (million ECU) | GDP 1991 (million PPS) | GDP per capita 1991 (ECU) | GDP per capita 1991 (PPS) | GDP per capita 1991 (PPS) EUR = 100 | GDP per capita 1980 (PPS) EUR = 100 |
|---|---|---|---|---|---|---|---|
| **United Kingdom** | **57 561** | **816 535** | **848 001** | **14 186** | **14 732** | **98** | **96** |
| North | 3083 | 38 212 | 39 684 | 12 393 | 12 870 | 86 | 88 |
| *Cleveland, Durham* | 1155 | 14 050 | 14 591 | 12 169 | 12 638 | 84 | : |
| *Cumbria* | 493 | 7398 | 7683 | 14 995 | 15 573 | 104 | : |
| *Northumberland, Tyne and* | | | | | | | |
| *   Wear* | 1436 | 16 770 | 17 416 | 11 682 | 12 132 | 81 | : |
| Yorkshire and Humberside | 4965 | 63 326 | 65 766 | 12 755 | 13 246 | 88 | 89 |
| *Humberside* | 861 | 11 785 | 12 239 | 13 680 | 14 207 | 95 | : |
| *North Yorkshire* | 728 | 9662 | 10 034 | 13 266 | 13 777 | 92 | : |
| *South Yorkshire* | 1300 | 14 441 | 14 997 | 11 112 | 11 540 | 77 | : |
| *West Yorkshire* | 2076 | 27 438 | 28 496 | 13 220 | 13 729 | 92 | : |
| East Midlands | 4029 | 54 857 | 56 971 | 13 615 | 14 140 | 94 | 92 |
| *Derbyshire, Nottinghamshire* | 1955 | 25 442 | 26 423 | 13 016 | 13 518 | 90 | : |
| *Leics., Northamptonshire* | 1482 | 22 322 | 23 182 | 15 065 | 15 646 | 104 | : |
| *Lincolnshire* | 593 | 7093 | 7367 | 11 965 | 12 426 | 83 | : |
| East Anglia | 2064 | 29 476 | 30 611 | 14 278 | 14 828 | 99 | 93 |
| South East (UK) | 17 504 | 294 875 | 306 238 | 16 846 | 17 496 | 117 | 114 |
| *Bedfordshire, Hertfordshire* | 1528 | 22 187 | 23 042 | 14 518 | 15 078 | 101 | : |
| *Berks., Bucks., Oxfordshire* | 1989 | 31 105 | 32 304 | 15 640 | 16 243 | 108 | : |
| *Surrey, East-West Sussex* | 2426 | 34 157 | 35 474 | 14 078 | 14 620 | 98 | : |
| *Essex* | 1538 | 18 909 | 19 637 | 12 298 | 12 772 | 85 | : |
| *Greater London* | 6812 | 145 663 | 151 277 | 21 383 | 22 207 | 148 | : |
| *Hampshire, Isle of Wight* | 1681 | 23 317 | 24 215 | 13 869 | 14 404 | 96 | : |
| *Kent* | 1529 | 19 537 | 20 290 | 12 774 | 13 266 | 89 | : |
| South West (UK) | 4679 | 63 695 | 66 149 | 13 614 | 14 138 | 94 | 90 |
| *Avon, Gloucs., Wiltshire* | 2051 | 31 423 | 32 634 | 15 324 | 15 914 | 106 | : |
| *Cornwall, Devon* | 1502 | 17 308 | 17 975 | 11 524 | 11 968 | 80 | : |
| *Dorset, Somerset* | 1126 | 14 962 | 15 538 | 13 286 | 13 798 | 92 | : |
| West Midlands | 5233 | 67 597 | 70 202 | 12 918 | 13 415 | 89 | 89 |
| *Hereford-Worcs., Warwicks.* | 1162 | 14 509 | 15 069 | 12 488 | 12 970 | 87 | : |
| *Shropshire, Staffordshire* | 1450 | 17 529 | 18 204 | 12 091 | 12 557 | 84 | : |
| *West Midlands (County)* | 2621 | 35 556 | 36 926 | 13 563 | 14 086 | 94 | : |
| North West (UK) | 6405 | 83 451 | 86 666 | 13 028 | 13 531 | 90 | 93 |
| *Cheshire* | 962 | 14 475 | 15 033 | 15 054 | 15 635 | 104 | : |
| *Greater Manchester* | 2597 | 34 434 | 35 761 | 13 258 | 13 769 | 92 | : |
| *Lancashire* | 1399 | 18 440 | 19 150 | 13 181 | 13 689 | 91 | : |
| *Merseyside* | 1447 | 16 100 | 16 720 | 11 123 | 11 551 | 77 | : |
| Wales | 2889 | 34 638 | 35 973 | 11 990 | 12 452 | 83 | 80 |
| *Clwyd, Dyfed, Gwynedd, Powys* | 1127 | 13 180 | 13 688 | 11 692 | 12 143 | 81 | : |
| *Gwent, Mid-S-W Glamorgan* | 1762 | 21 458 | 22 285 | 12 180 | 12 649 | 84 | : |
| Scotland | 5116 | 69 282 | 71 952 | 13 543 | 14 065 | 94 | 91 |
| *Bord.-Centr.-Fife-Loth.-Tay.* | 1870 | 25 702 | 26 693 | 13 745 | 14 274 | 95 | : |
| *Dumfr.-Galloway, Strathclyde* | 2461 | 31 793 | 33 018 | 12 919 | 13 417 | 90 | : |
| *Highlands, Islands* | 278 | 3108 | 3228 | 11 199 | 11 631 | 78 | : |
| *Grampian* | 507 | 8679 | 9013 | 17 104 | 17 763 | 119 | : |
| Northern Ireland | 1594 | 17 127 | 17 787 | 10 748 | 11 162 | 74 | 74 |

# Further reading

## General

Allum, P. (1995) *State and Society in Western Europe*, Cambridge: Polity Press.

Heisler, M. O. and Kvavik, R. B. (1974) 'Patterns of European politics: the "European polity" model' in *Politics in Europe* Heisler, M. O. (ed.), New York: McKay.

Mény, Y. (1993) *Government and Politics in Western Europe*, Oxford: Oxford University Press.

Smith, G. (1990) *Politics in Western Europe*, Aldershot: Dartmouth.

## Bureaucratic elites

Aberbach, J. D., Putnam, R. A. and Rockman, B. A. (1981) *Bureaucrats and Politicians in Western Democracies*, New Haven: Harvard University Press.

Ardagh, J. (1988) *France Today*, London: Penguin.

Beetham, D. (1987) *Bureaucracy*, Milton Keynes: Open University Press.

Blondel, J. and Müller-Rommel, F. (1988) *Cabinets in W. Europe*, London: Macmillan.

Dogan, M. (ed.) (1975) *The Mandarins of Western Europe: the Political Roles of the Top Civil Servants*, London: Sage.

Elliott, M. (1988) *Time for a New Constitutional Change*, London.

Hennessy, P. (1990) *Whitehall*, London: Fontana.

Hooper, J. (1995) *The New Spaniards*, London: Penguin.

Howorth, J. and Cerny, P. (1981) *Elites in France Origins, Reproduction and Power*, London: Pinter.

Perfil de una Decada, *El Pais extra* : 28/10/92.

Part, A. (1990) *The Making of a Mandarin*, London: André Deutsch.

Plowden, W. (1988) 'Whitehall and the Civil Service', in *1688–1988, Time for a New Constitution*, Holme, R. and Elliott, M.

Richardson, J. J. (1982) *Policy Styles in Western Europe*, London: Allen & Unwin.

Richardson J. J. (1990) *Government & Groups in Britain: Changing Styles*, Glasgow: Strathclyde University Press.

Roberts, G. K. (1989) 'Party System Change in West Germany: Land – Federal Linkages' *WEP* 12 (4) pp. 98–113.

Smith, G. (1986) *Democracy in Western Germany*, Aldershot: Gower.

Suleiman, E. (1978) *Elites in French Society*, New Jersey: Princeton University Press.

Urwin, D. W. and Paterson W. E. (eds) (1990) *Politics in Western Europe today: Perspectives, policies and problems since 1980*, London: Longman.

Wright, V. (1990) *The Government and Politics of France*, London: Unwin Hyman.

## Parliaments

Liebert, U. and Cotta, M. (eds) (1990) *Parliament and Democratic Consolidation in Southern Europe*, London: Pinter.

Norton, P. (ed.) (1985) *Parliament in the 1980s*, Oxford: Blackwell.

Thomas, G. (1994) *Parliament: resurgence or decline?* Sheffield: Hallam University.

# Lobbying

Ball, A. and Millard, F. (1986) *Pressure Politics in Industrial Societies*, London: Macmillan.

Berry, S. (1992) 'Lobbyists: techniques of the political insiders' *Parliamentary Affairs* 45 (2) pp. 220–231.

Berry, S. (1993) 'The rise of the professional lobbyist: a cause for concern?' *Political Quarterly* 64 (3) pp. 344–51.

Committee on the Rules of Procedure, the Verification of Credentials and Immunities Report (1992) *European Parliament*, Doc EN/CM/204513 16/03/92.

Halloran, P. and Hollingsworth, M. (1994) *A Bit on the Side*, London: Simon & Schuster.

Jordan, A. G. and Richardson, J. J. (1987) *Government and Pressure Groups in Britain*, Oxford: Clarendon Press.

Mazey, S. and Richardson, J. J. (1993) *Lobbying in the European Community*, Oxford: Oxford University Press.

Richardson, J. J. (1993) *Pressure Groups*, Oxford: Oxford University Press.

Streeck, W. and Schmitter, P. (1991) 'From national corporatism to transnational pluralism: organised interests in the single European market' *Politics and Society* 19 (2) pp. 133–64.

Wilson, G. K. (1990) *Interest Groups*, Oxford: Blackwell.

# The regions

Anderson, B. (1991) *Imagined Communities*, London: Verso.

Aurrecoechea, I. (1989) 'The role of the autonomous communities in the implementation of EC law in Spain' *International and Comparative Law Quarterly* 38 (1) p. 87.

Bulpitt, J. (1983) *Territory and Power in the United Kingdom. An Interpretation*, Manchester: Manchester University Press.

Dunford, M. and Kafkalas, G. (1992) *Cities and Regions in the New Europe*, Brighton: Belhaven Press.

Focus/Devolution in Europe. *The Guardian* 21/01/95.

Harvie, C. (1993) *The Rise of Regional Europe*, London: Routledge.

Hechter, M. (1975) *Internal Colonialism. The Celtic Fringe in British National Development, 1536–1966*, London: RKP.

Hine, D. (1993) 'Regional and local government' in *Governing Italy the Politics of Bargained Pluralism*, Oxford: Oxford University Press.

Humes IV, S. (1991) *Local Governance and National Power*, Hemel Hempstead: Harvester Wheatsheaf.

Keating, M. (1988) *State and Regional Nationalism*, Hemel Hempstead: Harvester Wheatsheaf.

Kingdom, J. (1991) *Local Government and Politics in Britain*, London: Philip Allan.

Loughlin, J. and Mazey, S. (1994) Special Issue: 'Regionalisation in France' *Regional Politics and Policy* 4 (3).

Nairn, T. (1981) *The Break-Up of Britain*, London: Verso.

Newton, M. (1983) 'The peoples and regions of Spain' in *Democratic Politics in Spain* Bell, D. S. (ed.), London: Pinter.

Parkinson, M. (1992) *EC Report on City and Relationship to Regions*, Liverpool: John Moores University.

Rokkan, S. and Urwin, D. (eds) (1982) *The Politics of Territorial Identity. Studies in European Regionalism*, London: Sage.

Rokkan, S. and Urwin, D. (1983) *Economy, Territory, Identity. Politics of West European Peripheries*, London: Sage.

Schmidt, V. (1990) *Democratizing France. The Political and Administrative History of Decentralization*, Cambridge: Cambridge University Press.

Spotts, F. and Wieser, M. (1991) 'Regional devolution and the problem of the South' in *Italy: A Difficult Democracy*, Cambridge: Cambridge University Press.

## Notes

1. Policy style is also defined as the interaction between (a) the government's approach to policy problem-solving and (b) the relationship between government and other actors in the policy process. See Richardson, J. (1982) *Policy Styles in Western Europe*, London: Allen & Unwin. One of the first attempts to consider this issue of a common European 'policy style' was in Heisler and Kvavik (1974).
2. Hayward in Richardson, 1982.
3. For example, there is a provision within the German Basic Law (constitution) (*Grundgesetz*) forbidding the participation of German troops outside Europe's borders (Article 24, Clause 2). This article was drafted in the immediate aftermath of the Second World War. As Germany has grown in economic importance and particularly after the unification of the country in 1990, there were more and more calls for the country to take its full share of political responsibility in the world commensurate with its economic power. The Gulf War in early 1991 and other events have forced the German government to rethink its position on this aspect of the Constitution. In 1994 The Federal Constitutional Court (**Bundesverfassunsgericht**), decided that German troops could participate in peace-keeping units with the United Nations.
4. The system of Administrative Trainees (ATs) in the British Civil Service is the method by which the 'super-elite' is selected and trained in the 'fast track' for the most senior administrative positions.
5. Beetham, 1987, p. 58.
6. *Ibid.*, p. 59.
7. The role of these 'cabinets', in effect ministerial think-tanks made up of chosen and trusted advisers, has been contrasted with British ministers' position where there is still over-reliance on the civil service for counsel in general. One change in British system has been the growth of private think-tanks, such as the right-wing Adam Smith Institute and the more left-inclined Institute for Public Policy Research, which both major political parties have relied on to float ideas on all aspects of policy.
8. Wright, 1989, p. 112. The presence of civil servants in office contrasts with the British situation where many local government employees are barred from participating in politics.
9. The British system of vetting candidates for higher level posts in the civil service consisted of a committee of three wise men, whose job was to weed out those with dubious political affiliations or homosexuals.
10. Smith, 1986, pp. 69–72.
11. House of Commons Treasury and Civil Service Committee Interim Report, July (1993) quoted in *Economist* 19/03/94.
12. *Guardian*, 09/01/91.
13. Wright, 1989, p. 122.
14. Ardagh, 1988, pp. 88–98.
    But not all Enarques lead a charmed life as the example of Jean-Yves Haberer, chairman of Crédit Lyonnais, illustrates. Under his chairmanship Crédit Lyonnais lost about £20 bn. Their network is pervasive. For example, Jacques Chirac, leader of the RPR, handed over

the premiership to Michel Rocard from the PS in 1988 and addressed him as 'tu', since they had been in the same class at ENA. Others of the 50 or so annual graduates include the historian Bernard Minc, whose latest work *Le nouveau moyen âge* has become a popular analysis of contemporary societies, and Jacques Attali, former head of the European Bank for Reconstruction and Development. Source: Nicholas Faith, *Independent on Sunday*, 8/5/94.

15. *Ibid.*, p. 166.
16. Anne Stevens in Howorth and Cerny, 1981, p. 117.
17. Wright, 1989, p. 121.
18. *Ibid.*, p. 113.
19. Hine, 1993, p. 240.
20. Furlong, P. (1994) *Modern Italy. Representation and Reform*, London: Routledge.
21. Gillespie in Urwin and Paterson, 1990, p. 237.
22. Part of the explanation for this occupation of administrative posts by PSOE was to offset the continued influence of the *Franquistas* who had not been purged from their posts in government departments by the Suarez government in the late 1970s.
23. Hooper, 1995, Chapter 17.
24. These reforms were introduced as a result of two main initiatives during the 1980s. The first was The Financial Management Initiative set up in 1982 to improve financial management in Whitehall departments, and the second stemmed from Sir Robin Ibbs' report *The Next Steps* (1988), which proposed the creation of agencies. The effect of the creation of agencies has been to split the civil service into two distinct parts with a core of secure and relatively well-paid middle to senior rank civil servants, and a periphery of a much larger number of civil servants working under more insecure and less well-paid conditions of service. The whole emphasis of the reforms fits in with the neo-liberal market approach of creating a more flexible service, less unified and cheaper labour force. Dowding, K. (1993) 'Managing the Civil Service' in *Managing the United Kingdom* Maidment, R. and Thompson, G. (eds) Milton Keynes: Open University.
25. *Guardian*, 30/04/91.
26. Plowden, W. (1992) in *New Anatomy of Britain* Sampson, A. (ed.) London: Hodder & Stoughton questions whether civil servants are guardians of the public interest.
27. Wright, 1989, p. 123.
28. *Guardian*, 28/4/94 and 07/03/95.
29. *Guardian*, 17/05/94 and 08/09/94.
30. Lintner, V. and Mazey, S. (1991) *The European Community: Economic and Political Aspects*, London: McGraw-Hill, pp. 160–1.
31. Liebert, U. (1990) 'Parliament as a central site in democratic consolidation: a preliminary exploration' in *Parliament and Democratic Consolidation in Southern Europe* Liebert, U. and Cotta, M. (eds) London: Pinter, p. 3.
32. *Ibid.*, p. 13.
33. 'One of the most striking characteristics of the Fifth Republic is the relatively weak position of parliament'. Wright, 1989, p. 132. See also references in the section on lobbying, where most writers argue that within the British system the role of the MP and parliament have been reduced.
34. Liebert and Cotta, 1990, p. 13.
35. Norton, P. (ed.) (1985) *Parliament in the 1980s*, Oxford: Blackwell.
36. Berry, S. (1993) 'The rise of the professional lobbyist: a cause for concern?' *Political Quarterly* 64 (3) pp. 344–51. The whole question of the role and influence of interest groups and lobbying is not new in the United Kingdom. Writing in 1958 Samuel Finer noted: 'Their day-to-day activities pervade every sphere of domestic policy, every day, every way, at

every nook and cranny of government'. Finer, S. (1958) *Anonymous Empire* London: Pall Mall in Sampson, A. (1971) *The New Anatomy of Britain*, London: Hodder & Stoughton.

37. Hollingsworth, M. (1991) *MPs for Hire – The secret world of political lobbying*, London: Bloomsbury.
38. Berry, S. (1992) 'Lobbyists: Techniques of the political insiders' *Parliamentary Affairs* 45 (2) pp. 220–31.
39. Wilson, 1990, p. 1.
40. Gillespie in Urwin and Paterson, 1990, p. 244.
41. The National Economic Development Organisation (NEDO) or 'Neddy' as it was affectionately called, brought together the government, the Employers and Trade Unions. It was a forum to discuss the national economic picture, and as a consultative body was an indication of the partnership of the three main groups. It played less and less role after 1979, and is no longer a functioning body.
42. *Guardian*, 10/12/93.
43. *Independent on Sunday*, 06/03/94.
44. The case of opposition to the M11 extension in East London and M77 bypass in Glasgow show that groups can promote self-organisation. *Independent on Sunday*, 12/02/95.
45. Mazey and Richardson, 1993.
46. This figure includes not only those members of respective federations but also those working for lobby firms. Report on Open and Structured Dialogue. OJEC 93/C 63/02. This report is concerned first with establishing a code of conduct for officials in their dealings with lobbyists, to prevent a conflict of interests arising from the 'revolving door' syndrome, whereby Commission officials may leave their civil service employment for more lucrative positions in the commercial sector. This has become a profitable route both for former senior civil servants and former government ministers in the United Kingdom, particularly in the case of ministers who have exchanged their seats in the Cabinet for one in the boardroom of those newly privatised public utility industries which they were themselves instrumental in selling off. See also Report on Increased Transparency, OJEC 93/C 63/03. The Commission is also attempting to reduce the 'democratic deficit' of the Commission by opening up the process of the legislative process.
47. Mazey and Richardson, 1993, p. 7.
48. For a full discussion of the relative importance of the *Länder* and the EU, see the special issue of *German Politics* 'Federalism, Unification and European Integration' 1 (3).
49. Cole, A. (1993) 'The Presidential Party and the Vth Republic' *WEP* 16 (2), pp. 62–74.
50. Wright, 1990, p. 12.
51. Mitterrand invoked this article during a televised broadcast in 1986, to demonstrate his central role within the political system.
52. Wright, 1990, p. 71.
53. Although a reduction in the term from 7 to 5 years was part of Mitterrand's campaign during the 1988 Presidential elections there was no attempt to institute this reform once elected. It was also part of the campaign promises of the Balladur candidacy during the 1995 presidential elections.
54. Whenever Chirac was about to launch a major policy intitiative, Mitterrand would don his international statesman's hat and fly off to some meeting abroad to distract media attention from the prime minister. Mitterrand also challenged the basis of the Gaullists' nationalisation programme by wrapping himself in the national flag, and refusing to sign the necessary *ordonnances*.
55. W. Hennis in the 1950s characterised the Chancellor's position in the following terms: 'The powers of the office leave nothing to be desired. At the moment of this election his stallion

is bridled and saddled; he only needs to be able to ride it'. Hennis had a different view in 1984, saying that the term originated out of an overconcentration on Adenauer's chancellorship, and was devised as a warning of too much executive power.

56. Edinger, L. (1977) *Politics in West Germany*, New York: Little Brown, p. 189.

57. It is a feature of government ministers that most stay within their various ministries for long periods of time, and tend to have some kind of technical competence in their particular post. The finance minister will normally have studied some economics, and for example, Klaus Kinkel, the Foreign Minister from 1992–94, was a career diplomat. This contrasts with the more 'musical chairs' scenario of the British Cabinet reshuffle, and the continued notion of the 'gifted amateur'.

58. Paterson, W. (1981) 'The Chancellor and his Party: political leadership in the Federal Republic' *West European Politics*, vol. 4 no. 2, pp. 3–17.

59. Webber, D. (1992) 'Kohl's **Wendepolitik** after a decade' *German Politics* 1 (2), pp. 149–80.

60. *Guardian*, 09/07/90; *Die Zeit*, 2–6/1/89.

61. Smith, G. (1986) *Democracy in Western Germany*, Aldershot: Gower, pp. 202–4.

62. Kenneth Clarke, who became Chancellor of the Exchequer after the sacking of Norman Lamont in 1992, has in his time also been Secretary of State for Education and Secretary of State for Health and Social Services. Another example is Stephen Dorrell, Financial Secretary to the Treasury from 1992–94 (the third most important political position in that department) who said: 'I am glad to say, as an ex-Treasury minister, that I have never attended an economics lecture in my life'. *Guardian*, 14/11/94.

63. It is ironic in this context to note that during the 1980s, Thatcher was forced to rely on the traditional loyalty of large numbers of unrepresentative 'good chaps' in the House of Lords to carry through some of the most contentious aspects of her programme, particularly over the abolition of the GLC and the Inner London Education Authority.

64. Lord Hailsham, for a long time the most senior judicial figure in the country, had warned during the Labour government of the late 1970s that the United Kingdom faced the danger of authoritarianism from that party's style and content of government. He was remarkably silent during the 1980s when he held high office, as one representative institution after another was abolished.

65. *Financial Times*, 09/11/94.

66. Concern over the use or misuse of taxpayers' money has surfaced on numerous occasions, with allegations that money in Wales was channelled to marginal constituencies to ensure support for the Conservative party. *Financial Times*, 01/06/94.

67. Stewart, J. (1994) in *Ego Trip: Extra-governmental Organisations in the UK and their Accountability* Weir, S. and Hall, W. (eds) London: Democratic Audit and Charter 88 Trust.

68. *Independent*, 3/4/94.

69. William Waldegrave, *Independent*, 22/5/94.

70. The legacy can also be traced back to the time of unification when, despite some federalist movements, the fear was that any great devolution of power would threaten the integrity of the new state. It is also interesting to note that it was the DC which was most in favour of devolution in the late 1940s, whereas the PCI and PSI were both in favour of a more centralised state structure. In fact it has been the left-wing parties that have gained from the regional level of government and provided it with its best successes.

71. See Capo Giol *et al* in Liebert and Cotta, 1990.

72. The authors are grateful to Nigel Nicholson for permission to quote from his final year dissertation on corruption in the Spanish political system for this section. This highly original work uses extensive print media analysis to analyse the current situation of corruption within the Spanish state.

73. As we have explained elsewhere in this chapter, one of the main reasons for PSOE's rapid takeover of state institutions was the need to counteract the continued presence of ex-Franco appointees still in leading positions within government ministries.

74. The deputy leader of PSOE Alfonso Guerra had declared in 1985 that Montesquieu was dead, prompting several commentators to urge the electorate in the 1993 General Election to consider those classic Montesquieu principles of separation of powers when they came to decide how to vote.

75. *El Mundo*, 22/3/90, p. 21.

76. The result has been that the opposition parties get equal time coverage but not equal quality, 'with the highlights of a speech by Gonzalez followed by a standing ovation cut to scenes of Aznar picking his nose'. Nicholson, unpublished dissertation, p. 41. PSOE does not have a total monopoly of media control, as the examples of Galician and Catalan broadcast media indicate.

77. The predominance of Paris and its Ile-de-France region has been a constant problem for real and effective decentralisation in France. Jean-François Gravier's book **Paris et le désert français**, published in 1947, highlighted this huge disequilibrium, and the evidence is that despite all the attempts to promote regional government, Paris remains pre-eminent. See also Scargill, I. (1995) 'L'aménagement du territoire: the great debate' *Modern and Contemporary France* NS 3 (1) pp. 19–28.

78. There are 22 regions in Metropolitan France and four overseas regions: Guadeloupe, Guyana, Martinique and Réunion.

79. Another issue concerning these 'pôles' of development is that they create the same effect at a regional level that Paris does at a national level (see note 14). The cities act as magnets for investment and employment, causing further rural depopulation and desertification, with each surrounding area becoming a 'désert' of its own.

80. This acceptance by all parties of the key role of the state is explored by Hazareesingh in Chapter 6 'The strengths and limits of the **étatiste** tradition' Hazareesingh, S. *Political Traditions in Modern France* Oxford: Oxford University Press. Citing De Tocqueville, who saw this tradition of strong interventionist role for the state originating in the period of absolute monarchies in France, Hazareesingh notes its all encompassing role in French life (Louis XIV 'L'État, c'est moi'). In France, most large new roadbuilding schemes have a large sign with words to the effect that here the state is investing for your future (*Ici l'État investit pour votre avenir*). This image and reality of the state as a benign influence has been reinforced by the almost 'hegemonic position' of the bureaucratic elite in France formed in the *Grandes Écoles*. This has been based on the extremely centralised nature of the French state, which was established by the Jacobins after the Revolution and which Napoleon consolidated. 'From the apex of the administration to its lowest level, a firm chain of command was conceived within the state, locking all its agents into a rigidly centralised system' (p. 159). The key symbol of this central power was the **préfet**.

81. Wright, 1989, p. 322.

82. Schmidt, V. (1990) *Democratizing France. The Political and Administrative History of Decentralization*, Cambridge: Cambridge University Press.

83. See Loughlin, J. and Mazey, S. (1995) *The End of the French Unitary State? Ten Years of Regionalisation in France 1982–1992*, London: Frank Cass.

84. Roberts, C. (1987) 'Local government decentralisation in France: the power of local notables and the limits of reform' *Modern and Contemporary France* 31, pp. 19–29.

85. See further Church, C. (1995) 'The effects of the Channel Tunnel – a provisional balance sheet' *Modern and Contemporary France* NS 3 (1) pp. 29–39.

86. Ardagh, J. (1988) *Germany and the Germans*, Harmondsworth: Penguin, p. 25.

87. 'One great advantage of the Bundesrat is that since it is composed of active local politicians and has an integral function in central government, it has managed to avoid the fate of other upper houses, namely becoming more and more of a final resting home for elder statesman'. von Beyme, K. (1980) *Das Politische System der Bundesrepublik Deutschland*, Bonn: Piper & Co. Verlag.

88. Under article 2 of the German ratification law of the Maastricht Treaty, the *Länder* must be informed by the *Bund* of all EC proposals in which they have an interest, and they have the right to attend Community meetings in those policy areas where they have competence. They attend those meetings as full members of the German delegation. The *Bundesrat* has also set up a special committee to monitor all legislation emanating from Brussels (a similar committee exists in the House of Lords). For further details of the nature of this relationship see Christiansen Thomas (1992) 'The Länder between Bonn and Brussels: the dilemma of German Federalism in the 1990s' *German Politics* 1 (2), pp. 239–63.

89. This section on Belgium relies heavily on Bart Deelen's (1994) article 'Will Belgium survive its Constitutional Reforms?' in *Dutch Crossing, A Journal of Low Country Studies* 18 (1), pp. 3–19.

90. Once the tax revenue falls below a certain threshold the Federal Government is obliged to intervene to help the region, known as 'the federal solidarity mechanism' *Ibid.*, p. 14. This is a common feature of federal systems. See section on economics of regions.

91. Communities and regions can sign international treaties, maintain separate representation abroad and have a range of new powers in undertaking foreign trade. For example, the Dutch government now deals directly with the Flemish government in discussion concerning the route of the high-speed rail link between Amsterdam and Brussels; Deelen, 1994, p. 10.

92. This 'alarm bell procedure' can be instituted if three-quarters of the Francophone group considers that any law is against its interests.

93. 'A nation is splitting apart – will anyone notice?'. The title of an article in the *Independent*, 20/05/95, suggested that the dissolution of the Belgian state was now an inevitable process, and by its peaceful nature could point a useful way for future break-ups of nation states in Europe.

94. Church, C. (1993) The Not so Model Republic? The relevance of Swiss federalism to the European Community, Centre for Federal Studies, University of Leicester Discussion Paper No. FS93/4.

95. *Ibid.*, p. 10.

96. Britain, or Great Britain refers to the island comprising England, Scotland and Wales. The United Kingdom of Great Britain and Northern Ireland is the nation state form (UK).

97. In order to introduce a tramway in Croydon, for example, the local authority had to have the necessary legislation passed in parliament.

98. England now comprises 10 regions: London, South-East, Eastern, South-West, West Midlands, East Midlands, Merseyside, North-West, Yorkshire and Humberside and the North-East. Scotland, Wales and Northern Ireland remain separate regions.

99. This is, of course, not the only indicator of regional difference, and readers should bear in mind that there is considerable debate in the United Kingdom about the measurement of unemployment, many observers claiming that official data seriously underestimates the true level of joblessness.

100. Certain parts of London, for example, are extremely poor, while the South-East is one of the richest parts of the United Kingdom.

101. *Economist*, 14/08/93.

102. Crouch, C. and Marquand, D. (eds) (1989) *The New Centralism: Britain out of step in Europe?*

Oxford: Blackwell. The process has also been referred to as 'authoritarian populism' (Stuart Hall).

103. Coyle, C. and Sinnott, R. (1992) 'Europe and the Regions in Ireland: A View from Below'. Working Paper no. 5, Centre for European Economic and Public Affairs. University College, Dublin.

104. The five special regions were Sicilia, Sardegna, Trentino-Alto Adige, Friuli-Venezia Giulia and the Valle d'Aosta.

105. Spotts and Wieser, 1991, p. 227.

106. Hine, 1993, p. 258.

107. 'Italy remains a country of countries, a land of contrasts far greater than that of any other European nation'. Spotts and Wieser, 1991, p. 222.

108. Clark, R. P. (1983) 'The question of regional autonomy in Spain's democratic transition' in Bell, D. S. (ed.) *Democratic Politics in Spain*, London: Pinter. Clark notes the reluctance of the Socialist government in the mid-1980s to pursue further devolution of powers based on a desire to ensure uniformity of provision for all ACs, avoiding special treatment particularly for Catalonia and the Basque province, and the need to maintain 'residual sovereignty' at the centre; p. 151.

109. Preston, P. (1990) *The Triumph of Democracy in Spain*, London: Routledge, pp. 135–6, 163.

110. For a fuller treatment of recent developments and the EU dimension see Morata, F. (1993) 'Regions and the European Community: a comparative analysis of four Spanish regions' in *The Regions in the European Community* Leonardi, R. (ed.), London: Cass.

111. The AC parliaments are elected usually every 4 years by a system of proportional representation. Municipal elections also take place on a 4-yearly cycle, when councillors are elected for the 8000 municipalities. These councillors in turn elect a mayor, and also choose the provincial deputies, who then elect the presidents of the Provincial Deputations, the executive organ of each province. Another form of local government organisation has been established since 1987, the *mancomunicad* which are associations of local authorities which work together usually in the larger cities like Barcelona and Valencia to cooperate in the areas of public works and services.

112. Black, M. (1994) Regions and Localities, CES unpublished Dissertation, University of North London.

113. *El Mundo*, 14/09/94.

## CHAPTER ELEVEN

# The social dimension

Think globally, act locally

GANDHI

## 11.1   Introduction

This chapter provides the substantive evidence for some of the theoretical perspectives presented in Chapter 4. Within this context, issues concerning the welfare state in Europe are considered first. This is followed by a presentation of demographic factors and a focus on the role of the family (provision of child care and domestic roles) as it affects the position of women. The growing participation of women in the labour force is also analysed. In previous chapters we have looked at economic growth and development in some European countries and the relative affluence of European societies. We now consider the other side of the coin with a brief section on inequality and poverty, which relates back to the debate about the growth of an underclass (see Section 4.3 in Chapter 4). The section on ethnicity and racism develops some of the issues raised in Chapter 4. Finally, we examine briefly social policy at the EU level and then provide a conclusion.

In considering changing class composition we shall analyse the way in which those societies have managed issues concerning the welfare state in terms of employment, income distribution and social security. Our focus is on the nature of European societies, concentrating on the unity and diversity that exist in the respective societies.[1]

## 11.2   Issues in social policy: challenges to the welfare state

The changing social composition of all European societies and demographic trends have had important effects on employment, income, income distribution and social welfare provisions. The history and rationale for the welfare state is presented first, followed by an analysis of its current state.

Ever since Bismarck's reforms in the late nineteenth century, industrialised societies faced the need to provide some kind of social insurance to cope with the effects of the free market economy. Reform or revolution has been one of the key issues in the political and economic debate. The experience of the inter-war years and particularly the Great Depression of the 1930s led many people in the industrialised world to consider new ways in which the social cohesion of society could be maintained, and social tensions eased. The debate between equality and liberty, in terms of the role of the state or voluntary agencies or charities often in the form of employers' largesse in providing social welfare, became the great challenge between capitalism and communism.

Indeed, Bismarck's reforms need to be seen in the context of the growing influence of the labour movement in the political arena, through trade unions and socialist and social democratic parties. The reforms of Lloyd George in Britain in the early 1900s were influenced by the German experience, and are an indication of the concern to mitigate the worst effects of capitalism in order to forestall revolutionary tendencies in working class movements.

The major debate, then, was between a demand for equality from the communist camp based on a class analysis of society, and the concerns of other groups such as the socialist and social democratic movements for the liberal democratic state to provide some kind of equal rights which can be seen under the heading of citizenship rights. For Marxists these individual rights concealed the real nature of the capitalist system, while for other left and moderate right groups they represented the desired balance between individual freedoms and the state, between the regulated sphere of state activity and the more voluntary sphere of civil society (see Section 3.8 in Chapter 3).

As we indicated in Chapter 3, according to Marshall the arrival of social rights moderated the worst effects of capitalism, and greater equality of status has been introduced. In the consideration of the welfare state, we are concerned with notions about social citizenship. As Marshall underlined, the social aspect of citizen rights has been the most recent development; but even this notion of **social citizenship** is open to some criticism, on the grounds that it has only related to a specific group of people, namely working class men in employment, with a large degree of unionisation. Other groups such as women and people from ethnic communities have been excluded from some or all the benefits of the welfare system.[2]

The other side of the coin of social citizenship, that is being able to participate in a society by virtue of the enjoyment of certain rights, is social exclusion. In the European context the term 'social exclusion' comes primarily from the approach in France to the poor which focuses on 'relational' issues. This concerns a group or individual's lack of power stemming from the systematic way in which they are marginalised in their societies and unable to participate fully in them, as a result of unemployment, low pay and poor social facilities (poor housing, education and health care). In the Anglo-Saxon approach, poverty is seen as a question of 'distributional' issues concerning the availability or lack of material resources.[3] In the sections on gender and ethnicity, various data indicate that equality between men and women is still a long way off in many areas, and for ethnic minority women there exists a double discrimination.

In terms of our themes of unity and diversity in European societies, the welfare state provides an interesting picture of various different models. Esping-Andersen (1990) identifies three main models: the Scandinavian welfare states, the 'Bismarck' countries and the Anglo-Saxon countries. Leibfried (1993) adds a fourth model: the 'Latin rim' countries.

The Scandinavian system has been based on the view that everybody has the right to work, with the state seeing itself as the main facilitator of employment opportunities. The whole strategy is designed to provide full employment, underpinned by a wide provision of benefits. It is worthwhile noting that much of the opposition of the Scandinavian countries to entry into the European Union has been based on the concern that the EU welfare regime is substantially less developed and less generous than their own systems. This attitude contrasts vividly with the British Conservative Government opposition to the social provisions of the Maastricht treaty and other EU instruments, which are considered to be too generous. We see in this context the divide between traditional social democratic approaches to welfare, and the more recent neo-liberal approach of right-wing governments.

The 'Bismarck' countries' (Germany and Austria) systems of social welfare have developed around the world of work, rather than the poor. The protection has been geared towards the mainly male working class, concentrating on conditions at work and providing adequate compensation and support in the event of unemployment. The welfare state is seen not as the employer (cf. Scandinavian model), but 'the compensator of first resort' (Leibfried, 1993). It is the first part of this approach that has been prominent until recently in social policy developments at the EU level (see below).

Social welfare protection systems in the United Kingdom, Australia, New Zealand and the United States (the Anglo-Saxon model) have stressed the basic safety net approach, coupled with an element of coercion to force people back onto the labour market. This coercion has taken the form of setting very minimal benefit levels, rather than in the other two models above which relied on more positive training and employment provision to ease people back onto the labour market. The welfare state is seen more as a 'compensator of last resort' (Leibfried, 1993).

Finally, the 'Latin Rim' countries, which include Spain, Portugal, Greece, Southern Italy and, to a limited degree France, have 'rudimentary welfare states' (Leibfried, 1993). In most cases there is no right to welfare, but the systems operate in a context where the Catholic Church has provided and continues to provide much institutional support, and where the family is expected to participate in many areas of care, for example substitute-nursing in hospital. The increasing urbanisation of these societies means that family care is now no longer so readily available, and all these countries have attempted to institute more universal provision. Castles (1995), like Leibfried, considers that:

the nations of Southern Europe cannot be considered inherently different from the core countries of Western Europe in their potential for welfare development . . . and may be seen as having been prevented from achieving that potential by a syndrome of political and economic underdevelopment inherited from the past.[4]

In the late twentieth century the demands of the welfare state, which consumes an enormous percentage of public expenditure in all European countries, has reached a point of crisis. This has been due to a number of factors:

(a)   The increased demand for welfare provision that has resulted from increased unemployment (see Chapter 7), from social changes such as the increase that has taken place in the number of single parents (see below), and to an extent from increased expectations.

(b)   The prospect of even greater demand for welfare into the twenty-first century as European populations age (and live longer). This, coupled with low fertility rates in many European countries (see below), is likely to significantly increase dependency ratios.

(c)   An increasing reluctance on the part of tax payers in many countries to pay the contributions that are required to fund welfare systems. Added to this pressure are the attempts that many European countries are making to cut public spending in order to meet the Maastricht Treaty's convergence criteria (see Chapter 5) and thus qualify for any future EU monetary union. Funding pressures are likely to be exacerbated by the increases in dependency ratios referred to above.

(d)   The change that has taken place since the mid-1970s from a welfare model of capitalism towards a more free-market-based, neo-liberal approach to economic organisation (see Chapters 2, 5, 6 and 7). It will be recalled (Chapter 2) that many believe there to be a trade-off in market economies between equity and efficiency. Thus, in the eyes of neo-liberal economists, a generous system of welfare provides a disincentive to work and fosters what is often referred to as a 'dependency culture', which facilitates unemployment as well as having a deleterious effect on economic performance in general. There are thus ideological pressures to cut welfare as part of the neo-liberal agenda, which in turn has arguably increased demand for welfare by increasing unemployment. This whole issue is a contentious one. For example, Pfaller *et al.* (1991) suggest that the maintenance of welfare provisions may have some depressing effects on the international performance of some capitalist countries. This does not always hold, and some of the evidence points to countries like Sweden and Germany, for example, being able to maintain welfare expenditure and remain internationally competitive.

However, despite Pfaller's findings most West European countries are in the process of cutting back on welfare expenditure. The example of Germany is useful in illustrating the issues about the high cost of maintaining a welfare system, and its effect on the international competitiveness of a country's economy. The challenge from the NICs and the (partly) consequent move towards free market capitalism is one of the key forces driving this policy of retrenchment. It is not only the NICs in the Pacific Rim, but also countries in East/Central Europe, where wage rates are usually a tenth of those in western European countries. Recent proposals in Germany include measures to cut earnings related unemployment benefit to 2 years. In the United Kingdom this benefit was cut during the 1980s. These cuts are deemed necessary because otherwise, according to the government, unemployment pay-ments would have trebled from DM7.1 bn in 1991 to DM20 bn in 1995. Under the current system an unemployed worker with one child, and an unemployed worker with no children, get 67 per cent and 60 per cent, respectively, of their final net income for a period of between 6–32 months, after that dole money of 57 per cent and 53 per cent respectively. The new plans propose cutting this earnings-related factor to a maximum of 2 years. Furthermore, those with no entitlement would receive no dole.[5] A further indication of the extent to which welfare states in all European countries are now under pressure are the moves to shift pension provision from the public sector to the private sector – Europeans are now being urged (and often given incentives) to buy private pensions. Since these privatised pensions are almost invariably linked to stock market performance, we must hope that the long-term performance of such markets is sufficiently good to ensure the standard of living of future European pensioners.

## 11.3   Demography: migration and urbanisation

One of the most significant aspects of the development of European societies since 1945 has been the process of large-scale urbanisation, which has resulted from economic transformation. The effects of this process have been numerous, including the decline of rural communities, the break-up of extended family networks/relations, the increase in the number of women in paid employment in the cities, and the changing roles within families.

Tables 11.1 and 11.2 indicate the current situation as far as population in the EU is concerned. The most significant features are the continued fall in the birth rate and a declining fertility rate. Most of the countries in the EU now rely on in-migration for any population growth.

The great migrations of the 1960s and 1970s from outside and within the EU member states have declined, although there is still the concern that large-scale movements of people from East Central Europe and beyond, and from the North African countries may put pressure on some member states' infrastructure. Most of the worst-case scenarios have now been revised to suggest that there may be some in-migration but it will not be the flood that was predicted.[6] Nevertheless, it is clear that most of those people who have migrated to western Europe since 1945 will remain and form part of the changing composition of European populations.

Overall, European populations are increasingly urbanised, with more than two-thirds of western Europe's population living in urban areas with populations over 300 000.[7] The cycle of development has tended to be urbanisation, suburbanisation, deurbanisation and reurbanisation. This process has been most marked in the North European states but the pattern of development is starting to converge in the Southern states.

In France, for example, there has been a massive rural exodus since the 1950s reflected in the very low levels of population densities in some *départements* such as the Lozère in the centre of the country. This exodus has to some extent now stopped, and much of rural France is now being occupied by house buyers from Northern Europe. The long-term effects of this process, together with the Common Agricultural Policies of the EC in terms of 'set-aside', remain to be seen.[8] It could end in large parts of the country being turned back into forest, and thereby threaten the traditional

**Table 11.1** Population change in 1993 – EUR 12 and EEA²
Source: Eurostat.

| | Population 1.1.1994³ | Births | Deaths | Natural increase | Net migration | Total increase | Birth | Mortality | Natural increase | Net migration | Total increase |
|---|---|---|---|---|---|---|---|---|---|---|---|
| | | | (1000) | | | | | | (per 1000 inhabitants) | | |
| B | 10 101.0 | 120.0 | 107.0 | 13.0 | 19.0 | 32.7 | 11.9 | 10.6 | 1.3 | 1.9 | 3.2 |
| DK | 5196.6 | 67.4 | 62.9 | 4.5 | 11.1 | 16.0 | 13.0 | 12.1 | 0.9 | 2.1 | 3.1 |
| D | 81 352.6 | 795.0 | 890.9 | -95.9 | 473.9 | 378.0 | 9.8 | 11.0 | -1.2 | 5.8 | 4.7 |
| GR | 10 390.0 | 102.0 | 97.0 | 5.0 | 39.0 | 44.0 | 9.8 | 9.4 | 0.5 | 3.8 | 4.2 |
| E | 39 168.2 | 388.7 | 339.2 | 49.5 | 4.5* | 54.0 | 9.9 | 8.7 | 1.3 | 0.1 | 1.4 |
| F | 57 800.1 | 710.3 | 530.1 | 180.2 | 90.0 | 270.2 | 12.3 | 9.2 | 3.1 | 1.6 | 4.7 |
| IRL | 3571.0 | 48.9 | 31.0 | 17.8 | -6.0 | 11.0 | 13.7 | 8.7 | 5.0 | -1.7 | 3.1 |
| I | 57 153.7 | 537.5 | 541.2 | -3.6 | 194.0 | 193.4 | 9.4 | 9.5 | -0.1 | 3.4 | 3.4 |
| L | 400.9 | 5.4 | 3.9 | 1.4 | 4.2 | 5.7 | 13.4 | 9.8 | 3.6 | 10.7 | 14.3 |
| NL | 15 341.3 | 195.7 | 137.8 | 57.9 | 59.7 | 102.1 | 12.8 | 9.0 | 3.8 | 3.9 | 6.7 |
| P | 9868.0 | 114.0 | 106.4 | 7.6 | 0.8* | 8.4 | 11.6 | 10.8 | 0.8 | 0.1 | 0.9 |
| UK | 58 276.0 | 761.8 | 658.0 | 103.8 | 84.2* | 188.0 | 13.1 | 11.3 | 1.8 | 1.4 | 3.2 |
| **EUR 12** | **348 619.3** | **3846.7** | **3505.4** | **341.3** | **974.4** | **1303.5** | **11.1** | **10.1** | **1.0** | **2.8** | **3.7** |
| A | 8005.9 | 95.3 | 82.5 | 12.8 | 32.0 | 44.8 | 11.9 | 10.3 | 1.6 | 4.0 | 5.6 |
| FIN | 5077.9 | 65.0 | 51.0 | 14.0 | 9.1 | 22.9 | 12.8 | 10.1 | 2.8 | 1.8 | 4.5 |
| IS | 262.4¹ | 4.6¹ | 1.7¹ | 2.9¹ | -0.3¹ | 2.7¹ | 17.7¹ | 6.6¹ | 11.1¹ | -1.0¹ | 10.2¹ |
| N | 4324.8 | 59.7 | 46.1 | 13.5 | 12.5 | 25.6 | 13.8 | 10.7 | 3.1 | 2.9 | 5.9 |
| S | 8745.1 | 117.8 | 97.0 | 20.9 | 31.9 | 53.1 | 13.5 | 11.1 | 2.4 | 3.7 | 6.1 |
| **EEA** | **375 038.1*** | **4189.1*** | **3783.7*** | **405.4*** | **1059.6*** | **1455.2** | **11.2** | **10.1** | **1.1** | **2.8** | **3.9** |
| CH | 6968.6 | 83.7 | 62.4 | 21.4 | 37.6 | 60.6 | 12.1 | 9.0 | 3.1 | 5.4 | 8.7 |
| FL | 30.5 | 0.4¹ | 0.2¹ | 0.2¹ | 0.3¹ | 0.6¹ | 12.4¹ | 6.0¹ | 6.5¹ | 9.5¹ | 19.8 |

(Rates)

* Eurostat estimate.
¹ 1992.
² Provisional data.
³ Resident population for Italy. Including administrative corrections for the Netherlands.

**Table 11.2** Main demographic indicators, 1993 – EUR 12 and EAA[7]
Source: Eurostat.

| | Average population 1993 (1000) | Fertility | | Marriages | | Divorces | | Mortality | | | |
|---|---|---|---|---|---|---|---|---|---|---|---|
| | | Total fertility[4] | % of births outside marriage (1000) | Marriages (1000) | Crude marriage rate[5] | Divorces (1000) | Divorces per 1000 population | Deaths under one year | Infant mortality rate[6] | Live expectancy at birth Males (years) | Females (years) |
| B | 10 084.7 | 1.61* | 11.3[3] | 54.2 | 5.4 | 21.6 | 2.1 | 962 | 8.0 | 73.1[1] | 79.8[1] |
| DK | 5189.4 | 1.75* | 46.4[1] | 30.5 | 5.9 | 12.6 | 2.4 | 444[1] | 6.6[1] | 72.6[1] | 77.9[1] |
| D | 81 187.3 | 1.30 | 14.6 | 441.3 | 5.4 | 135.0[1] | 1.7[1] | 4600 | 5.8 | 72.9 | 79.3 |
| GR | 10 368.0 | 1.38 | 2.7 | 61.0 | 5.9 | 7.2 | 0.7 | 850 | 8.3 | 74.6[1] | 79.8[1] |
| E | 39 141.2 | 1.24 | 10.0[2] | 201.7 | 5.2 | 26.8[1] | 0.7[1] | 2971 | 7.6 | 73.3[2] | 80.5[2] |
| F | 57 664.9 | 1.65 | 33.2[1] | 253.3 | 4.4 | 108.1[2] | 1.9[2] | 4557 | 6.4 | 73.3 | 81.5 |
| IRL | 3563.3 | 2.03[1] | 18.0[1] | 16.1[1] | 4.5[1] | — | — | 344[1] | 6.7[1] | 72.6[1] | 78.2[1] |
| I | 57 057.0 | 1.21 | 7.2 | 292.2 | 5.1 | 22.4 | 0.4 | 3963 | 7.4 | 73.6[2] | 80.3[2] |
| B | 398.1 | 1.70* | 12.9 | 2.4 | 6.0 | 0.7[1] | 1.8[1] | 44[1] | 8.5[1] | 71.9[1] | 78.4[1] |
| NL | 15 290.2 | 1.57 | 13.1 | 88.3 | 5.8 | 30.6 | 2.0 | 1222 | 6.2 | 74.0 | 80.0 |
| P | 9863.8 | 1.53* | 17.0 | 68.2 | 6.9 | 12.3 | 1.2 | 996 | 8.7 | 70.7[1] | 78.1[1] |
| UK | 58 182.0 | 1.82* | 30.8[1] | 349.7[2] | 6.1[2] | 173.5[2] | 3.0[2] | 5141[1] | 6.6[1] | 73.6 | 79.1 |
| **EUR 12** | **347 989.9** | **1.44*** | **20.0[1]** | **1838.6*** | **5.3*** | **556.8[1]** | **1.6[1]** | **25 900*** | **6.7[1]** | **72.9[2]** | **79.5[2]** |
| A | 7986.0 | 1.51 | 26.3 | 45.0 | 5.6 | 16.4 | 2.1 | 619 | 6.5 | 73.2 | 79.7 |
| FIN | 5066.4 | 1.82 | 28.9[1] | 23.7 | 4.7 | 12.3 | 2.4 | 285 | 4.4 | 71.7[1] | 79.4[1] |
| IS | 261.1[1] | 2.21[1] | 57.3[1] | 1.2[1] | 4.7[1] | 0.5[1] | 2.0[1] | 22[1] | 4.8[1] | 76.7[1] | 80.7[1] |
| N | 4312.0 | 1.82* | 44.4 | 19.3[1] | 4.5[1] | 10.2[1] | 2.4[1] | 346[1] | 5.8[1] | 74.2[1] | 80.3[1] |
| S | 8718.6 | 2.00 | 49.6 | 33.9 | 3.9 | 21.7 | 2.5 | 648 | 5.5 | 75.5 | 80.8 |
| **EEA** | **374 333.9** | **1.50*** | **21.4[1]** | **1961.7*** | **5.2*** | **617.9*** | **1.7*** | **27 800*** | **6.6*** | **73.3[2]** | **79.9[2]** |
| CH | 6938.3 | 1.48* | 6.3 | 42.9 | 6.2 | 15.1 | 2.2 | 470 | 5.6 | 74.5[1] | 81.3[1] |
| FL | 30.2 | : | 14.7[1] | 0.2[1] | 6.3[1] | 0.0[1] | 1.3[1] | 4[1] | 10.7[1] | : | : |

* Eurostat estimate.
[1] 1992.
[2] 1991.
[3] 1989.
[4] Children per women.
[5] Per 1000 average population.
[6] Per 1000 live births.
[7] Provisional data.

reliance of rural people on agriculture. However, diversification in terms of building leisure centres and golf courses may be one way of maintaining livelihoods, although this may fundamentally alter the nature of that countryside so beloved by tourists.

We have already touched elsewhere in this book on the kinds of changes that urbanisation has brought to Europe. The migration that this entailed, both internally and on an international scale, has wrought immense changes in the structure of European societies. The pace and nature of rural life, steeped as it was in centuries-old traditions, has been totally revolutionised by the introduction of mechanisation and modern fertilisers in farming methods. The consequence has been a massive increase not only in productivity, but also the depopulation of the countryside, as labour has been replacd by machinery and people have moved to the large urban agglomerations in search of work.

This migration has had enormous effects on the family, both in terms of its structure, with more nuclear and less extended types of families, and in terms of its nature with traditional roles being challenged by increasing women's participation in the labour market and demands for emancipation. In contrast to rural life where women were just as involved in farming work as men, urbanisation has provided women with some kind of escape from those ties by enabling financial independence to be achieved and a more independent lifestyle to be chosen. This has also been a result of declining religious belief, with its strictly ordered notions of women's positions and roles, that has been superseded by a growing secularisation and consumerism (children are expensive and so their numbers are restricted, in order for adults to enjoy all the benefits of a mass consumer society). However, as we shall see below the practical measures, for example universal child care facilities, needed to underpin this independence are still a long way off. Women are still expected to carry out much of the child care and domestic chores. Gender inequality is still a predominant feature of societies in western Europe.[9]

## 11.4 Poverty and inequality

Although overall incomes and standards of living have improved enormously for most of the population in the EU since 1945, there are still about 40 million in the EU who live in poverty.[10] Even in the richest EU countries poverty seems to be on the increase,[11] while income inequality has increased in the wake of the increased reliance on markets as allocators of resources. This is particularly true in the United Kingdom, where the neo-liberal economic agenda has been implemented with the greatest enthusiasm. The extent of increasing inequality in the United Kingdom has recently been highlighted by the Rowntree Report (see Chapter 12), and also by Peter Townsend (1993).

Our focus on poverty relates to issues of social inequality and the incidence of social exclusion. People are usually defined as being in poverty in the United Kingdom if they are on 50 per cent of average income, dependent solely on income support or family credit. Similar criteria are applied in other EU countries. However, the definition of poverty is a contentious issue. There are in essence two ways of approaching the measurement and definition of poverty: one can take an **absolute** approach or a **relative** approach.

The absolute approach implies that there is a minimum level of income that is required for people to survive, regardless of the social context in which they live. It is the approach that was adopted in early studies of poverty, for example Rowntree's study of poverty in York (United Kingdom) in 1899, and it usually involves estimating minimum physical requirements of food, clothing, shelter, etc. and then expressing these requirements in monetary form. If your income is less than that required for subsistence, then you are officially poor. The problem with this approach is that need is in fact inevitably related to the social context in which people live – what we require to live 'decent' lives varies according to where we live and changes over time.[12] Thus modern measures of poverty are usually relative; that is, the poverty line is expressed in terms of a proportion of the average income in a society. This can be calculated either on a national basis or on an international basis, for example calculating a European poverty line on the basis of average incomes throughout Europe. The problem with the relative approach, however, is that the definition of poverty increases as standards of living increase, and thus in one sense poverty continues to exist no matter how rich a society becomes. One can then be faced with a situation where somebody who is considered poor in Europe might well be rather rich by third world standards.

Tables 11.3 and 11.4 give an indication of the extent of inequality and poverty in European countries.

It can be seen from these tables that the United Kingdom has been one of the more equal societies in Europe. However, the evidence suggests that this has changed during the course of the 1980s, following the change in economic policy towards more market-orientated policies. This is evident, for example, from the Rowntree Report (Chapter 12), and in addition from *Households Below Average Income* (HMSO 1993/94).

***Table 11.3*** Income inequality in European countries
*Source:* Bailey (1992).

|  | Gini index | Rank order |
|---|---|---|
| Austria | 0.369 | 8 |
| Belgium | 0.340 | 4 |
| Denmark | 0.380 | 9 |
| FR Germany | 0.383 | 10 |
| France | 0.417 | 13 |
| Greece | 0.460 | 14 |
| Ireland | 0.361 | 7 |
| Italy | 0.398 | 11 |
| Netherlands | 0.354 | 5 |
| Norway | 0.307 | 2 |
| Spain | 0.355 | 6 |
| Sweden | 0.302 | 1 |
| Switzerland | 0.401 | 12 |
| UK | 0.318 | 3 |

*Source:* Bailey, J. (1992).

**Table 11.4** Poverty in the EC, 1985: people with incomes less than 50 per cent of national averages
*Source:* Bailey (1992).

|  | % Households | % People |
|---|---|---|
| Belgium | 6.3 | 7.1 |
| Denmark | 8.0 | 7.9 |
| FR Germany | 10.3 | 10.5 |
| Greece | 20.5 | 21.5 |
| Spain | 20.3 | 20.9 |
| France | 18.0 | 19.1 |
| Ireland | 18.5 | 18.4 |
| Italy | 12.0 | 14.1 |
| Netherlands | 6.9 | 9.6 |
| Portugal | 31.4 | 32.4 |
| UK | 14.1 | 14.6 |
| EUR 12 | 14.1 | 15.5 |

*Source:* Eurostat, 1990; figures for Luxembourg unavailable.

The latter suggests that one in three children are living in poverty in the United Kingdom, largely as a result of persistent high unemployment. In 1979 1.4 m children (10 per cent) were living below the unofficial poverty line of half the national income, but by 1991/92 this had increased to 4.1 m children (32 per cent). In 1979 5 m (9 per cent of the population) people were living below half the average income, yet by 1991/92 this had increased to 13.9 m people (25 per cent of the population). Between 1979 and 1991/92 the poorest one-tenth of the population suffered a fall of 17 per cent in their real incomes. Furthermore, between 1979 and 1991/92 the richest one-tenth of the population enjoyed an increase of 62 per cent in their real incomes.

Thus poverty is a growing problem. As yet, however, the supranational dimension to policy towards poverty has been very limited in scope. The European Union has initiated three anti-poverty programmes, the first between 1975 and 1980, the second from 1986 to 1989 and the last from 1990 to 1994. These were designed primarily to develop a cross-national research perspective. It seems clear that this is an area in which the EU might become more involved in the future.

## 11.5 Women, work and the family

The increase in the number of women now going out to work is having perhaps the greatest effect on changes in the relationship between men and women. Figures from all EU countries emphasise this phenomenon, which stems from structural economic factors and the desire of women for more financial independence.[13] Women tend to be employed on a part-time basis, in the service sector, characterised by low pay, poor conditions and few rights.[14] The deregulation of the labour market has been particularly marked in the United Kingdom (Deakin and Wilkinson, 1991/92).

However, the difficulties that women encounter in this area are revealed by numerous surveys, and the inescapable fact that despite all kinds of social advances women are still expected to give up career and promotion to take the major share in child rearing and household tasks.[15] The presence of children is seen as the single most important obstacle in preventing women starting or resuming a career.

In the labour market from 1985–90 employment in the Community increased by over 9 m, two-thirds of the additional jobs were taken by women, part of a longer-term trend of women taking an increasing share of the employment in the Community. Women in the 25–49 age range are coming into employment to offset the longer time spent in education by young people and earlier retirement at the other end of the age scale. More than 80 per cent of this increase is a result of part-time employment.

There are large variations between member states, with a high level of economic activity in:

| Denmark, Portugal | = | More than 75 per cent of mothers economically active |
| Germany, France, Belgium | = | 60–69 per cent of mothers economically active |
| Italy, United Kingdom | = | 50–59 per cent of mothers economically active |
| Ireland, Spain, Luxembourg Greece, the Netherlands | = | Less than 50 per cent of mothers economically active |

Most of this new employment is in part-time work (increase of 32 per cent from 1985 to 1991, compared to an increase of only 5 per cent in the same period for full-time work). These figures tend to indicate that mothers either by choice (to spend more time with their children) or necessity (the lack of comprehensive child care facilities) are concentrated in this sector of employment. Furthermore, this type of employment is useful for employers since it permits greater flexibility in terms of matching the number of employees with the amount of work available, and avoids expensive national insurance payments.

Among the obstacles to women entering the labour market, nearly 60 per cent of women said that children were the major obstacle, compared to less than 10 per cent of men (Eurobarometer, 1994). In fact, men's participation rate in the labour market is highest precisely at the time when their children are young. This is compared to women, who find it very difficult to enter the labour market as mothers and particularly when they have more than one child ('mother' is defined as having one or more children aged 0–9, 'father' = one child 0–9).[16] The most common reason expressed by mothers for their inability to start work or pursue full-time work is the practical difficulty of child care arrangements and facilities. The onus on women to arrange all the childcare is evident from Table 11.5 on maternity and paternity leave. In Germany, the group of women with the lowest participation rates are those with two or more children under 6 years old.[17]

Other issues about women and work concern the kind of work that is being done by women, which is not new. There have always been women employed in the service sector, for instance in domestic service until the Second World War in the United Kingdom and in most other European countries. This so-called new work is characterised by much of the same kind of low wages, poor conditions and lack of employment rights as domestic service and other kinds of previous female

**Table 11.5** Maternity and paternity leave
             *Source: Eurostat.*

| | | |
|---|---|---|
| BEL | ML: | 15 weeks: 1 week before birth, 8 weeks after, 6 weeks before or after. Paid at 82 per cent of earnings for first month, then 75 per cent up to maximum level. |
| | PL: | No statutory leave. Workers can take 6–12 months 'career breaks' from employment, subject to employer's agreement. Paid at flat rate (10 928 BF a month); higher rate if taken within 6 years of birth of second or third child. |
| DA | ML: | 18 weeks: 4 weeks before birth, 14 weeks after. Paid at flat rate (DKK 2556 a week, equal to approximately 65 per cent of average earnings for industrial worker). |
| | PL: | 10 weeks. Paid as for ML. In addition, workers can take 13–35 weeks of leave, subject to employer's agreement. Paid at flat rate (DKK 2045 a week). |
| DE | ML: | 14 weeks: 6 weeks before birth, 8 weeks after. Paid at 100 per cent of earnings. |
| | PL: | Until child reaches 36 months. Paid at flat rate (600 DM a month) for first 6 months, then income-related benefit until child is 24 months, last 12 months unpaid. |
| EL | ML: | 14 weeks: 3 weeks before birth, 7 weeks after, 4 weeks before or after. Paid at 100 per cent of earnings. |
| | PL: | 3 months *per parent*, not transferable from one parent to the other. Unpaid. |
| ES | ML: | 16 weeks: 6 weeks after birth, 10 weeks before or after. Paid at 75 per cent of earnings. |
| | PL: | 12 months. Unpaid. |
| FR | ML: | 16 weeks: 4 weeks before birth, 10 weeks after, 2 weeks before or after. Extra leave for a third or higher order birth). Paid at 84 per cent of earnings, but not taxed. |
| | PL: | Until child reaches 36 months. Unpaid for first and second child, then flat rate (2738 FF a month in July 1991). |
| IRL | ML: | 14 weeks: 4 weeks before birth, 10 weeks before or after. Mother can request extra 4 weeks. First 14 weeks paid at 70 per cent of earnings, but not taxed; extra 4 weeks unpaid. |
| | PL: | None. |
| IT | ML: | 5 months: 2 months before birth, 3 months after. Paid at 80 per cent of earnings. |
| | PL: | 6 months. Paid at 30 per cent of earnings. |
| LUX | ML: | 14 weeks: 6 weeks before birth, 8 weeks after. Paid at 100 per cent of earnings. |
| | PL: | None. |
| NL | ML: | 16 weeks: 4 weeks before birth, 10 weeks after, 2 weeks before or after. Paid at 100 per cent of earnings. |
| | PL: | 6 months of reduced hours *per parent* (minimum of 20 hours a week): not transferable between parents. Unpaid. |
| PT | ML: | 90 days: 60 days after birth, 30 days before or after. Paid at 100 per cent of earnings. |
| | PL: | 24 months. Unpaid. |
| UK | ML: | 40 weeks: 11 weeks before birth, 20 weeks after. Paid at 90 per cent of earnings for 6 weeks, flat rate for 12 weeks and unpaid for remaining period. |
| | PL: | None. |

ML = Statutory Maternity Leave; PL: = Statutory Parental Leave.
In many countries, statutory leave conditions are improved for many workers due to collective agreements (for example, most workers in Italy receive full pay while on Maternity Leave); these additional benefits are not included.

employment used to be. What is new is the scale at which the current changes are taking place and in particular the loss of full-time permanent employment (Cousins, 1994).

In Spain, as in all other European countries, there has been an increase in the participation rates of women, primarily in the same sectors of the economy as in other

European countries. The difference to the UK is that women in Spain have a high participation rate in their twenties but which then goes into a steady decline. In the United Kingdom, there is a high participation rate in the early twenties, followed by a dip in the late twenties and early thirties, and then a rise again until the fifties. However, this Spanish situation may change as better child care facilities are introduced, and increasing urbanisation and secularisation reduces the legacy of the Franco era. Several factors explain the lower level of participation rates for Spanish women, notably late industrialisation, and conservative and religious ideologies stressing subordination of women and their duties at home. Under the labour laws of the Franco regime women were expected to give up work on marriage and had to obtain permission from their husbands if they wanted to work.[18] There have, however, been enormous advances since the demise of the Franco regime in the mid-1970s, and currently about 70 per cent of all 3–5-year-olds are in some form of state funded nursery or school, compared to about 42 per cent of the children in the same age group in the United Kingdom.[19]

## Rights at work

Many European countries have enacted special legislation to protect the rights of women at work. In the United Kingdom the Sex Discrimination Act in 1975 and the Equal Pay Act in 1975 were attempts to redress the imbalance in treatment of women in the area of employment. Their success has been mixed but it has, nevertheless, raised the issue and caused many discriminatory practices to end. However the 'glass ceiling' remains, where equality of opportunity is subscribed to but where it is still difficult for women to reach senior positions within organisations.

The rights of pregnant women at work has also been an important issue at the European level, with the Commission attempting to pressure governments to improve the level of protection.[20] In June 1994 the Advocate-General of the European Court of Justice, whose opinion the Court accepted, stated that pregnancy could not be equated with an illness, and so could not put women at an employment disadvantage. Dismissal on the grounds of pregnancy or any normal consequences of pregnancy, therefore, was unlawful.[21]

A collective agreement signed in Greece between the social partners attempts to improve the conditions of women's employment. Entitlement to maternity leave will be increased from 15 to 16 weeks, the right for breast-feeding mothers to be absent from work for 1 hour a day will be extended from 1 year to 2, and parental leave will be increased from 3 to 3½ months for each parent, to be taken before the child reaches their third birthday (the last provision applies to companies with more than 50 employees).[22]

It has been the European Court of Justice in Luxembourg which has done more for the protection of women's rights at work than many individual member states. Since a landmark judgment in *SABENA* v. *Defrenne* in 1975, where an air hostess for the Belgian national airline claimed that she had been paid less than her male colleagues over a period of years, the Court has tried to force the pace by ensuring an end to this particular form of unequal treatment.[23]

## Family size and structure

The size of families in European societies has been falling dramatically over the past few decades. In most EU states, the fertility rate has fallen so low that populations are beginning to shrink. Even in countries in eastern Europe, the birth rate is declining rapidly. This decline is most rapid in the new German Federal States (the former East Germany), with a dramatic fall since 1989. The main reasons for this decline are job insecurity and the disappearance of the comprehensive child care facilities provided for by the previous regime.[24] In early 1994 the unemployment rate among women in the new Federal States stood at 23 per cent, whereas in the western part of the country it was 9.3 per cent. Despite the addition of around 18 m people to the West German population by the unification with East Germany, the overall birth rate is declining rapidly, and within 10 years Germany will once again have a falling population.

Fertility rates in the Southern states are also now approaching Northern rates. In Italy, Spain, Greece and Portugal the fertility rate is below the 2.1 necessary to maintain a stable population level (see Figure 11.1). This process is taking place despite the strong opposition of the Catholic and Orthodox churches. There are two important effects for women of the decline in the number of children. First, they do not have to spend so much time in bearing and rearing their offspring and secondly, the result is that they have more time to pursue their own careers and gain financial and social independence.

## Lone parents

There have been numerous attempts to estimate the number of lone parent families in each member state, but the method of statistical collection differs: comparisons are difficult to be wholly accurate.[25] Nevertheless, despite the varying definitions there is clear evidence to show that the number of such families is increasing in the EU.

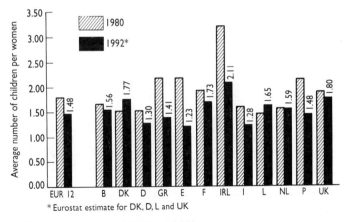

**Figure 11.1**  The total fertility rate, 1980 and 1992
*Source: Eurostat.*

The highest number of lone parent families is in the United Kingdom, where about 17 per cent of all families are in this category, followed by Denmark with about 15 per cent. Germany and France each have about 12 per cent, then a cluster of countries including Belgium, Ireland, Luxembourg, the Netherlands and Portugal. There is a much lower percentage of lone parent families in Italy, Spain and Greece. There has also been an important change in causes of the rise in lone parent families. The effects of war and accidents have decreased and the rise is attributable to personal choice, divorce, separation and births outside marriage.

Births outside marriage have shown a huge increase in the EU, particularly in Denmark and Sweden where almost half of all births take place outside marriage (see Figure 11.2). However, many Danish couples choose to cohabit rather than marry (only about 4–6 per cent of births were to women without a partner), and so this does not necessarily mean any greater increase in the number of lone parent families. France and the United Kingdom follow with about 30 per cent of all births taking place outside marriage. The average in Europe is 24.1 per cent.[26]

In France the regional variation in the 1980 figures, with many births outside marriage concentrated in the metropolitan areas, has now become a broadly spread phenomenon throughout the country, except in very rural areas.[27] It is also spread fairly evenly across social classes, again except among women engaged in agriculture, and is much higher among French nationals than in other ethnic groups. However, among the Portuguese and Algerian communities the figure is much higher for those women living in France than in their countries of origin. There is usually a gap of about 10 years between the host community and other groups, and so we can expect that births outside marriage among other ethnic groups will equal the host community over the next decade.

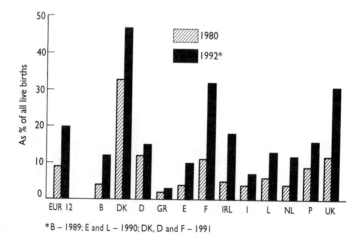

*Figure 11.2*  Births outside marriage, 1980 and 1992
*Source: Eurostat.*

## Divorce

The divorce rate is seen as another indicator of lone parent family increase but this ignores the remarriage rate, which for example is very high in the United Kingdom. The United Kingdom has the highest rate of divorce, but also the second highest rate of marriage after Portugal, with Sweden having the lowest rate. Italy has the lowest divorce rate (Tables 11.6 and 11.7).

## Abortion

The debate over abortion continues to dominate social policy in the EU. The unification of Germany has led to a fierce argument over the rights of women to terminate pregnancies. The 1972 East German abortion law permitted abortion on demand, but in the Federal Republic of Germany (FRG), West Germany, abortion was placed among 'crimes against life' in the penal code: a punishment that a Bavarian doctor underwent in the late 1980s.[28]

*Table 11.6* Marriages per 1000 people
Source: Eurostat.

| | 1983 | 1984 | 1985 | 1986 | 1987 | 1988 | 1989 | 1990 | 1991 | 1992 | 1993 |
|---|---|---|---|---|---|---|---|---|---|---|---|
| EUR12 | 6.0 | 5.9 | 5.9 | 5.9 | 6.0 | 6.0 | 6.1 | 6.0 | 5.7 | 5.4 | 5.3* |
| B | 6.1 | 6.0 | 5.8 | 5.8 | 5.7 | 6.0 | 6.4 | 6.5 | 6.1 | 5.8 | 5.4 |
| DK | 5.3 | 5.6 | 5.7 | 6.0 | 6.1 | 6.3 | 6.0 | 6.1 | 6.0 | 6.2 | 5.9 |
| D | 6.3 | 6.4 | 6.4 | 6.6 | 6.7 | 6.8 | 6.7 | 6.5 | 5.7 | 5.6 | 5.5 |
| GR | 6.7 | 5.8 | 6.4 | 5.8 | 6.6 | 4.8 | 6.2 | 5.9 | 6.4 | 4.7 | 5.9 |
| E | 5.1 | 5.2 | 5.2 | 5.4 | 5.6 | 5.6 | 5.7 | 5.7 | 5.6 | 5.5 | 5.2 |
| F | 5.5 | 5.1 | 4.9 | 4.8 | 4.8 | 4.8 | 5.0 | 5.1 | 4.9 | 4.7 | 4.4 |
| IRL | 5.6 | 5.2 | 5.3 | 5.2 | 5.2 | 5.2 | 5.2 | 5.1 | 4.9 | 4.5 | : |
| I | 5.4 | 5.3 | 5.3 | 5.2 | 5.4 | 5.6 | 5.7 | 5.6 | 5.5 | 5.3 | 5.1 |
| L | 5.4 | 5.4 | 5.3 | 5.1 | 5.3 | 5.6 | 5.8 | 6.1 | 6.7 | 6.4 | 6.0 |
| NL | 5.5 | 5.7 | 5.7 | 6.0 | 6.0 | 6.0 | 6.1 | 6.4 | 6.3 | 6.2 | 5.8 |
| P | 7.6 | 7.1 | 6.9 | 7.0 | 7.2 | 7.2 | 7.4 | 7.3 | 7.3 | 7.1 | 6.9 |
| UK | 6.9 | 7.0 | 6.9 | 6.9 | 7.0 | 6.9 | 6.8 | 6.5 | 6.1 | 6.1 | : |
| A | 7.4 | 6.1 | 5.9 | 6.1 | 10.1 | 4.7 | 5.6 | 5.9 | 5.6 | 5.8 | 5.6 |
| FIN | 6.1 | 5.8 | 5.3 | 5.2 | 5.3 | 5.2 | 4.9 | 5.0 | 4.9 | 4.7 | 4.7 |
| IS | 5.9 | 5.9 | 5.2 | 5.1 | 4.7 | 5.2 | 4.7 | 4.5 | 4.8 | 4.8 | : |
| N | 5.0 | 5.0 | 4.9 | 4.9 | 5.0 | 5.2 | 4.9 | 5.2 | 4.7 | 4.5 | : |
| S | 4.3 | 4.4 | 4.6 | 4.6 | 4.9 | 5.2 | 12.8 | 4.7 | 4.3 | 4.3 | 3.9 |
| EEA | 6.0 | 5.8 | 5.8 | 5.8 | 6.0 | 6.0 | 6.2 | 5.9 | 5.6 | 5.4 | 5.2* |
| CH | 5.9 | 6.0 | 6.0 | 6.2 | 6.6 | 6.9 | 6.8 | 6.9 | 7.0 | 6.6 | 6.2 |
| USA | 10.4 | 10.5 | 10.1 | 9.9 | 9.9 | 9.8 | 9.7 | 9.8 | 9.4 | 9.3 | 9.0 |
| CDN | 7.4 | 7.4 | 7.3 | 6.9 | 7.1 | 7.2 | 7.3 | 7.1 | : | : | : |
| J | 6.4 | 6.2 | 6.1 | 5.9 | 5.7 | 5.8 | 5.8 | 5.8 | 6.0 | 6.1 | 6.4 |

Source: Demographic statistics, 1995. Eurostat.
D: includes in all years data on the former GDR.

***Table 11.7***   Divorces per 1000 people
               Source: Eurostat.

|       | 1983 | 1984 | 1985 | 1986 | 1987 | 1988 | 1989 | 1990 | 1991 | 1992 | 1993 |
|-------|------|------|------|------|------|------|------|------|------|------|------|
| EUR12 | 1.6  | 1.7  | 1.7  | 1.7  | 1.7  | 1.7  | 1.7  | 1.6  | 1.6  | 1.6* | :    |
| B     | 1.7  | 1.8  | 1.9  | 1.9  | 2.0  | 2.1  | 2.0  | 2.0  | 2.1  | 2.2  | 2.1  |
| DK    | 2.9  | 2.8  | 2.8  | 2.8  | 2.8  | 2.9  | 3.0  | 2.7  | 2.5  | 2.5  | 2.4  |
| D     | 2.2  | 2.3  | 2.3  | 2.3  | 2.3  | 2.3  | 2.2  | 2.0  | 1.7  | 1.7  | :    |
| GR    | 0.6  | 0.9  | 0.8  | 0.9  | 0.9  | 0.9  | 0.6  | 0.6  | 0.6  | 0.6  | 0.7  |
| E     | 0.5  | 0.5  | 0.5  | 0.5  | 0.5  | 0.6  | 0.6  | 0.6  | 0.7  | 0.7  | :    |
| F     | 1.8  | 1.9  | 1.9  | 2.0  | 1.9  | 1.9  | 1.9  | 1.9  | 1.9  | :    | :    |
| IRL   | –    | –    | –    | –    | –    | –    | –    | –    | –    | –    | –    |
| I     | 0.2  | 0.3  | 0.3  | 0.3  | 0.5  | 0.5  | 0.5  | 0.5  | 0.5  | 0.5  | 0.4  |
| L     | 1.6  | 1.7  | 1.8  | 1.8  | 2.0  | 2.1  | 2.3  | 2.0  | 2.0  | 1.8  | :    |
| NL    | 2.3  | 2.4  | 2.3  | 2.0  | 1.9  | 1.9  | 1.9  | 1.9  | 1.9  | 2.0  | 2.0  |
| P     | 0.8  | 0.7  | 0.9  | 0.8  | 0.9  | 0.9  | 1.0  | 0.9  | 1.1  | 1.3  | 1.2  |
| UK    | 2.9  | 2.8  | 3.1  | 3.0  | 2.9  | 2.9  | 2.9  | 2.9  | 3.0  | :    | :    |
| A     | 1.9  | 2.0  | 2.0  | 1.9  | 1.9  | 2.0  | 2.0  | 2.1  | 2.1  | 2.1  | 2.1  |
| FIN   | 2.0  | 2.0  | 1.8  | 2.0  | 2.0  | 2.5  | 2.9  | 2.6  | 2.6  | 2.6  | 2.4  |
| IS    | 2.1  | 1.9  | 2.2  | 2.0  | 1.9  | 1.8  | 2.1  | 1.9  | 2.1  | 2.0  | :    |
| N     | 1.9  | 1.9  | 2.0  | 1.9  | 2.0  | 2.1  | 2.2  | 2.4  | 2.4  | 2.4  | :    |
| S     | 2.5  | 2.4  | 2.4  | 2.3  | 2.2  | 2.1  | 2.2  | 2.3  | 2.3  | 2.5  | 2.5  |
| EEA   | 1.6  | 1.7  | 1.7  | 1.7  | 1.7  | 1.7  | 1.7  | 1.7  | 1.6  | 1.7* | :    |
| CH    | 1.8  | 1.7  | 1.8  | 1.8  | 1.8  | 1.9  | 1.9  | 2.0  | 2.0  | 2.1  | 2.2  |
| USA   | 4.9  | 4.9  | 5.0  | 4.8  | 4.8  | 4.7  | 4.7  | 4.7  | 4.7  | 4.8  | 4.6  |
| CDN   | 2.8  | 2.6  | 2.4  | :    | 3.1  | :    | 3.1  | 2.9  | :    | :    | :    |
| J     | 1.5  | 1.5  | 1.4  | 1.4  | 1.3  | 1.3  | 1.3  | 1.3  | 1.4  | 1.4  | :    |

*Source:* Demographic statistics, 1995. *Eurostat.*
D: includes in all years data on the former GDR; IRL: divorce is not allowed.

    The issue of abortion became a sticking point between the former GDR and the Federal Republic in hammering out the terms of the Treaty of Unification. The agreement allowed for a new law to be introduced, and after a long debate in the *Bundestag* in 1991–92 the 1992 Abortion Reform Act was eventually passed, based on principles of support and assistance rather than punishment. Abortion was permitted up to the twelfth week, provided the woman had asked for it and had undergone counselling in the 3 days prior to termination. Medical and eugenic grounds remain the same. The only *Land* to vote against the bill in the *Bundesrat* was Bavaria, Germany's most heavily Catholic federal state. As soon as the President had signed the bill into law a sufficient number of MPs and the Bavarian state government appealed to the Constitutional Court on the constitutionality of the the new legislation. The Court accepted that the appeal was well founded and granted an interim injunction against Sections 218 and 219 of the law.

    The ensuing debate split the East CDU from the West CDU, and highlighted the Catholic and Protestant divide in the country. The Court rejected many parts of the reform by a 6:2 majority.[29] It outlawed abortions on social grounds, and accepted the appeal of the Bavarian government against financing those abortions by the federal state. The effect of this decision is that:

German women will have to pass a time-comsuming, emotionally stressful and possibly humiliating counselling hurdle before they can proceed with an abortion, and furthermore most women will have to pay for an abortion.[30]

The effect will be that a two-class system will develop, with richer women able to pay for trips to other countries ('abortion tourism'), and poorer women at the mercy of the back-street clinics. The overall effects of the Court's decision may well be to reduce public respect for its position and lead, particularly among women from the East, to a kind of *Systemverdrossenheit* (alienation from the political system) on top of the aready well documented *Parteiverdrossenheit* (see Chapter 3).

In Italy, the 1978 Law permitting abortion on demand in the first 3 months of pregnancy was endorsed by the 1981 referendum. Despite assurances from the main party, *Forza Italia*, in the new Italian government in 1994 that this law would not be reviewed, certain members of the government called for the repeal of this legislation. The main party in favour of repeal was the neo-Fascist National Alliance, and the Speaker of the lower house of the Italian Parliament the Chamber of Deputies, Irene Pivetti, a member of the Northern League. The leader of the Northern League, Umberto Bossi, disowned these statements, warning against the dangers of religious fundamentalism.[31]

Other European countries have various restrictions on abortion, and in Poland there is a debate led by the Catholic church to restrict further the rights women gained in this area under the previous communist regime.

## Family roles

There is still considerable debate as to how much roles in the family have really changed. Most studies tend to show that despite the real increases in women's earning capacities and attendant financial freedoms, expectations are much slower to change. Furthermore the number of women who are able to enjoy this lifestyle is very limited in industrialised countries. Women, therefore, still shoulder a disproportionate share and responsibility for household chores from child care to shopping.

Although it may appear that men want to spend more time with their children, little of practical change has taken place. The socialisation of men is still predominantly based on the authoritative father-figure breadwinner model. Changes that are occurring are a result of economic and social pressures. The economic pressure is, on the one hand, high unemployment among men, and the increasing participation of women on the labour market. The social pressures result from growing emancipation of women and reluctance to be left always at the kitchen sink with children, and changing attitudes towards parenting. However, until there is a more widely supported attitude both from men themselves and from employers towards equal dual-role parenting, men will tend to remain in full-time employment wherever possible because they tend to be better paid, and old habits die hard.

The European Commission is attempting to redress the balance, and proposed unsuccessfully a directive in 1983 on parental leave which would have allowed fathers and mothers alike to take 3 months' leave.[32]

## Different families

One other type of new family is created when parents are of the same sex. There has been fierce debate in the United Kingdom, for example, concerning adoption, and whether such couples can provide the accepted pattern of parenting.[33] Since opinions on the issue of child rearing are so varied it is unlikely that there is any one form of correct parenting. If gay or lesbian couples fulfil the same criteria concerning parenting as heterosexual couples, then many social service departments consider that they have as much right as any other type of couple to adopt.

Another aspect to this debate is that the market forces at the centre of neo-liberal ideology have devastated precisely those traditional communities which reflected the mythic ideal of the traditional family. For example, the mining communities of South Wales were tightly knit areas of social solidarity, where employment in paid activities concerned mainly men working down the mines and where women were employed predominantly in household tasks and child rearing. The destruction of the mining industry by unbridled market forces has also destroyed this 'traditional' family structure, so that in many of these areas the sole breadwinner is a woman usually employed in some part-time occupation. Furthermore, the effect of this change has not only been in terms of paid employment but also in terms of the roles men now have to perform. The question being asked is whether men are not only redundant outside the home but also inside the home?

## Equality between men and women – how wide is the gap?

This section has shown the way in which issues concerning the family and women's situation in society are important factors in analysing how society is organised. If equality is the goal, whether in terms of equal pay, equal promotion and equal status, then it is quite clear that gender is still a prime source of inequality in European societies. The changes that are occurring to redress the balance are a result not only of economic but also social and political developments.

The decline in family values resulting from the break-up of the traditional family set-up has been blamed for many of the current ills in society, from increased juvenile delinquency and crime to poor school performance and by extension to poor economic performance, because young people have not learnt the value of good old-fashioned discipline.

There are a number of problems with this kind of analysis, the main one being the creation of a mythic past when the 'ideal' family existed. In Victorian Britain there was no universal free schooling, no national health service and if circumstances became too difficult then the workhouse was the destination which broke up many families. Huge numbers of people had to leave the land in order to find work in the cities at home and abroad, which also disrupted 'traditional' family life. War and disease also had a major disruptive effect on family stability. Increasing mobility both in geographic terms, with migration, and in social terms with the huge growth in a middle class, has led to many changes in perceptions about family cohesion.

## 11.6  Ethnicity and racism

Nation states in western Europe have been created and maintained on the basis of territorial and/or ethnic identities. They are in many senses also 'imagined communities' (Anderson, 1991). In all cases, however, territorial and ethnic units are subject to change. The borders of Germany now, for example, are very recent. The Unification Treaty which brought this new territorial unit into being was signed only in 1990, and these borders have changed often over the last 100 years. Similarly the United Kingdom as a nation state in its present territorial configuration is a twentieth century creation, after the formation of the Republic of Ireland in 1922. Furthermore, the United Kingdom is a nation state made up of four different nations, Northern Ireland, Scotland, Wales and England, which at one time or another have been subjugated to dominant English power.

The twofold pressure of social tensions arising from the growing presence of other ethnic groups within their societies, and the demands for equal treatment from these groups, forced the major labour-importing countries of western Europe to consider ways of reducing these social divisions to maintain social order and cohesion.

The key words in the debate have been integration, assimilation and multiculturalism, which are linked to notions of being full citizens. In all these countries the issue of how best to integrate these new groups of people began in earnest in the late 1960s. In all these countries integration can be considered in terms of many factors, such as employment, education, culture and location. It seems clear that members of ethnic communities are much more likely to be unemployed, suffer poor education, have difficulties in maintaining cultural identity and be located in 'ghettos' than members of the host community. In other words they tend to suffer much more from social exclusion (see below). This is not to say that indices of deprivation do not also affect members of the host community, and that the distinction between the two groups is blurred in many inner city areas in Britain or in the French *banlieues* ( suburbs = high-rise flats grouped together usually on the edge of most medium- to large-sized French towns and cities, which are home to many different ethnic groups).

### Policies of regulation

Until the crisis provoked by the oil price rise in the early 1970s governments generally welcomed the influx of this labour as it was cheap, flexible, and helped to reduce the power of the trade unions. The 'rotation principle' underlined the German approach of allowing restricted time limits on work permits to emphasise the temporariness of their stay, which was similar to the procedure in France known as the 'lemon squeezer': extract as much as possible of their useful labour and then discard them and find a new group of workers. These people were seen primarily in terms of their economic function, with the social issues concerning family life, for example, ignored.

For most governments it was difficult to repatriate these groups. There were three main reasons; first, for the former colonial powers such as Britain, France, Belgium and the Netherlands, historic links meant that most of the people overseas actually had a right to come to Europe to seek work and then stay on and eventually gain permanent residence status. The second reason concerned obligations that states have under international law to protect and facilitate family life and family reunification.[34] Finally it became clear to employers, for example in the car industry, that to continually dismiss and then recruit new workers was very expensive in terms of administering new work permits, finding accommodation and above all in terms of retraining. These three factors meant that increasingly during the 1960s and early 1970s the population increasingly took on the characteristics of the host country. Family reunification occurred, children attended school and became socialised into the norms and values of that country. The situation in the 1990s is that more than 75 per cent of all immigrant workers and their families living in western Europe have been settled for at least 20 years or more. In Castle's (1984) words, they are 'here for good'.

Governments have subsequently followed a dual if contradictory policy, which is based on a stated policy of promoting integration while at the same time preventing large-scale family reunification and encouraging repatriation. There have been a number of different measures designed to integrate or assimilate those many groups who have become settled populations.

After 1973 many countries introduced restrictions and bans on the recruitment of new workers. Since then more and more restrictions have been imposed, to the extent that very few long-term work permits are issued by any West European country, and most immigration is either a result of limited family reunification or entry of asylum seekers and refugees.[35]

Regulations to control the immigration of people into the United Kingdom, particularly from the former colonies in the Caribbean, Africa and the Indian subcontinent, began a full decade before the oil crisis with Commonwealth Immigrants Act 1962. Prior to this Act any member of the old (usually white) Commonwealth and new (largely black and Asian) Commonwealth, could settle freely in the United Kingdom. Restrictions were now introduced equally on both groups. At the same time, attempts were made to integrate the populations into the host community. Subsequent legislation then tightened up procedure for entry and acquisition of nationality.[36]

A similar process was pursued by the French and German governments, which led to the introduction of a complete ban on further recruitment of foreign workers, and then attempts to persuade those remaining to return 'home' (Edye, 1987). In France these have been followed by a wide public discussion concerning the relative ease with which immigrants can become naturalised as French nationals. Under pressure from the electoral success of the far-right *Front National*, mainstream politicians on both the left and the right of French politics have discussed whether the nationality laws should be changed. After the election of the right coalition government in 1993, the interior minister Charles Pasqua undertook a reform of the laws relating to family reunification, which now make it extremely difficult for any non-EU citizen to join their family in France.[37] Table 11.8 sets out the kinds of approaches that various governments have towards the integration on other ethnic groups. The positions are represented in terms of a continuum.

**Table 11.8** Integration, assimilation and multiculturalism.

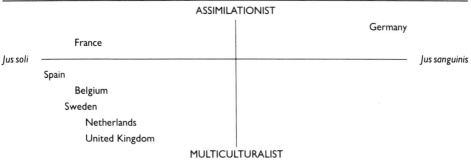

Another crucial aspect of integration is the ease with which a member of an ethnic community can naturalise and take on the nationality of the host country, and become a full citizen of that country. Although this is only at the formal legal level it is an important factor in allowing a secure form of permanent settlement. Nationality law is based either on a notion of *jus soli* (law of the soil) or *jus sanguinis* (blood descent).

### Jus soli

Under this provision anyone born in a country or who lives a substantial part of their lives there can become a national with full citizenship rights. This was the case in Britain and France until recently. In 1983, the 700-year-old tradition of nationality being granted to anyone born in Britain was abolished. Together with the 'patriality' clause in the Immigration Act 1971, and the increasing restrictions of the British Nationality Act 1981, the United Kingdom is moving towards nationality based more on *jus sanguinis*.

### Jus sanguinis

This second approach allows naturalisation, provided the person can show a blood descent, that is through kinship ties to a country. For example, in Germany it is extremely difficult to become a German national unless you can show this close blood link. After the fall of communism, many ethnic Germans from the Volga region of the former Soviet Union, whose forebears had emigrated over 200 years ago to that region, were welcomed back to Germany and granted full citizenship.[38] For the sons and daughters of Turkish people born and brought up in Germany since the 1960s the process is much more difficult.[39] This also has to do with the fact that neither Germany nor Turkey permit their citizens to hold dual nationality.[40]

In 1967 the British Home Secretary, Roy Jenkins, stated that it was not the intention of the government to initiate a flattening process of assimilation, but to let each ethnic community maintain its own cultural traditions within the framework of the wider society. The analogy was to a salad bowl with several ingredients rather than a melting pot. This was a change to the previous notion that the new communities would slowly become absorbed into British society, lose their original identity and become assimilated. This policy is best referred to as integration, and was followed by a series of attempts to facilitate this process, including the Race Relations Act 1965 and the establishment of the Commission for Racial Equality in 1976. However, at the same time that this attempt at integration was taking place, increasingly restrictive measures concerning rights of entry and settlement in the United Kingdom were being introduced.

The buzzword of the 1970s and 1980s in the United Kingdom was 'multicultural-ism', which involved respect and expression of the different cultures within the schools, and support from local authority-funded projects and central government money for educational projects. However, the feeling among many ethnic com-munities was that it was all very well to have bhajis on the menu, and council grants for Caribbean steel bands, but the much deeper issues of discrimination in the housing and job market and social provision were being ignored. A new approach was proposed that included the implementation of equal opportunities policies and the introduction of anti-racist policies. These were designed to tackle the deeper structural issues of continuing discrimination in all sectors of society. It is this policy, albeit in a much truncated form, that characterises most of the current British approach to integration. State support and recognition for religious schools remains an unresolved issue, particularly for Muslim schools; Christian and Jewish schools are state-aided.[41]

The Netherlands has followed a very similar process of integration to the United Kingdom based on the multicultural model. Rex considers that part of the reason that the Netherlands has developed this kind of pluralistic policy relates to its own long-term division into different religious groups (*verzuiling* – see Chapter 8 on the political cleavages in Dutch society).[42] Two main immigrant groups are present, those from the former Dutch Empire and those from Turkey and Morocco. In the first case, policies were designed to facilitate their integration into Dutch society without total loss of their own cultural identity. For the second group the attitude was similar to the German policy of guest-workers, that is, they were only in the Netherlands for a short time. Subsequent realisation that these groups were becoming permanently settled has altered policy.

Despite Belgium being one of Europe's most pluralistic societies, divided as it is into two distinct parts (see Chapter 10), the integration of certain ethnic groups poses problems for Belgian society. There are also strong extreme right-wing movements such as the *Vlaams Blok*, much of whose programme is based on overt racism.

In France you have an individual and universal relationship with the state. Either you are French or you are a foreigner, defined as your civil status. The state in terms of the public sphere cannot recognise particular groups, such as ethnic communities, as this could lead to an intermediate level between the state and the individual. Particularism and favouritism could arise and therefore go against an equal society, in terms of equal treatment for all. You cannot have French people who may also have a particular community affiliation based around, for example, an Algerian or Senegalese cultural identity.

The notion of the lay state (*laïcité*) is crucial to understanding how society is structured in France. The process of integration of this secular or lay state is seen to take place primarily in the classroom. This idea stems from the history since the French revolution of keeping religion out of the classroom (cf. the United States), of an anti-clericalism based around the notion of this individual contract that someone has with the state. It is also important to bear in mind the difference between the public and private spheres in France. In the public sphere, of which the state education system is a prime example, the idea is that everyone is equal and any preference given to one group or another suggests a particularism, while the emphasis of the Revolution was universalist. Anyone who becomes a French citizen is automatically part and parcel of being French, highly assimilationist, and explains why the notion of a multicultural society and ethnic community is very difficult to be accepted in France. The committee of nine wise people who sit on the *Haut Conseil à l'Intégration*, created in March 1990, have expressed the difficulty of accepting that there is a Jewish or Islamic community, given the preamble to the French constitution that France is 'indivisible'. The notion of a multicultural society which was part of the slogans of the 1980s now appears very distant.[43]

In the private sphere the Law of Associations (1901) permits any individual or group to set up an Association to further their interests. Organisations such as Trade Unions and Anglers' Associations derive their legal status from this law, which acknowledges such activity in the private sphere. It was only after the election of Mitterrand in 1981 that new minority ethnic groups were permitted to establish such associations.

The issue is still fraught within France, summed up by the seemingly contradictory statement of the Education Minister in 1994, François Bayrou:

Our choice is integration: to make a single nation, a country, a republic composed of different types of people.[44]

In Germany government ministers and officials still maintain the fiction that Germany is not a country of immigration (*Kein Einwanderungsland*). Despite the huge inflow of immigrant workers and their families since the 1950s and the more recent waves of asylum seekers and refugees, Germany still maintains this official position. According to Faist, it is 'remarkable that the government of the Federal Republic has clung to the idea that Germany is not a country of immigration', when it received around 18 m immigrants between 1945–89[45] (during the same period the United States received around 16 m immigrants). The country also operates a highly assimilationist policy basing the acquisition of nationality on a strict folk or ethnic model of integration. The government is attempting to modify its policy with a restricted granting of nationality to third generation children born in Germany, one of whose parents was also born in Germany or where both parents lived in Germany for at least 10 years before the birth of their child.[46] Despite all these proposals, the rate of naturalisation is very low. Table 11.9 shows comparative models of integration.

**Table 11.9**   Models of integration

| United Kingdom | France | F.R. Germany |
|---|---|---|
| Liberal | Republican | Ethno-cultural |
| Pluralist | Secular | *Kein Einwanderungsland* = 'Not a |
| | Egalitarian | country of immigration' |
| Anti-racist | Individual identity and mobility | |
| UK view of French model = Ethnocentric, coercive assimilation | | |
| French view of UK model = Communitarian | | |
| Multiculturalist | | |
| Particularism (danger of fundamentalism) | | |

*Comment:* The British and French models have developed very much as a result of the history of the two countries and particularly of the way in which their colonialism was managed. Their common histories of empire have allowed some kind of notion of difference, but very much along the lines of the subject peoples fitting into the dominant metropolitan society. The German model, on the other hand, excludes practically everyone from becoming German who cannot show some kind of direct family or cultural link.
*Source:* Adapted from Faist, Weil and Crowley in Baldwin-Edwards and Schain, 1994.

Whatever the type of integration practised and length of residence in any one country, substantial evidence exists to show that members of ethnic minority groups still undergo systematic discrimination in terms of their situation in society. The Child Poverty Action Group (CPAG) survey on poverty in 1990 concluded that black people and other minority ethnic groups were more at risk of unemployment, low pay, shift work and poor social security rights.[47]

Recent data from the United Kingdom indicate that the unemployment rate among ethnic minority groups is almost twice the rate for the white population, but there are big differences among the various groups. The Pakistani and Bangladeshi communities suffer an unemployment rate of over 30 per cent, Afro-Caribbeans around 25 per cent, while for the Indian Community it is at 13 per cent, about the same as for the white population, and for Chinese and African Asians lower at around 10 per cent.[48]

Research in the United Kingdom, using 1991 census information, has shown that women from minority ethnic groups suffer at work from double discrimination: their gender and their race.[49] Unemployment among white women is around 6 per cent, for ethnic minority women it stands at around 16 per cent, and for Bangladeshi women it is more than 30 per cent. Their type of work is also different to that of white women, with particular concentrations of women from these groups in ancillary jobs such as cleaning and cooking in the Health Service, and in the hotel and catering sector. Moreover, within certain occupations minority ethnic women are concentrated in work with the elderly and the mentally ill as nurses. Homeworking is another area where women from India and Pakistan and South East Europe (Turkey) are employed producing garments for the 'rag trade'.[50] This kind of work is obviously very flexible and can be fitted around child care arrangements, but given more accessible child care facilities it is likely that many of these women would be able to go out to work, and may even pursue further education opportunities. Educational attainment is the main factor in ensuring the likelihood of more secure and permanent employment, but highly qualified women from ethnic minorities still suffer higher rates of unemployment than white women.

In the provision of housing, Ginsburg demonstrates that in the private sector overt racial prejudice and discrimination was practised by vendors, landlords and estate agents.[51] In the public sector, local councils have attempted to respond to the needs of ethnic minority communities, which represents a change from earlier practices where families had to wait longer for a council house or usually a flat, and tended to receive inferior accommodation.[52]

The **Swann Report** (1985) recognised that 'prejudice' (preconceived or irrational evaluation of a person or a group based on assumed not actual characteristics) and 'institutional racism' ('a range of long-established practices, systems and procedures') existed in the education system. These two factors had the effect (not intentionally) of depriving ethnic groups of equality of opportunity. According to the Education Department's statistics on examination results, Afro-Caribbean pupils were doing less well than Asian or white pupils. The causes were manifold and included:

- socioeconomic status;
- family structure (higher rate of single-parent families), low teacher expectations;
- racism in general; and
- discrimination of parents in the labour and housing markets, consequent social deprivation resulting from this discrimination.

The report mentioned teacher racism as a factor which could discriminate against ethnic minority pupil achievement. The report considered various solutions, including greater language resources, multicultural religious education, separate schools, better teacher education, more ethnic minority teachers and increased funding for schools with a high number of ethnic minority pupils.[53]

Studies in numerous other countries reveal a similar pattern of social exclusion for people from ethnic minority groups. In Germany, for example, there is clear evidence of social exclusion for the Turkish community, which forms the largest minority ethnic group. As Sen notes:

The greatest problems for the Turkish parents during the 1970s and 1980s arose in the preschool education of their children. The fact that this concept does not exist in Turkey, and that most of the German nursery schools were run by Protestant or Catholic churches meant that Turkish parents did not send their children to German kindergartens.[54]

The fear of discrimination and Christian influence meant that many Turkish parents kept their children at home, and this lack of any preschool experience has had a knock-on effect in terms of later school performance. Fest estimates that until the mid-1980s, the vast majority of Turkish children did not receive a certificate of school completion and were to be found in 'special needs' schools or schools for children with multiple handicaps.[55] An additional important factor has been language, but overall the school performance of young Turkish people has been poor with more than 60 per cent of Turks aged 20 in 1991 having no completion of school certificate or certificate of apprenticeship, compounding their already existing exclusion from the job market.[56] However, the number of Turkish students attending a high school is showing signs of increase, and entries to universities are expanding.[57]

In France, despite the universalism of the Constitution, there is clear evidence that members of the various ethnic communities, whether they are French nationals or not, face social exclusion of one sort or another. The main issue has been the huge increase in unemployment which, as in most other EU countries, has particularly affected young people. According to some writers the lack of work has had other consequences. In particular, the sense of class solidarity has diminished, so young people no longer wish to change their society, merely become members of a society which does not seem to want them.[58] It is worth remembering, however, that the sense of class solidarity between the working class and the new immigrant workers was never really strong.[59] The official statistical office in France, L'INSEE (*Institut National de la Statistique et des Études Économiques*), has consistently shown in its studies that the level of unemployment in the suburbs, or *banlieues*, where most ethnic communities are located, is twice as high as the national average.[60]

The French education system with its insistence on the republican model of developing equal citizens has been the focus of fierce debate concerning its ability to reflect and respond to the needs of ethnic communities. In 1990, the government created priority education areas (ZEP: *Zones d'éducation en priorité*) as a way of trying to deal with these particular needs. These ZEPs were located in areas with high ethnic community density, usually the *banlieues* and with the geographical separation of the *banlieues* from the main urban centres, the divide between the pupils of French and non-French origin was further reinforced. In addition, there seems to be the same attitude among the teachers in these ZEPs towards their pupils in terms of low expectations of performance, as the **Swann Report** suggested exists among teachers in Britain.[61]

Economic growth in Italy and Spain since the 1960s has led, for significant numbers of immigrants, to the need to change from their position in countries of emigration in this century, with large numbers going to Northern Europe, the United States and Latin America.[62] Italy began to attract back many of its former emigrants to Northern Europe, as did Spain after the death of Franco in 1975. Spain has also witnessed a great deal of reverse immigration from Latin America, and these flows have been facilitated by long-standing links with those countries. For both countries the newer immigration has come from Morocco in Spain's case, and other parts of North and West Africa.[63] The labour market position of the more recent arrivals is comparable to that of similar groups in other European countries, and they face the same problems of exclusion.[64] One particular sector of employment in Spain is domestic work, almost exclusively undertaken by women, from Morocco and the Dominican Republic. Another area with a high percentage of immigrant labour is the textile industry.[65] Given their labour market location, and the prevailing wage rates in those sectors, there is evidence to suggest that many of these workers are living in precarious situations characterised by some degree of exclusion.[66]

## The EU: integration, immigration and asylum policy

There is a contradiction among the member states of the EU between a continued maintenance of the ideology of the nation state and yet at the same time a recognition that the nation state is no longer the secure base in which the accumulation of capital can be most effectively continued, given the globalisation of production and deregulation of finance (Miles, 1993). Each EU member state has jealously guarded its right to define who is, or who can, become a citizen. In terms of immigration entry and control, however, there have been several changes to member states' policy as a result of initiatives at the EU level. Furthermore, under Article 8a of the Maastricht Treaty a 'European citizen' is defined which may eventually undermine each individual nation state's attempts to hold exclusively to its own definition of nationality; but that day is a long way off.

All institutions at the EU level have become increasingly involved in issues concerning ethnicity and racism. In this section we will examine policies on integration, then look at the development of immigration and asylum policy.

## Trevi

A forum for Immigration and Justice ministers of the EC, established in 1975, with the remit to examine issues outside Community competence. It is not part of the formal institutions of the EU, although membership of the group is confined to EU countries. Initially the group concerned itself with terrorism, but it has widened its scope of interest to include drug trafficking and illegal immigration.

## Ad hoc *Group on Immigration (Politicians and civil servants from the Home Office and Interior Ministries of the EC).*

The group was set up to consider the immigration proposals for a Europe without internal frontiers. The European Commission has observer status at meetings of this group, which deals specifically with issues relating to frontier controls, visa policies, bogus travel documents and abuse of asylum procedures. A special Subgroup on Asylum has been formed to deal specifically with asylum issues.

## Schengen

A treaty between, initially, the Benelux countries, France and the FRG now includes Italy, Spain and Portugal but not Denmark, the United Kingdom or Ireland. The aim was to abolish frontier controls between their countries by 1 January 1990. The actual removal of all controls between the signatory countries took place on 26 March 1995. Austria, a new EU member, has confirmed that it will bring its policies into line with the agreement. The EU has, therefore, sealed its East and South borders. However, the reality of keeping to the letter of Schengen has proved difficult for the French government which reintroduced border controls with other EU countries shortly after the election of the new President Chirac in May 1995.

The scope of the treaty is wide: it contains short-term measures and provides for long-term measures in a variety of areas: drugs, firearms and ammunition, mutual judicial assistance, frontier controls, frontier surveillance, visas, rules on stays of less than 3 months by aliens and the grant of asylum. The agreement, then, contains measures for more stringent controls at the external borders, with provisions for more frontier guards, stricter controls on entrants from non-EC countries and mandatory refusal at the borders of aliens who do not meet all conditions of entry. A second strand to the agreement is a 'harmonised' visa policy, which Groenendijk considers is a 'euphemism for the re-introduction of visa obligations for virtually all Third World countries'.[67]

The situation for asylum seekers has become more difficult. The Interior Ministers signed a draft declaration on the treatment of asylum seekers and refugees in London on 30 November 1992. These proposals are as restrictive as any already in existence in individual member states. The meeting followed the recommendations of the *Ad Hoc* Group on Immigration which produced a draft on 1 July 1992, in which it was clear that the preferred option was the German proposal to produce an EU-wide definition of 'manifestly unfounded applications for asylum'.[68] The ministers, meeting in secret and outside any direct accountable framework, agreed to harmonise their national laws by 1995.

These measures would mean that asylum seekers should stay in the first safe country they reach, usually a neighbouring country, to prevent the intercontinental movements characteristic of recent years. If they actually arrive at an EU entry point they may make a claim for asylum to that country, and if refused by that country are unable to apply elsewhere in the EU for 6 months. This measure has led to the phenomenon of Refugees in Orbit (RIO), who shuttle from one place to another as governments seek to avoid any responsibility for them. There is also the proposal that asylum seekers should exhaust all local channels of redress before fleeing! The ministers found themselves unable to agree to the improvements in asylum law suggested by the UN High Commissioner for Refugees.[69]

As a result of increasing concern that a large number of asylum seekers from Algeria will attempt to come to France, the French government has proposed that the EU should adopt a much more restrictive definition of asylum seeker than the 1951 Geneva Convention. Whereas the Convention states that asylum should be offered to anyone fleeing because of 'well-founded reasons of persecution' on a number of grounds, the French proposal would limit asylum being offered only to those fleeing from organs of the state. In the case of Algeria, therefore, those who are fleeing as a result of fear of persecution from groups opposed to the government in Algeria would not be eligible for asylum.[70]

The European Parliament has been a consistent champion of the need for the EU's policy on immigration and asylum to be consonant with the European Convention on Human Rights, and the UN Declaration of Human Rights[71]. It is clear, however, that the Commission and the Council of Ministers are in the process of developing a very restrictive policy in this area. Furthermore, the EP's approach to an EU refugee policy arguing that it should be situated firmly within a human rights context would only be effective if there was a competent executive to implement this policy. The current approach of the EU is:

intergovernmental . . . piece-meal and haphazard, where the human rights angle is completely lost, as is demonstrated by present practice.[72]

The first concern for many interested organisations about the Schengen Treaty is over the way in which the information is being collected. The Home Office has informed the Data Protection Registrar that it intends to use as a source of information 'people making a complaint or enquiry', which implies, as Jenkins notes, 'that the immigration service is quite entitled to store anonymous, damaging, and possibly malicious information on computer without any checks on its accuracy'.[73]

The second concern is whether access will be permitted under the Data Protection Act. There are already concerns being expressed by the independent data protection authorities in the Schengen countries about the implications of the SIS. These authorities are not opposed in principle to closer cooperation between police forces, but point out that: 'the planned information system can impinge in a very sensitive way on the civil rights of citizens', by the way in which information may be collected, stored and divulged without an individual's knowledge. The authorities also point out that Belgium, one of the Schengen countries, has no data protection authority, two of the other signatory parties have no specific regulations governing collection of information by the police and five other EC countries still have no data protection legislation.

There could have been positive effects of the Schengen agreement, by permitting non-EU nationals, refugees and asylum seekers already resident in the EU to enjoy the same rights as EU nationals in terms of travel, looking for work and other civil and political liberties. However, the implications of Schengen will be more significant in terms of creating a negative climate of opinion around the whole issue of non-EC nationals, refugee and asylum seekers. The removal of internal border controls and the possible use of ID cards to guard against illegitimate entry is likely to lead to increased police powers to stop and check individuals on the streets, in the workplace, in schools and elsewhere. Such 'trawling' operations have already become a familiar part of immigration practice in the United Kingdom. The increase in racial discrimination from the need to check those most identifiably different also has to be considered in this context. The likelihood of ID cards being introduced, particularly in the United Kingdom, has implications for civil liberties. Although there is no ID card system as such in the United Kingdom, the gathering and collecting of computerised information by official agencies is increasing.

In 1988 the Home Office began to collect 'detailed statistics' on the nationality of asylum seekers. The Immigration Service in Britain acquired a new computer system in 1987 which with a wry sense of bureaucratic humour was called HOLMES (Home Office Large Major Enquiry System). This system is designed to assist the service in its detection of people who evade immigration control by overstaying or entering Britain illegally. Most of the information in the system is provided by anonymous letters and phone calls about alleged immigration offences. These types of systems mean that it will be very easy for the British government to link into the SIS.

The Trevi Group convenes in secret and there is little information about the content of its discussions. Much of the work being done on harmonisation of the conditions for granting visas and other immigration matters is being carried out by a subgroup of Trevi, the *Ad Hoc* Immigration Working Group, which is composed of EU ministers, civil servants and police officials from all member states. Its overall aim is to formulate combined action against terrorism, drug trafficking and illegal immigration. A major criticism of this group is that it is formulating EU policy outside any democratically accountable framework, thereby preventing public discussion about the issues involved.

The desire for secrecy still continues as MEPs become increasingly critical of the way in which this aspect of EU policy, and in particular the French proposal of April 1995 on tightening up the Geneva Convention, is being formulated:

If we are to be seen as a decent civilised part of the world, we should obey international standards on human rights. Instead we are continuing to build a wall around Europe.[74]

In addition, many organisations are concerned that refugee and immigration policy is being linked with other unrelated matters by the way in which the EU presents the issues. In many official publications and statements by EU officials and national political figures the three areas of terrorism, drug trafficking and illegal immigration are combined in one sentence or succeeding sentences.

The Schengen group have reached agreement on visa requirements for around 125 countries, which are likely to be adopted by all EU member states. Most of these countries are ACP states, many of them part of the new Commonwealth. In 1989 in Madrid a report (Palma Document) was agreed on, drawing up a 'positive' list of countries whose nationals would not require visas to enter the EU. The effect of these measures is to break traditional historical links between countries and create a division between those countries with which the Union has close relations and whose nationals do not 'give rise to problems', and countries whose nationals 'do give problems'.[75]

This terminology barely hides the division of the world into rich countries (EFTA, Canada and Japan) and the rest, the third world or two-thirds world (ACP states). The imposition of these visa requirements will add to race discrimination by making entry to the United Kingdom, even for short periods of time, more difficult for friends and relatives of Britain's settled black and Asian communities.[76] In addition the extension of visa requirements will be a major hurdle for refugees and asylum seekers, since in many cases now such people arrive first as visitors and then later claim asylum. This avenue is currently being severely curtailed, since visitors will become subject to much closer initial scrutiny and control. The Trevi group is using as a model for its proposals the work done by the those involved in drawing up the Schengen agreement, which is considered by the Commission:

as invaluable in formulating its ideas in the wider Community context.[77]

## 11.7   EU social policy

In the social chapter of the Maastricht Treaty, there is a very narrow definition of what constitutes the 'social'. The focus concerns mainly work-related issues such as health and safety, equal opportunities and vocational training. This view has been consistently expressed at this European-wide level since the early 1950s, in the relevant articles of the European Coal and Steel Community, the Euratom Treaty and the Rome Treaty establishing the European Economic Community. It is also found in the 1981 European Social Charter and in all subsequent EC developments up to the present day. More recent initiatives, however, concerning women's and ethnic minority rights, suggest that the Commission is beginning to broaden the notion of the social.

Critics of the EU's social policy such as Bailey (1992) consider that this reflects a 'narrow official understanding' of the 'social', and is a result of the predominance given to economic matters in the recent construction of Europe, with most discussions of the 'social' appearing as an afterthought. The whole area is at the heart of the current debate about the future of Europe, and discussion about the nature, scope and extent of the 'social' reflect long-standing ideological differences which have been apparent in every discussion of the social dimension at national and EC level.

Other writers, such as Meehan, consider that the EU has played a progressive role in championing a wider range of social issues, and despite the supposed narrow focus of its social policy there have been substantial 'spillovers' into other areas of policy.[78]

The domain of the 'social' is, however, infinitely more vast than the current EC interpretation of it, and concerns the entire domain of society in contemporary Europe. The current preoccupation at the political and economic level is the creation of a 'Europe', but what is ignored is if and how a 'European society' is being created at the same time. The important issues concern what kind of social change is taking place, and is the end result likely to be the standardised and harmonised social reality that reflects the political and economic form?

Other writers, such as Leibfried (1993), define the social in Europe in terms of a 'European social citizenship'. Leibfried is concerned with the development of a European welfare state that would underpin any further process of integration.

For some countries, notably the United Kingdom under its Conservative Government, the attempt to introduce a social dimension at the EU level is tantamount to implementation of a 'socialist' agenda, which implies government intervention and regulation. This kind of interventionist strategy is totally at odds with the neo-liberal policy of non-intervention and free market forces. This argument rejects such provisions on the grounds that they increase labour costs, thereby reducing the competitiveness of the United Kingdom's industry and in the final analysis increasing unemployment, since either British goods are too expensive and so no-one will buy them, or causing foreign investors to locate to countries with lower labour costs. At the other end of the spectrum, one of the main reasons for the vote against EU entry by the Norwegian people in November 1994 was the fear that the EU would undermine the generous provisions of Norway's social welfare benefits and hinder the continued emancipation of women. These fears were also expressed by other Nordic countries and Austria as they prepared for EU entry in January 1995.

The EU was set up in 1958 as the EEC (European Economic Community), then became the EC (European Community), before transforming into its current status. Each successive name change has reflected the growing desire of many politicians to turn the merely economic organisation into a political force with an attendant social dimension. However, it still remains primarily an organisation of nation states where the economic predominates, although as this book indicates the transformation into something beyond the narrowly economic is already under way. As far as the social dimension is concerned, the main Treaty provisions in this area are the free movement of workers (Articles 48–51), the right to establishment (Articles 52–58), freedom to provide services (Articles 59–66), social provisions (Articles 117–122), the European Social Fund (ESF) (Articles 123–128) and economic and social cohesion (Articles 130A–130E).

In the negotiations surrounding the original Rome Treaty France raised its concerns that its legislation on equal pay, holiday pay and overtime, which it considered were more generous than in other member states, would place it at a competitive disadvantage. The Treaty recognised the first two concerns in Articles 119 (equal pay) and Article 120 (holiday pay), but not on overtime. Issues such as minimum pay, working time and employee participation were not included.[79]

The Community Charter of Fundamental Social Rights was adopted by all EU member states, except one (the United Kingdom), at the Strasbourg summit in December 1989.[80] This document is referred to as the **Social Charter**, and was designed to establish a set of rights for all workers and other marginalised groups (elderly, disabled and children) in the EU. Under its social action programme, 47 measures were drawn up to cover such areas as employment and remuneration, social protection and vocational training. This charter then formed the basis of the social action programme of the Maastricht Treaty, which the UK government refused to accept and so exercised its opt-out. Nevertheless, other countries are concened to create more of a citizens' Europe, which implies a much greater emphasis in this area of policy.

## 11.8   Summary

The aim of this chapter has been to analyse the whole domain of the social, and to outline the most important trends in European societies. The issue of the maintenance of some kind of welfare state is crucial in this area. Every society seeks to ensure social cohesion, and any substantial reduction in welfare provision which entails leaving such support mainly to the private sector is likely to lead to increased marginalisation and social exclusion. The experience of the 1980s has shown that incidences of poverty have increased in several countries, which reinforces the need to develop a more adequate system of social protection. However, as Beveridge noted in the 1940s, it is unemployment that is the greatest scourge in society and so these issues of social provision are inextricably connected to economic and political events.

Other changes in European societies to which we have referred are the increased role and participation of women and different ethnic groups at all levels. Emancipation is a key factor, whether it comes from greater occupational equality or from increased social opportunities. For example, in the case of women the provision of adequate child care provision is a first step in this direction.

Our social identity is dependent on a dynamic relation between our background (culture), our place in the socioeconomic hierarchy (social class) and the possibility of social mobility. At present, there are several obstacles in the way of all individuals being able to climb the ladder of opportunity. The challenge to Europe is to find a way of permitting all its inhabitants to extend their talents in order to create a harmonious social identity, recognising diversity and not conformity, plurality and not singularity. The big problem is, however, how to fund such welfare provision given changing age structures and a general reluctance to pay more taxes.

## Further reading

### General

Bailey, J. (ed.) (1992) *Social Europe*, London: Longman.

Bocock, R. and Thompson, K. (eds) (1992) *Social and Cultural Forms of Modernity*, Cambridge: Polity Press.

Esping-Andersen, G. (1990) *The Three Worlds of Welfare Capitalism*, Cambridge: Polity Press.

Eurobarometer (1994) *Women in the Labour Market*, Brussels: Commission.

Hall, S., Held, D. and McGrew, A. (1992) *Modernity and its Futures*, Cambridge: Polity Press.

INSEE (1993) *Les Données Sociales*, Paris: Hachette.

Jones, G. (1992) *Youth Family and Citizenship*, Milton Keynes: Open University Press.

Leibfried, S. (1993) 'Towards a European welfare state?' *New Perspectives on the Welfare State in Europe* Jones, C. (ed.), London: Routledge.

Marchand, A. (ed.) (1993) *L'Europe Sociale*, Paris: L'Harmattan.

Meehan, E. (1993) *Citizenship and the European Community*, London: Sage.

Pfaller, A., Gough, I. and Therborn, G. (1991) *Can the Welfare State compete? A Comparative Study of Five Advanced Capitalist Countries*, London: Macmillan.

Teague, P. (1989) *The European Community; the Social Dimension*, London: Kogan Page.

### Poverty and inequality

Abrahamson, P. E. (1991) 'Welfare and Poverty in the Europe of the 1990s: Social Progress or Social Dumping?' *International Journal of Health Services* 21 (2) pp. 237–64.

Frayman, H. (1991) *Breadline Britain in the 1990s*, London: HarperCollins.

Jowell, R., Brook, L. and Dowds, L. (eds) (1993) *International Social Attitudes. The 10th BSA Report*, Aldershot: Dartmouth.

Oppenheim, C. (1990) *Poverty: the Facts*, London: CPAG.

Townsend, P. (1993) *The International Analysis of Poverty*, Hemel Hempstead: Harvester Wheatsheaf.

### Women

Boa, E. and Wharton, J. (1994) *Women and the Wende: Social Effects and Cultural Reflections of the German Unification Process*, Amsterdam: Rodopi.

Cousins, C. (1994) 'A comparison of the labour market position of women in Spain and the UK with reference to the "flexible" labour debate' *Work, Employment and Society* 8 (1) pp. 45–67.

Deakin, S. and Wilkinson, F. (1991/2) 'Social policy and economic efficiency: the deregulation of the labour market in Britain' *Critical Social Policy* 33 pp. 40–61.

Maruani, M. (1992) 'The position of women on the labour market' *Women of Europe. Supplement No. 36*, Brussels: European Commission (DGX).

Randzio-Plath, C. (1992) *The EC Internal Market – A Challenge for Women* European Parliament PE/GS/239/92.

Rolf, H.-H. and Schäfer, U. (1993) *Jahrbuch der Bundesrepublik Deutschland 1993/4*, Munich: Beck/dtv.

Roll, J. (1992) *Lone Parent Families in the European Community: 1992 Report*, Brussels: European Commission (DGV).

Sianne, G. and Wilkinson, H. (1995) *Gender, Feminism and the Future*, London: Demos.

## Ethnicity and racism

Anderson, B. (1991) *Imagined Communities*, London: Verso.

Braham, P., Rattansi, A. and Skellington, R. (eds) (1992) *Racism and Anti-Racism*, London: Sage.

Castles, S. and Kosack, G. (1985) *Immigrant Workers and Class Structure in Western Europe*, Oxford: Oxford University Press.

Castles, S., and Miller, M. (1994) *The Age of Migration. International Population Movements in the Modern World*, New York: The Guilford Press.

Castles, S., Wallace, T. and Booth, H. (1984) *Here for Good*, London: Pluto Press.

Collinson, D., Knight, D. and Collinson, M. (1990) *Managing to Discriminate*, London: Routledge.

Donald, J. and Rattansi, A. (eds) (1993) *'Race' Culture and Difference*, London: Sage.

Fryer, P. (1984) *Staying Power: The History of Black People in Britain*, London: Pluto Press.

Gijsels, H., Hobin, V., Boukhviss, H. and Brewaeys, P. (eds) (1988) *Les barbares – Les immigrés et le racisme dans la politique belge*, Bruxelles: epo/halt/celsius.

Hammar, T. (ed.) (1985) *European Immigration Policy: A Comparative Study*, Cambridge: Cambridge University Press.

Lapeyronnie, D. *et al.* (eds) (1990) *L'intégration des minorités immigrées. Étude comparative: France: Grande-Bretagne*, ADRI, 27 Boulevard Gambetta, 92130 Issy-les-Moulineaux, France.

Miles, R. (1993) *Race after 'Race Relations'*, London: Routledge.

O'Donnell, M. (1994) *Race and Ethnicity*, Harlow: Longman.

Rattansi, A. and Westwood, S. (1994) *Racism, Modernity and Identity on the Western Front*, Cambridge: Polity Press.

Rex, J. (1986) *Race and Ethnicity*, Milton Keynes: Open University Press.

Rex, J. (1992) 'Race and Ethnicity in Europe' in *Social Europe* in Bailey, J. (ed.) London: Longman.

Shukra, K. (1995) 'From Black Power to Black Perspectives: The Reconstruction of a Black Political Identity' *Youth and Policy*, 49, pp. 15–25.

Sivanandan, A. (1992) *Communities of Resistance*, London: Verso.

Skellington, R., Morris, P. and Gordon, P. (1992) *Race in Britain Today*, London: Sage.

Solomos, J. (1989) *Race and Racism in Contemporary Britain*, London: Macmillan.

Wieviorka, M. (1992) *La France Raciste*, Paris: Seuil.

## Notes

1. We are aware that in using the term 'society' to suggest a 'totalising concept' we may be ignoring the whole post-modernist debate about the redundancy of such a concept. We are not aiming to construct universal and objective accounts of society, but to attempt to locate

developments within European social formations that are responsive to and reflect a global social formation. See Archer, M. S. (1991) 'Sociology for one world: unity and diversity' *International Sociology*, 6 (2) pp. 131–47.

2. Walby, S. (1994) 'Is Citizenship Gendered?' *Sociology* 28 (2) pp. 379–95. See also Bauböck, R. (1991) 'Migration and Citizenship' *New Community* 18 (1) pp. 27–48.
3. Room, G. (1995) 'Poverty in Europe: competing paradigms of analysis', *Policy and Politics* 23 (2) pp. 14–21.
4. Castles, F. (1995) 'Welfare State Development in Southern Europe' *West European Politics* 18 (2) pp. 291–313.
5. *Guardian*, 15/07/94.
6. The fears that economic and political instability coupled with a population explosion in North Africa could lead to a huge wave of migrants wanting to enter the EU has now been shown to be exaggerated. Most of the recent estimates of population growth in Morocco, Algeria and Tunisia reveal a steady and continuing decline; *Financial Times*, 15/02/95.

    Various estimates in recent years have been shown to be exaggerated, from figures such as 127 million in 2025 to Brunetta's figures which range from the present 65 million to 202 million in 2035. *Libération*'s special issue on 'Migrations' (22/6/91) indicates that the birth rate is falling in most of these countries, but there is still none the less high unemployment: Algeria 22.5 per cent, Morocco 16.6 per cent, Tunisia 16.4 per cent. These two factors, together with political instability, may cause people to move in search of work and security and could become critical for the EU if there is no commitment to offering substantial aid and development packages to North Africa. Brunetta, R. (1988) '*La Mediterranée: une approche "multirivages"*' in *La Question Mediterranée. L'Événement Européen*, Naïr, S. (ed.), Paris: Seuil.
7. Parkinson, J. (1992) 'Urbanisation and the Functions of Cities in the European Community', European Institute of Urban Affairs, Liverpool John Moores University, for the EC Directorate General for Regional Policies Brussels.
8. Hilary Winchester (1993) in her *Contemporary France* (London: Longman), points to evidence that there is now some kind of reverse migration, but it is mainly relocation from the inner city to quieter suburban locations and retirement migration. Remote rural communes are still losing population although rural communes on the edge of industrial urban agglomerations are gaining population.
9. In the United Kingdom, for example, women form 2.8 per cent of senior managers, and 9 per cent of managers. Similar percentages are repeated throughout the EU, except for the Scandinavian countries.
10. *Guardian*, 02/02/94.
11. According to a report in 1994 by the German trade union congress (DGB) and welfare organisations, about 7 million people in Germany are living in poverty. *Guardian*, 21/01/94.
12. Also, it is well established that the poor tend to pay more for basic products, and that they are not very good at linear programming. That is, they are not necessarily efficient at, for example, working out the cheapest way of achieving a satisfactory diet.
13. The data on employment in this section comes from the Labour Force Survey (LFS) undertaken annually by each Member State using sample of households (640 000 in 1990).
14. In Spain the increase in the number of women working went from 27.4 per cent in 1984 to 32.5 per cent in 1989.
15. According to a survey on the amount of time spent on various household tasks undertaken by the *Instituto de la Mujer* in Madrid, part of the *Ministerio de Asuntos Sociales*, in 1988, working women still perform the traditional tasks of shopping, looking after children and cleaning the house, while the men take care of the car, the family pets and the household accounts. Overall, working women spent over 6 hours a day in these household-associated

tasks, whereas housewives spent just over 8 hours. Men on the other hand spent an average of 3 hours a day on their tasks, a third of which was connected somehow to driving, although an average of 24 minutes a day was spent looking after the children.

16. *Mothers, Fathers and Employment 1985–1991*, V/5787/93-EN DG V.B.4, Equal Opportunities Unit, March 1993. Report limited to mothers and fathers of children under 10.
17. Rolf and Schäfer, 1993, p. 29.
18. Cousins, 1994, pp. 48–52.
19. European Commission (1990) *Employment in Europe*, Luxembourg: Office for Official Publications of the European Communities.
20. The Directive lays down a minimum of 14 weeks maternity benefit as the right of all women no matter what their status. In the United Kingdom, the 1994 Trade Union and Employment Act incorporated this piece of Community legislation within domestic legislation, but at the same time as protection for one section of the population was being increased, another section was destined to become more vulnerable. The Wages Councils, which set minimum wages for the very lowest-paid sectors of society, were abolished in the same Act (see Chapter 7).
21. *Guardian*, 08/06/1994.
22. Bulletin on Women and Employment in the EU, No. 4, April 1994. Available from Dr Rubery, Manchester School of Management, UMIST, PO Box 88, Sackville Street, Manchester M60 1QD, UK.
23. The Court decided not only that SABENA was in breach of Community law in terms of unfair treatment but that it should also have to compensate her for all the back-pay she lost while working at the lower rate of pay.
24. In order to encourage women to have children the Communist authorities provided day-care centres free, allowed women either a year's maternity leave on full pay with the same job guaranteed on return, or 3 years' substantial state support and the guarantee of the same job at the end. The consequence was that over 90 per cent of the female population worked, compared to only 49 per cent in West Germany; *Financial Times*, 12/08/94.
25. Lone parent families are usually defined as having one parent with dependent children under the age of 18.
26. Cronin, N. (1994) *Families in the European Union*, London: Family Policy Studies Centre.
27. INSEE, *Les Données Sociales*, 1993, Paris: Hachette.
28. Horst Theissen was sentenced to 2½ years in prison for not following the formal procedures laid down in the Act. The law has been liberalised since 1970, with abortion permitted on medical, eugenic, ethical/criminological and social grounds. About 90 per cent of all abortions are carried out under the last provision, which has caused concern in the Catholic Church. Prützel-Thomas, M. 'The abortion issue and the Federal Constitutional Court' *German Politics* 2 (3) pp. 467–84.
29. *Independent*, 29/05/93.
30. Prützel-Thomas, 1993, p. 481.
31. *Guardian*, 30/08/94.
32. 'Fathers and their role in tomorrow's family' (1994) *The European Union and the Family. Social Europe*, Brussels: Commission.
33. Cosis Brown, H. (1992) 'Gender, sex and sexuality in the assessment of prospective carers' *Adoption and Fostering* 16 (2), pp. 3–7.
    Cosis Brown, H. (1991) 'Competent child-focused practice: working with lesbian and gay carers' *Adoption and Fostering* 15 (2), pp. 5–9.
34. The European Convention on Human Rights and various United Nations and International Labour Organisation Conventions would have made it impossible to forcibly repatriate these people.

35. France and Germany both introduced a voluntary repatriation programme with the promise of financial inducements if people agreed to leave and not return. Collinson, S. (1993) *Beyond Borders, West European Migration Policy Towards the 21st Century*, London: RIIA, pp. 60–61.
36. The second Commonwealth Immigrants Act 1968, the Immigration Act 1971, and the British Nationality Act 1981.
37. *Actualités Migrations*, Revue Bimensuelle de l'Office des migrations Internationales No. 447–448 du 16 Septembre au 15 Octobre 1994.
38. The German government is now considering restricting this right.
39. The German government is in the process of trying to adjust its nationality laws to cope with the presence of more and more 'non-ethnic' Germans. In a proposal to the *Bundestag* by the joint CDU–CSU–FDP coalition on 14 November 1994, it is proposed to allow third-generation children a kind of 'German child nationality'.
40. Koslowski, R. (1994) 'Intra-EU migration, citizenship and political union' *Journal of Common Market Studies* 32 (3), pp. 369–402.
41. Dwyer, C. (1993) 'Constructions of Muslim identity and the contesting of power: the debate over Muslim schools in the United Kingdom' in *Race, Place and Nation*, Jackson, P. and Penrose, J. (eds), London: UCL.
42. Rex, J. (1992) 'Race and Ethnicity in Europe' in *Social Europe*, Bailey, J. (ed.), Harlow: Longman.
43. Solé, R. 'Un modéle français d'intégration', *Le Monde*, 19/02/91.
44. *Guardian*, 06/10/94.
45. Faist, T. (1994) 'How to define a foreigner? The symbolic politics of immigration in German Partisan Discourse, 1978–1992, in Baldwin-Edwards and Schain (eds) *The Politics of Immigration in Western Europe*, London: Frank Cass.
46. These new proposals on acquisition of German nationality form part of the agreement between the CDU–CSU–FDP coalition partners in the new government after the October 1994 general elections. *Koalitionsvereinbarung*, Bonn, 11/11/94.
47. Oppenheim, C. (1990) *Poverty: the facts*, London: CPAG.
48. Roberts, B. (1994) *Minority Ethnic Women: Work, Unemployment and Education*, Equal Opportunities Commission. See also 'Britain's Ethnic Minorities' (1993) Policy Studies Institute in *Independent on Sunday*, 29/08/93.
49. Roberts, B. (1994) *Minority Ethnic Women: Work, Unemployment and Education*, Equal Opportunities Commission Research Unit, Overseas House, Quay Street, Manchester M3 3HN.
50. Homeworkers' rates of pay and rights are virtually nonexistent, and their super-exploitation is reflected in the pay they receive, often 50p. per garment, and the price the same dress or skirt then fetches in a high street shop, which can be as much as £50.
51. Ginsburg, N. (1992) 'Racism and housing: concepts and reality' in *Racism and Anti-Racism: Inequalities, Opportunities and Policies*, Braham, P. *et al.* (eds).
52. Simpson, A. (1981) Stacking the Decks: A Study of Race, Inequality and Council Housing in Nottingham, Nottingham: Spokesman.
53. See also Solomos, J. (1988) 'Institutional racism: policies of marginalisation in education and training' in *Multi-racist Britain*, Cohen, P. and Bains, H. (eds), London: Macmillan.
54. Sen, F. (1989) 'Problems and integration constraints of migrants in the Federal Republic of Germany', Centre for Turkish Studies, Essen in Czerniawski, G. (1995) 'The Turkish Community and Integration in Germany' Unpublished Dissertation, LES, University of North London.
55. Fest, J. *et al.* (1993) 'Migration movements from Turkey to the European Community' Forum des Migrants des C.E., Bruxelles.

56. Martin, P. (1991) 'The Unfinished Story: Turkish labour migration to Western Europe', Geneva: ILO.
57. Goldberg, A. (1993) *Turkish Immigrants – Future Prospects for the Europe of the 1990s*, Bonn: ZfT.
58. Dubet, F. (1993) 'Les temps d'exclusions', *Le Monde Diplomatique*, November.
59. For a consideration of the lack of trade union support in France for immigrant workers, see Edye, D. (1987) *Government Policy and Immigrant Labour*, Aldershot: Gower.
60. Insee, 1991 – Les étrangers en France, dossier, Économie et Statistique, no. 242, avril 1991. See also the INSEE annual reports on *La Société Française, données sociales*. For attitudes on integration see *Faire France* (1995) Paris: La Découverte.
61. Bauer, H. (1995) 'Banlieues-Lieux de Ban? Étude sur l'Exclusion des Maghrébins en France', unpublished dissertation, LES, University of North London.
62. Ochoa de Michelena, C. (1993) La immigración hacia España de los naturales de países teerceros a la CEE: un nuevo fenómeno. *Política y Sociedad*, 12, pp. 97–120.
63. Bernabé, F. *et al.* (1993) Immigración magrebí en España. Mapfie. colc. 'El Maghreb'. See also special issue on migration in *El Pais*, 20/06/91. For official statistics and government policy on immigration, see the annual reports of the Direccion General de Migraciones at the Ministerio de Trabajo y Seguridad Social, Madrid.
64. Nuevas Dinamicas Migratorias en Europa y sus Efectos sobre los Procesos de Insercion-Exclusion Social, Madrid 28/03/92 (Part of the EU's 3rd Anti-Poverty Programme).
65. Gregorio Gil, C. (1993) Mujeres Inmigrantes Marroquíes en la CAM, in Bernabé *et al.*
66. Gregorio, C. (1992) Mujeres inmigrantes de América Latina y Africa: su doble discriminación, *Rev. de Sodepaz*, 9. See also various issues of the Madrid based bimonthly review *Sin Fronteras*.
67. Groenendijk, C. (1989) 'Racism in Europe' in *Fortress Europe*, Gordon, P. (ed) London: Runnymede Trust.
68. *Independent*, 22/10/92.
69. *Guardian*, 01/12/92.
70. *Independent*, 22/04/95.
71. The Vetter report (OJ C99/170). See also the Malangre report EP A3-0199/91, 2/7/91.
72. Zwamborn, M. (1989) 'The scope for a refugee policy of the European Communities as part of an overall Human Rights policy', SIM. Netherlands Institute of Human Rights 'Refugees in the World: The European Community's response'. The Hague (Dec. 1989). See also: EC Commission – Communications on Immigration and Asylum: SEC (91) 1857 of 11/10/91 (Asylum); SEC (91) 1855 of 23/10/91 (Immigration); ISEC /B6/92 of 10/3/92.
73. Jenkins, J. (1989) 'Foreign Exchange' *New Statesman and Society*, 28 July 1989.
74. Hedy d'Ancona, MEP; *Independent*, 22/04/95.
75. Migration Newssheet (1989) *Fortress Europe*, in Gordon, P. (ed.), London: Runnymede Trust.
76. The expulsion of Jamaican tourists coming to visit families over the Christmas holiday by the UK Immigration Authorities in 1993 was one example of what is likely to become a more frequent occurrence; *Independent*, 24/12/93.
77. Commission communication on the abolition of controls of persons at intra-Community borders. COM (88) 640 final.
78. Meehan, E. (1993) *Citizenship and the European Community*, London: Sage, p. 9.
79. Collins, D. (1975) 'The European Communities – the Social Policy of the First Phase', vol. 2 *The European Economic Community 1958–1972*, London: Martin Robertson. M. Gold, EC Social and Labour Policy NIESR Working Paper no. 12.
80. Community Charter of the Fundamental Social Rights of Workers (1992) in *Social Europe* 1/92, Commission of the European Communities Brussels, pp. 7–11.

# CHAPTER TWELVE

# Conclusion: prospects for the new Europe

Only connect

E. M. FORSTER

## 12.1  Introductory comment

The purpose of this book has been to give a current analysis of contemporary Europe from an economic, political and social perspective. Our interest has not been with the position of any one ethnic group, nation or state, but with the overall interests of the inhabitants of Europe as a whole. In this conclusion we intend to evaluate the present situation and to discuss future prospects in the light of what seems both possible and desirable.

## 12.2  Where we are now: an evaluation of contemporary European societies

The policy-making process and the respective institutions that encompass it in the economic, political and social arenas have remained rooted in traditional practices and ways of thinking that no longer reflect the reality of contemporary Europe. In particular:

- there is the assumption that Europeans are still predominantly male and exclusively white;
- governments assume that they are still autonomous economic policy-makers;
- liberal democracy is still based on elitist forms; and
- most importantly, thought and practice is still moulded largely by the nation state and the accompanying nationalism that emerged with modernism.

It is our contention that this state of affairs is now profoundly unsatisfactory: it is both anachronistic and perpetuates injustice to the inhabitants of Europe on the basis of their class, ethnicity, gender and geographical location. The task for the future is to identify the way forward on the basis of best practice and underlying developments.

In Chapter 6 we examined the different models of economic organisation that can be found in European countries. We concluded that although all countries (at least in the post cold-war scenario) operate mixed economies, there have been different 'cultures of capitalism' offering differing mixes between market and state. Largely because of external pressures,[1] the cultures of European capitalism have tended to polarise into two camps: the so-called 'British model', based (to the extent that is politically possible) on free markets and other aspects of the neo-liberal economic agenda (see Chapters 2, 5 and 6); and the 'social market', based largely on the German approach to economic organisation: regulated markets, comprehensive social provision, devolved power, all in the context of a tight macroeconomic framework. On the whole the social market approach has probably prevailed, given German leadership of the Continent and the consequent modelling of much of the European integration project on German social market principles. However, it is also clear that the social market model itself is changing, broadly becoming more market and less social, as a reaction to changing external parameters.

Most countries seem to be choosing a version of the social market model, often at the expense of their own specific national approaches to economic organisation which have developed over many years.[2] The rationale behind this is clear: the social market economies have been by far the most successful in Europe during the post-war period,[3] providing a mixture of economic success and social protection and cohesion[4] (see the national income data presented in the Statistical Appendix). The United Kingdom's experiment with neo-liberalism, on the other hand, has proved to be a very mixed blessing, and has certainly failed to fulfil the pre-1979 promises of increasing the trend rate of growth in the United Kingdom by around 1 per cent. The increased rate of growth in the United Kingdom after the exit from the ERM in 1992 is probably the result of the 'quick fix' that follows a devaluation, and the medium-term prospects for the United Kingdom economy remain distinctly uncertain.[5] At the same time the United Kingdom has experienced increased inequality, a deterioration in the work experience of those still in jobs,[6] and potential threats to its very social fabric (see Chapter 6, and below).

However, the critique that proponents of the UK model might make of the social market approach concerns the view that the success of the social market approach has been due to a mixture of:

(a)  Particular favourable historical circumstances during the post-war period, which were conducive to economic success (see Chapter 1).

(b)  The particular features of the social market economies, which again rendered economic growth possible within the context of such structures. For example, the United Kingdom is sometimes seen as having been in secular economic decline after the end of its imperial days, while countries such as Germany are seen to have benefited from the ability to reconstruct their economies after defeat in the Second World War.

The argument here would be that times have changed, we are no longer in the post-war boom years, we are facing serious challenges of the type outlined in Chapter 5 and in this context the neo-liberal model represents the best way forward for European societies, given especially its propensity for rapid reaction to changing external parameters.

These are clearly opposing views which it is not possible to test empirically. We can, however, make a few observations:

1.  Although it may be necessary to change the emphasis of the mixed economy towards more market in order to render the European economies more able to meet the challenge of, for example, NIC competition there must be a limit to the extent to which this is desirable. For example, do we really believe that we can compete with countries such as Korea, or even Poland, on the basis of wage costs? If we did, what sort of society would we be creating in the process? Surely the answer lies elsewhere, possibly in competing on the basis of the human capital embedded in the European labour force,[7] and on the basis of technology and innovation.

2.  If we do choose the neo-liberal approach there are costs to be borne, in terms of both economic equality and justice, and indeed the very social fabric of our societies (see Chapter 4). This should come as no surprise, as is directly predictable from economic theory (see Chapter 2): freeing markets increases economic inequality. The United Kingdom's neo-liberal experiment provides a good case study in this context. We have seen how the United Kingdom has experienced the emergence of the 40:30:30 society (Hutton, 1995) with the creation of an underclass, widespread social dislocation and economic precariousness even among the luckier elements in society (Chapters 4, 6 and 7). All this in the context of widespread public disquiet at the growing salaries and 'perks' of top executives in the UK private sector in general, and in the privatised utilities in particular. This growing inequality in the distribution of income in the United Kingdom has been documented recently by the report of the Rowntree Commission, set up by the Joseph Rowntree Foundation and published in February 1995. This shows that income inequality in the United Kingdom has grown faster over the last decade or so than in any other similar industrial country (the only country to 'outdo' the United Kingdom is New Zealand, which has been the subject of a similar neo-liberal experiment). Income distribution in the United Kingdom is now more unequal than at any time since 1945, the poorest 20–30 per cent of the population not having benefited at all from economic growth. The Conservative Government would claim that this is a price worth paying for increased incentives to work, and that the poor will eventually benefit from economic growth through the 'trickle-down effect'. The Rowntree Report, however, finds no evidence that this has actually taken place, perhaps because the United Kingdom's trend rate of growth did not in fact increase during the 1980s. It further claims that increasing inequality threatens the fabric of society, increasing the propensity for crime, social unrest and drug abuse. The main findings of the Rowntree Report (and of some of the debate in this area) are summarised in Figure 12.1.

3.  Similarly, if we go along the road of freeing markets then we can also expect some of the other consequences that this implies (see Chapter 2). These might include:

    (a)  under-provision of certain basic goods and services (examples might include education, health, public transport), and over-provision of others (for example environmentally damaging activities) as a result of the switch from production

# While the rich get richer . . .

A fierce debate is now raging over the rights and wrongs of vast pay awards to the heads of Britain's largest industries

**Share options – The chief executive of a privatised water company, for example, may have the option to buy 500,000 shares in his company at a price of £1 a share. If the current price were £3 a share, he could exercise his option, pay £500,000 for the shares and then sell them immediately for £1,500,000. He would realise an instant profit of £1,000,000.**

The huge pay increases given to the people who run some of Britain's biggest industries have been the cause of a political row in recent months. For while the wages of millions of workers in factories, offices, schools and hospitals have struggled to keep pace with the increase in prices, some senior executives have been enjoying rises over 15 or 20 times the current rate of inflation.

Iain Vallence, who earns £663,000 a year as the chairman of British Telecom, had to apologise after joking to a House of Commons committee that he would not mind swapping jobs with a junior hospital doctor because it might be relaxing. More than half of all junior doctors work 72-hour weeks for pay as low as £12,500 a year.

In another celebrated case, the chief executive of British Gas, the company responsible for delivering gas to every home in Britain, was awarded a salary increase of 75 per cent to £475,000 a year. A couple of weeks later, it was revealed that British Gas intended to cut the wages of the people running its showrooms to bring them into line with other people working in high street shops and stores.

British Gas, together with the companies that supply electricity and water to our homes, were "nationalised" – owned by the Government – until a few years ago. But they were then sold off – or privatised. Shares in the companies were sold on the stock market, raising billions of pounds for the Government; but, as a result, control passed out of the hands of ministers to the new owners in the private sector.

When the industries were nationalised, the salaries of the senior staff were controlled by ministers, and they tended to be lower than for the chief executives of leading private sector companies.

This was partly because job security was greater in the nationalised industries, but also because the Government wanted to set an example to its five million public sector workers. Since then, there has been a rapid catching-up process, with the heads of the newly privatised industries securing hefty increases every year.

The jumps in basic pay are merely one aspect of the total package offered to senior figures. Most also have a clause in their contracts giving them share options – the right to buy shares in their company at a much lower price than that currently on offer in the market. This can be extremely lucrative.

In addition, Many chief executives have the added cushion of what are known as three-year rolling contracts. The way these operate is that the executive has a three-year contract to run a firm, but it "rolls forward" to begin afresh every day. If, for any reason, the executive were to be dismissed from his job, he would thus have a full three years of his contract to run, and be entitled to three years' pay in compensation. In the case of an executive on £335,000 a year, this would amount to a million pounds.

Even this is not the end of the story. Executives enjoy a range of perks, including chauffeur-driven limousines and help to pay for their children when they go to university. There are also generous payments into pension plans for their retirement. Since pensions are often based on the salary when they retire, some firms give a big boost to salaries for the last year of service.

One argument backing this system is that top-class executives differ from the bulk of the working population in that they are in short supply. Executives say that if there was less demand for their services, they would have to be prepared to work for less.

The Government has imposed tough pay limits on workers in the public sector – nurses, teachers and police officers, for example – because it is confident that there are plenty of people available to work in hospitals, schools and police stations. The same principle of supply and demand applies to workers in the private sector.

In addition, some say that the deals offered are justified by the performance of the companies. And it is also argued that British executives would be enticed overseas unless their packages matches those offered in the United States, Germany and France.

All these points are disputed, in most companies in Britain, pay and conditions of senior executives are set by what is known as a remuneration committee. This is normally a group of directors with no day-to-day responsibility for running the firm. However, executives tend to sit on several remuneration committees, and often a person who has been fixing the conditions for director X one week finds director X helping to fix his own pay the next. It is argued that this arrangement is far too cosy and encourages high awards.

Even more contentious is the claim that salary increases have been warranted by performance. Many privatised firms, for example are monopolies: they face no competition from rivals in the way that, say, Sainsbury's, Tesco, Gateway and Waitrose compete to sell us food.

Although prices of public utilities – water, gas and electricity – are regulated, the firms are still guaranteed enormous profits. Additionally, every former nationalised industry has increased its profitability by reducing its workforce, in some cases by at least 50 per cent. A smaller wage bill has meant higher profits,

***Figure 12.1*** The main findings of the Rowntree report
*Source: Guardian, 21/2/95*

# . . . the poor get poorer

### Investment in education and training is seen as the most reliable way to prevent poverty and create more jobs.

leading to higher pay for executives and an increase in the company share price, making share options even more valuable.

Finally, it is argued that there is no convincing evidence that foreign companies are lining up to poach underpaid British executives. Indeed, the gap between directors and workers on average earnings is already far higher in Britain than in countries which are usually considered to have more successful economies, such as Germany and Japan.

The gap between the incomes of the rich and poor in Britain grew rapidly between the late 1970s and the early 1990s, ending a process of increasing equality that stretches back for several centuries.

A report earlier this month by the Joseph Rowntree Foundation, which funds research into economic and social issues, said that between 1979 and 1992 the poorest 20–30 per cent of the population failed to benefit from economic growth. It warned that the way in which the living standards of a sizeable minority of people had lagged behind over the past 15 years was not only a problem for those affected directly, but also damaged "the social fabric and so affects us all".

The Rowntree report found that there had been a sharp increase in the number of people living on incomes less than half the level of the national average. The number fell from 10 per cent in the 1960s to a low of 6 per cent in 1977 but has since risen to over 20 per cent.

Government ministers dispute that the growing divide between high and low incomes has left poorer people worse off than when the Conservative Party came to power in 1979. Both the Prime Minister and the Social Security secretary, Peter Lilley, said last week that all groups in society had seen their standards of living rise, even though the Department of Social Security's own figures show that the poorest 10 per cent of the population saw their incomes fall by more than 15 per cent between 1979 and 1992, once the cost of housing was taken into account.

To some extent, the widening gap has been caused by trends in the global economy. Firms are increasingly able to shift production to countries in the developing world, where wages are lower. At the same time, governments in the Western industrialised countries have followed policies that have been aimed at preventing prices from rising too quickly. They did this by making it more expensive for individuals and firms to borrow money, which in turn meant consumers bought less in the shops and firms took on fewer workers. As a result the number of people without a job has doubled since 1979. And many of the new jobs created have been part-time rather than full-time.

The trend towards greater inequality has also been encouraged by government policies. The Conservative Party says cutting the taxes of the wealthy encourages people to set up new businesses. These businesses will then hire new workers, who will benefit from an increase in wages. Eventually, according to this philosophy, the gains from cutting the taxes of the rich would "trickle down" to the less well-off. The Rowntree report concluded, however, that there was "no evidence that this has occurred in Britain".

It argued that increasingly inequality over the past 15 years has not been accompanied by higher growth and could harm the long-term prospects for the economy. With competition from the rest of the world becoming more intense, it said the key to economic success was having a pool of highly-skilled and well educated workers, not a significant minority on the margins of society.

There are a number of ways to reverse the trends of the past 15 years. One suggestion is that the Government could set the levels of taxes and benefits to help the lower paid. Increasing taxation on the better off to increase benefits for the less well-off should, in theory, lead to less inequality. But ministers argue that hitting the incomes of the rich merely discourages people from setting up businesses and in the long run makes everybody worse off.

Most economists believe, however, that the most reliable way to distribute income more evenly would be to increase the demand for workers. This would involve economic policies that deliver strong rates of growth and investing more money in education and training to ensure that everybody who wanted a job could find one.

Most industrial nations enjoyed full employment for the three decades after the end of the war in 1945. Employees knew that if they left one job they could quickly find another, so employers were forced to pay high wages to keep their workers. Nowadays, high levels of unemployment, accompanied by curbs on unions, have tipped the balance in favour of employers who know that their staff will think twice before leaving a job in today's uncertain employment climate.

***Figure 12.1*** Continued

based on the social calculus towards production based on a private calculus following privatisation or deregulation;

(b) greater unemployment, at an even higher level than it currently exists (see Chapter 7);

(c) greater instability, especially in financial markets, as well as more acute business cycles; and

(d)   greater regional inequalities.

The exact nature of the above, of course, depends on the precise way in which the neo-liberal agenda is implemented. However, at the very least all this represents a salutary warning of some of the consequences we might expect from the adoption of the neo-liberal economic model in European countries.

On a political level some form of liberal democracy is a common feature of all European societies, but how those systems are run varies as a result of historical and other factors. Overall, however, there seems to be a crisis in liberal democracies over the nature of representation, participation, the degree of responsiveness to new forms of politics and the ability for democratically elected governments to fully represent the people, and control many areas of policy-making. According to Hirst (1994) liberal democracy is failing to cope with new demands. It has become 'atrophied', and merely legitimises a centralised and bureaucratic government rather than acting as a check on it. Furthermore, western societies are becoming less homogeneous and more multicultural with different ethnic groups. In other words a new kind of pluralism is developing with which centralised state structures cannot cope, and which demands new political forms.

Within Europe there is a difference of the degree of centralisation of state power. It seems clear that the tendency within Europe is a move towards more devolved national structures. Even countries such as France and Spain, both historically highly centralised states, have initiated steps towards more regional autonomy. It appears that highly centralised states such as Ireland, the United Kingdom and Greece do not have the necessary flexibility to respond to changing economic and political conditions in the same way that more devolved federal states such as Germany, Austria and Belgium possess. The formal process of devolving political power will not necessarily lead to any greater local autonomy if it is not accompanied by some kind of economic democracy.

There is a further element to this argument and that concerns the best possible form of representation that modern industrialised liberal democracies can offer. The contemporary cry is for more participation, and those states with meaningful devolved regional and local structures are by necessity closer to their populations.[8] At the same time, however, further European integration may imply that supranational bodies, like the European Commission and the European Parliament, become increasingly important. Most European states use some form of PR in their elections. The major exceptions are the United Kingdom and France (although PR is used in France for regional and European elections, and in Northern Ireland for the European elections). It would appear from all available evidence that PR systems, despite some drawbacks, are a fairer way of electing representatives than the majority system. Certainly those groups which have traditionally been excluded from the political process, for instance women, are assured greater degree of representation under PR systems. However, it is not simply a PR system *per se* that will guarantee better representation, it is also the general levels of social attitudes and the practical support which determines participation from a wider cross-section of society. The figures in Chapter 3 on representation indicate that it is the Scandinavian countries which score highest in this area.

A key part of increasing participation is the amount of transparency at all levels of government. As we have indicated, most executive power has a tendency to want to operate in secret, but the experience of the Stalinist bureaucracies of eastern Europe and the Soviet Union in the post-1945 period are clear reminders of the dangers in that approach. As far as open government is concerned, those states with a more devolved state structure, such as Germany, or a political culture of more open consultation, for example the Scandinavian countries and the Netherlands, are less secretive and therefore more responsive to their citizens' needs.

The need for transparency is reflected in the never-ending round of corruption scandals that affect every European state. The classic formulation of the strength of liberal democracy is the balance of powers between the various organs of the state: the legislative, executive and judiciary. Pluralist theory emphasises competing centres with a degree of transparency, and the strength of liberal democracies is that the issues of corruption have reached the light of day through diligent work by, in the Italian case, the judicial arm of the state (see below).

An endemic feature of all political power seems to be its tendency to become corrupt. In the former states of eastern Europe, the persistence of one ruling party over a long period of time led to all kinds of abuses of power: nepotism through the system of nomenclatura and accumulation of privileges and wealth by leading party figures. Newer states such as Zimbabwe have also had their corruption scandals. In western Europe we can observe the same process taking place, which may give some substance to the old adage that 'power corrupts, absolute power corrupts absolutely'. By this we mean that a governing party or elite which remains too long in power tends over a period of time to institutionalise its position by conferring privileges on its supporters, either in terms of favouring contracts or via appointments to positions of prestige and influence. In all the states that we have observed, such practices exist to a greater or lesser extent.

In the United Kingdom we can observe the process whereby democratic local government has been reduced in significance to be replaced by QUANGOs, run by ministerial appointees, many of whom have been contributors to Conservative Party funds or are Conservative Party supporters. As we have indicated in Chapter 10, these groups control large sums of tax-payers' money without any of the usual accountability checks, whether by public audit or public accounts. In France Mény (1992) has analysed the way in which the institutions of the Fifth Republic are conducive to less than democratic control. In Spain the socialist government, led by Felipe González since it came to power in 1982, has been accused of abuse of executive power and appointing party members to leading positions within the public sector. In Italy, the power of patronage and abuse of executive power were part and parcel of the operation of the Italian political system for more than 40 years between 1948 and the early 1990s. In Germany there was the Flick scandal in 1984, where the allegations centred on large sums of money paid to party leaders and parties to grant favourable tax exemptions on overseas investments by the Flick organisation. Many of the new parties elected in Italy in March 1994 gained from an electorate unable to countenance the kind of corruption practised by the DC.

The exposure of malpractice and corruption has thrust the judiciary, or more particularly the magistrates into the limelight in many European countries. The most widespread example of this high profile role is the investigation by magistrates in Italy, and increasingly in France.[9] The Italian magistrates have become known as the *mani puliti* (clean hands) in contrast to those people that are the subject of their investigations. The intense scrutiny that the judiciary are placing the executive branch of government under, underlines the importance of the separation of powers in the modern state. A truly independent judiciary is an absolute defence against executive or legislative malpractice.

The argument is not quite as simple as that, where in the United Kingdom the judiciary, although nominally independent, is much more a reflection of the ruling elite than in France or Italy where lawyers and magistrates are organised into trade unions, and guard a degree of social and professional distance from their political masters.[10] This structural difference is also a result of the nature of the constitutional systems that operate in most Continental countries, whereby the independence is guaranteed by the Constitution. In the United Kingdom, there is a more voluntaristic tradition whereby judges display independence, through a certain mannered eccentricity, rather than a strong and clear separation of power. The executive has a strong grip on the organisation and running of the state in the United Kingdom not least, as we have explained, by the concept of 'parliamentary sovereignty', which in principle makes the people's representatives the supreme decision-makers but in reality allows any government with a moderate majority to act arbitrarily.

On most indicators of social progress fair distribution of income, good living conditions, generous welfare benefits, participation of all groups in society at all levels of society, the Scandinavian countries seem to come out at the top of the list. However, the stronger forces of social cohesion in this part of northern Europe mask a continent divided in many countries along the traditional lines of class, as well as gender and race.

All societies have undergone enormous changes since 1945 in terms of the effects of greater levels of industrialisation, which have provoked urbanisation on a massive scale, breaking down traditional structures of family, employment and gender roles. There has been some kind of social mobility, reflected in the decline of the traditional working class, and a growing middle class. While everyone has become richer the distribution of income has remained the same, perpetuating the same kind of inequalities.

For women there has no doubt been a massive increase in participation in the labour market (see Chapter 11), but in many cases, the work is low-paid and with poor conditions. Nevertheless, there has been some kind of emancipation, as we indicated in Chapters 4 and 11. Substantial inequalities remain in terms of job security, career enhancement, child care facilities and changing the ingrained habits of centuries of patriarchy in the nature of who does what in the domestic environment.

Migration has always been an integral part of industrial societies, and there has been an added dimension in terms of the very different cultures that post-1945 migrants brought with them to Europe. The response of European states to the presence of these settled communities has been one ranging from some kind of welcome to outright hostility. Some countries, notably Germany, have maintained a dogged defence of notions of ethnic purity, but recent indications point to a relaxation in this attitude. There is no doubt that the issue of a socially cohesive Europe will depend to some extent on how it treats those from other cultures. The nature of the relationship with Islam is crucial in this context.

## 12.3 Where we are going: future prospects for Europe

We now consider what the future might hold for Europe. In essence, the economic future of Europe will be determined by the extent to which it manages to meet the internal and external challenges we have discussed above and in Chapter 5. Needless to say, economic success will require a successful political framework,[11] and it will to a large extent condition the future social agenda.[12] A central part of this issue concerns how European countries deal with the growing problem of unemployment (see Chapter 7), for until we find a way of reaching the nirvana of the leisure society for all, employment[13] for as great a proportion of the population as possible holds the key to the creation of what Galbraith refers to as the 'good society', in which citizens are not deprived or excluded.

At the basis of this issue is how we choose to structure our economies, and the principles by which we choose to operate them. The fundamental question for the future concerns, as we have discussed in Chapter 6, whether the two models discussed above, the neo-liberal model and the social market model, are compatible and can be fused over time into a single 'European model' that is acceptable to most nation states and that meets future challenges which will face the European economies. Another possibility is that one approach will prove so superior to the other that it will eventually prevail. A third possibility is that the two approaches are so incompatible that the European economies will polarise, possibly with the bulk of Europe continuing to integrate around the German model, and with the United Kingdom going its own way. The outcome will naturally depend on the political situation, particularly in the United Kingdom, as much as on the inherent features of the two models. Polarisation is probably an outcome that is less than likely, given that all countries are engaged in a general process of movement towards more of the market, and that in many ways the future may well be about emphases rather than absolutes. We shall see.

New forms of democracy are necessary which build on local, regional and cross-national initiatives and which move beyond traditional parties and institutions. Despite the way in which national systems of government may operate, there is also evidence to suggest that national parliaments are declining in importance, as other supranational institutions take over running Europe. This development in the organisation of the 'Eurostate' has great consequences for representation and participation. At present the European Parliament is restricted in its powers and without substantial extension of its powers the future for democracy and open government is under serious question. Countervailing centres of power and more transparency in local, regional, national and EU government via such measures as a Freedom of Information Act and overall greater public access to official documents would reduce the dangers of over-bureaucratisation and the growth of an unaccountable and secret Eurostate.

A new political theory is necessary that can encompass new forms of representation and participation for all Europeans, whatever their cultural origins. In Chapter 3 we began by considering the debate concerning the end of history. It has not ended, and Europe faces numerous challenges both internally and externally. The cancer of violent nationalism using mythic notions of pure ethnicities and rigid boundaries, propagated by extreme right-wing parties and which finds its expression in the ethnic cleansing horror of former Yugoslavia, presents a formidable challenge to the chosen European ideals of protection of human rights.

The experience of *Verdrossenheit* which refers to the lack of involvement in the formal political process by young people has led some commentators to suggest that the mechanisms of representation need a thorough overhaul. The measures outlined above may be one way to overcome the increasing alienation of people from the political system. However, the lack of involvement in the formal political system does not mean an overall general apathy. The high level of interest and membership of pressure groups, in some cases such as Greenpeace actually larger than many political parties, suggest a different kind of participation in the political arena. This may be a useful way of diverting attention and effort away from the real centres of influence and power contained within the higher echelons of the executive, boards of companies and financial institutions.

The new political theory would be based on the realisation that the traditional opposition between left and right has diminished. The whole notion of a radical left needs to be examined. This entails a thorough examination within the socialist framework of issues such as violence, tradition, nationalism and fundamentalism (Giddens 1992). The best way for these issues to be resolved is through dialogue, rather than through the existing established channels of power. More participation in decision making needs to take place which means including different kinds of groups such as community organisations and new social movements into the process of communicating about programmes and policy. This kind of democracy, which Giddens refers to as 'dialogic democracy', will involve all those groups which are active in civil society, not only the leading groups such as trade unions and employers' organisations and their close ties with the state. This is the only way to counter the way in which the global economy is developing. This theory would accept diversity, heterogeneity and multiculturality, but not monoculturality.

The concomitant political structures would reflect to some extent the hybridity and fragmented nature of nation states where cities and regions are becoming as important in terms of defining experience and engendering loyalties. Some other aspects of this new theory would include the recognition of creating countervailing powers – in institutional terms via greater powers of inquiry to elected representatives both at national and local levels, to increase accountability and a greater plurality of media scrutiny, through a system of regulation of monopoly control of print and broadcast media. Public service broadcasting systems, provided they do not become mouth-pieces of the government of the day, are one way, together with greater access to the various media.

Another consideration is the degree of alternance that a political system can provide. The importance of alternance lies in the prevention of one party dominating the political landscape for too long; but given the nature of the democratic system with the people's will as supreme, this would be difficult.

The development of globalisation in terms of the world economic system has led to a consideration of what may be happening at the other end of the spectrum, namely the local level. The term 'glocalisation' defines the global–local nexus in terms of economics, politics and society. Within the European context this is linked to the growth of the dynamic cities on their own or as part of regions connected by an integrated transport structure of high speed rail links and (TENs: Trans European Networks). What is evolving is a heterogeneity of cities, along lines last seen in the Italian city states during the Renaissance or in the medieval North European Hanseatic League. The prospect is a mosaic of European regions, so that the uniform homogeneous nation state evolves into a more fragmented and less unified form, but will remain important as possible mediators between the global and the local.[14]

Europe is witnessing a challenge to the concept of the nation state from the success of decentralised states such as Germany and the Netherlands with strong regional and city centres (Hamburg, Munich, Rotterdam and Amsterdam), and similar developments in formerly centralised states such as Belgium, France, Italy and Spain which have attempted to create stronger regional structures with countervailing powers to the central authority. In contrast, the state remains very centralised in Portugal, Ireland and Greece and in the United Kingdom the last 15 years have seen a recentralisation of the state.

One issue that is raised in this context is federalism–subsidiarity. From the examples we have given of how federalism works within some of the states of western Europe, it seems clear that it provides one of the most effective ways in which to devolve government down to the lowest possible level, and thereby make government more immediate to the people. This means that not only do people experience government more directly but that they can also influence the decisions of government in a more immediate way. The days of a large highly centralised nation state are slowly coming to an end within Europe. The concept of subsidiarity defines the nature of how this devolution of power should take place. The definition, however, refers to real and effective devolution, not to the total misunderstanding of the term that the British government has had whereby it has meant more power to central government at the nation state level.

Most writers have considered federalism as the only way in which power in a large state can be brought to more manageable levels. There is a long anarchist tradition in support of federal structures of government, based on spontaneous and individualised structures which caused them to oppose many of Marx's ideas of centralised state power and collective structures. The split between the two groups occurred in the 1870s.[15] Pierre-Joseph Proudhon, in *Du Principe Fédératif* published in 1863, proposed the model of the Swiss Confederation as one of the best ways to ensure that 'the organs of administration are local and lie as near the direct control of people as possible'.[16] Bakunin called in 1867 for a 'United States of Europe' to prevent an outbreak of civil war among the nations of Europe,[17] and Kropotkin at the beginning of this century, commenting on the centralised Tsarist state, saw a 'federation of independent units' as the best way for Russia to be governed.[18]

Those opposed to federalism tend to be either those who seek to maintain centralised state structures and hold to notions of the strong state or those who, like the SNP in an initial phase, consider that their status as a region within Europe is insufficient for their expression as full nation. This position is not necessarily opposed to some form of regional government but on Scottish, not English, terms.

The EU has always had a regional policy, designed to improve the economic performance of those areas with poor infrastructure and low levels of industrialisation. Within the institutions of the EU there has also been a committee of local authorities and regions. The Maastricht treaty (Article 198) established a new body, the Committee of the Regions (COR), whose function it is to represent the views of all subnational levels of government within member states to the respective institutions of the EU.[19] According to Bruce Millan, the Commissioner responsible for Regional Policy in the negotiations leading to the Maastricht Treaty, the COR is intended to be the forum of representation for local and regional government rather than for regions as territories.

European societies are divided along many cleavages. In the Introduction we focused on the nature of the class structure of the international economic system. There are business, political and social elites who in many countries may not form a class, as such, that own all the economic wealth, but are sufficiently linked within networks which connect and which operate in the running of many aspects of economic, political and social organisations. This is not to suggest a conspiracy approach to an analysis of contemporary European societies, merely to recognise which groups are the key decision makers within those societies. The question of power is as problematic as ever. In a traditional view of power, then we could say that these groups possess more power than other groups in that they can get other people to do their will. In the Foucault sense of power, where power exists at all levels of personal and social relations and is more like a web, it is more difficult to locate such centres of power.

This debate reflects in one way the whole nature of the modernist versus post-modernist argument, namely, whether totalising ways of analysing the world such as Marxism or Freudianism are more useful than more eclectic and local approaches. The irony is that just as these modernist views with their universalising theories are in relative decline, so the world through the process of globalisation is becoming just the kind of 'one society' the dynamics of which Marxist theory, for example, aims to explain.

Our examination of contemporary Europe has considered the cleavages in society arising from class, gender and race divisions. In conclusion we would emphasise that any analysis of society needs to evaluate all these cleavages, as well as other experiences of exclusion such as age, sexual orientation and geographical location.

One of the major changes, then, taking place within all European societies concerns the role of women. In many areas of society the decline in the influence of religion, the increase in employment and housing opportunities and the changing attitudes towards women has resulted in women taking positions previously restricted to men.

Although it is true that many of these jobs tend to be in lower-paid and less-protected areas of the labour market, they are none the less significant in the potential that is unlocked by larger numbers of women than men in employment. There is no clear overall progress, as Chapter 9 indicates. It appears that in the Scandinavian countries the most significant advances have been made, but even in what have been considered more 'traditional' societies, such as Spain and Italy, the influence of women in political, economic and social areas has increased enormously in the last two decades. There is still a rearguard action by certain sections of society to reverse this process, but overall it seems that it is irreversible.

This issue reflects a central concern of this book, namely that in order to understand modern European societies it is important to combine a political, economic and social analysis. The change in the role and status of women in these areas is not simply a result of greater economic opportunities, but also a result of the demands of women themselves for a greater degree of participation in all areas of society. Changing attitudes in a society are a result of changes in the ways people think, stemming from more educational opportunities, a decline in religious belief and its teachings on the role and status of women as mothers and domestic providers:

We are in the middle of an historic change in the relations between men and women: a shift in power and values that is unravelling many of the assumptions not only of 200 years of industrial society, but also of millenia of traditions and beliefs.[20]

Another major change in western European societies is the changing nature of their ethnic mix. These societies have now become multicultural and recognition is being made, but not without substantial opposition particularly from neo-Fascist groups, that cultures are ongoing and dynamic and created by people in their interaction on a daily basis with other human beings. The need is being constantly made to underline the inescapable hybridity and intermixture of ideas.[21]

Old notions of solidarity and community can once more become part of the primary focus of socialist movements. As Mulgan (1994) argues these were in fact the mainspring of the original socialist movements in the nineteenth century, reflected in organisations such as the mutual societies, Rochdale pioneers and the cooperative movement. These are ethical concerns, about the importance of values in politics as much as economics being the guiding force behind the politics of the industrial revolution and capitalism and communism. As these old structures of nation states become increasingly anachronistic, with their hierarchical structures, so it becomes possible for movements on the left to return the core of their values, and promote democracy based on local and regional areas.

Ideas about community and communitarianism would seem to be the context in which some commentators are articulating the major problems of social cohesion. The outlines of the arguments were sketched out in Chapter 3, and we can conclude that any notion of communitarianism will need to consider issues about and ownership of property and unequal distribution of wealth. In other words, since the macro and micro nature of the world is so interconnected, any analysis and prescription for society's ills that ignores that dynamic will fall short of useful solutions.

An attempt to define and put into practice a new concept of citizenship may be one way in which the gap between the state and civil society may be bridged in favour new groups and their participation within the political process. At the EU level the Maastricht Treaty states that all nationals of the member states are now citizens of the European Union. Some writers such as Meehan (1993) consider that these rights will form the basis of a new kind of Europe, but this concept needs to be broad enough to include in a meaningful sense those non-EU nationals, mainly immigrant workers and their families, who are excluded from this category of 'Euro-citizens'.

What emerges from much of the above discussion, and indeed from much of this book, is that the future of Europe is inevitably bound up with the future of the European integration project. We therefore need to examine the possible scenarios for the future of the EU. These might be summarised as follows:

1. That the process of integration will slow down and eventually go into reverse, as national and regional imperatives overwhelm the momentum towards integration.
2. That the EU will continue to develop along the lines it has followed since the mid-1980s,[22] emphasising the process of deepening rather than widening. This would probably involve the succesful implementation of the Maastricht Treaty (see Chapter 5), perhaps suitably amended in the light of the experiences of the last few years.
3. That the EU will continue to develop, but with an emphasis on widening over deepening. This would naturally involve further enlargement.
4. That the EU will continue to develop, placing more or less equal emphasis on both deepening and widening.

Our view is that the balance of probabilities discounts the first scenario, since the forces that are propelling European nation states into ever-closer cooperation and integration, as well as the net advantages of further integration (see Chapter 5), are probably too powerful for the project to fall apart, despite the fierce and vocal opposition of groups such as the so-called 'Eurosceptics' in the United Kingdom. We also feel it unlikely that the deepening process can continue at the pace it has done in recent years, given the problems that surround the Maastricht Treaty, the monetary union provisions of which are unlikely to be implemented in the form or on the timescale envisaged in the Treaty (see Chapter 5). Nevertheless, we feel that the deepening process will probably continue in a form and on a timescale yet to be determined.[23] We also feel that the the impetus towards and net advantages of widening will also be difficult to resist, although the timing of any further enlargements is difficult to predict, given the problems that these would entail.

We therefore feel that on balance scenario 4 represents the most likely way forward, albeit with uncertain timescales attached to both the deepening and the widening processes.

This then begs the question of what sort of European Union is likely to emerge. Again, there are a number of possibilities, aspects of which are discussed above and in various other parts of the book:

- A loose federation of independent nation states, or a tightly organised federal Europe on something akin to the USA model. The latter might be based on the principle of subsidiarity, with a federal government excercising powers over such domains as macroeconomic policy, defence, foreign policy, social security; and national or regional governments controlling most other functions.

■ An EU based on the current principle that all members have to accept the entire *acquis communautaire*,[24] and the EU develops *en masse* or not at all; or a 'variable speed', 'variable geometry' or *à la carte* EU, in which members each can choose to get involved in the deepening process at the speed which they think appropriate for their own needs, and in which each member can opt in and out of (or indeed be excluded from) different aspects of the integation process.

Table 12.1 illustrates the potential future enlargement position, as it looks after the accession of the EFTA countries Austria, Sweden and Finland in 1995.[25] The membership aspirants, actual or potential, can be conveniently divided into three groups of states that, albeit diverse, have certain characteristics in common.

***Table 12.1*** Applicants and potential applicants for EU membership

| Actual/potential applicants | Existing arrangements | Path towards membership |
|---|---|---|
| **I. EFTA** | | |
| Norway | Member of European Economic Area | Full membership rejected by referendum. |
| **II. MEDITERRANEAN STATES** | | |
| Turkey | Association Agreement | Full application blocked by Greece. Member of European customs union. |
| Malta Cyprus | Association Agreements | Have applied. Possible eventual membership. |
| **III. EX-COMECON:** | | |
| Poland Hungary Czech Republic Slovak Republic | European Agreements: Interim Agreements signed Dec 1991 not yet ratified. | Principal of eventual membership established at Copenhagen Summit. |
| Romania Bulgaria | Negotiations on Europe Agreement from May 1992. | |
| Slovenia Baltic States | Possible Europe Agreements | Possible eventual membership |
| Croatia Serbia Macedonia Bosnia-Herzegovina | None | Possibly an issue within next decade |
| **IV. FORMER SOVIET UNION:** | | |
| Russian Federation Kazakstan Ukraine Belarus | Negotiation of bilateral Partnership and Cooperation Agreements from 1993. | Full membership less likely |

The EFTA enlargement was probably the last of the traditional or 'classical' enlargements, in that it involves the integration into the EU of economies that have broadly similar characteristics to the existing members, and it was thus a relatively uncontroversial and economically logical enlargement. In fact the EFTA countries are considerably richer than the 12 countries that they joined: in the early 1990s Austrian per capita GDP was $16 592, Finland's $23 196,[26] and Sweden's $22 443, compared with the EC average of $14 805. They are all small countries of between 4 and 8.5 m inhabitants, with open economies in which trade accounts for 35–40 per cent of GDP, most of it (55–60 per cent) with the Union.[27]

The integration of the three former EFTA economies into the EU should prove to be relatively unproblematic and should on the whole lead to positive economic effects. Many of the trade effects of EU membership have already been experienced, given the close relations that already exist between the EU and EFTA, but there is likely to be substantial welfare enhancement as a result of the removal of NTBs. The Centre for Economic Policy Research (CEPR) has recently estimated that the EEA will increase EFTA's GDP by up to 5 per cent,[28] and interestingly enough the distribution of welfare gains that arise from the removal of NTBs are likely to be skewed in favour of the EFTA countries.

The potential enlargements after the EFTA group are an altogether different proposition. The first group of these are the Mediterranean states of Turkey, Cyprus and Malta, which have been referred to somewhat unfortunately by Jacques Delors as the 'Mediterranean orphans'. The next group of potential applicants consists of the former non-Soviet Union members of the COMECON bloc, sovereign states that became independent following the collapse of the Soviet empire in the late 1980s. Arguably, the first ex-COMECON state has already been integrated into the Union with the unification of Germany. These states have new and fragile pluralist democracies, and are almost universally attempting to establish market economies in a hurry. They are at present poor: average per capita GDP of the six potential East/Central members is around 13 per cent of the EU average.

The EU has as yet no concerted policy towards these countries, but it has negotiated a number of 'Europe Agreements' with them. So far Poland, Hungary, the Czech Republic and the Slovak Republic have concluded Interim Agreements (in December 1991), although at the time of writing these have yet to be ratified. Negotiation on Europe Agreements with Romania and Bulgaria have been in progress since May 1992. Full membership is clearly out of the question for these states at present. The economic impact would be devastating for the nascent and fragile economies of the entrants, and there would be potentially enormous problems for existing members. In fact, the CEPR has estimated that annual budget transfers to the East/Central applicants might amount to ECU 13 bn, and that this may preclude membership for another 20 years, although this may be an unduly pessimistic view. The potential economic and political benefits of accession are such that membership at some stage, perhaps in the late 1990s, is likely, assuming that the transition towards a market economy continues successfully in these states. Next in the queue from this part of Europe are Slovenia and the Baltic States, and conceivably even Croatia, Serbia, Bosnia and Macedonia if the war in the former Yugoslavia can be acceptably concluded. Membership for these countries is a more unlikely, but not inconceivable, prospect early in the twenty-first century. The same might also be said for the former Soviet Union itself, although at present the prospects of Russian or Ukrainian accession seem to be remote.[29]

## 12.4  Concluding remarks

Class politics (the conflict between capital and labour over the share of the fruits of the society, expressed in the struggle between socialist and communist parties (left-wing) and their right-wing Christian Democrat or conservative opponents has been replaced by identity politics. For Hobsbawm, these politics are:

generally ethnic, national or religious, and militantly nostalgic movements seeking to recover a hypothetical past age of unproblematic order and security. Such movements are cries for help rather than carriers of programmes, calls for some community to belong to in an anomic world, some family to belong to in a world of social isolates, some refuge in the jungle.[30]

The point is that many movements hark back to a mythic past, where in a 'romantic' vision everything was perfect, people were united and everyone knew their place. The problem with most 'romantics' is that they are prepared to pursue very unromantic means to secure these romantic ends. In fact much romanticism is very reactionary, as the experience of inter-war Fascist movements demonstrated. Similar movements in contemporary Europe share these ideal goals and are similarly engaged in a backward march. The effects of all this ideology can be seen in attacks on immigrants, who are considered foreign and therefore a threat to notions of 'racial' or cultural purity, on women for rising above their subordinate status, and on lesbians and gays for challenging the traditional notions of the family.

Europe east and west has to find a way, in Peter Glotz's words, to avoid the violent and tragic consequences of predominantly 'old men kissing old flags', and then persuading others that those flags are worth dying for. Whatever emerges in the Europe of the future our firm hope is that, as well as a Europe that is materially prosperous and inclusive, it is a Europe that heeds such lessons from the past.

## Further reading

Amin, A. and Dietrich, M. (1991) *Towards a New Europe? Structural Change in the European Economy*, Aldershot: Edward Elgar.

Andrews, G. (ed.) (1993) *Citizenship* London: Lawrence & Wishart.

Bauböck, R. (1991) 'Migration and Citizenship' *New Community* 18 (1).

Brouwer, F., Lintner, V. and Newman, M. (eds) (1994) *Economic Policy and the European Union*, London: Federal Trust.

Castles, S. and Miller, M. J. (1993) *The Age of Migration: International Population Movements in the Modern World*, New York: Guilford Press.

Centre for Economic Policy Research (1992) 'Is bigger better: the economics of EC enlargement' *Monitoring European Integration* 3, pamphlet.

Church, C. (1991) 'EFTA and the European Community' *PNL European Dossier 21*.

Costa-Lascoux, J. (1989) *De l'Immigré au Citoyen*, Paris: La Documentation Française.

Dummett, A. and Nicol, A. (1990) *Subjects, citizens, aliens and others*, London: Weidenfeld and Nicholson.

Giddens, A. (1992) *Beyond Left and Right – the future of radical politics*, Cambridge: Polity Press.

Gordon, M. (1978) *Human Nature, Class and Ethnicity*, New York: Oxford University Press.

Hammar, T. (1990) *Democracy and the Nation–State: Aliens, Denizens and Citizens in a World of International Migration*, Aldershot: Avebury.

Hirst, P. (1994) *Associative Demography, new forms of economic and social governance*, Cambridge: Polity Press.

*International Migration Review* (1985) Special Issue: 'Civil rights and the sociopolitical participation of migrants' 19 (3).

Kilz, H. and Preuss, J. (1985) *Flick: Die gekaufte Republik*, Hamburg: Rowohlt Reinbek.

Leonardi, R. and Nanetti, R. (1990) *The Regions and European Integration. The case of Emilia-Romagna*, London: Pinter.

Lintner, V. (1995) 'The economic implications of enlarging the European Union' in *The Economics of the New Europe*, Healey, N. M. (ed.), London: Routledge.

Lintner, V. and Mazey, S. (1991) *The European Community: Economic and Political Aspects*, Maidenhead: McGraw-Hill.

McGrew, A. and Lewis, P. (1994) *Global Politics Globalisation and the Nation State*, Cambridge: Polity Press.

Meehan, E. (1993) *Citizenship and the European Community*, London: Sage.

Mény, Y (1992) *La Corruption de la République*, Paris: Fayard.

Mulgan, G. (1994) *Politics in an Antipolitical Age*, Cambridge: Polity Press.

Newman, M. (1996) *Democracy, Sovereignty and the European Union*, London: Hurst.

Rex, J. and Drury, B. (1994) *Ethnic Mobilisation in a Multi-Cultural Society*, Aldershot: Avebury.

Rootes, C. and Davis, H. (eds) (1994) *Social Change and Political Transformation*, London: UCL.

Soysal, Y. N. (1995) *Limits of Citizenship: Migrants and Postnational Membership in Europe*, Chichester: John Wiley.

Spencer, S. (ed.) (1994) *Strangers and Citizens: A positive approach to Migrants and Refugees*, IPPR/Rivers Oram Press.

van Steenburgen, B. (1994) *The condition of citizenship*, London: Sage.

Wenden, C. de (1987) *Citoyenneté, Nationalité et Immigration*, Paris: Arcantère Editions.

## Notes

1. Greatly increased capital mobility, increased trade, competition from the NICs, etc.
2. The United Kingdom itself may well move in the same direction if the current Conservative government is replaced by 'new' Labour at the next general election, which must take place by Spring 1997.
3. Including the French economy, if we consider this to be in some way a social market economy (see Chapter 6).
4. Cynics might also argue that German leadership within the EU, and the consequent modelling of much of the Maastricht agenda for monetary union (see Chapter 5), is also forcing countries into adopting aspects of the German model. On the other hand, German leadership is itself a product of the country's economic success.
5. Italy, whose currency was ejected from the ERM at the same time as sterling, experienced an annual rate of increase in its level of GDP of nearly 25 per cent during some of 1994–95.

6. Employees are generally having to work harder, sometimes for lower wages (see Chapter 7), and are increasingly worried about job security. This is one of the reasons behind the lack of the so-called 'feel-good factor', which threatens the re-election prospects of the Conservative government, and behind the lack of consumer demand that has restricted the scope for economic recovery in the United Kingdom over the last few years.

7. See the literature on 'endogenous growth' theory.

8. Countries like Denmark with no regional tier of government nevertheless maintain some distinctive local autonomy. Regions are not the only level of responsive government at the non-national, it rather depends on the quality of second- or third-tier levels of government.

9. *Financial Times*, 31/10/94.

10. Griffith, J. A. G. (1991) *The Politics of the Judiciary*, London: Fontana Press.

11. However we define this.

12. Wealth creation will permit social expenditure to take place, while the choice of economic model which is adopted will to an extent determine how much social expenditure might be required! (see 12.2 above).

13. And preferably socially useful and personally fulfilling employment.

14. See Alain Touraine in Rootes and Davis, 1994.

15. Most of the following section relies on Woodcock, G. (1971) *Anarchism*, London: Pelican; and Colin Ward on an 'Alternative European Diversity', *New Statesman and Society*, 02/06/89.

16. Richard Vernon's (1979) translation of Proudhon's *The Principle of Federation*, University of Toronto Press.

17. Woodcock, G. *Anarchism*, London: Pelican, 1971, p. 262.

18. Berneri, C. (1943) *Peter Kropotkin, His Federalist Ideas*, London: Freedom Press.

19. The term 'regions' includes all subnational levels of elected government, that is provincial councils, county councils, city councils, district councils and communes. There was a great deal of debate in the member states between these various tiers as to who should be sent as representatives to the COR, particularly in Germany, where the regional tier is such an important part of the administrative and political structure of the country. A full regional tier of government exists in about half the member states of the EU: Austria, Belgium, France, Germany, Spain.

20. Mulgan, G. (1995) in Wilkinson, H. (ed.) *No Turning Back, Generations and the Genderquake*, London: Demos. See also Martin Kettle on representation of women in parliament; *Guardian*, 15/04/95.

21. Gilroy, P. (1993) *The Black Atlantic*, London: Verso, p. xi.

22. Despite the 1995 EFTA enlargement.

23. Starting at the 1996 Inter-Governmental Conference (IGC).

24. The full diet of EU rules and regulations, with no opting out of particular policies by individual members (despite the British and Danish opt-outs from parts of the Maastricht Treaty).

25. As mentioned in Chapter 1, Norway rejected membership at a referendum while Switzerland rejected membership of the European Economic Area (EEA) and thus the possibility of entry in 1995. Iceland, on the other hand, has shown no interest in membership.

26. Although Finland's per capita GDP subsequently declined because of the loss of the Soviet market, and was below the EU average at the time of entry.

27. See Church (1991).

28. CEPR (1992). This report, however, includes Norway.

29. For a more detailed analysis of the consequences of EU enlargement see Lintner (1995).

30. *Guardian*, 15/10/94.

# Statistical appendix

The source of all the data in this appendix is either *Eurostat* or *European Economy*

## Contents

## Symbols and abbreviations

| | |
|---|---|
| – | nil |
| : | not available |
| % | per cent or percentage |
| Mio | million |
| Mrd | 1000 million |
| ECU | European currency unit |
| EUA | European unit of account |
| UA | unit of account |
| PPS | purchasing power standard |
| GDP | gross domestic product, at market prices |
| EUR 12– | Member countries, including West Germany |
| EUR +12 | Member countries, including unified Germany |
| EEA | European economic area |

**Table A1** Population, total. National accounts definition.

(1000)

| | B | DK | WD | D | GR | E | F | IRL | I | L | NL | P[a] | UK | EUR 12− | EUR 12+ | USA | J |
|---|---|---|---|---|---|---|---|---|---|---|---|---|---|---|---|---|---|
| 1960 | 9154 | 4581.0 | 55433 | : | 8327 | 30279 | 45684 | 2834 | 50348 | 314.9 | 11483 | 8286 | 53372 | 279097 | : | 180671 | 94118 |
| 1961 | 9184 | 4612.0 | 56185 | : | 8398 | 30568 | 46163 | 2819 | 50675 | 316.9 | 11637 | 8368 | 52807 | 281733 | : | 183691 | 94965 |
| 1962 | 9221 | 4684.0 | 56837 | : | 8448 | 30893 | 46998 | 2825 | 50996 | 320.8 | 11801 | 8357 | 53292 | 284636 | : | 186538 | 95583 |
| 1963 | 9290 | 4685.0 | 57389 | : | 8480 | 31221 | 47836 | 2843 | 51352 | 324.1 | 11964 | 8415 | 53625 | 287425 | : | 189242 | 96772 |
| 1964 | 9378 | 4772.0 | 57971 | : | 8510 | 31553 | 48330 | 2863 | 51756 | 327.8 | 12125 | 8452 | 53991 | 289979 | : | 191889 | 97791 |
| 1965 | 9464 | 4760.0 | 58619 | : | 8551 | 31888 | 48778 | 2876 | 52144 | 331.5 | 12293 | 8458 | 54350 | 292512 | : | 194303 | 98851 |
| 1966 | 9528 | 4800.0 | 59148 | : | 8614 | 32228 | 49184 | 2884 | 52489 | 333.9 | 12455 | 8440 | 54643 | 294746 | : | 196560 | 99769 |
| 1967 | 9581 | 4838.0 | 59286 | : | 8716 | 32569 | 49568 | 2900 | 52825 | 335.0 | 12597 | 8435 | 54959 | 296609 | : | 198712 | 100839 |
| 1968 | 9619 | 4865.0 | 59500 | : | 8741 | 32916 | 49915 | 2913 | 53146 | 335.9 | 12726 | 8445 | 55214 | 298336 | : | 200706 | 101999 |
| 1969 | 9646 | 4892.0 | 60067 | : | 8773 | 33266 | 50318 | 2926 | 53477 | 337.5 | 12873 | 8429 | 55461 | 300465 | : | 202677 | 103261 |
| 1970 | 9651 | 4929.0 | 60651 | : | 8793 | 33619 | 50772 | 2950 | 53822 | 339.2 | 13032 | 8350 | 55632 | 302571 | : | 205052 | 104674 |
| 1971 | 9673 | 4963.0 | 61284 | : | 8769 | 33976 | 51251 | 2978 | 54073 | 342.4 | 13194 | 8330 | 55928 | 304762 | : | 207661 | 105713 |
| 1972 | 9709 | 4992.0 | 61672 | : | 8889 | 34471 | 51701 | 3024 | 54381 | 346.6 | 13330 | 8311 | 56097 | 306924 | : | 209896 | 107156 |
| 1973 | 9739 | 5022.0 | 61976 | : | 8929 | 34783 | 52118 | 3073 | 54751 | 350.5 | 13438 | 8316 | 56223 | 308719 | : | 211909 | 108660 |
| 1974 | 9768 | 5045.0 | 62054 | : | 8962 | 35119 | 52460 | 3124 | 55111 | 355.1 | 13543 | 8408 | 56236 | 310186 | : | 213854 | 110160 |
| 1975 | 9795 | 5060.0 | 61829 | : | 9046 | 35487 | 52699 | 3177 | 55441 | 359.0 | 13660 | 8687 | 56226 | 311466 | : | 215973 | 111520 |
| 1976 | 9811 | 5073.0 | 61531 | : | 9167 | 35909 | 52909 | 3228 | 55718 | 360.7 | 13773 | 8879 | 56216 | 312574 | : | 218035 | 112770 |
| 1977 | 9822 | 5088.0 | 61400 | : | 9309 | 36338 | 53145 | 3272 | 55955 | 361.3 | 13856 | 8958 | 56190 | 313695 | : | 220239 | 113880 |
| 1978 | 9830 | 5104.0 | 61327 | : | 9430 | 36749 | 53376 | 3314 | 56155 | 362.0 | 13939 | 9065 | 56178 | 314829 | : | 222585 | 114920 |
| 1979 | 9837 | 5117.0 | 61359 | : | 9548 | 37079 | 53606 | 3368 | 56318 | 362.9 | 14034 | 9169 | 56240 | 316038 | : | 225056 | 115880 |
| 1980 | 9847 | 5123.0 | 61566 | : | 9642 | 37356 | 53880 | 3401 | 56434 | 364.2 | 14148 | 9272 | 56330 | 317364 | : | 227757 | 116800 |
| 1981 | 9853 | 5122.0 | 61682 | : | 9730 | 37726 | 54182 | 3443 | 56510 | 365.3 | 14247 | 9358 | 56352 | 318571 | : | 230138 | 117650 |
| 1982 | 9856 | 5119.0 | 61638 | : | 9790 | 37950 | 54493 | 3480 | 56579 | 365.5 | 14312 | 9368 | 56306 | 319256 | : | 232520 | 118450 |
| 1983 | 9855 | 5114.0 | 61423 | : | 9847 | 38142 | 54772 | 3505 | 56626 | 365.5 | 14368 | 9388 | 56347 | 319753 | : | 234799 | 119260 |
| 1984 | 9855 | 5112.0 | 61175 | : | 9896 | 38311 | 55026 | 3529 | 56652 | 365.8 | 14423 | 9402 | 56460 | 320207 | : | 237001 | 120020 |
| 1985 | 9858 | 5114.0 | 61024 | : | 9934 | 38474 | 55284 | 3540 | 56674 | 366.6 | 14488 | 9409 | 56618 | 320784 | : | 239279 | 120750 |
| 1986 | 9862 | 5121.0 | 61066 | : | 9964 | 38604 | 55547 | 3541 | 56675 | 368.3 | 14567 | 9408 | 56763 | 321486 | : | 241625 | 121490 |
| 1987 | 9870 | 5127.0 | 61077 | : | 9984 | 38716 | 55824 | 3542 | 56674 | 370.7 | 14664 | 9405 | 56930 | 322184 | : | 243942 | 122090 |
| 1988 | 9921 | 5130.0 | 61449 | : | 10005 | 38809 | 56118 | 3538 | 56688 | 373.9 | 14760 | 9399 | 57065 | 323256 | : | 246307 | 122610 |
| 1989 | 9938 | 5132.0 | 62063 | : | 10038 | 38888 | 56423 | 3515 | 56705 | 377.6 | 14846 | 9391 | 57236 | 324553 | : | 248781 | 123120 |
| 1990 | 9967 | 5141.0 | 63253 | : | 10140 | 38959 | 56735 | 3503 | 56737 | 381.9 | 14947 | 9377 | 57411 | 326552 | : | 249951 | 125540 |
| 1991 | 10005 | 5152.0 | 64074 | 79984 | 10200 | 38902 | 57055 | 3524 | 56760 | 387.1 | 15068 | 9362 | 57649 | 328138 | 344048 | 252699 | 123920 |
| 1992 | 10045 | 5169.0 | 64865 | 80595 | 10280 | 38988 | 57372 | 3547 | 56859 | 392.4 | 15182 | 9345 | 57848 | 329892 | 345622 | 255472 | 124336 |
| 1993 | 10070 | 5187.0 | 65540 | 81200 | 10362 | 39068 | 57665 | 3560 | 57057 | 393.9 | 15297 | 9351 | 58018 | 331568 | 347228 | 258254 | 124664 |
| 1994 | 10095 | 5203.0 | 66114 | 81731 | 10414 | 39150 | 57953 | 3573 | 57114 | 395.1 | 15416 | 9359 | 58188 | 332975 | 348591 | 260891 | 125038 |

EUR 12−: incl. WD; EUR 12+: incl. D.
a Continental Portugal.

**Table A2**   Population by age and sex – yearly average 1992.

(1000)

| Country | Under 15 | | From 15 to 64 | | 65 and over | | Total | |
|---|---|---|---|---|---|---|---|---|
| | Male | Female | Male | Female | Male | Female | Male | Female |
| EUR 12 | 31 845.4 | 30 180.8 | 116 812.7 | 115 805.1 | 18 889.0 | 31 282.2 | 168 547.1 | 177 268.2 |
| 1. Belgique/België | 934.9 | 809.4 | 3365.5 | 3316.5 | 611.0 | 926.9 | 4911.4 | 5133.8 |
| 2. Danmark | 449.2 | 428.3 | 1768.3 | 1725.1 | 331.7 | 467.7 | 2549.1 | 2621.1 |
| 3. Deutschland[1] | 6677.9 | 6335.1 | 27 927.6 | 27 075.0 | 4052.2 | 7916.5 | 38.657.7 | 41.326.5 |
| 4. Ελλάδα | 953.8 | 893.5 | 3479.0 | 3495.4 | 651.1 | 840.4 | 5083.9 | 5229.3 |
| 5. España | 3723.1 | 3482.1 | 13 214.4 | 13 209.1 | 2249.6 | 3206.9 | 19 187.0 | 19 898.0 |
| 6. France | 5863.2 | 5594.4 | 18 796.5 | 18 838.8 | 3282.3 | 4998.4 | 27 942.0 | 29 431.6 |
| 7. Ireland | 476.0 | 451.2 | 1115.5 | 1102.7 | 174.7 | 231.7 | 1766.1 | 1785.6 |
| 8. Italia | 4598.9 | 4344.0 | 19 524.0 | 19 679.6 | 3516.0 | 5196.6 | 27 638.9 | 29 220.2 |
| 9. Luxembourg | 35.8 | 34.1 | 137.1 | 132.3 | 19.8 | 33.5 | 192.7 | 199.8 |
| 10. Nederland | 1419.9 | 1358.1 | 5300.6 | 5132.8 | 787.2 | 1185.3 | 7507.8 | 7676.2 |
| 11. Portugal | 965.0 | 920.6 | 3215.4 | 3379.1 | 571.2 | 806.2 | 4751.6 | 5105.9 |
| 12. United Kingdom | 5747.8 | 5449.2 | 18,969.0 | 18 718.7 | 3642.1 | 5472.2 | 28 358.9 | 29 640.1 |
| 13. Österreich | 711.4 | 671.6 | 2661.8 | 2640.4 | 422.4 | 777.7 | 3795.5 | 4089.6 |
| 14. Suomi/Finland | 494.1 | 472.8 | 1707.9 | 1677.1 | 248.2 | 441.8 | 2450.2 | 2591.8 |
| 15. Ísland | 33.1 | 31.6 | 85.2 | 82.9 | 12.6 | 15.6 | 130.9 | 130.1 |
| 16. Norge | 418.1 | 399.0 | 1405.8 | 1360.8 | 296.0 | 406.7 | 2119.9 | 2166.5 |
| 17. Sverige | 816.8 | 774.8 | 2814.8 | 2728.6 | 651.1 | 882.1 | 4282.6 | 4385.5 |
| EEA | 34 318.8*. | 32 530.7* | 125 488.2* | 124 292.9* | 21 519.2* | 33 806.2* | 181 326.2* | 190 631.8* |
| 18. Schweiz/Suisse | 611.1 | 581.5 | 2348.2 | 2327.3 | 398.4 | 603.4 | 3357.7 | 3512.2 |
| 19. Türkiye[2] | 10 469.0 | 10 032.0 | 17 602.0 | 17 156.0 | 1115.0 | 1333.0 | 29 186.0 | 28 521.0 |
| 20. USA[3] | 27 209.9 | 26 283.0 | 81 177.0 | 82 601.4 | 12 492.8 | 18 586.1 | 121 239.3 | 127 470.5 |
| 21. Canada[1&2] | 2896.6 | 2756.6 | 9096.8 | 9371.2 | 1309.0 | 1831.2 | 13 302.4 | 13 689.2 |
| 22. Nippon (Japan)[3] | 11 517.8 | 10 968.5 | 42 968.5 | 42 935.5 | 5987.6 | 8907.0 | 60 696.7 | 62 914.5 |

1. Provisional.
2. 1991.
3. 1990.

**Table A3**   Population by age and sex – yearly average 1992.

(% of total)

| Country | Under 15 | | From 15 to 64 | | 65 and over | | Total | |
|---|---|---|---|---|---|---|---|---|
| | Male | Female | Male | Female | Male | Female | Male | Female |
| EUR 12 | 9.2 | 8.7 | 33.8 | 33.5 | 5.8 | 9.0 | 48.7 | 51.3 |
| 1. Belgique/België | 9.3 | 8.9 | 33.5 | 33.0 | 6.1 | 9.2 | 48.9 | 51.1 |
| 2. Danmark | 8.7 | 8.3 | 34.2 | 33.4 | 6.4 | 9.0 | 49.3 | 50.7 |
| 3. Deutschland[2] | 8.3 | 7.9 | 34.9 | 33.9 | 5.1 | 9.9 | 48.3 | 51.7 |
| 4. Ελλάδα | 9.2 | 8.7 | 33.7 | 33.9 | 6.3 | 8.1 | 49.3 | 50.7 |
| 5. España | 9.5 | 8.9 | 33.8 | 33.8 | 5.8 | 8.2 | 49.1 | 50.9 |
| 6. France | 10.2 | 9.8 | 32.8 | 32.8 | 5.7 | 8.7 | 48.7 | 51.3 |
| 7. Ireland | 13.4 | 12.7 | 31.4 | 31.0 | 4.9 | 6.5 | 49.7 | 50.3 |
| 8. Italia | 8.1 | 7.6 | 34.3 | 34.6 | 6.2 | 9.1 | 48.6 | 51.4 |
| 9. Luxembourg | 9.1 | 8.7 | 34.9 | 33.7 | 5.1 | 8.5 | 49.1 | 50.9 |
| 10. Nederland | 9.4 | 8.9 | 34.9 | 33.8 | 5.2 | 7.8 | 49.4 | 50.6 |
| 11. Portugal | 9.8 | 9.3 | 32.6 | 34.3 | 5.8 | 8.2 | 48.2 | 51.8 |
| 12. United Kingdom | 9.9 | 9.4 | 32.7 | 32.3 | 6.3 | 9.4 | 48.9 | 51.1 |
| 13. Österreich | 9.0 | 8.5 | 33.8 | 33.5 | 5.4 | 9.9 | 48.1 | 51.9 |
| 14. Suomi/Finland | 9.8 | 9.4 | 33.9 | 33.3 | 4.9 | 8.8 | 48.6 | 51.4 |
| 15. Ísland | 12.7 | 12.1 | 32.6 | 31.7 | 4.8 | 6.0 | 50.2 | 49.8 |
| 16. Norge | 9.8 | 9.3 | 32.8 | 31.7 | 6.9 | 9.5 | 49.5 | 50.5 |
| 17. Sverige | 9.4 | 8.9 | 32.5 | 31.5 | 7.5 | 10.2 | 49.4 | 50.6 |
| EEA | 9.2* | 8.7* | 33.7* | 33.4* | 5.8* | 9.1* | 48.8* | 51.3* |
| 18. Schweiz/Suisse | 8.9 | 8.5 | 34.2 | 33.9 | 5.8 | 8.8 | 48.9 | 51.1 |
| 19. Türkiye[2] | 18.1 | 17.4 | 30.5 | 29.7 | 1.9 | 2.3 | 50.6 | 49.4 |
| 20. USA[1] | 10.9 | 10.6 | 32.6 | 33.2 | 5.0 | 7.5 | 48.7 | 51.3 |
| 21. Canada[1&2] | 10.7 | 10.2 | 33.7 | 34.7 | 4.8 | 6.8 | 49.3 | 50.7 |
| 22. Nippon (Japan)[3] | 9.3 | 8.9 | 34.8 | 34.7 | 4.8 | – | 49.1 | 50.9 |

1. Provisional.
2. 1991.
3. 1990.

**Table A4**   Area, population, density per square kilometre – 1992.

| Total area km² |                | Population | Inhab/km² |
|---|---|---|---|
| 30 500 | Belgique/Belgie | | 329.9[3] |
| 43 100 | Danmark | | 120.3[3] |
| 356 900 | Deutschland | | 225.9[3] |
| 132 000 | Ελλάδα | | 78.4[3] |
| 504 800 | España | | 77.5[3] |
| 544 000 | France | | 105.8[3] |
| 70 300 | Ireland | | 50.7[3] |
| 301 300 | Italia | | 189.0[3] |
| 2600 | Luxembourg | | 152.8[3] |
| 41 200 | Nederland | | 369.9[4] |
| 92 400 | Portugal | | 106.7[4] |
| 244 100 | United Kingdom | | 237.4[4] |
| 2 363 100 | EUR 12 | | 146.8[4] |
| 83 900 | Österrich | | 94.3[3] |
| 337 100 | Suomi/Finland | | 15.0[3] |
| 103 000 | Island | | 2.5[3] |
| 323 900 | Norge | | 13.3[3] |
| 450 000 | Sverige | | 19.3[3] |
| 3 660 900 | EEA | | 101.9[5] |
| 41 300 | Schweiz/Suisse | | 167.3 |
| 779 500 | Turkiye | | 75.4 |
| 9 372 600 | USA | | 27.2 |
| 9 976 100 | Canada | | 2.8 |
| 377 800 | Nippon (Japan) | | 329.1 |

100 90 80 70 60 50 40 30 20 10 0%          Mio  0  10  20  30  40  60  0  0  0

Agricultural area in use

[1] Provisional.   [2] Annual average.   [3] 1.1.1993.   [4] Including Leichenstein.   [5] 1991.

**Table B1**  Gross domestic product at current market prices.

(Mrd ECU)

| | B | DK | WD | D | GR | E | F | IRL | I | L | NL | P | UK | EUR 12− | EUR 12+ | USA | J |
|---|---|---|---|---|---|---|---|---|---|---|---|---|---|---|---|---|---|
| 1960 | 10.5 | 5.6 | 68.2 | : | 3.3 | 11.1 | 57.7 | 1.7 | 37.6 | 0.5 | 11.3 | 2.4 | 68.6 | 278.5 | : | 487.3 | 42.1 |
| 1961 | 11.1 | 6.2 | 77.0 | : | 3.7 | 12.6 | 62.2 | 1.9 | 41.3 | 0.5 | 12.2 | 2.5 | 71.9 | 303.2 | : | 499.4 | 50.3 |
| 1962 | 11.8 | 7.0 | 84.3 | : | 3.9 | 14.5 | 69.3 | 2.0 | 46.3 | 0.5 | 13.3 | 2.7 | 75.4 | 331.1 | : | 535.8 | 57.0 |
| 1963 | 12.7 | 7.4 | 89.4 | : | 4.4 | 17.1 | 77.7 | 2.2 | 53.1 | 0.5 | 14.4 | 2.9 | 80.0 | 361.7 | : | 565.3 | 65.2 |
| 1964 | 14.3 | 8.5 | 98.2 | : | 4.9 | 19.3 | 86.2 | 2.5 | 58.1 | 0.6 | 16.9 | 3.1 | 87.4 | 400.0 | : | 607.2 | 76.7 |
| 1965 | 15.5 | 9.5 | 107.3 | : | 5.6 | 22.5 | 92.8 | 2.6 | 62.5 | 0.7 | 18.9 | 3.5 | 94.1 | 435.5 | : | 658.1 | 85.3 |
| 1966 | 16.7 | 10.4 | 114.1 | : | 6.2 | 26.0 | 100.5 | 2.8 | 67.7 | 0.7 | 20.6 | 3.8 | 100.2 | 469.7 | : | 720.9 | 99.1 |
| 1967 | 17.9 | 11.4 | 116.1 | : | 6.8 | 28.8 | 109.1 | 3.0 | 75.0 | 0.7 | 22.7 | 4.3 | 104.0 | 499.6 | : | 765.5 | 116.7 |
| 1968 | 19.9 | 12.2 | 129.6 | : | 7.6 | 29.1 | 122.7 | 3.0 | 84.1 | 0.8 | 26.0 | 4.9 | 101.9 | 541.8 | : | 865.0 | 143.0 |
| 1969 | 22.2 | 14.0 | 148.3 | : | 8.7 | 33.4 | 134.3 | 3.5 | 93.4 | 0.9 | 29.7 | 5.4 | 110.4 | 604.2 | : | 940.2 | 169.1 |
| 1970 | 24.7 | 15.5 | 180.5 | : | 9.7 | 37.2 | 139.8 | 4.0 | 105.1 | 1.1 | 33.3 | 6.1 | 121.2 | 678.1 | : | 989.6 | 199.3 |
| 1971 | 27.2 | 16.9 | 205.7 | : | 10.5 | 41.3 | 153.2 | 4.5 | 112.7 | 1.1 | 38.0 | 6.7 | 134.4 | 752.1 | : | 1048.1 | 221.8 |
| 1972 | 31.3 | 19.4 | 230.1 | : | 11.2 | 48.8 | 174.6 | 5.2 | 122.0 | 1.3 | 43.6 | 7.6 | 143.6 | 838.7 | : | 1076.8 | 272.0 |
| 1973 | 36.7 | 23.3 | 280.0 | : | 13.1 | 59.0 | 206.6 | 5.6 | 135.0 | 1.6 | 52.2 | 9.3 | 147.5 | 970.0 | : | 1096.4 | 337.7 |
| 1974 | 44.8 | 26.9 | 318.8 | : | 15.8 | 75.4 | 229.6 | 6.1 | 154.3 | 2.0 | 64.1 | 11.3 | 163.0 | 1112.1 | : | 1215.0 | 395.2 |
| 1975 | 49.8 | 30.4 | 336.7 | : | 16.8 | 86.7 | 276.0 | 7.1 | 171.2 | 1.9 | 71.4 | 12.0 | 188.6 | 1248.5 | : | 1279.5 | 411.2 |
| 1976 | 59.7 | 37.2 | 398.0 | : | 20.2 | 98.1 | 318.2 | 7.8 | 188.0 | 2.3 | 86.7 | 13.9 | 201.1 | 1431.1 | : | 1583.4 | 502.9 |
| 1977 | 68.1 | 40.7 | 451.3 | : | 22.9 | 107.1 | 342.1 | 9.1 | 213.0 | 2.5 | 99.9 | 14.3 | 222.8 | 1593.9 | : | 1731.1 | 607.0 |
| 1978 | 74.6 | 44.4 | 502.2 | : | 24.8 | 116.8 | 380.3 | 10.6 | 234.7 | 2.8 | 109.7 | 14.1 | 253.3 | 1768.1 | : | 1749.9 | 765.3 |
| 1979 | 79.4 | 48.1 | 552.9 | : | 28.1 | 144.7 | 425.6 | 12.3 | 272.2 | 3.0 | 116.9 | 14.8 | 306.1 | 2004.2 | : | 1813.9 | 737.4 |
| 1980 | 85.0 | 47.8 | 583.2 | : | 28.8 | 154.3 | 478.5 | 14.5 | 326.0 | 3.3 | 124.1 | 18.1 | 386.4 | 2249.7 | : | 1945.1 | 762.4 |
| 1981 | 86.6 | 51.5 | 610.6 | : | 33.3 | 167.3 | 524.0 | 17.2 | 367.4 | 3.4 | 129.3 | 21.9 | 459.7 | 2472.2 | : | 2719.2 | 1051.3 |
| 1982 | 87.0 | 56.9 | 668.4 | : | 39.4 | 184.0 | 563.8 | 20.3 | 411.8 | 3.6 | 143.5 | 23.7 | 496.5 | 2698.8 | : | 3217.8 | 1111.1 |
| 1983 | 90.8 | 63.0 | 734.9 | : | 39.4 | 176.3 | 591.7 | 21.6 | 469.2 | 3.8 | 152.7 | 23.3 | 517.1 | 2883.9 | : | 3812.9 | 1333.2 |
| 1984 | 97.5 | 69.4 | 782.3 | : | 43.0 | 200.6 | 634.8 | 23.6 | 525.4 | 4.3 | 161.3 | 24.3 | 550.0 | 3116.6 | : | 4769.7 | 1606.4 |
| 1985 | 105.6 | 76.7 | 818.9 | : | 43.7 | 218.4 | 691.7 | 26.0 | 559.8 | 4.6 | 169.4 | 27.1 | 604.7 | 3346.4 | : | 5263.7 | 1774.6 |
| 1986 | 113.9 | 84.0 | 904.7 | : | 40.1 | 235.2 | 745.5 | 26.9 | 615.6 | 5.1 | 182.3 | 30.1 | 571.3 | 3554.5 | : | 4298.8 | 2028.0 |
| 1987 | 121.0 | 88.8 | 960.9 | : | 40.1 | 254.2 | 770.2 | 27.2 | 658.1 | 5.3 | 188.8 | 31.8 | 598.8 | 3745.1 | : | 3895.0 | 2091.4 |
| 1988 | 128.1 | 92.1 | 1010.4 | : | 45.2 | 291.8 | 815.1 | 29.2 | 710.2 | 5.8 | 195.9 | 35.3 | 707.0 | 4066.1 | : | 4104.9 | 2452.3 |
| 1989 | 139.0 | 95.3 | 1074.5 | : | 49.3 | 345.4 | 877.0 | 32.4 | 790.1 | 6.5 | 207.5 | 41.1 | 763.8 | 4422.0 | : | 4723.9 | 2607.6 |
| 1990 | 151.2 | 101.7 | 1181.8 | : | 52.4 | 387.3 | 940.9 | 35.1 | 862.1 | 7.1 | 223.3 | 47.0 | 769.6 | 4759.4 | : | 4291.4 | 2311.5 |
| 1991 | 158.8 | 104.6 | 1284.9 | 1373.1 | 56.8 | 426.7 | 967.5 | 36.4 | 923.3 | 7.6 | 234.5 | 55.5 | 815.7 | 5081.3 | 5169.5 | 4527.9 | 2707.6 |
| 1992 | 169.1 | 109.4 | 1383.1 | 1498.6 | 60.1 | 444.1 | 1021.7 | 38.9 | 942.8 | 8.2 | 247.6 | 65.1 | 805.5 | 5295.5 | 5411.0 | 4560.7 | 2831.1 |
| 1993 | 176.2 | 115.5 | 1462.5 | 1604.8 | 62.8 | 408.3 | 1072.2 | 39.2 | 847.3 | 8.6 | 263.9 | 64.3 | 802.6 | 5323.3 | 5465.6 | 5338.2 | 3619.4 |
| 1994 | 186.3 | 122.4 | 1509.9 | 1671.3 | 65.2 | 403.2 | 1111.4 | 42.6 | 876.8 | 9.2 | 273.5 | 65.0 | 861.4 | 5526.8 | 5688.2 | 5799.2 | 3993.7 |

EUR 12−: incl. WD; EUR 12+: incl. D.

**Table B2**  Gross domestic product at current market prices.

(Mrd PPS)

| | B | DK | WD | D | GR | E | F | IRL | I | L | NL | P | UK | EUR 12− | EUR 12+ | USA | J |
|---|---|---|---|---|---|---|---|---|---|---|---|---|---|---|---|---|---|
| 1960 | 9.0 | 5.3 | 68.2 | : | 2.9 | 17.8 | 48.4 | 1.7 | 43.5 | 0.5 | 13.2 | 3.1 | 64.7 | 278.5 | : | 327.7 | 51.2 |
| 1961 | 9.7 | 5.8 | 73.6 | : | 3.3 | 20.6 | 52.7 | 1.8 | 48.6 | 0.5 | 14.1 | 3.4 | 69.0 | 303.2 | : | 347.0 | 59.2 |
| 1962 | 10.6 | 6.4 | 80.3 | : | 3.5 | 23.5 | 58.7 | 2.0 | 53.8 | 0.5 | 15.3 | 3.8 | 72.7 | 331.1 | : | 380.7 | 67.2 |
| 1963 | 11.6 | 6.8 | 86.3 | : | 4.1 | 26.7 | 64.6 | 2.2 | 59.4 | 0.5 | 16.5 | 4.2 | 78.9 | 361.7 | : | 414.1 | 76.2 |
| 1964 | 13.0 | 7.7 | 96.2 | : | 4.6 | 29.6 | 71.9 | 2.3 | 63.8 | 0.6 | 18.7 | 4.7 | 86.9 | 400.0 | : | 456.7 | 88.9 |
| 1965 | 14.0 | 8.4 | 105.8 | : | 5.2 | 32.8 | 78.6 | 2.5 | 68.7 | 0.7 | 20.5 | 5.3 | 92.9 | 435.5 | : | 503.3 | 98.2 |
| 1966 | 15.0 | 9.0 | 112.9 | : | 5.8 | 36.5 | 85.8 | 2.6 | 75.6 | 0.7 | 21.9 | 5.7 | 98.3 | 469.7 | : | 553.9 | 112.8 |
| 1967 | 16.0 | 9.6 | 115.8 | : | 6.3 | 39.1 | 92.4 | 2.8 | 83.4 | 0.7 | 23.7 | 6.3 | 103.4 | 499.6 | : | 586.1 | 128.9 |
| 1968 | 17.2 | 10.3 | 125.7 | : | 6.9 | 43.0 | 99.3 | 3.2 | 95.5 | 0.8 | 26.0 | 7.1 | 110.8 | 541.8 | : | 628.1 | 149.9 |
| 1969 | 19.3 | 11.5 | 142.1 | : | 7.9 | 49.3 | 111.7 | 3.5 | 102.1 | 0.9 | 29.1 | 7.7 | 119.0 | 604.2 | : | 678.2 | 117.2 |
| 1970 | 22.0 | 12.6 | 160.0 | : | 9.2 | 55.0 | 126.6 | 3.9 | 115.3 | 1.1 | 33.0 | 8.9 | 130.5 | 678.1 | : | 725.3 | 210.4 |
| 1971 | 24.5 | 13.8 | 177.2 | : | 10.6 | 61.9 | 142.6 | 4.3 | 125.9 | 1.1 | 36.9 | 10.2 | 143.0 | 752.1 | : | 801.4 | 235.8 |
| 1972 | 27.6 | 15.6 | 197.5 | : | 12.3 | 71.4 | 159.2 | 4.9 | 138.2 | 1.2 | 40.8 | 11.8 | 158.2 | 838.7 | : | 897.0 | 272.7 |
| 1973 | 31.9 | 17.6 | 225.4 | : | 14.4 | 83.8 | 182.8 | 5.6 | 161.3 | 1.5 | 46.5 | 14.3 | 185.0 | 970.0 | : | 1026.8 | 319.7 |
| 1974 | 37.3 | 19.6 | 253.9 | : | 15.6 | 99.2 | 211.9 | 6.6 | 191.1 | 1.9 | 54.4 | 16.2 | 204.4 | 1112.1 | : | 1146.2 | 357.2 |
| 1975 | 41.6 | 22.1 | 284.1 | : | 18.8 | 113.0 | 239.4 | 7.9 | 210.8 | 1.8 | 61.6 | 17.6 | 229.9 | 1248.4 | : | 1285.9 | 416.3 |
| 1976 | 48.1 | 25.7 | 327.6 | : | 21.8 | 127.8 | 273.3 | 8.7 | 246.0 | 2.0 | 70.8 | 20.6 | 258.6 | 1431.1 | : | 1475.8 | 475.0 |
| 1977 | 52.3 | 28.3 | 364.8 | : | 24.5 | 142.5 | 305.4 | 10.2 | 275.3 | 2.1 | 78.5 | 23.5 | 286.5 | 1593.8 | : | 1670.0 | 538.5 |
| 1978 | 57.8 | 30.9 | 404.0 | : | 28.1 | 155.4 | 339.4 | 11.8 | 307.0 | 2.4 | 86.5 | 26.0 | 318.9 | 1768.1 | : | 1882.8 | 607.3 |
| 1979 | 64.6 | 35.0 | 461.0 | : | 31.9 | 170.0 | 383.6 | 13.3 | 356.2 | 2.7 | 96.9 | 30.1 | 358.9 | 2004.2 | : | 2112.8 | 701.7 |
| 1980 | 74.7 | 38.6 | 515.9 | : | 35.9 | 190.7 | 432.0 | 15.2 | 411.5 | 3.0 | 108.3 | 34.8 | 389.0 | 2249.7 | : | 2332.0 | 805.9 |
| 1981 | 81.2 | 42.0 | 567.1 | : | 39.5 | 208.8 | 480.0 | 17.3 | 454.3 | 3.3 | 118.2 | 38.9 | 421.6 | 2472.2 | : | 2617.1 | 916.6 |
| 1982 | 89.3 | 46.9 | 608.3 | : | 42.9 | 228.9 | 533.1 | 19.1 | 493.1 | 3.6 | 126.1 | 43.0 | 464.5 | 2698.8 | : | 2773.0 | 1024.0 |
| 1983 | 94.3 | 50.5 | 650.8 | : | 45.3 | 245.0 | 564.3 | 20.1 | 523.4 | 3.8 | 134.5 | 45.1 | 506.8 | 2883.9 | : | 3020.5 | 1105.7 |
| 1984 | 101.8 | 55.7 | 706.8 | : | 49.2 | 263.5 | 603.9 | 22.1 | 567.7 | 4.2 | 146.5 | 46.8 | 548.5 | 3116.6 | : | 3403.0 | 1217.7 |
| 1985 | 107.5 | 60.9 | 755.8 | : | 53.1 | 282.5 | 644.8 | 23.9 | 610.5 | 4.6 | 157.5 | 50.4 | 595.0 | 3346.5 | : | 3678.7 | 1339.8 |
| 1986 | 112.5 | 65.1 | 798.3 | : | 55.7 | 300.9 | 682.2 | 24.6 | 648.4 | 5.1 | 167.0 | 54.1 | 640.6 | 3554.5 | : | 3902.1 | 1419.1 |
| 1987 | 117.5 | 66.9 | 829.5 | : | 56.8 | 325.5 | 714.3 | 26.3 | 684.8 | 5.1 | 173.0 | 58.4 | 687.2 | 3745.1 | : | 4118.8 | 1512.7 |
| 1988 | 128.4 | 70.5 | 896.0 | : | 61.8 | 356.5 | 777.3 | 28.5 | 742.1 | 5.7 | 184.9 | 63.2 | 751.3 | 4066.1 | : | 4458.3 | 1673.1 |
| 1989 | 139.8 | 74.5 | 975.6 | : | 67.2 | 392.3 | 851.6 | 31.8 | 802.7 | 6.6 | 203.4 | 69.8 | 806.6 | 4422.0 | : | 4812.6 | 1841.1 |
| 1990 | 150.9 | 79.0 | 1078.0 | : | 69.5 | 424.9 | 912.8 | 36.3 | 857.0 | 7.0 | 221.3 | 76.1 | 846.5 | 4759.4 | : | 5071.5 | 2017.2 |
| 1991 | 161.4 | 85.0 | 1186.3 | 1267.8 | 74.9 | 468.0 | 976.8 | 39.5 | 921.0 | 7.6 | 233.9 | 85.0 | 848.7 | 5088.1 | 5169.5 | 5393.7 | 2258.1 |
| 1992 | 172.2 | 86.4 | 1251.4 | 1355.9 | 80.8 | 474.4 | 1008.6 | 42.9 | 954.1 | 8.1 | 244.0 | 91.0 | 892.7 | 5306.5 | 5411.0 | 5796.4 | 2396.7 |
| 1993 | 172.3 | 88.5 | 1236.8 | 1357.1 | 81.7 | 475.9 | 1015.3 | 44.6 | 960.6 | 8.4 | 248.1 | 91.1 | 922.0 | 5345.3 | 5465.6 | 6052.3 | 2430.8 |
| 1994 | 178.7 | 94.1 | 1271.4 | 1407.3 | 84.3 | 492.7 | 1056.6 | 47.6 | 998.7 | 8.8 | 257.4 | 94.3 | 967.6 | 5552.3 | 5688.2 | 6425.8 | 2508.2 |

EUR 12−: incl. WD; EUR 12+: incl. D.

**Table B3** Gross domestic product at current market prices per head of population.

(ECU; EUR 12− =100)

| | B | DK | WD | D | GR | E | F | IRL | I | L | NL | P | UK | EUR 12− | EUR 12+ | USA | J |
|---|---|---|---|---|---|---|---|---|---|---|---|---|---|---|---|---|---|
| 1960 | 115.5 | 123.4 | 123.4 | : | 39.9 | 36.9 | 126.5 | 61.8 | 74.7 | 157.3 | 98.2 | 28.5 | 131.2 | 100.0 | : | 270.3 | 44.8 |
| 1961 | 112.3 | 124.8 | 127.4 | : | 41.0 | 38.2 | 125.3 | 61.4 | 75.8 | 143.5 | 97.7 | 27.8 | 126.6 | 100.0 | : | 252.6 | 49.2 |
| 1962 | 110.5 | 128.8 | 127.5 | : | 40.0 | 40.3 | 126.8 | 61.2 | 78.1 | 137.8 | 96.6 | 27.4 | 121.7 | 100.0 | : | 247.0 | 51.1 |
| 1963 | 108.9 | 125.7 | 123.7 | : | 41.1 | 43.5 | 129.1 | 60.4 | 82.1 | 134.5 | 95.5 | 27.2 | 118.5 | 100.0 | : | 237.4 | 53.5 |
| 1964 | 110.2 | 130.1 | 122.8 | : | 41.9 | 44.4 | 129.3 | 62.3 | 81.4 | 138.5 | 101.2 | 26.8 | 117.3 | 100.0 | : | 229.4 | 56.9 |
| 1965 | 110.1 | 134.3 | 122.9 | : | 44.0 | 47.3 | 127.8 | 61.2 | 80.5 | 132.9 | 103.3 | 27.7 | 116.3 | 100.0 | : | 227.5 | 58.0 |
| 1966 | 109.8 | 136.5 | 121.0 | : | 45.4 | 50.6 | 128.2 | 60.1 | 81.0 | 129.6 | 103.7 | 28.5 | 115.1 | 100.0 | : | 230.1 | 62.3 |
| 1967 | 111.2 | 140.2 | 116.2 | : | 46.1 | 52.4 | 130.6 | 60.8 | 84.2 | 123.6 | 106.9 | 30.3 | 112.3 | 100.0 | : | 228.7 | 68.7 |
| 1968 | 113.8 | 138.4 | 119.9 | : | 47.9 | 48.7 | 135.3 | 57.3 | 87.1 | 129.4 | 112.7 | 32.1 | 101.6 | 100.0 | : | 237.3 | 77.2 |
| 1969 | 114.4 | 142.3 | 122.8 | : | 49.3 | 49.9 | 132.7 | 59.9 | 86.9 | 135.6 | 114.7 | 32.1 | 99.0 | 100.0 | : | 230.7 | 81.4 |
| 1970 | 114.2 | 140.1 | 132.8 | : | 49.5 | 49.4 | 122.8 | 60.1 | 87.2 | 141.7 | 114.0 | 32.2 | 97.2 | 100.0 | : | 215.3 | 85.0 |
| 1971 | 113.8 | 138.1 | 136.0 | : | 48.6 | 49.2 | 121.1 | 61.4 | 84.5 | 130.4 | 116.6 | 32.7 | 97.3 | 100.0 | : | 204.5 | 85.0 |
| 1972 | 118.0 | 141.9 | 136.5 | : | 46.2 | 51.8 | 123.6 | 63.0 | 82.1 | 135.2 | 119.7 | 33.5 | 93.7 | 100.0 | : | 187.7 | 92.9 |
| 1973 | 120.0 | 147.7 | 143.8 | : | 46.7 | 54.0 | 126.2 | 58.1 | 78.5 | 145.9 | 123.7 | 35.7 | 83.5 | 100.0 | : | 164.7 | 98.9 |
| 1974 | 127.9 | 148.8 | 143.3 | : | 49.1 | 59.9 | 122.1 | 54.2 | 78.1 | 160.2 | 132.0 | 37.6 | 80.9 | 100.0 | : | 158.5 | 100.1 |
| 1975 | 126.9 | 149.7 | 135.8 | : | 46.4 | 60.9 | 130.6 | 55.5 | 77.1 | 132.3 | 130.3 | 34.5 | 83.7 | 100.0 | : | 147.8 | 92.0 |
| 1976 | 133.0 | 160.0 | 141.3 | : | 48.1 | 59.6 | 131.3 | 52.8 | 73.7 | 140.0 | 137.5 | 34.3 | 78.1 | 100.0 | : | 158.6 | 97.4 |
| 1977 | 136.5 | 157.6 | 144.7 | : | 48.3 | 58.0 | 126.7 | 54.8 | 74.9 | 136.7 | 141.9 | 31.5 | 78.0 | 100.0 | : | 154.7 | 104.9 |
| 1978 | 135.1 | 154.8 | 145.8 | : | 46.9 | 56.6 | 126.8 | 57.1 | 74.4 | 137.8 | 140.1 | 27.7 | 80.3 | 100.0 | : | 140.0 | 118.6 |
| 1979 | 127.3 | 148.3 | 142.1 | : | 46.5 | 61.5 | 125.2 | 57.8 | 76.2 | 132.1 | 131.4 | 25.5 | 85.8 | 100.0 | : | 127.1 | 100.3 |
| 1980 | 121.8 | 131.5 | 133.6 | : | 42.1 | 58.3 | 125.3 | 60.0 | 81.5 | 126.8 | 123.7 | 27.5 | 96.8 | 100.0 | : | 120.5 | 92.1 |
| 1981 | 113.3 | 129.5 | 127.6 | : | 44.1 | 57.1 | 124.6 | 64.2 | 83.8 | 121.1 | 117.0 | 30.2 | 105.1 | 100.0 | : | 152.3 | 115.1 |
| 1982 | 104.4 | 131.6 | 128.3 | : | 47.6 | 57.3 | 122.4 | 68.9 | 86.1 | 114.9 | 118.6 | 30.0 | 104.3 | 100.0 | : | 163.7 | 111.0 |
| 1983 | 102.1 | 136.6 | 132.6 | : | 44.4 | 51.3 | 119.8 | 68.3 | 91.9 | 116.6 | 117.9 | 27.5 | 101.7 | 100.0 | : | 180.0 | 123.9 |
| 1984 | 101.7 | 139.5 | 131.4 | : | 44.7 | 53.8 | 118.5 | 68.7 | 95.3 | 119.7 | 114.9 | 26.6 | 100.1 | 100.0 | : | 206.8 | 137.5 |
| 1985 | 102.6 | 143.8 | 128.6 | : | 42.1 | 54.4 | 119.9 | 70.3 | 94.7 | 119.5 | 112.1 | 27.6 | 102.4 | 100.0 | : | 210.9 | 140.9 |
| 1986 | 104.5 | 148.3 | 134.0 | : | 36.4 | 55.1 | 121.4 | 68.6 | 98.2 | 125.2 | 113.2 | 28.9 | 91.0 | 100.0 | : | 160.9 | 151.0 |
| 1987 | 105.5 | 148.9 | 135.3 | : | 34.6 | 56.5 | 118.7 | 66.0 | 99.9 | 122.7 | 110.7 | 29.1 | 90.5 | 100.0 | : | 134.7 | 147.4 |
| 1988 | 102.7 | 142.7 | 130.7 | : | 35.9 | 59.8 | 115.5 | 65.6 | 99.6 | 122.5 | 105.5 | 29.9 | 98.5 | 100.0 | : | 132.5 | 159.0 |
| 1989 | 102.6 | 136.3 | 127.1 | : | 36.1 | 65.2 | 114.1 | 67.6 | 102.3 | 126.7 | 102.6 | 32.1 | 97.9 | 100.0 | : | 139.4 | 155.4 |
| 1990 | 104.1 | 135.7 | 128.2 | : | 35.4 | 68.2 | 113.8 | 68.8 | 104.2 | 127.2 | 102.5 | 34.4 | 92.0 | 100.0 | : | 117.8 | 128.4 |
| 1991 | 102.5 | 131.1 | 129.5 | 110.9 | 36.0 | 70.8 | 109.5 | 66.7 | 106.1 | 126.0 | 100.5 | 38.3 | 94.1 | 100.0 | 97.0 | 115.7 | 141.1 |
| 1992 | 104.9 | 131.8 | 132.8 | 115.8 | 36.4 | 71.0 | 110.9 | 68.4 | 103.3 | 129.6 | 101.6 | 43.4 | 86.7 | 100.0 | 97.5 | 111.2 | 148.1 |
| 1993 | 109.0 | 138.7 | 139.0 | 123.1 | 37.7 | 65.1 | 115.8 | 68.5 | 92.5 | 136.1 | 107.5 | 42.8 | 86.2 | 100.0 | 98.0 | 128.7 | 180.8 |
| 1994 | 111.2 | 141.8 | 137.6 | 123.2 | 37.7 | 62.1 | 115.5 | 71.8 | 92.5 | 139.7 | 106.9 | 41.8 | 89.2 | 100.0 | 98.3 | 133.9 | 192.4 |

EUR 12−: incl. WD; EUR 12+: incl. D.

**Table B4** Gross domestic product at current market prices per head of population.

(PPS; EUR 12− =100)

| | B | DK | WD | D | GR | E | F | IRL | I | L | NL | P | UK | EUR 12− | EUR 12+ | USA | J |
|---|---|---|---|---|---|---|---|---|---|---|---|---|---|---|---|---|---|
| 1960 | 98.1 | 116.6 | 123.3 | : | 34.9 | 59.0 | 106.3 | 60.0 | 86.6 | 153.4 | 115.5 | 37.9 | 123.9 | 100.0 | : | 181.8 | 54.5 |
| 1961 | 98.2 | 117.9 | 121.8 | : | 36.8 | 62.5 | 106.1 | 60.6 | 89.1 | 145.1 | 112.4 | 37.8 | 121.4 | 100.0 | : | 175.6 | 57.9 |
| 1962 | 99.2 | 119.2 | 121.5 | : | 35.9 | 65.3 | 107.3 | 60.2 | 90.7 | 136.3 | 111.2 | 38.9 | 117.2 | 100.0 | : | 175.5 | 60.3 |
| 1963 | 99.3 | 115.0 | 119.5 | : | 38.0 | 67.8 | 107.3 | 60.5 | 91.9 | 133.5 | 109.8 | 39.5 | 116.9 | 100.0 | : | 173.9 | 62.6 |
| 1964 | 100.3 | 118.8 | 120.3 | : | 39.1 | 68.0 | 107.8 | 59.4 | 89.4 | 135.9 | 111.8 | 40.2 | 116.7 | 100.0 | : | 172.5 | 65.9 |
| 1965 | 99.5 | 119.1 | 121.2 | : | 41.1 | 69.1 | 108.2 | 58.3 | 88.5 | 132.2 | 112.2 | 41.8 | 114.9 | 100.0 | : | 174.0 | 66.7 |
| 1966 | 98.9 | 117.7 | 119.7 | : | 42.0 | 71.0 | 109.5 | 56.9 | 90.4 | 128.0 | 110.3 | 42.2 | 112.9 | 100.0 | : | 176.8 | 70.9 |
| 1967 | 99.4 | 117.6 | 115.9 | : | 42.6 | 71.3 | 110.7 | 58.3 | 93.7 | 125.5 | 111.8 | 44.4 | 111.7 | 100.0 | : | 175.1 | 75.9 |
| 1968 | 98.6 | 116.1 | 116.4 | : | 43.3 | 72.0 | 109.5 | 60.0 | 94.8 | 125.5 | 112.5 | 46.3 | 110.5 | 100.0 | : | 172.3 | 80.9 |
| 1969 | 99.6 | 116.6 | 117.6 | : | 45.0 | 73.7 | 110.4 | 60.0 | 95.0 | 134.2 | 112.4 | 45.5 | 106.7 | 100.0 | : | 166.4 | 85.4 |
| 1970 | 101.8 | 113.6 | 117.7 | : | 46.7 | 73.0 | 111.3 | 58.8 | 95.6 | 138.2 | 112.9 | 47.4 | 104.6 | 100.0 | : | 157.8 | 89.7 |
| 1971 | 102.8 | 113.1 | 117.2 | : | 48.9 | 73.8 | 112.7 | 58.8 | 94.3 | 128.2 | 113.5 | 49.6 | 103.6 | 100.0 | : | 156.4 | 90.4 |
| 1972 | 104.1 | 114.2 | 117.2 | : | 50.7 | 75.8 | 112.7 | 59.6 | 93.0 | 130.6 | 112.0 | 51.8 | 103.2 | 100.0 | : | 156.4 | 93.1 |
| 1973 | 104.1 | 111.5 | 115.8 | : | 51.4 | 76.7 | 111.6 | 58.1 | 93.7 | 139.4 | 110.2 | 54.6 | 104.7 | 100.0 | : | 154.2 | 93.6 |
| 1974 | 106.4 | 108.3 | 114.1 | : | 48.6 | 78.8 | 112.7 | 58.7 | 96.7 | 149.3 | 112.0 | 53.8 | 101.4 | 100.0 | : | 149.5 | 90.4 |
| 1975 | 106.0 | 108.7 | 114.6 | : | 51.7 | 79.4 | 113.3 | 61.9 | 94.9 | 124.3 | 112.4 | 50.5 | 102.0 | 100.0 | : | 148.5 | 93.1 |
| 1976 | 107.1 | 110.7 | 116.3 | : | 52.0 | 77.7 | 112.8 | 59.2 | 96.4 | 123.7 | 112.3 | 50.6 | 100.5 | 100.0 | : | 147.8 | 92.0 |
| 1977 | 104.8 | 109.4 | 116.9 | : | 51.7 | 77.2 | 113.1 | 61.6 | 96.8 | 115.3 | 111.5 | 51.6 | 100.4 | 100.0 | : | 149.2 | 93.1 |
| 1978 | 104.7 | 107.7 | 117.3 | : | 53.0 | 75.3 | 113.2 | 63.4 | 97.3 | 117.6 | 110.4 | 51.0 | 101.1 | 100.0 | : | 150.6 | 94.1 |
| 1979 | 103.6 | 107.8 | 118.5 | : | 52.6 | 72.3 | 112.9 | 62.4 | 99.7 | 116.2 | 108.9 | 51.7 | 100.6 | 100.0 | : | 148.0 | 95.5 |
| 1980 | 107.0 | 106.3 | 118.2 | : | 52.6 | 72.0 | 113.1 | 63.1 | 102.9 | 116.0 | 108.0 | 53.0 | 97.4 | 100.0 | : | 144.4 | 97.3 |
| 1981 | 106.2 | 105.7 | 118.5 | : | 52.3 | 71.3 | 114.2 | 64.6 | 103.6 | 114.9 | 106.9 | 53.5 | 96.4 | 100.0 | : | 146.5 | 100.4 |
| 1982 | 107.2 | 108.3 | 116.7 | : | 51.8 | 71.4 | 115.7 | 65.0 | 103.1 | 116.8 | 104.3 | 54.3 | 97.6 | 100.0 | : | 141.1 | 102.3 |
| 1983 | 106.1 | 109.5 | 117.5 | : | 51.0 | 71.2 | 114.2 | 63.5 | 102.5 | 116.6 | 103.8 | 53.3 | 99.7 | 100.0 | : | 142.6 | 102.8 |
| 1984 | 106.1 | 112.0 | 118.7 | : | 51.0 | 70.7 | 112.8 | 64.4 | 103.0 | 118.7 | 104.3 | 51.1 | 99.8 | 100.0 | : | 147.5 | 104.2 |
| 1985 | 104.6 | 114.1 | 118.7 | : | 51.3 | 70.4 | 111.8 | 64.7 | 103.3 | 120.2 | 104.2 | 51.3 | 100.7 | 100.0 | : | 147.4 | 106.4 |
| 1986 | 103.2 | 115.0 | 118.2 | : | 50.6 | 70.5 | 111.1 | 62.7 | 103.5 | 124.7 | 103.7 | 52.1 | 102.1 | 100.0 | : | 146.1 | 105.6 |
| 1987 | 102.4 | 112.2 | 116.8 | : | 48.9 | 72.3 | 110.1 | 63.8 | 103.9 | 119.2 | 101.5 | 53.4 | 103.8 | 100.0 | : | 145.3 | 106.6 |
| 1988 | 102.9 | 109.2 | 115.9 | : | 49.1 | 73.0 | 110.1 | 64.1 | 104.1 | 121.8 | 99.6 | 53.4 | 104.7 | 100.0 | : | 143.9 | 108.5 |
| 1989 | 103.2 | 106.5 | 115.4 | : | 49.1 | 74.0 | 110.8 | 66.5 | 103.9 | 127.5 | 100.6 | 54.5 | 103.4 | 100.0 | : | 142.0 | 109.8 |
| 1990 | 103.9 | 105.4 | 116.9 | : | 47.0 | 74.8 | 110.4 | 71.1 | 103.6 | 126.3 | 101.6 | 55.7 | 101.2 | 100.0 | : | 139.2 | 112.0 |
| 1991 | 104.0 | 106.4 | 119.4 | 102.2 | 47.3 | 77.6 | 110.4 | 72.3 | 104.7 | 126.8 | 100.1 | 58.5 | 94.9 | 100.0 | 96.9 | 137.7 | 117.5 |
| 1992 | 106.6 | 103.9 | 119.9 | 104.6 | 48.8 | 75.6 | 109.3 | 75.3 | 104.3 | 128.0 | 99.9 | 60.5 | 95.9 | 100.0 | 97.3 | 141.1 | 119.8 |
| 1993 | 106.1 | 105.8 | 117.1 | 103.7 | 48.9 | 75.6 | 109.2 | 77.7 | 104.4 | 131.9 | 100.6 | 60.4 | 98.6 | 100.0 | 97.6 | 145.4 | 120.9 |
| 1994 | 106.2 | 108.5 | 115.3 | 103.3 | 48.5 | 75.5 | 109.3 | 79.9 | 104.9 | 133.6 | 100.1 | 60.4 | 99.7 | 100.0 | 97.9 | 147.7 | 120.3 |

EUR 12−: incl. WD; EUR 12+: incl. D.

**Table B5**  Gross domestic product at 1985 market prices.

(Annual percentage change)

| | B | DK | WD | D | GR | E | F | IRL | I | L | NL | P | UK | EUR 12− | EUR 12+ | USA | J |
|---|---|---|---|---|---|---|---|---|---|---|---|---|---|---|---|---|---|
| 1961 | 5.0 | 6.4 | 4.6 | : | 11.1 | 11.8 | 5.5 | 5.0 | 8.2 | 3.8 | 3.1 | 5.2 | 3.3 | 5.5 | : | 2.7 | 12.0 |
| 1962 | 5.2 | 5.7 | 4.7 | : | 1.5 | 9.3 | 6.7 | 3.2 | 6.2 | 1.4 | 4.0 | 6.6 | 1.0 | 4.7 | : | 5.2 | 8.9 |
| 1963 | 4.4 | 0.6 | 2.8 | : | 10.1 | 8.8 | 5.3 | 4.7 | 5.6 | 3.4 | 3.6 | 5.9 | 3.8 | 4.5 | : | 4.1 | 8.5 |
| 1964 | 7.0 | 9.3 | 6.7 | : | 8.3 | 6.2 | 6.5 | 3.8 | 2.8 | 7.9 | 8.3 | 7.3 | 5.4 | 5.8 | : | 5.6 | 11.7 |
| 1965 | 3.6 | 4.6 | 5.4 | : | 9.4 | 6.3 | 4.8 | 1.9 | 3.3 | 1.9 | 5.2 | 7.6 | 2.5 | 4.3 | : | 5.6 | 5.8 |
| 1966 | 3.2 | 2.7 | 2.8 | : | 6.1 | 7.1 | 5.2 | 0.9 | 6.0 | 1.1 | 2.7 | 3.9 | 1.9 | 3.9 | : | 6.0 | 10.6 |
| 1967 | 3.9 | 3.4 | −0.3 | : | 5.5 | 4.3 | 4.7 | 5.8 | 7.2 | 0.2 | 5.3 | 8.1 | 2.3 | 3.4 | : | 2.9 | 11.1 |
| 1968 | 4.2 | 4.0 | 5.5 | : | 6.7 | 6.8 | 4.3 | 8.2 | 6.5 | 4.2 | 6.4 | 9.2 | 4.1 | 5.3 | : | 4.0 | 12.9 |
| 1969 | 6.6 | 6.3 | 7.5 | : | 9.9 | 8.9 | 7.0 | 5.9 | 6.1 | 10.0 | 6.4 | 3.4 | 2.1 | 6.0 | : | 2.7 | 12.5 |
| 1970 | 6.4 | 2.0 | 5.0 | : | 8.0 | 4.1 | 5.7 | 2.7 | 5.3 | 1.7 | 5.7 | 7.6 | 2.3 | 4.7 | : | −0.3 | 10.7 |
| 1961-70 | 4.9 | 4.5 | 4.4 | : | 7.6 | 7.3 | 5.6 | 4.2 | 5.7 | 3.5 | 5.1 | 6.4 | 2.9 | 4.8 | : | 3.8 | 10.5 |
| 1971 | 3.7 | 2.7 | 3.1 | : | 7.1 | 4.6 | 4.8 | 3.5 | 1.6 | 2.7 | 4.2 | 6.6 | 2.0 | 3.2 | : | 2.8 | 4.3 |
| 1972 | 5.3 | 5.3 | 4.3 | : | 8.9 | 8.0 | 4.4 | 6.5 | 2.7 | 6.6 | 3.3 | 8.0 | 3.5 | 4.3 | : | 4.7 | 8.2 |
| 1973 | 5.9 | 3.6 | 4.8 | : | 7.3 | 7.7 | 5.4 | 4.7 | 7.1 | 8.3 | 4.7 | 11.2 | 7.4 | 6.2 | : | 5.1 | 7.6 |
| 1974 | 4.1 | −0.9 | 0.2 | : | −3.6 | 5.3 | 3.1 | 4.3 | 5.4 | 4.2 | 4.0 | 1.1 | −1.7 | 2.0 | : | −0.7 | −0.6 |
| 1975 | −1.5 | −0.7 | −1.3 | : | 6.1 | 0.5 | −0.3 | 5.7 | −2.7 | −6.6 | −0.1 | −4.3 | −0.7 | −0.9 | : | −1.0 | 2.9 |
| 1976 | 5.6 | 6.5 | 5.3 | : | 6.4 | 3.3 | 4.2 | 1.4 | 6.6 | 2.5 | 5.1 | 6.9 | 2.7 | 4.7 | : | 4.8 | 4.2 |
| 1977 | 0.5 | 1.6 | 2.8 | : | 3.4 | 3.0 | 3.2 | 8.2 | 3.4 | 1.6 | 2.3 | 5.5 | 2.3 | 2.9 | : | 4.5 | 4.7 |
| 1978 | 2.7 | 1.5 | 3.0 | : | 6.7 | 1.4 | 3.4 | 7.2 | 3.7 | 4.1 | 2.5 | 2.8 | 3.5 | 3.2 | : | 4.8 | 4.9 |
| 1979 | 2.1 | 3.5 | 4.2 | : | 3.7 | −0.1 | 3.2 | 3.1 | 6.0 | 2.3 | 2.4 | 5.6 | 2.8 | 3.5 | : | 2.5 | 5.5 |
| 1980 | 4.3 | −0.4 | 1.0 | : | 1.8 | 1.2 | 1.6 | 3.1 | 4.2 | 0.8 | 0.9 | 4.6 | −2.2 | 1.3 | : | −0.4 | 3.6 |
| 1971-80 | 3.2 | 2.2 | 2.7 | : | 4.7 | 3.5 | 3.3 | 4.7 | 3.8 | 2.6 | 2.9 | 4.7 | 1.9 | 3.0 | : | 2.7 | 4.5 |
| 1981 | −1.0 | −0.9 | 0.1 | : | 0.1 | −0.2 | 1.2 | 3.3 | 0.6 | −0.6 | −0.6 | 1.6 | −1.3 | 0.1 | : | 2.2 | 3.6 |
| 1982 | 1.5 | 3.0 | −0.9 | : | 0.4 | 1.2 | 2.5 | 2.3 | 0.2 | 1.1 | −1.4 | 2.1 | 1.7 | 0.8 | : | −2.2 | 3.2 |
| 1983 | 0.4 | 2.5 | 1.8 | : | 0.4 | 1.8 | 0.7 | −0.2 | 1.0 | 3.0 | 1.4 | −0.2 | 3.8 | 1.6 | : | 3.6 | 2.7 |
| 1984 | 2.2 | 4.4 | 2.8 | : | 2.8 | 1.8 | 1.3 | 4.4 | 2.7 | 6.2 | 3.1 | −1.9 | 2.5 | 2.3 | : | 6.7 | 4.3 |
| 1985 | 0.8 | 4.3 | 2.0 | : | 3.1 | 2.3 | 1.9 | 3.1 | 2.6 | 2.9 | 2.6 | 2.8 | 3.5 | 2.5 | : | 3.1 | 5.0 |
| 1986 | 1.4 | 3.6 | 2.3 | : | 1.6 | 3.2 | 2.5 | −0.4 | 2.9 | 4.8 | 2.7 | 4.1 | 4.3 | 2.9 | : | 2.8 | 2.6 |
| 1987 | 2.0 | 0.3 | 1.5 | : | −0.5 | 5.6 | 2.3 | 4.5 | 3.1 | 2.9 | 1.2 | 5.3 | 4.8 | 2.9 | : | 3.1 | 4.1 |
| 1988 | 5.0 | 1.2 | 3.7 | : | 4.4 | 5.2 | 4.5 | 4.2 | 4.1 | 5.7 | 2.6 | 3.9 | 5.0 | 4.3 | : | 3.9 | 6.2 |
| 1989 | 3.6 | 0.6 | 3.6 | : | 3.5 | 4.7 | 4.3 | 6.2 | 2.9 | 6.7 | 4.7 | 5.2 | 2.2 | 3.5 | : | 2.7 | 4.7 |
| 1990 | 3.2 | 1.4 | 5.7 | : | −1.1 | 3.6 | 2.5 | 9.0 | 2.1 | 3.2 | 4.1 | 4.4 | 0.4 | 3.0 | : | 0.8 | 4.8 |
| 1981-90 | 1.9 | 2.0 | 2.2 | : | 1.5 | 2.9 | 2.4 | 3.6 | 2.2 | 3.6 | 2.0 | 2.7 | 2.7 | 2.4 | : | 2.7 | 4.1 |
| 1991 | 1.8 | 1.0 | 4.5 | : | 3.3 | 2.2 | 0.7 | 2.6 | 1.2 | 3.1 | 2.1 | 2.1 | −2.3 | 1.5 | : | −1.1 | 4.0 |
| 1992 | 1.4 | 1.2 | 1.6 | 2.1 | 0.9 | 0.8 | 1.4 | 4.8 | 0.7 | 1.9 | 1.4 | 1.1 | −0.5 | 1.0 | 1.1 | 2.6 | 1.3 |
| 1993 | −1.3 | 1.1 | −1.9 | −1.2 | −0.2 | −1.0 | −0.7 | 2.5 | −0.7 | 0.3 | 0.3 | −1.2 | 1.9 | −0.5 | −0.3 | 3.0 | 0.1 |
| 1994 | 1.3 | 3.8 | 0.7 | 1.3 | 0.7 | 1.1 | 1.6 | 4.2 | 1.5 | 1.6 | 1.3 | 1.1 | 2.5 | 1.5 | 1.6 | 3.7 | 0.8 |

EUR: PPS weighted. EUR−: WD; EUR+: incl. D.

**Table B6**  Gross domestic product at 1985 market prices per person employed.

(Annual percentage change)

| | B | DK | WD | D | GR | E | F | IRL | I | L | NL | P | UK | EUR 12− | EUR 12+ | USA | J |
|---|---|---|---|---|---|---|---|---|---|---|---|---|---|---|---|---|---|
| 1961 | 4.1 | 4.8 | 3.2 | : | 10.7 | 11.6 | 5.4 | 5.2 | 7.9 | 2.7 | 1.6 | 4.7 | 2.1 | 4.8 | : | 3.1 | 10.5 |
| 1962 | 3.5 | 4.1 | 4.3 | : | 2.6 | 8.4 | 6.5 | 2.5 | 7.3 | 1.1 | 1.9 | 6.1 | 0.3 | 4.4 | : | 3.1 | 7.5 |
| 1963 | 3.6 | −0.6 | 2.6 | : | 11.7 | 8.2 | 4.3 | 4.2 | 7.3 | 3.8 | 2.2 | 6.0 | 3.7 | 4.5 | : | 3.2 | 7.6 |
| 1964 | 5.5 | 7.1 | 6.6 | : | 9.6 | 5.0 | 5.4 | 3.3 | 3.4 | 6.0 | 6.4 | 7.4 | 4.2 | 5.3 | : | 3.7 | 10.2 |
| 1965 | 3.4 | 2.7 | 4.8 | : | 10.2 | 5.8 | 4.4 | 2.1 | 5.1 | 1.0 | 4.4 | 7.2 | 1.6 | 4.1 | : | 2.2 | 4.1 |
| 1966 | 2.7 | 2.2 | 3.1 | : | 7.1 | 6.5 | 4.4 | 1.2 | 7.6 | 0.6 | 1.9 | 4.4 | 1.3 | 3.9 | : | 1.4 | 8.4 |
| 1967 | 4.2 | 4.1 | 3.0 | : | 6.8 | 3.5 | 4.4 | 6.4 | 6.0 | 1.3 | 5.6 | 8.7 | 3.8 | 4.2 | : | 0.3 | 9.0 |
| 1968 | 4.3 | 3.1 | 5.4 | : | 7.9 | 5.9 | 4.6 | 7.9 | 6.6 | 4.6 | 5.4 | 9.8 | 4.7 | 5.4 | : | 1.6 | 11.0 |
| 1969 | 4.9 | 5.0 | 5.8 | : | 10.3 | 8.0 | 5.4 | 5.6 | 5.6 | 8.5 | 4.7 | 4.0 | 1.6 | 5.0 | : | 0.2 | 11.6 |
| 1970 | 6.8 | 1.3 | 3.7 | : | 8.1 | 3.4 | 4.2 | 3.9 | 5.3 | −0.3 | 4.5 | 2.2 | 3.1 | 4.0 | : | 0.5 | 9.5 |
| 1961-70 | 4.3 | 3.4 | 4.2 | : | 8.5 | 6.6 | 4.9 | 4.2 | 6.2 | 2.9 | 3.9 | 6.0 | 2.6 | 4.6 | : | 1.9 | 8.9 |
| 1971 | 3.0 | 2.1 | 2.6 | : | 6.8 | 4.0 | 3.9 | 1.7 | −0.5 | 3.7 | 6.3 | 2.9 | 3.1 | | : | 3.3 | 3.5 |
| 1972 | 5.5 | 3.1 | 3.8 | : | 8.3 | 7.7 | 3.8 | 6.2 | 3.3 | 3.8 | 4.2 | 8.4 | 3.6 | 4.2 | : | 2.2 | 7.7 |
| 1973 | 5.0 | 2.3 | 3.6 | : | 6.2 | 5.6 | 4.0 | 3.2 | 4.9 | 6.3 | 4.6 | 11.8 | 5.0 | 4.5 | : | 0.7 | 5.2 |
| 1974 | 2.4 | −0.6 | 1.4 | : | −3.8 | 4.6 | 2.2 | 2.8 | 3.4 | 1.4 | 3.8 | 1.6 | −2.0 | 1.6 | : | −2.2 | −0.2 |
| 1975 | −0.1 | 0.6 | 1.5 | : | 6.0 | 2.2 | 0.6 | 6.5 | −2.8 | −7.7 | 0.6 | −1.7 | −0.3 | 0.2 | : | 1.1 | 3.1 |
| 1976 | 6.1 | 4.6 | 5.9 | : | 5.1 | 4.4 | 3.4 | 2.3 | 5.0 | 2.7 | 5.1 | 7.2 | 3.6 | 4.7 | : | 2.0 | 3.4 |
| 1977 | 0.9 | 0.8 | 2.7 | : | 2.6 | 3.7 | 2.4 | 6.3 | 2.3 | 1.6 | 2.1 | 4.7 | 2.2 | 2.5 | : | 1.0 | 3.5 |
| 1978 | 2.6 | 0.4 | 2.2 | : | 6.2 | 3.2 | 2.8 | 4.6 | 3.1 | 4.7 | 1.7 | 4.4 | 2.9 | 2.8 | : | −0.2 | 3.9 |
| 1979 | 1.2 | 2.3 | 2.5 | : | 2.6 | 1.6 | 3.0 | −0.1 | 4.4 | 1.8 | 1.1 | 3.5 | 1.3 | 2.5 | : | −0.7 | 4.5 |
| 1980 | 4.5 | 0.0 | −0.6 | : | 0.4 | 4.4 | 1.5 | 2.1 | 2.2 | 0.1 | 0.1 | 4.9 | −1.9 | 0.9 | : | −0.6 | 2.9 |
| 1971-80 | 3.1 | 1.6 | 2.6 | : | 4.0 | 4.1 | 2.8 | 3.8 | 2.7 | 1.4 | 2.7 | 5.0 | 1.7 | 2.7 | : | 0.6 | 3.7 |
| 1981 | 0.9 | 0.4 | 0.2 | : | −4.9 | 2.4 | 1.7 | 4.2 | 0.6 | −0.9 | 0.8 | 0.6 | 2.7 | 1.2 | : | 1.3 | 2.8 |
| 1982 | 2.9 | 2.6 | 0.3 | : | 1.2 | 2.2 | 2.3 | 2.3 | −0.3 | 1.4 | 1.1 | 4.1 | 3.6 | 1.6 | : | −0.5 | 2.3 |
| 1983 | 1.5 | 2.2 | 3.2 | : | −0.7 | 2.3 | 0.8 | 1.7 | 0.3 | 3.3 | 3.3 | 1.0 | 5.1 | 2.3 | : | 2.6 | 1.2 |
| 1984 | 2.3 | 2.6 | 2.6 | : | 2.4 | 4.3 | 2.2 | 6.3 | 2.3 | 5.6 | 3.2 | −0.4 | 0.5 | 2.2 | : | 1.7 | 3.9 |
| 1985 | 0.2 | 1.7 | 1.3 | : | 2.1 | 3.7 | 2.2 | 5.4 | 1.7 | 1.5 | 1.0 | 2.8 | 2.2 | 1.9 | : | 0.7 | 4.4 |
| 1986 | 0.7 | 1.0 | 0.9 | : | 1.3 | 1.8 | 2.1 | −0.6 | 2.1 | 2.1 | 0.7 | 7.0 | 4.4 | 2.2 | : | 1.0 | 1.8 |
| 1987 | 1.5 | −0.6 | 0.7 | : | −0.4 | 0.5 | 1.9 | 3.7 | 2.7 | 0.1 | −0.5 | 4.7 | 3.0 | 1.7 | : | −0.4 | 3.2 |
| 1988 | 3.4 | 1.8 | 2.9 | : | 2.7 | 2.3 | 3.6 | 4.2 | 3.1 | 2.6 | 1.0 | 3.9 | 1.7 | 2.7 | : | 1.1 | 4.5 |
| 1989 | 2.0 | 1.1 | 2.1 | : | 3.2 | 1.3 | 2.9 | 6.4 | 2.8 | 2.9 | 2.7 | 4.1 | −0.4 | 1.9 | : | 0.8 | 2.7 |
| 1990 | 1.8 | 2.5 | 2.7 | : | −2.3 | 0.1 | 1.5 | 4.6 | 1.2 | −1.0 | 1.7 | 3.5 | −0.7 | 1.2 | : | −0.4 | 2.6 |
| 1981-90 | 1.7 | 1.5 | 1.7 | : | 2.1 | 2.1 | 2.1 | 3.8 | 1.6 | 1.8 | 1.5 | 3.1 | 2.2 | 1.9 | : | 0.8 | 2.9 |
| 1991 | 1.6 | 2.8 | 1.9 | : | 5.7 | 1.7 | 0.7 | 2.6 | 0.4 | −1.1 | 0.6 | 1.2 | 0.8 | 1.3 | : | −0.1 | 2.0 |
| 1992 | 1.8 | 1.3 | 0.7 | 3.8 | −0.5 | 2.0 | 1.8 | 4.4 | 1.8 | 0.0 | 0.6 | 1.7 | 1.8 | 1.5 | 2.3 | 2.4 | 0.2 |
| 1993 | 0.2 | 1.6 | −0.3 | 0.7 | 0.6 | 3.4 | 0.6 | 1.8 | 2.2 | −1.4 | 0.6 | 1.1 | 3.2 | 1.4 | 1.6 | 1.6 | −0.1 |
| 1994 | 2.1 | 2.9 | 2.2 | 2.7 | 0.7 | 2.3 | 2.2 | 2.5 | 2.8 | 0.6 | 1.9 | 2.5 | 1.6 | 2.2 | 2.3 | 1.3 | 0.8 |

EUR: PPS weighted. EUR−: incl. WD; EUR+: incl. D.

**Table B7** Gross domestic product at market prices per head
(at current prices and purchasing power parities).

(PPS)

| Country | 1988 | 1989 | 1990 | 1991 | 1992 |
|---|---|---|---|---|---|
| EUR 12 | 12 555* | 13 597* | 14 549*[1] | 14 976* | 15 616* |
| 13. Österreich | 13 132* | 14 293* | 15 446* | 15 801* | 17 067* |
| 14. Suomi/Finland | 13 317* | 14 713* | 15 397* | 14 628* | 13 853* |
| 15. Island | 14 310* | 14 881* | 15 528* | 15 761* | 15 727* |
| 16. Norge | 13 339* | 14 062* | 14 941* | 15 457* | 16 912* |
| 17. Sverige | 14 039* | 15 023* | 15 732* | 15 297* | 15 820* |
| EEA | 12 625* | 13 669* | 14 612* | 15 002* | : |
| 18. Schweiz/Suisse | 17 035* | 18 479* | 19 589* | 19 885* | : |
| 19. Türkiye | 2693* | 2800* | 3134* | 3192* | : |
| 20. USA | 17 929* | 19 304* | 20 338* | 20 939* | 22 257* |
| 21. Canada | 16 267* | 17 289* | 17 752* | 17 536* | : |
| 22. Nippon (Japan) | 13 511* | 14 293* | 16 272* | 17 707* | 18 771* |

1. Break in series owing to the reunification of 3.10.1990.

**Table B8** Volume indices of gross domestic product at market prices.

(1995=100)

| Country | 1988 | 1989 | 1990 | 1991 | 1992 |
|---|---|---|---|---|---|
| EUR 12 | 110.5* | 114.3* | 117.7 | 121.7* | 123.1* |
| 13. Österreich | 105.0 | 107.8 | 111.0 | 114.4 | 116.3 |
| 14. Suomi/Finland | 109.2 | 113.7 | 117.6 | 119.6 | 115.1 |
| 15. Island | 120.5 | 125.1 | 129.0 | 132.6 | 127.7 |
| 16. Norge | 109.5 | 111.1 | 112.9 | 114.7 | 118.5 |
| 17. Sverige | 107.3 | 109.8 | 112.2 | 113.7 | 111.5 |
| EEA | 110.2* | 113.9* | 117.4* | 121.1* | 122.4* |
| 18. Schweiz/Suisse | 108.1 | 111.2 | 114.4 | 117.0 | – |
| 19. Türkiye | 124.5 | 130.8 | 138.6 | 146.0 | – |
| 20. USA | 109.8* | 113.1* | 114.3* | 113.4* | 116.1* |
| 21. Canada | 111.5 | 115.6 | 118.9 | 121.3 | – |
| 22. Nippon (Japan) | 113.5 | 118.8 | 124.5 | 129.6 | 131.3* |

**Table B9** Annual rates of growth of gross domestic product at market prices (at constant prices) – 1987-1992.

(%)

| Country | Total | Per head of total population | Per head of occupied population |
|---|---|---|---|
| EUR 12 | 2.9* | 1.7 | 1.2* |
| 1. Belgique/Belgié | 2.8 | 2.6 | 2.1 |
| 2. Danmark | 1.1 | 0.9 | 1.4 |
| 3. Deutschland[1] | 4.7* | 1.0* | 1.0* |
| 4. Ελλάδα | 1.8* | 1.2* | 1.4* |
| 5. España | 3.7* | 3.5* | 1.6* |
| 6. France | 2.4 | 1.9* | 1.7 |
| 7. Ireland | 5.3 | 5.2ᶜ | 4.6 |
| 8. Italia | 2.4 | 2.2 | 2.1 |
| 9. Luxembourg | 3.9 | 2.8 | 0.5 |
| 10. Nederland | 2.7* | 2.0* | 1.0* |
| 11. Portugal | 3.5* | 3.6* | 2.3* |
| 12. United Kingdom | 1.6* | 1.2* | 1.0* |
| 13. Österreich | 3.5 | 3.5[1] | : |
| 14. Suomi/Finland | 2.3 | 3.5[1] | : |
| 15. Island | –0.8 | –1.4[1] | : |
| 16. Norge | 0.9 | –0.2[1] | : |
| 17. Sverige | 1.0 | 1.2[1] | : |
| EEA | 3.2* | 1.9* | : |
| 18. Schweiz/Suisse | 2.5 | 1.7 | : |
| 19. Türkiye | 5.4 | 3.1 | : |
| 20. USA | 2.1* | 1.1* | 0.6* |
| 21. Canada | 3.4 | 2.2 | : |
| 22. Nippon (Japan) | 4.2* | 3.8* | 2.4* |

1. OECD de 1987 a 1991.

**Table B10** Gross value-added at market prices by branch – 1991.

(%)

| Country | Agriculture, forestry and fishing | Industry (incl. construction) | Services and general government | Gross value-added at market prices |
|---|---|---|---|---|
| EUR 12 | 2.7 | 33.5 | 63.7 | 99.9 |
| 1. Belgique/Belgié | 2.1 | 33.1 | 68.9 | 104.1 |
| 2. Danmark[1] | 4.2 | 28.5 | 71.7 | 104.4 |
| 3. Deutschland | 1.4 | 42.0 | 64.1 | 107.5 |
| 4. Ελλάδα[1] | 16.3 | 27.4 | 56.3 | 100.0 |
| 5. España | 4.2 | 36.2 | 59.6 | 100.0 |
| 6. France | 3.5 | 32.6 | 68.6 | 104.7 |
| 7. Ireland | 8.1 | 35.8 | 56.1 | 100.0 |
| 8. Italia | 3.8 | 37.2 | 67.4 | 108.4 |
| 9. Luxembourg | 1.7 | 39.8 | 63.7 | 105.2 |
| 10. Nederland | 4.6 | 34.4 | 68.1 | 107.1 |
| 11. Portugal | 7.3 | 46.5 | 62.6 | 116.4 |
| 12. United Kingdom | 1.5 | 36.2 | 66.3 | 104.0 |
| 13. Österreich | 3.4 | 43.9 | 52.7 | 100.0 |
| 14. Suomi/Finland | 6.7 | 38.0 | 55.2 | 99.9 |
| 15. Island[2] | 14.9 | 34.3 | 50.8 | 100.0 |
| 16. Norge | 3.8 | 44.7 | 51.6 | 100.1 |
| 17. Sverige | 3.1 | 40.4 | 56.4 | 99.9 |
| EEA | 2.8 | 34.1 | 63.0 | 99.9 |
| 18. Schweiz/Suisse[3] | 4.0 | 39.7 | 56.3 | 100.0 |
| 19. Türkiye[2] | 17.8 | 38.1 | 44.1 | 100.0 |
| 20. USA[4] | 2.2 | 32.2 | 64.0 | 98.4 |
| 21. Canada[5] | 3.3 | 39.6 | 57.2 | 100.1 |
| 22. Nippon (Japan) | 2.4 | 44.8 | 53.8 | 100.0 |

1. At factor cost.
2. 1990.
3. 1989.
4. 1987.
5. 1986.

420 *Contemporary Europe*

**Table B11** Cost structure of gross domestic product at market prices – 1992.  (%)

| Country | Remuneration of employees | Taxes linked to production and imports minus subsidies | Consumption of fixed capital | Net operating surplus | Gross domestic product at market prices |
|---|---|---|---|---|---|
| EUR 12 | 52.6* | 11.0* | 12.3* | 24.0* | 100.0* |
| 1. Belgique/Belgié | 55.0 | 9.5 | 9.5 | 26.6 | 100.6 |
| 2. Danmark | 53.6 | 13.6 | 9.1 | 23.6 | 100.0 |
| 3. Deutschland | 57.1 | 10.8 | 14.1* | 17.9* | 100.0 |
| 4. Ελλάδα | 36.7 | 15.0 | 8.3 | 40.0 | 100.0 |
| 5. España | 46.2 | 8.8 | 10.8 | 34.2 | 100.0 |
| 6. France | 52.5 | 12.4 | 13.1 | 22.0 | 100.0 |
| 7. Ireland | 51.3 | 10.3 | 10.3 | 28.2 | 100.0 |
| 8. Italia | 45.9 | 9.1 | 12.5 | 14.4 | 99.9 |
| 9. Luxembourg | 62.5 | 12.5 | 12.5 | 12.5 | 100.0 |
| 10. Nederland | 53.2* | 10.1* | 11.7 | 25.4 | 100.4 |
| 11. Portugal | 48.6* | 12.2* | 4.1* | 36.5* | 101.4 |
| 12. United Kingdom | 57.4 | 13.4 | 10.8 | 18.4 | 100.0 |
| 13. Österreich[1] | 53.3 | 13.1 | 12.3 | 21.4 | 100.1 |
| 14. Suomi/Finland[1] | 58.0 | 11.6 | 16.8 | 13.7 | 100.1 |
| 15. Island[1] | 51.6 | 19.2 | 11.5 | 14.1 | 96.4 |
| 16. Norge[1] | 51.9 | 10.6 | 14.9 | 22.6 | 100.0 |
| 17. Sverige[1] | 61.6 | 12.9 | 11.5 | 14.0 | 100.0 |
| EEA[1] | 52.3 | 11.2* | 11.9* | 24.6* | 100.0 |
| 18. Schweiz/Suisse[1] | 63.6 | 4.7 | 10.3 | 21.4 | 100.0* |
| 19. Türkiye[1] | 44.3* | 12.1* | 5.5* | 38.1 | 100.0 |
| 20. USA | 60.4 | 7.9 | 12.6 | 18.7 | 99.6 |
| 21. Canada[1] | 57.4 | 12.2 | 11.9 | 18.2 | 99.7 |
| 22. Nippon (Japan) | 55.9* | 6.8* | 15.2* | 22.2* | 100.0 |

1. 1991.

**Table B12** Use of gross domestic product at market prices – 1992.  (%)

| Country | National private consumption | Collective consumption of general government | Gross fixed capital formation | Change in stocks | Balance of exports and imports of goods and services | Gross domestic product at market prices |
|---|---|---|---|---|---|---|
| EUR 12 | 62.7* | 16.4* | 20.3* | 0.0* | 0.0* | 99.4* |
| 1. Belgique/Belgié | 63.2 | 14.8 | 19.2 | 0.1 | 2.9 | 99.9 |
| 2. Danmark | 51.8 | 25.5 | 15.5 | 0.0 | 7.3 | 100.0 |
| 3. Deutschland | 63.9 | 10.7* | 23.4 | −0.2 | −0.1 | 97.7 |
| 4. Ελλάδα | 71.7 | 20.0 | 18.3 | 1.7 | −10.0 | 101.7 |
| 5. España | 63.2 | 16.8 | 22.0 | 0.9 | −2.9 | 100.0 |
| 6. France | 60.5 | 18.6 | 20.0 | 0.3 | 1.2 | 100.0 |
| 7. Ireland | 56.4 | 15.4 | 15.4 | 0.0 | 10.1 | 97.4 |
| 8. Italia | 63.0 | 17.5 | 19.2 | 0.3 | 0.2 | 100.1 |
| 9. Luxembourg | 62.5 | 12.5 | 25.0 | 0.0 | 0.0 | 100.0 |
| 10. Nederland | 60.1 | 14.5 | 20.6 | 0.4 | 4.4 | 100.0 |
| 11. Portugal | 63.7 | 16.8 | 27.1 | 1.1 | 11.3 | 97.3 |
| 12. United Kingdom | 64.0 | 22.3 | 15.6 | 0.4 | 1.6 | 100.0 |
| 13. Österreich[1] | 55.3 | 18.2 | 25.2 | 0.4 | 0.9 | 100.0 |
| 14. Suomi/Finland[1] | 55.1 | 23.9 | 22.1 | −1.8 | 0.9 | 100.2 |
| 15. Island[1] | 62.3 | 19.5 | 19.0 | 0.3 | −1.1 | 100.0 |
| 16. Norge[1] | 50.9 | 21.5 | 18.5 | 0.3 | 8.8 | 100.0 |
| 17. Sverige[1] | 54.2 | 27.0 | 18.9 | −1.7 | 1.6 | 100.0 |
| EEA | 60.8 | 17.2 | 20.4 | 0.0 | 1.7* | 100.1 |
| 18. Schweiz/Suisse[1] | 57.5 | 14.0 | 25.5 | 1.7 | 1.4 | 100.1 |
| 19. Türkiye[1] | 57.2* | 22.5* | 22.8* | 2.5* | 0.0* | 100.0 |
| 20. USA | 67.1 | 17.7 | 15.7 | 0.1 | −0.7 | 100.0 |
| 21. Canada[1] | 60.5 | 21.0 | 19.9 | 0.1 | 1.0 | 100.3 |
| 22. Nippon (Japan) | 56.8* | 9.2* | 31.0* | 0.6* | 2.3* | 100.0 |

1. 1991.

**Table C1**  Private consumption at current prices.

(Mrd ECU)

| | B | DK | WD | D | GR | E | F | IRL | I | L | NL | P | UK | EUR 12- | EUR 12+ | USA | J |
|---|---|---|---|---|---|---|---|---|---|---|---|---|---|---|---|---|---|
| 1960 | 7.3 | 3.5 | 40.5 | : | 2.7 | 7.5 | 34.4 | 1.4 | 22.4 | 0.3 | 6.6 | 1.7 | 44.9 | 173.2 | .: | 310.6 | 24.7 |
| 1961 | 7.5 | 3.8 | 45.8 | : | 2.8 | 8.4 | 37.3 | 1.4 | 24.2 | 0.3 | 7.3 | 1.8 | 46.7 | 187.6 | : | 317.4 | 28.7 |
| 1962 | 7.9 | 4.3 | 50.2 | : | 3.0 | 9.6 | 41.6 | 1.5 | 27.3 | 0.3 | 8.0 | 1.9 | 49.4 | 205.0 | : | 336.4 | 32.9 |
| 1963 | 8.6 | 4.6 | 53.2 | : | 3.3 | 11.5 | 47.0 | 1.6 | 31.9 | 0.3 | 8.9 | 2.0 | 52.7 | 225.6 | : | 354.7 | 38.4 |
| 1964 | 9.1 | 5.1 | 57.4 | : | 3.6 | 12.8 | 51.3 | 1.8 | 34.6 | 0.4 | 10.1 | 2.1 | 56.2 | 244.7 | : | 380.6 | 44.2 |
| 1965 | 10.0 | 5.6 | 63.5 | : | 4.1 | 15.1 | 54.8 | 1.9 | 37.0 | 0.4 | 11.3 | 2.4 | 59.9 | 265.8 | : | 409.9 | 50.0 |
| 1966 | 10.7 | 6.2 | 68.1 | : | 4.5 | 17.3 | 59.2 | 2.0 | 40.8 | 0.4 | 12.3 | 2.6 | 63.3 | 287.5 | : | 443.7 | 57.5 |
| 1967 | 11.3 | 6.8 | 70.6 | : | 4.9 | 19.1 | 64.4 | 2.1 | 45.4 | 0.4 | 13.4 | 2.8 | 65.6 | 306.9 | : | 470.5 | 66.3 |
| 1968 | 12.7 | 7.2 | 77.8 | : | 5.5 | 19.2 | 72.8 | 2.2 | 50.2 | 0.5 | 15.1 | 3.4 | 63.8 | 330.3 | : | 534.5 | 78.2 |
| 1969 | 13.8 | 8.0 | 87.7 | : | 6.0 | 21.4 | 79.3 | 2.5 | 55.4 | 0.5 | 17.4 | 3.8 | 68.2 | 364.0 | : | 581.6 | 90.5 |
| 1970 | 14.8 | 8.9 | 105.3 | : | 6.7 | 23.8 | 80.9 | 2.8 | 62.6 | 0.5 | 19.5 | 4.0 | 74.3 | 404.3 | : | 621.8 | 104.2 |
| 1971 | 16.4 | 9.4 | 120.7 | : | 7.1 | 26.5 | 88.6 | 3.2 | 67.4 | 0.6 | 22.0 | 4.6 | 82.9 | 449.5 | : | 656.7 | 118.8 |
| 1972 | 18.8 | 10.3 | 136.6 | : | 7.4 | 31.2 | 100.8 | 3.5 | 73.3 | 0.7 | 25.1 | 4.9 | 89.5 | 502.0 | : | 672.5 | 146.9 |
| 1973 | 22.2 | 12.7 | 164.7 | : | 8.3 | 37.5 | 118.0 | 3.7 | 81.6 | 0.8 | 29.7 | 6.0 | 91.4 | 576.7 | : | 676.6 | 181.0 |
| 1974 | 26.8 | 14.6 | 190.1 | : | 10.7 | 48.4 | 132.1 | 4.3 | 93.0 | 0.9 | 36.5 | 8.2 | 103.2 | 668.9 | : | 757.4 | 214.7 |
| 1975 | 30.5 | 16.8 | 211.7 | : | 11.4 | 55.7 | 162.1 | 4.7 | 106.2 | 1.1 | 42.0 | 9.3 | 116.4 | 767.9 | : | 809.3 | 235.0 |
| 1976 | 36.4 | 21.0 | 248.7 | : | 13.3 | 64.4 | 185.9 | 5.2 | 114.4 | 1.3 | 51.1 | 10.5 | 112.9 | 874.0 | : | 1002.5 | 289.2 |
| 1977 | 42.2 | 23.2 | 284.6 | : | 15.1 | 69.7 | 199.3 | 6.0 | 128.3 | 1.5 | 59.9 | 10.3 | 132.5 | 972.6 | : | 1092.8 | 350.1 |
| 1978 | 45.9 | 24.9 | 314.3 | : | 16.2 | 74.6 | 220.2 | 7.0 | 139.6 | 1.6 | 66.4 | 9.6 | 150.5 | 1070.8 | : | 1090.3 | 441.5 |
| 1979 | 49.9 | 27.2 | 344.3 | : | 17.8 | 93.2 | 247.4 | 8.3 | 162.5 | 1.8 | 71.5 | 10.0 | 183.5 | 1217.3 | : | 1128.9 | 432.9 |
| 1980 | 53.5 | 26.7 | 367.8 | : | 18.6 | 100.8 | 281.7 | 9.8 | 199.0 | 1.9 | 76.1 | 12.2 | 230.3 | 1378.3 | : | 1226.9 | 448.6 |
| 1981 | 56.5 | 28.9 | 390.9 | : | 22.4 | 111.2 | 315.8 | 11.6 | 224.9 | 2.1 | 78.4 | 15.3 | 277.4 | 1534.4 | : | 1690.5 | 611.3 |
| 1982 | 57.0 | 31.3 | 428.2 | : | 26.5 | 121.8 | 342.2 | 12.5 | 253.4 | 2.1 | 86.6 | 16.5 | 300.3 | 1678.7 | : | 2058.7 | 660.4 |
| 1983 | 59.2 | 34.4 | 468.6 | : | 26.3 | 115.8 | 359.7 | 13.2 | 286.8 | 2.3 | 92.5 | 16.2 | 314.1 | 1789.2 | : | 2473.4 | 802.9 |
| 1984 | 63.3 | 37.8 | 497.6 | : | 27.8 | 128.9 | 385.8 | 14.3 | 320.9 | 2.5 | 95.8 | 17.2 | 334.4 | 1926.3 | : | 3044.1 | 954.8 |
| 1985 | 69.2 | 42.1 | 518.8 | : | 28.6 | 140.0 | 422.5 | 15.9 | 344.0 | 2.7 | 100.7 | 18.4 | 366.7 | 2069.5 | : | 3405.2 | 1045.4 |
| 1986 | 73.1 | 46.2 | 559.7 | : | 27.1 | 148.7 | 450.4 | 16.5 | 377.5 | 2.9 | 108.4 | 19.6 | 357.3 | 2187.4 | : | 2809.2 | 1187.7 |
| 1987 | 78.1 | 47.9 | 597.9 | : | 27.9 | 160.8 | 469.0 | 16.6 | 406.0 | 3.1 | 114.8 | 20.5 | 374.2 | 2316.6 | : | 2564.5 | 1228.0 |
| 1988 | 80.9 | 48.9 | 624.1 | : | 30.7 | 183.0 | 489.5 | 17.9 | 436.4 | 3.3 | 116.3 | 23.0 | 448.1 | 2502.1 | : | 2704.6 | 1420.3 |
| 1989 | 86.7 | 50.2 | 656.2 | : | 34.6 | 217.5 | 522.8 | 19.6 | 490.1 | 3.6 | 121.8 | 26.1 | 483.5 | 2712.6 | : | 3104.6 | 1503.8 |
| 1990 | 94.3 | 52.8 | 715.4 | : | 37.4 | 241.7 | 562.5 | 20.5 | 530.0 | 3.9 | 131.1 | 29.6 | 484.2 | 2903.5 | : | 2853.6 | 1326.5 |
| 1991 | 100.1 | 54.4 | 777.6 | 875.7 | 40.6 | 266.3 | 582.5 | 21.3 | 577.0 | 4.3 | 139.8 | 35.1 | 518.0 | 3117.1 | 3215.2 | 3036.6 | 1533.6 |
| 1992 | 106.8 | 56.6 | 836.7 | 957.6 | 43.1 | 280.5 | 617.1 | 22.7 | 593.5 | 4.6 | 149.3 | 40.9 | 516.1 | 3267.9 | 3388.8 | 3072.8 | 1613.6 |
| 1993 | 111.3 | 60.8 | 902.1 | 1037.2 | 45.0 | 256.0 | 656.3 | 22.4 | 524.3 | 4.9 | 160.8 | 40.8 | 517.8 | 3302.5 | 3437.6 | 3613.0 | 2080.7 |
| 1994 | 117.0 | 65.0 | 918.7 | 1061.5 | 46.6 | 252.1 | 678.0 | 24.3 | 539.9 | 5.2 | 166.4 | 41.0 | 555.1 | 3409.3 | 3552.1 | 3917.3 | 2327.7 |

EUR 12-: incl. WD; EUR 12+: incl. D.

**Table C2**  Private consumption at current prices.

(Mrd PPS)

| | B | DK | WD | D | GR | E | F | IRL | I | L | NL | P | UK | EUR 12- | EUR 12+ | USA | J |
|---|---|---|---|---|---|---|---|---|---|---|---|---|---|---|---|---|---|
| 1960 | 6.2 | 3.3 | 40.5 | : | 2.3 | 12.0 | 28.9 | 1.3 | 26.0 | 0.3 | 7.8 | 2.3 | 42.4 | 173.4 | : | 208.9 | 30.0 |
| 1961 | 6.6 | 3.6 | 43.8 | : | 2.6 | 13.8 | 31.6 | 1.4 | 28.5 | 0.3 | 8.4 | 2.5 | 44.8 | 187.9 | : | 220.6 | 33.8 |
| 1962 | 7.1 | 4.0 | 47.8 | : | 2.7 | 15.6 | 35.2 | 1.5 | 31.7 | 0.3 | 9.2 | 2.6 | 47.6 | 206.4 | : | 239.0 | 38.8 |
| 1963 | 7.8 | 4.2 | 51.5 | : | 3.0 | 18.0 | 39.0 | 1.6 | 35.7 | 0.3 | 10.3 | 2.9 | 52.0 | 226.3 | : | 259.8 | 44.8 |
| 1964 | 8.3 | 4.7 | 56.2 | : | 3.4 | 19.7 | 42.8 | 1.8 | 38.0 | 0.3 | 11.1 | 3.2 | 55.9 | 245.4 | : | 286.3 | 51.3 |
| 1965 | 9.0 | 5.0 | 62.6 | : | 3.8 | 22.0 | 46.4 | 1.8 | 40.7 | 0.4 | 12.2 | 3.6 | 59.1 | 266.6 | : | 313.5 | 57.5 |
| 1966 | 9.6 | 5.4 | 67.4 | : | 4.2 | 24.3 | 50.6 | 1.9 | 45.6 | 0.4 | 13.0 | 3.9 | 62.1 | 288.3 | : | 340.9 | 65.4 |
| 1967 | 10.1 | 5.7 | 70.4 | : | 4.5 | 26.0 | 54.6 | 2.1 | 50.5 | 0.4 | 14.0 | 4.1 | 65.2 | 307.7 | : | 360.2 | 73.2 |
| 1968 | 11.0 | 6.0 | 75.5 | : | 4.9 | 28.4 | 58.9 | 2.3 | 54.6 | 0.4 | 15.1 | 4.9 | 69.4 | 331.6 | : | 388.1 | 82.0 |
| 1969 | 12.0 | 6.6 | 84.0 | : | 5.5 | 31.6 | 66.0 | 2.5 | 60.5 | 0.5 | 17.1 | 5.3 | 73.5 | 365.2 | : | 419.6 | 94.8 |
| 1970 | 13.2 | 7.2 | 93.4 | : | 6.4 | 35.3 | 73.3 | 2.8 | 68.6 | 0.5 | 19.3 | 5.9 | 80.0 | 406.9 | : | 455.7 | 110.0 |
| 1971 | 14.8 | 7.7 | 104.1 | : | 7.2 | 39.7 | 82.4 | 3.0 | 75.3 | 0.6 | 21.4 | 7.0 | 88.2 | 451.5 | : | 502.1 | 126.3 |
| 1972 | 16.6 | 8.3 | 117.3 | : | 8.1 | 45.6 | 91.9 | 3.3 | 83.0 | 0.7 | 23.5 | 7.6 | 98.5 | 504.3 | : | 560.2 | 147.3 |
| 1973 | 19.3 | 9.6 | 132.6 | : | 9.1 | 53.2 | 104.4 | 3.7 | 97.5 | 0.8 | 26.5 | 9.2 | 114.7 | 580.6 | : | 633.6 | 171.4 |
| 1974 | 22.3 | 10.6 | 151.5 | : | 10.6 | 63.7 | 121.9 | 4.6 | 115.2 | 0.9 | 30.1 | 11.8 | 129.4 | 673.4 | : | 714.5 | 194.0 |
| 1975 | 25.5 | 12.2 | 178.6 | : | 12.7 | 72.7 | 140.6 | 5.2 | 130.7 | 1.0 | 36.2 | 13.6 | 141.9 | 771.0 | : | 813.4 | 237.9 |
| 1976 | 29.3 | 14.5 | 204.7 | : | 14.4 | 84.0 | 159.7 | 5.8 | 149.7 | 1.2 | 41.8 | 15.4 | 156.8 | 877.1 | : | 934.3 | 273.2 |
| 1977 | 32.4 | 16.1 | 230.0 | : | 16.1 | 92.7 | 177.9 | 6.8 | 165.9 | 1.3 | 47.1 | 16.9 | 170.4 | 973.5 | : | 1054.3 | 310.6 |
| 1978 | 35.6 | 17.3 | 252.9 | : | 18.3 | 99.3 | 196.6 | 7.7 | 182.6 | 1.4 | 52.4 | 17.7 | 189.5 | 1071.2 | : | 1173.1 | 350.4 |
| 1979 | 40.6 | 19.8 | 287.1 | : | 20.2 | 109.5 | 223.0 | 9.0 | 212.8 | 1.5 | 59.2 | 20.3 | 215.2 | 1218.0 | : | 1314.9 | 412.0 |
| 1980 | 47.0 | 21.6 | 325.4 | : | 23.2 | 124.6 | 254.4 | 10.3 | 251.1 | 1.8 | 66.4 | 23.4 | 231.9 | 1381.1 | : | 1471.0 | 474.2 |
| 1981 | 53.0 | 23.6 | 363.1 | : | 26.6 | 138.9 | 289.3 | 11.7 | 278.1 | 2.0 | 71.7 | 27.1 | 254.4 | 1539.3 | : | 1627.0 | 533.0 |
| 1982 | 58.6 | 25.8 | 389.8 | : | 28.9 | 151.6 | 323.5 | 11.8 | 303.4 | 2.2 | 76.1 | 29.9 | 281.0 | 1682.5 | : | 1774.1 | 608.6 |
| 1983 | 61.5 | 27.6 | 415.0 | : | 30.2 | 160.9 | 343.1 | 12.3 | 319.9 | 2.3 | 81.4 | 31.3 | 307.9 | 1793.3 | : | 1959.4 | 665.9 |
| 1984 | 66.0 | 30.3 | 449.5 | : | 31.8 | 169.3 | 367.1 | 13.4 | 346.7 | 2.5 | 87.0 | 33.1 | 333.5 | 1930.2 | : | 2171.8 | 723.8 |
| 1985 | 70.4 | 33.4 | 478.8 | : | 34.8 | 181.1 | 393.9 | 14.6 | 375.1 | 2.7 | 93.6 | 34.2 | 360.8 | 2073.6 | : | 2379.8 | 789.3 |
| 1986 | 72.2 | 35.8 | 493.9 | : | 37.6 | 190.2 | 412.2 | 15.1 | 397.6 | 2.9 | 99.3 | 35.2 | 400.7 | 2192.8 | : | 2549.9 | 831.1 |
| 1987 | 75.8 | 36.1 | 516.1 | : | 39.4 | 205.8 | 434.9 | 16.0 | 422.4 | 3.0 | 105.2 | 37.6 | 429.4 | 2322.0 | : | 2711.9 | 888.2 |
| 1988 | 81.1 | 37.4 | 553.4 | : | 42.0 | 223.5 | 466.9 | 17.4 | 456.0 | 3.3 | 109.8 | 41.1 | 476.1 | 2508.1 | : | 2937.5 | 969.0 |
| 1989 | 87.2 | 39.2 | 595.8 | : | 47.1 | 247.1 | 507.6 | 19.3 | 497.9 | 3.6 | 119.4 | 44.3 | 510.6 | 2719.1 | : | 3162.9 | 1061.7 |
| 1990 | 91.4 | 41.0 | 652.6 | : | 49.7 | 265.2 | 545.7 | 21.2 | 526.9 | 3.9 | 130.0 | 48.0 | 532.6 | 2910.8 | : | 3372.3 | 1157.6 |
| 1991 | 101.8 | 44.2 | 718.0 | 808.5 | 53.4 | 292.1 | 588.1 | 23.2 | 570.1 | 4.4 | 139.4 | 53.8 | 539.0 | 3127.3 | 3217.3 | 3617.8 | 1279.0 |
| 1992 | 108.8 | 44.7 | 757.0 | 866.4 | 57.9 | 299.7 | 609.2 | 25.0 | 600.6 | 4.5 | 147.1 | 57.2 | 571.9 | 3283.7 | 3393.1 | 3905.4 | 1366.0 |
| 1993 | 108.9 | 46.6 | 762.9 | 877.1 | 58.5 | 298.4 | 621.4 | 25.5 | 594.4 | 4.8 | 151.2 | 57.9 | 594.8 | 3325.3 | 3439.5 | 4096.3 | 1397.4 |
| 1994 | 112.2 | 50.0 | 773.6 | 893.9 | 60.2 | 308.1 | 644.6 | 27.1 | 615.0 | 5.0 | 156.6 | 59.6 | 623.5 | 3435.5 | 3555.8 | 4340.5 | 1461.9 |

EUR: 12-: incl. WD; EUR+: incl. D.

**Table C3**　Private consumption at current prices.

(Percentage of gross domestic product at market prices)

| | B | DK | WD | D | GR | E | F | IRL | I | L | NL | P | UK | EUR 12− | EUR 12+ | USA | J |
|---|---|---|---|---|---|---|---|---|---|---|---|---|---|---|---|---|---|
| 1960 | 69.2 | 62.0 | 59.4 | : | 80.3 | 67.5 | 59.7 | 78.8 | 59.7 | 54.0 | 58.7 | 73.1 | 65.5 | 62.2 | | 63.7 | 58.7 |
| 1961 | 67.9 | 62.1 | 59.5 | : | 76.8 | 66.9 | 60.0 | 77.2 | 58.6 | 56.9 | 59.9 | 73.6 | 65.0 | 61.9 | : | 63.6 | 57.0 |
| 1962 | 66.6 | 61.9 | 59.5 | : | 76.4 | 66.4 | 60.0 | 76.8 | 58.9 | 56.9 | 60.6 | 69.7 | 65.5 | 61.9 | : | 62.8 | 57.7 |
| 1963 | 67.1 | 61.4 | 59.6 | : | 74.3 | 67.5 | 60.5 | 76.2 | 60.2 | 57.5 | 62.0 | 69.4 | 65.9 | 62.4 | : | 62.7 | 58.8 |
| 1964 | 64.1 | 60.3 | 58.4 | : | 73.6 | 66.5 | 59.5 | 74.7 | 59.6 | 56.7 | 62.0 | 68.2 | 64.3 | 61.2 | : | 62.7 | 57.6 |
| 1965 | 64.3 | 58.9 | 59.2 | : | 72.8 | 67.1 | 59.0 | 73.8 | 59.2 | 58.2 | 59.6 | 67.9 | 63.6 | 61.0 | : | 62.3 | 58.5 |
| 1966 | 63.9 | 59.6 | 59.7 | : | 72.3 | 66.5 | 58.9 | 73.8 | 60.3 | 58.2 | 59.6 | 67.9 | 63.2 | 61.2 | : | 61.6 | 58.0 |
| 1967 | 62.9 | 59.9 | 60.8 | : | 72.4 | 66.4 | 59.1 | 72.1 | 60.6 | 59.1 | 59.0 | 65.4 | 63.1 | 61.4 | : | 61.5 | 56.8 |
| 1968 | 63.7 | 58.8 | 60.1 | : | 71.9 | 66.0 | 59.3 | 73.0 | 59.7 | 57.7 | 58.1 | 68.5 | 62.6 | 61.0 | : | 61.8 | 54.7 |
| 1969 | 62.2 | 57.5 | 59.1 | : | 69.2 | 64.1 | 59.1 | 71.7 | 59.3 | 53.4 | 58.7 | 69.1 | 61.8 | 60.3 | : | 61.9 | 53.5 |
| 1970 | 59.8 | 57.4 | 58.4 | : | 69.2 | 64.0 | 57.9 | 70.8 | 59.5 | 50.5 | 58.7 | 65.9 | 61.3 | 59.6 | : | 62.8 | 52.3 |
| 1961-70 | 64.3 | 59.8 | 59.4 | : | 72.9 | 66.1 | 59.3 | 74.0 | 59.6 | 56.5 | 59.6 | 68.6 | 63.6 | 61.6 | : | 62.4 | 56.5 |
| 1971 | 60.3 | 55.8 | 58.7 | : | 68.0 | 64.3 | 57.8 | 70.0 | 59.8 | 54.8 | 58.0 | 68.3 | 61.7 | 59.8 | : | 62.7 | 53.6 |
| 1972 | 60.2 | 53.4 | 59.4 | : | 65.7 | 63.8 | 57.7 | 66.8 | 60.1 | 53.6 | 57.6 | 64.2 | 62.3 | 59.9 | : | 62.5 | 54.0 |
| 1973 | 60.6 | 54.5 | 58.8 | : | 63.4 | 63.5 | 57.1 | 66.2 | 60.5 | 48.9 | 56.9 | 64.8 | 62.0 | 59.5 | : | 61.7 | 53.6 |
| 1974 | 59.8 | 54.3 | 59.7 | : | 67.7 | 64.2 | 57.5 | 70.4 | 60.3 | 46.1 | 57.0 | 72.7 | 63.3 | 60.1 | : | 62.3 | 54.3 |
| 1975 | 61.2 | 55.4 | 62.9 | : | 67.5 | 64.3 | 58.7 | 66.0 | 62.0 | 57.8 | 58.8 | 77.1 | 61.7 | 61.5 | : | 63.3 | 57.1 |
| 1976 | 60.9 | 56.6 | 62.5 | : | 65.8 | 65.7 | 58.4 | 66.4 | 60.8 | 56.6 | 59.0 | 75.0 | 60.6 | 61.1 | : | 63.3 | 57.5 |
| 1977 | 61.9 | 56.9 | 63.1 | : | 65.9 | 65.0 | 58.2 | 66.0 | 60.3 | 59.6 | 60.0 | 72.0 | 59.5 | 61.0 | : | 63.1 | 57.7 |
| 1978 | 61.6 | 56.2 | 62.6 | : | 65.2 | 63.9 | 57.9 | 65.6 | 59.5 | 57.9 | 60.6 | 68.0 | 59.4 | 60.6 | : | 62.3 | 57.7 |
| 1979 | 62.8 | 56.4 | 62.3 | : | 63.3 | 64.5 | 58.1 | 67.2 | 59.7 | 57.8 | 61.1 | 67.5 | 59.9 | 60.7 | : | 62.2 | 58.7 |
| 1980 | 62.9 | 55.9 | 63.1 | : | 64.6 | 65.3 | 58.9 | 67.7 | 61.0 | 58.7 | 61.3 | 67.3 | 59.6 | 61.3 | : | 63.1 | 58.8 |
| 1971-80 | 61.2 | 55.5 | 61.3 | : | 65.7 | 64.5 | 58.0 | 67.2 | 60.4 | 55.2 | 59.0 | 69.7 | 61.0 | 60.5 | : | 62.6 | 56.3 |
| 1981 | 65.2 | 56.0 | 64.0 | : | 67.5 | 66.5 | 60.3 | 67.8 | 61.2 | 60.9 | 60.7 | 69.6 | 60.3 | 62.1 | : | 62.2 | 58.1 |
| 1982 | 65.6 | 55.0 | 64.1 | : | 67.4 | 66.2 | 60.7 | 61.5 | 61.5 | 60.3 | 60.4 | 69.6 | 60.5 | 62.2 | : | 64.0 | 59.4 |
| 1983 | 65.2 | 54.6 | 63.8 | : | 66.7 | 65.7 | 60.8 | 61.3 | 61.1 | 59.6 | 60.6 | 69.3 | 60.8 | 62.0 | : | 64.9 | 60.2 |
| 1984 | 64.9 | 54.5 | 63.6 | : | 64.7 | 64.3 | 60.8 | 60.5 | 61.1 | 58.1 | 59.4 | 70.7 | 60.8 | 61.8 | : | 63.8 | 59.4 |
| 1985 | 65.5 | 54.8 | 63.4 | : | 65.5 | 64.1 | 61.1 | 61.3 | 61.4 | 58.7 | 59.5 | 67.9 | 60.6 | 61.8 | : | 64.7 | 58.9 |
| 1986 | 64.2 | 55.0 | 61.9 | : | 67.4 | 63.2 | 60.4 | 61.6 | 61.3 | 56.5 | 59.5 | 65.1 | 62.5 | 61.5 | : | 65.3 | 58.6 |
| 1987 | 64.5 | 54.0 | 62.2 | : | 69.5 | 63.2 | 60.9 | 61.0 | 61.7 | 59.2 | 60.8 | 64.5 | 62.5 | 61.9 | : | 65.8 | 58.7 |
| 1988 | 63.1 | 53.1 | 61.8 | : | 68.1 | 62.7 | 60.1 | 61.2 | 61.4 | 57.4 | 59.4 | 65.1 | 63.4 | 61.5 | : | 65.9 | 57.9 |
| 1989 | 62.4 | 52.6 | 61.1 | : | 70.1 | 63.0 | 59.6 | 60.5 | 62.0 | 54.7 | 58.7 | 63.5 | 63.3 | 61.3 | : | 65.7 | 57.7 |
| 1990 | 62.4 | 51.9 | 60.5 | : | 71.5 | 62.4 | 59.8 | 58.4 | 61.5 | 55.4 | 58.7 | 63.1 | 62.9 | 61.0 | : | 66.5 | 57.4 |
| 1981-90 | 64.3 | 54.2 | 62.6 | : | 67.8 | 64.1 | 60.4 | 61.5 | 61.4 | 58.1 | 59.7 | 66.8 | 61.8 | 61.7 | : | 64.9 | 58.6 |
| 1991 | 63.1 | 52.0 | 60.5 | 63.8 | 71.4 | 62.4 | 60.2 | 58.6 | 61.9 | 57.3 | 59.6 | 63.3 | 65.5 | 61.3 | 62.2 | 67.1 | 56.6 |
| 1992 | 63.2 | 51.8 | 60.5 | 63.9 | 71.7 | 63.2 | 60.4 | 58.3 | 62.9 | 56.3 | 60.3 | 62.9 | 64.1 | 61.7 | 62.6 | 67.4 | 57.0 |
| 1993 | 63.2 | 52.6 | 61.7 | 64.6 | 71.6 | 62.7 | 61.2 | 57.3 | 61.9 | 56.9 | 60.9 | 63.5 | 64.5 | 62.0 | 62.9 | 67.7 | 57.5 |
| 1994 | 62.8 | 53.1 | 60.8 | 63.5 | 71.5 | 62.5 | 61.0 | 57.0 | 61.6 | 56.9 | 60.8 | 63.2 | 64.4 | 61.7 | 62.4 | 67.5 | 58.3 |

EUR 12−: incl. WD; EUR 12+: incl. D.

**Table C4**　Private consumption at 1985 prices.

(Annual percentage change)

| | B | DK | WD | D | GR | E | F | IRL | I | L | NL | P | UK | EUR 12− | EUR 12+ | USA | J |
|---|---|---|---|---|---|---|---|---|---|---|---|---|---|---|---|---|---|
| 1961 | 1.6 | 7.3 | 6.0 | : | 6.8 | 11.0 | 5.9 | 3.1 | 7.5 | 5.0 | 5.2 | 7.8 | 2.2 | 5.5 | : | 2.3 | 10.4 |
| 1962 | 3.9 | 5.9 | 5.6 | : | 4.3 | 8.8 | 7.1 | 3.5 | 7.1 | 4.4 | 6.1 | -1.2 | 2.2 | 5.4 | : | 4.5 | 7.5 |
| 1963 | 4.4 | 0.0 | 3.0 | : | 5.1 | 11.3 | 6.9 | 4.2 | 9.3 | 4.6 | 7.0 | 6.9 | 4.9 | 6.0 | : | 3.7 | 8.8 |
| 1964 | 2.6 | 7.8 | 5.4 | : | 8.8 | 4.3 | 5.6 | 4.3 | 3.3 | 9.2 | 5.9 | 5.8 | 3.0 | 4.5 | : | 5.6 | 10.8 |
| 1965 | 4.3 | 3.4 | 7.0 | : | 7.7 | 6.9 | 4.0 | 0.8 | 3.3 | 4.0 | 7.5 | 6.0 | 1.5 | 4.4 | : | 5.7 | 5.8 |
| 1966 | 2.7 | 4.3 | 3.8 | : | 6.8 | 6.9 | 4.8 | 1.5 | 7.2 | 1.6 | 3.2 | 4.0 | 1.7 | 4.2 | : | 5.2 | 10.0 |
| 1967 | 2.8 | 2.9 | 1.5 | : | 6.2 | 6.0 | 5.1 | 3.8 | 7.4 | 0.0 | 5.4 | 6.0 | 2.4 | 4.0 | : | 3.0 | 10.4 |
| 1968 | 5.3 | 1.9 | 4.9 | : | 6.9 | 6.0 | 4.0 | 9.0 | 5.2 | 4.3 | 6.6 | 11.1 | 2.8 | 4.6 | : | 5.2 | 8.5 |
| 1969 | 5.4 | 6.3 | 7.6 | : | 6.2 | 7.0 | 6.0 | 5.4 | 6.6 | 5.2 | 7.9 | 5.4 | 0.6 | 5.5 | : | 3.7 | 10.3 |
| 1970 | 4.4 | 3.5 | 7.4 | : | 8.8 | 4.2 | 4.3 | -1.0 | 7.6 | 6.1 | 7.4 | 2.9 | 2.9 | 5.4 | : | 2.2 | 7.4 |
| 1961-70 | 3.7 | 4.3 | 5.2 | : | 6.7 | 7.2 | 5.4 | 3.4 | 6.4 | 4.4 | 6.2 | 5.4 | 2.4 | 4.9 | : | 4.1 | 9.0 |
| 1971 | 4.7 | -0.8 | 5.8 | : | 5.6 | 5.1 | 4.9 | 3.2 | 3.5 | 5.6 | 3.3 | 8.4 | 3.2 | 4.4 | : | 3.3 | 5.6 |
| 1972 | 6.0 | 1.7 | 5.1 | : | 7.0 | 8.3 | 4.9 | 5.1 | 3.3 | 4.8 | 3.5 | 2.9 | 6.2 | 5.1 | : | 5.7 | 9.1 |
| 1973 | 7.8 | 4.8 | 3.4 | : | 7.6 | 7.8 | 5.3 | 7.2 | 7.0 | 5.8 | 4.0 | 13.0 | 5.5 | 5.6 | : | 4.6 | 9.1 |
| 1974 | 2.6 | -2.9 | 1.2 | : | 0.7 | 5.1 | 1.2 | 1.6 | 3.7 | 4.5 | 3.7 | 9.1 | -1.4 | 1.7 | : | -0.9 | -0.1 |
| 1975 | 0.6 | 3.7 | 3.8 | : | 5.5 | 1.8 | 2.9 | 0.8 | 0.2 | 5.3 | 3.3 | 1.7 | -0.3 | 1.9 | : | 2.0 | 4.5 |
| 1976 | 4.8 | 7.9 | 4.1 | : | 5.3 | 5.6 | 4.9 | 2.8 | 5.0 | 3.1 | 5.3 | 2.3 | 0.5 | 4.0 | : | 5.3 | 3.1 |
| 1977 | 2.4 | 1.1 | 4.1 | : | 4.6 | 1.5 | 2.7 | 6.8 | 3.3 | 2.3 | 4.6 | 0.6 | -0.3 | 2.6 | : | 4.0 | 4.1 |
| 1978 | 2.3 | 0.7 | 3.7 | : | 5.7 | 0.9 | 3.7 | 9.1 | 3.1 | 2.9 | 4.3 | -2.0 | 5.3 | 3.5 | : | 4.1 | 5.4 |
| 1979 | 4.8 | 1.4 | 3.3 | : | 2.6 | 1.3 | 3.0 | 4.4 | 7.1 | 3.5 | 3.0 | 0.0 | 4.4 | 3.8 | : | 2.2 | 6.5 |
| 1980 | 2.0 | -3.7 | 1.5 | : | 0.2 | 0.6 | 1.2 | 0.4 | 6.2 | 2.8 | 0.0 | 3.7 | 0.0 | 1.8 | : | -0.2 | 1.1 |
| 1971-80 | 3.8 | 1.3 | 3.6 | : | 4.4 | 3.7 | 3.5 | 4.1 | 4.2 | 4.1 | 3.5 | 3.9 | 2.3 | 3.4 | : | 3.0 | 4.8 |
| 1981 | -1.1 | -2.3 | -0.2 | : | 2.0 | -0.6 | 2.1 | 1.7 | 1.8 | 1.7 | -2.0 | 2.9 | 0.1 | 0.5 | : | 1.3 | 1.6 |
| 1982 | 1.3 | 1.4 | -1.3 | : | 3.9 | 0.2 | 3.5 | -7.1 | 0.9 | 0.4 | -1.4 | 2.4 | 1.0 | 0.7 | : | 0.9 | 4.4 |
| 1983 | -1.6 | 2.6 | 1.4 | : | 0.3 | 0.3 | 0.9 | 0.9 | 0.6 | 0.5 | 0.7 | -1.4 | 4.5 | 1.4 | : | 4.5 | 3.4 |
| 1984 | 1.2 | 3.4 | 2.2 | : | 1.7 | -0.4 | 1.1 | 2.0 | 2.2 | 1.4 | 0.8 | -2.9 | 2.0 | 1.5 | : | 5.0 | 2.7 |
| 1985 | 1.9 | 5.0 | 1.9 | : | 3.9 | 2.4 | 2.4 | 4.6 | 3.1 | 2.7 | 2.4 | 0.7 | 3.8 | 2.7 | : | 4.4 | 3.4 |
| 1986 | 2.3 | 5.7 | 3.4 | : | 0.7 | 3.3 | 3.9 | 2.0 | 4.4 | 3.4 | 2.6 | 5.6 | 6.8 | 4.2 | : | 3.8 | 3.4 |
| 1987 | 3.0 | -1.5 | 3.3 | : | 1.2 | 5.8 | 2.9 | 3.1 | 4.5 | 5.0 | 2.7 | 5.4 | 5.3 | 3.9 | : | 2.9 | 4.2 |
| 1988 | 2.9 | -1.0 | 3.1 | : | 3.6 | 4.9 | 3.3 | 4.8 | 4.6 | 3.9 | 0.8 | 6.6 | 7.5 | 4.3 | : | 3.8 | 5.2 |
| 1989 | 3.6 | -0.4 | 1.9 | : | 4.5 | 5.7 | 3.1 | 6.0 | 3.6 | 3.9 | 3.5 | 3.3 | 3.2 | 3.2 | : | 2.1 | 4.3 |
| 1990 | 2.6 | 0.0 | 5.1 | : | 2.3 | 3.6 | 2.9 | 1.9 | 2.9 | 4.0 | 4.2 | 5.3 | 0.6 | 3.1 | : | 1.1 | 3.9 |
| 1981-90 | 1.6 | 1.3 | 2.1 | : | 2.4 | 2.5 | 2.6 | 1.9 | 2.8 | 2.7 | 1.4 | 2.7 | 3.5 | 2.5 | : | 3.0 | 3.7 |
| 1991 | 3.1 | 1.4 | 4.6 | : | 2.2 | 2.9 | 1.4 | 1.6 | 2.6 | 6.5 | 3.0 | 5.2 | -2.2 | 2.0 | : | -0.6 | 2.2 |
| 1992 | 2.9 | 0.7 | 1.9 | 2.8 | 1.7 | 2.1 | 1.7 | 2.8 | 1.7 | 1.7 | 2.1 | 3.7 | 0.0 | 1.6 | 1.8 | 2.6 | 1.7 |
| 1993 | -1.4 | 2.6 | 0.1 | -0.1 | -0.2 | -2.3 | 0.8 | 1.9 | -3.0 | 0.2 | 0.9 | 0.8 | 2.5 | -0.1 | -0.1 | 3.3 | 1.1 |
| 1994 | 0.8 | 4.4 | -1.0 | -0.8 | 0.6 | 0.0 | 1.1 | 4.0 | 0.5 | 1.7 | 0.9 | 0.3 | 2.2 | 0.6 | 0.6 | 3.9 | 1.8 |

EUR: PPS weighted. EUR 12−: incl. WD; EUR 12+: incl. D.

**Table C5** Private consumption at current prices per head of population.

(ECU; EUR 12− =100)

| | B | DK | WD | D | GR | E | F | IRL | I | L | NL | P | UK | EUR 12− | EUR 12+ | USA | J |
|---|---|---|---|---|---|---|---|---|---|---|---|---|---|---|---|---|---|
| 1960 | 128.4 | 122.9 | 117.8 | : | 51.6 | 40.0 | 112.5 | 78.2 | 71.7 | 136.6 | 92.7 | 33.4 | 138.1 | 100.0 | : | 277.0 | 42.3 |
| 1961 | 123.2 | 125.1 | 122.4 | : | 50.9 | 41.3 | 121.4 | 76.5 | 71.8 | 132.0 | 94.6 | 33.1 | 132.9 | 100.0 | : | 259.9 | 45.4 |
| 1962 | 118.9 | 128.7 | 122.6 | : | 49.3 | 43.2 | 122.9 | 75.9 | 74.3 | 126.6 | 94.5 | 30.8 | 128.7 | 100.0 | : | 250.3 | 47.6 |
| 1963 | 117.3 | 123.8 | 118.2 | : | 48.9 | 47.1 | 125.1 | 73.8 | 79.2 | 124.0 | 95.0 | 30.3 | 125.1 | 100.0 | : | 238.8 | 50.5 |
| 1964 | 115.5 | 128.1 | 117.3 | : | 50.4 | 48.2 | 125.9 | 76.0 | 79.3 | 128.4 | 98.6 | 29.9 | 123.4 | 100.0 | : | 235.0 | 53.6 |
| 1965 | 115.9 | 129.5 | 119.2 | : | 52.5 | 52.0 | 123.6 | 74.0 | 78.1 | 126.7 | 100.9 | 30.9 | 121.2 | 100.0 | : | 232.2 | 55.6 |
| 1966 | 114.7 | 132.9 | 118.1 | : | 53.6 | 55.0 | 123.5 | 72.5 | 79.7 | 123.1 | 101.0 | 31.6 | 118.8 | 100.0 | : | 231.5 | 59.1 |
| 1967 | 113.9 | 136.8 | 115.0 | : | 54.3 | 56.7 | 125.6 | 71.4 | 83.1 | 118.8 | 102.6 | 32.2 | 115.4 | 100.0 | : | 228.9 | 63.5 |
| 1968 | 118.9 | 133.5 | 118.2 | : | 56.4 | 52.8 | 131.7 | 68.6 | 85.3 | 122.5 | 107.4 | 36.1 | 104.4 | 100.0 | : | 240.5 | 69.3 |
| 1969 | 118.2 | 135.8 | 120.5 | : | 56.6 | 53.1 | 130.1 | 71.3 | 85.5 | 120.2 | 118.8 | 36.8 | 101.5 | 100.0 | : | 236.9 | 72.3 |
| 1970 | 114.6 | 134.8 | 130.0 | : | 57.4 | 53.0 | 119.3 | 71.4 | 87.0 | 120.0 | 112.2 | 35.6 | 100.0 | 100.0 | : | 227.0 | 74.5 |
| 1971 | 114.8 | 128.9 | 133.6 | : | 55.2 | 52.9 | 117.2 | 71.9 | 84.6 | 119.7 | 113.2 | 37.3 | 101.4 | 100.0 | : | 214.4 | 76.2 |
| 1972 | 118.7 | 126.5 | 135.4 | : | 50.7 | 55.3 | 119.2 | 70.3 | 82.4 | 121.0 | 115.0 | 35.9 | 97.5 | 100.0 | : | 195.5 | 83.8 |
| 1973 | 122.3 | 135.4 | 142.2 | : | 49.8 | 57.7 | 121.2 | 64.7 | 79.8 | 120.0 | 184.4 | 38.9 | 87.1 | 100.0 | : | 170.9 | 89.2 |
| 1974 | 127.2 | 134.5 | 142.1 | : | 55.2 | 63.9 | 116.8 | 63.5 | 78.3 | 122.9 | 125.0 | 45.4 | 85.1 | 100.0 | : | 164.2 | 90.4 |
| 1975 | 126.4 | 135.0 | 138.9 | : | 50.9 | 63.7 | 124.8 | 59.5 | 77.4 | 124.3 | 124.7 | 43.2 | 84.0 | 100.0 | : | 152.0 | 85.5 |
| 1976 | 132.7 | 148.2 | 144.5 | : | 51.8 | 64.2 | 125.6 | 57.4 | 73.4 | 129.8 | 132.8 | 42.1 | 77.5 | 100.0 | : | 164.4 | 91.7 |
| 1977 | 138.5 | 146.9 | 149.5 | : | 52.2 | 61.8 | 120.9 | 59.2 | 74.0 | 133.4 | 139.5 | 37.2 | 76.1 | 100.0 | : | 160.0 | 99.2 |
| 1978 | 137.3 | 143.5 | 150.7 | : | 50.4 | 59.7 | 121.3 | 61.8 | 73.1 | 131.8 | 140.1 | 31.1 | 78.8 | 100.0 | : | 144.0 | 113.0 |
| 1979 | 131.6 | 137.8 | 145.7 | : | 48.5 | 65.3 | 119.8 | 63.9 | 74.9 | 125.8 | 132.2 | 28.3 | 84.7 | 100.0 | : | 130.2 | 97.0 |
| 1980 | 125.1 | 119.9 | 137.6 | : | 44.4 | 62.1 | 120.4 | 66.2 | 81.2 | 121.6 | 123.9 | 30.2 | 94.1 | 100.0 | : | 124.0 | 88.4 |
| 1981 | 119.0 | 116.9 | 131.5 | : | 47.9 | 61.2 | 120.9 | 70.1 | 82.6 | 118.7 | 114.2 | 33.8 | 102.1 | 100.0 | : | 152.4 | 107.8 |
| 1982 | 110.1 | 116.4 | 132.1 | : | 51.6 | 61.0 | 119.4 | 68.1 | 85.2 | 111.4 | 115.1 | 33.5 | 101.4 | 100.0 | : | 168.4 | 106.0 |
| 1983 | 107.3 | 120.3 | 136.4 | : | 47.7 | 54.2 | 117.4 | 67.5 | 90.5 | 112.1 | 115.0 | 30.8 | 99.6 | 100.0 | : | 188.3 | 120.3 |
| 1984 | 106.8 | 122.9 | 135.2 | : | 46.8 | 55.9 | 116.6 | 67.2 | 94.2 | 112.6 | 110.4 | 30.4 | 98.4 | 100.0 | : | 213.5 | 132.2 |
| 1985 | 108.7 | 127.5 | 131.8 | : | 44.6 | 56.4 | 118.5 | 67.9 | 94.1 | 113.5 | 107.8 | 30.3 | 100.4 | 100.0 | : | 220.6 | 134.2 |
| 1986 | 109.0 | 132.6 | 134.7 | : | 39.9 | 56.6 | 119.2 | 68.7 | 97.9 | 115.0 | 109.4 | 30.5 | 92.5 | 100.0 | : | 170.9 | 143.7 |
| 1987 | 110.0 | 130.0 | 136.1 | : | 38.8 | 57.8 | 116.8 | 65.0 | 99.6 | 117.4 | 108.9 | 30.3 | 91.4 | 100.0 | : | 146.2 | 139.9 |
| 1988 | 105.3 | 123.1 | 131.2 | : | 39.7 | 60.9 | 112.7 | 65.2 | 99.5 | 114.3 | 101.8 | 31.6 | 101.4 | 100.0 | : | 141.9 | 149.7 |
| 1989 | 104.4 | 117.0 | 126.5 | : | 41.2 | 66.9 | 110.9 | 66.7 | 103.4 | 112.9 | 98.2 | 33.3 | 101.1 | 100.0 | : | 149.3 | 146.1 |
| 1990 | 106.4 | 115.6 | 127.2 | : | 41.5 | 69.8 | 111.5 | 65.9 | 105.1 | 115.6 | 98.6 | 35.6 | 94.9 | 100.0 | : | 128.4 | 120.8 |
| 1991 | 105.4 | 111.1 | 127.8 | 115.3 | 41.9 | 72.1 | 107.5 | 63.7 | 107.0 | 117.6 | 97.6 | 35.9 | 94.6 | 100.0 | 98.4 | 126.5 | 130.3 |
| 1992 | 107.4 | 110.6 | 130.2 | 119.9 | 42.3 | 72.6 | 108.6 | 64.6 | 105.4 | 118.1 | 99.2 | 44.2 | 90.1 | 100.0 | 99.0 | 121.4 | 131.0 |
| 1993 | 111.0 | 117.6 | 138.2 | 128.2 | 43.6 | 65.8 | 114.3 | 63.3 | 92.3 | 124.9 | 105.6 | 43.9 | 89.6 | 100.0 | 99.4 | 140.5 | 167.6 |
| 1994 | 113.2 | 122.0 | 135.7 | 126.8 | 43.7 | 62.9 | 114.3 | 66.4 | 92.3 | 128.8 | 105.4 | 42.8 | 93.2 | 100.0 | 99.5 | 146.6 | 181.8 |

EUR 12−: incl. WD; EUR 12+: incl. D.

**Table C6** Private consumption at current prices per head of population.

(PPS; EUR 12− =100)

| | B | DK | WD | D | GR | E | F | IRL | I | L | NL | P | UK | EUR 12− | EUR 12+ | USA | J |
|---|---|---|---|---|---|---|---|---|---|---|---|---|---|---|---|---|---|
| 1960 | 109.0 | 116.0 | 117.7 | : | 45.0 | 64.0 | 102.0 | 75.9 | 83.0 | 133.1 | 108.9 | 44.5 | 130.4 | 100.0 | : | 186.1 | 51.4 |
| 1961 | 107.5 | 118.0 | 116.8 | : | 45.7 | 67.6 | 102.7 | 75.4 | 84.3 | 133.4 | 108.6 | 44.9 | 127.3 | 100.0 | : | 180.1 | 53.3 |
| 1962 | 106.6 | 119.0 | 116.6 | : | 44.2 | 69.8 | 103.8 | 74.5 | 86.2 | 125.1 | 108.6 | 43.7 | 123.8 | 100.0 | : | 177.6 | 56.1 |
| 1963 | 106.6 | 112.9 | 113.9 | : | 45.1 | 73.2 | 103.7 | 73.7 | 88.4 | 122.8 | 108.8 | 43.9 | 123.1 | 100.0 | : | 174.4 | 58.8 |
| 1964 | 104.8 | 116.7 | 114.6 | : | 46.9 | 73.7 | 104.6 | 72.3 | 86.8 | 125.6 | 108.6 | 44.7 | 122.3 | 100.0 | : | 176.3 | 61.9 |
| 1965 | 104.4 | 114.6 | 117.1 | : | 48.9 | 75.7 | 104.3 | 70.3 | 85.7 | 125.6 | 109.3 | 46.3 | 119.3 | 100.0 | : | 177.0 | 63.8 |
| 1966 | 102.9 | 114.3 | 116.5 | : | 49.5 | 76.9 | 105.2 | 68.4 | 88.8 | 121.3 | 107.1 | 46.7 | 116.2 | 100.0 | : | 177.3 | 67.0 |
| 1967 | 101.6 | 114.4 | 114.4 | : | 50.1 | 76.9 | 106.2 | 68.2 | 92.2 | 120.4 | 107.0 | 47.2 | 114.4 | 100.0 | : | 174.8 | 70.0 |
| 1968 | 102.7 | 111.6 | 114.2 | : | 50.9 | 77.6 | 106.1 | 71.5 | 92.5 | 118.4 | 106.9 | 51.8 | 113.2 | 100.0 | : | 174.0 | 72.3 |
| 1969 | 102.5 | 110.9 | 115.1 | : | 51.6 | 78.2 | 107.9 | 71.3 | 93.1 | 118.6 | 109.2 | 52.0 | 109.0 | 100.0 | : | 170.3 | 75.6 |
| 1970 | 101.8 | 108.9 | 114.8 | : | 54.0 | 78.2 | 107.7 | 69.6 | 95.1 | 116.6 | 110.7 | 52.2 | 107.2 | 100.0 | : | 165.7 | 78.3 |
| 1971 | 103.2 | 105.1 | 114.6 | : | 55.4 | 79.0 | 108.6 | 68.8 | 94.0 | 117.1 | 109.7 | 56.4 | 106.4 | 100.0 | : | 163.2 | 80.6 |
| 1972 | 104.2 | 101.4 | 115.7 | : | 55.4 | 80.5 | 108.2 | 66.2 | 92.9 | 116.3 | 107.2 | 55.3 | 106.9 | 100.0 | : | 162.4 | 83.7 |
| 1973 | 105.4 | 101.5 | 113.7 | : | 54.4 | 81.4 | 106.5 | 64.3 | 94.7 | 113.9 | 104.8 | 59.1 | 108.5 | 100.0 | : | 159.0 | 83.9 |
| 1974 | 105.2 | 97.2 | 112.4 | : | 54.3 | 83.5 | 107.0 | 68.3 | 96.3 | 113.7 | 105.4 | 64.5 | 106.0 | 100.0 | : | 153.9 | 81.1 |
| 1975 | 105.1 | 97.7 | 116.7 | : | 56.6 | 82.7 | 107.8 | 66.1 | 95.3 | 116.3 | 107.1 | 63.0 | 102.0 | 100.0 | : | 152.1 | 86.2 |
| 1976 | 106.5 | 102.2 | 118.5 | : | 55.8 | 83.3 | 107.5 | 64.1 | 95.7 | 114.3 | 108.1 | 61.9 | 99.4 | 100.0 | : | 152.7 | 86.3 |
| 1977 | 106.3 | 101.9 | 120.7 | : | 55.8 | 82.2 | 107.9 | 66.6 | 95.5 | 112.4 | 109.5 | 60.8 | 97.7 | 100.0 | : | 154.3 | 87.9 |
| 1978 | 106.4 | 99.8 | 121.2 | : | 57.0 | 79.4 | 108.2 | 68.7 | 95.6 | 112.5 | 110.4 | 57.3 | 99.1 | 100.0 | : | 154.9 | 89.6 |
| 1979 | 107.1 | 100.2 | 121.4 | : | 54.8 | 76.7 | 107.9 | 69.0 | 98.0 | 110.6 | 109.5 | 57.4 | 99.3 | 100.0 | : | 151.6 | 92.3 |
| 1980 | 109.7 | 96.7 | 121.5 | : | 55.3 | 76.6 | 108.5 | 69.6 | 102.3 | 111.0 | 107.9 | 58.1 | 94.6 | 100.0 | : | 148.4 | 93.3 |
| 1981 | 111.3 | 95.2 | 121.8 | : | 56.6 | 76.2 | 110.5 | 70.4 | 101.8 | 112.4 | 104.1 | 59.9 | 93.4 | 100.0 | : | 146.3 | 93.8 |
| 1982 | 112.7 | 95.6 | 120.0 | : | 56.0 | 75.8 | 112.7 | 64.1 | 101.8 | 113.0 | 101.0 | 60.6 | 94.7 | 100.0 | : | 144.8 | 97.5 |
| 1983 | 111.2 | 96.2 | 120.5 | : | 54.7 | 75.2 | 111.7 | 62.6 | 100.7 | 111.8 | 101.0 | 59.4 | 97.4 | 100.0 | : | 148.8 | 99.6 |
| 1984 | 111.2 | 98.5 | 121.9 | : | 53.3 | 73.3 | 110.7 | 62.9 | 101.5 | 111.4 | 100.0 | 58.3 | 98.0 | 100.0 | : | 152.0 | 100.0 |
| 1985 | 110.6 | 101.0 | 121.4 | : | 54.2 | 72.8 | 110.2 | 64.0 | 102.4 | 113.9 | 100.0 | 56.3 | 98.6 | 100.0 | : | 153.9 | 101.1 |
| 1986 | 107.3 | 102.6 | 118.6 | : | 55.3 | 72.3 | 108.8 | 62.6 | 102.9 | 114.2 | 99.9 | 54.9 | 100.5 | 100.0 | : | 154.7 | 100.3 |
| 1987 | 106.6 | 97.7 | 117.2 | : | 54.8 | 73.8 | 108.1 | 62.7 | 103.4 | 113.8 | 99.6 | 55.5 | 104.7 | 100.0 | : | 154.3 | 100.9 |
| 1988 | 105.3 | 94.0 | 116.1 | : | 54.2 | 74.2 | 107.2 | 63.6 | 103.7 | 113.4 | 95.9 | 56.4 | 107.5 | 100.0 | : | 153.7 | 101.9 |
| 1989 | 104.8 | 91.2 | 114.6 | : | 56.0 | 75.8 | 107.4 | 65.4 | 104.8 | 113.3 | 96.0 | 56.3 | 106.5 | 100.0 | : | 151.7 | 102.9 |
| 1990 | 105.9 | 89.5 | 115.7 | : | 55.0 | 76.4 | 107.9 | 67.9 | 104.2 | 114.4 | 97.5 | 57.5 | 104.1 | 100.0 | : | 157.4 | 105.1 |
| 1991 | 106.7 | 89.9 | 117.6 | 106.1 | 55.0 | 78.8 | 108.2 | 68.9 | 105.4 | 118.2 | 97.1 | 60.3 | 98.1 | 100.0 | 98.1 | 150.2 | 108.3 |
| 1992 | 108.8 | 86.9 | 117.2 | 108.1 | 56.6 | 77.2 | 106.7 | 70.9 | 106.1 | 116.3 | 97.3 | 61.5 | 99.3 | 100.0 | 98.6 | 153.6 | 110.4 |
| 1993 | 107.8 | 89.5 | 116.1 | 107.1 | 56.3 | 76.2 | 107.5 | 71.6 | 103.9 | 120.7 | 98.6 | 61.7 | 102.2 | 100.0 | 98.8 | 158.2 | 111.8 |
| 1994 | 107.8 | 93.1 | 113.4 | 106.0 | 56.0 | 76.3 | 107.8 | 73.6 | 104.4 | 122.8 | 98.5 | 61.7 | 103.9 | 100.0 | 98.9 | 161.3 | 113.3 |

EUR 12−: incl. WD; EUR+: incl. D.

**Table C7**   Public consumption at 1985 prices.

(Annual percentage change)

| | B | DK | WD | D | GR | E | F | IRL | I | L | NL | P | UK | EUR 12− | EUR 12+ | USA | J |
|---|---|---|---|---|---|---|---|---|---|---|---|---|---|---|---|---|---|
| 1961 | 1.9 | 5.3 | 6.6 | : | 4.4 | 5.6 | 4.8 | 2.1 | 4.4 | 1.3 | 2.8 | 26.7 | 3.5 | 4.8 | : | 5.8 | 5.9 |
| 1962 | 8.6 | 9.9 | 10.5 | : | 6.7 | 6.7 | 4.7 | 3.1 | 3.9 | 2.4 | 3.3 | 8.5 | 3.1 | 5.6 | : | 4.0 | 8.7 |
| 1963 | 11.6 | 2.9 | 6.4 | : | 4.2 | 9.7 | 3.4 | 4.0 | 4.3 | 5.8 | 4.7 | 3.0 | 1.8 | 4.3 | : | 1.4 | 8.3 |
| 1964 | 4.2 | 7.3 | 0.8 | : | 9.3 | 1.3 | 4.2 | 3.0 | 4.2 | −0.8 | 1.7 | 6.8 | 1.6 | 2.6 | : | 2.3 | 3.3 |
| 1965 | 5.5 | 3.4 | 4.0 | : | 9.0 | 3.7 | 3.2 | 3.7 | 4.0 | 2.5 | 1.5 | 7.4 | 2.6 | 3.5 | : | 2.9 | 3.8 |
| 1966 | 4.7 | 5.8 | 1.1 | : | 6.3 | 1.7 | 2.7 | 1.0 | 4.0 | 5.8 | 1.7 | 6.6 | 2.7 | 2.7 | : | 10.7 | 5.7 |
| 1967 | 5.7 | 7.6 | 3.0 | : | 8.5 | 2.3 | 4.3 | 4.5 | 4.4 | 4.2 | 2.4 | 13.6 | 5.7 | 4.5 | : | 7.5 | 4.0 |
| 1968 | 3.5 | 4.7 | −1.3 | : | 1.3 | 1.8 | 5.6 | 5.8 | 5.2 | 5.6 | 2.2 | 8.4 | 0.4 | 2.3 | : | 2.0 | 6.4 |
| 1969 | 6.3 | 6.8 | 4.5 | : | 7.7 | 4.2 | 4.1 | 6.9 | 2.8 | 3.3 | 4.5 | 3.2 | −1.8 | 2.6 | : | 0.0 | 5.9 |
| 1970 | 3.1 | 6.9 | 4.2 | : | 5.9 | 5.3 | 4.2 | 11.3 | 2.6 | 4.1 | 6.0 | 12.7 | 1.7 | 3.7 | : | −1.0 | 7.1 |
| 1961-70 | 5.5 | 6.0 | 3.9 | : | 6.3 | 4.2 | 4.1 | 4.5 | 4.0 | 3.4 | 3.1 | 9.5 | 2.1 | 3.6 | : | 3.5 | 5.9 |
| 1971 | 5.5 | 5.5 | 3.8 | : | 4.9 | 4.3 | 4.0 | 8.6 | 5.2 | 3.0 | 4.4 | 6.4 | 3.0 | 4.1 | : | −3.4 | 5.3 |
| 1972 | 5.9 | 5.7 | 2.3 | : | 5.7 | 5.2 | 3.5 | 7.5 | 5.1 | 4.2 | 0.8 | 8.6 | 4.4 | 3.9 | : | 1.3 | 5.4 |
| 1973 | 5.3 | 4.0 | 3.7 | : | 6.8 | 6.4 | 3.4 | 6.7 | 2.7 | 3.4 | 0.8 | 7.8 | 4.4 | 3.8 | : | −0.9 | 5.3 |
| 1974 | 3.4 | 3.5 | 2.4 | : | 12.1 | 9.3 | 1.2 | 7.6 | 2.4 | 3.8 | 2.2 | 17.3 | 1.8 | 2.8 | : | 2.8 | 3.2 |
| 1975 | 4.5 | 2.0 | 1.6 | : | 11.9 | 5.2 | 4.3 | 8.7 | 2.4 | 3.3 | 4.1 | 6.6 | 5.4 | 3.9 | : | 1.0 | 7.8 |
| 1976 | 3.7 | 4.5 | −0.2 | : | 5.1 | 6.9 | 4.1 | 2.6 | 2.1 | 2.8 | 4.1 | 7.0 | 1.3 | 2.4 | : | 1.1 | 4.5 |
| 1977 | 2.3 | 2.4 | 1.7 | : | 6.5 | 3.9 | 2.4 | 2.1 | 3.0 | 2.9 | 3.4 | 12.2 | −1.7 | 1.7 | : | 1.2 | 4.1 |
| 1978 | 6.0 | 6.2 | 3.7 | : | 3.5 | 5.4 | 5.1 | 7.9 | 3.5 | 1.8 | 3.9 | 4.4 | 2.2 | 3.9 | : | 1.3 | 5.1 |
| 1979 | 2.5 | 5.9 | 3.6 | : | 5.8 | 4.2 | 3.0 | 4.6 | 3.0 | 2.2 | 2.8 | 6.4 | 1.9 | 3.1 | : | 2.5 | 4.3 |
| 1980 | 1.5 | 4.3 | 2.2 | : | 0.2 | 4.2 | 2.5 | 7.1 | 2.1 | 3.1 | 0.6 | 8.0 | 1.7 | 2.3 | : | 2.6 | 3.3 |
| 1971-80 | 4.1 | 4.4 | 2.5 | : | 6.2 | 5.5 | 3.4 | 6.3 | 3.1 | 3.0 | 2.7 | 8.4 | 2.4 | 3.2 | : | 0.9 | 4.8 |
| 1981 | 0.3 | 2.6 | 1.2 | : | 6.8 | 1.9 | 3.1 | 0.3 | 2.3 | 1.4 | 2.5 | 5.5 | 0.3 | 1.8 | : | 1.7 | 4.8 |
| 1982 | −1.4 | 3.1 | −0.7 | : | 2.3 | 4.9 | 3.7 | 3.2 | 2.6 | 1.5 | 0.4 | 3.7 | 0.9 | 1.8 | : | 2.4 | 2.0 |
| 1983 | 0.1 | 0.0 | 0.1 | : | 2.7 | 3.9 | 2.1 | −0.4 | 3.5 | 1.9 | 1.0 | 3.8 | 2.1 | 1.9 | : | 2.2 | 3.0 |
| 1984 | 0.2 | −0.4 | 1.1 | : | 3.0 | 2.9 | 1.1 | −0.7 | 2.2 | 2.2 | −0.8 | 0.2 | 0.8 | 1.2 | : | 3.6 | 2.7 |
| 1985 | 2.4 | 2.5 | 1.5 | : | 3.2 | 4.6 | 2.3 | 1.8 | 3.4 | 2.0 | 1.3 | 6.4 | −0.1 | 2.0 | : | 4.9 | 1.7 |
| 1986 | 1.7 | 0.5 | 2.3 | : | −0.8 | 5.4 | 1.7 | 2.6 | 2.6 | 3.1 | 3.6 | 7.2 | 1.6 | 2.3 | : | 4.9 | 4.5 |
| 1987 | 0.3 | 2.5 | 1.2 | : | 0.9 | 8.6 | 2.8 | −4.8 | 3.5 | 2.7 | 2.6 | 4.9 | 1.0 | 2.5 | : | 3.9 | 0.4 |
| 1988 | −1.0 | 0.9 | 0.1 | : | 5.7 | 4.0 | 3.4 | −5.0 | 2.8 | 3.8 | 1.4 | 5.3 | 0.7 | 1.9 | : | 1.4 | 2.1 |
| 1989 | 0.0 | −0.6 | 0.4 | : | 2.8 | 8.3 | 0.5 | −1.0 | 0.8 | 1.9 | 1.5 | 2.8 | 1.4 | 1.4 | : | −0.2 | 2.0 |
| 1990 | 1.0 | −0.4 | 1.0 | : | 1.3 | 5.6 | 2.0 | 5.7 | 1.2 | 3.2 | 1.6 | 1.5 | 2.5 | 2.0 | : | 1.5 | 1.9 |
| 1981-90 | 0.4 | 1.1 | 0.8 | : | 2.8 | 5.0 | 2.3 | 0.1 | 2.5 | 2.4 | 1.5 | 4.1 | 1.1 | 1.9 | : | 2.6 | 2.5 |
| 1991 | 1.8 | 0.0 | −2.7 | : | 3.6 | 5.4 | 2.5 | 2.4 | 1.5 | 3.8 | 1.3 | 3.0 | 2.5 | 1.6 | : | 2.0 | 1.7 |
| 1992 | 1.3 | 0.7 | 2.6 | 2.3 | 0.0 | 3.8 | 2.7 | 2.2 | 0.9 | 3.5 | 1.3 | 1.4 | 0.2 | 1.7 | 1.6 | −0.1 | 2.4 |
| 1993 | 1.5 | 2.9 | −2.5 | 0.0 | 1.0 | 1.6 | 1.6 | 2.4 | 0.8 | 2.2 | 0.7 | 0.5 | −0.5 | 0.3 | 0.7 | −1.5 | 3.0 |
| 1994 | 0.7 | 1.1 | −0.5 | −0.5 | 0.5 | 0.6 | 1.4 | 3.4 | 0.5 | 0.9 | 0.2 | 1.0 | 0.7 | 0.6 | 0.6 | −0.6 | 2.5 |

EUR: PPS weighted. EUR 12−: incl. WD; EUR 12+: incl. D.

**Table C8**   Public consumption at current prices.

(Percentage of gross domestic product at market prices)

| | B | DK | WD | D | GR | E | F | IRL | I | L | NL | P | UK | EUR 12− | EUR 12+ | USA | J |
|---|---|---|---|---|---|---|---|---|---|---|---|---|---|---|---|---|---|
| 1960 | 12.4 | 13.3 | 10.7 | : | 11.7 | 8.3 | 14.2 | 11.9 | 12.0 | 9.8 | 12.3 | 10.5 | 16.8 | 13.2 | : | 16.8 | 8.0 |
| 1961 | 11.9 | 14.4 | 11.1 | : | 11.3 | 8.2 | 14.4 | 11.9 | 11.9 | 9.9 | 12.8 | 12.5 | 17.1 | 13.4 | : | 17.7 | 7.7 |
| 1962 | 12.3 | 15.2 | 11.9 | : | 11.6 | 8.1 | 14.5 | 12.0 | 12.3 | 10.9 | 13.3 | 12.9 | 17.4 | 13.7 | : | 17.8 | 8.0 |
| 1963 | 13.0 | 15.4 | 12.6 | : | 11.3 | 8.5 | 14.7 | 12.1 | 13.1 | 12.3 | 14.0 | 12.3 | 17.3 | 14.1 | : | 17.5 | 8.2 |
| 1964 | 12.5 | 15.6 | 11.9 | : | 11.7 | 8.2 | 14.5 | 12.8 | 13.5 | 10.8 | 14.2 | 12.3 | 16.8 | 13.8 | : | 17.2 | 8.0 |
| 1965 | 12.8 | 16.3 | 12.1 | : | 11.7 | 8.4 | 14.4 | 13.0 | 14.2 | 10.9 | 14.1 | 12.0 | 17.1 | 14.0 | : | 16.7 | 8.2 |
| 1966 | 13.1 | 17.1 | 12.1 | : | 11.8 | 8.7 | 14.2 | 13.0 | 14.0 | 11.4 | 14.5 | 12.1 | 17.5 | 14.0 | : | 17.7 | 8.0 |
| 1967 | 13.5 | 17.8 | 12.6 | : | 13.0 | 9.5 | 14.2 | 12.8 | 13.6 | 12.1 | 14.8 | 13.1 | 18.4 | 14.4 | : | 18.9 | 7.6 |
| 1968 | 13.6 | 18.6 | 11.8 | : | 12.9 | 9.2 | 14.8 | 12.8 | 13.6 | 12.1 | 14.5 | 13.1 | 18.0 | 14.2 | : | 18.7 | 7.4 |
| 1969 | 13.6 | 18.9 | 11.9 | : | 12.7 | 9.3 | 14.6 | 13.0 | 13.4 | 11.0 | 14.6 | 12.9 | 17.5 | 14.0 | : | 18.4 | 7.3 |
| 1970 | 13.4 | 20.0 | 12.0 | : | 12.6 | 9.6 | 14.7 | 14.0 | 13.0 | 10.5 | 15.0 | 13.8 | 17.9 | 14.1 | : | 18.7 | 7.4 |
| 1961-70 | 13.0 | 16.9 | 12.0 | : | 12.1 | 8.8 | 14.5 | 12.7 | 13.3 | 11.2 | 14.2 | 12.7 | 17.5 | 14.0 | : | 17.9 | 7.8 |
| 1971 | 14.1 | 21.3 | 12.7 | : | 12.5 | 9.7 | 14.9 | 14.6 | 14.6 | 11.7 | 15.6 | 13.5 | 18.3 | 14.7 | : | 18.1 | 8.0 |
| 1972 | 14.5 | 21.3 | 12.7 | : | 12.2 | 9.6 | 14.9 | 14.7 | 15.1 | 11.8 | 15.4 | 13.4 | 18.7 | 14.8 | : | 18.0 | 8.2 |
| 1973 | 14.5 | 21.3 | 13.0 | : | 11.5 | 9.6 | 14.8 | 15.0 | 14.4 | 11.3 | 15.1 | 12.8 | 18.6 | 14.6 | : | 17.4 | 8.3 |
| 1974 | 14.7 | 23.4 | 13.9 | : | 13.8 | 10.0 | 15.4 | 16.5 | 13.8 | 11.5 | 15.8 | 14.1 | 20.5 | 15.3 | : | 18.0 | 9.1 |
| 1975 | 16.4 | 24.6 | 14.4 | : | 15.2 | 10.6 | 16.6 | 17.8 | 14.1 | 14.9 | 16.9 | 15.0 | 22.4 | 16.3 | : | 18.6 | 10.0 |
| 1976 | 16.4 | 24.1 | 13.7 | : | 15.1 | 11.4 | 16.9 | 17.3 | 13.4 | 14.7 | 16.8 | 13.7 | 22.2 | 16.0 | : | 18.0 | 9.9 |
| 1977 | 16.8 | 23.9 | 13.7 | : | 16.0 | 11.6 | 17.2 | 16.3 | 13.8 | 15.9 | 16.9 | 14.0 | 20.7 | 15.9 | : | 17.5 | 9.8 |
| 1978 | 17.4 | 24.5 | 13.7 | : | 15.9 | 12.1 | 17.6 | 16.4 | 14.1 | 15.6 | 17.2 | 13.9 | 20.3 | 16.1 | : | 17.0 | 9.7 |
| 1979 | 17.6 | 25.0 | 13.7 | : | 16.3 | 12.6 | 17.6 | 17.3 | 14.5 | 16.0 | 17.6 | 13.9 | 20.0 | 16.2 | : | 16.9 | 9.7 |
| 1980 | 17.8 | 26.7 | 14.0 | : | 16.4 | 13.3 | 18.1 | 19.0 | 14.7 | 16.7 | 17.4 | 14.5 | 21.6 | 16.9 | : | 17.6 | 9.8 |
| 1971-80 | 16.0 | 23.6 | 13.6 | : | 14.5 | 11.1 | 16.4 | 16.5 | 14.3 | 14.0 | 16.5 | 13.9 | 20.3 | 15.7 | : | 17.7 | 9.2 |
| 1981 | 18.6 | 27.8 | 14.3 | : | 18.0 | 13.9 | 18.8 | 19.1 | 16.0 | 17.4 | 17.3 | 15.0 | 22.2 | 17.6 | : | 17.4 | 9.9 |
| 1982 | 18.0 | 28.2 | 14.2 | : | 18.3 | 14.1 | 19.3 | 18.9 | 16.0 | 16.4 | 17.2 | 14.9 | 22.2 | 17.7 | : | 18.4 | 9.9 |
| 1983 | 17.5 | 27.4 | 13.9 | : | 18.8 | 14.6 | 19.5 | 18.5 | 16.4 | 15.8 | 17.0 | 15.1 | 22.2 | 17.7 | : | 18.3 | 9.9 |
| 1984 | 17.0 | 25.9 | 13.6 | : | 19.5 | 14.4 | 19.6 | 17.9 | 16.3 | 15.4 | 16.1 | 15.0 | 21.9 | 17.4 | : | 17.8 | 9.8 |
| 1985 | 17.1 | 25.3 | 13.6 | : | 20.4 | 14.7 | 19.4 | 17.8 | 16.4 | 15.7 | 15.5 | 15.5 | 21.1 | 17.3 | : | 18.1 | 9.6 |
| 1986 | 16.8 | 23.9 | 13.4 | : | 19.4 | 14.7 | 18.9 | 18.0 | 16.2 | 15.7 | 15.5 | 15.4 | 21.1 | 17.0 | : | 18.5 | 9.7 |
| 1987 | 16.2 | 25.2 | 13.4 | : | 19.5 | 15.1 | 18.7 | 17.0 | 16.7 | 16.8 | 15.8 | 15.2 | 20.6 | 17.0 | : | 18.5 | 9.5 |
| 1988 | 15.2 | 25.7 | 13.0 | : | 20.2 | 14.8 | 18.5 | 15.6 | 16.9 | 16.1 | 15.3 | 16.0 | 19.9 | 16.7 | : | 18.1 | 9.2 |
| 1989 | 14.6 | 25.6 | 12.6 | : | 20.6 | 15.2 | 18.0 | 14.6 | 16.6 | 15.4 | 14.8 | 16.1 | 19.8 | 16.4 | : | 17.6 | 9.2 |
| 1990 | 14.5 | 25.3 | 12.1 | : | 21.1 | 15.5 | 17.9 | 15.1 | 17.4 | 16.4 | 14.5 | 16.7 | 20.6 | 16.5 | : | 17.9 | 9.1 |
| 1981-90 | 16.5 | 26.0 | 13.4 | : | 19.6 | 14.7 | 18.9 | 17.3 | 16.5 | 16.1 | 15.9 | 15.5 | 21.2 | 17.1 | : | 18.0 | 9.6 |
| 1991 | 14.8 | 25.4 | 11.4 | 12.9 | 19.9 | 16.1 | 18.3 | 15.9 | 17.5 | 17.1 | 14.4 | 17.8 | 21.7 | 16.6 | 16.9 | 18.2 | 9.2 |
| 1992 | 14.8 | 25.4 | 11.5 | 13.0 | 19.7 | 16.8 | 18.6 | 16.1 | 17.6 | 17.1 | 14.5 | 18.3 | 22.3 | 16.8 | 17.1 | 17.8 | 9.4 |
| 1993 | 15.4 | 25.9 | 11.3 | 13.1 | 20.0 | 17.2 | 19.2 | 16.3 | 17.7 | 17.6 | 14.5 | 18.3 | 21.8 | 16.8 | 17.2 | 17.1 | 9.7 |
| 1994 | 15.5 | 25.3 | 11.1 | 12.8 | 20.0 | 16.8 | 19.3 | 16.6 | 17.5 | 17.6 | 14.4 | 18.3 | 21.4 | 16.4 | 17.0 | 16.6 | 10.0 |

EUR 12−: incl. WD; EUR 12+: incl. D.

**Table C9** Final consumption of households per inhabitant, by purpose – 1991. (ECU)

| Country | Food beverages, tobacco | Clothing and footwear | Gross rent, fuel and power | Furniture, furnishings and household equipment and operation | Medical care and health expenses |
|---|---|---|---|---|---|
| EUR 12 | 1963 | 719 | 1611 | 720 | 722 |
| 1. Belgique/België | 1842 | 790 | 1662 | 1084 | 1131 |
| 2. Danmark | 2233 | 574 | 2926 | 669 | 239 |
| 3. Deutschland | 1535 | 693 | 1730 | 800 | 1367 |
| 4. Ελλάδα | 1502 | 354 | 506 | 324 | 143 |
| 5. España | 1493 | 626 | 895 | 466 | 295 |
| 6. France | 1977 | 651 | 2083 | 788 | 1010 |
| 7. Ireland | 1985 | 394 | 563 | 436 | 217 |
| 8. Italia | 2031 | 999 | 1550 | 953 | 670 |
| 9. Luxembourg | 2136 | 674 | 2279 | 1242 | 844 |
| 10. Nederland | 1409 | 639 | 1685 | 660 | 1168 |
| 11. Portugal[1] | 803 | 222 | 107 | 186 | 97 |
| 12. United Kingdom | 1914 | 520 | 1630 | 564 | 138 |
| 13. Österreich | 1728 | 807 | 1570 | 667 | 465 |
| 14. Suomi/Finland | 1858 | 420 | 1616 | 542 | 472 |
| 15. Island | 2542 | 808 | 1527 | 857 | 477 |
| 16. Norge | 2063 | 554 | 1575 | 543 | 425 |
| 17. Sverige | 1748 | 558 | 2431 | 508 | 225 |
| EEA | 1953 | 711 | 1629 | 709 | 695 |
| 18. Schweiz/Suisse | 3406 | 493 | 2293 | 562 | 4204 |
| 19. Türkiye | | | | | |
| 20. USA[2] | 1618 | 815 | 2382 | 690 | 1894 |
| 21. Canada | 1734 | 575 | 2564 | 936 | 458 |
| 22. Nippon (Japan) | 2066 | 595 | 1853 | 651 | 1043 |

1. 1989.  2. 1986.

**Table C10** Final consumption of households per inhabitant by purpose – 1991 (ECU)

| Country | Transport and communications | Recreation, entertainment, education and cultural services | Miscellaneous goods and services | Total | Total (PPS) |
|---|---|---|---|---|---|
| EUR 12 | 1319 | 752 | 1228 | 9035 | : |
| 1. Belgique/België | 1335 | 652 | 1549 | 9936 | : |
| 2. Danmark | 1685 | 1079 | 1140 | 10 546 | : |
| 3. Deutschland | 1574 | 855 | 940 | 940 | 9494: |
| 4. Ελλάδα | 606 | 230 | 392 | 4058 | : |
| 5. España | 1084 | 469 | 1806 | 7134 | : |
| 6. France | 1654 | 784 | 1469 | 10 415 | : |
| 7. Ireland | 733 | 605 | 520 | 5453 | : |
| 8. Italia | 1218 | 916 | 1726 | 10 063 | : |
| 9. Luxembourg | 2197 | 480 | 1650 | 11 503 | : |
| 10. Nederland | 1161 | 965 | 1473 | 9159 | : |
| 11. Portugal | 332 | 124 | 290 | 2162 | : |
| 12. United Kingdom | 1501 | 864 | 1619 | 8751 | : |
| 13. Österreich | 1482 | 640 | 1412 | 8771 | 8333 |
| 14. Suomi/Finland | 1349 | 889 | 1067 | 8080 | 7297 |
| 15. Island | 1586 | 1462 | 1888 | 9851 | 7910 |
| 16. Norge | 1008 | 740 | 977 | 7875 | 6153 |
| 17. Sverige | 1440 | 766 | 641 | 8326 | 5847 |
| EEA | 1322 | 752 | 1213 | 8989 | : |
| 18. Schweiz/Suisse | 1341 | 1481 | 1272 | 11 463 | 8501 |
| 19. Türkiye | | | | 1832 | : |
| 20. USA[1] | 1790 | 1242 | 1993 | 12 364 | : |
| 21. Canada | 1564 | 1181 | 1639 | 10 641 | : |
| 22. Nippon (Japan) | 1092 | 1030 | 1610 | 9941 | : |

1. 1989.  2. 1986.

**Table D1**   Gross fixed capital formation at current prices; total economy.

(Percentage of gross domestic product at market prices)

| | B | DK | WD | D | GR | E | F | IRL | I | L | NL | P | UK | EUR 12- | EUR 12+ | USA | J |
|---|---|---|---|---|---|---|---|---|---|---|---|---|---|---|---|---|---|
| 1960 | 19.3 | 21.6 | 24.3 | : | 19.0 | 20.4 | 20.9 | 14.1 | 26.0 | 20.9 | 24.8 | 23.2 | 16.4 | 21.3 | : | 18.0 | 29.0 |
| 1961 | 20.7 | 23.2 | 25.2 | : | 18.2 | 21.4 | 22.0 | 15.9 | 26.8 | 24.2 | 25.5 | 23.2 | 17.3 | 22.4 | : | 17.5 | 31.9 |
| 1962 | 21.3 | 23.1 | 25.7 | : | 20.1 | 21.9 | 22.2 | 17.4 | 27.2 | 25.9 | 25.1 | 22.4 | 17.0 | 22.7 | : | 17.6 | 32.2 |
| 1963 | 20.7 | 22.0 | 25.6 | : | 19.2 | 22.1 | 23.0 | 19.1 | 27.7 | 30.1 | 24.4 | 23.7 | 16.8 | 22.8 | : | 18.1 | 31.6 |
| 1964 | 22.4 | 24.5 | 26.6 | : | 21.0 | 23.6 | 23.8 | 20.0 | 25.6 | 33.7 | 26.2 | 22.8 | 18.3 | 23.6 | : | 18.5 | 31.7 |
| 1965 | 22.4 | 24.1 | 26.1 | : | 21.6 | 24.8 | 24.2 | 20.9 | 22.2 | 28.0 | 25.8 | 22.8 | 18.4 | 23.1 | : | 19.0 | 29.8 |
| 1966 | 22.9 | 24.1 | 25.4 | : | 21.7 | 25.1 | 24.6 | 19.3 | 21.6 | 26.6 | 26.9 | 25.1 | 18.4 | 23.1 | : | 18.8 | 30.3 |
| 1967 | 22.9 | 24.2 | 23.1 | : | 20.3 | 25.4 | 24.8 | 19.6 | 22.5 | 23.9 | 27.0 | 26.6 | 19.1 | 22.8 | : | 18.1 | 31.9 |
| 1968 | 21.5 | 23.4 | 22.4 | : | 23.2 | 26.0 | 24.3 | 20.4 | 23.4 | 22.1 | 27.6 | 22.2 | 19.5 | 22.9 | : | 18.4 | 33.2 |
| 1969 | 21.3 | 24.6 | 23.3 | : | 24.6 | 26.5 | 24.4 | 22.7 | 24.2 | 22.2 | 25.2 | 22.6 | 18.8 | 23.1 | : | 18.6 | 34.5 |
| 1970 | 22.7 | 24.7 | 25.5 | : | 23.6 | 26.4 | 24.3 | 22.2 | 24.6 | 23.1 | 26.5 | 23.2 | 18.9 | 23.8 | : | 18.0 | 35.5 |
| 1961-70 | 21.9 | 23.8 | 24.9 | : | 21.4 | 24.3 | 23.8 | 19.7 | 24.6 | 26.0 | 26.0 | 23.4 | 18.3 | 23.0 | : | 18.3 | 32.2 |
| 1971 | 22.1 | 24.2 | 26.2 | : | 25.2 | 24.2 | 24.7 | 23.1 | 23.9 | 28.4 | 26.0 | 24.7 | 18.9 | 23.9 | : | 18.5 | 34.2 |
| 1972 | 21.3 | 24.6 | 25.4 | : | 27.8 | 25.3 | 24.7 | 23.1 | 23.1 | 27.8 | 24.2 | 27.1 | 18.5 | 23.6 | : | 19.2 | 34.1 |
| 1973 | 21.4 | 24.8 | 23.9 | : | 28.0 | 26.8 | 25.2 | 24.6 | 24.9 | 27.3 | 23.7 | 26.8 | 19.9 | 23.9 | : | 19.5 | 36.4 |
| 1974 | 22.7 | 24.0 | 21.6 | : | 22.2 | 28.3 | 25.8 | 24.0 | 25.9 | 24.6 | 22.5 | 26.0 | 20.9 | 23.7 | : | 18.9 | 34.8 |
| 1975 | 22.5 | 21.1 | 20.4 | : | 20.8 | 26.8 | 24.1 | 22.2 | 24.9 | 27.7 | 21.6 | 25.9 | 19.9 | 22.5 | : | 17.6 | 32.5 |
| 1976 | 22.1 | 23.0 | 20.1 | : | 21.2 | 25.3 | 23.9 | 24.4 | 23.9 | 24.9 | 19.9 | 25.1 | 19.6 | 22.0 | : | 17.9 | 31.2 |
| 1977 | 21.6 | 22.1 | 20.3 | : | 23.0 | 24.3 | 22.9 | 24.2 | 23.5 | 25.1 | 21.6 | 26.5 | 18.6 | 21.6 | : | 19.3 | 30.2 |
| 1978 | 21.7 | 21.7 | 20.6 | : | 23.9 | 23.0 | 22.4 | 27.0 | 22.7 | 24.1 | 21.9 | 27.9 | 18.5 | 21.4 | : | 20.7 | 30.4 |
| 1979 | 20.7 | 20.9 | 21.7 | : | 25.8 | 21.9 | 22.4 | 29.7 | 22.8 | 24.4 | 21.6 | 26.6 | 18.7 | 21.6 | : | 21.3 | 31.7 |
| 1980 | 21.1 | 18.8 | 22.6 | : | 24.2 | 22.5 | 23.0 | 27.9 | 24.3 | 27.1 | 21.6 | 28.6 | 18.0 | 22.2 | : | 20.2 | 31.6 |
| 1971-80 | 21.7 | 22.5 | 22.3 | : | 24.2 | 24.8 | 23.9 | 25.0 | 24.0* | 26.1 | 22.4 | 26.5 | 19.1 | 22.6 | : | 19.3 | 32.7 |
| 1981 | 18.0 | 15.6 | 21.6 | : | 22.3 | 22.1 | 22.1 | 28.9 | 23.9 | 25.4 | 19.6 | 30.8 | 16.2 | 20.9 | : | 19.9 | 30.6 |
| 1982 | 17.3 | 16.1 | 20.4 | : | 19.9 | 21.6 | 21.4 | 25.9 | 22.3 | 25.0 | 18.7 | 31.1 | 16.1 | 20.0 | : | 18.7 | 29.5 |
| 1983 | 16.2 | 16.0 | 20.4 | : | 20.3 | 20.9 | 20.2 | 22.6 | 21.3 | 21.2 | 18.7 | 29.2 | 16.0 | 19.5 | : | 18.5 | 28.0 |
| 1984 | 16.0 | 17.2 | 20.0 | : | 18.5 | 19.0 | 19.3 | 20.9 | 21.0 | 20.0 | 19.0 | 23.6 | 17.0 | 19.2 | : | 19.3 | 27.7 |
| 1985 | 15.6 | 18.7 | 19.5 | : | 19.1 | 19.2 | 19.3 | 18.6 | 20.7 | 17.7 | 19.7 | 21.8 | 17.0 | 19.1 | : | 19.5 | 27.5 |
| 1986 | 15.7 | 20.8 | 19.4 | : | 18.5 | 19.5 | 19.3 | 17.5 | 19.7 | 22.1 | 20.4 | 22.1 | 17.0 | 19.0 | : | 19.1 | 27.3 |
| 1987 | 16.0 | 19.7 | 19.4 | : | 17.1 | 20.8 | 19.8 | 16.4 | 19.7 | 25.5 | 20.8 | 24.2 | 17.8 | 19.3 | : | 18.5 | 28.5 |
| 1988 | 17.7 | 18.1 | 19.6 | : | 17.4 | 22.6 | 20.7 | 15.7 | 20.1 | 27.0 | 21.3 | 26.8 | 19.4 | 20.1 | : | 18.3 | 29.9 |
| 1989 | 19.3 | 18.1 | 20.2 | : | 19.2 | 24.1 | 21.3 | 17.0 | 20.2 | 27.1 | 21.5 | 26.4 | 20.3 | 20.8 | : | 17.7 | 31.0 |
| 1990 | 20.2 | 17.4 | 20.9 | : | 19.6 | 24.6 | 21.4 | 18.1 | 20.3 | 26.9 | 20.9 | 26.4 | 19.4 | 20.9 | : | 16.8 | 32.2 |
| 1981-90 | 17.2 | 17.8 | 20.1 | : | 19.2 | 21.4 | 20.5 | 20.2 | 20.9 | 23.8 | 20.1 | 26.2 | 17.6 | 19.9 | : | 18.6 | 29.2 |
| 1991 | 19.4 | 16.4 | 21.4 | 23.2 | 18.6 | 23.9 | 20.9 | 16.8 | 19.7 | 29.0 | 20.5 | 26.0 | 16.9 | 20.3 | 20.8 | 15.4 | 31.7 |
| 1992 | 19.2 | 15.2 | 21.2 | 23.4 | 18.0 | 22.0 | 20.0 | 15.8 | 19.1 | 27.7 | 20.4 | 26.2 | 15.6 | 19.6 | 20.2 | 15.4 | 30.6 |
| 1993 | 17.9 | 14.8 | 20.0 | 22.7 | 17.0 | 20.0 | 19.1 | 15.4 | 17.1 | 28.5 | 19.4 | 25.6 | 15.0 | 18.4 | 19.2 | 16.1 | 29.8 |
| 1994 | 17.9 | 15.3 | 19.7 | 22.8 | 17.1 | 19.5 | 19.0 | 15.6 | 17.0 | 27.7 | 19.0 | 25.7 | 15.0 | 18.2 | 19.2 | 16.7 | 28.9 |

EUR 12-: incl. WD; EUR 12+: incl. D.

**Table D2**   Gross fixed capital formation at 1985 prices; total economy.

(Annual percentage charge)

| | B | DK | WD | D | GR | E | F | IRL | I | L | NL | P | UK | EUR 12- | EUR 12+ | USA | J |
|---|---|---|---|---|---|---|---|---|---|---|---|---|---|---|---|---|---|
| 1961 | 12.4 | 13.9 | 6.5 | : | 8.1 | 17.9 | 10.9 | 16.9 | 11.6 | 9.0 | 6.0 | 6.7 | 9.8 | 9.8 | : | 1.3 | 23.4 |
| 1962 | 5.9 | 6.7 | 3.8 | : | 8.4 | 11.4 | 8.5 | 14.8 | 9.8 | 7.8 | 3.4 | 1.7 | 0.7 | 5.8 | : | 7.1 | 14.3 |
| 1963 | 0.1 | -2.4 | 1.2 | : | 5.5 | 11.4 | 8.8 | 12.0 | 8.1 | 14.2 | 1.1 | 15.3 | 1.4 | 4.7 | : | 7.4 | 11.9 |
| 1964 | 14.7 | 23.5 | 11.2 | : | 20.7 | 15.0 | 10.5 | 10.8 | -5.8 | 22.1 | 19.2 | 4.0 | 16.6 | 9.6 | : | 8.1 | 15.7 |
| 1965 | 4.1 | 4.7 | 4.7 | : | 12.8 | 16.6 | 7.0 | 10.5 | -8.4 | -13.9 | 5.3 | 10.3 | 5.2 | 4.0 | : | 8.6 | 4.6 |
| 1966 | 6.8 | 4.3 | 1.2 | : | 3.2 | 12.7 | 7.3 | -3.0 | 4.3 | -5.1 | 8.0 | 17.9 | 2.6 | 4.8 | : | 4.2 | 14.0 |
| 1967 | 2.9 | 5.4 | -7.0 | : | -1.6 | 6.0 | 6.0 | 6.8 | 11.7 | -7.9 | 8.5 | 5.2 | 8.7 | 3.8 | : | -1.6 | 18.3 |
| 1968 | -1.3 | 1.9 | 3.3 | : | 21.4 | 9.4 | 5.5 | 13.2 | 10.8 | -4.2 | 11.2 | -9.3 | 6.3 | 6.3 | : | 5.8 | 20.5 |
| 1969 | 5.3 | 11.8 | 9.6 | : | 18.6 | 9.8 | 9.2 | 20.5 | 7.8 | 10.5 | -2.2 | 8.1 | -0.6 | 6.8 | : | 2.7 | 18.9 |
| 1970 | 8.4 | 2.2 | 8.9 | : | -1.4 | 3.0 | 4.6 | -3.3 | 3.0 | 7.5 | 7.5 | 11.4 | 2.5 | 5.0 | : | -3.4 | 16.9 |
| 1961-70 | 5.8 | 7.0 | 4.2 | : | 9.3 | 11.2 | 7.8 | 9.6 | 5.1 | 3.4 | 6.7 | 6.9 | 5.2 | 6.0 | : | 3.9 | 15.7 |
| 1971 | -1.9 | 1.9 | 5.9 | : | 14.0 | -3.0 | 7.3 | 8.9 | 0.2 | 10.7 | 1.5 | 10.2 | 1.8 | 3.4 | : | 5.4 | 4.4 |
| 1972 | 3.4 | 9.3 | 2.7 | : | 15.4 | 14.2 | 6.0 | 7.8 | 1.3 | 7.0 | -2.3 | 14.0 | -0.2 | 3.9 | : | 8.9 | 9.7 |
| 1973 | 7.0 | 3.5 | -0.3 | : | 7.7 | 13.0 | 8.5 | 16.2 | 8.8 | 11.8 | 4.2 | 10.3 | 6.5 | 6.1 | : | 7.0 | 11.6 |
| 1974 | 6.9 | -8.9 | -9.7 | : | -25.6 | 6.2 | 1.3 | -11.6 | 2.0 | -7.0 | -4.0 | -6.1 | -2.4 | -2.2 | : | -6.0 | -8.3 |
| 1975 | -1.9 | -12.4 | -5.4 | : | 0.2 | -4.5 | -6.4 | -3.6 | -7.3 | -7.4 | -4.4 | -10.6 | -2.0 | -5.3 | : | -10.9 | -1.0 |
| 1976 | 4.0 | 17.1 | 3.6 | : | 6.8 | -0.8 | 3.3 | 13.6 | 0.0 | -4.2 | -2.2 | 1.3 | 1.7 | 2.1 | : | 7.4 | 2.7 |
| 1977 | 0.0 | -2.4 | 3.6 | : | 7.8 | -0.9 | -1.8 | 4.1 | 1.8 | -0.1 | 9.7 | 11.5 | -1.8 | 1.0 | : | 12.1 | 2.8 |
| 1978 | 2.8 | 1.1 | 4.1 | : | 6.0 | -2.7 | 2.1 | 18.9 | 0.6 | 1.1 | 2.5 | 6.2 | 3.0 | 2.2 | : | 9.3 | 7.8 |
| 1979 | -2.7 | -0.4 | 6.7 | : | 8.8 | -4.4 | 3.1 | 13.6 | 5.7 | 3.8 | -1.7 | -1.3 | 2.8 | 3.2 | : | 4.2 | 4.2 |
| 1980 | 4.6 | -12.6 | 2.2 | : | -6.5 | 0.7 | 2.6 | -4.7 | 8.7 | 12.7 | -0.9 | 8.5 | -5.4 | 1.8 | : | -6.7 | 0.0 |
| 1971-80 | 2.2 | -0.8 | 1.2 | : | 2.8 | 1.6 | 2.5 | 5.9 | 2.1 | 2.6 | 0.2 | 4.1 | 0.4 | 1.6 | : | 2.8 | 3.4 |
| 1981 | -16.1 | -19.2 | -5.0 | : | -7.5 | -3.3 | -1.9 | 9.5 | -3.1 | -7.4 | -10.0 | 5.5 | -9.6 | -5.0 | : | 0.6 | 2.4 |
| 1982 | -1.7 | 7.1 | -5.4 | : | -1.9 | 0.5 | -1.4 | -3.4 | -4.7 | -0.5 | -4.3 | 2.3 | 5.4 | -1.9 | : | -7.2 | -0.1 |
| 1983 | -4.4 | 1.9 | 3.1 | : | -1.3 | -2.5 | -3.6 | -9.3 | -0.6 | -11.8 | 1.9 | -7.1 | 5.0 | 0.0 | : | 5.8 | -1.0 |
| 1984 | 1.7 | 12.9 | 0.1 | : | -5.7 | -5.8 | -2.6 | -2.5 | 3.6 | 0.1 | 5.2 | -17.4 | 8.9 | 0.9 | : | 14.7 | 4.7 |
| 1985 | 0.7 | 12.6 | -0.5 | : | 5.2 | 4.1 | 3.2 | -7.7 | 0.6 | -9.5 | 6.7 | -3.5 | 4.2 | 2.1 | : | 5.5 | 5.3 |
| 1986 | 4.4 | 17.1 | 3.3 | : | -6.2 | 9.9 | 4.5 | -2.8 | 2.2 | 31.2 | 6.9 | 10.9 | 2.6 | 4.2 | : | 0.6 | 4.8 |
| 1987 | 5.6 | -3.8 | 1.8 | : | -5.1 | 14.0 | 4.8 | -2.3 | 5.0 | 14.7 | 0.9 | 15.1 | 10.2 | 5.5 | : | 1.0 | 9.6 |
| 1988 | 15.4 | -6.6 | 4.4 | : | 8.9 | 13.9 | 9.6 | -1.6 | 6.9 | 14.1 | 4.5 | 15.0 | 13.5 | 8.7 | : | 3.7 | 11.9 |
| 1989 | 13.4 | 1.0 | 6.3 | : | 10.1 | 13.6 | 7.9 | 13.6 | 4.3 | 8.9 | 4.9 | 5.6 | 5.5 | 6.9 | : | 1.4 | 9.3 |
| 1990 | 8.5 | -1.7 | 8.5 | : | 9.4 | 7.1 | 2.9 | 12.6 | 3.8 | 2.5 | 1.6 | 5.9 | -3.4 | 3.8 | : | -1.8 | 8.8 |
| 1981-90 | 2.4 | 1.6 | 1.6 | : | 0.4 | 4.9 | 2.3 | 0.3 | 1.7 | 3.5 | 1.7 | 2.7 | 4.1 | 2.4 | : | 2.3 | 5.5 |
| 1991 | -1.7 | -5.4 | 6.1 | : | -4.4 | 1.7 | -1.5 | -7.3 | 0.6 | 9.8 | 0.4 | 2.4 | -9.8 | -0.4 | : | -6.7 | 3.0 |
| 1992 | 1.0 | -8.2 | 1.1 | 4.2 | 1.2 | -3.9 | -2.1 | -1.9 | -2.0 | -2.1 | 1.1 | 5.4 | -1.1 | -1.0 | -0.1 | 6.2 | -1.0 |
| 1993 | -7.0 | -1.8 | -6.9 | -3.3 | -3.4 | -10.3 | -5.0 | 0.3 | -11.1 | 4.0 | -3.8 | -3.9 | 0.8 | -6.2 | -5.1 | 9.6 | -1.3 |
| 1994 | 1.4 | 7.3 | -0.3 | 2.2 | 1.9 | -1.3 | 1.5 | 5.7 | 0.6 | -1.8 | -0.4 | 1.1 | 3.6 | 0.9 | 1.6 | 9.6 | -0.9 |

EUR: PPS weighted. EUR 12-: incl. WD; EUR 12+: incl. D.

**Table D3**   Net stockbuilding at current prices; total economy.

(Percentage of gross domestic product at market prices)

| | B | DK | WD | D | GR | E | F | IRL | I | L | NL | P | UK | EUR 12- | EUR 12+ | USA | J |
|---|---|---|---|---|---|---|---|---|---|---|---|---|---|---|---|---|---|
| 1960 | -0.1 | 4.4 | 3.0 | : | -0.4 | -0.5 | 3.0 | 2.0 | 2.1 | 2.4 | 3.3 | 1.4 | 2.2 | 2.4 | : | 0.7 | 3.9 |
| 1961 | 0.5 | 1.9 | 2.0 | : | 1.8 | 1.7 | 1.7 | 1.4 | 2.3 | 2.2 | 2.7 | 3.9 | 1.0 | 1.7 | : | 0.4 | 5.0 |
| 1962 | 0.0 | 2.9 | 1.6 | : | 1.1 | 3.6 | 2.3 | 1.6 | 1.7 | 5.6 | 1.5 | 1.8 | 0.0 | 1.4 | : | 1.1 | 2.0 |
| 1963 | 0.4 | 0.8 | 0.7 | : | 2.1 | 3.4 | 1.5 | 0.9 | 1.0 | -0.1 | 1.1 | 2.0 | 0.5 | 1.0 | : | 0.9 | 2.2 |
| 1964 | 1.5 | 1.7 | 1.5 | : | 4.7 | 2.6 | 2.4 | 1.2 | 0.5 | -1.2 | 3.0 | 3.3 | 2.1 | 1.8 | : | 0.7 | 2.9 |
| 1965 | 0.8 | 2.3 | 2.3 | : | 4.7 | 3.0 | 1.6 | 2.3 | 0.7 | 2.1 | 1.9 | 4.4 | 1.3 | 1.7 | : | 1.2 | 2.1 |
| 1966 | 1.0 | 0.8 | 1.1 | : | 0.6 | 2.9 | 2.0 | 0.8 | 0.8 | 1.7 | 1.3 | 1.8 | 0.8 | 1.3 | : | 1.5 | 2.1 |
| 1967 | 0.4 | 0.0 | -0.1 | : | 2.0 | 1.4 | 1.8 | -0.4 | 1.1 | -3.0 | 0.9 | 0.6 | 0.7 | 0.8 | : | 1.2 | 3.4 |
| 1968 | 0.9 | 0.6 | 2.1 | : | -0.1 | 0.8 | 1.8 | 1.1 | 0.0 | -1.9 | 0.6 | 3.1 | 1.0 | 1.3 | : | 1.0 | 3.6 |
| 1969 | 1.9 | 1.3 | 2.9 | : | 1.3 | 2.5 | 2.6 | 2.4 | 0.7 | -1.2 | 2.1 | 1.8 | 1.1 | 2.0 | : | 1.1 | 3.1 |
| 1970 | 1.6 | 1.0 | 2.1 | : | 4.5 | 0.8 | 2.5 | 1.7 | 2.8 | 2.7 | 2.0 | 5.9 | 0.7 | 2.0 | : | 0.1 | 3.5 |
| 1961-70 | 0.9 | 1.3 | 1.6 | : | 2.3 | 2.3 | 2.0 | 1.3 | 1.2 | 0.7 | 1.7 | 2.9 | 0.9 | 1.5 | : | 0.9 | 3.0 |
| 1971 | 1.4 | 0.6 | 0.6 | : | 2.7 | 0.9 | 1.5 | 0.3 | 1.0 | 1.3 | 1.1 | 3.2 | 0.2 | 0.9 | : | 0.7 | 1.5 |
| 1972 | 0.5 | 0.2 | 0.5 | : | 1.8 | 0.9 | 1.6 | 1.4 | 0.9 | 0.7 | 0.5 | 3.6 | 0.0 | 0.8 | : | 0.7 | 1.4 |
| 1973 | 1.3 | 1.3 | 1.3 | : | 7.8 | 0.8 | 2.0 | 1.6 | 2.3 | -0.2 | 1.4 | 5.9 | 2.1 | 1.8 | : | 1.2 | 1.7 |
| 1974 | 2.2 | 1.2 | 0.4 | : | 7.1 | 2.2 | 2.3 | 4.4 | 4.2 | -3.4 | 2.3 | 5.2 | 1.2 | 1.9 | : | 0.9 | 2.5 |
| 1975 | -0.6 | -0.2 | -0.6 | : | 6.2 | 2.1 | -0.7 | 0.6 | -1.0 | -4.8 | -0.4 | -3.3 | -1.3 | -0.5 | : | -0.3 | 0.3 |
| 1976 | 0.2 | 1.0 | 1.4 | : | 5.1 | 2.0 | 1.4 | 0.4 | 3.0 | -2.2 | 1.2 | 1.8 | 0.7 | 1.5 | : | 0.9 | 0.7 |
| 1977 | 0.3 | 0.8 | 0.6 | : | 3.5 | 1.1 | 1.5 | 3.2 | 1.4 | -4.7 | 0.6 | 2.5 | 1.3 | 1.1 | : | 1.3 | 0.7 |
| 1978 | 0.1 | -0.2 | 0.6 | : | 3.7 | 0.2 | 0.8 | 1.4 | 1.4 | 0.9 | 0.6 | 2.6 | 1.1 | 0.8 | : | 1.3 | 0.5 |
| 1979 | 0.7 | 0.5 | 1.7 | : | 4.3 | 0.8 | 1.3 | 2.5 | 1.8 | -2.3 | 0.5 | 2.9 | 1.1 | 1.4 | : | 0.6 | 0.8 |
| 1980 | 0.7 | -0.3 | 0.8 | : | 4.4 | 1.2 | 1.2 | -0.8 | 2.7 | -1.9 | 0.5 | 4.2 | -1.1 | 0.9 | : | -0.2 | 0.7 |
| 1971-80 | 0.7 | 0.5 | 0.7 | : | 4.6 | 1.2 | 1.3 | 1.5 | 1.8 | -1.7 | 0.8 | 2.9 | 0.5 | 1.1 | : | 0.7 | 1.1 |
| 1981 | -0.1 | -0.2 | -0.7 | : | 3.1 | -0.3 | -0.2 | -1.3 | 0.9 | -0.9 | -0.9 | 3.7 | -1.1 | -0.3 | : | 1.0 | 0.6 |
| 1982 | 0.1 | 0.2 | -1.0 | : | 1.2 | -0.1 | 0.5 | 1.3 | 1.2 | -0.1 | -0.3 | 3.0 | -0.4 | 0.0 | : | -0.4 | 0.4 |
| 1983 | -0.7 | 0.0 | -0.1 | : | 1.6 | -0.5 | -0.4 | 0.7 | 0.5 | 3.1 | 0.1 | -0.9 | 0.5 | 0.1 | : | 0.0 | 0.1 |
| 1984 | 0.4 | 1.2 | 0.3 | : | 1.0 | 0.0 | -0.3 | 1.3 | 1.9 | 4.7 | 0.5 | -1.3 | 0.4 | 0.5 | : | 1.9 | 0.3 |
| 1985 | -0.7 | 0.8 | 0.1 | : | 2.2 | 0.0 | -0.4 | 0.9 | 1.8 | 2.6 | 0.3 | -1.2 | 0.2 | 0.3 | : | 0.7 | 0.7 |
| 1986 | -0.6 | 0.8 | 0.2 | : | 1.4 | 0.5 | 0.3 | 0.6 | 1.2 | 1.4 | 0.9 | 0.2 | 0.2 | 0.4 | : | 0.4 | 0.5 |
| 1987 | 0.2 | -0.7 | 0.0 | : | 0.5 | 0.7 | 0.4 | 0.1 | 1.3 | -0.7 | -0.1 | 3.3 | 0.3 | 0.4 | : | 0.6 | 0.2 |
| 1988 | 0.4 | -0.2 | 0.5 | : | 1.9 | 1.0 | 0.7 | -0.1 | 1.4 | 0.0 | 0.1 | 2.8 | 1.0 | 0.8 | : | 0.2 | 0.7 |
| 1989 | 0.5 | 0.2 | 0.7 | : | 1.7 | 1.0 | 1.0 | 0.9 | 1.2 | 0.5 | 1.1 | 2.7 | 0.7 | 0.9 | : | 0.7 | 0.8 |
| 1990 | 0.2 | -0.1 | 0.5 | : | 0.3 | 0.9 | 0.9 | 2.4 | 0.7 | 1.4 | 1.3 | 2.7 | -0.2 | 0.6 | : | 0.2 | 0.5 |
| 1981-90 | 0.0 | 0.2 | 0.0 | : | 1.5 | 0.3 | 0.3 | 0.7 | 1.2 | 1.2 | 0.3 | 1.5 | 0.2 | 0.4 | : | 0.5 | 0.5 |
| 1991 | -0.1 | -0.3 | 0.3 | 0.2 | 1.8 | 0.7 | 0.3 | 2.2 | 0.7 | 2.4 | 0.6 | 2.3 | -0.9 | 0.3 | 0.3 | -0.1 | 0.7 |
| 1992 | -0.1 | 0.0 | -0.2 | -0.2 | 1.8 | 0.9 | -0.4 | -0.2 | 0.3 | 2.5 | 0.4 | 2.3 | -0.3 | 0.0 | 0.0 | 0.1 | 0.5 |
| 1993 | -0.2 | -1.1 | -0.9 | -0.8 | 0.9 | 0.8 | -1.6 | -0.1 | -0.2 | -0.6 | 0.6 | 1.0 | 0.1 | -0.5 | -0.5 | 0.3 | 0.2 |
| 1994 | -0.1 | -0.4 | -0.3 | -0.2 | 0.9 | 0.8 | -1.5 | -0.1 | -0.1 | -1.7 | 0.2 | 1.0 | 0.2 | -0.3 | -0.3 | 0.4 | 0.3 |

EUR 12-: incl. WD; EUR 12+: incl. D.

**Table E1**   Price deflator gross domestic product at market prices.

(National currency; annual percentage change)

| | B | DK | WD | D | GR | E | F | IRL | I | L | NL | P | UK | EUR 12- | EUR 12+ | USA | J |
|---|---|---|---|---|---|---|---|---|---|---|---|---|---|---|---|---|---|
| 1961 | 1.3 | 4.3 | 4.7 | : | 1.5 | 1.8 | 3.4 | 2.5 | 2.8 | -3.7 | 2.4 | 2.3 | 2.7 | 3.2 | : | 0.9 | 7.8 |
| 1962 | 1.7 | 6.6 | 3.9 | : | 4.6 | 5.7 | 4.7 | 4.9 | 5.8 | 3.9 | 3.5 | -0.2 | 4.0 | 4.4 | : | 2.2 | 4.2 |
| 1963 | 3.0 | 5.8 | 3.1 | : | 1.4 | 8.5 | 6.4 | 2.7 | 8.5 | 3.1 | 4.7 | 2.5 | 2.1 | 4.8 | : | 1.4 | 5.5 |
| 1964 | 4.6 | 4.6 | 3.0 | : | 3.7 | 6.3 | 4.1 | 9.7 | 6.5 | 5.8 | 8.7 | 1.1 | 3.7 | 4.5 | : | 1.7 | 5.3 |
| 1965 | 5.1 | 7.4 | 3.7 | : | 4.0 | 9.4 | 2.7 | 4.5 | 4.2 | 2.8 | 6.1 | 3.8 | 5.1 | 4.6 | : | 2.6 | 5.1 |
| 1966 | 4.2 | 6.8 | 3.4 | : | 4.9 | 8.1 | 2.9 | 4.4 | 2.2 | 3.9 | 6.0 | 5.5 | 4.5 | 4.0 | : | 3.3 | 5.0 |
| 1967 | 3.1 | 6.3 | 1.6 | : | 2.4 | 7.7 | 3.2 | 3.2 | 2.8 | 0.4 | 4.2 | 3.4 | 2.9 | 3.1 | : | 2.8 | 5.5 |
| 1968 | 2.7 | 7.0 | 2.3 | : | 1.7 | 5.0 | 4.2 | 4.2 | 1.7 | 5.0 | 4.2 | 1.4 | 4.1 | 3.3 | : | 5.0 | 4.9 |
| 1969 | 4.0 | 7.0 | 4.2 | : | 3.4 | 4.4 | 6.6 | 9.1 | 4.1 | 5.3 | 6.4 | 6.1 | 5.4 | 5.1 | : | 5.2 | 4.4 |
| 1970 | 4.6 | 8.3 | 7.7 | : | 3.9 | 6.8 | 5.6 | 9.7 | 6.9 | 15.1 | 6.2 | 3.4 | 7.4 | 6.8 | : | 5.5 | 6.5 |
| 1961-70 | 3.4 | 6.4 | 3.8 | : | 3.1 | 6.4 | 4.4 | 5.5 | 4.5 | 4.1 | 5.2 | 2.9 | 4.2 | 4.4 | : | 3.0 | 5.4 |
| 1971 | 5.6 | 7.7 | 7.7 | : | 3.2 | 7.9 | 6.3 | 10.5 | 6.9 | -0.8 | 8.1 | 5.1 | 9.4 | 7.5 | : | 5.6 | 5.5 |
| 1972 | 6.2 | 9.2 | 5.3 | : | 5.0 | 8.6 | 7.0 | 13.4 | 6.5 | 5.8 | 9.4 | 7.8 | 8.2 | 7.0 | : | 5.0 | 5.8 |
| 1973 | 7.2 | 10.7 | 6.4 | : | 19.4 | 12.0 | 8.5 | 15.3 | 13.2 | 12.2 | 9.0 | 9.4 | 7.0 | 9.0 | : | 6.4 | 13.1 |
| 1974 | 12.6 | 13.1 | 7.1 | : | 20.9 | 16.3 | 11.8 | 6.1 | 19.8 | 17.0 | 9.2 | 18.9 | 15.0 | 13.2 | : | 8.9 | 20.1 |
| 1975 | 12.1 | 12.4 | 5.7 | : | 12.3 | 16.8 | 13.0 | 20.1 | 16.5 | -0.9 | 10.2 | 16.2 | 27.1 | 14.7 | : | 9.8 | 7.4 |
| 1976 | 7.6 | 9.1 | 3.6 | : | 15.4 | 16.5 | 11.1 | 21.0 | 18.4 | 12.2 | 9.0 | 16.3 | 15.2 | 11.8 | : | 6.4 | 7.8 |
| 1977 | 7.5 | 9.4 | 3.7 | : | 13.0 | 23.2 | 9.3 | 13.3 | 18.6 | 1.2 | 6.7 | 26.5 | 13.9 | 11.8 | : | 6.7 | 6.4 |
| 1978 | 4.4 | 9.9 | 4.3 | : | 12.9 | 20.6 | 10.1 | 10.5 | 14.1 | 5.1 | 5.4 | 22.3 | 11.5 | 10.4 | : | 7.7 | 5.0 |
| 1979 | 4.5 | 7.6 | 3.8 | : | 18.6 | 17.1 | 10.1 | 13.7 | 15.3 | 6.4 | 3.9 | 19.4 | 14.5 | 10.7 | : | 8.8 | 2.7 |
| 1980 | 3.8 | 8.2 | 5.0 | : | 17.7 | 14.2 | 11.4 | 14.7 | 20.0 | 7.9 | 5.7 | 20.9 | 19.5 | 12.8 | : | 9.4 | 4.6 |
| 1971-80 | 7.1 | 9.7 | 5.2 | : | 13.7 | 15.2 | 9.8 | 13.8 | 14.8 | 6.5 | 7.6 | 16.1 | 14.0 | 10.9 | : | 7.5 | 7.7 |
| 1981 | 4.7 | 10.1 | 4.2 | : | 19.8 | 12.0 | 11.4 | 17.4 | 19.0 | 7.2 | 5.5 | 17.6 | 11.4 | 10.9 | : | 9.7 | 3.7 |
| 1982 | 7.1 | 10.6 | 4.4 | : | 25.1 | 13.8 | 11.7 | 15.2 | 17.2 | 10.8 | 6.1 | 20.7 | 7.6 | 10.5 | : | 6.1 | 1.6 |
| 1983 | 5.6 | 7.6 | 3.2 | : | 19.1 | 11.6 | 9.7 | 10.6 | 15.1 | 6.8 | 1.9 | 24.6 | 5.1 | 8.4 | : | 3.9 | 1.4 |
| 1984 | 5.2 | 5.7 | 2.1 | : | 20.3 | 10.9 | 7.5 | 6.4 | 11.6 | 4.4 | 1.9 | 24.7 | 4.4 | 6.8 | : | 4.0 | 2.3 |
| 1985 | 6.1 | 4.3 | 2.1 | : | 17.7 | 8.5 | 5.8 | 5.2 | 8.9 | 3.0 | 1.8 | 21.7 | 5.9 | 6.0 | : | 3.5 | 1.6 |
| 1986 | 3.9 | 4.6 | 3.2 | : | 17.5 | 11.1 | 5.2 | 6.5 | 7.9 | 3.8 | 0.1 | 20.5 | 3.2 | 5.5 | : | 2.5 | 1.8 |
| 1987 | 2.3 | 4.7 | 1.9 | : | 14.3 | 5.8 | 3.0 | 2.3 | 6.0 | -1.0 | -0.5 | 11.2 | 5.0 | 4.0 | : | 3.1 | 0.0 |
| 1988 | 1.8 | 3.4 | 1.5 | : | 15.6 | 5.7 | 2.8 | 3.1 | 6.6 | 4.0 | 1.2 | 11.6 | 6.1 | 4.3 | : | 3.9 | 0.4 |
| 1989 | 4.6 | 4.2 | 2.4 | : | 12.5 | 7.1 | 3.0 | 4.6 | 6.2 | 6.0 | 1.2 | 13.0 | 7.1 | 4.9 | : | 4.4 | 1.9 |
| 1990 | 3.0 | 2.7 | 3.1 | : | 20.9 | 7.4 | 3.0 | -1.6 | 7.6 | 2.9 | 2.3 | 14.3 | 6.4 | 5.2 | : | 4.2 | 2.2 |
| 1981-90 | 4.4 | 5.8 | 2.8 | : | 18.2 | 9.4 | 6.3 | 6.8 | 10.5 | 4.8 | 2.1 | 17.9 | 6.2 | 6.6 | : | 4.5 | 1.7 |
| 1991 | 2.7 | 2.5 | 3.9 | : | 17.6 | 7.0 | 3.0 | 1.0 | 7.7 | 3.0 | 2.8 | 14.1 | 6.5 | 5.4 | : | 3.9 | 2.1 |
| 1992 | 3.4 | 1.9 | 4.4 | 5.3 | 14.9 | 6.5 | 2.3 | 1.1 | 4.5 | 4.5 | 2.5 | 13.4 | 4.4 | 4.3 | 4.6 | 2.9 | 1.8 |
| 1993 | 2.7 | 1.6 | 3.3 | 3.9 | 13.8 | 4.5 | 2.4 | 3.3 | 4.4 | 2.3 | 1.6 | 7.9 | 3.4 | 3.5 | 3.7 | 2.5 | 1.3 |
| 1994 | 2.8 | 1.7 | 2.3 | 2.7 | 10.4 | 4.0 | 1.6 | 3.1 | 3.4 | 3.1 | 2.0 | 5.4 | 3.3 | 2.9 | 2.9 | 3.1 | 1.1 |

EUR: PPS weighted. EUR 12-: incl. WD; EUR 12+: incl. D.

**Table E2**   Price deflator private consumption.

(National currency; annual percentage change)

| | B | DK | WD | D | GR | E | F | IRL | I | L | NL | P | UK | EUR 12− | EUR 12+ | USA | J |
|---|---|---|---|---|---|---|---|---|---|---|---|---|---|---|---|---|---|
| 1961 | 2.7 | 3.5 | 3.5 | : | 1.1 | 1.8 | 3.3 | 2.3 | 1.7 | 0.5 | 2.4 | 0.6 | 2.9 | 2.8 | | 0.9 | 6.4 |
| 1962 | 1.1 | 6.2 | 3.0 | : | 1.3 | 5.3 | 4.4 | 4.1 | 5.3 | 0.8 | 2.6 | 2.0 | 3.7 | 3.9 | | 1.6 | 6.7 |
| 1963 | 3.7 | 5.6 | 3.1 | : | 3.4 | 7.8 | 5.7 | 2.4 | 7.0 | 3.1 | 3.8 | 1.1 | 1.6 | 4.3 | | 1.6 | 7.3 |
| 1964 | 4.2 | 4.0 | 2.2 | : | 2.2 | 6.7 | 3.4 | 7.0 | 4.9 | 3.0 | 6.8 | 0.8 | 3.6 | 3.9 | | 1.6 | 4.1 |
| 1965 | 4.6 | 6.1 | 3.4 | : | 4.6 | 9.7 | 2.6 | 4.4 | 3.6 | 3.4 | 4.0 | 4.8 | 4.9 | 4.3 | | 1.9 | 6.8 |
| 1966 | 4.1 | 6.5 | 3.4 | : | 3.5 | 7.3 | 3.2 | 3.9 | 2.9 | 3.4 | 5.4 | 5.5 | 4.0 | 4.0 | | 2.9 | 4.6 |
| 1967 | 2.5 | 7.4 | 1.5 | : | 1.9 | 5.8 | 3.0 | 2.8 | 3.2 | 2.3 | 3.0 | 1.5 | 2.6 | 2.9 | | 2.4 | 3.9 |
| 1968 | 2.9 | 7.1 | 1.6 | : | 0.7 | 5.1 | 5.0 | 4.8 | 1.5 | 2.5 | 2.6 | 4.3 | 4.7 | 3.4 | | 4.3 | 5.1 |
| 1969 | 2.8 | 4.6 | 2.3 | : | 3.0 | 3.4 | 7.1 | 7.8 | 2.9 | 1.9 | 6.1 | 4.9 | 5.5 | 4.3 | | 4.3 | 4.2 |
| 1970 | 2.5 | 6.6 | 3.9 | : | 3.1 | 6.6 | 5.0 | 12.4 | 5.0 | 4.3 | 4.4 | 3.2 | 5.9 | 5.0 | | 4.6 | 7.2 |
| 1961-70 | 3.1 | 5.8 | 2.8 | : | 2.5 | 5.9 | 4.3 | 5.1 | 3.8 | 2.5 | 4.1 | 2.8 | 3.9 | 3.9 | | 2.6 | 5.6 |
| 1971 | 5.3 | 8.3 | 5.6 | : | 2.9 | 7.8 | 6.0 | 9.4 | 5.5 | 4.7 | 7.9 | 7.0 | 8.7 | 6.6 | | 4.7 | 6.8 |
| 1972 | 5.4 | 8.2 | 5.6 | : | 3.3 | 7.6 | 6.3 | 9.7 | 6.3 | 5.1 | 8.3 | 6.3 | 6.5 | 6.4 | | 3.7 | 5.8 |
| 1973 | 6.1 | 11.7 | 6.7 | : | 15.0 | 11.4 | 7.4 | 11.6 | 13.9 | 4.9 | 8.5 | 8.9 | 8.4 | 9.2 | | 5.6 | 10.8 |
| 1974 | 12.8 | 15.0 | 7.5 | : | 23.5 | 17.8 | 14.8 | 15.7 | 21.4 | 10.0 | 9.5 | 23.5 | 17.0 | 15.0 | | 10.2 | 21.0 |
| 1975 | 12.3 | 9.9 | 6.0 | : | 12.7 | 15.5 | 11.8 | 18.0 | 16.5 | 10.2 | 10.1 | 16.0 | 23.5 | 13.9 | | 8.1 | 11.2 |
| 1976 | 7.8 | 9.9 | 4.2 | : | 13.4 | 16.5 | 9.9 | 20.0 | 17.8 | 9.3 | 9.0 | 18.1 | 15.7 | 11.7 | | 6.0 | 9.6 |
| 1977 | 7.2 | 10.6 | 3.4 | : | 11.9 | 23.7 | 9.4 | 14.1 | 17.6 | 5.7 | 6.1 | 27.3 | 14.7 | 11.8 | | 7.0 | 7.4 |
| 1978 | 4.2 | 9.2 | 2.7 | : | 12.8 | 19.0 | 9.1 | 7.9 | 13.2 | 3.4 | 4.5 | 21.3 | 9.5 | 9.2 | | 7.0 | 4.5 |
| 1979 | 3.9 | 10.4 | 4.2 | : | 16.5 | 16.5 | 10.7 | 14.9 | 14.5 | 4.9 | 4.3 | 25.2 | 13.7 | 10.7 | | 8.9 | 3.6 |
| 1980 | 6.4 | 10.7 | 5.8 | : | 21.9 | 16.5 | 13.3 | 18.6 | 20.4 | 7.5 | 6.9 | 21.6 | 16.3 | 13.4 | | 10.7 | 7.5 |
| 1971-80 | 7.1 | 10.4 | 5.2 | : | 13.2 | 15.1 | 7.8 | 13.9 | 14.6 | 6.5 | 7.5 | 17.3 | 13.3 | 10.7 | | 7.2 | 8.7 |
| 1981 | 8.7 | 12.0 | 6.1 | : | 22.7 | 14.3 | 13.0 | 19.6 | 18.0 | 8.6 | 5.8 | 20.2 | 11.2 | 12.0 | | 9.1 | 4.5 |
| 1982 | 7.8 | 10.2 | 4.9 | : | 20.7 | 14.5 | 11.5 | 14.9 | 17.0 | 10.6 | 5.5 | 20.3 | 8.7 | 10.7 | | 5.9 | 2.7 |
| 1983 | 7.1 | 6.0 | 3.2 | : | 10.1 | 12.3 | 9.7 | 9.2 | 14.8 | 8.3 | 2.9 | 25.8 | 4.8 | 8.5 | : | 4.8 | 2.0 |
| 1984 | 5.7 | 6.4 | 2.4 | : | 17.9 | 11.0 | 7.7 | 7.3 | 12.1 | 6.5 | 2.2 | 28.5 | 5.0 | 7.2 | : | 3.9 | 2.5 |
| 1985 | 5.9 | 4.3 | 1.8 | : | 18.3 | 8.2 | 5.7 | 5.0 | 9.0 | 4.3 | 2.2 | 19.4 | 5.3 | 5.8 | | 3.6 | 2.2 |
| 1986 | 0.7 | 2.9 | -0.3 | : | 22.1 | 9.4 | 2.7 | 4.6 | 6.2 | 1.3 | 0.3 | 13.8 | 4.0 | 3.8 | | 2.5 | 0.4 |
| 1987 | 1.9 | 4.6 | 0.7 | : | 15.7 | 5.7 | 3.2 | 2.6 | 5.3 | 1.7 | 0.2 | 10.0 | 4.3 | 3.6 | | 4.1 | 0.2 |
| 1988 | 1.6 | 4.0 | 1.4 | : | 14.2 | 5.0 | 2.7 | 2.9 | 5.7 | 2.7 | 0.5 | 10.0 | 5.0 | 3.8 | | 4.1 | -0.1 |
| 1989 | 3.4 | 4.3 | 3.0 | : | 14.7 | 6.6 | 3.4 | 3.6 | 6.5 | 3.6 | 1.2 | 12.1 | 5.9 | 4.9 | | 4.8 | 1.8 |
| 1990 | 3.6 | 2.7 | 2.8 | : | 19.2 | 6.5 | 2.9 | 1.6 | 5.9 | 3.6 | 2.2 | 12.6 | 5.5 | 4.7 | | 5.0 | 2.6 |
| 1981-90 | 4.6 | 5.8 | 2.6 | : | 18.3 | 9.3 | 6.2 | 7.0 | 9.9 | 5.1 | 2.3 | 17.1 | 6.0 | 6.5 | | 4.7 | 1.9 |
| 1991 | 2.5 | 2.2 | 3.8 | : | 18.5 | 6.3 | 3.0 | 2.3 | 6.9 | 2.9 | 3.4 | 11.1 | 7.4 | 5.4 | | 4.1 | 2.5 |
| 1992 | 2.1 | 2.1 | 4.0 | 4.8 | 14.6 | 6.4 | 2.3 | 2.6 | 5.2 | 2.8 | 3.0 | 9.8 | 4.8 | 4.4 | 4.6 | 3.4 | 2.0 |
| 1993 | 2.8 | 1.7 | 3.3 | 3.9 | 13.7 | 5.1 | 2.2 | 2.0 | 5.1 | 3.6 | 2.1 | 6.8 | 3.5 | 3.8 | 3.9 | 2.6 | 1.1 |
| 1994 | 2.6 | 2.0 | 2.7 | 3.0 | 10.2 | 4.8 | 1.8 | 2.8 | 3.9 | 2.9 | 2.3 | 5.6 | 3.5 | 3.2 | 3.3 | 2.7 | 1.4 |

EUR: PPS weighted. EUR 12−: incl. WD; EUR 12+: incl. D.

**Table F1**   Nominal compensation per employee; total economy.

(National currency; annual percentage change)

| | B | DK | WD | D | GR | E | F | IRL | I | L | NL | P | UK | EUR 12− | EUR 12+ | USA | J |
|---|---|---|---|---|---|---|---|---|---|---|---|---|---|---|---|---|---|
| 1961 | 3.2 | 12.9 | 10.2 | : | 4.6 | 12.9 | 10.6 | 8.3 | 8.2 | 2.9 | 7.4 | 5.1 | 6.8 | 8.8 | | 3.2 | 13.2 |
| 1962 | 7.2 | 11.1 | 9.1 | : | 6.6 | 15.2 | 11.6 | 8.5 | 13.5 | 4.8 | 6.8 | 4.9 | 4.7 | 9.0 | | 4.3 | 14.1 |
| 1963 | 8.0 | 4.6 | 6.1 | : | 7.7 | 21.1 | 11.4 | 5.2 | 19.7 | 8.0 | 9.3 | 8.6 | 5.0 | 9.7 | | 4.0 | 13.2 |
| 1964 | 9.7 | 10.7 | 8.2 | : | 13.3 | 12.6 | 9.2 | 13.7 | 12.3 | 13.3 | 16.5 | 8.3 | 7.1 | 9.5 | | 5.1 | 13.1 |
| 1965 | 9.5 | 13.8 | 9.5 | : | 12.2 | 15.6 | 6.5 | 5.3 | 7.7 | 4.2 | 11.7 | 10.5 | 6.8 | 8.6 | | 3.7 | 11.9 |
| 1966 | 8.6 | 10.2 | 7.6 | : | 12.6 | 18.1 | 6.0 | 8.5 | 7.9 | 5.0 | 11.1 | 10.5 | 6.4 | 8.1 | | 5.1 | 11.2 |
| 1967 | 7.4 | 10.9 | 3.3 | : | 9.5 | 14.7 | 6.9 | 8.0 | 8.4 | 2.8 | 9.3 | 13.8 | 6.2 | 6.8 | | 4.3 | 12.1 |
| 1968 | 6.3 | 10.0 | 6.7 | : | 9.8 | 8.8 | 11.3 | 10.6 | 7.4 | 5.9 | 8.6 | 3.6 | 7.8 | 8.2 | | 7.4 | 13.7 |
| 1969 | 8.4 | 11.0 | 9.5 | : | 9.6 | 11.8 | 11.1 | 13.9 | 7.6 | 5.6 | 13.2 | 10.0 | 6.8 | 9.3 | | 7.4 | 15.8 |
| 1970 | 9.2 | 11.0 | 16.0 | : | 8.8 | 9.4 | 10.3 | 16.8 | 15.7 | 15.1 | 12.4 | 18.2 | 13.4 | 13.2 | | 7.6 | 16.7 |
| 1961-70 | 7.7 | 10.6 | 8.6 | : | 9.4 | 14.0 | 9.5 | 9.8 | 10.8 | 6.7 | 10.6 | 9.3 | 7.1 | 9.1 | | 5.2 | 13.5 |
| 1971 | 12.3 | 11.6 | 11.4 | : | 8.0 | 13.6 | 11.3 | 14.8 | 13.4 | 7.8 | 13.8 | 15.3 | 11.3 | 12.1 | | 7.2 | 14.6 |
| 1972 | 14.2 | 8.0 | 9.6 | : | 12.6 | 17.7 | 10.1 | 15.8 | 10.6 | 9.7 | 12.8 | 16.0 | 13.1 | 11.6 | | 7.4 | 14.2 |
| 1973 | 13.6 | 13.1 | 11.9 | : | 17.2 | 18.3 | 12.4 | 18.8 | 17.7 | 11.4 | 15.4 | 17.5 | 13.2 | 14.0 | | 7.0 | 21.0 |
| 1974 | 18.0 | 18.4 | 11.4 | : | 19.3 | 21.3 | 17.8 | 18.0 | 22.6 | 22.9 | 15.7 | 34.9 | 18.8 | 17.6 | | 8.1 | 25.7 |
| 1975 | 16.5 | 13.9 | 7.0 | : | 20.3 | 22.5 | 18.7 | 28.9 | 20.8 | 12.3 | 13.3 | 38.1 | 31.3 | 19.1 | | 9.0 | 16.2 |
| 1976 | 15.8 | 11.7 | 7.7 | : | 23.2 | 23.4 | 14.8 | 19.6 | 20.9 | 11.1 | 10.8 | 24.3 | 14.8 | 14.8 | | 8.2 | 11.1 |
| 1977 | 9.0 | 9.7 | 6.6 | : | 22.0 | 26.8 | 12.2 | 14.9 | 20.8 | 9.9 | 8.5 | 23.2 | 10.7 | 13.0 | | 7.5 | 10.1 |
| 1978 | 7.2 | 9.2 | 5.5 | : | 23.1 | 24.8 | 12.4 | 15.5 | 16.5 | 5.9 | 7.2 | 18.7 | 13.4 | 12.3 | | 7.8 | 7.5 |
| 1979 | 5.8 | 9.4 | 5.8 | : | 22.1 | 19.0 | 12.8 | 18.9 | 19.9 | 6.7 | 6.0 | 20.0 | 15.3 | 12.7 | | 8.8 | 6.0 |
| 1980 | 9.7 | 10.0 | 6.8 | : | 15.7 | 17.3 | 15.0 | 21.1 | 21.4 | 9.0 | 5.5 | 25.6 | 19.7 | 14.6 | | 10.0 | 6.5 |
| 1971-80 | 12.1 | 11.5 | 8.3 | : | 18.3 | 20.4 | 13.7 | 18.6 | 18.4 | 10.6 | 10.8 | 23.1 | 16.0 | 14.2 | | 8.1 | 13.1 |
| 1981 | 6.2 | 9.2 | 4.8 | : | 21.3 | 15.3 | 14.1 | 18.1 | 22.6 | 8.5 | 3.5 | 21.0 | 14.7 | 12.6 | | 9.5 | 6.4 |
| 1982 | 7.9 | 11.9 | 4.2 | : | 27.6 | 13.7 | 13.8 | 14.2 | 16.2 | 6.9 | 5.8 | 21.6 | 8.5 | 10.6 | | 7.7 | 3.8 |
| 1983 | 6.3 | 8.2 | 3.6 | : | 21.5 | 13.8 | 9.9 | 12.8 | 16.0 | 6.9 | 3.2 | 21.8 | 8.7 | 9.3 | | 5.1 | 2.2 |
| 1984 | 6.6 | 5.5 | 3.4 | : | 20.5 | 10.0 | 8.1 | 10.7 | 11.8 | 7.1 | 0.2 | 21.2 | 5.9 | 7.2 | | 4.3 | 3.9 |
| 1985 | 4.5 | 4.7 | 2.9 | : | 23.2 | 9.4 | 6.4 | 8.9 | 10.1 | 4.5 | 1.4 | 22.5 | 7.6 | 6.7 | | 4.2 | 2.9 |
| 1986 | 4.8 | 4.4 | 3.6 | : | 12.8 | 9.5 | 4.1 | 5.3 | 7.5 | 3.7 | 2.1 | 21.6 | 8.1 | 6.0 | | 4.0 | 3.2 |
| 1987 | 1.5 | 7.9 | 3.2 | : | 11.5 | 6.7 | 3.6 | 5.4 | 8.2 | 4.9 | 1.4 | 17.9 | 7.3 | 5.4 | | 3.3 | 3.2 |
| 1988 | 2.4 | 5.0 | 3.0 | : | 18.6 | 7.1 | 4.2 | 6.4 | 8.7 | 2.7 | 0.9 | 13.4 | 7.9 | 5.6 | | 5.2 | 3.6 |
| 1989 | 3.1 | 3.8 | 2.9 | : | 18.1 | 6.4 | 4.3 | 6.9 | 8.7 | 6.7 | 0.7 | 12.8 | 9.0 | 5.8 | | 4.0 | 4.6 |
| 1990 | 7.5 | 4.6 | 4.7 | : | 17.4 | 8.6 | 5.1 | 5.3 | 10.7 | 7.0 | 3.2 | 18.7 | 9.0 | 7.3 | | 4.8 | 5.3 |
| 1981-90 | 5.1 | 6.5 | 3.6 | : | 19.2 | 10.0 | 7.3 | 9.3 | 12.0 | 5.9 | 2.2 | 19.2 | 8.6 | 7.6 | | 5.2 | 3.9 |
| 1991 | 8.0 | 4.7 | 5.8 | : | 16.1 | 8.2 | 4.4 | 4.7 | 8.5 | 4.3 | 4.3 | 17.2 | 8.1 | 6.9 | | 4.5 | 4.5 |
| 1992 | 5.8 | 2.8 | 5.4 | 10.0 | 11.2 | 8.5 | 3.6 | 5.5 | 5.7 | 5.8 | 4.6 | 15.9 | 5.9 | 5.6 | 6.9 | 5.1 | 1.8 |
| 1993 | 4.8 | 2.2 | 3.2 | 4.6 | 11.7 | 7.2 | 2.7 | 5.8 | 3.7 | 5.7 | 3.1 | 7.5 | 4.2 | 3.9 | 4.3 | 2.8 | 0.7 |
| 1994 | 3.3 | 2.4 | 2.2 | 3.0 | 11.2 | 4.6 | 2.1 | 4.0 | 3.3 | 4.6 | 2.4 | 6.3 | 3.6 | 3.0 | 3.2 | 3.3 | 1.0 |

EUR: PPS weighted. EUR 12−: incl. WD; EUR 12+: incl. D.

**Table F2** Real compensation per employee; total economy; deflator GDP.

(Annual percentage change)

| | B | DK | WD | D | GR | E | F | IRL | I | L | NL | P | UK | EUR 12- | EUR 12+ | USA | J |
|---|---|---|---|---|---|---|---|---|---|---|---|---|---|---|---|---|---|
| 1961 | 1.9 | 8.2 | 5.2 | : | 3.1 | 10.9 | 6.9 | 5.6 | 5.3 | 6.8 | 4.9 | 2.8 | 4.0 | 5.4 | : | 2.3 | 5.1 |
| 1962 | 5.5 | 4.2 | 5.0 | : | 1.9 | 9.0 | 6.6 | 3.4 | 7.3 | 0.9 | 3.2 | 5.1 | 0.6 | 4.4 | : | 2.1 | 9.5 |
| 1963 | 4.8 | -1.1 | 2.9 | : | 6.2 | 11.6 | 4.7 | 2.4 | 10.4 | 4.7 | 4.4 | 6.0 | 2.8 | 4.6 | : | 2.6 | 7.3 |
| 1964 | 4.8 | 5.8 | 5.0 | : | 9.2 | 5.9 | 4.8 | 3.7 | 5.5 | 7.1 | 7.2 | 7.1 | 3.3 | 4.8 | : | 3.3 | 7.4 |
| 1965 | 4.2 | 5.9 | 5.5 | : | 7.9 | 5.6 | 3.7 | 0.8 | 3.4 | 1.3 | 5.2 | 6.5 | 1.7 | 3.9 | : | 1.0 | 6.4 |
| 1966 | 4.3 | 3.1 | 4.0 | : | 7.3 | 9.3 | 3.0 | 3.9 | 5.5 | 1.0 | 4.8 | 4.8 | 1.9 | 3.9 | : | 1.7 | 5.9 |
| 1967 | 4.1 | 4.4 | 1.7 | : | 6.9 | 6.5 | 3.6 | 4.6 | 5.5 | 2.3 | 4.8 | 10.0 | 3.1 | 3.6 | : | 1.5 | 6.2 |
| 1968 | 3.5 | 2.8 | 4.3 | : | 8.0 | 3.7 | 6.8 | 6.1 | 5.5 | 0.8 | 4.2 | 2.2 | 3.6 | 4.7 | : | 2.3 | 8.4 |
| 1969 | 4.2 | 3.7 | 5.1 | : | 6.0 | 7.1 | 4.2 | 4.4 | 3.4 | 0.3 | 6.3 | 3.7 | 1.3 | 4.0 | : | 2.1 | 10.9 |
| 1970 | 4.4 | 2.4 | 7.7 | : | 4.7 | 2.4 | 4.5 | 6.5 | 8.2 | 0.0 | 5.9 | 14.3 | 5.6 | 6.0 | : | 2.0 | 9.6 |
| 1961-70 | 4.2 | 3.9 | 4.6 | : | 6.1 | 7.2 | 4.9 | 4.1 | 6.0 | 2.5 | 5.1 | 6.2 | 2.8 | 4.5 | : | 2.1 | 7.7 |
| 1971 | 6.3 | 3.7 | 3.4 | : | 4.7 | 5.3 | 4.7 | 3.8 | 6.0 | 8.7 | 5.3 | 9.7 | 1.8 | 4.2 | : | 1.6 | 8.6 |
| 1972 | 7.5 | -1.1 | 4.1 | : | 7.2 | 8.4 | 2.9 | 2.1 | 3.9 | 3.7 | 3.2 | 7.6 | 4.5 | 4.3 | : | 2.2 | 8.0 |
| 1973 | 5.9 | 2.2 | 5.2 | : | -1.9 | 5.7 | 3.6 | 3.1 | 4.0 | -0.7 | 5.8 | 7.4 | 5.8 | 4.6 | : | 0.6 | 6.9 |
| 1974 | 4.8 | 4.7 | 4.1 | : | -1.3 | 4.3 | 5.4 | 11.2 | 2.3 | 5.1 | 6.0 | 13.5 | 3.4 | 3.9 | : | -0.7 | 4.7 |
| 1975 | 3.9 | 1.3 | 1.3 | : | 7.1 | 4.9 | 5.1 | 7.3 | 3.7 | 13.3 | 2.8 | 18.8 | 3.3 | 3.8 | : | -0.7 | 8.2 |
| 1976 | 7.6 | 2.3 | 3.9 | : | 6.8 | 5.9 | 3.3 | -1.2 | 2.2 | -1.0 | 1.7 | 6.9 | -0.4 | 2.7 | : | 1.7 | 3.1 |
| 1977 | 1.4 | 0.3 | 2.8 | : | 8.0 | 2.9 | 2.7 | 1.4 | 1.8 | 8.6 | 1.7 | -2.6 | -2.8 | 1.1 | : | 0.7 | 3.5 |
| 1978 | 2.7 | -0.6 | 1.2 | : | 9.0 | 3.5 | 2.1 | 4.5 | 2.1 | 0.7 | 1.6 | -3.0 | 1.7 | 1.7 | : | 0.1 | 2.3 |
| 1979 | 1.2 | 1.7 | 1.9 | : | 2.9 | 1.6 | 2.4 | 4.6 | 4.0 | 0.3 | 2.0 | 0.5 | 0.7 | 1.8 | : | 0.0 | 3.2 |
| 1980 | 5.7 | 1.7 | 1.7 | : | -1.7 | 2.7 | 3.3 | 5.6 | 1.2 | 1.0 | -0.2 | 3.9 | 0.2 | 1.6 | : | 0.6 | 1.8 |
| 1971-80 | 4.7 | 1.6 | 2.9 | : | 4.0 | 4.5 | 3.5 | 4.2 | 3.1 | 3.9 | 3.0 | 6.1 | 1.8 | 3.0 | : | 0.6 | 5.0 |
| 1981 | 1.5 | -0.8 | 0.6 | : | 1.3 | 3.0 | 2.4 | 0.6 | 3.0 | 1.2 | -1.9 | 2.9 | 2.3 | 1.5 | : | -0.2 | 2.6 |
| 1982 | 0.7 | 1.2 | -0.2 | : | 2.0 | -0.1 | 1.9 | -0.8 | -0.9 | -3.5 | -0.3 | 0.7 | 0.8 | 0.1 | : | 1.5 | 2.1 |
| 1983 | 0.7 | 0.5 | 0.3 | : | 2.0 | 1.9 | 0.1 | 1.9 | 0.8 | 0.1 | 1.3 | -2.3 | 3.4 | 0.8 | : | 1.1 | 0.8 |
| 1984 | 1.3 | -0.1 | 1.3 | : | 0.2 | -0.9 | 0.6 | 4.1 | 0.2 | 2.6 | -1.6 | -2.8 | 1.4 | 0.3 | : | 0.3 | 1.6 |
| 1985 | -1.5 | 0.4 | 0.9 | : | 4.7 | 0.8 | 0.6 | 3.5 | 1.1 | 1.5 | -0.4 | 0.6 | 1.6 | 0.7 | : | 0.7 | 1.3 |
| 1986 | 0.9 | -0.2 | 0.4 | : | -4.1 | -1.4 | -1.0 | -1.2 | -0.3 | -0.1 | 1.9 | 0.9 | 4.7 | 0.5 | : | 1.4 | 1.4 |
| 1987 | -08 | 3.0 | 1.3 | : | -2.4 | 0.8 | 0.6 | 3.0 | 2.1 | 5.9 | 2.0 | 6.0 | 2.2 | 1.3 | : | 0.2 | 3.1 |
| 1988 | 0.6 | 1.5 | 1.5 | : | 2.6 | 1.4 | 1.3 | 3.2 | 1.9 | -1.3 | -0.3 | 1.5 | 1.7 | 1.2 | : | 1.3 | 3.3 |
| 1989 | -1.4 | -0.4 | 0.4 | : | 5.0 | -0.6 | 1.2 | 2.2 | 2.4 | 0.7 | -0.5 | -0.2 | 1.7 | 0.9 | : | -0.4 | 2.7 |
| 1990 | 4.3 | 1.9 | 1.5 | : | -2.8 | 1.2 | 2.0 | 7.1 | 2.9 | 3.9 | 0.9 | 3.9 | 2.4 | 1.9 | : | 0.7 | 3.0 |
| 1981-90 | 0.6 | 0.7 | 0.8 | : | 0.8 | 0.6 | 1.0 | 2.3 | 1.3 | 1.1 | 0.1 | 1.1 | 2.2 | 0.9 | : | 0.7 | 2.2 |
| 1991 | 5.1 | 2.2 | 1.8 | : | -1.3 | 1.1 | 1.4 | 3.7 | 0.8 | 1.3 | 1.5 | 2.7 | 1.5 | 1.5 | : | 0.6 | 2.4 |
| 1992 | 2.3 | 0.8 | 0.9 | 4.4 | -3.2 | 1.9 | 1.3 | 4.4 | 1.2 | 1.2 | 2.0 | 2.2 | 1.4 | 1.3 | 2.2 | 2.2 | 0.0 |
| 1993 | 2.0 | 0.6 | -0.1 | 0.6 | -1.8 | 2.6 | 0.3 | 2.5 | -0.7 | 3.3 | 1.5 | -0.3 | 0.7 | 0.4 | 0.6 | 0.3 | -0.6 |
| 1994 | 0.5 | 0.7 | -0.1 | 0.3 | 0.7 | 0.6 | 0.5 | 0.9 | -0.1 | 1.5 | 0.4 | 0.9 | 0.3 | 0.2 | 0.3 | 0.2 | -0.1 |

EUR: PPS weighted. EUR 12-: incl. WD; EUR 12+: incl. D.

**Table F3** Real compensation per employee; total economy; deflator private consumption.

(Annual percentage change)

| | B | DK | WD | D | GR | E | F | IRL | I | L | NL | P | UK | EUR 12- | EUR 12+ | USA | J |
|---|---|---|---|---|---|---|---|---|---|---|---|---|---|---|---|---|---|
| 1961 | 0.6 | 9.0 | 6.5 | : | 3.5 | 10.9 | 7.0 | 5.9 | 6.4 | 2.4 | 4.9 | 4.5 | 3.7 | 5.8 | : | 2.3 | 6.5 |
| 1962 | 6.1 | 4.7 | 5.9 | : | 5.3 | 9.4 | 7.0 | 4.2 | 7.8 | 4.0 | 4.1 | 2.9 | 0.9 | 4.9 | : | 2.7 | 7.0 |
| 1963 | 4.2 | -0.9 | 2.9 | : | 4.2 | 12.4 | 5.4 | 2.7 | 11.8 | 4.7 | 5.3 | 7.4 | 3.3 | 5.2 | : | 2.3 | 5.5 |
| 1964 | 5.3 | 6.4 | 5.8 | : | 10.8 | 5.5 | 5.6 | 6.3 | 7.1 | 10.0 | 9.1 | 7.4 | 3.3 | 5.5 | : | 3.4 | 8.7 |
| 1965 | 4.7 | 7.3 | 5.9 | : | 7.3 | 5.4 | 3.9 | 0.9 | 4.0 | 0.8 | 7.4 | 5.4 | 1.8 | 4.1 | : | 1.8 | 4.7 |
| 1966 | 4.3 | 3.4 | 4.0 | : | 8.8 | 10.0 | 2.8 | 4.4 | 4.8 | 1.6 | 5.4 | 4.8 | 2.4 | 4.0 | : | 2.1 | 6.3 |
| 1967 | 4.7 | 3.2 | 1.7 | : | 7.4 | 8.4 | 3.7 | 5.1 | 5.1 | 0.5 | 6.1 | 12.0 | 3.5 | 3.9 | : | 1.8 | 7.8 |
| 1968 | 3.3 | 2.7 | 5.0 | : | 9.0 | 3.5 | 6.0 | 5.5 | 5.8 | 3.3 | 5.9 | -0.7 | 3.1 | 4.7 | : | 3.0 | 8.2 |
| 1969 | 5.4 | 6.1 | 7.0 | : | 6.4 | 8.1 | 3.7 | 5.7 | 4.5 | 3.7 | 6.7 | 4.9 | 1.2 | 4.8 | : | 3.0 | 11.2 |
| 1970 | 6.5 | 4.1 | 11.6 | : | 5.5 | 2.7 | 5.0 | 4.0 | 10.1 | 10.3 | 7.7 | 14.5 | 7.0 | 7.9 | : | 2.9 | 8.9 |
| 1961-70 | 4.5 | 4.6 | 5.6 | : | 6.8 | 7.6 | 5.0 | 4.4 | 6.7 | 4.1 | 6.3 | 6.2 | 3.0 | 5.1 | : | 2.5 | 7.5 |
| 1971 | 6.7 | 3.1 | 5.5 | : | 5.0 | 5.4 | 5.0 | 4.9 | 7.4 | 3.0 | 5.4 | 7.8 | 2.4 | 5.1 | : | 2.4 | 7.3 |
| 1972 | 8.4 | -0.2 | 3.8 | : | 9.0 | 9.4 | 3.5 | 5.6 | 4.0 | 4.4 | 4.2 | 9.1 | 6.2 | 4.9 | : | 3.6 | 7.9 |
| 1973 | 7.1 | 1.3 | 4.8 | : | 1.9 | 6.2 | 4.7 | 6.5 | 3.3 | 6.2 | 6.3 | 7.9 | 4.5 | 4.5 | : | 1.3 | 9.2 |
| 1974 | 4.7 | 3.0 | 3.6 | : | -3.4 | 3.0 | 2.6 | 1.9 | 0.9 | 11.7 | 5.6 | 9.2 | 1.5 | 2.3 | : | -1.9 | 3.9 |
| 1975 | 3.8 | 3.6 | 0.9 | : | 6.8 | 6.0 | 6.2 | 9.3 | 3.7 | 1.9 | 2.9 | 19.0 | 6.3 | 4.6 | : | 0.8 | 4.5 |
| 1976 | 7.4 | 1.6 | 3.4 | : | 8.6 | 5.9 | 4.5 | -0.4 | 2.6 | 1.7 | 1.7 | 5.2 | -0.8 | 2.8 | : | 2.1 | 1.4 |
| 1977 | 1.7 | -0.8 | 3.1 | : | 9.0 | 2.4 | 2.5 | 0.6 | 2.7 | 4.0 | 2.2 | -3.2 | -3.5 | 1.1 | : | 0.5 | 2.6 |
| 1978 | 2.8 | -0.1 | 2.7 | : | 9.1 | 4.8 | 3.0 | 7.0 | 2.9 | 2.4 | 2.5 | -2.2 | 3.6 | 2.9 | : | 0.7 | 2.9 |
| 1979 | 1.8 | -0.9 | 1.5 | : | 4.8 | 2.1 | 1.8 | 3.5 | 4.7 | 1.6 | 1.6 | -4.1 | 1.4 | 1.8 | : | -0.1 | 2.4 |
| 1980 | 3.1 | -0.6 | 0.9 | : | -5.1 | 0.6 | 1.6 | 2.1 | 0.8 | 1.4 | -1.3 | 3.3 | 3.0 | 1.1 | : | -0.6 | -0.9 |
| 1971-80 | 4.7 | 1.0 | 3.0 | : | 4.4 | 4.6 | 3.5 | 4.1 | 3.3 | 3.8 | 3.1 | 5.0 | 2.4 | 3.1 | : | 0.9 | 4.1 |
| 1981 | -2.2 | -2.5 | -1.2 | : | -1.2 | 0.8 | 0.9 | -1.3 | 3.9 | -0.1 | -2.2 | 0.7 | 2.5 | 0.6 | : | 0.4 | 1.9 |
| 1982 | 0.0 | 1.5 | -0.6 | : | 5.7 | -0.7 | 2.1 | -0.6 | -0.8 | -3.3 | 0.2 | 1.1 | -0.2 | -0.1 | : | 1.8 | 1.1 |
| 1983 | -0.8 | 1.3 | 0.4 | : | 2.9 | 1.3 | 0.2 | 3.2 | 1.1 | -1.2 | 0.2 | -3.2 | 3.7 | 0.8 | : | 0.6 | 0.2 |
| 1984 | 0.8 | -0.8 | 1.0 | : | 2.2 | -0.9 | 0.4 | 3.2 | -0.3 | 0.5 | -1.9 | -5.6 | 0.9 | -0.1 | : | 0.3 | 1.4 |
| 1985 | -1.3 | 0.4 | 1.1 | : | 4.1 | 1.1 | 0.6 | 3.7 | 1.0 | 0.2 | -0.8 | 2.6 | 2.2 | 0.9 | : | 0.5 | 0.7 |
| 1986 | 4.0 | 1.5 | 4.0 | : | -7.7 | 0.1 | 1.4 | 0.7 | 1.3 | 2.4 | 1.8 | 6.8 | 4.0 | 2.2 | : | 1.4 | 2.8 |
| 1987 | -0.3 | 3.1 | 2.5 | : | -3.6 | 0.9 | 0.4 | 2.7 | 2.8 | 3.1 | 1.2 | 7.2 | 2.8 | 1.7 | : | -0.8 | 3.0 |
| 1988 | 0.8 | 1.0 | 1.6 | : | 3.8 | 2.0 | 1.5 | 3.3 | 2.8 | 0.0 | 0.3 | 3.1 | 2.7 | 1.7 | : | 1.1 | 3.7 |
| 1989 | -0.2 | -0.5 | -0.1 | : | 3.0 | -0.2 | 0.8 | 3.2 | 2.1 | 3.0 | -0.5 | 0.6 | 2.9 | 0.8 | : | -0.7 | 2.7 |
| 1990 | 3.8 | 1.8 | 1.9 | : | -1.5 | 2.0 | 2.1 | 3.6 | 4.6 | 3.3 | 1.0 | 5.4 | 3.3 | 1.5 | : | -0.2 | 2.6 |
| 1981-90 | 0.4 | 0.7 | 1.0 | : | 0.7 | 0.6 | 1.0 | 2.2 | 1.8 | 0.8 | -0.1 | 1.8 | 2.5 | 1.1 | : | 0.4 | 2.0 |
| 1991 | 5.3 | 2.5 | 2.0 | : | -2.1 | 1.8 | 1.4 | 2.4 | 1.5 | 1.4 | 0.9 | 5.5 | 0.7 | 1.5 | : | 0.3 | 1.9 |
| 1992 | 3.6 | 0.6 | 1.3 | 4.9 | -3.0 | 1.9 | 1.3 | 2.8 | 0.4 | 2.9 | 1.6 | 5.6 | 1.0 | 1.2 | 2.2 | 1.7 | -0.2 |
| 1993 | 1.9 | 0.5 | -0.1 | 0.7 | -1.8 | 2.0 | 0.5 | 3.8 | -1.3 | 2.0 | 1.0 | 0.7 | 0.6 | 0.2 | 0.4 | 0.2 | -0.4 |
| 1994 | 0.7 | 0.4 | -0.5 | 0.0 | 0.9 | -0.1 | 0.3 | 1.2 | -0.6 | 1.7 | 0.2 | 0.7 | 0.1 | -0.2 | -0.1 | 0.6 | -0.4 |

EUR: PPS weighted. EUR 12-: incl. WD; EUR 12+: incl. D.

Contemporary Europe

**Table F4**  Adjust wage share; total economy.

(Percentage of gross domestic product at factor cost.)

| | B | DK | WD | D | GR | E | F | IRL | I | L | NL | P | UK | EUR 12− | EUR 12+ | USA | J |
|---|---|---|---|---|---|---|---|---|---|---|---|---|---|---|---|---|---|
| 1960 | 68.8 | 71.4 | 70.6 | : | 107.0 | 71.5 | 72.8 | 84.3 | 74.2 | 66.1 | 63.5 | 70.0 | 71.2 | 74.6 | : | 72.4 | 80.0 |
| 1961 | 68.0 | 72.4 | 72.1 | : | 99.1 | 70.9 | 73.7 | 83.8 | 72.6 | 68.9 | 65.8 | 69.0 | 72.4 | 75.1 | : | 71.9 | 76.0 |
| 1962 | 69.3 | 73.0 | 72.5 | : | 99.8 | 71.0 | 73.7 | 84.3 | 72.3 | 68.3 | 66.6 | 68.8 | 72.8 | 75.1 | : | 71.2 | 77.1 |
| 1963 | 70.0 | 73.4 | 72.6 | : | 95.2 | 73.3 | 74.2 | 83.5 | 74.3 | 68.7 | 68.1 | 68.7 | 72.1 | 75.1 | : | 70.8 | 76.8 |
| 1964 | 69.6 | 72.6 | 71.4 | : | 94.8 | 74.1 | 74.1 | 84.3 | 75.6 | 68.9 | 68.6 | 68.7 | 71.7 | 74.8 | : | 70.5 | 74.5 |
| 1965 | 69.8 | 75.4 | 71.6 | : | 92.7 | 74.1 | 73.3 | 83.4 | 74.3 | 69.4 | 69.3 | 68.3 | 72.1 | 74.6 | : | 69.6 | 75.9 |
| 1966 | 71.4 | 76.6 | 72.2 | : | 93.4 | 76.3 | 72.4 | 86.7 | 72.8 | 69.5 | 71.5 | 68.7 | 72.9 | 74.6 | : | 69.4 | 73.9 |
| 1967 | 71.8 | 77.4 | 71.5 | : | 93.8 | 78.5 | 71.4 | 84.7 | 72.8 | 70.3 | 71.1 | 70.1 | 72.7 | 74.2 | : | 70.3 | 71.9 |
| 1968 | 70.9 | 78.0 | 70.0 | : | 94.6 | 76.4 | 72.1 | 83.4 | 71.7 | 67.7 | 70.7 | 65.2 | 72.3 | 73.2 | : | 71.0 | 70.0 |
| 1969 | 70.3 | 77.1 | 70.5 | : | 91.4 | 76.2 | 71.8 | 83.1 | 69.9 | 62.7 | 71.1 | 65.3 | 73.1 | 73.0 | : | 72.5 | 69.4 |
| 1970 | 68.5 | 78.1 | 72.1 | : | 88.2 | 75.4 | 71.4 | 85.4 | 71.8 | 63.3 | 72.5 | 73.5 | 74.7 | 74.0 | : | 73.8 | 69.6 |
| 1961-70 | 70.0 | 75.4 | 71.6 | : | 94.4 | 74.6 | 72.8 | 84.3 | 72.8 | 67.8 | 69.5 | 68.6 | 72.7 | 74.4 | : | 71.1 | 73.5 |
| 1971 | 70.6 | 79.4 | 72.7 | : | 85.4 | 76.0 | 71.5 | 85.6 | 74.5 | 69.9 | 74.0 | 75.5 | 73.0 | 74.6 | : | 72.7 | 73.0 |
| 1972 | 71.1 | 76.0 | 72.8 | : | 84.5 | 76.6 | 71.0 | 81.9 | 74.4 | 70.4 | 73.4 | 74.8 | 72.8 | 74.3 | : | 72.5 | 73.1 |
| 1973 | 71.3 | 75.2 | 73.6 | : | 77.1 | 77.0 | 70.5 | 81.4 | 73.6 | 65.6 | 73.7 | 71.7 | 72.7 | 74.2 | : | 72.3 | 74.4 |
| 1974 | 73.1 | 78.0 | 75.2 | : | 77.7 | 75.9 | 72.3 | 86.7 | 72.8 | 67.1 | 74.7 | 79.3 | 75.3 | 75.6 | : | 73.5 | 77.5 |
| 1975 | 75.6 | 78.9 | 75.0 | : | 80.1 | 77.4 | 75.4 | 85.1 | 75.7 | 83.6 | 76.6 | 96.3 | 77.9 | 77.5 | : | 72.1 | 81.1 |
| 1976 | 76.9 | 77.6 | 73.6 | : | 81.2 | 78.5 | 75.7 | 84.5 | 74.3 | 80.0 | 74.0 | 96.6 | 75.3 | 76.5 | : | 71.7 | 81.0 |
| 1977 | 77.3 | 77.9 | 73.7 | : | 86.2 | 77.9 | 75.2 | 77.6 | 74.3 | 85.4 | 74.3 | 89.6 | 72.4 | 76.0 | : | 71.3 | 81.3 |
| 1978 | 77.4 | 77.9 | 73.0 | : | 88.5 | 77.2 | 75.0 | 75.7 | 73.4 | 82.8 | 74.3 | 81.9 | 71.6 | 75.4 | : | 71.2 | 80.0 |
| 1979 | 77.3 | 78.3 | 72.7 | : | 89.2 | 77.5 | 74.9 | 78.8 | 72.6 | 81.4 | 74.6 | 79.4 | 72.4 | 75.3 | : | 71.4 | 79.5 |
| 1980 | 78.3 | 79.3 | 74.5 | : | 85.5 | 76.2 | 76.4 | 83.5 | 72.2 | 83.1 | 74.5 | 79.8 | 74.5 | 74.4 | : | 72.5 | 78.6 |
| 1971-80 | 74.9 | 77.9 | 73.7 | : | 83.6 | 77.0 | 73.8 | 82.1 | 73.8 | 76.9 | 74.4 | 82.5 | 73.8 | 75.6 | : | 72.1 | 78.0 |
| 1981 | 78.8 | 78.3 | 74.8 | : | 89.3 | 77.2 | 76.6 | 82.3 | 73.7 | 84.1 | 72.3 | 81.6 | 75.0 | 76.9 | : | 71.7 | 78.6 |
| 1982 | 77.4 | 76.4 | 74.3 | : | 91.0 | 75.5 | 76.7 | 80.6 | 73.3 | 80.7 | 71.0 | 80.4 | 73.3 | 76.0 | : | 73.1 | 78.5 |
| 1983 | 76.7 | 75.2 | 72.3 | : | 94.5 | 75.8 | 76.0 | 81.0 | 74.1 | 79.7 | 69.6 | 78.7 | 71.8 | 75.1 | : | 72.0 | 78.0 |
| 1984 | 75.7 | 73.4 | 71.3 | : | 92.8 | 72.2 | 74.9 | 78.8 | 72.6 | 78.0 | 66.3 | 76.5 | 72.1 | 73.8 | : | 71.0 | 76.6 |
| 1985 | 74.4 | 72.9 | 70.7 | : | 93.9 | 70.8 | 73.8 | 76.4 | 72.2 | 78.4 | 65.4 | 75.1 | 71.6 | 73.1 | : | 71.0 | 74.6 |
| 1986 | 74.4 | 73.1 | 70.0 | : | 90.2 | 69.8 | 71.2 | 76.2 | 70.6 | 76.5 | 66.6 | 73.1 | 72.6 | 72.1 | : | 71.2 | 74.2 |
| 1987 | 73.4 | 75.5 | 70.4 | : | 89.4 | 70.0 | 70.4 | 75.6 | 70.7 | 81.1 | 68.2 | 73.0 | 72.2 | 72.1 | : | 71.6 | 74.7 |
| 1988 | 71.3 | 74.7 | 69.3 | : | 89.2 | 69.0 | 69.3 | 74.4 | 70.4 | 78.4 | 67.4 | 72.3 | 72.2 | 71.3 | : | 71.6 | 74.0 |
| 1989 | 69.3 | 72.8 | 68.5 | : | 89.2 | 67.9 | 68.1 | 73.3 | 70.3 | 77.1 | 65.2 | 68.9 | 73.3 | 70.4 | : | 70.9 | 73.9 |
| 1990 | 71.0 | 71.9 | 67.8 | : | 90.3 | 68.4 | 68.5 | 73.2 | 71.9 | 80.7 | 64.9 | 69.2 | 74.6 | 70.7 | : | 71.8 | 74.1 |
| 1981-90 | 74.3 | 74.4 | 70.9 | : | 91.0 | 71.7 | 72.6 | 77.2 | 72.0 | 79.5 | 67.7 | 74.9 | 72.9 | 73.1 | : | 71.6 | 75.7 |
| 1991 | 73.2 | 71.4 | 68.2 | 70.1 | 85.4 | 68.0 | 68.7 | 73.8 | 72.6 | 83.3 | 65.4 | 70.0 | 75.6 | 71.1 | 71.4 | 72.6 | 74.2 |
| 1992 | 73.8 | 70.6 | 68.6 | 70.9 | 84.6 | 68.4 | 68.1 | 74.6 | 72.3 | 85.2 | 66.9 | 70.3 | 75.3 | 71.1 | 71.6 | 72.4 | 73.9 |
| 1993 | 75.5 | 69.8 | 69.0 | 71.1 | 85.3 | 67.1 | 68.0 | 74.4 | 70.8 | 90.3 | 67.5 | 68.4 | 73.3 | 71.0 | 71.5 | 71.5 | 73.5 |
| 1994 | 74.6 | 68.8 | 67.7 | 69.5 | 86.4 | 66.1 | 67.2 | 73.9 | 68.8 | 90.8 | 66.8 | 67.7 | 72.6 | 70.0 | 70.4 | 70.7 | 72.9 |

EUR 12−: incl. WD; EUR 12+: incl. D.

**Table F5**  Nominal unit labour costs; total economy[a].

(National currency; 1980 = 100)

| | B | DK | WD | GR | E | F | IRL | I | L | NL | P | UK | EUR 12− | USA | J |
|---|---|---|---|---|---|---|---|---|---|---|---|---|---|---|---|
| 1960 | 31.1 | 20.1 | 38.5 | 25.3 | 12.0 | 23.8 | 15.6 | 15.9 | 29.2 | 24.9 | 15.1 | 17.5 | 22.7 | 35.6 | 27.9 |
| 1961 | 30.9 | 21.6 | 41.1 | 23.9 | 12.2 | 25.0 | 16.1 | 15.9 | 29.2 | 26.3 | 15.2 | 18.3 | 23.5 | 35.6 | 28.6 |
| 1962 | 32.0 | 23.0 | 43.0 | 24.9 | 12.9 | 26.2 | 17.0 | 16.8 | 30.3 | 27.6 | 15.0 | 19.1 | 24.6 | 36.1 | 30.3 |
| 1963 | 33.3 | 24.3 | 44.4 | 24.0 | 14.5 | 27.9 | 17.2 | 18.8 | 31.5 | 29.5 | 15.4 | 19.4 | 25.8 | 36.4 | 31.9 |
| 1964 | 34.6 | 25.1 | 45.1 | 24.8 | 15.5 | 28.9 | 18.9 | 20.4 | 33.7 | 32.3 | 15.5 | 19.9 | 26.8 | 36.9 | 32.8 |
| 1965 | 36.7 | 27.8 | 47.1 | 25.2 | 16.9 | 29.5 | 19.5 | 20.9 | 34.7 | 34.6 | 16.0 | 20.9 | 28.0 | 37.4 | 35.2 |
| 1966 | 38.8 | 30.0 | 49.2 | 26.5 | 18.8 | 30.0 | 20.9 | 21.0 | 36.2 | 37.7 | 16.9 | 22.0 | 29.1 | 38.7 | 36.1 |
| 1967 | 40.0 | 31.9 | 49.3 | 27.2 | 20.8 | 30.7 | 21.2 | 21.5 | 36.7 | 39.0 | 17.7 | 22.5 | 29.8 | 40.3 | 37.1 |
| 1968 | 40.8 | 34.0 | 49.9 | 27.7 | 21.4 | 32.7 | 21.7 | 21.6 | 37.2 | 40.1 | 16.7 | 23.2 | 30.6 | 42.6 | 38.0 |
| 1969 | 42.1 | 36.0 | 51.7 | 27.5 | 22.1 | 34.4 | 23.5 | 22.0 | 36.2 | 43.4 | 17.7 | 24.3 | 31.9 | 45.6 | 39.4 |
| 1970 | 43.1 | 39.4 | 57.8 | 27.7 | 23.4 | 36.5 | 26.4 | 24.2 | 41.8 | 46.7 | 20.4 | 26.8 | 34.7 | 48.9 | 42.0 |
| 1971 | 47.0 | 43.1 | 62.7 | 28.0 | 25.6 | 38.9 | 29.2 | 27.0 | 45.3 | 51.2 | 22.1 | 28.9 | 37.7 | 50.8 | 46.5 |
| 1972 | 50.8 | 45.1 | 66.2 | 29.1 | 28.0 | 41.2 | 31.8 | 28.9 | 47.9 | 55.4 | 23.7 | 31.6 | 40.4 | 53.3 | 49.3 |
| 1973 | 55.0 | 49.9 | 71.5 | 32.1 | 31.3 | 44.6 | 36.6 | 32.4 | 50.2 | 61.1 | 24.9 | 34.1 | 44.0 | 56.7 | 56.7 |
| 1974 | 63.3 | 59.4 | 78.5 | 39.8 | 36.3 | 51.4 | 42.0 | 38.4 | 60.9 | 68.1 | 33.0 | 41.3 | 51.0 | 62.7 | 71.4 |
| 1975 | 73.9 | 67.3 | 82.8 | 45.2 | 43.5 | 60.6 | 50.8 | 47.7 | 74.0 | 76.7 | 46.4 | 54.4 | 60.6 | 67.6 | 80.5 |
| 1976 | 80.6 | 71.8 | 84.2 | 52.9 | 51.5 | 67.3 | 59.4 | 55.0 | 80.2 | 80.9 | 53.8 | 60.3 | 66.5 | 71.7 | 86.5 |
| 1977 | 87.1 | 78.2 | 87.4 | 62.9 | 62.9 | 73.8 | 64.2 | 64.9 | 86.7 | 86.0 | 63.3 | 65.2 | 73.3 | 76.3 | 92.0 |
| 1978 | 91.1 | 85.0 | 90.2 | 72.9 | 76.0 | 80.6 | 70.8 | 73.3 | 87.7 | 90.6 | 72.0 | 71.9 | 80.1 | 82.4 | 95.2 |
| 1979 | 95.2 | 90.9 | 93.1 | 86.8 | 89.0 | 88.2 | 84.3 | 84.2 | 91.9 | 94.9 | 83.5 | 81.9 | 88.1 | 90.3 | 96.7 |
| 1980 | 100.0 | 100.0 | 100.0 | 100.0 | 100.0 | 100.0 | 100.0 | 100.0 | 100.0 | 100.0 | 100.0 | 100.0 | 100.0 | 100.0 | 100.0 |
| 1981 | 105.3 | 108.8 | 104.6 | 127.5 | 112.6 | 112.2 | 113.3 | 121.9 | 109.4 | 102.6 | 120.3 | 111.0 | 111.3 | 108.1 | 103.5 |
| 1982 | 110.4 | 118.7 | 108.8 | 160.7 | 125.3 | 124.9 | 126.5 | 142.1 | 115.4 | 107.4 | 140.5 | 116.2 | 121.2 | 117.1 | 105.1 |
| 1983 | 115.7 | 125.6 | 109.1 | 196.6 | 139.4 | 136.1 | 140.3 | 164.3 | 119.5 | 107.2 | 169.4 | 120.0 | 129.5 | 120.0 | 106.1 |
| 1984 | 120.5 | 129.1 | 110.0 | 231.3 | 147.0 | 143.9 | 146.1 | 179.5 | 121.2 | 104.1 | 206.1 | 126.7 | 135.8 | 123.0 | 106.1 |
| 1985 | 125.7 | 132.9 | 111.8 | 279.0 | 155.1 | 149.8 | 151.0 | 194.4 | 124.8 | 104.5 | 245.5 | 133.3 | 142.2 | 127.2 | 104.6 |
| 1986 | 130.8 | 137.4 | 114.7 | 310.7 | 166.9 | 152.8 | 159.9 | 204.7 | 126.7 | 106.0 | 278.8 | 138.0 | 147.5 | 130.9 | 106.1 |
| 1987 | 130.8 | 149.1 | 117.5 | 347.9 | 177.1 | 155.3 | 162.7 | 215.6 | 132.7 | 108.1 | 314.0 | 143.8 | 152.8 | 135.8 | 106.0 |
| 1988 | 129.4 | 153.8 | 117.6 | 401.6 | 185.4 | 156.2 | 166.0 | 227.2 | 132.8 | 107.9 | 342.7 | 152.5 | 157.1 | 141.4 | 105.2 |
| 1989 | 130.9 | 157.8 | 118.5 | 459.9 | 194.9 | 158.3 | 166.7 | 240.2 | 137.7 | 105.8 | 371.3 | 166.9 | 163.1 | 145.9 | 107.1 |
| 1990 | 138.2 | 161.1 | 120.9 | 552.9 | 211.6 | 164.0 | 167.9 | 262.8 | 148.7 | 107.4 | 426.0 | 183.2 | 172.8 | 153.5 | 109.9 |
| 1991 | 146.8 | 164.1 | 125.6 | 606.9 | 225.1 | 170.1 | 171.3 | 284.1 | 156.8 | 111.4 | 493.1 | 196.5 | 182.4 | 160.5 | 112.6 |
| 1992 | 152.6 | 166.4 | 131.4 | 678.3 | 239.5 | 173.1 | 173.2 | 295.0 | 165.8 | 115.8 | 562.1 | 204.3 | 189.8 | 164.9 | 114.3 |
| 1993 | 159.6 | 167.3 | 136.0 | 753.1 | 248.3 | 176.6 | 180.2 | 299.3 | 177.7 | 118.8 | 597.6 | 206.2 | 194.5 | 166.9 | 115.3 |
| 1994 | 161.6 | 166.5 | 136.0 | 832.1 | 253.8 | 176.4 | 183.0 | 300.8 | 184.8 | 119.4 | 620.0 | 210.2 | 196.2 | 170.1 | 115.6 |

EUR: PPS weighted. EUR 12−: incl. WD;
[a] Compensation of employees adjusted for the share of self-employed in occupied population, per unit of GDP at constant prices.

**Table F6**   Real unit labour cots; total economy[a].

(1980 = 100)

| | B | DK | WD | GR | E | F | IRL | I | L | NL | P | UK | EUR 12- | USA | J |
|---|---|---|---|---|---|---|---|---|---|---|---|---|---|---|---|
| 1960 | 86.7 | 94.3 | 92.7 | 124.6 | 91.7 | 93.4 | 96.8 | 98.5 | 81.4 | 86.5 | 89.5 | 97.8 | 97.9 | 98.6 | 99.6 |
| 1961 | 84.8 | 97.3 | 94.5 | 116.1 | 91.1 | 94.7 | 97.1 | 96.1 | 84.6 | 89.3 | 87.9 | 99.6 | 98.4 | 97.9 | 94.7 |
| 1962 | 86.4 | 97.4 | 95.1 | 115.3 | 91.6 | 94.9 | 98.0 | 96.0 | 84.5 | 90.4 | 87.1 | 99.9 | 98.4 | 97.0 | 96.5 |
| 1963 | 87.4 | 96.9 | 95.4 | 109.7 | 94.5 | 95.2 | 96.3 | 98.9 | 85.2 | 92.3 | 87.1 | 99.0 | 98.5 | 96.4 | 96.3 |
| 1964 | 86.8 | 95.7 | 94.0 | 109.3 | 95.3 | 94.7 | 96.7 | 100.9 | 86.0 | 92.9 | 86.8 | 98.1 | 98.1 | 96.0 | 93.8 |
| 1965 | 87.5 | 98.8 | 94.8 | 107.0 | 95.2 | 94.1 | 95.4 | 99.2 | 86.2 | 93.7 | 86.3 | 98.2 | 97.8 | 94.9 | 95.8 |
| 1966 | 88.9 | 99.7 | 95.6 | 107.3 | 97.6 | 92.9 | 98.0 | 97.3 | 86.6 | 96.4 | 86.5 | 98.8 | 97.8 | 95.2 | 93.6 |
| 1967 | 88.8 | 100.0 | 94.3 | 107.4 | 100.4 | 92.1 | 96.4 | 96.8 | 87.5 | 95.7 | 87.5 | 99.2 | 97.2 | 96.3 | 91.2 |
| 1968 | 88.1 | 99.6 | 93.4 | 107.4 | 98.3 | 94.0 | 94.7 | 95.9 | 84.4 | 94.6 | 81.5 | 97.1 | 96.6 | 97.0 | 89.1 |
| 1969 | 87.5 | 98.4 | 92.8 | 103.2 | 97.5 | 93.0 | 93.7 | 93.9 | 78.0 | 96.1 | 81.2 | 96.8 | 95.7 | 98.8 | 88.5 |
| 1970 | 85.6 | 99.5 | 96.4 | 100.0 | 96.6 | 93.2 | 96.0 | 96.4 | 78.2 | 97.3 | 90.8 | 99.1 | 97.6 | 100.3 | 88.5 |
| 1971 | 88.3 | 101.1 | 97.1 | 98.0 | 97.7 | 93.5 | 95.9 | 100.5 | 85.5 | 98.8 | 93.7 | 98.0 | 98.6 | 98.7 | 92.9 |
| 1972 | 90.0 | 96.9 | 97.3 | 97.0 | 98.3 | 92.7 | 92.3 | 101.1 | 85.4 | 97.7 | 93.0 | 98.9 | 98.6 | 98.7 | 93.4 |
| 1973 | 90.8 | 96.8 | 98.7 | 89.5 | 98.4 | 92.3 | 92.1 | 100.3 | 79.8 | 98.9 | 89.3 | 99.7 | 98.7 | 98.6 | 94.6 |
| 1974 | 92.9 | 102.0 | 101.3 | 91.8 | 98.2 | 95.2 | 99.6 | 99.2 | 82.7 | 101.0 | 99.7 | 105.1 | 100.9 | 100.1 | 99.2 |
| 1975 | 96.7 | 102.7 | 101.1 | 92.8 | 100.8 | 99.4 | 100.3 | 105.8 | 101.4 | 103.3 | 120.6 | 108.9 | 104.5 | 98.3 | 104.1 |
| 1976 | 98.1 | 100.5 | 99.2 | 94.2 | 102.2 | 99.3 | 96.9 | 103.0 | 97.9 | 99.9 | 120.3 | 104.7 | 102.6 | 98.1 | 103.8 |
| 1977 | 98.6 | 100.0 | 99.3 | 99.2 | 101.4 | 99.6 | 92.5 | 102.4 | 104.6 | 99.5 | 111.9 | 99.6 | 101.2 | 97.8 | 103.8 |
| 1978 | 98.7 | 98.9 | 98.3 | 101.8 | 101.6 | 98.8 | 92.4 | 101.5 | 100.6 | 99.5 | 104.0 | 98.4 | 100.0 | 98.1 | 102.3 |
| 1979 | 98.8 | 98.4 | 97.8 | 102.1 | 101.7 | 98.2 | 96.7 | 101.1 | 99.1 | 100.3 | 101.0 | 97.9 | 99.4 | 98.8 | 101.1 |
| 1980 | 100.0 | 100.0 | 100.0 | 100.0 | 100.0 | 100.0 | 100.0 | 100.0 | 100.0 | 100.0 | 100.0 | 100.0 | 100.0 | 100.0 | 100.0 |
| 1981 | 100.6 | 98.8 | 100.4 | 106.5 | 100.5 | 100.7 | 96.5 | 102.4 | 102.1 | 97.3 | 102.3 | 99.6 | 100.3 | 98.6 | 99.9 |
| 1982 | 98.5 | 97.5 | 100.0 | 107.3 | 98.3 | 100.4 | 93.5 | 101.8 | 97.2 | 96.0 | 99.0 | 97.0 | 98.9 | 100.6 | 99.7 |
| 1983 | 97.7 | 95.9 | 97.2 | 110.1 | 98.0 | 99.7 | 93.7 | 102.3 | 94.2 | 94.1 | 95.8 | 95.4 | 97.5 | 99.2 | 99.3 |
| 1984 | 96.8 | 93.3 | 95.9 | 107.8 | 93.1 | 98.1 | 91.7 | 100.2 | 91.5 | 89.7 | 93.5 | 96.3 | 95.6 | 97.8 | 97.0 |
| 1985 | 95.1 | 92.1 | 95.5 | 110.5 | 90.6 | 96.5 | 90.1 | 99.6 | 91.5 | 88.4 | 91.4 | 95.7 | 94.5 | 97.7 | 94.2 |
| 1986 | 95.3 | 91.0 | 95.0 | 104.7 | 87.7 | 93.6 | 89.6 | 97.3 | 89.5 | 86.2 | | 95.9 | 92.9 | 98.1 | 93.9 |
| 1987 | 93.2 | 94.3 | 95.5 | 102.6 | 88.0 | 92.4 | 89.0 | 96.7 | 94.6 | 91.8 | 87.3 | 95.2 | 92.5 | 98.8 | 93.8 |
| 1988 | 90.6 | 94.1 | 94.2 | 102.5 | 87.2 | 90.4 | 88.1 | 95.5 | 91.1 | 90.6 | 85.4 | 95.2 | 91.2 | 99.0 | 92.7 |
| 1989 | 87.6 | 92.6 | 92.6 | 104.3 | 85.6 | 88.9 | 84.6 | 95.1 | 89.1 | 87.7 | 81.9 | 97.2 | 90.2 | 97.9 | 92.7 |
| 1990 | 89.8 | 92.1 | 91.6 | 103.7 | 86.5 | 89.4 | 86.6 | 96.7 | 93.5 | 87.0 | 82.2 | 100.3 | 90.9 | 98.9 | 93.0 |
| 1991 | 92.8 | 91.5 | 91.6 | 96.9 | 86.0 | 90.0 | 87.5 | 97.1 | 95.7 | 87.8 | 83.4 | 101.0 | 91.0 | 99.6 | 93.4 |
| 1992 | 93.3 | 91.0 | 91.8 | 94.2 | 85.9 | 89.5 | 87.6 | 96.5 | 96.8 | 89.1 | 83.8 | 100.6 | 90.8 | 99.4 | 93.1 |
| 1993 | 95.0 | 90.1 | 92.0 | 91.9 | 85.2 | 89.3 | 88.2 | 93.8 | 101.5 | 89.9 | 82.6 | 98.2 | 89.9 | 98.2 | 92.7 |
| 1994 | 93.6 | 88.2 | 89.9 | 92.0 | 83.8 | 87.8 | 86.8 | 91.2 | 102.4 | 88.6 | 81.3 | 96.9 | 88.1 | 97.0 | 92.0 |

EUR: PPS weighted. EUR 12-: incl. WD; EUR 12+: incl. D.
a Nominal unit labour costs deflated by the DGP price deflator.

**Table F7**   Relative nominal unit labour costs in a common currency; total economy[a].
Performance relative to 19 industrial countries; double export weights.

(USD; 1980 = 100)

| | B | DK | WD | GR | E | F | IRL | I | NL | P | UK | EUR 12-[b] | USA | J |
|---|---|---|---|---|---|---|---|---|---|---|---|---|---|---|
| 1960 | 94.6 | 78.0 | 81.2 | 174.8 | 66.7 | 102.8 | 95.7 | 108.4 | 66.0 | 123.5 | 98.4 | 76.9 | 167.2 | 68.0 |
| 1961 | 89.1 | 80.3 | 87.5 | 158.5 | 65.0 | 103.7 | 94.8 | 103.9 | 69.5 | 119.5 | 99.7 | 80.2 | 162.2 | 67.8 |
| 1962 | 88.7 | 82.3 | 88.0 | 158.0 | 66.6 | 104.5 | 96.7 | 105.6 | 70.4 | 114.0 | 100.8 | 81.7 | 159.5 | 70.2 |
| 1963 | 88.3 | 83.7 | 87.2 | 147.1 | 71.8 | 107.2 | 95.5 | 113.7 | 72.5 | 112.4 | 97.9 | 83.1 | 154.9 | 72.2 |
| 1964 | 88.6 | 83.7 | 85.3 | 147.2 | 74.6 | 107.2 | 101.9 | 119.4 | 76.8 | 109.4 | 96.9 | 83.8 | 151.8 | 72.1 |
| 1965 | 90.4 | 89.0 | 85.0 | 144.0 | 78.4 | 104.7 | 100.5 | 117.5 | 79.0 | 108.4 | 98.1 | 84.4 | 146.9 | 75.3 |
| 1966 | 91.6 | 91.9 | 85.1 | 145.7 | 83.6 | 101.6 | 102.9 | 113.0 | 82.4 | 110.1 | 99.0 | 84.7 | 146.2 | 74.1 |
| 1967 | 92.1 | 94.3 | 82.7 | 145.6 | 88.6 | 101.1 | 100.7 | 112.6 | 83.7 | 112.1 | 96.3 | 82.7 | 146.9 | 73.8 |
| 1968 | 91.6 | 93.9 | 82.3 | 146.5 | 78.6 | 106.4 | 93.6 | 111.8 | 85.0 | 106.2 | 84.6 | 78.5 | 154.6 | 74.1 |
| 1969 | 90.4 | 94.7 | 83.6 | 139.7 | 77.6 | 102.3 | 96.2 | 108.5 | 88.3 | 108.1 | 84.8 | 77.8 | 158.7 | 73.3 |
| 1970 | 85.5 | 95.6 | 95.1 | 128.1 | 75.7 | 92.1 | 99.5 | 109.4 | 86.4 | 115.3 | 86.5 | 81.4 | 156.5 | 72.2 |
| 1971 | 86.3 | 96.0 | 98.5 | 117.0 | 76.0 | 88.6 | 102.4 | 112.3 | 88.5 | 115.4 | 87.0 | 83.3 | 146.7 | 76.7 |
| 1972 | 90.2 | 94.8 | 99.9 | 107.0 | 79.5 | 90.1 | 101.8 | 112.2 | 91.3 | 114.2 | 86.0 | 85.6 | 135.0 | 85.2 |
| 1973 | 90.9 | 102.7 | 109.3 | 99.8 | 83.4 | 92.2 | 100.8 | 102.3 | 95.7 | 112.5 | 76.1 | 87.8 | 120.2 | 95.7 |
| 1974 | 93.4 | 107.3 | 109.5 | 108.5 | 86.7 | 86.6 | 96.7 | 97.8 | 98.4 | 128.1 | 77.8 | 86.4 | 115.6 | 99.0 |
| 1975 | 97.2 | 108.7 | 101.0 | 97.8 | 88.5 | 98.4 | 92.6 | 103.2 | 99.7 | 150.7 | 81.8 | | 107.3 | 96.2 |
| 1976 | 101.0 | 109.1 | 99.2 | 100.8 | 89.0 | 97.6 | 89.6 | 92.0 | 100.5 | 147.1 | 73.3 | 83.4 | 110.5 | 100.9 |
| 1977 | 107.2 | 109.2 | 102.1 | 108.1 | 88.2 | 94.3 | 86.5 | 93.3 | 104.5 | 125.5 | 70.1 | 84.2 | 108.1 | 110.6 |
| 1978 | 107.8 | 110.7 | 103.2 | 106.3 | 89.9 | 95.0 | 89.0 | 92.6 | 105.6 | 105.6 | 72.5 | 85.8 | 99.9 | 112.9 |
| 1979 | 106.1 | 109.5 | 103.0 | 111.0 | 106.5 | 97.1 | 97.3 | 96.0 | 104.7 | 96.1 | 81.6 | 94.0 | 99.4 | 112.2 |
| 1980 | 100.0 | 100.0 | 100.0 | 100.0 | 100.0 | 100.0 | 100.0 | 100.0 | 100.0 | 100.0 | 100.0 | 100.0 | 100.0 | 100.0 |
| 1981 | 91.1 | 92.3 | 89.6 | 105.1 | 93.0 | 93.6 | 94.7 | 98.7 | 90.1 | 106.0 | 102.4 | 85.7 | 112.1 | 107.6 |
| 1982 | 80.6 | 89.8 | 90.1 | 113.4 | 90.0 | 88.9 | 97.8 | 99.9 | 92.4 | 100.2 | 95.1 | 80.3 | 127.1 | 95.7 |
| 1983 | 78.7 | 90.7 | 89.1 | 108.4 | 79.1 | 86.1 | 100.0 | 107.2 | 90.1 | 91.1 | 87.6 | 75.6 | 132.9 | 103.4 |
| 1984 | 77.8 | 86.9 | 84.9 | 105.5 | 78.6 | 83.9 | 96.3 | 107.0 | 83.1 | 88.5 | 85.4 | 69.7 | 143.2 | 106.0 |
| 1985 | 79.1 | 87.3 | 83.2 | 103.5 | 78.1 | 85.2 | 97.0 | 106.5 | 80.7 | 90.1 | 86.9 | 69.5 | 150.3 | 103.6 |
| 1986 | 84.2 | 92.4 | 91.2 | 87.8 | 80.1 | 87.5 | 103.1 | 112.6 | 85.1 | 91.1 | 80.6 | 76.2 | 121.4 | 129.3 |
| 1987 | 85.0 | 101.0 | 96.7 | 86.0 | 82.5 | 86.9 | 99.4 | 116.5 | 88.5 | 92.3 | 80.7 | 81.7 | 107.9 | 134.9 |
| 1988 | 81.3 | 99.4 | 93.4 | 90.1 | 86.8 | 83.2 | 97.2 | 116.0 | 86.2 | 93.2 | 88.5 | 79.9 | 103.3 | 142.8 |
| 1989 | 79.3 | 95.8 | 89.6 | 92.6 | 92.2 | 80.5 | 92.7 | 119.8 | 81.1 | 94.6 | 91.2 | 77.2 | 108.1 | 134.3 |
| 1990 | 84.2 | 99.8 | 91.4 | 97.7 | 99.9 | 83.8 | 93.4 | 129.8 | 81.4 | 101.9 | 95.0 | 86.1 | 101.8 | 117.3 |
| 1991 | 85.2 | 95.0 | 89.2 | 90.3 | 100.7 | 80.7 | 89.5 | 131.4 | 79.8 | 112.9 | 97.7 | 83.8 | 101.2 | 124.6 |
| 1992 | 87.6 | 96.1 | 89.3 | 90.1 | 101.8 | 82.1 | 89.4 | 128.4 | 82.1 | 129.1 | 95.1 | 87.3 | 98.9 | 129.0 |
| 1993 | 90.4 | 96.7 | 97.6 | 88.6 | 89.8 | 83.5 | 86.3 | 105.8 | 84.7 | 124.2 | 85.5 | 80.4 | 102.9 | 154.5 |
| 1994 | 91.7 | 94.7 | 95.6 | 89.8 | 84.5 | 82.1 | 86.8 | 102.6 | 84.0 | 120.2 | 86.6 | 77.4 | 104.3 | 163.8 |

EUR: PPS weighted. EUR 12-: incl. WD.
a Compensation of employees adjusted for the share of self-employed in occupied population, per unit of GDP at constant prices.
b EUR 12 relative to nine industrial non-member countries.

**Table G1**  Occupied population, total economy. National accounts definition.

(Annual percentage change)

| | B | DK | WD | D | GR | E | F | IRL | I | L | NL | P | UK | EUR 12− | EUR 12+ | USA | J |
|---|---|---|---|---|---|---|---|---|---|---|---|---|---|---|---|---|---|
| 1961 | 0.8 | 1.5 | 1.4 | : | 0.4 | 0.2 | 0.1 | -0.2 | 0.2 | 1.1 | 1.5 | 0.5 | 1.2 | 0.7 | : | -0.4 | 1.4 |
| 1962 | 1.6 | 1.5 | 0.3 | : | -1.0 | 0.9 | 0.2 | 0.7 | -1.1 | 0.3 | 2.0 | 0.5 | 0.7 | 0.3 | : | 2.1 | 1.3 |
| 1963 | 0.7 | 1.2 | 0.2 | : | -1.4 | 0.5 | 1.0 | 0.6 | -1.5 | -0.4 | 1.4 | -0.2 | 0.1 | 0.1 | : | 0.9 | 0.9 |
| 1964 | 1.3 | 2.1 | 0.1 | : | -1.3 | 1.2 | 1.1 | 0.5 | -0.6 | 1.7 | 1.8 | -0.1 | 1.1 | 0.5 | : | 1.8 | 1.3 |
| 1965 | 0.2 | 1.8 | 0.6 | : | -0.7 | 0.5 | 0.4 | -0.2 | -1.7 | 0.9 | 0.9 | 0.4 | 0.9 | 0.2 | : | 3.3 | 1.6 |
| 1966 | 0.5 | 0.5 | -0.3 | : | -0.9 | 0.5 | 0.8 | -0.3 | -1.5 | 0.5 | 0.8 | -0.6 | 0.6 | 0.0 | : | 4.5 | 2.1 |
| 1967 | -0.3 | -0.6 | -3.3 | : | -1.2 | 0.8 | 0.3 | -0.6 | 1.1 | -1.1 | -0.3 | -0.6 | -1.4 | -0.8 | : | 2.5 | 1.9 |
| 1968 | -0.1 | 0.8 | 0.1 | : | -1.2 | 0.8 | -0.3 | 0.3 | 0.0 | -0.4 | 0.9 | -0.6 | -0.6 | -0.1 | : | 2.4 | 1.7 |
| 1969 | 1.7 | 1.2 | 1.6 | : | -0.3 | 0.9 | 1.5 | 0.3 | 0.5 | 1.4 | 1.7 | -0.6 | 0.4 | 0.9 | : | 2.5 | 0.8 |
| 1970 | -0.4 | 0.7 | 1.3 | : | -0.1 | 0.7 | 1.5 | -1.2 | 0.0 | 2.0 | 1.1 | 5.2 | -0.8 | 0.6 | : | -0.8 | 1.1 |
| 1961-70 | 0.6 | 1.1 | 0.2 | : | -0.8 | 0.7 | 0.6 | 0.0 | -0.5 | 0.6 | 1.2 | 0.4 | 0.2 | 0.3 | : | 1.9 | 1.4 |
| 1971 | 0.6 | 0.6 | 0.4 | : | 0.3 | 0.5 | 0.5 | -0.4 | -0.1 | 3.2 | 0.5 | 0.3 | -0.9 | 0.1 | : | -0.4 | 0.7 |
| 1972 | -0.2 | 2.1 | 0.4 | : | 0.5 | 0.3 | 0.6 | 0.3 | -0.6 | 2.7 | -0.9 | -0.3 | -0.2 | 0.1 | : | 2.5 | 0.5 |
| 1973 | 0.9 | 1.3 | 1.1 | : | 1.0 | 2.0 | 1.4 | 1.4 | 2.2 | 1.9 | 0.1 | -0.5 | 2.3 | 1.5 | : | 4.3 | 2.3 |
| 1974 | 1.6 | -0.3 | -1.2 | : | 0.1 | 0.7 | 0.9 | 1.4 | 2.0 | 2.8 | 0.2 | -0.5 | 0.3 | 0.4 | : | 1.6 | -0.4 |
| 1975 | -1.4 | -1.3 | -2.7 | : | 0.1 | -1.6 | -0.9 | -0.8 | 0.1 | 1.2 | -0.7 | -2.6 | -0.4 | -1.1 | : | -2.1 | -0.2 |
| 1976 | -0.5 | 1.8 | -0.5 | : | 1.2 | -1.1 | 0.8 | -0.8 | 1.5 | -0.1 | 0.0 | -0.2 | -0.9 | 0.0 | : | 2.8 | 0.8 |
| 1977 | -0.4 | 0.8 | 0.1 | : | 0.8 | -0.7 | 0.8 | 1.8 | 1.0 | -0.1 | 0.2 | 0.8 | 0.1 | 0.4 | : | 3.5 | 1.2 |
| 1978 | 0.2 | 1.0 | 0.8 | : | 0.4 | -1.7 | 0.5 | 2.5 | 0.5 | -0.6 | 0.7 | -1.5 | 0.6 | 0.3 | : | 5.0 | 1.0 |
| 1979 | 1.0 | 1.2 | 1.7 | : | 1.1 | -1.7 | 0.2 | 3.2 | 1.5 | 0.5 | 1.3 | 2.1 | 1.5 | 1.0 | : | 3.2 | 1.0 |
| 1980 | -0.1 | -0.5 | 1.6 | : | 1.4 | -3.0 | 0.2 | 1.0 | 1.9 | 0.7 | 0.7 | -0.3 | -0.3 | 0.4 | : | 0.2 | 0.7 |
| 1971-80 | 0.2 | 0.7 | 0.2 | : | 0.7 | -0.6 | 0.5 | 0.9 | · 1.0 | 1.2 | 0.2 | -0.3 | 0.2 | 0.3 | : | 2.0 | 0.7 |
| 1981 | -1.9 | -1.3 | -0.1 | : | 5.2 | -2.6 | -0.5 | -0.9 | 0.0 | -0.3 | -1.5 | 1.0 | -3.9 | -1.1 | : | 0.9 | 0.8 |
| 1982 | -1.3 | 0.4 | -1.2 | : | -0.8 | -0.9 | 0.3 | 0.0 | 0.6 | -0.3 | -2.5 | -1.9 | -1.8 | -0.8 | : | -1.6 | 0.8 |
| 1983 | -1.0 | 0.3 | -1.4 | : | 1.1 | -0.5 | -0.1 | -1.9 | 0.6 | -0.3 | -1.9 | -1.1 | -1.2 | -0.6 | : | 1.0 | 1.5 |
| 1984 | -0.2 | 1.7 | 0.2 | : | 0.4 | -2.4 | -0.9 | -1.9 | 0.4 | 0.6 | -0.1 | -1.5 | 1.9 | 0.0 | : | 4.9 | 0.3 |
| 1985 | 0.6 | 2.5 | 0.7 | : | 1.0 | -1.3 | -0.3 | -2.2 | 0.9 | 1.4 | 1.5 | 0.0 | 1.3 | 0.5 | : | 2.4 | 0.6 |
| 1986 | 0.6 | 2.6 | 1.4 | : | 0.4 | 1.4 | 0.4 | 0.2 | 0.8 | 2.6 | 2.1 | -2.7 | -0.1 | 0.7 | : | 1.7 | 0.9 |
| 1987 | 0.5 | 0.9 | 0.7 | : | -0.1 | 5.1 | 0.3 | 0.8 | 0.4 | 2.8 | 1.7 | 0.5 | 1.8 | 1.2 | : | 3.5 | 0.9 |
| 1988 | 1.5 | -0.6 | 0.8 | : | 1.7 | 2.8 | 0.9 | 0.0 | 0.9 | 3.1 | 1.6 | 0.1 | 3.2 | 1.5 | : | 2.8 | 1.7 |
| 1989 | 1.6 | -0.6 | 1.5 | : | 0.4 | 3.4 | 1.3 | -0.2 | 0.2 | 3.7 | 1.9 | 1.0 | 2.5 | 1.5 | : | 1.9 | 2.0 |
| 1990 | 1.4 | -1.0 | 3.0 | : | 1.3 | 3.5 | 1.0 | 4.2 | 0.9 | 4.2 | 2.3 | 0.9 | 1.1 | 1.7 | : | 1.2 | 2.1 |
| 1981-90 | 0.2 | 0.5 | 0.5 | : | 1.0 | 0.8 | 0.2 | -0.2 | 0.6 | 1.8 | 0.5 | -0.4 | 0.5 | 0.5 | : | 1.9 | 1.1 |
| 1991 | 0.1 | -1.8 | 2.6 | : | -2.3 | 0.5 | 0.0 | 0.0 | 0.8 | 4.2 | 1.5 | 0.9 | -3.1 | 0.1 | : | -1.1 | 2.1 |
| 1992 | -0.4 | -0.1 | 0.9 | -1.7 | 1.5 | -1.2 | -0.5 | 0.4 | -1.0 | 1.8 | 0.8 | -0.6 | -2.2 | -0.6 | -1.1 | 0.2 | 1.1 |
| 1993 | -1.4 | -0.5 | -1.6 | -1.9 | -0.8 | -4.3 | -1.3 | 0.7 | -2.8 | 1.7 | -0.2 | -2.3 | -1.2 | -1.8 | -1.9 | 1.4 | 0.2 |
| 1994 | -0.8 | 0.9 | -1.4 | -1.4 | 0.0 | -1.2 | -0.6 | 1.7 | -1.2 | 1.0 | -0.6 | -1.4 | 0.8 | -0.6 | -0.7 | 2.3 | 0.0 |

EUR 12−: incl. WD; EUR 12+: incl. D.

**Table G2**  Unemployment rate, total. Eurostat definition.

(Percentage of civilian labour force)

| | B | DK | WD | GR | E | F | IRL | I | L | NL | P | UK | EUR 9−ᵃ | EUR 12− | USAᵇ | Jᵇ |
|---|---|---|---|---|---|---|---|---|---|---|---|---|---|---|---|---|
| 1960 | 3.1 | 1.6 | 1.0 | : | : | 0.7 | 4.7 | 7.2 | 0.1 | 0.7 | : | 1.6 | 2.5 | : | 5.5 | 1.6 |
| 1961 | 2.5 | 1.2 | 0.7 | : | : | 0.6 | 4.3 | 6.6 | 0.1 | 0.5 | : | 1.4 | 2.2 | : | 6.7 | 1.4 |
| 1962 | 2.0 | 1.1 | 0.6 | 5.1 | : | 0.7 | 4.2 | 5.5 | 0.1 | 0.5 | : | 1.9 | 2.0 | : | 5.5 | 1.3 |
| 1963 | 1.5 | 1.5 | 0.7 | 5.0 | : | 0.7 | 4.5 | 5.1 | 0.2 | 0.6 | : | 2.3 | 2.1 | : | 5.7 | 1.3 |
| 1964 | 1.5 | 0.9 | 0.6 | 4.7 | 2.8 | 0.6 | 4.3 | 5.2 | 0.0 | 0.5 | 2.5 | 1.6 | 1.9 | 1.9 | 5.2 | 1.2 |
| 1964 | 1.4 | 1.2 | 0.5 | 4.7 | 2.8 | 1.2 | 5.2 | 4.0 | 0.0 | 0.5 | 2.5 | 1.4 | 1.7 | 1.9 | 5.2 | 1.2 |
| 1965 | 1.6 | 0.9 | 0.4 | 4.8 | 2.6 | 1.5 | 5.0 | 5.0 | 0.0 | 0.6 | 2.5 | 1.2 | 1.8 | 2.0 | 4.5 | 1.2 |
| 1966 | 1.7 | 1.1 | 0.5 | 5.0 | 2.2 | 1.6 | 5.1 | 5.4 | 0.0 | 0.8 | 2.5 | 1.1 | 1.9 | 2.1 | 3.8 | 1.3 |
| 1967 | 2.4 | 1.0 | 1.4 | 5.4 | 3.0 | 2.1 | 5.5 | 5.0 | 0.0 | 1.7 | 2.5 | 2.0 | 2.5 | 2.6 | 3.8 | 1.3 |
| 1968 | 2.8 | 1.0 | 1.0 | 5.6 | 3.0 | 2.6 | 5.8 | 5.3 | 0.0 | 1.5 | 2.6 | 2.1 | 2.6 | 2.7 | 3.6 | 1.2 |
| 1969 | 2.2 | 0.9 | 0.6 | 5.3 | 2.5 | 2.3 | 5.5 | 5.3 | 0.0 | 1.1 | 2.6 | 2.0 | 2.3 | 2.4 | 3.5 | 1.1 |
| 1970 | 1.8 | 0.6 | 0.5 | 4.2 | 2.6 | 2.4 | 6.3 | 5.1 | 0.0 | 1.0 | 2.6 | 2.2 | 2.3 | 2.4 | 4.9 | 1.2 |
| 1964-70 | 2.0 | 1.0 | 0.7 | 5.0 | 2.7 | 2.0 | 5.5 | 5.0 | 0.0 | 1.0 | 2.5 | 1.7 | 2.2 | 2.3 | 4.2 | 1.2 |
| 1971 | 1.7 | 0.9 | 0.6 | 3.1 | 3.4 | 2.7 | 6.0 | 5.1 | 0.0 | 1.3 | 2.5 | 2.7 | 2.5 | 2.6 | 6.0 | 1.2 |
| 1972 | 2.2 | 0.8 | 0.8 | 2.1 | 2.9 | 2.8 | 6.7 | 6.0 | 0.0 | 2.3 | 2.5 | 3.1 | 2.9 | 2.9 | 5.6 | 1.4 |
| 1973 | 2.2 | 0.7 | 0.8 | 2.0 | 2.6 | 2.7 | 6.2 | 5.9 | 0.0 | 2.4 | 2.6 | 2.2 | 2.7 | 2.6 | 4.9 | 1.3 |
| 1974 | 2.3 | 2.8 | 1.8 | 2.1 | 3.1 | 2.8 | 5.8 | 5.0 | 0.0 | 2.9 | 1.7 | 2.0 | 2.8 | 2.8 | 5.6 | 1.4 |
| 1975 | 4.2 | 3.9 | 3.3 | 2.3 | 4.5 | 4.0 | 7.9 | 5.5 | 0.0 | 5.5 | 4.4 | 3.2 | 4.0 | 4.1 | 8.5 | 1.9 |
| 1976 | 5.5 | 5.1 | 3.3 | 1.9 | 4.9 | 4.4 | 9.8 | 6.2 | 0.0 | 5.8 | 6.2 | 4.8 | 4.7 | 4.7 | 7.7 | 2.0 |
| 1977 | 6.3 | 5.9 | 3.2 | 1.7 | 5.3 | 4.9 | 9.7 | 6.7 | 0.0 | 5.6 | 7.3 | 5.1 | 5.0 | 5.0 | 7.1 | 2.0 |
| 1978 | 6.8 | 6.7 | 3.1 | 1.8 | 7.1 | 5.1 | 9.0 | 6.7 | 1.2 | 5.6 | 7.9 | 5.0 | 5.1 | 5.3 | 6.1 | 2.3 |
| 1979 | 7.0 | 4.8 | 2.7 | 1.9 | 8.8 | 5.8 | 7.8 | 7.2 | 2.4 | 5.7 | 7.9 | 4.6 | 5.1 | 5.4 | 5.8 | 2.2 |
| 1980 | 7.4 | 5.2 | 2.7 | 2.8 | 11.6 | 6.2 | 8.0 | 7.1 | 2.4 | 6.4 | 7.6 | 5.6 | 5.4 | 6.0 | 7.1 | 2.0 |
| 1971-80 | 4.6 | 3.7 | 2.2 | 2.2 | 5.4 | 4.1 | 7.7 | 6.1 | 0.6 | 4.4 | 5.1 | 3.8 | 4.0 | 4.2 | 6.4 | 1.8 |
| 1981 | 9.5 | 8.3 | 3.9 | 4.0 | 14.4 | 7.3 | 10.8 | 7.4 | 2.4 | 8.9 | 7.3 | 8.9 | 7.1 | 7.7 | 7.6 | 2.2 |
| 1982 | 11.2 | 8.9 | 5.6 | 5.8 | 16.3 | 8.0 | 12.5 | 8.0 | 2.4 | 11.9 | 7.2 | 10.3 | 8.3 | 9.0 | 9.7 | 2.4 |
| 1983 | 12.5 | 9.2 | 6.9 | 7.9 | 17.7 | 8.2 | 15.2 | 8.9 | 3.5 | 12.1 | 7.8 | 11.0 | 9.1 | 9.9 | 9.6 | 2.7 |
| 1984 | 12.5 | 8.7 | 7.1 | 8.1 | 20.0 | 9.7 | 16.8 | 9.5 | 3.1 | 11.6 | 8.5 | 11.0 | 9.6 | 10.5 | 7.5 | 2.7 |
| 1985 | 11.8 | 7.2 | 7.1 | 7.8 | 21.1 | 10.1 | 18.2 | 10.1 | 2.9 | 10.5 | 8.6 | 11.4 | 9.8 | 10.8 | 7.2 | 2.6 |
| 1986 | 11.7 | 5.5 | 6.5 | 7.4 | 21.1 | 10.3 | 18.2 | 10.6 | 2.6 | 10.2 | 8.3 | 11.4 | 9.7 | 10.7 | 7.0 | 2.8 |
| 1987 | 11.3 | 5.6 | 6.3 | 7.4 | 20.5 | 10.4 | 18.0 | 10.3 | 2.5 | 10.0 | 6.8 | 10.4 | 9.5 | 10.4 | 6.2 | 2.8 |
| 1988 | 10.2 | 6.4 | 6.3 | 7.7 | 19.4 | 9.9 | 17.3 | 10.9 | 2.0 | 9.3 | 5.7 | 8.5 | 8.9 | 9.8 | 5.5 | 2.5 |
| 1989 | 8.6 | 7.7 | 5.6 | 7.5 | 17.1 | 9.4 | 15.7 | 10.9 | 1.8 | 8.5 | 5.0 | 7.1 | 8.2 | 9.0 | 5.3 | 2.3 |
| 1990 | 7.6 | 8.1 | 4.8 | 7.0 | 16.2 | 9.0 | 14.5 | 10.0 | 1.7 | 7.5 | 4.6 | 7.0 | 7.6 | 8.4 | 5.5 | 2.1 |
| 1981-90 | 10.7 | 7.6 | 6.0 | 7.1 | 18.4 | 9.2 | 15.7 | 9.7 | 2.5 | 10.1 | 7.0 | 9.7 | 8.8 | 9.6 | 7.1 | 2.5 |
| 1991 | 7.5 | 8.9 | 4.2 | 7.7 | 16.4 | 9.5 | 16.2 | 10.1 | 1.6 | 7.1 | 4.0 | 8.9 | 8.0 | 8.7 | 6.7 | 2.1 |
| 1992 | 8.2 | 9.5 | 4.5 | 8.7 | 18.2 | 10.0 | 17.8 | 10.3 | 1.9 | 7.2 | 3.9 | 10.2 | 8.6 | 9.4 | 7.4 | 2.2 |
| 1993 | 9.4 | 10.4 | 5.6 | 9.8 | 21.5 | 10.8 | 18.4 | 11.1 | 2.6 | 8.8 | 5.0 | 10.5 | 9.4 | 10.5 | 6.8 | 2.5 |
| 1994 | 10.3 | 9.9 | 6.9 | 10.1 | 23.3 | 11.5 | 17.8 | 12.0 | 3.0 | 10.2 | 6.5 | 9.9 | 10.0 | 11.3 | 6.3 | 3.1 |

EUR 12−: incl. WD
a EUR 12−: excl. GR, E, P.
b OECD.

**Table H1** Gross national saving.

(Percentage of gross domestic product at market prices)

| | B | DK | WD | D | GR | E | F | IRL | I | L | NL | P | UK | EUR 12- | EUR 12+ | USA | J |
|---|---|---|---|---|---|---|---|---|---|---|---|---|---|---|---|---|---|
| 1960 | 19.4 | 24.9 | 28.9 | : | 12.7 | 24.3 | 25.9 | 15.3 | 29.7 | 35.8 | 30.8 | 18.3 | 18.0 | 24.8 | : | 19.3 | 33.4 |
| 1961 | 21.1 | 23.4 | 28.2 | : | 16.8 | 25.6 | 25.4 | 16.8 | 31.1 | 32.9 | 29.3 | 14.1 | 18.2 | 24.9 | : | 18.7 | 35.2 |
| 1962 | 21.9 | 22.9 | 27.3 | : | 17.6 | 26.0 | 26.0 | 16.6 | 30.2 | 32.1 | 27.4 | 18.8 | 17.5 | 24.6 | : | 19.4 | 34.3 |
| 1963 | 20.5 | 22.9 | 26.4 | : | 20.2 | 24.6 | 25.3 | 16.6 | 30.3 | | 25.9 | 20.5 | 17.4 | 23.8 | : | 19.8 | 32.7 |
| 1964 | 24.0 | 24.0 | 28.3 | : | 20.3 | 26.1 | 26.4 | 17.1 | 27.7 | 32.4 | 27.8 | 25.2 | 19.2 | 25.2 | : | 20.3 | 34.1 |
| 1965 | 23.7 | 24.6 | 27.2 | : | 21.0 | 25.1 | 27.1 | 18.1 | 27.4 | 30.8 | 27.5 | 26.1 | 19.7 | 25.2 | : | 21.2 | 33.0 |
| 1966 | 23.6 | 22.9 | 26.8 | : | 21.4 | 25.3 | 27.2 | 17.8 | 26.5 | 30.0 | 26.9 | 26.4 | 19.5 | 24.9 | : | 20.8 | 33.7 |
| 1967 | 24.2 | 21.8 | 25.2 | : | 19.8 | 24.5 | 27.1 | 19.7 | 26.5 | 28.3 | 27.3 | 29.9 | 18.6 | 24.3 | : | 19.7 | 35.3 |
| 1968 | 23.3 | 22.3 | 26.8 | : | 20.4 | 25.2 | 26.0 | 19.4 | 27.5 | 29.9 | 28.1 | 26.3 | 19.3 | 24.9 | : | 19.6 | 37.6 |
| 1969 | 24.4 | 23.0 | 27.6 | : | 23.1 | 27.3 | 26.4 | 19.6 | 28.4 | 35.0 | 27.5 | 27.5 | 20.9 | 25.9 | : | 19.9 | 38.9 |
| 1970 | 27.1 | 21.8 | 28.1 | : | 23.4 | 27.3 | 27.6 | 19.2 | 28.2 | 41.3 | 27.0 | 31.2 | 21.1 | 26.4 | : | 18.5 | 40.0 |
| 1961-70 | 23.4 | 23.0 | 27.2 | : | 20.4 | 25.7 | 26.5 | 18.1 | 28.1 | 32.3 | 27.5 | 24.6 | 19.1 | 25.0 | : | 19.8 | 35.5 |
| 1971 | 25.6 | 22.4 | 27.1 | : | 26.1 | 27.1 | 27.1 | 18.9 | 26.4 | 36.3 | 26.7 | 29.9 | 20.3 | 25.6 | : | 19.3 | 38.3 |
| 1972 | 25.5 | 24.4 | 26.5 | : | 29.2 | 27.6 | 27.3 | 21.5 | 25.6 | 39.1 | 27.4 | 36.2 | 19.2 | 25.4 | : | 19.6 | 37.8 |
| 1973 | 24.6 | 24.4 | 26.7 | : | 32.3 | 28.3 | 27.8 | 21.9 | 25.6 | 43.5 | 28.9 | 35.8 | 19.9 | 26.0 | : | 21.3 | 38.1 |
| 1974 | 25.3 | 22.1 | 24.7 | : | 25.2 | 26.9 | 26.8 | 18.0 | 26.0 | 47.7 | 27.9 | 22.9 | 16.7 | 24.4 | : | 20.3 | 36.4 |
| 1975 | 21.8 | 19.4 | 21.0 | : | 23.6 | 25.8 | 24.3 | 20.5 | 23.8 | 39.9 | 23.6 | 13.2 | 15.5 | 21.7 | : | 18.6 | 32.7 |
| 1976 | 22.5 | 19.1 | 22.4 | : | 25.5 | 23.2 | 24.5 | 18.8 | 25.7 | 44.3 | 24.0 | 15.6 | 16.7 | 22.6 | : | 19.3 | 32.5 |
| 1977 | 20.8 | 18.9 | 21.7 | : | 24.7 | 23.5 | 24.4 | 21.1 | 26.0 | 42.1 | 22.8 | 19.7 | 19.0 | 22.6 | : | 20.1 | 32.4 |
| 1978 | 20.6 | 18.8 | 22.6 | : | 24.6 | 24.2 | 24.6 | 20.8 | 26.3 | 44.6 | 21.4 | 24.8 | 19.4 | 23.0 | : | 21.5 | 32.6 |
| 1979 | 18.6 | 16.6 | 22.8 | : | 26.2 | 23.0 | 24.6 | 18.4 | 26.3 | 43.8 | 20.7 | 27.8 | 19.8 | 22.9 | : | 21.9 | 31.6 |
| 1980 | 17.5 | 14.9 | 21.7 | : | 24.9 | 21.1 | 23.6 | 15.1 | 24.7 | 44.2 | 20.5 | 26.9 | 18.0 | 21.6 | : | 20.3 | 31.2 |
| 1971-80 | 22.3 | 20.1 | 23.7 | : | 26.2 | 25.1 | 25.5 | 19.5 | 25.6 | 42.5 | 24.4 | 25.3 | 18.5 | 23.6 | : | 20.2 | 34.4 |
| 1981 | 14.1 | 12.4 | 20.3 | : | 20.3 | 18.9 | 21.1 | 12.8 | 22.5 | 45.8 | 20.9 | 22.4 | 17.1 | 19.8 | : | 21.2 | 31.6 |
| 1982 | 13.7 | 12.1 | 20.2 | : | 20.2 | 18.9 | 19.7 | 16.1 | 22.0 | 59.3 | 21.5 | 20.6 | 17.0 | 19.4 | : | 18.3 | 30.6 |
| 1983 | 14.7 | 13.4 | 21.2 | : | 19.7 | 18.8 | 19.1 | 15.9 | 22.2 | 63.8 | 21.9 | 20.0 | 17.1 | 19.7 | : | 17.4 | 29.9 |
| 1984 | 15.8 | 15.1 | 21.7 | : | 20.0 | 20.4 | 19.0 | 15.9 | 22.3 | 63.8 | 23.7 | 18.8 | 17.2 | 20.1 | : | 18.7 | 30.9 |
| 1985 | 15.2 | 14.9 | 22.0 | : | 17.5 | 20.6 | 18.9 | 15.0 | 21.6 | 64.1 | 24.3 | 21.0 | 17.6 | 20.1 | : | 17.3 | 31.8 |
| 1986 | 17.2 | 16.1 | 23.8 | : | 16.5 | 21.6 | 20.1 | 14.9 | 21.4 | 62.2 | 24.4 | 24.7 | 16.0 | 20.8 | : | 16.1 | 32.1 |
| 1987 | 17.5 | 16.1 | 23.5 | : | 15.2 | 21.6 | 20.0 | 16.3 | 20.8 | 55.1 | 22.6 | 27.1 | 15.9 | 20.5 | : | 15.6 | 32.3 |
| 1988 | 19.7 | 16.6 | 24.3 | : | 16.2 | 22.6 | 21.1 | 15.6 | 20.8 | 57.8 | 24.2 | 25.3 | 15.5 | 21.0 | : | 16.0 | 33.4 |
| 1989 | 21.5 | 16.9 | 25.7 | : | 13.3 | 21.9 | 21.8 | 16.2 | 20.0 | 61.6 | 26.1 | 26.8 | 15.5 | 21.4 | : | 16.6 | 33.8 |
| 1990 | 21.4 | 17.8 | 25.0 | : | 12.3 | 21.8 | 21.4 | 19.9 | 19.6 | 62.5 | 26.0 | 26.6 | 14.7 | 21.1 | : | 15.7 | 34.1 |
| 1981-90 | 17.1 | 15.1 | 22.8 | : | 17.1 | 20.7 | 20.2 | 15.9 | 21.3 | 59.6 | 23.6 | 23.3 | 16.4 | 20.4 | : | 17.3 | 32.0 |
| 1991 | 21.1 | 17.4 | 23.1 | 22.2 | 14.1 | 21.0 | 20.7 | 20.9 | 18.6 | 59.4 | 24.7 | 25.4 | 13.5 | 20.0 | 19.8 | 15.4 | 34.4 |
| 1992 | 20.9 | 18.2 | 22.7 | 22.0 | 14.1 | 19.1 | 19.8 | 19.2 | 17.2 | 60.2 | 24.0 | 25.3 | 12.8 | 19.2 | 19.1 | 14.6 | 34.4 |
| 1993 | 20.8 | 17.3 | 21.0 | 20.7 | 14.1 | 19.1 | 18.3 | 19.4 | 18.0 | 58.6 | 23.5 | 24.1 | 12.6 | 18.6 | 18.6 | 14.8 | 33.4 |
| 1994 | 20.7 | 17.9 | 21.7 | 21.7 | 14.0 | 19.6 | 18.4 | 19.0 | 18.6 | 57.9 | 23.8 | 24.1 | 13.7 | 19.1 | 19.2 | 15.7 | 32.3 |

EUR 12-: incl. WD; EUR 12+: incl. D.

**Table H2** Gross private saving.

(Percentage of gross domestic product at market prices)

| | B | DK | WD | D | GR | E | F | IRL | I | L | NL | P | UK | EUR 12- | EUR 12+ | USA | J |
|---|---|---|---|---|---|---|---|---|---|---|---|---|---|---|---|---|---|
| 1960 | 20.2 | 19.0 | 21.6 | : | 9.0 | : | 21.9 | 15.2 | 27.1 | 29.2 | 25.5 | 15.5 | 17.6 | : | : | 16.2 | : |
| 1961 | 20.2 | 20.2 | 20.1 | : | 12.1 | : | 21.1 | 17.0 | 28.3 | 24.7 | 23.7 | 12.8 | 17.3 | : | : | 16.9 | : |
| 1962 | 20.7 | 18.9 | 19.7 | : | 12.8 | : | 22.6 | 16.8 | 27.6 | 26.3 | 23.1 | 17.1 | 15.5 | : | : | 17.5 | : |
| 1963 | 19.9 | 17.7 | 19.7 | : | 15.7 | : | 21.7 | 16.2 | 25.6 | 25.5 | 22.6 | 18.4 | 16.9 | : | : | 17.0 | : |
| 1964 | 21.7 | 18.8 | 21.2 | : | 16.1 | : | 21.8 | 16.8 | 25.2 | 27.2 | 24.5 | 23.0 | 17.6 | : | : | 18.1 | : |
| 1965 | 22.6 | 19.1 | 21.9 | : | 17.9 | : | 22.5 | 17.8 | 28.0 | 25.5 | 23.8 | 23.0 | 17.4 | : | : | 18.5 | : |
| 1966 | 21.6 | 16.8 | 21.4 | : | 17.7 | : | 22.5 | 16.3 | 27.2 | 25.5 | 23.0 | 22.9 | 16.4 | : | : | 18.5 | : |
| 1967 | 22.1 | 17.1 | 21.6 | : | 17.2 | : | 22.9 | 18.2 | 25.5 | 26.3 | 23.6 | 27.0 | 15.5 | : | : | 18.7 | : |
| 1968 | 22.1 | 16.7 | 22.5 | : | 16.6 | : | 22.6 | 18.0 | 26.9 | 28.3 | 23.5 | 22.7 | 15.0 | : | : | 17.3 | : |
| 1969 | 22.7 | 16.9 | 21.1 | : | 18.4 | : | 21.7 | 18.3 | 28.3 | 31.2 | 22.8 | 22.5 | 14.1 | : | : | 16.2 | : |
| 1970 | 24.8 | 11.8 | 21.8 | : | 19.0 | 23.3 | 22.5 | 17.4 | 27.7 | 33.6 | 22.6 | 25.6 | 13.1 | 21.3 | : | 16.2 | 32.9 |
| 1961-70 | 21.8 | 17.4 | 21.1 | : | 16.4 | : | 22.2 | 17.3 | 27.0 | 27.4 | 23.3 | 21.5 | 15.9 | : | : | 17.6 | : |
| 1971 | 23.5 | 12.9 | 21.1 | : | 22.2 | 23.9 | 22.4 | 16.9 | 27.9 | 28.4 | 22.0 | 24.7 | 14.1 | 21.3 | : | 18.7 | 31.1 |
| 1972 | 24.5 | 15.6 | 21.3 | : | 24.7 | 24.0 | 22.6 | 20.0 | 29.2 | 31.3 | 22.6 | 31.8 | 16.1 | 22.2 | : | 17.5 | 31.3 |
| 1973 | 23.7 | 14.9 | 20.1 | : | 28.0 | 24.0 | 23.4 | 20.9 | 29.0 | 33.6 | 23.1 | 31.4 | 17.3 | 22.3 | : | 18.5 | 30.9 |
| 1974 | 23.6 | 14.2 | 20.3 | : | 23.2 | 23.5 | 22.5 | 19.2 | 29.1 | 36.4 | 23.6 | 21.6 | 15.0 | 21.7 | : | 17.9 | 29.7 |
| 1975 | 22.3 | 16.1 | 21.1 | : | 22.9 | 22.3 | 22.3 | 26.1 | 29.9 | 31.2 | 21.0 | 13.9 | 15.0 | 21.6 | : | 20.0 | 29.1 |
| 1976 | 23.6 | 14.7 | 20.4 | : | 23.4 | 20.4 | 20.5 | 21.5 | 30.0 | 35.1 | 21.6 | 16.8 | 16.8 | 21.3 | : | 19.1 | 30.1 |
| 1977 | 22.2 | 15.2 | 18.9 | : | 23.8 | 20.4 | 21.5 | 23.2 | 29.6 | 32.2 | 20.4 | 20.0 | 18.4 | 21.2 | : | 18.8 | 29.6 |
| 1978 | 22.6 | 14.9 | 20.1 | : | 24.4 | 22.8 | 23.3 | 24.6 | 31.0 | 32.9 | 20.1 | 27.1 | 20.3 | 22.6 | : | 19.2 | 30.7 |
| 1979 | 21.3 | 14.0 | 20.2 | : | 25.4 | 21.9 | 21.8 | 23.3 | 30.7 | 35.6 | 19.8 | 29.1 | 20.0 | 22.1 | : | 19.2 | 28.7 |
| 1980 | 21.8 | 14.1 | 19.2 | : | 25.0 | 20.6 | 19.9 | 20.2 | 29.3 | 36.0 | 19.0 | 29.1 | 18.5 | 21.0 | : | 19.2 | 28.0 |
| 1971-80 | 22.9 | 14.7 | 20.3 | : | 24.3 | 22.4 | 22.0 | 21.6 | 29.6 | 33.3 | 21.3 | 24.6 | 17.1 | 21.7 | : | 18.8 | 29.9 |
| 1981 | 22.3 | 15.2 | 19.2 | : | 27.1 | 18.8 | 19.4 | 19.2 | 29.5 | 40.3 | 20.6 | 26.6 | 17.6 | 20.7 | : | 20.0 | 28.0 |
| 1982 | 20.6 | 17.5 | 19.1 | : | 24.9 | 19.4 | 18.8 | 23.5 | 29.1 | 52.4 | 23.2 | 25.8 | 17.3 | 20.7 | : | 19.6 | 27.2 |
| 1983 | 22.5 | 17.4 | 19.8 | : | 24.3 | 18.7 | 18.7 | 22.1 | 29.0 | 53.4 | 23.3 | 24.2 | 17.8 | 21.0 | : | 19.4 | 26.9 |
| 1984 | 21.8 | 16.5 | 19.7 | : | 25.4 | 21.1 | 18.4 | 21.1 | 29.4 | 53.5 | 24.7 | 26.9 | 18.3 | 21.4 | : | 19.6 | 27.0 |
| 1985 | 21.0 | 14.1 | 19.4 | : | 26.6 | 22.0 | 18.4 | 21.6 | 28.5 | 51.3 | 23.4 | 27.3 | 18.1 | 21.0 | : | 18.2 | 26.9 |
| 1986 | 23.7 | 10.4 | 21.4 | : | 23.8 | 22.1 | 19.5 | 21.5 | 28.2 | 52.0 | 24.6 | 28.3 | 16.6 | 21.6 | : | 17.1 | 27.3 |
| 1987 | 22.6 | 11.4 | 21.8 | : | 23.1 | 19.9 | 18.5 | 21.8 | 27.0 | 46.1 | 23.6 | 29.8 | 15.6 | 20.9 | : | 15.8 | 26.0 |
| 1988 | 23.9 | 13.4 | 23.0 | : | 26.3 | 20.8 | 19.2 | 18.3 | 26.9 | 47.4 | 24.5 | 26.4 | 13.4 | 21.0 | : | 16.0 | 25.9 |
| 1989 | 25.8 | 15.1 | 22.1 | : | 26.1 | 19.0 | 19.4 | 16.3 | 25.5 | 50.0 | 27.1 | 26.0 | 12.9 | 20.6 | : | 15.9 | 25.4 |
| 1990 | 25.1 | 17.5 | 23.7 | : | 27.2 | 19.7 | 18.8 | 20.7 | 25.8 | 54.2 | 27.6 | 27.6 | 12.6 | 21.2 | : | 16.0 | 25.1 |
| 1981-90 | 22.9 | 14.8 | 20.9 | : | 25.5 | 20.2 | 18.9 | 20.6 | 27.9 | 50.1 | 24.3 | 26.9 | 16.0 | 21.0 | : | 17.8 | 26.5 |
| 1991 | 25.7 | 18.2 | 22.0 | 20.9 | 24.7 | 20.2 | 19.3 | 22.0 | 24.6 | 51.2 | 24.3 | 27.3 | 13.4 | 20.7 | 20.4 | 16.5 | 25.3 |
| 1992 | 25.5 | 18.0 | 21.1 | 20.2 | 24.6 | 18.4 | 20.3 | 20.4 | 24.7 | 53.5 | 24.4 | 25.2 | 16.3 | 21.0 | 20.8 | 16.8 | : |
| 1993 | 25.6 | 18.9 | 20.1 | 19.7 | 27.4 | 21.0 | 20.4 | 20.1 | 23.9 | 50.8 | 23.4 | 27.0 | 17.6 | 21.0 | 20.9 | 15.9 | : |
| 1994 | 24.4 | 19.6 | 20.6 | 20.9 | 28.6 | 21.6 | 20.2 | 19.5 | 24.3 | 51.8 | 24.0 | 26.9 | 17.2 | 21.1 | 21.2 | 15.7 | : |

EUR 12-: incl. WD; EUR 12+: incl. D.

**Table H3**   Gross saving; general government.

(Percentage of gross domestic product at market prices)

| | B | DK | WD | D | GR | E[a] | F | IRL | I | L[b] | NL[c] | P | UK | EUR 12− | EUR 12+ | USA | J |
|---|---|---|---|---|---|---|---|---|---|---|---|---|---|---|---|---|---|
| 1960 | −0.8 | 5.9 | 7.3 | : | 3.7 | : | 4.1 | 0.1 | 2.6 | 6.7 | 5.3 | 2.8 | 0.4 | : | : | 3.1 | : |
| 1961 | 1.0 | 3.2 | 8.0 | : | 4.7 | : | 4.3 | −0.2 | 2.8 | 8.2 | 5.6 | 1.3 | 0.9 | : | : | 1.7 | : |
| 1962 | 1.2 | 3.9 | 7.5 | : | 4.8 | : | 3.4 | −0.2 | 2.6 | 5.9 | 4.3 | 1.7 | 2.0 | : | : | 2.0 | : |
| 1963 | 0.6 | 5.3 | 6.7 | : | 4.5 | : | 3.5 | 0.4 | 2.0 | 4.8 | 3.3 | 2.0 | 0.6 | : | : | 2.8 | : |
| 1964 | 2.4 | 5.2 | 7.1 | : | 4.2 | : | 4.6 | 0.3 | 2.4 | 5.2 | 3.3 | 2.2 | 1.6 | : | : | 2.2 | : |
| 1965 | 1.1 | 5.5 | 5.3 | : | 3.1 | : | 4.7 | 0.3 | −0.5 | 5.3 | 3.7 | 3.1 | 2.4 | : | : | 2.7 | : |
| 1966 | 2.0 | 6.2 | 5.3 | : | 3.7 | : | 4.7 | 1.5 | −0.6 | 4.4 | 3.9 | 3.5 | 3.1 | : | : | 2.3 | : |
| 1967 | 2.1 | 4.7 | 3.7 | : | 2.6 | : | 4.2 | 1.5 | 1.0 | 2.1 | 3.7 | 2.9 | 3.1 | : | : | 1.0 | : |
| 1968 | 1.2 | 5.6 | 4.2 | : | 3.8 | : | 3.4 | 1.5 | 0.6 | 1.6 | 4.6 | 3.5 | 4.2 | : | : | 2.3 | : |
| 1969 | 1.7 | 6.0 | 6.5 | : | 4.7 | : | 4.6 | 1.3 | 0.1 | 3.8 | 4.7 | 4.9 | 6.7 | : | : | 3.7 | : |
| 1970 | 2.2 | 10.0 | 6.3 | : | 4.4 | 4.0 | 5.2 | 1.7 | 0.5 | 7.7 | 4.4 | 5.5 | 7.9 | 5.1 | : | 1.3 | 7.1 |
| 1961-70 | 1.5 | 5.6 | 6.1 | : | 4.0 | : | 4.3 | 0.8 | 1.1 | 4.9 | 4.2 | 3.1 | 3.3 | : | : | 2.2 | : |
| 1971 | 2.0 | 9.4 | 6.1 | : | 3.9 | 3.2 | 4.7 | 2.0 | −1.6 | 7.9 | 4.7 | 5.2 | 6.3 | 4.3 | : | 0.6 | 7.2 |
| 1972 | 1.0 | 8.8 | 5.2 | : | 4.6 | 3.7 | 4.8 | 1.5 | −3.6 | 7.7 | 4.8 | 4.4 | 3.1 | 3.2 | : | 2.1 | 6.4 |
| 1973 | 0.9 | 9.5 | 6.6 | : | 4.3 | 4.3 | 4.4 | 1.0 | −3.4 | 9.9 | 5.7 | 4.4 | 2.6 | 3.7 | : | 2.9 | 7.2 |
| 1974 | 1.7 | 7.9 | 4.5 | : | 2.0 | 3.4 | 4.3 | −1.2 | −3.2 | 11.3 | 4.3 | 1.3 | 1.7 | 2.8 | : | 2.4 | 6.7 |
| 1975 | −0.5 | 3.3 | −0.1 | : | 0.7 | 3.5 | 2.1 | −5.7 | −6.1 | 8.7 | 2.6 | −0.7 | 0.6 | 0.1 | : | −1.4 | 3.6 |
| 1976 | −1.1 | 4.3 | 1.9 | : | 2.1 | 2.8 | 4.1 | −2.7 | −4.3 | 9.2 | 2.4 | −1.3 | −0.1 | 1.3 | : | 0.3 | 2.5 |
| 1977 | −1.4 | 3.7 | 2.8 | : | 0.8 | 3.1 | 2.9 | −2.1 | −3.6 | 9.8 | 2.4 | −0.3 | 0.6 | 1.4 | : | 1.3 | 2.8 |
| 1978 | −2.0 | 3.9 | 2.5 | : | 0.2 | 1.3 | 1.3 | −3.8 | −4.7 | 11.7 | 1.4 | −2.3 | −0.8 | 0.4 | : | 2.3 | 1.9 |
| 1979 | −2.7 | 2.6 | 2.6 | : | 0.9 | 1.1 | 2.8 | −4.9 | −4.4 | 8.1 | 0.9 | −1.4 | −0.2 | 0.7 | : | 2.7 | 2.9 |
| 1980 | −4.3 | 0.8 | 2.4 | : | −0.1 | 0.6 | 3.8 | −5.2 | −4.5 | 8.2 | 1.5 | −2.3 | −0.5 | 0.6 | : | 1.1 | 3.2 |
| 1971-80 | −0.7 | 5.4 | 3.5 | : | 1.9 | 2.7 | 3.5 | −2.1 | −3.9 | 9.3 | 3.1 | 0.7 | 1.3 | 1.9 | : | 1.4 | 4.4 |
| 1981 | −8.2 | −2.7 | 1.1 | : | −6.8 | 0.1 | 1.7 | −6.4 | −7.0 | 5.6 | 0.2 | −4.2 | −0.5 | −1.0 | : | 1.2 | 3.7 |
| 1982 | −6.9 | −5.4 | 1.1 | : | −4.7 | −0.5 | 0.9 | 7.4 | 7.0 | 6.9 | −1.7 | −5.2 | −0.4 | −1.3 | : | −1 3 | 3 4 |
| 1983 | −7.8 | −4.0 | 1.4 | : | −4.6 | 0.0 | 0.4 | −6.2 | −6.8 | 10.4 | −1.4 | −4.2 | −0.7 | −1.3 | : | −2.0 | 3.0 |
| 1984 | −6.0 | −1.4 | 2.0 | : | −5.4 | −0.7 | 0.6 | −5.2 | −7.1 | 10.3 | −1.0 | −8.1 | −1.1 | −1.3 | : | −0.9 | 3.9 |
| 1985 | −5.8 | 0.9 | 2.6 | : | −9.1 | −1.4 | 0.5 | −6.6 | −6.9 | 12.8 | 0.9 | −6.3 | −0.5 | −0.9 | : | −0.9 | 4.9 |
| 1986 | −6.6 | 5.7 | 2.4 | : | −7.4 | −0.5 | 0.6 | −6.6 | −6.8 | 10.2 | −0.3 | −3.6 | −0.6 | −0.8 | : | −1.0 | 4.7 |
| 1987 | −5.1 | 4.7 | 1.7 | : | −7.9 | 1.7 | 1.5 | −5.5 | −6.2 | 9.0 | −0.9 | −2.7 | 0.3 | −0.4 | : | −0.2 | 6.3 |
| 1988 | −4.2 | 3.1 | 1.3 | : | −10.1 | 1.8 | 1.9 | −2.7 | −6.1 | 10.4 | −0.4 | −1.1 | 2.2 | −0.1 | : | 0.0 | 7.5 |
| 1989 | −4.3 | 1.8 | 3.6 | : | −12.8 | 2.9 | 2.4 | −0.1 | −5.5 | 11.6 | −1.0 | 0.9 | 2.7 | 0.8 | : | 0.7 | 8.5 |
| 1990 | −3.7 | 0.3 | 1.3 | : | −14.8 | 2.1 | 2.5 | −0.8 | −6.2 | 8.3 | −1.6 | −0.9 | 2.2 | −0.1 | : | −0.3 | 9.0 |
| 1981-90 | −5.9 | 0.3 | 1.8 | : | −8.4 | 0.5 | 1.3 | −4.7 | −6.6 | 9.6 | −0.7 | −3.5 | 0.3 | −0.6 | : | −0.5 | 5.5 |
| 1991 | −4.5 | −0.7 | 1.0 | 1.4 | −10.5 | 0.9 | 1.5 | −1.0 | −6.1 | 8.2 | 0.4 | −2.0 | 0.2 | −0.7 | −0.6 | −1.1 | 9.5 |
| 1992 | −4.6 | 0.1 | 1.6 | 1.7 | −10.6 | 0.7 | −0.5 | −1.1 | −7.5 | 6.8 | −0.4 | 0.1 | −3.5 | −1.8 | −1.6 | −2.1 | : |
| 1993 | −4.8 | −1.6 | 0.9 | 0.9 | −13.3 | −2.0 | −2.1 | −0.7 | −5.9 | 7.8 | 0.1 | −2.9 | −5.0 | −2.4 | −2.3 | −1.1 | : |
| 1994 | −3.6 | −1.7 | 1.1 | 0.7 | −14.6 | −2.0 | −1.8 | −0.5 | −5.7 | 6.1 | −0.3 | −2.8 | −3.5 | −2.0 | −2.0 | −0.1 | : |

EUR 12−: incl. WD; EUR 12+: incl. D.        b Break in 1990/91.
a Break in 1979/80 and 1984/85.       c Break in 1968/69 and 1984/85.

**Table I1**   Nominal short-term interest rates.

(%)

| | B | DK | WD | GR | E | F | IRL | I | NL | P | UK | EUR 12− | USA | J |
|---|---|---|---|---|---|---|---|---|---|---|---|---|---|---|
| 1960 | : | : | 5.1 | : | : | 4.1 | : | 3.5 | 2.1 | : | : | : | : | : |
| 1961 | 4.6 | 6.3 | 3.6 | : | : | 3.7 | : | 3.5 | 1.1 | : | 5.2 | 4.0 | 2.4 | : |
| 1962 | 3.4 | 6.5 | 3.4 | : | : | 3.6 | : | 3.5 | 1.9 | : | 4.1 | 3.6 | 2.8 | : |
| 1963 | 3.6 | 6.1 | 4.0 | : | : | 4.0 | : | 3.5 | 2.0 | : | 3.7 | 3.7 | 3.2 | : |
| 1964 | 4.9 | 6.2 | 4.1 | : | : | 4.7 | : | 3.5 | 3.5 | : | 5.0 | 4.4 | 3.6 | : |
| 1965 | 5.0 | 6.5 | 5.1 | : | : | 4.2 | : | 3.5 | 4.0 | : | 6.8 | 5.0 | 4.0 | : |
| 1966 | 5.6 | 6.5 | 6.6 | : | : | 4.8 | : | 3.5 | 4.9 | 3.0 | 7.0 | 5.6 | 4.9 | : |
| 1967 | 5.5 | 6.6 | 4.3 | : | : | 4.8 | : | 3.5 | 4.7 | 3.1 | 6.3 | 4.8 | 4.3 | : |
| 1968 | 4.5 | 6.6 | 3.8 | : | : | 6.2 | : | 3.5 | 4.6 | 3.4 | 7.9 | 5.3 | 5.4 | : |
| 1969 | 7.3 | 8.2 | 5.8 | : | : | 9.3 | : | 3.7 | 5.7 | 3.4 | 9.2 | 6.9 | 6.7 | : |
| 1970 | 8.1 | 9.0 | 9.4 | : | : | 8.6 | : | 5.3 | 6.2 | 4.0 | 8.1 | 7.8 | 6.3 | : |
| 1961-70 | 5.2 | 6.8 | 5.0 | : | : | 5.4 | : | 3.7 | 3.8 | : | 6.3 | 5.1 | 4.3 | : |
| 1971 | 5.4 | 7.6 | 7.1 | : | : | 6.0 | 6.6 | 5.7 | 4.5 | 4.3 | 6.2 | 6.2 | 4.3 | 6.5 |
| 1972 | 4.2 | 7.3 | 5.7 | : | : | 5.3 | 7.1 | 5.2 | 2.7 | 4.4 | 6.8 | 5.5 | 4.2 | 5.2 |
| 1973 | 6.6 | 7.6 | 12.2 | : | : | 9.3 | 12.2 | 7.0 | 7.5 | 4.4 | 11.8 | 9.8 | 7.2 | 8.3 |
| 1974 | 10.6 | 10.0 | 9.8 | : | : | 13.0 | 14.6 | 14.9 | 10.4 | 5.3 | 13.4 | 12.2 | 7.9 | 14.7 |
| 1975 | 7.0 | 8.0 | 4.9 | : | : | 7.6 | 10.9 | 10.4 | 5.4 | 6.8 | 10.6 | 7.9 | 5.8 | 10.1 |
| 1976 | 10.1 | 8.9 | 4.3 | : | : | 8.7 | 11.7 | 16.0 | 7.4 | 8.4 | 11.6 | 9.5 | 5.0 | 7.3 |
| 1977 | 7.3 | 14.5 | 4.3 | : | 15.5 | 9.1 | 8.4 | 14.0 | 4.8 | 11.1 | 8.0 | 9.0 | 5.3 | 6.4 |
| 1978 | 7.3 | 15.4 | 3.7 | : | 17.6 | 7.8 | 9.9 | 11.5 | 7.0 | 15.5 | 9.4 | 8.8 | 7.4 | 5.1 |
| 1979 | 10.9 | 12.5 | 6.9 | : | 15.5 | 9.7 | 16.0 | 12.0 | 9.6 | 16.1 | 13.9 | 10.9 | 10.1 | 5.9 |
| 1980 | 14.2 | 16.9 | 9.5 | 16.4 | 16.5 | 12.0 | 16.2 | 16.9 | 10.6 | 16.3 | 16.8 | 13.8 | 11.6 | 10.7 |
| 1971-80 | 8.4 | 10.9 | 6.9 | : | : | 8.8 | 11.4 | 11.3 | 7.0 | 9.3 | 10.8 | 9.4 | 6.9 | 8.0 |
| 1981 | 15.6 | 14.9 | 12.4 | 16.8 | 16.2 | 15.3 | 16.7 | 19.3 | 11.8 | 16.0 | 14.1 | 15.1 | 14.0 | 7.4 |
| 1982 | 14.1 | 16.4 | 8.8 | 18.9 | 16.3 | 14.6 | 17.5 | 19.9 | 8.2 | 16.8 | 12.2 | 13.8 | 10.6 | 6.9 |
| 1983 | 10.5 | 12.0 | 5.8 | 16.6 | 20.1 | 12.5 | 14.0 | 18.3 | 5.7 | 20.9 | 10.1 | 12.0 | 8.7 | 6.5 |
| 1984 | 11.5 | 11.5 | 6.0 | 15.7 | 14.9 | 11.7 | 13.2 | 17.3 | 6.1 | 22.5 | 10.0 | 11.3 | 9.5 | 6.3 |
| 1985 | 9.6 | 10.0 | 5.4 | 17.0 | 12.2 | 10.0 | 12.0 | 15.0 | 6.3 | 21.0 | 12.2 | 10.5 | 7.5 | 6.5 |
| 1986 | 8.1 | 9.1 | 4.6 | 19.8 | 11.7 | 7.7 | 12.4 | 12.8 | 5.7 | 15.6 | 10.9 | 9.1 | 6.0 | 5.0 |
| 1987 | 7.1 | 9.9 | 4.0 | 14.9 | 15.8 | 8.3 | 11.1 | 11.4 | 5.4 | 13.9 | 9.7 | 8.8 | 5.9 | 3.9 |
| 1988 | 6.7 | 8.3 | 4.3 | 15.9 | 11.6 | 7.9 | 8.1 | 11.3 | 4.8 | 13.0 | 10.3 | 8.5 | 6.9 | 4.0 |
| 1989 | 8.7 | 9.7 | 7.1 | 18.7 | 15.0 | 9.4 | 9.8 | 12.7 | 7.4 | 14.9 | 13.9 | 10.9 | 8.4 | 5.4 |
| 1990 | 9.8 | 11.0 | 8.4 | 19.9 | 15.2 | 10.3 | 11.4 | 12.3 | 8.7 | 16.9 | 14.8 | 11.6 | 7.8 | 7.8 |
| 1981-90 | 10.2 | 11.3 | 6.7 | 17.4 | 14.9 | 10.8 | 12.6 | 15.0 | 7.0 | 17.2 | 11.8 | 11.1 | 8.5 | 6.0 |
| 1991 | 9.4 | 9.9 | 9.2 | 22.7 | 13.2 | 9.6 | 10.4 | 12.2 | 9.3 | 17.7 | 11.5 | 10.9 | 5.5 | 7.4 |
| 1992 | 9.4 | 11.5 | 9.5 | 23.5 | 13.3 | 10.4 | 12.4 | 14.0 | 9.4 | 16.2 | 9.6 | 11.2 | 3.5 | 4.4 |
| 1993 | 8.2 | 10.8 | 7.2 | 23.5 | 11.7 | 8.6 | 9.3 | 10.2 | 6.9 | 12.2 | 5.9 | 8.6 | 3.1 | 3.0 |
| 1994 | 5.7 | 6.0 | 5.4 | 19.3 | 7.9 | 5.8 | 5.8 | 7.9 | 5.2 | 10.6 | 5.2 | 6.4 | 4.3 | 2.2 |

EUR: PPS weighted. EUR 12−: incl. WD.
B: 1961-84 four-month certificates of Foods des rentes; 1985-88 three-month Treasury certificates; 1989-1993 three-month interbank deposits. DK: 1961-76 discount rate; 1977-88 call money; 1989-93 three-month interbank deposits. D: three-month interbank deposits. GR: 1960-April 1980 credit for working capital to industry; May 1980-87 interbank sight deposits; 1988-93: one-month interbank deposits. E: three-month interbank deposits. F: 1960-68 call money; 1969-81 one-month sale and repurchase agreements on private sector paper, 1982-1993 three-month sale and repurchase agreements on private sector paper (PIBOR). IRL: 1961-70 three-month interbank deposits in London; 1971-93 three-month interbank deposits in Dublin. I: 1960-70 12-month Treasury bills; 1971-84 interbank sight deposits; 1985-93 three-month interbank deposits. NL: 1960-September 1972 three-month Treasury bills; October 1972-93 three-month interbank deposits. P: 1966-July 1985 six-month deposits; August 1985-93 three-month Treasury bills. UK: 1961-September 1964 three-month Treasury bills; October 1964-93 three-month interbank deposits. EUR 12: weighted geometric mean; weights: gross domestic product at current market prices and PPS. USA: three-month Treasury bills. J: bonds traded with three-month repurchase agreements; from January 1989 three-months Certificates of Deposit.

***Table 12***  Nominal long-term interest rates.

(%)

| | B | DK | WD | GR | E | F | IRL | I | L | NL | P | UK | EUR 12- | USA | J |
|---|---|---|---|---|---|---|---|---|---|---|---|---|---|---|---|
| 1960 | : | : | 6.3 | : | : | 5.7 | : | 5.3 | : | 4.2 | : | 5.4 | : | : | : |
| 1961 | 5.9 | 6.6 | 5.9 | : | : | 5.5 | : | 5.2 | : | 3.9 | : | 6.3 | 5.7 | 3.9 | : |
| 1962 | 5.2 | 6.6 | 5.9 | : | : | 5.4 | : | 5.8 | : | 4.2 | : | 5.9 | 5.7 | 3.9 | : |
| 1963 | 5.0 | 6.5 | 6.1 | : | : | 5.3 | : | 6.1 | : | 4.2 | : | 5.4 | 5.6 | 4.0 | : |
| 1964 | 5.6 | 7.1 | 6.2 | : | : | 5.5 | : | 7.4 | : | 4.9 | : | 6.0 | 6.1 | 4.1 | : |
| 1965 | 6.4 | 8.6 | 7.1 | : | : | 6.2 | : | 6.9 | : | 5.2 | : | 6.6 | 6.7 | 4.2 | : |
| 1966 | 6.7 | 8.7 | 8.1 | : | : | 6.6 | : | 6.5 | : | 6.2 | : | 6.9 | 7.1 | 4.7 | : |
| 1967 | 6.7 | 9.1 | 7.0 | : | : | 6.7 | : | 6.6 | : | 6.0 | : | 6.8 | 6.8 | 4.9 | : |
| 1968 | 6.6 | 8.7 | 6.5 | : | : | 7.0 | : | 6.7 | : | 6.2 | : | 7.6 | 6.9 | 5.3 | : |
| 1969 | 7.3 | 9.7 | 6.8 | : | : | 7.9 | : | 6.9 | : | 7.0 | : | 9.1 | 7.6 | 6.2 | : |
| 1970 | 7.8 | 11.1 | 8.3 | : | : | 8.6 | : | 9.0 | : | 7.8 | : | 9.3 | 8.7 | 6.6 | : |
| 1961-70 | 6.3 | 8.3 | 6.8 | : | : | 6.5 | : | 6.7 | : | 5.6 | : | 7.0 | 6.7 | 4.8 | : |
| 1971 | 7.3 | 11.0 | 8.0 | : | : | 8.4 | 9.2 | 8.3 | : | 7.1 | : | 8.9 | 8.3 | 5.7 | : |
| 1972 | 7.0 | 11.0 | 7.9 | : | : | 8.0 | 9.1 | 7.5 | : | 6.7 | : | 9.0 | 8.0 | 5.6 | 6.9 |
| 1973 | 7.5 | 12.6 | 9.3 | 9.3 | : | 9.0 | 10.7 | 7.4 | 6.8 | 7.3 | : | 10.8 | 9.1 | 6.3 | 7.0 |
| 1974 | 8.8 | 15.9 | 10.4 | 10.5 | : | 11.0 | 14.6 | 9.9 | 7.3 | 10.7 | : | 15.0 | 11.4 | 7.0 | 8.1 |
| 1975 | 8.5 | 12.7 | 8.5 | 9.4 | : | 10.3 | 14.0 | 11.5 | 6.7 | 9.2 | : | 14.5 | 10.8 | 7.0 | 8.4 |
| 1976 | 9.1 | 14.9 | 7.8 | 10.2 | : | 10.5 | 14.6 | 13.1 | 7.2 | 9.2 | : | 14.6 | 11.1 | 6.8 | 8.2 |
| 1977 | 8.8 | 16.2 | 6.2 | 9.5 | : | 11.0 | 12.9 | 14.6 | 7.0 | 8.5 | : | 12.5 | 10.6 | 7.1 | 7.4 |
| 1978 | 8.5 | 16.8 | 5.7 | 10.0 | : | 10.6 | 12.8 | 13.7 | 6.6 | 8.1 | : | 12.6 | 10.2 | 7.9 | 6.3 |
| 1979 | 9.7 | 16.7 | 7.4 | 11.2 | 13.3 | 10.9 | 15.1 | 14.1 | 6.8 | 9.2 | : | 13.0 | 11.2 | 8.7 | 8.3 |
| 1980 | 12.2 | 18.7 | 8.5 | 17.1 | 16.0 | 13.1 | 15.4 | 16.1 | 7.4 | 10.7 | : | 13.9 | 13.0 | 10.8 | 8.9 |
| 1971-80 | 8.7 | 14.6 | 8.0 | : | : | 10.3 | 12.8 | 11.6 | : | 8.7 | : | 12.5 | 10.4 | 7.3 | : |
| 1981 | 13.8 | 19.3 | 10.4 | 17.7 | 15.8 | 15.9 | 17.3 | 20.6 | 8.7 | 12.2 | : | 14.8 | 15.1 | 12.9 | 8.4 |
| 1982 | 13.5 | 20.5 | 9.0 | 15.4 | 16.0 | 15.7 | 17.0 | 20.9 | 10.4 | 10.5 | : | 12.7 | 14.3 | 12.2 | 8.3 |
| 1983 | 11.8 | 14.4 | 7.9 | 18.2 | 16.9 | 13.6* | 13.9 | 18.0 | 9.8 | 8.8 | : | 10.8 | 12.6 | 10.8 | 7.8 |
| 1984 | 12.0 | 14.0 | 7.8 | 18.5 | 16.5 | 12.5 | 14.6 | 15.0 | 10.3 | 8.6 | : | 10.7 | 11.8 | 12.0 | 7.3 |
| 1985 | 10.6 | 11.6 | 6.9 | 15.8 | 13.4 | 10.9 | 12.7 | 14.3 | 9.5 | 7.3 | 27.7 | 10.6 | 10.9 | 10.8 | 6.5 |
| 1986 | 7.9 | 10.6 | 5.9 | 15.8 | 11.4 | 8.4 | 11.1 | 11.7 | 8.7 | 6.4 | 19.5 | 9.8 | 9.2 | 8.1 | 5.2 |
| 1987 | 7.8 | 11.9 | 5.8 | 17.4 | 12.8 | 9.4 | 11.3 | 11.3 | 8.0 | 6.4 | 16.8 | 9.5 | 9.3 | 8.7 | 4.7 |
| 1988 | 7.9 | 10.6 | 6.1 | 16.6 | 11.7 | 9.0 | 9.4 | 12.1 | 7.1 | 6.3 | 15.5 | 9.3 | 9.3 | 9.0 | 4.7 |
| 1989 | 8.7 | 10.2 | 7.0 | : | 13.7 | 8.8 | 9.0 | 12.2 | 7.7 | 7.2 | 16.3 | 9.6 | 9.8 | 8.5 | 5.2 |
| 1990 | 10.1 | 11.0 | 8.9 | : | 14.7 | 9.9 | 10.1 | 13.4 | 8.6 | 9.0 | 16.8 | 11.1 | 11.0 | 8.6 | 7.5 |
| 1981-90 | 10.4 | 13.4 | 7.6 | : | 14.3 | 11.4 | 12.6 | 15.0 | 8.9 | 8.3 | : | 10.9 | 11.3 | 10.2 | 6.6 |
| 1991 | 9.3 | 10.1 | 8.6 | : | 12.4 | 9.0 | 9.2 | 13.0 | 8.2 | 8.7 | 18.3 | 9.9 | 10.3 | 8.1 | 6.7 |
| 1992 | 8.6 | 10.1 | 8.0 | : | 12.2 | 8.6 | 9.1 | 13.7 | 7.9 | 8.1 | 15.4 | 9.1 | 9.9 | 7.7 | 5.3 |
| 1993 | 7.2 | 8.8 | 6.3 | : | 10.2 | 6.8 | 7.7 | 11.3 | 6.9 | 6.7 | 12.5 | 7.8 | 8.1 | 6.6 | 4.0 |
| 1994 | 7.5 | 8.1 | 6.3 | : | 8.8 | 6.9 | 9.4 | 6.4 | 6.9 | 6.9 | 10.0 | 8.2 | 7.7 | 7.2 | 3.8 |

EUR: PPS weighted. EUR 12-: incl. WD.
B: State bonds over five years, secondary market. DK: State bonds. D: Public sector bonds outstanding. GR: State bonds. E: 1979-87 State bonds of two to four years; State bonds of more than two years. F: 1960-79 public sector bonds; 1980-93 State bonds of seven to 10 years. IRL: 1960-70 State bonds 20 years in London; 1971-93 State bonds 15 years in Dublin. I: 1960-84 Crediop bonds; 1985-91 rate of specialised industrial credit institutions (gross rate); from January 1992: public sector bonds outstanding. NL: 1960-73 3.25% State bonds 1948; 1974-84 private loans to public enterprises; 1985-93 yield of five State bonds with the longest maturity. P: Weighted average of public and private bonds over 5 years. UK: State bonds 20 years. EUR 12: weighted geometric mean; weights: gross domestic product at current market prices and PPS. USA: 1960-88 Federal government bonds over 10 years; 1989-93 Federal government bonds over 30 years. J: 1961-78 State bonds; 1979-June 1987; over-the-counter sales of State bonds; 1987-April 1989: Benchmark: bond No 111 (1998); 1989-August 1992: Benchmark: bond No 119 (1999); from September 1992: Benchmark bond No 145 (maturity in 2002).

***Table J1***  Money supply (M2/M3).

(End year: annual percentage change)

| | B/L | DK | WD | GR | E | F | IRL | I | NL | P | UK | EUR 10-[a] | EUR 12- | USA | J |
|---|---|---|---|---|---|---|---|---|---|---|---|---|---|---|---|
| 1960 | 4.3 | 8.0 | 11.1 | 20.2 | : | 16.7 | 5.5 | 19.6 | 7.0 | : | : | : | : | 4.9 | 20.1 |
| 1961 | 9.9 | 9.8 | 12.9 | 17.0 | : | 17.2 | 7.3 | 14.9 | 5.4 | : | : | : | : | 7.4 | 20.2 |
| 1962 | 7.4 | 8.5 | 10.4 | 21.5 | : | 18.7 | 9.6 | 17.0 | 6.6 | : | : | : | : | 8.1 | 20.3 |
| 1963 | 10.3 | 12.5 | 9.9 | 21.4 | : | 14.1 | 5.8 | 13.5 | 9.8 | : | : | : | : | 8.4 | 24.0 |
| 1964 | 7.6 | 11.1 | 9.4 | 16.1 | : | 9.8 | 9.4 | 12.7 | 10.4 | : | 7.6 | 9.7 | : | 8.0 | 18.7 |
| 1965 | 9.6 | 9.7 | 10.6 | 12.9 | : | 10.9 | 6.7 | 15.2 | 6.2 | : | 9.4 | 10.9 | : | 8.1 | 18.0 |
| 1966 | 8.2 | 12.8 | 8.3 | 18.2 | : | 10.6 | 10.6 | 13.0 | 5.9 | : | 6.5 | 9.3 | : | 4.5 | 16.3 |
| 1967 | 7.1 | 9.8 | 12.0 | 16.1 | : | 13.1 | 12.7 | 13.7 | 10.9 | 11.7 | 12.8 | 12.5 | : | 9.2 | 15.5 |
| 1968 | 8.6 | 14.5 | 11.8 | 17.8 | : | 11.6 | 16.9 | 13.1 | 14.8 | 14.1 | 8.5 | 11.5 | : | 8.0 | 14.8 |
| 1969 | 7.0 | 10.2 | 9.4 | 16.2 | : | 6.1 | 11.2 | 12.5 | 10.2 | 17.8 | 5.1 | 8.4 | : | 4.1 | 18.5 |
| 1970 | 10.0 | 3.3 | 9.1 | 19.3 | 15.4 | 15.3 | 14.0 | 15.9 | 11.0 | 12.4 | 12.0 | 12.5 | 12.7 | 6.6 | 16.9 |
| 1961-70 | 8.6 | 10.2 | 10.4 | 17.6 | : | 12.7 | 10.4 | 14.1 | 9.1 | : | : | : | : | 7.2 | 18.3 |
| 1971 | 12.9 | 8.5 | 13.5 | 22.4 | 23.2 | 18.0 | 12.9 | 17.2 | 9.0 | 21.0 | 16.2 | 15.4 | 16.2 | 13.5 | 24.3 |
| 1972 | 17.0 | 15.0 | 14.4 | 23.6 | 23.1 | 18.8 | 14.2 | 19.0 | 11.9 | 23.4 | 23.2 | 18.1 | 18.6 | 13.0 | 24.7 |
| 1973 | 15.4 | 12.6 | 10.1 | 14.5 | 25.6 | 14.7 | 26.0 | 23.1 | 21.9 | 28.9 | 21.8 | 17.0 | 17.9 | 6.9 | 16.8 |
| 1974 | 14.0 | 8.9 | 8.5 | 20.9 | 19.2 | 15.6 | 20.6 | 15.7 | 20.7 | 12.1 | 10.8 | 13.0 | 13.5 | 5.5 | 11.5 |
| 1975 | 15.1 | 25.1 | 8.6 | 26.5 | 19.2 | 18.1 | 18.9 | 23.7 | 5.7 | 13.1 | 11.7 | 14.9 | 15.2 | 12.6 | 16.5 |
| 1976 | 14.3 | 10.9 | 8.4 | 26.7 | 18.6 | 12.3 | 14.5 | 20.8 | 22.7 | 16.4 | 11.3 | 13.6 | 14.1 | 13.7 | 15.4 |
| 1977 | 10.3 | 9.8 | 11.2 | 22.7 | 19.2 | 14.2 | 17.1 | 21.7 | 3.6 | 21.8 | 14.8 | 14.3 | 14.9 | 10.6 | 13.4 |
| 1978 | 10.2 | 8.3 | 11.0 | 26.0 | 19.9 | 12.4 | 29.0 | 22.6 | 4.2 | 26.0 | 15.0 | 14.3 | 15.0 | 8.0 | 14.0 |
| 1979 | 8.2 | 9.7 | 6.0 | 18.4 | 19.3 | 14.0 | 18.7 | 20.8 | 6.9 | 31.0 | 14.4 | 12.8 | 13.7 | 7.8 | 10.8 |
| 1980 | 6.5 | 8.8 | 6.2 | 24.7 | 16.6 | 9.6 | 17.7 | 12.7 | 4.4 | 28.4 | 17.1 | 10.7 | 11.5 | 8.9 | 9.5 |
| 1971-80 | 12.4 | 11.8 | 9.8 | 22.6 | 20.4 | 14.8 | 19.0* | 19.7 | 11.0 | 22.2 | 15.6 | 14.4 | 15.1 | 10.1 | 15.7 |
| 1981 | 5.9 | 10.0 | 5.0 | 34.7 | 16.7 | 11.1 | 17.4 | 10.0 | 5.3 | 24.0 | 20.4 | 11.0 | 11.7 | 10.1 | 11.0 |
| 1982 | 5.5 | 11.4 | 7.1 | 29.0 | 17.9 | 12.4 | 13.0 | 18.0 | 7.6 | 24.1 | 12.0 | 11.9 | 12.6 | 8.8 | 7.9 |
| 1983 | 9.0 | 25.4 | 5.3 | 20.3 | 15.9 | 13.1 | 5.6 | 12.3 | 5.1 | 16.9 | 13.2 | 10.7 | 11.3 | 11.8 | 7.3 |
| 1984 | 5.6 | 17.8 | 4.7 | 29.4 | 15.1 | 11.0 | 10.1 | 12.1 | 5.8 | 24.8 | 13.5 | 10.1 | 10.7 | 8.7 | 7.8 |
| 1985 | 7.8 | 15.8 | 7.6 | 26.8 | 13.8 | 7.4 | 5.3 | 11.1 | 9.0 | 28.5 | 13.0 | 9.9 | 10.5 | 8.3 | 8.7 |
| 1986 | 12.8 | 10.8 | 6.6 | 19.0 | 14.1 | 6.8 | -1.0 | 10.7 | 7.1 | 26.3 | 16.2 | 9.9 | 10.5 | 9.4 | 9.2 |
| 1987 | 10.2 | 4.3 | 5.9 | 24.0 | 15.0 | 9.8 | 10.9 | 7.2 | 4.1 | 19.7 | 16.2 | 9.4 | 10.1 | 3.6 | 10.8 |
| 1988 | 7.8 | 3.4 | 6.9 | 23.2 | 13.9 | 8.4 | 6.3 | 7.6 | 9.8 | 17.8 | 17.4 | 9.9 | 10.4 | 5.5 | 10.2 |
| 1989 | 13.1 | 6.1 | 5.5 | 24.2 | 13.7 | 9.6 | 5.0 | 9.9 | 12.0 | 10.4 | 18.8 | 10.9 | 11.2 | 5.1 | 12.0 |
| 1990 | 4.5 | 7.1 | 4.2 | 15.3 | 16.4 | 8.9 | 15.4 | 8.1 | 7.7 | 11.2 | 12.0 | 8.1 | 8.9 | 3.5 | 7.4 |
| 1981-90 | 8.2 | 11.2 | 5.9 | 24.6 | 15.2 | 9.8 | 8.8 | 10.7 | 7.3 | 20.4 | 15.3 | 10.2 | 10.8 | 7.5 | 9.2 |
| 1991 | 5.9 | 6.4 | 6.3 | 12.3 | 10.8 | 2.5 | 3.1 | 9.1 | 5.2 | 18.7 | 5.8 | 5.9 | 6.6 | 3.1 | 2.3 |
| 1992 | 6.2 | -0.1 | 7.6 | 14.4 | 5.0 | 5.2 | 9.0 | 4.5 | 6.3 | 12.7 | 3.5 | 5.6 | 5.6 | 1.6 | 0.2 |
| 1993 | : | 14.6 | 10.9 | 15.2 | 7.5 | -1.7 | 23.3 | 7.8 | 7.7 | 6.6 | 5.8 | 6.6 | 6.7 | 1.5 | 2.2 |

EUR: PPS weighted. EUR 12-: incl. WD.
B: M3H; DK: M2; D: M3, until 1990 WD, from 1991 onwards D; GR: M3; E: ALP; F: M3; IRL: M3; I: M2; NL: M3; P: L-; UK: M4; EUR: chain-weighted arithmetic mean; weights: GDP at current market prices and PPS; USA: M2; J: M2 plus certificates of deposit.
a EUR 12- excl. E, P.

***Table K1***   Current receipts; general government.

(Percentage of gross domestic product at market prices)

| | B | DK | WD | D | GR | E[a] | F | IRL | I | L[a] | NL[a] | P | UK | EUR 10–[a] | EUR 12– | EUR 12+ | USA | J |
|---|---|---|---|---|---|---|---|---|---|---|---|---|---|---|---|---|---|---|
| 1960 | 27.9 | 27.3 | 35.5 | : | 21.1 | : | 34.9 | 24.8 | 28.8 | 31.0 | 33.9 | 19.1 | 29.9 | 32.2 | : | : | 27.6 | : |
| 1961 | 29.0 | 26.6 | 36.6 | | 22.0 | : | 36.2 | 25.7 | 28.2 | 33.4 | 34.9 | 20.0 | 31.3 | 33.2 | | : | 27.7 | |
| 1962 | 29.8 | 28.2 | 37.0 | | 23.2 | : | 36.3 | 25.2 | 29.1 | 31.7 | 34.4 | 20.8 | 32.8 | 33.9 | | : | 27.9 | |
| 1963 | 30.0 | 29.9 | 37.3 | | 23.2 | : | 37.1 | 26.1 | 29.5 | 31.8 | 35.6 | 20.5 | 31.5 | 34.0 | | : | 28.5 | |
| 1964 | 30.6 | 29.7 | 36.8 | | 24.0 | : | 38.0 | 26.9 | 30.6 | 31.8 | 35.7 | 20.7 | 31.4 | 34.2 | | : | 27.4 | |
| 1965 | 31.3 | 31.2 | 36.1 | | 23.7 | : | 38.4 | 27.9 | 30.1 | 33.5 | 37.3 | 21.7 | 33.0 | 34.6 | | : | 27.3 | |
| 1966 | 33.1 | 33.5 | 36.7 | | 25.4 | : | 38.4 | 30.0 | 30.1 | 33.9 | 39.2 | 22.2 | 34.2 | 35.2 | | : | 28.0 | |
| 1967 | 33.9 | 34.1 | 37.4 | | 26.2 | : | 38.2 | 30.6 | 31.0 | 34.3 | 40.6 | 22.3 | 36.2 | 36.1 | | : | 28.6 | |
| 1968 | 34.5 | 36.9 | 38.3 | | 27.3 | : | 38.8 | 31.0 | 31.6 | 33.2 | 42.4 | 23.1 | 37.7 | 37.0 | | : | 30.2 | |
| 1969 | 35.0 | 37.2 | 39.6 | | 27.2 | : | 39.8 | 31.6 | 30.7 | 32.8 | 43.2 | 24.0 | 39.3 | 27.9 | | : | 31.4 | |
| 1970 | 35.9 | 41.7 | 38.7 | | 26.8 | : | 39.0 | 35.3 | 30.4 | 34.4 | 41.2 | 26.0 | 40.2 | 37.7 | | : | 30.5 | |
| 1961-70 | 32.3 | 32.9 | 37.4 | | 24.9 | : | 38.0 | 29.0 | 30.1 | 33.1 | 38.4 | 22.1 | 34.8 | 35.4 | | : | 28.7 | |
| 1970 | 39.1 | 46.1 | 38.7 | : | : | 22.1 | 39.0 | 31.8 | 28.8 | 36.4 | 41.2 | 26.0 | 39.8 | 37.5 | | : | 30.5 | 21.1 |
| 1971 | 39.8 | 46.8 | 39.8 | | : | 22.4 | 38.6 | 32.7 | 29.5 | 39.7 | 42.9 | 25.2 | 38.1 | 37.7 | | : | 29.6 | 22.0 |
| 1972 | 39.9 | 46.4 | 40.1 | | : | 22.8 | 38.9 | 31.5 | 29.4 | 39.8 | 44.0 | 25.3 | 36.0 | 37.6 | | : | 31.0 | 21.9 |
| 1973 | 41.1 | 46.0 | 42.5 | | : | 23.3 | 39.0 | 30.9 | 28.5 | 40.2 | 45.3 | 24.9 | 35.4 | 38.4 | | : | 31.2 | 22.9 |
| 1974 | 42.3 | 47.9 | 43.1 | | 26.7 | 22.8 | 39.7 | 35.3 | 28.0 | 41.3 | 46.3 | 25.0 | 39.3 | 39.5 | 38.2 | : | 32.0 | 24.9 |
| 1975 | 45.4 | 45.7 | 43.1 | | 27.1 | 24.4 | 41.4 | 33.0 | 28.5 | 49.9 | 48.7 | 27.7 | 40.0 | 40.3 | 39.0 | : | 30.4 | 24.5 |
| 1976 | 45.7 | 46.1 | 44.3 | | 29.2 | 25.3 | 43.5 | 36.4 | 29.7 | 51.4 | 49.0 | 30.7 | 39.4 | 41.5 | 40.2 | : | 31.3 | 24.0 |
| 1977 | 47.4 | 46.6 | 45.3 | | 29.6 | 26.5 | 43.2 | 35.2 | 30.6 | 55.4 | 49.9 | 30.5 | 38.5 | 41.9 | 40.7 | : | 31.4 | 25.i |
| 1978 | 48.4 | 48.4 | 44.8 | | 29.9 | 27.2 | 43.1 | 33.6 | 31.8 | 56.5 | 50.2 | 29.5 | 37.1 | 41.8 | 40.6 | : | 31.7 | 25.0 |
| 1979 | 49.4 | 49.8 | 44.6 | | 30.4 | 28.5 | 44.7 | 33.2 | 31.3 | 53.4 | 50.9 | 29.7 | 37.8 | 42.1 | 40.9 | : | 32.1 | 26.9 |
| 1980 | 48.8 | 51.5 | 45.1 | | 30.2 | 29.9 | 46.5 | 36.2 | 33.3 | 55.1 | 52.5 | 30.9 | 39.7 | 43.1 | 42.1 | : | 32.4 | 28.1 |
| 1971-80 | 44.8 | 47.5 | 43.3 | | : | 25.3 | 41.9 | 33.8 | 30.1 | 48.3 | 48.0 | 27.9 | 38.1 | 40.4 | | : | 31.3 | 24.5 |
| 1981 | 49.9 | 51.7 | 45.3 | | 28.8 | 31.3 | 47.3 | 37.1 | 34.3 | 55.8 | 53.1 | 32.4 | 41.7 | 43.8 | 42.8 | : | 33.2 | 29.6 |
| 1982 | 51.8 | 50.9 | 46.0 | | 32.0 | 31.5 | 48.2 | 39.4 | 36.1 | 55.6 | 53.4 | 33.4 | 42.2 | 44.6 | 43.6 | : | 33.0 | 30.0 |
| 1983 | 51.3 | 53.2 | 45.4 | | 33.2 | 33.6 | 48.8 | 40.9 | 37.9 | 58.3 | 54.7 | 37.0 | 41.5 | 44.9 | 44.1 | : | 32.7 | 30.3 |
| 1984 | 52.3 | 54.7 | 45.6 | | 34.2 | 33.5 | 49.8 | 41.4 | 37.7 | 56.3 | 53.4 | 34.6 | 41.4 | 45.1 | 44.2 | : | 32.7 | 30.8 |
| 1985 | 52.3 | 56.0 | 46.0 | | 34.2 | 35.2 | 49.9 | 40.7 | 38.3 | 58.6 | 54.4 | 33.4 | 41.3 | 45.3 | 44.5 | : | 33.3 | 31.5 |
| 1986 | 51.3 | 57.7 | 45.2 | | 35.1 | 35.9 | 49.4 | 40.8 | 39.1 | 55.5 | 52.8 | 37.3 | 40.1 | 45.0 | 44.3 | : | 33.6 | 31.7 |
| 1987 | 51.5 | 58.1 | 45.0 | | 36.0 | 37.7 | 49.8 | 41.0 | 39.2 | 57.5 | 53.5 | 36.2 | 39.5 | 45.0 | 44.4 | : | 34.3 | 33.3 |
| 1988 | 49.9 | 58.6 | 44.2 | | 33.8 | 37.7 | 49.2 | 41.8 | 39.6 | : | 53.0 | 37.6 | 39.1 | 44.4 | 43.8 | : | 33.8 | 33.7 |
| 1989 | 48.4 | 57.9 | 45.1 | | 32.8 | 39.5 | 48.6 | 38.3 | 41.4 | : | 50.1 | 39.5 | 38.6 | 44.5 | 44.0 | : | 34.3 | 34.0 |
| 1990 | 48.9 | 55.9 | 43.3 | | 35.1 | 39.5 | 49.0 | 38.0 | 42.2 | : | 49.9 | 34.0 | 38.8 | 44.2 | 43.7 | : | 34.3 | 35.2 |
| 1981-90 | 50.8 | 55.5 | 45.1 | | 33.5 | 35.6 | 49.0 | 40.0 | 38.6 | : | 52.8 | 35.6 | 40.4 | 44.7 | 43.9 | : | 33.5 | 32.0 |
| 1991 | 49.1 | 55.8 | 44.6 | 45.5 | 36.4 | 40.3 | 49.1 | 38.8 | 43.3 | 55.2 | 52.8 | 35.5 | 38.2 | 44.8 | 44.3 | 44.6 | 34.3 | 34.9 |
| 1992 | 49.5 | 57.1 | 45.5 | 46.8 | 39.4 | 42.0 | 48.6 | 39.1 | 44.0 | 53.0 | 52.6 | 39.5 | 37.0 | 45.1 | 44.7 | 45.1 | 34.2 | : |
| 1993 | 50.6 | 57.3 | 46.1 | 47.1 | 38.4 | 41.7 | 48.9 | 40.0 | 46.7 | 55.2 | 53.7 | 36.9 | 35.8 | 45.8 | 45.4 | 45.7 | 34.5 | : |
| 1994 | 51.1 | 58.1 | 46.8 | 47.7 | 39.4 | 41.6 | 49.7 | 39.8 | 45.6 | 53.3 | 52.3 | 36.6 | 36.7 | 46.0 | 45.6 | 45.9 | 34.7 | : |

EUR 12–: incl. WD; EUR 12+: incl. D.
a   Breaks: E in 1979/80 and 1984/85; L in 1990/91; NL in 1968/69 and 1981/85.
b   EUR 12– excl. GR, E.

***Table K2***   Total expenditure; general government.

(Percentage of gross domestic product at market prices)

| | B | DK | WD | D | GR | E[a] | F | IRL | I | L[a] | NL[a] | P | UK | EUR 10–[a] | EUR 12– | EUR 12+ | USA | J |
|---|---|---|---|---|---|---|---|---|---|---|---|---|---|---|---|---|---|---|
| 1960 | 30.7 | 24.8 | 32.5 | : | : | : | 34.6 | 28.0 | 30.1 | 29.1 | 33.7 | 18.5 | 32.2 | 32.2 | | : | 27.0 | : |
| 1961 | 30.1 | 27.1 | 33.8 | : | : | : | 35.7 | 29.7 | 29.4 | 29.7 | 35.4 | 20.9 | 33.1 | 33.1 | | : | 28.3 | : |
| 1962 | 30.9 | 28.1 | 35.6 | : | : | : | 37.0 | 29.5 | 30.5 | 30.5 | 35.6 | 20.3 | 33.9 | 34.2 | | : | 28.4 | : |
| 1963 | 31.9 | 28.6 | 36.4 | : | : | : | 37.8 | 30.5 | 31.1 | 30.4 | 37.6 | 21.8 | 35.4 | 35.2 | | : | 28.2 | : |
| 1964 | 31.3 | 28.4 | 36.1 | : | : | : | 38.0 | 31.8 | 31.8 | 30.7 | 37.8 | 21.8 | 33.5 | 34.8 | | : | 27.6 | : |
| 1965 | 32.7 | 29.9 | 36.7 | : | : | : | 38.4 | 33.1 | 34.3 | 31.6 | 38.7 | 21.5 | 35.9 | 36.2 | | : | 27.1 | : |
| 1966 | 33.9 | 31.7 | 36.8 | : | : | : | 38.5 | 33.6 | 34.3 | 33.1 | 40.7 | 21.7 | 35.2 | 36.2 | | : | 28.2 | : |
| 1967 | 35.0 | 34.3 | 38.8 | : | : | : | 39.0 | 34.8 | 33.7 | 36.0 | 42.5 | 22.2 | 38.3 | 37.7 | | : | 30.2 | : |
| 1968 | 36.9 | 36.4 | 39.1 | : | : | : | 40.3 | 35.2 | 34.7 | 35.8 | 43.9 | 22.4 | 39.3 | 38.6 | | : | 30.7 | : |
| 1969 | 36.7 | 36.3 | 38.5 | : | : | : | 39.6 | 36.6 | 34.2 | 32.6 | 44.4 | 22.4 | 41.0 | 38.6 | | : | 30.4 | : |
| 1970 | 37.0 | 40.2 | 38.5 | : | : | : | 38.9 | 39.6 | 34.2 | 32.5 | 42.4 | 23.2 | 38.8 | 38.0 | | : | 31.6 | : |
| 1961-70 | 33.7 | 32.1 | 37.0 | : | : | : | 38.3 | 33.5 | 32.8 | 32.3 | 39.9 | 21.8 | 36.5 | 36.3 | | : | 29.1 | : |
| 1970 | 41.7 | 42.0 | 38.5 | : | : | 21.4 | 38.1 | 35.9 | 32.1 | 33.2 | 42.4 | 23.2 | 36.8 | 37.3 | | : | 31.6 | 19.3 |
| 1971 | 43.5 | 42.9 | 39.9 | : | : | 22.9 | 38.0 | 36.7 | 34.3 | 37.1 | 43.9 | 23.0 | 36.7 | 38.2 | | : | 31.6 | 20.7 |
| 1972 | 44.7 | 42.5 | 40.7 | : | : | 22.5 | 38.3 | 35.4 | 36.4 | 37.5 | 44.4 | 24.5 | 37.3 | 39.1 | | : | 31.3 | 21.8 |
| 1973 | 45.2 | 40.8 | 41.3 | : | : | 22.2 | 38.4 | 35.3 | 35.0 | 36.4 | 44.6 | 23.3 | 38.1 | 39.3 | | : | 30.7 | 22.4 |
| 1974 | 45.4 | 44.8 | 44.4 | : | : | 22.6 | 39.4 | 43.1 | 34.4 | 36.0 | 46.6 | 26.4 | 43.1 | 41.5 | | : | 32.3 | 24.5 |
| 1975 | 50.9 | 47.0 | 48.7 | : | : | 24.4 | 43.8 | 45.0 | 39.1 | 48.7 | 51.5 | 31.9 | 44.7 | 45.4 | | : | 34.5 | 27.2 |
| 1976 | 51.9 | 46.4 | 47.7 | : | : | 25.6 | 44.3 | 44.6 | 37.8 | 49.4 | 51.7 | 36.6 | 44.4 | 45.2 | | : | 33.4 | 27.7 |
| 1977 | 53.7 | 47.2 | 47.7 | : | : | 27.1 | 44.1 | 42.5 | 37.7 | 52.1 | 51.6 | 35.2 | 41.9 | 44.9 | | : | 32.3 | 29.0 |
| 1978 | 55.2 | 48.7 | 47.2 | : | : | 28.9 | 45.2 | 42.9 | 40.4 | 51.5 | 52.9 | 36.4 | 41.5 | 45.5 | | : | 31.5 | 30.5 |
| 1979 | 56.9 | 51.4 | 47.2 | : | 33.0 | 30.1 | 45.6 | 44.1 | 39.7 | 52.6 | 54.6 | 35.8 | 41.0 | 45.6 | 44.3 | : | 31.7 | 31.6 |
| 1980 | 58.1 | 54.8 | 48.0 | : | 33.1 | 32.5 | 46.6 | 48.3 | 41.9 | 55.6 | 56.5 | : | 43.2 | 46.8 | 45.7 | : | 33.7 | 32.6 |
| 1971-80 | 50.6 | 46.7 | 45.3 | : | : | 25.9 | 42.3 | 41.8 | 37.7 | 45.7 | 49.8 | : | 41.2 | 43.2 | | : | 32.3 | 26.8 |
| 1981 | 63.4 | 58.6 | 49.0 | : | 39.0 | 35.2 | 49.2 | 49.9 | 45.8 | 59.4 | 58.6 | 41.7 | 45.7 | 49.1 | 48.0 | : | 34.2 | 33.4 |
| 1982 | 63.2 | 60.0 | 49.3 | : | 39.7 | 37.1 | 50.9 | 52.7 | 47.4 | 56.8 | 60.5 | 43.8 | 45.1 | 49.9 | 48.8 | : | 36.4 | 33.6 |
| 1982 | 63.2 | 60.4 | 48.0 | : | 41.7 | 38.4 | 52.0 | 52.1 | 48.6 | 56.0 | 61.0 | 46.1 | 44.8 | 49.9 | 49.1 | : | 36.8 | 33.9 |
| 1984 | 61.8 | 58.8 | 47.6 | : | 44.3 | 38.9 | 52.5 | 50.8 | 49.4 | 52.6 | 59.6 | 46.6 | 45.3 | 50.0 | 49.2 | : | 35.6 | 32.9 |
| 1985 | 61.4 | 58.1 | 47.2 | : | 48.3 | 42.2 | 52.7 | 51.5 | 50.9 | 50.9 | 58.0 | 43.5 | 44.1 | 49.9 | 49.3 | : | 36.4 | 32.3 |
| 1986 | 60.7 | 54.3 | 46.5 | : | 47.6 | 41.9 | 52.2 | 51.4 | 50.7 | 50.4 | 57.9 | 44.6 | 42.9 | 49.3 | 48.8 | : | 37.1 | 32.6 |
| 1987 | 59.0 | 55.7 | 46.9 | : | 47.6 | 40.8 | 51.7 | 49.4 | 50.2 | 54.2 | 59.4 | 43.0 | 40.8 | 48.9 | 48.3 | : | 36.8 | 32.8 |
| 1988 | 56.7 | 58.0 | 46.4 | : | 47.5 | 41.0 | 50.8 | 46.3 | 50.3 | : | 57.6 | 43.0 | 38.9 | 47.9 | 47.4 | : | 35.8 | 32.2 |
| 1989 | 54.9 | 58.4 | 45.0 | : | 49.4 | 42.3 | 49.9 | 39.9 | 51.3 | : | 54.8 | 42.9 | 38.6 | 47.2 | 46.8 | : | 35.8 | 31.5 |
| 1990 | 54.8 | 57.4 | 45.3 | : | 53.2 | 43.5 | 50.5 | 40.2 | 53.2 | : | 55.0 | 38.8 | 40.3 | 48.1 | 47.8 | : | 36.8 | 32.3 |
| 1981-90 | 59.9 | 58.0 | 47.1 | : | 45.8 | 40.1 | 51.2 | 48.4 | 49.8 | : | 58.2 | 43.4 | 42.7 | 49.0 | 48.4 | : | 36.2 | 32.8 |
| 1991 | 55.9 | 57.8 | 48.1 | 48.8 | 50.8 | 45.2 | 51.2 | 40.8 | 53.5 | 52.8 | 55.3 | 41.1 | 41.0 | 49.8 | 49.0 | 49.1 | 37.8 | 32.0 |
| 1992 | 56.5 | 59.5 | 47.8 | 49.4 | 53.7 | 46.4 | 52.5 | 41.4 | 53.6 | 53.3 | 56.1 | 42.8 | 43.3 | 50.0 | 49.8 | 50.2 | 38.7 | : |
| 1993 | 57.7 | 61.9 | 48.9 | 50.4 | 54.7 | 48.9 | 54.7 | 42.3 | 56.2 | 33.8 | 56.6 | 43.9 | 43.5 | 51.5 | 51.3 | 51.7 | 38.0 | : |
| 1994 | 56.5 | 62.7 | 49.0 | 50.8 | 57.3 | 48.8 | 55.3 | 42.2 | 55.1 | 53.6 | 55.9 | 42.8 | 42.7 | 51.2 | 51.1 | 51.6 | 37.2 | : |

EUR 12–: incl. WD; EUR 12+: incl. D.
a   Breaks: E in 179/80 and 1984/85; L in 1990/91; NL in 1968/69 and 1981/85.
b   EUR 12– excl. GR, E.

**Table K3** Net lending (+) or net borrowing (−); general government.

(Percentage of gross domestic product at market prices)

| | B | DK | WD | D | GR | E* | F | IRL | I | L* | NL* | P | UK | EUR 10-b | EUR 12- | EUR 12+ | USA | J |
|---|---|---|---|---|---|---|---|---|---|---|---|---|---|---|---|---|---|---|
| 1960 | -2.9 | 3.1 | 3.0 | : | : | : | 0.9 | -2.4 | -0.9 | 3.0 | 0.8 | 0.6 | -1.0 | 0.6 | : | : | 0.7 | : |
| 1961 | -1.3 | 0.1 | 2.8 | : | : | : | 1.0 | -3.2 | -0.8 | 4.7 | 0.1 | -0.9 | -0.7 | 0.6 | : | : | -0.6 | : |
| 1962 | -1.3 | 0.6 | 1.4 | : | : | : | -0.1 | -3.6 | -1.0 | 2.2 | -0.6 | 0.6 | 0.0 | 0.1 | : | : | -0.5 | : |
| 1963 | -2.2 | 1.9 | 0.9 | : | : | : | 0.1 | -3.6 | 1.2 | 2.5 | -1.3 | -1.3 | -2.8 | -0.7 | : | : | 0.3 | : |
| 1964 | -0.8 | 1.8 | 0.7 | : | : | : | 0.7 | -4.1 | -0.8 | 2.1 | -1.5 | -1.1 | -1.1 | -0.1 | : | : | -0.2 | : |
| 1965 | 1.6 | 1.8 | 0.6 | : | : | : | 0.7 | -4.3 | -3.8 | 2.8 | -0.8 | 0.3 | -1.9 | -1.1 | : | : | 0.2 | : |
| 1966 | 1.0 | 2.3 | 0.2 | : | : | : | 0.6 | -2.8 | -3.8 | 1.8 | -0.9 | 0.5 | 0.0 | -0.5 | : | : | -0.1 | : |
| 1967 | -1.3 | 0.4 | 1.4 | : | : | : | 0.0 | -3.3 | -2.2 | -0.7 | -1.3 | 0.1 | -1.0 | -1.1 | : | : | -1.7 | : |
| 1968 | 2.6 | 1.1 | 0.8 | : | : | : | -0.8 | -3.3 | -2.8 | -1.6 | -0.9 | 0.7 | -0.5 | -1.1 | : | : | -0.5 | : |
| 1969 | 1.8 | 1.4 | 1.1 | : | : | : | 0.9 | -4.2 | -3.1 | 1.1 | -0.5 | 1.6 | -0.6 | -0.2 | : | : | 1.0 | : |
| 1970 | 1.3 | 2.1 | 0.2 | : | : | : | 0.9 | -3.7 | -3.5 | 2.8 | -1.2 | 2.8 | 2.4 | 0.1 | : | : | -1.1 | : |
| 1961-70 | 1.5 | 1.3 | 0.4 | : | : | : | 0.4 | -3.6 | -2.3 | 1.8 | -0.9 | 0.3 | -0.6 | -0.4 | : | : | -0.3 | : |
| 1970 | 2.6 | 4.1 | 0.2 | : | : | 0.7 | 0.9 | -4.1 | -3.3 | 3.2 | -1.2 | 2.8 | 3.0 | 0.2 | : | : | -1.1 | 1.8 |
| 1971 | 3.7 | 3.9 | 0.2 | : | : | 0.5 | 0.6 | -4.0 | -4.8 | 2.6 | -1.0 | 2.3 | 1.3 | -1.5 | : | : | -1.8 | 1.3 |
| 1972 | 4.8 | 3.9 | 0.5 | : | : | 0.3· | 0.6 | -3.9 | -7.0 | 2.3 | -0.4 | 0.9 | -1.3 | -1.5 | : | : | -0.3 | 0.2 |
| 1973 | 4.2 | 5.2 | 1.2 | : | : | 1.1 | 0.6 | -4.4 | -6.5 | 3.8 | 0.8 | 1.6 | -2.7 | -0.9 | : | : | 0.5 | 0.5 |
| 1974 | 3.1 | 3.1 | 1.3 | : | : | 0.2 | 0.3 | -7.8 | -6.4 | 5.3 | -0.2 | -1.4 | -3.8 | -2.0 | : | : | -0.3 | 0.4 |
| 1975 | 5.5 | 1.4 | 5.6 | : | : | 0.0 | -2.4 | -12.0 | -10.6 | 1.1 | -2.9 | -4.1 | -4.7 | -5.2 | : | : | -4.1 | -2.8 |
| 1976 | 6.2 | 0.3 | 3.4 | : | : | 0.3 | 0.7 | -8.2 | -8.1 | 2.0 | -2.6 | -5.9 | -4.9 | -3.7 | : | : | -2.2 | -3.7 |
| 1977 | 6.4 | 0.6 | 2.4 | : | : | 0.6 | 0.8 | -7.3 | -7.0 | 3.3 | -1.8 | -4.7 | -3.4 | -3.0 | : | : | -0.9 | -3.8 |
| 1978 | 6.8 | 0.4 | 2.4 | : | : | 1.7 | -2.1 | -9.3 | -8.5 | 5.0 | -2.8 | -6.9 | -4.4 | -3.8 | : | : | 0.1 | -5.5 |
| 1979 | 7.5 | 1.7 | 2.6 | : | 2.6 | 1.6 | 0.8 | -11.0 | -8.3 | 0.7 | -3.7 | -6.1 | -3.3 | -3.5 | -3.3 | : | 0.4 | -4.7 |
| 1980 | 9.3 | 3.3 | 2.9 | : | 2.9 | 2.6 | 0.0 | -12.2 | -8.6 | -0.5 | -4.0 | : | -3.5 | -3.7 | -3.6 | : | -1.3 | -4.4 |
| 1971-80 | 5.7 | 0.9 | 2.0 | : | : | 0.6 | -0.5 | -8.0 | -7.6 | 2.6 | -1.9 | : | -3.1 | -2.8 | : | : | -1.0 | -2.3 |
| 1981 | 13.5 | 6.9 | 3.7 | : | 10.2 | 3.9 | -1.9 | -12.8 | -11.4 | -3.6 | -5.5 | -9.3 | -4.0 | -5.3 | -5.2 | : | -1.0 | -3.8 |
| 1982 | 11.5 | 9.1 | 3.3 | : | 7.7 | 5.6 | -2.8 | -13.2 | -11.3 | -1.2 | -7.1 | -10.4 | -2.9 | -5.3 | -5.3 | : | -3.4 | -3.6 |
| 1983 | 11.9 | 7.2 | 2.6 | : | 8.6 | 4.7 | 3.2 | -11.3 | -10.6 | 2.3 | -6.4 | -9.0 | -3.4 | -5.0 | -5.1 | : | -4.1 | -3.6 |
| 1984 | 9.6 | 4.1 | 1.9 | : | 10.1 | 5.4 | -2.8 | -9.4 | -11.6 | 3.7 | -6.3 | -12.0 | -3.9 | -5.0 | -5.1 | : | -2.9 | -2.1 |
| 1985 | 9.1 | 2.0 | 1.2 | : | 14.0 | 6.9 | -2.9 | -10.7 | -12.6 | 7.2 | -3.6 | -10.1 | -2.8 | -4.5 | -4.8 | : | -3.1 | -0.8 |
| 1986 | 9.4 | 3.4 | 1.3 | : | 12.5 | 6.0 | -2.7 | -10.6 | -11.6 | 5.1 | -5.1 | -7.2 | -2.8 | -4.3 | -4.5 | : | -3.5 | -0.9 |
| 1987 | 7.5 | 2.4 | 1.9 | : | 11.7 | 3.1 | -1.9 | -8.5 | -11.0 | 3.3 | -5.9 | -6.8 | -1.4 | -3.9 | -4.0 | : | -2.5 | 0.5 |
| 1988 | 6.8 | 0.6 | 2.2 | : | 13.7 | 3.3 | -1.7 | -4.5 | -10.7 | : | -4.6 | -5.4 | 0.1 | -3.5 | -3.6 | : | -2.0 | 1.5 |
| 1989 | 6.5 | 0.5 | 0.1 | : | 16.6 | 2.8 | -1.3 | -1.7 | -9.9 | : | -4.7 | -3.4 | -0.1 | -2.7 | -2.9 | : | -1.5 | 2.5 |
| 1990 | 5.9 | 1.5 | 2.1 | : | 18.1 | 3.9 | -1.5 | -2.2 | -10.9 | 5.9 | -5.1 | -5.5 | -1.5 | -3.9 | -4.1 | : | -2.5 | 2.9 |
| 1981-90 | 9.2 | 2.5 | 2.0 | : | 12.3 | 4.6 | -2.3 | -8.5 | -11.2 | : | -5.4 | -7.9 | -2.3 | -4.3 | -4.4 | : | -2.7 | -0.7 |
| 1991 | 6.8 | 2.1 | 3.5 | 3.2 | 14.4 | -4.9 | -2.1 | -2.0 | -10.2 | 2.3 | -2.5 | -6.6 | -2.8 | -4.5 | -4.6 | -4.6 | -3.5 | 3.0 |
| 1992 | 7.1 | 2.4 | 2.3 | 2.6 | 14.3 | -4.5 | -3.9 | -2.3 | -9.5 | -0.3 | -3.5 | -3.3 | -6.4 | -5.0 | -5.0 | -5.1 | -4.5 | : |
| 1993 | 7.0 | 4.6 | 2.8 | 3.3 | -16.3 | -7.3 | -5.7 | -2.3 | -9.5 | 1.4 | -2.9 | -7.1 | -7.7 | -5.7 | -5.9 | -6.0 | -3.5 | : |
| 1994 | 5.4 | 4.6 | 2.2 | 3.1 | 17.9 | -7.2 | -5.6 | -2.5 | -9.5 | -0.4 | -3.6 | -6.2 | -6.0 | -5.2 | -5.5 | -5.5 | -2.5 | : |

EUR 12 incl. WD, EUR 12+ incl. D

Belgium: net borrowing figures for 1993, 1994 and 1995 include the proceeds from the sale of public participation, the accounting treatment of which is currently being examined. Luxembourg and Portugal: net borrowing/lending figures for 1990 (Luxembourg and Portugal) and for 1991 (Portugal) are those reported in the context of the excessive deficit procedure. These balances do not correspond to the differences between receipts and expenditure

a Breaks: E in 1979/80 and 1984/85, L in 1990/91, NL in 1968/9 and 1981/85.
b EUR 12 excl. GR, E

**Table L1** Budgetary expenditure of the European Communities.

(Mio UA/EUA/ECU)a

| | ECSC operational budget | European development Fund | Euratom b | EC general budget | | | | | | | Total |
|---|---|---|---|---|---|---|---|---|---|---|---|
| | | | | EAGGF c | Social Fund | Regional Fund | Industry energy, research | Admini-stration d | Other | Total EC | |
| 1958 | 21.7 | – | 7.9 | – | – | – | – | 8.6 | 0.0 | 8.6 | 35.5 |
| 1959 | 30.7 | 51.2 | 39.1 | – | – | – | – | 20.3 | 4.9 | 25.2 | 146.2 |
| 1960 | 23.5 | 63.2 | 20.0 | – | – | – | – | 23.4 | 4.9 | 28.3 | 135.0 |
| 1961 | 26.5 | 172.0 | 72.5 | – | 8.6 | – | – | 27.9 | 2.9 | 39.4 | 305.0 |
| 1962 | 13.6 | 162.3 | 88.6 | – | 11.3 | – | – | 34.2 | 46.8 | 92.3 | 356.8 |
| 1963 | 21.9 | 55.5 | 106.4 | – | 4.6 | – | – | 37.2 | 42.3 | 84.1 | 267.9 |
| 1964 | 18.7 | 35.0 | 124.4 | – | 7.2 | – | – | 43.0 | 42.9 | 93.1 | 271.1 |
| 1965 | 37.3 | 248.8 | 120.0 | 102.7 | 42.9 | – | – | 48.1 | 7.4 | 201.1 | 607.2 |
| 1966 | 28.1 | 157.8 | 129.2 | 310.3 | 26.2 | – | – | 55.4 | 10.4 | 402.3 | 717.3 |
| 1967 | 10.4 | 105.8 | 158.5 | 562.0 | 35.6 | – | – | 60.4 | 17.1 | 675.1 | 949.8 |
| 1968 | 21.2 | 121.0 | 73.4 | 2250.4 | 43.0 | – | – | 91.8 | 23.5 | 2408.7 | 2624.2 |
| 1969 | 40.7 | 104.8 | 59.2 | 3818.0 | 50.5 | – | – | 105.6 | 77.1 | 4051.2 | 4255.9 |
| 1970 | 56.2 | 10.5 | 63.4 | 5228.3 | 64.0 | – | – | 114.7 | 41.4 | 5448.4 | 5578.5 |
| 1971 | 37.4 | 236.1 | – | 1883.6 | 56.5 | – | 65.0 | 132.1 | 152.2 | 2289.3 | 2562.8 |
| 1972 | 43.7 | 212.7 | – | 2477.6 | 97.5 | – | 75.1 | 177.2 | 247.1 | 3074.5 | 3330.9 |
| 1973 | 86.9 | 210.0 | – | 3768.8 | 269.2 | – | 69.1 | 239.4 | 294.4 | 4641.0 | 4937.9 |
| 1974 | 92.0 | 157.0 | – | 3651.3 | 292.1 | – | 82.8 | 336.7 | 675.2 | 5038.2 | 5287.2 |
| 1975 | 127.4 | 71.0 | – | 4586.6 | 360.2 | 150.0 | 99.0 | 375.0 | 642.8 | 6212.6 | 6412.0 |
| 1976 | 94.0 | 320.0 | – | 6033.3 | 176.7 | 300.0 | 113.3 | 419.7 | 909.5 | 7952.6 | 8366.6 |
| 1977 | 93.0 | 244.7 | – | 6464.5 | 325.2 | 372.5 | 163.3 | 497.0 | 883.4 | 8704.9 | 9042.6 |
| 1978 | 159.1 | 394.5 | – | 9602.2 | 284.8 | 254.9 | 227.2 | 676.7 | 1302.4 | 12348.2 | 12901.8 |
| 1979 | 173.9 | 480.0 | – | 10735.5 | 595.7 | 671.5 | 288.0 | 863.9 | 1447.9 | 14602.5 | 15256.4 |
| 1980 | 175.7 | 508.5 | – | 11596.1 | 502.0 | 751.8 | 212.8 | 938.8 | 2056.1 | 16057.5c | 16741.7 |
| 1981 | 261.0 | 658.0 | – | 11446.0 | 547.0 | 2264.0 | 217.6 | 1035.4 | 3024.6 | 18546.0f | 19465.0 |
| 1982 | 243.0 | 750.0 | – | 12792.0 | 910.0 | 2766.0e | 346.0 | 1103.3 | 3509.7 | 21427.0h | 22420.0 |
| 1983 | 300.0 | 752.0 | – | 16331.3 | 801.0 | 2265.5 | 1216.2 | 1161.6 | 2989.9 | 24765.5i | 25817.5 |
| 1984 | 408.0 | 703.0 | – | 18985.8 | 1116.4 | 1283.3 | 1346.4 | 1236.6 | 2150.8 | 26119.3j | 27230.3 |
| 1985 | 453.0 | 698.0 | – | 20546.4 | 1413.0 | 1624.3 | 706.9 | 1332.6 | 2599.8 | 28223.0k | 29374.0 |
| 1986 | 439.0 | 846.7 | – | 23067.7 | 2533.0 | 2373.0 | 760.1 | 1603.2 | 4526.2 | 34863.2 | 36148.9 |
| 1987 | 399.3 | 837.9 | – | 23939.4 | 2542.2 | 2562.3 | 964.8 | 1740.0 | 3720.5 | 35469.2 | 36706.4 |
| 1988 | 567.0 | 1196.3 | – | 27531.9 | 2298.8 | 3092.8 | 1203.7 | 1947.0 | 6186.8 | 42261.0 | 44024.3 |
| 1989 | 404.0 | 1297.0 | – | 25868.8 | 2676.1 | 3920.0 | 1353.0 | 2063.0 | 9978.9l | 45859.8 | 47560.8 |
| 1990 | 488.0 | 1256.5 | – | 27233.8 | 3212.0 | 4554.1 | 1738.7 | 2298.1 | 7567.9 | 46604.6m | 48349.1 |
| 1991 | 495.0 | 1191.0 | – | 33443.2 | 3869.3 | 5179.9 | 1918.8 | 2519.2 | 9655.6 | 56586.0m | 58272.0 |
| 1992 | 535.3 | 1910.0 | – | 38461.6 | 4817.2 | 7578.7 | 2423.7 | 2927.4 | 6619.0 | 62827.6m | 65272.9 |
| 1993 | 551.8 | 1750.0 | – | 38824.0 | 5536.0 | 8358.0 | 2892.6 | 3400.9 | 6511.1 | 65522.6n | 67824.4 |
| 1994 | 393.0 | 1960.0 | – | 40750.8 | 5939.9 | 7941.9 | 3194.3 | 3617.6 | 8569.0 | 70013.5o | 72366.5 |

a UA until 1977, EUA/ECU from 1978 onwards.
b Incorporated in the EC budget from 1971.
c This column includes for the years to 1970, substantial amounts carried forward to following years.
d Commission, Council, Parliament, Court of Justice and Court of Auditors.
e Including surplus of ECU 82.4 Mio carried forward to 1981.
f Including ECU 173 Mio carried forward to 1981.
g Including ECU 1 819 Mio UK special measures.
h Including ECU 2 211 Mio carried forward to 1983.
i Including ECU 1 707 Mio carried forward to 1984.
j There was a small deficit in 1984 in respect of the EC budget due largely to late payment of advances by some Member States.
k There was a cash deficit in 1985 of ECU 25 Mio due to late payment of advances by some Member States.
l Including a surplus of ECU 5080 Mio carried forward to 1990.
m 1990-92: Court of Auditors' Report.
n General budget of the Community for 1993.
o General budget of the European Union for 1994. The figures for Social and Regional Funds do not include Community initiatives as these have not yet been decided.
Source: 1958-89: Management accounts.

***Table L2***   Budgetary receipts of the European Communities.

(Mio UA/EUA/ECU)[a]

| | ECSC levies and other | European Development Fund contributions | Euratom contributions (research only) | EC budget | | | | | | Total |
| | | | | Miscellaneous and contributions under special keys | Own resources | | | | Total EC | Total |
| | | | | | Miscellaneous | Agricultural levies | Import duties | GNP contributions or VAT[b, c] | | |
|---|---|---|---|---|---|---|---|---|---|---|
| 1958 | 44.0 | 116.0 | 7.9 | 0.02 | – | – | – | 5.9 | 5.9 | 173.8 |
| 1959 | 49.6 | 116.0 | 39.1 | 0.1 | – | – | – | 25.1 | 25.2 | 229.9 |
| 1960 | 53.3 | 116.0 | 20.0 | 0.2 | – | – | – | 28.1 | 28.3 | 217.6 |
| 1961 | 53.1 | 116.0 | 72.5 | 2.8 | – | – | – | 31.2 | 34.0 | 275.6 |
| 1962 | 45.3 | 116.0 | 88.6 | 2.1 | – | – | – | 90.2 | 92.3 | 342.2 |
| 1963 | 47.1 | – | 106.4 | 6.7 | – | – | – | 77.4 | 84.1 | 237.5 |
| 1964 | 61.3 | – | 124.4 | 2.9 | – | – | – | 90.1 | 93.1 | 278.7 |
| 1965 | 66.1 | – | 98.8 | 3.5 | – | – | – | 197.6 | 201.1 | 366.0 |
| 1966 | 71.2 | – | 116.5 | 3.9 | – | – | – | 398.3 | 402.2 | 590.0 |
| 1967 | 40.3 | 40.0 | 158.5 | 4.2 | – | – | – | 670.9 | 675.1 | 913.9 |
| 1968 | 85.4 | 90.0 | 82.0 | – | – | – | – | – | 2408.6 | 2666.0 |
| 1969 | 106.8 | 110.0 | 62.7 | 78.6 | – | – | – | 3972.6 | 4051.2 | 4330.7 |
| 1970 | 100.0 | 130.0 | 67.7 | 121.1 | – | – | – | 5327.3 | 5448.4 | 5746.1 |
| 1971 | 57.9 | 170.0 | – | – | 69.5 | 713.8 | 582.2 | 923.8 | 2289.3 | 2517.2 |
| 1972 | 61.1 | 170.0 | – | – | 80.9 | 799.6 | 957.4 | 1236.6 | 3074.5 | 3305.6 |
| 1973 | 120.3 | 150.0 | – | – | 511.0 | 478.0 | 1564.7 | 2087.3 | 4641.0 | 4911.3 |
| 1974 | 124.6 | 150.0 | – | – | 65.3 | 323.6 | 2684.4 | 1964.8 | 5038.2 | 5312.8 |
| 1975 | 189.5 | 220.1 | – | – | 320.5 | 590.0 | 3151.0 | 2152.0 | 6213.6 | 6623.1 |
| 1976 | 129.6 | 311.0 | – | – | 282.8 | 1163.7 | 4064.6 | 2482.1 | 7993.1[d] | 8433.7 |
| 1977 | 123.0 | 410.0 | – | – | 504.7 | 1778.5 | 3927.2 | 2494.5 | 8704.9 | 9237.9 |
| 1978 | 164.9 | 147.5 | – | – | 344.4 | 2283.3 | 4390.9 | 5329.7 | 12348.2 | 12660.6 |
| 1979 | 168.4 | 480.0 | – | – | 230.3 | 2143.4 | 5189.1 | 7039.8 | 14602.5 | 15251.0 |
| 1980 | 226.2 | 555.0 | – | – | 1055.9[e] | 2002.3 | 5905.8 | 7093.5 | 16057.5[f] | 16838.7 |
| 1981 | 264.0 | 658.0 | – | – | 1219.0 | 1747.0 | 6392.0 | 9188.0 | 18546.0[g] | 19468.0 |
| 1982 | 243.0 | 750.0 | – | – | 187.0 | 2228.0 | 6815.0 | 12197.0 | 21427.0 | 22420.0 |
| 1983 | 300.0 | 700.0 | – | – | 1565.0 | 2295.0 | 6988.7 | 13916.8 | 24765.5[h] | 25765.5 |
| 1984 | 408.0 | 703.0 | – | – | 1060.7[i] | 2436.3 | 7960.8 | 14594.6 | 26052.4[j] | 27163.4 |
| 1985 | 453.0 | 698.0 | – | – | 2491.0[k] | 2179.0 | 8310.0 | 15218.0 | 28198.0 | 29349.0 |
| 1986 | 439.0 | 846.7 | – | – | 396.5 | 2287.0 | 8172.9 | 22810.8 | 33667.2 | 34952.9 |
| 1987 | 399.3 | 837.9 | – | – | 74.8 | 3097.9 | 8936.5 | 23674.1 | 35783.3 | 37020.5 |
| 1988 | 567.0 | 1196.3 | – | – | 1377.0 | 2606.0 | 9310.0 | 28968.0 | 42261.0 | 44024.3 |
| 1989 | 404.0 | 1297.0 | – | – | 4018.4 | 2397.9 | 10312.9 | 29170.6 | 45899.8 | 47600.8 |
| 1990 | 488.0 | 1256.5 | – | – | 5191.5 | 1675.7 | 10285.1 | 29252.4 | 46604.7[l] | 49349.1 |
| 1991 | 495.0 | 1191.0 | – | – | 3749.2 | 2486.8 | 11476.0 | 38874.5 | 56586.5[l] | 58272.5 |
| 1992 | 535.3 | 1910.0 | – | – | 385.9 | 2328.6 | 11599.9 | 48513.2 | 62827.6[l] | 65272.9 |
| 1993 | 551.8 | 1750.0 | – | – | 457.7 | 2239.3 | 13118.6 | 49707.0 | 65522.6[m] | 67824.4 |
| 1994 | 393.0 | – | – | – | 516.1 | 2038.9 | 12619.3 | 54839.2 | 70013.6[n] | 72366.5 |

a  UA until 1977, EUA/ECU from 1978 onwards.
b  GNP until 1978, VAT from 1979 until 1987. GNP from 1988 onwards.
c  This column includes for the years until 1970 surplus revenue from previous years carried forward to following years.
d  As a result of the calculations to establish the relative shares of the Member States in the 1976 budget, an excess of revenue over expenditure occurred amounting to 40.5 Mio UA. This was carried forward to 1977.
e  Including surplus brought forward from 1979 and balance of 1979 VAT and financial contributions.
f  Including surplus of ECU 82.4 Mio carried foward to 1981
g  Including surplus of ECU 661 Mio.
h  Including surplus of ECU 307 Mio.
i  Including ECU 593 Mio of repayable advances by Member States.
j  See note j to Table 63.
k  Including non-repayable advances by Member States of 1981. ECU 6 Mio
l  1990-92; Court of Auditors' Report.
m  General budget of the Community for 1993.
n  General budget of the European Union for 1994
Note: From 1988 onwards agricultural levies, sugar levies and customs duties are net of 10% collection costs previously included as an expenditure item.
Source: 1958-89: Management accounts.

***Table M1***   Price deflator exports of goods and services. National accounts definition.

(National currency; annual percentage change)

| | B | DK | WD | D | GR | E | F | IRL | I | L | NL | P | UK | EUR 12– | EUR 12+ | USA | J |
|---|---|---|---|---|---|---|---|---|---|---|---|---|---|---|---|---|---|
| 1960 | 0.6 | -1.2 | -0.9 | : | 0.2 | 2.0 | 0.3 | -0.1 | -0.8 | -3.0 | -1.7 | -1.1 | 1.2 | -0.1 | : | 1.4 | -0.7 |
| 1961 | 1.0 | 2.5 | 1.9 | : | 1.1 | 4.8 | 1.2 | 1.9 | 0.9 | -1.7 | -0.1 | -0.9 | 0.8 | 1.2 | : | -0.1 | -1.5 |
| 1963 | 2.1 | 2.8 | 1.0 | : | 8.0 | 6.3 | 2.8 | 2.1 | 3.3 | 0.0 | 2.6 | 3.2 | 4.2 | 2.8 | : | 0.1 | 2.5 |
| 1964 | 4.2 | 3.4 | 2.7 | : | 0.9 | 2.8 | 4.4 | 4.7 | 4.1 | 2.2 | 2.5 | 3.9 | 2.1 | 3.0 | : | 0.4 | 1.6 |
| 1965 | 1.4 | 2.2 | 2.7 | : | -1.1 | 5.6 | 1.1 | 1.9 | 0.0 | 1.4 | 2.3 | 3.0 | 2.0 | 1.9 | : | 3.1 | -0.4 |
| 1966 | 3.7 | 3.0 | 2.5 | : | 3.9 | 5.7 | 2.0 | 1.9 | 0.2 | 0.8 | 0.7 | -1.8 | 2.5 | 2.1 | : | 3.1 | -0.2 |
| 1967 | 0.5 | 1.2 | 0.2 | : | -2.7 | 7.9 | -0.4 | 0.6 | 1.1 | 0.4 | 0.0 | 3.7 | 2.7 | 1.1 | : | 3.2 | 0.2 |
| 1968 | 0.2 | 3.0 | 0.0 | : | -1.3 | 9.2 | -0.4 | 6.2 | 0.3 | 1.3 | -0.5 | 2.3 | 7.7 | 2.2 | : | 1.7 | 0.1 |
| 1969 | 4.6 | 6.7 | 4.0 | : | 0.5 | 1.6 | 4.8 | 6.1 | 2.7 | 6.5 | 2.2 | -1.5 | 2.2 | 3.3 | : | 2.0 | 1.5 |
| 1970 | 5.7 | 6.5 | 3.3 | : | 3.1 | 5.0 | 7.8 | -6.1 | 6.1 | 13.2 | 5.8 | 5.4 | 8.0 | 5.8 | : | 5.5 | 2.9 |
| 1961-70 | 2.4 | 3.0 | 1.7 | : | 1.2 | 5.1 | 2.3 | 1.9 | 1.8 | 2.0 | 1.3 | 1.6 | 3.3 | 2.3 | : | 2.0 | 0.6 |
| 1971 | 2.1 | 3.5 | 4.3 | : | 1.7 | 6.0 | 6.0 | 7.3 | 4.6 | -2.8 | 3.2 | 2.9 | 5.0 | 4.5 | : | 4.0 | 2.8 |
| 1972 | 1.7 | 6.9 | 2.1 | : | 5.7 | 6.1 | 1.5 | 11.5 | 4.3 | 0.7 | 1.8 | 5.2 | 4.1 | 3.1 | : | 4.0 | -0.6 |
| 1973 | 8.3 | 12.0 | 6.7 | : | 26.1 | 9.4 | 8.6 | 19.7 | 14.8 | 15.0 | 7.2 | 9.4 | 11.8 | 9.9 | : | 12.4 | 9.7 |
| 1974 | 24.5 | 20.5 | 15.8 | : | 31.6 | 22.4 | 24.7 | 23.0 | 38.2 | 26.5 | 26.0 | 39.5 | 24.9 | 24.5 | : | 22.4 | 31.3 |
| 1975 | 5.5 | 7.7 | 4.1 | : | 12.9 | 10.7 | 5.6 | 18.4 | 13.5 | -1.0 | 5.1 | 1.0 | 20.7 | 9.7 | : | 10.9 | 5.0 |
| 1976 | 5.8 | 7.0 | 3.5 | : | 10.0 | 16.4 | 10.0 | 23.0 | 23.0 | 8.6 | 6.6 | 7.1 | 19.8 | 12.0 | : | 4.7 | 2.0 |
| 1977 | 3.6 | 6.7 | 1.8 | : | 9.9 | 19.4 | 9.9 | 14.8 | 15.8 | -2.8 | 3.6 | 35.5 | 15.4 | 9.7 | : | 5.1 | -3.6 |
| 1978 | 1.1 | 6.3 | 1.6 | : | 8.2 | 15.8 | 7.1 | 6.6 | 9.0 | 2.7 | -1.3 | 25.9 | 7.6 | 5.8 | : | 6.9 | -6.3 |
| 1979 | 9.0 | 8.2 | 4.9 | : | 14.5 | 9.3 | 10.1 | 9.6 | 16.4 | 7.7 | 8.3 | 27.6 | 11.4 | 10.2 | : | 13.2 | 8.1 |
| 1980 | 9.3 | 14.6 | 6.3 | : | 34.0 | 19.3 | 11.7 | 10.8 | 23.6 | 7.5 | 12.3 | 25.2 | 13.9 | 13.4 | : | 11.5 | 9.7 |
| 1971-80 | 6.9 | 9.2 | 5.0 | : | 15.0 | 13.3 | 9.4 | 14.3 | 15.9 | 5.9 | 7.1 | 17.2 | 13.3 | 10.1 | : | 9.4 | 5.4 |
| 1981 | 9.6 | 12.7 | 5.7 | : | 25.5 | 17.9 | 14.0 | 16.4 | 20.0 | 9.6 | 13.4 | 18.5 | 8.4 | 12.0 | : | 6.5 | 2.6 |
| 1982 | 13.1 | 10.6 | 3.5 | : | 20.7 | 13.8 | 12.5 | 10.8 | 16.9 | 15.5 | 4.2 | 19.8 | 6.9 | 9.6 | : | 2.1 | 2.8 |
| 1983 | 7.3 | 5.2 | 1.9 | : | 19.3 | 16.8 | 9.9 | 9.1 | 9.1 | 5.9 | 0.1 | 30.0 | 7.6 | 7.1 | : | 1.5 | -4.8 |
| 1984 | 8.1 | 7.7 | 3.4 | : | 15.7 | 12.6 | 9.3 | 8.1 | 9.6 | 5.2 | 5.5 | 30.2 | 7.6 | 7.8 | : | 1.9 | 0.0 |
| 1985 | 2.9 | 3.6 | 2.8 | : | 17.0 | 6.7 | 4.7 | 3.1 | 8.7 | 3.9 | 1.5 | 17.6 | 5.1 | 4.8 | : | -1.5 | -2.5 |
| 1986 | -8.4 | -5.4 | -1.4 | : | 10.6 | -1.7 | -3.0 | -6.3 | -2.7 | -2.2 | -15.8 | 4.5 | -8.2 | -4.8 | : | -0.9 | -13.5 |
| 1987 | -3.8 | -1.9 | -1.1 | : | 7.5 | 2.5 | -0.5 | 0.5 | 1.1 | -6.5 | -4.6 | 11.4 | 2.8 | 0.0 | : | 2.5 | -5.0 |
| 1988 | 2.9 | 0.7 | 1.9 | : | 7.5 | 3.0 | 2.6 | 5.6 | 4.2 | 3.6 | 0.5 | 8.9 | 0.3 | 2.4 | : | 5.0 | -3.3 |
| 1989 | 7.1 | 6.5 | 2.7 | : | 10.6 | 4.5 | 4.8 | 7.3 | 7.3 | 7.3 | 4.5 | 10.7 | 8.2 | 5.6 | : | 2.1 | 3.6 |
| 1990 | -1.7 | 0.1 | 0.1 | : | 11.9 | 1.7 | -1.2 | -8.3 | 3.3 | -0.8 | -0.8 | 6.0 | 4.4 | 1.0 | : | 1.2 | 1.0 |
| 1981-90 | 3.5 | 3.8 | 1.9 | : | 14.5 | 7.6 | 5.2 | 4.4 | 7.5 | 4.0 | 0.6 | 15.4 | 4.2 | 4.4 | : | 2.0 | -2.0 |
| 1991 | -0.3 | 1.2 | 1.3 | : | 9.5 | 2.0 | 0.5 | -0.4 | 2.8 | -0.3 | -0.2 | 1.0 | 1.5 | 1.2 | : | 1.1 | -2.8 |
| 1992 | -1.0 | -1.2 | 1.0 | 0.7 | 17.2 | 3.2 | -1.4 | -2.1 | 1.9 | -0.7 | -2.4 | -1.7 | 1.6 | 0.5 | 0.4 | 0.1 | -3.5 |
| 1993 | 1.0 | -1.6 | 1.2 | 0.8 | 14.8 | 6.8 | -1.1 | 4.6 | 9.9 | 1.5 | -2.0 | 3.0 | 9.3 | 3.5 | 3.6 | 0.4 | -4.8 |
| 1994 | 2.4 | 1.8 | 1.6 | 1.9 | 10.6 | 5.6 | 1.7 | 2.2 | 5.0 | 4.6 | 1.9 | 5.4 | 1.7 | 2.7 | 2.8 | 2.2 | -3.0 |

EUR: PPS weighted. EUR 12–: incl. WD; EUR 12+: incl. D.

**Table M2** Price deflator imports of goods and services. National accounts definition.

(National currency; annual percentage change)

| | B | DK | WD | D | GR | E | F | IRL | I | L | NL | P | UK | EUR 12- | EUR 12+ | USA | J |
|---|---|---|---|---|---|---|---|---|---|---|---|---|---|---|---|---|---|
| 1961 | 2.6 | 0.1 | -2.4 | : | -1.7 | 2.0 | 0.1 | 1.1 | -2.2 | 1.4 | -1.9 | 1.0 | 0.0 | -0.7 | : | -0.2 | 1.2 |
| 1962 | 0.8 | -0.1 | -0.2 | : | -0.7 | 2.0 | 2.7 | 0.5 | 0.4 | 0.8 | -0.9 | -1.3 | -0.2 | 0.3 | : | -0.9 | -2.2 |
| 1963 | 4.0 | 1.9 | 2.4 | : | 3.0 | 2.0 | 1.1 | 1.9 | 1.5 | 1.2 | 1.4 | 1.6 | 4.8 | 2.6 | : | 2.2 | 1.8 |
| 1964 | 3.2 | 1.3 | 1.8 | : | 3.0 | 2.4 | 0.9 | 1.3 | 3.4 | 2.1 | 2.4 | 2.2 | 2.1 | 2.1 | : | 2.0 | 1.5 |
| 1965 | 0.2 | 1.6 | 2.9 | : | 0.3 | 0.2 | 1.4 | 2.6 | 0.6 | 1.7 | 0.5 | 2.8 | 1.1 | 1.4 | : | 1.6 | -0.7 |
| 1966 | 3.2 | 1.6 | 1.8 | : | 3.3 | 0.2 | 3.2 | 0.2 | 1.9 | 1.4 | 0.7 | 0.0 | 1.3 | 1.7 | : | 3.2 | 2.3 |
| 1967 | 0.5 | 2.5 | -1.4 | : | -3.0 | 2.8 | -1.3 | -0.3 | 0.7 | -0.7 | -0.9 | -2.4 | 1.4 | 0.0 | : | 1.6 | -0.1 |
| 1968 | 0.6 | 5.0 | 0.7 | : | 0.2 | 10.7 | -1.1 | 7.9 | 0.7 | 0.0 | -2.9 | -2.5 | 10.6 | 2.9 | : | 0.7 | 0.7 |
| 1969 | 3.2 | 2.9 | 1.9 | : | 0.0 | 3.0 | 4.9 | 4.2 | 1.4 | 3.1 | 3.3 | 0.9 | 2.5 | 2.7 | : | 1.9 | 2.9 |
| 1970 | 5.1 | 5.6 | -6.5 | : | 4.0 | 5.1 | 9.7 | 0.7 | 3.7 | 6.8 | 6.6 | 9.3 | 6.3 | 3.1 | : | 5.9 | 2.1 |
| 1961-70 | 2.3 | 2.2 | 0.0 | : | 0.8 | 3.0 | 2.1 | 2.0 | 1.2 | 1.8 | 0.8 | 1.1 | 2.9 | 1.6 | : | 1.8 | 1.0 |
| 1971 | 3.4 | 6.1 | 1.0 | : | 2.9 | 5.4 | 5.2 | 5.4 | 4.9 | 5.1 | 4.3 | 1.4 | 4.1 | 3.7 | : | 4.7 | -3.0 |
| 1972 | 0.4 | 2.0 | 1.7 | : | 7.7 | 1.5 | 0.9 | 5.7 | 4.5 | -0.1 | -0.4 | 3.4 | 2.7 | 2.0 | : | 6.3 | -4.7 |
| 1973 | 7.5 | 16.8 | 8.0 | : | 21.9 | 10.4 | 6.7 | 13.9 | 27.1 | 9.0 | 7.5 | 14.1 | 23.3 | 14.1 | : | 12.1 | 18.5 |
| 1974 | 27.5 | 32.7 | 24.2 | : | 41.6 | 41.9 | 47.0 | 44.4 | 55.9 | 22.4 | 32.7 | 43.8 | 41.5 | 38.9 | : | 43.1 | 64.2 |
| 1975 | 6.7 | 4.9 | 2.1 | : | 17.4 | 7.0 | 2.7 | 20.5 | 9.9 | 10.2 | 4.3 | 13.9 | 13.6 | 7.4 | : | 8.0 | 9.5 |
| 1976 | 6.4 | 8.5 | 6.2 | : | 11.2 | 14.9 | 12.2 | 19.0 | 25.3 | 6.2 | 6.4 | 11.2 | 21.1 | 13.8 | : | 3.2 | 5.3 |
| 1977 | 3.1 | 7.7 | 1.7 | : | 5.8 | 22.1 | 12.9 | 16.8 | 14.9 | 3.8 | 3.2 | 30.7 | 13.7 | 10.1 | : | 8.4 | -3.8 |
| 1978 | 1.1 | 2.7 | -1.8 | : | 9.7 | 7.6 | 3.5 | 4.7 | 7.7 | 1.8 | -1.6 | 22.1 | 3.0 | 3.0 | : | 8.7 | -15.7 |
| 1979 | 8.9 | 13.7 | 8.6 | : | 17.7 | 7.2 | 11.7 | 13.7 | 19.7 | 7.9 | 10.9 | 30.5 | 9.3 | 11.8 | : | 17.5 | 27.7 |
| 1980 | 13.5 | 21.7 | 12.8 | : | 35.2 | 37.9 | 21.7 | 18.0 | 29.0 | 7.6 | 14.5 | 31.3 | 9.6 | 18.6 | : | 24.6 | 37.5 |
| 1971-80 | 7.6 | 11.3 | 6.2 | : | 16.5 | 14.9 | 11.8 | 15.7 | 19.1 | 7.2 | 7.8 | 19.5 | 13.7 | 11.9 | : | 13.1 | 11.4 |
| 1981 | 13.9 | 17.7 | 11.7 | : | 19.5 | 29.8 | 19.1 | 18.6 | 24.7 | 10.1 | 14.3 | 25.6 | 7.7 | 16.5 | : | 4.3 | 2.1 |
| 1982 | 13.3 | 10.1 | 2.8 | : | 24.0 | 13.0 | 12.5 | 7.5 | 11.9 | 13.8 | 1.3 | 18.1 | 7.0 | 8.8 | : | -2.9 | 6.6 |
| 1983 | 7.4 | 3.7 | 0.9 | : | 17.6 | 21.5 | 8.5 | 5.2 | 4.8 | 7.9 | 0.4 | 29.9 | 7.6 | 6.6 | : | -3.0 | -5.4 |
| 1984 | 8.1 | 7.9 | 5.1 | : | 22.8 | 11.5 | 10.0 | 9.4 | 9.8 | 7.4 | 5.7 | 31.2 | 8.7 | 8.9 | : | -0.2 | -2.6 |
| 1985 | 2.1 | 3.2 | 2.7 | : | 17.8 | 3.8 | 2.0 | 2.6 | 8.2 | 3.1 | 1.2 | 13.0 | 4.0 | 4.0 | : | -2.2 | -2.3 |
| 1986 | -12.3 | -9.2 | -11.5 | : | 8.4 | -14.6 | -12.7 | -10.2 | -13.5 | -4.4 | -16.7 | -6.8 | -4.4 | -10.9 | : | -0.1 | -31.9 |
| 1987 | -4.6 | -2.4 | -4.8 | : | 0.4 | 0.8 | -0.6 | 1.3 | 0.6 | -2.6 | -3.0 | 12.6 | 2.4 | -0.9 | : | 5.9 | -5.7 |
| 1988 | 2.7 | 2.2 | 1.8 | : | 6.4 | 1.1 | 2.5 | 6.4 | 4.4 | 2.4 | -0.4 | 11.6 | -0.8 | 2.0 | : | 4.0 | -2.8 |
| 1989 | 6.6 | 6.4 | 5.2 | : | 10.7 | 2.3 | 6.6 | 6.8 | 9.1 | 5.0 | 4.8 | 8.5 | 6.5 | 6.3 | : | 1.6 | 7.6 |
| 1990 | -1.2 | -0.5 | -0.6 | : | 9.5 | -1.2 | -1.4 | -4.2 | 0.8 | 0.0 | -1.3 | 6.5 | 3.4 | 0.3 | : | 2.7 | 7.4 |
| 1981-90 | 3.3 | 3.7 | 1.2 | : | 13.5 | 6.1 | 4.3 | 4.1 | 5.7 | 4.1 | 0.3 | 14.5 | 4.1 | 3.9 | : | -1.0 | -3.4 |
| 1991 | -0.4 | 1.4 | 2.2 | : | 9.1 | -0.3 | -0.1 | 2.5 | -0.1 | 1.3 | 0.1 | 1.2 | 0.4 | 0.8 | : | -1.8 | -5.9 |
| 1992 | -2.4 | -1.3 | -1.6 | -1.7 | 14.3 | 1.4 | -2.1 | -1.1 | 2.0 | -1.5 | -2.0 | -3.3 | 0.2 | -0.6 | -0.6 | -0.8 | -6.1 |
| 1993 | 0.6 | -0.7 | -1.0 | -1.0 | 13.0 | 7.3 | -2.9 | 4.0 | 12.4 | -0.5 | -2.2 | 2.6 | 7.6 | 3.0 | 3.0 | -1.1 | -10.0 |
| 1994 | 2.4 | 2.4 | 1.6 | 1.4 | 9.7 | 5.6 | 2.3 | 2.1 | 6.5 | 3.2 | 2.0 | 5.9 | 1.2 | 3.0 | 3.0 | -1.5 | -3.3 |

EUR: PPS weighted. EUR 12-: incl. WD; EUR 12+: incl. D.

**Table M3** Terms of trade; goods and services. National accounts definition.

(1980=100)

| | B | DK | WD | GR | E | F | IRL | I | L | NL | P | UK | USA | J |
|---|---|---|---|---|---|---|---|---|---|---|---|---|---|---|
| 1960 | 106.0 | 112.1 | 94.5 | 109.8 | 93.9 | 122.2 | 114.7 | 123.4 | 110.8 | 101.9 | 116.8 | 99.7 | 136.6 | 181.5 |
| 1961 | 103.9 | 110.7 | 96.0 | 111.9 | 93.9 | 122.4 | 113.3 | 125.3 | 106.0 | 102.1 | 114.4 | 100.9 | 138.7 | 178.0 |
| 1962 | 104.1 | 113.5 | 98.1 | 114.0 | 96.4 | 120.5 | 114.9 | 125.9 | 103.4 | 102.9 | 114.9 | 102.0 | 140.0 | 179.1 |
| 1963 | 102.2 | 114.5 | 96.7 | 119.6 | 100.5 | 122.5 | 115.0 | 128.0 | 102.1 | 104.1 | 116.7 | 101.4 | 137.1 | 180.4 |
| 1964 | 103.2 | 116.9 | 97.5 | 117.1 | 100.9 | 126.8 | 118.9 | 128.9 | 102.2 | 104.2 | 118.6 | 101.3 | 135.1 | 180.5 |
| 1965 | 104.4 | 117.5 | 97.3 | 115.5 | 106.3 | 126.3 | 118.1 | 128.1 | 101.9 | 106.0 | 118.9 | 102.2 | 137.1 | 181.0 |
| 1966 | 105.0 | 119.1 | 98.0 | 116.1 | 112.1 | 124.8 | 120.0 | 126.0 | 101.3 | 106.0 | 116.7 | 103.5 | 137.0 | 176.6 |
| 1967 | 105.0 | 117.6 | 99.6 | 116.5 | 117.6 | 126.0 | 121.1 | 126.5 | 102.4 | 106.9 | 124.0 | 104.8 | 139.1 | 177.1 |
| 1968 | 104.5 | 115.4 | 99.0 | 114.7 | 116.0 | 126.9 | 119.3 | 126.0 | 103.7 | 109.4 | 130.1 | 102.1 | 140.5 | 176.0 |
| 1969 | 106.0 | 119.7 | 101.1 | 115.2 | 114.4 | 126.7 | 121.4 | 127.6 | 107.1 | 108.2 | 126.9 | 101.8 | 140.7 | 173.6 |
| 1970 | 106.6 | 120.7 | 111.8 | 114.2 | 114.3 | 124.4 | 113.2 | 130.6 | 113.6 | 107.3 | 122.3 | 103.5 | 140.1 | 174.9 |
| 1971 | 105.3 | 118.8 | 115.5 | 112.8 | 114.9 | 125.4 | 115.2 | 130.1 | 105.1 | 106.2 | 124.1 | 104.4 | 139.2 | 185.3 |
| 1972 | 106.7 | 123.5 | 115.8 | 110.7 | 120.2 | 126.2 | 121.5 | 129.9 | 105.9 | 108.6 | 126.2 | 105.8 | 136.2 | 193.1 |
| 1973 | 107.5 | 118.5 | 114.5 | 114.5 | 119.1 | 128.4 | 127.7 | 117.3 | 111.8 | 108.2 | 121.0 | 96.0 | 136.3 | 178.8 |
| 1974 | 104.9 | 107.6 | 106.7 | 106.4 | 102.7 | 109.0 | 108.8 | 104.0 | 115.5 | 102.8 | 117.3 | 84.7 | 116.8 | 143.0 |
| 1975 | 103.8 | 110.4 | 108.9 | 102.3 | 106.4 | 112.0 | 106.9 | 107.4 | 103.7 | 103.6 | 104.1 | 90.0 | 119.9 | 137.1 |
| 1976 | 103.2 | 108.9 | 106.1 | 101.2 | 107.7 | 109.9 | 110.5 | 105.4 | 106.1 | 103.7 | 100.3 | 89.0 | 121.7 | 132.9 |
| 1977 | 103.7 | 107.8 | 106.2 | 105.2 | 105.4 | 106.9 | 108.5 | 106.1 | 99.3 | 104.1 | 103.9 | 90.3 | 118.0 | 133.1 |
| 1978 | 103.7 | 111.5 | 109.9 | 103.7 | 113.4 | 110.6 | 110.5 | 107.4 | 100.2 | 104.4 | 107.2 | 94.4 | 116.0 | 148.0 |
| 1979 | 103.8 | 106.2 | 106.2 | 100.9 | 115.6 | 109.0 | 106.5 | 104.4 | 100.1 | 101.9 | 104.8 | 96.2 | 111.7 | 125.3 |
| 1980 | 100.0 | 100.0 | 100.0 | 100.0 | 100.0 | 100.0 | 100.0 | 100.0 | 100.0 | 100.0 | 100.0 | 100.0 | 100.0 | 100.0 |
| 1981 | 96.2 | 95.7 | 94.6 | 105.0 | 90.8 | 95.7 | 98.1 | 96.2 | 99.6 | 99.3 | 94.4 | 100.6 | 102.1 | 100.5 |
| 1982 | 96.0 | 96.1 | 95.3 | 102.2 | 91.5 | 95.8 | 101.1 | 100.5 | 101.0 | 102.0 | 95.7 | 100.5 | 107.4 | 96.9 |
| 1983 | 95.9 | 97.5 | 96.2 | 103.7 | 88.0 | 97.0 | 104.8 | 104.7 | 99.1 | 101.7 | 95.8 | 100.6 | 112.4 | 97.5 |
| 1984 | 95.9 | 97.3 | 94.6 | 97.6 | 88.9 | 96.4 | 103.5 | 104.5 | 97.1 | 101.5 | 95.1 | 99.6 | 114.7 | 100.0 |
| 1985 | 96.6 | 97.6 | 94.7 | 97.0 | 91.4 | 99.0 | 104.1 | 104.9 | 97.9 | 101.7 | 98.9 | 100.6 | 115.5 | 99.7 |
| 1986 | 100.9 | 101.8 | 105.5 | 99.0 | 105.1 | 110.0 | 108.6 | 117.9 | 100.1 | 102.9 | 110.9 | 96.6 | 114.6 | 126.6 |
| 1987 | 101.8 | 102.3 | 109.6 | 105.9 | 107.0 | 110.1 | 107.7 | 118.4 | 96.1 | 101.2 | 109.7 | 96.9 | 111.0 | 127.0 |
| 1988 | 102.0 | 100.8 | 109.7 | 107.1 | 109.0 | 110.2 | 106.9 | 118.2 | 97.3 | 102.2 | 107.1 | 98.1 | 112.1 | 127.0 |
| 1989 | 102.5 | 100.8 | 107.1 | 107.0 | 111.4 | 108.4 | 107.4 | 116.3 | 99.4 | 101.9 | 109.2 | 99.6 | 112.7 | 122.3 |
| 1990 | 101.9 | 101.5 | 107.9 | 109.3 | 114.6 | 108.6 | 102.9 | 119.2 | 98.6 | 102.4 | 108.8 | 100.6 | 111.0 | 115.1 |
| 1991 | 102.0 | 101.3 | 106.9 | 109.8 | 117.2 | 109.3 | 100.0 | 122.6 | 97.0 | 102.1 | 108.5 | 101.7 | 114.3 | 118.9 |
| 1992 | 103.5 | 101.4 | 109.8 | 112.6 | 119.3 | 110.1 | 99.0 | 122.5 | 97.8 | 101.6 | 110.2 | 103.1 | 115.3 | 122.3 |
| 1993 | 103.9 | 100.6 | 112.2 | 114.4 | 118.8 | 112.2 | 99.6 | 119.8 | 99.9 | 101.8 | 110.6 | 104.8 | 117.1 | 129.4 |
| 1994 | 104.0 | 100.0 | 112.1 | 115.3 | 118.7 | 111.5 | 99.6 | 118.2 | 101.3 | 101.8 | 110.0 | 105.3 | 121.4 | 129.8 |

*Contemporary Europe*

**Table M4** Exports of goods and services at current prices. National accounts definition.

(Percentage of gross domestic product at market prices)

| | B | DK | WD | D | GR | E | F | IRL | I | L | NL | P | UK | EUR 12- | EUR 12+ | USA | J |
|---|---|---|---|---|---|---|---|---|---|---|---|---|---|---|---|---|---|
| 1960 | 38.4 | 32.2 | 19.0 | : | 9.1 | 9.9 | 14.5 | 30.6 | 13.0 | 86.7 | 45.7 | 17.5 | 20.9 | 19.5 | : | 5.2 | 10.7 |
| 1961 | 39.6 | 29.9 | 18.0 | : | 9.3 | 9.6 | 14.0 | 33.2 | 13.3 | 86.9 | 43.5 | 16.4 | 20.6 | 19.0 | : | 5.1 | 9.3 |
| 1962 | 41.2 | 28.5 | 17.4 | : | 9.7 | 9.8 | 12.9 | 31.0 | 13.2 | 79.9 | 42.9 | 18.7 | 20.1 | 18.4 | : | 5.0 | 9.4 |
| 1963 | 42.4 | 30.3 | 17.8 | : | 10.0 | 9.2 | 12.7 | 32.2 | 12.7 | 77.7 | 43.0 | 19.1 | 20.0 | 18.3 | : | 5.1 | 9.0 |
| 1964 | 43.2 | 29.7 | 18.1 | : | 9.2 | 10.5 | 12.7 | 32.1 | 13.3 | 78.8 | 41.7 | 25.6 | 19.4 | 18.4 | : | 5.3 | 9.5 |
| 1965 | 42.6 | 29.2 | 18.0 | : | 9.0 | 10.2 | 13.3 | 33.4 | 14.9 | 80.7 | 41.1 | 26.8 | 19.2 | 18.7 | : | 5.2 | 10.5 |
| 1966 | 44.3 | 28.4 | 19.2 | : | 11.3 | 10.7 | 13.4 | 35.8 | 15.3 | 77.2 | 39.9 | 27.1 | 19.4 | 19.1 | : | 5.3 | 10.6 |
| 1967 | 43.4 | 27.2 | 20.4 | : | 10.7 | 9.8 | 13.2 | 36.3 | 15.0 | 78.5 | 38.8 | 27.2 | 19.1 | 19.1 | : | 5.3 | 9.6 |
| 1968 | 45.5 | 27.5 | 21.4 | : | 9.6 | 11.3 | 13.3 | 37.3 | 15.8 | 80.5 | 39.3 | 25.0 | 21.4 | 20.1 | : | 5.3 | 10.1 |
| 1969 | 49.5 | 27.4 | 21.7 | : | 9.7 | 11.6 | 14.1 | 35.8 | 16.5 | 84.3 | 40.7 | 24.4 | 22.3 | 20.9 | : | 5.3 | 10.5 |
| 1970 | 51.9 | 27.9 | 21.2 | : | 10.0 | 12.9 | 15.8 | 35.5 | 16.4 | 88.9 | 42.9 | 24.4 | 23.1 | 21.6 | : | 5.8 | 10.8 |
| 1961-70 | 44.4 | 28.6 | 19.3 | : | 9.8 | 10.5 | 13.5 | 34.3 | 14.6 | 81.3 | 41.4 | 23.5 | 20.5 | 19.3 | : | 5.3 | 9.9 |
| 1971 | 50.6 | 27.6 | 20.8 | : | 10.3 | 13.8 | 16.4 | 34.7 | 16.9 | 88.1 | 43.5 | 25.1 | 23.2 | 21.8 | : | 5.7 | 11.7 |
| 1972 | 51.1 | 27.1 | 20.6 | : | 11.7 | 14.2 | 16.7 | 33.2 | 17.7 | 82.9 | 43.1 | 27.2 | 21.7 | 21.8 | : | 5.8 | 10.6 |
| 1973 | 55.6 | 28.5 | 21.8 | : | 14.2 | 14.2 | 17.6 | 36.5 | 17.4 | 89.3 | 45.4 | 26.7 | 23.7 | 23.0 | : | 6.9 | 10.0 |
| 1974 | 61.3 | 31.8 | 26.4 | : | 16.1 | 14.0 | 20.7 | 40.9 | 20.2 | 102.6 | 51.7 | 26.9 | 28.0 | 26.8 | : | 8.6 | 13.6 |
| 1975 | 53.7 | 30.1 | 24.7 | : | 16.9 | 13.2 | 19.1 | 41.0 | 20.5 | 92.5 | 47.8 | 20.4 | 25.9 | 24.9 | : | 8.6 | 12.8 |
| 1976 | 57.1 | 28.8 | 25.7 | : | 17.6 | 13.4 | 19.6 | 44.4 | 22.1 | 88.1 | 48.8 | 17.4 | 28.5 | 26.2 | : | 8.3 | 13.6 |
| 1977 | 56.6 | 28.8 | 25.5 | : | 16.8 | 14.1 | 20.5 | 47.4 | 23.2 | 86.9 | 45.6 | 18.4 | 30.1 | 26.7 | : | 8.0 | 13.1 |
| 1978 | 55.1 | 27.8 | 24.8 | : | 17.6 | 14.8 | 20.4 | 48.0 | 23.4 | 83.8 | 43.0 | 20.1 | 28.5 | 26.1 | : | 8.3 | 11.1 |
| 1979 | 60.5 | 29.2 | 25.1 | : | 17.5 | 14.6 | 21.2 | 47.7 | 24.3 | 90.9 | 47.0 | 27.1 | 28.0 | 26.8 | : | 9.1 | 11.6 |
| 1980 | 62.9 | 32.7 | 26.4 | : | 20.9 | 15.4 | 21.5 | 47.6 | 21.9 | 88.5 | 50.3 | 27.4 | 27.3 | 27.1 | : | 10.2 | 13.7 |
| 1971-80 | 56.4 | 29.2 | 24.2 | : | 16.0 | 14.2 | 19.4 | 42.1 | 20.8 | 89.4 | 46.6 | 23.7 | 26.5 | 25.1 | : | 8.0 | 12.2 |
| 1981 | 68.2 | 36.5 | 28.7 | : | 20.6 | 17.6 | 22.6 | 46.5 | 23.3 | 86.6 | 55.6 | 25.9 | 26.7 | 28.5 | : | 9.9 | 14.7 |
| 1982 | 71.9 | 36.4 | 29.9 | : | 18.4 | 18.2 | 21.8 | 46.2 | 23.0 | 89.0 | 55.2 | 26.4 | 26.3 | 28.5 | : | 8.9 | 14.6 |
| 1983 | 74.7 | 36.4 | 28.7 | : | 19.8 | 20.7 | 22.5 | 50.4 | 22.1 | 90.2 | 55.3 | 31.3 | 26.5 | 28.6 | : | 8.0 | 13.9 |
| 1984 | 79.1 | 36.7 | 30.6 | : | 21.7 | 23.0 | 24.1 | 57.2 | 22.8 | 101.1 | 59.5 | 37.2 | 28.4 | 30.5 | : | 7.9 | 15.0 |
| 1985 | 76.9 | 36.7 | 32.5 | : | 21.2 | 22.7 | 23.9 | 58.0 | 22.8 | 108.6 | 60.8 | 37.3 | 28.8 | 30.9 | : | 7.4 | 14.5 |
| 1986 | 70.6 | 32.0 | 30.2 | : | 22.4 | 19.9 | 21.2 | 52.7 | 20.2 | 100.7 | 50.7 | 33.2 | 25.6 | 27.8 | : | 7.4 | 11.4 |
| 1987 | 69.3 | 31.4 | 29.0 | : | 24.5 | 19.4 | 20.6 | 56.3 | 19.5 | 98.4 | 49.8 | 34.3 | 25.3 | 27.1 | : | 7.9 | 10.4 |
| 1988 | 72.4 | 32.6 | 29.6 | : | 23.8 | 18.9 | 21.3 | 60.2 | 19.2 | 99.6 | 52.5 | 35.5 | 23.0 | 27.0 | : | 9.0 | 10.1 |
| 1989 | 76.8 | 34.5 | 31.5 | : | 22.9 | 18.1 | 22.9 | 64.1 | 20.4 | 101.1 | 55.2 | 37.5 | 23.8 | 28.3 | : | 9.6 | 10.7 |
| 1990 | 73.9 | 35.5 | 32.0 | : | 21.6 | 17.1 | 22.6 | 59.7 | 20.8 | 96.9 | 54.2 | 36.4 | 24.4 | 28.3 | : | 10.0 | 10.8 |
| 1981-90 | 73.4 | .34.9 | 30.3 | : | 21.7 | 19.5 | 22.4 | 55.1 | 21.4 | 97.2 | 54.9 | 33.5 | 25.9 | 28.6 | : | 8.6 | 12.6 |
| 1991 | 72.3 | 37.4 | 33.9 | 25.3 | 22.7 | 17.2 | 22.7 | 60.4 | 19.6 | 94.3 | 54.3 | 31.9 | 23.6 | 28.4 | 26.2 | 10.5 | 10.4 |
| 1992 | 69.3 | 37.1 | 33.5 | 23.7 | 23.2 | 17.6 | 23.2 | 63.1 | 20.0 | 89.1 | 52.3 | 29.1 | 23.7 | 28.5 | 25.9 | 10.6 | 10.2 |
| 1993 | 66.8 | 35.0 | 31.4 | 21.1 | 24.0 | 19.8 | 22.4 | 64.7 | 23.4 | 85.1 | 50.4 | 27.1 | 25.3 | 28.9 | 25.9 | 10.4 | 9.7 |
| 1994 | 67.9 | 35.1 | 32.4 | 21.9 | 24.9 | 21.7 | 22.9 | 64.8 | 25.1 | 87.2 | 51.7 | 28.5 | 25.4 | 29.9 | 26.9 | 10.5 | 9.3 |

EUR 12-: incl. WD; EUR 12+: incl. D.

**Table M5** Exports of goods and services at 1985 prices. National accounts definition.

(Annual percentage charge)

| | B | DK | WD | D | GR | E | F | IRL | I | L | NL | P | UK | EUR 12- | EUR 12+ | USA | J |
|---|---|---|---|---|---|---|---|---|---|---|---|---|---|---|---|---|---|
| 1961 | 9.2 | 4.3 | 5.0 | : | 14.5 | 7.9 | 5.1 | 17.2 | 14.7 | 3.5 | 2.3 | 1.9 | 3.1 | 5.7 | : | 0.6 | 5.3 |
| 1962 | 10.1 | 4.9 | 2.7 | : | 10.0 | 12.8 | 1.8 | -1.0 | 10.3 | -1.6 | 6.2 | 22.7 | 1.8 | 4.7 | : | 5.3 | 17.2 |
| 1963 | 8.2 | 10.0 | 7.9 | : | 6.7 | 3.8 | 7.1 | 9.6 | 6.5 | 3.8 | 6.0 | 7.2 | 1.2 | 5.7 | : | 6.9 | 7.0 |
| 1964 | 9.4 | 8.5 | 8.3 | : | 1.6 | 25.5 | 6.7 | 8.2 | 10.8 | 13.3 | 11.3 | 39.9 | 3.8 | 8.7 | : | 12.1 | 21.7 |
| 1965 | 6.1 | 7.9 | 6.4 | : | 12.7 | 6.9 | 11.5 | 8.9 | 20.0 | 5.8 | 7.6 | 13.5 | 4.4 | 8.5 | : | 2.9 | 23.7 |
| 1966 | 7.7 | 3.9 | 10.1 | : | 34.4 | 15.2 | 6.6 | 10.6 | 11.2 | -0.2 | 5.2 | 12.8 | 5.2 | 8.2 | : | 7.0 | 17.0 |
| 1967 | 4.3 | 4.0 | 7.7 | : | 5.1 | -4.7 | 7.3 | 10.3 | 7.2 | 1.9 | 6.6 | 8.3 | 1.0 | 5.1 | : | 3.0 | 6.7 |
| 1968 | 12.2 | 9.3 | 12.7 | : | -1.0 | 18.4 | 9.4 | 9.0 | 13.9 | 10.7 | 12.8 | -0.5 | 12.7 | 12.1 | : | 8.4 | 23.9 |
| 1969 | 15.3 | 6.2 | 9.3 | : | 14.6 | 15.6 | 15.7 | 4.6 | 11.8 | 13.8 | 14.9 | 8.7 | 9.3 | 11.6 | : | 6.1 | 20.8 |
| 1970 | 10.2 | 5.6 | 6.9 | : | 12.4 | 17.4 | 16.1 | 18.8 | 5.8 | 9.0 | 11.9 | 5.4 | 5.4 | 8.9 | : | 9.0 | 17.5 |
| 1961-70 | 9.2 | 6.4 | 7.7 | : | 10.7 | 11.6 | 8.6 | 9.5 | 11.1 | 5.9 | 8.4 | 11.5 | 4.7 | 7.9 | : | 6.1 | 15.9 |
| 1971 | 4.5 | 5.6 | 4.4 | : | 11.9 | 14.2 | 9.2 | 4.1 | 7.0 | 3.9 | 10.7 | 11.9 | 6.8 | 7.2 | : | 1.5 | 16.0 |
| 1972 | 11.1 | 5.6 | 6.8 | : | 22.9 | 13.4 | 12.0 | 3.6 | 9.5 | 5.3 | 10.0 | 20.2 | 0.8 | 7.9 | : | 8.1 | 4.1 |
| 1973 | 14.2 | 7.8 | 10.6 | : | 23.4 | 10.0 | 10.8 | 10.9 | 3.9 | 13.9 | 12.1 | 9.2 | 12.0 | 10.4 | : | 19.0 | 5.2 |
| 1974 | 3.8 | 3.5 | 12.0 | : | 0.1 | -1.0 | 8.8 | 0.7 | 5.9 | 10.7 | 2.6 | -13.3 | 6.9 | 6.6 | : | 8.9 | 23.2 |
| 1975 | -8.2 | -1.8 | -6.3 | : | 10.6 | -0.4 | -1.7 | 7.6 | 1.8 | -15.7 | -3.1 | -16.4 | -3.2 | -3.3 | : | -1.1 | -1.0 |
| 1976 | 14.1 | 4.1 | 9.7 | : | 16.4 | 5.0 | 8.2 | 8.1 | 10.2 | 0.9 | 9.9 | -0.8 | 8.8 | 9.2 | : | 3.1 | 16.6 |
| 1977 | 3.3 | 4.1 | 3.9 | : | 1.8 | 12.1 | 7.4 | 14.0 | 11.6 | 4.2 | -1.8 | 4.1 | 6.5 | 6.0 | : | 1.3 | 11.7 |
| 1978 | 3.3 | 1.2 | 2.9 | : | 16.4 | 10.7 | 5.9 | 12.3 | 9.4 | 2.7 | 3.3 | 9.1 | 1.6 | 4.8 | : | 9.7 | -0.3 |
| 1979 | 7.5 | 8.4 | 4.3 | : | 6.7 | 5.6 | 7.5 | 6.5 | 8.7 | 9.7 | 7.4 | 33.0 | 3.8 | 6.4 | : | 8.8 | 4.3 |
| 1980 | 2.9 | 5.2 | 5.2 | : | 6.9 | 2.3 | 2.7 | 6.4 | -8.5 | -1.4 | 1.5 | 2.2 | -0.2 | 0.9 | : | 9.5 | 17.0 |
| 1971-80 | 5.4 | 4.3 | 5.2 | : | 11.4 | 7.0 | 7.0 | 7.3 | 5.8 | 3.1 | 5.1 | 5.0 | 4.3 | 5.5 | : | 6.7 | 9.4 |
| 1981 | 2.6 | 8.2 | 7.2 | : | -5.9 | 8.4 | 3.7 | 2.0 | 6.3 | -4.8 | 2.1 | -4.4 | -0.8 | 3.9 | : | 2.0 | 12.5 |
| 1982 | 1.3 | 2.5 | 3.9 | : | -7.2 | 4.8 | -1.7 | 5.5 | -1.2 | -0.3 | -0.3 | 4.7 | 0.9 | 1.1 | : | -8.9 | 0.9 |
| 1983 | 2.7 | 4.9 | -0.8 | : | 8.0 | 10.1 | 3.7 | 10.5 | 2.6 | 5.3 | 3.3 | 13.6 | 2.0 | 2.7 | : | -4.1 | 4.8 |
| 1984 | 5.3 | 3.5 | 8.2 | : | 16.9 | 11.7 | 7.0 | 16.6 | 7.7 | 18.0 | 7.2 | 11.6 | 6.6 | 7.7 | : | 7.2 | 14.8 |
| 1985 | 1.1 | 5.0 | 7.6 | : | 1.3 | 2.7 | 1.9 | 6.6 | 3.1 | 9.5 | 5.3 | 6.7 | 5.8 | 4.6 | : | 1.0 | 5.4 |
| 1986 | 5.5 | 0.0 | -0.6 | : | 14.0 | 1.9 | -1.4 | 2.9 | 1.1 | 3.2 | 1.8 | 6.8 | 4.5 | 1.6 | : | 6.6 | -4.9 |
| 1987 | 6.5 | 5.1 | 0.4 | : | 16.0 | 6.3 | 3.1 | 13.7 | 4.6 | 6.5 | 3.6 | 8.6 | 5.8 | 4.1 | : | 11.1 | 0.1 |
| 1988 | 8.5 | 7.8 | 5.5 | : | 9.0 | 5.1 | 8.1 | 8.9 | 4.8 | 7.5 | 9.0 | 10.2 | 0.5 | 5.7 | : | 16.5 | 7.0 |
| 1989 | 7.3 | 4.2 | 10.2 | : | 1.3 | 3.0 | 10.2 | 10.3 | 7.8 | 6.9 | 6.7 | 13.3 | 4.7 | 7.8 | : | 12.3 | 9.0 |
| 1990 | 4.2 | 6.9 | 10.4 | : | 0.9 | 3.2 | 5.3 | 8.9 | 8.7 | 2.6 | 5.3 | 9.5 | 5.1 | 6.9 | : | 8.4 | 7.3 |
| 1981-90 | 4.5 | 4.8 | 5.1 | : | 5.1 | 5.7 | 3.9 | 8.5 | 4.5 | 5.3 | 4.4 | 7.9 | 3.5 | 4.6 | : | 4.9 | 5.6 |
| 1991 | 2.5 | 7.7 | 13.7 | : | 16.4 | 7.9 | 3.9 | 5.2 | -0.2 | 3.6 | 5.5 | 1.1 | -0.8 | 5.6 | : | 6.2 | 4.9 |
| 1992 | 1.6 | 3.7 | 3.7 | 0.1 | 0.9 | 6.7 | 7.2 | 12.9 | 5.4 | 1.3 | 2.4 | 6.1 | 2.6 | 4.3 | 3.5 | 6.4 | 4.9 |
| 1993 | -3.2 | -1.7 | -6.1 | -9.5 | 2.5 | 8.8 | -0.4 | 3.8 | 10.5 | -3.5 | 0.4 | -3.5 | 3.1 | 0.3 | -0.1 | 3.5 | 1.0 |
| 1994 | 3.2 | 4.2 | 4.8 | 5.9 | 4.1 | 9.2 | 3.8 | 5.2 | 7.0 | 2.5 | 3.9 | 6.4 | 4.7 | 5.0 | 5.3 | 5.4 | 1.3 |

EUR: PPS weighted. EUR 12-: incl. WD; EUR 12+: incl. D.

**Table M6**  Intra-EC exports of goods at current prices. Foreign trade statistics.

(Percentage of gross domestic products at market prices)

|  | B/L | DK | WD | GR | E | F | IRL | I | NL | P | UK | EUR 12− |
|---|---|---|---|---|---|---|---|---|---|---|---|---|
| 1960 | 19.6 | 14.1 | 6.4 | 2.5 | 3.6 | 4.3 | 18.8 | 3.7 | 20.7 | 5.1 | 3.3 | 6.0 |
| 1961 | 20.1 | 12.7 | 6.6 | 2.3 | 3.1 | 4.7 | 20.7 | 4.0 | 20.5 | 4.8 | 3.6 | 6.2 |
| 1962 | 21.7 | 12.0 | 6.6 | 2.8 | 2.7 | 4.6 | 17.7 | 4.3 | 20.9 | 5.3 | 3.7 | 6.3 |
| 1963 | 23.9 | 12.8 | 7.4 | 2.6 | 2.3 | 4.7 | 18.7 | 4.1 | 21.8 | 5.5 | 4.0 | 6.6 |
| 1964 | 25.0 | 12.3 | 7.4 | 2.7 | 2.7 | 4.9 | 19.5 | 4.7 | 22.2 | 6.5 | 3.8 | 6.8 |
| 1965 | 26.2 | 11.6 | 7.3 | 2.6 | 2.2 | 5.3 | 18.5 | 5.5 | 21.9 | 6.8 | 3.8 | 7.0 |
| 1966 | 26.2 | 10.9 | 7.9 | 2.7 | 2.2 | 5.4 | 18.2 | 5.7 | 21.0 | 6.6 | 3.8 | 7.2 |
| 1967 | 25.3 | 9.8 | 8.4 | 3.3 | 2.1 | 5.2 | 19.7 | 5.4 | 20.6 | 6.6 | 3.7 | 7.1 |
| 1968 | 27.5 | 9.5 | 8.9 | 3.2 | 2.3 | 5.3 | 19.9 | 5.9 | 21.8 | 6.4 | 4.2 | 7.7 |
| 1969 | 31.9 | 9.2 | 9.6 | 3.3 | 2.5 | 6.2 | 18.7 | 6.3 | 23.6 | 6.8 | 4.6 | 8.5 |
| 1970 | 33.1 | 9.1 | 9.2 | 3.5 | 3.1 | 7.2 | 19.5 | 6.4 | 25.1 | 6.7 | 5.0 | 8.9 |
| 1971 | 31.4 | 8.9 | 9.1 | 3.4 | 3.4 | 7.5 | 20.5 | 6.8 | 26.1 | 6.9 | 5.1 | 9.1 |
| 1972 | 33.4 | 8.9 | 9.1 | 3.7 | 3.4 | 8.0 | 21.2 | 7.4 | 26.5 | 7.5 | 5.0 | 9.4 |
| 1973 | 35.8 | 10.3 | 9.9 | 5.1 | 3.7 | 8.5 | 23.9 | 7.4 | 28.0 | 8.3 | 5.9 | 10.3 |
| 1974 | 36.1 | 10.7 | 11.3 | 5.7 | 4.0 | 9.6 | 27.6 | 8.2 | 31.0 | 8.5 | 7.2 | 11.6 |
| 1975 | 32.6 | 10.7 | 10.1 | 5.6 | 3.4 | 8.1 | 29.2 | 8.1 | 28.8 | 7.0 | 6.6 | 10.4 |
| 1976 | 35.8 | 10.1 | 11.2 | 5.8 | 4.0 | 8.6 | 29.3 | 9.1 | 30.6 | 6.3 | 7.9 | 11.6 |
| 1977 | 34.0 | 9.6 | 11.0 | 5.1 | 4.1 | 8.9 | 32.8 | 9.4 | 27.8 | 6.7 | 9.0 | 11.6 |
| 1978 | 33.3 | 10.0 | 10.8 | 5.5 | 4.4 | 8.9 | 33.1 | 9.7 | 26.2 | 7.9 | 9.0 | 11.5 |
| 1979 | 37.0 | 10.9 | 11.6 | 5.0 | 4.7 | 9.6 | 33.6 | 10.4 | 29.7 | 10.0 | 9.6 | 12.3 |
| 1980 | 38.3 | 12.6 | 12.1 | 6.2 | 5.1 | 9.2 | 32.1 | 8.8 | 31.5 | 10.8 | 9.5 | 12.3 |
| 1981 | 39.3 | 12.9 | 12.6 | 5.0 | 5.0 | 9.0 | 29.1 | 8.4 | 34.6 | 9.7 | 8.7 | 12.1 |
| 1982 | 42.3 | 13.1 | 13.5 | 5.3 | 5.5 | 8.8 | 29.4 | 8.8 | 34.9 | 10.9 | 8.8 | 12.5 |
| 1983 | 44.0 | 13.3 | 13.0 | 6.7 | 6.3 | 9.2 | 31.7 | 8.4 | 35.6 | 13.9 | 9.2 | 12.7 |
| 1984 | 45.0 | 12.3 | 13.9 | 7.9 | 7.5 | 9.8 | 36.2 | 8.4 | 37.9 | 16.8 | 10.2 | 13.4 |
| 1985 | 44.7 | 12.2 | 14.6 | 7.4 | 7.6 | 9.9 | 36.2 | 8.9 | 39.1 | 17.2 | 10.7 | 13.8 |
| 1986 | 42.9 | 11.3 | 13.9 | 9.1 | 7.1 | 9.4 | 34.3 | 8.6 | 33.6 | 16.5 | 9.1 | 12.9 |
| 1987 | 42.4 | 11.3 | 14.0 | 9.4 | 7.4 | 9.7 | 37.5 | 8.6 | 31.9 | 17.8 | 9.4 | 12.9 |
| 1988 | 42.0 | 11.9 | 14.7 | 6.2 | 7.7 | 10.3 | 40.2 | 8.7 | 31.4 | 18.9 | 8.7 | 13.0 |
| 1989 | 46.4 | 12.7 | 15.9 | 8.8 | 7.8 | 10.9 | 43.1 | 9.1 | 33.4 | 20.3 | 9.2 | 13.8 |
| 1990 | 44.1 | 13.2 | 14.4 | 7.7 | 7.8 | 11.0 | 39.8 | 9.0 | 33.3 | 20.3 | 10.0 | 13.5 |
| 1991 | 43.3 | 14.0 | 13.5 | 7.8 | 8.1 | 11.2 | 40.0 | 8.7 | 33.1 | 17.9 | 10.4 | 13.3 |
| 1992 | 40.2 | 14.3 | 12.8 | 8.2 | 7.9 | 10.9 | 41.7 | 8.4 | 31.0 | 16.5 | 10.2 | 12.9 |
| 1993 | 37.1 | 13.7 | 11.3 | 8.4 | 8.2 | 9.7 | 42.8 | 9.0 | 29.4 | 15.4 | 10.2 | 12.3 |
| 1994 | 37.2 | 13.5 | 11.7 | 8.6 | 8.9 | 9.9 | 42.4 | 9.1 | 29.9 | 16.1 | 10.1 | 12.6 |

EUR 12−: incl. WD.

**Table M7**  Extra-EC exports of goods at current prices. Foreign trade statistics.

(Percentage of gross domestic products at market prices)

|  | B/L | DK | WD | GR | E | F | IRL | I | NL | P | UK | EUR 12− |
|---|---|---|---|---|---|---|---|---|---|---|---|---|
| 1960 | 12.7 | 10.6 | 9.5 | 3.3 | 2.6 | 6.9 | 4.4 | 5.5 | 13.1 | 8.1 | 11.0 | 8.7 |
| 1961 | 11.6 | 10.2 | 8.9 | 3.4 | 2.2 | 6.2 | 4.7 | 5.5 | 12.5 | 7.4 | 10.4 | 8.1 |
| 1962 | 11.0 | 9.9 | 8.1 | 3.1 | 2.0 | 5.3 | 4.2 | 5.1 | 11.4 | 7.7 | 9.4 | 7.3 |
| 1963 | 10.1 | 10.8 | 7.9 | 3.6 | 1.7 | 5.0 | 4.5 | 4.8 | 10.5 | 8.0 | 9.4 | 7.0 |
| 1964 | 10.1 | 10.7 | 8.0 | 3.1 | 1.9 | 4.9 | 3.6 | 4.9 | 9.8 | 8.9 | 8.9 | 6.9 |
| 1965 | 10.7 | 10.7 | 8.3 | 2.9 | 1.9 | 4.9 | 3.3 | 5.2 | 9.7 | 8.6 | 9.3 | 7.1 |
| 1966 | 10.6 | 10.6 | 8.6 | 3.4 | 2.3 | 4.7 | 4.1 | 5.3 | 9.6 | 8.6 | 9.3 | 7.2 |
| 1967 | 10.2 | 10.6 | 9.2 | 3.6 | 2.4 | 4.6 | 4.3 | 5.5 | 9.6 | 8.7 | 8.8 | 7.1 |
| 1968 | 10.9 | 11.0 | 9.7 | 2.7 | 3.0 | 4.7 | 5.0 | 5.9 | 9.4 | 8.6 | 10.0 | 7.6 |
| 1969 | 10.7 | 11.4 | 9.5 | 3.0 | 3.0 | 4.6 | 5.1 | 6.0 | 9.3 | 8.6 | 10.3 | 7.6 |
| 1970 | 10.9 | 11.7 | 9.3 | 3.0 | 3.2 | 5.2 | 5.1 | 5.9 | 9.5 | 8.6 | 10.6 | 7.8 |
| 1971 | 10.4 | 11.4 | 9.0 | 2.6 | 3.4 | 5.2 | 6.6 | 6.0 | 9.0 | 8.1 | 10.8 | 7.8 |
| 1972 | 10.5 | 11.0 | 8.8 | 3.2 | 3.6 | 5.2 | 5.9 | 6.1 | 9.0 | 7.7 | 10.1 | 7.6 |
| 1973 | 11.7 | 11.0 | 9.6 | 3.9 | 3.4 | 5.5 | 6.9 | 6.0 | 9.3 | 7.9 | 10.9 | 8.0 |
| 1974 | 13.8 | 13.1 | 12.0 | 5.0 | 3.8 | 6.8 | 8.4 | 8.1 | 11.5 | 8.3 | 12.6 | 9.8 |
| 1975 | 12.2 | 12.3 | 11.4 | 5.3 | 3.7 | 7.0 | 7.1 | 8.3 | 10.7 | 6.0 | 12.1 | 9.4 |
| 1976 | 11.5 | 11.5 | 11.7 | 5.6 | 4.0 | 7.0 | 8.6 | 8.4 | 10.8 | 5.4 | 12.5 | 9.6 |
| 1977 | 12.4 | 11.7 | 11.9 | 5.4 | 4.2 | 7.4 | 9.5 | 9.2 | 10.5 | 5.6 | 13.6 | 10.1 |
| 1978 | 12.1 | 10.6 | 11.4 | 5.1 | 4.5 | 6.9 | 8.9 | 9.0 | 9.7 | 5.5 | 13.2 | 9.7 |
| 1979 | 12.6 | 10.8 | 11.0 | 5.0 | 4.5 | 7.2 | 8.8 | 9.0 | 10.0 | 6.6 | 11.9 | 9.5 |
| 1980 | 13.8 | 12.1 | 11.5 | 6.6 | 4.6 | 7.4 | 10.0 | 8.3 | 11.3 | 7.6 | 11.7 | 9.7 |
| 1981 | 15.6 | 14.4 | 13.1 | 6.4 | 5.9 | 8.3 | 11.6 | 10.0 | 13.0 | 7.4 | 11.2 | 10.7 |
| 1982 | 16.0 | 13.7 | 13.3 | 5.8 | 5.8 | 7.9 | 11.2 | 9.4 | 12.4 | 7.0 | 11.1 | 10.5 |
| 1983 | 17.3 | 14.5 | 12.8 | 5.9 | 6.3 | 8.1 | 13.1 | 9.0 | 12.7 | 8.3 | 10.7 | 10.5 |
| 1984 | 19.0 | 16.0 | 13.8 | 6.4 | 7.2 | 8.8 | 15.5 | 9.3 | 13.8 | 10.5 | 11.5 | 11.3 |
| 1985 | 18.7 | 15.9 | 14.7 | 6.2 | 7.0 | 8.5 | 16.2 | 9.6 | 13.7 | 10.3 | 11.2 | 11.4 |
| 1986 | 15.7 | 13.6 | 13.4 | 5.2 | 4.7 | 6.8 | 13.3 | 7.5 | 11.3 | 7.7 | 9.8 | 9.7 |
| 1987 | 14.5 | 12.8 | 12.5 | 4.6 | 4.2 | 6.4 | 13.4 | 6.7 | 10.7 | 7.2 | 9.6 | 9.1 |
| 1988 | 14.2 | 13.6 | 12.3 | 3.5 | 4.0 | 6.4 | 14.0 | 6.5 | 13.1 | 7.4 | 8.6 | 8.9 |
| 1989 | 16.4 | 14.0 | 12.9 | 4.7 | 3.9 | 6.9 | 14.9 | 7.0 | 13.8 | 8.0 | 9.0 | 9.3 |
| 1990 | 14.5 | 13.7 | 12.0 | 4.4 | 3.5 | 6.5 | 13.4 | 6.4 | 12.9 | 7.2 | 8.9 | 8.7 |
| 1991 | 14.1 | 13.5 | 11.1 | 4.5 | 3.3 | 6.6 | 13.7 | 6.0 | 12.9 | 5.9 | 7.9 | 8.2 |
| 1992 | 13.3 | 13.6 | 10.6 | 4.4 | 3.2 | 6.5 | 14.4 | 6.2 | 12.5 | 5.4 | 8.0 | 8.1 |
| 1993 | 14.1 | 13.1 | 9.5 | 4.7 | 4.2 | 6.6 | 15.3 | 8.0 | 12.6 | 5.0 | 9.3 | 8.5 |
| 1994 | 14.9 | 13.3 | 10.0 | 4.9 | 4.7 | 6.9 | 15.7 | 9.0 | 13.1 | 5.4 | 9.4 | 9.1 |

EUR 12−: incl. WD.

**Table M8**  Imports of goods and services at current prices. National accounts definition.

(Percentage of gross domestic product at market prices)

| | B | DK | WD | D | GR | E | F | IRL | I | L | NL | P | UK | EUR 12− | EUR 12+ | USA | J |
|---|---|---|---|---|---|---|---|---|---|---|---|---|---|---|---|---|---|
| 1960 | 39.3 | 33.4 | 16.5 | : | 16.7 | 7.2 | 12.4 | 35.9 | 13.5 | 73.7 | 43.8 | 23.7 | 22.3 | 18.9 | | 4.4 | 10.2 |
| 1961 | 40.6 | 31.5 | 15.8 | : | 16.4 | 9.1 | 12.2 | 38.4 | 13.5 | 80.2 | 43.3 | 27.7 | 29.9 | 18.4 | : | 4.3 | 10.9 |
| 1962 | 41.4 | 31.6 | 16.1 | : | 16.9 | 10.8 | 12.0 | 37.5 | 13.9 | 79.2 | 42.4 | 23.5 | 20.3 | 18.2 | : | 4.4 | 9.3 |
| 1963 | 43.5 | 30.0 | 16.3 | : | 18.0 | 11.5 | 12.3 | 39.3 | 15.1 | 77.5 | 43.5 | 24.3 | 20.4 | 18.6 | : | 4.3 | 9.8 |
| 1964 | 43.7 | 31.8 | 16.5 | : | 19.0 | 11.8 | 12.9 | 39.5 | 13.4 | 78.8 | 43.5 | 29.9 | 21.1 | 18.9 | : | 4.3 | 9.7 |
| 1965 | 42.9 | 30.7 | 17.8 | : | 20.3 | 13.5 | 12.4 | 42.3 | 12.7 | 79.9 | 41.6 | 31.5 | 20.0 | 18.8 | : | 4.5 | 9.1 |
| 1966 | 45.2 | 30.0 | 17.5 | : | 18.8 | 13.9 | 13.1 | 41.7 | 13.7 | 75.1 | 41.1 | 31.0 | 19.5 | 18.9 | : | 4.8 | 9.0 |
| 1967 | 43.1 | 29.2 | 16.8 | : | 18.0 | 12.3 | 13.0 | 39.5 | 14.2 | 70.6 | 39.5 | 29.5 | 20.2 | 18.6 | : | 4.9 | 9.4 |
| 1968 | 45.3 | 28.9 | 17.7 | : | 18.4 | 13.2 | 13.3 | 43.6 | 14.0 | 70.4 | 39.2 | 29.8 | 22.2 | 19.4 | : | 5.2 | 9.0 |
| 1969 | 48.6 | 29.6 | 18.9 | : | 18.7 | 13.8 | 14.6 | 44.7 | 15.3 | 69.7 | 40.8 | 28.6 | 21.8 | 20.4 | : | 5.3 | 8.9 |
| 1970 | 49.4 | 30.9 | 19.1 | : | 18.4 | 13.9 | 15.3 | 43.4 | 16.3 | 75.7 | 44.4 | 30.9 | 22.2 | 21.1 | : | 5.5 | 9.5 |
| 1961-70 | 44.4 | 30.4 | 17.3 | : | 18.3 | 12.4 | 13.1 | 41.0 | 14.2 | 75.7 | 41.9 | 28.7 | 20.9 | 19.1 | : | 4.7 | 9.5 |
| 1971 | 48.4 | 29.4 | 19.0 | : | 18.4 | 13.1 | 15.3 | 41.8 | 16.2 | 84.3 | 43.6 | 32.1 | 21.7 | 20.9 | : | 5.7 | 9.0 |
| 1972 | 47.6 | 26.5 | 18.6 | : | 20.0 | 14.1 | 15.7 | 38.5 | 16.9 | 76.7 | 40.3 | 31.9 | 21.8 | 20.8 | : | 6.1 | 8.3 |
| 1973 | 53.4 | 30.4 | 18.9 | : | 25.2 | 15.1 | 16.7 | 43.2 | 19.4 | 76.5 | 42.2 | 33.7 | 26.1 | 22.7 | : | 6.8 | 10.0 |
| 1974 | 60.7 | 34.7 | 22.0 | : | 25.6 | 18.8 | 21.7 | 55.2 | 24.3 | 81.4 | 48.9 | 42.2 | 33.0 | 27.6 | : | 8.7 | 14.3 |
| 1975 | 53.3 | 31.0 | 21.8 | : | 26.9 | 17.0 | 17.9 | 47.0 | 20.6 | 88.1 | 44.4 | 32.8 | 27.6 | 24.5 | : | 7.7 | 12.8 |
| 1976 | 56.7 | 33.5 | 23.4 | : | 25.8 | 17.8 | 20.3 | 52.3 | 23.2 | 82.2 | 45.4 | 30.9 | 29.6 | 26.5 | : | 8.5 | 12.8 |
| 1977 | 57.3 | 32.5 | 23.1 | : | 25.2 | 16.2 | 20.4 | 56.4 | 22.2 | 82.7 | 44.2 | 33.5 | 29.3 | 26.2 | : | 9.2 | 11.5 |
| 1978 | 55.9 | 29.9 | 22.3 | : | 24.6 | 14.1 | 19.1 | 57.7 | 21.2 | 82.3 | 42.8 | 32.5 | 27.1 | 24.9 | : | 9.5 | 9.4 |
| 1979 | 62.4 | 32.1 | 24.4 | : | 25.3 | 14.4 | 20.6 | 63.8 | 23.2 | 86.8 | 47.3 | 37.9 | 27.7 | 26.7 | : | 10.2 | 12.5 |
| 1980 | 65.4 | 33.8 | 26.9 | : | 26.2 | 17.8 | 22.7 | 60.8 | 24.6 | 89.2 | 50.6 | 42.0 | 25.0 | 28.1 | : | 10.9 | 14.6 |
| 1971-80 | 56.1 | 31.4 | 22.0 | : | 24.3 | 15.9 | 19.0 | 51.7 | 21.2 | 83.0 | 45.0 | 34.9 | 26.9 | 24.9 | : | 8.3 | 11.5 |
| 1981 | 69.8 | 35.8 | 27.9 | : | 27.1 | 19.8 | 23.5 | 60.4 | 25.3 | 89.5 | 52.0 | 45.2 | 23.8 | 28.6 | : | 10.5 | 13.9 |
| 1982 | 72.9 | 35.9 | 27.5 | : | 28.7 | 20.2 | 23.7 | 53.4 | 24.0 | 90.6 | 50.9 | 45.0 | 24.5 | 28.4 | : | 9.6 | 13.8 |
| 1983 | 72.8 | 34.4 | 26.7 | : | 30.1 | 21.4 | 22.6 | 53.3 | 21.4 | 90.0 | 51.4 | 44.1 | 25.6 | 27.9 | : | 9.7 | 12.2 |
| 1984 | 77.4 | 35.5 | 28.2 | : | 28.9 | 20.9 | 23.5 | 57.7 | 23.0 | 99.3 | 54.3 | 45.2 | 28.6 | 29.5 | : | 10.8 | 12.3 |
| 1985 | 74.4 | 36.3 | 29.0 | : | 32.8 | 20.8 | 23.2 | 56.4 | 23.2 | 103.3 | 56.0 | 41.4 | 27.8 | 29.5 | : | 10.4 | 11.1 |
| 1986 | 66.7 | 32.5 | 25.0 | : | 30.9 | 17.7 | 20.2 | 50.4 | 18.7 | 96.3 | 46.9 | 35.9 | 26.4 | 25.7 | : | 10.7 | 7.4 |
| 1987 | 66.3 | 29.6 | 23.9 | : | 31.8 | 19.2 | 20.5 | 50.7 | 18.9 | 99.2 | 47.1 | 41.5 | 26.6 | 25.7 | : | 11.3 | 7.2 |
| 1988 | 68.8 | 29.4 | 24.3 | : | 30.3 | 20.0 | 21.2 | 52.6 | 19.1 | 100.2 | 48.6 | 46.3 | 26.7 | 26.1 | : | 11.4 | 7.8 |
| 1989 | 73.6 | 31.1 | 26.1 | : | 31.9 | 21.4 | 22.8 | 57.1 | 20.4 | 98.8 | 51.3 | 46.2 | 27.9 | 27.7 | : | 11.3 | 9.3 |
| 1990 | 71.2 | 30.1 | 26.1 | : | 32.7 | 20.5 | 22.6 | 53.8 | 20.7 | 97.0 | 49.6 | 45.4 | 27.1 | 27.3 | : | 11.5 | 10.1 |
| 1981-90 | 71.4 | 33.1 | 26.5 | : | 30.6 | 20.2 | 22.4 | 54.6 | 21.5 | 96.4 | 50.8 | 43.6 | 26.5 | 27.7 | : | 10.7 | 10.5 |
| 1991 | 69.5 | 30.9 | 27.5 | 25.4 | 33.2 | 20.3 | 22.4 | 53.9 | 19.4 | 100.0 | 49.4 | 41.3 | 24.8 | 26.9 | 26.3 | 11.0 | 8.5 |
| 1992 | 66.4 | 29.4 | 26.5 | 23.8 | 33.0 | 20.4 | 21.8 | 53.1 | 19.9 | 92.7 | 47.8 | 38.8 | 25.2 | 26.6 | 25.8 | 11.3 | 7.8 |
| 1993 | 63.2 | 27.2 | 23.4 | 20.7 | 33.4 | 20.5 | 20.3 | 53.6 | 19.9 | 87.7 | 45.4 | 37.1 | 26.7 | 25.6 | 24.7 | 11.7 | 7.1 |
| 1994 | 64.0 | 28.5 | 23.6 | 20.6 | 34.1 | 21.4 | 20.8 | 54.0 | 21.0 | 87.8 | 46.1 | 37.9 | 26.5 | 26.1 | 25.2 | 11.9 | 7.0 |

EUR 12−: incl. WD; EUR 12+: incl. D.

**Table M9**  Imports of goods and services at 1985 prices. National accounts definition.

(Annual percentage change)

| | B | DK | WD | D | GR | E | F | IRL | I | L | NL | P | UK | EUR 12− | EUR 12+ | USA | J |
|---|---|---|---|---|---|---|---|---|---|---|---|---|---|---|---|---|---|
| 1961 | 7.2 | 4.4 | 7.7 | : | 12.7 | 40.1 | 6.9 | 13.7 | 13.7 | 7.3 | 6.4 | 24.9 | −0.6 | 6.8 | : | 0.5 | 26.4 |
| 1962 | 8.2 | 13.4 | 11.1 | : | 10.1 | 34.4 | 6.7 | 5.4 | 14.9 | 3.2 | 6.5 | −8.7 | 2.1 | 8.4 | : | 11.1 | −1.1 |
| 1963 | 8.6 | −1.1 | 4.9 | : | 15.4 | 23.5 | 14.1 | 10.6 | 22.5 | 3.1 | 9.8 | 10.4 | 1.7 | 9.0 | : | 2.4 | 19.5 |
| 1964 | 8.9 | 19.6 | 9.3 | : | 15.3 | 13.0 | 15.1 | 12.9 | −6.1 | 13.6 | 14.9 | 30.8 | 10.8 | 9.8 | : | 5.5 | 13.7 |
| 1965 | 6.6 | 6.9 | 14.2 | : | 21.2 | 33.1 | 2.2 | 11.0 | 2.0 | 4.5 | 6.1 | 14.3 | 1.1 | 7.3 | : | 10.5 | 5.6 |
| 1966 | 9.9 | 5.4 | 2.7 | : | −0.5 | 19.0 | 10.6 | 3.5 | 14.0 | −2.5 | 7.0 | 8.1 | 2.5 | 6.8 | : | 13.9 | 12.2 |
| 1967 | 1.6 | 4.5 | −1.3 | : | 7.1 | −3.3 | 8.3 | 3.7 | 13.5 | −4.8 | 6.3 | 8.9 | 7.2 | 4.9 | : | 6.0 | 22.7 |
| 1968 | 11.7 | 4.9 | 13.2 | : | 10.3 | 8.1 | 12.9 | 15.7 | 5.9 | 9.1 | 13.0 | 14.6 | 7.9 | 10.4 | : | 15.8 | 12.1 |
| 1969 | 15.5 | 13.1 | 17.0 | : | 15.5 | 15.7 | 19.5 | 13.4 | 19.3 | 11.2 | 14.1 | 4.3 | 2.9 | 13.4 | : | 6.5 | 13.7 |
| 1970 | 7.6 | 9.3 | 22.7 | : | 6.2 | 7.0 | 6.3 | 8.6 | 16.0 | 19.0 | 14.7 | 9.9 | 5.1 | 12.1 | : | 4.2 | 22.9 |
| 1961-70 | 8.5 | 7.9 | 9.9 | : | 11.2 | 18.3 | 10.2 | 9.8 | 11.3 | 6.1 | 9.8 | 11.3 | 4.0 | 8.9 | : | 7.4 | 14.5 |
| 1971 | 3.6 | −0.7 | 9.0 | : | 7.6 | 0.7 | 6.3 | 4.7 | 2.9 | 8.0 | 6.1 | 14.6 | 5.2 | 5.7 | : | 6.8 | 7.0 |
| 1972 | 9.6 | 1.5 | 5.8 | : | 15.4 | 24.3 | 13.2 | 5.1 | 9.1 | 2.7 | 4.8 | 12.1 | 9.4 | 9.3 | : | 12.0 | 10.5 |
| 1973 | 18.5 | 12.8 | 4.9 | : | 32.2 | 16.7 | 14.2 | 19.0 | 9.3 | 11.3 | 11.0 | 12.7 | 11.5 | 11.4 | : | 9.6 | 24.3 |
| 1974 | 4.4 | −3.8 | 0.4 | : | −16.3 | 8.0 | 1.9 | −2.3 | 1.4 | 5.9 | −0.8 | 4.6 | 0.8 | 1.2 | : | −2.3 | 4.2 |
| 1975 | −9.0 | −4.8 | 1.3 | : | 6.3 | −0.9 | −9.7 | −10.2 | −12.5 | −9.0 | −4.1 | −24.2 | −6.9 | −6.4 | : | −10.8 | −10.3 |
| 1976 | 13.5 | 15.6 | 10.5 | : | 6.1 | 9.8 | 17.4 | 14.7 | 13.4 | 1.2 | 10.1 | 5.2 | 4.7 | 10.8 | : | 19.3 | 6.7 |
| 1977 | 5.8 | 0.0 | 3.4 | : | 8.0 | −5.5 | 0.1 | 13.3 | 1.9 | −0.4 | 2.9 | 10.8 | 1.4 | 2.1 | : | 11.4 | 4.1 |
| 1978 | 3.6 | 0.1 | 5.5 | : | 7.2 | −1.0 | 3.0 | 15.7 | 4.9 | 7.0 | 6.3 | 0.2 | 3.8 | 4.2 | : | 7.0 | 6.9 |
| 1979 | 9.3 | 5.0 | 9.2 | : | 7.2 | 11.4 | 10.1 | 13.9 | 11.5 | 6.4 | 6.0 | 12.6 | 9.7 | 9.6 | : | 1.3 | 12.9 |
| 1980 | 0.0 | −6.8 | 3.6 | : | −8.0 | 3.3 | 2.5 | −4.5 | 3.1 | 3.9 | −0.4 | 6.9 | −3.5 | 0.9 | : | −6.7 | −7.8 |
| 1971-80 | 5.7 | 1.7 | 5.3 | : | 5.9 | 6.3 | 5.6 | 6.5 | 4.3 | 3.5 | 4.1 | 4.9 | 3.5 | 4.7 | : | 4.4 | 5.4 |
| 1981 | −2.9 | −1.7 | −3.1 | : | 3.6 | −4.2 | −2.1 | 1.7 | −1.4 | −2.9 | −5.8 | 2.3 | −2.8 | −2.6 | : | 3.6 | 0.4 |
| 1982 | 0.2 | 3.8 | −1.1 | : | 7.0 | 3.9 | 2.6 | −3.1 | −0.2 | −0.3 | 1.1 | 3.9 | 4.9 | 1.4 | : | −1.7 | −2.5 |
| 1983 | −1.3 | 1.8 | 1.4 | : | 6.6 | −0.6 | −2.7 | 4.7 | −1.3 | 1.2 | 3.9 | −6.1 | 6.3 | 0.8 | : | 11.6 | −3.0 |
| 1984 | 5.6 | 5.5 | 5.2 | : | 0.2 | −1.0 | 2.7 | 9.9 | 12.4 | 13.9 | 5.0 | −4.4 | 10.0 | 6.0 | : | 23.7 | 10.4 |
| 1985 | 0.7 | 8.1 | 4.5 | : | 12.8 | 6.2 | 4.5 | 3.2 | 4.0 | 7.0 | 6.5 | 1.4 | 2.5 | 4.2 | : | 5.4 | −1.4 |
| 1986 | 7.6 | 6.8 | 2.7 | : | 3.8 | 14.4 | 7.1 | 5.6 | 3.3 | 6.1 | 3.5 | 16.9 | 6.9 | 5.8 | : | 8.3 | 2.4 |
| 1987 | 8.8 | −2.0 | 4.2 | : | 16.6 | 20.1 | 7.7 | 6.2 | 9.7 | 7.8 | 4.2 | 20.0 | 8.1 | 8.0 | : | 6.0 | 7.8 |
| 1988 | 8.0 | 1.5 | 5.1 | : | 8.0 | 14.4 | 8.6 | 4.9 | 7.3 | 8.5 | 7.6 | 16.1 | 12.7 | 8.7 | : | 4.8 | 18.7 |
| 1989 | 8.8 | 4.5 | 8.3 | : | 10.8 | 17.3 | 8.1 | 12.7 | 7.2 | 6.1 | 6.7 | 9.1 | 7.4 | 8.5 | : | 4.8 | 17.6 |
| 1990 | 4.1 | 1.2 | 9.4 | : | 12.0 | 7.8 | 6.3 | 5.5 | 10.6 | 4.3 | 4.2 | 10.1 | 0.4 | 6.3 | : | 3.7 | 8.6 |
| 1981-90 | 3.9 | 2.9 | 3.6 | : | 8.0 | 7.5 | 4.2 | 5.1 | 5.0 | 5.1 | 3.6 | 6.6 | 5.5 | 4.6 | : | 6.8 | 5.6 |
| 1991 | 2.4 | 4.9 | 12.1 | : | 13.2 | 9.0 | 2.9 | 1.3 | 2.3 | 8.1 | 4.6 | 4.9 | −5.3 | 4.1 | : | 0.9 | −4.5 |
| 1992 | 2.7 | −0.5 | 3.9 | 2.6 | 0.7 | 6.6 | 3.1 | 5.4 | 5.8 | 0.2 | 2.6 | 11.1 | 5.7 | 4.3 | 4.0 | 8.7 | 0.0 |
| 1993 | −4.1 | −4.2 | −9.5 | −10.0 | 1.7 | −3.2 | −2.6 | 2.8 | −7.7 | −2.5 | −1.0 | −0.7 | 3.5 | −3.8 | −3.9 | 10.3 | 3.1 |
| 1994 | 2.9 | 7.9 | 2.4 | 2.3 | 3.6 | 3.6 | 3.4 | 5.8 | 4.1 | 1.6 | 2.8 | 2.9 | 3.9 | 3.4 | 3.4 | 10.7 | 3.2 |

EUR; PPS weighted. EUR 12−: incl. WD; EUR 12+: incl. D.

**Table M10**  Intra-EC exports of goods at current prices. Foreign trade statistics.

|  | B/L | DK | WD | GR | E | F | IRL | I | NL | P | UK | EUR 12– |
|---|---|---|---|---|---|---|---|---|---|---|---|---|
| 1960 | 19.2 | 16.5 | 5.6 | 9.0 | 2.2 | 3.6 | 21.9 | 4.4 | 20.6 | 11.3 | 3.9 | 6.0 |
| 1961 | 20.3 | 15.5 | 5.5 | 9.1 | 2.9 | 3.8 | 24.3 | 4.5 | 22.7 | 13.8 | 3.8 | 6.2 |
| 1962 | 20.8 | 15.1 | 5.7 | 9.5 | 4.2 | 4.2 | 24.0 | 4.9 | 22.2 | 11.0 | 3.8 | 6.4 |
| 1963 | 22.3 | 13.8 | 5.8 | 9.2 | 4.8 | 4.6 | 25.4 | 5.6 | 23.4 | 10.7 | 3.9 | 6.7 |
| 1964 | 23.2 | 14.5 | 6.1 | 9.2 | 5.0 | 5.0 | 25.2 | 4.8 | 23.7 | 11.5 | 4.2 | 7.0 |
| 1965 | 23.4 | 13.8 | 7.1 | 9.9 | 6.1 | 4.8 | 25.2 | 4.2 | 22.8 | 12.8 | 4.1 | 7.1 |
| 1966 | 25.0 | 13.2 | 6.9 | 9.7 | 6.3 | 5.4 | 23.8 | 4.7 | 22.5 | 13.1 | 4.3 | 7.3 |
| 1967 | 23.3 | 12.3 | 6.7 | 9.1 | 5.3 | 5.4 | 22.6 | 5.1 | 21.3 | 12.3 | 4.6 | 7.3 |
| 1968 | 25.1 | 12.2 | 7.4 | 9.7 | 5.1 | 6.0 | 25.9 | 5.1 | 21.7 | 12.1 | 5.2 | 7.8 |
| 1969 | 28.0 | 13.0 | 8.4 | 9.5 | 5.4 | 7.2 | 27.5 | 5.9 | 23.2 | 12.6 | 5.0 | 8.7 |
| 1970 | 28.6 | 13.5 | 8.4 | 10.0 | 5.1 | 7.4 | 27.9 | 6.6 | 24.9 | 13.6 | 5.0 | 9.0 |
| 1971 | 30.8 | 12.1 | 8.6 | 9.9 | 4.8 | 7.6 | 26.4 | 6.6 | 23.0 | 13.6 | 5.2 | 9.1 |
| 1972 | 31.0 | 11.1 | 8.7 | 10.4 | 5.3 | 8.0 | 25.4 | 7.2 | 22.1 | 13.3 | 5.7 | 9.4 |
| 1973 | 33.4 | 12.9 | 8.6 | 11.1 | 5.7 | 8.5 | 29.5 | 8.5 | 22.7 | 13.5 | 7.5 | 10.3 |
| 1974 | 35.3 | 14.3 | 9.1 | 10.2 | 6.2 | 9.6 | 36.3 | 9.7 | 24.5 | 16.4 | 9.7 | 11.5 |
| 1975 | 32.6 | 13.0 | 9.3 | 11.5 | 5.3 | 8.2 | 30.2 | 8.0 | 22.3 | 11.6 | 8.9 | 10.5 |
| 1976 | 35.0 | 14.5 | 10.0 | 11.1 | 5.2 | 9.5 | 33.9 | 9.3 | 22.8 | 12.8 | 9.6 | 11.6 |
| 1977 | 34.3 | 13.9 | 10.0 | 11.8 | 5.0 | 9.5 | 35.8 | 8.8 | 22.5 | 14.7 | 10.2 | 11.6 |
| 1978 | 34.4 | 13.2 | 9.8 | 11.1 | 4.9 | 9.3 | 37.4 | 8.8 | 22.4 | 15.0 | 10.4 | 11.5 |
| 1979 | 36.6 | 14.3 | 10.7 | 11.2 | 4.7 | 9.8 | 42.3 | 9.7 | 24.4 | 15.2 | 11.2 | 12.2 |
| 1980 | 37.3 | 14.4 | 11.2 | 10.7 | 4.9 | 10.0 | 39.9 | 10.1 | 24.4 | 16.7 | 9.5 | 12.1 |
| 1981 | 38.4 | 14.5 | 11.8 | 12.1 | 5.1 | 9.9 | 40.0 | 9.4 | 24.5 | 18.3 | 8.9 | 12.0 |
| 1982 | 41.6 | 14.9 | 11.8 | 12.3 | 5.5 | 10.7 | 34.8 | 9.3 | 24.7 | 19.4 | 9.6 | 12.3 |
| 1983 | 44.2 | 14.1 | 11.9 | 13.2 | 6.1 | 10.8 | 32.9 | 8.5 | 25.0 | 17.9 | 10.4 | 12.5 |
| 1984 | 46.9 | 14.4 | 12.4 | 13.8 | 6.2 | 11.3 | 34.4 | 9.2 | 26.9 | 17.9 | 11.6 | 13.2 |
| 1985 | 46.6 | 15.1 | 12.9 | 14.7 | 6.6 | 11.4 | 33.6 | 10.0 | 29.4 | 16.9 | 11.6 | 13.3 |
| 1986 | 42.3 | 14.2 | 11.2 | 16.7 | 7.7 | 10.5 | 29.4 | 9.2 | 26.9 | 18.7 | 11.6 | 12.7 |
| 1987 | 41.2 | 12.8 | 10.8 | 17.0 | 9.1 | 10.8 | 28.5 | 9.3 | 26.9 | 23.2 | 11.8 | 12.8 |
| 1988 | 42.1 | 12.4 | 10.8 | 14.0 | 10.0 | 11.1 | 29.8 | 9.5 | 27.4 | 28.8 | 11.9 | 13.0 |
| 1989 | 44.4 | 12.5 | 11.6 | 18.5 | 10.7 | 11.8 | 32.0 | 10.0 | 28.4 | 28.6 | 12.4 | 13.7 |
| 1990 | 43.6 | 12.5 | 11.9 | 19.0 | 10.6 | 11.6 | 30.9 | 9.4 | 27.9 | 29.2 | 12.0 | 13.5 |
| 1991 | 42.8 | 13.0 | 13.3 | 18.5 | 10.6 | 11.2 | 30.1 | 9.1 | 27.5 | 27.5 | 10.7 | 13.4 |
| 1992 | 39.9 | 12.5 | 12.4 | 18.9 | 10.5 | 10.7 | 29.6 | 9.0 | 26.6 | 26.6 | 11.1 | 13.1 |
| 1993 | 38.5 | 11.5 | 10.4 | 19.8 | 9.7 | 9.3 | 29.6 | 8.2 | 25.1 | 25.4 | 11.0 | 12.0 |
| 1994 | 39.3 | 12.0 | 10.4 | 20.5 | 10.0 | 9.6 | 29.2 | 8.2 | 25.4 | 25.9 | 10.7 | 12.1 |

EUR 12–: incl. WD.

**Table M11**  Extra-EC exports of goods at current prices. Foreign trade statistics.

|  | B/L | DK | WD | GR | E | F | IRL | I | NL | P | UK | EUR 12– |
|---|---|---|---|---|---|---|---|---|---|---|---|---|
| 1960 | 14.7 | 13.7 | 8.5 | 11.0 | 4.0 | 6.7 | 12.4 | 7.5 | 17.5 | .6 | 13.6 | 9.9 |
| 1961 | 13.8 | 12.7 | 7.9 | 9.0 | 5.3 | 6.2 | 12.6 | 7.4 | 16.5 | 10.7 | 12.2 | 9.1 |
| 1962 | 13.7 | 13.4 | 7.9 | 7.2 | 5.9 | 6.0 | 11.6 | 7.3 | 15.5 | 9.6 | 11.8 | 8.9 |
| 1963 | 13.7 | 12.9 | 7.8 | 8.0 | 5.9 | 5.9 | 11.7 | 7.7 | 15.4 | 10.6 | 11.9 | 8.9 |
| 1964 | 14.0 | 14.3 | 7.8 | 7.6 | 5.7 | 6.0 | 11.8 | 6.9 | 15.3 | 11.6 | 12.4 | 8.9 |
| 1965 | 13.4 | 13.8 | 8.1 | 9.1 | 6.4 | 5.6 | 11.9 | 6.8 | 14.1 | 11.9 | 11.9 | 8.8 |
| 1966 | 13.6 | 13.5 | 7.8 | 8.7 | 6.6 | 5.6 | 11.5 | 7.2 | 13.9 | 11.9 | 11.3 | 8.6 |
| 1967 | 12.8 | 13.4 | 7.4 | 7.3 | 6.0 | 5.2 | 11.3 | 7.1 | 13.2 | 10.8 | 11.4 | 8.3 |
| 1968 | 14.1 | 13.3 | 7.7 | 8.1 | 6.6 | 5.0 | 11.8 | 6.8 | 13.0 | 11.1 | 12.9 | 8.5 |
| 1969 | 14.3 | 13.6 | 8.0 | 8.5 | 7.0 | 5.3 | 11.7 | 7.2 | 13.1 | 10.7 | 12.7 | 8.8 |
| 1970 | 14.5 | 14.2 | 7.8 | 9.6 | 7.3 | 5.8 | 10.7 | 7.3 | 14.4 | 12.1 | 12.5 | 8.9 |
| 1971 | 12.6 | 13.8 | 7.4 | 9.1 | 6.6 | 5.6 | 12.4 | 6.9 | 14.5 | 12.3 | 11.8 | 8.5 |
| 1972 | 11.7 | 12.1 | 6.8 | 8.2 | 7.0 | 5.6 | 10.6 | 6.9 | 13.1 | 12.8 | 11.5 | 8.1 |
| 1973 | 13.0 | 14.0 | 7.2 | 10.4 | 7.4 | 6.1 | 10.9 | 8.3 | 14.2 | 13.2 | 13.9 | 9.0 |
| 1974 | 17.0 | 16.1 | 8.9 | 12.9 | 10.7 | 9.3 | 16.0 | 12.3 | 17.7 | 17.7 | 17.9 | 12.1 |
| 1975 | 14.5 | 14.4 | 8.5 | 14.0 | 9.7 | 7.5 | 12.8 | 9.8 | 16.5 | 14.4 | 13.9 | 10.3 |
| 1976 | 15.7 | 15.3 | 9.7 | 15.8 | 10.5 | 8.5 | 14.2 | 11.0 | 17.9 | 14.9 | 15.3 | 11.5 |
| 1977 | 15.5 | 14.6 | 9.6 | 14.5 | 9.5 | 8.5 | 16.0 | 10.4 | 17.4 | 15.6 | 14.8 | 11.2 |
| 1978 | 14.5 | 12.9 | 9.0 | 13.1 | 8.1 | 7.6 | 15.0 | 9.6 | 15.6 | 14.2 | 13.9 | 10.3 |
| 1979 | 16.7 | 13.6 | 10.1 | 13.6 | 8.1 | 8.5 | 15.9 | 10.7 | 17.6 | 16.8 | 13.2 | 11.1 |
| 1980 | 20.6 | 14.6 | 11.7 | 15.6 | 10.8 | 10.2 | 15.4 | 11.5 | 20.1 | 20.3 | 12.4 | 12.4 |
| 1981 | 22.7 | 16.0 | 12.1 | 11.6 | 12.1 | 10.6 | 15.3 | 12.3 | 21.2 | 22.4 | 10.8 | 12.6 |
| 1982 | 22.9 | 15.3 | 11.7 | 13.6 | 11.8 | 10.2 | 14.0 | 11.5 | 19.8 | 21.9 | 10.8 | 12.2 |
| 1983 | 19.5 | 14.7 | 11.3 | 13.8 | 12.3 | 9.2 | 14.8 | 10.2 | 20.3 | 21.9 | 11.2 | 11.7 |
| 1984 | 21.2 | 15.8 | 12.4 | 14.5 | 11.9 | 9.4 | 17.5 | 10.6 | 21.9 | 23.7 | 12.8 | 12.5 |
| 1985 | 19.6 | 15.7 | 12.4 | 15.8 | 11.4 | 9.0 | 17.1 | 10.7 | 21.0 | 20.1 | 12.1 | 12.2 |
| 1986 | 15.8 | 13.3 | 10.1 | 11.8 | 7.6 | 7.0 | 14.3 | 7.2 | 15.2 | 13.1 | 10.7 | 9.5 |
| 1987 | 15.5 | 11.9 | 9.7 | 10.8 | 7.6 | 6.9 | 14.9 | 6.8 | 15.0 | 13.4 | 10.5 | 9.2 |
| 1988 | 15.4 | 11.9 | 10.0 | 8.4 | 7.6 | 7.2 | 15.2 | 6.7 | 15.6 | 14.1 | 10.8 | 9.4 |
| 1989 | 17.6 | 12.8 | 11.1 | 11.1 | 8.0 | 7.9 | 16.8 | 7.2 | 17.2 | 13.4 | 11.3 | 10.1 |
| 1990 | 15.8 | 11.8 | 10.8 | 10.6 | 7.2 | 7.8 | 15.4 | 6.6 | 16.4 | 13.1 | 10.9 | 9.7 |
| 1991 | 15.9 | 11.8 | 10.8 | 12.1 | 7.0 | 8.0 | 15.9 | 6.3 | 15.8 | 10.8 | 10.0 | 9.5 |
| 1992 | 14.2 | 11.1 | 10.1 | 11.1 | 6.8 | 7.2 | 14.9 | 6.0 | 15.2 | 9.5 | 10.1 | 9.0 |
| 1993 | 12.7 | 10.3 | 8.5 | 10.9 | 6.7 | 6.6 | 15.6 | 6.5 | 14.6 | 9.1 | 11.4 | 8.7 |
| 1994 | 12.5 | 10.9 | 8.5 | 10.9 | 7.0 | 6.8 | 16.1 | 7.2 | 14.8 | 9.4 | 11.4 | 8.9 |

EUR 12–: incl. WD.

**Table M12**  Balance on current transactions with the rest of the world. National accounts definition.

(Percentage of gross domestic product at market prices)

|       | B    | DK   | WD   | D    | GR   | E    | F    | IRL   | I    | L    | NL   | P     | UK   | EUR 12- | EUR 12+ | USA  | J    |
|-------|------|------|------|------|------|------|------|-------|------|------|------|-------|------|---------|---------|------|------|
| 1960  | 0.1  | -1.1 | 1.6  | :    | -2.9 | 3.3  | 1.5  | -0.1  | 0.7  | 12.5 | 2.8  | -4.0  | -1.0 | 0.7     | :       | 0.6  | 0.5  |
| 1961  | -0.1 | -1.7 | 1.0  | :    | -2.2 | 1.6  | 1.1  | 0.2   | 1.1  | 6.5  | 1.3  | -9.9  | 0.0  | 0.6     | :       | 0.8  | -1.6 |
| 1962  | 0.6  | -3.2 | -0.1 | :    | -1.6 | -0.1 | 1.0  | -1.7  | 0.6  | 0.6  | 1.0  | -3.4  | 0.4  | 0.3     | :       | 0.7  | 0.1  |
| 1963  | -0.5 | 0.1  | 0.2  | :    | -2.2 | -1.3 | 0.3  | -2.7  | -1.3 | 0.2  | 0.6  | -3.3  | 0.3  | -0.1    | :       | 0.8  | -1.0 |
| 1964  | 0.2  | -2.2 | 0.2  | :    | -4.3 | 0.1  | -0.3 | -3.3  | 1.0  | -1.0 | 0.0  | -1.3  | -0.3 |         | :       | 1.2  | -0.5 |
| 1965  | 0.6  | -1.8 | -1.3 | :    | -5.8 | -2.0 | 0.8  | -4.2  | 3.4  | 0.7  | 0.1  | -0.4  | -0.4 | 0.0     | :       | 0.9  | 1.1  |
| 1966  | -0.3 | -1.9 | 0.2  | :    | -2.0 | -2.1 | 0.1  | -1.5  | 3.0  | 1.7  | -0.9 | 0.8   | 0.1  | 0.3     | :       | 0.5  | 1.3  |
| 1967  | 0.8  | -2.4 | 2.2  | :    | -2.2 | -1.5 | 0.0  | 1.3   | 2.1  | 7.4  | -0.3 | 3.6   | -0.9 | 0.5     | :       | 0.4  | 0.0  |
| 1968  | 0.9  | -1.7 | 2.3  | :    | -3.6 | -0.8 | -0.5 | -1.3  | 3.1  | 9.7  | 0.3  | 1.5   | -0.8 | 0.7     | :       | 0.2  | 0.8  |
| 1969  | 1.2  | -2.8 | 1.4  | :    | -4.0 | -1.1 | -1.1 | -4.6  | 2.5  | 14.0 | 0.2  | 3.6   | 0.6  | 0.5     | :       | 0.2  | 1.3  |
| 1970  | 2.8  | -3.9 | 0.6  | :    | -3.1 | 0.2  | 0.8  | -3.9  | 0.8  | 15.5 | -1.4 | 1.9   | 1.3  | 0.6     | :       | 0.4  | 1.0  |
| 1961-70 | 0.6 | -2.1 | 0.7 | :   | -3.1 | -0.7 | 0.2  | -2.2  | 1.6  | 5.6  | 0.0  | -0.6  | -0.1 | 0.3     | :       | 0.6  | 0.2  |
| 1971  | 2.1  | -2.4 | 0.4  | :    | -1.5 | 2.2  | 0.9  | -3.7  | 1.4  | 6.6  | -0.3 | 2.5   | 1.8  | 0.9     | :       | 0.1  | 2.5  |
| 1972  | 3.6  | -0.4 | 0.6  | :    | -1.2 | 1.5  | 1.0  | -2.1  | 1.6  | 10.6 | 2.8  | 5.5   | 0.1  | 1.0     | :       | -0.3 | 2.2  |
| 1973  | 2.0  | -1.7 | 1.5  | :    | -3.8 | 0.8  | 0.6  | -3.3  | -1.6 | 16.5 | 3.8  | 3.0   | -1.9 | 0.3     | :       | 0.6  | 0.0  |
| 1974  | 0.4  | -3.1 | 2.7  | :    | -2.8 | -3.5 | -1.3 | -9.4  | -4.2 | 26.5 | 3.1  | -6.2  | -4.5 | -0.9    | :       | 0.5  | -1.0 |
| 1975  | -0.1 | -1.5 | 1.2  | :    | -3.7 | -2.9 | 0.8  | -1.5  | -0.2 | 17.0 | 2.5  | -5.5  | -2.0 | 0.0     | :       | 1.3  | -0.1 |
| 1976  | 0.3  | -4.9 | 0.8  | :    | -1.9 | -3.9 | -0.9 | -5.1  | -1.2 | 21.6 | 2.9  | -8.0  | -1.6 | -0.6    | :       | 0.5  | 0.7  |
| 1977  | -1.1 | -4.0 | 0.8  | :    | -1.9 | -1.7 | -0.1 | -5.2  | 1.1  | 21.7 | 0.8  | -9.4  | 0.0  | 0.0     | :       | -0.5 | 1.5  |
| 1978  | -1.3 | -2.7 | 1.4  | :    | -1.3 | 1.0  | 1.4  | -6.5  | 2.2  | 19.7 | -0.9 | -5.7  | 0.5  | 0.9     | :       | -0.5 | 1.7  |
| 1979  | -2.9 | -4.7 | -0.5 | :    | -1.9 | 0.5  | 0.9  | -12.8 | 1.6  | 21.7 | -1.2 | -1.7  | 0.2  | 0.0     | :       | 0.0  | -0.9 |
| 1980  | -4.3 | -3.7 | -1.7 | :    | 0.5  | -2.4 | -0.6 | -11.3 | -2.2 | 19.0 | -1.4 | -5.9  | 1.5  | -1.2    | :       | 0.4  | -1.0 |
| 1971-80 | -0.1 | -2.9 | 0.7 | :  | -1.9 | -0.8 | 0.3  | -6.1  | -0.1 | 18.1 | 1.2  | -3.1  | -0.6 | 0.0     | :       | 0.2  | 0.6  |
| 1981  | -3.8 | -3.0 | -0.6 | :    | -0.7 | -2.7 | -0.8 | -14.1 | -2.2 | 21.3 | 2.2  | -12.2 | 2.5  | -0.6    | :       | 0.3  | 0.5  |
| 1982  | -3.7 | -4.2 | 0.8  | :    | -4.4 | -2.5 | -2.1 | -10.1 | -1.5 | 34.4 | 3.1  | -13.5 | 1.5  | -0.6    | :       | -0.1 | 0.7  |
| 1983  | -0.8 | -2.6 | 0.9  | :    | -5.0 | -1.5 | -0.8 | -6.6  | 0.3  | 39.5 | 3.1  | -8.3  | 0.8  | 0.1     | :       | -1.0 | 1.8  |
| 1984  | -0.6 | -3.3 | 1.4  | :    | -4.0 | 1.4  | 0.0  | -5.6  | -0.6 | 39.1 | 4.1  | -3.4  | -0.3 | 0.3     | :       | -2.5 | 2.8  |
| 1985  | 0.3  | -4.6 | 2.4  | :    | -8.2 | 1.4  | 0.1  | -3.8  | -0.9 | 43.8 | 4.3  | 0.4   | 0.3  | 0.6     | :       | -2.9 | 3.6  |
| 1986  | 2.1  | -5.4 | 4.3  | :    | -5.3 | 1.6  | 0.5  | -3.3  | 0.5  | 38.8 | 3.1  | 2.4   | -1.1 | 1.3     | :       | -3.3 | 4.3  |
| 1987  | 1.3  | -2.9 | 4.1  | :    | -3.1 | 0.1  | -0.2 | -0.2  | -0.2 | 30.3 | 1.9  | -0.4  | -2.2 | 0.7     | :       | -3.4 | 3.6  |
| 1988  | 1.7  | -1.3 | 4.3  | :    | -2.0 | -1.1 | -0.3 | 0.0   | -0.7 | 30.8 | 2.8  | -4.4  | -4.9 | 0.1     | :       | -2.4 | 2.8  |
| 1989  | 1.7  | -1.5 | 4.8  | :    | -5.0 | -3.2 | -0.5 | -1.7  | -1.3 | 34.0 | 3.5  | -2.3  | -5.5 | -0.2    | :       | -1.7 | 2.0  |
| 1990  | 0.9  | 0.5  | 3.6  | :    | -6.2 | -3.7 | -0.9 | -0.7  | -1.4 | 34.2 | 3.8  | -2.5  | -4.5 | -0.4    | :       | -1.4 | 1.3  |
| 1981-90 | -0.1 | -2.8 | 2.6 | :  | -4.4 | -1.0 | -0.5 | -4.6  | -0.8 | 34.6 | 3.2  | -4.4  | -1.3 | 0.1     | :       | -1.9 | 2.4  |
| 1991  | 1.8  | 1.3  | 1.4  | -1.2 | -5.1 | -3.6 | -0.5 | 2.0   | -1.8 | 27.9 | 3.6  | -2.9  | -2.4 | -0.6    | -1.2    | 0.2  | 2.5  |
| 1992  | 1.8  | 3.0  | 1.6  | -1.2 | -4.3 | -3.8 | 0.2  | 3.6   | -2.2 | 30.0 | 3.2  | -3.2  | -2.4 | -0.3    | -1.1    | -0.9 | 3.3  |
| 1993  | 3.0  | 3.6  | 1.9  | -1.2 | -3.6 | -1.8 | 0.9  | 4.1   | 1.1  | 28.3 | 4.0  | -3.5  | -2.5 | 0.7     | -0.2    | -1.7 | 3.1  |
| 1994  | 3.0  | 3.0  | 2.3  | -0.9 | -3.8 | -0.8 | 0.9  | 3.5   | 1.1  | 29.6 | 4.6  | -3.6  | -1.7 | 1.1     | 0.2     | -1.7 | 2.9  |

EUR 12-: incl. ED; EUR 12+: incl. D.

**Table M13**  Structure of EC exports by country and region, 1858 and 1992.

(Percentage of total exports)

| Export of → / to ↓ | B/L 1958 | B/L 1992 | DK 1958 | DK 1992 | D 1958 | D 1992 | GR 1958 | GR 1992 | E 1958 | E 1992 | F 1958 | F 1992 | IRL 1958 | IRL 1992 | I 1958 | I 1992 | NL 1958 | NL 1992 | P 1958 | P 1992 | UK 1958 | UK 1992 | EUR 12 1958 | EUR 12 1992 |
|---|---|---|---|---|---|---|---|---|---|---|---|---|---|---|---|---|---|---|---|---|---|---|---|---|
| B/L | – | – | 1.2 | 2.1 | 6.6 | 7.4 | 1.0 | 2.6 | 2.1 | 3.0 | 6.3 | 8.7 | 0.8 | 4.9 | 2.2 | 3.3 | 15.0 | 14.2 | 3.7 | 3.3 | 1.9 | 5.3 | 4.8 | 6.4 |
| D/K | 1.6 | 0.9 | – | – | 3.0 | 1.9 | 0.2 | 0.7 | 1.7 | 0.6 | 0.7 | 0.8 | 0.1 | 1.0 | 0.8 | 0.8 | 2.6 | 1.5 | 1.2 | 2.2 | 2.4 | 1.3 | 2.0 | 1.4 |
| D | 11.6 | 22.8 | 20.0 | 23.7 | – | – | 20.5 | 23.2 | 10.2 | 14.6 | 10.4 | 19.1 | 2.2 | 12.8 | 14.1 | 20.4 | 19.0 | 28.6 | 7.7 | 19.2 | 4.2 | 13.6 | 7.6 | 14.0 |
| GR | 0.8 | 0.6 | 0.3 | 0.9 | 1.3 | 1.1 | – | – | 0.1 | 0.7 | 0.6 | 0.8 | 0.1 | 0.5 | 1.9 | 1.8 | 0.6 | 1.1 | 0.6 | 0.5 | 0.7 | 0.7 | 0.8 | 1.0 |
| E | 0.7 | 2.7 | 0.8 | 1.9 | 1.2 | 4.1 | 0.2 | 2.3 | – | – | 1.6 | 6.8 | 0.8 | 2.3 | 0.7 | 5.1 | 0.8 | 2.6 | 0.7 | 14.5 | 0.8 | 4.1 | 1.0 | 4.2 |
| F | 10.6 | 19.3 | 3.0 | 5.8 | 7.6 | 12.9 | 12.8 | 7.2 | 10.1 | 18.9 | – | – | 0.8 | 9.7 | 5.3 | 14.6 | 4.9 | 10.5 | 6.6 | 14.1 | 2.4 | 10.5 | 4.7 | 10.9 |
| IRL | 0.3 | 0.3 | 0.3 | 0.5 | 0.3 | 0.4 | 0.4 | 0.2 | 0.3 | 0.3 | 0.2 | 0.4 | – | – | 0.1 | 0.3 | 0.4 | 0.6 | 0.3 | 0.5 | 3.5 | 5.3 | 1.1 | 1.0 |
| I | 2.3 | 5.9 | 5.3 | 4.5 | 5.0 | 9.2 | 6.0 | 18.0 | 2.7 | 10.2 | 3.4 | 11.0 | 0.4 | 4.1 | – | – | 2.7 | 6.3 | 4.3 | 3.9 | 2.1 | 5.6 | 3.1 | 7.2 |
| NL | 20.7 | 13.6 | 2.2 | 4.5 | 8.1 | 8.3 | 2.0 | 2.7 | 3.2 | 3.9 | 2.0 | 4.6 | 0.5 | 7.0 | 2.0 | 3.1 | – | – | 2.5 | 5.5 | 3.2 | 7.9 | 5.3 | 6.2 |
| P | 1.1 | 0.8 | 0.3 | 0.6 | 0.9 | 1.1 | 0.3 | 0.3 | 0.4 | 7.0 | 0.8 | 1.6 | 0.1 | 0.5 | 0.7 | 1.6 | 0.4 | 0.8 | – | – | 0.4 | 1.1 | 0.8 | 1.4 |
| UK | 5.7 | 7.8 | 25.9 | 10.1 | 3.9 | 7.7 | 7.6 | 7.0 | 15.9 | 7.0 | 4.9 | 9.2 | 76.8 | 31.5 | 6.8 | 6.6 | 11.9 | 9.1 | 11.3 | 11.3 | – | – | 5.9 | 7.5 |
| **Total intra-EC trade** | 55.4 | 74.8 | 59.3 | 54.5 | 37.9 | 54.1 | 50.9 | 64.2 | 46.8 | 66.3 | 30.9 | 63.0 | 82.4 | 74.2 | 34.5 | 57.7 | 58.3 | 75.4 | 38.9 | 74.8 | 21.7 | 55.5 | 37.2 | 61.3 |
| Other European OECD countries | 8.7 | 6.5 | 16.6 | 22.6 | 22.7 | 17.0 | 10.3 | 8.5 | 12.4 | 5.4 | 9.0 | 7.4 | 0.9 | 5.4 | 18.9 | 11.0 | 11.9 | 7.1 | 5.1 | 9.0 | 9.1 | 7.9 | 13.7 | 11.0 |
| USA | 9.4 | 3.9 | 9.3 | 5.0 | 7.3 | 6.4 | 13.6 | 4.0 | 10.1 | 4.5 | 5.9 | 6.2 | 5.7 | 8.2 | 9.9 | 7.0 | 5.6 | 4.1 | 8.3 | 3.5 | 8.8 | 11.5 | 7.9 | 6.5 |
| Canada | 1.1 | 0.3 | 0.7 | 0.5 | 1.2 | 0.6 | 0.3 | 0.5 | 1.3 | 0.5 | 0.8 | 0.9 | 0.7 | 1.0 | 1.2 | 0.7 | 0.8 | 0.4 | 1.1 | 0.7 | 5.8 | 1.5 | 2.3 | 0.7 |
| Japan | 0.6 | 1.0 | 0.2 | 3.6 | 0.9 | 2.2 | 1.4 | 0.9 | 1.7 | 0.7 | 0.3 | 1.7 | 0.0 | 2.9 | 0.3 | 1.9 | 0.4 | 0.9 | 0.5 | 0.8 | 2.1 | 0.6 | 1.8 | 1.8 |
| Australia | 0.5 | 0.3 | 0.3 | 0.4 | 1.0 | 0.6 | 0.1 | 0.5 | 0.3 | 0.2 | 0.5 | 0.4 | 0.1 | 0.6 | 0.8 | 0.5 | 0.7 | 0.4 | 0.6 | 0.2 | 7.2 | 1.3 | 2.4 | 0.6 |
| Developing countries | 18.0 | 10.4 | 9.3 | 9.9 | 20.9 | 11.6 | 7.2 | 14.0 | 18.4 | 20.0 | 46.9 | 17.2 | 1.6 | 5.5 | 26.2 | 15.8 | 17.6 | 8.4 | 42.3 | 9.0 | 33.6 | 16.2 | 27.4 | 13.4 |
| of which: OPEC | 3.3 | 2.2 | 2.3 | 2.1 | 4.8 | 3.5 | 0.9 | 3.4 | 2.6 | 3.4 | 21.3 | 4.5 | 0.2 | 1.4 | 7.5 | 5.2 | 4.5 | 2.3 | 2.0 | 0.6 | 7.0 | 5.0 | 7.6 | 3.7 |
| Other developing countries | 14.7 | 8.2 | 7.0 | 7.8 | 16.1 | 8.1 | 6.3 | 10.6 | 15.8 | 16.6 | 25.6 | 12.7 | 1.4 | 4.1 | 18.7 | 10.6 | 13.1 | 6.1 | 40.3 | 8.4 | 26.6 | 11.2 | 19.8 | 9.7 |
| Rest of the world and unspecified | 6.3 | 2.8 | 4.3 | 3.5 | 8.1 | 7.5 | 16.2 | 7.4 | 9.0 | 2.4 | 5.7 | 3.2 | 8.6 | 2.2 | 8.2 | 5.4 | 4.7 | 3.3 | 3.2 | 2.0 | 13.2 | 4.0 | 8.5 | 4.7 |
| **World (excl. EC)** | 44.6 | 25.2 | 40.7 | 45.5 | 62.1 | 45.9 | 49.1 | 35.8 | 53.2 | 33.7 | 69.1 | 37.0 | 17.6 | 25.8 | 65.5 | 42.3 | 41.7 | 24.6 | 61.1 | 25.2 | 78.3 | 44.5 | 62.8 | 38.7 |
| **World (incl. EC)** | 100 | 100 | 100 | 100 | 100 | 100 | 100 | 100 | 100 | 100 | 100 | 100 | 100 | 100 | 100 | 100 | 100 | 100 | 100 | 100 | 100 | 100 | 100 | 100 |

D: 1958: West Germany; 1992: unified Germany.

**Table M14** Structure of EC imports by country and region, 1958 and 1992.

(Percentage of total imports)

| Import of | B/L 1958 | B/L 1992 | DK 1958 | DK 1992 | D 1958 | D 1992 | GR 1958 | GR 1992 | E 1958 | E 1992 | F 1958 | F 1992 | IRL 1958 | IRL 1992 | I 1958 | I 1992 | NL 1958 | NL 1992 | P 1958 | P 1992 | UK 1958 | UK 1992 | EUR 12 1958 | EUR 12 1992 |
|---|---|---|---|---|---|---|---|---|---|---|---|---|---|---|---|---|---|---|---|---|---|---|---|---|
| to | | | | | | | | | | | | | | | | | | | | | | | | |
| B/L | – | – | 3.8 | 3.4 | 4.5 | 7.8 | 3.3 | 3.5 | 1.8 | 3.3 | 5.4 | 10.5 | 1.8 | 2.2 | 2.0 | 4.8 | 17.8 | 12.9 | 7.3 | 3.8 | 1.6 | 4.4 | 4.4 | 6.6 |
| D/K | 0.5 | 0.6 | – | – | 3.4 | 2.4 | 0.7 | 1.4 | 1.3 | 0.8 | 0.6 | 1.0 | 0.7 | 1.0 | 2.2 | 1.0 | 0.7 | 1.2 | 0.8 | 0.8 | 3.1 | 1.9 | 2.0 | 1.4 |
| D | 17.2 | 22.5 | 19.9 | 24.3 | – | – | 20.3 | 20.2 | 8.7 | 16.1 | 11.6 | 21.2 | 4.0 | 8.3 | 12.0 | 21.6 | 19.5 | 23.0 | 17.6 | 14.8 | 3.6 | 14.8 | 8.7 | 14.5 |
| GR | 0.1 | 0.1 | 0.0 | 0.2 | 0.7 | 0.6 | – | – | 0.2 | 0.2 | 0.6 | 0.3 | 0.2 | 0.2 | 0.4 | 0.9 | 0.2 | 0.2 | 0.1 | 0.1 | 0.2 | 0.3 | 0.4 | 0.4 |
| E | 0.5 | 1.5 | 0.7 | 1.1 | 1.6 | 2.6 | 0.1 | 2.2 | – | – | 1.2 | 5.1 | 0.4 | 0.7 | 0.4 | 3.4 | 0.4 | 1.5 | 0.4 | 16.6 | 1.0 | 2.3 | 0.9 | 2.9 |
| F | 11.6 | 15.5 | 3.4 | 5.5 | 7.6 | 12.0 | 5.4 | 7.9 | 6.8 | 16.2 | – | – | 1.6 | 4.5 | 4.8 | 14.4 | 2.8 | 7.2 | 7.7 | 12.7 | 2.7 | 9.6 | 4.4 | 9.8 |
| IRL | 0.1 | 0.6 | 0.0 | 0.8 | 0.1 | 1.0 | 0.0 | 0.6 | 0.6 | 0.7 | 0.0 | 1.2 | – | – | 0.0 | 0.7 | 0.0 | 1.0 | 0.1 | 0.4 | 2.9 | 4.0 | 0.9 | 1.3 |
| I | 2.1 | 4.3 | 1.7 | 3.9 | 5.5 | 9.1 | 8.8 | 14.2 | 1.8 | 9.4 | 2.4 | 10.9 | 0.8 | 2.2 | – | – | 1.8 | 3.3 | 3.7 | 10.2 | 2.1 | 5.3 | 2.7 | 6.7 |
| NL | 15.7 | 18.4 | 7.3 | 6.9 | 8.1 | 11.9 | 4.8 | 6.9 | 2.6 | 3.7 | 2.5 | 6.6 | 2.9 | 5.1 | 2.6 | 5.9 | – | – | 2.9 | 6.9 | 4.2 | 7.3 | 5.2 | 8.2 |
| P | 0.4 | 0.4 | 0.3 | 1.2 | 0.4 | 0.9 | 0.3 | 0.4 | 0.3 | 2.7 | 0.4 | 1.1 | 0.2 | 0.3 | 0.4 | 0.4 | 0.2 | 0.6 | – | – | 0.4 | 0.9 | 0.3 | 0.9 |
| UK | 7.4 | 7.2 | 22.8 | 8.1 | 4.3 | 6.6 | 9.9 | 5.5 | 7.8 | 7.1 | 3.5 | 7.9 | 56.3 | 47.5 | 5.5 | 5.7 | 7.4 | 7.9 | 12.9 | 7.2 | – | – | 5.4 | 6.6 |
| Total intra-EC trade | 55.5 | 71.2 | 60.0 | 55.4 | 36.3 | 54.7 | 53.7 | 62.7 | 31.8 | 60.3 | 28.3 | 65.6 | 68.9 | 71.9 | 30.2 | 58.8 | 50.7 | 58.8 | 53.4 | 73.6 | 21.8 | 50.7 | 35.2 | 59.3 |
| Other European OECD countries | 7.7 | 5.7 | 18.6 | 23.1 | 15.2 | 15.1 | 11.5 | 6.4 | 8.4 | 5.9 | 6.7 | 7.3 | 3.4 | 5.2 | 13.1 | 10.7 | 7.2 | 7.0 | 8.6 | 6.3 | 8.7 | 11.3 | 10.1 | 10.3 |
| USA | 9.9 | 5.8 | 9.1 | 5.1 | 13.6 | 6.0 | 13.7 | 3.7 | 21.6 | 7.4 | 10.0 | 7.3 | 7.0 | 11.9 | 16.4 | 5.3 | 11.3 | 8.2 | 7.0 | 3.0 | 9.4 | 11.7 | 11.4 | 7.2 |
| Canada | 1.4 | 0.5 | 0.2 | 0.5 | 3.1 | 0.6 | 0.8 | 0.2 | 0.5 | 0.6 | 1.0 | 0.6 | 3.0 | 0.4 | 1.5 | 0.8 | 1.4 | 0.6 | 0.5 | 0.6 | 8.2 | 1.6 | 3.6 | 0.7 |
| Japan | 0.6 | 3.8 | 1.5 | 3.3 | 0.6 | 5.0 | 2.0 | 6.4 | 0.7 | 4.4 | 0.2 | 2.9 | 1.1 | 3.3 | 0.4 | 2.3 | 0.8 | 5.4 | 0.0 | 3.1 | 0.9 | 5.7 | 0.7 | 4.3 |
| Australia | 1.7 | 0.3 | 0.0 | 0.2 | 1.2 | 0.3 | 0.3 | 0.1 | 0.8 | 0.3 | 2.4 | 0.4 | 1.2 | 0.0 | 3.0 | 0.5 | 0.2 | 0.4 | 0.9 | 0.1 | 5.4 | 0.8 | 2.6 | 0.4 |
| Developing countries of which: | 19.2 | 8.1 | 5.9 | 7.0 | 23.9 | 10.3 | 9.6 | 14.6 | 32.0 | 17.5 | 45.6 | 12.2 | 9.3 | 4.8 | 9.4 | 14.4 | 24.4 | 15.3 | 27.6 | 11.7 | 34.7 | 12.5 | 29.5 | 12.1 |
| OPEC | 5.7 | 1.2 | 0.3 | 0.5 | 6.7 | 2.4 | 1.7 | 6.9 | 17.7 | 5.8 | 19.7 | 4.1 | 0.7 | 0.4 | 13.9 | 6.2 | 11.5 | 5.6 | 6.3 | 3.9 | 11.3 | 2.2 | 10.8 | 3.5 |
| Other developing countries | 13.5 | 6.9 | 5.6 | 6.5 | 17.2 | 7.9 | 7.9 | 7.7 | 14.3 | 11.7 | 25.9 | 8.1 | 8.6 | 4.4 | 15.5 | 7.9 | 12.9 | 9.7 | 21.3 | 7.8 | 23.4 | 10.3 | 18.7 | 8.6 |
| Rest of the world and unspecified | 4.0 | 4.6 | 4.7 | 5.4 | 6.1 | 8.0 | 8.4 | 5.9 | 4.2 | 3.6 | 5.8 | 3.7 | 6.1 | 2.5 | 6.0 | 7.5 | 4.0 | 4.3 | 2.0 | 1.6 | 10.9 | 5.7 | 6.9 | 5.7 |
| World (excl. EC) | 44.5 | 28.8 | 40.0 | 44.6 | 63.7 | 45.3 | 46.3 | 37.3 | 68.2 | 39.7 | 71.7 | 34.4 | 31.1 | 28.1 | 69.8 | 41.2 | 49.3 | 41.2 | 46.6 | 26.4 | 78.2 | 49.3 | 64.8 | 40.7 |
| World (incl. EC) | 100 | 100 | 100 | 100 | 100 | 100 | 100 | 100 | 100 | 100 | 100 | 100 | 100 | 100 | 100 | 100 | 100 | 100 | 100 | 100 | 100 | 100 | 100 | 100 |

D: 1958: West Germany; 1992: unified Germany.

**Table M15** Importance of trade[1] – 1992

| Country | Imports Mio ECU | Imports % of GDP | Imports 1,000 ECU per head | Exports Mio ECU | Exports % of GDP | Exports 1000 ECU per head | Balance[2] (Mio ECU) |
|---|---|---|---|---|---|---|---|
| EUR 12 intra + extra) | 1 207 269 | 22.3* | 3.5 | 1 136 487 | 21.0* | 3.3 | −70 782 |
| EUR 12 (extra) | 487 730 | 9.0* | 1.4 | 435 660 | 8.0* | 1.3 | −52 070 |
| 1. Belg/Lux | 101 890 | 60.3 | 10.2 | 95 412 | 56.4 | 9.5 | −6478 |
| 2. Danmark | 26 753 | 24.3 | 5.2 | 31 063 | 28.2 | 6.0 | 4310 |
| 3. Deutschland | 315 745 | 21.1 | 3.9 | 331 009 | 22.1 | 4.1 | 15 264 |
| 4. Ελλάδα | 17 951 | 29.9 | 1.7 | 7338 | 12.2 | 0.7 | 10 163 |
| 5. España | 74 862 | 16.9 | 1.9 | 53 032 | 11.9 | 1.4 | 21 830 |
| 6. France | 199 361 | 19.5 | 3.5 | 192 361 | 18.9 | 3.4 | 7000 |
| 7. Ireland | 16 808 | 43.4 | 4.7 | 21 828 | 56.4 | 6.2 | 5020 |
| 8. Italia | 145 777 | 15.4 | 2.6* | 137 581 | 14.6 | 2.4 | 8196 |
| 9. Luxembourg | | | | | | | |
| 10. Nederland | 113 973 | 46.0 | 7.5 | 108 614 | 43.9 | 7.2 | 5359 |
| 11. Portugal | 22 739 | 30.6* | 2.3 | 13 727 | 18.5* | 1.4 | −9012 |
| 12. United Kingdom | 171 410 | 21.3 | 3.0* | 144 522 | 17.9 | 2.5 | 26 888 |
| 13. Österreich | 41 750 | 29.7[1] | 5.3 | 34 230 | 21.2[1] | 4.4 | −7520 |
| 14. Suomi/Finland | 16 333 | 17.1[1] | 3.2 | 18 474 | 18.1[1] | 3.7 | 2141 |
| 15. Island | 1298 | 25.3[1] | 5.0 | 1177 | 22.9[1] | 4.5 | −121 |
| 16. Norge | 20 039 | 23.3[1] | 4.7 | 27 055 | 31.4[1] | 6.3 | 7016 |
| 17. Sverige | 38 513 | 20.5[1] | 4.5 | 43 229 | 22.7[1] | 5.0 | 4716 |
| EEA | 1 325 202 | : | 3.6 | 1 260 652 | : | 3.4 | −78 748 |
| 18. Schweiz/Suisse | 50 586 | 28.0[1] | 7.4 | 50 483 | 25.9[1] | 7.9 | −103 |
| 19. Türkiye | 17 619 | 19.1[1] | 0.3 | 11 336 | 12.3[1] | 0.2 | 6283 |
| 20. USA | 409 292 | 8.9 | 1.6 | 344 715 | 7.5 | 1.4 | 64 577 |
| 21. Canada | 94 820 | 19.9[1] | 3.5 | 103 890 | 21.4[1] | 3.8 | 9070 |
| 22. Nippon (Japan) | 129 301 | 6.3* | 1.4 | 261 254 | 9.2* | 2.1 | 82 483 |

1. Trade with the rest of the world, including intra EUR 12 trade.
+ Denotes exports surplus.
* Denotes imports surplus.
2. 1991.

**Table M16** Evolution of total imports.

(Mio ECU)

| Country | 1984 | 1985 | 1986 | 1987 | 1988 | 1989 | 1990 | 1991 | 1992 Mio ECU | 1992 % |
|---|---|---|---|---|---|---|---|---|---|---|
| EUR 12 (intra + extra) | 809 357 | 874 675 | 796 004 | 829 134 | 930 594 | 1 073 552 | 1 127 583 | 1 999 583 | 1 207 269 | 41.5 |
| EUR 12 (extra) | | | | | | | | 461 521 | 493 990 | 487 730 | 16.8 |
| 13. Österreich | 24 836 | 27 470 | 27 165 | 28 219 | 30 919 | 35 308 | 37 734 | 40 985 | 41 750 | 1.4 |
| 14. Suomi/Finland | 15 750 | 17 222 | 15 589 | 17 194 | 18 619 | 22 326 | 21 221 | 17 583 | 16 333 | 0.6 |
| 15. Island | 1070 | 1186 | 1138 | 1377 | 1362 | 1271 | 1299 | 1385 | 1208 | 0.0 |
| 16. Norge | 17 565 | 20 304 | 20 628 | 19 548 | 19 608 | 21 313 | 21 325 | 20 390 | 20 039 | 0.7 |
| 17. Sverige | 33 383 | 37 322 | 33 238 | 35 263 | 38 650 | 44 527 | 42 797 | 40 329 | 38 513 | 1.3 |
| EEA | 901 961 | 978 179 | 893 735 | 930 735 | 1 039 742 | 1 198 297 | 1 251 965 | 1 320 255 | 1 325 202 | 45.5 |
| 18. Schweiz/Suisse | 37 231 | 39 888 | 41 543 | 43 666 | 47 620 | 52 824 | 54 825 | 53 480 | 50 586 | 1.7 |
| 19. Türkiye | 13 825 | 14 839 | 11 307 | 12 127 | 12 135 | 14 306 | 17 514 | 16 985 | 17 619 | 0.6 |
| 20. USA | 412 818 | 452 471 | 376 103 | 351 599 | 373 183 | 429 677 | 388 918 | 393 914 | 409 292 | 14.1 |
| 21. Canada | 93 791 | 100 670 | 82 237 | 75 866 | 90 335 | 103 599 | 91 593 | 95 387 | 94 820 | 3.3 |
| 22. Nippon (Japan) | 172 462 | 172 067 | 128 506 | 129 513 | 158 457 | 191 320 | 184 383 | 191 046 | 129 301 | 6.2 |
| | 2 518 999 | 2 629 499 | 2 234 614 | 2 214 732 | 2 459 941 | 2 863 118 | 2 797 948 | 2 836 144 | 2 911 246 | 100.0 |

General note on the external trade figures.
General trade for Norway, Sweden and Canada. Special trade in all other cases.
Imports of (United States and Canada = fob); exports fob.

**Table M17** Evolution of total exports.

(Mio ECU)

| Country | 1984 | 1985 | 1986 | 1987 | 1988 | 1989 | 1990 | 1991 | 1992 Mio ECU | 1992 % |
|---|---|---|---|---|---|---|---|---|---|---|
| EUR 12 (intra + extra) | 776 772 | 849 936 | 806 958 | 829 911 | 906 730 | 1 043 289 | 1 076 654 | 1 116 451 | 1 136 487 | 40.5 |
| EUR 12 (extra) | | | | | | | | 415 319 | 423 497 | 435 660 | 15.5 |
| 13. Osterreich | 19 921 | 22 562 | 22 805 | 23 462 | 26 246 | 29 451 | 28 101 | 33 177 | 34 230 | 1.2 |
| 14. Suomi/Finland | 17 065 | 17 775 | 16 603 | 17 239 | 18 810 | 21 131 | 20 871 | 18 576 | 18 474 | 0.7 |
| 15. Island | 942 | 1068 | 1116 | 1191 | 1210 | 1271 | 1249 | 1234 | 1177 | 1.2 |
| 16. Norge | 23 943 | 26 094 | 18 401 | 18 584 | 19 030 | 24 431 | 26 541 | 27 512 | 27 055 | 0.7 |
| 17. Sverige | 37 153 | 39 771 | 37 881 | 38 565 | 42 037 | 46 827 | 45 054 | 44 557 | 43 229 | 1.5 |
| EEA | 875 296 | 957 206 | 903 764 | 929 042 | 1 014 063 | 1 166 400 | 1 198 470 | 1 241 507 | 1 206 652 | 44.9 |
| 18. Schweiz/Suisse | 32 716 | 35 535 | 37 865 | 39 197 | 42 803 | 46 754 | 50 085 | 49 493 | 50 483 | 1.8 |
| 19. Turkiye | 9015 | 10 368 | 7551 | 8902 | 9862 | 10 553 | 10 175 | 49 493 | 11 336 | 1.8 |
| 20. USA | 226 146 | 279 320 | 220 912 | 219 038 | 270 943 | 330 171 | 308 596 | 340 435 | 344 715 | 12.3 |
| 21. Canada | 110 087 | 114 387 | 88 298 | 81 766 | 94 667 | 105 469 | 100 137 | 102 631 | 103 890 | 3.7 |
| 22. Nippon (Japan) | 215 171 | 232 211 | 212 623 | 200 340 | 224 057 | 249 817 | 225 337 | 253 822 | 261 754 | 9.3 |
| | 2 435 032 | 2 530 727 | 2 155 784 | 2 152 651 | 2 379 684 | 2 756 751 | 2 695 311 | 2 750 653 | 2 809 377 | 100.0 |

**Table M18** Evolution of trade balance[1].

(Mio ECU)

| Country | 1985 | 1986 | 1987 | 1988 | 1989 | 1990 | 1991 | 1992 |
|---|---|---|---|---|---|---|---|---|
| EUR 12 (intra + extra) | 24 739* | +10 954 | +777 | 23 864* | 30 263* | 50 935* | 83 132* | 70 782* |
| EUR 12 (extra) | | | | | | 46 202* | 70 493* | 52 070* |
| 13. Osterreich | 4908* | 4360* | 4757* | 4673* | 5857* | 9663* | 17 808* | 7520* |
| 14. Suomi/Finland | +553 | +1014 | +135 | +191 | 1195* | 350* | +993 | +2141 |
| 15. Island | 118* | 22* | 186* | 142* | 0 | 50 | 151* | 121* |
| 16. Norge | +5790 | 2227* | 964* | 578* | +3118 | +5216 | +7122 | +7016 |
| 17. Sverige | +2449 | +4643 | +3302 | +3387 | +2300 | +2257 | +4228 | +4716 |
| EEA | 15 465* | +14 362 | 1693* | 29 257* | 37 315* | 53 495* | 78 748* | 78 748* |
| 18. Schweiz/Suisse | 4353* | 3678* | 4469* | 4817* | 6070* | 4740* | 3987* | 103* |
| 19. Turkiye | 4171* | 3753* | 3233* | 2265* | 3753* | 7339* | 6015* | 6285* |
| 20. USA | 173 151* | 155 191* | 132 561* | 102 240* | 99 506* | 80 322* | 53 479* | 64 577* |
| 21. Canada | +13 717 | +6061 | +5900 | +4332 | +1870 | +8544 | +7244 | +9070 |
| 22. Nippon (Japan) | +60 144 | +83 834 | +70 827 | +65 600 | +58 497 | +40 954 | +62 776 | +82 453 |

1. + Denotes export surplus
* Denotes import surplus

**Table M19** Total imports by partner country – 1992.

(Mio ECU)

| Importing country | Total imports | EUR 12 | USA | Japan | Rest of world | Of which ACP |
|---|---|---|---|---|---|---|
| EUR 12 (intra + extra) | 1 207 269 | 715 997 | | | | |
| EUR 12 (extra) | 491 272 | | 86 776 | 51 511 | 352 985 | 17 954 |
| 1. Belg./Lux. | 101 890 | 72 587 | 5927 | 3904 | 19 472 | 2090 |
| 2. Danmark | 26 753 | 14 824 | 1359 | 870 | 9700 | 99 |
| 3. Deutschland | 315 745 | 172 828 | 19 056 | 15 944 | 107 917 | 2820 |
| 4. Ελλάδα | 17 951 | 11 264 | 655 | 1152 | 4880 | 155 |
| 5. España | 74 862 | 45 124 | 5548 | 3259 | 20 931 | 2009 |
| 6. France | 199 361 | 130 879 | 14 476 | 5744 | 48 262 | 3979 |
| 7. Ireland | 16 808 | 12 078 | 2003 | 558 | 2169 | 149 |
| 8. Italia | 145 777 | 85 693 | 7659 | 3411 | 49 014 | 1649 |
| 9. Luxembourg | | | | | | |
| 10. Nederland | 113 973 | 67 063 | 9390 | 6187 | 31 333 | 1706 |
| 11. Portugal | 22 739 | 16 725 | 687 | 695 | 4642 | 720 |
| 12. United Kingdom | 171 410 | 86 932 | 20 015 | 9787 | 54 676 | 2577 |
| 13. Osterreich | 41 750 | 28 342 | 1648 | 1965 | 9795 | 311 |
| 14. Suomi/Finland | 16 333 | 7705 | 997 | 897 | 6734 | 194 |
| 15. Island | 1298 | 956 | 108 | 75 | 159 | 1 |
| 16. Norge | 20 039 | 97 767 | 1713 | 1262 | 7297 | 364 |
| 17. Sverige | 38 513 | 21 384 | 3369 | 1947 | 11 814 | 139 |
| EEA | 1 325 202 | 784 151 | 94 610 | 57 657 | 388 784 | 18 963 |
| 18. Schweiz/Suisse | 50 586 | 36 515 | 3228 | 2482 | 8664 | 189 |
| 19. Türkiye | 17 619 | 7741 | 2003 | 857 | 7018 | |
| 20. USA | 409 292 | 72 463 | | 74 310 | 257 519 | 11 224 |
| 21. Canada | 94 820 | 9263 | 61 813 | 6906 | 16 838 | |
| 22. Nippon (Japan) | 129 301 | 24 179 | 40 564 | | 114 558 | 1410 |

**Table M20**  Total imports by partner country – 1992.

(%)

| Importing country | Total imports | Origin EUR 12 | USA | Japan | Rest of world | Of which ACP |
|---|---|---|---|---|---|---|
| EUR 12 (intra + extra) | 100.0 | 59.3 | | | | |
| EUR 12 (extra) | 40.7 | | 7.2 | 4.3 | 29.3 | 1.5 |
| 1. Belg./Lux. | 100.0 | 71.2 | 5.8 | 3.8 | 19.1 | 2.1 |
| 2. Danmark | 100.0 | 55.4 | 5.1 | 3.3 | 36.3 | 0.4 |
| 3. Deutschland | 100.0 | 54.7 | 6.0 | 5.0 | 34.2 | 0.9 |
| 4. Ελλάδα | 100.0 | 62.7 | 3.6 | 6.4 | 27.2 | 0.9 |
| 5. España | 100.0 | 60.3 | 7.4 | 4.4 | 28.0 | 2.7 |
| 6. France | 100.0 | 65.6 | 7.3 | 2.9 | 24.2 | 2.0 |
| 7. Ireland | 100.0 | 71.9 | 11.9 | 3.3 | 12.9 | 0.9 |
| 8. Italia | 100.0 | 58.8 | 5.3 | 2.3 | 33.6 | 1.1 |
| 9. Luxembourg | : | : | : | : | : | : |
| 10. Nederland | 100.0 | 58.8 | 8.2 | 5.4 | 27.5 | 1.5 |
| 11. Portugal | 100.0 | 73.6 | 3.8 | 3.1 | 20.4 | 3.2 |
| 12. United Kingdom | 100.0 | 50.7 | 11.7 | 5.7 | 31.9 | 1.5 |
| 13. Österreich | 100.0 | 67.9 | 3.9 | 4.7 | 23.5 | 7.4 |
| 14. Suomi/Finland | 100.0 | 47.2 | 6.1 | 5.5 | 41.2 | 1.2 |
| 15. Island | 100.0 | 73.7 | 8.3 | 5.8 | 12.2 | 0.1 |
| 16. Norge | 100.0 | 48.7 | 8.5 | 6.3 | 36.4 | 1.8 |
| 17. Sverige | 100.0 | 55.5 | 8.7 | 5.1 | 30.7 | 0.4 |
| EEA | 100.0 | 59.2 | 7.1 | 4.4 | 29.3 | 1.4 |
| 18. Schweiz/Suisse | 100.0 | 72.2 | 6.4 | 4.3 | 17.1 | 0.4 |
| 19. Türkiye | 100.0 | 43.9 | 11.4 | 4.9 | 39.8 | |
| 20. USA | 100.0 | 17.7 | | 18.2 | 62.9 | 2.9 |
| 21. Canada | 100.0 | 9.8 | 65.2 | 7.3 | 17.8 | |
| 22. Nippon (Japan) | 100.0 | 13.5 | 22.6 | | 63.9 | 0.8 |

**Table M21**  Total exports by partner country – 1992.

(Mio ECU)

| Exporting country | Total exports | Destination EUR 12 | USA | Japan | Rest of world | Of which ACP |
|---|---|---|---|---|---|---|
| EUR 12 (intra + extra) | 1 136 487 | 696 541 | | | | |
| EUR 12 (extra) | 439 946 | | 73 917 | 20 507 | 345 522 | 17 048 |
| 1. Belg./Lux. | 95 412 | 71 388 | 3686 | 988 | 19 350 | 1037 |
| 2. Danmark | 31 063 | 16 932 | 1560 | 1112 | 11 459 | 411 |
| 3. Deutschland | 331 009 | 179 165 | 21 126 | 7236 | 123 482 | 2508 |
| 4. Ελλάδα | 7338 | 4709 | 295 | 69 | 2265 | 99 |
| 5. España | 53 032 | 35 163 | 2368 | 394 | 15 107 | 986 |
| 6. France | 192 361 | 121 278 | 11 940 | 3309 | 55 834 | 5385 |
| 7. Ireland | 21 828 | 16 203 | 1792 | 630 | 3203 | 155 |
| 8. Italia | 137 581 | 79 388 | 9569 | 2647 | 45 977 | 1466 |
| 9. Luxembourg | : | : | : | : | : | : |
| 10. Nederland | 108 614 | 81 871 | 4448 | 989 | 21 306 | 1349 |
| 11. Portugal | 13 727 | 10 274 | 478 | 108 | 2867 | 822 |
| 12. United Kingdom | 144 522 | 80 172 | 16 653 | 3025 | 44 673 | 2830 |
| 13. Österreich | 34 230 | 22 622 | 904 | 526 | 10 178 | 155 |
| 14. Suomi/Finland | 18 474 | 9836 | 1109 | 236 | 7293 | 150 |
| 15. Island | 1177 | 809 | 133 | 89 | 146 | 12 |
| 16. Norge | 27 055 | 17 995 | 1451 | 46 | 7563 | 672 |
| 17. Sverige | 43 229 | 24 133 | 3598 | 877 | 14 621 | 224 |
| EEA | 1 260 652 | 771 936 | 81 112 | 22 281 | 385 323 | 171 261 |
| 18. Schweiz/Suisse | 50 483 | 29 741 | 4309 | 1890 | 14 543 | 361 |
| 19. Türkiye | 11 336 | 5855 | 666 | 125 | 4690 | : |
| 20. USA | 344 716 | 79 233 | | 36 795 | 228 688 | 6512 |
| 21. Canada | 103 890 | 7341 | 80 398 | 4782 | 11 369 | : |
| 22. Nippon (Japan) | 261 755 | 48 415 | 74 453 | | 138 887 | 3518 |

**Table M22**  Total exports by partner country – 1992.

(%)

| Exporting country | Total exports | Destination EUR 12 | USA | Japan | Rest of world | Of which ACP |
|---|---|---|---|---|---|---|
| EUR 12 (intra + extra) | 100.0 | 61.3 | | | | |
| EUR 12 (extra) | 38.7 | | 6.5 | 1.8 | 30.4 | 1.5 |
| 1. Belg./Lux. | 100.0 | 74.8 | 3.9 | 1.0 | 20.3 | 1.1 |
| 2. Danmark | 100.0 | 54.5 | 5.0 | 3.5 | 36.9 | 1.3 |
| 3. Deutschland | 100.0 | 54.1 | 6.4 | 2.2 | 37.3 | 0.8 |
| 4. Ελλάδα | 100.0 | 64.2 | 4.0 | 0.9 | 30.9 | 1.3 |
| 5. España | 100.0 | 66.3 | 4.5 | 0.7 | 28.5 | 1.9 |
| 6. France | 100.0 | 63.0 | 6.2 | 1.7 | 29.0 | 2.8 |
| 7. Ireland | 100.0 | 74.2 | 8.2 | 2.9 | 14.7 | 0.7 |
| 8. Italia | 100.0 | 57.7 | 7.0 | 1.9 | 33.4 | 1.1 |
| 9. Luxembourg | : | : | : | : | : | : |
| 10. Nederland | 100.0 | 75.4 | 4.1 | 0.9 | 19.6 | 1.2 |
| 11. Portugal | 100.0 | 74.6 | 3.5 | 0.8 | 20.9 | 6.0 |
| 12. United Kingdom | 100.0 | 55.5 | 11.5 | 2.1 | 30.9 | 2.0 |
| 13. Österreich | 100.0 | 66.1 | 2.6 | 1.5 | 29.7 | 0.5 |
| 14. Suomi/Finland | 100.0 | 53.2 | 6.0 | 1.3 | 39.5 | 0.8 |
| 15. Island | 100.0 | 68.7 | 11.3 | 7.6 | 12.4 | 1.0 |
| 16. Norge | 100.0 | 66.5 | 5.4 | 0.2 | 28.0 | 2.5 |
| 17. Sverige | 100.0 | 55.8 | 6.0 | 2.0 | 33.8 | 0.5 |
| EEA | 100.0 | 61.2 | 6.4 | 1.8 | 30.6 | 13.6 |
| 18. Schweiz/Suisse | 100.0 | 58.9 | 8.5 | 3.7 | 28.8 | 0.7 |
| 19. Türkiye | 100.0 | 51.6 | 5.9 | 1.1 | 41.4 | : |
| 20. USA | 100.0 | 23.0 | | 10.7 | 66.3 | 1.9 |
| 21. Canada | 100.0 | 7.1 | 77.4 | 4.6 | 10.9 | : |
| 22. Nippon (Japan) | 100.0 | 18.5 | 28.4 | – | 53.1 | 1.3 |

*Contemporary Europe*

**Table M23**  Imports by commodity class – 1992.

(Mio ECU)

| Importing country | Total imports | According to the Standard International Trade Classification (SITC, Rev. 3)[1] | | | | |
|---|---|---|---|---|---|---|
| | | Food, Beverages and tobacco (Sectors 0+1) | Mineral fuels, lubricants and related materials (Sector 3) | Crude materials, oils and fats (Sectors 2+4) | Machinery and equipment (Sector 7) | Other (Sectors 5+6+8+9) |
| EUR 12 (intra + extra) | 1 207 269 | 127 302 | 92 199 | 58 257 | 416 108 | 513 402 |
| EUR 12 (extra) | : | : | : | : | : | : |
| 1. Belg./Lux. | 101 890 | 10 146 | 7373 | 5341 | 27 045 | 51 985 |
| 2. Danmark | 26 753 | 3275 | 1235 | 1095 | 8057 | 10 091 |
| 3. Deutschland | 315 745 | 30 444 | 23 549 | 14 974 | 109 212 | 137 567 |
| 4. Ελλάδα | 17 951 | 2462 | 1706 | 632 | 6114 | 6977 |
| 5. España | 74 862 | 8347 | 7383 | 4079 | 27 974 | 27 078 |
| 6. France | 199 360 | 18 294 | 15 882 | 6977 | 28 229 | 29 430 |
| 7. Ireland | 46 808 | 1935 | 886 | 438 | 5617 | 7932 |
| 8. Italia | 145 777 | 17 170 | 12 305 | 10 552 | 46 509 | 59 241 |
| 9. Luxembourg | : | : | : | : | : | : |
| 10. Nederland | 113 973 | 14 146 | 10 588 | 6235 | 36 207 | 46 797 |
| 11. Portugal | 22 739 | 2516 | 1865 | 1044 | 8640 | 8673 |
| 12. United Kingdom | 171 410 | 18 067 | 9367 | 6891 | 62 456 | 74 630 |
| 13. Österreich | 41 750 | 2028 | 2132 | 1792 | 16 378 | 19 419 |
| 14. Suomi/Finland | 16 333 | 925 | 2046 | 1205 | 5265 | 6892 |
| 15. Island | 1298 | 122 | 107 | 65 | 446 | 558 |
| 16. Norge | 20 039 | 1250 | 672 | 1422 | 7412 | 9283 |
| 17. Sverige | 38 513 | 2726 | 3330 | 1445 | 13 723 | 17 254 |
| EEA | 1 325 202 | 134 353 | 100 477 | 64 186 | 459 337 | 566 808 |
| 18. Schweiz/Suisse | 50 586 | 3289 | 2154 | 1388 | 15 488 | 28 267 |
| 19. Türkiye | 17 619 | 708 | 2878 | 1726 | 6163 | 6144 |
| 20. USA | 409 292 | 23 253 | 44 913 | 12 551 | 181 505 | 147 070 |
| 21. Canada | 94 820 | 5739 | 4077 | 3105 | 47 406 | 34 493 |
| 22. Nippon (Japan) | 179 301 | 28 520 | 40 599 | 21 178 | 28 848 | 60 156 |

1. SITC, Rev 3, 1988.

**Table M24**  Imports by commodity class – 1992.

(%)

| Importing country | Total imports | According to the Standard International Trade Classification (SITC, Rev. 3)[1] | | | | |
|---|---|---|---|---|---|---|
| | | Food, Beverages and tobacco (Sectors 0+1) | Mineral fuels, lubricants and related materials (Sector 3) | Crude materials, oils and fats (Sectors 2+4) | Machinery and equipment (Sector 7) | Other (Sectors 5+6+8+9) |
| EUR 12 (intra + extra) | 100.0 | 105.0 | 7.6 | 4.8 | 34.5 | 42.5 |
| EUR 12 (extra) | : | : | : | : | : | : |
| 1. Belg./Lux. | 100.0 | 10.0 | 7.2 | 5.2 | 26.5 | 51.0 |
| 2. Danmark | 100.0 | 12.2 | 4.6 | 4.1 | 30.1 | 48.9 |
| 3. Deutschland | 100.0 | 9.6 | 7.5 | 4.7 | 34.6 | 43.6 |
| 4. Ελλάδα | 100.0 | 13.7 | 9.5 | 3.5 | 34.1 | 38.9 |
| 5. España | 100.0 | 11.1 | 9.9 | 5.4 | 37.4 | 36.2 |
| 6. France | 100.0 | 9.4 | 8.0 | 3.5 | 39.3 | 39.8 |
| 7. Ireland | 100.0 | 11.5 | 5.3 | 2.6 | 33.4 | 47.2 |
| 8. Italia | 100.0 | 11.8 | 8.4 | 7.2 | 31.9 | 40.6 |
| 9. Luxembourg | : | : | : | : | : | : |
| 10. Nederland | 100.0 | 12.4 | 9.3 | 5.5 | 31.8 | 41.1 |
| 11. Portugal | 100.0 | 11.1 | 8.2 | 4.6 | 38.0 | 38.1 |
| 12. United Kingdom | 100.0 | 10.5 | 5.5 | 4.0 | 36.4 | 43.5 |
| 13. Österreich | 100.0 | 4.9 | 5.1 | 4.3 | 39.2 | 46.5 |
| 14. Suomi/Finland | 100.0 | 5.7 | 12.5 | 7.4 | 32.2 | 42.2 |
| 15. Island | 100.0 | 9.4 | 8.2 | 5.0 | 34.4 | 43.0 |
| 16. Norge | 100.0 | 6.2 | 3.4 | 7.1 | 37.0 | 45.3 |
| 17. Sverige | 100.0 | 7.1 | 8.6 | 3.8 | 35.6 | 44.8 |
| EEA | 100.0 | 10.1 | 7.6 | 4.8 | 34.7 | 42.8 |
| 18. Schweiz/Suisse | 100.0 | 6.5 | 4.3 | 2.7 | 30.6 | 55.9 |
| 19. Türkiye | 100.0 | 4.0 | 16.3 | 9.8 | 35.0 | 34.9 |
| 20. USA | 100.0 | 5.7 | 11.0 | 3.1 | 44.3 | 35.9 |
| 21. Canada | 100.0 | 6.1 | 4.3 | 3.3 | 50.0 | 36.4 |
| 22. Nippon (Japan) | 100.0 | 15.9 | 22.6 | 11.8 | 16.1 | 33.6 |

1. SITC, Rev 3, 1988.

**Table M25** Exports by commodity class – 1992.

(Mio ECU)

| Importing country | Total imports | According to the Standard International Trade Classification (SITC, Rev. 3)[1] | | | | |
|---|---|---|---|---|---|---|
| | | Food, Beverages and tobacco (Sectors 0+1) | Mineral fuels, lubricants and related materials (Sector 3) | Crude materials, oils and fats (Sectors 2+4) | Machinery and equipment (Sector 7) | Other (Sectors 5+6+8+9) |
| EUR 12 (intra + extra) | 1 136 487 | 120 435 | 36 393 | 31 550 | 446 922 | 501 187 |
| EUR 12 (extra) | : | : | : | : | : | : |
| 1. Belg./Lux. | 95 412 | 9939 | 3299 | 2536 | 25 795 | 53 843 |
| 2. Danmark | 31 063 | 7817 | 1049 | 1317 | 8293 | 12 587 |
| 3. Deutschland | 331 009 | 16 948 | 4077 | 6751 | 164 426 | 138 807 |
| 4. Ελλάδα | 7338 | 2043 | 395 | 711 | 362 | 3827 |
| 5. España | 53 032 | 7568 | 1544 | 1848 | 22 061 | 20 011 |
| 6. France | 192 361 | 26 579 | 4151 | 5186 | 82 859 | 73 405 |
| 7. Ireland | 21 828 | 5315 | 127 | 635 | 5868 | 9883 |
| 8. Italia | 137 581 | 9139 | 2921 | 1945 | 50 630 | 72 946 |
| 9. Luxembourg | : | : | : | : | : | : |
| 10. Nederland | 108 614 | 22 210 | 9280 | 6975 | 25 888 | 44 262 |
| 11. Portugal | 13 727 | 979 | 357 | 974 | 2972 | 8445 |
| 12. United Kingdom | 144 522 | 11 719 | 9193 | 2671 | 57 769 | 63 171 |
| 13. Österreich | 34 230 | 1107 | 360 | 1404 | 13 233 | 18 126 |
| 14. Suomi/Finland | 18 474 | 448 | 587 | 1616 | 5244 | 10 579 |
| 15. Island | 1177 | 915 | 1 | 34 | 16 | 211 |
| 16. Norge | 27 055 | 2082 | 13 531 | 865 | 3833 | 6744 |
| 17. Sverige | 43 299 | 783 | 1359 | 3538 | 18 329 | 19 220 |
| EEA | 1 260 652 | 125 770 | 52 231 | 39 007 | 487 577 | 556 067 |
| 18. Schweiz/Suisse | 50 483 | 1463 | 54 | 569 | 15 357 | 33 040 |
| 19. Türkiye | 11 336 | 2388 | 178 | 550 | 988 | 7232 |
| 20. USA | 344 716 | 30 570 | 8515 | 20 530 | 153 840 | 131 261 |
| 21. Canada | 103 890 | 8945 | 10 569 | 12 245 | 38 530 | 33 601 |
| 22. Nippon (Japan) | 261 755 | 1441 | 1221 | 1761 | 186 134 | 71 198 |

1. SITC, Rev 3, 1988.

**Table M26** Exports by commodity class – 1992.

(%)

| Importing country | Total imports | According to the Standard International Trade Classification (SITC, Rev. 3)[1] | | | | |
|---|---|---|---|---|---|---|
| | | Food, Beverages and tobacco (Sectors 0+1) | Mineral fuels, lubricants and related materials (Sector 3) | Crude materials, oils and fats (Sectors 2+4) | Machinery and equipment (Sector 7) | Other (Sectors 5+6+8+9) |
| EUR 12 (intra + extra) | 100.0 | 10.6 | 3.2 | 2.8 | 39.3 | 44.1 |
| EUR 12 (extra) | : | : | : | : | : | : |
| 1. Belg./Lux. | 100.0 | 10.4 | 3.5 | 2.7 | 27.0 | 13.5 |
| 2. Danmark | 100.0 | 25.2 | 3.4 | 4.2 | 26.7 | 40.5 |
| 3. Deutschland | 100.0 | 5.1 | 1.2 | 2.0 | 49.7 | 41.9 |
| 4. Ελλάδα | 100.0 | 27.8 | 5.4 | 9.7 | 4.9 | 52.2 |
| 5. España | 100.0 | 14.3 | 2.9 | 3.5 | 41.6 | 37.7 |
| 6. France | 100.0 | 13.9 | 2.2 | 2.7 | 43.1 | 38.2 |
| 7. Ireland | 100.0 | 24.3 | 0.6 | 2.9 | 26.9 | 45.0 |
| 8. Italia | 100.0 | 6.6 | 2.1 | 1.4 | 36.8 | 53.0 |
| 9. Luxembourg | : | : | : | : | : | : |
| 10. Nederland | 100.0 | 20.4 | 8.5 | 6.4 | 23.8 | 40.8 |
| 11. Portugal | 100.0 | 7.1 | 2.6 | 7.1 | 21.7 | 61.5 |
| 12. United Kingdom | 100.0 | 8.1 | 6.4 | 1.8 | 40.0 | 43.7 |
| 13. Österreich | 100.0 | 3.3 | 1.1 | 4.1 | 38.7 | 53.0 |
| 14. Suomi/Finland | 100.0 | 2.4 | 3.2 | 8.7 | 28.4 | 57.3 |
| 15. Island | 100.0 | 77.7 | 0.1 | 2.9 | 1.4 | 17.9 |
| 16. Norge | 100.0 | 7.7 | 50.0 | 3.2 | 14.2 | 24.9 |
| 17. Sverige | 100.0 | 1.8 | 3.1 | 8.2 | 42.4 | 44.5 |
| EEA | 100.0 | 10.0 | 4.1 | 3.1 | 38.7 | 44.1 |
| 18. Schweiz/Suisse | 100.0 | 2.9 | 0.1 | 1.1 | 30.4 | 65.4 |
| 19. Türkiye | 100.0 | 21.1 | 1.6 | 4.9 | 8.7 | 63.3 |
| 20. USA | 100.0 | 8.9 | 2.5 | 6.0 | 44.6 | 38.1 |
| 21. Canada | 100.0 | 8.6 | 10.2 | 11.8 | 37.1 | 32.3 |
| 22. Nippon (Japan) | 100.0 | 0.6 | 0.5 | 0.7 | 71.1 | 27.2 |

1. SITC, Rev 3, 1988.

**Table M27**   EC (EUR 12) share in the trade of the main non-EC countries.

| Country | % of each country's total imports | | | % of each country's total exports | | | Country | % of each country's total imports | | | % of each country's total exports | | |
|---|---|---|---|---|---|---|---|---|---|---|---|---|---|
| | 1980 | 1991 | 1992 | 1980 | 1991 | 1992 | | 1980 | 1991 | 1992 | 1980 | 1991 | 1992 |
| Iceland | 51.0 | 52.4 | 48.6 | 46.9 | 67.1 | 68.7 | Cuba | 14.5 | 36.6 | 32.3 | 10.2 | 31.0 | 24.9 |
| Norway | 49.3 | 47.9 | 48.8 | 72.2 | 64.4 | 67.0 | Bahamas | 7.4 | 15.7 | 23.2 | 21.5 | 25.6 | 22.6 |
| Sweden | 50.2 | 55.0 | 55.6 | 51.3 | 55.2 | 55.8 | Dominican Republic | 10.4 | 13.6 | 12.2 | 10.2 | 21.4 | 22.8 |
| Finland | 34.9 | 45.8 | 47.2 | 40.4 | 51.0 | 53.2 | Jamaica | 11.4 | 13.5 | 9.8 | 25.3 | 27.6 | 24.0 |
| Austria | 62.1 | 67.8 | 67.9 | 56.2 | 65.9 | 66.1 | Trinidad and Tobago | 14.3 | 15.0 | 15.9 | 12.3 | 9.3 | 5.5 |
| Switzerland | 68.4 | 70.2 | 72.2 | 53.4 | 58.8 | 59.0 | Netherlands Antilles | 4.0 | 13.9 | 12.5 | 13.6 | 15.6 | 9.6 |
| Yugoslavia | 35.4 | 51.9 | 51.4 | 26.5 | 56.2 | 53.4 | Venezuela | 23.6 | 22.5 | 22.2 | 17.4 | 10.3 | 10.5 |
| Turkey | 35.2 | 43.8 | 43.7 | 45.9 | 51.6 | 51.7 | Ecuador | 17.9 | 23.7 | 20.9 | 8.0 | 16.8 | 17.8 |
| ex-Soviet Union | 17.1 | 35.8 | : | 22.6 | 42.8 | : | Peru | 17.9 | 17.8 | 13.9 | 20.0 | 27.2 | 27.7 |
| Poland | 19.7 | 49.9 | 52.9 | 22.8 | 55.6 | 55.7 | Brazil | 16.5 | 22.6 | 22.4 | 30.5 | 31.2 | 29.6 |
| Czechoslovakia | 14.1 | 32.1 | 24.8 | 13.1 | 20.8 | 11.4 | Chile | 19.9 | 18.4 | 19.3 | 37.1 | 32.0 | 28.7 |
| Hungary | 23.1 | 40.4 | 42.4 | 20.9 | 46.7 | 46.5 | Bolivia | 19.3 | 15.6 | 19.2 | 24.4 | 27.5 | 40.4 |
| Romania | 17.3 | 27.4 | 37.5 | 25.4 | 34.2 | 32.5 | Uruguay | 19.1 | 17.2 | 15.8 | 31.4 | 28.2 | 25.9 |
| Bulgaria | 11.7 | 50.9 | 51.6 | 15.0 | 39.7 | 41.3 | Argentina | 29.7 | 21.5 | 22.5 | 30.4 | 31.9 | 30.7 |
| Morocco | 53.7 | 63.4 | 62.8 | 63.8 | 64.7 | 64.5 | Syria | 38.6 | 36.8 | 38.1 | 64.0 | 47.9 | 61.5 |
| Algeria | 67.9 | 64.7 | 67.5 | 43.4 | 68.3 | 71.8 | Iraq | 44.3 | 18.5 | 21.8 | 42.0 | 42.4 | 32.9 |
| Tunisia | 67.3 | 69.5 | 70.1 | 72.1 | 74.4 | 74.9 | Iran | 42.0 | 45.6 | 48.8 | 32.1 | 43.9 | 41.8 |
| Libya | 68.4 | 62.9 | 59.0 | 44.2 | 84.7 | 82.5 | Israel | 28.1 | 47.5 | 48.7 | 41.0 | 34.4 | 33.6 |
| Egypt | 42.0 | 39.0 | 38.2 | 47.4 | 38.1 | 42.6 | Saudi Arabia | 36.8 | 34.4 | 37.2 | 38.0 | 20.7 | 21.9 |
| Sudan | 39.1 | 43.8 | 38.2 | 31.1 | 30.8 | 32.6 | Kuwait | 32.9 | 18.9 | 39.4 | 26.1 | 33.9 | 26.3 |
| Ivory Coast | 58.8 | 48.9 | 55.0 | 67.3 | 54.8 | 54.6 | Bahrain | 12.8 | 22.6 | 22.1 | 0.5 | 4.5 | 5.7 |
| Ghana | 41.6 | 46.1 | 45.1 | 42.4 | 60.1 | 56.6 | Pakistan | 21.9 | 25.6 | 25.5 | 19.8 | 29.5 | 28.1 |
| Nigeria | 58.0 | 52.2 | 57.0 | 38.0 | 43.7 | 39.5 | India | 21.8 | 28.3 | 30.9 | 23.0 | 27.1 | 27.5 |
| Cameroon | 66.5 | 64.3 | 67.8 | 59.2 | 80.9 | 73.1 | Bangladesh | 14.4 | 12.5 | 11.7 | 17.4 | 40.2 | 36.0 |
| Gabon | 79.2 | 64.9 | 59.4 | 45.5 | 48.4 | 39.5 | Sri Lanka | 22.0 | 17.9 | 17.1 | 20.9 | 30.6 | 31.6 |
| Zaire | 54.7 | 56.4 | 54.3 | 88.6 | 64.8 | 52.5 | Thailand | 13.4 | 14.6 | 14.4 | 26.0 | 21.4 | 19.6 |
| Angola | 53.9 | 67.5 | 79.4 | 16.3 | 32.8 | 31.1 | Indonesia | 13.6 | 18.2 | 20.1 | 6.5 | 12.9 | 13.8 |
| Kenya | 37.4 | 45.3 | 37.4 | 34.9 | 45.8 | 42.8 | Malaysia | 15.8 | 13.6 | 12.5 | 17.6 | 14.8 | 14.9 |
| Tanzania | 46.1 | 41.4 | 37.3 | 44.4 | 51.2 | 43.8 | Brunei Darussalam | 20.3 | 29.8 | 26.5 | : | 9.8 | 9.3 |
| Zambia | 36.7 | 25.2 | 26.7 | 51.1 | 28.2 | 23.7 | Singapore | 11.2 | 12.8 | 12.0 | 12.8 | 14.4 | 14.0 |
| Republic of South Africa[1] | 36.0 | 41.4 | : | 49.1 | 28.4 | 25.3 | Philippines | 10.2 | 10.2 | 12.7 | 17.4 | 18.6 | 17.9 |
| United States of America | 15.8 | 17.6 | 17.6 | 26.7 | 24.4 | 23.0 | China | 14.4 | 13.3 | 12.0 | 13.0 | 9.5 | 8.9 |
| Canada | 8.4 | 10.5 | 9.5 | 13.2 | 7.9 | 7.0 | South Korea | 7.3 | 12.1 | 11.8 | 15.0 | 13.7 | 12.3 |
| Mexico | 14.9 | 12.5 | 12.5 | 15.3 | 8.5 | 7.8 | Japan | 5.9 | 13.5 | 13.5 | 14.0 | 18.9 | 18.5 |
| Guatemala | 13.9 | 12.4 | 13.6 | 26.0 | 10.7 | 18.8 | Taiwan | 8.2 | : | : | 14.6 | : | : |
| El Salvador | 9.4 | 10.4 | 9.2 | : | 21.9 | 11.7 | Hong Kong | 12.3 | 9.2 | 9.5 | 22.9 | : | 15.8 |
| Nicaragua | 8.8 | 14.4 | 11.8 | 34.6 | 29.8 | 31.3 | Australia | 22.7 | 20.9 | 20.1 | 13.9 | 11.8 | 12.7 |
| Costa Rica | 13.4 | 12.4 | 12.7 | 23.7 | 27.4 | 20.5 | Papua New Guinea | 7.6 | 4.9 | 7.5 | 36.8 | 11.5 | 14.2 |
| Panama | 7.2 | 7.3 | 6.5 | 12.9 | 26.9 | 38.8 | New Zealand | 20.0 | 18.0 | 17.9 | 23.6 | 14.6 | 14.3 |

1. Estimate.

**Table N1**   Gross official reserves.

(End year; Mrd ECU)

| | B/L | DK | WD | GR | E | F | IRL | I | NL | P | UK | EUR 12− |
|---|---|---|---|---|---|---|---|---|---|---|---|---|
| 1960 | 1.44 | 0.27 | 6.67 | 0.23 | 0.51 | 2.17 | 0.31 | 3.10 | 1.78 | 0.61 | 3.55 | 20.62 |
| 1961 | 1.69 | 0.26 | 6.68 | 0.25 | 0.83 | 3.14 | 0.32 | 3.55 | 1.83 | 0.52 | 3.10 | 22.15 |
| 1962 | 1.64 | 0.24 | 6.49 | 0.27 | 0.97 | 3.78 | 0.33 | 3.79 | 1.81 | 0.63 | 3.09 | 23.03 |
| 1963 | 1.84 | 0.44 | 7.13 | 0.27 | 1.07 | 4.58 | 0.38 | 3.38 | 1.96 | 0.68 | 2.94 | 24.66 |
| 1964 | 2.08 | 0.60 | 7.36 | 0.26 | 1.41 | 5.35 | 0.42 | 3.57 | 2.19 | 0.81 | 2.16 | 26.21 |
| 1965 | 2.18 | 0.55 | 6.94 | 0.23 | 1.33 | 5.93 | 0.38 | 4.48 | 2.26 | 0.88 | 2.81 | 27.97 |
| 1966 | 2.21 | 0.56 | 7.53 | 0.26 | 1.18 | 6.32 | 0.46 | 4.60 | 2.30 | 1.01 | 2.91 | 29.33 |
| 1967 | 2.52 | 0.52 | 7.92 | 0.28 | 1.07 | 6.80 | 0.43 | 5.30 | 2.55 | 1.20 | 2.62 | 31.20 |
| 1968 | 2.42 | 0.46 | 10.55 | 0.34 | 1.27 | 4.83 | 0.55 | 5.76 | 2.72 | 1.49 | 2.64 | 33.03 |
| 1969 | 2.35 | 0.44 | 7.01 | 0.31 | 1.26 | 3.78 | 0.68 | 4.96 | 2.49 | 1.42 | 2.48 | 27.17 |
| 1970 | 2.87 | 0.48 | 13.54 | 0.31 | 1.81 | 5.07 | 0.68 | 5.41 | 3.28 | 1.53 | 2.85 | 37.82 |
| 1971 | 3.37 | 0.66 | 17.47 | 0.48 | 3.03 | 7.98 | 0.90 | 6.59 | 3.71 | 1.89 | 8.10 | 54.18 |
| 1972 | 4.56 | 0.82 | 24.44 | 1.02 | 4.90 | 11.54 | 1.03 | 7.53 | 5.66 | 2.75 | 5.64 | 69.91 |
| 1973 | 6.82 | 1.23 | 35.07 | 1.09 | 6.58 | 13.21 | 0.89 | 10.34 | 8.77 | 4.04 | 6.73 | 94.76 |
| 1974 | 9.10 | 0.95 | 39.32 | 1.16 | 6.81 | 18.63 | 1.06 | 14.99 | 11.78 | 5.07 | 7.95 | 116.81 |
| 1975 | 8.58 | 0.91 | 36.70 | 1.27 | 6.45 | 19.43 | 1.35 | 11.14 | 10.75 | 3.68 | 6.49 | 106.74 |
| 1976 | 8.12 | 0.96 | 40.61 | 1.22 | 5.87 | 17.03 | 1.66 | 12.76 | 11.07 | 3.46 | 5.50 | 108.24 |
| 1977 | 8.95 | 1.56 | 44.29 | 1.36 | 6.83 | 18.49 | 1.98 | 17.79 | 12.05 | 3.55 | 19.42 | 136.27 |
| 1978 | 9.89 | 2.60 | 54.76 | 1.57 | 9.74 | 23.52 | 2.02 | 21.75 | 12.71 | 4.27 | 15.41 | 158.23 |
| 1979 | 10.41 | 2.59 | 57.59 | 1.47 | 12.28 | 29.44 | 1.62 | 26.69 | 14.52 | 5.32 | 17.39 | 179.33 |
| 1980 | 20.54 | 3.28 | 76.57 | 2.49 | 15.26 | 57.10 | 2.25 | 45.94 | 27.50 | 10.03 | 23.69 | 284.62 |
| 1981 | 18.28 | 3.01 | 79.81 | 2.19 | 15.58 | 52.52 | 2.59 | 45.48 | 26.26 | 9.41 | 22.13 | 277.53 |
| 1982 | 16.24 | 2.94 | 82.14 | 2.31 | 13.27 | 46.30 | 2.84 | 39.02 | 26.52 | 8.57 | 19.71 | 259.85 |
| 1983 | 20.94 | 5.17 | 98.20 | 2.95 | 15.92 | 63.69 | 3.33 | 56.31 | 33.25 | 10.21 | 23.17 | 333.13 |
| 1984 | 21.97 | 4.99 | 100.90 | 3.21 | 23.51 | 66.18 | 3.03 | 59.67 | 32.89 | 9.95 | 22.51 | 348.82 |
| 1985 | 19.02 | 6.78 | 88.94 | 2.63 | 19.62 | 62.53 | 3.45 | 44.24 | 29.55 | 9.74 | 21.02 | 307.52 |
| 1986 | 17.70 | 4.79 | 84.32 | 2.64 | 17.97 | 59.71 | 3.16 | 43.34 | 26.52 | 8.69 | 23.44 | 292.28 |
| 1987 | 20.55 | 8.30 | 96.13 | 3.38 | 28.31 | 57.53 | 3.83 | 49.45 | 29.44 | 10.27 | 37.64 | 344.84 |
| 1988 | 19.92 | 9.80 | 85.10 | 4.36 | 36.71 | 50.82 | 4.41 | 53.44 | 29.27 | 10.07 | 45.32 | 349.21 |
| 1989 | 19.09 | 5.89 | 82.27 | 3.86 | 39.99 | 47.42 | 3.46 | 61.17 | 28.34 | 13.66 | 39.09 | 344.24 |
| 1990 | 17.60 | 8.31 | 77.74 | 3.56 | 42.62 | 50.75 | 3.88 | 66.08 | 25.40 | 15.18 | 34.06 | 345.19 |
| 1991 | 17.21 | 5.96 | 72.11 | 4.81 | 53.06 | 44.89 | 4.26 | 60.69 | 24.70 | 19.51 | 37.85 | 345.15 |
| 1992 | 15.43 | 9.60 | 98.09 | 4.95 | 42.07 | 44.90 | 2.85 | 44.53 | 26.23 | 20.21 | 39.76 | 348.60 |
| 1993 | 19.59 | 9.64 | 100.31 | 8.16 | 41.59 | 48.77 | 5.11 | 49.18 | 38.99 | 18.75 | 44.11 | 385.20 |

EUR 12−: incl. WD.
Source: IMF: International Financial Statistics, Bank for International Settlements (BIS) and Commission departments. Gold is valued at market-related prices.

**Table N2**  Exchange rates.

(Annual average; national currency units per ECU).

| | B | DK | WD | GR | E | F | IRL | I | L | NL | P | UK | USA | J |
|---|---|---|---|---|---|---|---|---|---|---|---|---|---|---|
| 1960 | 52.810 | 7.2954 | 4.4361 | 31.69 | 63.37 | 5.2145 | 0.37722 | 660.1 | 52.810 | 4.0136 | 30.37 | 0.37722 | 1.0562 | 380.23 |
| 1961 | 53.367 | 7.3722 | 4.3074 | 32.02 | 64.04 | 5.2695 | 0.38119 | 667.1 | 53.367 | 3.8985 | 30.69 | 0.38119 | 1.0673 | 384.24 |
| 1962 | 53.490 | 7.3893 | 4.2792 | 32.09 | 64.14 | 5.2817 | 0.38207 | 668.6 | 53.490 | 3.8727 | 30.76 | 0.38207 | 1.0698 | 385.13 |
| 1963 | 53.490 | 7.3893 | 4.2792 | 32.09 | 64.14 | 5.2817 | 0.38207 | 668.6 | 53.490 | 3.8727 | 30.76 | 0.38207 | 1.0698 | 385.13 |
| 1964 | 53.490 | 7.3893 | 4.2792 | 32.09 | 64.14 | 5.2817 | 0.38207 | 668.6 | 53.490 | 3.8727 | 30.76 | 0.38207 | 1.0698 | 385.13 |
| 1965 | 53.490 | 7.3893 | 4.2792 | 32.09 | 64.14 | 5.2817 | 0.38207 | 668.6 | 53.490 | 3.8727 | 30.76 | 0.38207 | 1.0698 | 385.13 |
| 1966 | 53.490 | 7.3893 | 4.2792 | 32.09 | 64.14 | 5.2817 | 0.38207 | 668.6 | 53.490 | 3.8727 | 30.76 | 0.38207 | 1.0698 | 385.13 |
| 1967 | 53.240 | 7.4229 | 4.2592 | 31.94 | 65.11 | 5.2570 | 0.38765 | 665.5 | 53.240 | 3.8546 | 30.61 | 0.38765 | 1.0648 | 383.33 |
| 1968 | 51.444 | 7.7166 | 4.1155 | 30.87 | 72.02 | 5.0797 | 0.42870 | 643.1 | 51.444 | 3.7246 | 29.58 | 0.42870 | 1.0289 | 370.40 |
| 1969 | 51.109 | 7.6664 | 4.0262 | 30.67 | 71.55 | 5.2903 | 0.42591 | 638.9 | 51.109 | 3.7003 | 29.39 | 0.42591 | 1.0222 | 367.99 |
| 1970 | 51.112 | 7.6668 | 3.7414 | 30.67 | 71.36 | 5.6777 | 0.42593 | 638.9 | 51.112 | 3.7005 | 29.38 | 0.42593 | 1.0222 | 368.00 |
| 1971 | 50.866 | 7.7526 | 3.6457 | 31.43 | 72.57 | 5.7721 | 0.42858 | 647.4 | 50.866 | 3.6575 | 29.64 | 0.42858 | 1.0478 | 363.83 |
| 1972 | 49.361 | 7.7891 | 3.5768 | 33.65 | 72.00 | 5.6572 | 0.44894 | 654.3 | 49.361 | 3.5999 | 30.48 | 0.44894 | 1.1218 | 339.72 |
| 1973 | 47.801 | 7.4160 | 3.2764 | 36.95 | 71.81 | 5.4678 | 0.50232 | 716.5 | 47.801 | 3.4285 | 30.27 | 0.50232 | 1.2317 | 333.17 |
| 1974 | 45.912 | 7.1932 | 3.0867 | 35.78 | 68.84 | 5.6745 | 0.51350 | 791.7 | 45.912 | 3.1714 | 29.93 | 0.51350 | 1.2021 | 339.68 |
| 1975 | 45.569 | 7.1227 | 3.0494 | 39.99 | 70.27 | 5.3192 | 0.55981 | 809.5 | 45.569 | 3.1349 | 31.44 | 0.56003 | 1.2408 | 360.73 |
| 1976 | 43.166 | 6.7618 | 2.8155 | 40.88 | 74.74 | 5.3449 | 0.62192 | 930.2 | 43.166 | 2.9552 | 33.62 | 0.62158 | 1.1180 | 331.21 |
| 1977 | 40.883 | 6.8557 | 2.6483 | 41.16 | 86.82 | 5.6061 | 0.65370 | 1006.8 | 40.883 | 2.8001 | 43.62 | 0.65370 | 1.1411 | 305.81 |
| 1978 | 40.061 | 7.0195 | 2.5561 | 46.80 | 97.42 | 5.7398 | 0.66389 | 1080.2 | 40.061 | 2.7541 | 55.87 | 0.66391 | 1.2741 | 267.08 |
| 1979 | 40.165 | 7.2079 | 2.5110 | 50.76 | 91.97 | 5.8298 | 0.66945 | 1138.4 | 40.165 | 2.7488 | 67.01 | 0.64630 | 1.3705 | 300.46 |
| 1980 | 40.598 | 7.8274 | 2.5242 | 59.42 | 99.70 | 5.8690 | 0.67600 | 1189.2 | 40.598 | 2.7603 | 69.55 | 0.59849 | 1.3923 | 315.04 |
| 1981 | 41.295 | 7.9226 | 2.5139 | 61.62 | 102.68 | 6.0399 | 0.69102 | 1263.2 | 41.295 | 2.7751 | 68.49 | 0.55311 | 1.1164 | 245.38 |
| 1982 | 44.712 | 8.1569 | 2.3760 | 65.34 | 107.56 | 6.4312 | 0.68961 | 1323.8 | 44.712 | 2.6139 | 78.01 | 0.56046 | 0.9797 | 243.55 |
| 1983 | 45.438 | 8.1319 | 2.2705 | 78.09 | 127.50 | 6.7708 | 0.71496 | 1349.9 | 45.438 | 2.5372 | 98.69 | 0.58701 | 0.8902 | 211.35 |
| 1984 | 45.442 | 8.1465 | 2.2381 | 88.42 | 126.57 | 6.8717 | 0.72594 | 1381.4 | 45.442 | 2.5234 | 115.68 | 0.59063 | 0.7890 | 187.09 |
| 1985 | 44.914 | 8.0188 | 2.2263 | 105.74 | 129.13 | 6.7950 | 0.71517 | 1448.0 | 44.914 | 2.5110 | 130.25 | 0.58898 | 0.7631 | 180.56 |
| 1986 | 43.798 | 7.9357 | 2.1282 | 137.42 | 137.46 | 6.7998 | 0.73353 | 1416.9 | 43.798 | 2.4009 | 147.09 | 0.67154 | 0.9842 | 165.00 |
| 1987 | 43.041 | 7.8847 | 2.0715 | 156.27 | 142.16 | 6.9291 | 0.77545 | 1494.9 | 43.041 | 2.3342 | 162.62 | 0.70457 | 1.1544 | 166.60 |
| 1988 | 43.429 | 7.9515 | 2.0744 | 167.58 | 137.60 | 7.0364 | 0.77567 | 1537.3 | 43.429 | 2.3348 | 170.06 | 0.66443 | 1.1825 | 151.46 |
| 1989 | 43.381 | 8.0493 | 2.0702 | 178.84 | 130.41 | 7.0239 | 0.77682 | 1510.5 | 43.381 | 2.3353 | 173.41 | 0.67330 | 1.1017 | 151.94 |
| 1990 | 42.426 | 7.8565 | 2.0521 | 201.41 | 129.41 | 6.9141 | 0.76777 | 1522.0 | 42.426 | 2.3121 | 181.11 | 0.71385 | 1.2734 | 183.66 |
| 1991 | 42.223 | 7.9086 | 2.0508 | 225.22 | 128.47 | 6.9733 | 0.76781 | 1533.2 | 42.223 | 2.3110 | 178.61 | 0.70101 | 1.2392 | 166.49 |
| 1992 | 41.593 | 7.8093 | 2.0203 | 247.03 | 132.53 | 6.8484 | 0.76072 | 1595.5 | 41.593 | 2.2748 | 174.71 | 0.73765 | 1.2981 | 164.22 |
| 1993 | 40.471 | 7.5936 | 1.9364 | 268.57 | 149.12 | 6.6337 | 0.79995 | 1841.2 | 40.471 | 2.1752 | 188.37 | 0.77999 | 1.1710 | 130.15 |
| 1994 | 39.826 | 7.5612 | 1.9329 | 287.61 | 158.75 | 6.6075 | 0.79059 | 1867.0 | 39.826 | 2.1689 | 198.65 | 0.76961 | 1.1525 | 120.10 |

**Table N3**  Central rates against the ecu.

(National currency units per ECU)

| | B/L | DK | D | GR[a] | E | F | IRL | I[b] | NL | P[c] | UK[d] |
|---|---|---|---|---|---|---|---|---|---|---|---|
| 13.3.1979[e] | 39.4582 | 7.08592 | 2.51064 | – | – | 5.79831 | 0.662638 | 1148.18 | 2.72077 | – | (0.663247) |
| 24.9.1979 | 39.8456 | 7.36594 | 2.48557 | – | – | 5.85522 | 0.669141 | 1159.42 | 2.74748 | – | (0.649821) |
| 30.11.1979 | 39.7897 | 7.72336 | 2.48208 | – | – | 5.84700 | 0.668201 | 1157.79 | 2.74362 | – | (0.648910) |
| 23.3.1981 | 40.7985 | 7.91917 | 2.54502 | – | – | 5.99526 | 0.685145 | 1262.92 | 2.81318 | – | (0.542122) |
| 5.10.1981 | 40.7572 | 7.91117 | 2.40989 | – | – | 6.17443 | 0.684452 | 1300.67 | 2.66382 | – | (0.601048) |
| 22.2.1982 | 44.6963 | 8.18382 | 2.41815 | – | – | 6.19564 | 0.686799 | 1305.13 | 2.67296 | – | (0.557037) |
| 14.6.1982 | 44.9704 | 8.23400 | 2.33379 | – | – | 6.61387 | 0.691011 | 1350.27 | 3.57971 | – | (0.560453) |
| 21.3.1983 | 44.3662 | 8.04412 | 2.21515 | – | – | 6.79271 | 0.717050 | 1386.78 | 2.49587 | – | (0.629848) |
| 18.5.1983 | 44.9008 | 8.14104 | 2.24184 | – | – | 6.87456 | 0.725690 | 1403.49 | 2.52595 | – | (0.587087) |
| 17.9.1984[f] | 44.9008 | 8.14104 | 2.24184 | (87.4813) | – | 5.87456 | 0.725690 | 1403.49 | 2.52595 | – | (0.585992) |
| 22.7.1985 | 44.8320 | 8.12857 | 2.23840 | (100.719) | – | 6.86402 | 0.724578 | 1520.60 | 2.52208 | – | (0.555312) |
| 7.4.1986 | 43.6761 | 7.91896 | 2.13834 | (135.659) | – | 6.96280 | 0.712956 | 1496.21 | 2.40935 | – | (0.630317) |
| 4.8.1986 | 43.1139 | 7.81701 | 2.11083 | (137.049) | – | 6.87316 | 0.764976 | 1476.95 | 2.37833 | – | (0.679256) |
| 21.1.1987 | 42.4582 | 7.85212 | 2.05853 | (150.792) | – | 6.90403 | 0.768411 | 1483.58 | 2.31943 | – | (0.739615) |
| 19.6.1989 | 42.4582 | 7.85212 | 2.05853 | (150.792) | 133.804 | 6.90403 | 0.768411 | 1483.58 | 2.31943 | – | (0.739615) |
| 21.9.1989[g] | 42.4582 | 7.85212 | 2.05853 | (150.792) | 133.804 | 6.90403 | 0.768411 | 1483.58 | 2.31943 | (172.085) | (0.728627) |
| 8.1.1990 | 42.1679 | 7.79845 | 2.04446 | (187.934) | 133.631 | 6.85684 | 0.763159 | 1529.70 | 2.30358 | (177.743) | (0.728615) |
| 8.10.1990[i] | 42.4032 | 7.84195 | 2.05586 | (205.311) | 133.631 | 6.89509 | 0.767417 | 1538.24 | 2.31643 | (178.735) | 0.696904 |
| 14.9.1992 | 42.0639 | 7.77921 | 2.03942 | (251.202) | 132.562 | 6.83992 | 0.761276 | 1636.61 | 2.29789 | 177.305 | 0.691328 |
| 17.9.1992[j] | 41.9547 | 7.75901 | 2.03412 | (250.550) | 139.176 | 6.82216 | 0.759300 | (1632.36) | 2.29193 | 176.844 | (0.689533) |
| 23.11.1992 | 40.6304 | 7.51410 | 1.96992 | (254.254) | 143.386 | 6.60683 | 0.735304 | (1690.76) | 2.21958 | 182.194 | (0.805748) |
| 1.2.1993 | 40.2802 | 7.44934 | 1.95294 | (259.306) | 142.150 | 6.54988 | 0.809996 | (1796.22) | 2.20045 | 180.624 | (0.808431) |
| 14.5.1993 | 40.2123 | 7.43679 | 1.94964 | (264.513) | 154.250 | 6.53883 | 0.808628 | (1793.19) | 2.19672 | 192.854 | (0.786749) |

a  Notional central rates.
b  Temporary notional central rates as from 17 September 1992.
c  Notional central rates until escudo entry into the exchange-rate mechanism (ERM) on 6 April 1992.
d  Notional central rates until 8 October 1990 (sterling entry into ERM) and as from 17 September 1992 (suspension of sterling participation in the ERM).
e  Initial parities at the start of the European Monetary System.
f  Revised composition of the ecu and inclusion of the drachma.
g  Revised composition of the ecu and inclusion of the peseta and the Portuguese escudo. The central rate of the Spanish peseta was fixed on 19 June when it entered the ERM.
h  Accompanied by a narrowing of the Italian lira fluctuation band from 6% to 2.25%.
i  Sterling entry into the ERM with a fluctuation margin of 6%.
j  Accompanied by a suspension of their participation in the ERM by the sterling and the Italian lira.

**Table N4**   Bilateral central rates and intervention limits in force since 2 August 1993.

| | Percentage margin | BFR 100/ LFR 100 | DKR 100 | DM 100 | PTA 100 | FF 100 | IRL 1 | HFL 100 | ESC 100 |
|---|---|---|---|---|---|---|---|---|---|
| Brussels | +16.1187 | 100 | 627.880 | 2395.20 | 30.2715 | 714.030 | 57.445 | 2125.60 | 24.2120 |
| in BLF | Central rate | 100 | 540.723 | 2062.55 | 26.0696 | 614.977 | 49.7289 | 1830.54 | 20.8512 |
| | −13.8813 | 100 | 465.665 | 1776.20 | 22.4510 | 529.660 | 42.8260 | 1576.45 | 17.9570 |
| Copenhagen | +16.1187 | 21.4747 | 100 | 442.968 | 5.59850 | 132.066 | 10.6792 | 393.105 | 4.47770 |
| in DKR | Central rate | 18.4938 | 100 | 381.443 | 4.82126 | 113.732 | 9.19676 | 338.537 | 3.85618 |
| | −13.8813 | 15.9266 | 100 | 328.461 | 4.15190 | 97.9430 | 7.92014 | 291.544 | 3.32090 |
| Frankfurt | +16.1187 | 5.63000 | 30.4450 | 100 | 1.46800 | 34.6250 | 2.80000 | 103.058 | 1.17400 |
| in DM | Central rate | 4.84837 | 26.2162 | 100 | 1.26395 | 29.8164 | 2.41105 | 88.7526 | 1.01094 |
| | −13.8813 | 4.17500 | 22.5750 | 100 | 1.08800 | 25.6750 | 2.07600 | 76.4326 | 0.87100 |
| Madrid | +16.1187 | 445.418 | 2408.50 | 9191.20 | 100 | 2739.30 | 221.503 | 8153.70 | 92.8760 |
| in PTA | Central rate | 383.589 | 2074.15 | 7911.72 | 100 | 2358.98 | 190.755 | 7021.83 | 79.9828 |
| | −13.8813 | 330.342 | 1786.20 | 6812.00 | 100 | 2031.50 | 164.276 | 6047.10 | 68.8800 |
| Paris | +16.1187 | 18.8800 | 102.100 | 389.480 | 4.92250 | 100 | 9.38950 | 345.650 | 3.93700 |
| in FF | Central rate | 16.2608 | 87.9257 | 335.386 | 4.23911 | 100 | 8.08631 | 297.661 | 3.39056 |
| | −13.8813 | 14.0050 | 75.7200 | 288.810 | 3.65050 | 100 | 6.96400 | 256.350 | 2.91990 |
| Dublin | +16.1187 | 2.33503 | 12.6261 | 48.1696 | 0.608731 | 14.3599 | 1 | 42.7439 | 0.486881 |
| in IRL | Central rate | 2.01090 | 10.8734 | 41.4757 | 0.524232 | 12.3666 | 1 | 36.8105 | 0.419295 |
| | −13.8813 | 1.73176 | 9.36403 | 35.7143 | 0.451462 | 10.6500 | 1 | 31.7007 | 0.361092 |
| Amsterdam | +16.1187 | 6.34340 | 34.3002 | 130.834 | 1.65368 | 39.0091 | 3.15450 | 100 | 1.32266 |
| in HFL | Central rate | 5.46286 | 29.5389 | 112.673 | 1.42413 | 33.5953 | 2.71662 | 100 | 1.13906 |
| | −13.8813 | 4.70454 | 25.4385 | 97.0325 | 1.22644 | 28.9381 | 2.33952 | 100 | 0.98094 |
| Lisbon | +16.1187 | 556.890 | 3011.20 | 11481.10 | 145.180 | 3424.80 | 276.938 | 10194.3 | 100 |
| in ESC | Central rate | 479.590 | 2593.24 | 9891.77 | 125.027 | 2949.37 | 238.495 | 8779.18 | 100 |
| | −13.8813 | 413.020 | 2233.30 | 8517.90 | 107.670 | 2540.00 | 205.389 | 7560.50 | 100 |

DR does not participate in the exchange-rate mechanism (ERM). LIT intervention limits temporarily not applicable and UKL participation in the ERM suspended as from 17 September 1992. Their notional central rates are DR 264.513, LIT 1793.19 and UKL 0.786749 respectively for ECU 1.

**Table N5**   Nominal effective exchange rates. Performance relative to 19 industrial countries; double export weights.

(1980-100)

| | B | DK | WD | GR | E | F | IRL | I | NL | P | UK | EUR 12−a | USA | J |
|---|---|---|---|---|---|---|---|---|---|---|---|---|---|---|
| 1960 | 82.6 | 104.1 | 52.8 | 192.6 | 150.4 | 117.1 | 149.1 | 196.9 | 74.8 | 214.5 | 158.6 | 98.4 | 125.0 | 71.8 |
| 1961 | 81.7 | 103.1 | 54.7 | 191.1 | 149.6 | 116.1 | 149.4 | 195.2 | 77.1 | 213.4 | 157.8 | 99.9 | 125.3 | 71.4 |
| 1962 | 81.7 | 103.1 | 54.9 | 190.9 | 150.0 | 116.1 | 149.8 | 195.0 | 77.6 | 213.8 | 158.3 | 100.5 | 126.3 | 71.5 |
| 1963 | 81.5 | 103.2 | 55.2 | 191.0 | 150.1 | 116.2 | 149.7 | 194.8 | 77.7 | 213.4 | 158.0 | 100.6 | 126.6 | 71.5 |
| 1964 | 81.7 | 103.0 | 55.3 | 191.0 | 150.1 | 116.2 | 149.5 | 193.9 | 77.5 | 212.9 | 157.5 | 100.5 | 126.7 | 71.4 |
| 1965 | 82.0 | 103.1 | 55.1 | 191.2 | 150.2 | 116.2 | 149.6 | 193.9 | 77.7 | 213.1 | 157.8 | 100.4 | 126.7 | 71.5 |
| 1966 | 81.9 | 103.3 | 55.1 | 191.4 | 150.2 | 116.1 | 149.6 | 194.3 | 77.4 | 213.3 | 157.8 | 100.3 | 126.8 | 71.4 |
| 1967 | 82.1 | 102.6 | 55.4 | 191.8 | 147.9 | 116.2 | 148.6 | 194.8 | 77.9 | 214.1 | 155.3 | 100.1 | 127.2 | 71.6 |
| 1968 | 82.9 | 99.0 | 56.4 | 195.1 | 132.2 | 117.9 | 139.5 | 198.7 | 79.1 | 222.8 | 137.1 | 96.5 | 130.0 | 73.1 |
| 1969 | 83.1 | 98.6 | 57.9 | 195.4 | 132.3 | 112.1 | 139.6 | 198.3 | 79.2 | 224.6 | 137.2 | 96.4 | 128.0 | 73.7 |
| 1970 | 83.2 | 97.8 | 62.8 | 192.6 | 131.8 | 103.1 | 139.4 | 196.1 | 78.0 | 223.4 | 136.7 | 97.5 | 128.5 | 73.3 |
| 1971 | 83.1 | 96.9 | 64.7 | 188.2 | 130.2 | 100.8 | 139.5 | 194.3 | 78.7 | 222.0 | 136.7 | 98.3 | 125.1 | 74.5 |
| 1972 | 85.5 | 97.6 | 66.4 | 176.2 | 132.6 | 103.2 | 136.7 | 193.0 | 79.8 | 219.6 | 131.8 | 100.3 | 116.7 | 82.8 |
| 1973 | 86.7 | 103.6 | 73.4 | 162.2 | 134.7 | 106.7 | 127.3 | 173.3 | 82.4 | 223.5 | 118.0 | 103.0 | 107.4 | 87.4 |
| 1974 | 87.9 | 104.0 | 77.4 | 162.6 | 138.7 | 99.5 | 124.1 | 156.4 | 86.7 | 220.5 | 113.9 | 101.1 | 109.6 | 81.6 |
| 1975 | 89.2 | 107.6 | 78.6 | 146.7 | 135.2 | 109.3 | 117.0 | 149.9 | 88.8 | 213.9 | 104.8 | 102.5 | 108.7 | 79.3 |
| 1976 | 91.3 | 110.0 | 83.1 | 138.7 | 124.2 | 105.2 | 105.1 | 124.3 | 91.2 | 195.4 | 89.7 | 92.8 | 114.4 | 83.3 |
| 1977 | 96.5 | 109.4 | 89.7 | 134.7 | 108.7 | 100.2 | 101.5 | 114.4 | 96.0 | 153.1 | 85.5 | 91.9 | 113.6 | 92.4 |
| 1978 | 99.3 | 109.4 | 95.0 | 122.4 | 98.3 | 98.9 | 102.0 | 107.3 | 98.3 | 121.9 | 85.7 | 92.4 | 103.1 | 112.5 |
| 1979 | 100.5 | 108.5 | 99.6 | 115.5 | 107.4 | 99.6 | 102.2 | 103.7 | 99.8 | 103.3 | 90.9 | 98.4 | 100.2 | 104.2 |
| 1980 | 100.0 | 100.0 | 100.0 | 100.0 | 100.0 | 100.0 | 100.0 | 100.0 | 100.0 | 100.0 | 100.0 | 100.0 | 100.0 | 100.0 |
| 1981 | 94.2 | 92.5 | 94.4 | 89.8 | 90.4 | 91.2 | 91.3 | 87.6 | 95.7 | 96.2 | 100.2 | 83.9 | 112.8 | 113.6 |
| 1982 | 85.5 | 88.4 | 99.1 | 82.7 | 84.9 | 83.6 | 90.3 | 81.6 | 100.5 | 83.8 | 95.8 | 78.0 | 126.3 | 107.9 |
| 1983 | 83.1 | 87.9 | 103.1 | 67.7 | 70.3 | 77.6 | 86.6 | 78.5 | 102.6 | 66.1 | 89.1 | 71.4 | 133.6 | 119.7 |
| 1984 | 81.3 | 84.7 | 101.4 | 58.0 | 68.6 | 73.9 | 82.9 | 73.9 | 101.0 | 54.6 | 84.9 | 64.8 | 144.0 | 126.6 |
| 1985 | 82.0 | 85.7 | 101.7 | 48.8 | 67.1 | 74.7 | 83.9 | 70.1 | 101.2 | 48.3 | 84.8 | 63.5 | 149.9 | 130.5 |
| 1986 | 86.5 | 91.1 | 112.6 | 38.4 | 66.0 | 78.0 | 87.0 | 72.7 | 109.0 | 44.6 | 78.6 | 69.7 | 121.3 | 166.0 |
| 1987 | 90.0 | 95.0 | 120.4 | 34.6 | 66.2 | 78.9 | 85.2 | 73.5 | 114.6 | 41.4 | 77.8 | 74.5 | 106.7 | 179.7 |
| 1988 | 88.9 | 93.2 | 119.5 | 32.1 | 68.2 | 77.0 | 84.0 | 70.9 | 114.1 | 39.3 | 82.3 | 73.3 | 100.2 | 198.4 |
| 1989 | 88.1 | 90.7 | 118.0 | 29.7 | 71.0 | 76.0 | 83.0 | 71.2 | 112.9 | 38.1 | 79.5 | 71.1 | 105.1 | 189.7 |
| 1990 | 92.7 | 97.6 | 124.7 | 27.3 | 74.7 | 80.7 | 87.8 | 73.9 | 117.3 | 37.6 | 78.8 | 79.3 | 98.6 | 170.3 |
| 1991 | 92.4 | 95.7 | 123.3 | 24.2 | 74.4 | 79.0 | 86.7 | 72.4 | 116.4 | 37.8 | 79.1 | 76.7 | 97.9 | 185.1 |
| 1992 | 94.5 | 98.4 | 127.4 | 22.3 | 73.0 | 81.8 | 89.1 | 70.4 | 119.3 | 39.2 | 76.3 | 78.5 | 95.7 | 194.3 |
| 1993 | 95.3 | 100.5 | 130.8 | 20.2 | 63.5 | 83.4 | 83.8 | 58.5 | 122.9 | 36.2 | 69.4 | 71.4 | 100.0 | 234.8 |
| 1994 | 96.1 | 99.6 | 129.5 | 18.6 | 58.9 | 82.9 | 83.8 | 57.0 | 122.3 | 34.0 | 69.5 | 69.0 | 100.1 | 251.7 |

EUR 12−: incl. WD.
a EUR 12− relative to nine industrial non-member countries.

***Table O1*** Main economic indicators 1961-94[a].
EUR 12[-b]

(Annual percentage change, unless otherwise stated)

| | 1961-73 | 1974-85 | 1986 | 1987 | 1988 | 1989 | 1990 | 1991 | 1992 | 1993 | 1994 |
|---|---|---|---|---|---|---|---|---|---|---|---|
| 1. Gross domestic product | | | | | | | | | | | |
| – at current market prices | 10.2 | 12.9 | 8.6 | 7.1 | 8.8 | 8.5 | 8.4 | 6.9 | 5.3 | 3.1 | 4.4 |
| – at 1985 market prices | | | | | | | | | | | |
| • incl. West Germany | 4.8 | 2.0 | 2.9 | 2.9 | 4.3 | 3.5 | 3.0 | 1.5 | 1.0 | -0.5 | 1.5 |
| • incl. unified Germany | : | : | : | : | : | : | : | : | 1.1 | -0.3 | 1.6 |
| 2. Gross fixed capital formation at 1985 prices | | | | | | | | | | | |
| – total | 5.7 | -0.1 | 4.2 | 5.5 | 8.7 | 6.9 | 3.8 | -0.4 | -1.0 | -6.2 | 0.9 |
| – construction[c] | : | -1.3 | 4.0 | 3.2 | 7.1 | 5.7 | 3.7 | 1.1 | 1.0 | -2.7 | 1.0 |
| – equipment[c] | : | 2.0 | 4.3 | 8.3 | 10.1 | 9.3 | 4.7 | 0.1 | -3.2 | -9.9 | 1.0 |
| 3. Gross fixed capital formation at current prices (% of GDP) | | | | | | | | | | | |
| – total | 23.2 | 21.1 | 19.0 | 19.3 | 20.1 | 20.8 | 20.9 | 20.3 | 19.6 | 18.4 | 18.2 |
| – general government[d] | : | 3.2 | 2.8 | 2.7 | 2.6 | 2.8 | 3.0 | 2.9 | 2.9 | 2.8 | 2.7 |
| – other sectors[d] | : | 17.9 | 16.2 | 16.7 | 17.5 | 18.0 | 17.9 | 17.4 | 16.7 | 15.6 | 15.5 |
| 4. Final national uses including stocks | | | | | | | | | | | |
| – at 1985 prices | 4.9 | 1.6 | 4.1 | 3.9 | 5.1 | 3.7 | 2.9 | 1.1 | 1.0 | -1.9 | 1.0 |
| – relative against nine other OECD countries | -0.5 | -0.9 | 0.5 | -0.3 | 0.2 | -0.1 | 1.4 | 1.6 | 0.2 | -2.8 | -1.4 |
| 5. Inflation | | | | | | | | | | | |
| – price deflator private consumption | 4.7 | 10.8 | 3.8 | 3.6 | 3.8 | 4.9 | 4.7 | 5.4 | 4.4 | 3.8 | 3.2 |
| – price deflator GDP | 5.2 | 10.7 | 5.5 | 4.0 | 4.3 | 4.9 | 5.2 | 5.4 | 4.3 | 3.5 | 2.9 |
| 6. Compensation per employee | | | | | | | | | | | |
| – nominal | 9.9 | 12.5 | 6.0 | 5.4 | 5.6 | 5.8 | 7.3 | 6.9 | 5.6 | 3.9 | 3.0 |
| – real, deflator private consumption | 5.0 | 1.5 | 2.2 | 1.7 | 1.7 | 0.8 | 2.5 | 1.5 | 1.2 | 0.2 | -0.2 |
| – real, deflator GDP | 4.5 | 1.7 | 0.5 | 1.3 | 1.2 | 0.9 | 1.9 | 1.5 | 1.3 | 0.4 | 0.2 |
| 7. GDP at 1985 market prices per person employed | 4.4 | 2.0 | 2.2 | 1.7 | 2.7 | 1.9 | 1.2 | 1.3 | 1.5 | 1.4 | 2.2 |
| 8. Real unit labour costs | | | | | | | | | | | |
| – 1961-73 = 100 | 100.0 | 101.8 | 94.9 | 94.5 | 93.2 | 92.2 | 92.9 | 93.0 | 92.8 | 91.8 | 90.0 |
| – annual % change | 0.1 | -0.4 | -1.7 | -0.4 | -1.4 | -1.0 | 0.7 | 0.2 | -0.3 | -1.0 | -2.0 |
| 9. Relative unit labour costs in common currency, against nine other OECD countries | | | | | | | | | | | |
| – 1961-73 = 100 | 100.0 | 101.4 | 92.1 | 98.8 | 96.6 | 93.4 | 104.2 | 101.3 | 105.5 | 97.2 | 93.5 |
| – annual % change | 1.0 | -1.9 | 9.6 | 7.2 | -2.2 | -3.4 | 11.6 | -2.7 | 4.2 | -7.9 | -3.8 |
| 10. Employment | | | | | | | | | | | |
| – incl. West Germany | 0.3 | 0.0 | 0.7 | 1.2 | 1.5 | 1.5 | 1.7 | 0.1 | -0.6 | 1.8 | -0.6 |
| – incl. unified Germany | : | : | : | : | : | : | : | : | -1.1 | -1.9 | -0.7 |
| 11. Unemployment rate (% of civilian labour force) | 2.1 | 6.8 | 10.7 | 10.4 | 9.8 | 9.0 | 8.4 | 8.7 | 9.4 | 10.5 | 11.3 |
| 12. Current balance (% of GDP) | | | | | | | | | | | |
| – incl. West Germany | 0.4 | -0.2 | 1.3 | 0.7 | 0.1 | -0.2 | -0.4 | -0.6 | -0.3 | 0.7 | 1.1 |
| – incl. unified Germany | : | : | : | : | : | : | : | -1.2 | -1.1 | -0.2 | 0.2 |
| 13. Net lending (+) or net borrowing (−) of general government (% of GDP)[f] | | | | | | | | | | | |
| – incl. West Germany | -0.5 | -4.1 | -4.5 | -4.0 | -3.6 | -2.9 | -4.1 | -4.6 | -5.0 | -5.9 | -5.5 |
| – incl. unified Germany | : | : | : | : | : | : | : | -4.6 | -5.1 | -6.0 | -5.6 |
| 14. General government gross debt (% of GDP) | | | | | | | | | | | |
| – incl. unified Germany | : | : | : | : | : | : | : | 57.0 | 60.8 | 66.0 | 69.8 |
| 15. Interest payment by general government (% of GDP) | : | 3.2 | 4.9 | 4.7 | 4.6 | 4.7 | 4.9 | 5.0 | 5.4 | 5.5 | 5.5 |
| 16. Money supply (end of year)[g] | 12.8 | 12.9 | 10.5 | 10.1 | 10.4 | 11.2 | 8.9 | 6.6 | 5.6 | 6.7 | : |
| 17. Long-term interest rate (%) | 7.1 | 11.9 | 9.2 | 9.3 | 9.3 | 9.8 | 11.0 | 10.3 | 9.9 | 8.1 | 7.7 |
| 18. Profitability (1961-73 = 100) | 100.0 | 76.0 | 81.2 | 82.7 | 87.7 | 91.2 | 90.1 | 89.0 | 89.0 | 87.2 | 91.3 |

a 1961-92: Eurostat and Commission services; 1992-94: economic forecast, May 1994.
b Incl. West Germany, otherwise stated.
c 1974-85: EUR 12 excl. Portugal.
d 1974-85: EUR 12 excl. Greece.

e 1961-73: EUR 12 excl. Greece, Spain and Portugal.
f 1961-73, 1974-85: EUR 12 excl. Greece and Spain.
g Broad money supply M2 or M3 according to country: 1961-73: EUR 12 excl. Spain, Portugal and United Kingdom.

***Table O2*** Main economic indicators 1961-94[a].
Belgium

(Annual percentage change, unless otherwise stated)

| | 1961-73 | 1974-85 | 1986 | 1987 | 1988 | 1989 | 1990 | 1991 | 1992 | 1993 | 1994 |
|---|---|---|---|---|---|---|---|---|---|---|---|
| 1. Gross domestic product | | | | | | | | | | | |
| – at current market prices | 9.2 | 8.6 | 5.3 | 4.3 | 6.8 | 8.4 | 6.4 | 4.5 | 4.9 | 1.4 | 4.1 |
| – at 1985 market prices | 4.9 | 1.8 | 1.4 | 2.0 | 5.0 | 3.6 | 3.2 | 1.8 | 1.4 | -1.3 | 1.3 |
| 2. Gross fixed capital formation at 1985 prices | | | | | | | | | | | |
| – total | 5.1 | -0.7 | 4.4 | 5.6 | 15.4 | 13.4 | 8.5 | -1.7 | 1.0 | -7.0 | 1.4 |
| – construction | : | -2.6 | 3.0 | 3.0 | 14.9 | 9.2 | 7.9 | 3.6 | 6.2 | -4.3 | 1.3 |
| – equipment | : | 3.3 | 5.3 | 7.1 | 16.1 | 17.4 | 9.9 | -2.5 | -5.8 | -11.0 | 1.5 |
| 3. Gross fixed capital formation at current prices (% of GDP) | | | | | | | | | | | |
| – total | 21.8 | 19.6 | 15.7 | 16.0 | 17.7 | 19.3 | 20.2 | 19.4 | 19.2 | 17.9 | 17.9 |
| – general government | : | 3.7 | 2.1 | 1.9 | 1.9 | 1.6 | 1.6 | 1.7 | 1.8 | 2.0 | 2.0 |
| – other sectors | : | 16.0 | 13.6 | 14.1 | 15.7 | 17.7 | 18.6 | 17.7 | 17.5 | 16.0 | 15.9 |
| 4. Final national uses including stocks | | | | | | | | | | | |
| – at 1985 prices | 4.8 | 1.2 | 2.8 | 3.8 | 4.5 | 4.9 | 3.3 | 1.7 | 2.5 | -2.1 | 1.0 |
| – relative against 19 competitors | -0.1 | -0.6 | -1.0 | 0.5 | 0.2 | 1.4 | 0.4 | 0.8 | 1.5 | -1.1 | -0.3 |
| – relative against other member countries | 0.0 | -0.4 | -1.1 | 0.6 | 0.2 | 1.4 | 0.1 | 0.4 | 1.5 | -0.4 | 0.1 |
| 5. Inflation | | | | | | | | | | | |
| – price deflator private consumption | 3.7 | 7.5 | 0.7 | 1.9 | 1.6 | 3.4 | 3.6 | 2.5 | 2.1 | 2.8 | 2.6 |
| – price deflator GDP | 4.1 | 6.7 | 3.9 | 2.3 | 1.8 | 4.6 | 3.0 | 2.7 | 3.4 | 2.7 | 2.8 |
| 6. Compensation per employee | | | | | | | | | | | |
| – nominal | 9.0 | 9.4 | 4.8 | 1.5 | 2.4 | 3.1 | 7.5 | 8.0 | 5.8 | 4.8 | 3.3 |
| – real, deflator private consumption | 5.1 | 1.8 | 4.0 | -0.3 | 0.8 | -0.2 | 3.8 | 5.3 | 3.6 | 1.9 | 0.7 |
| – real, deflator GDP | 4.7 | 2.5 | 0.9 | -0.8 | 0.6 | -1.4 | 4.3 | 5.1 | 2.3 | 2.0 | 0.5 |
| 7. GDP at 1985 market prices per person employed | 4.3 | 2.1 | 0.7 | 1.5 | 3.4 | 2.0 | 1.8 | 1.6 | 1.8 | 0.2 | 2.1 |
| 8. Real unit labour costs | | | | | | | | | | | |
| – 1961-73 = 100 | 100.0 | 111.3 | 108.6 | 106.1 | 103.2 | 99.8 | 102.3 | 105.8 | 106.3 | 108.2 | 106.6 |
| – annual % change | 0.4 | 0.4 | 0.2 | -2.3 | -2.8 | -3.3 | 2.5 | 3.4 | 0.5 | 1.9 | -1.5 |
| 9. Relative unit labour costs in common currency, against 19 competitors | | | | | | | | | | | |
| • 1961-73 = 100 | 100.0 | 104.3 | 94.0 | 94.9 | 90.8 | 88.6 | 94.1 | 95.2 | 97.9 | 101.0 | 102.4 |
| • annual % change | -0.3 | -1.2 | 6.4 | 1.0 | -4.4 | -2.4 | 6.2 | 1.1 | 2.9 | 3.2 | 1.4 |
| – against other member countries | | | | | | | | | | | |
| • 1961-73 = 100 | 100.0 | 102.9 | 95.5 | 94.7 | 91.0 | 89.6 | 92.7 | 94.4 | 96.1 | 101.0 | 103.4 |
| • annual % change | -0.7 | -0.6 | 3.9 | -0.9 | -3.9 | -1.5 | 3.4 | 1.8 | 1.7 | 5.1 | 2.4 |
| 10. Employment | 0.6 | -0.3 | 0.6 | 0.5 | 1.5 | 1.6 | 1.4 | 0.1 | -0.4 | -1.4 | -0.8 |
| 11. Unemployment rate (% of civilian labour force) | : | 8.1 | 11.7 | 11.3 | 10.2 | 8.6 | 7.6 | 7.5 | 8.2 | 9.4 | 10.3 |
| 12. Current balance (% of GDP) | 1.1 | -1.5 | 2.1 | 1.3 | 1.7 | 1.7 | 0.9 | 1.8 | 1.8 | 3.0 | 3.0 |
| 13. Net lending (+) or net borrowing (−) of general government (% of GDP) | -2.3 | -8.4 | -9.4 | -7.5 | -6.8 | -6.5 | -5.9 | -6.8 | -7.1 | -7.0 | -5.4 |
| 14. General government gross debt (% of GDP) | : | : | : | : | : | : | : | 131.0 | 133.6 | 135.1 | 142.1 | 142.6 |
| 15. Interest payment by general government (% of GDP) | 3.2 | 6.6 | 11.5 | 10.8 | 10.3 | 10.6 | 11.0 | 10.7 | 11.0 | 11.1 | 10.2 |
| 16. Money supply (end of year)[b] | 10.1 | 9.4 | 12.8 | 10.2 | 7.8 | 13.1 | 4.5 | 5.9 | 6.2 | 9.3 | : |
| 17. Long-term interest rate (%) | 6.5 | 10.6 | 7.9 | 7.8 | 7.9 | 8.7 | 10.1 | 9.3 | 8.6 | 7.2 | 7.5 |
| 18. Profitability (1961-73 = 100) | 100.0 | 65.7 | 69.3 | 74.9 | 81.4 | 90.0 | 85.4 | 77.9 | 75.8 | 69.5 | 71.8 |

a 1961-92: EUROSTAT and Commission services; 1993-94: Economic forecasts May 1994.
b M3H.

**Table O3**   Main economic indicators 1961-94[a].
Denmark

(Annual percentage change, unless otherwise stated)

| | 1961-73 | 1974-85 | 1986 | 1987 | 1988 | 1989 | 1990 | 1991 | 1992 | 1993 | 1994 |
|---|---|---|---|---|---|---|---|---|---|---|---|
| 1. Gross domestic product | | | | | | | | | | | |
| – at current market prices | 11.7 | 11.2 | 8.4 | 5.0 | 4.6 | 4.8 | 4.2 | 3.5 | 3.2 | 2.7 | 5.6 |
| – at 1985 market prices | 4.3 | 2.0 | 3.6 | 0.3 | 1.2 | 0.6 | 1.4 | 1.0 | 1.2 | 1.1 | 3.8 |
| 2. Gross fixed capital formation at 1985 prices | | | | | | | | | | | |
| – total | 6.5 | –0.9 | 17.1 | –3.8 | –6.6 | 1.0 | –1.7 | –5.4 | –8.2 | –1.8 | 7.3 |
| – construction | : | –3.4 | 18.0 | 1.1 | –5.5 | –6.1 | –5.6 | –12.9 | 0.2 | –6.4 | 6.0 |
| – equipment | : | 3.5 | 16.6 | –8.9 | –8.6 | 9.7 | 1.9 | 2.9 | –15.4 | 2.9 | 8.5 |
| 3. Gross fixed capital formation at current prices (% of GDP) | | | | | | | | | | | |
| – total | 24.0 | 19.6 | 20.8 | 19.7 | 18.1 | 18.1 | 17.4 | 16.4 | 15.2 | 14.8 | 15.3 |
| – general government | : | 3.2 | 1.6 | 1.8 | 1.9 | 1.7 | 1.6 | 1.2 | 1.9 | 2.2 | 2.2 |
| – other sectors | : | 16.4 | 19.1 | 17.9 | 16.2 | 16.4 | 15.8 | 15.2 | 13.2 | 12.6 | 13.1 |
| 4. Final national uses including stocks | | | | | | | | | | | |
| – at 1985 prices | 4.6 | 1.3 | 6.1 | –2.2 | –1.2 | 0.5 | –1.0 | –0.5 | –0.7 | 0.3 | 5.3 |
| – relative against 19 competitors | 0.1 | –0.6 | 2.2 | –5.4 | –5.2 | –2.7 | –3.2 | –0.8 | –1.4 | 1.2 | 4.0 |
| – relative against other member countries | 0.2 | –0.2 | 2.2 | –5.5 | –5.6 | –2.8 | –4.0 | –1.8 | –1,8 | 2.0 | 4.4 |
| 5. Inflation | | | | | | | | | | | |
| – price deflator private consumption | 6.6 | 9.6 | 2.9 | 4.6 | 4.0 | 4.3 | 2.7 | 2.2 | 2.1 | 1.7 | 2.0 |
| – price deflator GDP | 7.0 | 9.0 | 4.6 | 4.7 | 3.4 | 4.2 | 2.7 | 2.5 | 1.9 | 1.6 | 1.7 |
| 6. Compensation per employee | | | | | | | | | | | |
| – nominal | 10.7 | 10.1 | 4.4 | 7.9 | 5.0 | 3.8 | 4.6 | 4.7 | 2.8 | 2.2 | 2.4 |
| – real, deflator private consumption | 3.8 | 0.5 | 1.5 | 3.1 | 1.0 | –0.5 | 1.8 | 2.5 | 0.6 | 0.5 | 0.4 |
| – real, deflator GDP | 3.4 | 1.0 | –0.2 | 3.0 | 1.5 | –0.4 | 1.9 | 2.2 | 0.8 | 0.6 | 0.7 |
| 7. GDP at 1985 market prices per person employed | 3.2 | 1.5 | 1.0 | –0.6 | 1.8 | 1.1 | 2.5 | 2.8 | 1.3 | 1.6 | 2.9 |
| 8. Real unit labour costs | | | | | | | | | | | |
| – 1961-73 = 100 | 100.0 | 100.0 | 92.5 | 95.9 | 95.7 | 94.2 | 93.7 | 93.1 | 92.6 | 91.6 | 89.7 |
| – annual % change | 0.2 | –0.4 | –1.2 | 3.6 | –0.2 | –1.5 | –0.6 | –0.6 | –0.5 | –1.0 | –2.1 |
| 9. Relative unit labour costs in common currency, against 19 competitors | | | | | | | | | | | |
| • 1961-73 = 100 | 100.0 | 110.0 | 101.6 | 111.1 | 109.2 | 105.3 | 109.7 | 104.4 | 105.7 | 106.3 | 104.1 |
| • annual % change | 2.1 | –1.3 | 5.8 | 9.4 | –1.6 | –3.6 | 4.2 | –4.8 | 1.2 | 0.6 | –2.1 |
| – against other member countries | | | | | | | | | | | |
| • 1961-73 = 100 | 100.0 | 108.4 | 102.7 | 109.4 | 108.9 | 106.9 | 107.0 | 102.6 | 101.8 | 103.5 | 102.7 |
| • annual % change | 1.7 | –0.7 | 2.1 | 6.6 | –0.5 | –1.9 | 0.1 | –4.0 | –0.8 | 1.7 | –0.8 |
| 10. Employment | 1.1 | 0.5 | 2.6 | 0.9 | –0.6 | –0.6 | –1.0 | –1.8 | –0.1 | –0.5 | 0.9 |
| 11. Unemployment rate (% of civilian labour force) | : | 6.4 | 5.5 | 5.6 | 6.4 | 7.7 | 8.1 | 8.9 | 9.5 | 10.4 | 9.9 |
| 12. Current balance (% of GDP) | –2.0 | –3.5 | –5.4 | –2.9 | –1.3 | –1.5 | 0.5 | 1.3 | 3.0 | 3.6 | 3.0 |
| 13. Net lending (+) or net borrowing (–) of general government (% of GDP) | 2.2 | –2.8 | 3.4 | 2.4 | 0.6 | –0.5 | –1.5 | –2.1 | –2.4 | –4.6 | –4.6 |
| 14. General government gross debt (% of GDP) | : | : | : | : | : | : | : | 64.6 | 68.8 | 80.4 | 82.2 |
| 15. Interest payment by general government (% of GDP) | : | 4.5 | 8.8 | 8.3 | 8.0 | 7.5 | 7.3 | 7.4 | 6.9 | 7.6 | 7.7 |
| 16. Money supply (end of year)[b] | 10.6 | 13.5 | 10.8 | 4.3 | 3.4 | 6.1 | 7.1 | 6.4 | –0.1 | 14.6 | : |
| 17. Long-term interest rate (%) | 9.0 | 16.0 | 10.6 | 11.9 | 10.6 | 10.2 | 11.0 | 10.1 | 10.1 | 8.8 | 8.1 |
| 18. Profitability (1961-73 = 100) | 100.0 | 73.5 | 89.7 | 81.2 | 80.8 | 81.8 | 82.6 | 82.0 | 80.6 | 81.6 | 87.0 |

a 1961-92: EUROSTAT and Commission services; 1993-94: Economic forecasts May 1994.
b M3H.

**Table O4**   Main economic indicators 1961-94[a].
Federal Republic of Germany[b]

(Annual percentage change, unless otherwise stated)

| | 1961-73 | 1974-85 | 1986 | 1987 | 1988 | 1989 | 1990 | 1991 | 1992 | 1993 | 1994 |
|---|---|---|---|---|---|---|---|---|---|---|---|
| 1. Gross domestic product | | | | | | | | | | | |
| – at current market prices | 8.9 | 5.9 | 5.6 | 3.4 | 5.3 | 6.1 | 9.0 | 8.7 | 6.0 | 1.4 | 3.1 |
| – at 1985 market prices | | | | | | | | | | | |
| • West Germany | 4.3 | 1.7 | 2.3 | 1.5 | 3.7 | 3.6 | 5.7 | 4.5 | 1.6 | –1.9 | 0.7 |
| • Unified Germany | : | : | : | : | : | : | : | : | 2.1 | –1.2 | 1.3 |
| 2. Gross fixed capital formation at 1985 prices | | | | | | | | | | | |
| – total | 3.9 | –0.3 | 3.3 | 1.8 | 4.4 | 6.3 | 8.5 | 6.1 | 1.1 | –6.9 | –0.3 |
| – construction | : | –1.3 | 3.1 | 0.0 | 3.1 | 4.4 | 4.9 | 4.1 | 5.5 | –0.4 | 1.0 |
| – equipment | : | 1.9 | 4.5 | 5.0 | 6.7 | 9.2 | 13.1 | 10.3 | –3.9 | –15.1 | –2.2 |
| 3. Gross fixed capital formation at current prices (% of GDP) | | | | | | | | | | | |
| – total | 24.9 | 20.8 | 19.4 | 19.4 | 19.6 | 20.2 | 20.9 | 21.4 | 21.2 | 20.0 | 19.7 |
| – general government | 4.2 | 3.2 | 2.5 | 2.4 | 2.3 | 2.4 | 2.3 | 2.3 | 2.4 | 2.3 | 2.1 |
| – other sectors | 20.8 | 17.6 | 16.9 | 17.0 | 17.2 | 17.8 | 18.6 | 19.1 | 18.9 | 17.7 | 17.6 |
| 4. Final national uses including stocks | | | | | | | | | | | |
| – at 1985 prices | 4.5 | –1.3 | 3.3 | 2.4 | 3.6 | 2.9 | 5.2 | 3.6 | 1.5 | –2.6 | –0.2 |
| – relative against 19 competitors | –0.5 | –0.6 | –0.4 | –1.1 | –0.9 | –0.8 | 3.1 | 3.5 | 0.7 | –2.2 | –2.0 |
| – relative against other member countries | –0.4 | –0.3 | –0.8 | –1.2 | –1.2 | –0.9 | 2.9 | 3.2 | 0.6 | –1.2 | –1.7 |
| 5. Inflation | | | | | | | | | | | |
| – price deflator private consumption | 3.5 | 4.3 | –0.3 | 0.7 | 1.4 | 3.0 | 2.8 | 3.8 | 4.0 | 3.3 | 2.7 |
| – price deflator GDP | 4.4 | 4.1 | 3.2 | 1.9 | 1.5 | 2.4 | 3.1 | 3.9 | 4.4 | 3.3 | 2.3 |
| 6. Compensation per employee | | | | | | | | | | | |
| – nominal | 9.1 | 5.8 | 3.6 | 3.2 | 3.0 | 2.9 | 4.7 | 5.8 | 5.4 | 3.2 | 2.2 |
| – real, deflator private consumption | 5.4 | 1.4 | 4.0 | 2.5 | 1.6 | –0.1 | 1.9 | 2.0 | 1.3 | –0.1 | –0.5 |
| – real, deflator GDP | 4.5 | 1.6 | 0.4 | 1.3 | 1.5 | 0.4 | 1.5 | 1.8 | 0.9 | –0.1 | –0.1 |
| 7. GDP at 1985 market prices per person employed | 4.0 | 1.9 | 0.9 | 0.7 | 2.9 | 2.1 | 2.7 | 1.9 | 0.7 | –0.3 | 2.2 |
| 8. Real unit labour costs | | | | | | | | | | | |
| – 1961-73 = 100 | 100.0 | 103.7 | 99.7 | 100.2 | 98.8 | 97.1 | 96.1 | 96.1 | 96.3 | 96.5 | 94.3 |
| – annual % change | 0.5 | –0.3 | –0.5 | 0.5 | –1.4 | –1.7 | –1.1 | 0.0 | 0.2 | 0.2 | –2.2 |
| 9. Relative unit labour costs in common currency, against 19 competitors | | | | | | | | | | | |
| • 1961-73 = 100 | 100.0 | 107.0 | 101.4 | 107.5 | 103.8 | 99.6 | 101.6 | 99.1 | 104.0 | 108.5 | 106.2 |
| • annual % change | 2.3 | –2.2 | 9.6 | 6.0 | –3.4 | –4.0 | 2.0 | –2.5 | 5.0 | 4.3 | –2.1 |
| – against other member countries | | | | | | | | | | | |
| • 1961-73 = 100 | 100.0 | 107.9 | 106.3 | 110.1 | 106.6 | 103.3 | 100.7 | 99.0 | 102.7 | 112.0 | 111.3 |
| • annual % change | 2.2 | –1.6 | 6.6 | 3.6 | –3.1 | –3.1 | –2.6 | –1.7 | 3.7 | 9.1 | –0.6 |
| 10. Employment | | | | | | | | | | | |
| – West Germany | 0.3 | –0.2 | 1.4 | 0.7 | 0.8 | 1.5 | 3.0 | 2.6 | 0.9 | –1.6 | –1.4 |
| – Unified Germany | : | : | : | : | : | : | : | : | –1.7 | –1.9 | –1.4 |
| 11. Unemployment rate (% of civilian labour force) | : | 4.2 | 6.5 | 6.3 | 6.3 | 5.6 | 4.8 | 4.2 | 4.5 | 5.6 | 6.9 |
| 12. Current balance (% of GDP) | | | | | | | | | | | |
| – West Germany | 0.7 | 0.8 | 4.3 | 4.1 | 4.3 | 4.8 | 3.6 | 1.4 | 1.6 | 1.9 | 2.3 |
| – Unified Germany | : | : | : | : | : | : | : | –1.2 | –1.2 | –1.2 | –0.9 |
| 13. Net lending (+) or net borrowing (–) of general government (% of GDP) | | | | | | | | | | | |
| – West Germany | 0.4 | –2.8 | –1.3 | –1.9 | –2.2 | 0.1 | –2.1 | –3.5 | –2.3 | –2.8 | –2.2 |
| – Unified Germany | : | : | : | : | : | : | : | –3.2 | –2.6 | –3.3 | –3.1 |
| 14. General government gross debt (% of GDP) | : | : | : | : | : | : | : | 42.1 | 44.8 | 48.9 | 53.6 |
| 15. Interest payment by general government (% of GDP) | 0.9 | 2.1 | 3.0 | 2.9 | 2.9 | 2.7 | 2.6 | 2.8 | 3.0 | 3.3 | 3.7 |
| 16. Money supply (M3; end of year)[c] | 10.9 | 7.5 | 6.6 | 5.9 | 6.9 | 5.5 | 4.2 | 6.3 | 7.6 | 10.9 | : |
| 17. Long-term interest rate (%) | 7.2 | 8.0 | 5.9 | 5.8 | 6.1 | 7.0 | 8.9 | 8.6 | 8.0 | 6.3 | 6.3 |
| 18. Profitability (1961-73 = 100) | 100.0 | 71.5 | 74.0 | 73.0 | 77.3 | 81.3 | 85.4 | 86.0 | 84.4 | 79.3 | 83.0 |

a 1961-92: EUROSTAT and Commission services; 1993-94: Economic forecasts May 1994.
b West Germany unless otherwise stated.
c M3H.

**Table O5**  Main economic indicators 1961-94[a].

Greece

(Annual percentage change, unless otherwise stated)

| | 1961-73 | 1974-85 | 1986 | 1987 | 1988 | 1989 | 1990 | 1991 | 1992 | 1993 | 1994 |
|---|---|---|---|---|---|---|---|---|---|---|---|
| 1. Gross domestic product | | | | | | | | | | | |
| – at current market prices | 12.5 | 20.7 | 19.4 | 13.7 | 20.7 | 16.5 | 19.6 | 21.4 | 16.0 | 13.6 | 11.2 |
| – at 1985 market prices | 7.7 | 2.5 | 1.6 | −0.5 | 4.4 | 3.5 | −1.1 | 3.3 | 0.9 | −0.2 | 0.7 |
| 2. Gross fixed capital formation at 1985 prices | | | | | | | | | | | |
| – total | 10.0 | −1.6 | −6.2 | −5.1 | 8.9 | 10.1 | 9.4 | −4.4 | 1.2 | −3.4 | 1.9 |
| – construction | : | −3.2 | −0.8 | −5.0 | 9.2 | 4.0 | 5.7 | −6.5 | −4.2 | −7.5 | 2.4 |
| – equipment | : | 0.7 | −12.6 | −5.2 | 8.4 | 18.1 | 5.7 | 3.3 | 7.0 | 0.6 | 1.5 |
| 3. Gross fixed capital formation at current prices (% of GDP) | | | | | | | | | | | |
| – total | 22.7 | 21.8 | 18.5 | 17.1 | 17.4 | 19.2 | 19.6 | 18.6 | 18.0 | 17.0 | 17.1 |
| – general government | : | : | 4.1 | 3.2 | 3.2 | 3.4 | 3.1 | 3.8 | 4.0 | 3.6 | 3.9 |
| – other sectors | : | : | 14.3 | 13.9 | 14.2 | 15.8 | 16.5 | 14.8 | 14.0 | 13.4 | 13.2 |
| 4. Final national uses including stocks | | | | | | | | | | | |
| – at 1985 prices | 8.1 | 1.8 | −1.1 | −1.3 | 7.1 | 4.0 | 1.5 | 3.2 | 1.6 | −0.2 | 0.8 |
| – relative against 19 competitors | 3.1 | −0.1 | −4.7 | −4.6 | 2.6 | 0.6 | −1.3 | 2.2 | 0.5 | 1.0 | −0.4 |
| – relative against other member countries | 3.3 | 0.3 | −4.8 | −4.5 | 2.6 | 0.6 | −1.7 | 1.7 | 0.5 | 1.9 | 0.0 |
| 5. Inflation | | | | | | | | | | | |
| – price deflator private consumption | 3.5 | 17.5 | 22.1 | 15.7 | 14.2 | 14.7 | 19.2 | 18.5 | 14.6 | 13.7 | 10.2 |
| – price deflator GDP | 4.5 | 17.7 | 17.5 | 14.3 | 15.6 | 12.5 | 20.9 | 17.6 | 14.9 | 13.8 | 10.4 |
| 6. Compensation per employee | | | | | | | | | | | |
| – nominal | 10.1 | 21.6 | 12.8 | 11.5 | 18.6 | 18.1 | 17.4 | 16.1 | 11.2 | 11.7 | 11.2 |
| – real, deflator private consumption | 6.4 | 3.5 | −7.7 | −3.6 | 3.8 | 3.0 | −1.5 | −2.1 | −3.0 | −1.8 | 0.9 |
| – real, deflator GDP | 5.4 | 3.3 | −4.1 | −2.4 | 2.6 | 5.0 | −2.8 | −1.3 | −3.2 | −1.8 | 0.7 |
| 7. GDP at 1985 market prices per person employed | 8.1 | 1.6 | 1.3 | −0.4 | 2.7 | 3.2 | −2.3 | 5.7 | −0.5 | 0.6 | 0.7 |
| 8. Real unit labour costs | | | | | | | | | | | |
| – 1961-73 = 100 | 100.0 | 97.0 | 99.5 | 97.5 | 97.4 | 99.2 | 98.6 | 92.1 | 89.6 | 87.4 | 87.5 |
| – annual % change | −2.5 | 1.8 | −5.2 | −2.0 | −0.1 | 1.8 | −0.5 | −6.6 | −2.7 | −2.4 | 0.1 |
| 9. Relative unit labour costs in common currency, against 19 competitors | | | | | | | | | | | |
| ● 1961-73 = 100 | 100.0 | 77.0 | 64.0 | 62.7 | 65.6 | 67.5 | 71.1 | 65.8 | 65.7 | 64.5 | 65.4 |
| ● annual % change | −4.2 | 0.3 | −15.2 | −2.1 | 4.7 | 2.8 | 5.4 | −7.5 | −0.2 | −1.7 | 1.4 |
| – against other member countries | | | | | | | | | | | |
| ● 1961-73 = 100 | 100.0 | 76.3 | 66.0 | 63.2 | 66.6 | 69.2 | 70.6 | 65.8 | 64.8 | 65.4 | 67.1 |
| ● annual % change | −4.7 | 1.1 | −17.6 | −4.2 | 5.4 | 3.9 | 1.9 | −6.8 | −1.4 | 0.9 | 2.6 |
| 10. Employment | −0.5 | 1.0 | 0.4 | −0.1 | 1.7 | 0.4 | 1.3 | −2.3 | 1.5 | −0.8 | 0.0 |
| 11. Unemployment rate (% of civilian labour force) | : | 4.0 | 7.4 | 7.4 | 7.7 | 7.5 | 7.0 | 7.7 | 8.7 | 9.8 | 10.1 |
| 12. Current balance (% of GDP) | −2.9 | −2.9 | −5.3 | −3.1 | −2.0 | −5.0 | −6.2 | −5.1 | −4.3 | −3.6 | −3.8 |
| 13. Net lending (+) or net borrowing (−) of general government (% of GDP) | : | : | −12.5 | −11.7 | −13.7 | −16.6 | −18.1 | −14.4 | −14.3 | −16.3 | −17.9 |
| 14. General government gross debt (% of GDP) | : | : | : | : | : | : | 98.4 | 103.9 | 110.2 | 145.2 | 154.0 |
| 15. Interest payment by general government (% of GDP) | : | 2.6 | 5.7 | 7.2 | 7.8 | 8.3 | 11.9 | 11.6 | 14.5 | 16.2 | 18.2 |
| 16. Money supply (end of year)[b] | 18.2 | 25.5 | 19.0 | 24.0 | 23.2 | 24.2 | 15.3 | 12.3 | 14.4 | 15.2 | : |
| 17. Long-term interest rate (%) | : | 13.6 | 15.8 | 17.4 | 16.6 | : | : | : | : | : | : |
| 18. Profitability (1961-73 = 100) | 100.0 | 73.1 | 46.0 | 52.3 | 57.4 | 49.0 | 53.0 | 75.7 | 86.2 | 93.3 | 92.3 |

a 1961-92: EUROSTAT and Commission services; 1993-94: Economic forecasts May 1994.
b M3.


**Table O6**  Main economic indicators 1961-94[a].

Spain

(Annual percentage change, unless otherwise stated)

| | 1961-73 | 1974-85 | 1986 | 1987 | 1988 | 1989 | 1990 | 1991 | 1992 | 1993 | 1994 |
|---|---|---|---|---|---|---|---|---|---|---|---|
| 1. Gross domestic product | | | | | | | | | | | |
| – at current market prices | 14.8 | 17.1 | 14.6 | 11.8 | 11.1 | 12.2 | 11.3 | 9.4 | 7.4 | 3.4 | 5.1 |
| – at 1985 market prices | 7.2 | 1.8 | 3.2 | 5.6 | 5.2 | 4.7 | 3.6 | 2.2 | 0.8 | −1.0 | 1.1 |
| 2. Gross fixed capital formation at 1985 prices | | | | | | | | | | | |
| – total | 10.4 | −1.2 | 9.9 | 14.0 | 13.9 | 13.6 | 7.1 | 1.7 | −3.9 | −10.3 | −1.3 |
| – construction | : | −1.5 | 6.5 | 9.9 | 12.4 | 15.1 | 10.8 | 9.7 | −4.8 | −6.4 | −1.1 |
| – equipment | : | −0.5 | 15.7 | 23.2 | 16.6 | 12.9 | 1.4 | 1.4 | −2.5 | −16.6 | −1.7 |
| 3. Gross fixed capital formation at current prices (% of GDP) | | | | | | | | | | | |
| – total | 24.6 | 22.9 | 19.5 | 20.8 | 22.6 | 24.1 | 24.6 | 23.9 | 22.0 | 20.0 | 19.5 |
| – general government | : | 2.6 | 3.6 | 3.4 | 3.8 | 4.4 | 5.2 | 5.1 | 4.4 | 4.5 | 4.4 |
| – other sectors | : | 20.0 | 15.8 | 17.4 | 18.8 | 19.7 | 19.4 | 18.9 | 17.5 | 15.6 | 15.1 |
| 4. Final national uses including stocks | | | | | | | | | | | |
| – at 1985 prices | 7.6 | 1.2 | 5.4 | 8.1 | 7.0 | 7.8 | 4.7 | 2.8 | 1.1 | −3.6 | −0.1 |
| – relative against 19 competitors | 2.8 | −0.7 | 1.5 | 4.5 | 2.5 | 4.2 | 2.1 | 2.2 | 0.0 | −3.0 | −1.6 |
| – relative against other member countries | 2.9 | −0.4 | 1.3 | 4.6 | 2.4 | 4.2 | 1.6 | 1.6 | 0.1 | −2.0 | −1.1 |
| 5. Inflation | | | | | | | | | | | |
| – price deflator private consumption | 6.6 | 15.4 | 9.4 | 5.7 | 5.0 | 6.6 | 6.5 | 6.3 | 6.4 | 5.1 | 4.8 |
| – price deflator GDP | 7.1 | 15.1 | 11.1 | 5.8 | 5.7 | 7.1 | 7.4 | 7.0 | 6.5 | 4.5 | 4.0 |
| 6. Compensation per employee | | | | | | | | | | | |
| – nominal | 14.6 | 18.0 | 9.5 | 6.7 | 7.1 | 6.4 | 8.6 | 8.2 | 8.5 | 7.2 | 4.6 |
| – real, deflator private consumption | 7.4 | 2.2 | 0.1 | 0.9 | 2.0 | −0.2 | 2.0 | 1.8 | 1.9 | 2.0 | −0.1 |
| – real, deflator GDP | 7.0 | 2.5 | −1.4 | 0.8 | 1.4 | −0.6 | 1.2 | 1.1 | 1.9 | 2.6 | 0.6 |
| 7. GDP at 1985 market prices per person employed | 6.4 | 3.2 | 1.8 | 0.5 | 2.3 | 1.3 | 0.1 | 1.7 | 2.0 | 3.4 | 2.3 |
| 8. Real unit labour costs | | | | | | | | | | | |
| – 1961-73 = 100 | 100.0 | 102.6 | 91.0 | 91.3 | 90.5 | 88.8 | 89.8 | 89.2 | 89.1 | 88.4 | 86.9 |
| – annual % change | 0.5 | −0.7 | −3.2 | 0.3 | −0.9 | −1.8 | 1.1 | −0.6 | −0.1 | −0.8 | −1.7 |
| 9. Relative unit labour costs in common currency, against 19 competitors | | | | | | | | | | | |
| ● 1961-73 = 100 | 100.0 | 115.7 | 104.1 | 107.3 | 113.0 | 119.9 | 130.0 | 131.0 | 132.4 | 116.8 | 109.9 |
| ● annual % change | 1.7 | −0.5 | 2.4 | 3.0 | 5.3 | 6.1 | 8.4 | 0.8 | 1.0 | −11.8 | −5.9 |
| – against other member countries | | | | | | | | | | | |
| ● 1961-73 = 100 | 100.0 | 112.6 | 105.6 | 105.9 | 112.3 | 120.8 | 126.1 | 128.2 | 127.7 | 115.9 | 110.2 |
| ● annual % change | 1.2 | 0.2 | −1.4 | 0.3 | 6.0 | 7.6 | 4.3 | 1.7 | −0.4 | −9.3 | −4.9 |
| 10. Employment | 0.7 | −1.4 | 1.4 | 5.1 | 2.8 | 3.4 | 3.5 | 0.5 | −1.2 | −4.3 | −1.2 |
| 11. Unemployment rate (% of civilian labour force) | : | 11.2 | 21.1 | 20.5 | 19.4 | 17.1 | 16.2 | 16.4 | 18.2 | 21.5 | 23.3 |
| 12. Current balance (% of GDP) | −0.2 | −1.4 | 1.6 | 0.1 | −1.1 | −3.2 | −3.7 | −3.6 | −3.8 | −1.8 | −0.8 |
| 13. Net lending (+) or net borrowing (−) of general government (% of GDP) | : | −2.8 | −6.0 | −3.1 | −3.3 | −2.8 | −3.9 | −4.9 | −4.5 | −7.3 | −7.2 |
| 14. General government gross debt (% of GDP) | : | : | : | : | : | : | 44.0 | 45.2 | 48.2 | 55.9 | 61.4 |
| 15. Interest payment by general government (% of GDP) | : | 1.0 | 4.0 | 3.5 | 3.4 | 3.5 | 3.5 | 4.0 | 4.2 | 4.8 | 5.3 |
| 16. Money supply (end of year)[b] | : | 17.6 | 14.1 | 15.0 | 13.9 | 13.7 | 16.4 | 10.8 | 5.0 | 7.5 | : |
| 17. Long-term interest rate (%) | : | : | 11.4 | 12.8 | 11.7 | 13.7 | 14.7 | 12.4 | 12.2 | 10.2 | 8.8 |
| 18. Profitability (1961-73 = 100) | 100.0 | 72.8 | 102.3 | 107.4 | 112.1 | 121.5 | 119.7 | 121.2 | 122.0 | 117.5 | 119.9 |

a 1961-92: EUROSTAT and Commission services; 1993-94: Economic forecasts May 1994.
b ALP: liquid assets held by the public.

**Table O7**   Main economic indicators 1961-94[a].

Italy           (Annual percentage change, unless otherwise stated)

| | 1961-73 | 1974-85 | 1986 | 1987 | 1988 | 1989 | 1990 | 1991 | 1992 | 1993 | 1994 |
|---|---|---|---|---|---|---|---|---|---|---|---|
| 1. Gross domestic product | | | | | | | | | | | |
| – at current market prices | 11.0 | 19.4 | 11.0 | 9.3 | 11.0 | 9.3 | 9.9 | 8.9 | 5.2 | 3.7 | 4.9 |
| – at 1985 market prices | 5.3 | 2.8 | 2.9 | 3.1 | 4.1 | 2.9 | 2.1 | 1.2 | 0.7 | -0.7 | 1.5 |
| 2. Gross fixed capital formation at 1985 prices | | | | | | | | | | | |
| – total | 4.7 | 0.5 | 2.2 | 5.0 | 6.9 | 4.3 | 3.8 | 0.6 | -2.0 | -11.1 | 0.6 |
| – construction | : | -1.3 | 1.9 | -0.7 | 2.3 | 3.6 | 3.5 | 1.4 | -2.1 | -6.2 | -0.5 |
| – equipment | : | 3.4 | 2.6 | 11.9 | 11.6 | 5.2 | 4.0 | 0.1 | -2.0 | -15.6 | 1.8 |
| 3. Gross fixed capital formation at current prices (% of GDP) | | | | | | | | | | | |
| – total | 24.4 | 23.1 | 19.7 | 19.7 | 20.1 | 20.2 | 20.3 | 19.7 | 19.1 | 17.1 | 17.0 |
| – general government | : | 3.3 | 3.5 | 3.5 | 3.4 | 3.3 | 3.3 | 3.3 | 3.0 | 2.6 | 2.6 |
| – other sectors | : | 19.8 | 16.2 | 16.2 | 16.7 | 16.9 | 17.0 | 16.5 | 16.1 | 14.4 | 14.5 |
| 4. Final national uses including stocks | | | | | | | | | | | |
| – at 1985 prices | 5.3 | 2.4 | 3.4 | 4.3 | 4.7 | 2.9 | 2.8 | 1.8 | 1.0 | -5.6 | 0.7 |
| – relative against 19 competitors | 0.4 | 0.6 | -0.3 | 0.9 | 0.2 | -0.7 | 0.1 | 1.1 | 0.0 | -5.3 | -0.8 |
| – relative against other member countries | 0.6 | 0.9 | -0.5 | 1.1 | 0.1 | -0.7 | -0.4 | 0.5 | 0.0 | -4.4 | -0.2 |
| 5. Inflation | | | | | | | | | | | |
| – price deflator private consumption | 4.9 | 16.0 | 6.2 | 5.3 | 5.7 | 6.5 | 5.9 | 6.9 | 5.2 | 5.1 | 3.9 |
| – price deflator GDP | 5.5 | 16.2 | 7.9 | 6.0 | 6.6 | 6.2 | 7.6 | 7.7 | 4.5 | 4.4 | 3.4 |
| 6. Compensation per employee | | | | | | | | | | | |
| – nominal | 11.5 | 18.2 | 7.5 | 8.2 | 8.7 | 8.7 | 10.7 | 8.5 | 5.7 | 3.7 | 3.3 |
| – real, deflator private consumption | 6.3 | 1.9 | 1.3 | 2.8 | 2.8 | 2.1 | 4.6 | 1.5 | 0.4 | -1.3 | -0.6 |
| – real, deflator GDP | 5.7 | 1.8 | -0.3 | 2.1 | 1.9 | 2.4 | 2.9 | 0.8 | 1.2 | -0.7 | -0.1 |
| 7. GDP at 1985 market prices per person employed | 5.5 | 1.8 | 2.1 | 2.7 | 3.1 | 2.8 | 1.2 | 0.4 | 1.8 | 2.2 | 2.8 |
| 8. Real unit labour costs | | | | | | | | | | | |
| – 1961-73 = 100 | 100.0 | 103.7 | 99.3 | 98.7 | 95.5 | 97.1 | 98.7 | 99.1 | 98.5 | 95.7 | 93.1 |
| – annual % change | 0.1 | -0.1 | -2.4 | -0.6 | -1.2 | -0.4 | 1.6 | 0.4 | -0.6 | -2.8 | -2.8 |
| 9. Relative unit labour costs in common currency, against 19 competitors | | | | | | | | | | | |
| • 1961-73 = 100 | 100.0 | 98.6 | 101.4 | 104.9 | 104.4 | 107.8 | 116.9 | 118.3 | 115.6 | 95.2 | 92.4 |
| • annual % change | -0.3 | 0.2 | 5.8 | 3.5 | -0.5 | 3.2 | 8.4 | 1.2 | -2.3 | -17.6 | -3.0 |
| – against other member countries | | | | | | | | | | | |
| • 1961-73 = 100 | 100.0 | 89.1 | 105.6 | 106.2 | 106.5 | 111.7 | 116.4 | 119.1 | 114.2 | 96.6 | 94.9 |
| • annual % change | -0.8 | 1.1 | 1.8 | 0.6 | 0.3 | 4.9 | 4.1 | 2.4 | -4.0 | -15.6 | -1.7 |
| 10. Employment | -0.2 | 0.9 | 0.8 | 0.4 | 0.9 | 0.2 | 0.9 | 0.8 | -1.0 | -2.8 | -1.2 |
| 11. Unemployment rate (% of civilian labour force) | : | 7.4 | 10.6 | 10.8 | 10.9 | 10.9 | 10.0 | 10.1 | 10.3 | 11.1 | 12.0 |
| 12. Current balance (% of GDP) | 1.4 | -0.7 | 0.5 | -0.2 | -0.7 | -1.3 | -1.4 | -1.8 | -2.2 | 1.1 | 1.1 |
| 13. Net lending (+) or net borrowing (−) of general government (% of GDP) | -3.2 | -9.6 | -11.6 | -11.0 | -10.7 | -9.9 | -10.9 | -10.2 | -9.5 | -9.5 | -9.5 |
| 14. General government gross debt (% of GDP) | : | 62.7 | 86.3 | 90.5 | 92.6 | 95.6 | 97.8 | 101.2 | 108.2 | 118.3 | 123.3 |
| 15. Interest payment by general government (% of GDP) | : | 5.6 | 8.5 | 7.9 | 8.1 | 8.9 | 9.6 | 10.2 | 11.4 | 12.0 | 10.5 |
| 16. Money supply (end of year)[b] | 15.4 | 16.8 | 10.7 | 7.2 | 7.6 | 9.9 | 8.1 | 9.1 | 4.5 | 7.8 | : |
| 17. Long-term interest rate (%) | 7.0 | 15.1 | 11.7 | 11.3 | 12.1 | 12.9 | 13.4 | 13.0 | 13.7 | 11.3 | 9.4 |
| 18. Profitability (1961-73 = 100) | 100.0 | 64.5 | 76.4 | 80.3 | 85.6 | 87.2 | 83.7 | 83.3 | 83.1 | 86.8 | 92.5 |

a 1961-92: EUROSTAT and Commission services; 1993-94: Economic forecasts May 1994.
b M2.

**Table O8**   Main economic indicators 1961-94[a].

Luxembourg           (Annual percentage change, unless otherwise stated)

| | 1961-73 | 1974-85 | 1986 | 1987 | 1988 | 1989 | 1990 | 1991 | 1992 | 1993 | 1994 |
|---|---|---|---|---|---|---|---|---|---|---|---|
| 1. Gross domestic product | | | | | | | | | | | |
| – at current market prices | 8.7 | 8.5 | 8.8 | 1.9 | 10.0 | 13.0 | 6.2 | 6.1 | 6.5 | 2.6 | 4.7 |
| – at 1985 market prices | 4.0 | 1.8 | 4.8 | 2.9 | 5.7 | 6.7 | 3.2 | 3.1 | 1.9 | 0.3 | 1.6 |
| 2. Gross fixed capital formation at 1985 prices | | | | | | | | | | | |
| – total | 4.9 | -2.7 | 31.2 | 14.7 | 14.1 | 8.9 | 2.5 | 9.8 | -2.1 | 4.0 | -1.8 |
| – construction | : | -3.0 | 5.3 | 8.7 | 12.5 | 13.8 | 7.2 | 9.0 | 6.2 | 2.6 | -0.2 |
| – equipment | : | -2.6 | 87.2 | 18.7 | 16.0 | 4.4 | -6.0 | 11.2 | -12.0 | 6.0 | -3.9 |
| 3. Gross fixed capital formation at current prices (% of GDP) | | | | | | | | | | | |
| – total | 26.4 | 23.9 | 22.1 | 25.5 | 27.0 | 27.1 | 26.9 | 29.0 | 27.7 | 28.5 | 27.7 |
| – general government | : | 6.1 | 4.3 | 4.9 | 4.3 | 4.2 | 4.5 | 5.3 | 6.6 | 6.0 | 6.0 |
| – other sectors | : | 17.8 | 17.8 | 20.7 | 22.7 | 22.9 | 22.4 | 23.7 | 21.1 | 22.5 | 21.7 |
| 4. Final national uses including stocks | | | | | | | | | | | |
| – at 1985 prices | 4.1 | 1.5 | 8.0 | 4.2 | 6.8 | 5.7 | 5.1 | 8.0 | 0.5 | 1.3 | 0.6 |
| – relative against 19 competitors | : | : | : | : | : | : | : | : | : | : | : |
| – relative against other member countries | : | : | : | : | : | : | : | : | : | : | : |
| 5. Inflation | | | | | | | | | | | |
| – price deflator private consumption | 3.0 | 7.4 | 1.3 | 1.7 | 2.7 | 3.6 | 3.6 | 2.9 | 2.8 | 3.6 | 2.9 |
| – price deflator GDP | 4.4 | 6.7 | 3.8 | -1.0 | 4.0 | 6.0 | 2.9 | 3.0 | 4.5 | 2.3 | 3.1 |
| 6. Compensation per employee | | | | | | | | | | | |
| – nominal | 7.4 | 9.2 | 3.7 | 4.9 | 2.7 | 6.7 | 7.0 | 4.3 | 5.8 | 5.7 | 4.6 |
| – real, deflator private consumption | 4.2 | 1.7 | 2.4 | 3.1 | 0.0 | 3.0 | 3.3 | 1.4 | 2.9 | 2.0 | 1.7 |
| – real, deflator GDP | 2.8 | 2.4 | -0.1 | 5.9 | -1.3 | 0.7 | 3.9 | 1.3 | 1.2 | 3.3 | 1.5 |
| 7. GDP at 1985 market prices per person employed | 3.0 | 1.2 | 2.1 | 0.1 | 2.6 | 2.9 | -1.0 | -1.1 | 0.0 | -1.4 | 0.6 |
| 8. Real unit labour costs | | | | | | | | | | | |
| – 1961-73 = 100 | 100.0 | 115.4 | 106.5 | 112.7 | 108.4 | 106.1 | 111.3 | 114.0 | 115.3 | 120.8 | 121.9 |
| – annual % change | -0.2 | 1.1 | -2.2 | 5.8 | -3.8 | -2.2 | 4.9 | 2.4 | 1.2 | 4.8 | 0.9 |
| 9. Relative unit labour costs in common currency, against 19 competitors | | | | | | | | | | | |
| • 1961-73 = 100 | : | : | : | : | : | : | : | : | : | : | : |
| • annual % change | : | : | : | : | : | : | : | : | : | : | : |
| – against other member countries | | | | | | | | | | | |
| • 1961-73 = 100 | : | : | : | : | : | : | : | : | : | : | : |
| • annual % change | : | : | : | : | : | : | : | : | : | : | : |
| 10. Employment | 1.1 | 0.5 | 2.6 | 2.8 | 3.1 | 3.7 | 4.2 | 4.2 | 1.8 | 1.7 | 1.0 |
| 11. Unemployment rate (% of civilian labour force) | : | 1.7 | 2.6 | 2.5 | 2.0 | 1.8 | 1.7 | 1.6 | 1.9 | 2.6 | 3.0 |
| 12. Current balance (% of GDP) | 6.9 | 27.1 | 38.8 | 30.3 | 30.8 | 34.0 | 34.2 | 27.9 | 30.0 | 28.3 | 29.6 |
| 13. Net lending (+) or net borrowing (−) of general government (% of GDP) | 2.0 | 2.1 | 5.1 | 3.3 | : | : | 5.9 | 2.3 | -0.3 | 1.4 | -0.4 |
| 14. General government gross debt (% of GDP) | : | : | : | : | : | : | 5.4 | 4.9 | 5.8 | 6.8 | 7.9 |
| 15. Interest payment by general government (% of GDP) | : | 1.2 | 1.1 | 1.2 | 1.0 | 0.7 | 0.6 | 0.5 | 0.5 | 0.4 | 0.4 |
| 16. Money supply (end of year) | : | : | : | : | : | : | : | : | : | : | : |
| 17. Long-term interest rate (%) | : | 8.1 | 8.7 | 8.0 | 7.1 | 7.7 | 8.6 | 8.2 | 7.9 | 6.9 | 6.4 |
| 18. Profitability (1961-73 = 100) | 100.0 | 52.8 | 71.2 | 55.9 | 68.1 | 76.9 | 65.8 | 58.5 | 54.7 | 42.6 | 39.3 |

a 1961-92: EUROSTAT and Commission services; 1993-94: Economic forecasts May 1994.

**Table O9**   Main economic indicators 1961-94[a].

Portugal                                 (Annual percentage change, unless otherwise stated)

| | 1961-73 | 1974-85 | 1986 | 1987 | 1988 | 1989 | 1990 | 1991 | 1992 | 1993 | 1994 |
|---|---|---|---|---|---|---|---|---|---|---|---|
| 1. Gross domestic product | | | | | | | | | | | |
| – at current market prices | 11.1 | 23.4 | 25.4 | 17.1 | 16.0 | 18.8 | 19.3 | 16.5 | 14.7 | 6.6 | 6.5 |
| – at 1985 market prices | 6.9 | 2.2 | 4.1 | 5.3 | 3.9 | 5.2 | 4.4 | 2.1 | 1.1 | –1.2 | 1.1 |
| 2. Gross fixed capital formation at 1985 prices | | | | | | | | | | | |
| – total | 7.9 | –1.3 | 10.9 | 15.1 | 15.0 | 5.6 | 5.9 | 2.4 | 5.4 | –3.9 | 1.1 |
| – construction | : | : | 8.7 | 9.4 | 10.1 | 3.5 | 5.3 | 4.5 | 3.5 | 0.7 | 0.0 |
| – equipment | : | : | 14.2 | 26.8 | 23.2 | 10.0 | 5.8 | 1.0 | 5.6 | –7.5 | 2.0 |
| 3. Gross fixed capital formation at current prices (% of GDP) | | | | | | | | | | | |
| – total | 24.1 | 26.9 | 22.1 | 24.2 | 26.8 | 26.4 | 26.4 | 26.0 | 26.2 | 25.6 | 25.7 |
| – general government | 2.7 | 3.2 | 2.6 | 2.7 | 2.9 | 3.1 | 3.4 | 3.5 | 4.0 | 4.1 | 4.3 |
| – other sectors | 21.4 | 23.7 | 19.5 | 21.5 | 23.9 | 23.3 | 22.9 | 22.5 | 22.2 | 21.5 | 21.5 |
| 4. Final national uses including stocks | | | | | | | | | | | |
| – at 1985 prices | 7.3 | 1.1 | 8.3 | 10.4 | 7.4 | 4.3 | 5.4 | 4.1 | 4.7 | –0.5 | 0.6 |
| – relative against 19 competitors | 2.6 | –0.6 | 4.2 | 6.6 | 2.9 | 0.6 | 2.8 | 3.6 | 3.8 | 0.6 | –0.7 |
| – relative against other member countries | 2.7 | –0.3 | 4.1 | 6.7 | 2.7 | 0.6 | 2.4 | 3.0 | 3.7 | 1.2 | –0.4 |
| 5. Inflation | | | | | | | | | | | |
| – price deflator private consumption | 3.9 | 22.2 | 13.8 | 10.0 | 10.0 | 12.1 | 12.6 | 11.1 | 9.8 | 6.8 | 5.6 |
| – price deflator GDP | 3.9 | 20.8 | 20.5 | 11.2 | 11.6 | 13.0 | 14.3 | 14.1 | 13.4 | 7.9 | 5.4 |
| 6. Compensation per employee | | | | | | | | | | | |
| – nominal | 10.8 | 24.3 | 21.6 | 17.9 | 13.4 | 12.8 | 18.7 | 17.2 | 15.9 | 7.5 | 6.3 |
| – real, deflator private consumption | 6.7 | 1.7 | 6.8 | 7.2 | 3.1 | 0.6 | 5.4 | 5.5 | 5.6 | 0.7 | 0.7 |
| – real, deflator GDP | 6.7 | 2.9 | 0.9 | 6.0 | 1.5 | –0.2 | 3.9 | 2.7 | 2.2 | –0.3 | 0.9 |
| 7. GDP at 1985 market prices per person employed | 6.7 | 2.7 | 7.0 | 4.7 | 3.9 | 4.1 | 3.5 | 1.2 | 1.7 | 1.1 | 2.5 |
| 8. Real unit labour costs | | | | | | | | | | | |
| – 1961-73 = 100 | 100.0 | 117.9 | 98.4 | 99.7 | 97.4 | 93.5 | 93.8 | 95.2 | 95.7 | 94.3 | 92.8 |
| – annual % change | 0.0 | 0.2 | –5.7 | 1.3 | –2.2 | –4.1 | 0.4 | 1.5 | 0.5 | –1.4 | –1.6 |
| 9. Relative unit labour costs in common currency, against 19 competitors | | | | | | | | | | | |
| • 1961-73 = 100 | 100.0 | 98.8 | 81.2 | 82.3 | 83.1 | 84.4 | 90.8 | 100.7 | 115.1 | 110.8 | 107.2 |
| • annual % change | –0.7 | –1.8 | 1.2 | 1.3 | 1.0 | 1.5 | 7.6 | 10.8 | 14.4 | –3.8 | –3.2 |
| – against other member countries | | | | | | | | | | | |
| • 1961-73 = 100 | 100.0 | 97.0 | 82.0 | 81.4 | 82.7 | 85.0 | 89.1 | 99.4 | 112.1 | 109.3 | 106.7 |
| • annual % change | –1.2 | –1.3 | –1.6 | –0.6 | 1.6 | 2.7 | 4.8 | 11.6 | 12.9 | –2.6 | –2.4 |
| 10. Employment | 0.2 | 0.5 | –2.7 | 0.5 | 0.1 | 1.0 | 0.9 | 0.9 | –0.6 | –2.3 | –1.4 |
| 11. Unemployment rate (% of civilian labour force) | : | 6.9 | 8.3 | 6.8 | 5.7 | 5.0 | 4.6 | 4.0 | 3.9 | 5.0 | 6.5 |
| 12. Current balance (% of GDP) | 0.4 | –6.6 | 2.4 | –0.4 | –4.4 | –2.3 | –2.5 | –2.9 | –3.2 | –3.5 | –3.6 |
| 13. Net lending (+) or net borrowing (–) of general government (% of GDP) | 0.6 | : | –7.2 | –6.8 | –5.4 | –3.4 | –5.5 | –6.6 | –3.3 | –7.1 | –6.2 |
| 14. General government gross debt (% of GDP) | : | : | : | : | : | : | 67.7 | 69.4 | 61.7 | 66.6 | 70.2 |
| 15. Interest payment by general government (% of GDP) | 0.6 | 3.7 | 9.2 | 7.8 | 7.8 | 7.2 | 7.1 | 7.4 | 7.6 | 6.7 | 5.8 |
| 16. Money supply (end of year)[b] | : | 22.3 | 26.3 | 19.7 | 17.8 | 10.4 | 11.2 | 18.7 | 12.7 | 6.6 | : |
| 17. Long-term interest rate (%) | : | : | 19.5 | 16.8 | 15.5 | 16.3 | 16.8 | 18.3 | 15.4 | 12.5 | 10.0 |
| 18. Profitability (1961-73 = 100) | 100.0 | 38.7 | 53.6 | 53.1 | 55.0 | 60.5 | 60.9 | 58.9 | 58.2 | 56.0 | 55.5 |

a 1961-92: EUROSTAT and Commission services; 1993-94: Economic forecasts May 1994.
b L-: liquid assets of the residents.


**Table O10**   Main economic indicators 1961-94[a].

United Kingdom                             (Annual percentage change, unless otherwise stated)

| | 1961-73 | 1974-85 | 1986 | 1987 | 1988 | 1989 | 1990 | 1991 | 1992 | 1993 | 1994 |
|---|---|---|---|---|---|---|---|---|---|---|---|
| 1. Gross domestic product | | | | | | | | | | | |
| – at current market prices | 8.4 | 14.0 | 7.7 | 10.0 | 11.3 | 9.5 | 6.8 | 4.1 | 3.9 | 5.4 | 5.9 |
| – at 1985 market prices | 3.2 | 1.4 | 4.3 | 4.8 | 5.0 | 2.2 | 0.4 | –2.3 | –0.5 | 1.9 | 2.5 |
| 2. Gross fixed capital formation at 1985 prices | | | | | | | | | | | |
| – total | 4.6 | 0.7 | 2.6 | 10.2 | 13.5 | 5.5 | –3.4 | –9.8 | –1.1 | 0.8 | 3.6 |
| – construction | : | –0.8 | 6.1 | 11.0 | 13.4 | 5.4 | –0.6 | –8.3 | 0.8 | 0.1 | 4.0 |
| – equipment | : | 2.2 | –0.9 | 8.7 | 13.0 | 11.6 | –3.6 | –11.5 | –3.5 | 2.1 | 4.9 |
| 3. Gross fixed capital formation at current prices (% of GDP) | | | | | | | | | | | |
| – total | 18.5 | 18.0 | 17.0 | 17.8 | 19.4 | 20.3 | 19.4 | 16.9 | 15.6 | 15.0 | 15.0 |
| – general government | : | 2.9 | 1.9 | 1.7 | 1.3 | 1.8 | 2.3 | 2.2 | 2.1 | 1.8 | 1.7 |
| – other sectors | : | 15.1 | 15.1 | 16.1 | 18.1 | 18.5 | 17.1 | 14.7 | 13.5 | 13.2 | 13.3 |
| 4. Final national uses including stocks | | | | | | | | | | | |
| – at 1985 prices | 3.2 | 1.2 | 4.9 | 5.3 | 7.9 | 2.9 | –0.6 | –3.3 | 0.4 | 2.0 | 2.3 |
| – relative against 19 competitors | –1.8 | –0.8 | 1.3 | 2.0 | 3.7 | –0.7 | –3.3 | –4.1 | –0.7 | 2.6 | 0.7 |
| – relative against other member countries | –1.8 | –0.4 | 1.1 | 2.3 | 3.9 | –0.8 | –4.3 | –5.3 | –0.7 | 4.4 | 1.5 |
| 5. Inflation | | | | | | | | | | | |
| – price deflator private consumption | 4.8 | 12.0 | 4.0 | 4.3 | 5.0 | 5.9 | 5.5 | 7.4 | 4.8 | 3.5 | 3.5 |
| – price deflator GDP | 5.1 | 12.4 | 3.2 | 5.0 | 6.1 | 7.1 | 6.4 | 6.5 | 4.4 | 3.4 | 3.3 |
| 6. Compensation per employee | | | | | | | | | | | |
| – nominal | 8.3 | 13.9 | 8.1 | 7.3 | 7.9 | 9.0 | 9.0 | 8.1 | 5.9 | 4.2 | 3.6 |
| – real, deflator private consumption | 3.3 | 1.7 | 4.0 | 2.8 | 2.7 | 2.9 | 3.3 | 0.7 | 1.0 | 0.6 | 0.1 |
| – real, deflator GDP | 3.1 | 1.3 | 4.7 | 2.2 | 1.7 | 1.7 | 2.4 | 1.5 | 1.4 | 0.7 | 0.3 |
| 7. GDP at 1985 market prices per person employed | 2.9 | 1.6 | 4.4 | 3.0 | 1.7 | –0.4 | –0.7 | 0.8 | 1.8 | 3.2 | 1.6 |
| 8. Real unit labour costs | | | | | | | | | | | |
| – 1961-73 = 100 | 100.0 | 101.3 | 97.3 | 96.6 | 96.6 | 98.6 | 101.8 | 102.5 | 102.0 | 99.6 | 98.3 |
| – annual % change | 0.1 | 0.3 | 0.3 | –0.7 | 0.0 | 2.1 | 3.2 | 0.7 | –0.4 | –2.3 | –1.4 |
| 9. Relative unit labour costs in common currency, against 19 competitors | | | | | | | | | | | |
| • 1961-73 = 100 | 100.0 | 92.2 | 87.7 | 87.9 | 96.4 | 99.3 | 103.4 | 106.4 | 103.6 | 93.1 | 94.3 |
| • annual % change | –1.9 | 1.1 | –7.3 | 0.1 | 9.7 | 3.0 | 4.2 | 2.9 | –2.7 | –10.1 | 1.3 |
| – against other member countries | | | | | | | | | | | |
| • 1961-73 = 100 | 100.0 | 89.1 | 87.9 | 84.4 | 94.4 | 99.7 | 98.3 | 102.7 | 97.5 | 90.4 | 93.2 |
| • annual % change | –3.0 | 2.3 | –13.2 | –3.9 | 11.8 | 5.6 | –1.4 | 4.5 | –5.1 | –7.3 | 3.2 |
| 10. Employment | 0.3 | –0.2 | –0.1 | 1.8 | 3.2 | 2.5 | 1.1 | –3.1 | –2.2 | –1.2 | 0.8 |
| 11. Unemployment rate (% of civilian labour force) | : | 6.9 | 11.4 | 10.4 | 8.5 | 7.1 | 7.0 | 8.9 | 10.2 | 10.5 | 9.9 |
| 12. Current balance (% of GDP) | –0.1 | –0.1 | –1.1 | –2.2 | –4.9 | –5.5 | –4.5 | –2.4 | –2.4 | –2.5 | –1.7 |
| 13. Net lending (+) or net borrowing (–) of general government (% of GDP) | –0.6 | –3.7 | –2.8 | –1.4 | 0.1 | –0.1 | –1.5 | –2.8 | –6.4 | –7.7 | –6.0 |
| 14. General government gross debt (% of GDP) | : | : | : | : | : | : | : | 35.8 | 41.7 | 48.2 | 50.5 |
| 15. Interest payment by general government (% of GDP) | : | 4.5 | 4.5 | 4.2 | 3.9 | 3.7 | 3.4 | 3.0 | 2.9 | 2.9 | 3.2 |
| 16. Money supply (end of year)[b] | : | 13.9 | 16.2 | 16.2 | 17.4 | 18.8 | 12.0 | 5.8 | 3.5 | 5.8 | : |
| 17. Long-term interest rate (%) | 7.6 | 13.0 | 9.8 | 9.5 | 9.3 | 9.6 | 11.1 | 9.9 | 9.1 | 7.8 | 8.2 |
| 18. Profitability (1961-73 = 100) | 100.0 | 76.4 | 92.3 | 98.2 | 100.8 | 94.6 | 85.2 | 84.6 | 90.9 | 100.0 | 105.3 |

a 1961-92: EUROSTAT and Commission services; 1993-94: Economic forecasts May 1994.
b M4.

# Index